DC THROUGH THE '80S

VOLUME TWO

THE EXPERIMENTS

Edited by **PAUL LEVITZ**

Additional essays by **BARBARA SLATE**
MARV WOLFMAN
DAVE GIBBONS

SUPERMAN created by **JERRY SIEGEL** and **JOE SHUSTER**
By special arrangement with the Jerry Siegel family

KAREN BERGER
DAVE MANAK
ALAN GOLD
MARK WAID
MICHAEL EURY
NICOLA CUTI
ROY THOMAS
ROBERT GREENBERGER
FRANK MILLER
MIKE GOLD

Associate Editors – Original Series   JANICE RACE
ART YOUNG

Assistant Editor – Original Series   JONATHAN PETERSON

Editor – Collected Edition   PAUL LEVITZ

Design Director – Books   STEVE COOK

Publication Design   CURTIS KING JR.

Publication Production   SUZANNAH ROWNTREE

Editor-in-Chief, DC Comics   MARIE JAVINS

Senior VP – General Manager   DANIEL CHERRY III

Publisher & Chief Creative Officer   JIM LEE

VP – Global Brand & Creative Services   JOEN CHOE

*VP – Manufacturing Operations
& Workflow Management*   DON FALLETTI

VP – Talent Services   LAWRENCE GANEM

Senior VP – Manufacturing & Operations   ALISON GILL

VP – Manufacturing Administration & Design   NICK J. NAPOLITANO

VP – Revenue   NANCY SPEARS

Interior color reconstruction by
MICHAEL KELLEHER

DC THROUGH THE '80S: THE EXPERIMENTS

Published by DC Comics. Compilation and all new material Copyright © 2021 DC Comics. All Rights Reserved. Originally published in single magazine form in *Camelot 3000* 1, *Warlord* 48, 55, *Legion of Super-Heroes* 298, *The New Teen Titans* 16, *Angel Love* 1, *Nathaniel Dusk* 1, *Secret Origins* 48, *The Best of DC* 58, *Infinity Inc.* 14, *Swamp Thing* 40, *Doom Patrol* 25, *The Sandman* 8, *Watchmen* 1, *Batman: The Dark Knight Returns* 1, *The History of the DC Universe* 1-2, *Who's Who* 1, 2, 4, 9, 10, 15, 17, 19. Copyright © 1981-1989 DC Comics and *Ronin* 1 © 1983 Frank Miller, Inc. All Rights Reserved. All characters, their distinctive likenesses, and related elements featured in this publication are trademarks of DC Comics. The stories, characters, and incidents featured in this publication are entirely fictional. DC Comics does not read or accept unsolicited submissions of ideas, stories, or artwork. DC – a WarnerMedia Company.

DC COMICS

2900 West Alameda Ave., Burbank, CA 91505
Printed by Transcontinental Interglobe,
Beauceville, QC, Canada. 4/16/21.
First Printing. 978-1-77950-709-9

Library of Congress Cataloging-in-Publication Data is available.

CONTENTS

PART THREE: 50 YEARS AND ONWARD

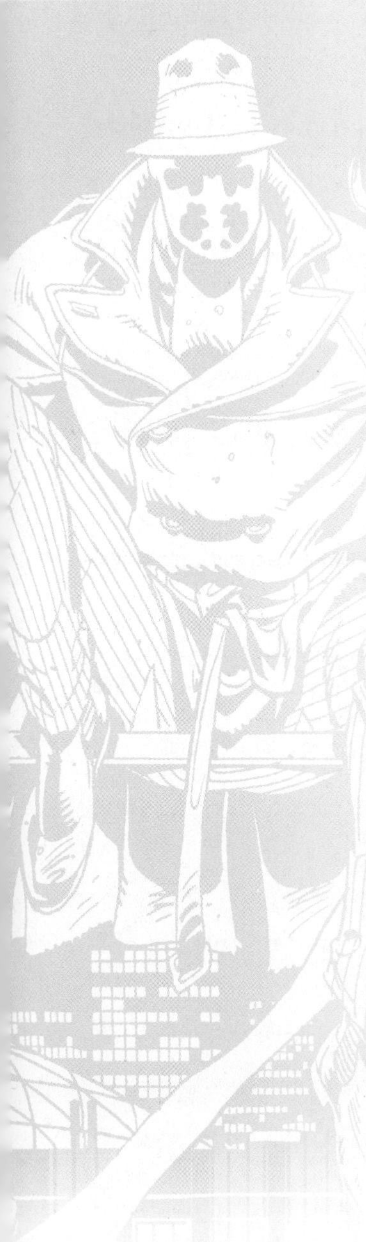

INTRODUCTION

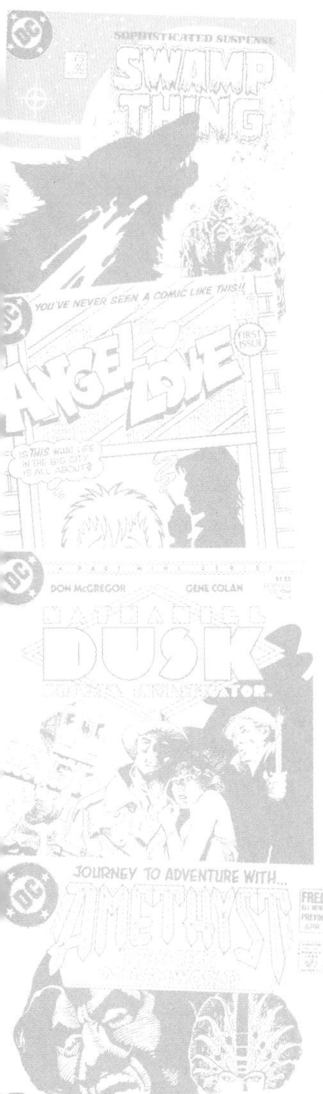
SOPHISTICATED SUSPENSE
SWAMP THING
YOU'VE NEVER SEEN A COMIC LIKE THIS!!
ANGEL LOVE
FIRST ISSUE
IS THIS WHAT LIFE IN THE BIG CITY IS ALL ABOUT?
DON McGREGOR
GENE COLAN
NATHANIEL DUSK
JOURNEY TO ADVENTURE WITH...
AMETHYST

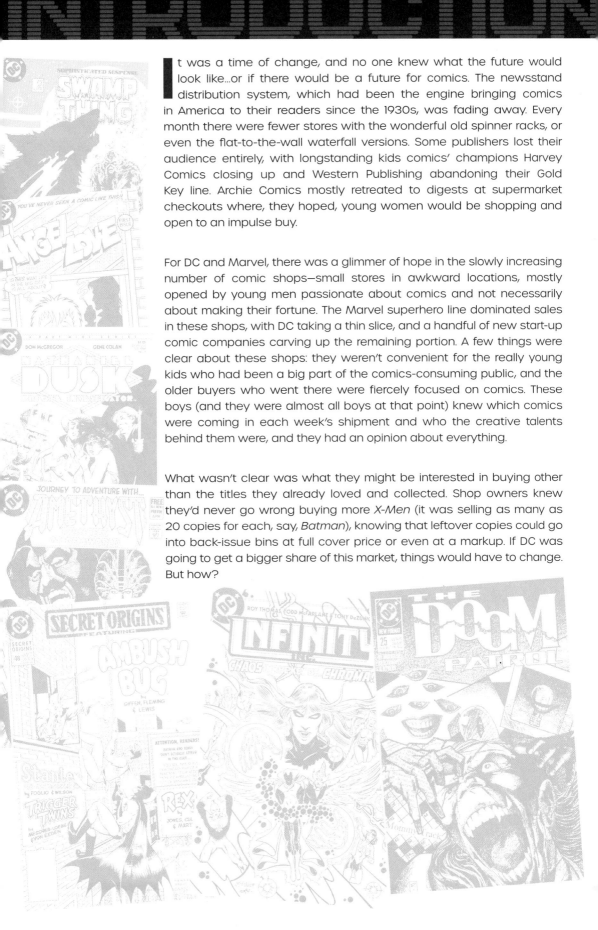

It was a time of change, and no one knew what the future would look like...or if there would be a future for comics. The newsstand distribution system, which had been the engine bringing comics in America to their readers since the 1930s, was fading away. Every month there were fewer stores with the wonderful old spinner racks, or even the flat-to-the-wall waterfall versions. Some publishers lost their audience entirely, with longstanding kids comics' champions Harvey Comics closing up and Western Publishing abandoning their Gold Key line. Archie Comics mostly retreated to digests at supermarket checkouts where, they hoped, young women would be shopping and open to an impulse buy.

For DC and Marvel, there was a glimmer of hope in the slowly increasing number of comic shops—small stores in awkward locations, mostly opened by young men passionate about comics and not necessarily about making their fortune. The Marvel superhero line dominated sales in these shops, with DC taking a thin slice, and a handful of new start-up comic companies carving up the remaining portion. A few things were clear about these shops: they weren't convenient for the really young kids who had been a big part of the comics-consuming public, and the older buyers who went there were fiercely focused on comics. These boys (and they were almost all boys at that point) knew which comics were coming in each week's shipment and who the creative talents behind them were, and they had an opinion about everything.

What wasn't clear was what they might be interested in buying other than the titles they already loved and collected. Shop owners knew they'd never go wrong buying more *X-Men* (it was selling as many as 20 copies for each, say, *Batman*), knowing that leftover copies could go into back-issue bins at full cover price or even at a markup. If DC was going to get a bigger share of this market, things would have to change. But how?

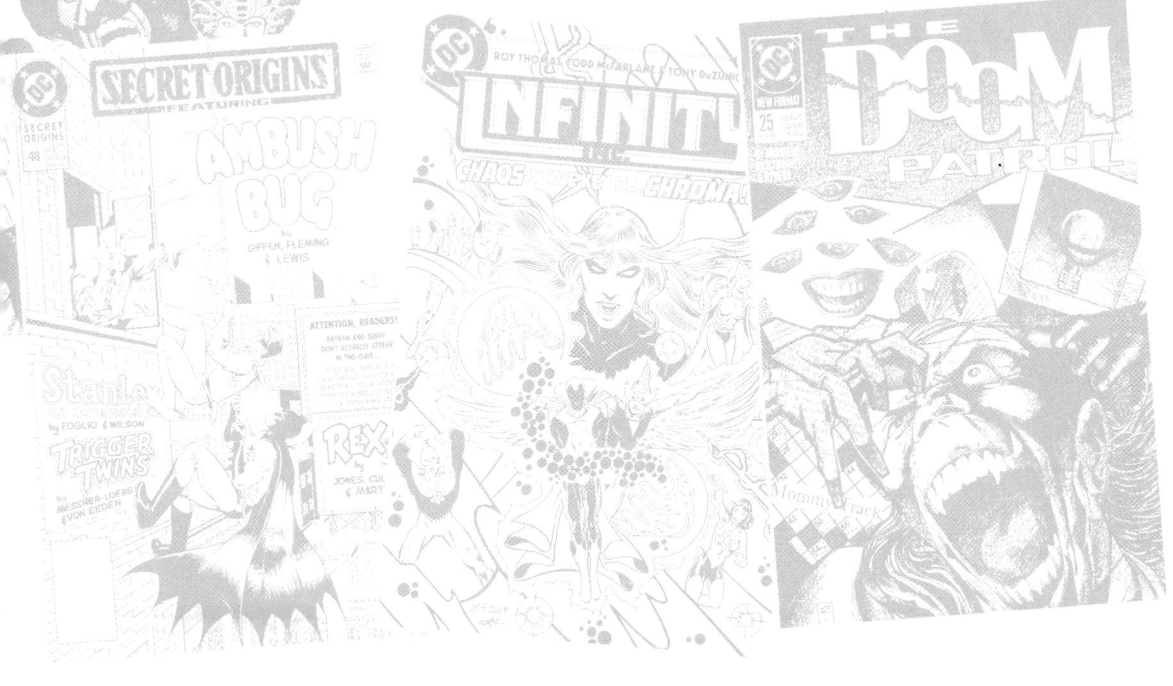
SECRET ORIGINS
FEATURING
AMBUSH BUG
by GIFFEN, FLEMING & LEWIS
ATTENTION, READERS!
by FOGLIO & WILSON
TRIGGER TWINS
REX
JONES, GIL & MART
ROY THOMAS TODD McFARLANE TONY DeZUNIGA
INFINITY INC.
CHAOS
CHROMA!
THE DOOM PATROL
NEW FORMAT

Going head on against Marvel only went so far. *The New Teen Titans* by Marv Wolfman and George Pérez became DC's bestseller and reached some of the so-called Marvel Zombies, as did *Legion of Super-Heroes* by Keith Giffen and me, but neither shook Marvel's dominance. So the change had to go deeper. Experiments would need to be conducted. Radical experiments.

A vital part of the new formula was a tidal shift in how the talent was treated. Royalties were established based on sales, incentivizing writers and artists to create new titles and characters, and to put their absolute best work forward. This was largely invisible to readers, but other aspects of the shifts were more obvious: new formats (*Camelot 3000* becoming the first series to be printed using the far sharper offset presses, whiter and sturdier paper, and brighter colors; and escaping the limitations of the Comics Code by avoiding the newsstands entirely), credits on the covers, and a steady flow of new titles unlike what staid DC had offered for decades. No more talking gorillas or strange transformations for our heroes. Instead...well, maybe anything?

Welcome to a magic moment.

Paul Levitz
January 2021

Paul Levitz was managing DC's business activities in the early 1980s in addition to writing comics. Over the course of his career, he served on the editorial side of the company as well, and he ended his time on staff as DC's president and publisher. For his efforts, he was inducted into the Will Eisner Hall of Fame in 2019.

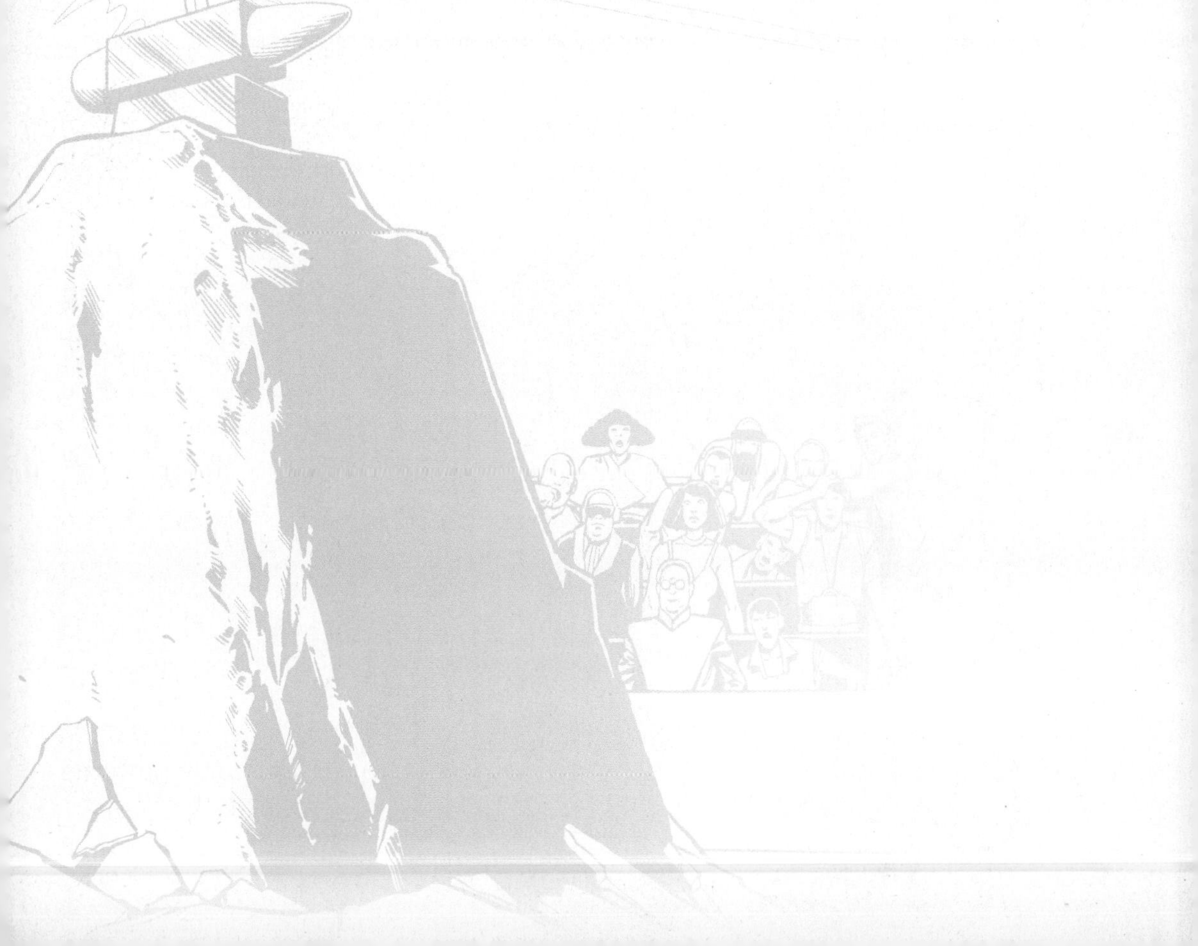

ANYTHING GOES

The traditional genres that had served DC were fading away with the newsstands—no more mystery comics, no more Nazis to battle in the endless war; even the remaining Westerns and SF titles were ending their runs. Replacing them were some conventional superhero comics, but also a steady stream of the unconventional. Rule-breaking experiments like *Camelot 3000*, reversals of the traditions like *Arak, Son of Thunder* (a Native American as the hero?), bait for new audiences (would young girls come into comic shops if offered *Amethyst, Princess of Gemworld*?), mash-ups of old genres (*Captain Carrot and His Amazing Zoo Crew*), and on and on.

One change begat others. The shift to offset printing offered the possibility of breaking away from the mass-production approach of breaking down the artists' responsibilities into pencillers and inkers, and a first experiment was with the magnificent pencil work of Gene Colan. Colan's work shined when inked by talents as varied as Tom Palmer, Jack

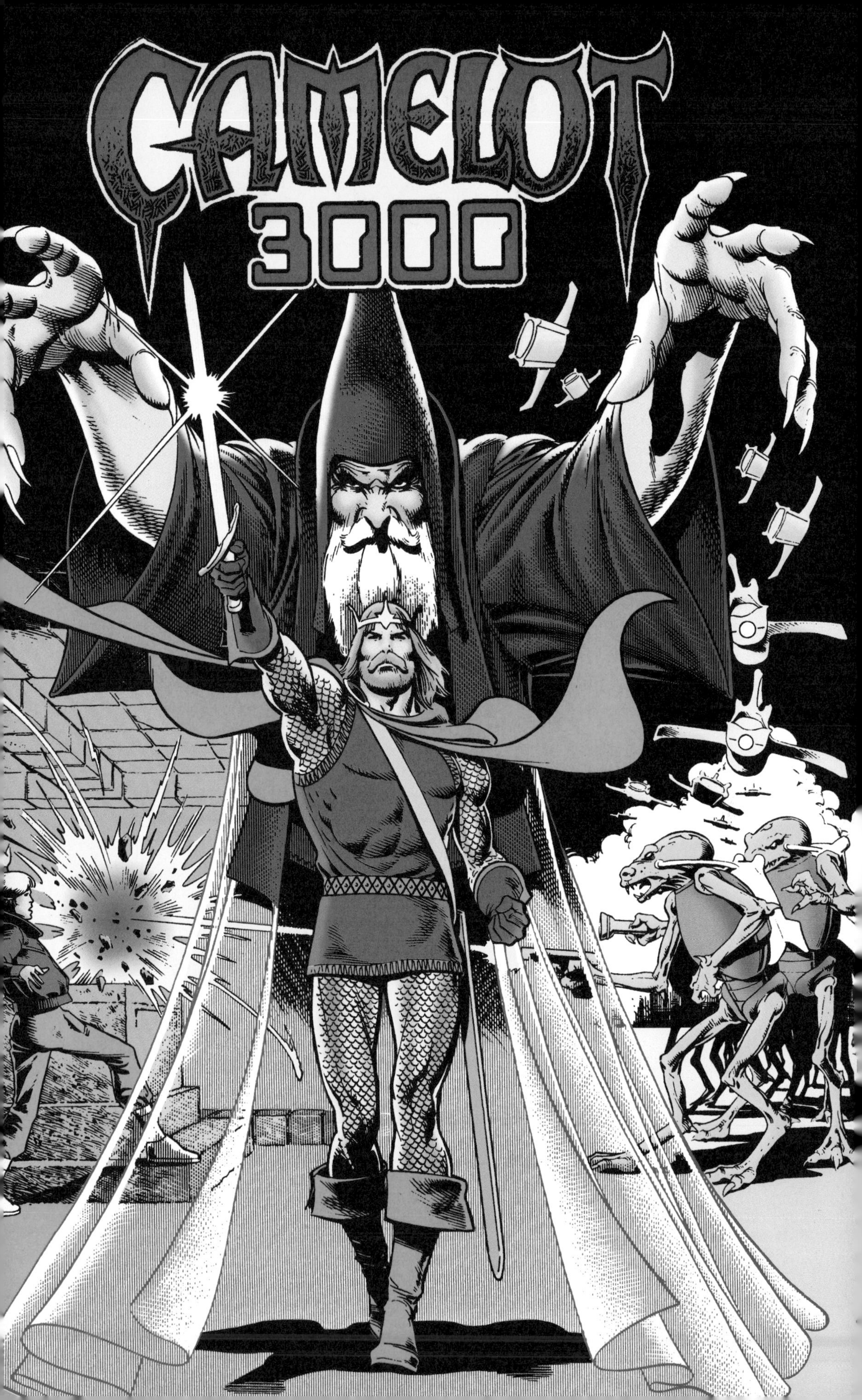
CAMELOT
3000

THE PAST AND FUTURE KING

Story by
MIKE W. BARR

Pencils by
BRIAN BOLLAND

Inks by
BRUCE D. PATTERSON

Colors by
TATJANA WOOD

Letters by
JOHN COSTANZA

CAMELOT 3000 created by **MIKE W. BARR** and **BRIAN BOLLAND**

The Past And Future King

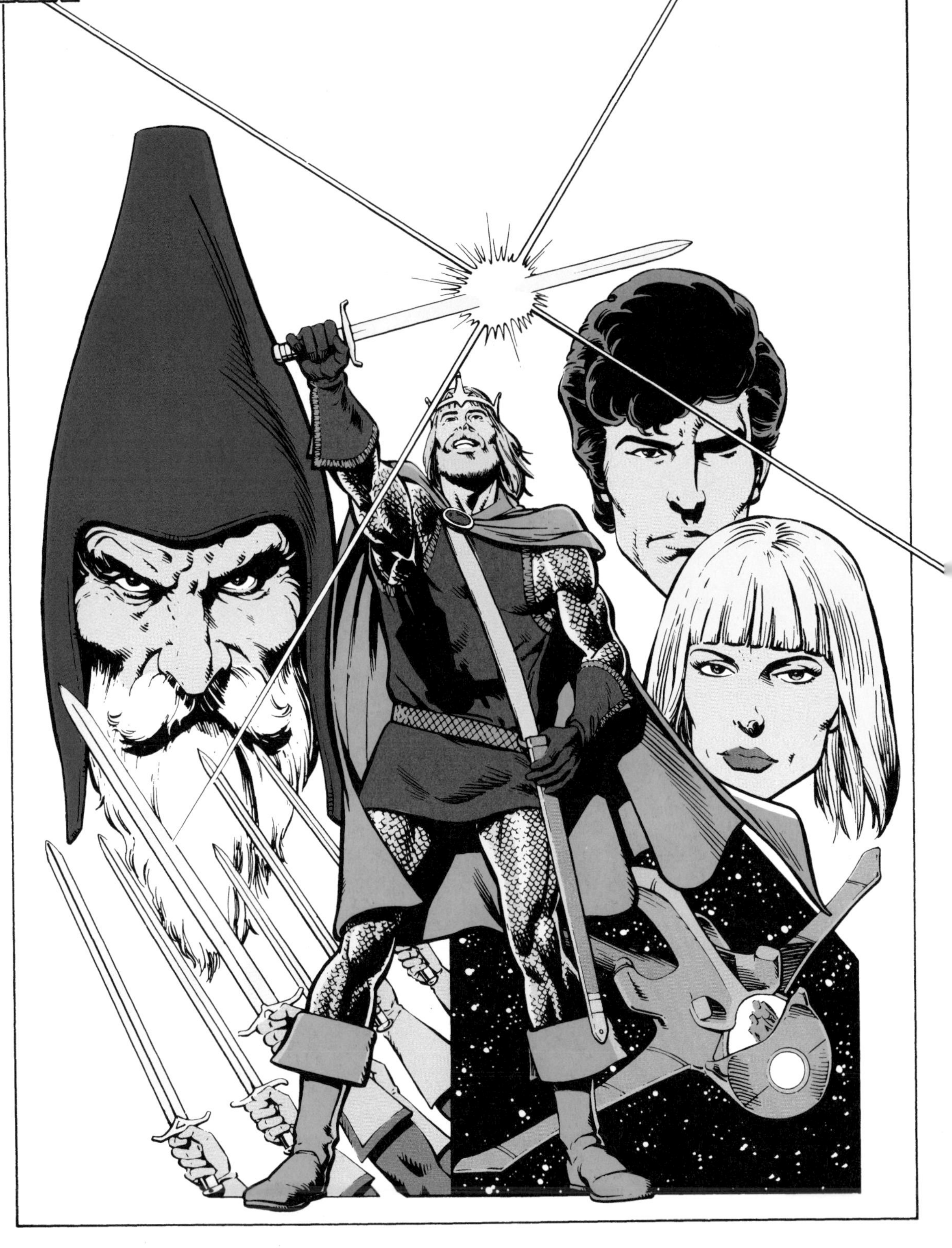

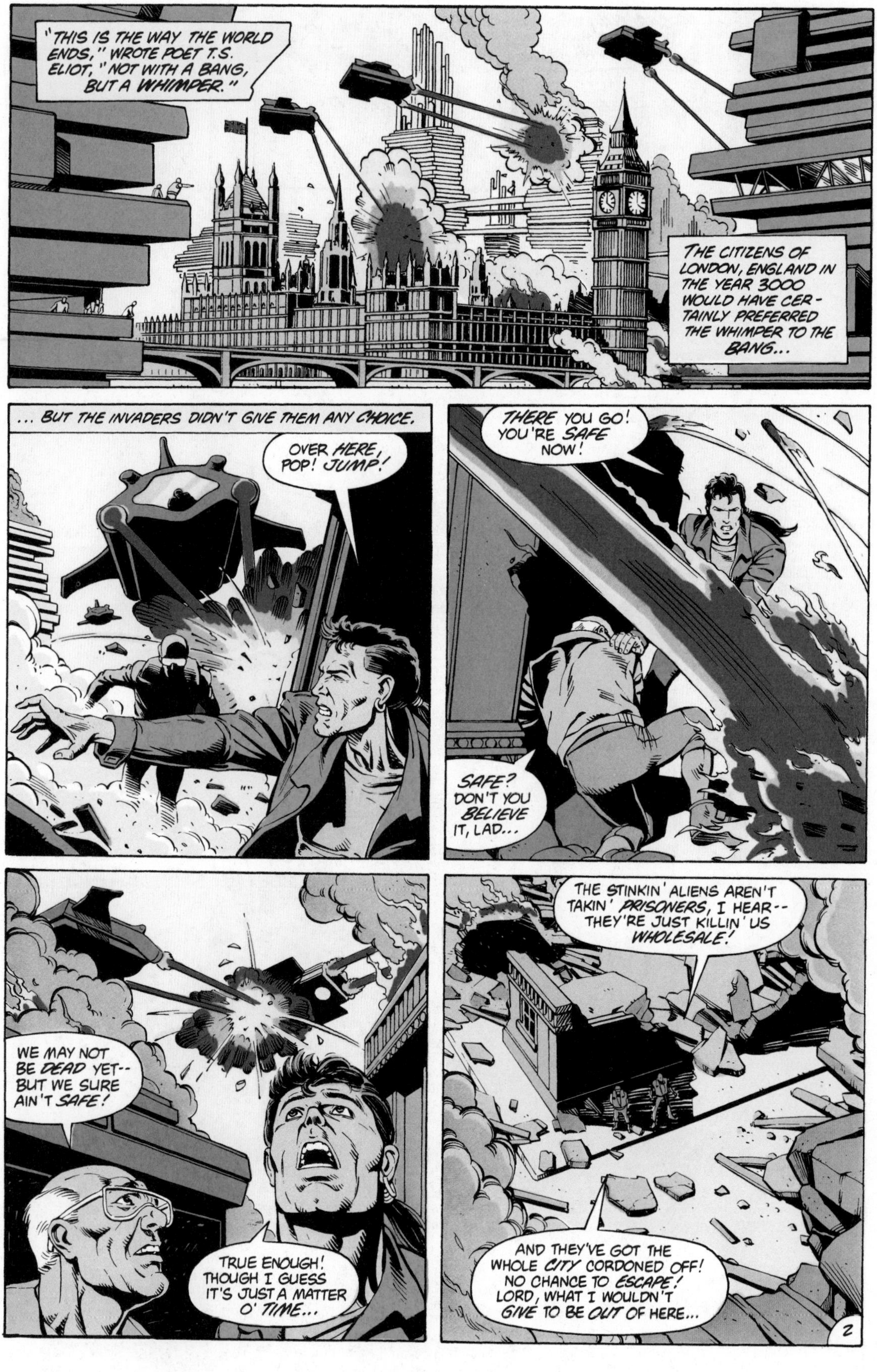
"THIS IS THE WAY THE WORLD ENDS," WROTE POET T.S. ELIOT, "NOT WITH A BANG, BUT A WHIMPER."
THE CITIZENS OF LONDON, ENGLAND IN THE YEAR 3000 WOULD HAVE CERTAINLY PREFERRED THE WHIMPER TO THE BANG...
... BUT THE INVADERS DIDN'T GIVE THEM ANY CHOICE.
OVER HERE, POP! JUMP!
THERE YOU GO! YOU'RE SAFE NOW!
SAFE? DON'T YOU BELIEVE IT, LAD...
WE MAY NOT BE DEAD YET-- BUT WE SURE AIN'T SAFE!
TRUE ENOUGH! THOUGH I GUESS IT'S JUST A MATTER O' TIME...
THE STINKIN' ALIENS AREN'T TAKIN' PRISONERS, I HEAR-- THEY'RE JUST KILLIN' US WHOLESALE!
AND THEY'VE GOT THE WHOLE CITY CORDONED OFF! NO CHANCE TO ESCAPE! LORD, WHAT I WOULDN'T GIVE TO BE OUT OF HERE...
2

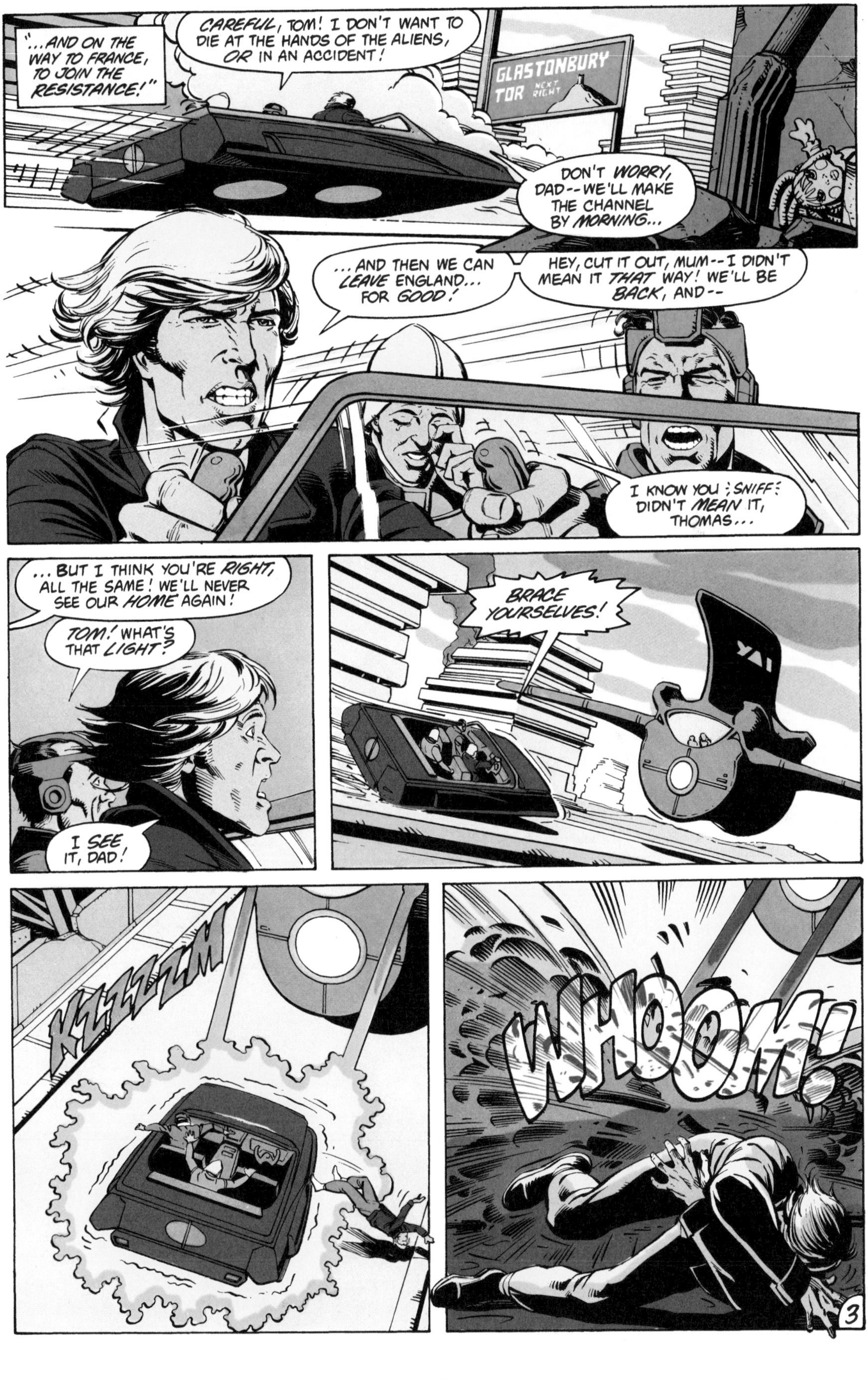
"...AND ON THE WAY TO FRANCE, TO JOIN THE RESISTANCE!"
CAREFUL, TOM! I DON'T WANT TO DIE AT THE HANDS OF THE ALIENS, OR IN AN ACCIDENT!
GLASTONBURY TOR NEXT RIGHT
DON'T WORRY, DAD--WE'LL MAKE THE CHANNEL BY MORNING...
...AND THEN WE CAN LEAVE ENGLAND... FOR GOOD!
HEY, CUT IT OUT, MUM--I DIDN'T MEAN IT THAT WAY! WE'LL BE BACK, AND--
I KNOW YOU :SNIFF: DIDN'T MEAN IT, THOMAS...
...BUT I THINK YOU'RE RIGHT, ALL THE SAME! WE'LL NEVER SEE OUR HOME AGAIN!
TOM! WHAT'S THAT LIGHT?
I SEE IT, DAD!
BRACE YOURSELVES!
KZZZZZM
WHOOM!
3

TO AN OBJECTIVE OBSER-VER, IT IS OBVIOUS THAT YOUNG TOM COULD NOT POSSIBLY HAVE SAVED HIS PARENTS' LIVES.

BUT UNTIL HE HIMSELF ACKNOWLEDGES THIS TRUTH, HE WILL *RUN*...

...*AND RUN*...

...AND *RUN....!*

GLASTONBURY TOR: FOR AEONS, A REGION THICK-SWATHED IN MAGIC AND MYSTERY...

...YET THE PEOPLE OF THE YEAR 3000 DON'T MUCH BELIEVE IN *MAGIC*, AND THE ONLY *MYSTERY* IN TOM'S MIND--

--IS WHETHER HE'LL SURVIVE THE *NIGHT!*

DIG PERSONNEL ONLY-- PROVIDE VOCAL IDENTI-FICATION.

GLASTONBURY HISTORICAL DIG-- NO TRESPASSING

PRENTICE, THOMAS. :PUFF: JUNIOR MEMBER OF DIG.

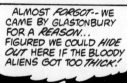

ALMOST *FORGOT*-- WE CAME BY GLASTONBURY FOR A *REASON*... FIGURED WE COULD *HIDE OUT* HERE IF THE BLOODY ALIENS GOT TOO *THICK!*

I CAN LAY LOW FOR *DAYS* IF I HAVE TO...

I JUST HOPE THEY DIDN'T SEE ME *COME IN* HERE!

4

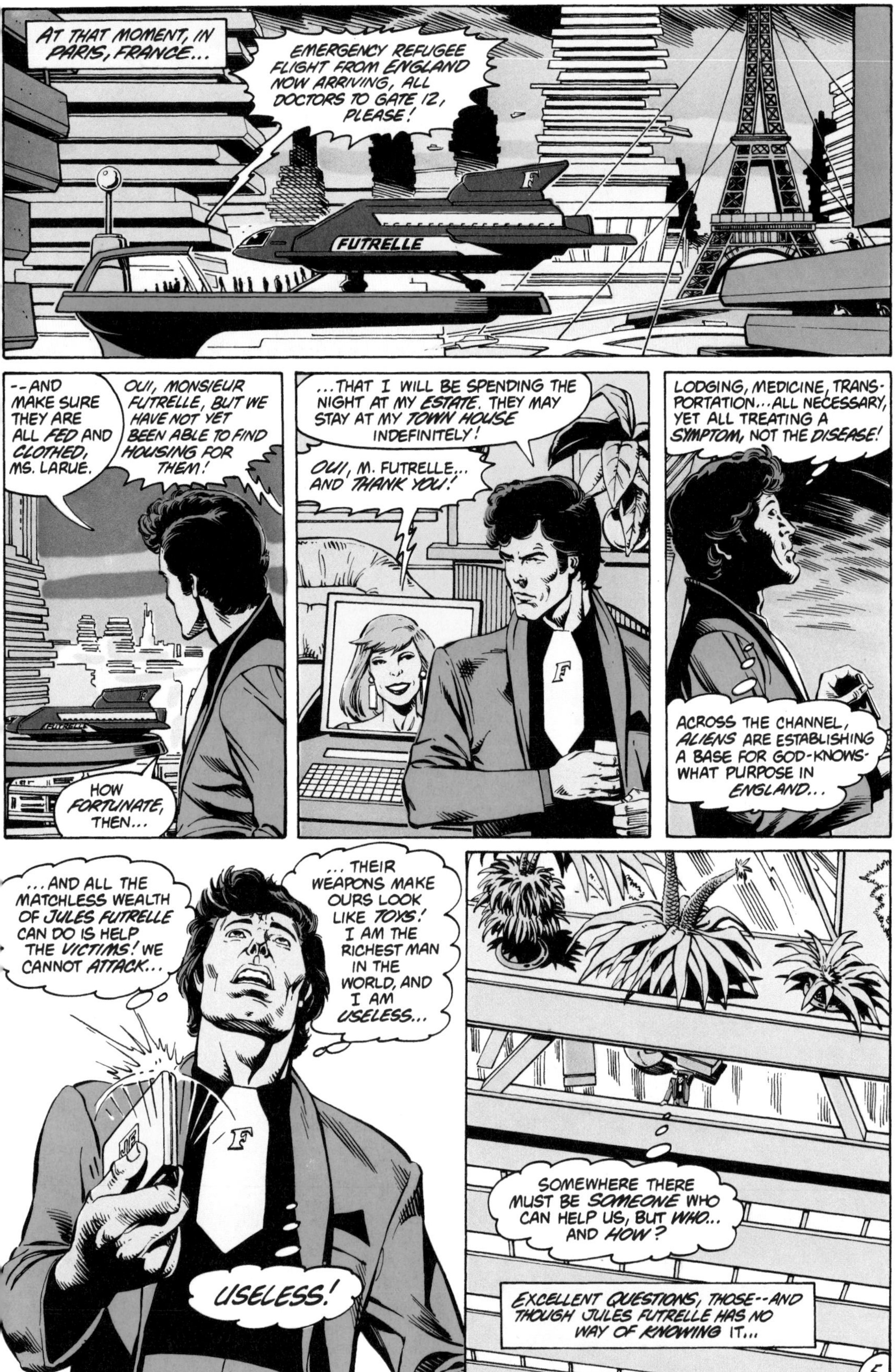
AT THAT MOMENT, IN PARIS, FRANCE...
EMERGENCY REFUGEE FLIGHT FROM ENGLAND NOW ARRIVING, ALL DOCTORS TO GATE 12, PLEASE!
FUTRELLE
--AND MAKE SURE THEY ARE ALL FED AND CLOTHED, MS. LARUE.
OUI, MONSIEUR FUTRELLE, BUT WE HAVE NOT YET BEEN ABLE TO FIND HOUSING FOR THEM!
HOW FORTUNATE, THEN...
...THAT I WILL BE SPENDING THE NIGHT AT MY ESTATE. THEY MAY STAY AT MY TOWN HOUSE INDEFINITELY!
OUI, M. FUTRELLE... AND THANK YOU!
LODGING, MEDICINE, TRANSPORTATION... ALL NECESSARY, YET ALL TREATING A SYMPTOM, NOT THE DISEASE!
ACROSS THE CHANNEL, ALIENS ARE ESTABLISHING A BASE FOR GOD-KNOWS-WHAT PURPOSE IN ENGLAND...
...AND ALL THE MATCHLESS WEALTH OF JULES FUTRELLE CAN DO IS HELP THE VICTIMS! WE CANNOT ATTACK...
...THEIR WEAPONS MAKE OURS LOOK LIKE TOYS! I AM THE RICHEST MAN IN THE WORLD, AND I AM USELESS...
USELESS!
SOMEWHERE THERE MUST BE SOMEONE WHO CAN HELP US, BUT WHO... AND HOW?
EXCELLENT QUESTIONS, THOSE--AND THOUGH JULES FUTRELLE HAS NO WAY OF KNOWING IT...
5

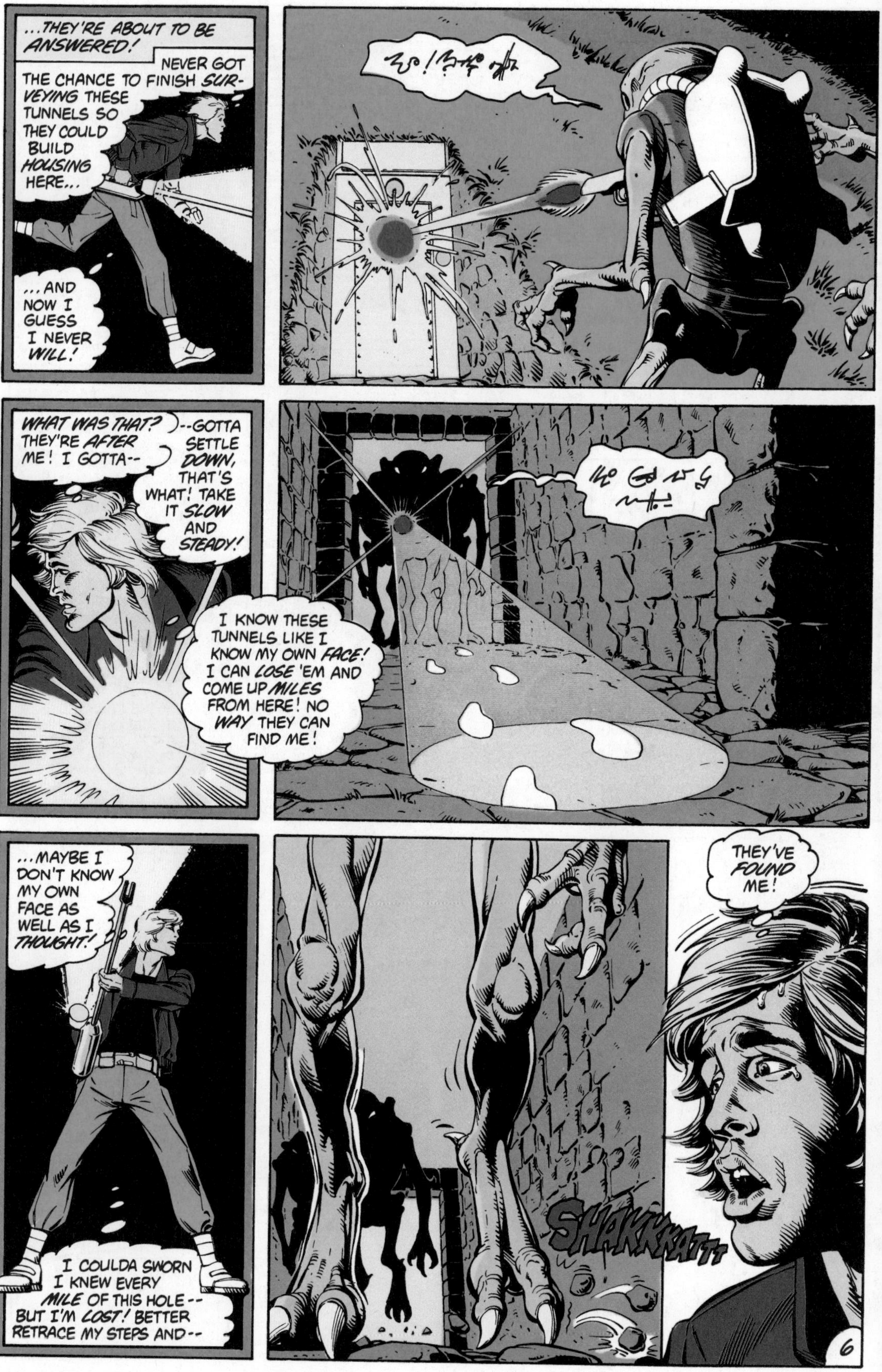
...THEY'RE ABOUT TO BE ANSWERED!
NEVER GOT THE CHANCE TO FINISH SURVEYING THESE TUNNELS SO THEY COULD BUILD HOUSING HERE...
...AND NOW I GUESS I NEVER WILL!
WHAT WAS THAT? THEY'RE AFTER ME! I GOTTA--
--GOTTA SETTLE DOWN, THAT'S WHAT! TAKE IT SLOW AND STEADY!
I KNOW THESE TUNNELS LIKE I KNOW MY OWN FACE! I CAN LOSE 'EM AND COME UP MILES FROM HERE! NO WAY THEY CAN FIND ME!
...MAYBE I DON'T KNOW MY OWN FACE AS WELL AS I THOUGHT!
I COULDA SWORN I KNEW EVERY MILE OF THIS HOLE--BUT I'M LOST! BETTER RETRACE MY STEPS AND--
THEY'VE FOUND ME!
SHAKKKATTT
6

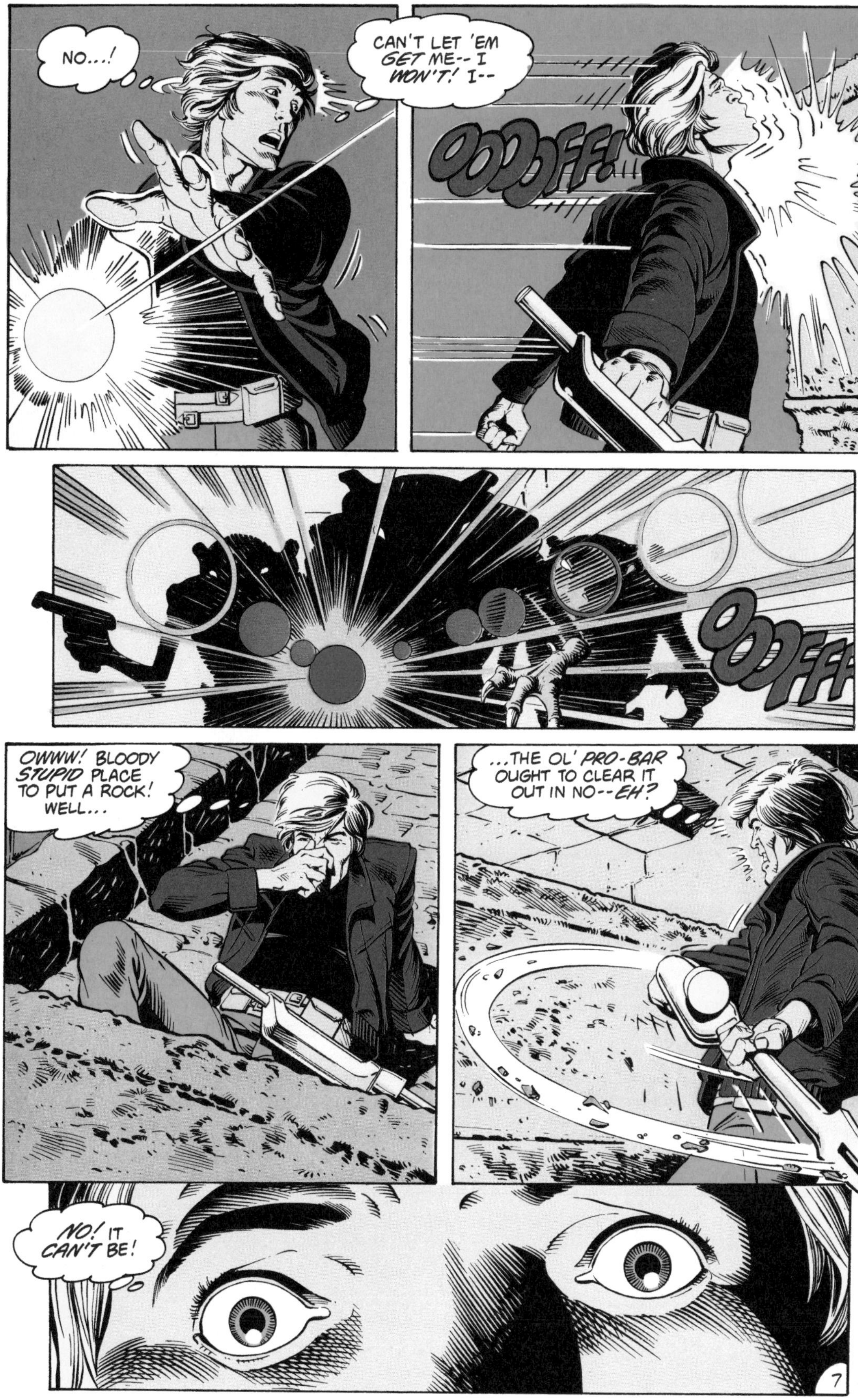
NO...!
CAN'T LET 'EM GET ME-- I WON'T! I--
OOOOFF!
OOOFFF
OWWW! BLOODY STUPID PLACE TO PUT A ROCK! WELL...
...THE OL' PRO-BAR OUGHT TO CLEAR IT OUT IN NO--EH?
NO! IT CAN'T BE!
7

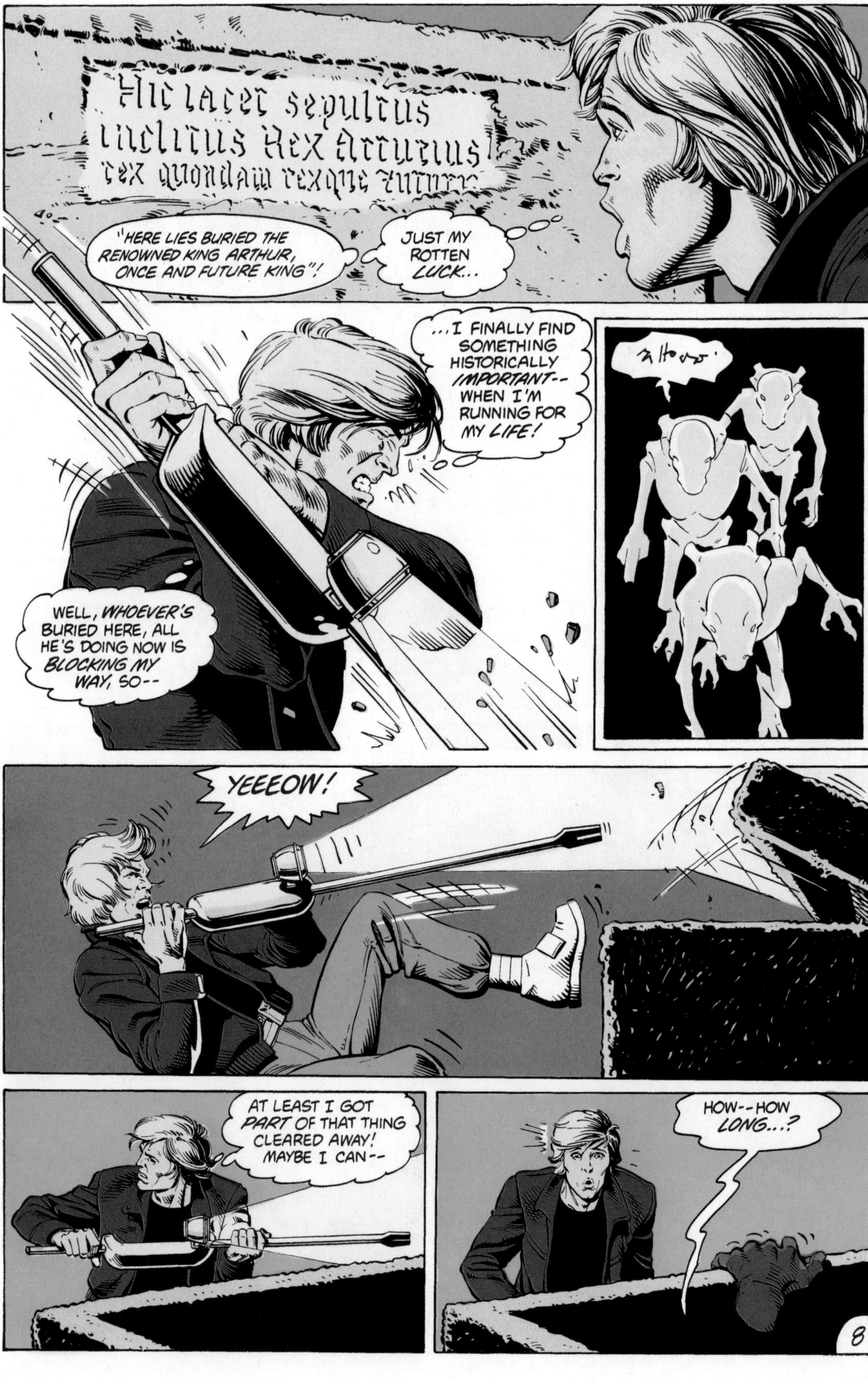
Hic iacet sepultus
inclitus Rex Arturius
rex quondam rexque futurus
"HERE LIES BURIED THE RENOWNED KING ARTHUR, ONCE AND FUTURE KING"!
JUST MY ROTTEN LUCK...
...I FINALLY FIND SOMETHING HISTORICALLY IMPORTANT-- WHEN I'M RUNNING FOR MY LIFE!
WELL, WHOEVER'S BURIED HERE, ALL HE'S DOING NOW IS BLOCKING MY WAY, SO--
YEEEOW!
AT LEAST I GOT PART OF THAT THING CLEARED AWAY! MAYBE I CAN--
HOW--HOW LONG...?
8

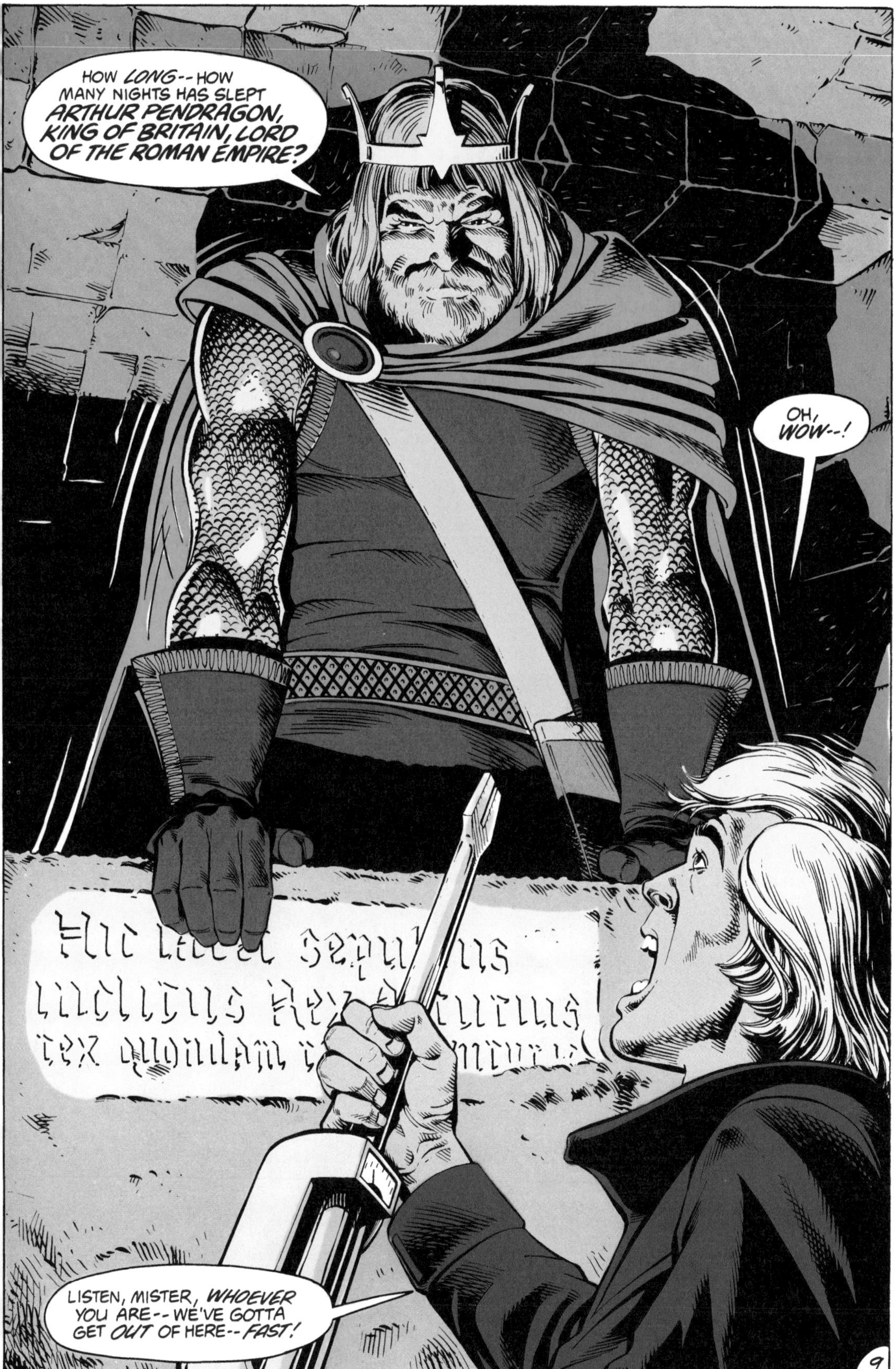
HOW LONG--HOW MANY NIGHTS HAS SLEPT ARTHUR PENDRAGON, KING OF BRITAIN, LORD OF THE ROMAN EMPIRE?
OH, WOW--!
LISTEN, MISTER, WHOEVER YOU ARE--WE'VE GOTTA GET OUT OF HERE--FAST!
9

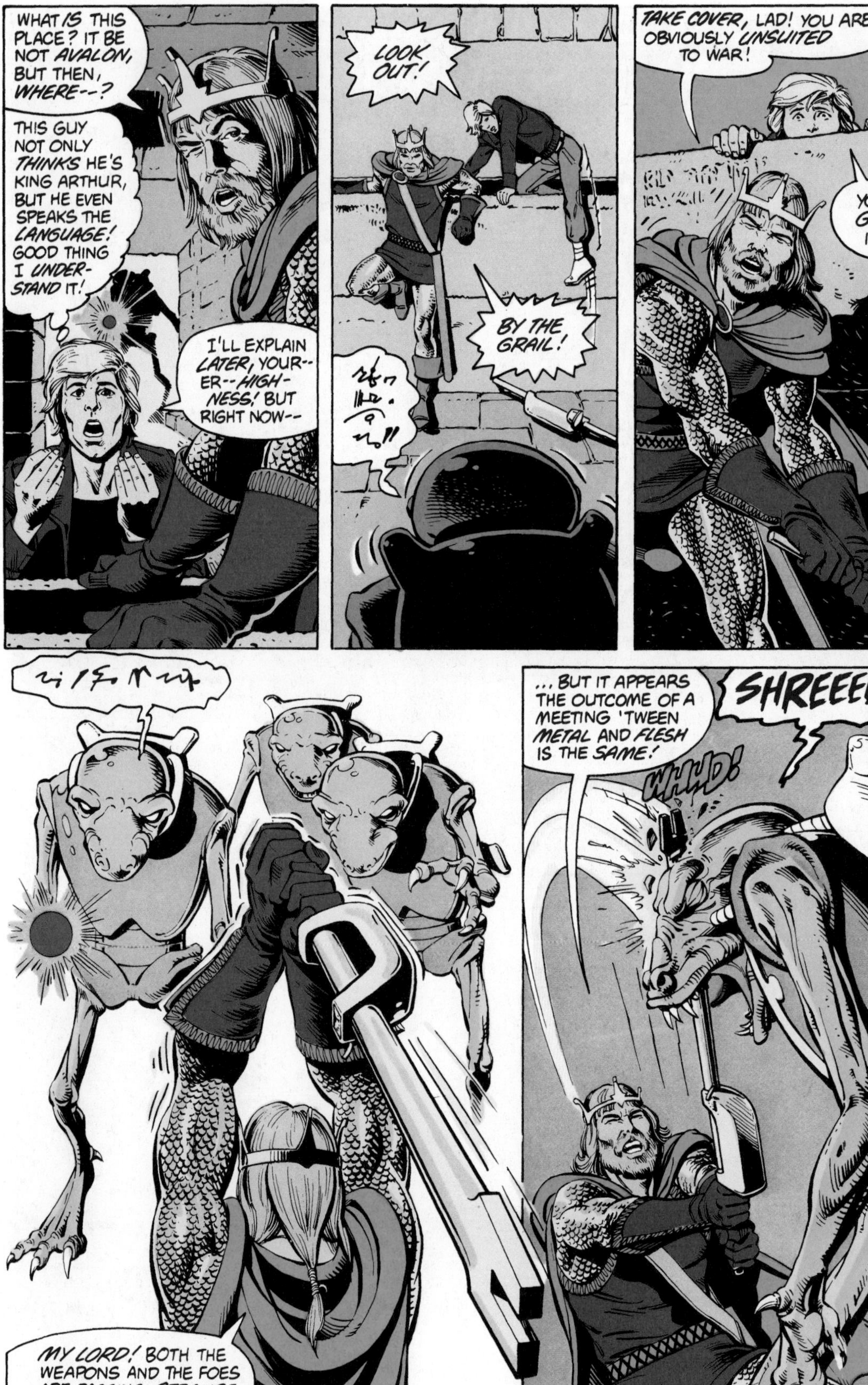
WHAT IS THIS PLACE? IT BE NOT AVALON, BUT THEN, WHERE--?
THIS GUY NOT ONLY THINKS HE'S KING ARTHUR, BUT HE EVEN SPEAKS THE LANGUAGE! GOOD THING I UNDERSTAND IT!
I'LL EXPLAIN LATER, YOUR-- ER--HIGHNESS! BUT RIGHT NOW--
LOOK OUT!
BY THE GRAIL!
TAKE COVER, LAD! YOU ARE OBVIOUSLY UNSUITED TO WAR!
YOU GOT IT!
MY LORD! BOTH THE WEAPONS AND THE FOES ARE PASSING STRANGE IN THIS LAND...
..., BUT IT APPEARS THE OUTCOME OF A MEETING 'TWEEN METAL AND FLESH IS THE SAME!
SHREEEEE
WHUD!
10

AWAY WITH THAT WEIRD *TORCH!* *AWAY* WITH IT, I SAY!

OR *BETTER:* IF YE SO *DEARLY* WISH TO SEE IT REND *FLESH...*

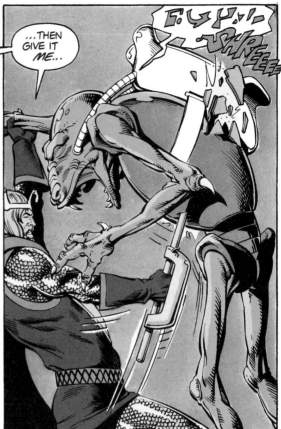

...THEN GIVE IT *ME...*

...AND I SHALL *GRANT* THY BOON...

...THOUGH NOT IN THE MANNER YE *INTENDED!*

I AM SORE TEMPTED TO KEEP THIS WEAPON-- AND *WHY NOT?*

ITS *OWNER* HAS NO FURTHER USE FOR IT!

TH-THAT WAS *AMAZING!*

AMAZING? NO, LAD, THE DIMMEST SQUIRE OF THE *TABLE ROUND* COULD EASILY VANQUISH SUCH FOES AS *THESE!*

BUT TELL ME NOW... WHAT *PLACE* AND *TIME* IS THIS?

WELL, WE'RE UNDER *GLASTONBURY TOR,* AND--AND IT'S THE YEAR *3000!*

THE YEAR *3000,* YE SAY? BY JESU, I SLEPT FOR SOMEWHAT LONGER THAN I *THOUGHT...*

...BUT IT SEEMS TO HAVE SERVED ITS PURPOSE, FOR THE WOUND GIVEN ME BY THE EVIL *MODRED* IS *HEALED!*

...IN THE BATTLE... AT *SALISBURY DOWN?*

WHAT? THEN MY MENTOR DID NOT *FAIL* ME! HE *SAID* THE WORLD WOULD KNOW OF *KING ARTHUR AND THE TABLE ROUND!*

I MUST *FIND* HIM, LAD! WOULD YOU *COME* WITH ME? I'LL *NEED* A SQUIRE IN THIS STRANGE ERA!

I--I'M *SORRY,* YOUR...ER...MAJESTY, I *CAN'T!*

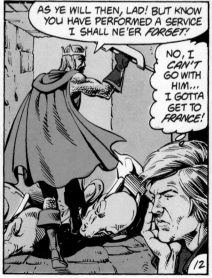

AS YE WILL THEN, LAD! BUT KNOW YOU HAVE PERFORMED A SERVICE I SHALL NE'ER *FORGET!*

NO, I *CAN'T* GO WITH HIM... I GOTTA GET TO *FRANCE!*

12

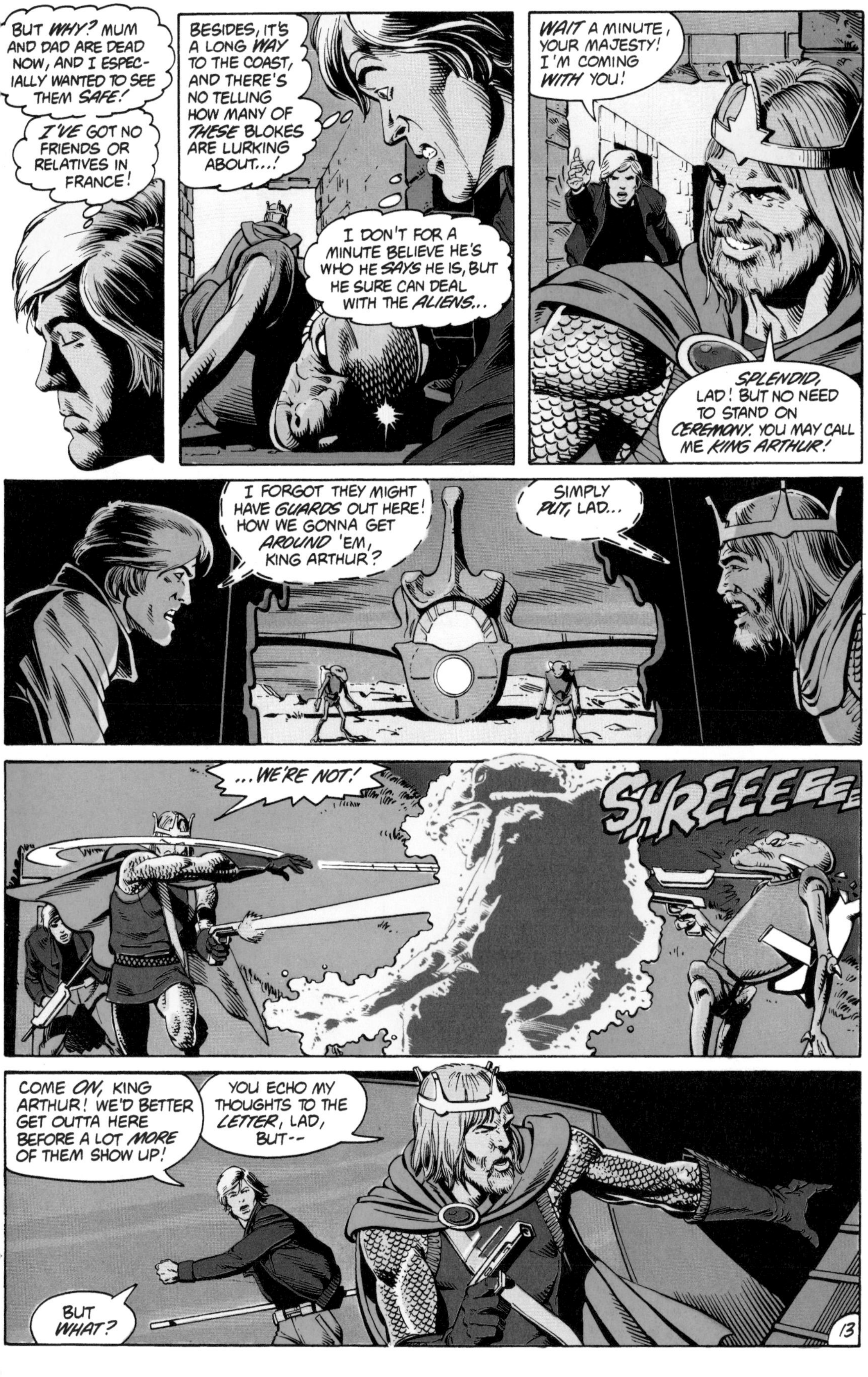

BUT WHY? MUM AND DAD ARE DEAD NOW, AND I ESPECIALLY WANTED TO SEE THEM SAFE!
I'VE GOT NO FRIENDS OR RELATIVES IN FRANCE!
BESIDES, IT'S A LONG WAY TO THE COAST, AND THERE'S NO TELLING HOW MANY OF THESE BLOKES ARE LURKING ABOUT...!
I DON'T FOR A MINUTE BELIEVE HE'S WHO HE SAYS HE IS, BUT HE SURE CAN DEAL WITH THE ALIENS...
WAIT A MINUTE, YOUR MAJESTY! I'M COMING WITH YOU!
SPLENDID, LAD! BUT NO NEED TO STAND ON CEREMONY. YOU MAY CALL ME KING ARTHUR!
I FORGOT THEY MIGHT HAVE GUARDS OUT HERE! HOW WE GONNA GET AROUND 'EM, KING ARTHUR?
SIMPLY PUT, LAD...
...WE'RE NOT!
SHREEEEEE
COME ON, KING ARTHUR! WE'D BETTER GET OUTTA HERE BEFORE A LOT MORE OF THEM SHOW UP!
YOU ECHO MY THOUGHTS TO THE LETTER, LAD, BUT--
BUT WHAT?
13

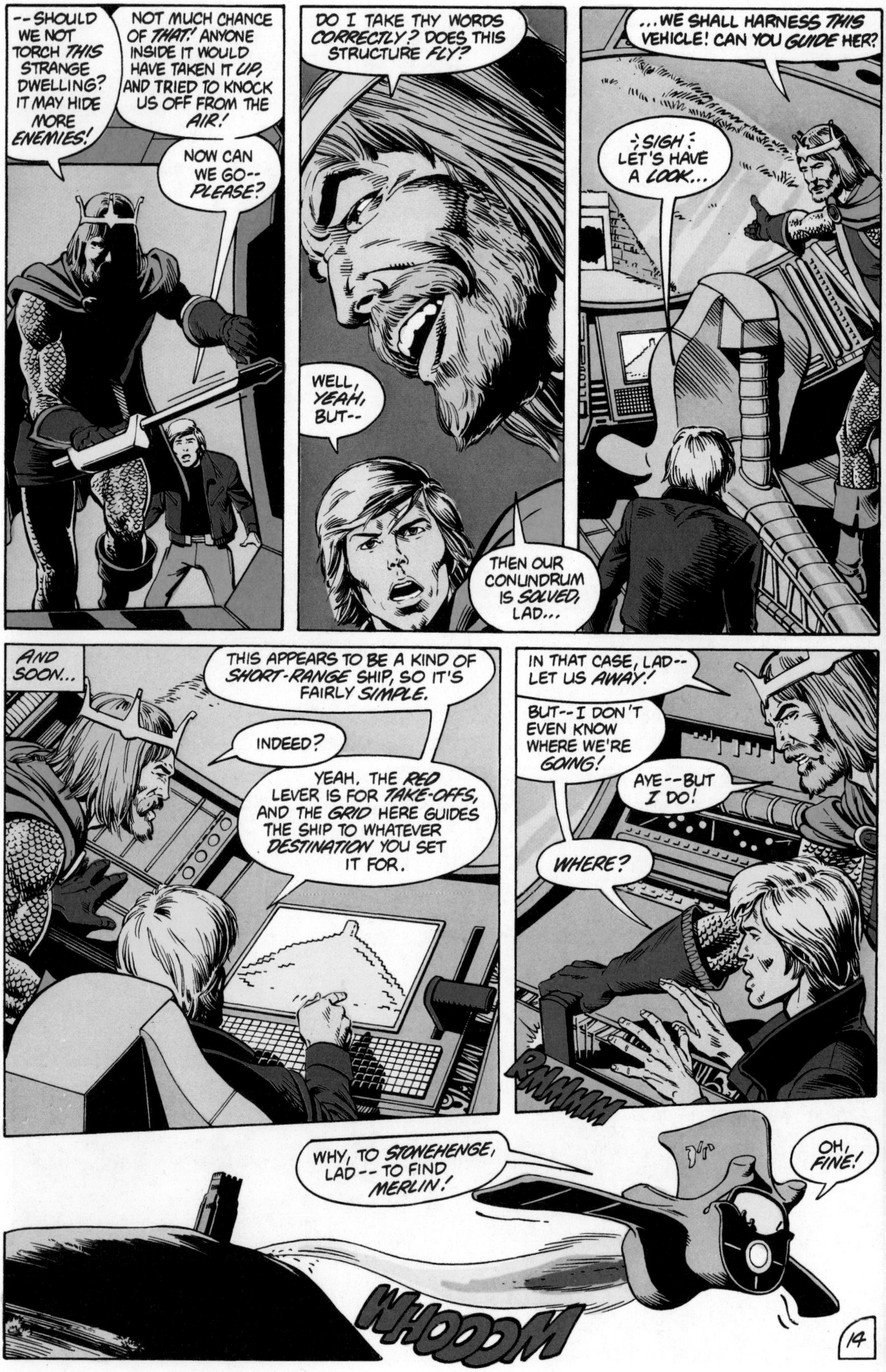
--SHOULD WE NOT TORCH THIS STRANGE DWELLING? IT MAY HIDE MORE ENEMIES!
NOT MUCH CHANCE OF THAT! ANYONE INSIDE IT WOULD HAVE TAKEN IT UP, AND TRIED TO KNOCK US OFF FROM THE AIR!
NOW CAN WE GO-- PLEASE?
DO I TAKE THY WORDS CORRECTLY? DOES THIS STRUCTURE FLY?
WELL, YEAH, BUT--
THEN OUR CONUNDRUM IS SOLVED, LAD...
...WE SHALL HARNESS THIS VEHICLE! CAN YOU GUIDE HER?
-SIGH- LET'S HAVE A LOOK...
AND SOON...
THIS APPEARS TO BE A KIND OF SHORT-RANGE SHIP, SO IT'S FAIRLY SIMPLE.
INDEED?
YEAH, THE RED LEVER IS FOR TAKE-OFFS, AND THE GRID HERE GUIDES THE SHIP TO WHATEVER DESTINATION YOU SET IT FOR.
IN THAT CASE, LAD-- LET US AWAY!
BUT--I DON'T EVEN KNOW WHERE WE'RE GOING!
AYE--BUT I DO!
WHERE?
RMMMM
WHY, TO STONEHENGE, LAD--TO FIND MERLIN!
OH, FINE!
WHOOOM
14

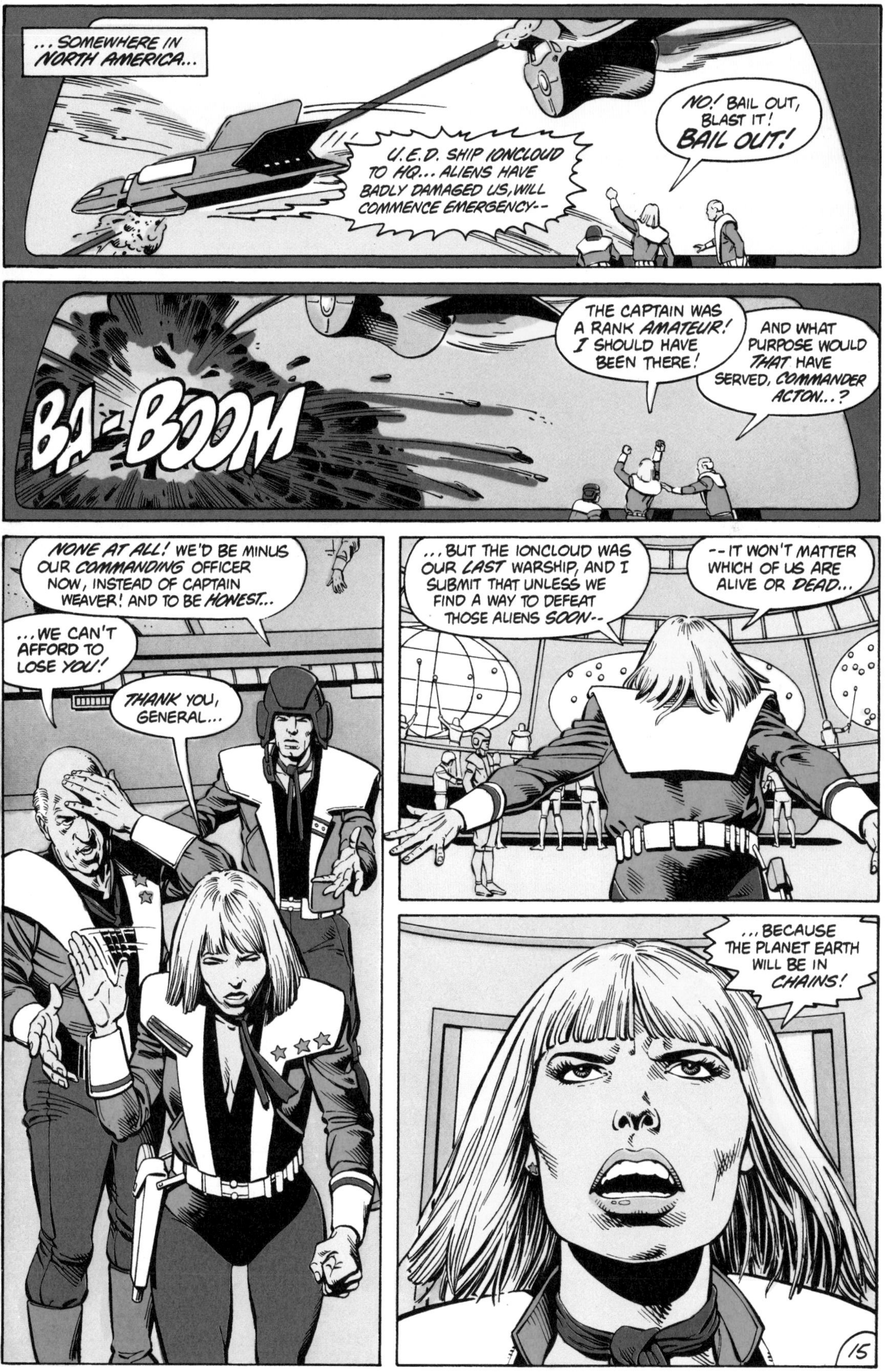
...SOMEWHERE IN NORTH AMERICA...
U.E.D. SHIP IONCLOUD TO HQ... ALIENS HAVE BADLY DAMAGED US, WILL COMMENCE EMERGENCY--
NO! BAIL OUT, BLAST IT! BAIL OUT!
BA-BOOM
THE CAPTAIN WAS A RANK AMATEUR! I SHOULD HAVE BEEN THERE!
AND WHAT PURPOSE WOULD THAT HAVE SERVED, COMMANDER ACTON...?
NONE AT ALL! WE'D BE MINUS OUR COMMANDING OFFICER NOW, INSTEAD OF CAPTAIN WEAVER! AND TO BE HONEST...
...WE CAN'T AFFORD TO LOSE YOU!
THANK YOU, GENERAL...
...BUT THE IONCLOUD WAS OUR LAST WARSHIP, AND I SUBMIT THAT UNLESS WE FIND A WAY TO DEFEAT THOSE ALIENS SOON--
--IT WON'T MATTER WHICH OF US ARE ALIVE OR DEAD...
...BECAUSE THE PLANET EARTH WILL BE IN CHAINS!
15

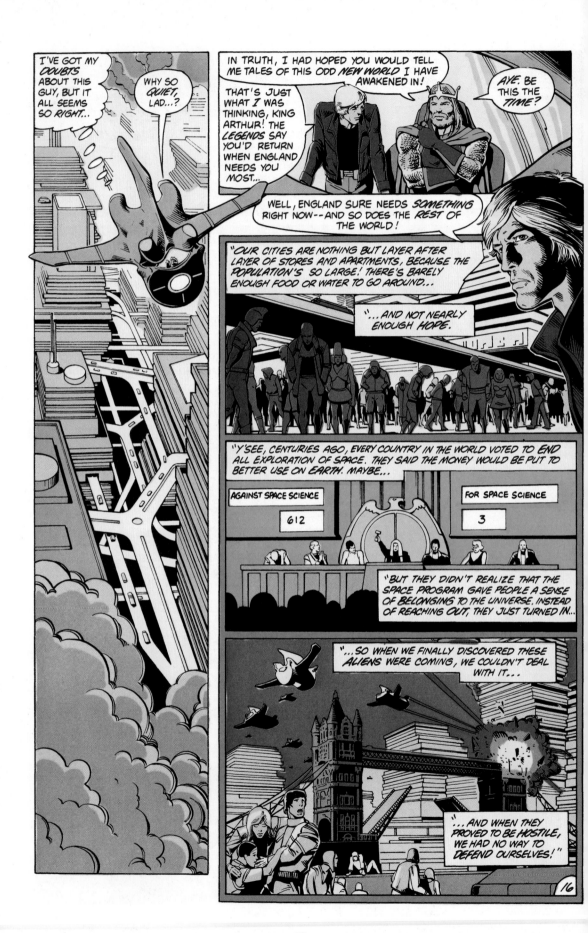

I'VE GOT MY *DOUBTS* ABOUT THIS GUY, BUT IT ALL SEEMS SO *RIGHT*...

WHY SO *QUIET*, LAD...?

IN TRUTH, I HAD HOPED YOU WOULD TELL ME TALES OF THIS ODD *NEW WORLD* I HAVE AWAKENED IN!

AYE. BE THIS THE *TIME*?

THAT'S JUST WHAT *I* WAS THINKING, KING ARTHUR! THE *LEGENDS* SAY YOU'D RETURN WHEN ENGLAND NEEDS YOU MOST...

WELL, ENGLAND SURE NEEDS *SOMETHING* RIGHT NOW -- AND SO DOES THE *REST OF THE WORLD*!

"OUR CITIES ARE NOTHING BUT LAYER AFTER LAYER OF STORES AND APARTMENTS, BECAUSE THE *POPULATION'S* SO LARGE! THERE'S BARELY ENOUGH FOOD OR WATER TO GO AROUND...

"...AND NOT NEARLY ENOUGH *HOPE*.

"Y'SEE, CENTURIES AGO, EVERY COUNTRY IN THE WORLD VOTED TO *END* ALL EXPLORATION OF SPACE. THEY SAID THE MONEY WOULD BE PUT TO BETTER USE ON *EARTH*. MAYBE...

AGAINST SPACE SCIENCE	FOR SPACE SCIENCE
612	3

"BUT THEY DIDN'T REALIZE THAT THE SPACE PROGRAM GAVE PEOPLE A SENSE OF *BELONGING* TO THE UNIVERSE. INSTEAD OF REACHING *OUT*, THEY JUST TURNED IN...

"...SO WHEN WE FINALLY DISCOVERED THESE *ALIENS* WERE COMING, WE COULDN'T DEAL WITH IT...

"...AND WHEN THEY PROVED TO BE HOSTILE, WE HAD NO WAY TO DEFEND OURSELVES!"

16

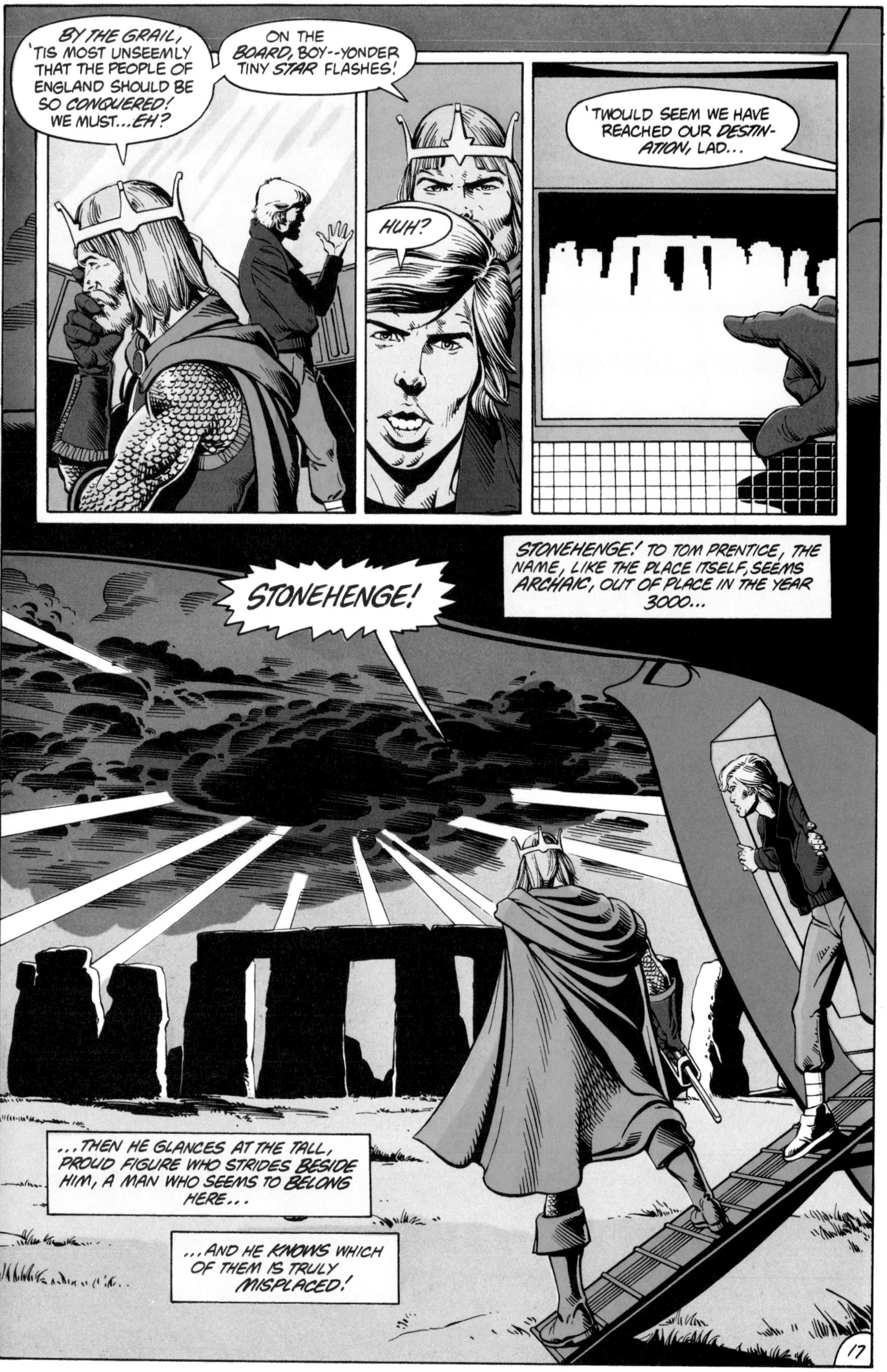
BY THE GRAIL, 'TIS MOST UNSEEMLY THAT THE PEOPLE OF ENGLAND SHOULD BE SO CONQUERED! WE MUST...EH?
ON THE BOARD, BOY--YONDER TINY STAR FLASHES!
HUH?
'TWOULD SEEM WE HAVE REACHED OUR DESTINATION, LAD...
STONEHENGE!
STONEHENGE! TO TOM PRENTICE, THE NAME, LIKE THE PLACE ITSELF, SEEMS ARCHAIC, OUT OF PLACE IN THE YEAR 3000...
...THEN HE GLANCES AT THE TALL, PROUD FIGURE WHO STRIDES BESIDE HIM, A MAN WHO SEEMS TO BELONG HERE...
...AND HE KNOWS WHICH OF THEM IS TRULY MISPLACED!
17

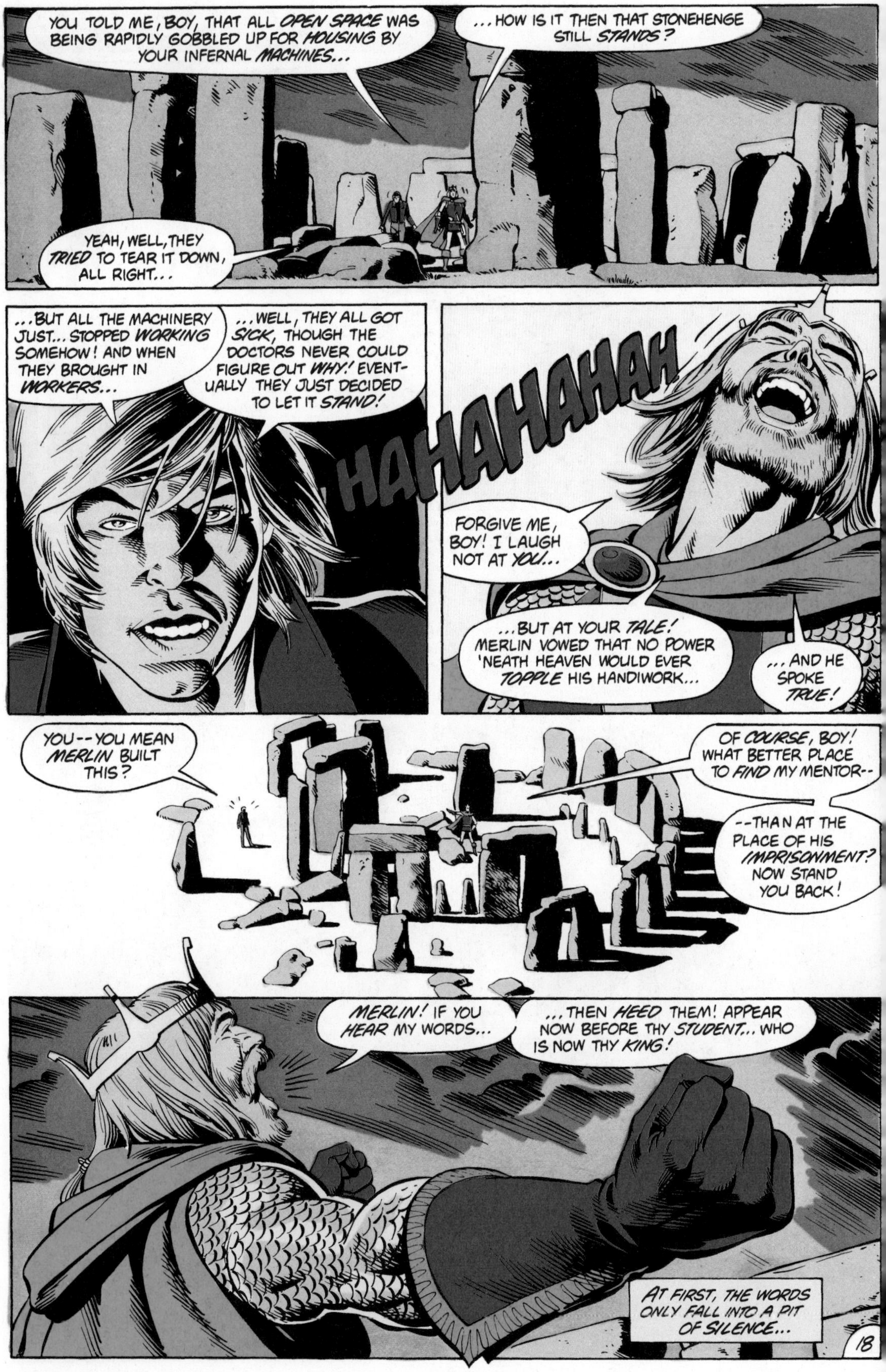
YOU TOLD ME, BOY, THAT ALL OPEN SPACE WAS BEING RAPIDLY GOBBLED UP FOR HOUSING BY YOUR INFERNAL MACHINES...
...HOW IS IT THEN THAT STONEHENGE STILL STANDS?
YEAH, WELL, THEY TRIED TO TEAR IT DOWN, ALL RIGHT...
...BUT ALL THE MACHINERY JUST... STOPPED WORKING SOMEHOW! AND WHEN THEY BROUGHT IN WORKERS...
...WELL, THEY ALL GOT SICK, THOUGH THE DOCTORS NEVER COULD FIGURE OUT WHY! EVENT-UALLY THEY JUST DECIDED TO LET IT STAND!
HAHAHAHAHAH
FORGIVE ME, BOY! I LAUGH NOT AT YOU...
...BUT AT YOUR TALE! MERLIN VOWED THAT NO POWER 'NEATH HEAVEN WOULD EVER TOPPLE HIS HANDIWORK...
...AND HE SPOKE TRUE!
YOU--YOU MEAN MERLIN BUILT THIS?
OF COURSE, BOY! WHAT BETTER PLACE TO FIND MY MENTOR--
--THAN AT THE PLACE OF HIS IMPRISONMENT? NOW STAND YOU BACK!
MERLIN! IF YOU HEAR MY WORDS...
...THEN HEED THEM! APPEAR NOW BEFORE THY STUDENT... WHO IS NOW THY KING!
AT FIRST, THE WORDS ONLY FALL INTO A PIT OF SILENCE...
18

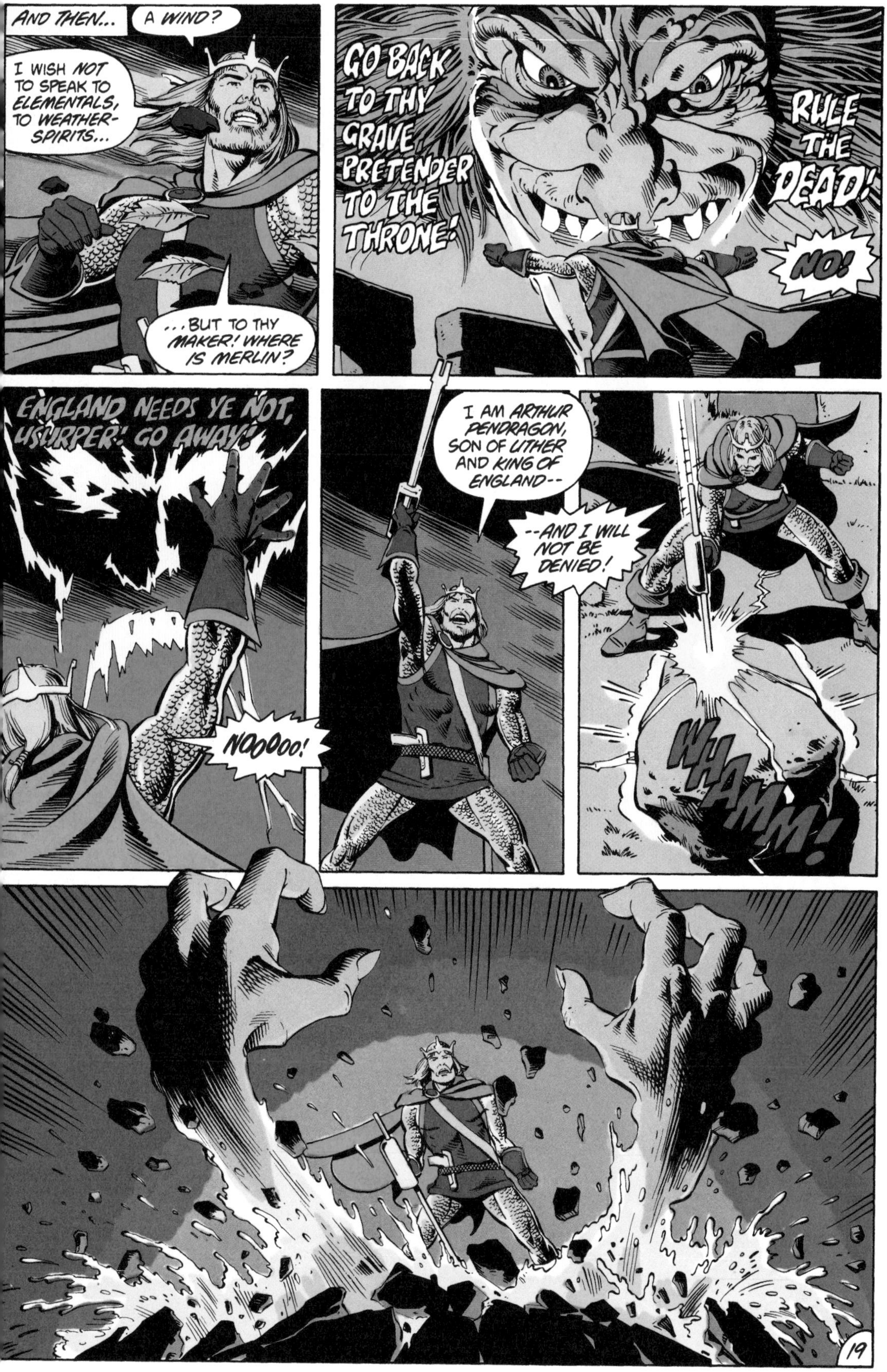
AND THEN...
A WIND?
I WISH NOT TO SPEAK TO ELEMENTALS, TO WEATHER-SPIRITS...
...BUT TO THY MAKER! WHERE IS MERLIN?
GO BACK TO THY GRAVE PRETENDER TO THE THRONE!
RULE THE DEAD!
NO!
ENGLAND NEEDS YE NOT, USURPER! GO AWAY!
NOOOOO!
I AM ARTHUR PENDRAGON, SON OF UTHER AND KING OF ENGLAND--
--AND I WILL NOT BE DENIED!
WHAMM!
19

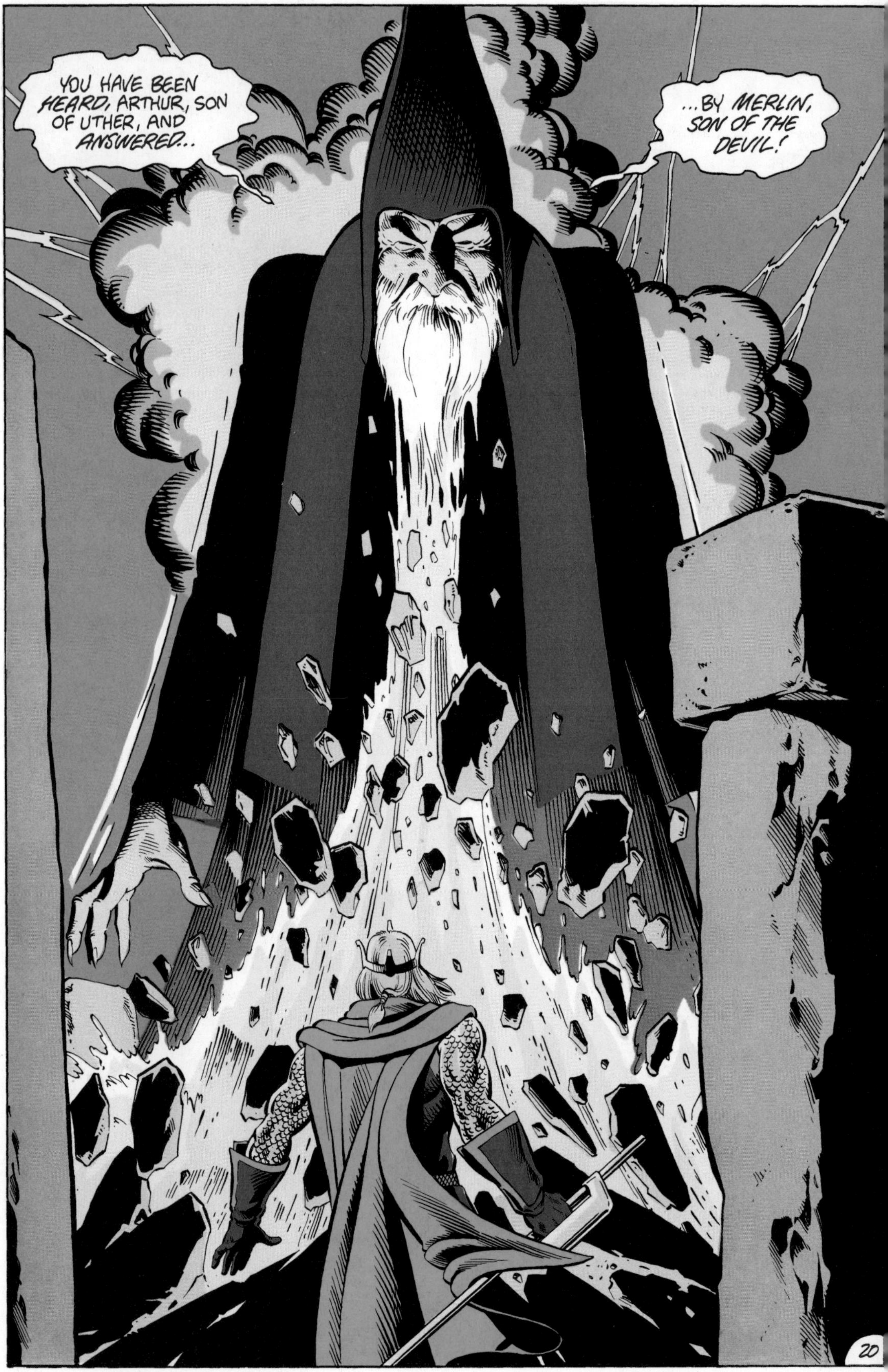
YOU HAVE BEEN HEARD, ARTHUR, SON OF UTHER, AND ANSWERED...
...BY MERLIN, SON OF THE DEVIL!
20

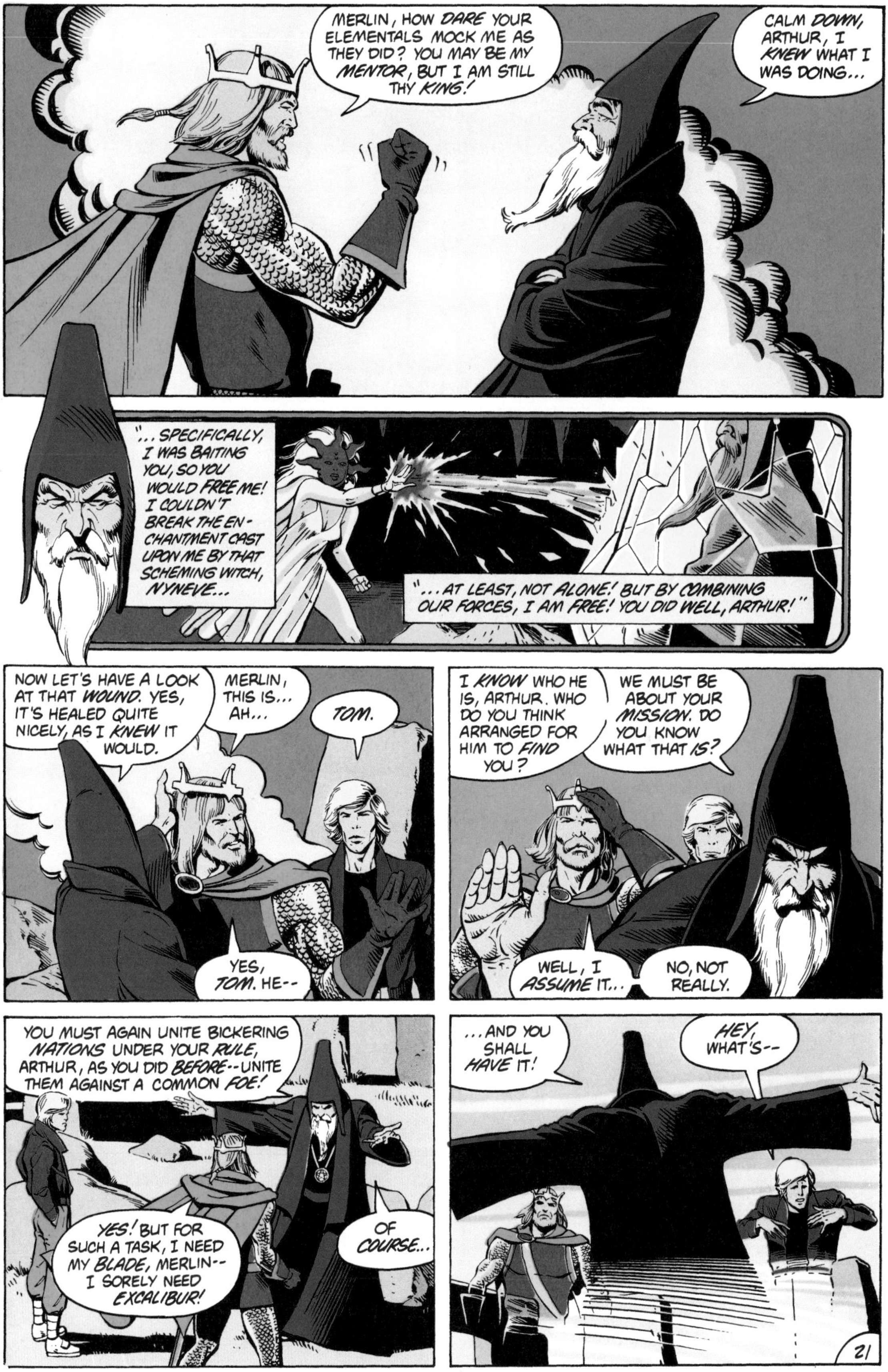
MERLIN, HOW DARE YOUR ELEMENTALS MOCK ME AS THEY DID? YOU MAY BE MY MENTOR, BUT I AM STILL THY KING!
CALM DOWN, ARTHUR, I KNEW WHAT I WAS DOING...
"...SPECIFICALLY, I WAS BAITING YOU, SO YOU WOULD FREE ME! I COULDN'T BREAK THE EN-CHANTMENT CAST UPON ME BY THAT SCHEMING WITCH, NYNEVE...
"...AT LEAST, NOT ALONE! BUT BY COMBINING OUR FORCES, I AM FREE! YOU DID WELL, ARTHUR!"
NOW LET'S HAVE A LOOK AT THAT WOUND. YES, IT'S HEALED QUITE NICELY, AS I KNEW IT WOULD.
MERLIN, THIS IS... AH...
TOM.
YES, TOM. HE--
I KNOW WHO HE IS, ARTHUR. WHO DO YOU THINK ARRANGED FOR HIM TO FIND YOU?
WE MUST BE ABOUT YOUR MISSION. DO YOU KNOW WHAT THAT IS?
WELL, I ASSUME IT...
NO, NOT REALLY.
YOU MUST AGAIN UNITE BICKERING NATIONS UNDER YOUR RULE, ARTHUR, AS YOU DID BEFORE--UNITE THEM AGAINST A COMMON FOE!
YES! BUT FOR SUCH A TASK, I NEED MY BLADE, MERLIN-- I SORELY NEED EXCALIBUR!
OF COURSE...
...AND YOU SHALL HAVE IT!
HEY, WHAT'S--
21

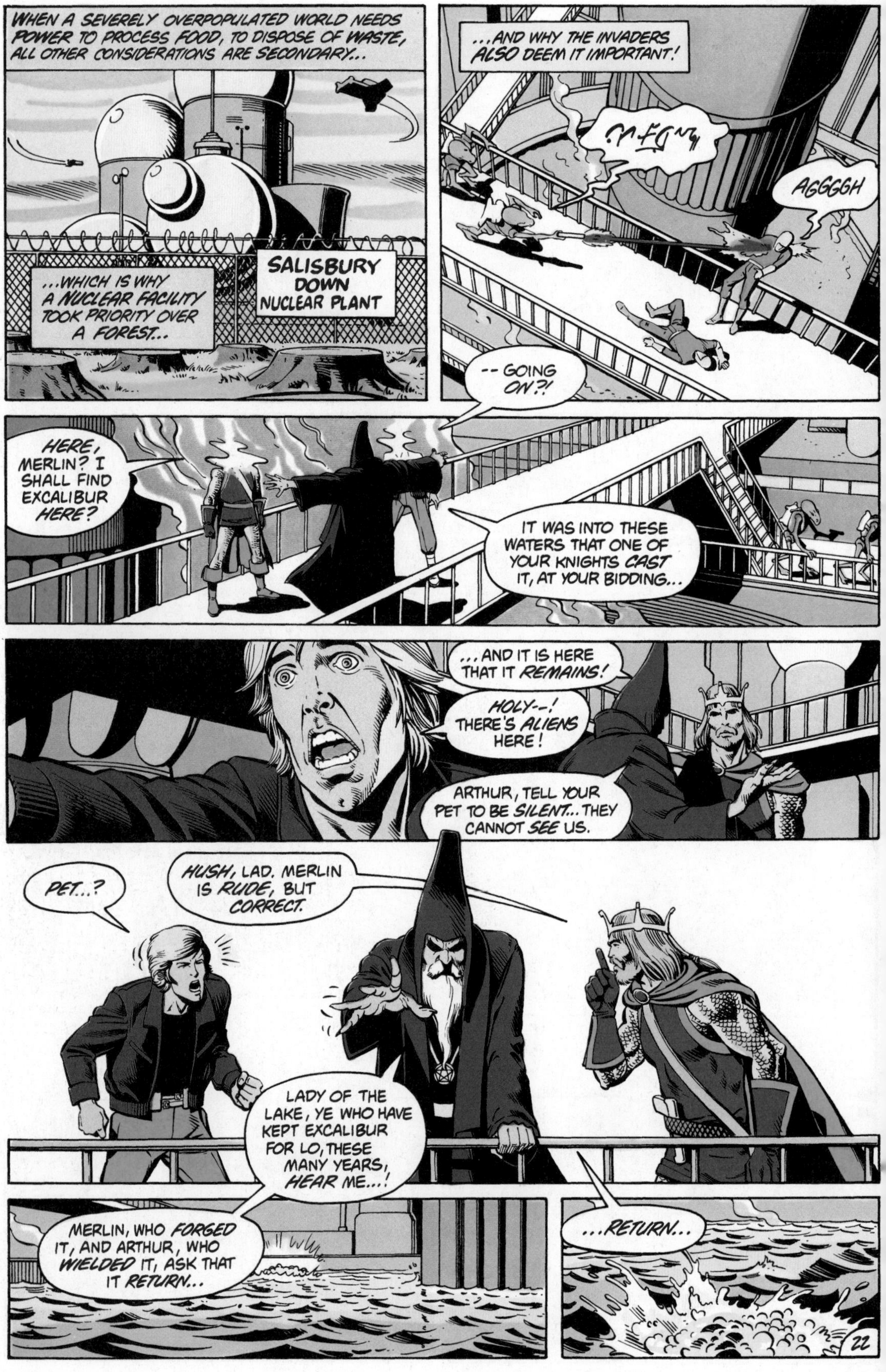

WHEN A SEVERELY OVERPOPULATED WORLD NEEDS POWER TO PROCESS FOOD, TO DISPOSE OF WASTE, ALL OTHER CONSIDERATIONS ARE SECONDARY...
...WHICH IS WHY A NUCLEAR FACILITY TOOK PRIORITY OVER A FOREST...
SALISBURY DOWN NUCLEAR PLANT
...AND WHY THE INVADERS ALSO DEEM IT IMPORTANT!
AGGGGH
-- GOING ON?!
HERE, MERLIN? I SHALL FIND EXCALIBUR HERE?
IT WAS INTO THESE WATERS THAT ONE OF YOUR KNIGHTS CAST IT, AT YOUR BIDDING...
...AND IT IS HERE THAT IT REMAINS!
HOLY--! THERE'S ALIENS HERE!
ARTHUR, TELL YOUR PET TO BE SILENT... THEY CANNOT SEE US.
PET...?
HUSH, LAD. MERLIN IS RUDE, BUT CORRECT.
LADY OF THE LAKE, YE WHO HAVE KEPT EXCALIBUR FOR LO, THESE MANY YEARS, HEAR ME...!
MERLIN, WHO FORGED IT, AND ARTHUR, WHO WIELDED IT, ASK THAT IT RETURN...
...RETURN...
22

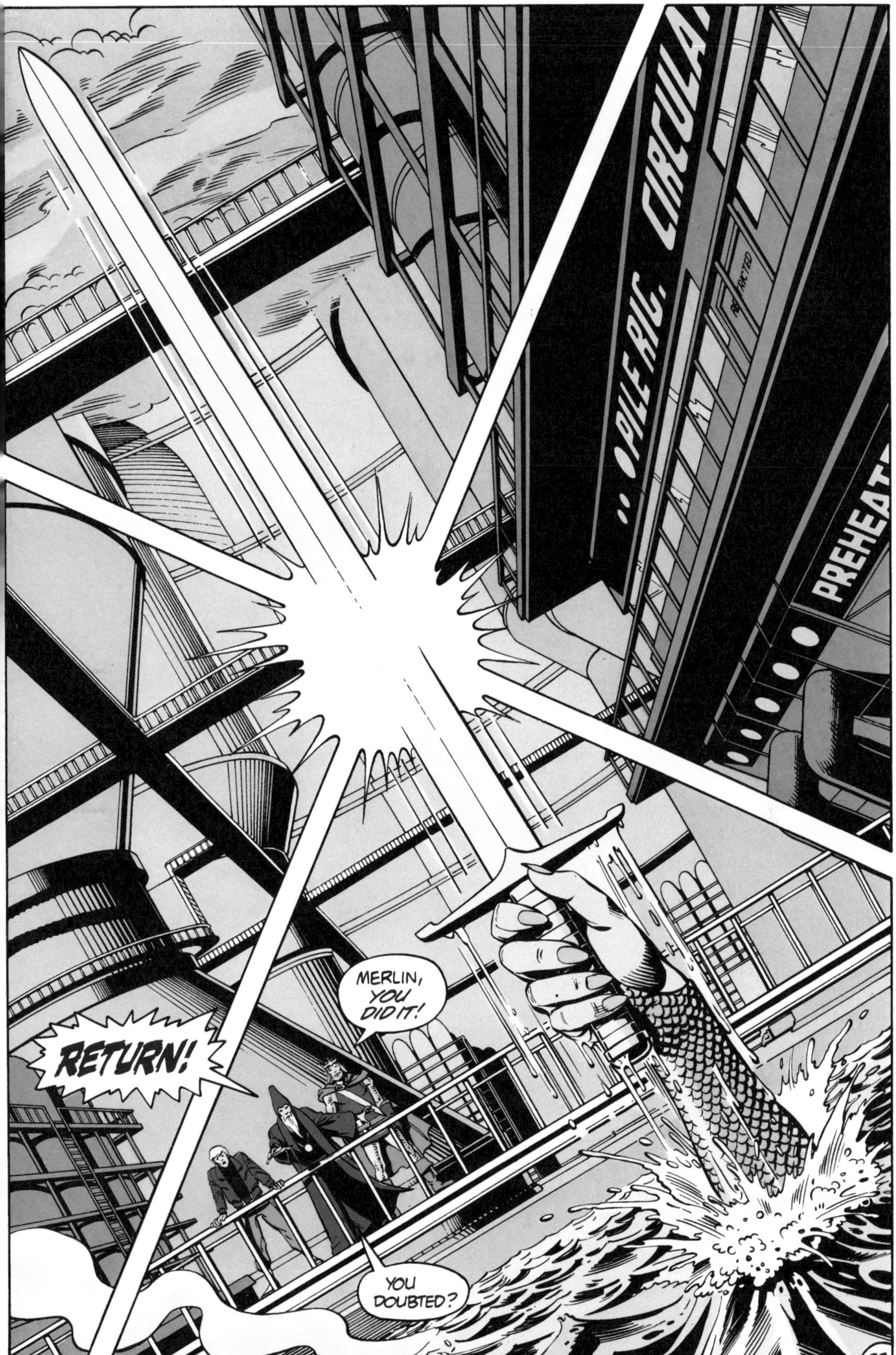
PILE RIG. CIRCULA
RESTRICTED
PREHEAT
MERLIN, YOU DID IT!
RETURN!
YOU DOUBTED?
23

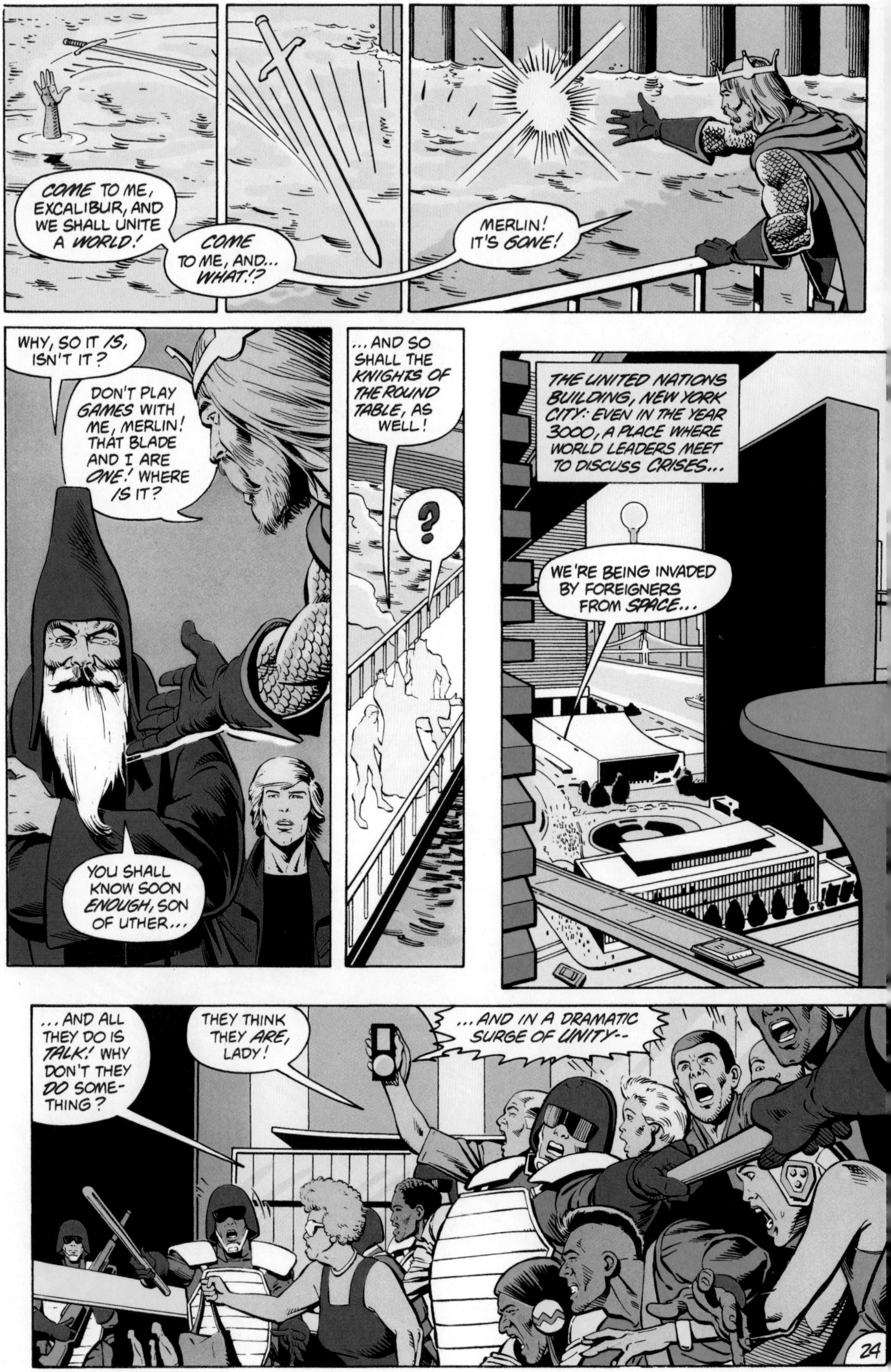
COME TO ME, EXCALIBUR, AND WE SHALL UNITE A WORLD!
COME TO ME, AND... WHAT!?
MERLIN! IT'S GONE!
WHY, SO IT IS, ISN'T IT?
DON'T PLAY GAMES WITH ME, MERLIN! THAT BLADE AND I ARE ONE! WHERE IS IT?
YOU SHALL KNOW SOON ENOUGH, SON OF UTHER...
...AND SO SHALL THE KNIGHTS OF THE ROUND TABLE, AS WELL!
?
THE UNITED NATIONS BUILDING, NEW YORK CITY: EVEN IN THE YEAR 3000, A PLACE WHERE WORLD LEADERS MEET TO DISCUSS CRISES...
WE'RE BEING INVADED BY FOREIGNERS FROM SPACE...
...AND ALL THEY DO IS TALK! WHY DON'T THEY DO SOMETHING?
THEY THINK THEY ARE, LADY!
...AND IN A DRAMATIC SURGE OF UNITY--
24

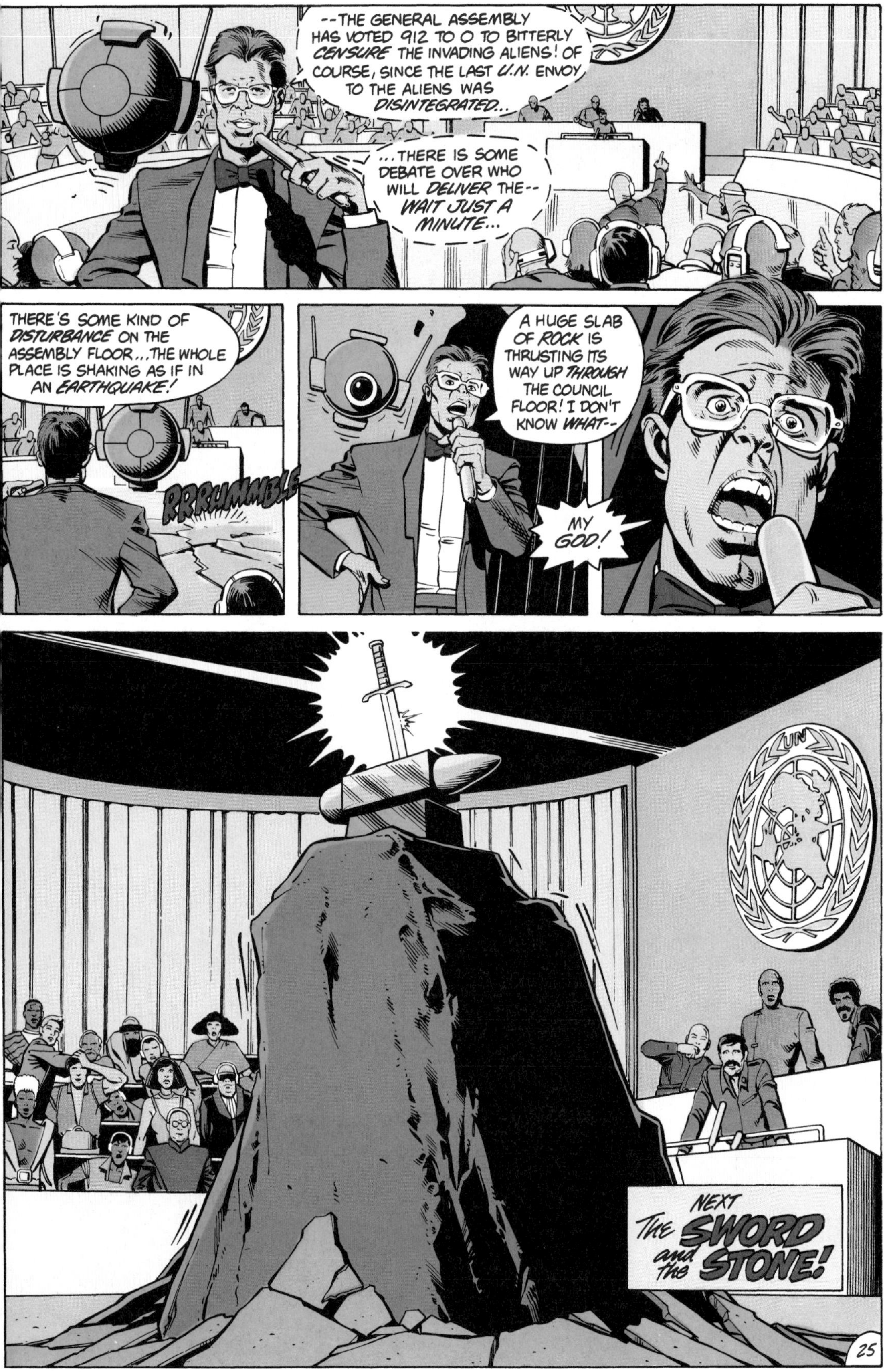
--THE GENERAL ASSEMBLY HAS VOTED 912 TO 0 TO BITTERLY CENSURE THE INVADING ALIENS! OF COURSE, SINCE THE LAST U.N. ENVOY TO THE ALIENS WAS DISINTEGRATED...
...THERE IS SOME DEBATE OVER WHO WILL DELIVER THE--WAIT JUST A MINUTE...
THERE'S SOME KIND OF DISTURBANCE ON THE ASSEMBLY FLOOR...THE WHOLE PLACE IS SHAKING AS IF IN AN EARTHQUAKE!
RRRUMMBLE
A HUGE SLAB OF ROCK IS THRUSTING ITS WAY UP THROUGH THE COUNCIL FLOOR! I DON'T KNOW WHAT--
MY GOD!
UN
NEXT The SWORD and the STONE!
25

Eye of the hunter, piercing the morn...

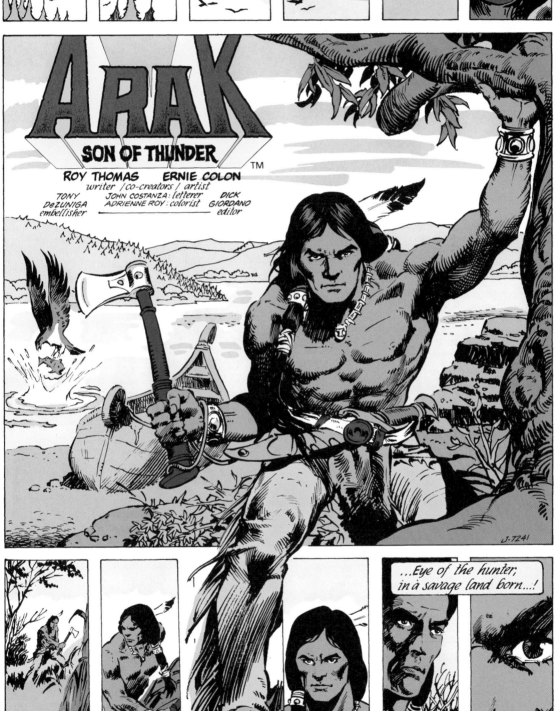

ARAK
SON OF THUNDER ™

ROY THOMAS   ERNIE COLON
writer /co-creators / artist

TONY DeZUNIGA   JOHN COSTANZA: letterer   DICK GIORDANO
embellisher   ADRIENNE ROY: colorist   editor

J-7241

...Eye of the hunter, in a savage land born....!

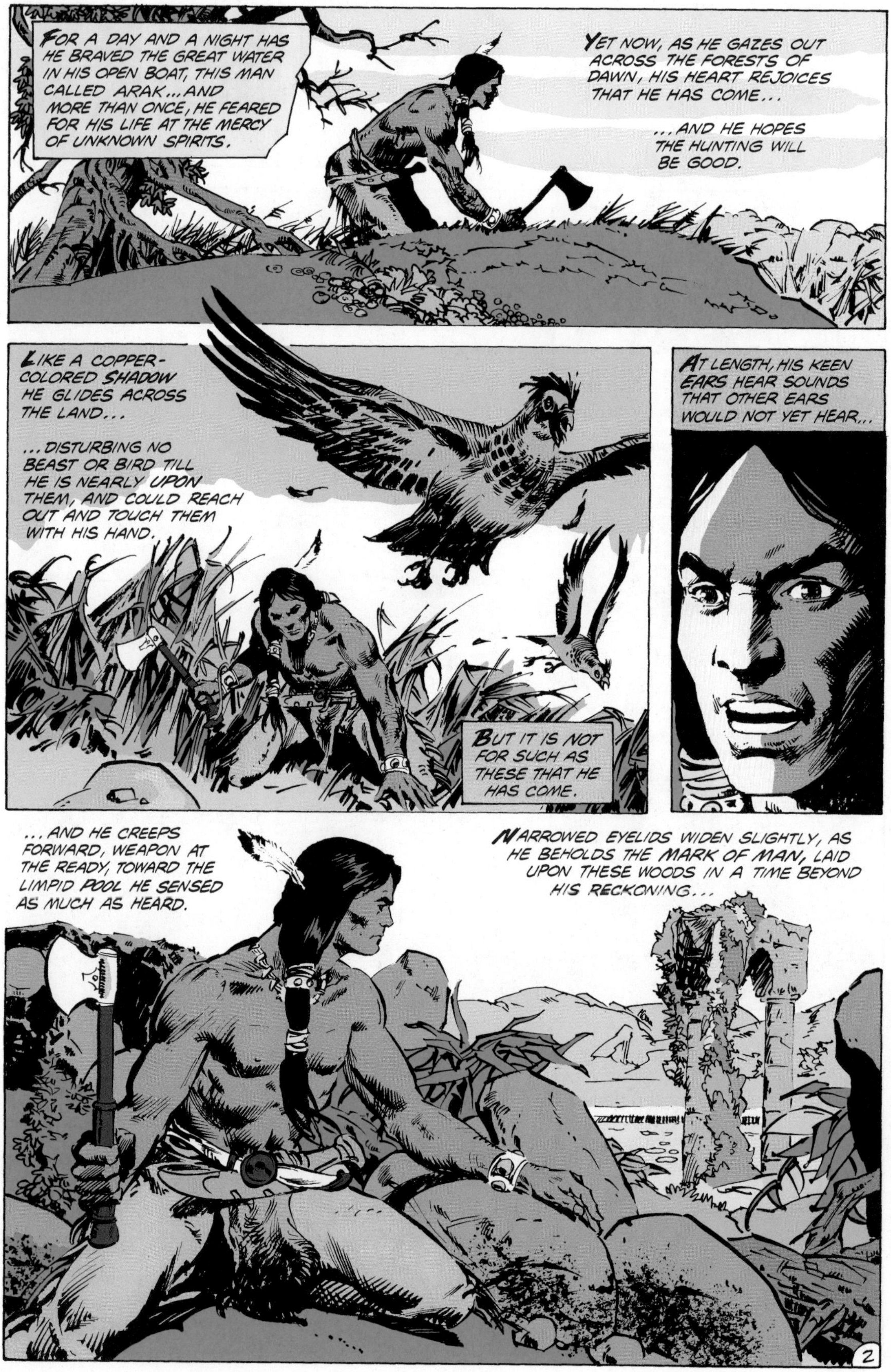
FOR A DAY AND A NIGHT HAS HE BRAVED THE GREAT WATER IN HIS OPEN BOAT, THIS MAN CALLED ARAK...AND MORE THAN ONCE, HE FEARED FOR HIS LIFE AT THE MERCY OF UNKNOWN SPIRITS.
YET NOW, AS HE GAZES OUT ACROSS THE FORESTS OF DAWN, HIS HEART REJOICES THAT HE HAS COME...
...AND HE HOPES THE HUNTING WILL BE GOOD.
LIKE A COPPER-COLORED SHADOW HE GLIDES ACROSS THE LAND...
...DISTURBING NO BEAST OR BIRD TILL HE IS NEARLY UPON THEM, AND COULD REACH OUT AND TOUCH THEM WITH HIS HAND.
BUT IT IS NOT FOR SUCH AS THESE THAT HE HAS COME.
AT LENGTH, HIS KEEN EARS HEAR SOUNDS THAT OTHER EARS WOULD NOT YET HEAR...
...AND HE CREEPS FORWARD, WEAPON AT THE READY, TOWARD THE LIMPID POOL HE SENSED AS MUCH AS HEARD.
NARROWED EYELIDS WIDEN SLIGHTLY, AS HE BEHOLDS THE MARK OF MAN, LAID UPON THESE WOODS IN A TIME BEYOND HIS RECKONING...
2

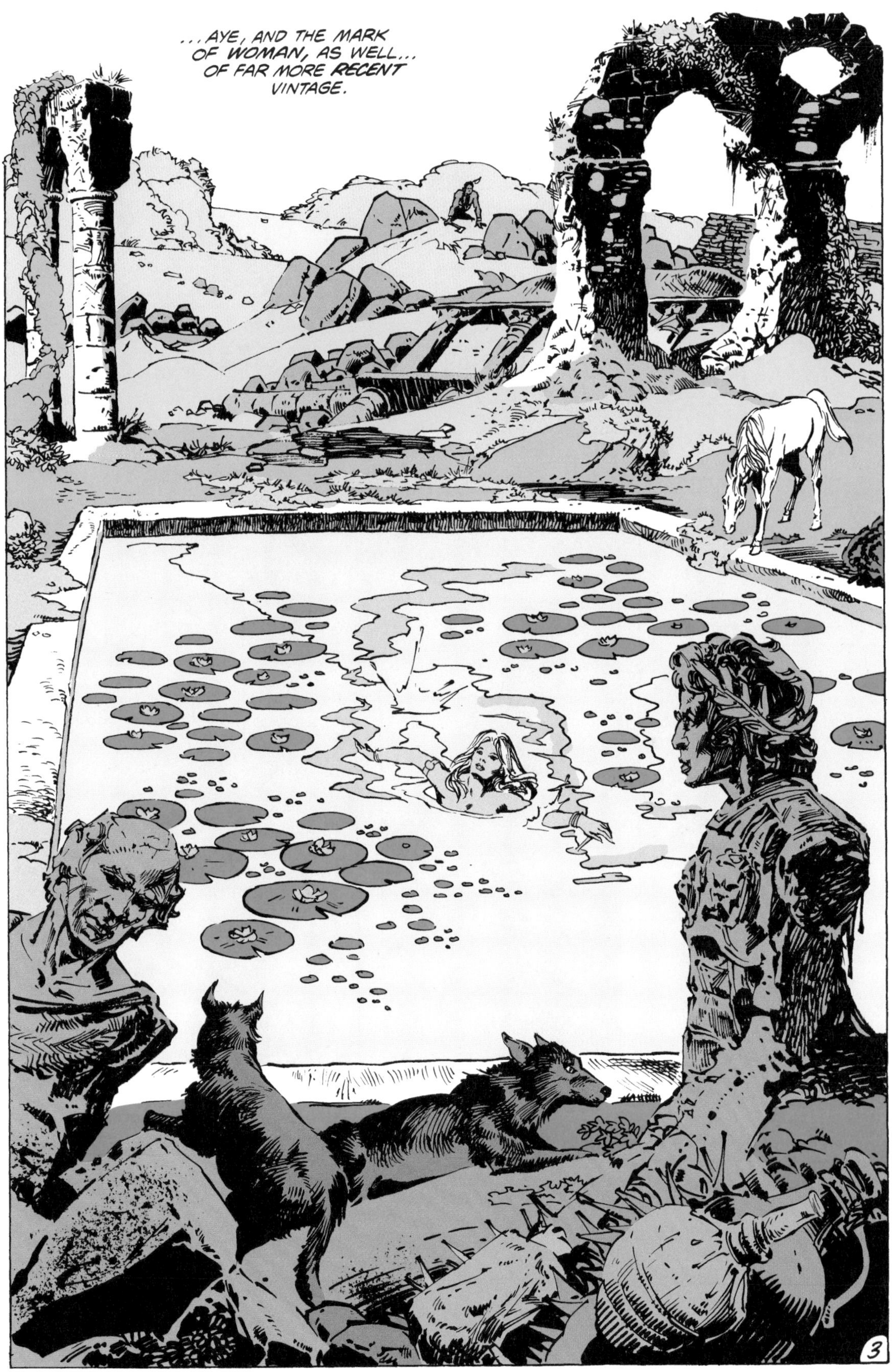
...AYE, AND THE MARK OF WOMAN, AS WELL... OF FAR MORE RECENT VINTAGE.
3

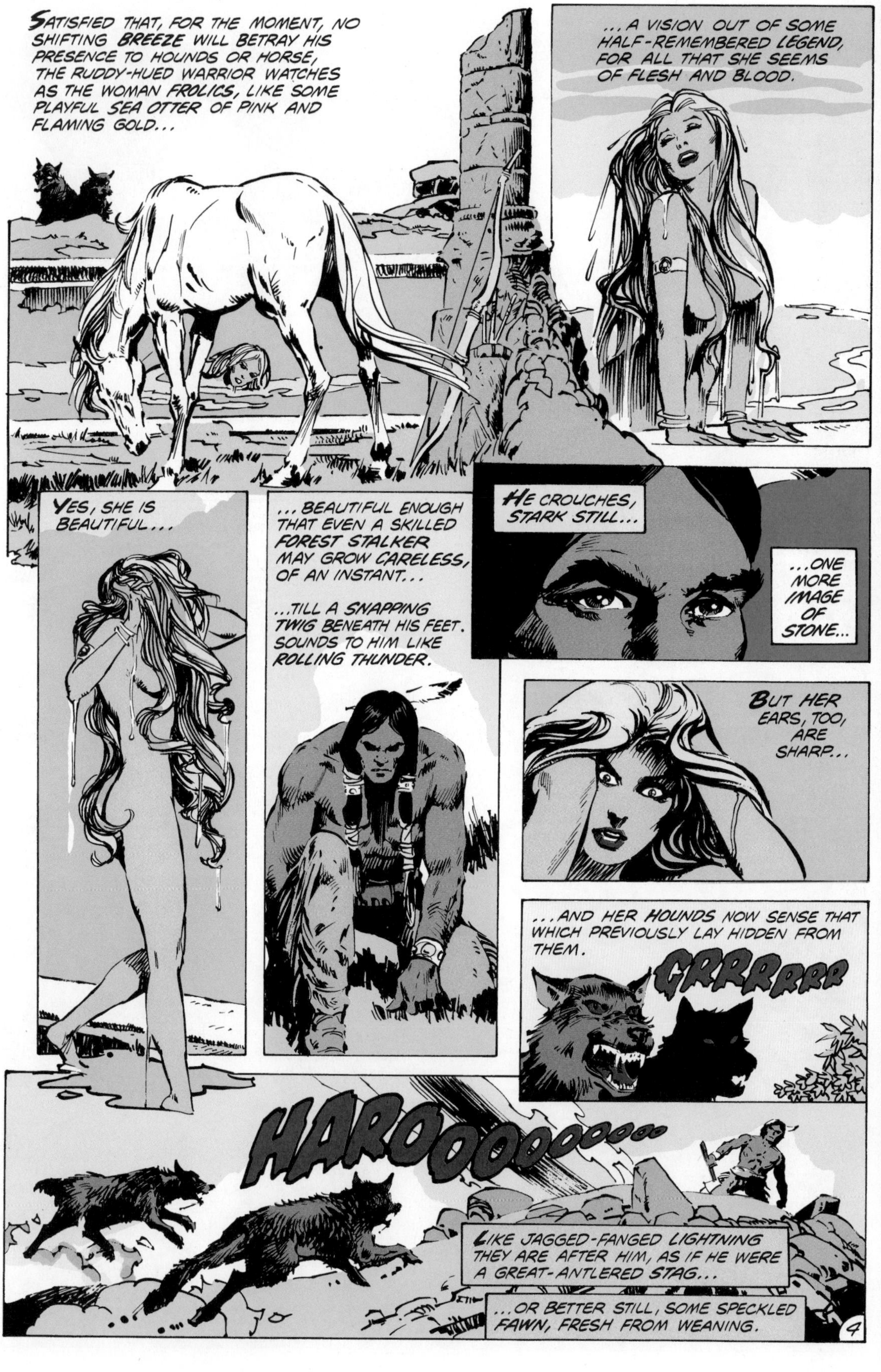
SATISFIED THAT, FOR THE MOMENT, NO SHIFTING BREEZE WILL BETRAY HIS PRESENCE TO HOUNDS OR HORSE, THE RUDDY-HUED WARRIOR WATCHES AS THE WOMAN FROLICS, LIKE SOME PLAYFUL SEA OTTER OF PINK AND FLAMING GOLD...
...A VISION OUT OF SOME HALF-REMEMBERED LEGEND, FOR ALL THAT SHE SEEMS OF FLESH AND BLOOD.
YES, SHE IS BEAUTIFUL...
...BEAUTIFUL ENOUGH THAT EVEN A SKILLED FOREST STALKER MAY GROW CARELESS, OF AN INSTANT...
...TILL A SNAPPING TWIG BENEATH HIS FEET. SOUNDS TO HIM LIKE ROLLING THUNDER.
HE CROUCHES, STARK STILL...
...ONE MORE IMAGE OF STONE...
BUT HER EARS, TOO, ARE SHARP...
...AND HER HOUNDS NOW SENSE THAT WHICH PREVIOUSLY LAY HIDDEN FROM THEM.
GRRRRRR
HAROOOOOOOOO
LIKE JAGGED-FANGED LIGHTNING THEY ARE AFTER HIM, AS IF HE WERE A GREAT-ANTLERED STAG...
...OR BETTER STILL, SOME SPECKLED FAWN, FRESH FROM WEANING.
4

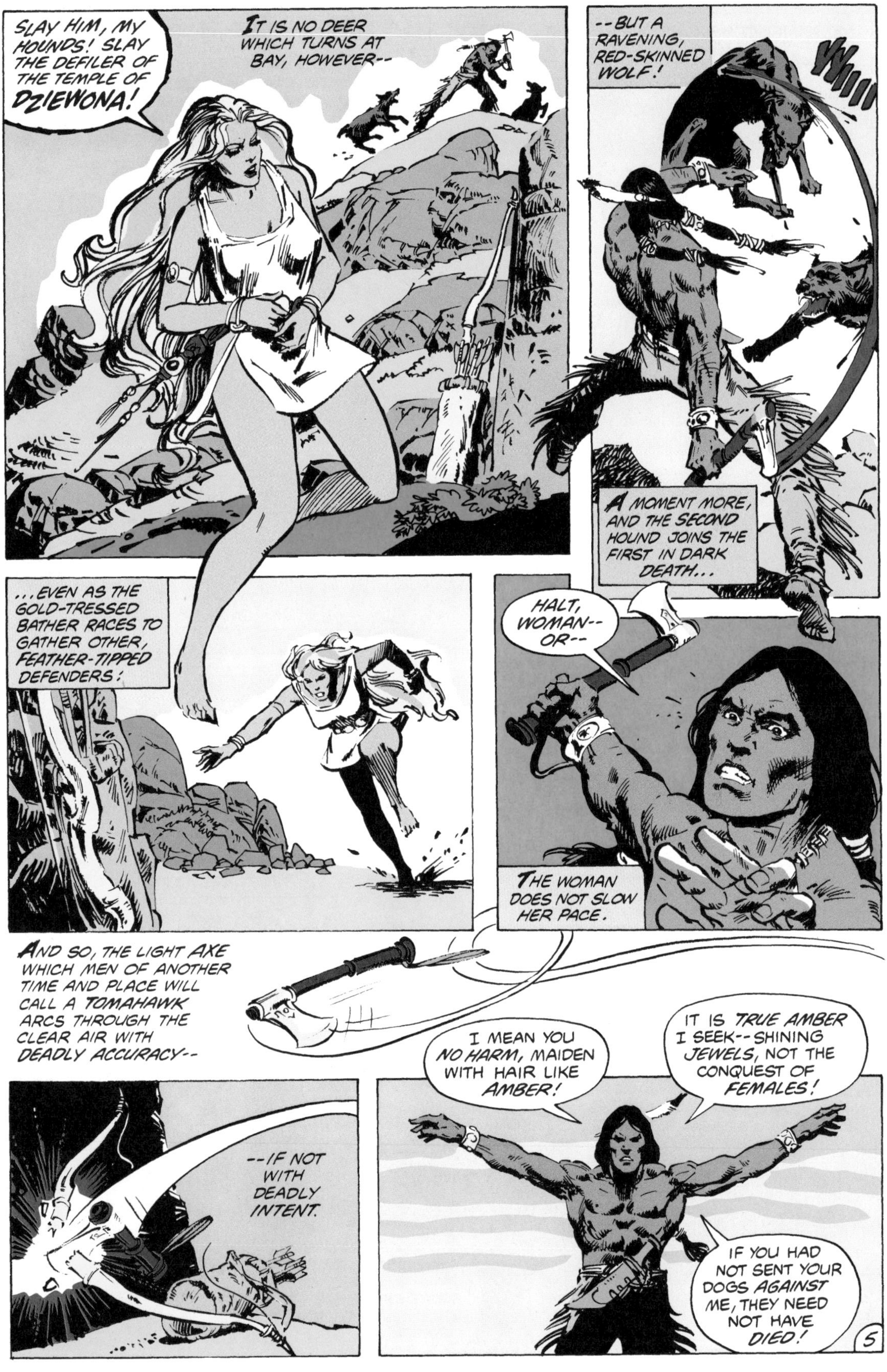
SLAY HIM, MY HOUNDS! SLAY THE DEFILER OF THE TEMPLE OF DZIEWONA!
IT IS NO DEER WHICH TURNS AT BAY, HOWEVER--
--BUT A RAVENING, RED-SKINNED WOLF!
VVIII
A MOMENT MORE, AND THE SECOND HOUND JOINS THE FIRST IN DARK DEATH...
...EVEN AS THE GOLD-TRESSED BATHER RACES TO GATHER OTHER, FEATHER-TIPPED DEFENDERS:
HALT, WOMAN-- OR--
THE WOMAN DOES NOT SLOW HER PACE.
AND SO, THE LIGHT AXE WHICH MEN OF ANOTHER TIME AND PLACE WILL CALL A TOMAHAWK ARCS THROUGH THE CLEAR AIR WITH DEADLY ACCURACY--
--IF NOT WITH DEADLY INTENT.
I MEAN YOU NO HARM, MAIDEN WITH HAIR LIKE AMBER!
IT IS TRUE AMBER I SEEK--SHINING JEWELS, NOT THE CONQUEST OF FEMALES!
IF YOU HAD NOT SENT YOUR DOGS AGAINST ME, THEY NEED NOT HAVE DIED!
5

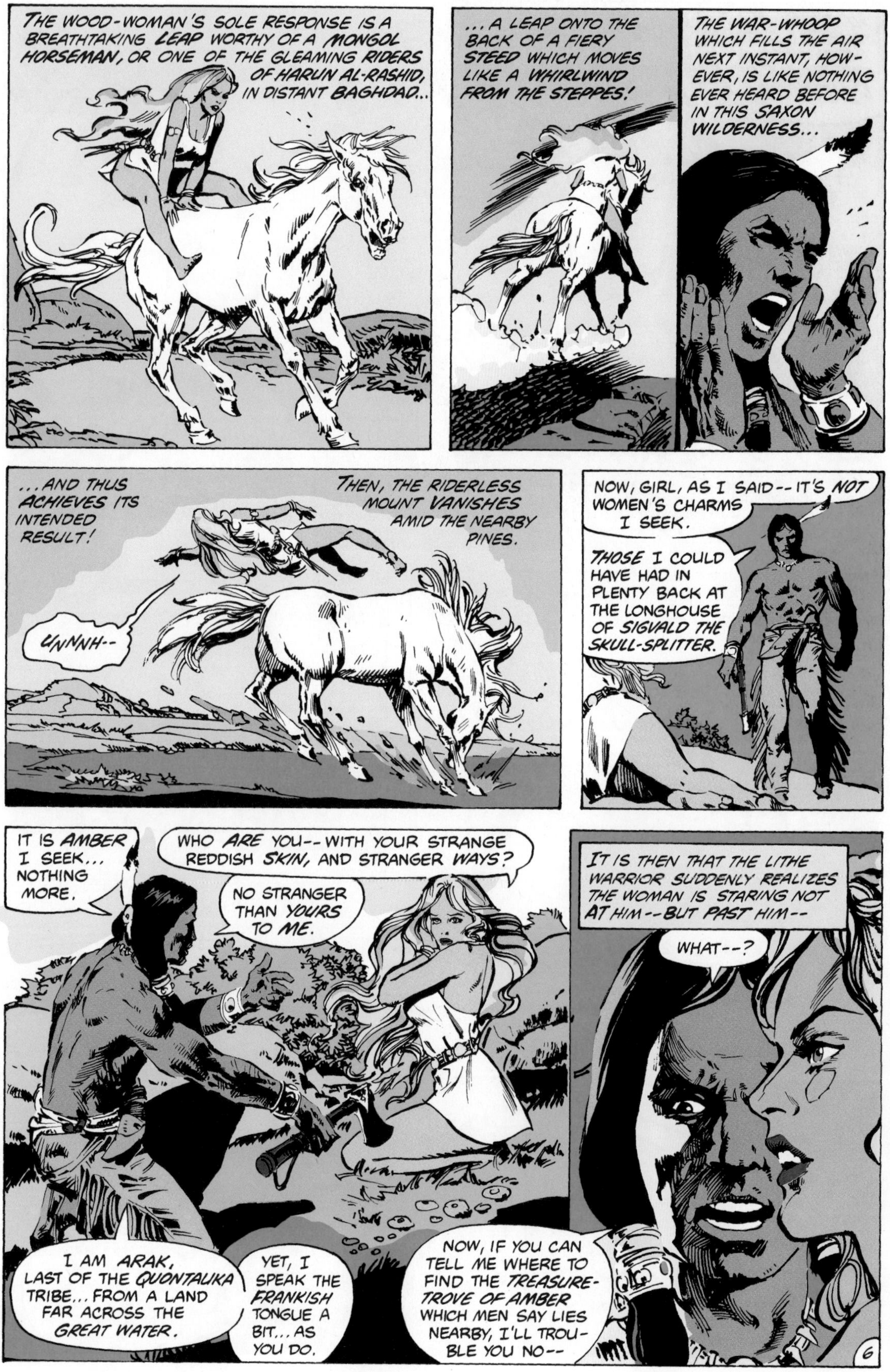

THE WOOD-WOMAN'S SOLE RESPONSE IS A BREATHTAKING LEAP WORTHY OF A MONGOL HORSEMAN, OR ONE OF THE GLEAMING RIDERS OF HARUN AL-RASHID, IN DISTANT BAGHDAD...
...A LEAP ONTO THE BACK OF A FIERY STEED WHICH MOVES LIKE A WHIRLWIND FROM THE STEPPES!
THE WAR-WHOOP WHICH FILLS THE AIR NEXT INSTANT, HOW-EVER, IS LIKE NOTHING EVER HEARD BEFORE IN THIS SAXON WILDERNESS...
...AND THUS ACHIEVES ITS INTENDED RESULT!
THEN, THE RIDERLESS MOUNT VANISHES AMID THE NEARBY PINES.
UNNNH--
NOW, GIRL, AS I SAID--IT'S NOT WOMEN'S CHARMS I SEEK.
THOSE I COULD HAVE HAD IN PLENTY BACK AT THE LONGHOUSE OF SIGVALD THE SKULL-SPLITTER.
IT IS AMBER I SEEK... NOTHING MORE.
WHO ARE YOU--WITH YOUR STRANGE REDDISH SKIN, AND STRANGER WAYS?
NO STRANGER THAN YOURS TO ME.
I AM ARAK, LAST OF THE QUONTAUKA TRIBE... FROM A LAND FAR ACROSS THE GREAT WATER.
YET, I SPEAK THE FRANKISH TONGUE A BIT... AS YOU DO.
IT IS THEN THAT THE LITHE WARRIOR SUDDENLY REALIZES THE WOMAN IS STARING NOT AT HIM--BUT PAST HIM--
WHAT--?
NOW, IF YOU CAN TELL ME WHERE TO FIND THE TREASURE-TROVE OF AMBER WHICH MEN SAY LIES NEARBY, I'LL TROU-BLE YOU NO--
6

--AT SHADOWS CONVERGING FROM THE TREES--

WHAT *TREACHERY* IS THIS, WITCH?

--SHADOWS ARMED WITH *SPEARS!*

NONE! I DID NOT KNOW--!

MOVING WITH THE SPEED OF A CRIMSON THUNDERBOLT, THE AGILE YOUTH EVADES THE POINT OF A WELL-HURLED SPEAR--

ARRRH

--BUT NOT, ALAS, ITS *SHAFT!*

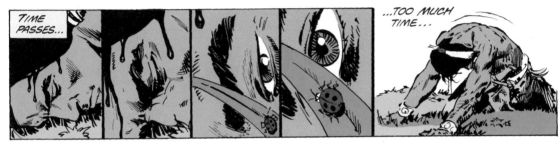

TIME PASSES...

...TOO MUCH TIME...

AND WHEN HE AWAKENS, TO THE DRUMLIKE POUNDING IN HIS SKULL, HE IS *ALONE* AMID THE RUINS OF A MIGHTY, LONG-FALLEN *EMPIRE* WHICH ONCE HELD SWAY OVER HALF THE WORLD.

WHOEVER HIS STEALTHY ASSAILANTS WERE, THEY WANTED ONLY THE WOMAN... AND LEFT HER APPARENT DEFENDER FOR DEAD.

BUT THEY WERE *WRONG...*

...AND THEY SHALL PAY!

YOUNG ARAK'S FOREBEARS WERE TRACKERS... AS MUCH AT HOME IN THICK FOREST AS ARE FISH IN THE WINE-DARK SEA...

...WHILE HIS RECENT ATTACKERS HAVE LEFT A TRAIL, IT SEEMS, WHICH EVEN A BLIND VIKING COULD FOLLOW.

7

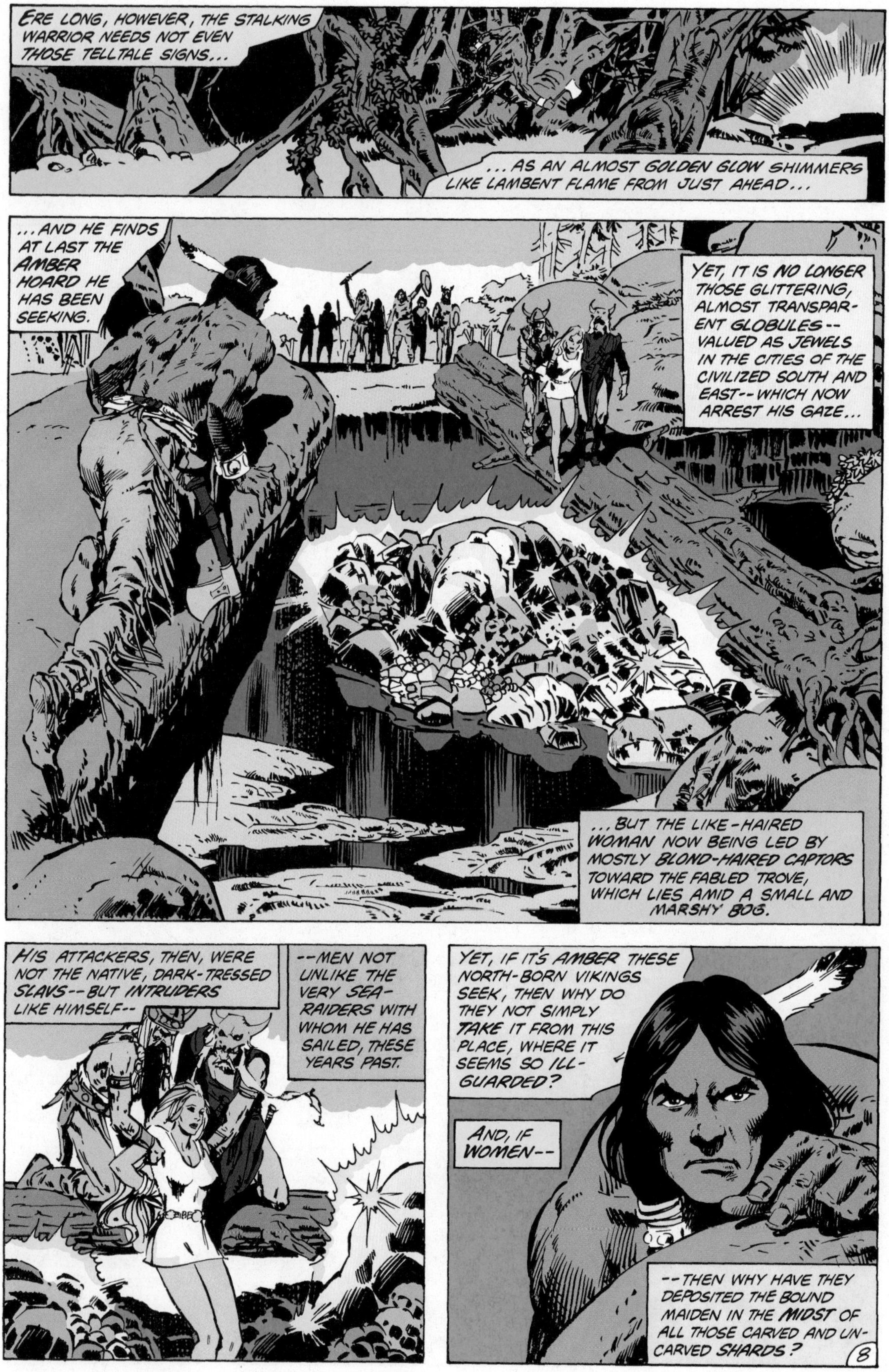
ERE LONG, HOWEVER, THE STALKING WARRIOR NEEDS NOT EVEN THOSE TELLTALE SIGNS...
...AS AN ALMOST GOLDEN GLOW SHIMMERS LIKE LAMBENT FLAME FROM JUST AHEAD...
...AND HE FINDS AT LAST THE AMBER HOARD HE HAS BEEN SEEKING.
YET, IT IS NO LONGER THOSE GLITTERING, ALMOST TRANSPARENT GLOBULES--VALUED AS JEWELS IN THE CITIES OF THE CIVILIZED SOUTH AND EAST--WHICH NOW ARREST HIS GAZE...
...BUT THE LIKE-HAIRED WOMAN NOW BEING LED BY MOSTLY BLOND-HAIRED CAPTORS TOWARD THE FABLED TROVE, WHICH LIES AMID A SMALL AND MARSHY BOG.
HIS ATTACKERS, THEN, WERE NOT THE NATIVE, DARK-TRESSED SLAVS--BUT INTRUDERS LIKE HIMSELF--
--MEN NOT UNLIKE THE VERY SEA-RAIDERS WITH WHOM HE HAS SAILED, THESE YEARS PAST.
YET, IF IT'S AMBER THESE NORTH-BORN VIKINGS SEEK, THEN WHY DO THEY NOT SIMPLY TAKE IT FROM THIS PLACE, WHERE IT SEEMS SO ILL-GUARDED?
AND, IF WOMEN--
--THEN WHY HAVE THEY DEPOSITED THE BOUND MAIDEN IN THE MIDST OF ALL THOSE CARVED AND UNCARVED SHARDS?
8

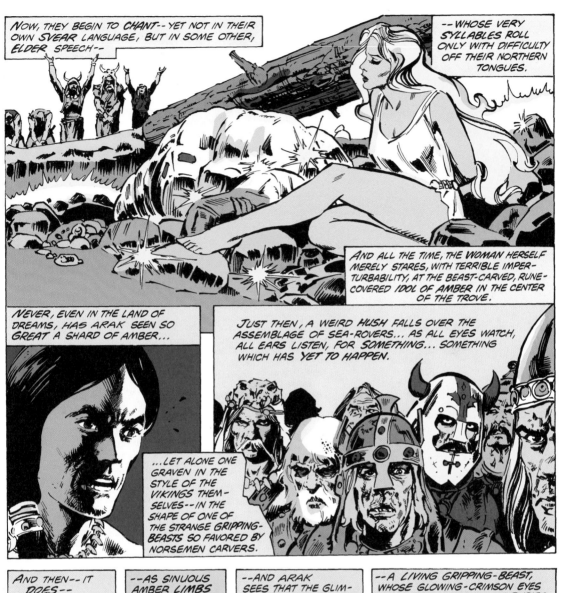

NOW, THEY BEGIN TO *CHANT*-- YET NOT IN THEIR OWN *SVEAR* LANGUAGE, BUT IN SOME OTHER, *ELDER* SPEECH--

--WHOSE VERY *SYLLABLES* ROLL ONLY WITH DIFFICULTY OFF THEIR NORTHERN *TONGUES.*

AND ALL THE TIME, THE *WOMAN* HERSELF MERELY STARES, WITH TERRIBLE IMPERTURBABILITY, AT THE BEAST-CARVED, RUNE-COVERED *IDOL* OF AMBER IN THE CENTER OF THE TROVE.

NEVER, EVEN IN THE LAND OF DREAMS, HAS *ARAK* SEEN SO GREAT A SHARD OF AMBER...

JUST THEN, A WEIRD *HUSH* FALLS OVER THE ASSEMBLAGE OF SEA-ROVERS... AS ALL EYES WATCH, ALL EARS LISTEN, FOR *SOMETHING... SOMETHING* WHICH HAS YET TO *HAPPEN.*

...LET ALONE ONE GRAVEN IN THE STYLE OF THE *VIKINGS* THEMSELVES-- IN THE SHAPE OF ONE OF THE STRANGE *GRIPPING-BEASTS* SO FAVORED BY NORSEMEN CARVERS.

AND THEN-- IT *DOES*--

--AS SINUOUS AMBER *LIMBS* BEGIN, SNAKE-LIKE, TO *UNWIND*--

--AND ARAK SEES THAT THE GLIMMERING IMAGE WAS *ALIVE,* ALL THE WHILE--

--A *LIVING* GRIPPING-BEAST, WHOSE GLOWING-CRIMSON EYES MAY BE MADE EITHER OF RUBIES FROM THE MAGIC-HAUNTED EAST--

--OR ELSE TWIN GATEWAYS TO THE RAGING *FIRES* OF SOME FORGOTTEN HELL!

9

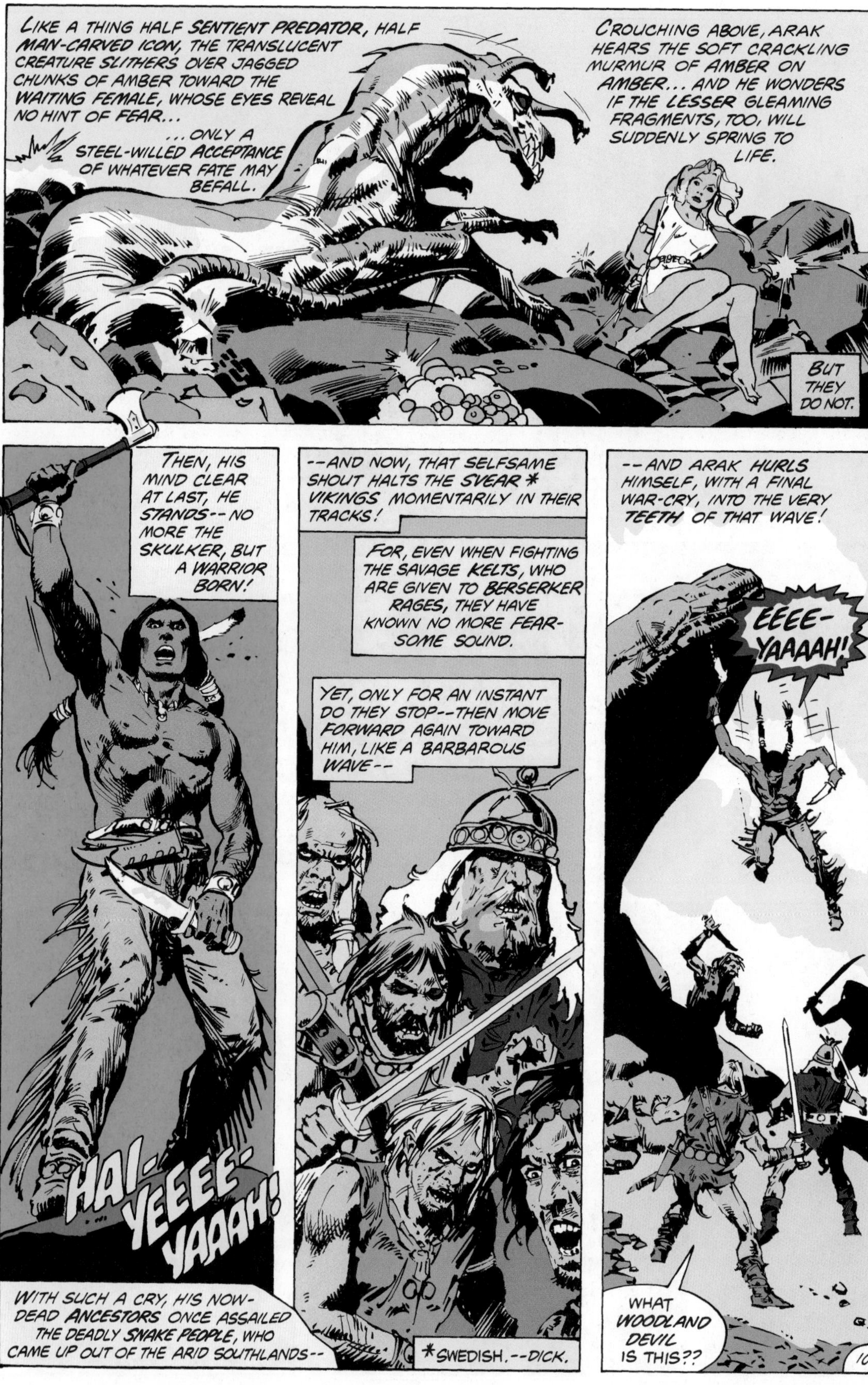
LIKE A THING HALF SENTIENT PREDATOR, HALF MAN-CARVED ICON, THE TRANSLUCENT CREATURE SLITHERS OVER JAGGED CHUNKS OF AMBER TOWARD THE WAITING FEMALE, WHOSE EYES REVEAL NO HINT OF FEAR...
...ONLY A STEEL-WILLED ACCEPTANCE OF WHATEVER FATE MAY BEFALL.
CROUCHING ABOVE, ARAK HEARS THE SOFT CRACKLING MURMUR OF AMBER ON AMBER... AND HE WONDERS IF THE LESSER GLEAMING FRAGMENTS, TOO, WILL SUDDENLY SPRING TO LIFE.
BUT THEY DO NOT.
THEN, HIS MIND CLEAR AT LAST, HE STANDS--NO MORE THE SKULKER, BUT A WARRIOR BORN!
HAI-YEEEE-YAAAH!
WITH SUCH A CRY, HIS NOW-DEAD ANCESTORS ONCE ASSAILED THE DEADLY SNAKE PEOPLE, WHO CAME UP OUT OF THE ARID SOUTHLANDS--
--AND NOW, THAT SELFSAME SHOUT HALTS THE SVEAR* VIKINGS MOMENTARILY IN THEIR TRACKS!
FOR, EVEN WHEN FIGHTING THE SAVAGE KELTS, WHO ARE GIVEN TO BERSERKER RAGES, THEY HAVE KNOWN NO MORE FEARSOME SOUND.
YET, ONLY FOR AN INSTANT DO THEY STOP--THEN MOVE FORWARD AGAIN TOWARD HIM, LIKE A BARBAROUS WAVE--
*SWEDISH.--DICK.
--AND ARAK HURLS HIMSELF, WITH A FINAL WAR-CRY, INTO THE VERY TEETH OF THAT WAVE!
EEEE-YAAAAH!
WHAT WOODLAND DEVIL IS THIS??
10

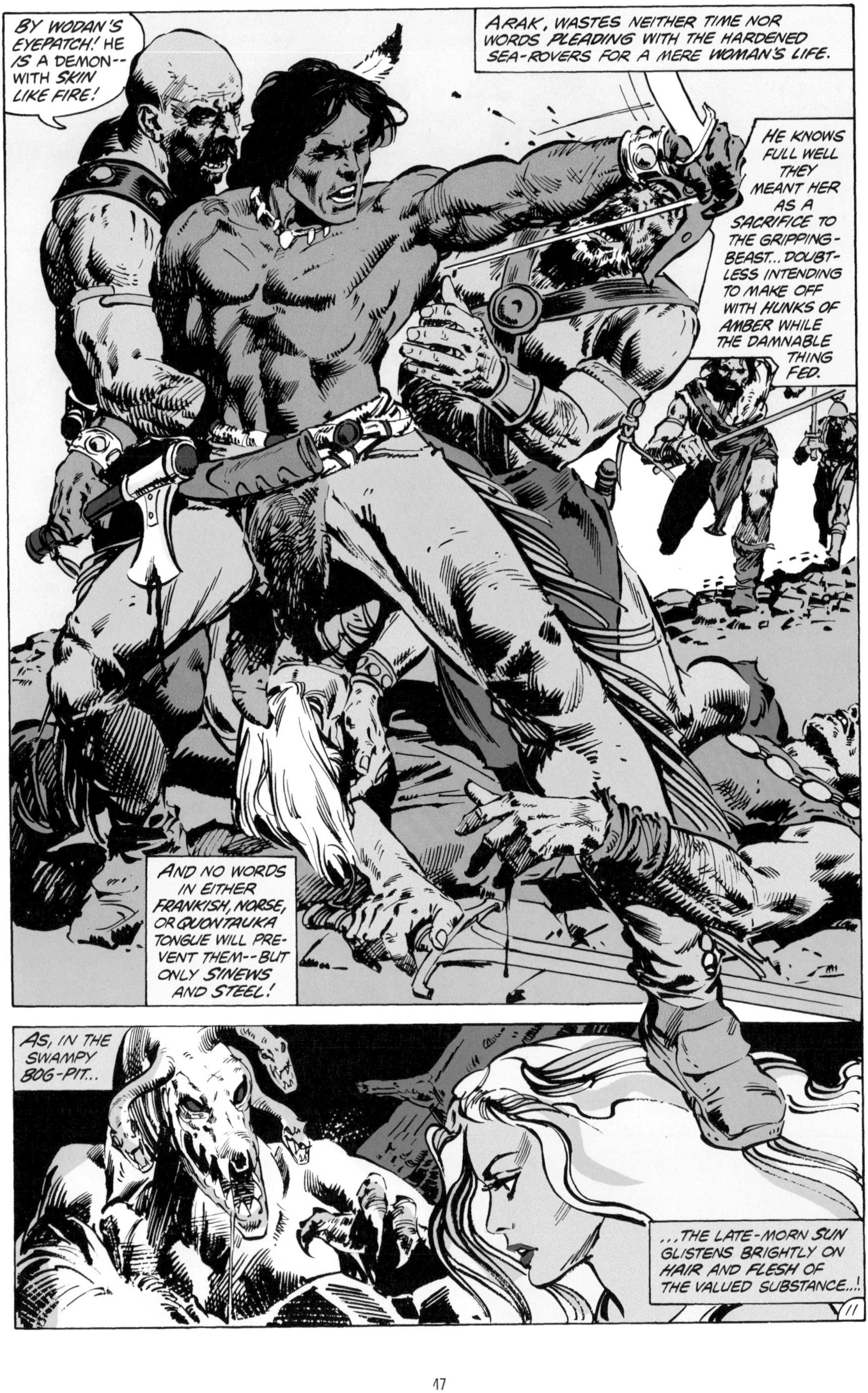
BY WODAN'S EYEPATCH! HE IS A DEMON-- WITH SKIN LIKE FIRE!
ARAK, WASTES NEITHER TIME NOR WORDS PLEADING WITH THE HARDENED SEA-ROVERS FOR A MERE WOMAN'S LIFE.
HE KNOWS FULL WELL THEY MEANT HER AS A SACRIFICE TO THE GRIPPING-BEAST... DOUBTLESS INTENDING TO MAKE OFF WITH HUNKS OF AMBER WHILE THE DAMNABLE THING FED.
AND NO WORDS IN EITHER FRANKISH, NORSE, OR QUONTAUKA TONGUE WILL PREVENT THEM--BUT ONLY SINEWS AND STEEL!
AS, IN THE SWAMPY BOG-PIT...
...THE LATE-MORN SUN GLISTENS BRIGHTLY ON HAIR AND FLESH OF THE VALUED SUBSTANCE...!
11

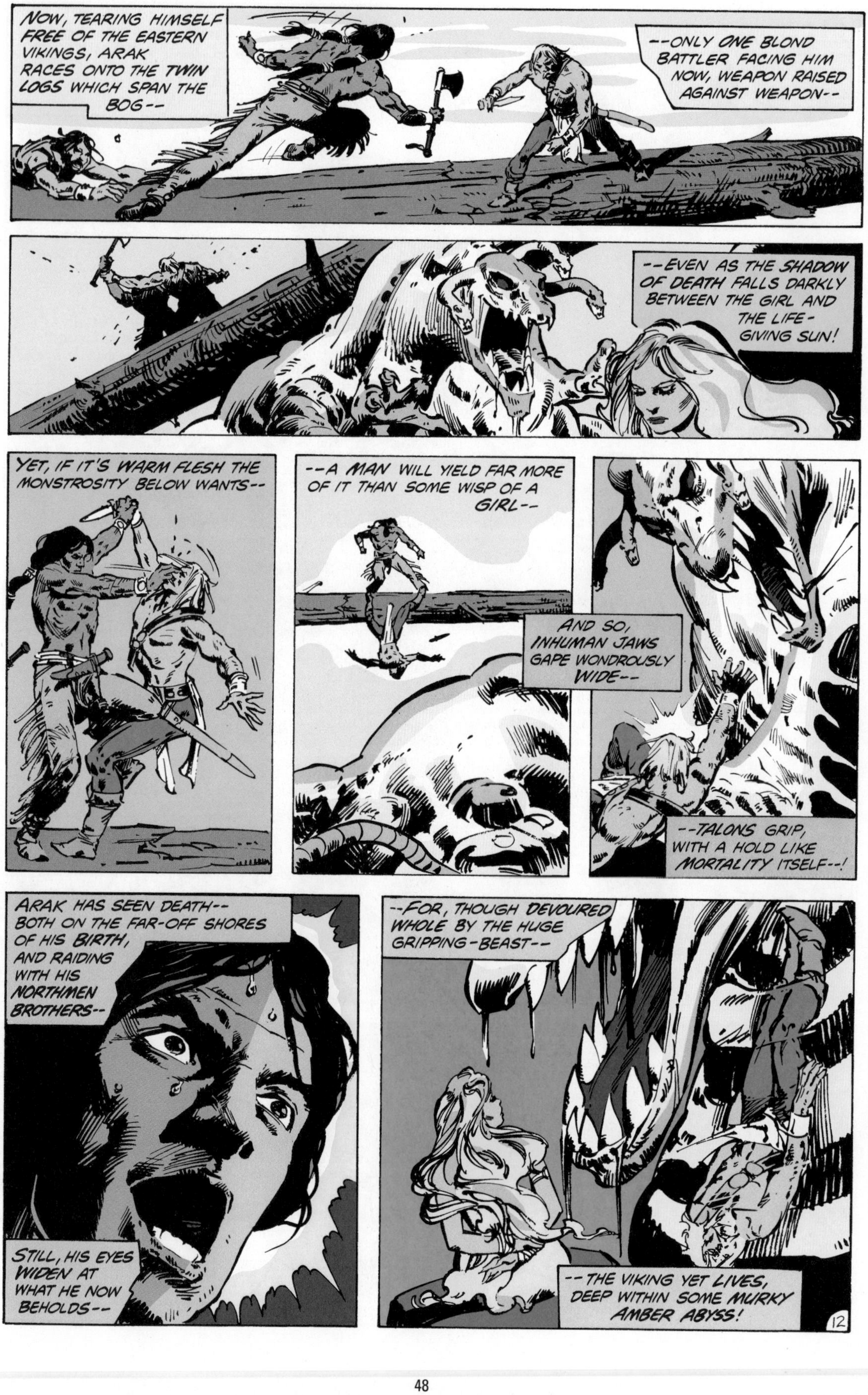
NOW, TEARING HIMSELF FREE OF THE EASTERN VIKINGS, ARAK RACES ONTO THE TWIN LOGS WHICH SPAN THE BOG--
--ONLY ONE BLOND BATTLER FACING HIM NOW, WEAPON RAISED AGAINST WEAPON--
--EVEN AS THE SHADOW OF DEATH FALLS DARKLY BETWEEN THE GIRL AND THE LIFE-GIVING SUN!
YET, IF IT'S WARM FLESH THE MONSTROSITY BELOW WANTS--
--A MAN WILL YIELD FAR MORE OF IT THAN SOME WISP OF A GIRL--
AND SO, INHUMAN JAWS GAPE WONDROUSLY WIDE--
--TALONS GRIP, WITH A HOLD LIKE MORTALITY ITSELF--!
ARAK HAS SEEN DEATH-- BOTH ON THE FAR-OFF SHORES OF HIS BIRTH, AND RAIDING WITH HIS NORTHMEN BROTHERS--
STILL, HIS EYES WIDEN AT WHAT HE NOW BEHOLDS--
--FOR, THOUGH DEVOURED WHOLE BY THE HUGE GRIPPING-BEAST--
--THE VIKING YET LIVES, DEEP WITHIN SOME MURKY AMBER ABYSS!
12

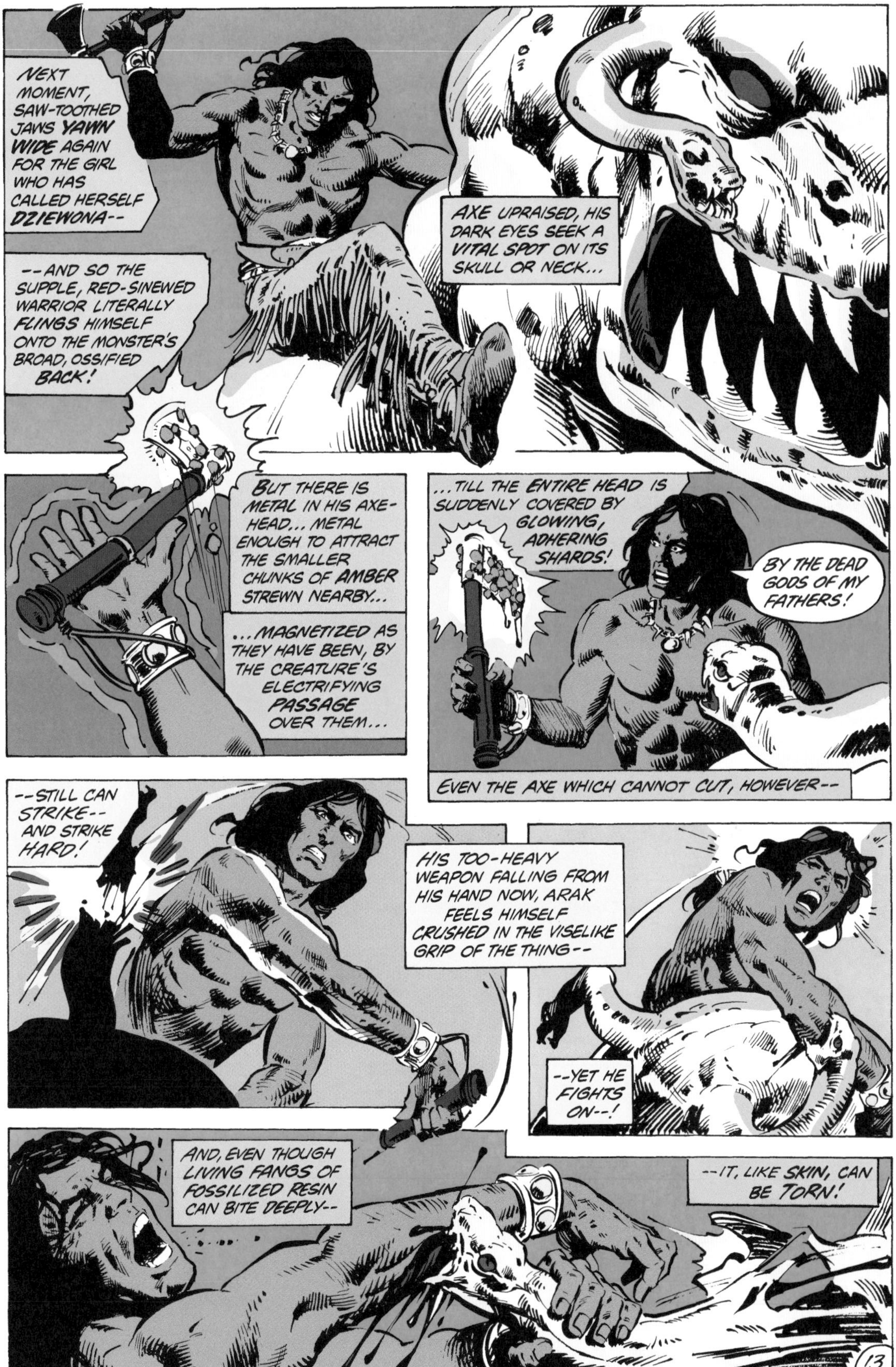
NEXT MOMENT, SAW-TOOTHED JAWS YAWN WIDE AGAIN FOR THE GIRL WHO HAS CALLED HERSELF DZIEWONA--
--AND SO THE SUPPLE, RED-SINEWED WARRIOR LITERALLY FLINGS HIMSELF ONTO THE MONSTER'S BROAD, OSSIFIED BACK!
AXE UPRAISED, HIS DARK EYES SEEK A VITAL SPOT ON ITS SKULL OR NECK...
BUT THERE IS METAL IN HIS AXE-HEAD... METAL ENOUGH TO ATTRACT THE SMALLER CHUNKS OF AMBER STREWN NEARBY...
...MAGNETIZED AS THEY HAVE BEEN, BY THE CREATURE'S ELECTRIFYING PASSAGE OVER THEM...
...TILL THE ENTIRE HEAD IS SUDDENLY COVERED BY GLOWING, ADHERING SHARDS!
BY THE DEAD GODS OF MY FATHERS!
EVEN THE AXE WHICH CANNOT CUT, HOWEVER--
--STILL CAN STRIKE-- AND STRIKE HARD!
HIS TOO-HEAVY WEAPON FALLING FROM HIS HAND NOW, ARAK FEELS HIMSELF CRUSHED IN THE VISELIKE GRIP OF THE THING--
--YET HE FIGHTS ON--!
AND, EVEN THOUGH LIVING FANGS OF FOSSILIZED RESIN CAN BITE DEEPLY--
--IT, LIKE SKIN, CAN BE TORN!
13

NOW, STRONG SINEWS FLEX AND *PULL*-- MIGHTY TENDONS HEAVE AND *PUSH*--

FOR *ARAK* KNOWS THAT TO *RELAX* HIS HERCULEAN STRUGGLE, EVEN FOR AN INSTANT, MEANS CERTAIN *DOOM!*

MEANWHILE, THE WILLOWY-GOWNED *GIRL* STARES STRAIGHT AHEAD, AS IF GAZING WITH SOME SECRET INNER *KEN* ON OTHER WORLDS, OTHER SHORES.

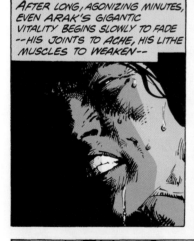

AFTER LONG, AGONIZING MINUTES, EVEN *ARAK'S* GIGANTIC *VITALITY* BEGINS SLOWLY TO *FADE* --HIS JOINTS TO *ACHE*, HIS LITHE MUSCLES TO *WEAKEN*--

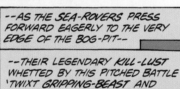

--AS THE *SEA-ROVERS* PRESS FORWARD EAGERLY TO THE VERY EDGE OF THE *BOG-PIT*--

--THEIR LEGENDARY *KILL-LUST* WHETTED BY THIS PITCHED BATTLE 'TWIXT *GRIPPING-BEAST* AND *UNKNOWN WARRIOR.*

VOLOS! YARULUS KUPALA PIORUN!

FOR A MOMENT, NOTHING HAPPENS...

THEN--

--AMAZINGLY, THE *MANY-FANGED* THING BEGINS TO *STIFFEN*--

--TO BECOME AGAIN A MERE ICON OF SHINING *AMBER*--

--YET *POISED*, LIKE SOME HUGE PRAYING *MANTIS*, TO SPRING ONCE MORE UPON ANY MEN SO PRESUMPTUOUS AS TO COVET THE *PRICELESS HOARD* OVER WHICH IT STANDS ETERNAL, UNENDING *GUARD!* (14)

THE SVEAR VIKINGS, HOWEVER, HAVE THIS DAY SEEN A *CARVEN IMAGE* COME SUDDENLY, HORRIBLY TO LIFE--AND A STRANGE, RED-HUED *SAVAGE* APPEAR TO GIVE IT *BATTLE.*

THERE ARE, THEY DECIDE, EASIER TREASURE-TROVES TO LOOT IN THIS AGE OF DARKNESS.

SOON, ARAK AWAKENS--FROM DREAMS OF A GODDESS NAMED DZIEWONA-- VIRGIN HUNTRESS, AND PATRONESS OF WARRIORS--

--WHOM SHE PROTECTS WITH HER LONG VEIL-- OR WAS IT, HER *GOSSAMER-THIN GOWN?*

YOU--WERE *NEVER* IN DANGER FROM THE *THING* OF AMBER, WERE YOU?

ONLY FROM THE *RAIDERS...*

...NOT FROM THE *GRIPPING-BEAST,* WHO GUARDS ME...JUST AS, BY KEEPING HIS HOARD'S LOCATION A SECRET, I GUARD *HIM.*

YET YOU ARE *REAL*-- NO TRUE *"GODDESS"*--!

NOT IF, BY THAT, YOU MEAN ONE WHO *WALKS THE WIND,* OR BENDS THE TALL TREETOPS LIKE STALKS OF GRAIN.

STILL, I HAVE MY *WAYS...*!

A RAISING OF HER *ARM,* THEN, AND HER *STALLION* IS THERE...AS IF IT HAD WAITED THERE, ALL ALONG, FOR HER *SIGNAL.*

YOU WOULD NOT *UNDERSTAND* IF I SAID MORE... NOT NOW, NOT YET.

BUT PERHAPS, ONE DAY, YOU *SHALL.*

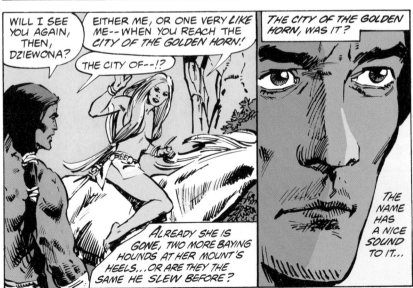

WILL I SEE YOU AGAIN, THEN, DZIEWONA?

EITHER ME, OR ONE VERY *LIKE* ME--WHEN YOU REACH THE *CITY OF THE GOLDEN HORN!*

THE CITY OF--!?

ALREADY SHE IS GONE, TWO MORE BAYING HOUNDS AT HER MOUNT'S HEELS...OR ARE THEY THE SAME HE SLEW BEFORE?

THE CITY OF THE GOLDEN HORN, WAS IT?

THE NAME HAS A NICE SOUND TO IT...

AND SOMEHOW, YOUNG ARAK DOUBTS NOT AT ALL THAT HE WILL *FIND* THAT CITY...

...WHETHER HE *SEEKS* IT OR *NOT...*!

Fin

15

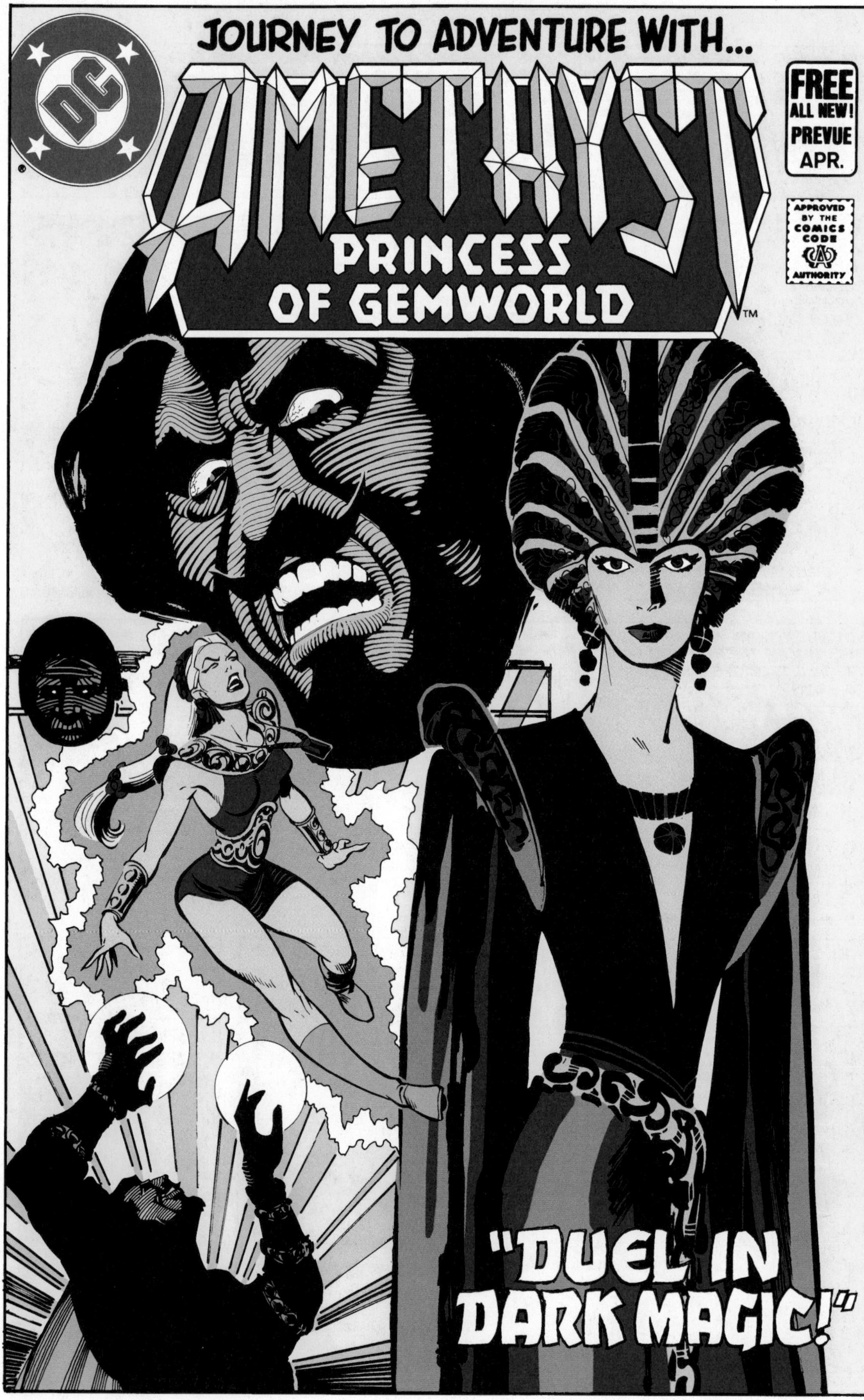
JOURNEY TO ADVENTURE WITH...
DC
AMETHYST
PRINCESS OF GEMWORLD
TM
FREE
ALL NEW!
PREVUE
APR.
APPROVED BY THE COMICS CODE AUTHORITY
"DUEL IN DARK MAGIC!"

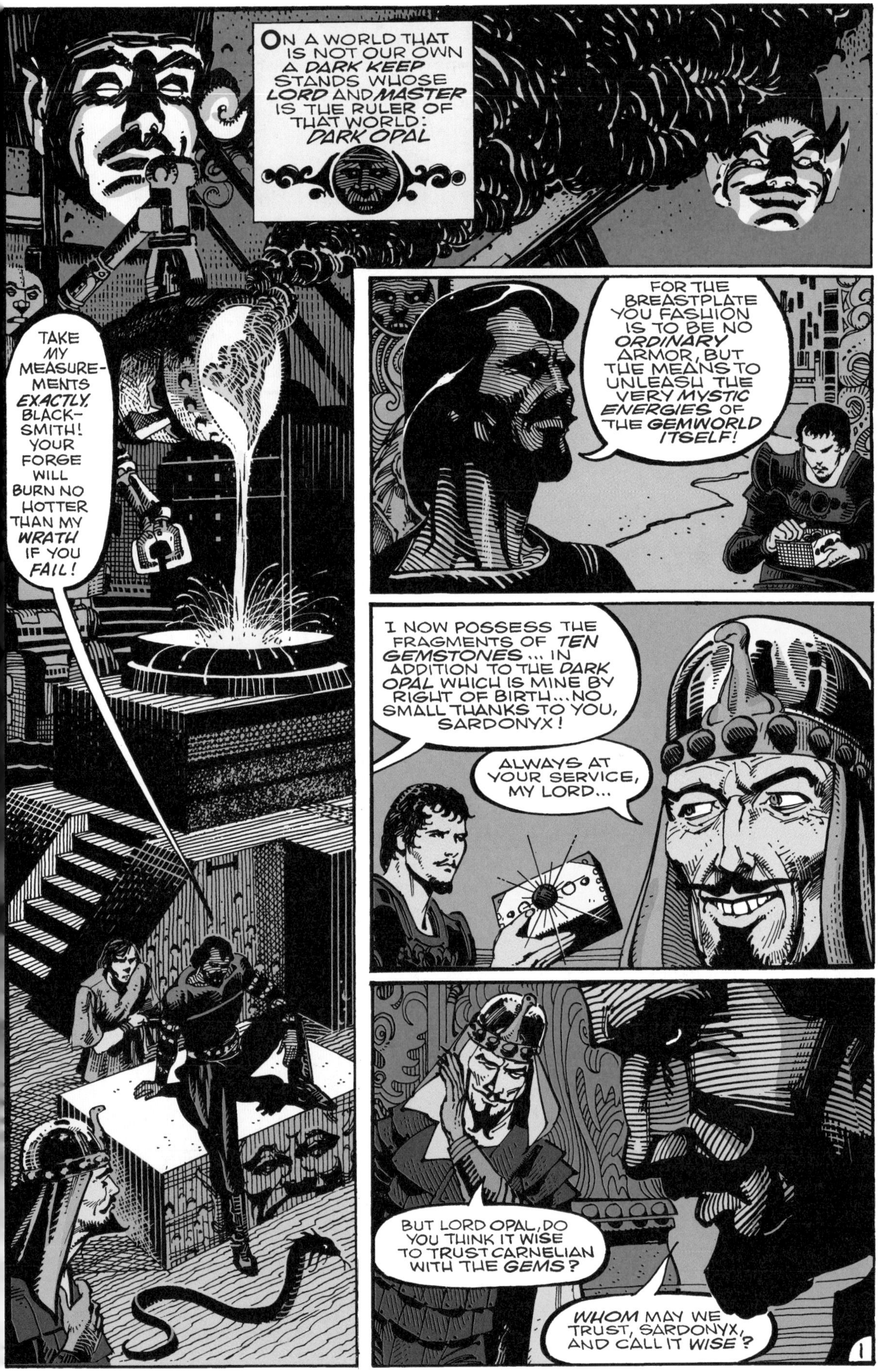

ON A WORLD THAT IS NOT OUR OWN A DARK KEEP STANDS WHOSE LORD AND MASTER IS THE RULER OF THAT WORLD: DARK OPAL
TAKE MY MEASUREMENTS EXACTLY, BLACKSMITH! YOUR FORGE WILL BURN NO HOTTER THAN MY WRATH IF YOU FAIL!
FOR THE BREASTPLATE YOU FASHION IS TO BE NO ORDINARY ARMOR, BUT THE MEANS TO UNLEASH THE VERY MYSTIC ENERGIES OF THE GEMWORLD ITSELF!
I NOW POSSESS THE FRAGMENTS OF TEN GEMSTONES... IN ADDITION TO THE DARK OPAL WHICH IS MINE BY RIGHT OF BIRTH...NO SMALL THANKS TO YOU, SARDONYX!
ALWAYS AT YOUR SERVICE, MY LORD...
BUT LORD OPAL, DO YOU THINK IT WISE TO TRUST CARNELIAN WITH THE GEMS?
WHOM MAY WE TRUST, SARDONYX, AND CALL IT WISE?
1

BUT CARNELIAN IS MY SON AND *CHOSEN HEIR*... I FEAR HIM NOT! AND NO POWER...NOT YOURS, AND LEAST OF ALL HIS...WILL CHALLENGE ME WHEN I GAIN THE TWELFTH AND *FINAL GEMSTONE*... *THE AMETHYST!*

MY LORD! MY LORD! I BRING YOU NEWS OF *GREAT MOMENT!*

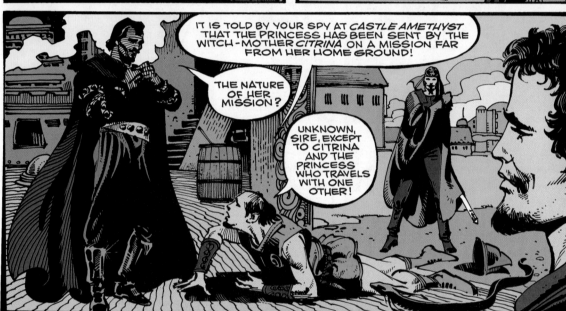

IT IS TOLD BY YOUR SPY AT *CASTLE AMETHYST* THAT THE PRINCESS HAS BEEN SENT BY THE WITCH-MOTHER *CITRINA* ON A MISSION FAR FROM HER HOME GROUND!

THE NATURE OF HER MISSION?

UNKNOWN, SIRE, EXCEPT TO CITRINA AND THE PRINCESS WHO TRAVELS WITH ONE OTHER!

WHAT IS YOUR OPINION, SARDONYX?

IT'S A RARE OPPORTUNITY TO FIND HER AT SUCH DISADVANTAGE-- FAR FROM CITRINA AND HER CASTLE AND WITH BUT ONE COMPANION... I SAY GO!

AGREED! YOU AND MY SON WILL OVERSEE THE SMITH IN THE COMPLETION OF HIS WORK...AND CARE WELL FOR MY PRECIOUS OPAL! I WILL RETURN WITH THE *VIOLET GEM*.....

J-8/73

AMETHYST™
PRINCESS OF GEMWORLD

"DUEL IN DARK MAGIC!"

DAN MISHKIN & GARY COHN * ERNIE COLÓN
WRITERS   ARTIST & LETTERER

TOM ZIUKO * KAREN BERGER & DAVE MANAK
COLORIST   EDITORS

②

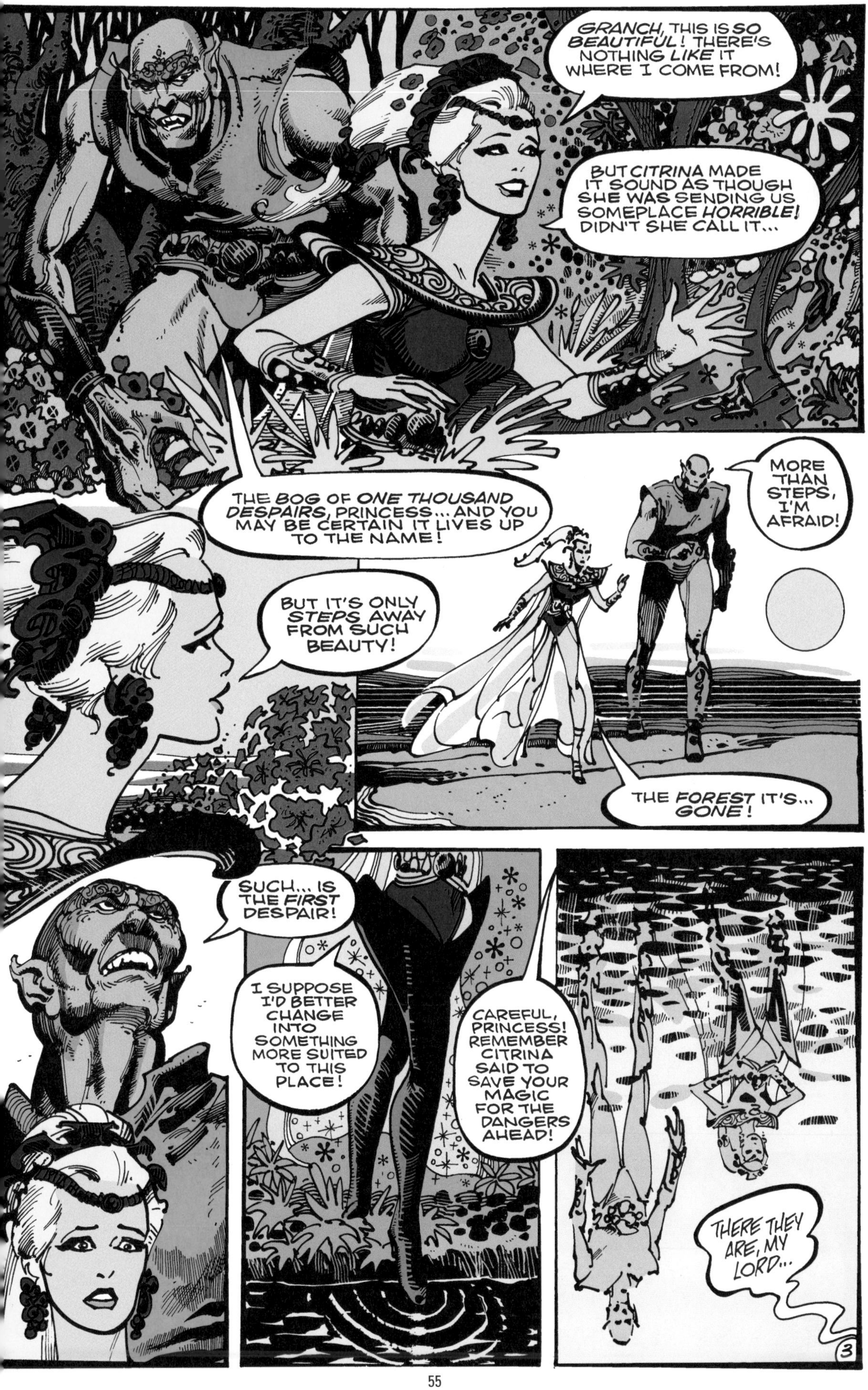
GRANCH, THIS IS SO BEAUTIFUL! THERE'S NOTHING LIKE IT WHERE I COME FROM!
BUT CITRINA MADE IT SOUND AS THOUGH SHE WAS SENDING US SOMEPLACE HORRIBLE! DIDN'T SHE CALL IT...
THE BOG OF ONE THOUSAND DESPAIRS, PRINCESS... AND YOU MAY BE CERTAIN IT LIVES UP TO THE NAME!
BUT IT'S ONLY STEPS AWAY FROM SUCH BEAUTY!
MORE THAN STEPS, I'M AFRAID!
THE FOREST IT'S... GONE!
SUCH... IS THE FIRST DESPAIR!
I SUPPOSE I'D BETTER CHANGE INTO SOMETHING MORE SUITED TO THIS PLACE!
CAREFUL, PRINCESS! REMEMBER CITRINA SAID TO SAVE YOUR MAGIC FOR THE DANGERS AHEAD!
THERE THEY ARE, MY LORD...
3

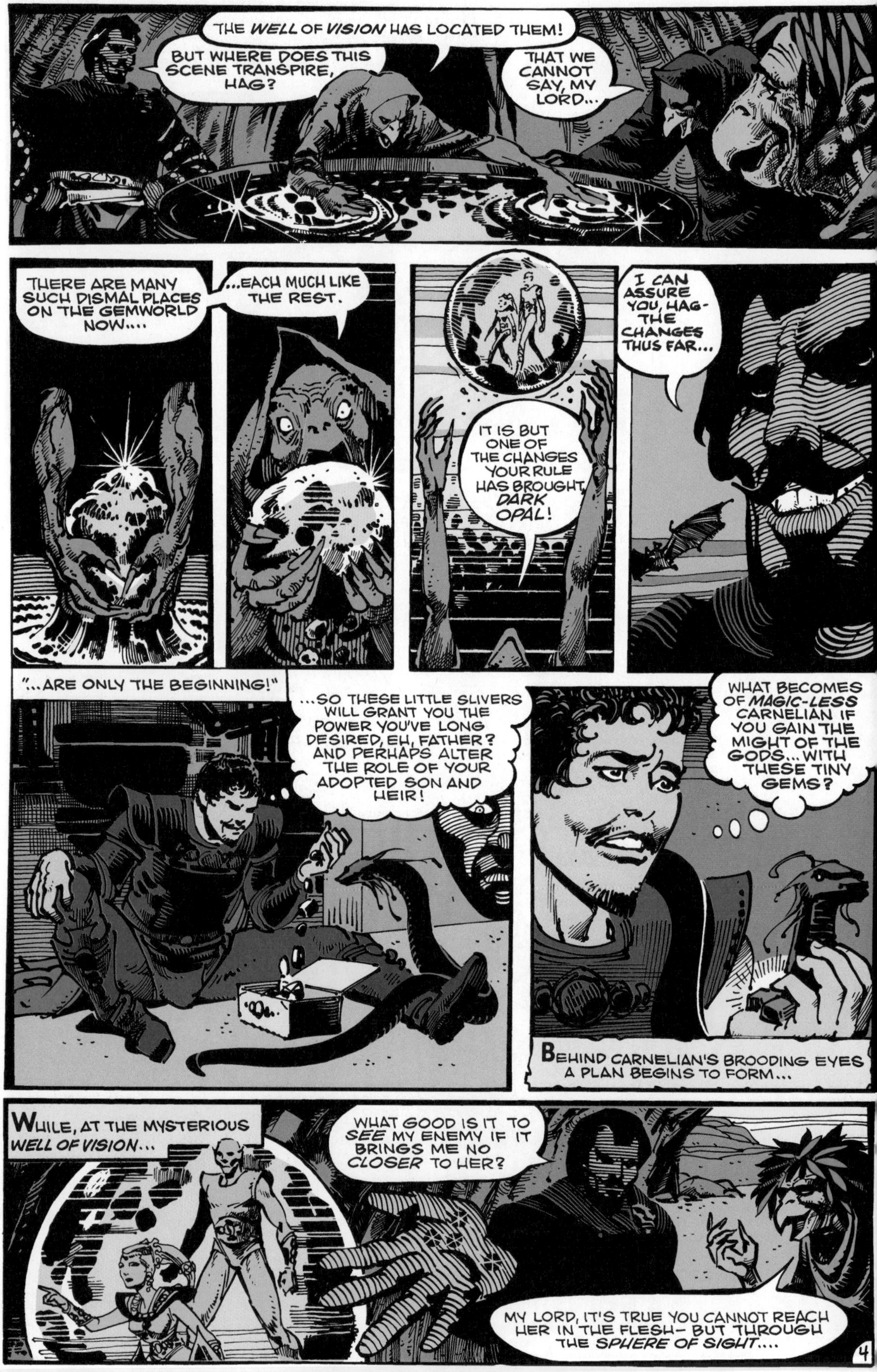
THE WELL OF VISION HAS LOCATED THEM!
BUT WHERE DOES THIS SCENE TRANSPIRE, HAG?
THAT WE CANNOT SAY, MY LORD...
THERE ARE MANY SUCH DISMAL PLACES ON THE GEMWORLD NOW....
...EACH MUCH LIKE THE REST.
IT IS BUT ONE OF THE CHANGES YOUR RULE HAS BROUGHT, DARK OPAL!
I CAN ASSURE YOU, HAG- THE CHANGES THUS FAR...
"...ARE ONLY THE BEGINNING!"
...SO THESE LITTLE SLIVERS WILL GRANT YOU THE POWER YOU'VE LONG DESIRED, EH, FATHER? AND PERHAPS ALTER THE ROLE OF YOUR ADOPTED SON AND HEIR!
WHAT BECOMES OF MAGIC-LESS CARNELIAN IF YOU GAIN THE MIGHT OF THE GODS... WITH THESE TINY GEMS?
BEHIND CARNELIAN'S BROODING EYES A PLAN BEGINS TO FORM...
WHILE, AT THE MYSTERIOUS WELL OF VISION...
WHAT GOOD IS IT TO SEE MY ENEMY IF IT BRINGS ME NO CLOSER TO HER?
MY LORD, IT'S TRUE YOU CANNOT REACH HER IN THE FLESH- BUT THROUGH THE SPHERE OF SIGHT....
4

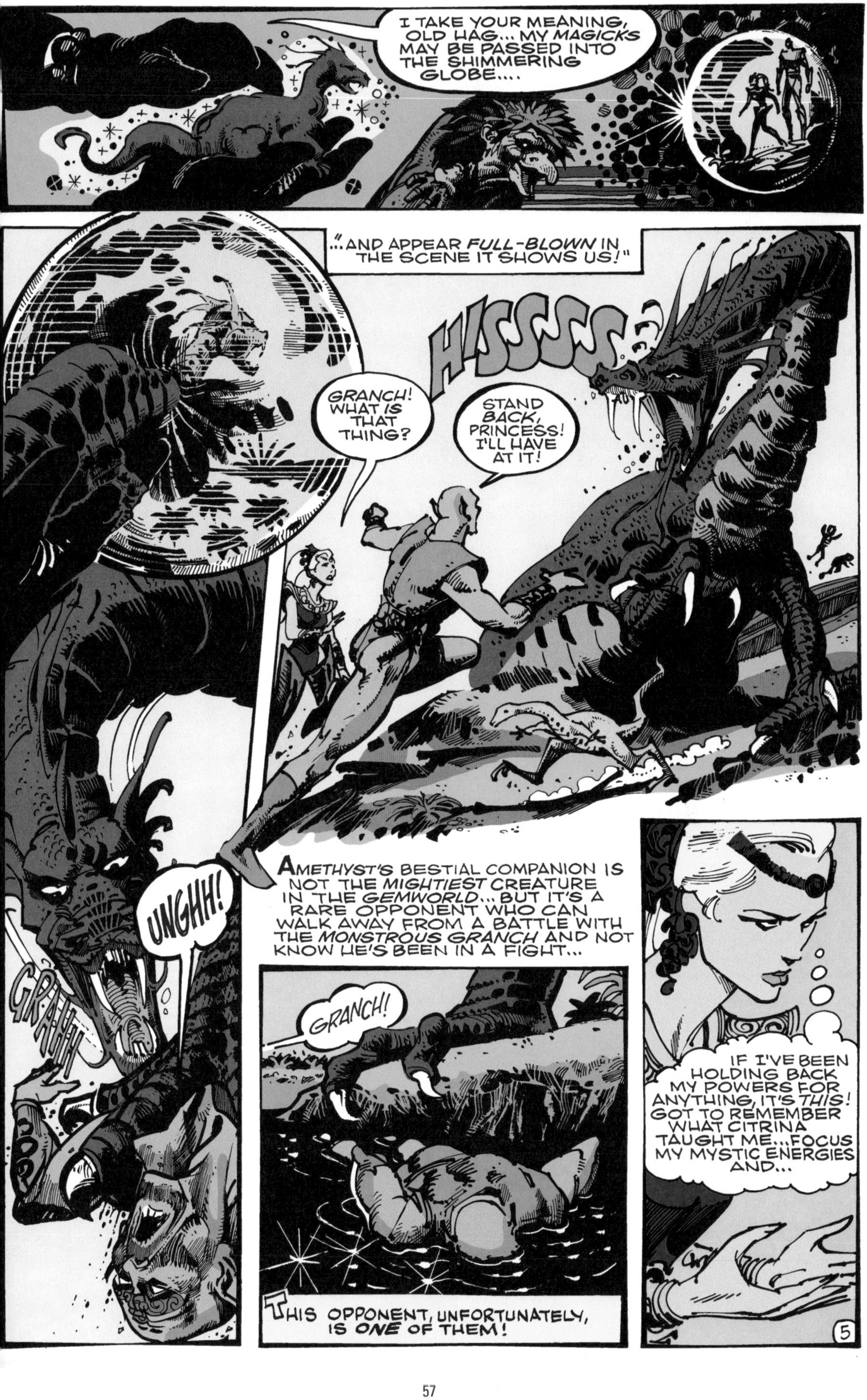
I TAKE YOUR MEANING, OLD HAG... MY MAGICKS MAY BE PASSED INTO THE SHIMMERING GLOBE....
"...AND APPEAR FULL-BLOWN IN THE SCENE IT SHOWS US!"
HISSSS
GRANCH! WHAT IS THAT THING?
STAND BACK, PRINCESS! I'LL HAVE AT IT!
AMETHYST'S BESTIAL COMPANION IS NOT THE MIGHTIEST CREATURE IN THE GEMWORLD... BUT IT'S A RARE OPPONENT WHO CAN WALK AWAY FROM A BATTLE WITH THE MONSTROUS GRANCH AND NOT KNOW HE'S BEEN IN A FIGHT...
UNGHH!
GRAHHH
GRANCH!
THIS OPPONENT, UNFORTUNATELY, IS ONE OF THEM!
IF I'VE BEEN HOLDING BACK MY POWERS FOR ANYTHING, IT'S THIS! GOT TO REMEMBER WHAT CITRINA TAUGHT ME...FOCUS MY MYSTIC ENERGIES AND...
5

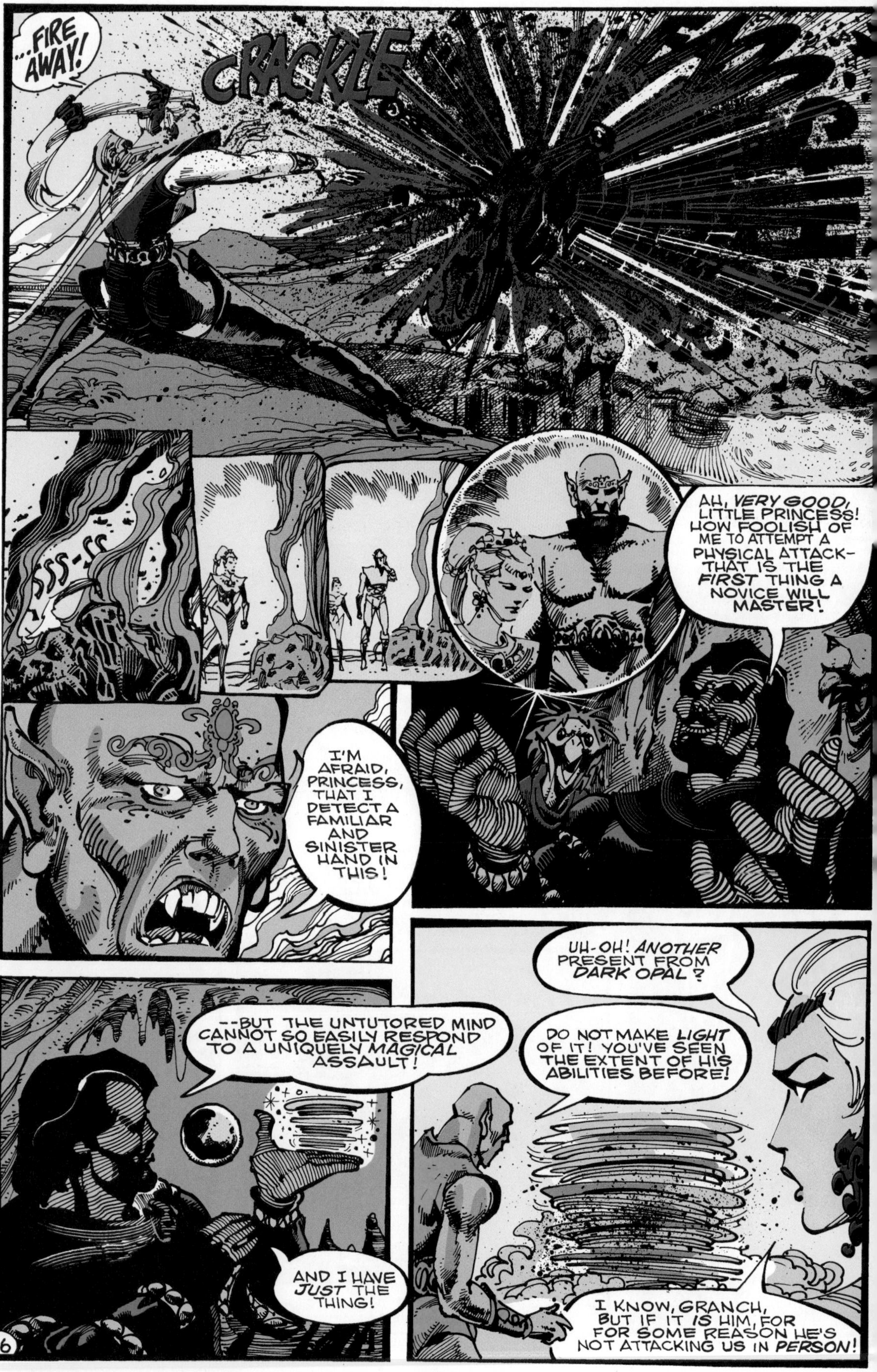
...FIRE AWAY!
CRACKLE
SSS-SS
AH, VERY GOOD, LITTLE PRINCESS! HOW FOOLISH OF ME TO ATTEMPT A PHYSICAL ATTACK-- THAT IS THE FIRST THING A NOVICE WILL MASTER!
I'M AFRAID, PRINCESS, THAT I DETECT A FAMILIAR AND SINISTER HAND IN THIS!
--BUT THE UNTUTORED MIND CANNOT SO EASILY RESPOND TO A UNIQUELY MAGICAL ASSAULT!
AND I HAVE JUST THE THING!
UH-OH! ANOTHER PRESENT FROM DARK OPAL?
DO NOT MAKE LIGHT OF IT! YOU'VE SEEN THE EXTENT OF HIS ABILITIES BEFORE!
I KNOW, GRANCH, BUT IF IT IS HIM, FOR FOR SOME REASON HE'S NOT ATTACKING US IN PERSON!
6

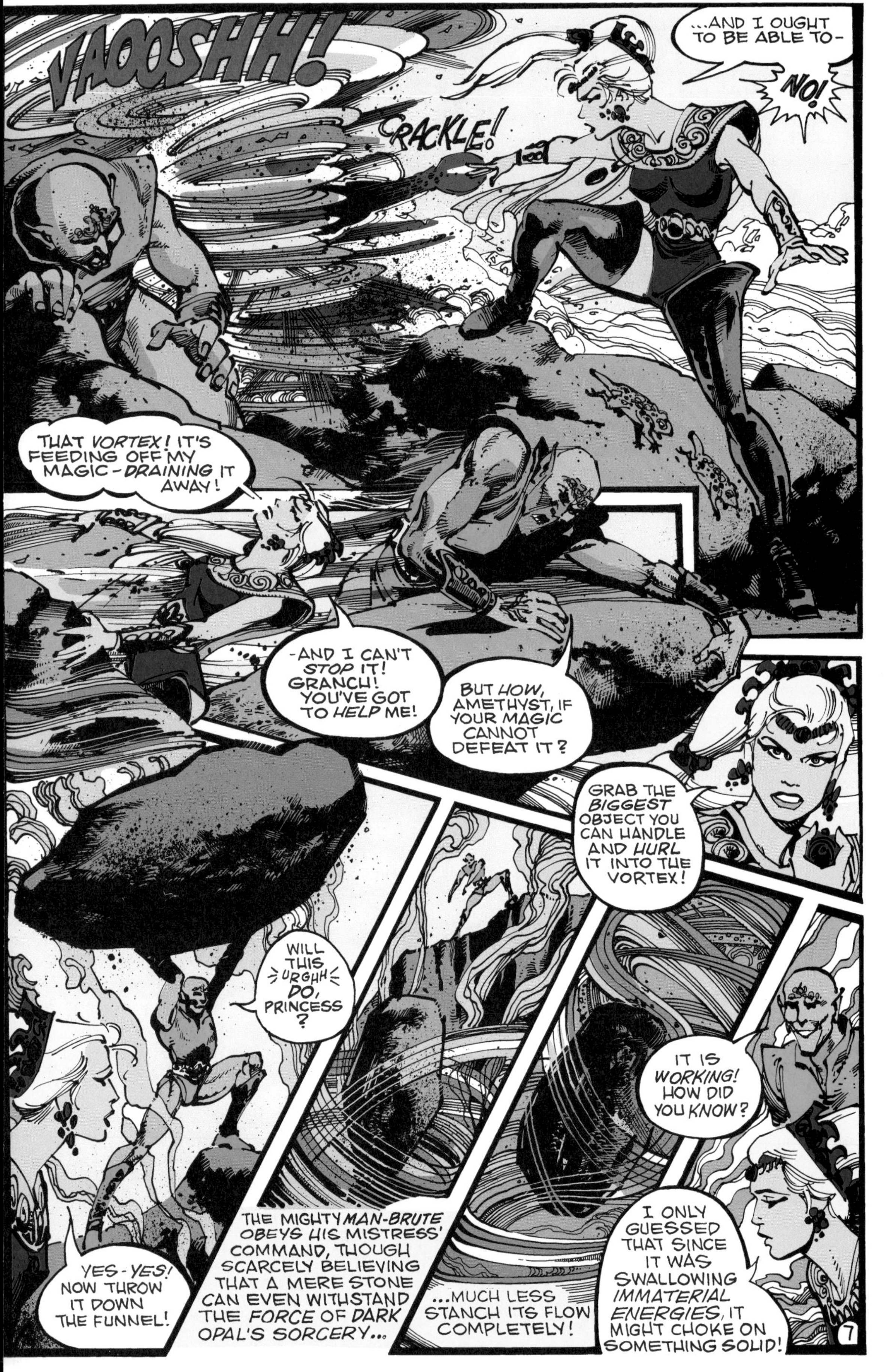
VAOOSHH!
...AND I OUGHT TO BE ABLE TO-
NO!
CRACKLE!
THAT VORTEX! IT'S FEEDING OFF MY MAGIC-DRAINING IT AWAY!
-AND I CAN'T STOP IT! GRANCH! YOU'VE GOT TO HELP ME!
BUT HOW, AMETHYST, IF YOUR MAGIC CANNOT DEFEAT IT?
GRAB THE BIGGEST OBJECT YOU CAN HANDLE AND HURL IT INTO THE VORTEX!
WILL THIS URGHH DO, PRINCESS?
YES-YES! NOW THROW IT DOWN THE FUNNEL!
THE MIGHTY MAN-BRUTE OBEYS HIS MISTRESS' COMMAND, THOUGH SCARCELY BELIEVING THAT A MERE STONE CAN EVEN WITHSTAND THE FORCE OF DARK OPAL'S SORCERY...
...MUCH LESS STANCH ITS FLOW COMPLETELY!
IT IS WORKING! HOW DID YOU KNOW?
I ONLY GUESSED THAT SINCE IT WAS SWALLOWING IMMATERIAL ENERGIES, IT MIGHT CHOKE ON SOMETHING SOLID!
7

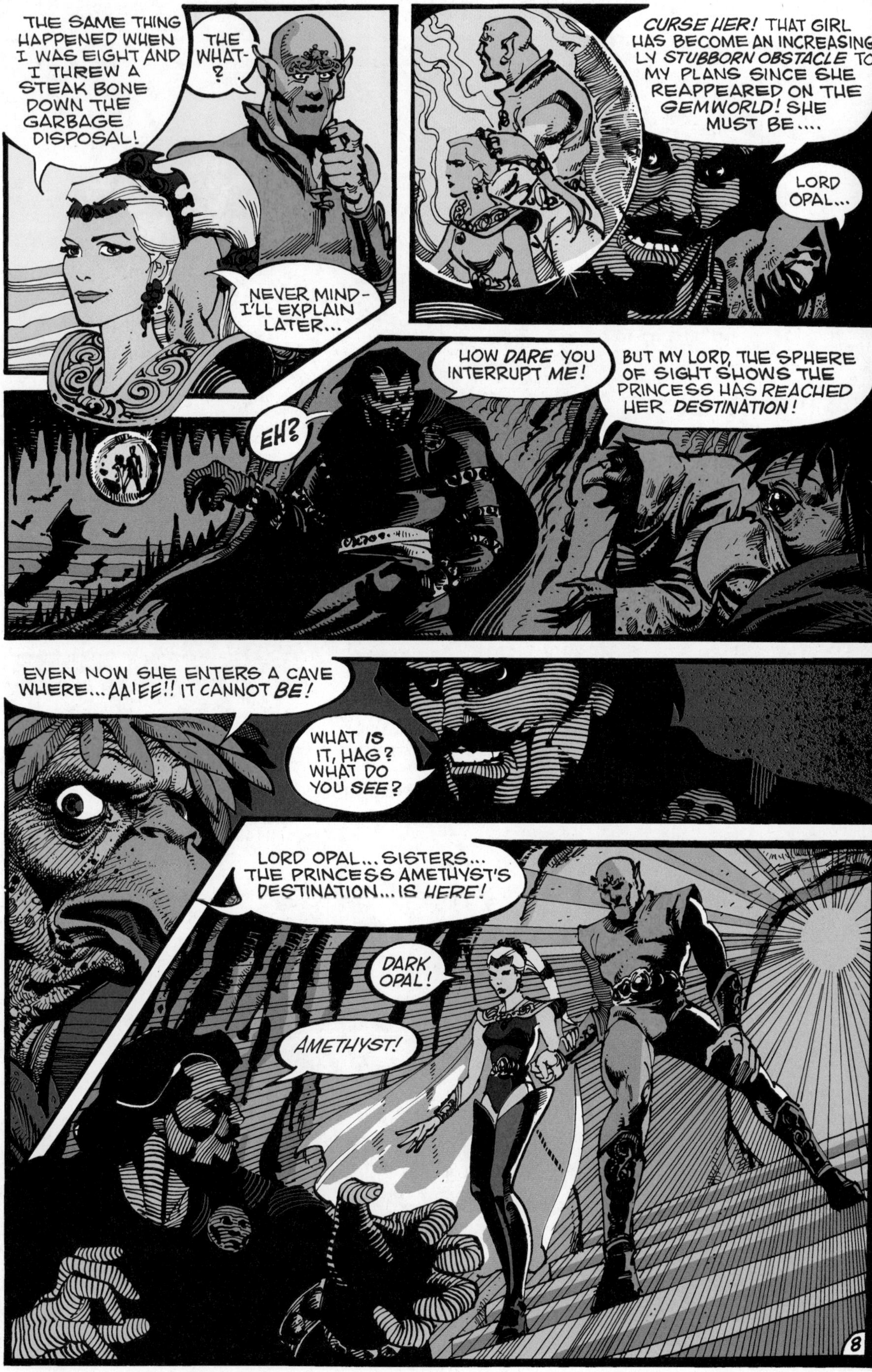
THE SAME THING HAPPENED WHEN I WAS EIGHT AND I THREW A STEAK BONE DOWN THE GARBAGE DISPOSAL!
THE WHAT-?
NEVER MIND- I'LL EXPLAIN LATER...
CURSE HER! THAT GIRL HAS BECOME AN INCREASINGLY STUBBORN OBSTACLE TO MY PLANS SINCE SHE REAPPEARED ON THE GEMWORLD! SHE MUST BE....
LORD OPAL...
EH?
HOW DARE YOU INTERRUPT ME!
BUT MY LORD, THE SPHERE OF SIGHT SHOWS THE PRINCESS HAS REACHED HER DESTINATION!
EVEN NOW SHE ENTERS A CAVE WHERE... AAIEE!! IT CANNOT BE!
WHAT IS IT, HAG? WHAT DO YOU SEE?
LORD OPAL... SISTERS... THE PRINCESS AMETHYST'S DESTINATION... IS HERE!
DARK OPAL!
AMETHYST!
8

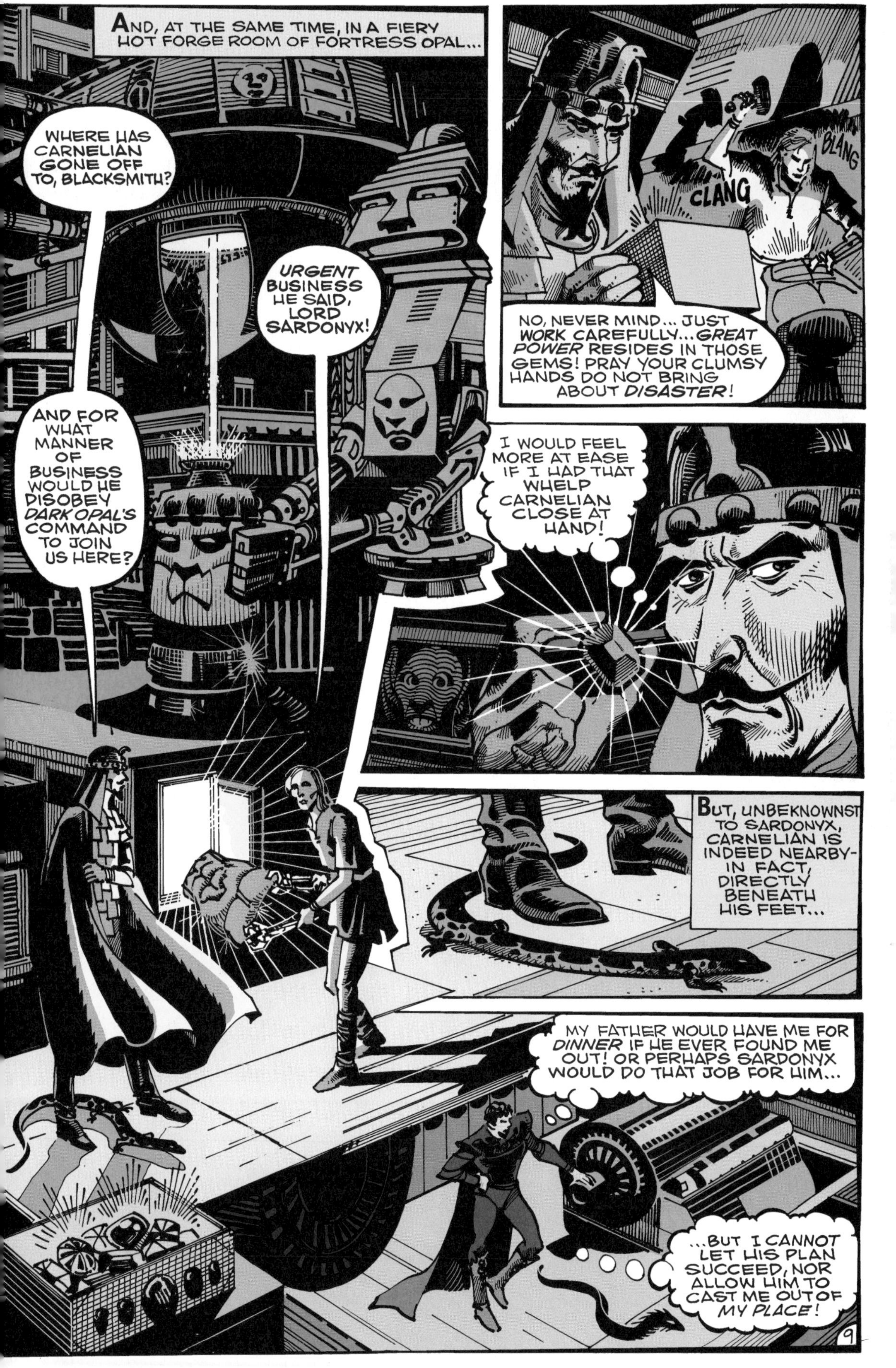
AND, AT THE SAME TIME, IN A FIERY HOT FORGE ROOM OF FORTRESS OPAL...
WHERE HAS CARNELIAN GONE OFF TO, BLACKSMITH?
URGENT BUSINESS HE SAID, LORD SARDONYX!
AND FOR WHAT MANNER OF BUSINESS WOULD HE DISOBEY DARK OPAL'S COMMAND TO JOIN US HERE?
CLANG
BLANG
NO, NEVER MIND... JUST WORK CAREFULLY... GREAT POWER RESIDES IN THOSE GEMS! PRAY YOUR CLUMSY HANDS DO NOT BRING ABOUT DISASTER!
I WOULD FEEL MORE AT EASE IF I HAD THAT WHELP CARNELIAN CLOSE AT HAND!
BUT, UNBEKNOWNST TO SARDONYX, CARNELIAN IS INDEED NEARBY- IN FACT, DIRECTLY BENEATH HIS FEET...
MY FATHER WOULD HAVE ME FOR DINNER IF HE EVER FOUND ME OUT! OR PERHAPS SARDONYX WOULD DO THAT JOB FOR HIM...
...BUT I CANNOT LET HIS PLAN SUCCEED, NOR ALLOW HIM TO CAST ME OUT OF MY PLACE!
9

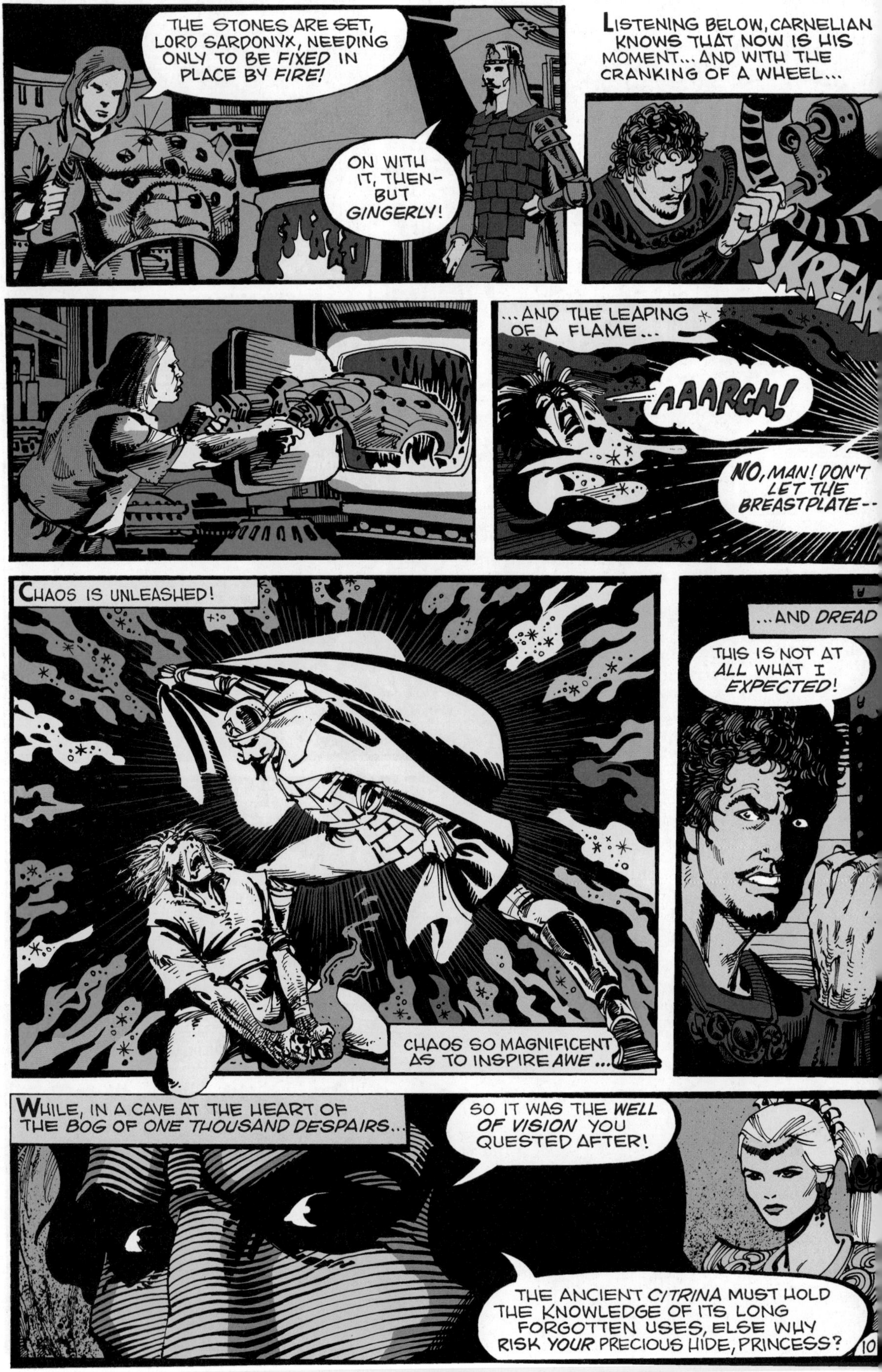
THE STONES ARE SET, LORD SARDONYX, NEEDING ONLY TO BE FIXED IN PLACE BY FIRE!
ON WITH IT, THEN- BUT GINGERLY!
LISTENING BELOW, CARNELIAN KNOWS THAT NOW IS HIS MOMENT... AND WITH THE CRANKING OF A WHEEL...
...AND THE LEAPING OF A FLAME...
AAARGH!
NO, MAN! DON'T LET THE BREASTPLATE--
CHAOS IS UNLEASHED!
CHAOS SO MAGNIFICENT AS TO INSPIRE AWE...
...AND DREAD
THIS IS NOT AT ALL WHAT I EXPECTED!
WHILE, IN A CAVE AT THE HEART OF THE BOG OF ONE THOUSAND DESPAIRS...
SO IT WAS THE WELL OF VISION YOU QUESTED AFTER!
THE ANCIENT CITRINA MUST HOLD THE KNOWLEDGE OF ITS LONG FORGOTTEN USES, ELSE WHY RISK YOUR PRECIOUS HIDE, PRINCESS?
10

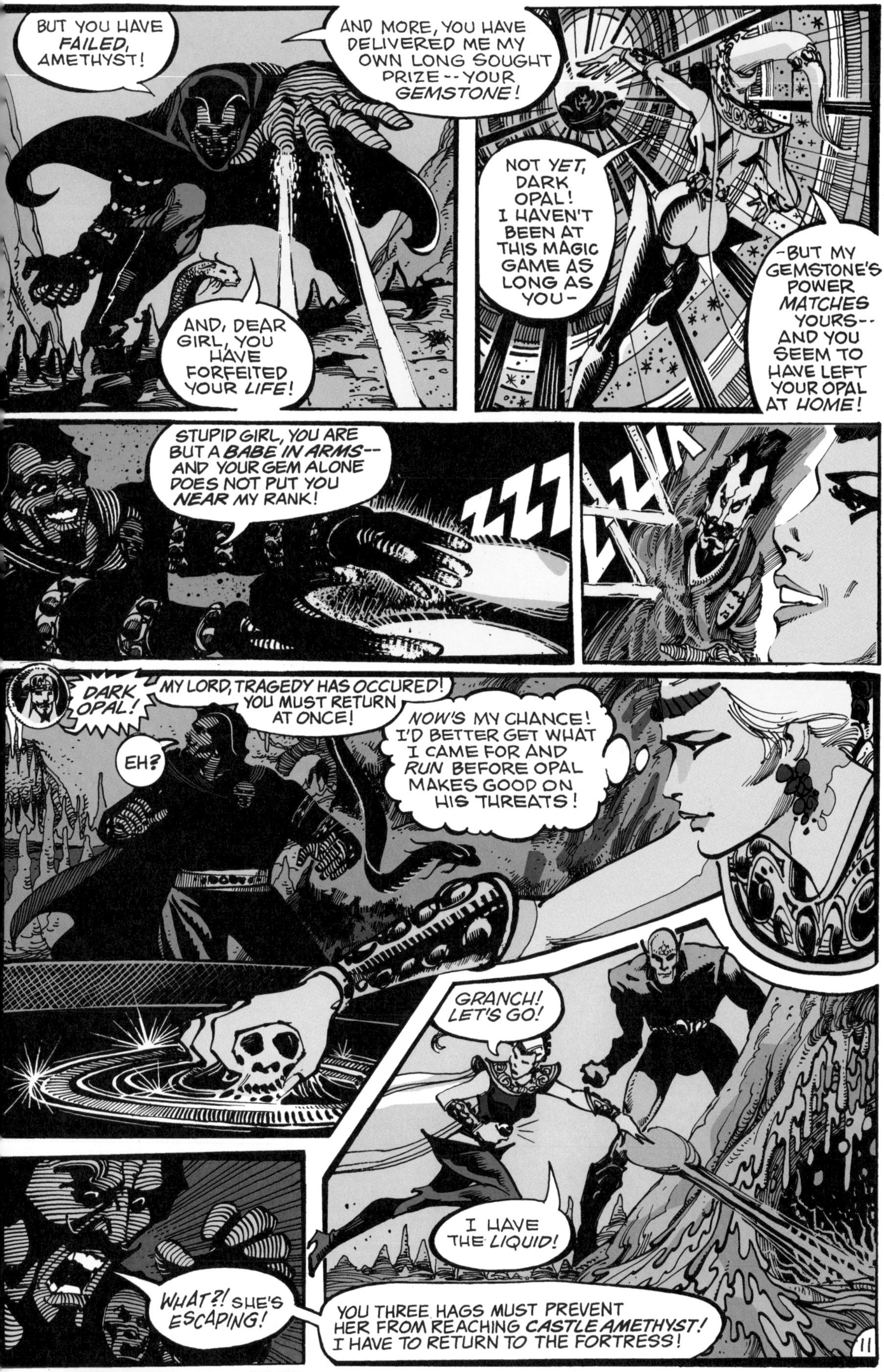
BUT YOU HAVE FAILED, AMETHYST!
AND MORE, YOU HAVE DELIVERED ME MY OWN LONG SOUGHT PRIZE--YOUR GEMSTONE!
AND, DEAR GIRL, YOU HAVE FORFEITED YOUR LIFE!
NOT YET, DARK OPAL! I HAVEN'T BEEN AT THIS MAGIC GAME AS LONG AS YOU-
-BUT MY GEMSTONE'S POWER MATCHES YOURS--AND YOU SEEM TO HAVE LEFT YOUR OPAL AT HOME!
STUPID GIRL, YOU ARE BUT A BABE IN ARMS--AND YOUR GEM ALONE DOES NOT PUT YOU NEAR MY RANK!
ZZZZZZ
DARK OPAL!
MY LORD, TRAGEDY HAS OCCURED! YOU MUST RETURN AT ONCE!
EH?
NOW'S MY CHANCE! I'D BETTER GET WHAT I CAME FOR AND RUN BEFORE OPAL MAKES GOOD ON HIS THREATS!
GRANCH! LET'S GO!
I HAVE THE LIQUID!
WHAT?! SHE'S ESCAPING!
YOU THREE HAGS MUST PREVENT HER FROM REACHING CASTLE AMETHYST! I HAVE TO RETURN TO THE FORTRESS!
11

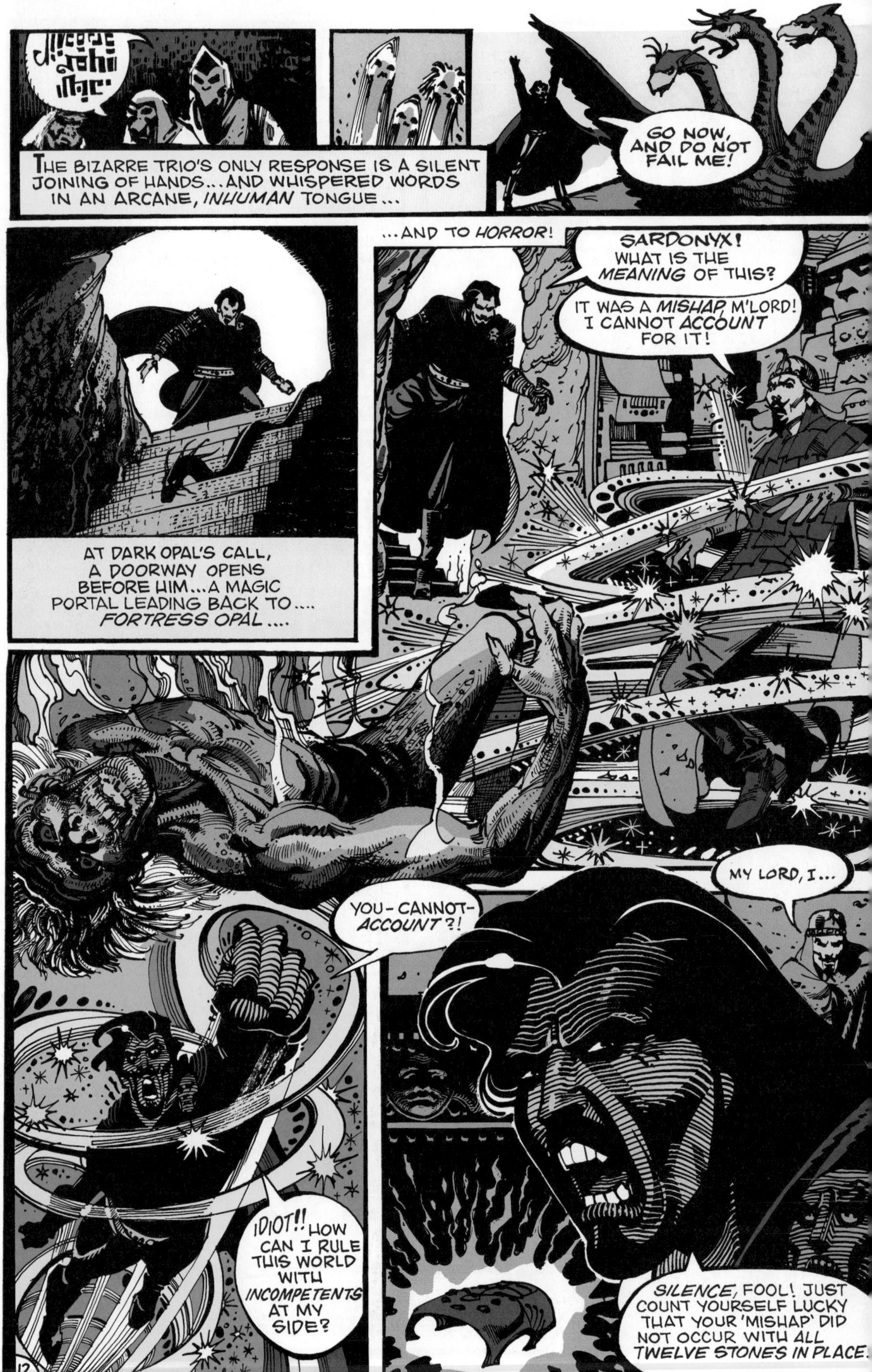
THE BIZARRE TRIO'S ONLY RESPONSE IS A SILENT JOINING OF HANDS...AND WHISPERED WORDS IN AN ARCANE, INHUMAN TONGUE...
GO NOW, AND DO NOT FAIL ME!
AT DARK OPAL'S CALL, A DOORWAY OPENS BEFORE HIM...A MAGIC PORTAL LEADING BACK TO.... FORTRESS OPAL....
...AND TO HORROR!
SARDONYX! WHAT IS THE MEANING OF THIS?
IT WAS A MISHAP, M'LORD! I CANNOT ACCOUNT FOR IT!
YOU-CANNOT-ACCOUNT?!
IDIOT!! HOW CAN I RULE THIS WORLD WITH INCOMPETENTS AT MY SIDE?
MY LORD, I...
SILENCE, FOOL! JUST COUNT YOURSELF LUCKY THAT YOUR 'MISHAP' DID NOT OCCUR WITH ALL TWELVE STONES IN PLACE.

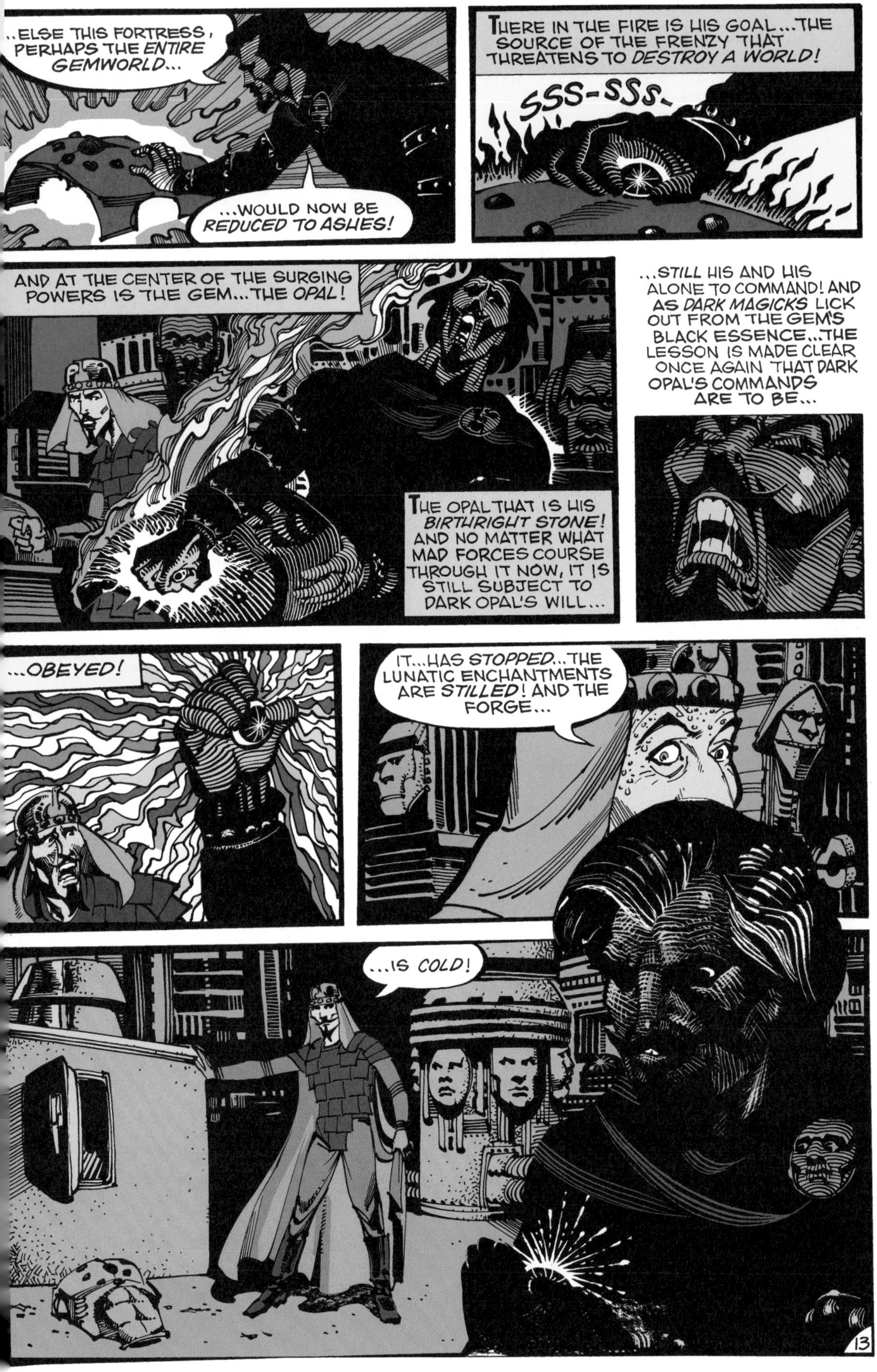

..ELSE THIS FORTRESS, PERHAPS THE ENTIRE GEMWORLD...
...WOULD NOW BE REDUCED TO ASHES!
THERE IN THE FIRE IS HIS GOAL...THE SOURCE OF THE FRENZY THAT THREATENS TO DESTROY A WORLD!
SSS-SSS-
AND AT THE CENTER OF THE SURGING POWERS IS THE GEM...THE OPAL!
THE OPAL THAT IS HIS BIRTHRIGHT STONE! AND NO MATTER WHAT MAD FORCES COURSE THROUGH IT NOW, IT IS STILL SUBJECT TO DARK OPAL'S WILL...
...STILL HIS AND HIS ALONE TO COMMAND! AND AS DARK MAGICKS LICK OUT FROM THE GEM'S BLACK ESSENCE...THE LESSON IS MADE CLEAR ONCE AGAIN THAT DARK OPAL'S COMMANDS ARE TO BE...
...OBEYED!
IT...HAS STOPPED...THE LUNATIC ENCHANTMENTS ARE STILLED! AND THE FORGE...
...IS COLD!
13

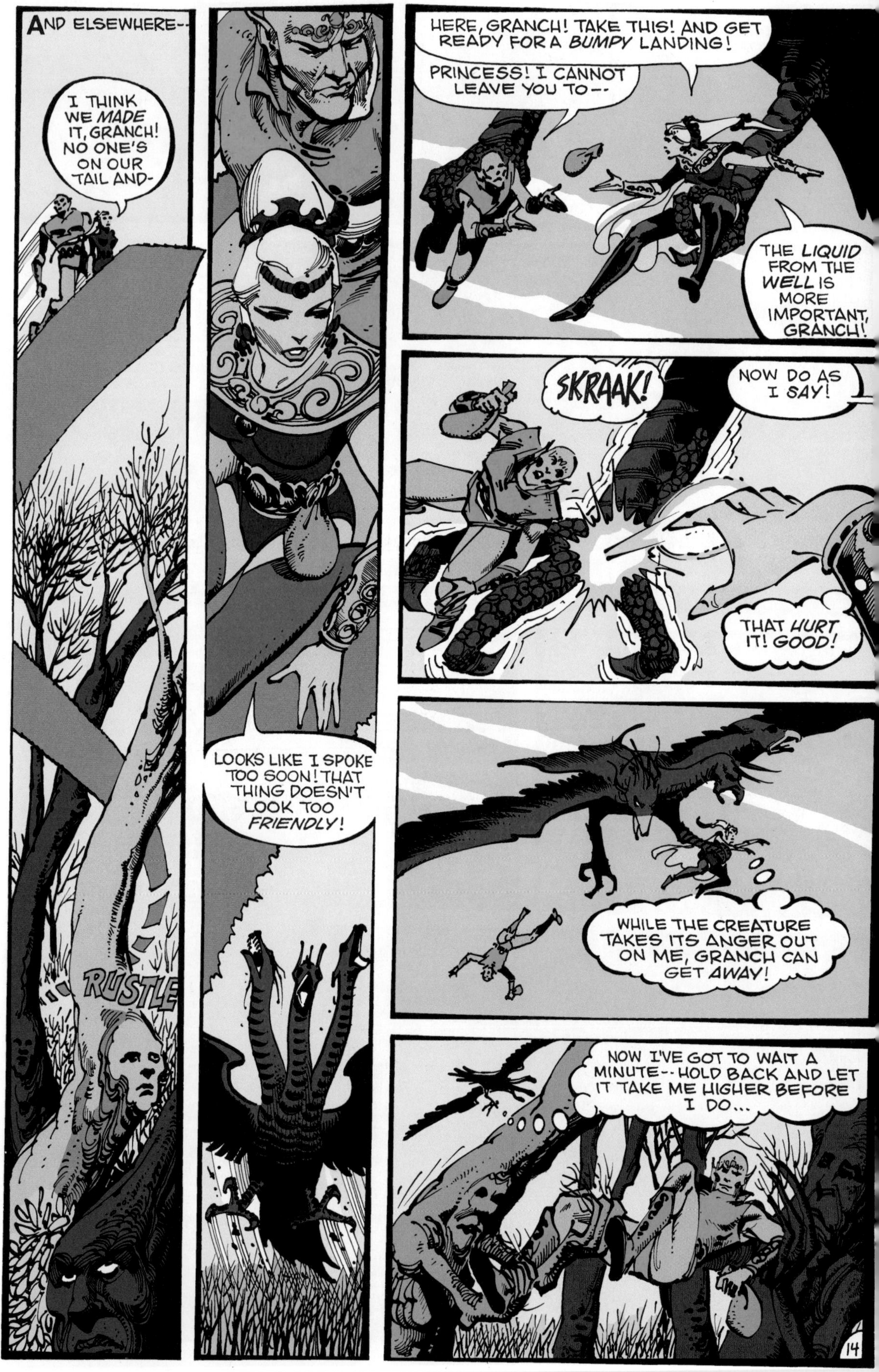
AND ELSEWHERE--
I THINK WE MADE IT, GRANCH! NO ONE'S ON OUR TAIL AND-
RUSTLE
LOOKS LIKE I SPOKE TOO SOON! THAT THING DOESN'T LOOK TOO FRIENDLY!
HERE, GRANCH! TAKE THIS! AND GET READY FOR A BUMPY LANDING!
PRINCESS! I CANNOT LEAVE YOU TO--
THE LIQUID FROM THE WELL IS MORE IMPORTANT, GRANCH!
SKRAAK!
NOW DO AS I SAY!
THAT HURT IT! GOOD!
WHILE THE CREATURE TAKES ITS ANGER OUT ON ME, GRANCH CAN GET AWAY!
NOW I'VE GOT TO WAIT A MINUTE--HOLD BACK AND LET IT TAKE ME HIGHER BEFORE I DO...
14

...THIS!

HUH? THE CREATURE IS REALLY THOSE *BIRD WITCHES!* WEIRD! I DON'T CARE WHAT *CITRINA* SAYS - I'M *NEVER* GONNA GET USED TO *THIS* PLACE!

CAN'T WORRY ABOUT THAT, *NOW,* THOUGH! I DID WHAT I *CAME* HERE FOR--SO BEFORE THOSE WITCHES *CHANGE BACK,* I'D BETTER *USE* THE *AMETHYST* TO TAKE ME *HOME!*

MOM AND DAD MIGHT BE WORRIED ABOUT--

AMY? AMY, DEAR, ARE YOU *ALL RIGHT?*

UH, YEAH, MOM - I'M OKAY...

I WAS JUST HAVING A *BAD DREAM.*

FWUP!

OOF

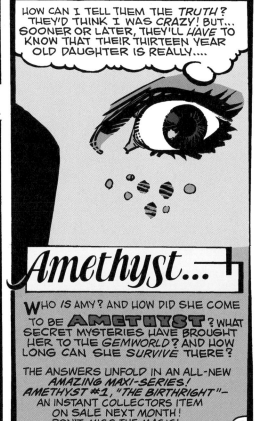

HOW CAN I TELL THEM THE *TRUTH?* THEY'D THINK I WAS *CRAZY!* BUT... SOONER OR LATER, THEY'LL *HAVE* TO KNOW THAT THEIR THIRTEEN YEAR OLD DAUGHTER IS REALLY....

Amethyst...

WHO IS AMY? AND HOW DID SHE COME TO BE **AMETHYST?** WHAT SECRET MYSTERIES HAVE BROUGHT HER TO THE *GEMWORLD?* AND HOW LONG CAN SHE *SURVIVE* THERE?

THE ANSWERS UNFOLD IN AN ALL-NEW *AMAZING MAXI-SERIES!* AMETHYST #1, "THE BIRTHRIGHT"-- AN INSTANT COLLECTORS ITEM ON SALE NEXT MONTH! DON'T MISS THE MAGIC!

15

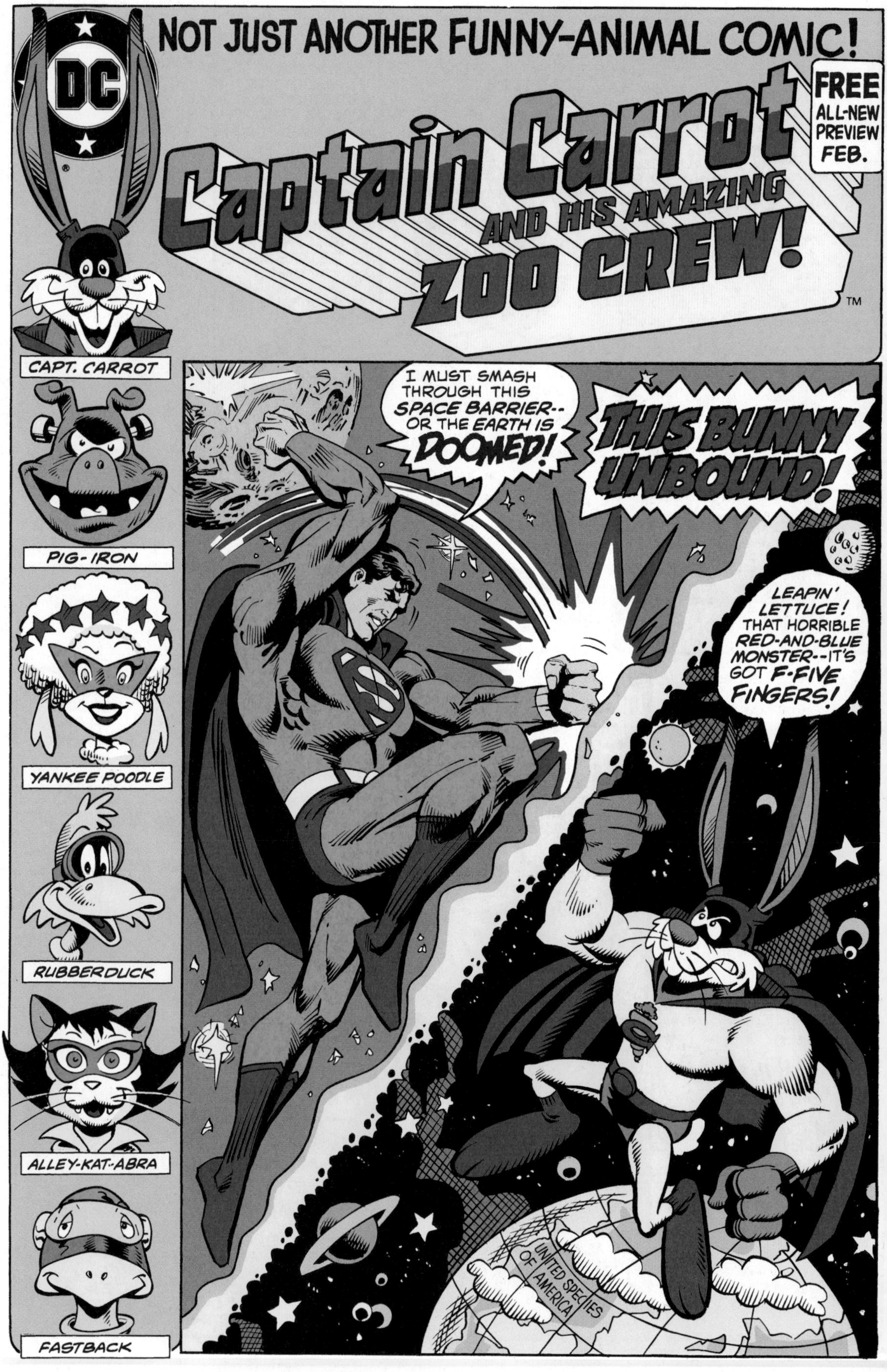
NOT JUST ANOTHER FUNNY-ANIMAL COMIC!
DC
FREE ALL-NEW PREVIEW FEB.
Captain Carrot AND HIS AMAZING ZOO CREW!
TM
CAPT. CARROT
PIG-IRON
YANKEE POODLE
RUBBERDUCK
ALLEY-KAT-ABRA
FASTBACK
I MUST SMASH THROUGH THIS SPACE BARRIER-- OR THE EARTH IS DOOMED!
THIS BUNNY UNBOUND!
LEAPIN' LETTUCE! THAT HORRIBLE RED-AND-BLUE MONSTER--IT'S GOT F-FIVE FINGERS!
UNITED SPECIES OF AMERICA

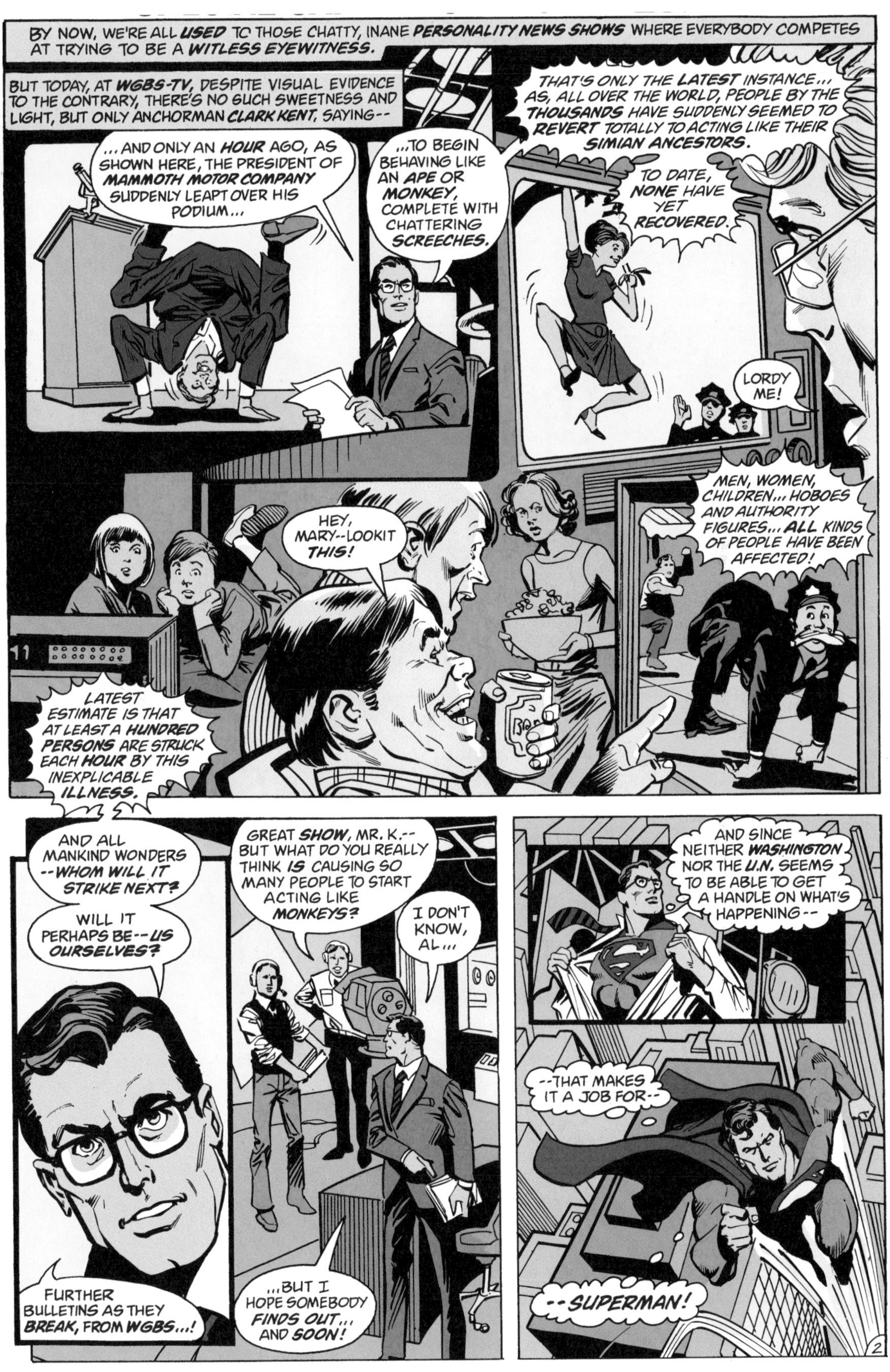
BY NOW, WE'RE ALL USED TO THOSE CHATTY, INANE PERSONALITY NEWS SHOWS WHERE EVERYBODY COMPETES AT TRYING TO BE A WITLESS EYEWITNESS.
BUT TODAY, AT WGBS-TV, DESPITE VISUAL EVIDENCE TO THE CONTRARY, THERE'S NO SUCH SWEETNESS AND LIGHT, BUT ONLY ANCHORMAN CLARK KENT, SAYING--
...AND ONLY AN HOUR AGO, AS SHOWN HERE, THE PRESIDENT OF MAMMOTH MOTOR COMPANY SUDDENLY LEAPT OVER HIS PODIUM...
...TO BEGIN BEHAVING LIKE AN APE OR MONKEY, COMPLETE WITH CHATTERING SCREECHES.
THAT'S ONLY THE LATEST INSTANCE... AS, ALL OVER THE WORLD, PEOPLE BY THE THOUSANDS HAVE SUDDENLY SEEMED TO REVERT TOTALLY TO ACTING LIKE THEIR SIMIAN ANCESTORS.
TO DATE, NONE HAVE YET RECOVERED.
LORDY ME!
HEY, MARY--LOOKIT THIS!
MEN, WOMEN, CHILDREN... HOBOES AND AUTHORITY FIGURES... ALL KINDS OF PEOPLE HAVE BEEN AFFECTED!
LATEST ESTIMATE IS THAT AT LEAST A HUNDRED PERSONS ARE STRUCK EACH HOUR BY THIS INEXPLICABLE ILLNESS.
AND ALL MANKIND WONDERS --WHOM WILL IT STRIKE NEXT?
WILL IT PERHAPS BE--US OURSELVES?
FURTHER BULLETINS AS THEY BREAK, FROM WGBS...!
GREAT SHOW, MR. K.--BUT WHAT DO YOU REALLY THINK IS CAUSING SO MANY PEOPLE TO START ACTING LIKE MONKEYS?
I DON'T KNOW, AL...
...BUT I HOPE SOMEBODY FINDS OUT... AND SOON!
AND SINCE NEITHER WASHINGTON NOR THE U.N. SEEMS TO BE ABLE TO GET A HANDLE ON WHAT'S HAPPENING--
--THAT MAKES IT A JOB FOR--
--SUPERMAN!
2

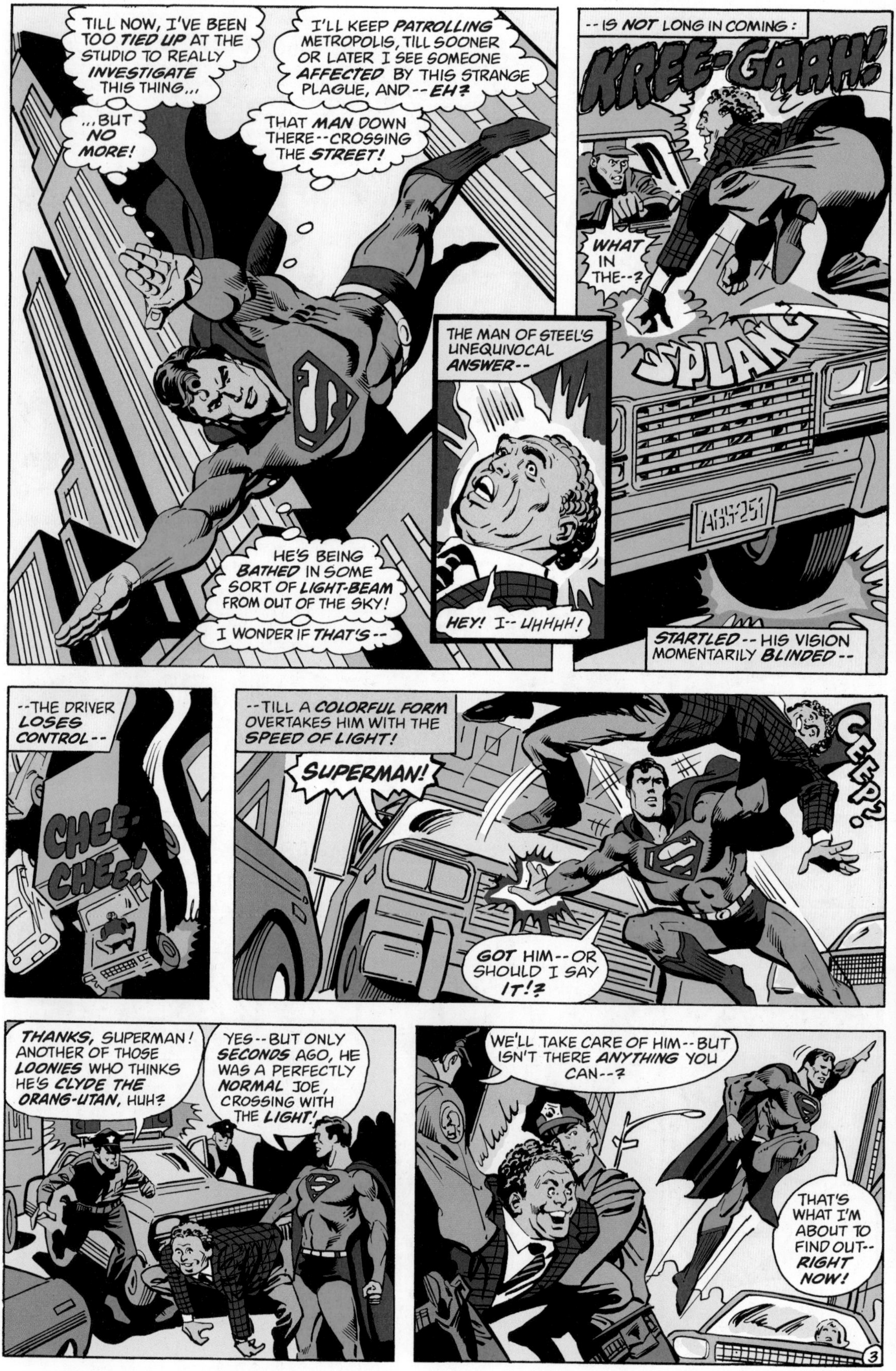

TILL NOW, I'VE BEEN TOO TIED UP AT THE STUDIO TO REALLY INVESTIGATE THIS THING...
...BUT NO MORE!
I'LL KEEP PATROLLING METROPOLIS, TILL SOONER OR LATER I SEE SOMEONE AFFECTED BY THIS STRANGE PLAGUE, AND--EH?
THAT MAN DOWN THERE--CROSSING THE STREET!
HE'S BEING BATHED IN SOME SORT OF LIGHT-BEAM FROM OUT OF THE SKY!
I WONDER IF THAT'S--
THE MAN OF STEEL'S UNEQUIVOCAL ANSWER--
HEY! I--UHHHH!
--IS NOT LONG IN COMING:
KREE-GAAH!
WHAT IN THE--?
SPLANG
STARTLED--HIS VISION MOMENTARILY BLINDED--
--THE DRIVER LOSES CONTROL--
CHEE-CHEE!
--TILL A COLORFUL FORM OVERTAKES HIM WITH THE SPEED OF LIGHT!
SUPERMAN!
CEEP?
GOT HIM--OR SHOULD I SAY IT!?
THANKS, SUPERMAN! ANOTHER OF THOSE LOONIES WHO THINKS HE'S CLYDE THE ORANG-UTAN, HUH?
YES--BUT ONLY SECONDS AGO, HE WAS A PERFECTLY NORMAL JOE, CROSSING WITH THE LIGHT!
WE'LL TAKE CARE OF HIM--BUT ISN'T THERE ANYTHING YOU CAN--?
THAT'S WHAT I'M ABOUT TO FIND OUT--RIGHT NOW!
3

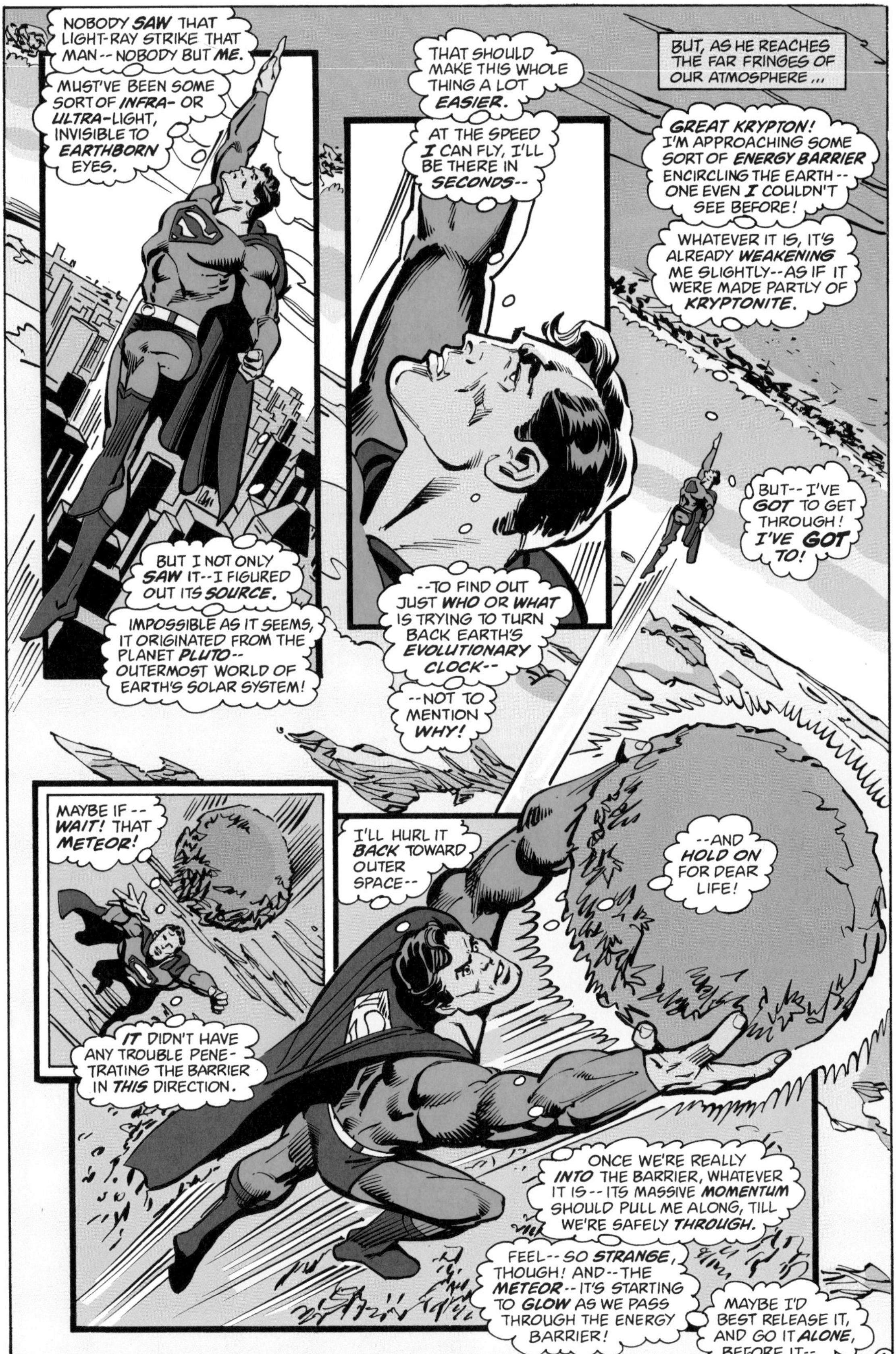
NOBODY SAW THAT LIGHT-RAY STRIKE THAT MAN -- NOBODY BUT ME.
MUST'VE BEEN SOME SORT OF INFRA- OR ULTRA-LIGHT, INVISIBLE TO EARTHBORN EYES.
BUT I NOT ONLY SAW IT -- I FIGURED OUT ITS SOURCE.
IMPOSSIBLE AS IT SEEMS, IT ORIGINATED FROM THE PLANET PLUTO -- OUTERMOST WORLD OF EARTH'S SOLAR SYSTEM!
THAT SHOULD MAKE THIS WHOLE THING A LOT EASIER.
AT THE SPEED I CAN FLY, I'LL BE THERE IN SECONDS--
--TO FIND OUT JUST WHO OR WHAT IS TRYING TO TURN BACK EARTH'S EVOLUTIONARY CLOCK--
--NOT TO MENTION WHY!
BUT, AS HE REACHES THE FAR FRINGES OF OUR ATMOSPHERE ...
GREAT KRYPTON! I'M APPROACHING SOME SORT OF ENERGY BARRIER ENCIRCLING THE EARTH -- ONE EVEN I COULDN'T SEE BEFORE!
WHATEVER IT IS, IT'S ALREADY WEAKENING ME SLIGHTLY -- AS IF IT WERE MADE PARTLY OF KRYPTONITE.
BUT -- I'VE GOT TO GET THROUGH! I'VE GOT TO!
MAYBE IF -- WAIT! THAT METEOR!
IT DIDN'T HAVE ANY TROUBLE PENE-TRATING THE BARRIER IN THIS DIRECTION.
I'LL HURL IT BACK TOWARD OUTER SPACE--
--AND HOLD ON FOR DEAR LIFE!
ONCE WE'RE REALLY INTO THE BARRIER, WHATEVER IT IS -- ITS MASSIVE MOMENTUM SHOULD PULL ME ALONG, TILL WE'RE SAFELY THROUGH.
FEEL -- SO STRANGE, THOUGH! AND -- THE METEOR -- IT'S STARTING TO GLOW AS WE PASS THROUGH THE ENERGY BARRIER!
MAYBE I'D BEST RELEASE IT, AND GO IT ALONE, BEFORE IT--
4

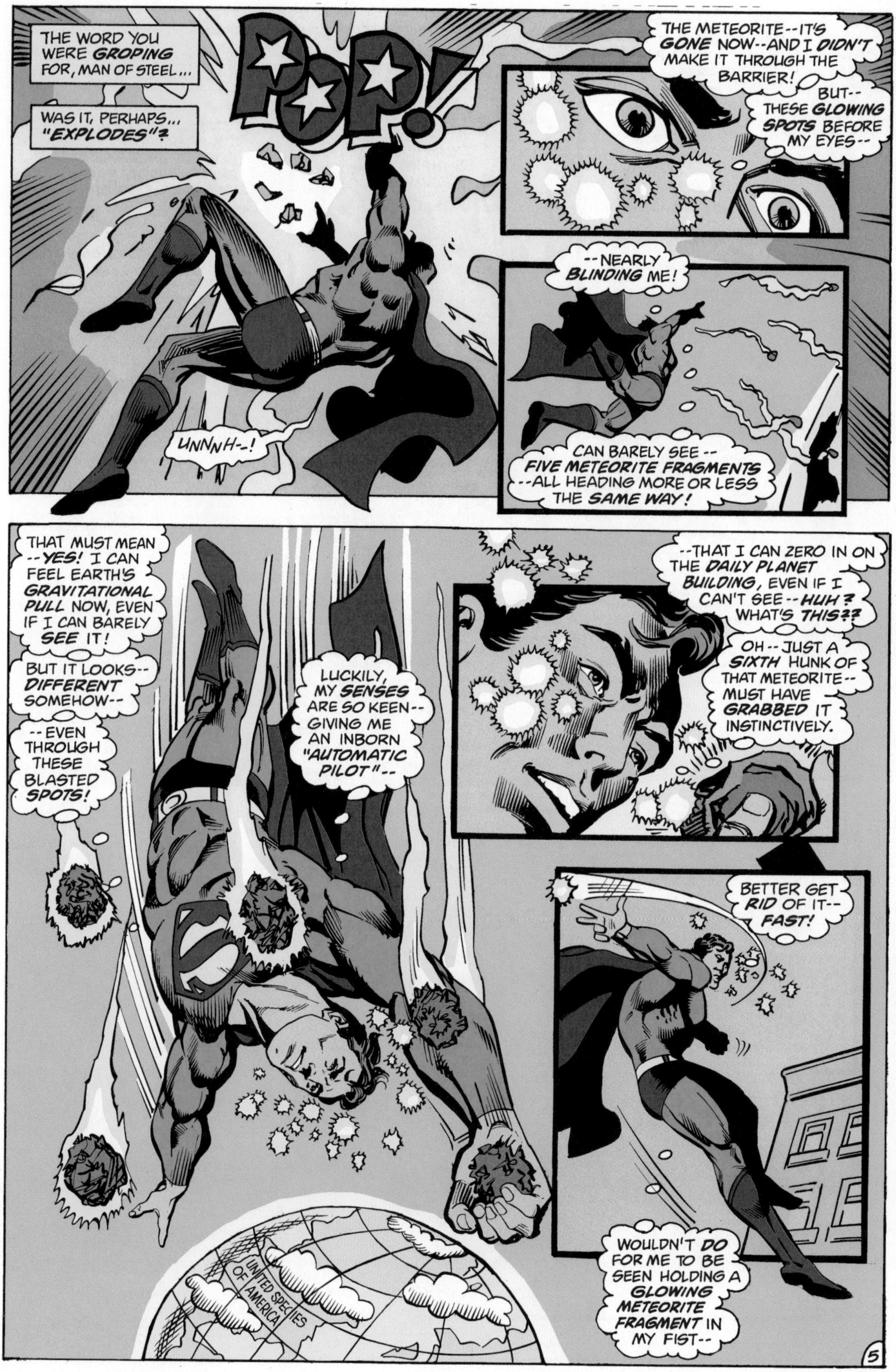
THE WORD YOU WERE GROPING FOR, MAN OF STEEL...
WAS IT, PERHAPS... "EXPLODES"?
POP!
UNNNH--!
THE METEORITE--IT'S GONE NOW--AND I DIDN'T MAKE IT THROUGH THE BARRIER!
BUT--THESE GLOWING SPOTS BEFORE MY EYES--
--NEARLY BLINDING ME!
CAN BARELY SEE--FIVE METEORITE FRAGMENTS--ALL HEADING MORE OR LESS THE SAME WAY!
THAT MUST MEAN--YES! I CAN FEEL EARTH'S GRAVITATIONAL PULL NOW, EVEN IF I CAN BARELY SEE IT!
BUT IT LOOKS--DIFFERENT SOMEHOW--
--EVEN THROUGH THESE BLASTED SPOTS!
LUCKILY, MY SENSES ARE SO KEEN--GIVING ME AN INBORN "AUTOMATIC PILOT"--
--THAT I CAN ZERO IN ON THE DAILY PLANET BUILDING, EVEN IF I CAN'T SEE--HUH? WHAT'S THIS??
OH--JUST A SIXTH HUNK OF THAT METEORITE--MUST HAVE GRABBED IT INSTINCTIVELY.
UNITED SPECIES OF AMERICA
BETTER GET RID OF IT--FAST!
WOULDN'T DO FOR ME TO BE SEEN HOLDING A GLOWING METEORITE FRAGMENT IN MY FIST--
5

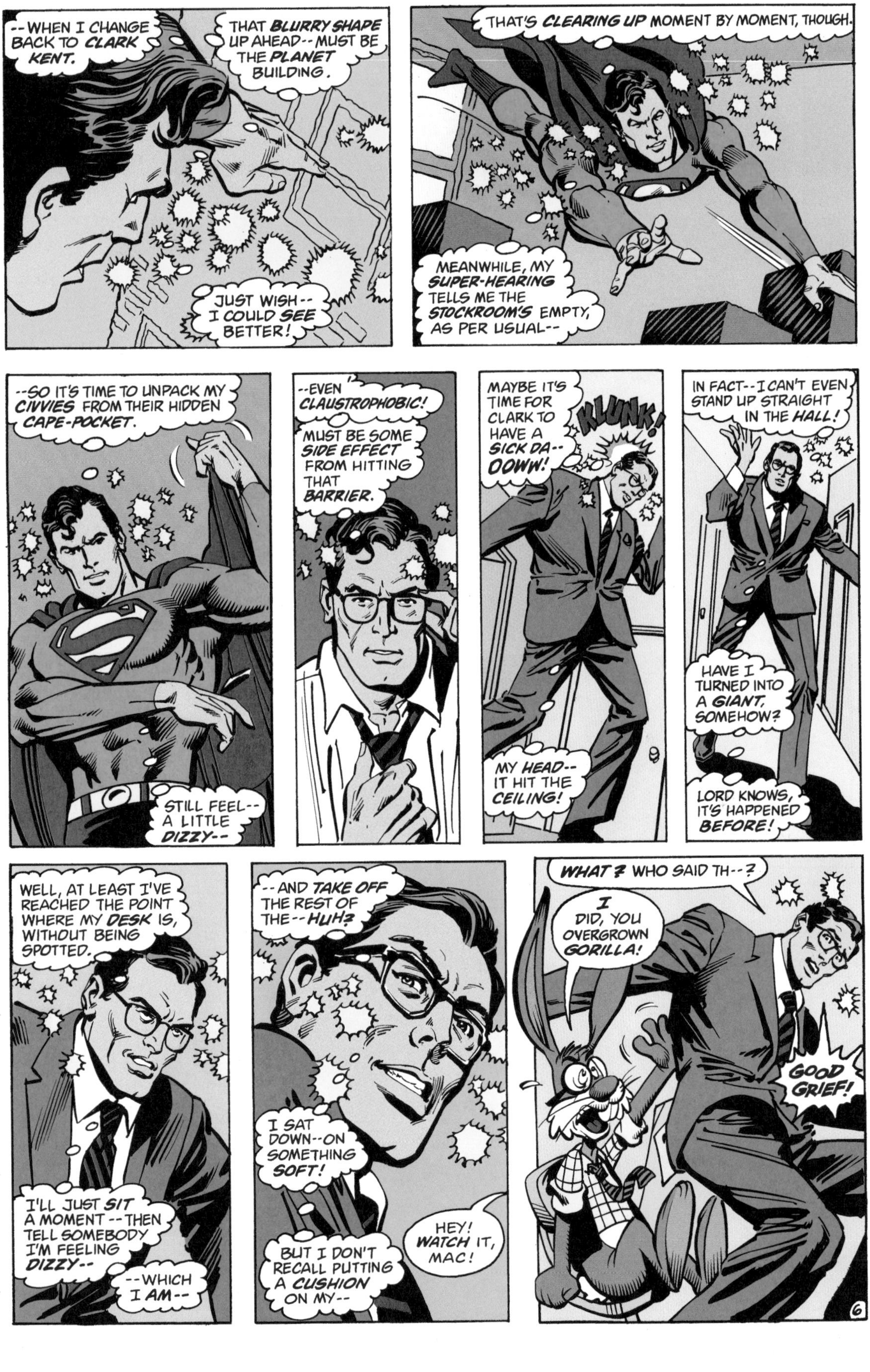
--WHEN I CHANGE BACK TO CLARK KENT.
THAT BLURRY SHAPE UP AHEAD--MUST BE THE PLANET BUILDING.
JUST WISH--I COULD SEE BETTER!
THAT'S CLEARING UP MOMENT BY MOMENT, THOUGH.
MEANWHILE, MY SUPER-HEARING TELLS ME THE STOCKROOM'S EMPTY, AS PER USUAL--
--SO IT'S TIME TO UNPACK MY CIVVIES FROM THEIR HIDDEN CAPE-POCKET.
STILL FEEL--A LITTLE DIZZY--
--EVEN CLAUSTROPHOBIC!
MUST BE SOME SIDE EFFECT FROM HITTING THAT BARRIER.
MAYBE IT'S TIME FOR CLARK TO HAVE A SICK DA--OOWW!
KLUNK!
MY HEAD--IT HIT THE CEILING!
IN FACT--I CAN'T EVEN STAND UP STRAIGHT IN THE HALL!
HAVE I TURNED INTO A GIANT, SOMEHOW?
LORD KNOWS, IT'S HAPPENED BEFORE!
WELL, AT LEAST I'VE REACHED THE POINT WHERE MY DESK IS, WITHOUT BEING SPOTTED.
I'LL JUST SIT A MOMENT--THEN TELL SOMEBODY I'M FEELING DIZZY--
--WHICH I AM--
--AND TAKE OFF THE REST OF THE--HUH?
I SAT DOWN--ON SOMETHING SOFT!
BUT I DON'T RECALL PUTTING A CUSHION ON MY--
HEY! WATCH IT, MAC!
WHAT? WHO SAID TH--?
I DID, YOU OVERGROWN GORILLA!
GOOD GRIEF!
6

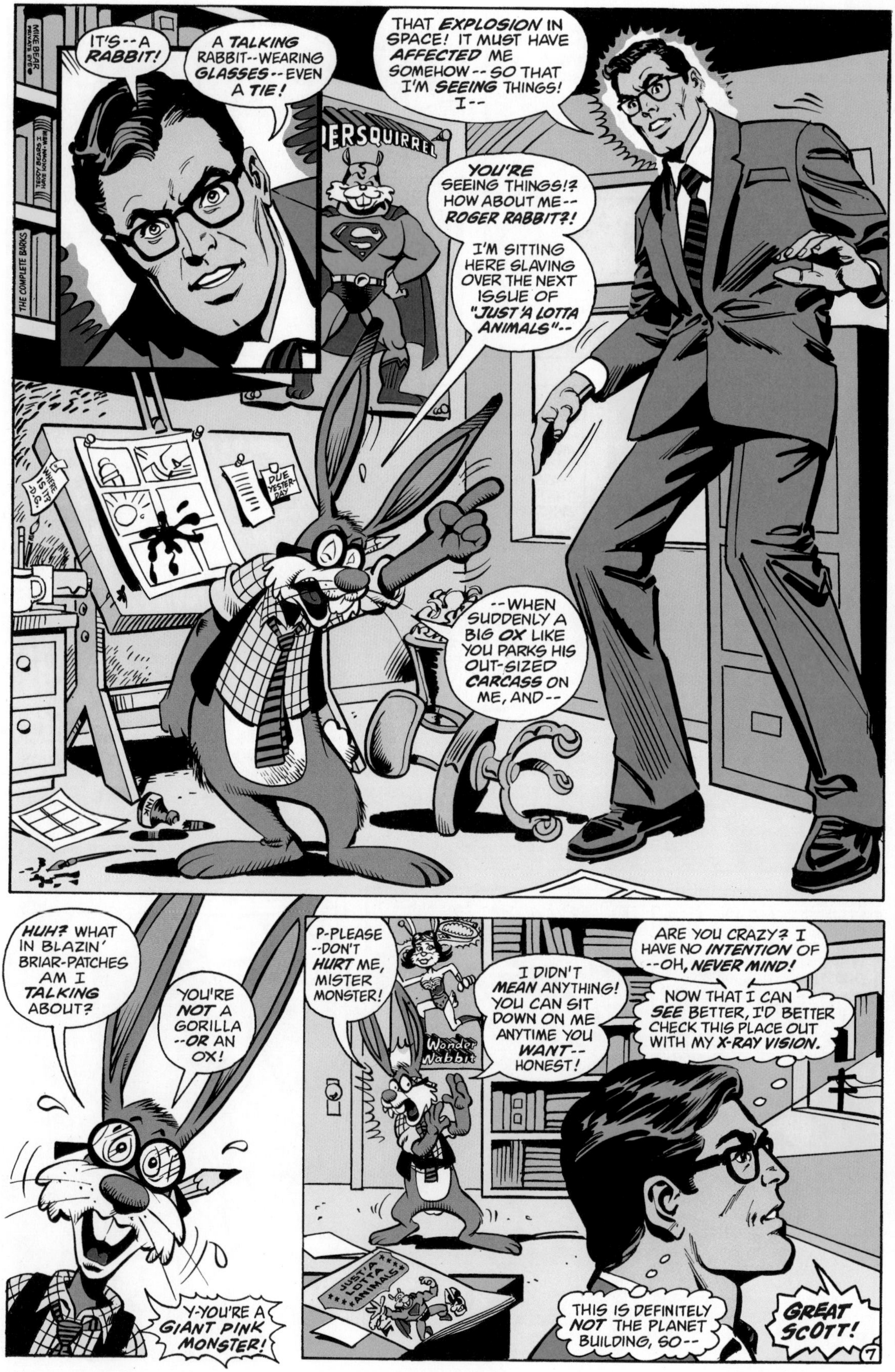
IT'S--A RABBIT!
A TALKING RABBIT--WEARING GLASSES--EVEN A TIE!
THAT EXPLOSION IN SPACE! IT MUST HAVE AFFECTED ME SOMEHOW--SO THAT I'M SEEING THINGS! I--
YOU'RE SEEING THINGS!? HOW ABOUT ME--ROGER RABBIT?!
I'M SITTING HERE SLAVING OVER THE NEXT ISSUE OF "JUST'A LOTTA ANIMALS"--
--WHEN SUDDENLY A BIG OX LIKE YOU PARKS HIS OUT-SIZED CARCASS ON ME, AND--
MIKE BEAR PRIVATE EYE
TEDDY BEARS I HAVE KNOWN
THE COMPLETE BARKS
WHERE IS IT? R.G.
DUE YESTER-DAY
INK
HUH? WHAT IN BLAZIN' BRIAR-PATCHES AM I TALKING ABOUT?
YOU'RE NOT A GORILLA --OR AN OX!
Y-YOU'RE A GIANT PINK MONSTER!
P-PLEASE --DON'T HURT ME, MISTER MONSTER!
I DIDN'T MEAN ANYTHING! YOU CAN SIT DOWN ON ME ANYTIME YOU WANT--HONEST!
ARE YOU CRAZY? I HAVE NO INTENTION OF --OH, NEVER MIND!
NOW THAT I CAN SEE BETTER, I'D BETTER CHECK THIS PLACE OUT WITH MY X-RAY VISION.
Wonder Wabbit
JUST'A LOTTA ANIMALS
THIS IS DEFINITELY NOT THE PLANET BUILDING, SO--
GREAT SCOTT!
7

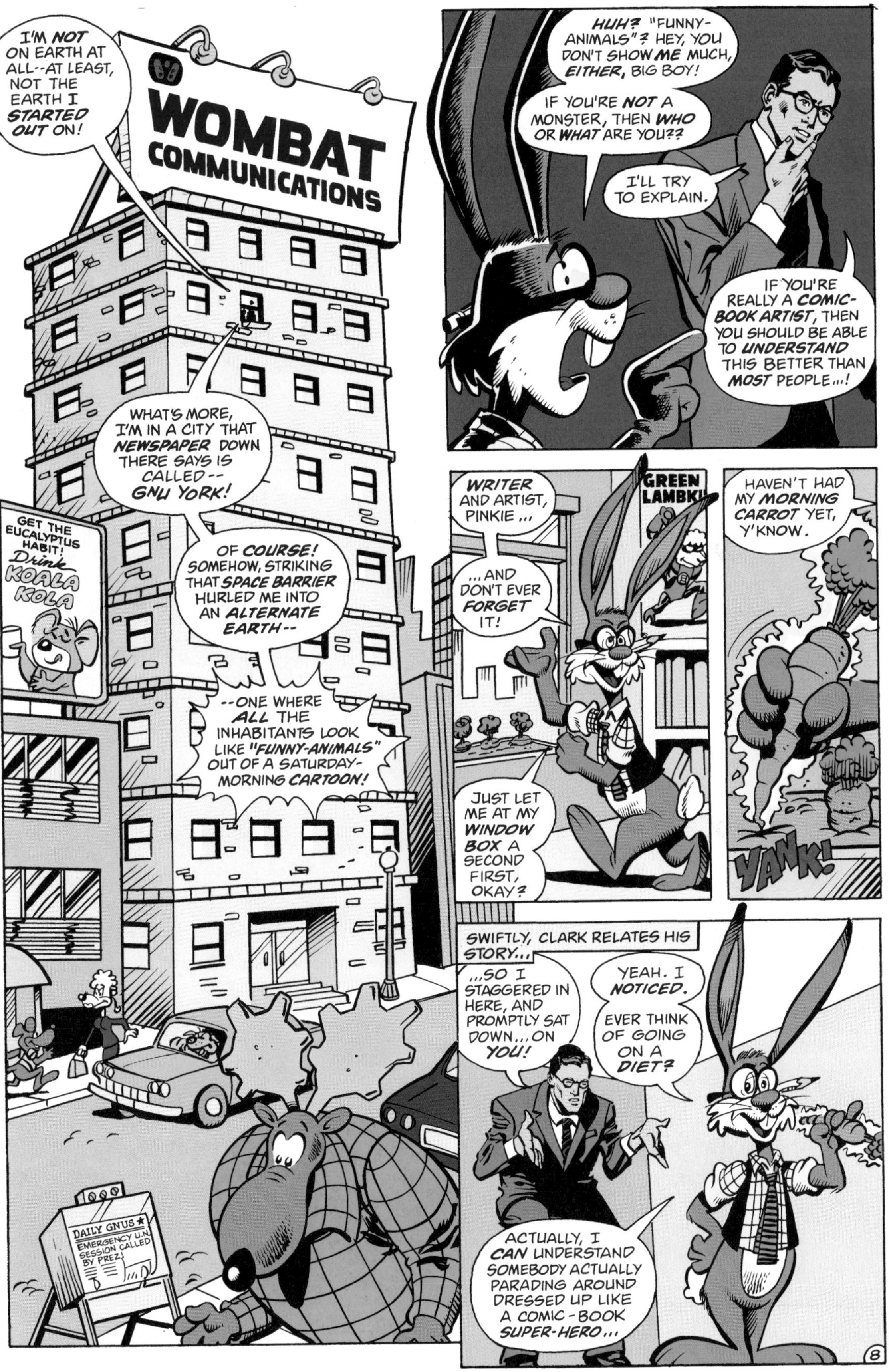
I'M NOT ON EARTH AT ALL--AT LEAST, NOT THE EARTH I STARTED OUT ON!
WOMBAT COMMUNICATIONS
WHAT'S MORE, I'M IN A CITY THAT NEWSPAPER DOWN THERE SAYS IS CALLED-- GNU YORK!
OF COURSE! SOMEHOW, STRIKING THAT SPACE BARRIER HURLED ME INTO AN ALTERNATE EARTH--
--ONE WHERE ALL THE INHABITANTS LOOK LIKE "FUNNY-ANIMALS" OUT OF A SATURDAY-MORNING CARTOON!
GET THE EUCALYPTUS HABIT! Drink KOALA KOLA
DAILY GNUS
EMERGENCY U.N. SESSION CALLED BY PREZ!
HUH? "FUNNY-ANIMALS"? HEY, YOU DON'T SHOW ME MUCH, EITHER, BIG BOY!
IF YOU'RE NOT A MONSTER, THEN WHO OR WHAT ARE YOU??
I'LL TRY TO EXPLAIN.
IF YOU'RE REALLY A COMIC-BOOK ARTIST, THEN YOU SHOULD BE ABLE TO UNDERSTAND THIS BETTER THAN MOST PEOPLE...!
WRITER AND ARTIST, PINKIE...
...AND DON'T EVER FORGET IT!
GREEN LAMBKI
JUST LET ME AT MY WINDOW BOX A SECOND FIRST, OKAY?
HAVEN'T HAD MY MORNING CARROT YET, Y'KNOW.
YANK!
SWIFTLY, CLARK RELATES HIS STORY...
...SO I STAGGERED IN HERE, AND PROMPTLY SAT DOWN... ON YOU!
YEAH. I NOTICED.
EVER THINK OF GOING ON A DIET?
ACTUALLY, I CAN UNDERSTAND SOMEBODY ACTUALLY PARADING AROUND DRESSED UP LIKE A COMIC-BOOK SUPER-HERO...
8

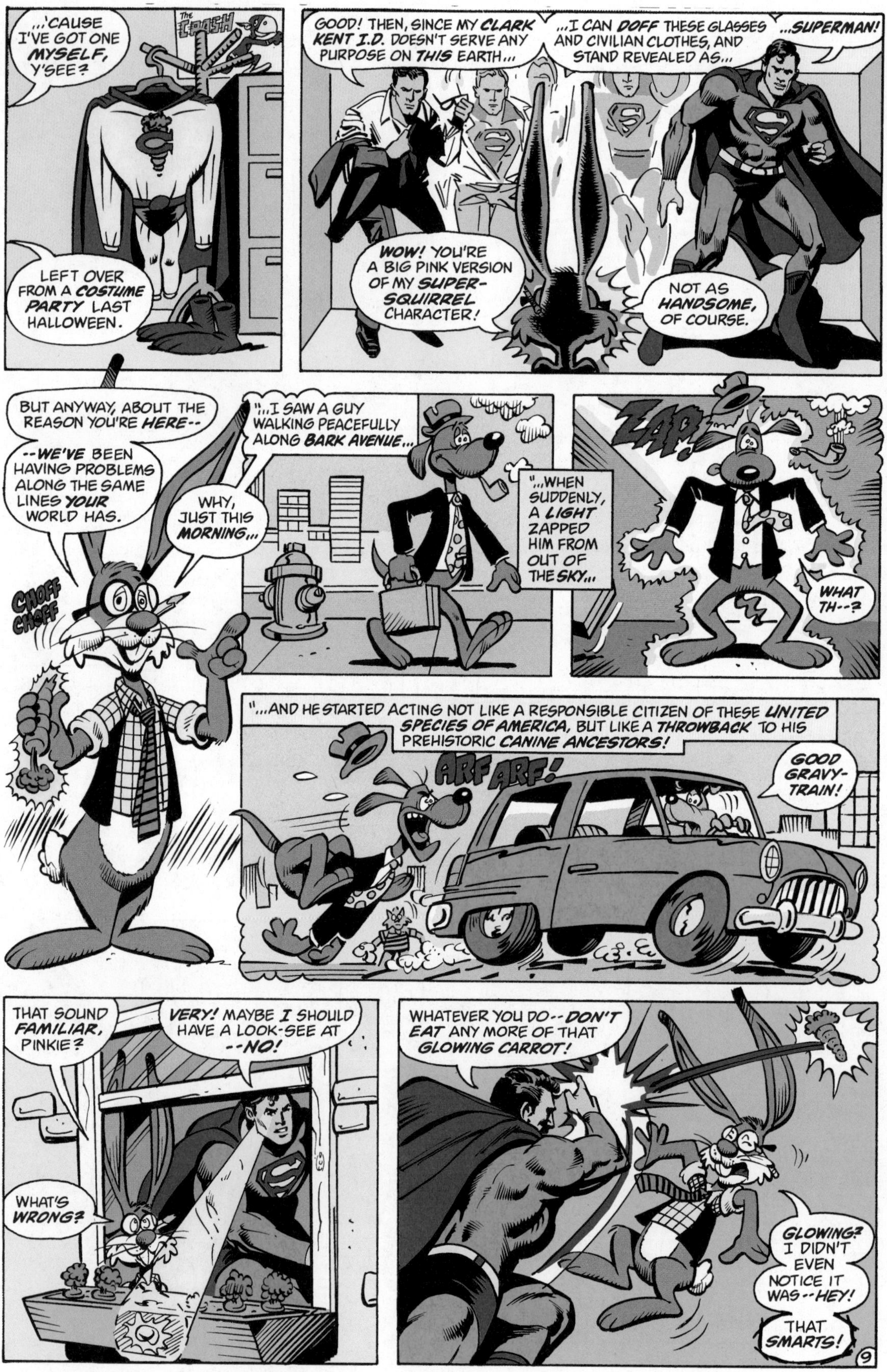

...'CAUSE I'VE GOT ONE MYSELF, Y'SEE?
The CRASH
LEFT OVER FROM A COSTUME PARTY LAST HALLOWEEN.
GOOD! THEN, SINCE MY CLARK KENT I.D. DOESN'T SERVE ANY PURPOSE ON THIS EARTH...
...I CAN DOFF THESE GLASSES AND CIVILIAN CLOTHES, AND STAND REVEALED AS...
...SUPERMAN!
WOW! YOU'RE A BIG PINK VERSION OF MY SUPER-SQUIRREL CHARACTER!
NOT AS HANDSOME, OF COURSE.
BUT ANYWAY, ABOUT THE REASON YOU'RE HERE--
--WE'VE BEEN HAVING PROBLEMS ALONG THE SAME LINES YOUR WORLD HAS.
WHY, JUST THIS MORNING...
CHOFF CHOFF
"...I SAW A GUY WALKING PEACEFULLY ALONG BARK AVENUE...
"...WHEN SUDDENLY, A LIGHT ZAPPED HIM FROM OUT OF THE SKY...
ZAP!
WHAT TH--?
"...AND HE STARTED ACTING NOT LIKE A RESPONSIBLE CITIZEN OF THESE UNITED SPECIES OF AMERICA, BUT LIKE A THROWBACK TO HIS PREHISTORIC CANINE ANCESTORS!
ARF ARF!
GOOD GRAVY-TRAIN!
THAT SOUND FAMILIAR, PINKIE?
VERY! MAYBE I SHOULD HAVE A LOOK-SEE AT --NO!
WHAT'S WRONG?
WHATEVER YOU DO--DON'T EAT ANY MORE OF THAT GLOWING CARROT!
GLOWING? I DIDN'T EVEN NOTICE IT WAS--HEY!
THAT SMARTS!
9

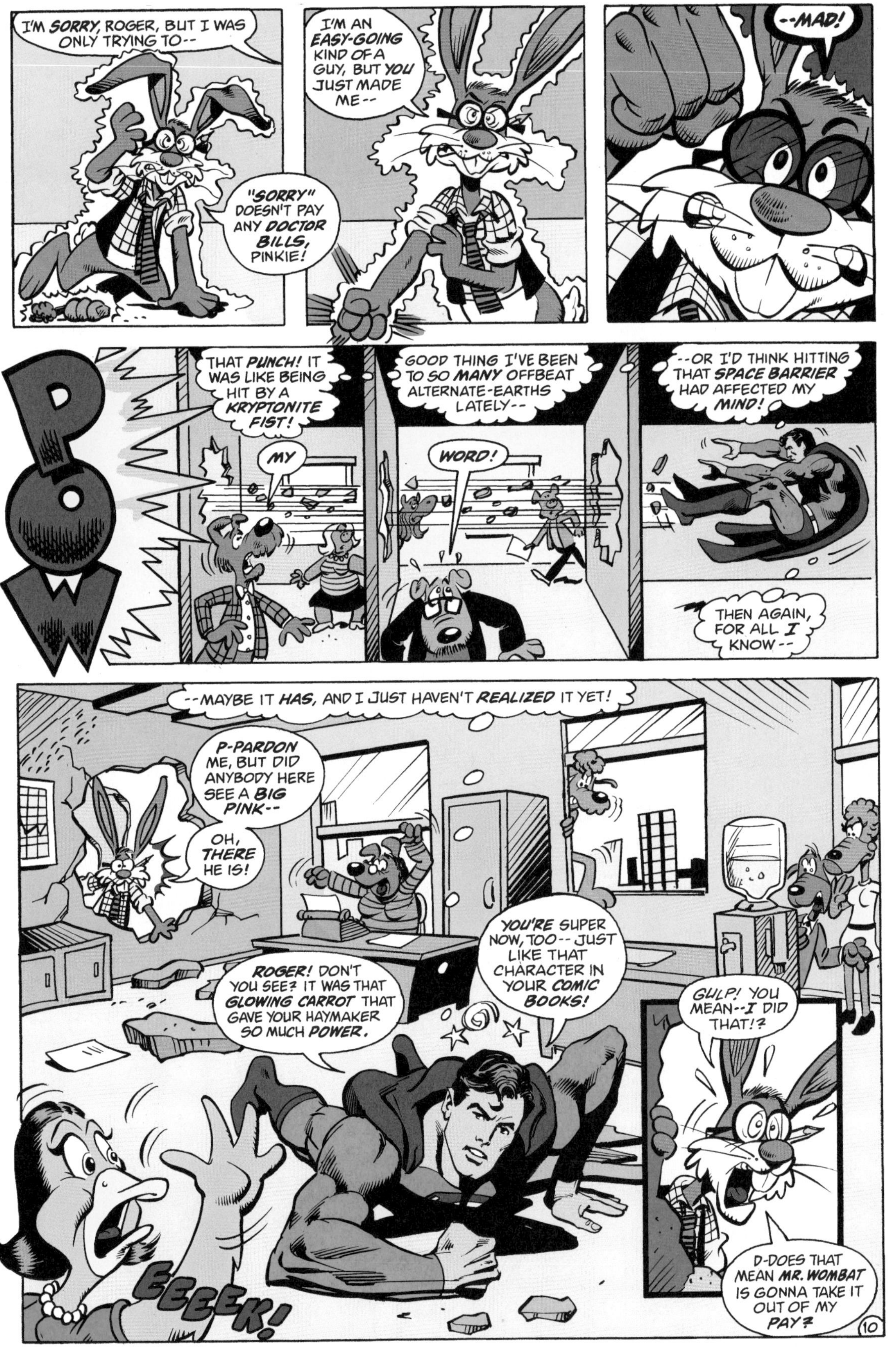
I'M SORRY, ROGER, BUT I WAS ONLY TRYING TO--
I'M AN EASY-GOING KIND OF A GUY, BUT YOU JUST MADE ME--
"SORRY" DOESN'T PAY ANY DOCTOR BILLS, PINKIE!
--MAD!
POW
THAT PUNCH! IT WAS LIKE BEING HIT BY A KRYPTONITE FIST!
MY
GOOD THING I'VE BEEN TO SO MANY OFFBEAT ALTERNATE-EARTHS LATELY--
WORD!
--OR I'D THINK HITTING THAT SPACE BARRIER HAD AFFECTED MY MIND!
THEN AGAIN, FOR ALL I KNOW--
--MAYBE IT HAS, AND I JUST HAVEN'T REALIZED IT YET!
P-PARDON ME, BUT DID ANYBODY HERE SEE A BIG PINK--
OH, THERE HE IS!
YOU'RE SUPER NOW, TOO-- JUST LIKE THAT CHARACTER IN YOUR COMIC BOOKS!
ROGER! DON'T YOU SEE? IT WAS THAT GLOWING CARROT THAT GAVE YOUR HAYMAKER SO MUCH POWER.
GULP! YOU MEAN--I DID THAT!?
EEEEK!
D-DOES THAT MEAN MR. WOMBAT IS GONNA TAKE IT OUT OF MY PAY?
10

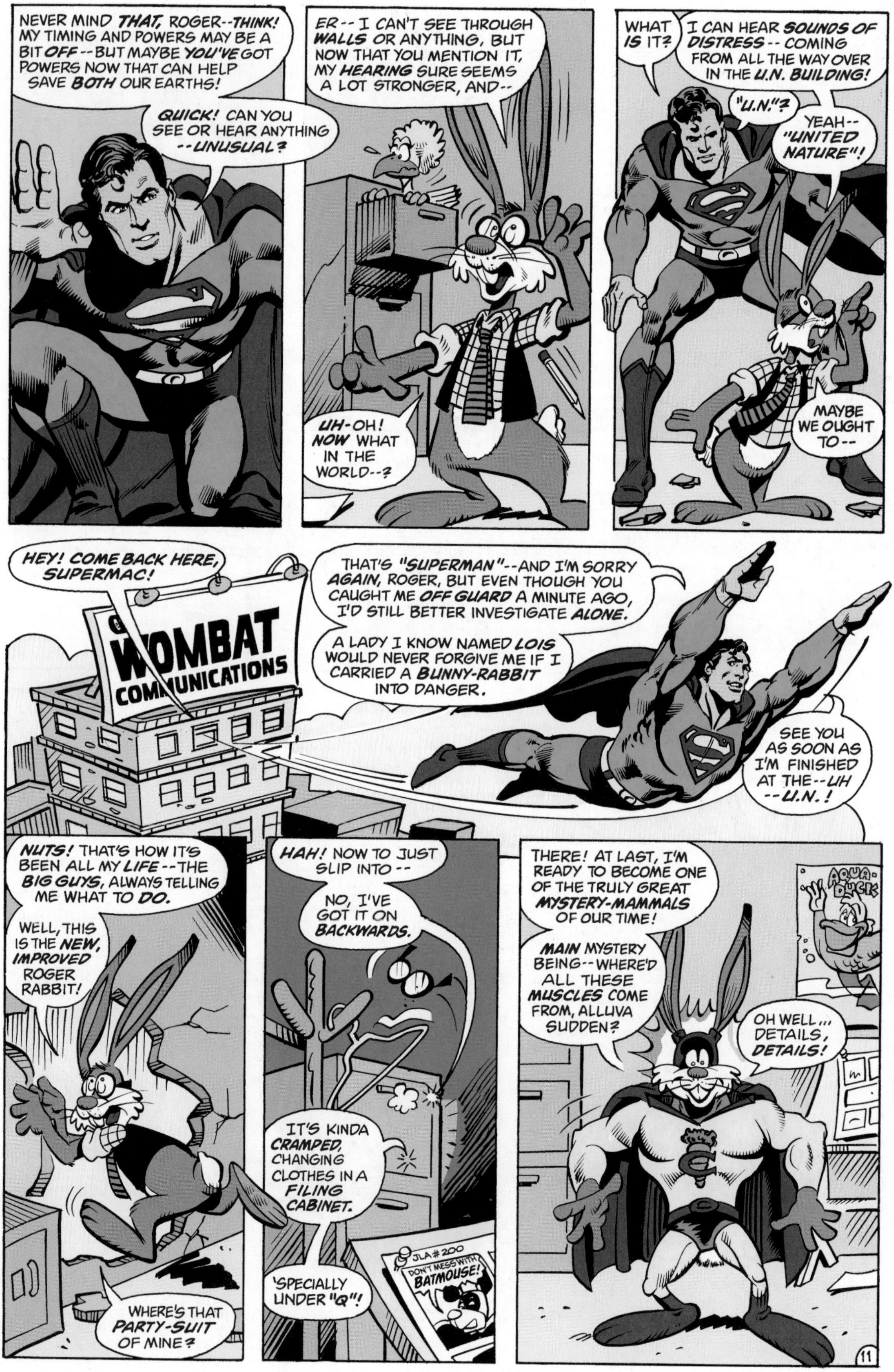
NEVER MIND THAT, ROGER--THINK! MY TIMING AND POWERS MAY BE A BIT OFF--BUT MAYBE YOU'VE GOT POWERS NOW THAT CAN HELP SAVE BOTH OUR EARTHS!
QUICK! CAN YOU SEE OR HEAR ANYTHING --UNUSUAL?
ER--I CAN'T SEE THROUGH WALLS OR ANYTHING, BUT NOW THAT YOU MENTION IT, MY HEARING SURE SEEMS A LOT STRONGER, AND--
UH-OH! NOW WHAT IN THE WORLD--?
WHAT IS IT?
I CAN HEAR SOUNDS OF DISTRESS--COMING FROM ALL THE WAY OVER IN THE U.N. BUILDING!
"U.N."?
YEAH-- "UNITED NATURE"!
MAYBE WE OUGHT TO--
HEY! COME BACK HERE, SUPERMAC!
WOMBAT COMMUNICATIONS
THAT'S "SUPERMAN"--AND I'M SORRY AGAIN, ROGER, BUT EVEN THOUGH YOU CAUGHT ME OFF GUARD A MINUTE AGO, I'D STILL BETTER INVESTIGATE ALONE.
A LADY I KNOW NAMED LOIS WOULD NEVER FORGIVE ME IF I CARRIED A BUNNY-RABBIT INTO DANGER.
SEE YOU AS SOON AS I'M FINISHED AT THE--UH --U.N.!
NUTS! THAT'S HOW IT'S BEEN ALL MY LIFE--THE BIG GUYS, ALWAYS TELLING ME WHAT TO DO.
WELL, THIS IS THE NEW, IMPROVED ROGER RABBIT!
WHERE'S THAT PARTY-SUIT OF MINE?
HAH! NOW TO JUST SLIP INTO--
NO, I'VE GOT IT ON BACKWARDS.
IT'S KINDA CRAMPED, CHANGING CLOTHES IN A FILING CABINET.
'SPECIALLY UNDER "Q"!
JLA #200
DON'T MESS WITH BATMOUSE!
THERE! AT LAST, I'M READY TO BECOME ONE OF THE TRULY GREAT MYSTERY-MAMMALS OF OUR TIME!
MAIN MYSTERY BEING--WHERE'D ALL THESE MUSCLES COME FROM, ALLUVA SUDDEN?
OH WELL... DETAILS, DETAILS!
AQUA-DUCK
11

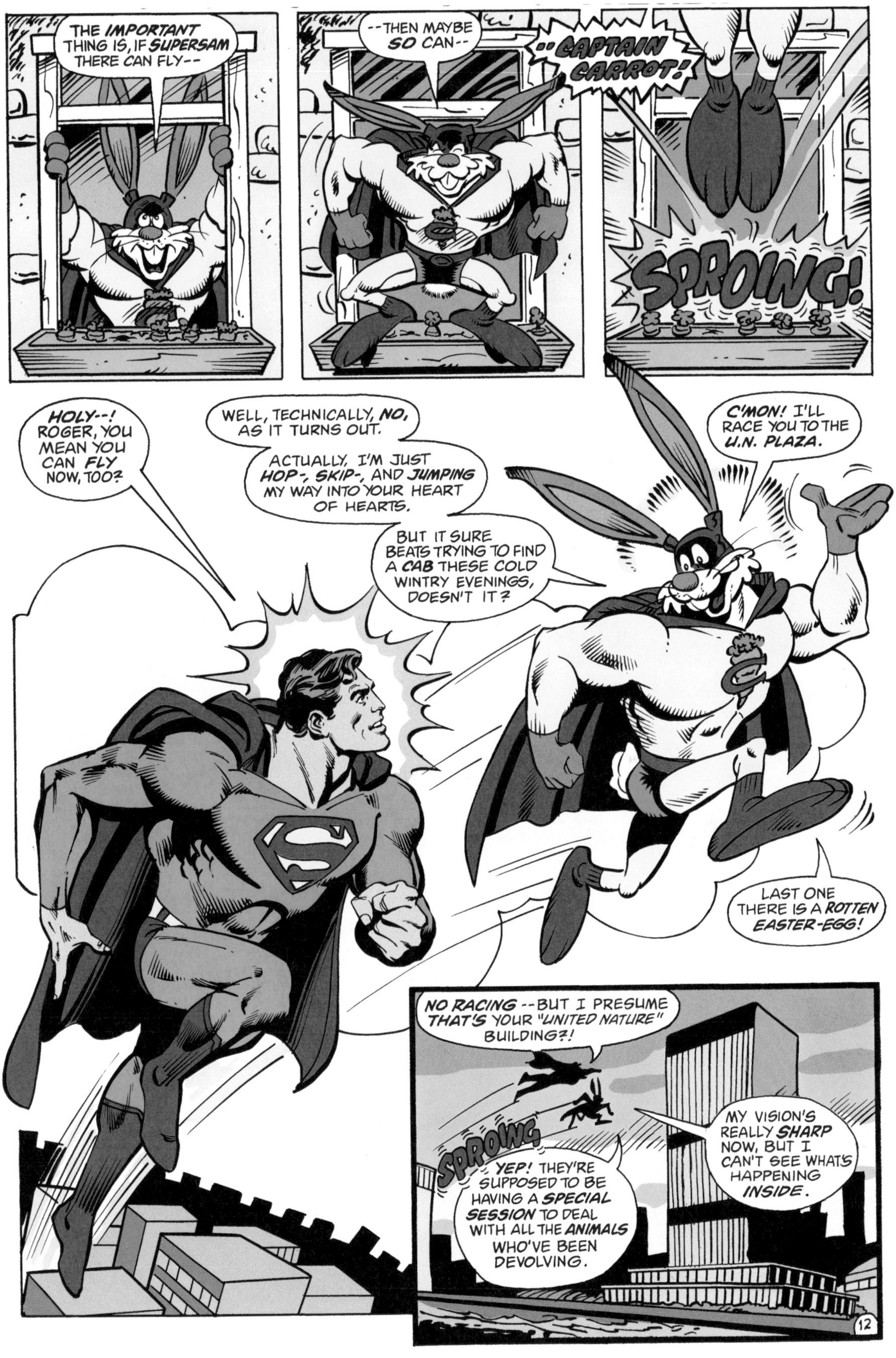

THE IMPORTANT THING IS, IF SUPERSAM THERE CAN FLY--
--THEN MAYBE SO CAN--
--CAPTAIN CARROT!
SPROING!
HOLY--! ROGER, YOU MEAN YOU CAN FLY NOW, TOO?
WELL, TECHNICALLY, NO, AS IT TURNS OUT.
ACTUALLY, I'M JUST HOP-, SKIP-, AND JUMPING MY WAY INTO YOUR HEART OF HEARTS.
BUT IT SURE BEATS TRYING TO FIND A CAB THESE COLD WINTRY EVENINGS, DOESN'T IT?
C'MON! I'LL RACE YOU TO THE U.N. PLAZA.
LAST ONE THERE IS A ROTTEN EASTER-EGG!
NO RACING --BUT I PRESUME THAT'S YOUR "UNITED NATURE" BUILDING?!
SPROING
YEP! THEY'RE SUPPOSED TO BE HAVING A SPECIAL SESSION TO DEAL WITH ALL THE ANIMALS WHO'VE BEEN DEVOLVING.
MY VISION'S REALLY SHARP NOW, BUT I CAN'T SEE WHAT'S HAPPENING INSIDE.
12

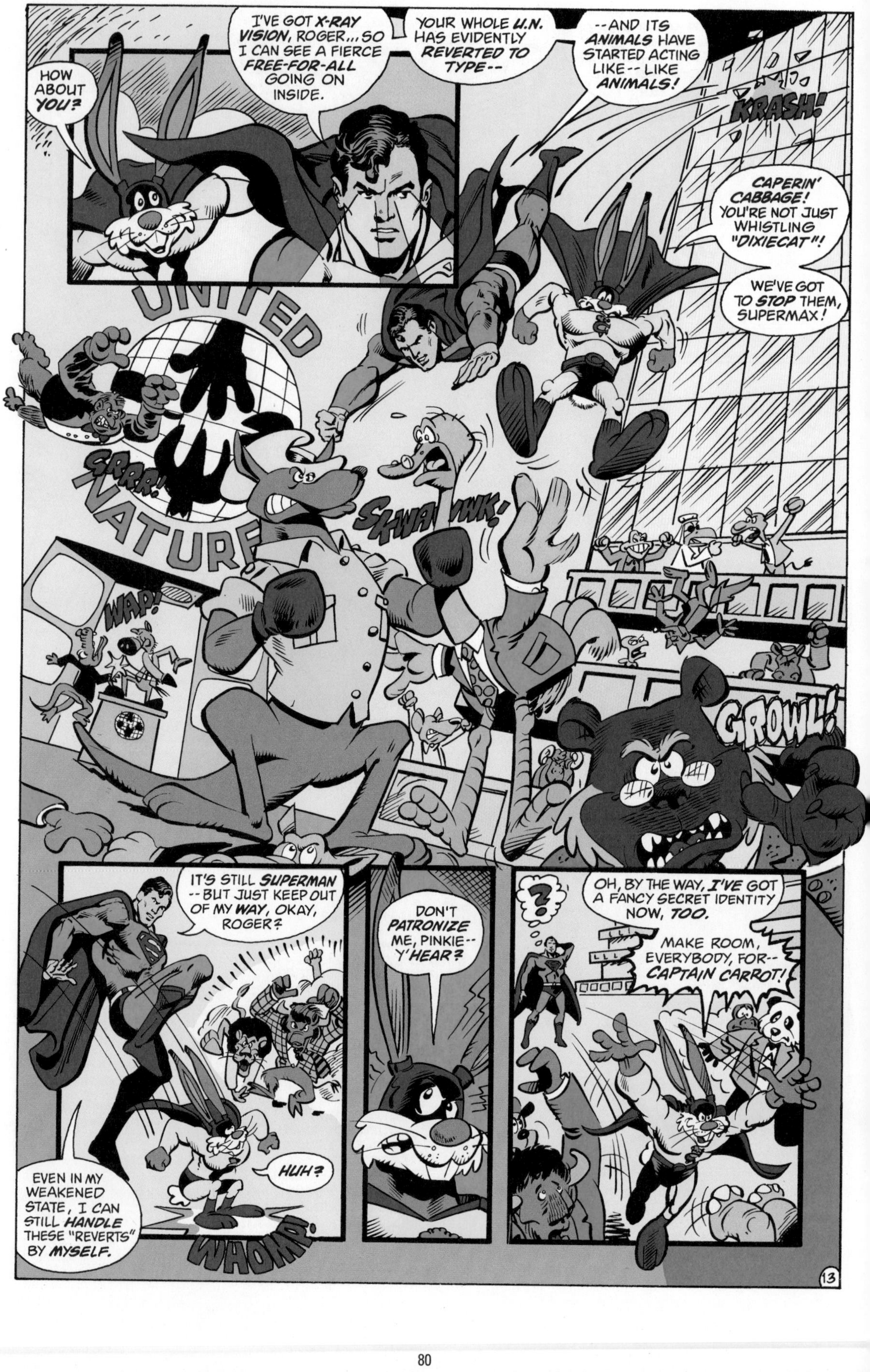
HOW ABOUT YOU?
I'VE GOT X-RAY VISION, ROGER... SO I CAN SEE A FIERCE FREE-FOR-ALL GOING ON INSIDE.
YOUR WHOLE U.N. HAS EVIDENTLY REVERTED TO TYPE--
--AND ITS ANIMALS HAVE STARTED ACTING LIKE-- LIKE ANIMALS!
KRASH!
CAPERIN' CABBAGE! YOU'RE NOT JUST WHISTLING "DIXIECAT"!
WE'VE GOT TO STOP THEM, SUPERMAX!
UNITED NATURE
SRRR!
SKWAWWK!
WAP!
GROWL!
IT'S STILL SUPERMAN --BUT JUST KEEP OUT OF MY WAY, OKAY, ROGER?
HUH?
EVEN IN MY WEAKENED STATE, I CAN STILL HANDLE THESE "REVERTS" BY MYSELF.
WHOMP!
DON'T PATRONIZE ME, PINKIE-- Y'HEAR?
?
OH, BY THE WAY, I'VE GOT A FANCY SECRET IDENTITY NOW, TOO.
MAKE ROOM, EVERYBODY, FOR-- CAPTAIN CARROT!
13

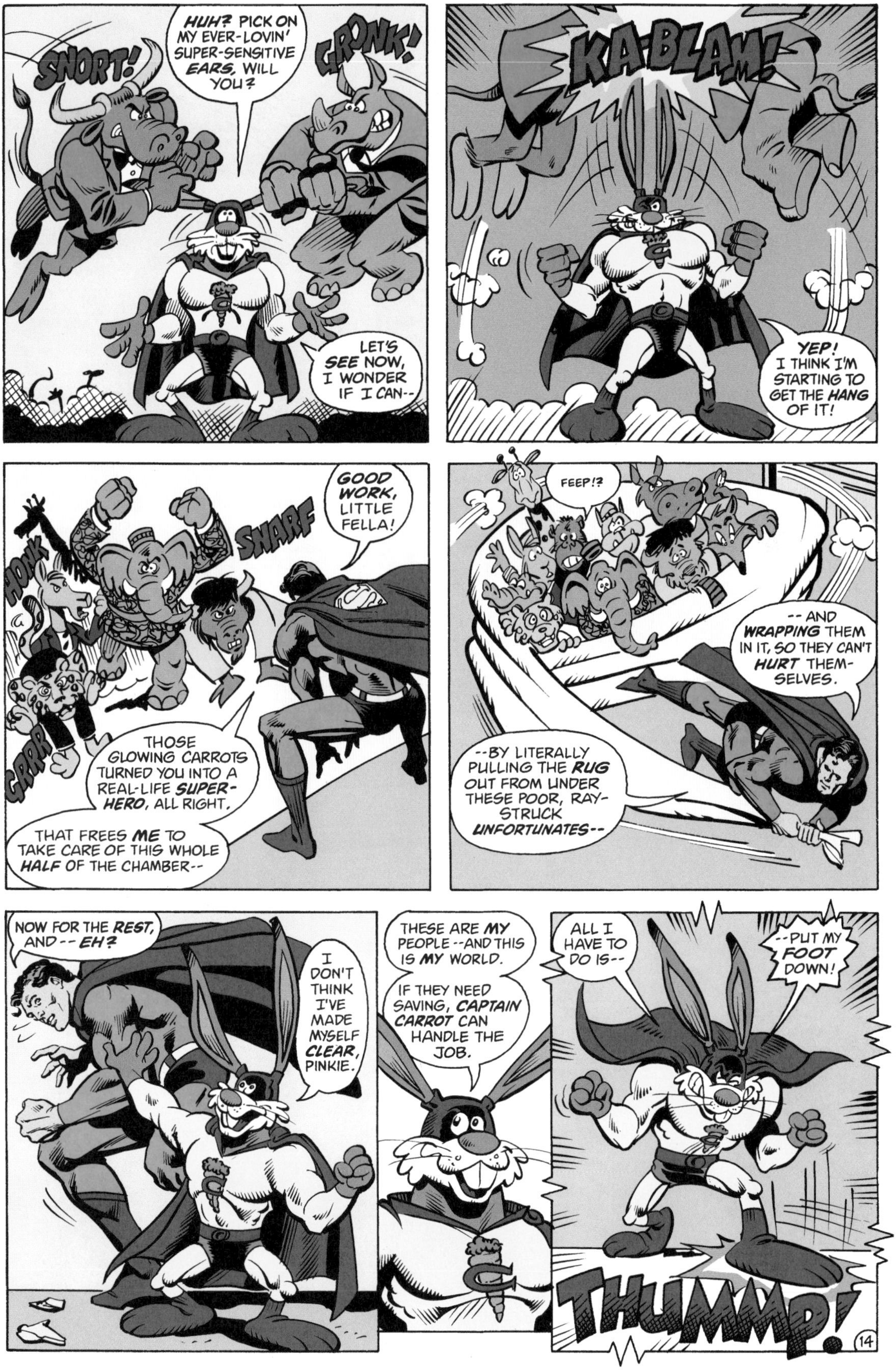
SNORT!
HUH? PICK ON MY EVER-LOVIN' SUPER-SENSITIVE EARS, WILL YOU?
GRONK!
LET'S SEE NOW, I WONDER IF I CAN--
KA-BLAM!
YEP! I THINK I'M STARTING TO GET THE HANG OF IT!
GOOD WORK, LITTLE FELLA!
SNARF
HONK
GRRR
THOSE GLOWING CARROTS TURNED YOU INTO A REAL-LIFE SUPER-HERO, ALL RIGHT.
THAT FREES ME TO TAKE CARE OF THIS WHOLE HALF OF THE CHAMBER--
FEEP!?
--BY LITERALLY PULLING THE RUG OUT FROM UNDER THESE POOR, RAY-STRUCK UNFORTUNATES--
-- AND WRAPPING THEM IN IT, SO THEY CAN'T HURT THEM-SELVES.
NOW FOR THE REST, AND -- EH?
I DON'T THINK I'VE MADE MYSELF CLEAR, PINKIE.
THESE ARE MY PEOPLE --AND THIS IS MY WORLD.
IF THEY NEED SAVING, CAPTAIN CARROT CAN HANDLE THE JOB.
ALL I HAVE TO DO IS--
--PUT MY FOOT DOWN!
THUMMP!
14

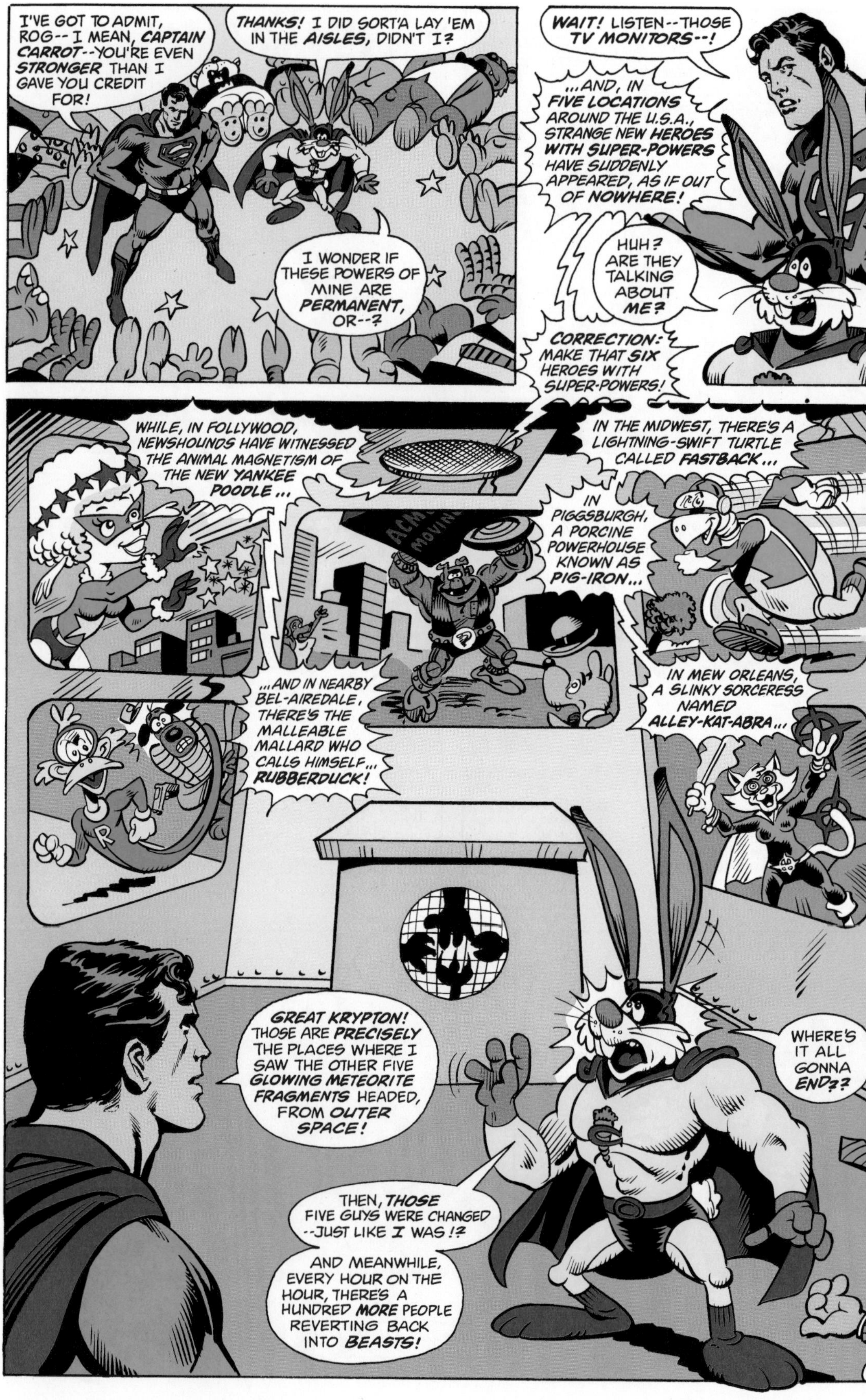
I'VE GOT TO ADMIT, ROG-- I MEAN, CAPTAIN CARROT--YOU'RE EVEN STRONGER THAN I GAVE YOU CREDIT FOR!
THANKS! I DID SORT'A LAY 'EM IN THE AISLES, DIDN'T I?
I WONDER IF THESE POWERS OF MINE ARE PERMANENT, OR--?
WAIT! LISTEN--THOSE TV MONITORS--!
...AND, IN FIVE LOCATIONS AROUND THE U.S.A., STRANGE NEW HEROES WITH SUPER-POWERS HAVE SUDDENLY APPEARED, AS IF OUT OF NOWHERE!
HUH? ARE THEY TALKING ABOUT ME?
CORRECTION: MAKE THAT SIX HEROES WITH SUPER-POWERS!
WHILE, IN FOLLYWOOD, NEWSHOUNDS HAVE WITNESSED THE ANIMAL MAGNETISM OF THE NEW YANKEE POODLE...
IN THE MIDWEST, THERE'S A LIGHTNING-SWIFT TURTLE CALLED FASTBACK...
IN PIGGSBURGH, A PORCINE POWERHOUSE KNOWN AS PIG-IRON...
...AND IN NEARBY BEL-AIREDALE, THERE'S THE MALLEABLE MALLARD WHO CALLS HIMSELF... RUBBERDUCK!
IN MEW ORLEANS, A SLINKY SORCERESS NAMED ALLEY-KAT-ABRA...
GREAT KRYPTON! THOSE ARE PRECISELY THE PLACES WHERE I SAW THE OTHER FIVE GLOWING METEORITE FRAGMENTS HEADED, FROM OUTER SPACE!
WHERE'S IT ALL GONNA END??
THEN, THOSE FIVE GUYS WERE CHANGED --JUST LIKE I WAS!?
AND MEANWHILE, EVERY HOUR ON THE HOUR, THERE'S A HUNDRED MORE PEOPLE REVERTING BACK INTO BEASTS!
15

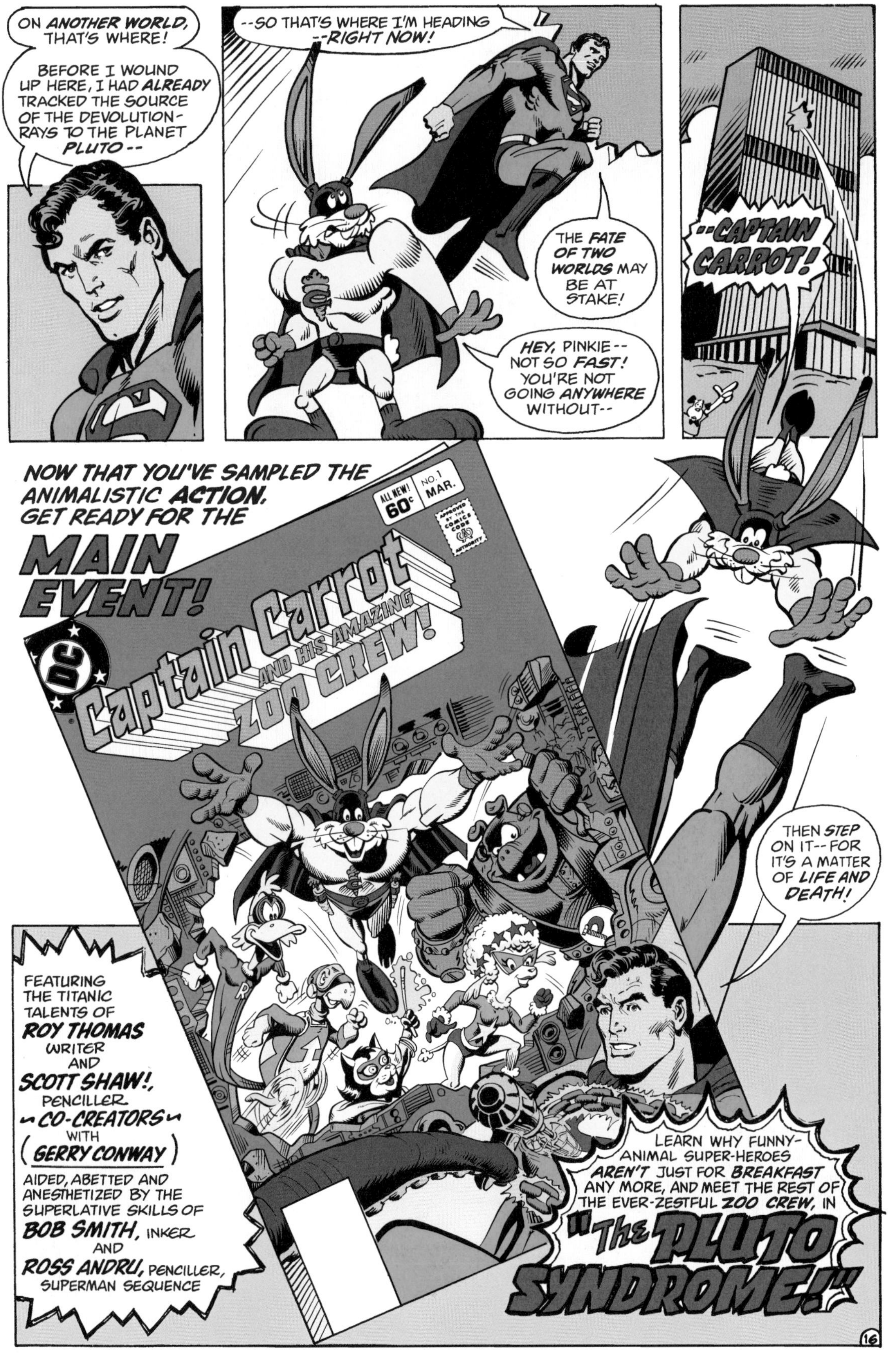

ON ANOTHER WORLD, THAT'S WHERE!
BEFORE I WOUND UP HERE, I HAD ALREADY TRACKED THE SOURCE OF THE DEVOLUTION-RAYS TO THE PLANET PLUTO --
--SO THAT'S WHERE I'M HEADING --RIGHT NOW!
THE FATE OF TWO WORLDS MAY BE AT STAKE!
HEY, PINKIE-- NOT SO FAST! YOU'RE NOT GOING ANYWHERE WITHOUT--
--CAPTAIN CARROT!
NOW THAT YOU'VE SAMPLED THE ANIMALISTIC ACTION, GET READY FOR THE
MAIN EVENT!
ALL NEW! 60¢
NO. 1 MAR.
APPROVED BY THE COMICS CODE AUTHORITY
DC
Captain Carrot AND HIS AMAZING ZOO CREW!
THEN STEP ON IT-- FOR IT'S A MATTER OF LIFE AND DEATH!
FEATURING THE TITANIC TALENTS OF ROY THOMAS WRITER AND SCOTT SHAW!, PENCILLER ~CO-CREATORS~ WITH (GERRY CONWAY)
AIDED, ABETTED AND ANESTHETIZED BY THE SUPERLATIVE SKILLS OF BOB SMITH, INKER AND ROSS ANDRU, PENCILLER, SUPERMAN SEQUENCE
LEARN WHY FUNNY-ANIMAL SUPER-HEROES AREN'T JUST FOR BREAKFAST ANY MORE, AND MEET THE REST OF THE EVER-ZESTFUL ZOO CREW, IN
"The PLUTO SYNDROME!"
16

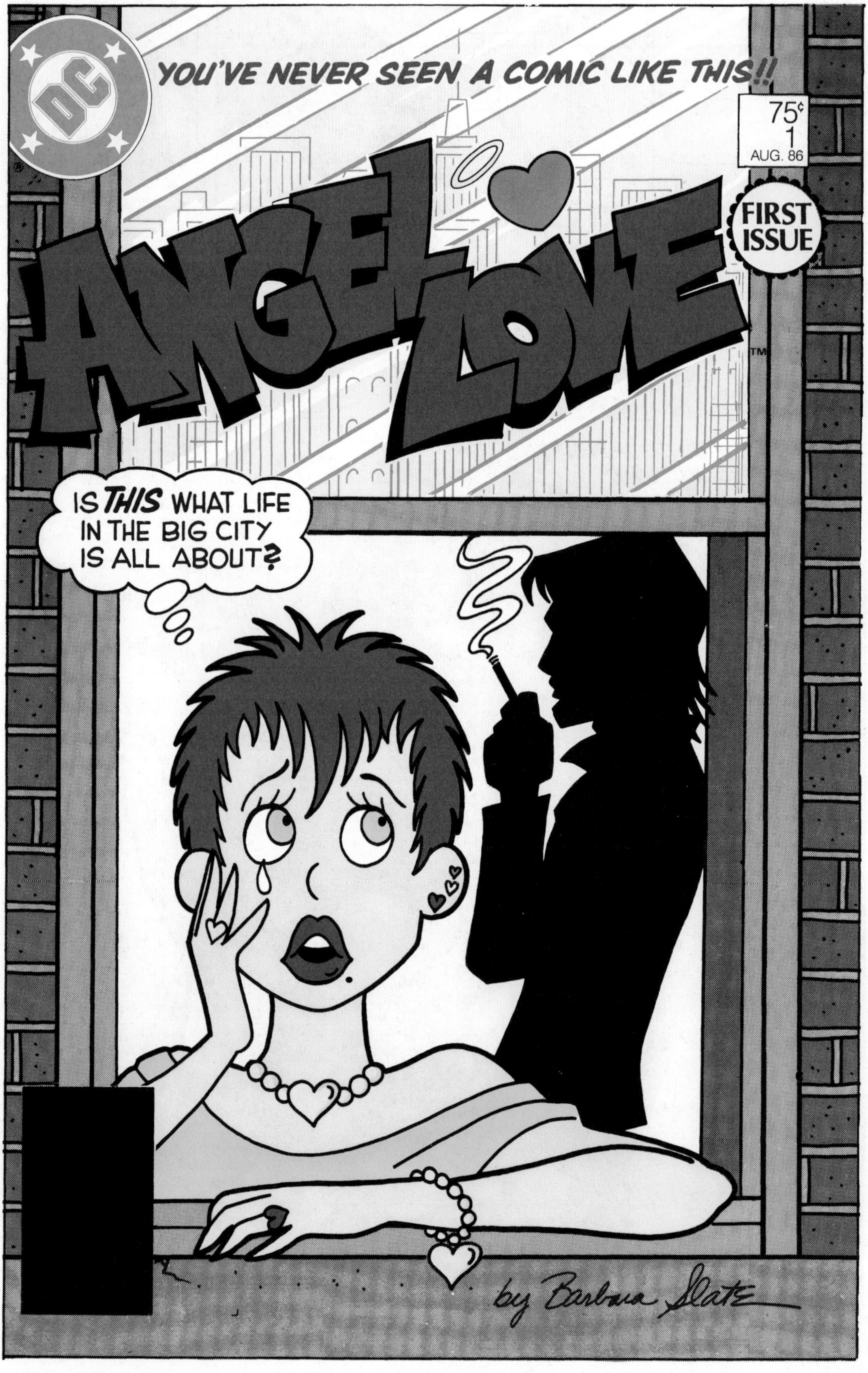
DC
YOU'VE NEVER SEEN A COMIC LIKE THIS!!
75¢
1
AUG. 86
ANGEL LOVE
FIRST ISSUE
IS *THIS* WHAT LIFE IN THE BIG CITY IS ALL ABOUT?
by Barbara Slate

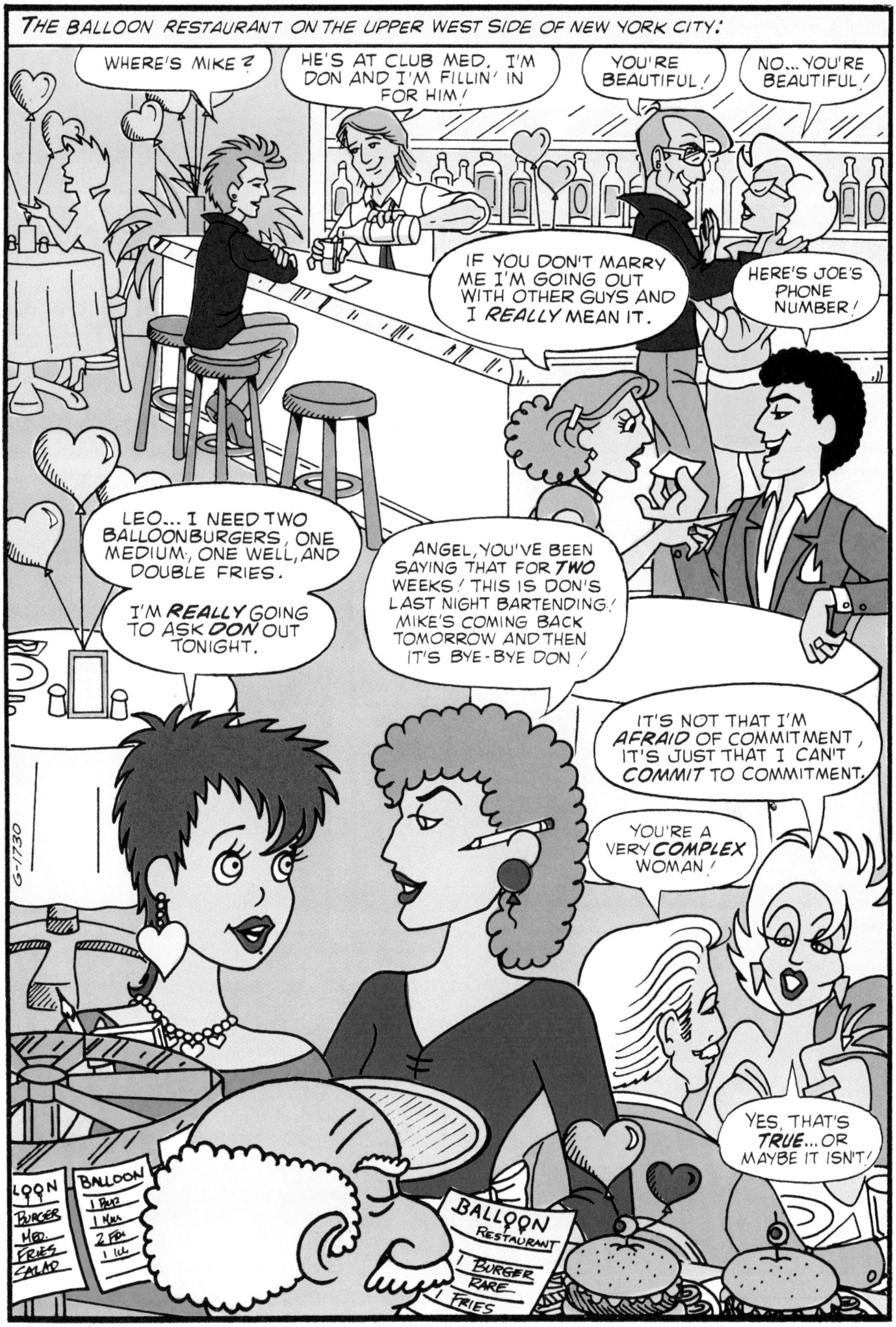
THE BALLOON RESTAURANT ON THE UPPER WEST SIDE OF NEW YORK CITY:
WHERE'S MIKE?
HE'S AT CLUB MED. I'M DON AND I'M FILLIN' IN FOR HIM!
YOU'RE BEAUTIFUL!
NO... YOU'RE BEAUTIFUL!
IF YOU DON'T MARRY ME I'M GOING OUT WITH OTHER GUYS AND I REALLY MEAN IT.
HERE'S JOE'S PHONE NUMBER!
LEO... I NEED TWO BALLOONBURGERS, ONE MEDIUM, ONE WELL, AND DOUBLE FRIES.
I'M REALLY GOING TO ASK DON OUT TONIGHT.
ANGEL, YOU'VE BEEN SAYING THAT FOR TWO WEEKS! THIS IS DON'S LAST NIGHT BARTENDING! MIKE'S COMING BACK TOMORROW AND THEN IT'S BYE-BYE DON!
IT'S NOT THAT I'M AFRAID OF COMMITMENT, IT'S JUST THAT I CAN'T COMMIT TO COMMITMENT.
YOU'RE A VERY COMPLEX WOMAN!
YES, THAT'S TRUE... OR MAYBE IT ISN'T!
G-1730
BALLOON RESTAURANT
1 BURGER RARE
1 FRIES

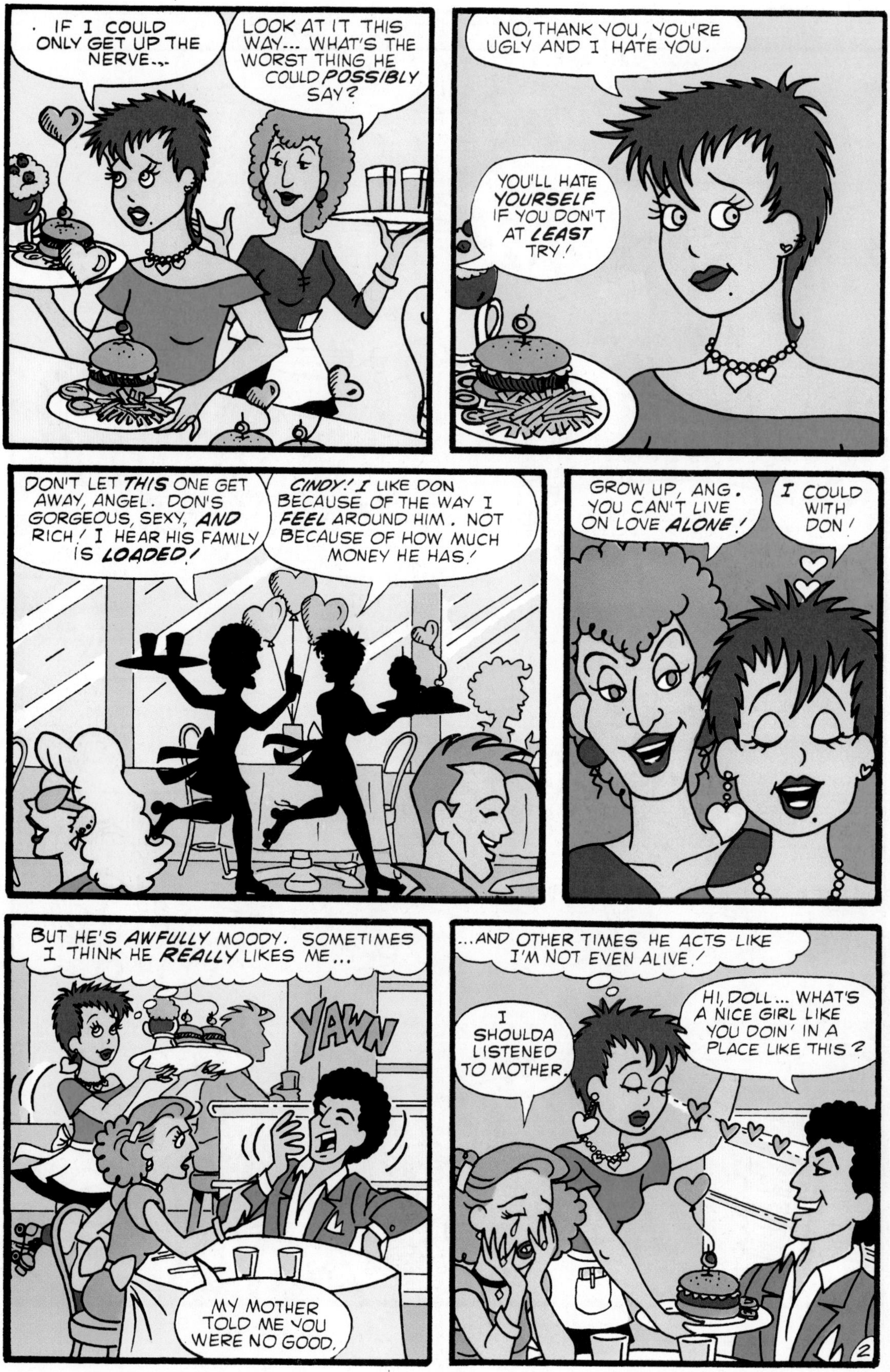

. IF I COULD ONLY GET UP THE NERVE...
LOOK AT IT THIS WAY... WHAT'S THE WORST THING HE COULD POSSIBLY SAY?
NO, THANK YOU, YOU'RE UGLY AND I HATE YOU.
YOU'LL HATE YOURSELF IF YOU DON'T AT LEAST TRY!
DON'T LET THIS ONE GET AWAY, ANGEL. DON'S GORGEOUS, SEXY, AND RICH! I HEAR HIS FAMILY IS LOADED!
CINDY! I LIKE DON BECAUSE OF THE WAY I FEEL AROUND HIM. NOT BECAUSE OF HOW MUCH MONEY HE HAS!
GROW UP, ANG. YOU CAN'T LIVE ON LOVE ALONE!
I COULD WITH DON!
BUT HE'S AWFULLY MOODY. SOMETIMES I THINK HE REALLY LIKES ME...
YAWN
MY MOTHER TOLD ME YOU WERE NO GOOD.
...AND OTHER TIMES HE ACTS LIKE I'M NOT EVEN ALIVE!
I SHOULDA LISTENED TO MOTHER.
HI, DOLL... WHAT'S A NICE GIRL LIKE YOU DOIN' IN A PLACE LIKE THIS?
2

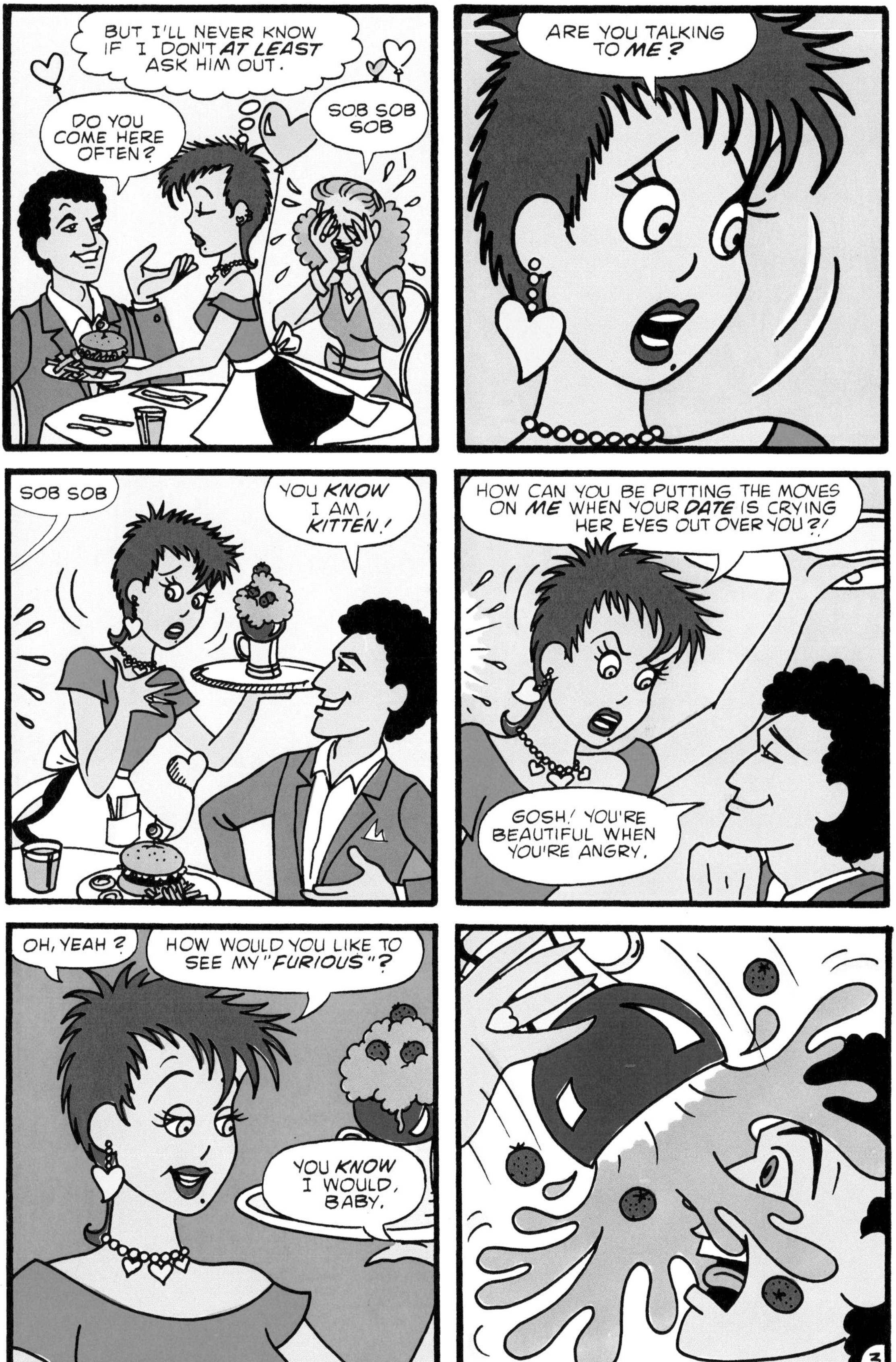
BUT I'LL NEVER KNOW IF I DON'T AT LEAST ASK HIM OUT.
DO YOU COME HERE OFTEN?
SOB SOB SOB
ARE YOU TALKING TO ME?
SOB SOB
YOU KNOW I AM, KITTEN!
HOW CAN YOU BE PUTTING THE MOVES ON ME WHEN YOUR DATE IS CRYING HER EYES OUT OVER YOU?!
GOSH! YOU'RE BEAUTIFUL WHEN YOU'RE ANGRY.
OH, YEAH?
HOW WOULD YOU LIKE TO SEE MY "FURIOUS"?
YOU KNOW I WOULD, BABY.
3

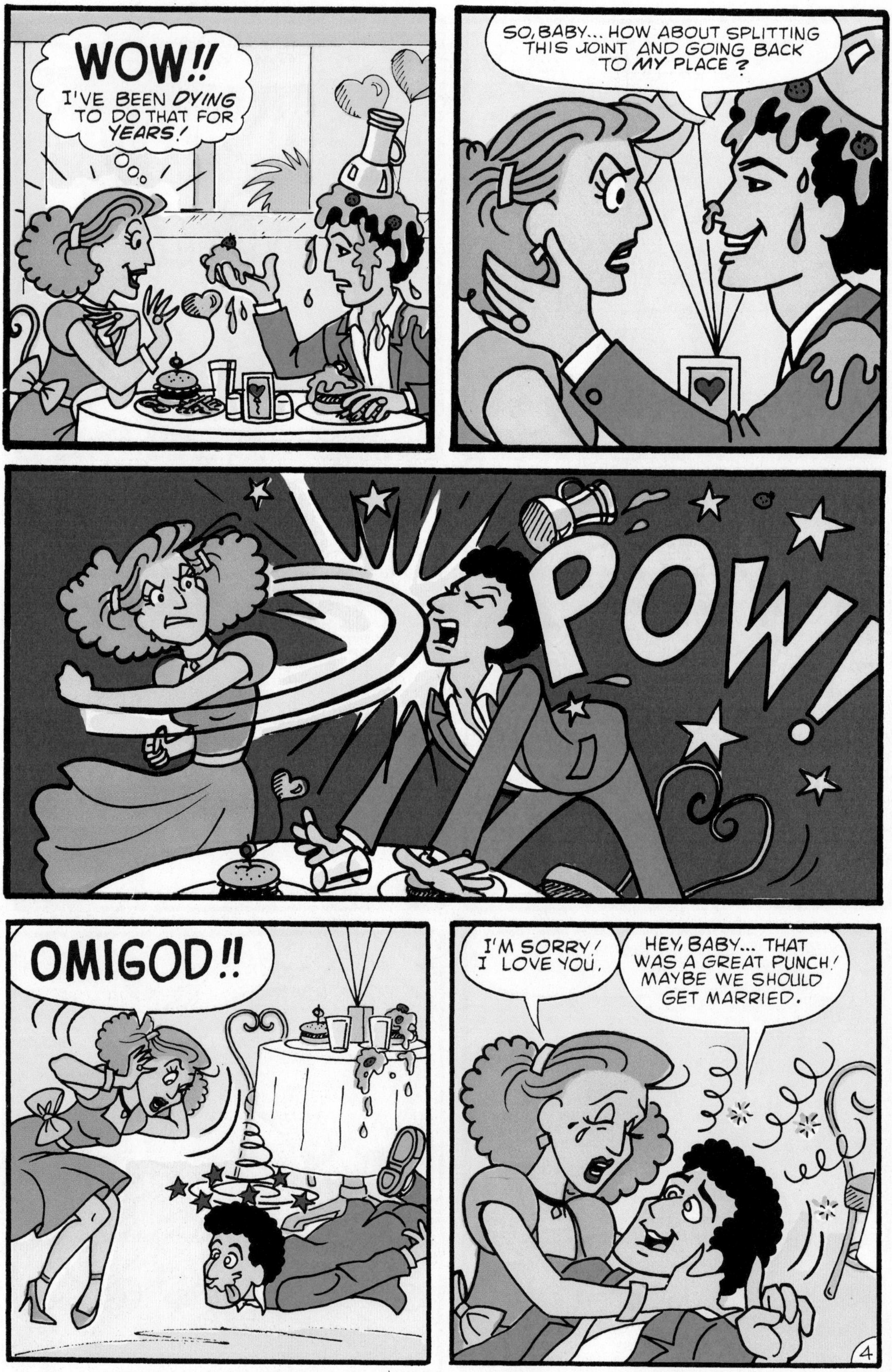
WOW!! I'VE BEEN DYING TO DO THAT FOR YEARS!
SO, BABY... HOW ABOUT SPLITTING THIS JOINT AND GOING BACK TO MY PLACE?
POW!
OMIGOD!!
I'M SORRY! I LOVE YOU.
HEY, BABY... THAT WAS A GREAT PUNCH! MAYBE WE SHOULD GET MARRIED.
4

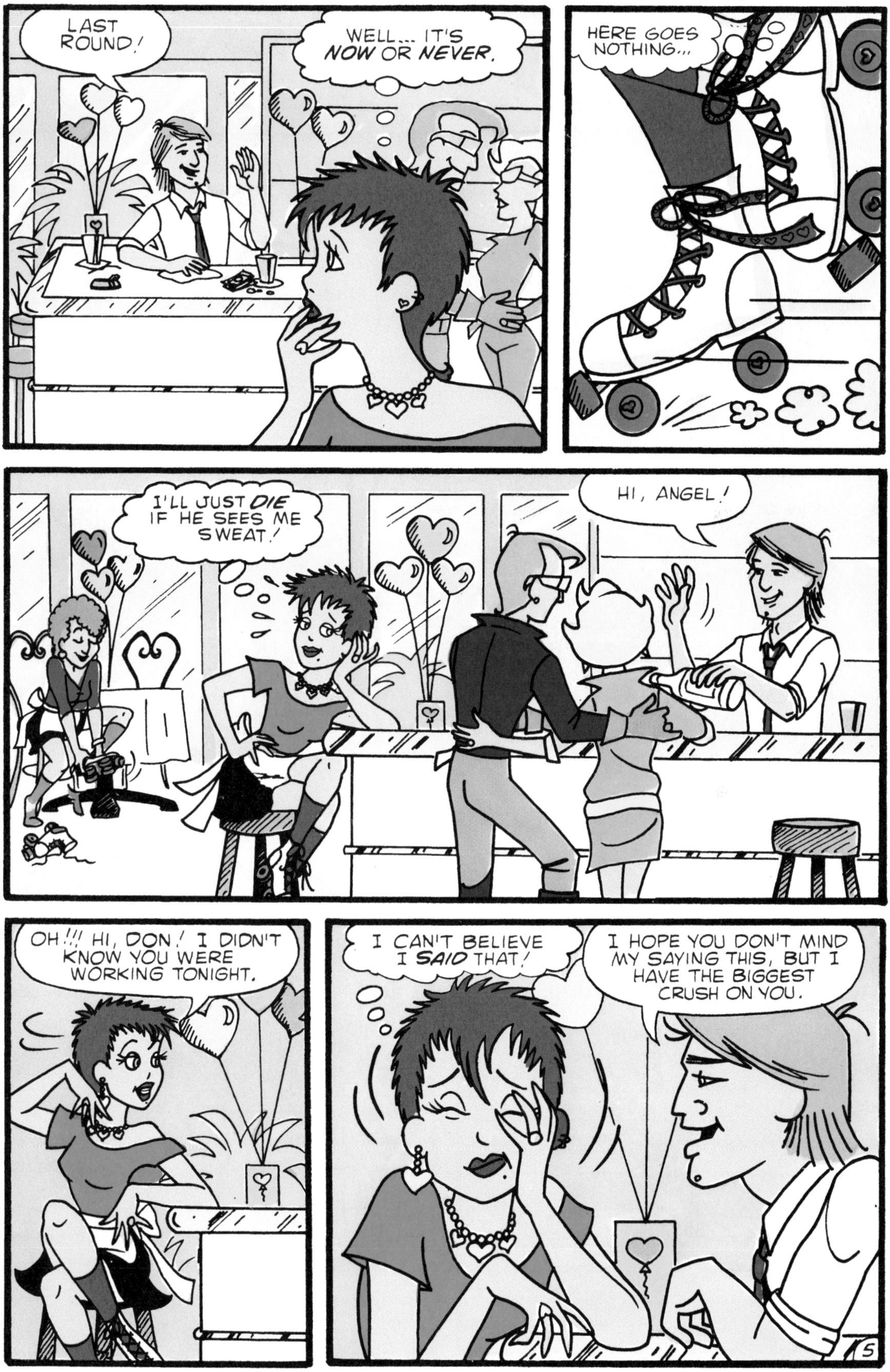
LAST ROUND!
WELL... IT'S NOW OR NEVER.
HERE GOES NOTHING...
I'LL JUST DIE IF HE SEES ME SWEAT!
HI, ANGEL!
OH!!! HI, DON! I DIDN'T KNOW YOU WERE WORKING TONIGHT.
I CAN'T BELIEVE I SAID THAT!
I HOPE YOU DON'T MIND MY SAYING THIS, BUT I HAVE THE BIGGEST CRUSH ON YOU.
5

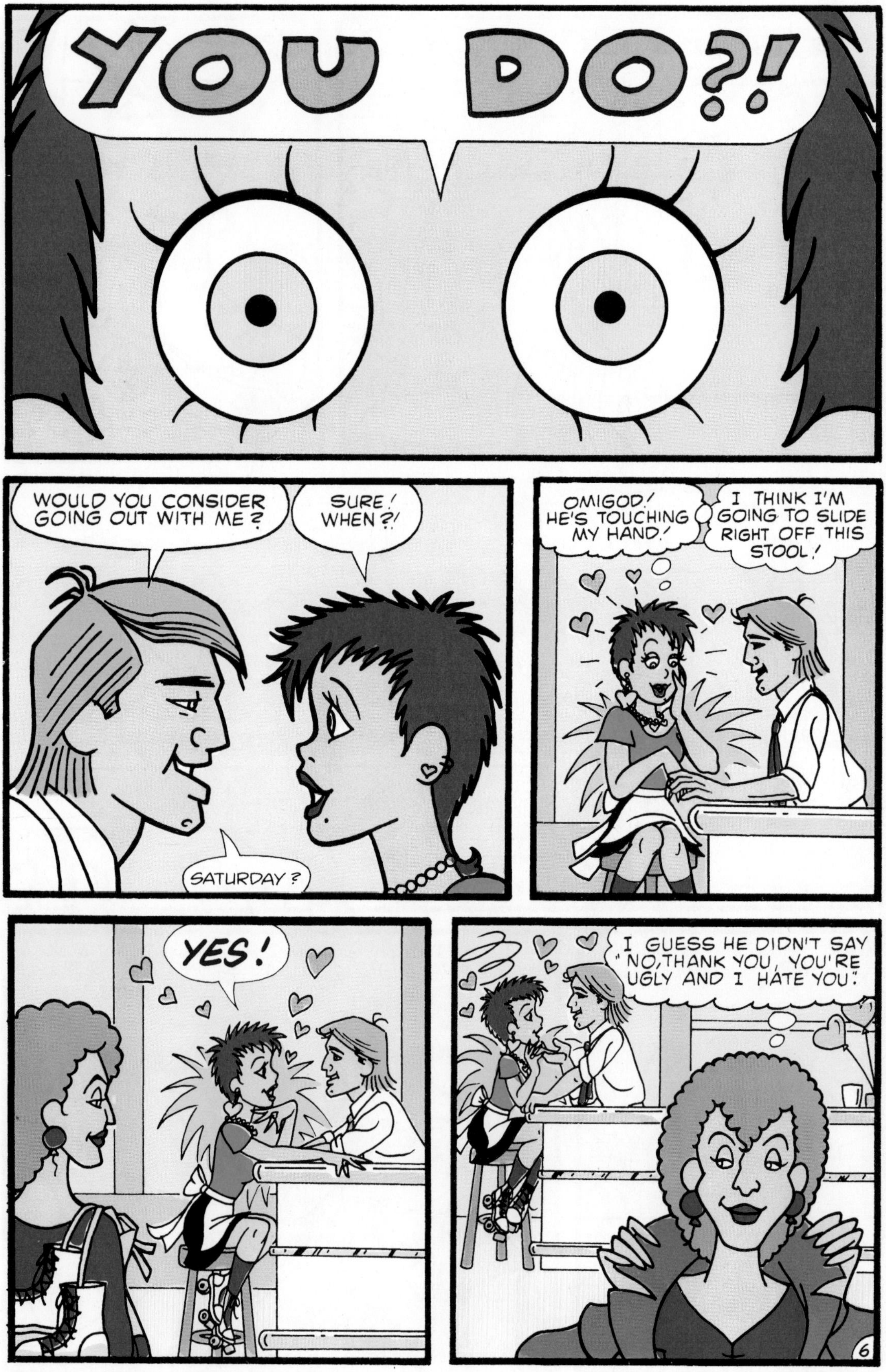
YOU DO?!
WOULD YOU CONSIDER GOING OUT WITH ME?
SURE! WHEN?!
SATURDAY?
OMIGOD! HE'S TOUCHING MY HAND!
I THINK I'M GOING TO SLIDE RIGHT OFF THIS STOOL!
YES!
I GUESS HE DIDN'T SAY "NO, THANK YOU, YOU'RE UGLY AND I HATE YOU".
6

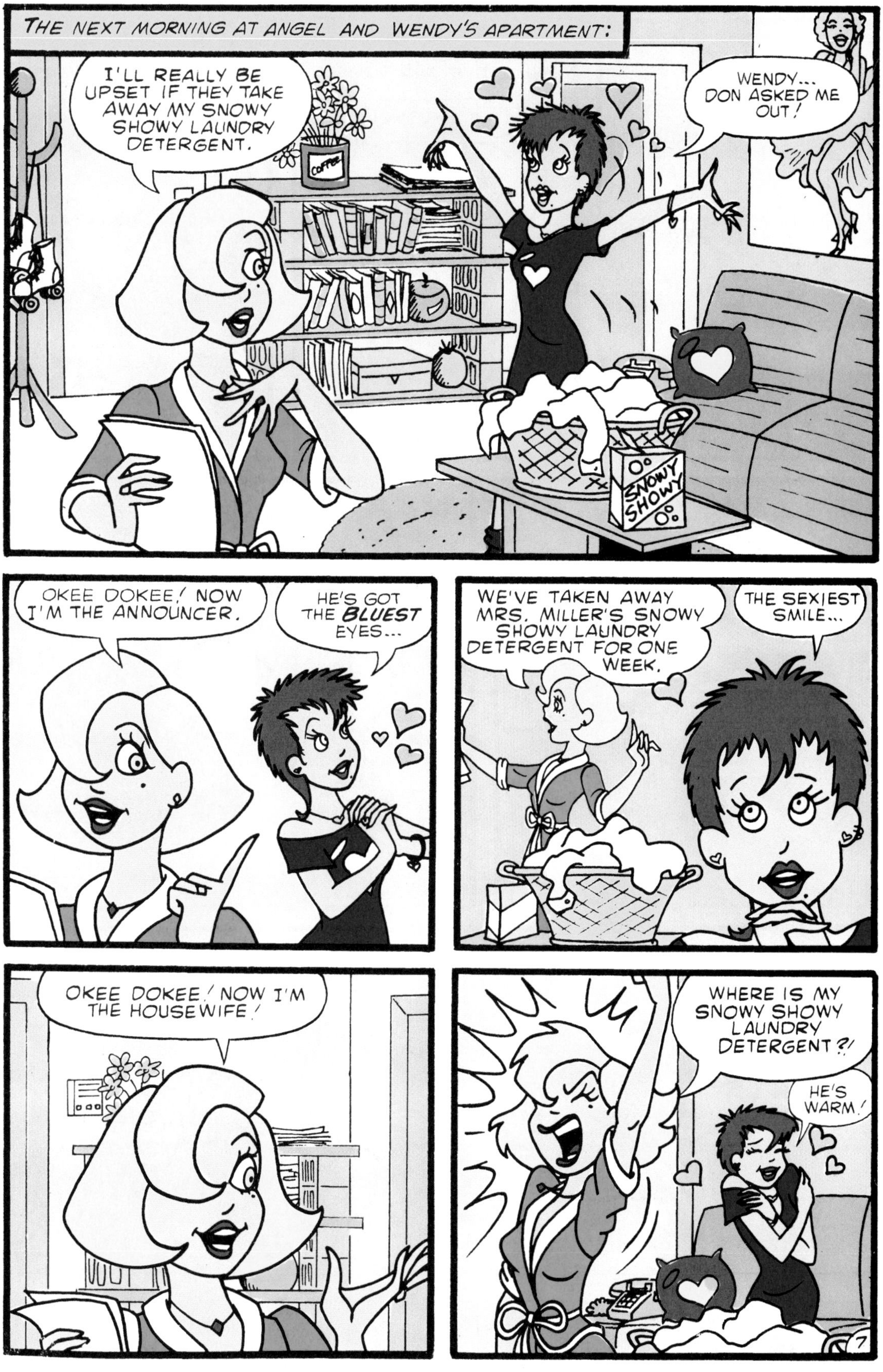
THE NEXT MORNING AT ANGEL AND WENDY'S APARTMENT:
I'LL REALLY BE UPSET IF THEY TAKE AWAY MY SNOWY SHOWY LAUNDRY DETERGENT.
WENDY... DON ASKED ME OUT!
COFFEE
SNOWY SHOWY
OKEE DOKEE! NOW I'M THE ANNOUNCER.
HE'S GOT THE BLUEST EYES...
WE'VE TAKEN AWAY MRS. MILLER'S SNOWY SHOWY LAUNDRY DETERGENT FOR ONE WEEK.
THE SEXIEST SMILE...
OKEE DOKEE! NOW I'M THE HOUSEWIFE!
WHERE IS MY SNOWY SHOWY LAUNDRY DETERGENT?!
HE'S WARM!
7

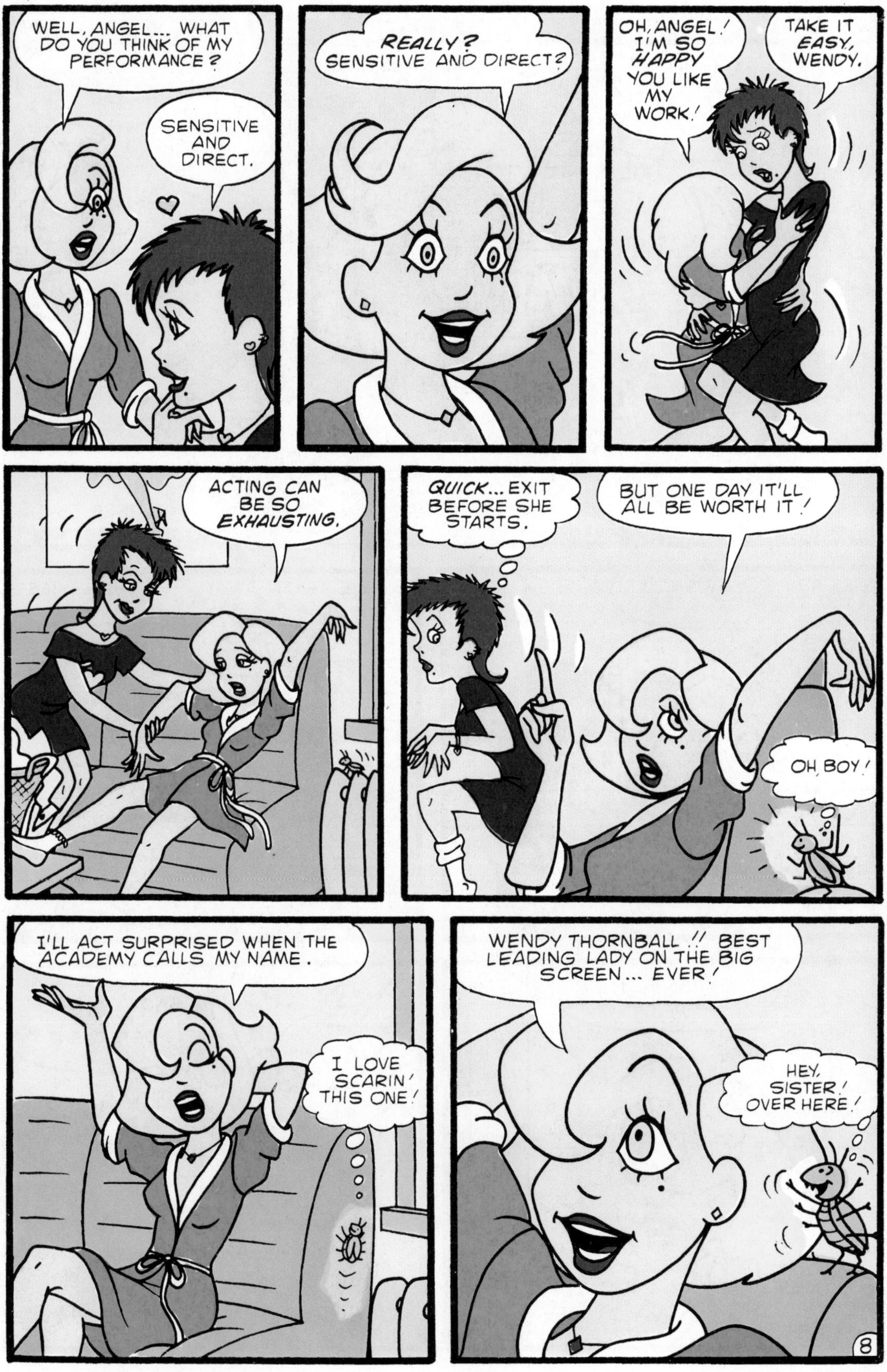
WELL, ANGEL... WHAT DO YOU THINK OF MY PERFORMANCE?
SENSITIVE AND DIRECT.
REALLY? SENSITIVE AND DIRECT?
OH, ANGEL! I'M SO HAPPY YOU LIKE MY WORK!
TAKE IT EASY, WENDY.
ACTING CAN BE SO EXHAUSTING.
QUICK... EXIT BEFORE SHE STARTS.
BUT ONE DAY IT'LL ALL BE WORTH IT!
OH, BOY!
I'LL ACT SURPRISED WHEN THE ACADEMY CALLS MY NAME.
I LOVE SCARIN' THIS ONE!
WENDY THORNBALL!! BEST LEADING LADY ON THE BIG SCREEN... EVER!
HEY, SISTER! OVER HERE!
8

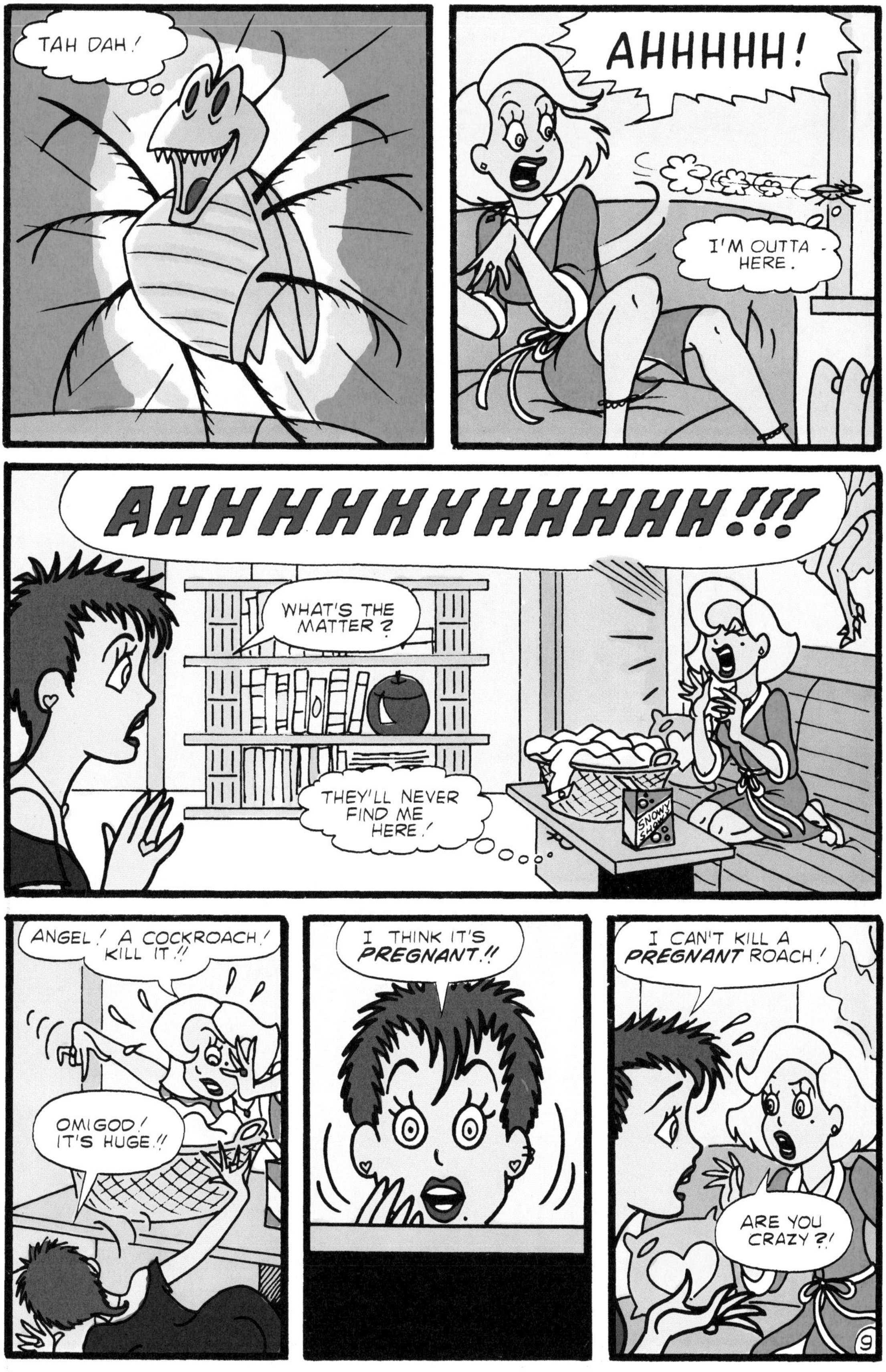

TAH DAH!
AHHHHH!
I'M OUTTA - HERE.
AHHHHHHHHHHHH!!!
WHAT'S THE MATTER?
THEY'LL NEVER FIND ME HERE!
SNOWY SHOW
ANGEL! A COCKROACH! KILL IT!!
OMIGOD! IT'S HUGE!!
I THINK IT'S *PREGNANT*!!
I CAN'T KILL A *PREGNANT* ROACH!
ARE YOU CRAZY?!
9

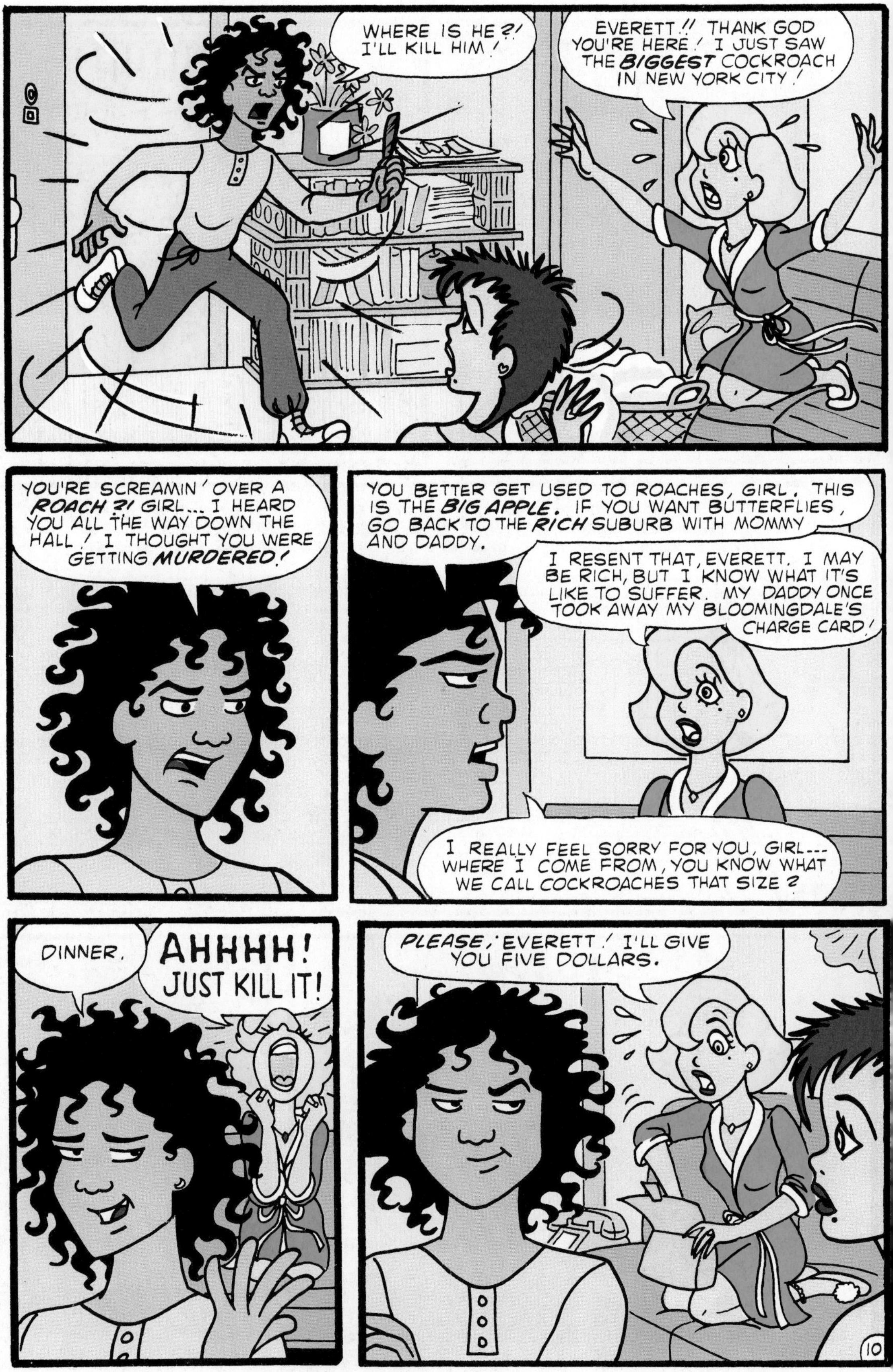
WHERE IS HE?! I'LL KILL HIM!
EVERETT!! THANK GOD YOU'RE HERE! I JUST SAW THE BIGGEST COCKROACH IN NEW YORK CITY!
YOU'RE SCREAMIN' OVER A ROACH?! GIRL... I HEARD YOU ALL THE WAY DOWN THE HALL! I THOUGHT YOU WERE GETTING MURDERED!
YOU BETTER GET USED TO ROACHES, GIRL. THIS IS THE BIG APPLE. IF YOU WANT BUTTERFLIES, GO BACK TO THE RICH SUBURB WITH MOMMY AND DADDY.
I RESENT THAT, EVERETT. I MAY BE RICH, BUT I KNOW WHAT IT'S LIKE TO SUFFER. MY DADDY ONCE TOOK AWAY MY BLOOMINGDALE'S CHARGE CARD!
I REALLY FEEL SORRY FOR YOU, GIRL--- WHERE I COME FROM, YOU KNOW WHAT WE CALL COCKROACHES THAT SIZE?
DINNER.
AHHHH! JUST KILL IT!
PLEASE, EVERETT! I'LL GIVE YOU FIVE DOLLARS.
10

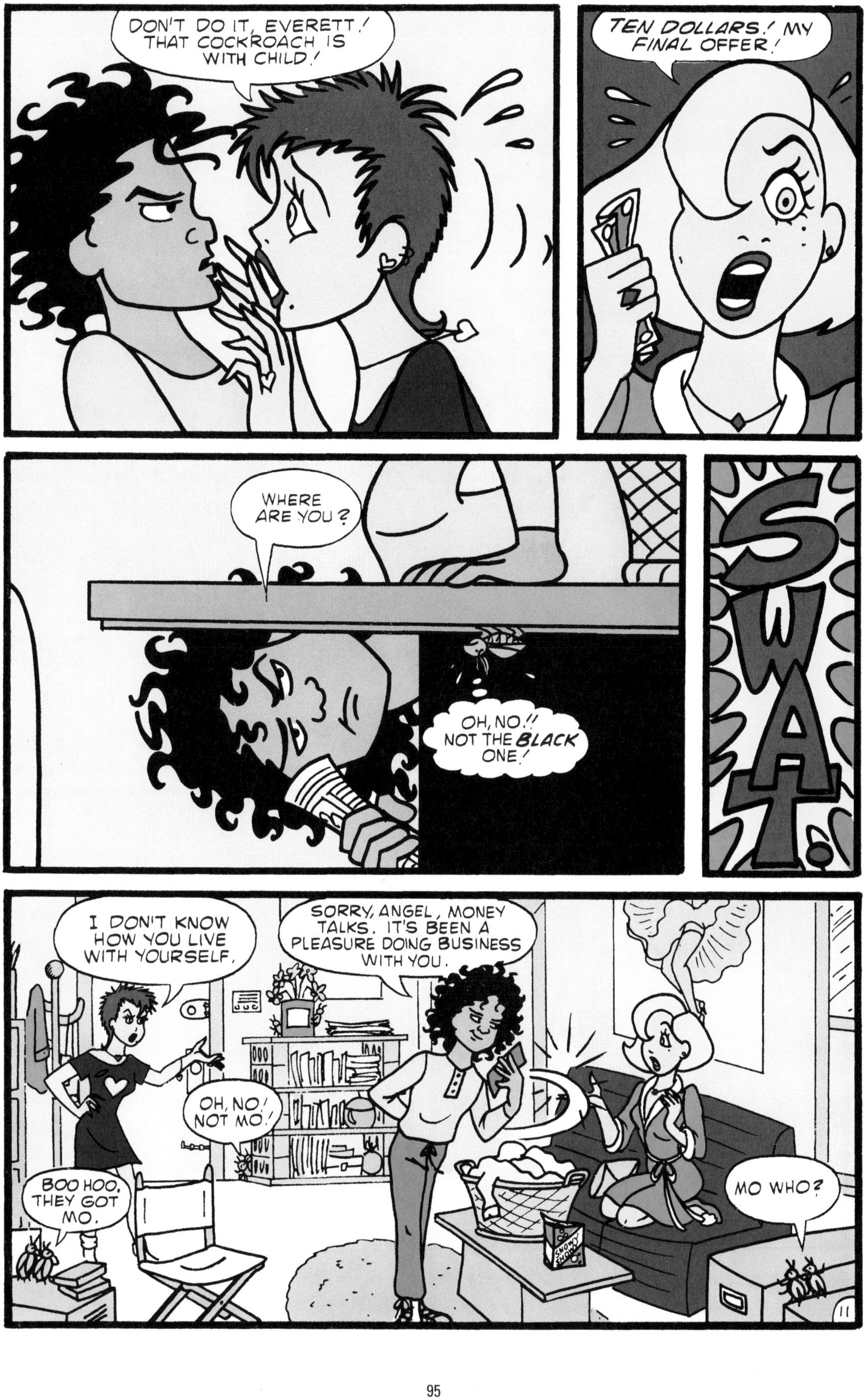
DON'T DO IT, EVERETT! THAT COCKROACH IS WITH CHILD!
TEN DOLLARS! MY FINAL OFFER!
WHERE ARE YOU?
OH, NO!! NOT THE BLACK ONE!
SWAT.
I DON'T KNOW HOW YOU LIVE WITH YOURSELF.
SORRY, ANGEL, MONEY TALKS. IT'S BEEN A PLEASURE DOING BUSINESS WITH YOU.
OH, NO! NOT MO!
BOO HOO, THEY GOT MO.
MO WHO?
SNOWY SHOW
11

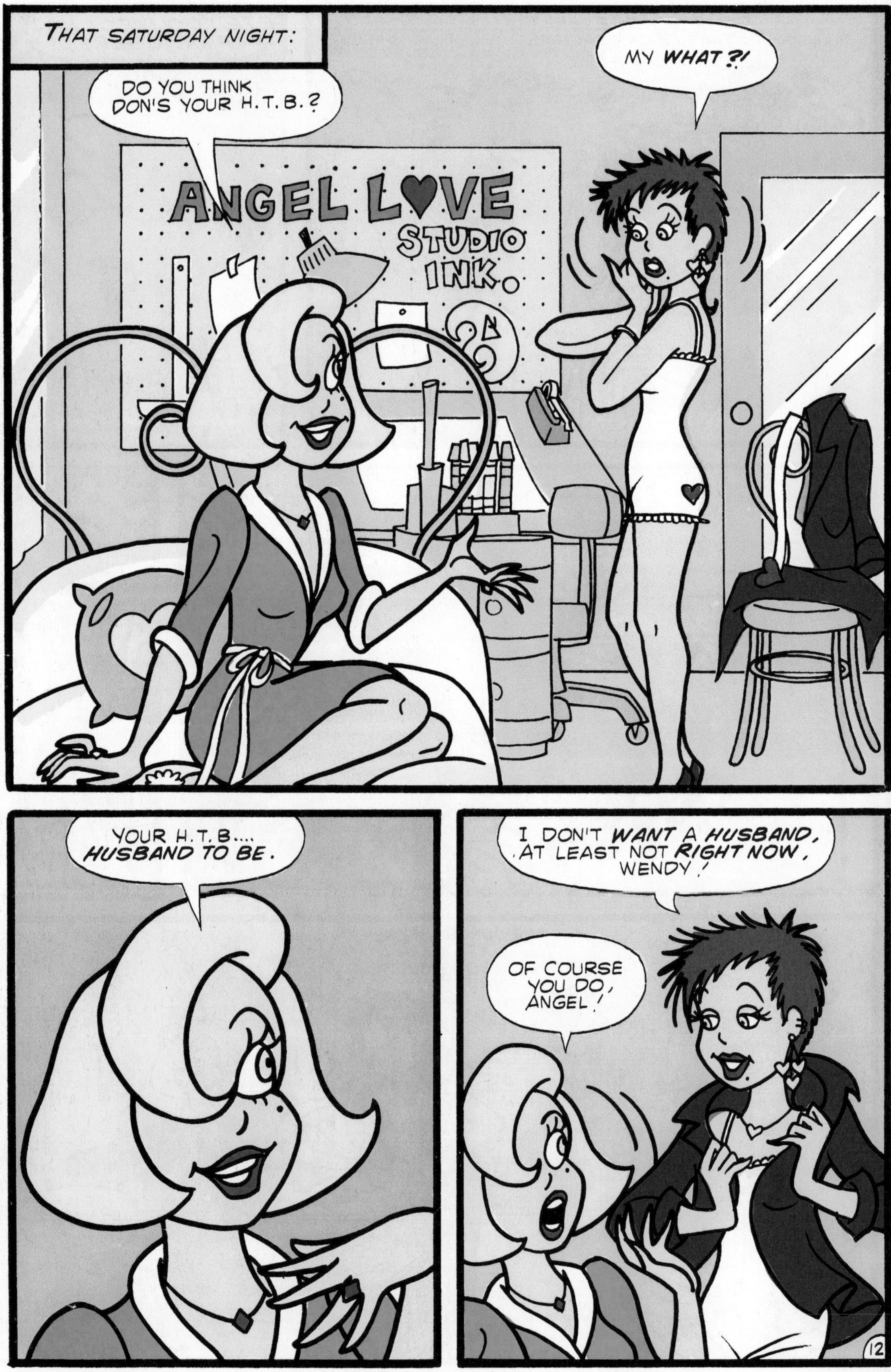
THAT SATURDAY NIGHT:
DO YOU THINK DON'S YOUR H.T.B.?
MY WHAT?!
ANGEL LOVE STUDIO INK.
YOUR H.T.B.... HUSBAND TO BE.
I DON'T WANT A HUSBAND, AT LEAST NOT RIGHT NOW, WENDY!
OF COURSE YOU DO, ANGEL!
12

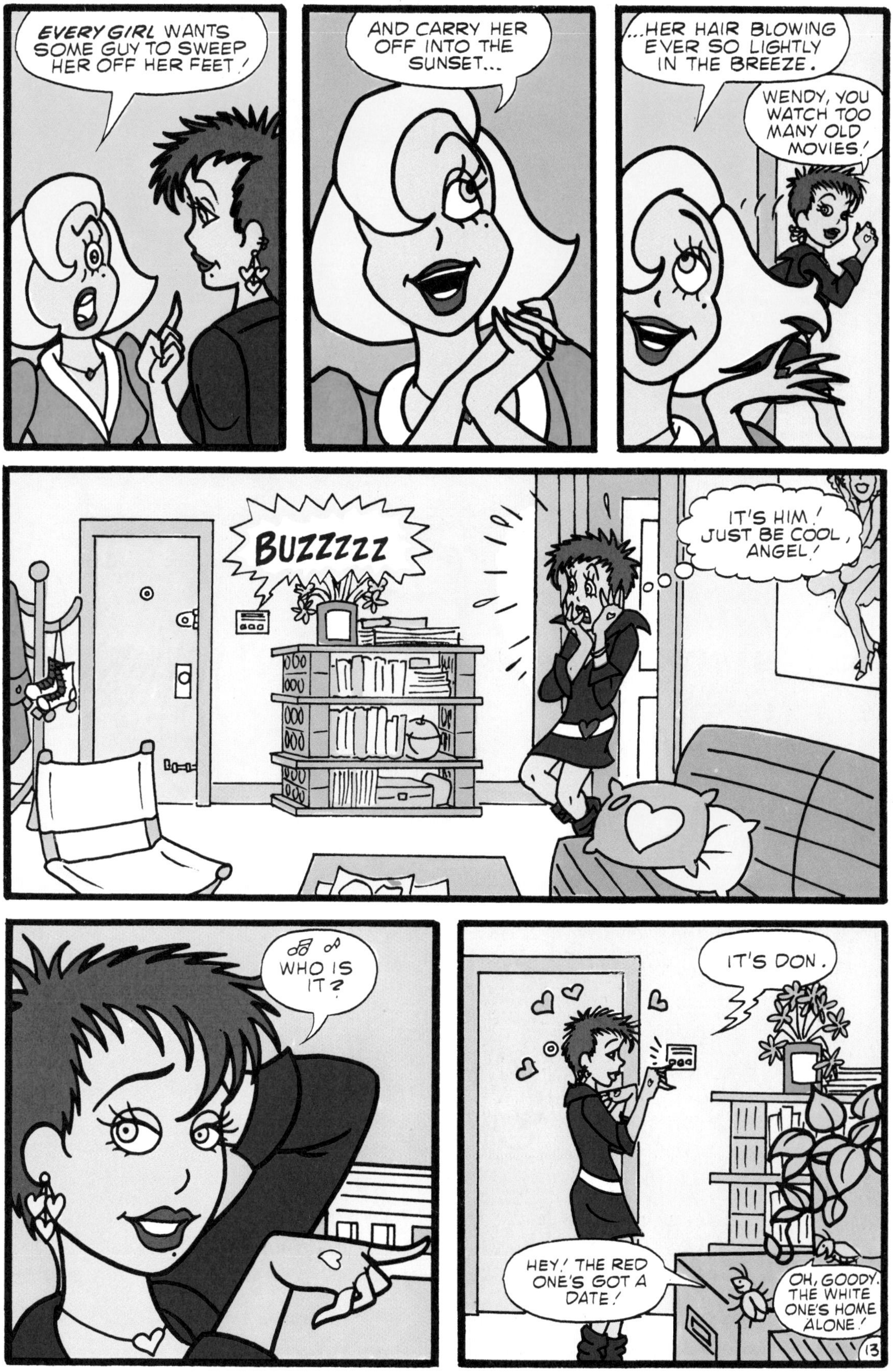
EVERY GIRL WANTS SOME GUY TO SWEEP HER OFF HER FEET!
AND CARRY HER OFF INTO THE SUNSET...
...HER HAIR BLOWING EVER SO LIGHTLY IN THE BREEZE.
WENDY, YOU WATCH TOO MANY OLD MOVIES!
BUZZZZZ
IT'S HIM! JUST BE COOL, ANGEL!
WHO IS IT?
IT'S DON.
HEY! THE RED ONE'S GOT A DATE!
OH, GOODY. THE WHITE ONE'S HOME ALONE!
13

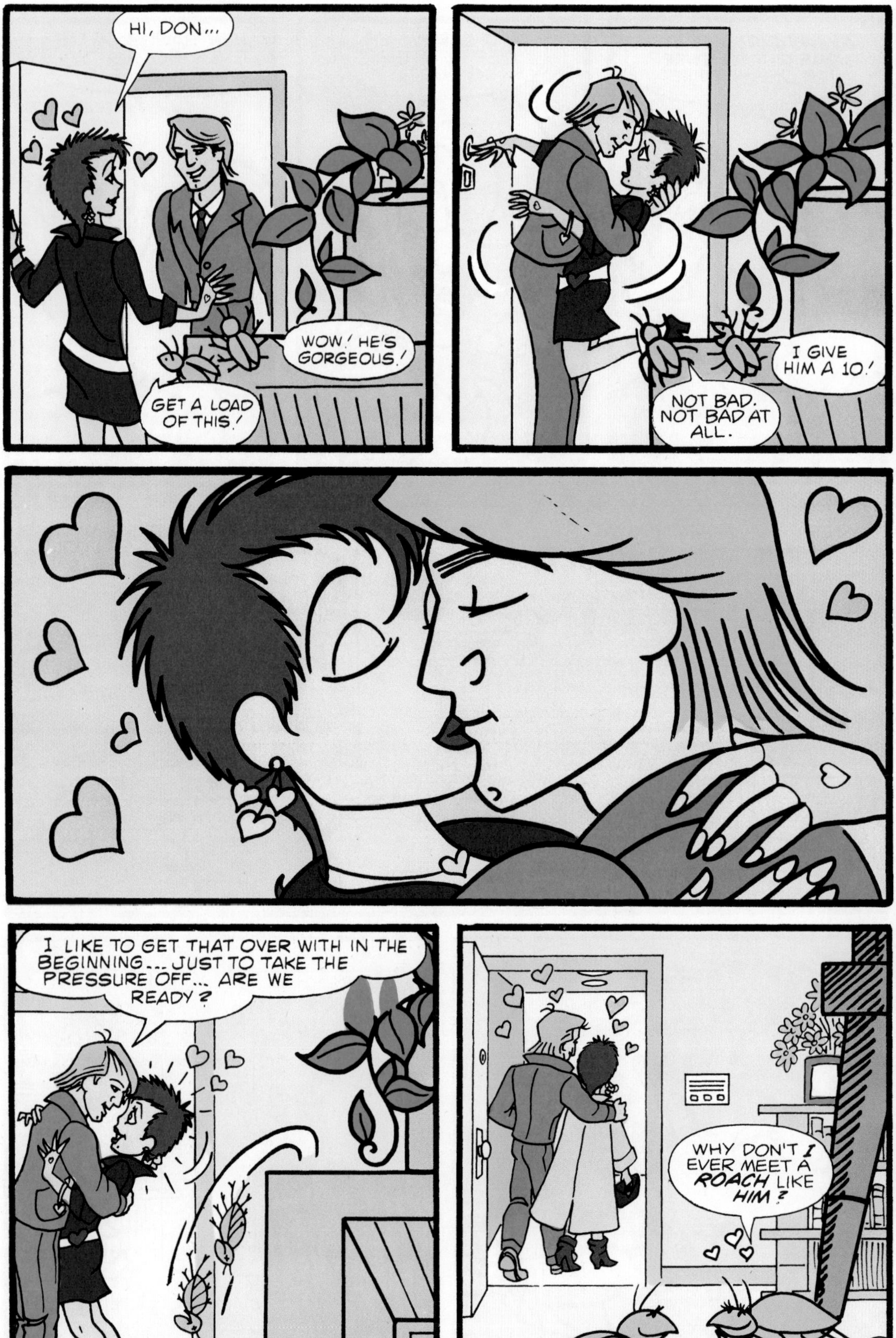
HI, DON...
WOW! HE'S GORGEOUS!
GET A LOAD OF THIS!
I GIVE HIM A 10!
NOT BAD. NOT BAD AT ALL.
I LIKE TO GET THAT OVER WITH IN THE BEGINNING... JUST TO TAKE THE PRESSURE OFF... ARE WE READY?
WHY DON'T I EVER MEET A ROACH LIKE HIM?
14

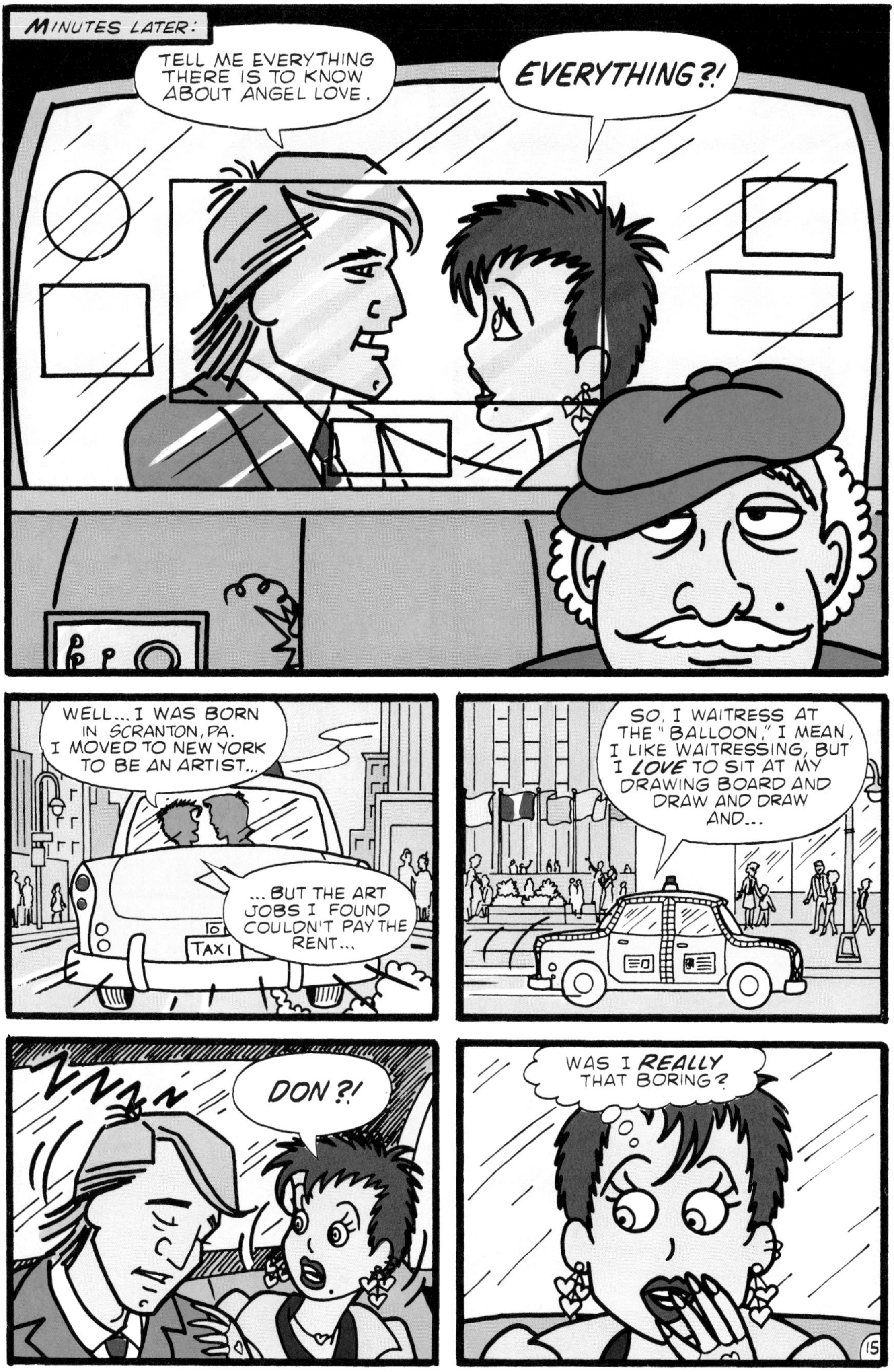
MINUTES LATER:
TELL ME EVERYTHING THERE IS TO KNOW ABOUT ANGEL LOVE.
EVERYTHING?!
WELL... I WAS BORN IN SCRANTON, PA. I MOVED TO NEW YORK TO BE AN ARTIST...
...BUT THE ART JOBS I FOUND COULDN'T PAY THE RENT...
TAXI
SO, I WAITRESS AT THE "BALLOON." I MEAN, I LIKE WAITRESSING, BUT I LOVE TO SIT AT MY DRAWING BOARD AND DRAW AND DRAW AND...
ZZZZ
DON?!
WAS I REALLY THAT BORING?
15

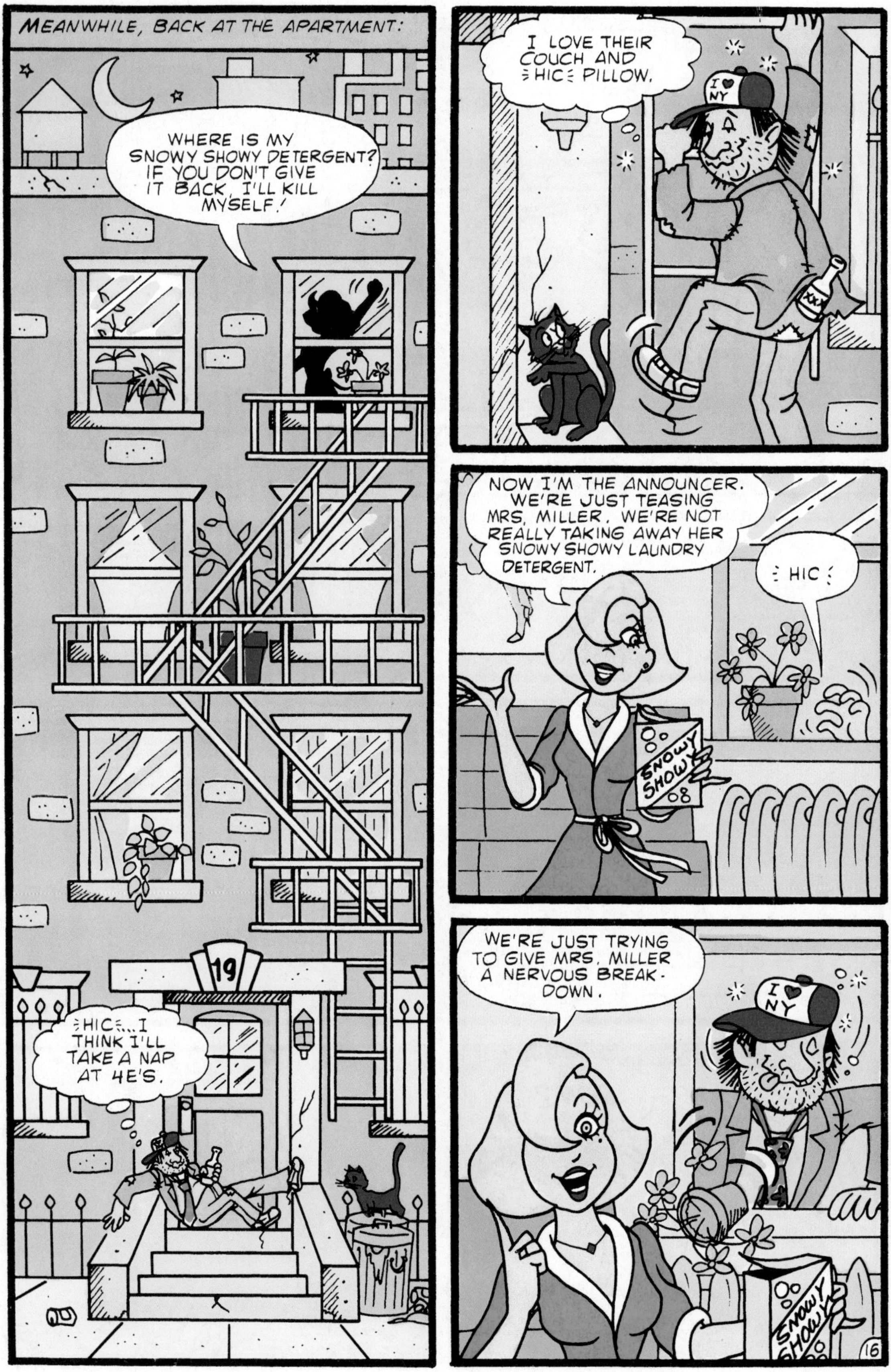
MEANWHILE, BACK AT THE APARTMENT:
WHERE IS MY SNOWY SHOWY DETERGENT? IF YOU DON'T GIVE IT BACK, I'LL KILL MYSELF!
HIC...I THINK I'LL TAKE A NAP AT 4E'S.
19
I LOVE THEIR COUCH AND HIC PILLOW.
I ♥ NY
NOW I'M THE ANNOUNCER. WE'RE JUST TEASING MRS. MILLER. WE'RE NOT REALLY TAKING AWAY HER SNOWY SHOWY LAUNDRY DETERGENT.
HIC
SNOWY SHOWY
WE'RE JUST TRYING TO GIVE MRS. MILLER A NERVOUS BREAK-DOWN.
I ♥ NY
16

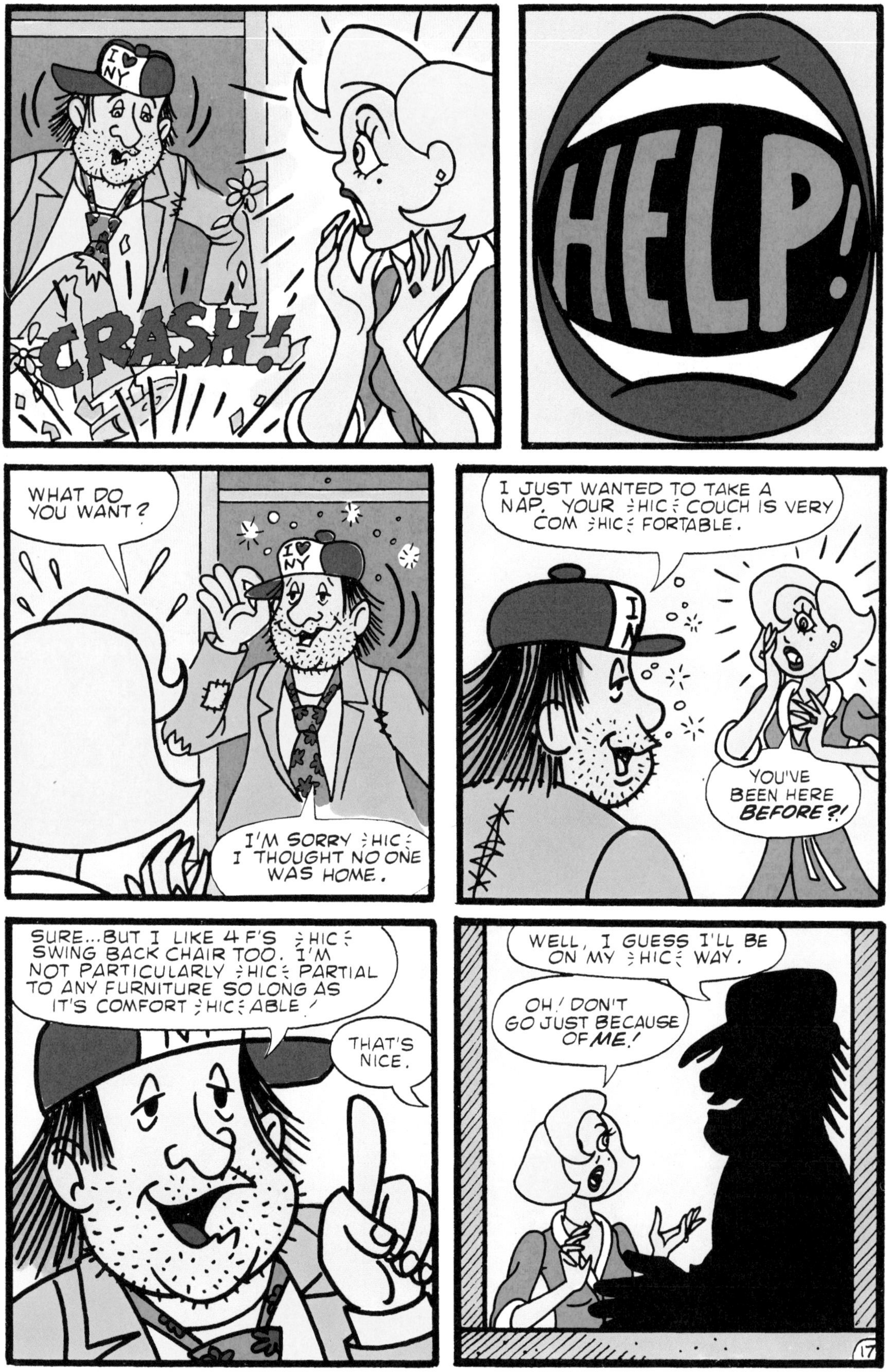
CRASH!
HELP!
WHAT DO YOU WANT?
I'M SORRY HIC I THOUGHT NO ONE WAS HOME.
I JUST WANTED TO TAKE A NAP. YOUR HIC COUCH IS VERY COM HIC FORTABLE.
YOU'VE BEEN HERE BEFORE?!
SURE...BUT I LIKE 4 F'S HIC SWING BACK CHAIR TOO. I'M NOT PARTICULARLY HIC PARTIAL TO ANY FURNITURE SO LONG AS IT'S COMFORT HIC ABLE!
THAT'S NICE.
WELL, I GUESS I'LL BE ON MY HIC WAY.
OH! DON'T GO JUST BECAUSE OF ME!
17

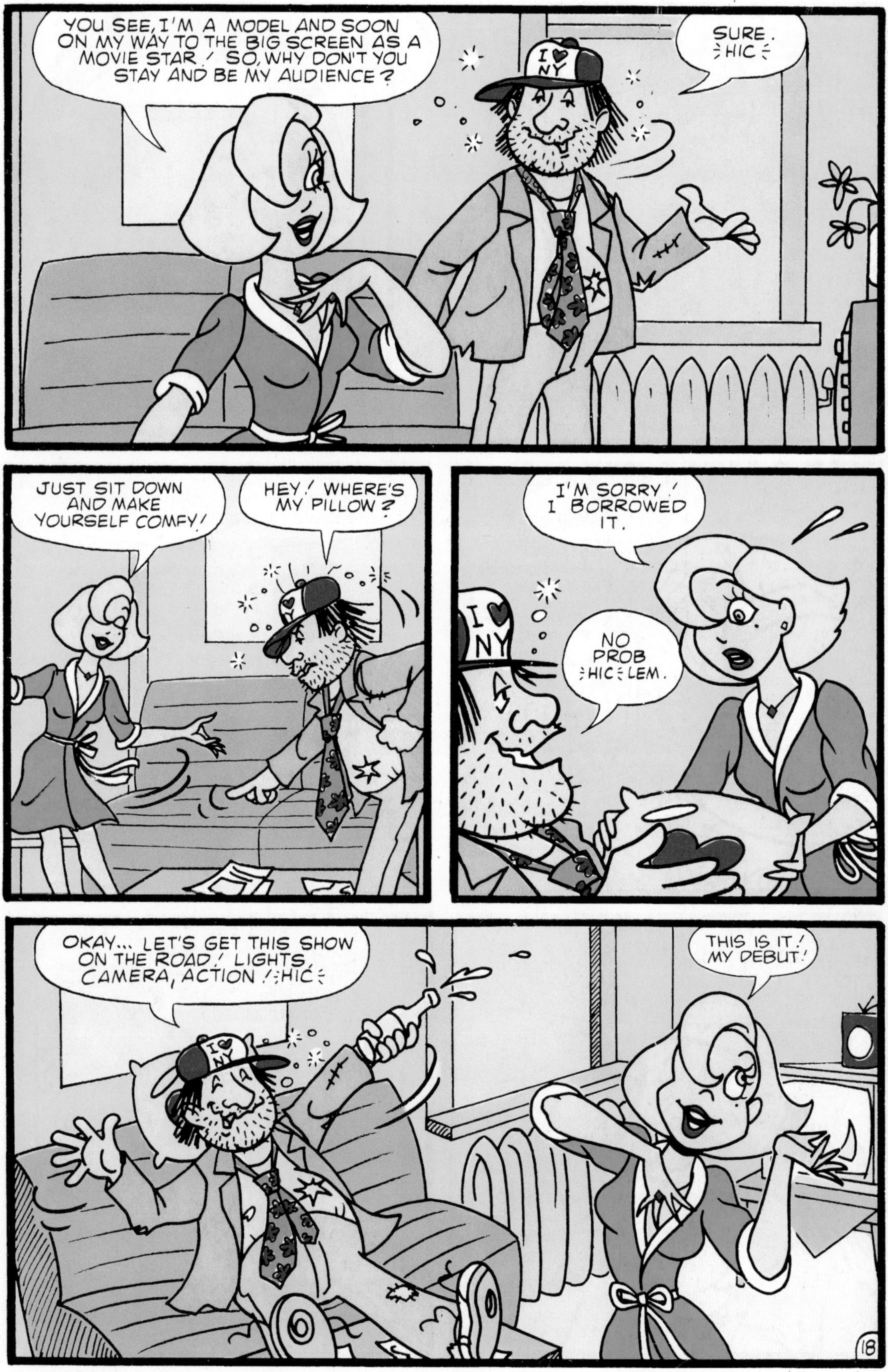
YOU SEE, I'M A MODEL AND SOON ON MY WAY TO THE BIG SCREEN AS A MOVIE STAR! SO, WHY DON'T YOU STAY AND BE MY AUDIENCE?
SURE. HIC
JUST SIT DOWN AND MAKE YOURSELF COMFY!
HEY! WHERE'S MY PILLOW?
I'M SORRY! I BORROWED IT.
NO PROB HIC LEM.
OKAY... LET'S GET THIS SHOW ON THE ROAD! LIGHTS, CAMERA, ACTION! HIC
THIS IS IT! MY DEBUT!
I ♥ NY
18

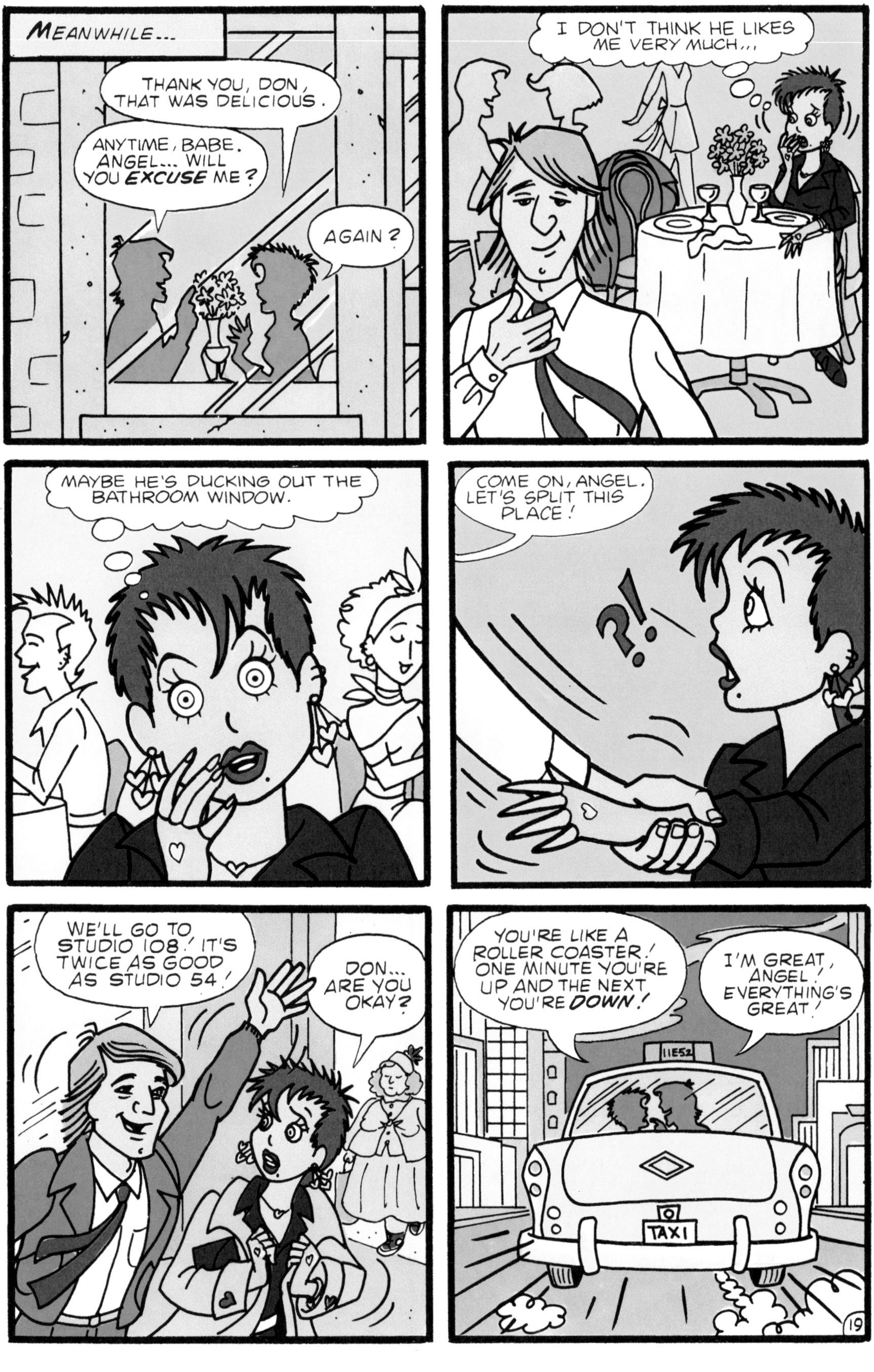
MEANWHILE...
THANK YOU, DON, THAT WAS DELICIOUS.
ANYTIME, BABE. ANGEL... WILL YOU EXCUSE ME?
AGAIN?
I DON'T THINK HE LIKES ME VERY MUCH...
MAYBE HE'S DUCKING OUT THE BATHROOM WINDOW.
COME ON, ANGEL. LET'S SPLIT THIS PLACE!
?!
WE'LL GO TO STUDIO 108! IT'S TWICE AS GOOD AS STUDIO 54!
DON... ARE YOU OKAY?
YOU'RE LIKE A ROLLER COASTER! ONE MINUTE YOU'RE UP AND THE NEXT YOU'RE DOWN!
I'M GREAT, ANGEL! EVERYTHING'S GREAT!
TAXI
19

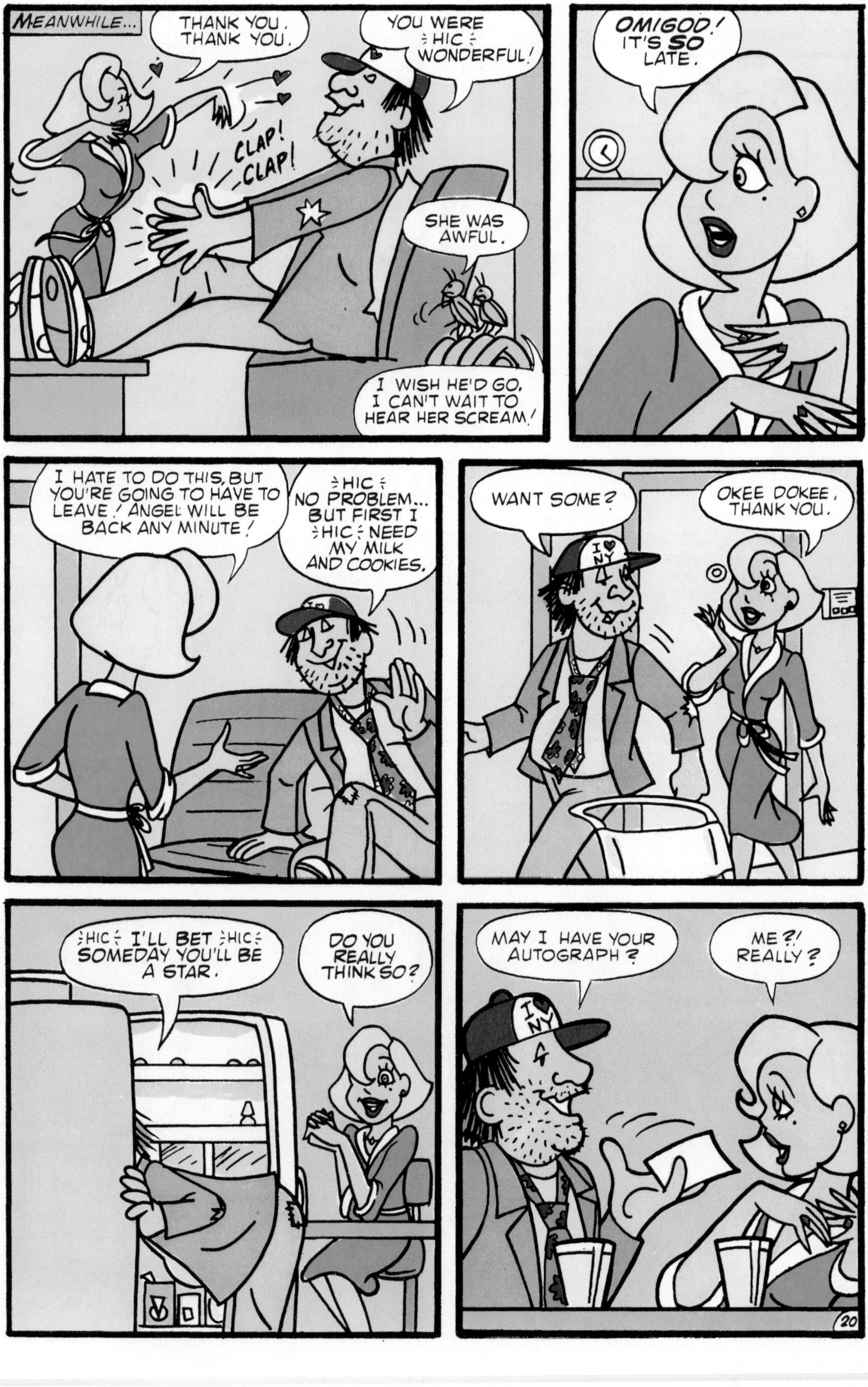
MEANWHILE...
THANK YOU. THANK YOU.
YOU WERE ⁝HIC⁝ WONDERFUL!
CLAP! CLAP!
SHE WAS AWFUL.
I WISH HE'D GO. I CAN'T WAIT TO HEAR HER SCREAM!
OMIGOD! IT'S SO LATE.
I HATE TO DO THIS, BUT YOU'RE GOING TO HAVE TO LEAVE! ANGEL WILL BE BACK ANY MINUTE!
⁝HIC⁝ NO PROBLEM... BUT FIRST I ⁝HIC⁝ NEED MY MILK AND COOKIES.
WANT SOME?
OKEE DOKEE, THANK YOU.
⁝HIC⁝ I'LL BET ⁝HIC⁝ SOMEDAY YOU'LL BE A STAR.
DO YOU REALLY THINK SO?
MAY I HAVE YOUR AUTOGRAPH?
ME?! REALLY?
20

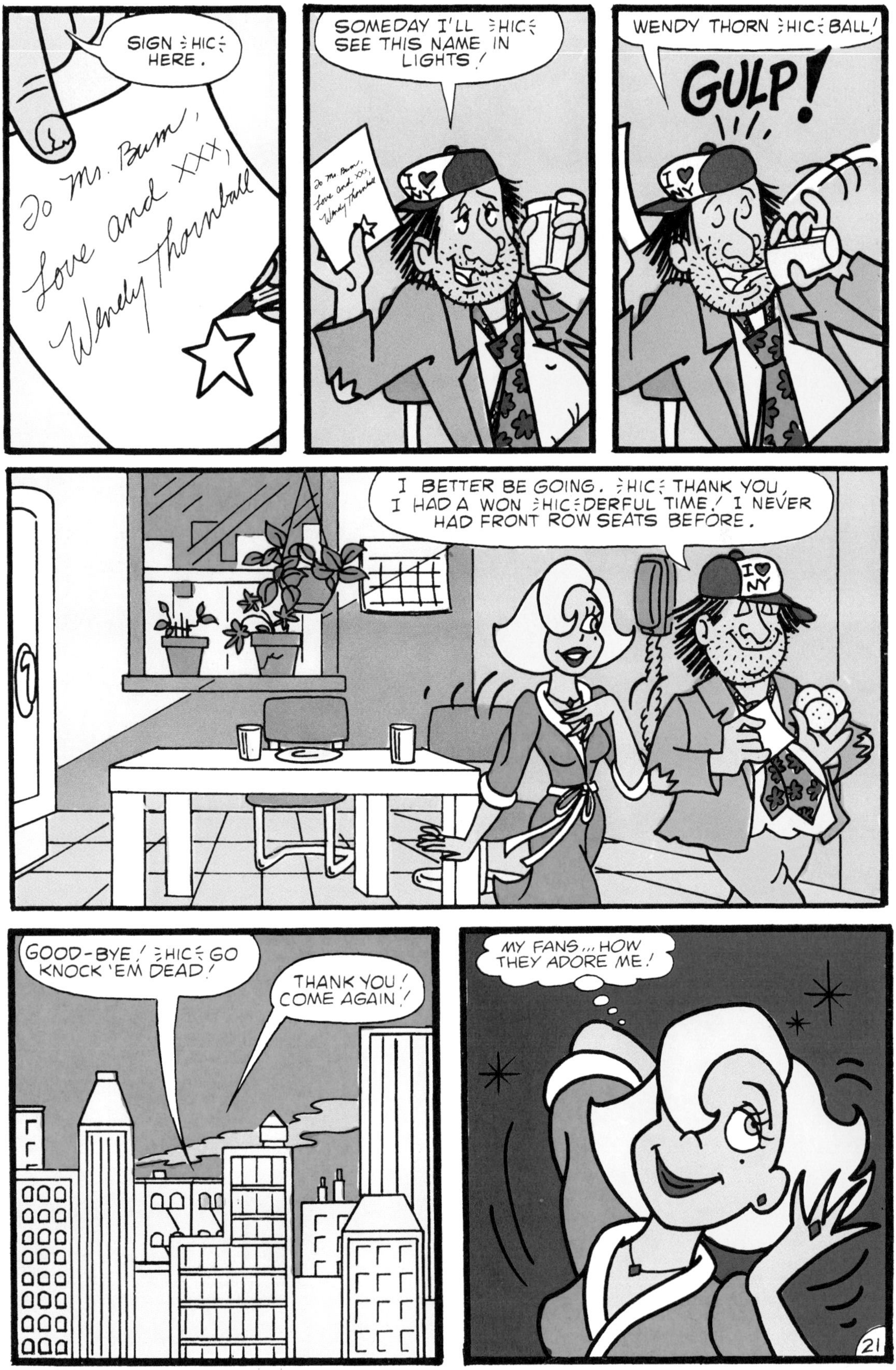
SIGN ⁝HIC⁝ HERE.
To Ms. Bum, Love and XXX, Wendy Thornball
SOMEDAY I'LL ⁝HIC⁝ SEE THIS NAME IN LIGHTS!
WENDY THORN ⁝HIC⁝ BALL!
GULP!
I ♥ NY
I BETTER BE GOING. ⁝HIC⁝ THANK YOU, I HAD A WON ⁝HIC⁝ DERFUL TIME! I NEVER HAD FRONT ROW SEATS BEFORE.
GOOD-BYE! ⁝HIC⁝ GO KNOCK 'EM DEAD!
THANK YOU! COME AGAIN!
MY FANS... HOW THEY ADORE ME!
21

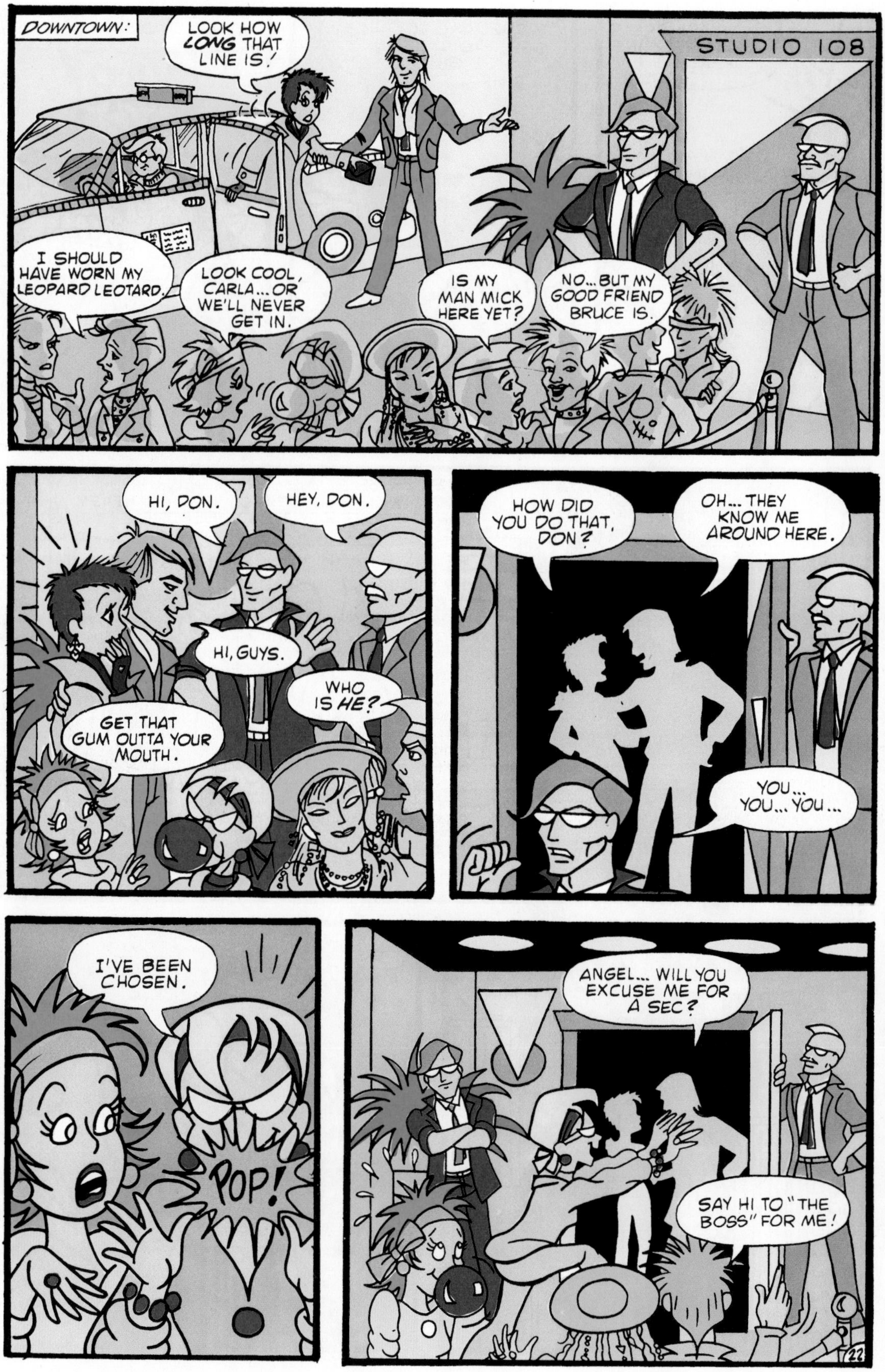
DOWNTOWN:
LOOK HOW LONG THAT LINE IS!
STUDIO 108
I SHOULD HAVE WORN MY LEOPARD LEOTARD.
LOOK COOL, CARLA... OR WE'LL NEVER GET IN.
IS MY MAN MICK HERE YET?
NO... BUT MY GOOD FRIEND BRUCE IS.
HI, DON.
HEY, DON.
HI, GUYS.
WHO IS HE?
GET THAT GUM OUTTA YOUR MOUTH.
HOW DID YOU DO THAT, DON?
OH... THEY KNOW ME AROUND HERE.
YOU... YOU... YOU...
I'VE BEEN CHOSEN.
POP!
ANGEL... WILL YOU EXCUSE ME FOR A SEC?
SAY HI TO "THE BOSS" FOR ME!
22

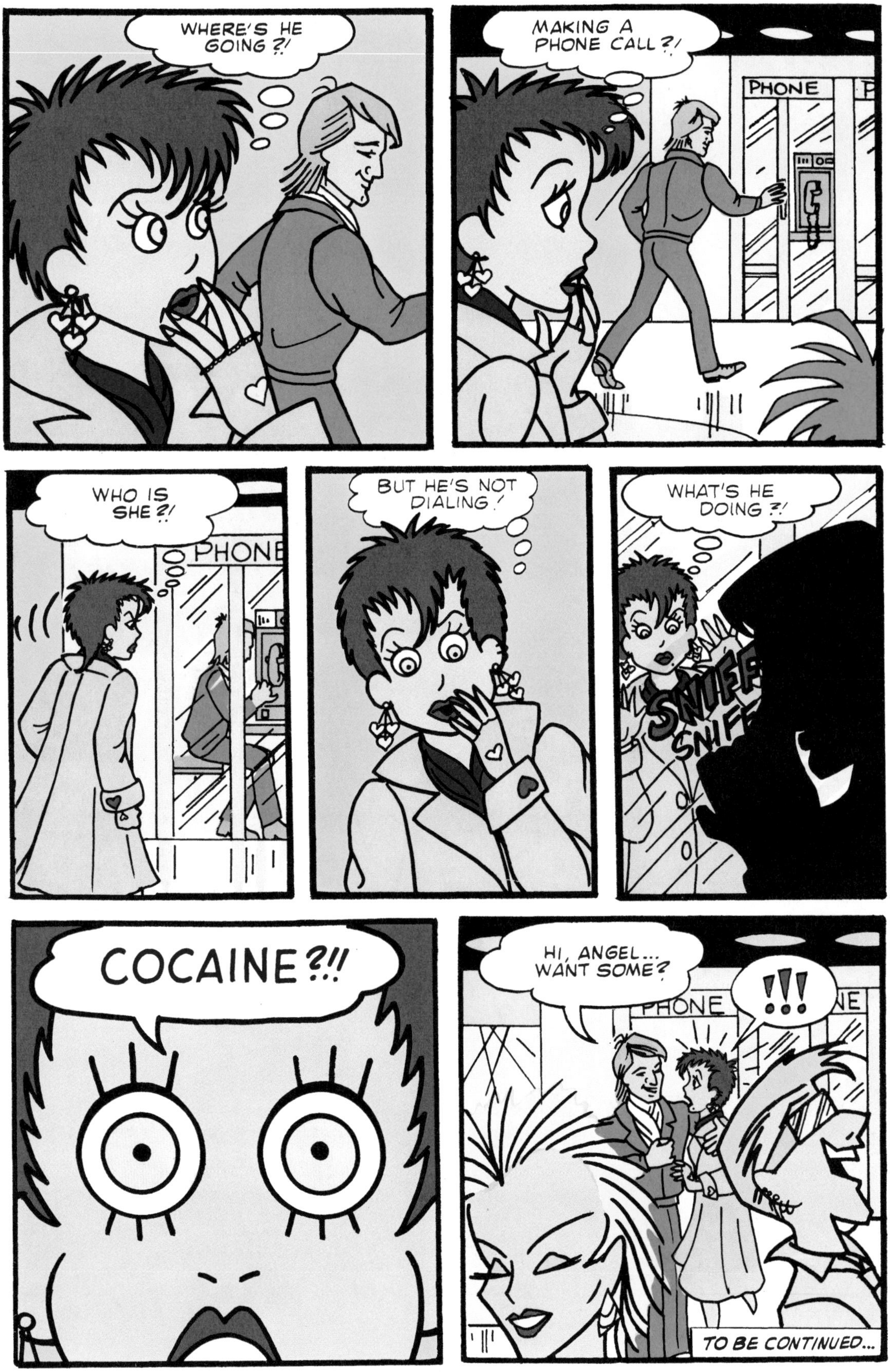
WHERE'S HE GOING ?!
MAKING A PHONE CALL ?!
PHONE
WHO IS SHE ?!
PHONE
BUT HE'S NOT DIALING !
WHAT'S HE DOING ?!
SNIFF
SNIFF
COCAINE ?!!
HI, ANGEL... WANT SOME ?
PHONE
!!!
TO BE CONTINUED...

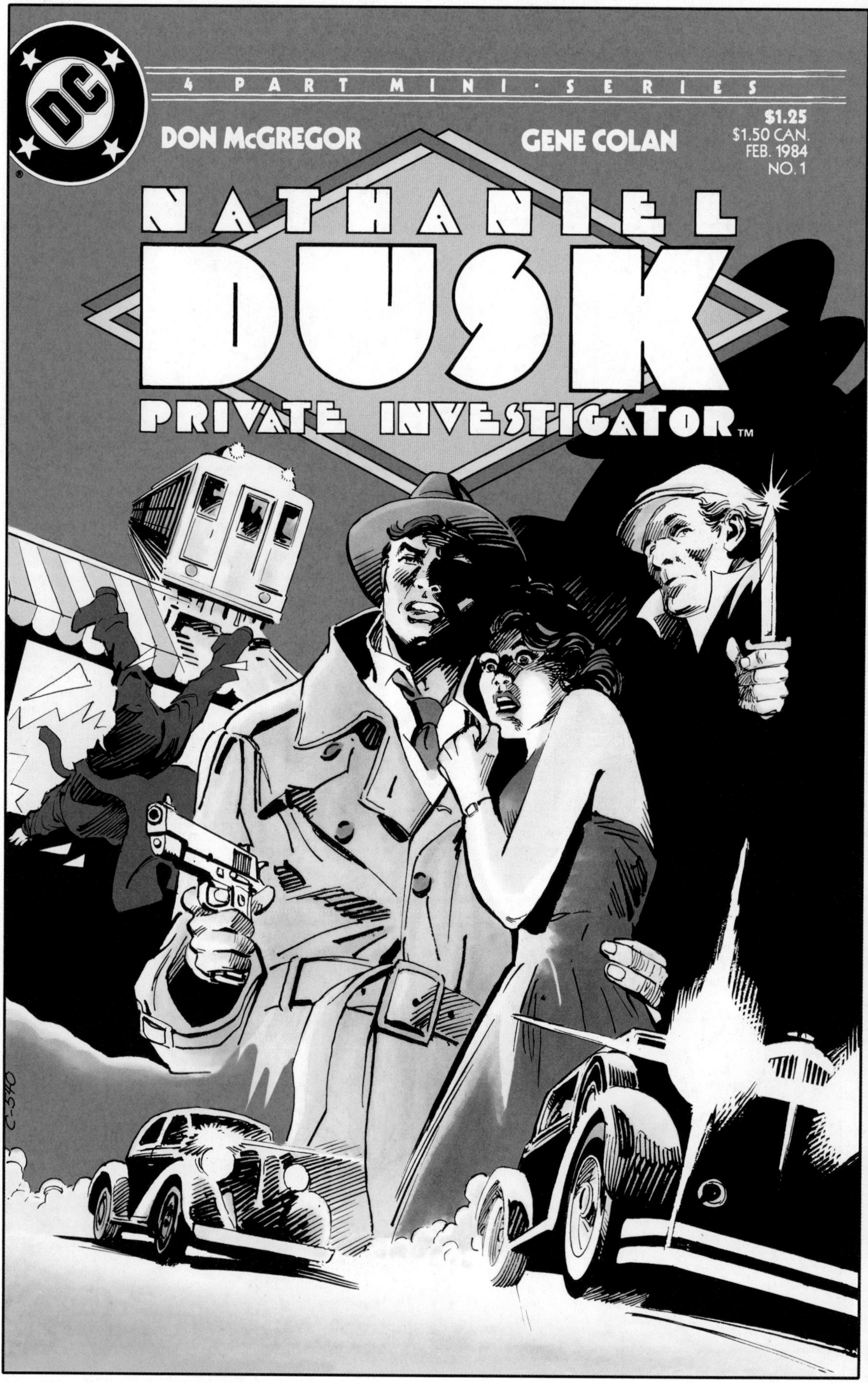
4 PART MINI-SERIES
DON McGREGOR
GENE COLAN
$1.25
$1.50 CAN.
FEB. 1984
NO. 1
NATHANIEL
DUSK
PRIVATE INVESTIGATOR™
C-340

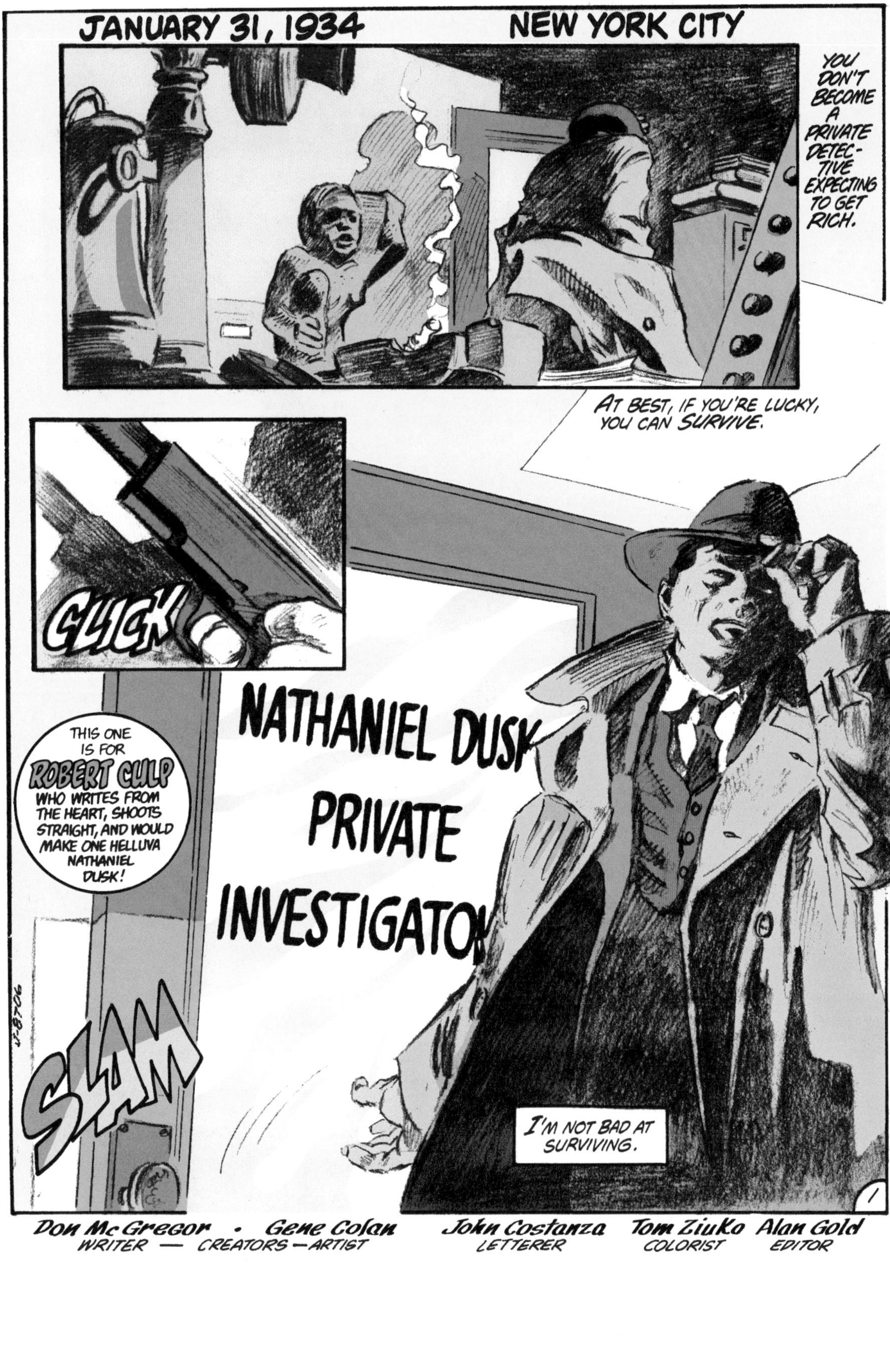
JANUARY 31, 1934
NEW YORK CITY
YOU DON'T BECOME A PRIVATE DETECTIVE EXPECTING TO GET RICH.
AT BEST, IF YOU'RE LUCKY, YOU CAN SURVIVE.
CLICK
THIS ONE IS FOR ROBERT CULP WHO WRITES FROM THE HEART, SHOOTS STRAIGHT, AND WOULD MAKE ONE HELLUVA NATHANIEL DUSK!
NATHANIEL DUSK
PRIVATE
INVESTIGATOR
SLAM
I'M NOT BAD AT SURVIVING.
1
Don McGregor · Gene Colan
WRITER — CREATORS — ARTIST
John Costanza
LETTERER
Tom Ziuko
COLORIST
Alan Gold
EDITOR

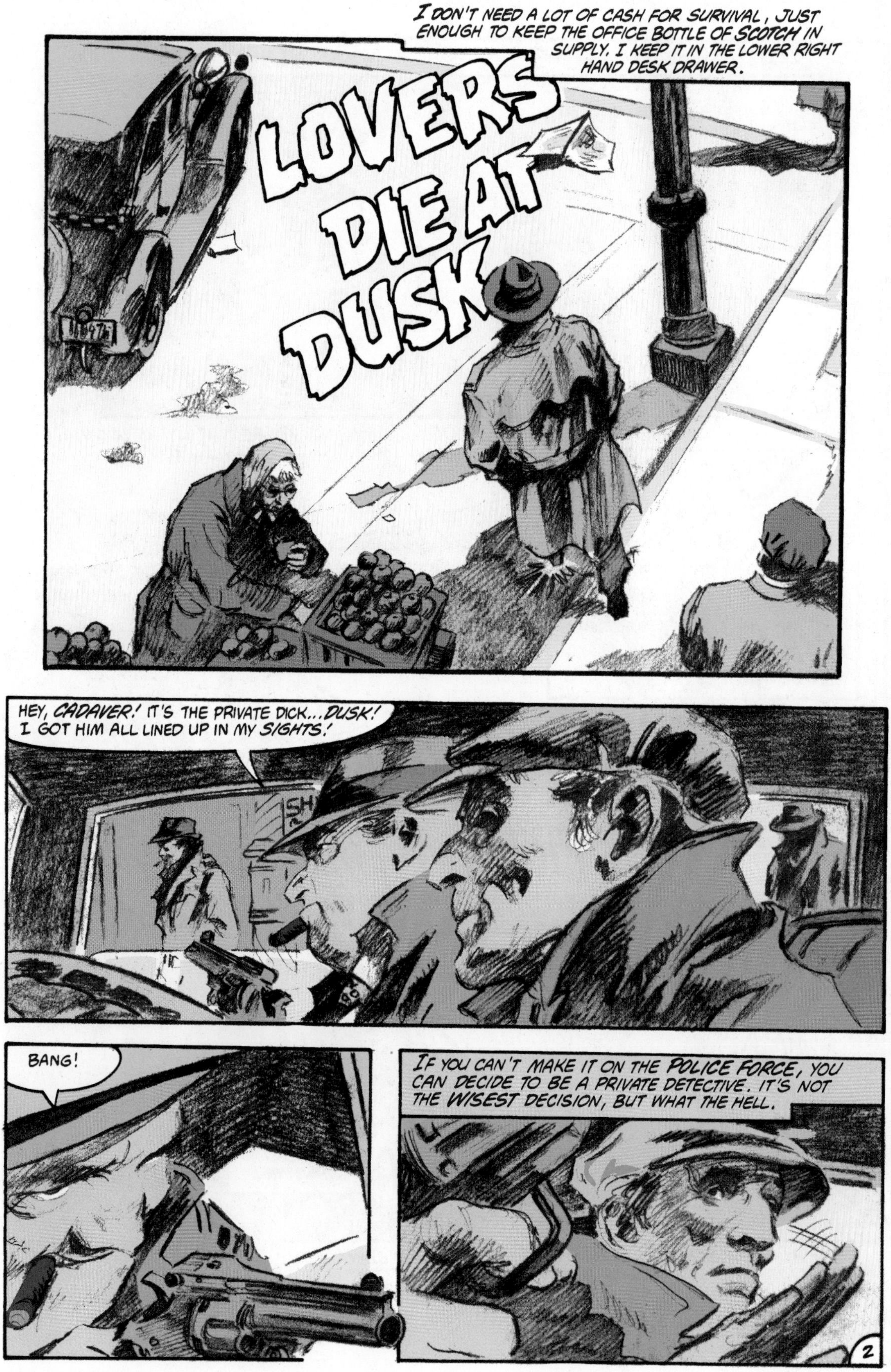
I DON'T NEED A LOT OF CASH FOR SURVIVAL, JUST ENOUGH TO KEEP THE OFFICE BOTTLE OF SCOTCH IN SUPPLY. I KEEP IT IN THE LOWER RIGHT HAND DESK DRAWER.
LOVERS DIE AT DUSK
HEY, CADAVER! IT'S THE PRIVATE DICK... DUSK! I GOT HIM ALL LINED UP IN MY SIGHTS!
BANG!
IF YOU CAN'T MAKE IT ON THE POLICE FORCE, YOU CAN DECIDE TO BE A PRIVATE DETECTIVE. IT'S NOT THE WISEST DECISION, BUT WHAT THE HELL.
2

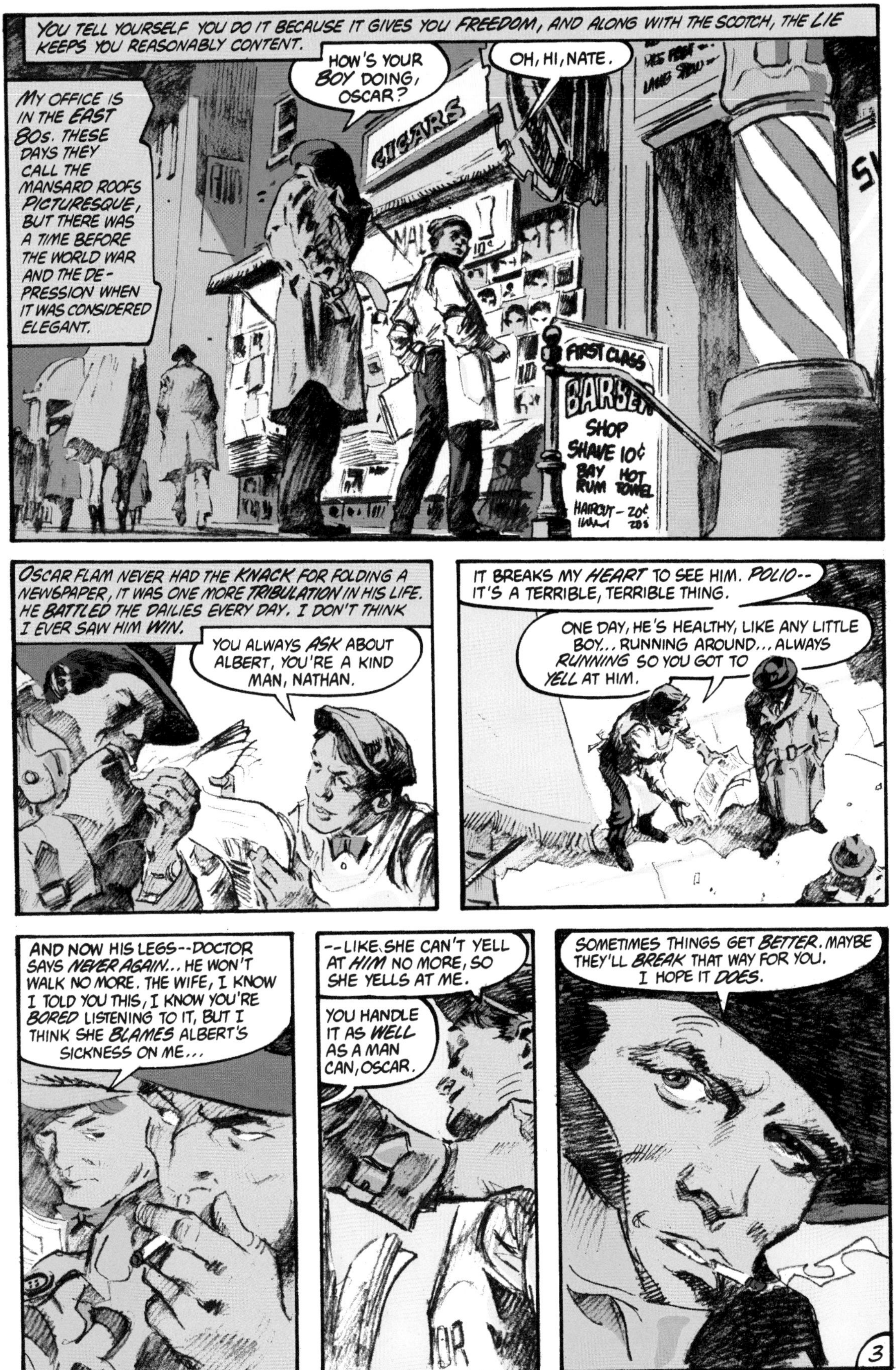
YOU TELL YOURSELF YOU DO IT BECAUSE IT GIVES YOU FREEDOM, AND ALONG WITH THE SCOTCH, THE LIE KEEPS YOU REASONABLY CONTENT.
HOW'S YOUR BOY DOING, OSCAR?
OH, HI, NATE.
MY OFFICE IS IN THE EAST 80s. THESE DAYS THEY CALL THE MANSARD ROOFS PICTURESQUE, BUT THERE WAS A TIME BEFORE THE WORLD WAR AND THE DE-PRESSION WHEN IT WAS CONSIDERED ELEGANT.
CIGARS
FIRST CLASS BARBER SHOP SHAVE 10¢ BAY RUM HOT TOWEL HAIRCUT - 20¢
OSCAR FLAM NEVER HAD THE KNACK FOR FOLDING A NEWSPAPER, IT WAS ONE MORE TRIBULATION IN HIS LIFE. HE BATTLED THE DAILIES EVERY DAY. I DON'T THINK I EVER SAW HIM WIN.
YOU ALWAYS ASK ABOUT ALBERT, YOU'RE A KIND MAN, NATHAN.
IT BREAKS MY HEART TO SEE HIM. POLIO-- IT'S A TERRIBLE, TERRIBLE THING.
ONE DAY, HE'S HEALTHY, LIKE ANY LITTLE BOY... RUNNING AROUND... ALWAYS RUNNING SO YOU GOT TO YELL AT HIM.
AND NOW HIS LEGS--DOCTOR SAYS NEVER AGAIN... HE WON'T WALK NO MORE. THE WIFE, I KNOW I TOLD YOU THIS, I KNOW YOU'RE BORED LISTENING TO IT, BUT I THINK SHE BLAMES ALBERT'S SICKNESS ON ME...
--LIKE SHE CAN'T YELL AT HIM NO MORE, SO SHE YELLS AT ME.
YOU HANDLE IT AS WELL AS A MAN CAN, OSCAR.
SOMETIMES THINGS GET BETTER. MAYBE THEY'LL BREAK THAT WAY FOR YOU. I HOPE IT DOES.
3

HMM.

DAILY MIRROR

TAXI DRIVERS THREATEN STRIKE

SHE WAS *WAITING* FOR ME. MRS. GRANT MORRISON, A TRANSPLANTED MIDWESTERN WOMAN...

NATHANIEL
PRIVATE
INVESTIGA

... WHO WANTED TO FIND OUT IF HER HUSBAND WAS AN ADULTERER.

YOU TOOK YOUR *SWEET TIME*, MR. DUSK, I'VE BEEN COOLING MY *HEELS* FOR FIFTEEN MINUTES!

THE *PHOTO LAB* WAS LATE. TAKE IT OUT ON THEM.

HER EYES DENIED THE POSSIBILITY, BUT SHE ALREADY KNEW THE REAL ANSWER. HUSBANDS OR WIVES, IT DOESN'T MATTER, THEY ALL WANT THE SAME THING. THEY WANT YOU TO TELL THEM THEY HAVEN'T BEEN DECEIVED.

SHE LOOKED AT THE PICTURES WITH COLD, CRUEL EYES. I HAD JUST BEEN *MIDWIFE* TO A LITTLE MORE *HATE* IN THE WORLD.

THE *SONOFABITCH!* THAT VILE LOWLIFE!

4

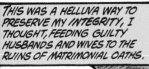

THIS WAS A HELLUVA WAY TO PRESERVE MY *INTEGRITY,* I THOUGHT, FEEDING GUILTY HUSBANDS AND WIVES TO THE RUINS OF MATRIMONIAL OATHS.

HOW *COULD* HE?

SHE LOOKED LIKE SHE MIGHT LOSE BREAKFAST AND LUNCH.

IF YOU *BREAK* THE FURNITURE, MRS. MORRISON, IT DOESN'T CHANGE ANY- THING. IT ONLY GETS ADDED ON THE BILL.

SMASH

JOYCE GULINO ENTERED THE OFFICE. SHE DIDN'T KNOCK, SHE DIDN'T HAVE TO. HER DARK BEAUTY *BRIGHTENED* THE PLACE.

SHE DIDN'T LOOK AS IF SHE HAD JUST SPENT THE DAY ON HER *FEET,* SELLING *CHEAP* PERFUMES AT THE FIVE-AND-DIME TO OVERWEIGHT LADIES WHO HAD MONEY FOR SUCH *DEBATABLE* LUXURIES. WE'D MET TWO MONTHS AGO WHEN SHE WAS PINCH-HITTING BEHIND THE *LUNCH* COUNTER.

A QUICK LOOK OF *SORROW* PASSED ACROSS JOYCE'S FACE, AND OF SOMETHING *MORE*--SOMETHING I COULD NOT QUITE FATHOM... A KIND OF *KINSHIP,* PERHAPS... AS IF SHE *IDENTIFIED* WITH EVELYN MORRISON'S HURT AND RAGE.

PERHAPS YOU HAD TO BE A PART OF THE *FEMALE SORORITY* TO BE A PART OF IT. I SUDDENLY FELT LIKE AN *OUTSIDER.*

YOU CAN *SURVIVE* THIS. IT MIGHT NOT SEEM LIKE IT, RIGHT THIS MINUTE. BUT YOU CAN GET PAST THIS.

WHAT THE HELL DO YOU KNOW ABOUT IT?

HERE'S YOUR FEE, MR. DUSK. YOU CAN BE SURE I'LL GIVE YOU MY *HIGHEST* RECOMMENDATIONS TO MY FRIENDS.

5

113

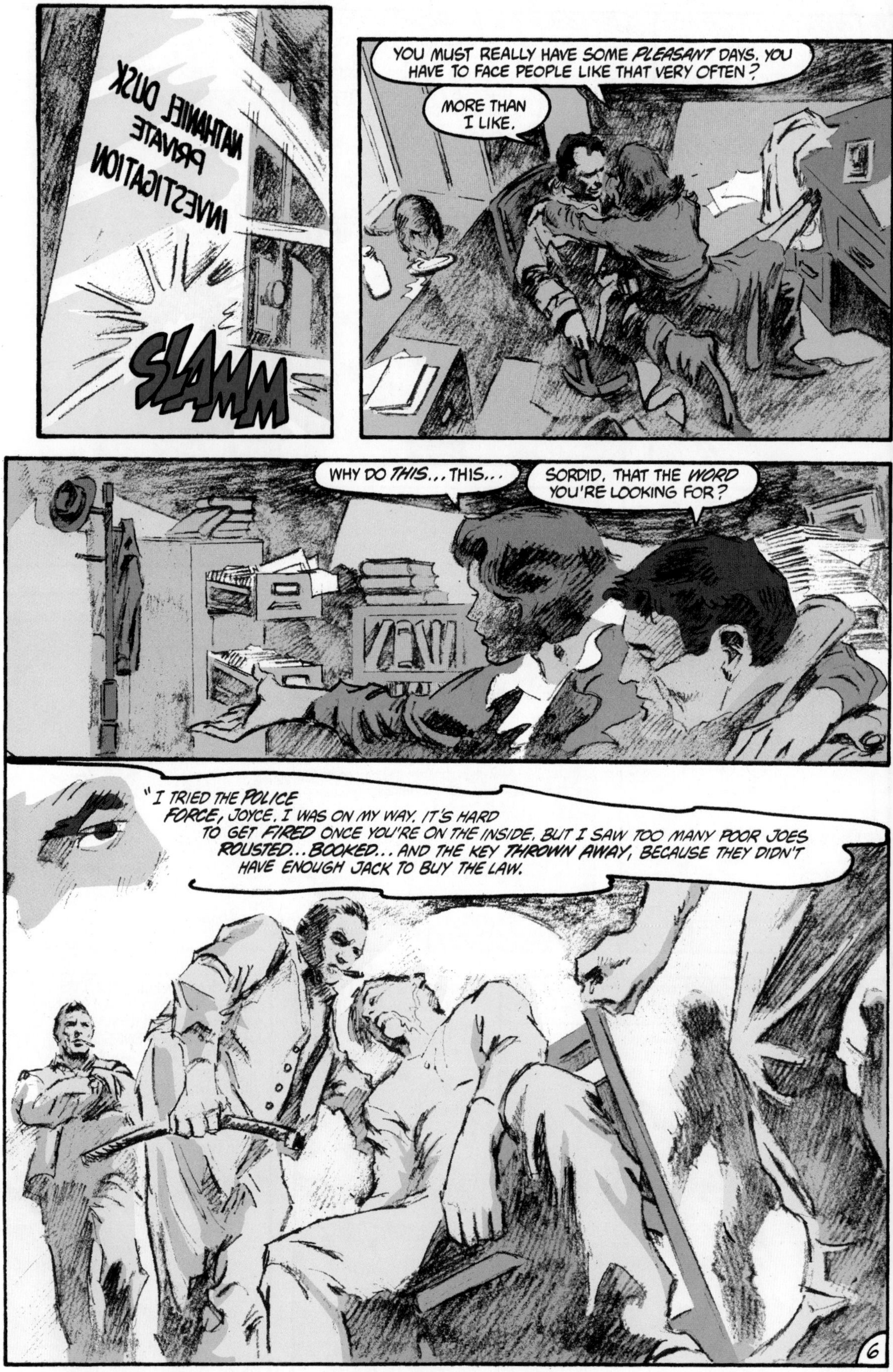
NATHANIEL DUSK
PRIVATE
INVESTIGATION
SLAMM
YOU MUST REALLY HAVE SOME *PLEASANT* DAYS. YOU HAVE TO FACE PEOPLE LIKE THAT VERY OFTEN?
MORE THAN I LIKE.
WHY DO *THIS*... THIS...
SORDID, THAT THE *WORD* YOU'RE LOOKING FOR?
"I TRIED THE *POLICE FORCE*, JOYCE. I WAS ON MY WAY. IT'S HARD TO GET *FIRED* ONCE YOU'RE ON THE INSIDE. BUT I SAW TOO MANY POOR JOES *ROUSTED*... *BOOKED*... AND THE KEY *THROWN AWAY*, BECAUSE THEY DIDN'T HAVE ENOUGH JACK TO BUY THE LAW.
6

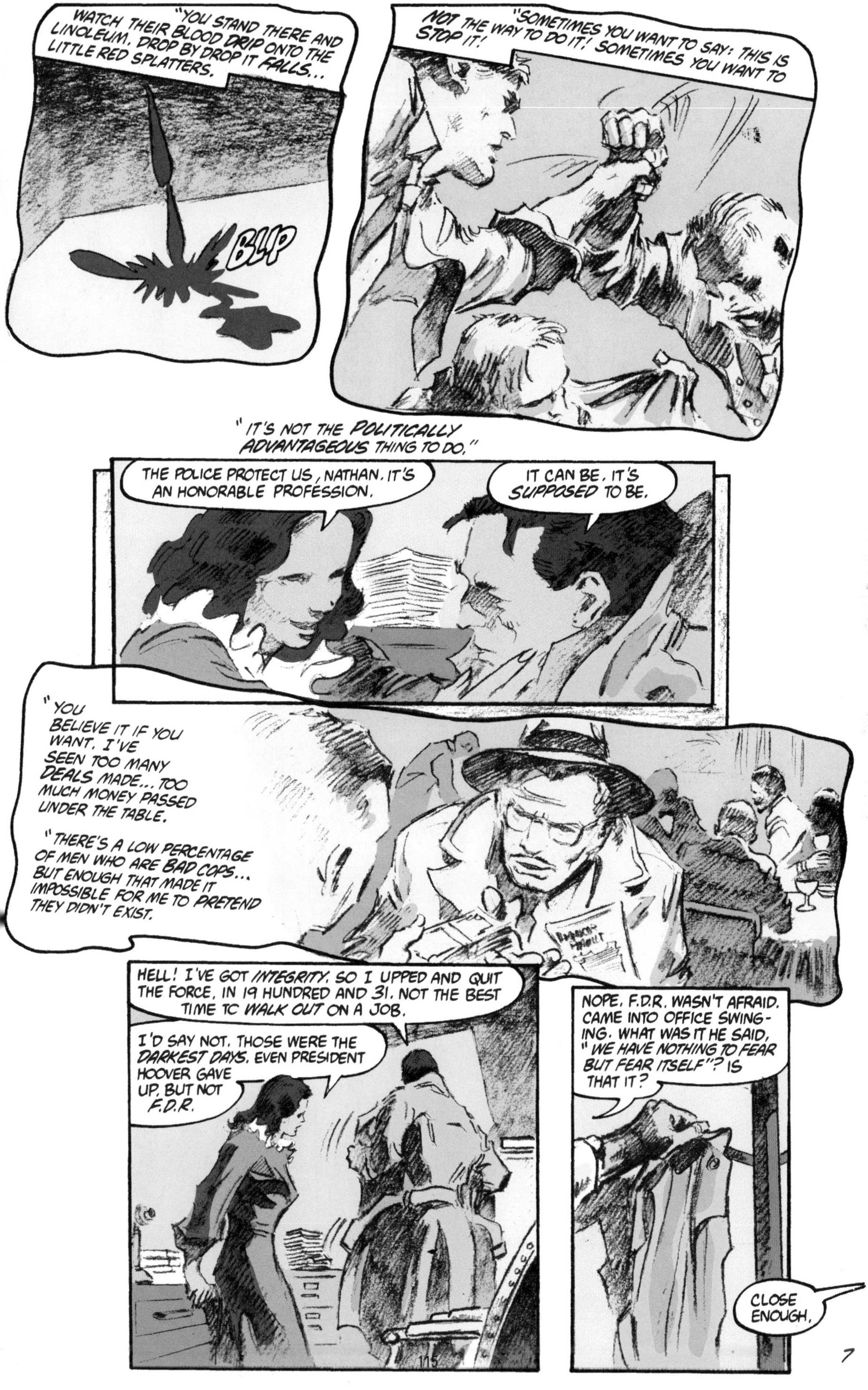
"YOU STAND THERE AND WATCH THEIR BLOOD DRIP ONTO THE LINOLEUM. DROP BY DROP IT FALLS... LITTLE RED SPLATTERS.
BLIP
"SOMETIMES YOU WANT TO SAY: THIS IS NOT THE WAY TO DO IT! SOMETIMES YOU WANT TO STOP IT!
"IT'S NOT THE POLITICALLY ADVANTAGEOUS THING TO DO."
THE POLICE PROTECT US, NATHAN. IT'S AN HONORABLE PROFESSION.
IT CAN BE. IT'S SUPPOSED TO BE.
"YOU BELIEVE IT IF YOU WANT. I'VE SEEN TOO MANY DEALS MADE... TOO MUCH MONEY PASSED UNDER THE TABLE.
"THERE'S A LOW PERCENTAGE OF MEN WHO ARE BAD COPS... BUT ENOUGH THAT MADE IT IMPOSSIBLE FOR ME TO PRETEND THEY DIDN'T EXIST.
HELL! I'VE GOT INTEGRITY. SO I UPPED AND QUIT THE FORCE, IN 19 HUNDRED AND 31. NOT THE BEST TIME TO WALK OUT ON A JOB.
I'D SAY NOT. THOSE WERE THE DARKEST DAYS. EVEN PRESIDENT HOOVER GAVE UP, BUT NOT F.D.R.
NOPE. F.D.R. WASN'T AFRAID. CAME INTO OFFICE SWINGING. WHAT WAS IT HE SAID, "WE HAVE NOTHING TO FEAR BUT FEAR ITSELF"? IS THAT IT?
CLOSE ENOUGH.

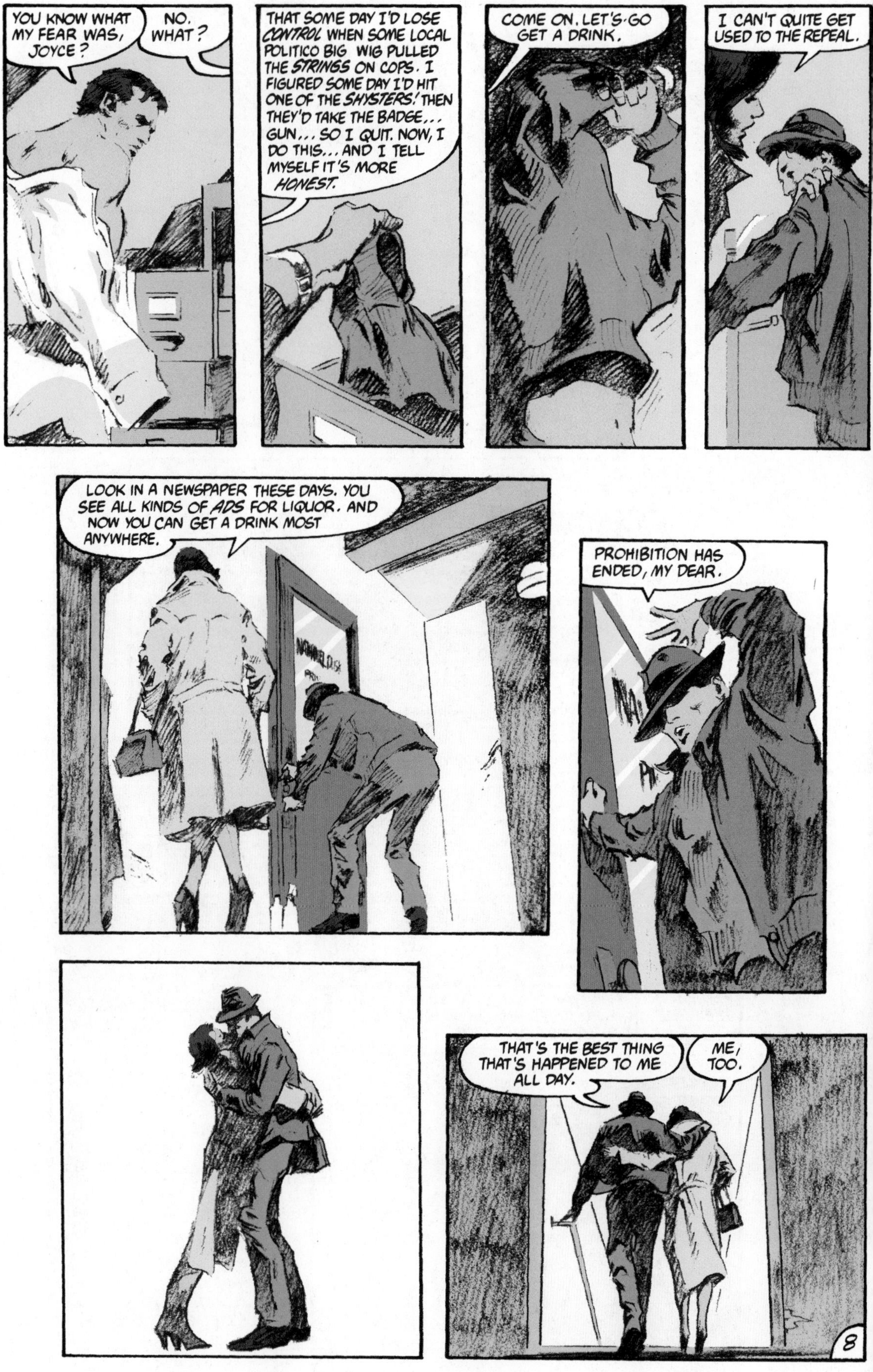
YOU KNOW WHAT MY FEAR WAS, JOYCE?
NO. WHAT?
THAT SOME DAY I'D LOSE CONTROL WHEN SOME LOCAL POLITICO BIG WIG PULLED THE STRINGS ON COPS. I FIGURED SOME DAY I'D HIT ONE OF THE SHYSTERS! THEN THEY'D TAKE THE BADGE... GUN... SO I QUIT. NOW, I DO THIS... AND I TELL MYSELF IT'S MORE HONEST.
COME ON. LET'S GO GET A DRINK.
I CAN'T QUITE GET USED TO THE REPEAL.
LOOK IN A NEWSPAPER THESE DAYS. YOU SEE ALL KINDS OF ADS FOR LIQUOR. AND NOW YOU CAN GET A DRINK MOST ANYWHERE.
PROHIBITION HAS ENDED, MY DEAR.
THAT'S THE BEST THING THAT'S HAPPENED TO ME ALL DAY.
ME, TOO.
8

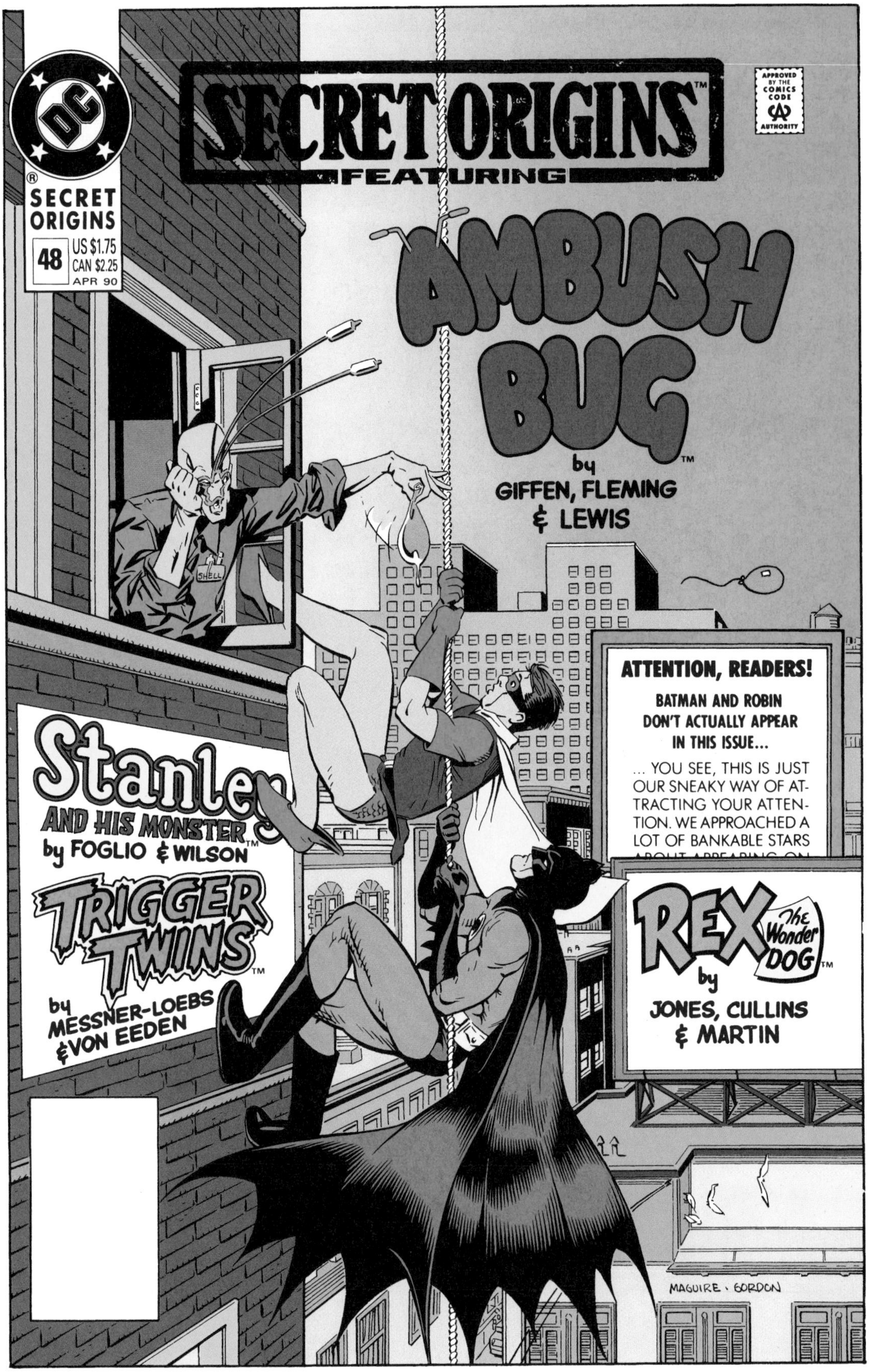

SECRET ORIGINS
SECRET ORIGINS
48
US $1.75
CAN $2.25
APR 90
FEATURING
AMBUSH BUG
by
GIFFEN, FLEMING
& LEWIS
SHELL
ATTENTION, READERS!
BATMAN AND ROBIN
DON'T ACTUALLY APPEAR
IN THIS ISSUE...
... YOU SEE, THIS IS JUST
OUR SNEAKY WAY OF AT-
TRACTING YOUR ATTEN-
TION. WE APPROACHED A
LOT OF BANKABLE STARS
Stanley
AND HIS MONSTER
by FOGLIO & WILSON
TRIGGER TWINS
by
MESSNER-LOEBS
& VON EEDEN
REX The Wonder DOG
by
JONES, CULLINS
& MARTIN
MAGUIRE · GORDON

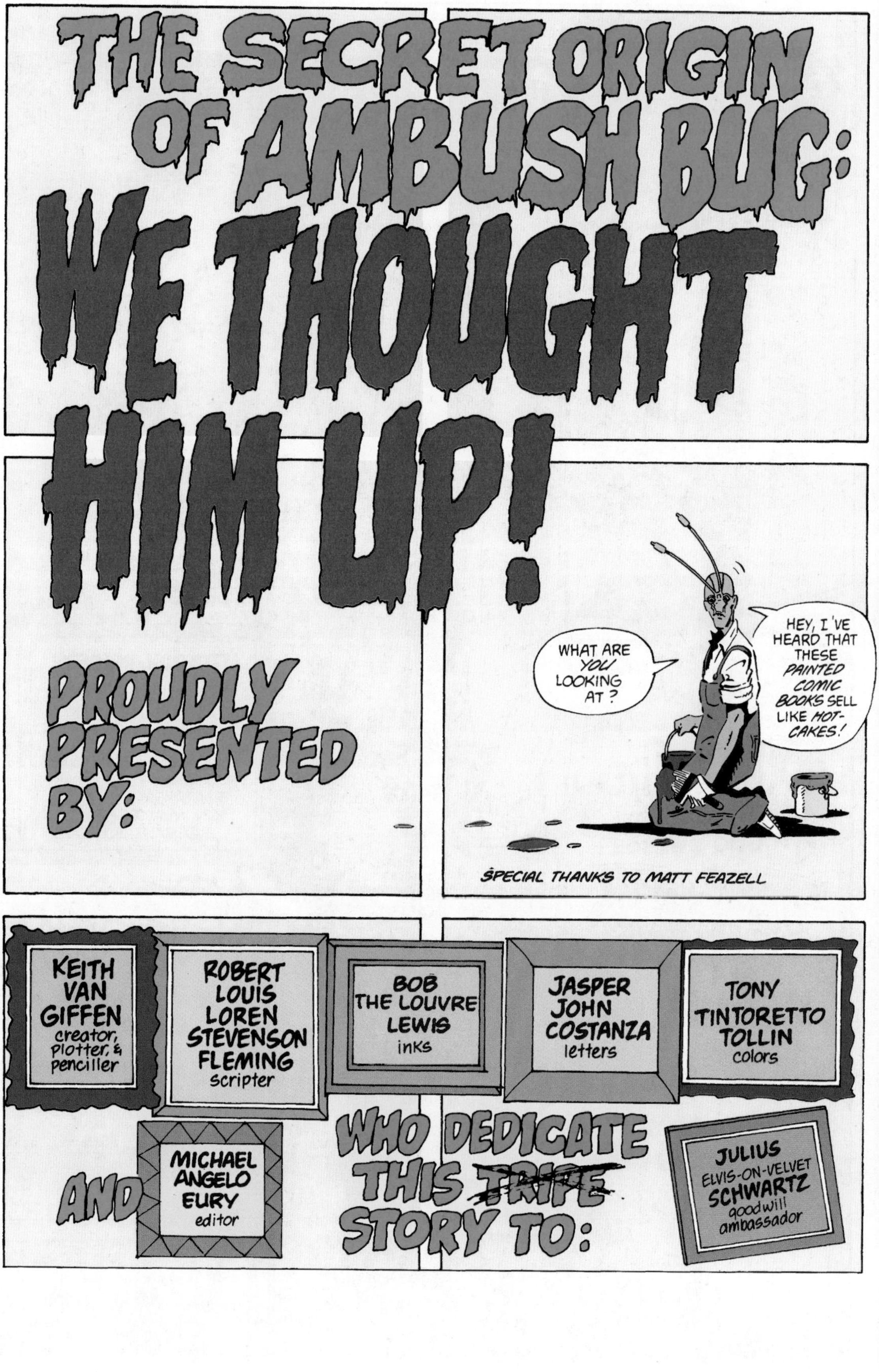
THE SECRET ORIGIN OF AMBUSH BUG: WE THOUGHT HIM UP!
PROUDLY PRESENTED BY:
WHAT ARE YOU LOOKING AT?
HEY, I'VE HEARD THAT THESE PAINTED COMIC BOOKS SELL LIKE HOT-CAKES!
SPECIAL THANKS TO MATT FEAZELL
KEITH VAN GIFFEN creator, plotter, & penciller
ROBERT LOUIS LOREN STEVENSON FLEMING scripter
BOB THE LOUVRE LEWIS inks
JASPER JOHN COSTANZA letters
TONY TINTORETTO TOLLIN colors
AND
MICHAEL ANGELO EURY editor
WHO DEDICATE THIS ~~TRIPE~~ STORY TO:
JULIUS ELVIS-ON-VELVET SCHWARTZ goodwill ambassador

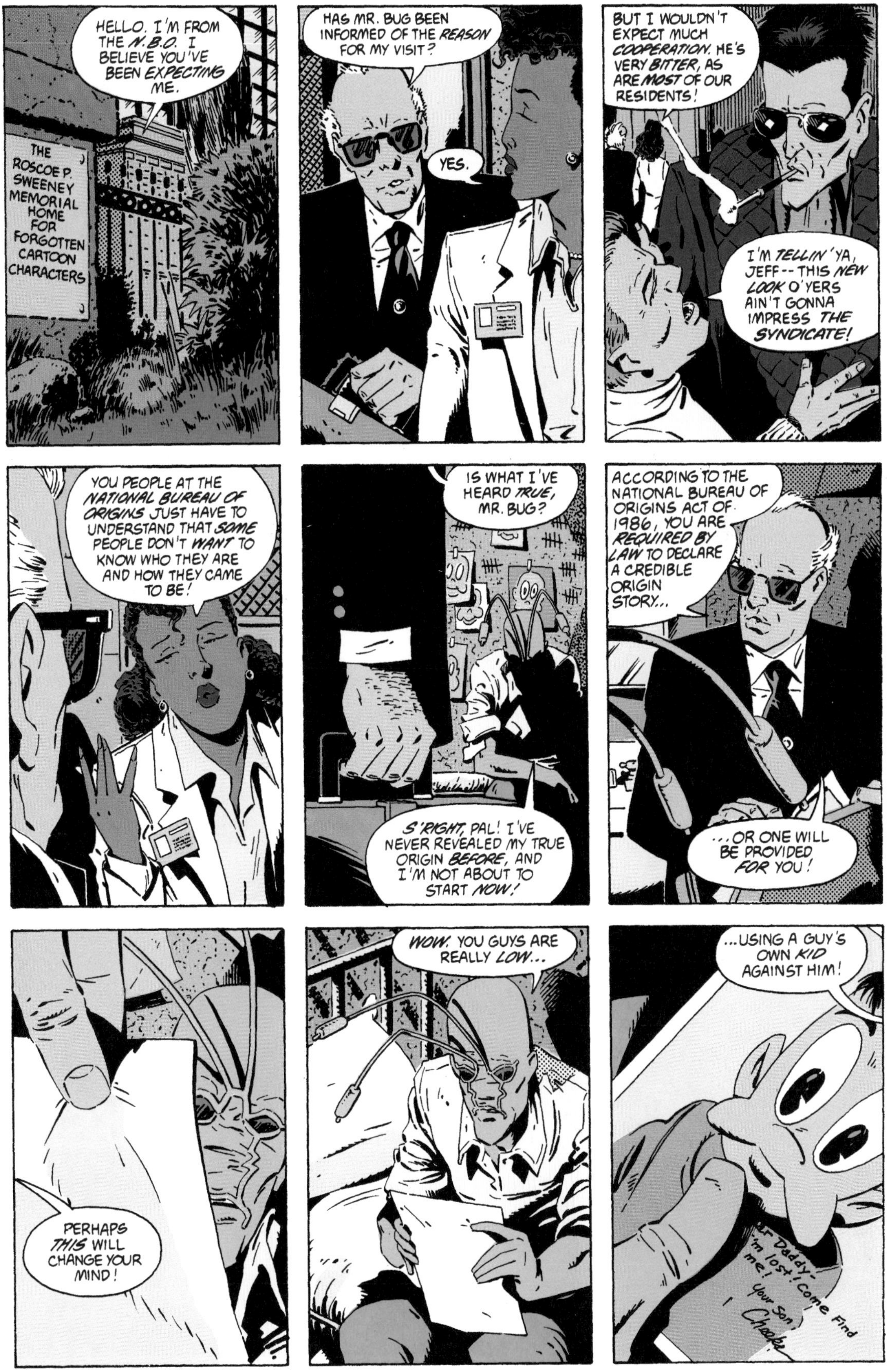
HELLO. I'M FROM THE N.B.O. I BELIEVE YOU'VE BEEN EXPECTING ME.
THE ROSCOE P. SWEENEY MEMORIAL HOME FOR FORGOTTEN CARTOON CHARACTERS
HAS MR. BUG BEEN INFORMED OF THE REASON FOR MY VISIT?
YES.
BUT I WOULDN'T EXPECT MUCH COOPERATION. HE'S VERY BITTER, AS ARE MOST OF OUR RESIDENTS!
I'M TELLIN' YA, JEFF -- THIS NEW LOOK O'YERS AIN'T GONNA IMPRESS THE SYNDICATE!
YOU PEOPLE AT THE NATIONAL BUREAU OF ORIGINS JUST HAVE TO UNDERSTAND THAT SOME PEOPLE DON'T WANT TO KNOW WHO THEY ARE AND HOW THEY CAME TO BE!
IS WHAT I'VE HEARD TRUE, MR. BUG?
S'RIGHT, PAL! I'VE NEVER REVEALED MY TRUE ORIGIN BEFORE, AND I'M NOT ABOUT TO START NOW!
ACCORDING TO THE NATIONAL BUREAU OF ORIGINS ACT OF 1986, YOU ARE REQUIRED BY LAW TO DECLARE A CREDIBLE ORIGIN STORY...
...OR ONE WILL BE PROVIDED FOR YOU!
PERHAPS THIS WILL CHANGE YOUR MIND!
WOW. YOU GUYS ARE REALLY LOW...
...USING A GUY'S OWN KID AGAINST HIM!
'm lost! Come Find
me!
Your Son

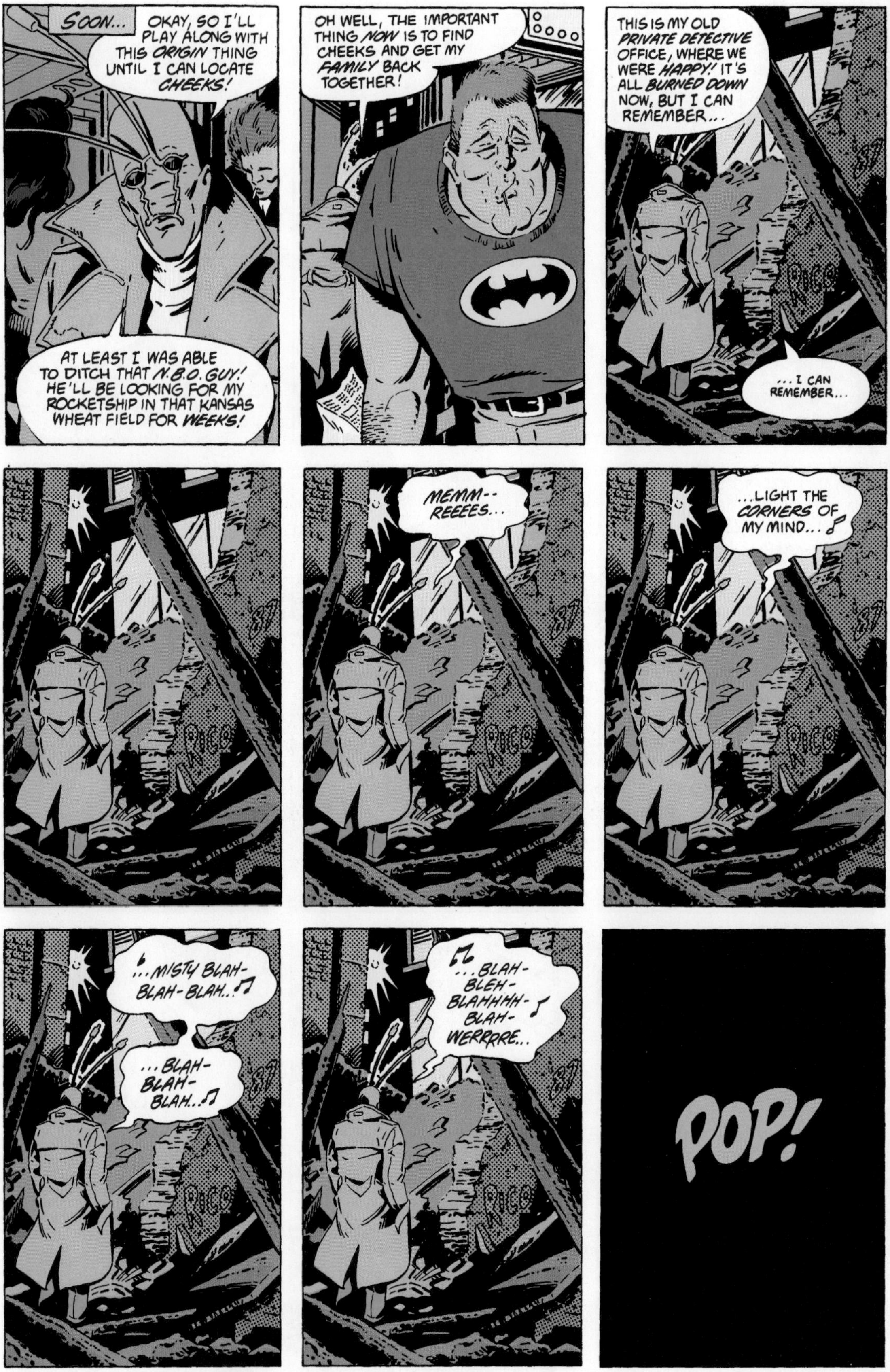
SOON...
OKAY, SO I'LL PLAY ALONG WITH THIS ORIGIN THING UNTIL I CAN LOCATE CHEEKS!
AT LEAST I WAS ABLE TO DITCH THAT N.B.O. GUY! HE'LL BE LOOKING FOR MY ROCKETSHIP IN THAT KANSAS WHEAT FIELD FOR WEEKS!
OH WELL, THE IMPORTANT THING NOW IS TO FIND CHEEKS AND GET MY FAMILY BACK TOGETHER!
THIS IS MY OLD PRIVATE DETECTIVE OFFICE, WHERE WE WERE HAPPY! IT'S ALL BURNED DOWN NOW, BUT I CAN REMEMBER...
...I CAN REMEMBER...
MEMM-- REEEES...
...LIGHT THE CORNERS OF MY MIND...
...MISTY BLAH-BLAH-BLAH...
...BLAH-BLAH-BLAH...
...BLAH-BLEH-BLAHHHH-BLAH-WERRRRE...
POP!

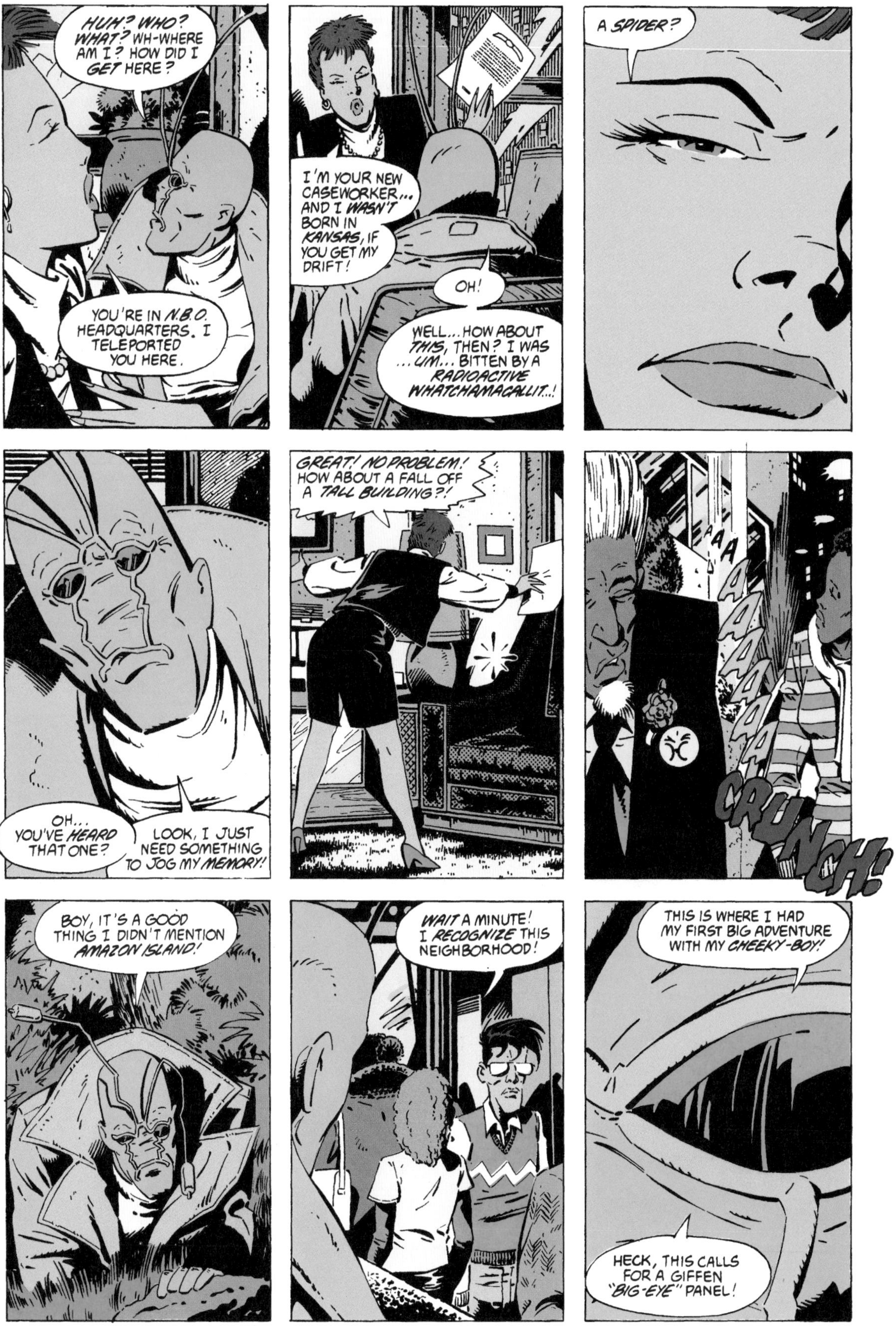
HUH? WHO? WHAT? WH-WHERE AM I? HOW DID I GET HERE?
YOU'RE IN N.B.O. HEADQUARTERS. I TELEPORTED YOU HERE.
I'M YOUR NEW CASEWORKER... AND I WASN'T BORN IN KANSAS, IF YOU GET MY DRIFT!
OH!
WELL... HOW ABOUT THIS, THEN? I WAS ...UM... BITTEN BY A RADIOACTIVE WHATCHAMAGALLIT...!
A SPIDER?
OH... YOU'VE HEARD THAT ONE?
LOOK, I JUST NEED SOMETHING TO JOG MY MEMORY!
GREAT! NO PROBLEM! HOW ABOUT A FALL OFF A TALL BUILDING?!
AAAAAAAAAAAA
CRUNCH!
BOY, IT'S A GOOD THING I DIDN'T MENTION AMAZON ISLAND!
WAIT A MINUTE! I RECOGNIZE THIS NEIGHBORHOOD!
THIS IS WHERE I HAD MY FIRST BIG ADVENTURE WITH MY CHEEKY-BOY!
HECK, THIS CALLS FOR A GIFFEN "BIG-EYE" PANEL!

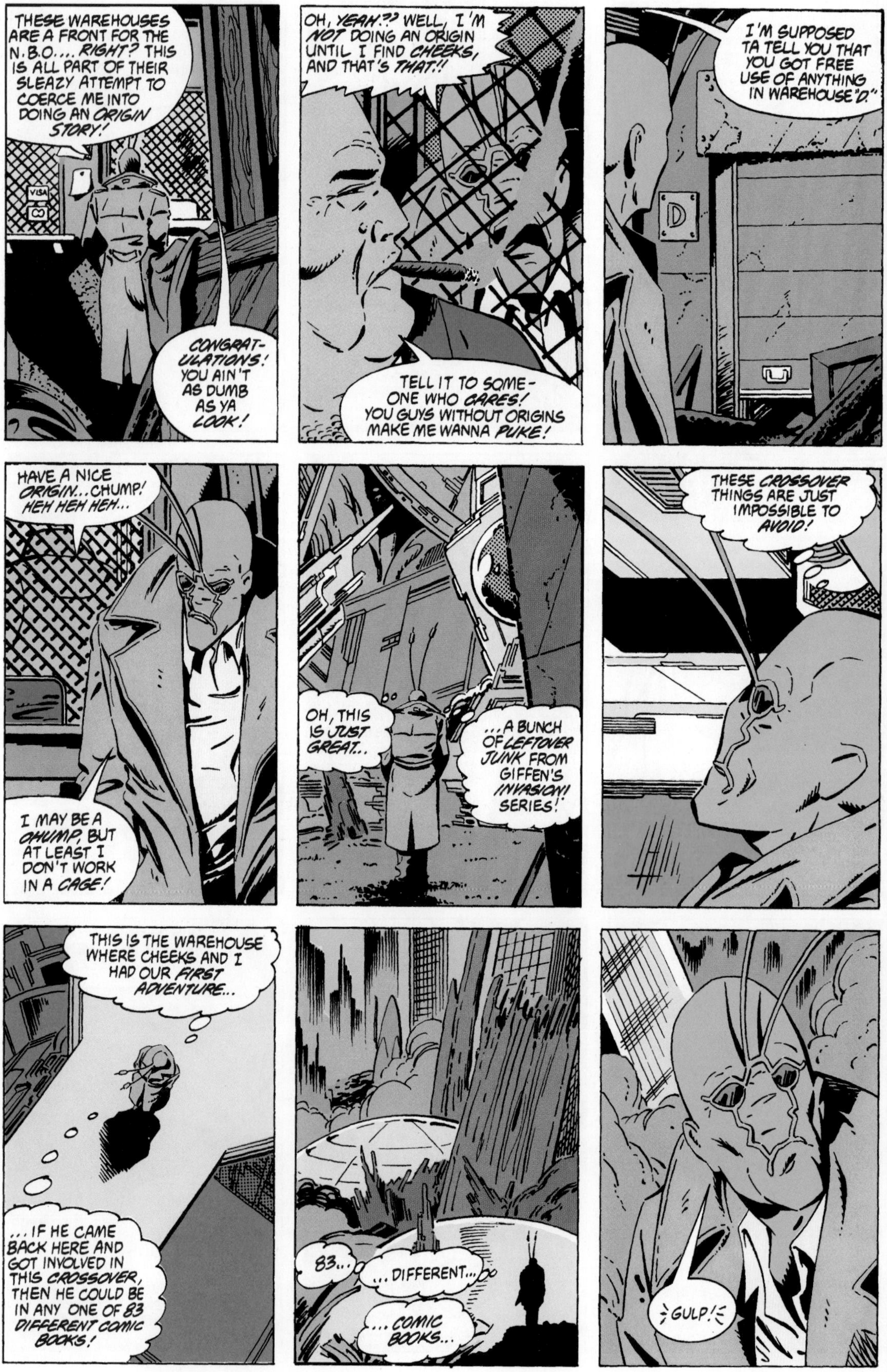
THESE WAREHOUSES ARE A FRONT FOR THE N.B.O.... RIGHT? THIS IS ALL PART OF THEIR SLEAZY ATTEMPT TO COERCE ME INTO DOING AN ORIGIN STORY!
CONGRATULATIONS! YOU AIN'T AS DUMB AS YA LOOK!
OH, YEAH?? WELL, I'M NOT DOING AN ORIGIN UNTIL I FIND CHEEKS, AND THAT'S THAT!!
TELL IT TO SOME-ONE WHO CARES! YOU GUYS WITHOUT ORIGINS MAKE ME WANNA PUKE!
I'M SUPPOSED TA TELL YOU THAT YOU GOT FREE USE OF ANYTHING IN WAREHOUSE "D."
HAVE A NICE ORIGIN... CHUMP! HEH HEH HEH...
I MAY BE A CHUMP, BUT AT LEAST I DON'T WORK IN A CAGE!
OH, THIS IS JUST GREAT...
...A BUNCH OF LEFTOVER JUNK FROM GIFFEN'S INVASION! SERIES!
THESE CROSSOVER THINGS ARE JUST IMPOSSIBLE TO AVOID!
THIS IS THE WAREHOUSE WHERE CHEEKS AND I HAD OUR FIRST ADVENTURE...
...IF HE CAME BACK HERE AND GOT INVOLVED IN THIS CROSSOVER, THEN HE COULD BE IN ANY ONE OF 83 DIFFERENT COMIC BOOKS!
83...
...DIFFERENT...
...COMIC BOOKS...
GULP!

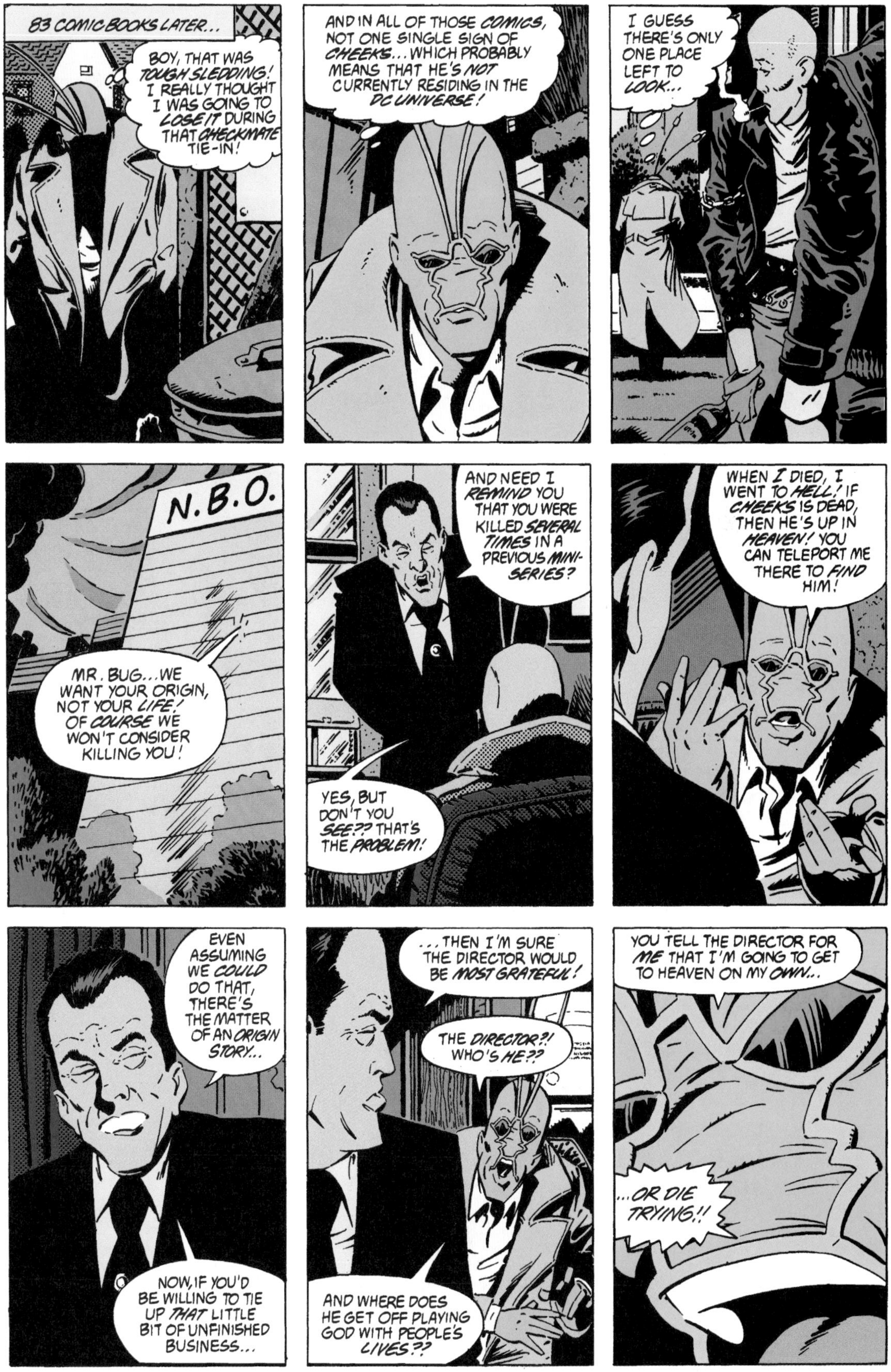
83 COMIC BOOKS LATER...
BOY, THAT WAS TOUGH SLEDDING! I REALLY THOUGHT I WAS GOING TO LOSE IT DURING THAT CHECKMATE TIE-IN!
AND IN ALL OF THOSE COMICS, NOT ONE SINGLE SIGN OF CHEEKS... WHICH PROBABLY MEANS THAT HE'S NOT CURRENTLY RESIDING IN THE DC UNIVERSE!
I GUESS THERE'S ONLY ONE PLACE LEFT TO LOOK...
N.B.O.
MR. BUG...WE WANT YOUR ORIGIN, NOT YOUR LIFE! OF COURSE WE WON'T CONSIDER KILLING YOU!
AND NEED I REMIND YOU THAT YOU WERE KILLED SEVERAL TIMES IN A PREVIOUS MINI-SERIES?
YES, BUT DON'T YOU SEE?? THAT'S THE PROBLEM!
WHEN I DIED, I WENT TO HELL! IF CHEEKS IS DEAD, THEN HE'S UP IN HEAVEN! YOU CAN TELEPORT ME THERE TO FIND HIM!
EVEN ASSUMING WE COULD DO THAT, THERE'S THE MATTER OF AN ORIGIN STORY...
NOW, IF YOU'D BE WILLING TO TIE UP THAT LITTLE BIT OF UNFINISHED BUSINESS...
...THEN I'M SURE THE DIRECTOR WOULD BE MOST GRATEFUL!
THE DIRECTOR?! WHO'S HE??
AND WHERE DOES HE GET OFF PLAYING GOD WITH PEOPLE'S LIVES??
YOU TELL THE DIRECTOR FOR ME THAT I'M GOING TO GET TO HEAVEN ON MY OWN...
...OR DIE TRYING!!

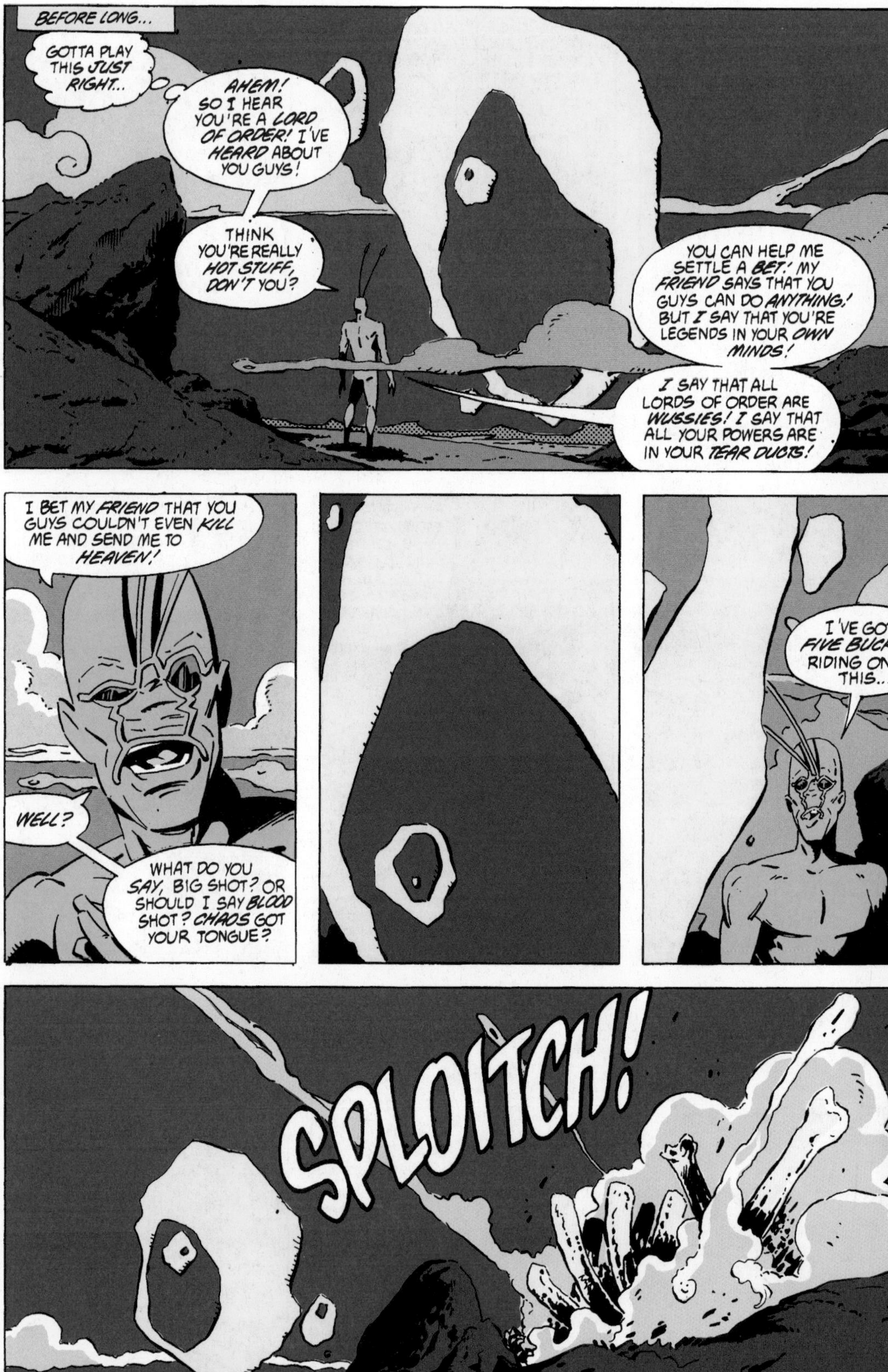
BEFORE LONG...
GOTTA PLAY THIS JUST RIGHT...
AHEM! SO I HEAR YOU'RE A LORD OF ORDER! I'VE HEARD ABOUT YOU GUYS!
THINK YOU'RE REALLY HOT STUFF, DON'T YOU?
YOU CAN HELP ME SETTLE A BET! MY FRIEND SAYS THAT YOU GUYS CAN DO ANYTHING! BUT I SAY THAT YOU'RE LEGENDS IN YOUR OWN MINDS!
I SAY THAT ALL LORDS OF ORDER ARE WUSSIES! I SAY THAT ALL YOUR POWERS ARE IN YOUR TEAR DUCTS!
I BET MY FRIEND THAT YOU GUYS COULDN'T EVEN KILL ME AND SEND ME TO HEAVEN!
WELL?
WHAT DO YOU SAY, BIG SHOT? OR SHOULD I SAY BLOOD SHOT? CHAOS GOT YOUR TONGUE?
I'VE GOT FIVE BUCKS RIDING ON THIS...
SPLOITCH!

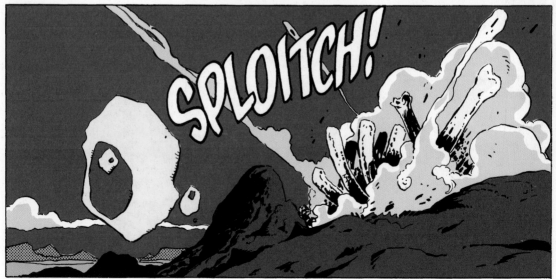

THE ORIGIN OF AMBUSH BUG
A TYPICAL, BORING ALGEBRA NOTEBOOK.
SUDDENLY...
RAR!
GRR
IEEE!
ARGH!
BANZAI!
SIEG HEIL
IRWIN! QUIT DRAWING AND FINISH YOUR HOMEWORK!
BAP!
OW!
WHAT IS THIS? DINOSAURS? SPACE SHIPS? NAZI TANKS? HOW INFANTILE!
I'M VERY DISAPPOINTED IN YOU, IRWIN! HOW DO YOU EXPECT TO EVER MAKE SOMETHING OF YOURSELF IF YOU WASTE YOUR TIME DRAWING SUCH NONSENSE?!
RAR
WHAT THE--?
GLOMP!
MR. FRF!
I'LL SAVE YOU, MR. PLANCK!
BWA-HA-HA!
PLEP!
BAF!
KEEP DRAWING, IRWIN! THE WORLD NEEDS YOU!
BOINT!
CLASS DISMISSED.
END.

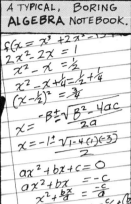

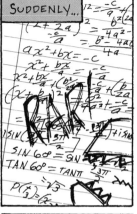

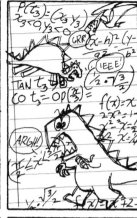

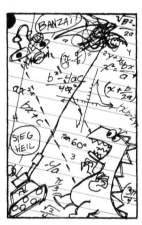

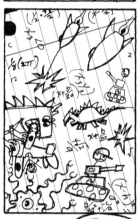

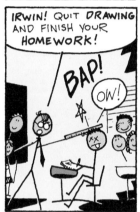

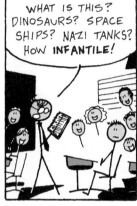

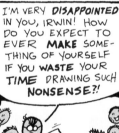

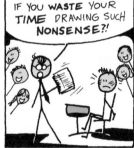

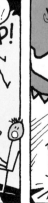

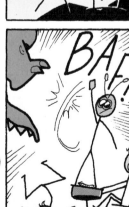

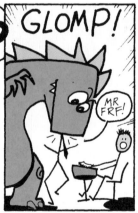

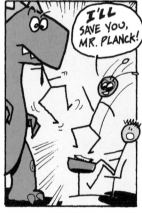

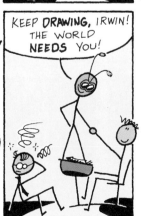

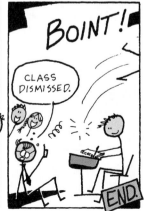

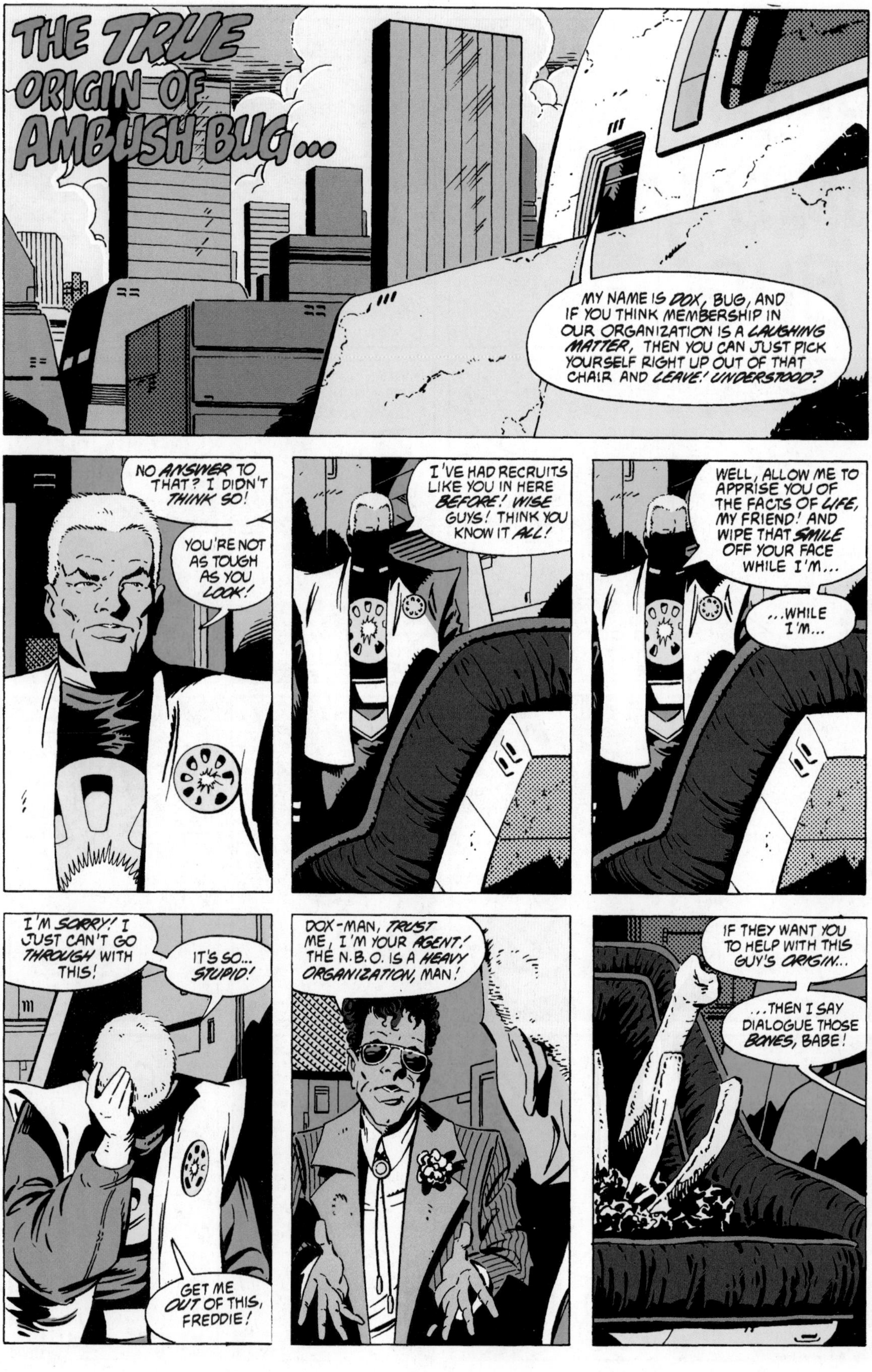
THE TRUE ORIGIN OF AMBUSH BUG...
MY NAME IS DOX, BUG, AND IF YOU THINK MEMBERSHIP IN OUR ORGANIZATION IS A LAUGHING MATTER, THEN YOU CAN JUST PICK YOURSELF RIGHT UP OUT OF THAT CHAIR AND LEAVE! UNDERSTOOD?
NO ANSWER TO THAT? I DIDN'T THINK SO!
YOU'RE NOT AS TOUGH AS YOU LOOK!
I'VE HAD RECRUITS LIKE YOU IN HERE BEFORE! WISE GUYS! THINK YOU KNOW IT ALL!
WELL, ALLOW ME TO APPRISE YOU OF THE FACTS OF LIFE, MY FRIEND! AND WIPE THAT SMILE OFF YOUR FACE WHILE I'M...
...WHILE I'M...
I'M SORRY! I JUST CAN'T GO THROUGH WITH THIS!
IT'S SO... STUPID!
GET ME OUT OF THIS, FREDDIE!
DOX-MAN, TRUST ME, I'M YOUR AGENT! THE N.B.O. IS A HEAVY ORGANIZATION, MAN!
IF THEY WANT YOU TO HELP WITH THIS GUY'S ORIGIN...
...THEN I SAY DIALOGUE THOSE BONES, BABE!

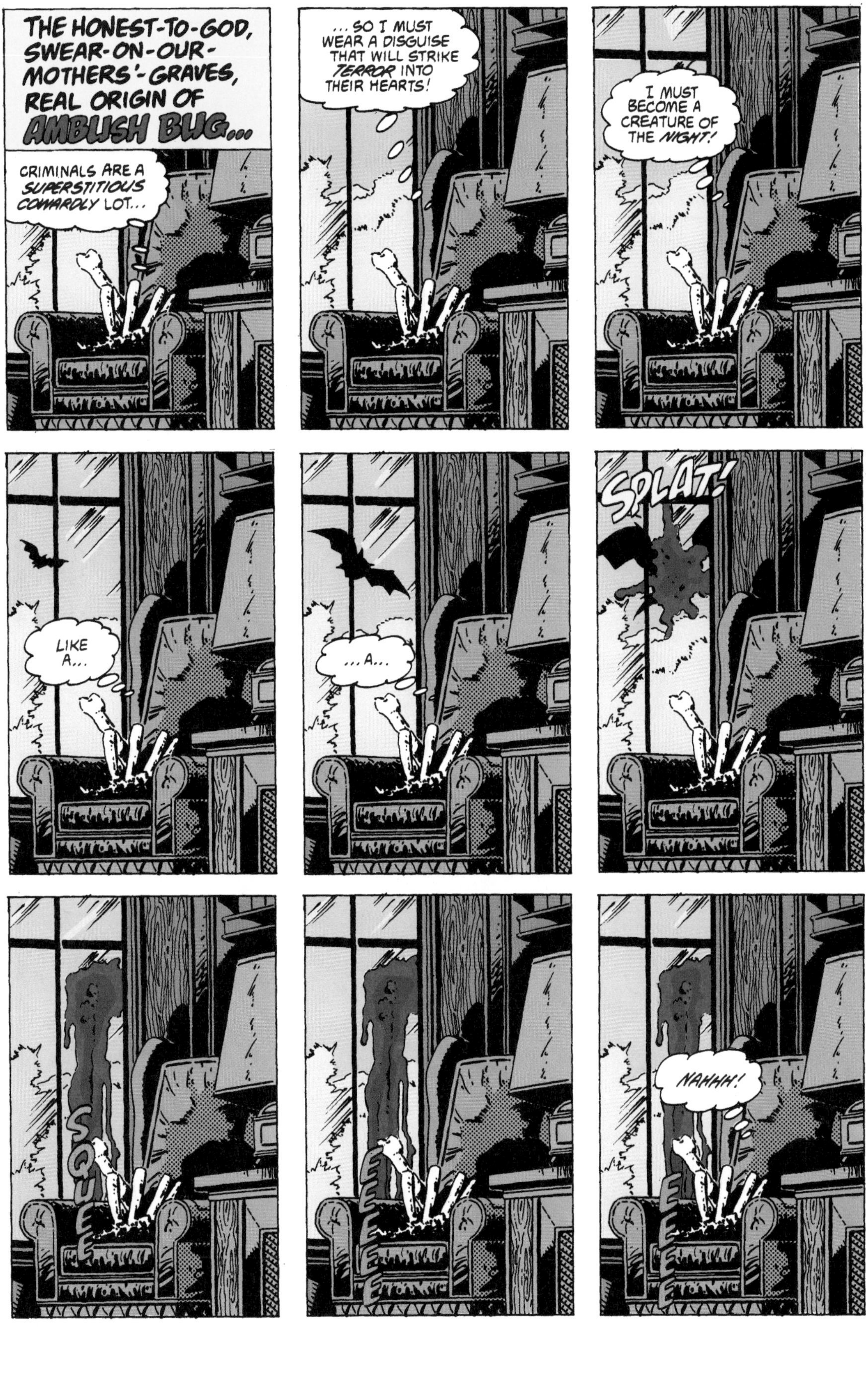
THE HONEST-TO-GOD, SWEAR-ON-OUR-MOTHERS'-GRAVES, REAL ORIGIN OF AMBUSH BUG...
CRIMINALS ARE A SUPERSTITIOUS COWARDLY LOT...
...SO I MUST WEAR A DISGUISE THAT WILL STRIKE TERROR INTO THEIR HEARTS!
I MUST BECOME A CREATURE OF THE NIGHT!
LIKE A...
...A...
SPLAT!
SQUEEEEEEEEEEEEEE
NAHHH!

MEANWHILE...

HEAVEN?

I'M IN HEAVEN?

"AND HIS HEART BEAT SO THAT HE COULD HARDLY SPEAK!"

♫ But I'll never find the happiness I SEEK... ♫

...till I'm REUNITED WITH MY little CHEEKS!

RED EYE EXPRESS TO MINNEAPOLIS... NOW BOARDING AT GATE 12!

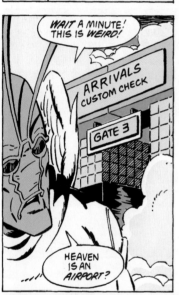

WAIT A MINUTE! THIS IS WEIRD!

ARRIVALS CUSTOM CHECK

GATE 3

HEAVEN IS AN AIRPORT?

DEPARTURES

I ALWAYS THOUGHT OF AIRPORTS AS PURGATORY! ALL THAT WAITING TO GET SOMEWHERE BETTER...

DO YOU HAVE ANY DISTINGUISHING SCARS OR MOLES?

BEG YOUR PARDON?

SCARS? MOLES? DISEASES? NEXT OF KIN?

WAIT BEHIND RED LINE UNTIL NEXT REPRESENTATIVE IS AVAILABLE

WELL...NO.

GOOD!

SCARS MOLES DIS

DUTY FREE SHOP

YOUR FLIGHT LEAVES FROM GATE 7!

YOU HAVE PLENTY OF TIME TO MAKE PURCHASES FROM OUR DUTY FREE SHOP!

HAVE A PLEASANT NEW LIFE, SIR!

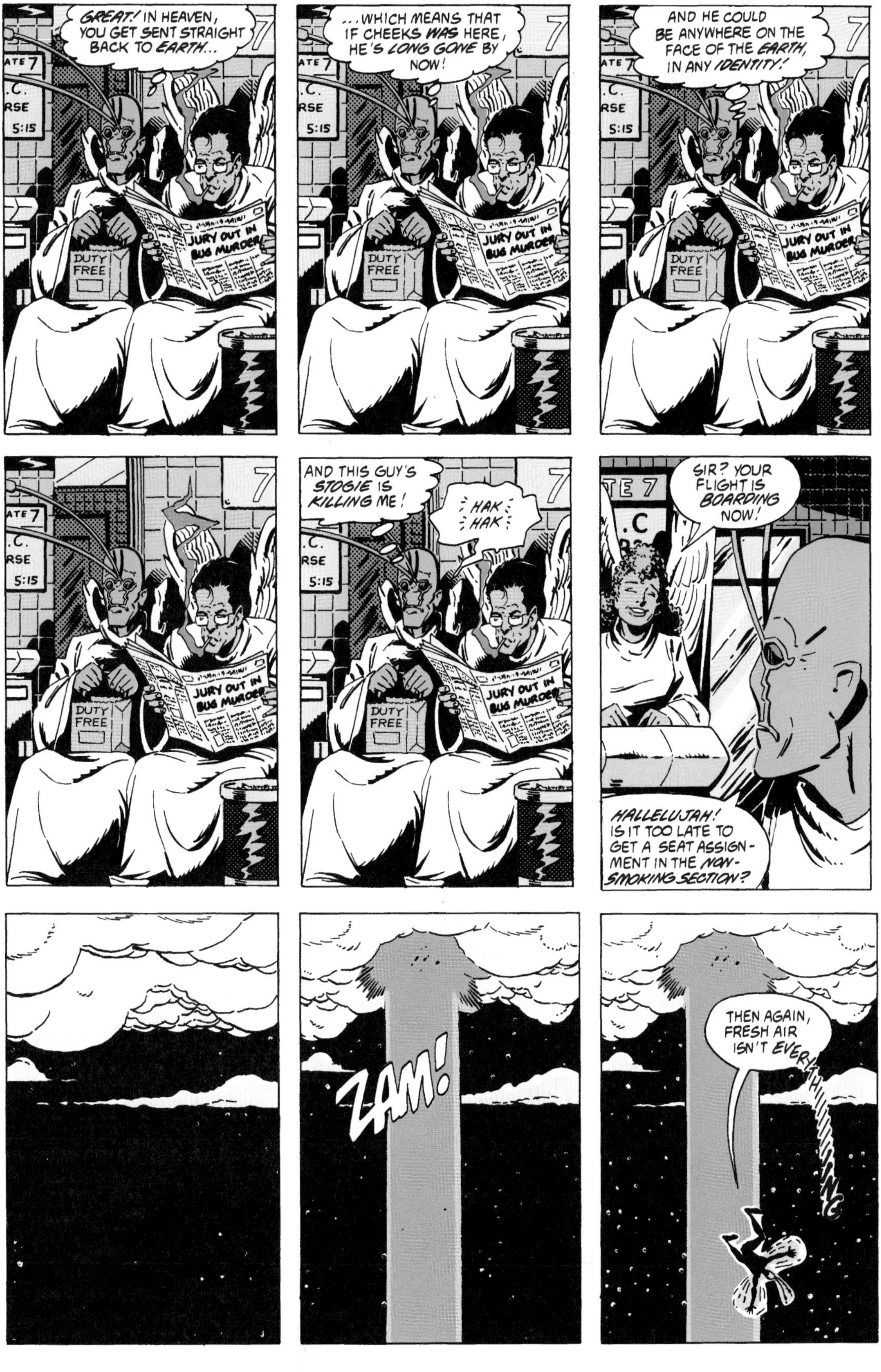
GREAT! IN HEAVEN, YOU GET SENT STRAIGHT BACK TO EARTH...
ATE 7
.C.
RSE
5:15
JURY OUT IN BUG MURDER
DUTY FREE
...WHICH MEANS THAT IF CHEEKS WAS HERE, HE'S LONG GONE BY NOW!
AND HE COULD BE ANYWHERE ON THE FACE OF THE EARTH, IN ANY IDENTITY!
AND THIS GUY'S STOGIE IS KILLING ME!
HAK HAK
SIR? YOUR FLIGHT IS BOARDING NOW!
HALLELUJAH! IS IT TOO LATE TO GET A SEAT ASSIGNMENT IN THE NON-SMOKING SECTION?
ZAM!
THEN AGAIN, FRESH AIR ISN'T EVERYTHING

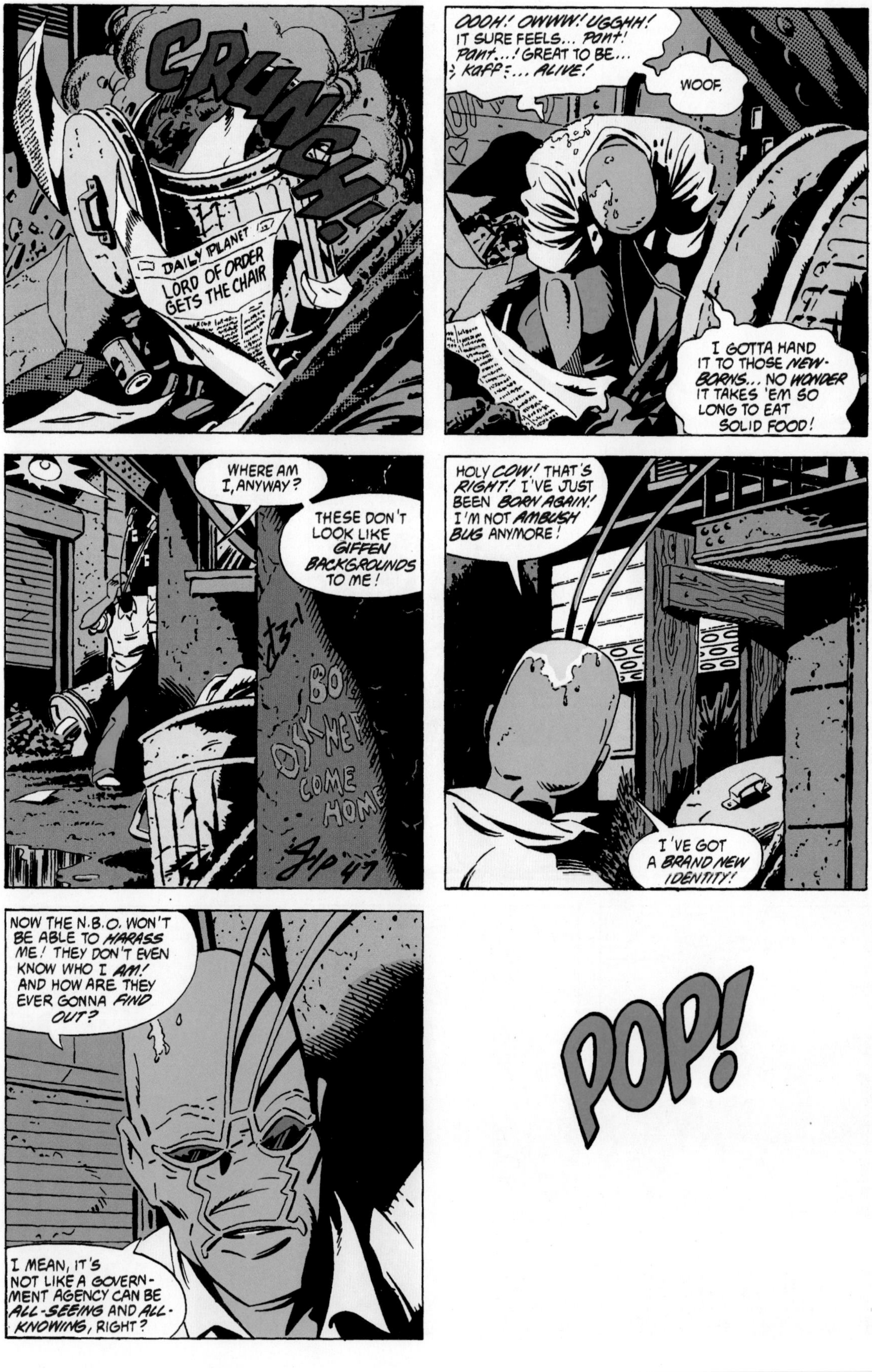
CRUNCH!
DAILY PLANET
LORD OF ORDER GETS THE CHAIR
OOOH! OWWW! UGGHH! IT SURE FEELS... Pant! Pant...! GREAT TO BE... kaff... ALIVE!
WOOF.
I GOTTA HAND IT TO THOSE NEW-BORNS... NO WONDER IT TAKES 'EM SO LONG TO EAT SOLID FOOD!
WHERE AM I, ANYWAY?
THESE DON'T LOOK LIKE GIFFEN BACKGROUNDS TO ME!
COME HOME
HOLY COW! THAT'S RIGHT! I'VE JUST BEEN BORN AGAIN! I'M NOT AMBUSH BUG ANYMORE!
I'VE GOT A BRAND NEW IDENTITY!
NOW THE N.B.O. WON'T BE ABLE TO HARASS ME! THEY DON'T EVEN KNOW WHO I AM! AND HOW ARE THEY EVER GONNA FIND OUT?
I MEAN, IT'S NOT LIKE A GOVERNMENT AGENCY CAN BE ALL-SEEING AND ALL-KNOWING, RIGHT?
POP!

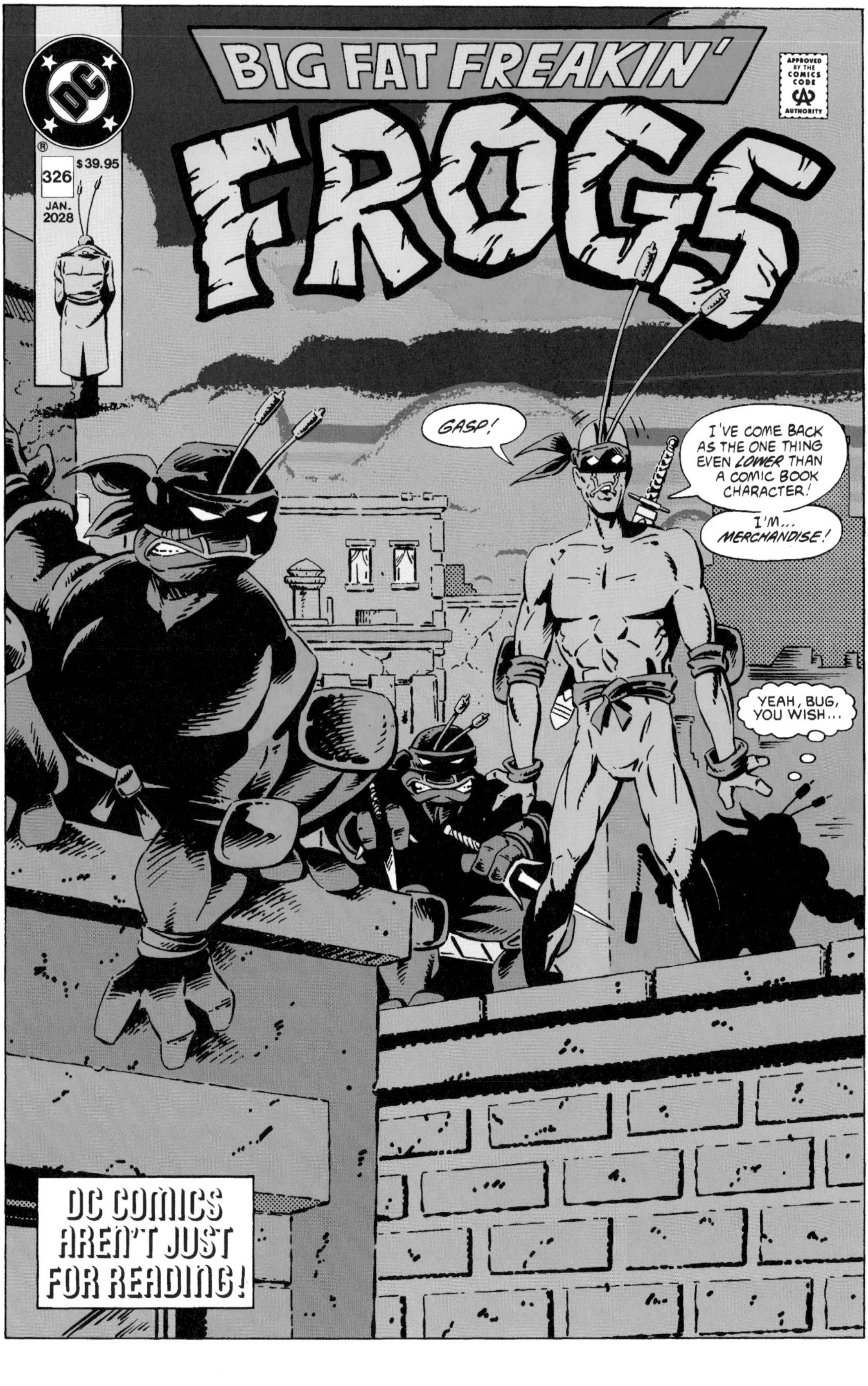

326
$39.95
JAN. 2028
APPROVED BY THE COMICS CODE AUTHORITY
BIG FAT FREAKIN'
FROGS
GASP!
I'VE COME BACK AS THE ONE THING EVEN LOWER THAN A COMIC BOOK CHARACTER!
I'M... MERCHANDISE!
YEAH, BUG, YOU WISH...
DC COMICS AREN'T JUST FOR READING!

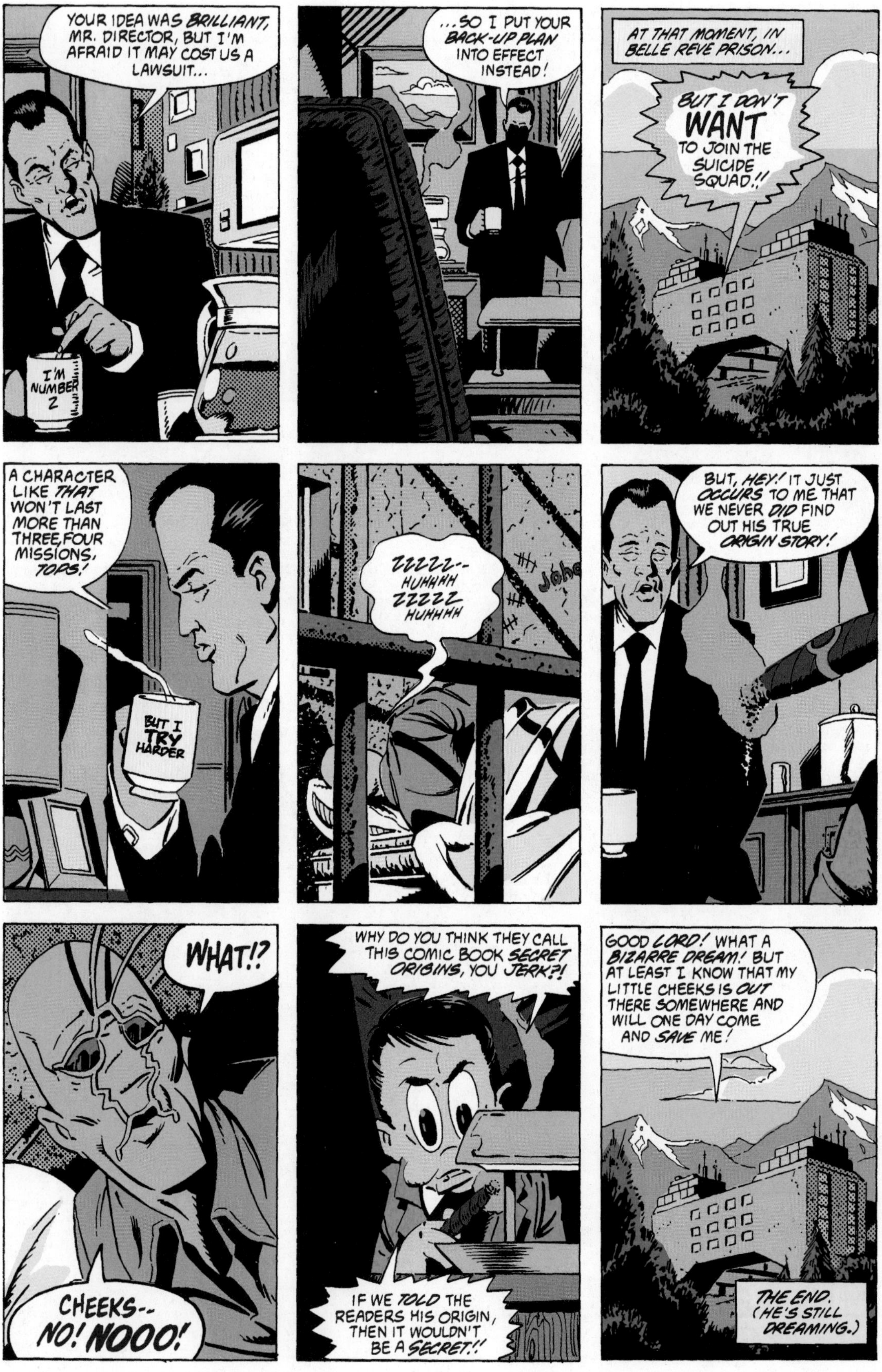
YOUR IDEA WAS BRILLIANT, MR. DIRECTOR, BUT I'M AFRAID IT MAY COST US A LAWSUIT...
I'M NUMBER 2
...SO I PUT YOUR BACK-UP PLAN INTO EFFECT INSTEAD!
AT THAT MOMENT, IN BELLE REVE PRISON...
BUT I DON'T WANT TO JOIN THE SUICIDE SQUAD!!
A CHARACTER LIKE THAT WON'T LAST MORE THAN THREE, FOUR MISSIONS, TOPS!
BUT I TRY HARDER
ZZZZZ-- HUHHHH ZZZZZ HUHHHH
BUT, HEY! IT JUST OCCURS TO ME THAT WE NEVER DID FIND OUT HIS TRUE ORIGIN STORY!
WHAT!?
CHEEKS-- NO! NOOO!
WHY DO YOU THINK THEY CALL THIS COMIC BOOK SECRET ORIGINS, YOU JERK?!
IF WE TOLD THE READERS HIS ORIGIN, THEN IT WOULDN'T BE A SECRET!!
GOOD LORD! WHAT A BIZARRE DREAM! BUT AT LEAST I KNOW THAT MY LITTLE CHEEKS IS OUT THERE SOMEWHERE AND WILL ONE DAY COME AND SAVE ME!
THE END. (HE'S STILL DREAMING.)

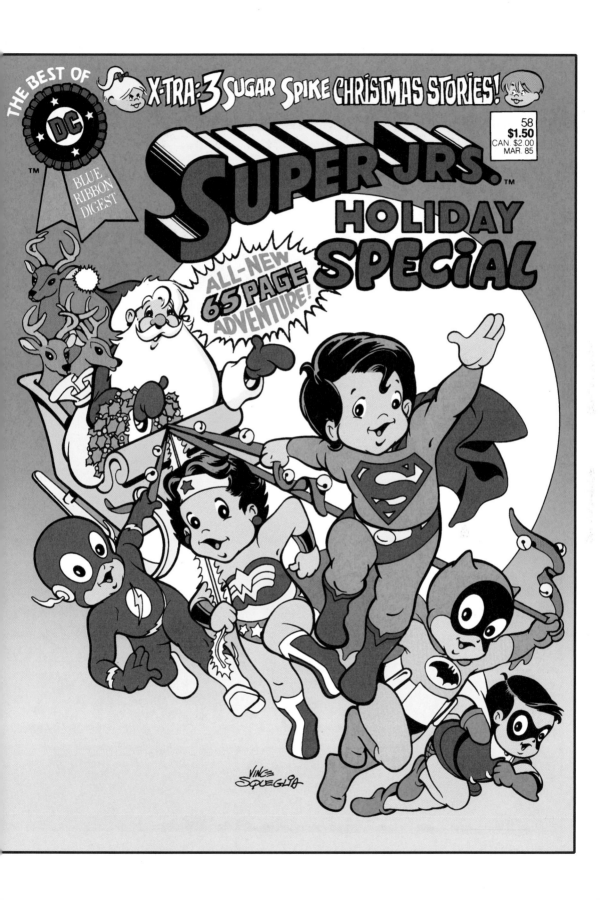

THE BEST OF DC
TM
BLUE RIBBON DIGEST

X-TRA: 3 SUGAR SPIKE CHRISTMAS STORIES!

58
$1.50
CAN. $2.00
MAR. 85

SUPER JRS. TM
HOLIDAY SPECIAL

ALL-NEW 65 PAGE ADVENTURE!

VINCE SQUEGLIA

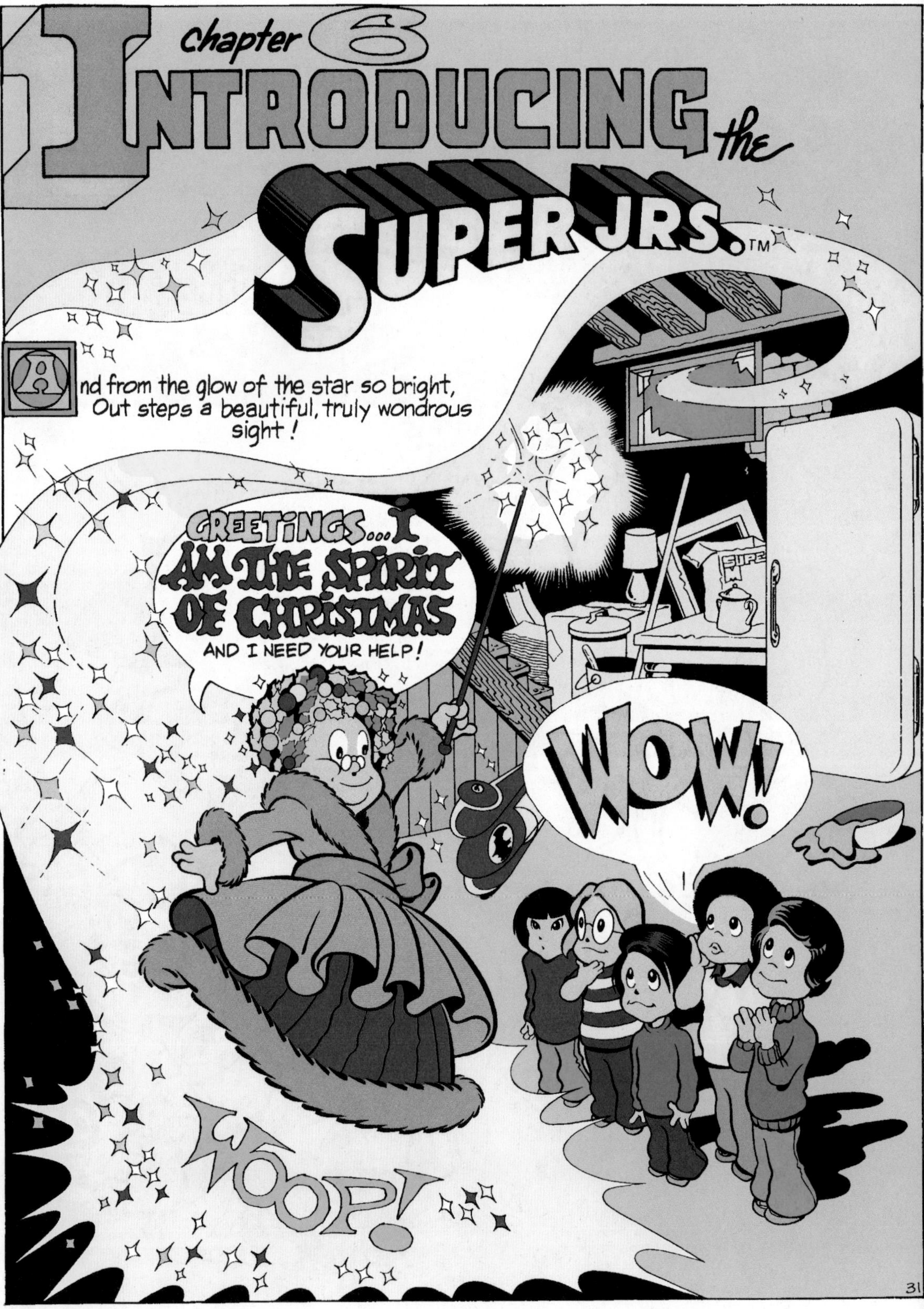

Chapter 6
INTRODUCING the
SUPER JRS.™
And from the glow of the star so bright, Out steps a beautiful, truly wondrous sight!
GREETINGS... I AM THE SPIRIT OF CHRISTMAS AND I NEED YOUR HELP!
WOW!
WOOP!
31

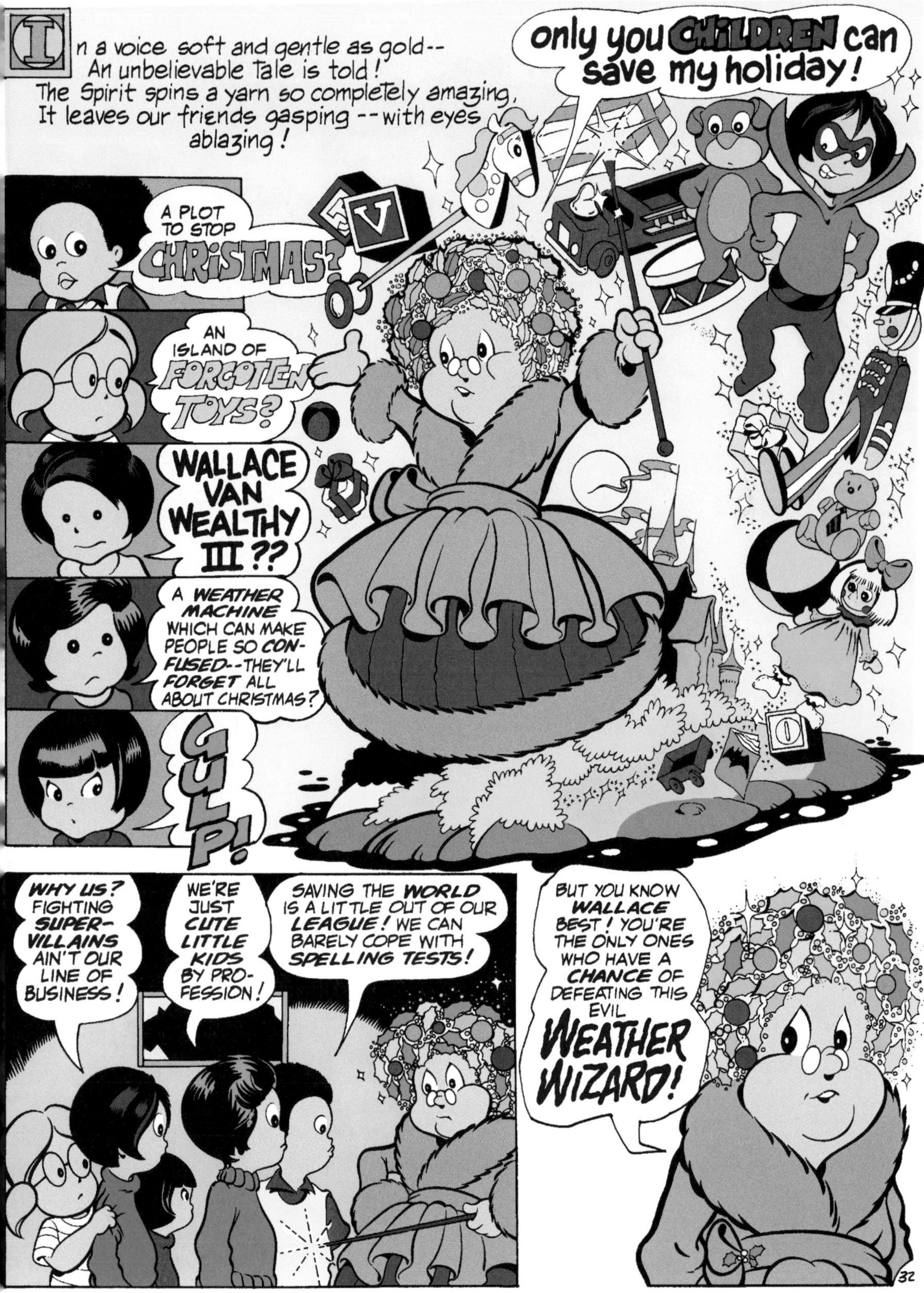
In a voice soft and gentle as gold--
An unbelievable Tale is told!
The Spirit spins a yarn so completely amazing,
It leaves our friends gasping --with eyes ablazing!
only you CHILDREN can save my holiday!
A PLOT TO STOP CHRISTMAS?
AN ISLAND OF FORGOTTEN TOYS?
WALLACE VAN WEALTHY III ??
A WEATHER MACHINE WHICH CAN MAKE PEOPLE SO CON-FUSED--THEY'LL FORGET ALL ABOUT CHRISTMAS?
GULP!
WHY US? FIGHTING SUPER-VILLAINS AIN'T OUR LINE OF BUSINESS!
WE'RE JUST CUTE LITTLE KIDS BY PRO-FESSION!
SAVING THE WORLD IS A LITTLE OUT OF OUR LEAGUE! WE CAN BARELY COPE WITH SPELLING TESTS!
BUT YOU KNOW WALLACE BEST! YOU'RE THE ONLY ONES WHO HAVE A CHANCE OF DEFEATING THIS EVIL WEATHER WIZARD!
32

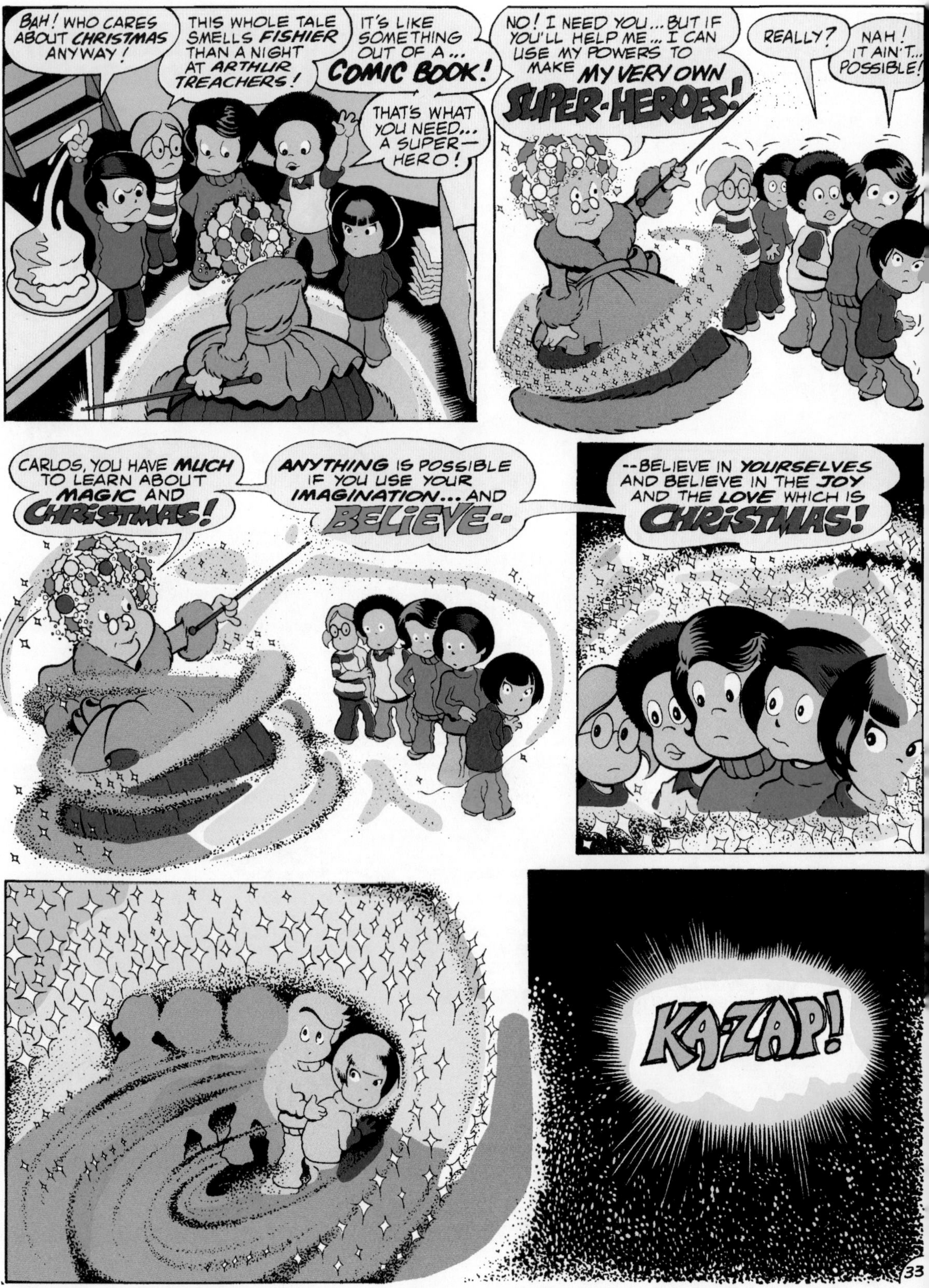
BAH! WHO CARES ABOUT CHRISTMAS ANYWAY!
THIS WHOLE TALE SMELLS FISHIER THAN A NIGHT AT ARTHUR TREACHERS!
IT'S LIKE SOMETHING OUT OF A... COMIC BOOK!
THAT'S WHAT YOU NEED... A SUPER-HERO!
NO! I NEED YOU... BUT IF YOU'LL HELP ME... I CAN USE MY POWERS TO MAKE MY VERY OWN SUPER-HEROES!
REALLY?
NAH! IT AIN'T... POSSIBLE!
CARLOS, YOU HAVE MUCH TO LEARN ABOUT MAGIC AND CHRISTMAS!
ANYTHING IS POSSIBLE IF YOU USE YOUR IMAGINATION... AND BELIEVE--
--BELIEVE IN YOURSELVES AND BELIEVE IN THE JOY AND THE LOVE WHICH IS CHRISTMAS!
KA-ZAP!
33

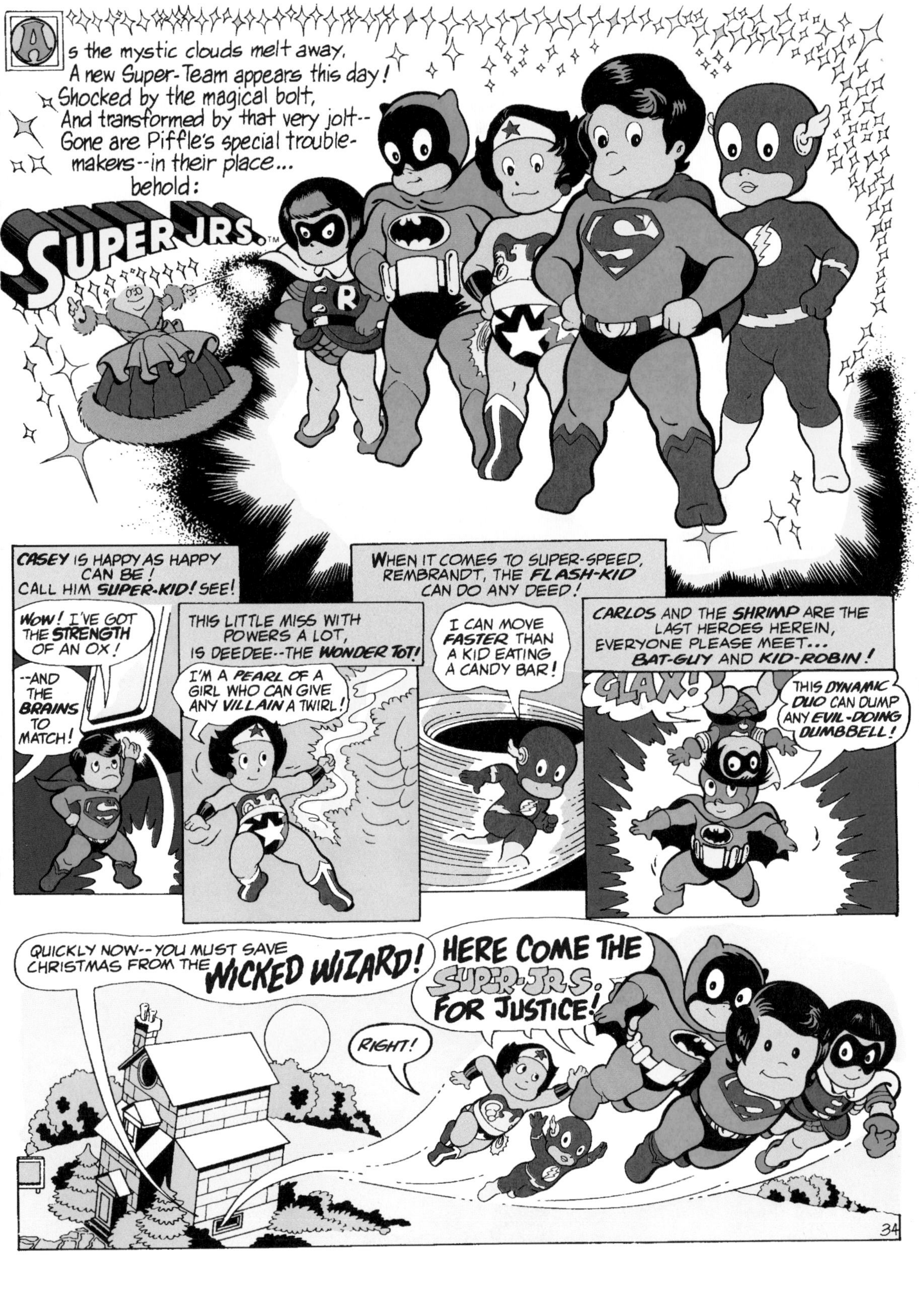
As the mystic clouds melt away,
A new Super-Team appears this day!
Shocked by the magical bolt,
And transformed by that very jolt--
Gone are Piffle's special trouble-makers--in their place...
behold:
SUPER JRS.™
CASEY IS HAPPY AS HAPPY CAN BE! CALL HIM SUPER-KID! SEE!
WOW! I'VE GOT THE STRENGTH OF AN OX!
--AND THE BRAINS TO MATCH!
THIS LITTLE MISS WITH POWERS A LOT, IS DEEDEE--THE WONDER TOT!
I'M A PEARL OF A GIRL WHO CAN GIVE ANY VILLAIN A TWIRL!
WHEN IT COMES TO SUPER-SPEED, REMBRANDT, THE FLASH-KID CAN DO ANY DEED!
I CAN MOVE FASTER THAN A KID EATING A CANDY BAR!
CARLOS AND THE SHRIMP ARE THE LAST HEROES HEREIN, EVERYONE PLEASE MEET... BAT-GUY AND KID-ROBIN!
GLAX!
THIS DYNAMIC DUO CAN DUMP ANY EVIL-DOING DUMBBELL!
QUICKLY NOW--YOU MUST SAVE CHRISTMAS FROM THE WICKED WIZARD!
HERE COME THE SUPER-JRS. FOR JUSTICE!
RIGHT!
34

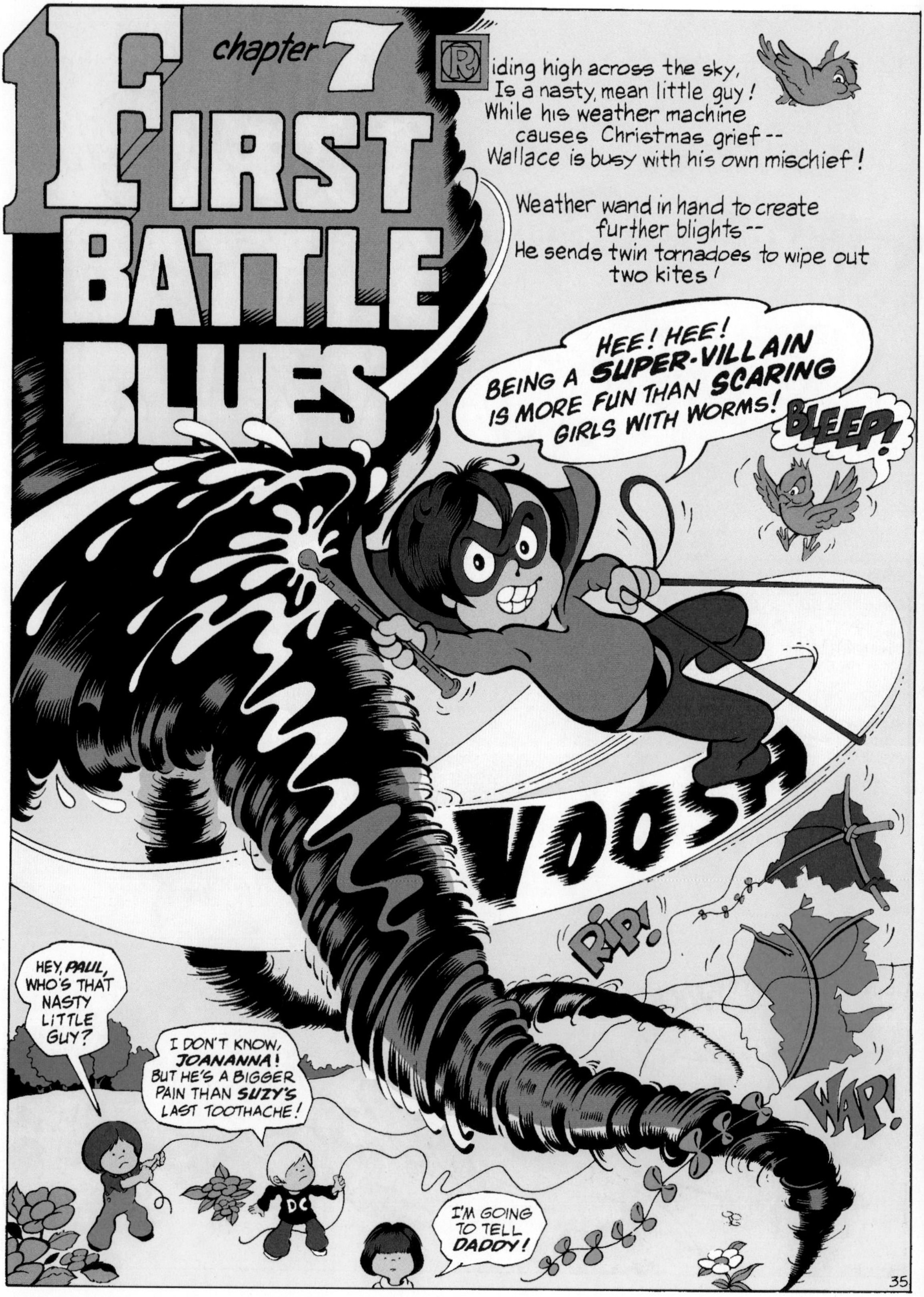

chapter 7
FIRST BATTLE BLUES
Riding high across the sky, Is a nasty, mean little guy! While his weather machine causes Christmas grief -- Wallace is busy with his own mischief!
Weather wand in hand to create further blights -- He sends twin tornadoes to wipe out two kites!
HEE! HEE! BEING A SUPER-VILLAIN IS MORE FUN THAN SCARING GIRLS WITH WORMS!
BLEEP!
VOOSH
RIP!
WAP!
HEY, PAUL, WHO'S THAT NASTY LITTLE GUY?
I DON'T KNOW, JOANANNA! BUT HE'S A BIGGER PAIN THAN SUZY'S LAST TOOTHACHE!
I'M GOING TO TELL DADDY!
35

Strange sounds creep up to the Wizard's ear! Strange sounds which fill him up with fear! Slowly, he twists his neck and turns his head, And his body is suddenly struck with dread!

GASP!

VOOSH!

For streaking toward him with proud glory, Are the **SUPER-HEROES** of this story!

SURRENDER, WALLACE! WE STAND FOR TRUTH, JUSTICE AND THE CHRISTMAS WAY!

☆GROAN☆

I KNEW CASEY WAS GONNA GET CORNY! I JUST KNEW IT!

VOOOSH!

BAH! YOU DINGBATS COULDN'T PLAY SUPER-HEROES ON THE **GONG SHOW!**

WATCH THE WAND, WEIRDOS!

GLUB!

VOOSH!

And so a raging thundercloud makes the scene, An event the Weather Wizard considers routine!

THAT'S A LOUD CLOUD!

IT'S MAKING ME SOGGY AND GROGGY!

GLUP!

BA-BOOM!

36

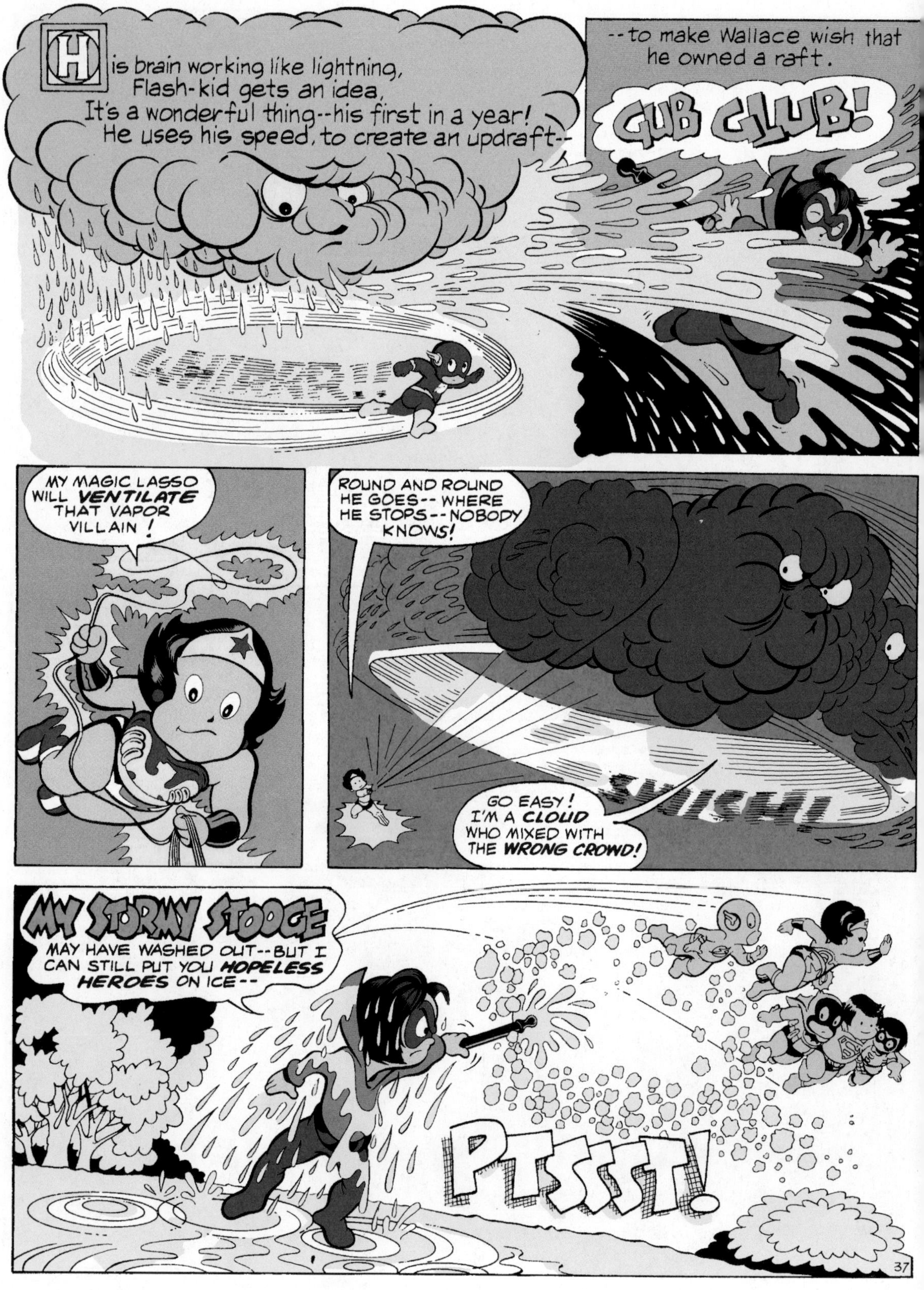
His brain working like lightning,
Flash-kid gets an idea,
It's a wonderful thing--his first in a year!
He uses his speed, to create an updraft--
--to make Wallace wish that he owned a raft.
GUB GLUB!
MY MAGIC LASSO WILL VENTILATE THAT VAPOR VILLAIN!
ROUND AND ROUND HE GOES-- WHERE HE STOPS--NOBODY KNOWS!
SWISH!
GO EASY! I'M A CLOUD WHO MIXED WITH THE WRONG CROWD!
MY STORMY STOOGE MAY HAVE WASHED OUT--BUT I CAN STILL PUT YOU HOPELESS HEROES ON ICE--
PTSSST!
37

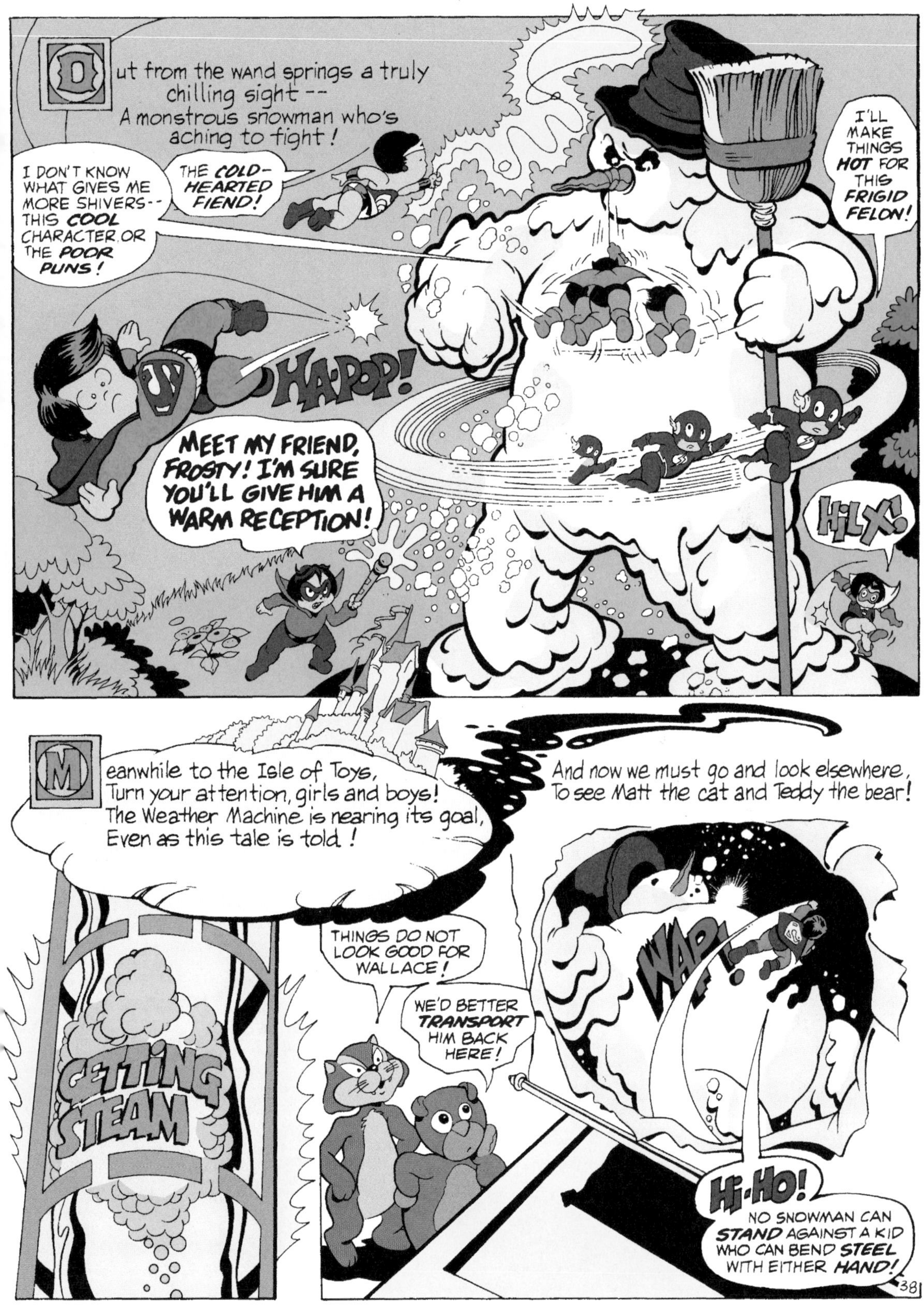
Out from the wand springs a truly chilling sight -- A monstrous snowman who's aching to fight!
I DON'T KNOW WHAT GIVES ME MORE SHIVERS-- THIS COOL CHARACTER OR THE POOR PUNS!
THE COLD-HEARTED FIEND!
I'LL MAKE THINGS HOT FOR THIS FRIGID FELON!
HA-POP!
MEET MY FRIEND, FROSTY! I'M SURE YOU'LL GIVE HIM A WARM RECEPTION!
HiLX!
Meanwhile to the Isle of Toys, Turn your attention, girls and boys! The Weather Machine is nearing its goal, Even as this tale is told!
And now we must go and look elsewhere, To see Matt the cat and Teddy the bear!
GETTING STEAM
THINGS DO NOT LOOK GOOD FOR WALLACE!
WE'D BETTER TRANSPORT HIM BACK HERE!
HI-HO! NO SNOWMAN CAN STAND AGAINST A KID WHO CAN BEND STEEL WITH EITHER HAND!
38

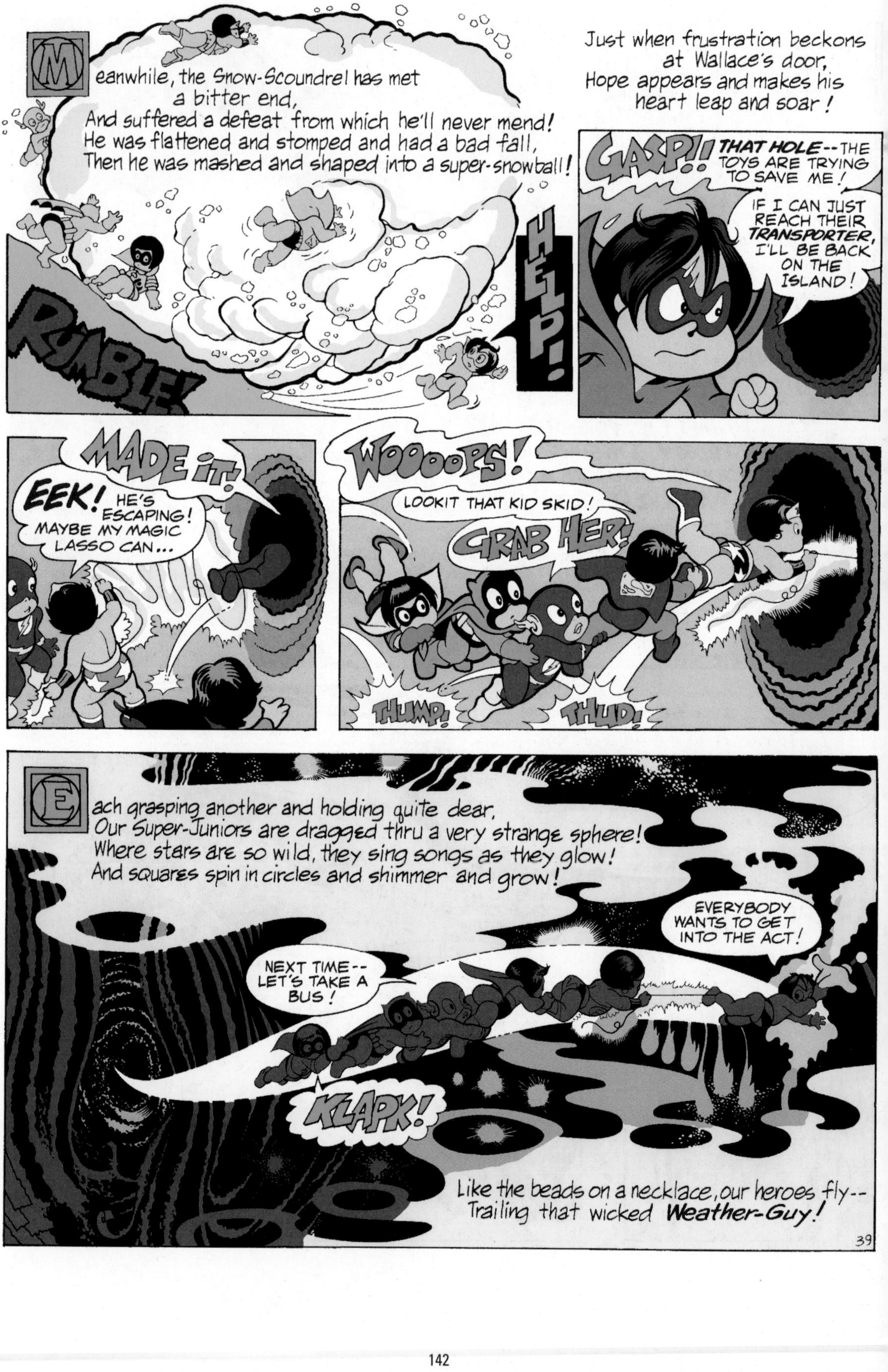
Meanwhile, the Snow-Scoundrel has met a bitter end,
And suffered a defeat from which he'll never mend!
He was flattened and stomped and had a bad fall,
Then he was mashed and shaped into a super-snowball!
RUMBLE!
HELP!
Just when frustration beckons at Wallace's door,
Hope appears and makes his heart leap and soar!
GASP!!
THAT HOLE -- THE TOYS ARE TRYING TO SAVE ME!
IF I CAN JUST REACH THEIR TRANSPORTER, I'LL BE BACK ON THE ISLAND!
MADE IT!
EEK! HE'S ESCAPING! MAYBE MY MAGIC LASSO CAN...
WOOOOOPS!
LOOKIT THAT KID SKID!
GRAB HER!
THUMP!
THUD!
Each grasping another and holding quite dear,
Our Super-Juniors are dragged thru a very strange sphere!
Where stars are so wild, they sing songs as they glow!
And squares spin in circles and shimmer and grow!
EVERYBODY WANTS TO GET INTO THE ACT!
NEXT TIME -- LET'S TAKE A BUS!
KLAPK!
Like the beads on a necklace, our heroes fly --
Trailing that wicked Weather-Guy!
39

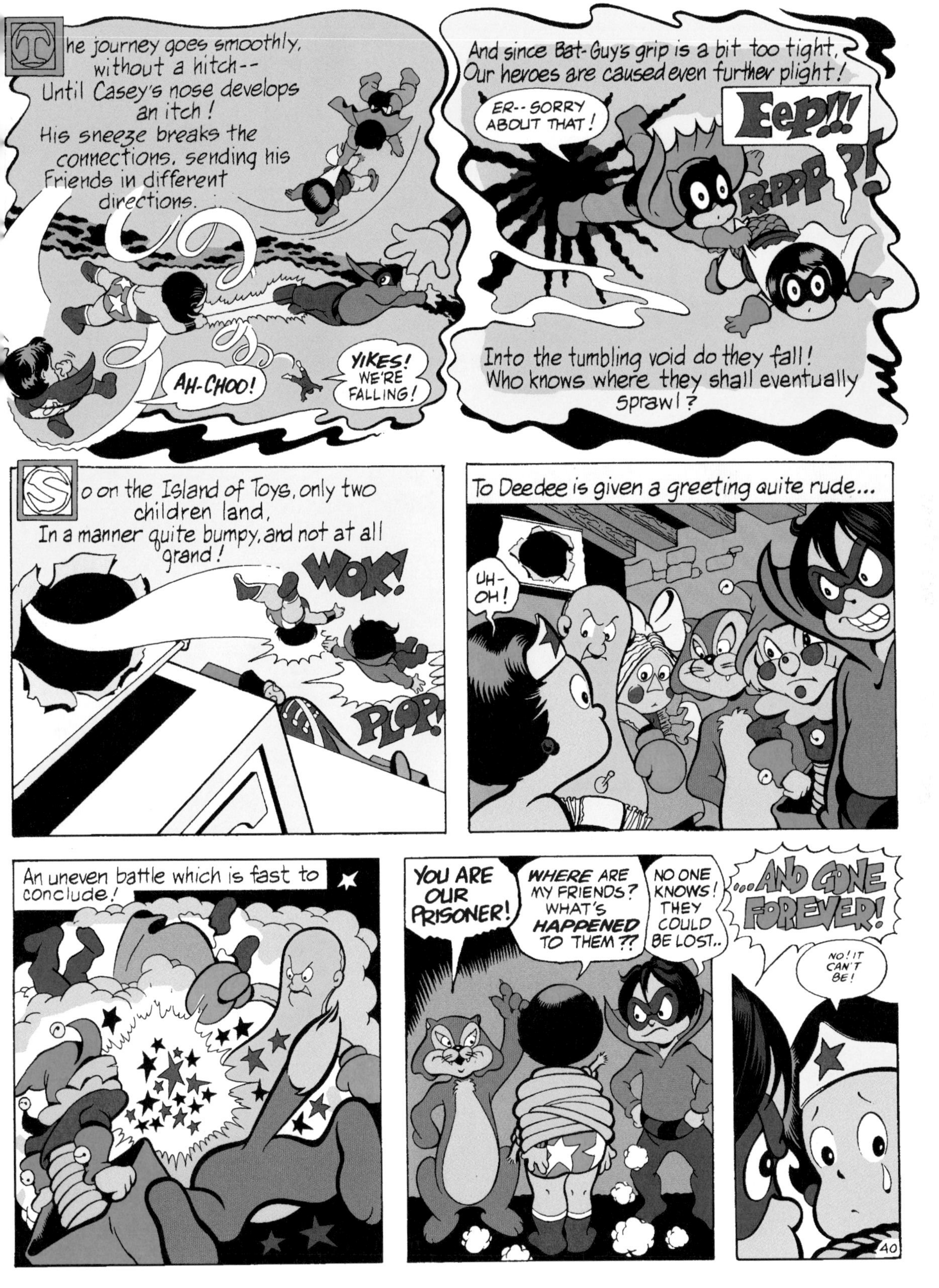
The journey goes smoothly, without a hitch--
Until Casey's nose develops an itch!
His sneeze breaks the connections, sending his Friends in different directions.
AH-CHOO!
YIKES! WE'RE FALLING!
And since Bat-Guy's grip is a bit too tight,
Our heroes are caused even further plight!
ER-- SORRY ABOUT THAT!
EEP!!!
RIPPP ?!
Into the tumbling void do they fall!
Who knows where they shall eventually sprawl?
So on the Island of Toys, only two children land,
In a manner quite bumpy, and not at all grand!
WOK!
PLOP!
To Deedee is given a greeting quite rude...
UH-OH!
An uneven battle which is fast to conclude!
YOU ARE OUR PRISONER!
WHERE ARE MY FRIENDS? WHAT'S HAPPENED TO THEM??
NO ONE KNOWS! THEY COULD BE LOST..
...AND GONE FOREVER!
NO! IT CAN'T BE!
40

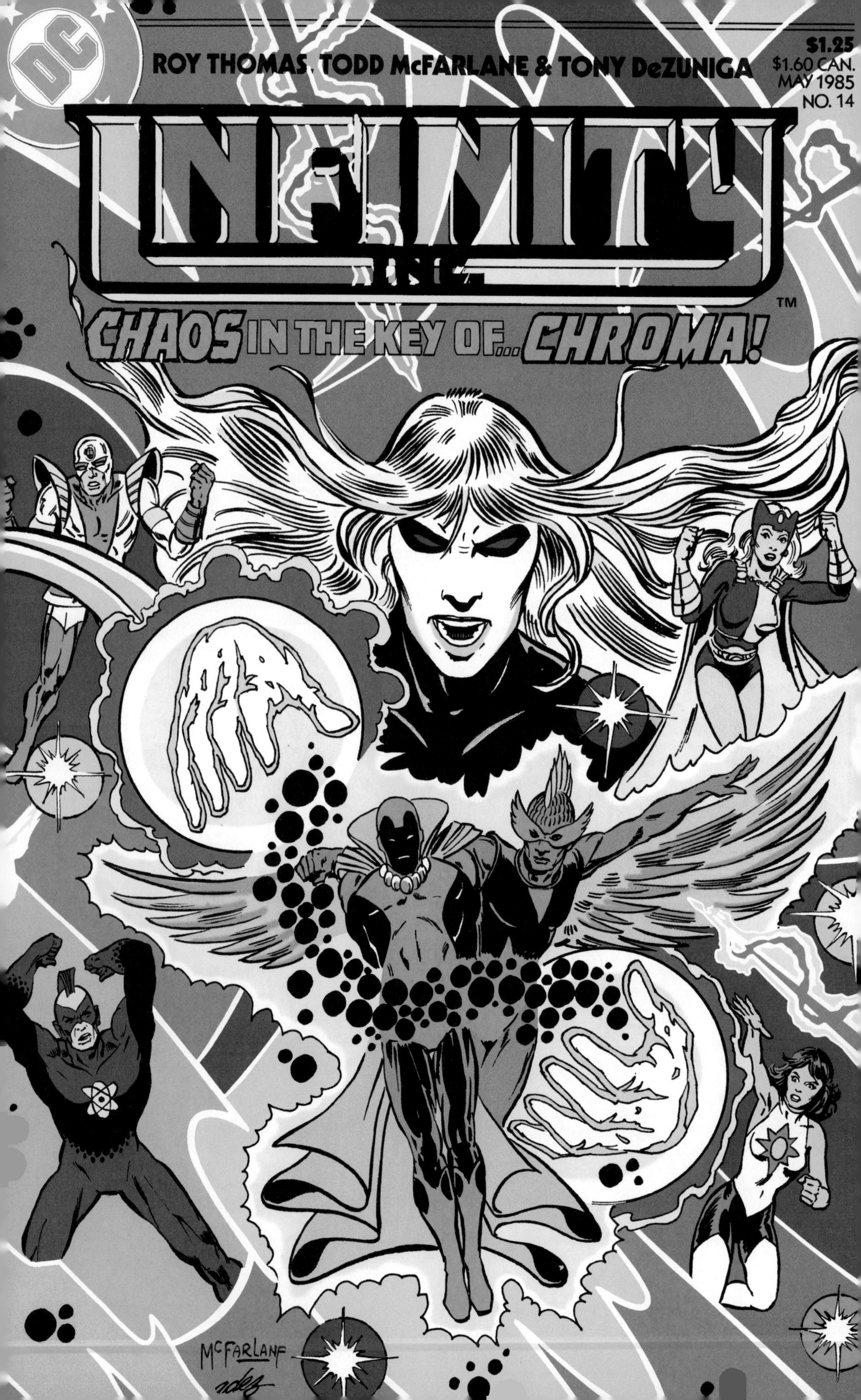
DC
ROY THOMAS, TODD McFARLANE & TONY DeZUNIGA
$1.25
$1.60 CAN.
MAY 1985
NO. 14
INFINITY INC.
TM
CHAOS IN THE KEY OF... CHROMA!
McFARLANE

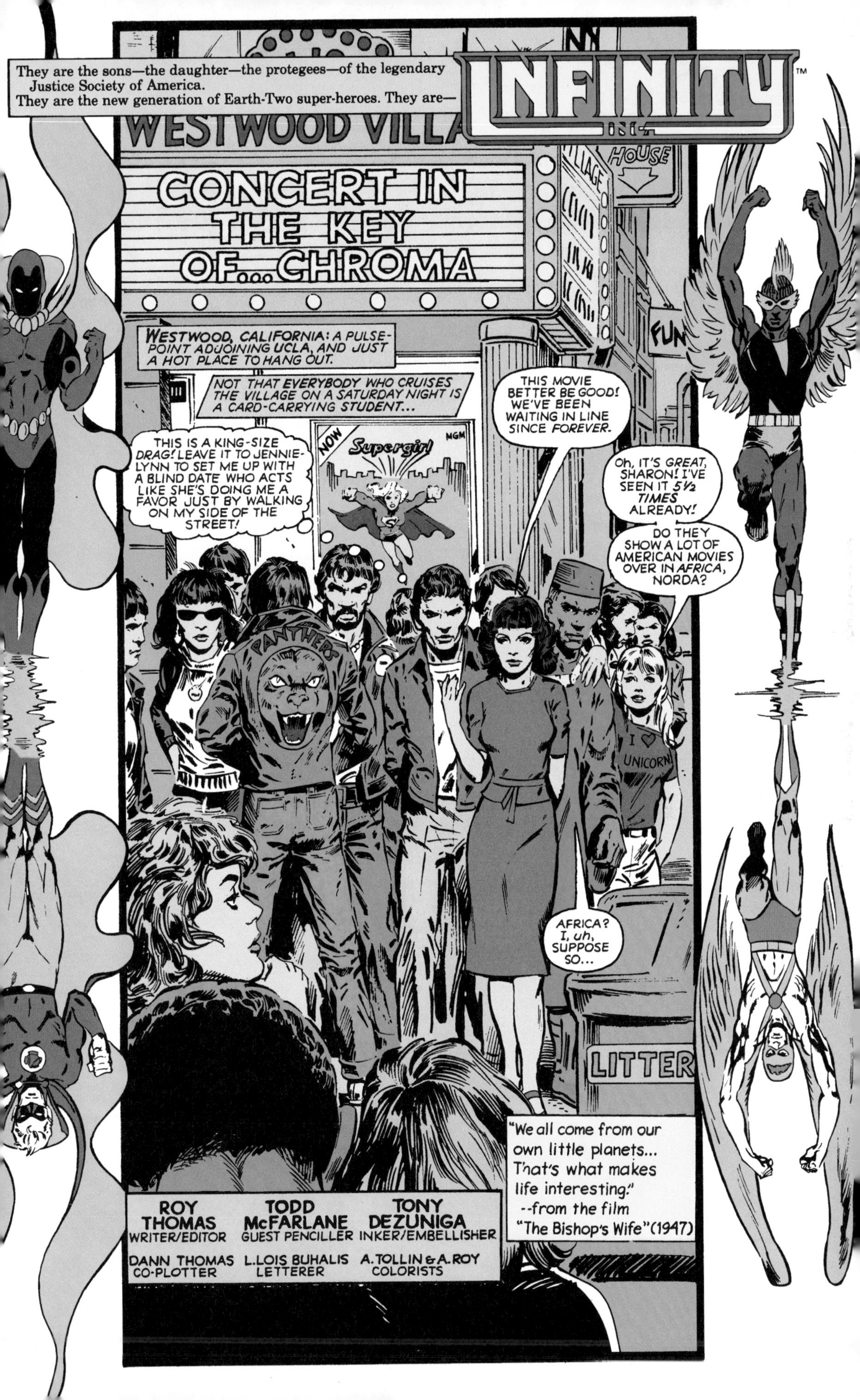

They are the sons—the daughter—the protegees—of the legendary Justice Society of America.
They are the new generation of Earth-Two super-heroes. They are—
INFINITY INC.
WESTWOOD VILLA
CONCERT IN THE KEY OF...CHROMA
HOUSE
FUN
WESTWOOD, CALIFORNIA: A PULSE-POINT ADJOINING UCLA, AND JUST A HOT PLACE TO HANG OUT.
NOT THAT EVERYBODY WHO CRUISES THE VILLAGE ON A SATURDAY NIGHT IS A CARD-CARRYING STUDENT...
NOW Supergirl MGM
THIS IS A KING-SIZE DRAG! LEAVE IT TO JENNIE-LYNN TO SET ME UP WITH A BLIND DATE WHO ACTS LIKE SHE'S DOING ME A FAVOR JUST BY WALKING ON MY SIDE OF THE STREET!
THIS MOVIE BETTER BE GOOD! WE'VE BEEN WAITING IN LINE SINCE FOREVER.
Oh, IT'S GREAT, SHARON! I'VE SEEN IT 5½ TIMES ALREADY!
DO THEY SHOW A LOT OF AMERICAN MOVIES OVER IN AFRICA, NORDA?
PANTHERS
I ♥ UNICORN
AFRICA? I, uh, SUPPOSE SO...
LITTER
"We all come from our own little planets... That's what makes life interesting." --from the film "The Bishop's Wife" (1947)
ROY THOMAS WRITER/EDITOR
TODD McFARLANE GUEST PENCILLER
TONY DEZUNIGA INKER/EMBELLISHER
DANN THOMAS CO-PLOTTER
L.LOIS BUHALIS LETTERER
A.TOLLIN & A.ROY COLORISTS

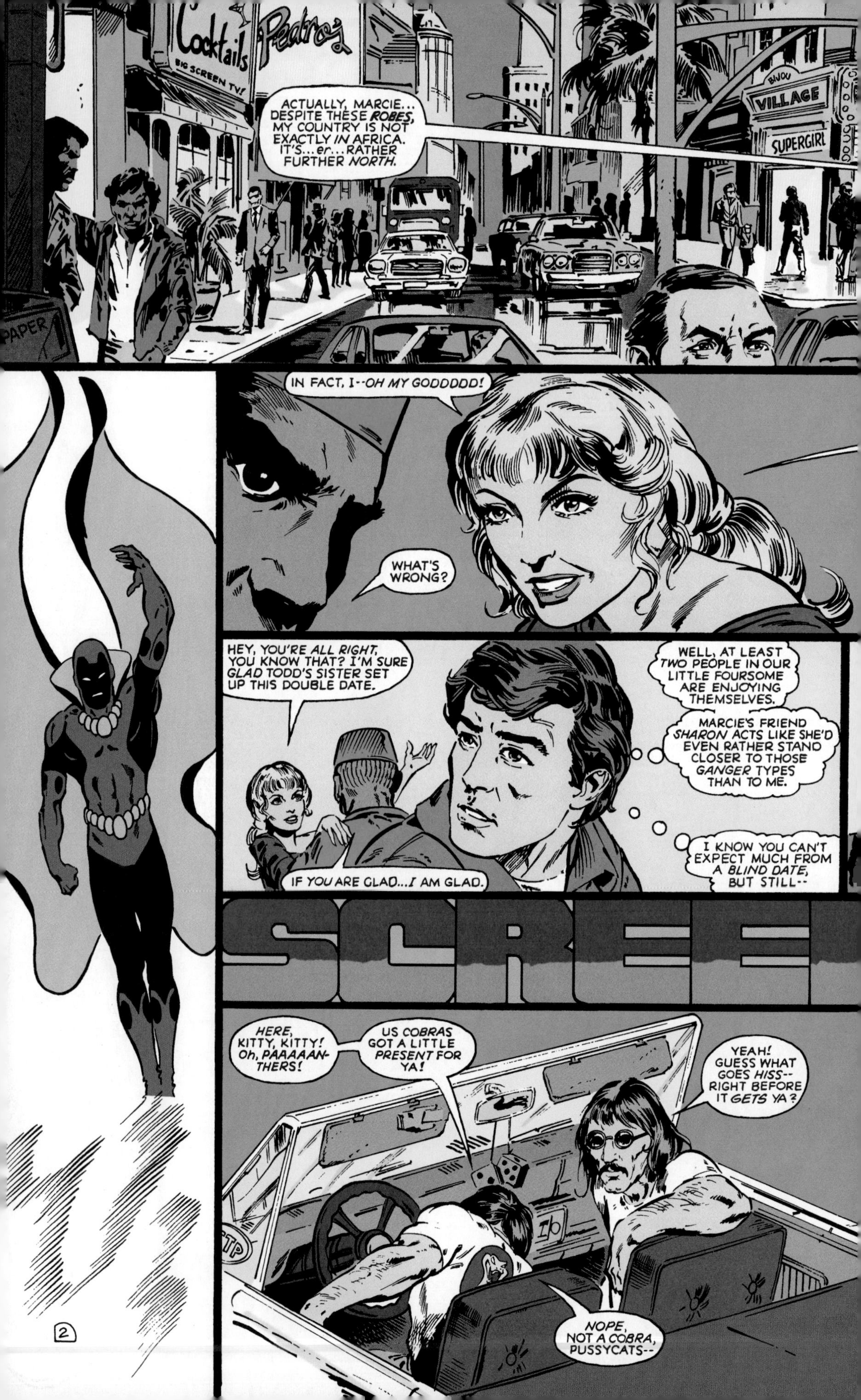
Cocktails
BIG SCREEN TV!
Pedro's
BIJOU
VILLAGE
SUPERGIRL
PAPER
ACTUALLY, MARCIE... DESPITE THESE ROBES, MY COUNTRY IS NOT EXACTLY IN AFRICA. IT'S...er...RATHER FURTHER NORTH.
IN FACT, I--OH MY GODDDDD!
WHAT'S WRONG?
HEY, YOU'RE ALL RIGHT, YOU KNOW THAT? I'M SURE GLAD TODD'S SISTER SET UP THIS DOUBLE DATE.
IF YOU ARE GLAD...I AM GLAD.
WELL, AT LEAST TWO PEOPLE IN OUR LITTLE FOURSOME ARE ENJOYING THEMSELVES.
MARCIE'S FRIEND SHARON ACTS LIKE SHE'D EVEN RATHER STAND CLOSER TO THOSE GANGER TYPES THAN TO ME.
I KNOW YOU CAN'T EXPECT MUCH FROM A BLIND DATE, BUT STILL--
SCREE
HERE, KITTY, KITTY! Oh, PAAAAAN-THERS!
US COBRAS GOT A LITTLE PRESENT FOR YA!
YEAH! GUESS WHAT GOES HISS--RIGHT BEFORE IT GETS YA?
NOPE, NOT A COBRA, PUSSYCATS--

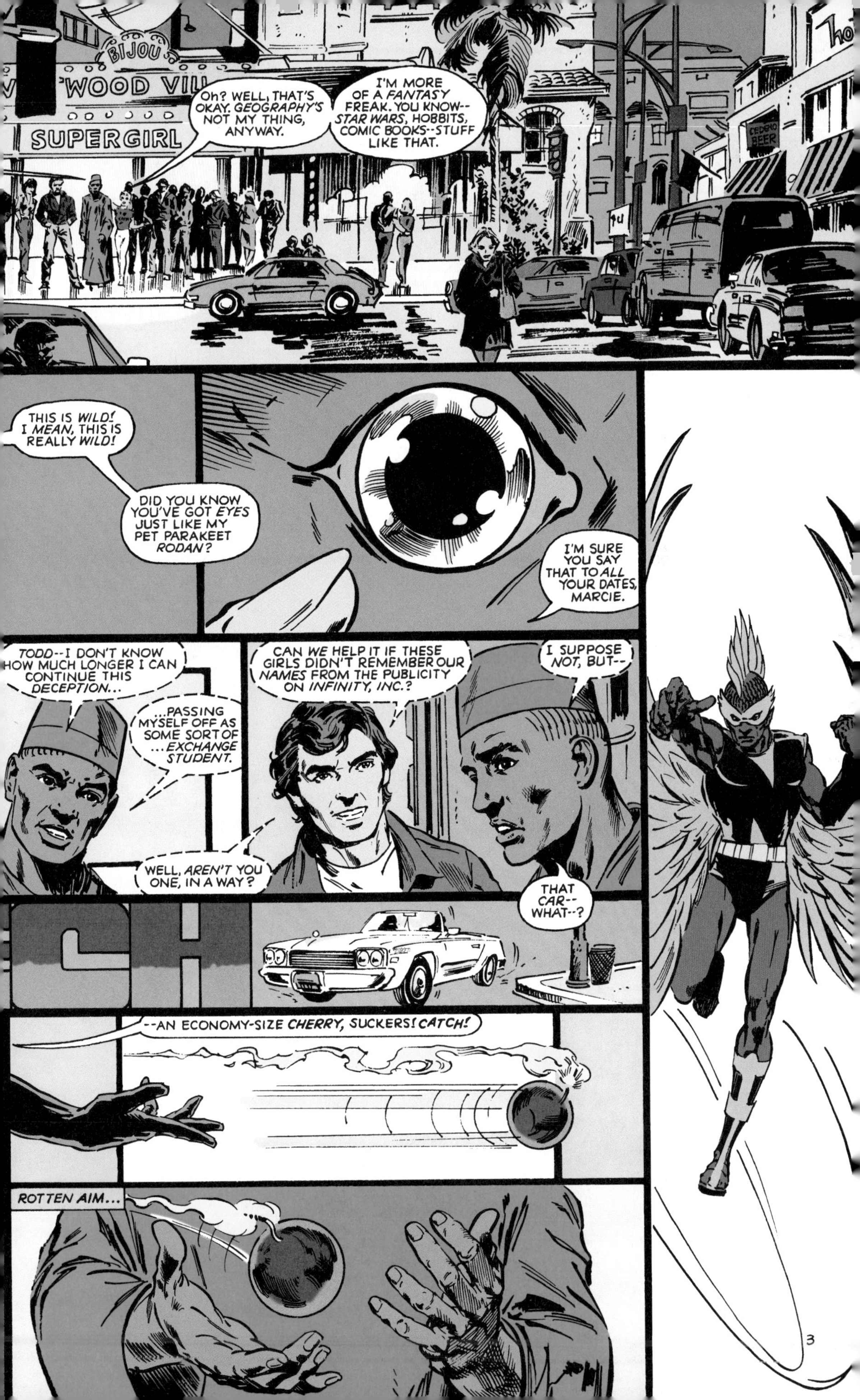
BIJOU
WOOD VIL
SUPERGIRL
Oh? WELL, THAT'S OKAY. GEOGRAPHY'S NOT MY THING, ANYWAY.
I'M MORE OF A FANTASY FREAK. YOU KNOW-- STAR WARS, HOBBITS, COMIC BOOKS--STUFF LIKE THAT.
THIS IS WILD! I MEAN, THIS IS REALLY WILD!
DID YOU KNOW YOU'VE GOT EYES JUST LIKE MY PET PARAKEET RODAN?
I'M SURE YOU SAY THAT TO ALL YOUR DATES, MARCIE.
TODD--I DON'T KNOW HOW MUCH LONGER I CAN CONTINUE THIS DECEPTION...
...PASSING MYSELF OFF AS SOME SORT OF ...EXCHANGE STUDENT.
WELL, AREN'T YOU ONE, IN A WAY?
CAN WE HELP IT IF THESE GIRLS DIDN'T REMEMBER OUR NAMES FROM THE PUBLICITY ON INFINITY, INC.?
I SUPPOSE NOT, BUT--
THAT CAR-- WHAT--?
--AN ECONOMY-SIZE CHERRY, SUCKERS! CATCH!
ROTTEN AIM...

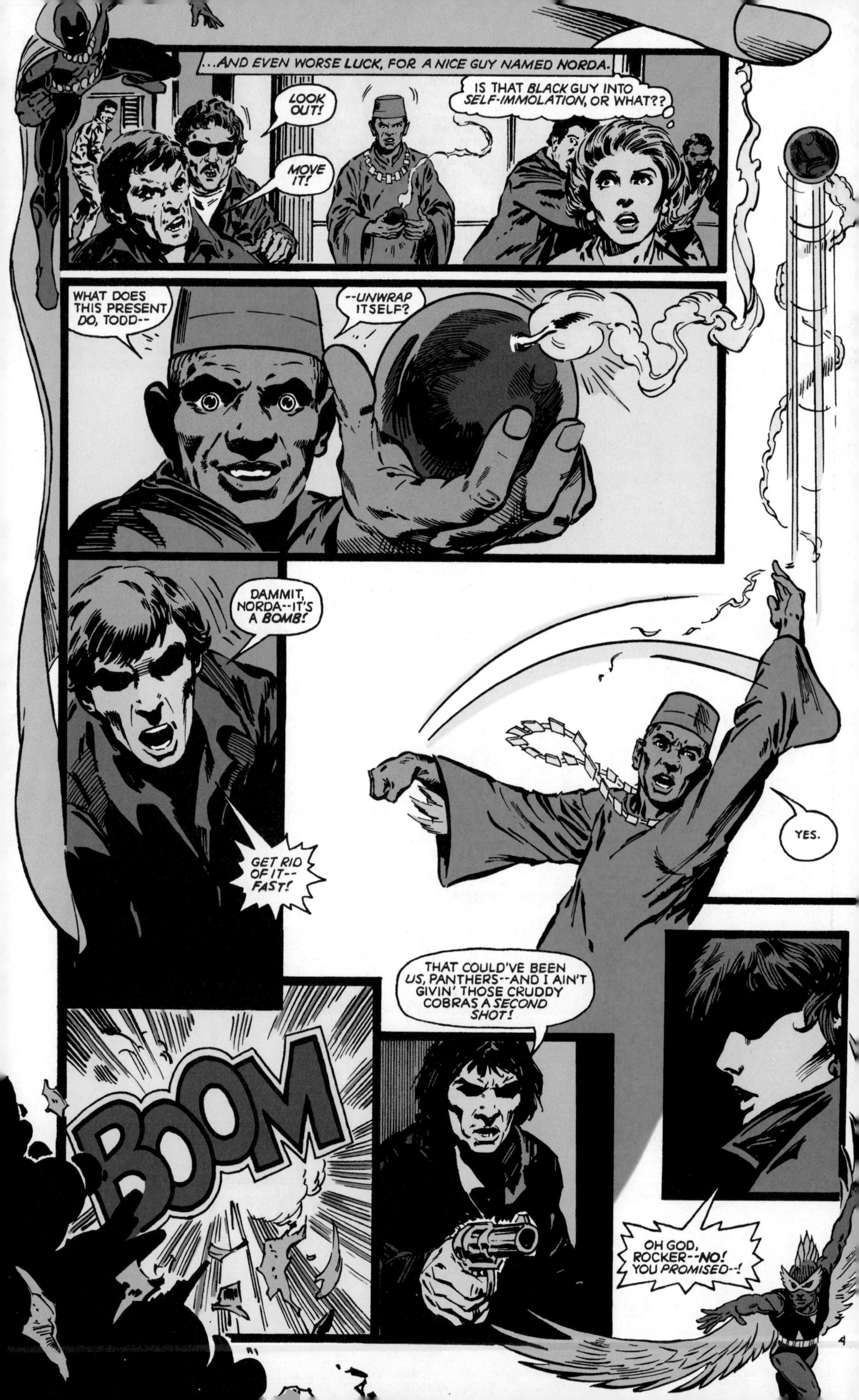
...AND EVEN WORSE LUCK, FOR A NICE GUY NAMED NORDA.
LOOK OUT!
MOVE IT!
IS THAT BLACK GUY INTO SELF-IMMOLATION, OR WHAT??
WHAT DOES THIS PRESENT DO, TODD--
--UNWRAP ITSELF?
DAMMIT, NORDA--IT'S A BOMB!
GET RID OF IT--FAST!
YES.
BOOM
THAT COULD'VE BEEN US, PANTHERS--AND I AIN'T GIVIN' THOSE CRUDDY COBRAS A SECOND SHOT!
OH GOD, ROCKER--NO! YOU PROMISED--!

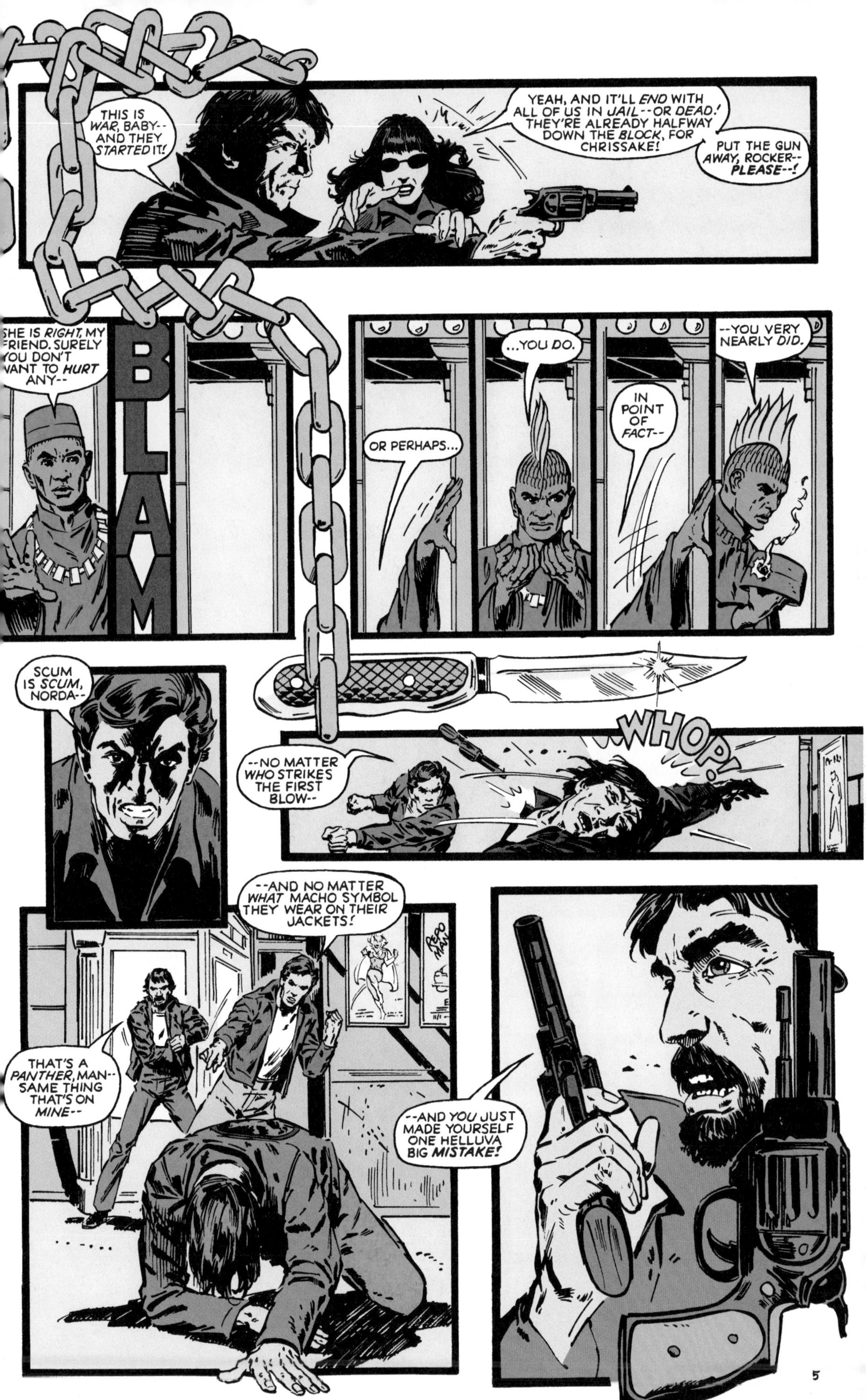
THIS IS WAR, BABY--AND THEY STARTED IT!
YEAH, AND IT'LL END WITH ALL OF US IN JAIL--OR DEAD! THEY'RE ALREADY HALFWAY DOWN THE BLOCK, FOR CHRISSAKE!
PUT THE GUN AWAY, ROCKER--PLEASE--!
SHE IS RIGHT, MY FRIEND. SURELY YOU DON'T WANT TO HURT ANY--
BLAM
OR PERHAPS...
...YOU DO.
IN POINT OF FACT--
--YOU VERY NEARLY DID.
SCUM IS SCUM, NORDA--
--NO MATTER WHO STRIKES THE FIRST BLOW--
WHOP!
--AND NO MATTER WHAT MACHO SYMBOL THEY WEAR ON THEIR JACKETS!
REPO MAN
THAT'S A PANTHER, MAN--SAME THING THAT'S ON MINE--
--AND YOU JUST MADE YOURSELF ONE HELLUVA BIG MISTAKE!

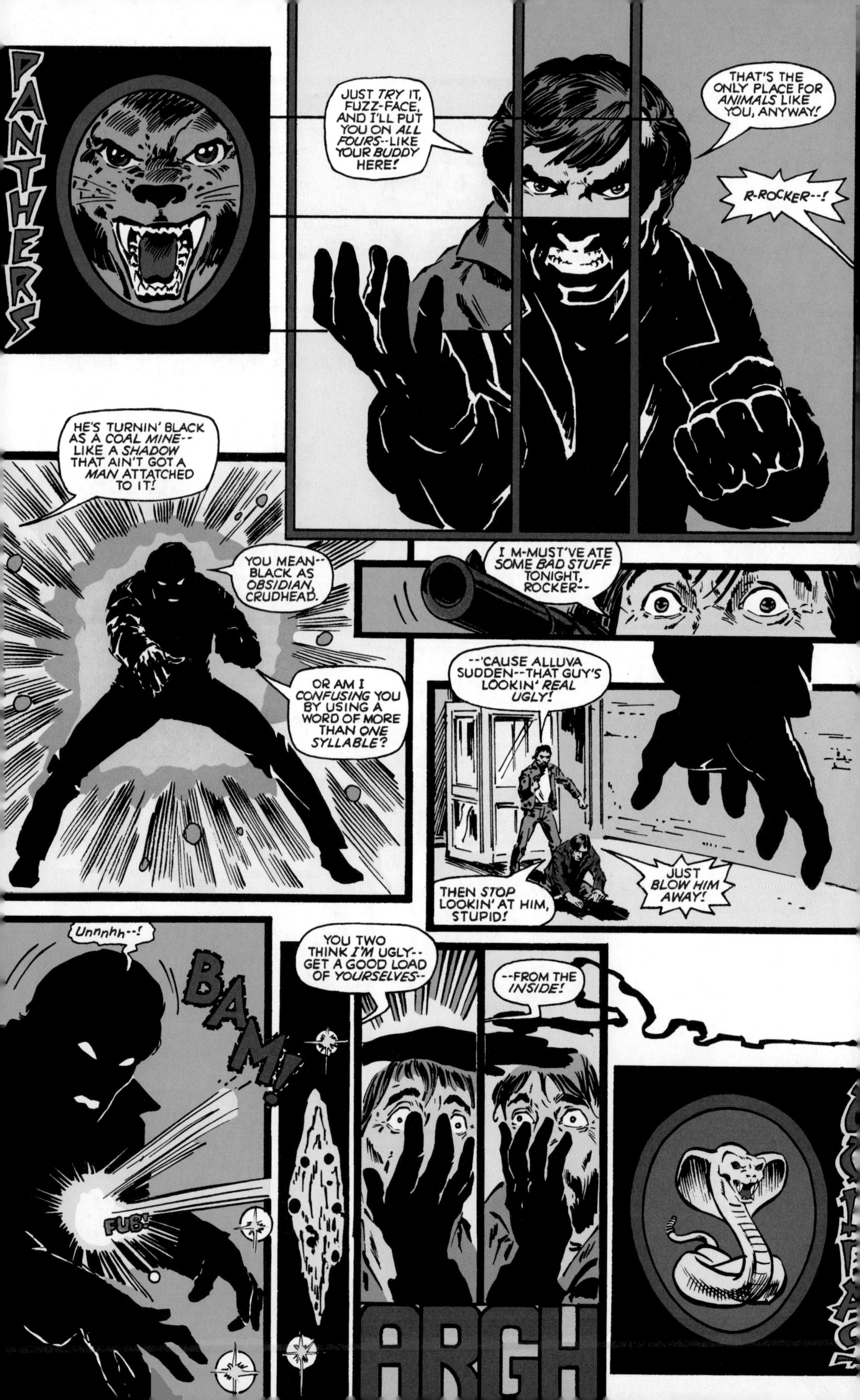
PANTHERS
JUST TRY IT, FUZZ-FACE, AND I'LL PUT YOU ON ALL FOURS--LIKE YOUR BUDDY HERE!
THAT'S THE ONLY PLACE FOR ANIMALS LIKE YOU, ANYWAY!
R-ROCKER--!
HE'S TURNIN' BLACK AS A COAL MINE--LIKE A SHADOW THAT AIN'T GOT A MAN ATTATCHED TO IT!
YOU MEAN--BLACK AS OBSIDIAN, CRUDHEAD.
OR AM I CONFUSING YOU BY USING A WORD OF MORE THAN ONE SYLLABLE?
I M-MUST'VE ATE SOME BAD STUFF TONIGHT, ROCKER--
--'CAUSE ALLUVA SUDDEN--THAT GUY'S LOOKIN' REAL UGLY!
THEN STOP LOOKIN' AT HIM, STUPID!
JUST BLOW HIM AWAY!
Unnnhh--!
BAM!
FUB!
YOU TWO THINK I'M UGLY--GET A GOOD LOAD OF YOURSELVES--
--FROM THE INSIDE!
ARGH

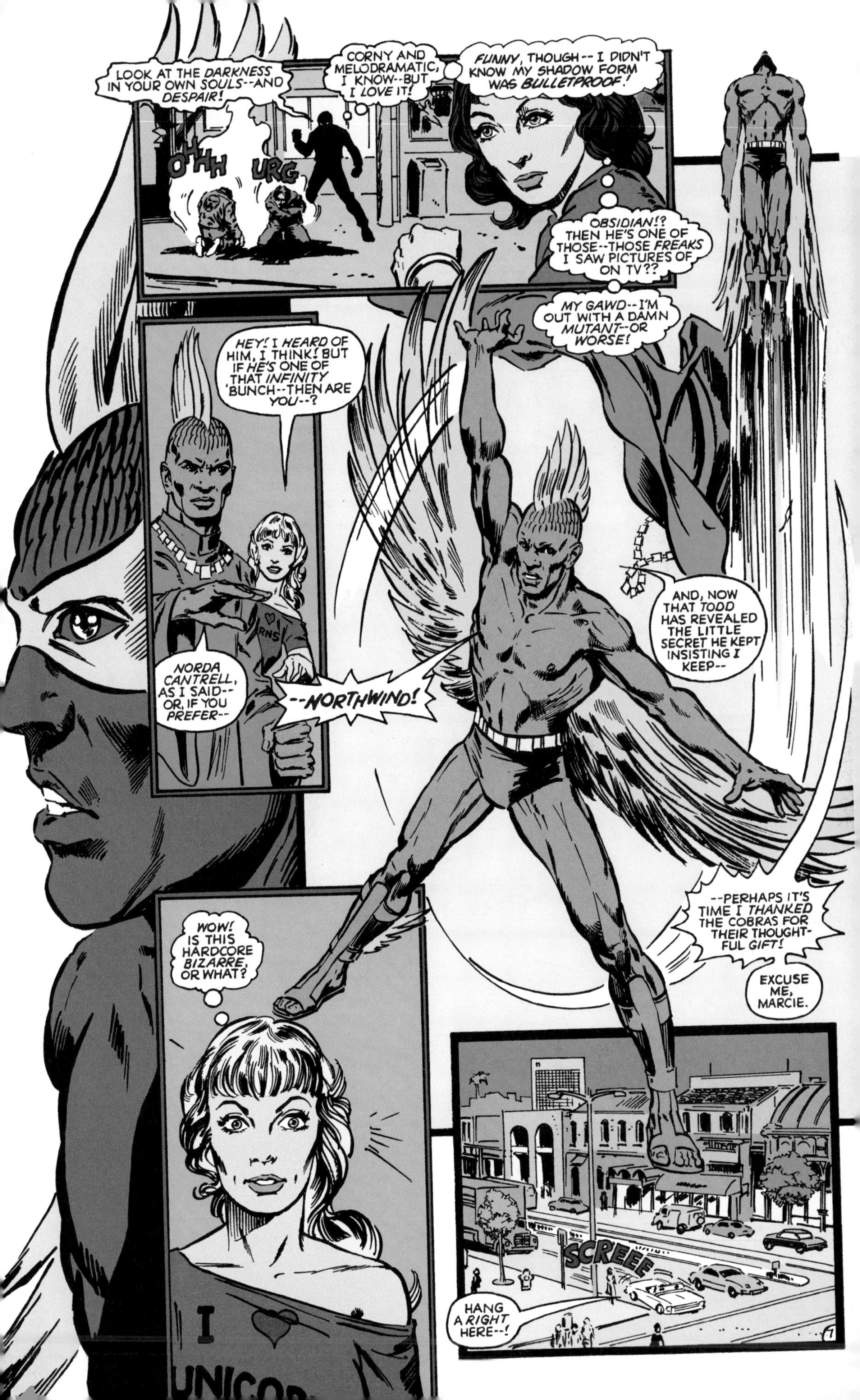

LOOK AT THE DARKNESS IN YOUR OWN SOULS--AND DESPAIR!
CORNY AND MELODRAMATIC, I KNOW--BUT I LOVE IT!
FUNNY, THOUGH--I DIDN'T KNOW MY SHADOW FORM WAS BULLETPROOF!
OHHH
URG
OBSIDIAN!? THEN HE'S ONE OF THOSE--THOSE FREAKS I SAW PICTURES OF ON TV??
MY GAWD--I'M OUT WITH A DAMN MUTANT--OR WORSE!
HEY! I HEARD OF HIM, I THINK! BUT IF HE'S ONE OF THAT INFINITY BUNCH--THEN ARE YOU--?
NORDA CANTRELL, AS I SAID--OR, IF YOU PREFER--
--NORTHWIND!
AND, NOW THAT TODD HAS REVEALED THE LITTLE SECRET HE KEPT INSISTING I KEEP--
--PERHAPS IT'S TIME I THANKED THE COBRAS FOR THEIR THOUGHTFUL GIFT!
EXCUSE ME, MARCIE.
WOW! IS THIS HARDCORE BIZARRE, OR WHAT?
SCREEE
HANG A RIGHT HERE--!
7

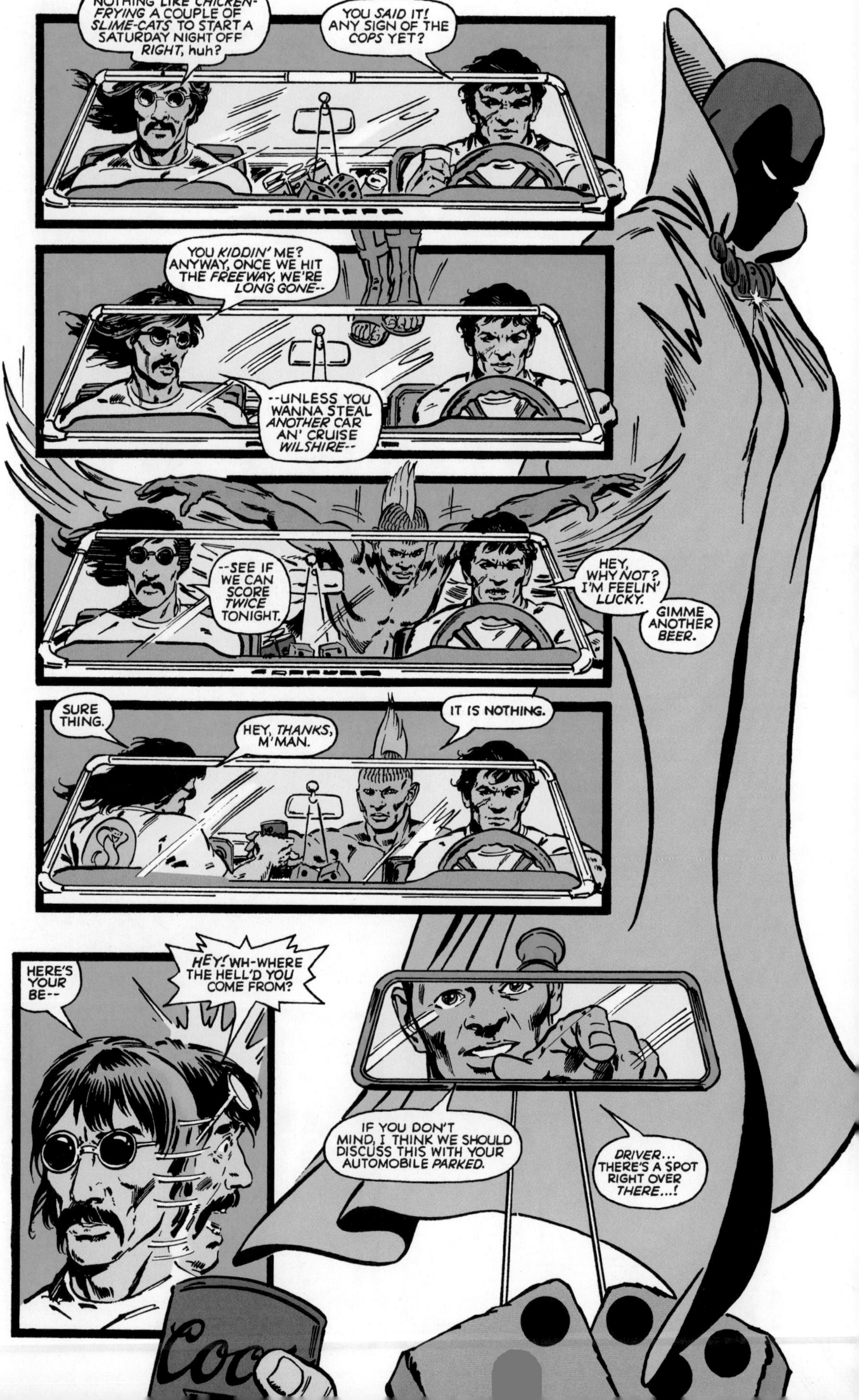
NOTHING LIKE CHICKEN-FRYING A COUPLE OF SLIME-CATS TO START A SATURDAY NIGHT OFF RIGHT, huh?
YOU SAID IT! ANY SIGN OF THE COPS YET?
YOU KIDDIN' ME? ANYWAY, ONCE WE HIT THE FREEWAY, WE'RE LONG GONE--
--UNLESS YOU WANNA STEAL ANOTHER CAR AN' CRUISE WILSHIRE--
--SEE IF WE CAN SCORE TWICE TONIGHT.
HEY, WHY NOT? I'M FEELIN' LUCKY.
GIMME ANOTHER BEER.
SURE THING.
HEY, THANKS, M'MAN.
IT IS NOTHING.
HERE'S YOUR BE--
HEY! WH-WHERE THE HELL'D YOU COME FROM?
IF YOU DON'T MIND, I THINK WE SHOULD DISCUSS THIS WITH YOUR AUTOMOBILE PARKED.
DRIVER... THERE'S A SPOT RIGHT OVER THERE...!

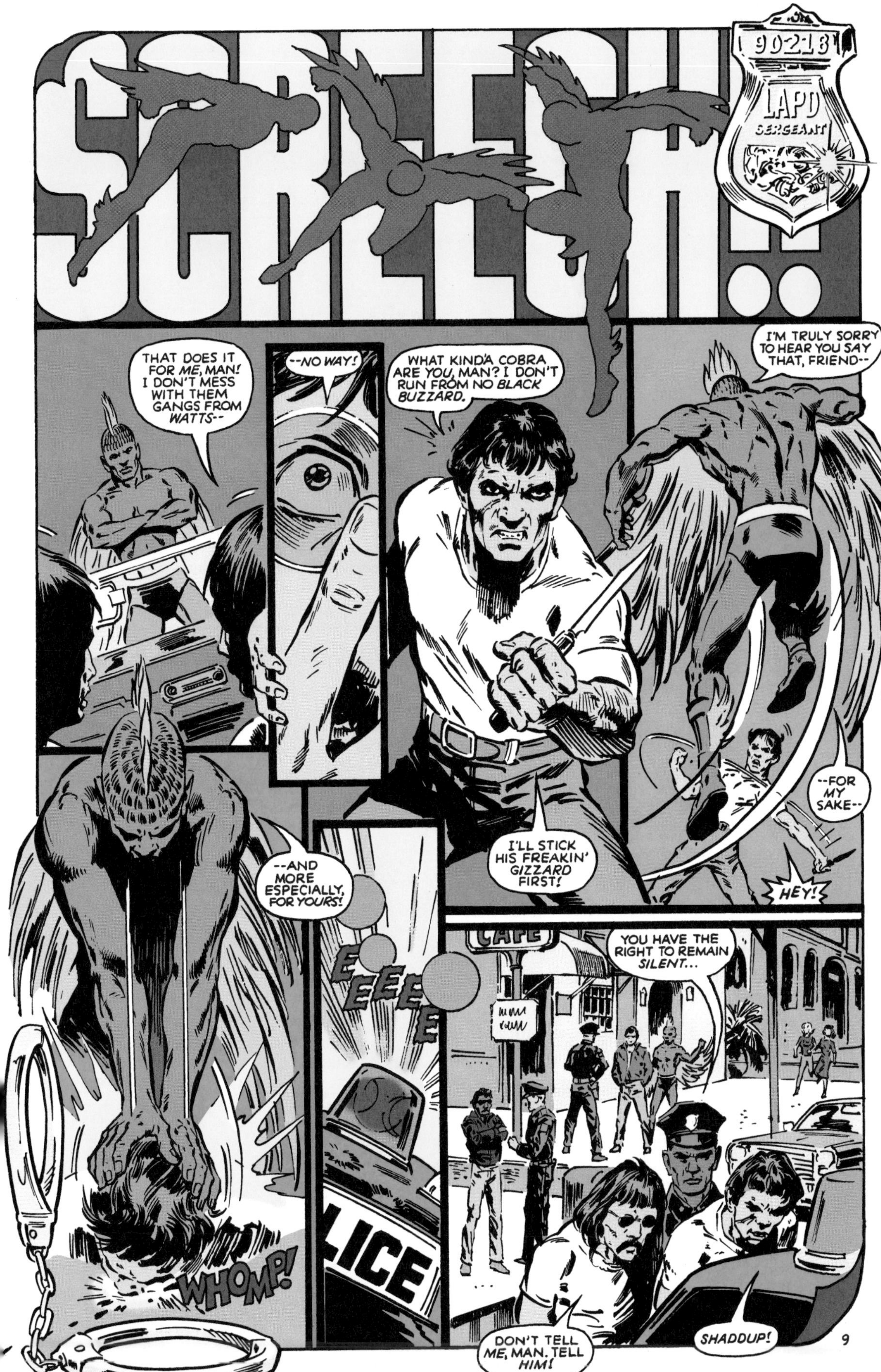
SCREECH!!
90218
LAPD
SERGEANT
THAT DOES IT FOR ME, MAN! I DON'T MESS WITH THEM GANGS FROM WATTS--
--NO WAY!
WHAT KIND'A COBRA ARE YOU, MAN? I DON'T RUN FROM NO BLACK BUZZARD.
I'M TRULY SORRY TO HEAR YOU SAY THAT, FRIEND--
--FOR MY SAKE--
I'LL STICK HIS FREAKIN' GIZZARD FIRST!
HEY!
--AND MORE ESPECIALLY, FOR YOURS!
WHOMP!
EEEEEE
LICE
CAFE
YOU HAVE THE RIGHT TO REMAIN SILENT...
DON'T TELL ME, MAN. TELL HIM!
SHADDUP!

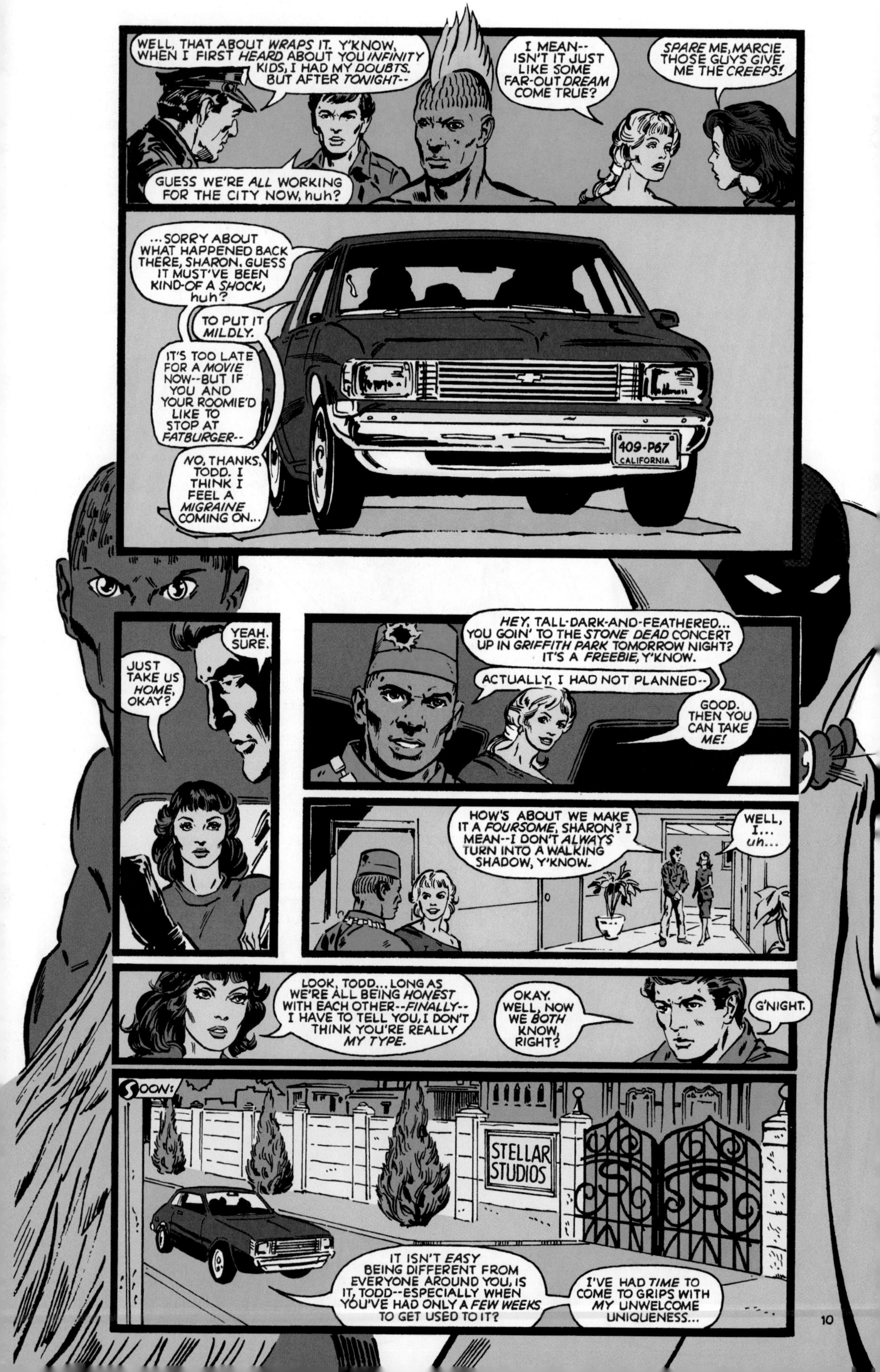
WELL, THAT ABOUT WRAPS IT. Y'KNOW, WHEN I FIRST HEARD ABOUT YOU INFINITY KIDS, I HAD MY DOUBTS. BUT AFTER TONIGHT--
GUESS WE'RE ALL WORKING FOR THE CITY NOW, huh?
I MEAN-- ISN'T IT JUST LIKE SOME FAR-OUT DREAM COME TRUE?
SPARE ME, MARCIE. THOSE GUYS GIVE ME THE CREEPS!
...SORRY ABOUT WHAT HAPPENED BACK THERE, SHARON. GUESS IT MUST'VE BEEN KIND-OF A SHOCK, huh?
TO PUT IT MILDLY.
IT'S TOO LATE FOR A MOVIE NOW--BUT IF YOU AND YOUR ROOMIE'D LIKE TO STOP AT FATBURGER--
NO, THANKS, TODD. I THINK I FEEL A MIGRAINE COMING ON...
409-P67
CALIFORNIA
YEAH. SURE.
JUST TAKE US HOME, OKAY?
HEY, TALL-DARK-AND-FEATHERED... YOU GOIN' TO THE STONE DEAD CONCERT UP IN GRIFFITH PARK TOMORROW NIGHT? IT'S A FREEBIE, Y'KNOW.
ACTUALLY, I HAD NOT PLANNED--
GOOD. THEN YOU CAN TAKE ME!
HOW'S ABOUT WE MAKE IT A FOURSOME, SHARON? I MEAN--I DON'T ALWAYS TURN INTO A WALKING SHADOW, Y'KNOW.
WELL, I... uh...
LOOK, TODD... LONG AS WE'RE ALL BEING HONEST WITH EACH OTHER--FINALLY-- I HAVE TO TELL YOU, I DON'T THINK YOU'RE REALLY MY TYPE.
OKAY. WELL, NOW WE BOTH KNOW, RIGHT?
G'NIGHT.
SOON:
STELLAR STUDIOS
IT ISN'T EASY BEING DIFFERENT FROM EVERYONE AROUND YOU, IS IT, TODD--ESPECIALLY WHEN YOU'VE HAD ONLY A FEW WEEKS TO GET USED TO IT?
I'VE HAD TIME TO COME TO GRIPS WITH MY UNWELCOME UNIQUENESS...

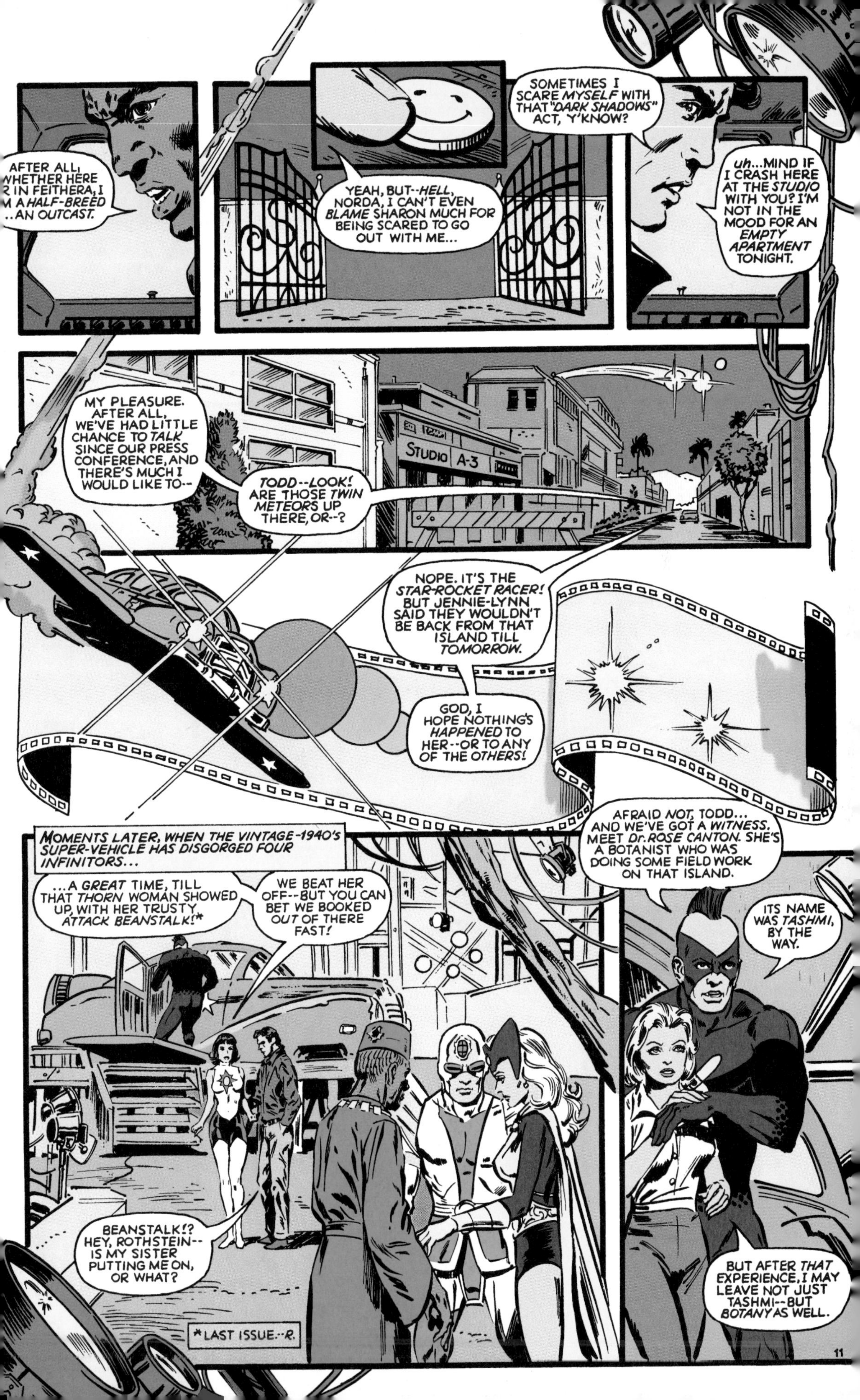
AFTER ALL, WHETHER HERE OR IN FEITHERA, I AM A HALF-BREED ...AN OUTCAST.
YEAH, BUT--HELL, NORDA, I CAN'T EVEN BLAME SHARON MUCH FOR BEING SCARED TO GO OUT WITH ME...
SOMETIMES I SCARE MYSELF WITH THAT "DARK SHADOWS" ACT, Y'KNOW?
uh...MIND IF I CRASH HERE AT THE STUDIO WITH YOU? I'M NOT IN THE MOOD FOR AN EMPTY APARTMENT TONIGHT.
MY PLEASURE. AFTER ALL, WE'VE HAD LITTLE CHANCE TO TALK SINCE OUR PRESS CONFERENCE, AND THERE'S MUCH I WOULD LIKE TO--
STUDIO A-3
TODD--LOOK! ARE THOSE TWIN METEORS UP THERE, OR--?
NOPE. IT'S THE STAR-ROCKET RACER! BUT JENNIE-LYNN SAID THEY WOULDN'T BE BACK FROM THAT ISLAND TILL TOMORROW.
GOD, I HOPE NOTHING'S HAPPENED TO HER--OR TO ANY OF THE OTHERS!
MOMENTS LATER, WHEN THE VINTAGE-1940's SUPER-VEHICLE HAS DISGORGED FOUR INFINITORS...
...A GREAT TIME, TILL THAT THORN WOMAN SHOWED UP, WITH HER TRUSTY ATTACK BEANSTALK!*
WE BEAT HER OFF--BUT YOU CAN BET WE BOOKED OUT OF THERE FAST!
BEANSTALK!? HEY, ROTHSTEIN--IS MY SISTER PUTTING ME ON, OR WHAT?
*LAST ISSUE.--R.
AFRAID NOT, TODD... AND WE'VE GOT A WITNESS. MEET Dr. ROSE CANTON. SHE'S A BOTANIST WHO WAS DOING SOME FIELD WORK ON THAT ISLAND.
ITS NAME WAS TASHMI, BY THE WAY.
BUT AFTER THAT EXPERIENCE, I MAY LEAVE NOT JUST TASHMI--BUT BOTANY AS WELL.

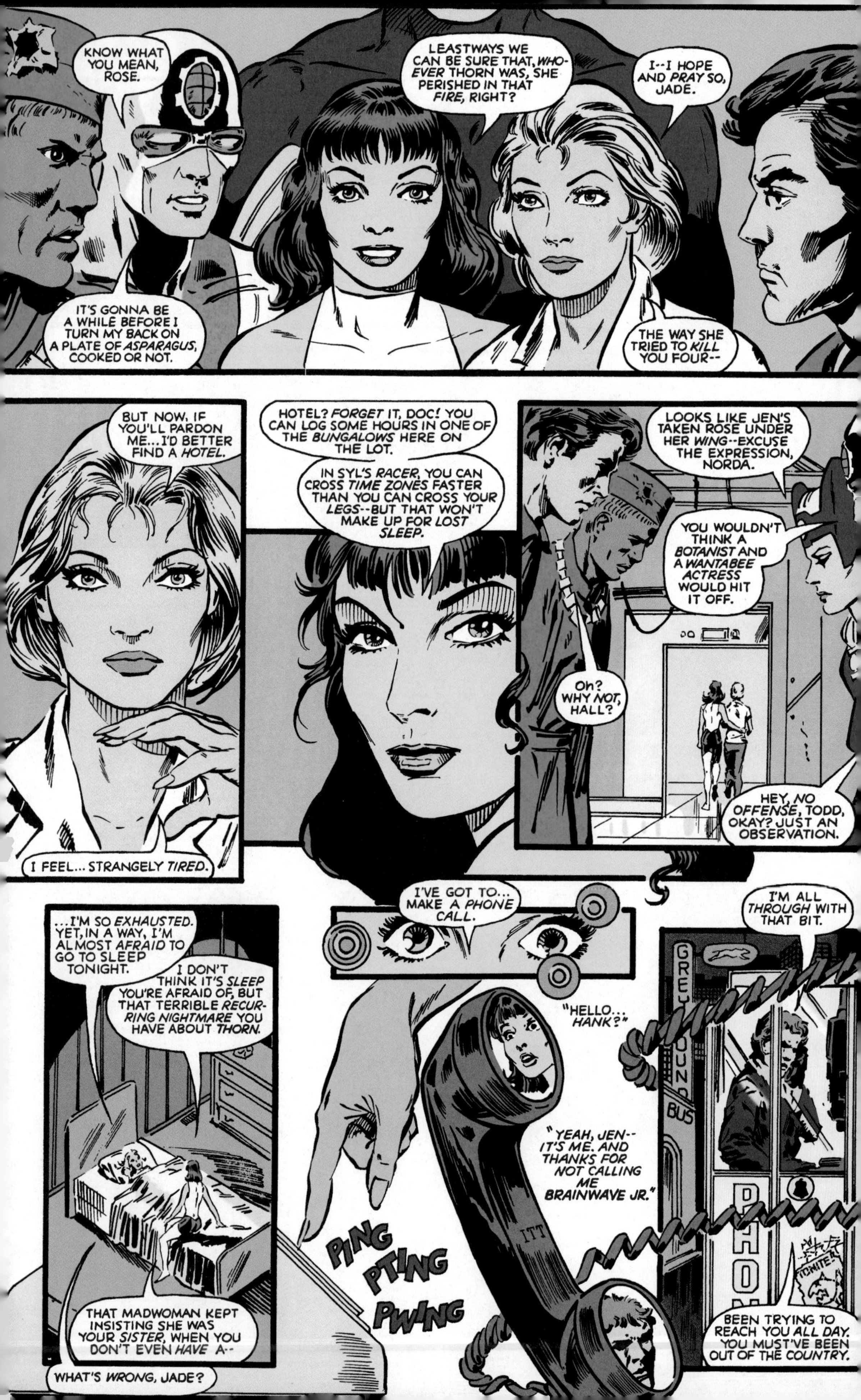
KNOW WHAT YOU MEAN, ROSE.
IT'S GONNA BE A WHILE BEFORE I TURN MY BACK ON A PLATE OF ASPARAGUS, COOKED OR NOT.
LEASTWAYS WE CAN BE SURE THAT, WHOEVER THORN WAS, SHE PERISHED IN THAT FIRE, RIGHT?
I--I HOPE AND PRAY SO, JADE.
THE WAY SHE TRIED TO KILL YOU FOUR--
BUT NOW, IF YOU'LL PARDON ME... I'D BETTER FIND A HOTEL.
I FEEL... STRANGELY TIRED.
HOTEL? FORGET IT, DOC! YOU CAN LOG SOME HOURS IN ONE OF THE BUNGALOWS HERE ON THE LOT.
IN SYL'S RACER, YOU CAN CROSS TIME ZONES FASTER THAN YOU CAN CROSS YOUR LEGS--BUT THAT WON'T MAKE UP FOR LOST SLEEP.
LOOKS LIKE JEN'S TAKEN ROSE UNDER HER WING--EXCUSE THE EXPRESSION, NORDA.
YOU WOULDN'T THINK A BOTANIST AND A WANTABEE ACTRESS WOULD HIT IT OFF.
Oh? WHY NOT, HALL?
HEY, NO OFFENSE, TODD, OKAY? JUST AN OBSERVATION.
...I'M SO EXHAUSTED. YET, IN A WAY, I'M ALMOST AFRAID TO GO TO SLEEP TONIGHT.
I DON'T THINK IT'S SLEEP YOU'RE AFRAID OF, BUT THAT TERRIBLE RECURRING NIGHTMARE YOU HAVE ABOUT THORN.
THAT MADWOMAN KEPT INSISTING SHE WAS YOUR SISTER, WHEN YOU DON'T EVEN HAVE A--
WHAT'S WRONG, JADE?
I'VE GOT TO... MAKE A PHONE CALL.
PING
PTING
PWING
"HELLO... HANK?"
"YEAH, JEN--IT'S ME. AND THANKS FOR NOT CALLING ME BRAINWAVE JR."
I'M ALL THROUGH WITH THAT BIT.
BEEN TRYING TO REACH YOU ALL DAY. YOU MUST'VE BEEN OUT OF THE COUNTRY.
GREYHOUND BUS
PHON
TONITE!

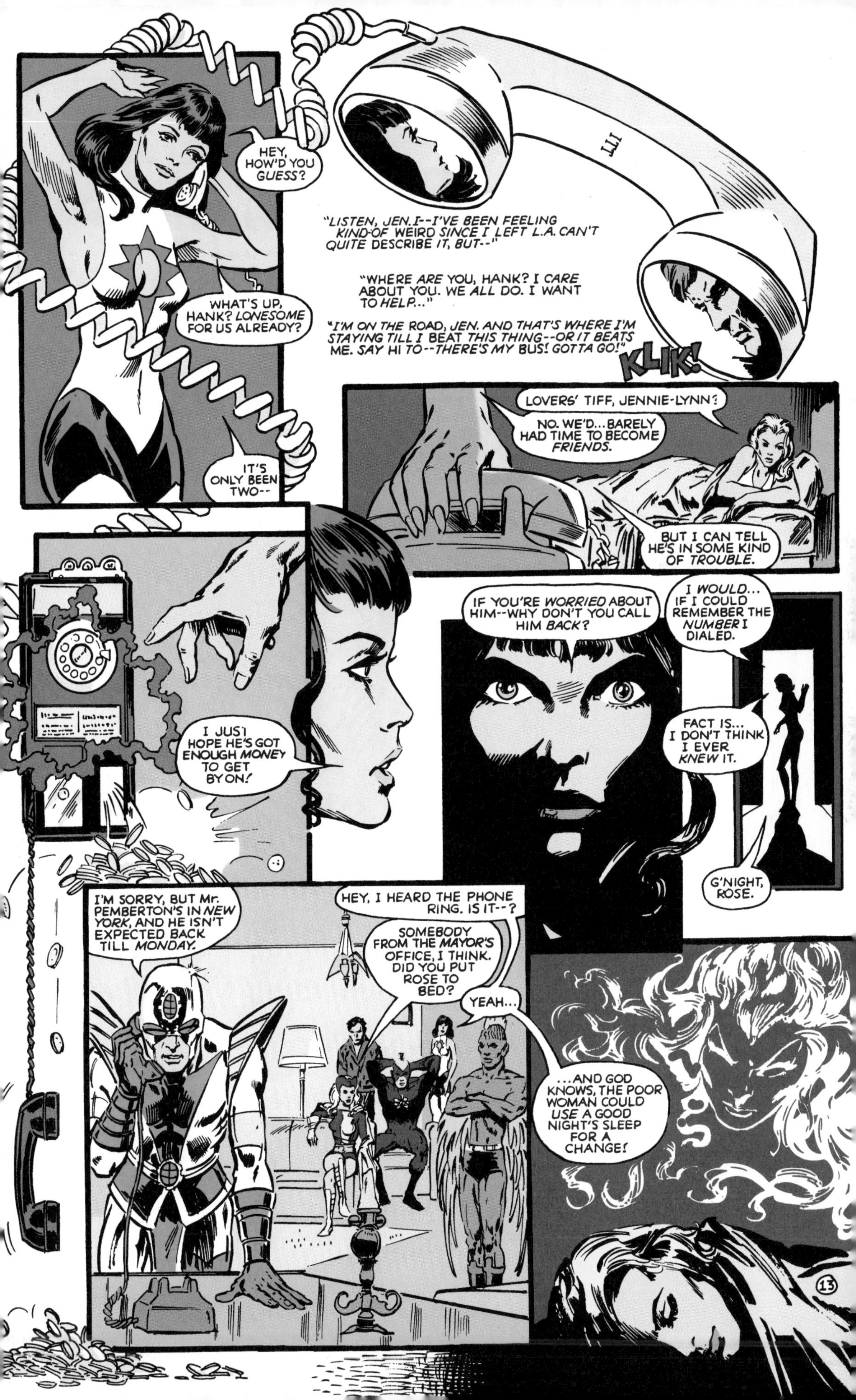

HEY, HOW'D YOU GUESS?
"LISTEN, JEN. I--I'VE BEEN FEELING KIND-OF WEIRD SINCE I LEFT L.A. CAN'T QUITE DESCRIBE IT, BUT--"
WHAT'S UP, HANK? LONESOME FOR US ALREADY?
IT'S ONLY BEEN TWO--
"WHERE ARE YOU, HANK? I CARE ABOUT YOU. WE ALL DO. I WANT TO HELP..."
"I'M ON THE ROAD, JEN. AND THAT'S WHERE I'M STAYING TILL I BEAT THIS THING--OR IT BEATS ME. SAY HI TO--THERE'S MY BUS! GOTTA GO!"
KLIK!
LOVERS' TIFF, JENNIE-LYNN?
NO. WE'D... BARELY HAD TIME TO BECOME FRIENDS.
BUT I CAN TELL HE'S IN SOME KIND OF TROUBLE.
I JUST HOPE HE'S GOT ENOUGH MONEY TO GET BY ON!
IF YOU'RE WORRIED ABOUT HIM--WHY DON'T YOU CALL HIM BACK?
I WOULD... IF I COULD REMEMBER THE NUMBER I DIALED.
FACT IS... I DON'T THINK I EVER KNEW IT.
G'NIGHT, ROSE.
I'M SORRY, BUT Mr. PEMBERTON'S IN NEW YORK, AND HE ISN'T EXPECTED BACK TILL MONDAY.
HEY, I HEARD THE PHONE RING. IS IT--?
SOMEBODY FROM THE MAYOR'S OFFICE, I THINK. DID YOU PUT ROSE TO BED?
YEAH...
...AND GOD KNOWS, THE POOR WOMAN COULD USE A GOOD NIGHT'S SLEEP FOR A CHANGE!
ITT

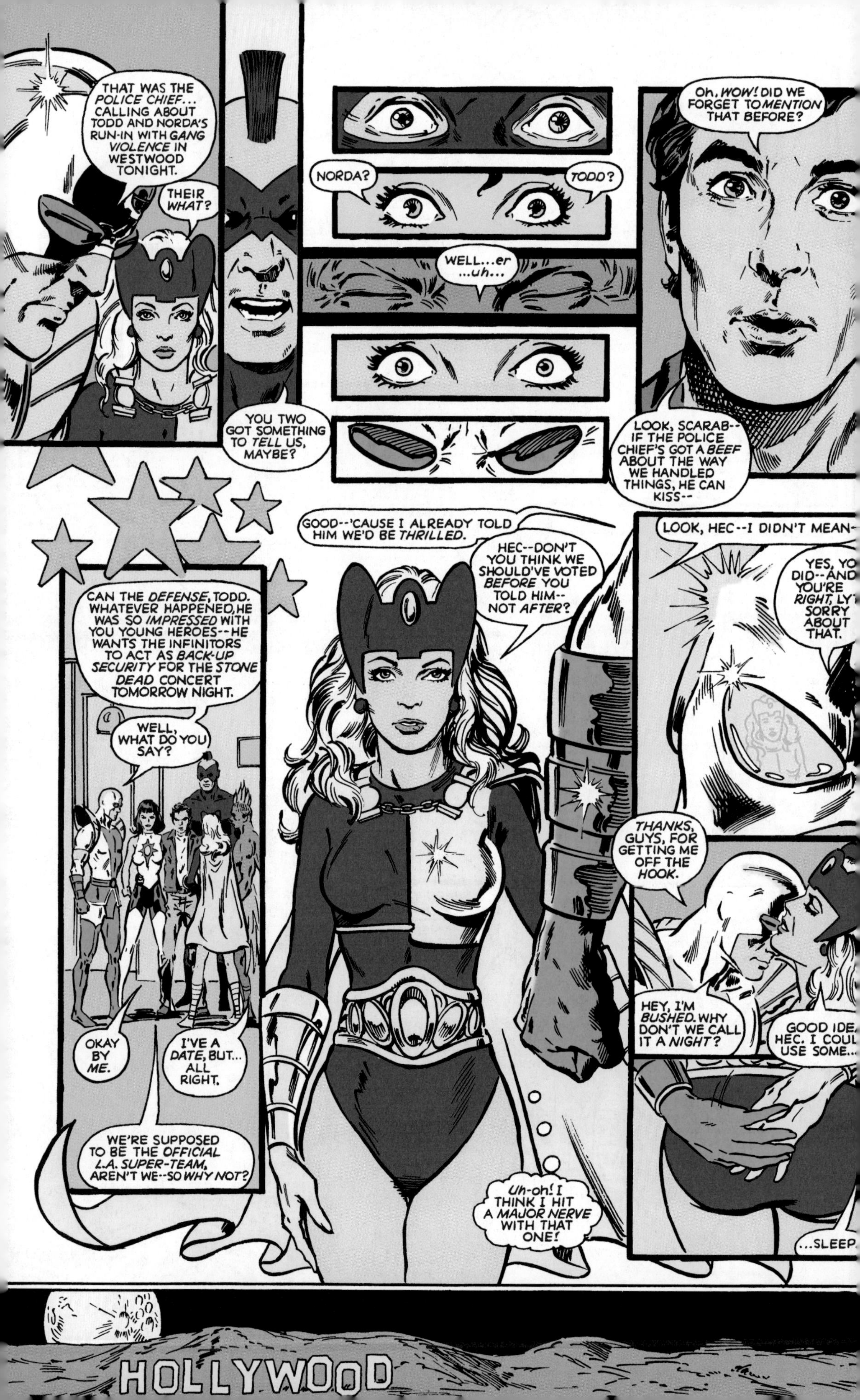
THAT WAS THE POLICE CHIEF... CALLING ABOUT TODD AND NORDA'S RUN-IN WITH GANG VIOLENCE IN WESTWOOD TONIGHT.
THEIR WHAT?
NORDA?
TODD?
WELL...er ...uh...
YOU TWO GOT SOMETHING TO TELL US, MAYBE?
Oh, WOW! DID WE FORGET TO MENTION THAT BEFORE?
LOOK, SCARAB-- IF THE POLICE CHIEF'S GOT A BEEF ABOUT THE WAY WE HANDLED THINGS, HE CAN KISS--
CAN THE DEFENSE, TODD. WHATEVER HAPPENED, HE WAS SO IMPRESSED WITH YOU YOUNG HEROES--HE WANTS THE INFINITORS TO ACT AS BACK-UP SECURITY FOR THE STONE DEAD CONCERT TOMORROW NIGHT.
WELL, WHAT DO YOU SAY?
OKAY BY ME.
I'VE A DATE, BUT... ALL RIGHT.
WE'RE SUPPOSED TO BE THE OFFICIAL L.A. SUPER-TEAM, AREN'T WE--SO WHY NOT?
GOOD--'CAUSE I ALREADY TOLD HIM WE'D BE THRILLED.
HEC--DON'T YOU THINK WE SHOULD'VE VOTED BEFORE YOU TOLD HIM-- NOT AFTER?
Uh-oh! I THINK I HIT A MAJOR NERVE WITH THAT ONE!
LOOK, HEC--I DIDN'T MEAN-
YES, YO DID--AND YOU'RE RIGHT, LY SORRY ABOUT THAT.
THANKS, GUYS, FOR GETTING ME OFF THE HOOK.
HEY, I'M BUSHED. WHY DON'T WE CALL IT A NIGHT?
GOOD IDE HEC. I COUL USE SOME...
...SLEEP.
HOLLYWOOD

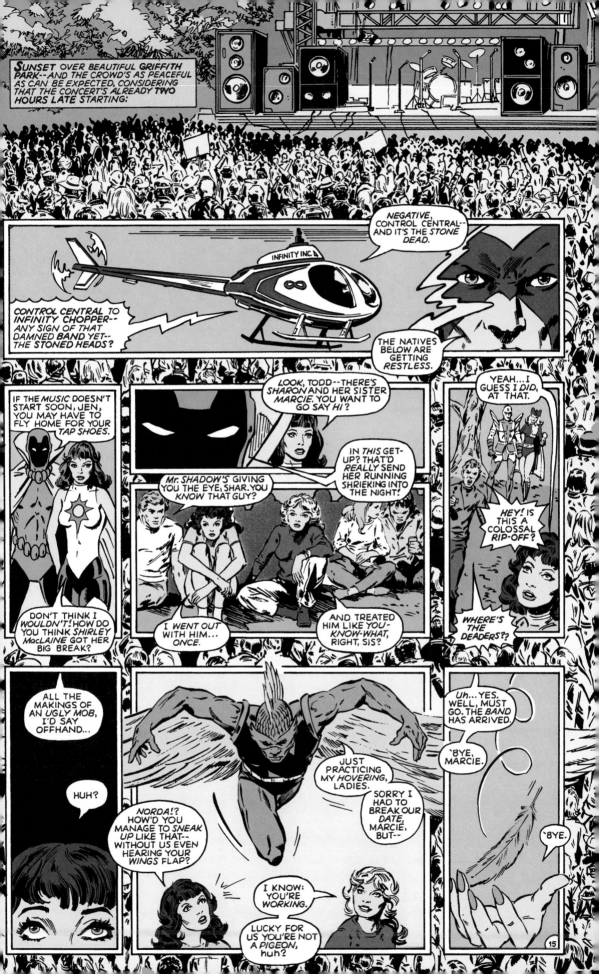

SUNSET OVER BEAUTIFUL GRIFFITH PARK--AND THE CROWD'S AS PEACEFUL AS CAN BE EXPECTED, CONSIDERING THAT THE CONCERT'S ALREADY *TWO* HOURS LATE STARTING:

INFINITY INC.

NEGATIVE, CONTROL CENTRAL-- AND IT'S THE *STONE DEAD.*

CONTROL CENTRAL TO INFINITY CHOPPER-- ANY SIGN OF THAT *DAMNED BAND* YET-- THE *STONED HEADS?*

THE NATIVES BELOW ARE GETTING *RESTLESS.*

IF THE *MUSIC* DOESN'T START SOON, JEN, YOU MAY HAVE TO FLY HOME FOR YOUR *TAP SHOES.*

LOOK, TODD--THERE'S *SHARON* AND HER SISTER *MARCIE.* YOU WANT TO GO SAY *HI?*

YEAH... I GUESS I *DID,* AT THAT.

IN *THIS* GET-UP? THAT'D *REALLY* SEND HER RUNNING SHRIEKING INTO THE NIGHT!

MR. SHADOW'S GIVING YOU THE EYE, SHAR. YOU *KNOW* THAT GUY?

DON'T THINK I *WOULDN'T!* HOW DO YOU THINK *SHIRLEY MacLAINE* GOT HER BIG BREAK?

I WENT OUT WITH HIM... *ONCE.*

AND TREATED HIM LIKE YOU- *KNOW-WHAT,* RIGHT, SIS?

HEY! IS THIS A COLOSSAL *RIP-OFF?*

WHERE'S THE *DEADERS??*

ALL THE MAKINGS OF AN *UGLY MOB,* I'D SAY OFFHAND...

HUH?

NORDA!? HOW'D YOU MANAGE TO *SNEAK UP* LIKE THAT-- WITHOUT US EVEN *HEARING* YOUR WINGS FLAP?

JUST PRACTICING MY *HOVERING,* LADIES.

SORRY I HAD TO *BREAK* OUR DATE, MARCIE, BUT--

UH...YES, WELL, MUST GO. THE *BAND* HAS ARRIVED.

'BYE, MARCIE.

'BYE.

I *KNOW:* YOU'RE *WORKING.*

LUCKY FOR US YOU'RE NOT A *PIGEON,* HUH?

15

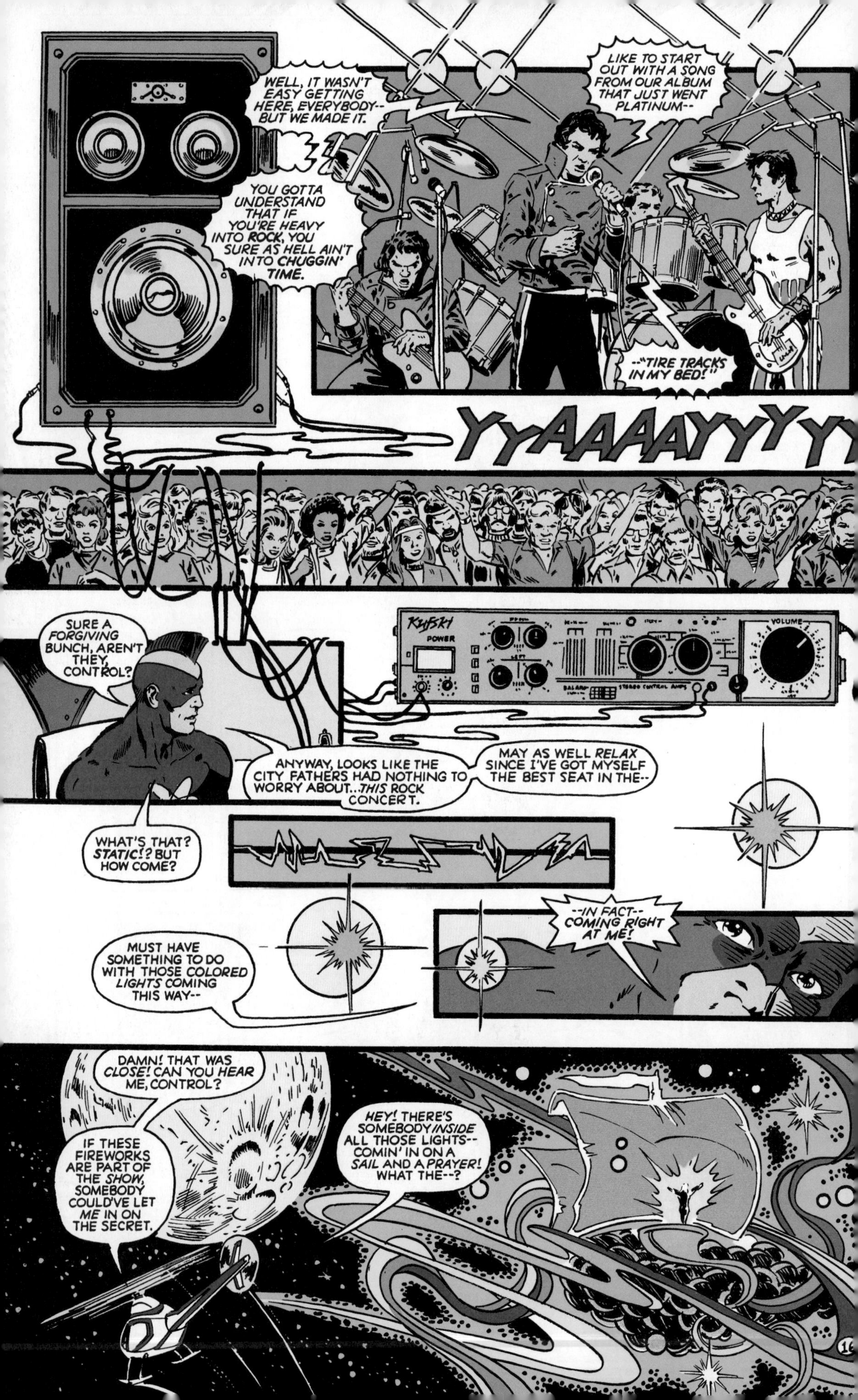
WELL, IT WASN'T EASY GETTING HERE, EVERYBODY-- BUT WE MADE IT.
YOU GOTTA UNDERSTAND THAT IF YOU'RE HEAVY INTO ROCK, YOU SURE AS HELL AIN'T INTO CHUGGIN' TIME.
LIKE TO START OUT WITH A SONG FROM OUR ALBUM THAT JUST WENT PLATINUM--
--"TIRE TRACKS IN MY BED!"
YYAAAAYYYYY
SURE A FORGIVING BUNCH, AREN'T THEY, CONTROL?
POWER
VOLUME
ANYWAY, LOOKS LIKE THE CITY FATHERS HAD NOTHING TO WORRY ABOUT...THIS ROCK CONCERT.
MAY AS WELL RELAX SINCE I'VE GOT MYSELF THE BEST SEAT IN THE--
WHAT'S THAT? STATIC!? BUT HOW COME?
MUST HAVE SOMETHING TO DO WITH THOSE COLORED LIGHTS COMING THIS WAY--
--IN FACT-- COMING RIGHT AT ME!
DAMN! THAT WAS CLOSE! CAN YOU HEAR ME, CONTROL?
IF THESE FIREWORKS ARE PART OF THE SHOW, SOMEBODY COULD'VE LET ME IN ON THE SECRET.
HEY! THERE'S SOMEBODY INSIDE ALL THOSE LIGHTS-- COMIN' IN ON A SAIL AND A PRAYER! WHAT THE--?

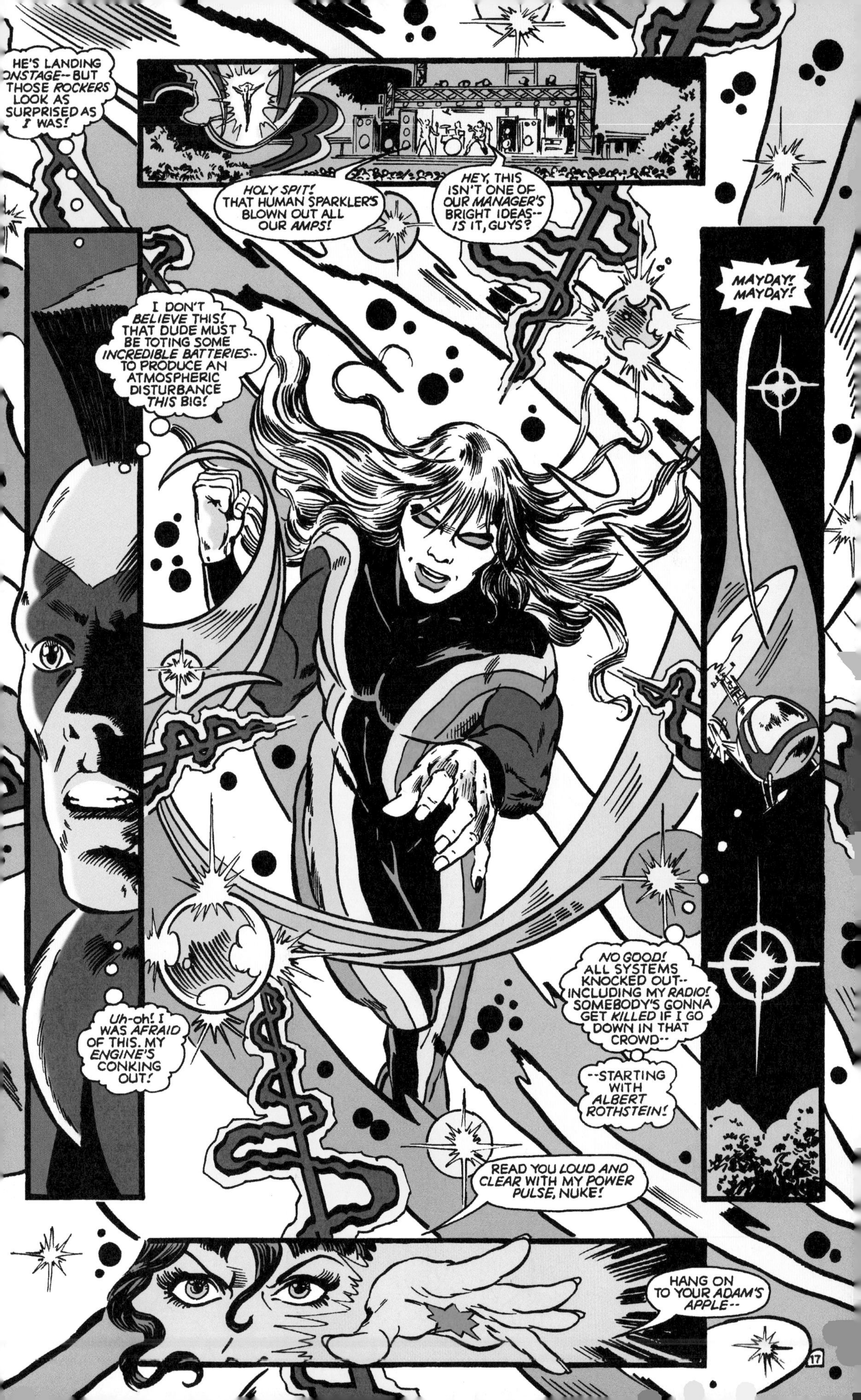
HE'S LANDING ONSTAGE-- BUT THOSE ROCKERS LOOK AS SURPRISED AS I WAS!
HOLY SPIT! THAT HUMAN SPARKLER'S BLOWN OUT ALL OUR AMPS!
HEY, THIS ISN'T ONE OF OUR MANAGER'S BRIGHT IDEAS-- IS IT, GUYS?
I DON'T BELIEVE THIS! THAT DUDE MUST BE TOTING SOME INCREDIBLE BATTERIES-- TO PRODUCE AN ATMOSPHERIC DISTURBANCE THIS BIG!
MAYDAY! MAYDAY!
Uh-oh! I WAS AFRAID OF THIS. MY ENGINE'S CONKING OUT!
NO GOOD! ALL SYSTEMS KNOCKED OUT-- INCLUDING MY RADIO! SOMEBODY'S GONNA GET KILLED IF I GO DOWN IN THAT CROWD--
--STARTING WITH ALBERT ROTHSTEIN!
READ YOU LOUD AND CLEAR WITH MY POWER PULSE, NUKE!
HANG ON TO YOUR ADAM'S APPLE--

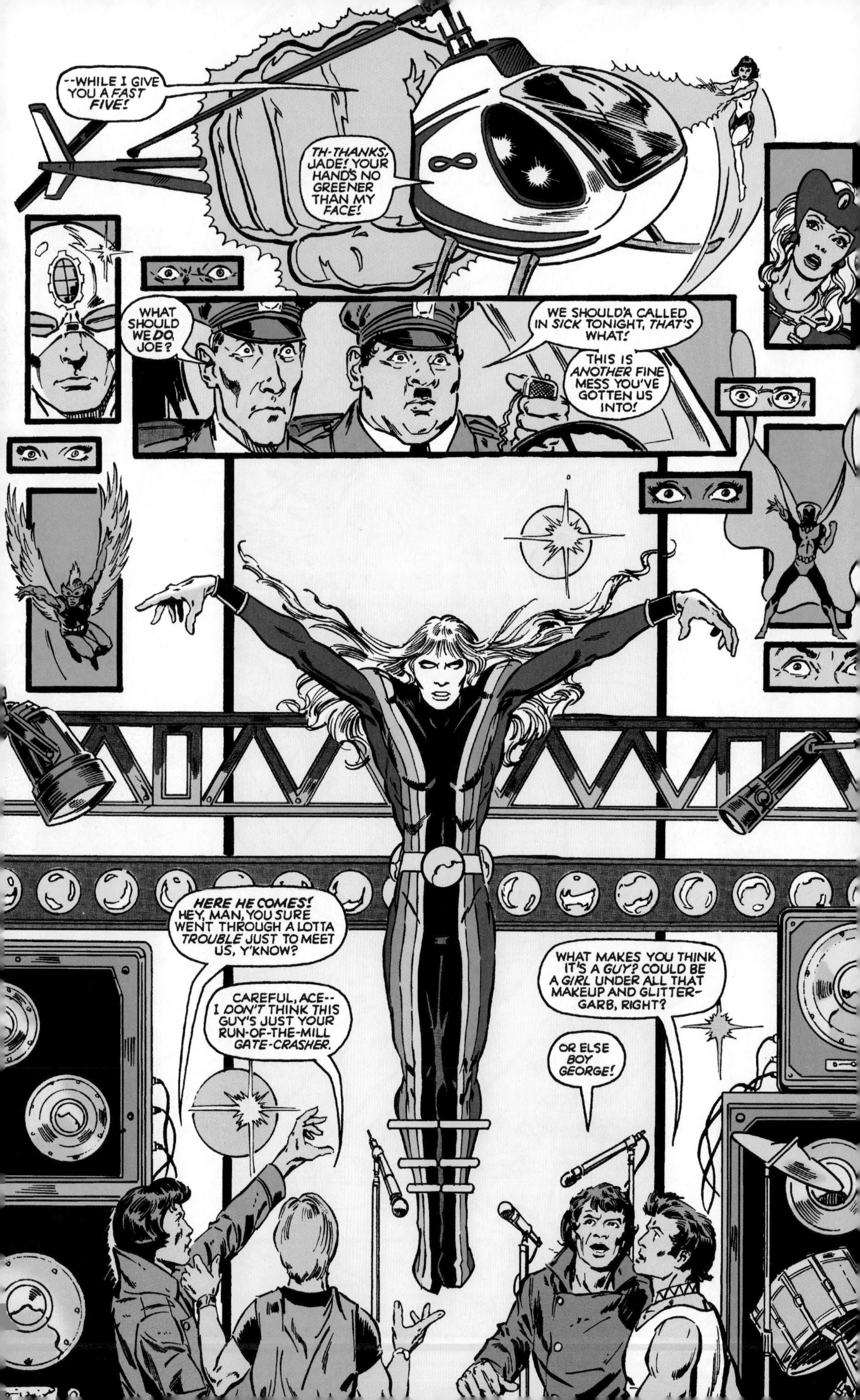
--WHILE I GIVE YOU A FAST FIVE!
TH-THANKS, JADE! YOUR HAND'S NO GREENER THAN MY FACE!
WHAT SHOULD WE DO, JOE?
WE SHOULD'A CALLED IN SICK TONIGHT, THAT'S WHAT!
THIS IS ANOTHER FINE MESS YOU'VE GOTTEN US INTO!
HERE HE COMES! HEY, MAN, YOU SURE WENT THROUGH A LOTTA TROUBLE JUST TO MEET US, Y'KNOW?
CAREFUL, ACE-- I DON'T THINK THIS GUY'S JUST YOUR RUN-OF-THE-MILL GATE-CRASHER.
WHAT MAKES YOU THINK IT'S A GUY? COULD BE A GIRL UNDER ALL THAT MAKEUP AND GLITTER-GARB, RIGHT?
OR ELSE BOY GEORGE!

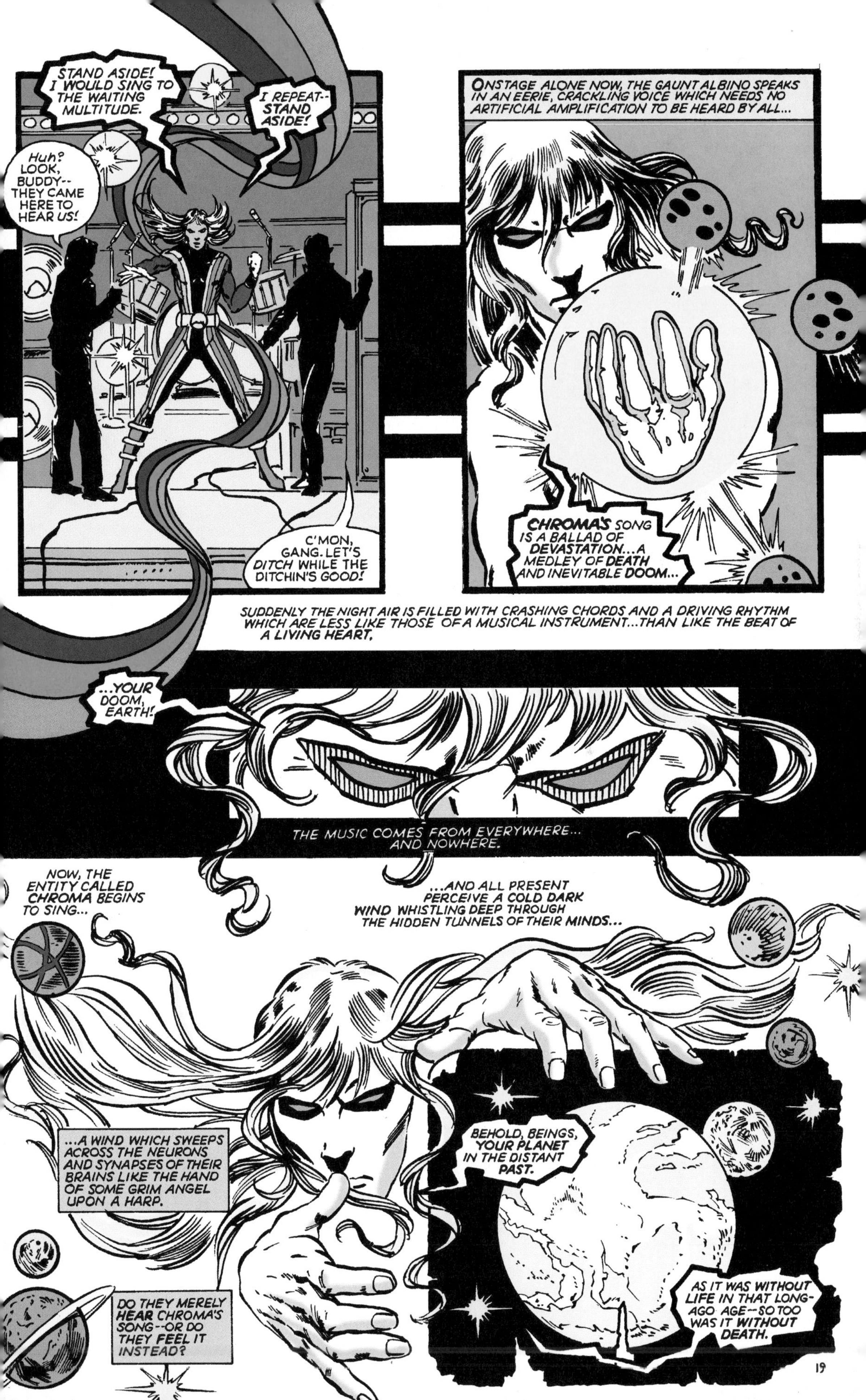
STAND ASIDE! I WOULD SING TO THE WAITING MULTITUDE.
I REPEAT-- STAND ASIDE!
Huh? LOOK, BUDDY-- THEY CAME HERE TO HEAR US!
C'MON, GANG. LET'S DITCH WHILE THE DITCHIN'S GOOD!
ONSTAGE ALONE NOW, THE GAUNT ALBINO SPEAKS IN AN EERIE, CRACKLING VOICE WHICH NEEDS NO ARTIFICIAL AMPLIFICATION TO BE HEARD BY ALL...
CHROMA'S SONG IS A BALLAD OF DEVASTATION... A MEDLEY OF DEATH AND INEVITABLE DOOM...
SUDDENLY THE NIGHT AIR IS FILLED WITH CRASHING CHORDS AND A DRIVING RHYTHM WHICH ARE LESS LIKE THOSE OF A MUSICAL INSTRUMENT...THAN LIKE THE BEAT OF A LIVING HEART.
...YOUR DOOM, EARTH!
THE MUSIC COMES FROM EVERYWHERE... AND NOWHERE.
NOW, THE ENTITY CALLED CHROMA BEGINS TO SING...
...AND ALL PRESENT PERCEIVE A COLD DARK WIND WHISTLING DEEP THROUGH THE HIDDEN TUNNELS OF THEIR MINDS...
...A WIND WHICH SWEEPS ACROSS THE NEURONS AND SYNAPSES OF THEIR BRAINS LIKE THE HAND OF SOME GRIM ANGEL UPON A HARP.
BEHOLD, BEINGS, YOUR PLANET IN THE DISTANT PAST.
DO THEY MERELY HEAR CHROMA'S SONG--OR DO THEY FEEL IT INSTEAD?
AS IT WAS WITHOUT LIFE IN THAT LONG-AGO AGE--SO TOO WAS IT WITHOUT DEATH.

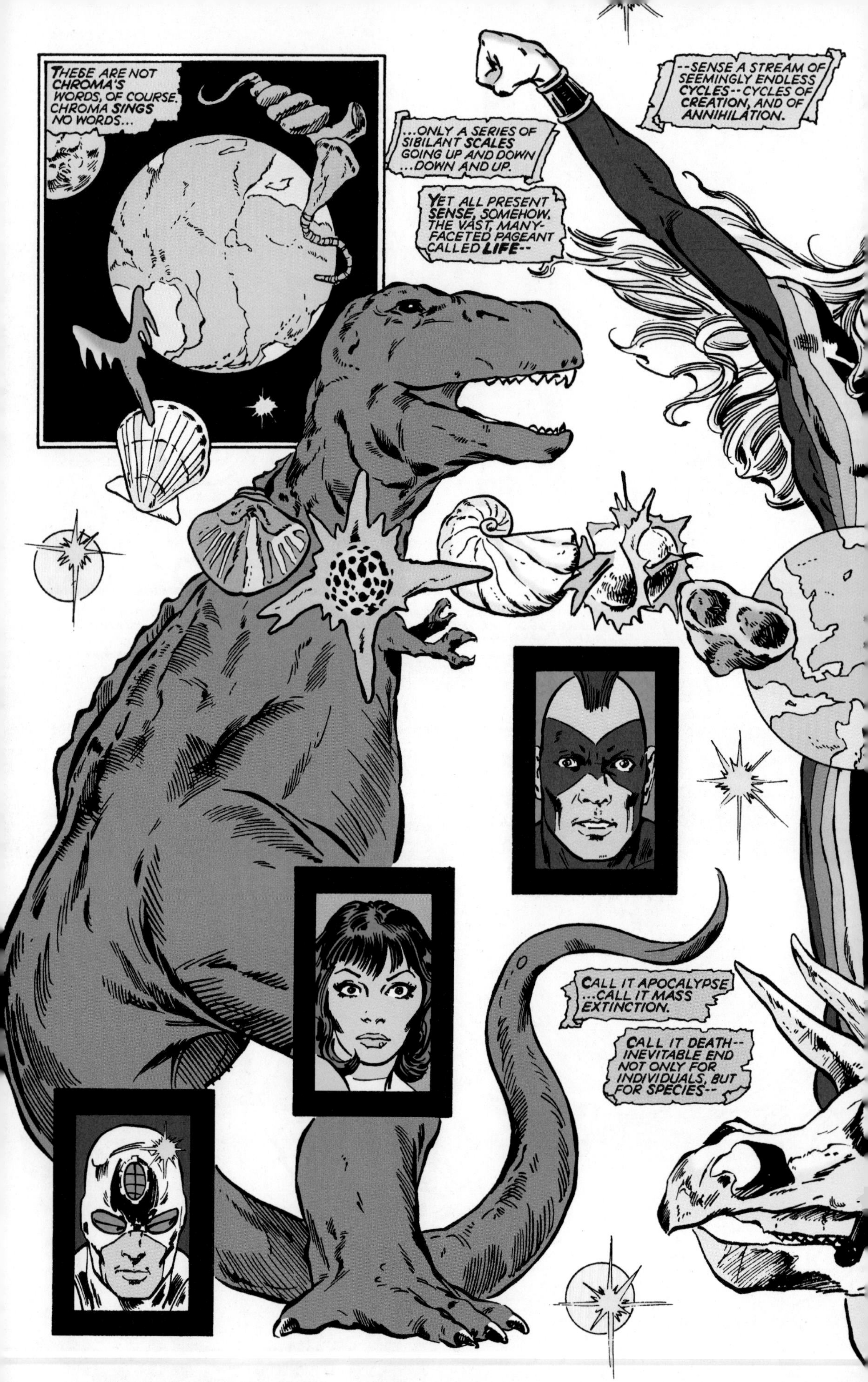
THESE ARE NOT CHROMA'S WORDS, OF COURSE. CHROMA SINGS NO WORDS...
...ONLY A SERIES OF SIBILANT SCALES GOING UP AND DOWN ...DOWN AND UP.
YET ALL PRESENT SENSE, SOMEHOW, THE VAST, MANY-FACETED PAGEANT CALLED LIFE--
--SENSE A STREAM OF SEEMINGLY ENDLESS CYCLES--CYCLES OF CREATION, AND OF ANNIHILATION.
CALL IT APOCALYPSE ...CALL IT MASS EXTINCTION.
CALL IT DEATH--INEVITABLE END NOT ONLY FOR INDIVIDUALS, BUT FOR SPECIES--

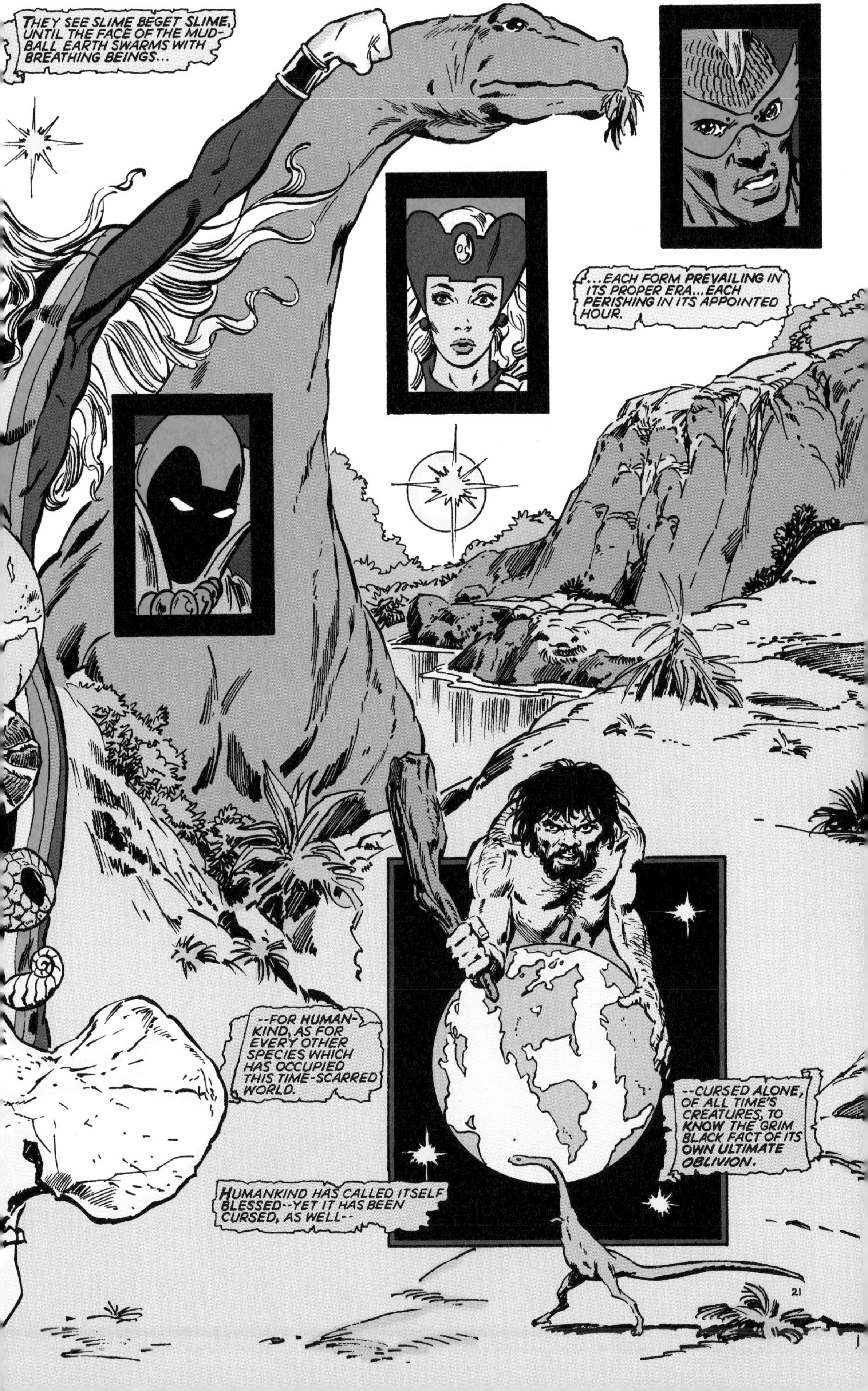
THEY SEE SLIME BEGET SLIME, UNTIL THE FACE OF THE MUD-BALL EARTH SWARMS WITH BREATHING BEINGS...
...EACH FORM PREVAILING IN ITS PROPER ERA...EACH PERISHING IN ITS APPOINTED HOUR.
HUMANKIND HAS CALLED ITSELF BLESSED--YET IT HAS BEEN CURSED, AS WELL--
--FOR HUMAN-KIND, AS FOR EVERY OTHER SPECIES WHICH HAS OCCUPIED THIS TIME-SCARRED WORLD.
--CURSED ALONE, OF ALL TIME'S CREATURES, TO KNOW THE GRIM BLACK FACT OF ITS OWN ULTIMATE OBLIVION.

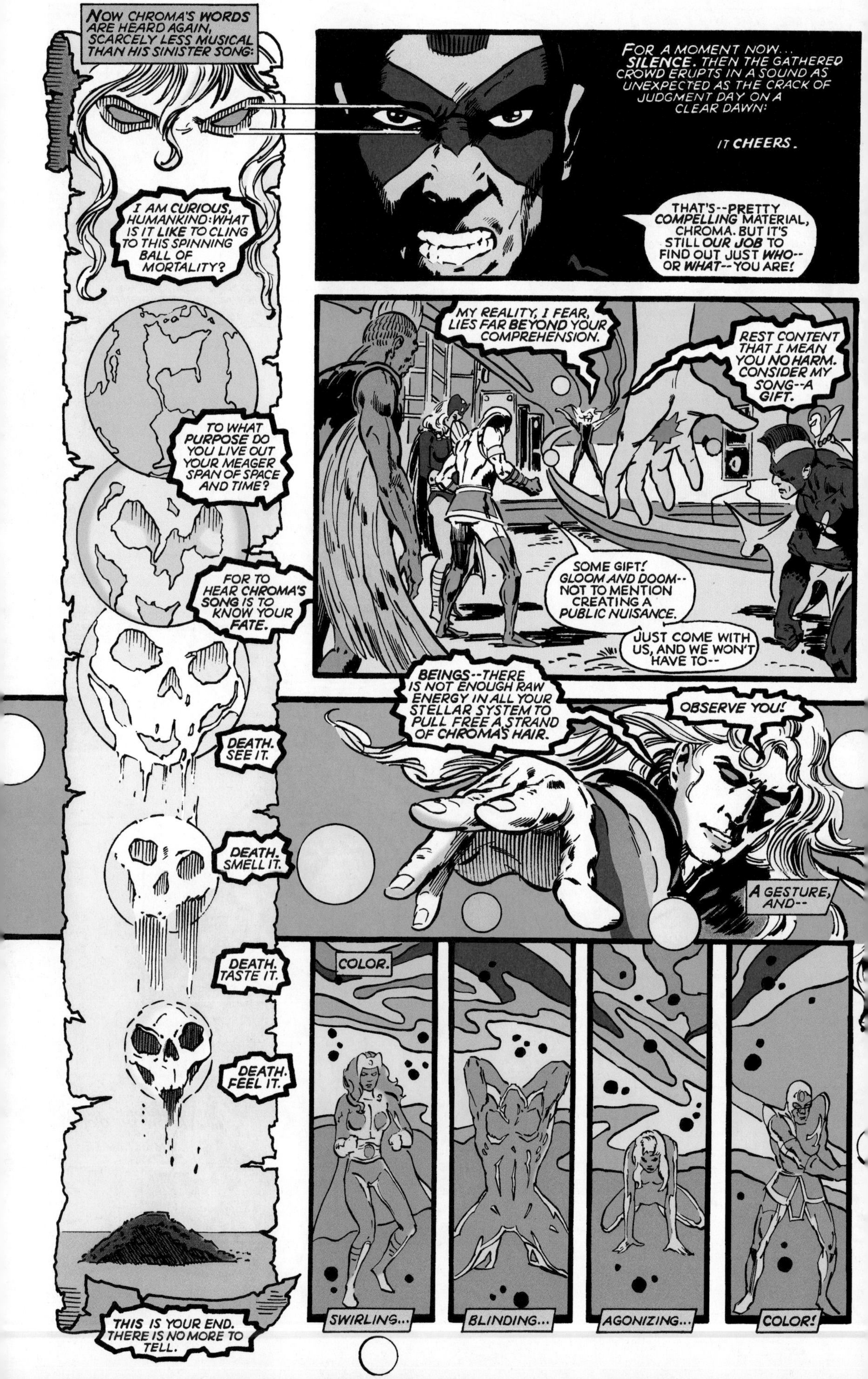

NOW CHROMA'S WORDS ARE HEARD AGAIN, SCARCELY LESS MUSICAL THAN HIS SINISTER SONG:
FOR A MOMENT NOW... SILENCE. THEN THE GATHERED CROWD ERUPTS IN A SOUND AS UNEXPECTED AS THE CRACK OF JUDGMENT DAY ON A CLEAR DAWN:
IT CHEERS.
I AM CURIOUS, HUMANKIND: WHAT IS IT LIKE TO CLING TO THIS SPINNING BALL OF MORTALITY?
THAT'S--PRETTY COMPELLING MATERIAL, CHROMA. BUT IT'S STILL OUR JOB TO FIND OUT JUST WHO-- OR WHAT--YOU ARE!
MY REALITY, I FEAR, LIES FAR BEYOND YOUR COMPREHENSION.
REST CONTENT THAT I MEAN YOU NO HARM. CONSIDER MY SONG--A GIFT.
TO WHAT PURPOSE DO YOU LIVE OUT YOUR MEAGER SPAN OF SPACE AND TIME?
SOME GIFT! GLOOM AND DOOM-- NOT TO MENTION CREATING A PUBLIC NUISANCE.
JUST COME WITH US, AND WE WON'T HAVE TO--
FOR TO HEAR CHROMA'S SONG IS TO KNOW YOUR FATE.
BEINGS--THERE IS NOT ENOUGH RAW ENERGY IN ALL YOUR STELLAR SYSTEM TO PULL FREE A STRAND OF CHROMA'S HAIR.
OBSERVE YOU!
DEATH. SEE IT.
DEATH. SMELL IT.
A GESTURE, AND--
DEATH. TASTE IT.
COLOR.
DEATH. FEEL IT.
SWIRLING...
BLINDING...
AGONIZING...
COLOR!
THIS IS YOUR END. THERE IS NO MORE TO TELL.

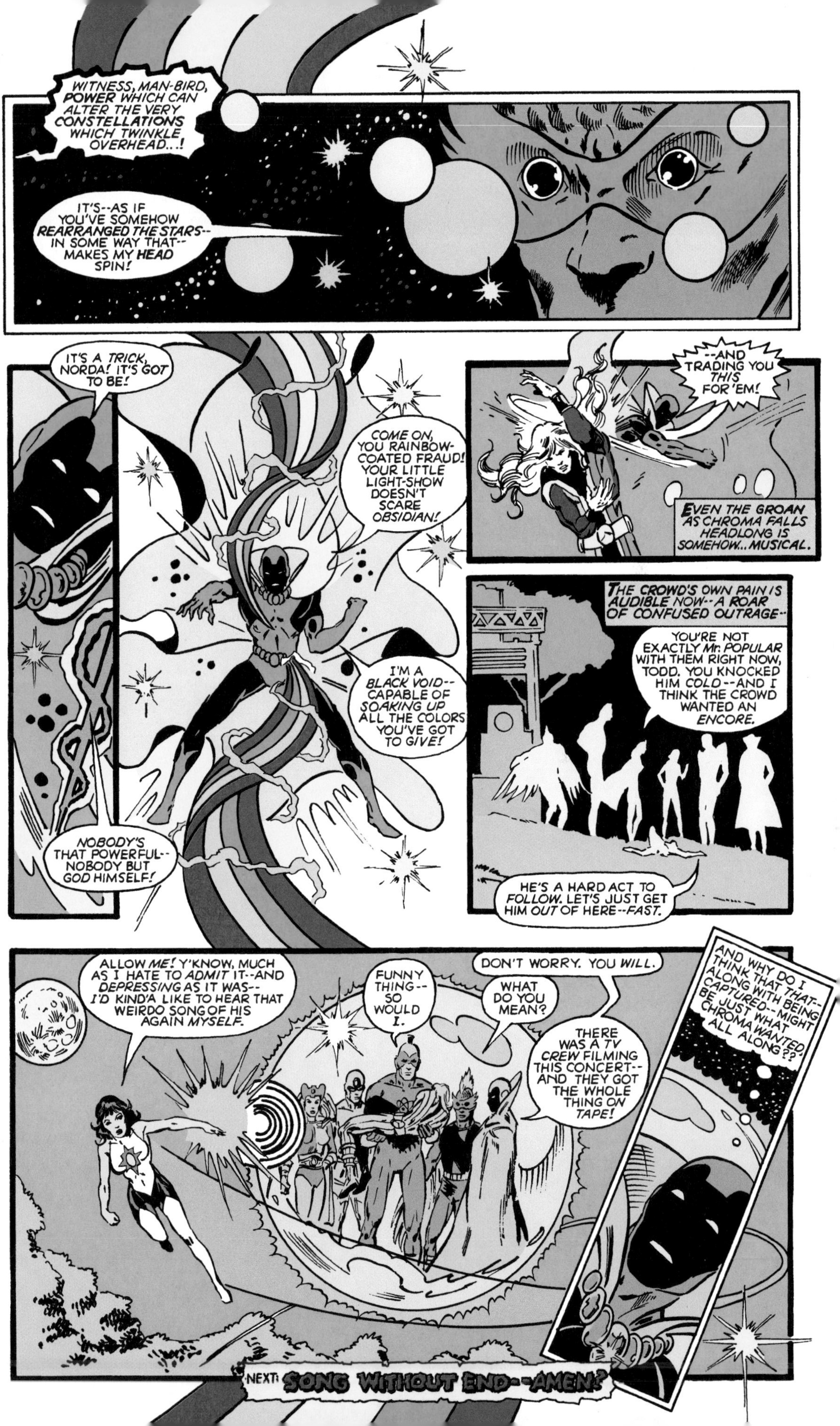
WITNESS, MAN-BIRD, POWER WHICH CAN ALTER THE VERY CONSTELLATIONS WHICH TWINKLE OVERHEAD...!
IT'S--AS IF YOU'VE SOMEHOW REARRANGED THE STARS--IN SOME WAY THAT--MAKES MY HEAD SPIN!
IT'S A TRICK, NORDA! IT'S GOT TO BE!
COME ON, YOU RAINBOW-COATED FRAUD! YOUR LITTLE LIGHT-SHOW DOESN'T SCARE OBSIDIAN!
I'M A BLACK VOID--CAPABLE OF SOAKING UP ALL THE COLORS YOU'VE GOT TO GIVE!
NOBODY'S THAT POWERFUL--NOBODY BUT GOD HIMSELF!
--AND TRADING YOU THIS FOR 'EM!
EVEN THE GROAN AS CHROMA FALLS HEADLONG IS SOMEHOW... MUSICAL.
THE CROWD'S OWN PAIN IS AUDIBLE NOW--A ROAR OF CONFUSED OUTRAGE--
YOU'RE NOT EXACTLY Mr. POPULAR WITH THEM RIGHT NOW, TODD. YOU KNOCKED HIM COLD--AND I THINK THE CROWD WANTED AN ENCORE.
HE'S A HARD ACT TO FOLLOW. LET'S JUST GET HIM OUT OF HERE--FAST.
ALLOW ME! Y'KNOW, MUCH AS I HATE TO ADMIT IT--AND DEPRESSING AS IT WAS--I'D KIND'A LIKE TO HEAR THAT WEIRDO SONG OF HIS AGAIN MYSELF.
FUNNY THING--SO WOULD I.
WHAT DO YOU MEAN?
DON'T WORRY. YOU WILL.
THERE WAS A TV CREW FILMING THIS CONCERT--AND THEY GOT THE WHOLE THING ON TAPE!
AND WHY DO I THINK THAT THAT--ALONG WITH BEING CAPTURED--MIGHT BE JUST WHAT CHROMA WANTED ALL ALONG??
NEXT: SONG WITHOUT END--AMEN?

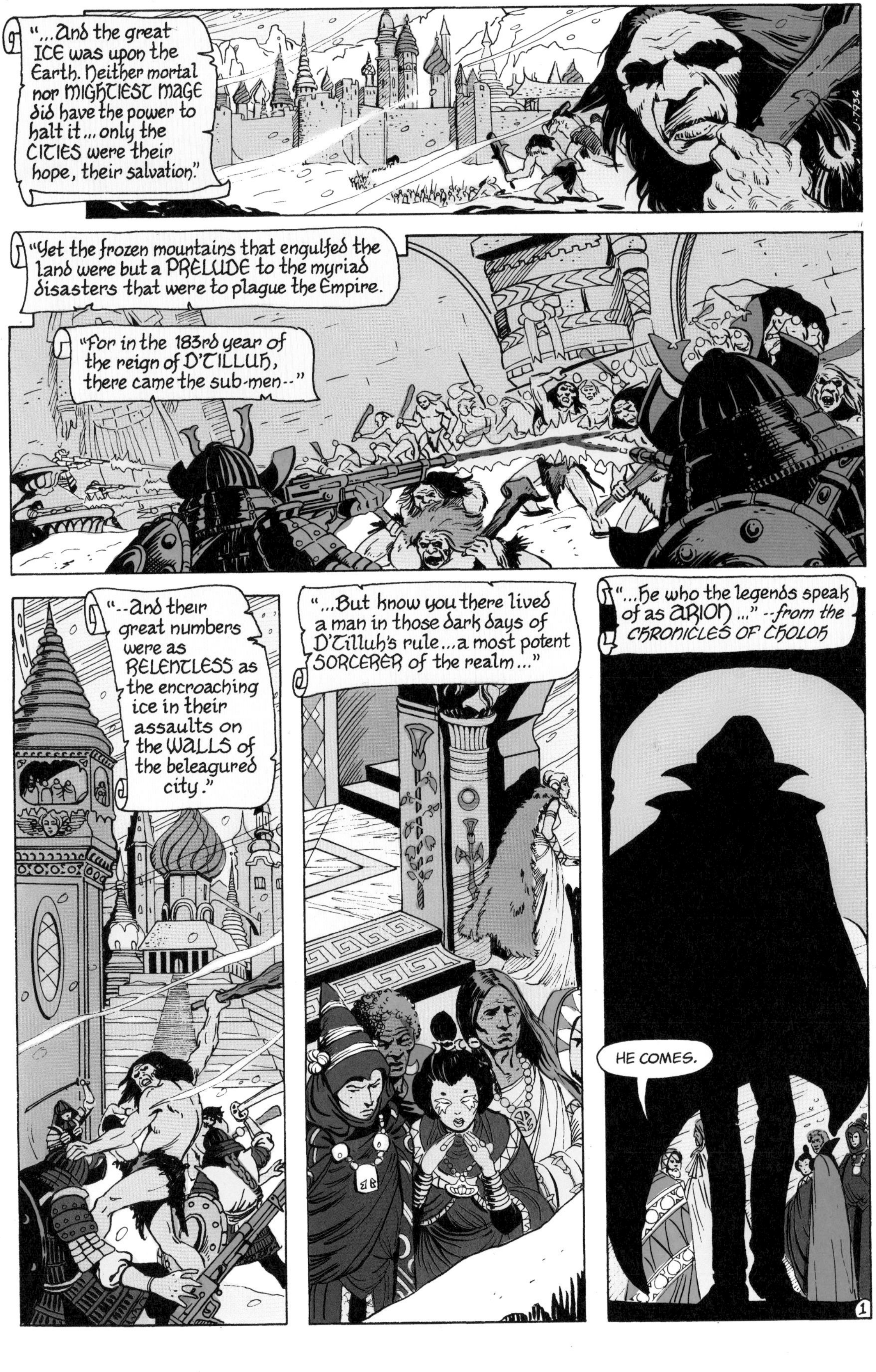
"...And the great ICE was upon the Earth. Neither mortal nor MIGHTIEST MAGE did have the power to halt it... only the CITIES were their hope, their salvation."
"Yet the frozen mountains that engulfed the land were but a PRELUDE to the myriad disasters that were to plague the Empire.
"For in the 183rd year of the reign of D'TILLUH, there came the sub-men--"
"--And their great numbers were as RELENTLESS as the encroaching ice in their assaults on the WALLS of the beleagured city."
"...But know you there lived a man in those dark days of D'Tilluh's rule...a most potent SORCERER of the realm..."
"...He who the legends speak of as ARION..." --from the CHRONICLES OF CHOLOH
HE COMES.
1

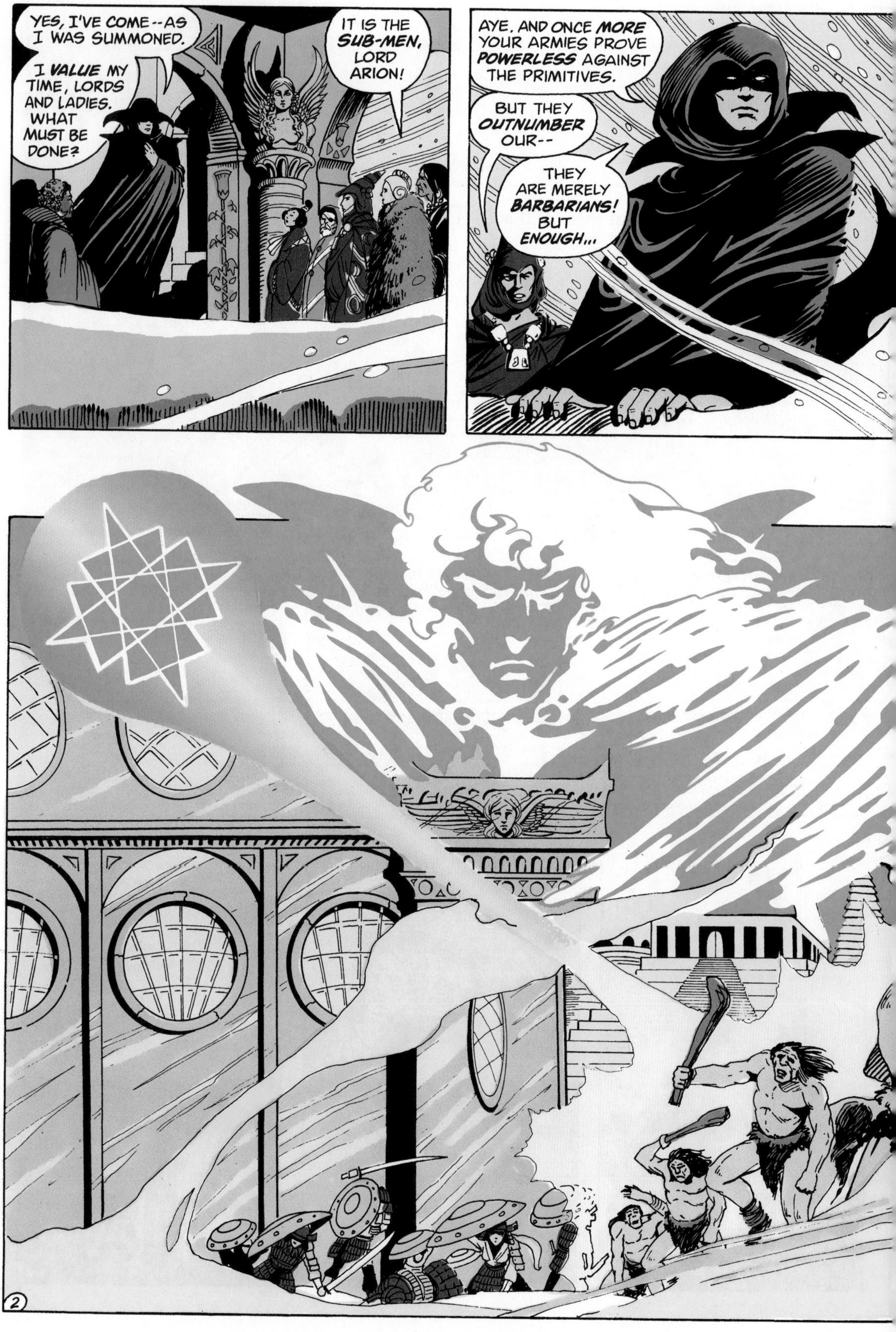
YES, I'VE COME--AS I WAS SUMMONED.
I VALUE MY TIME, LORDS AND LADIES. WHAT MUST BE DONE?
IT IS THE SUB-MEN, LORD ARION!
AYE. AND ONCE MORE YOUR ARMIES PROVE POWERLESS AGAINST THE PRIMITIVES.
BUT THEY OUTNUMBER OUR--
THEY ARE MERELY BARBARIANS! BUT ENOUGH...
2

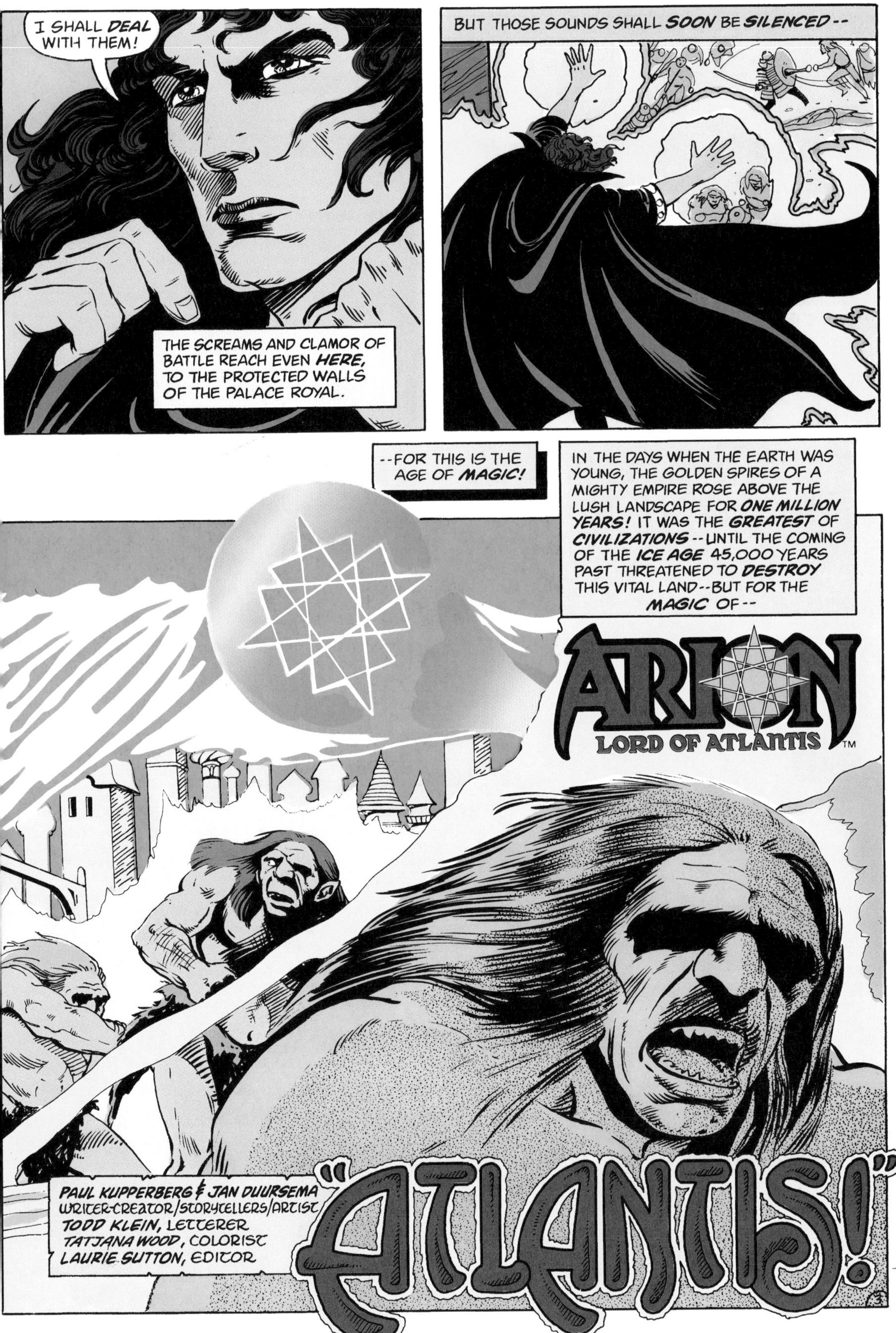
I SHALL DEAL WITH THEM!
THE SCREAMS AND CLAMOR OF BATTLE REACH EVEN HERE, TO THE PROTECTED WALLS OF THE PALACE ROYAL.
BUT THOSE SOUNDS SHALL SOON BE SILENCED--
--FOR THIS IS THE AGE OF MAGIC!
IN THE DAYS WHEN THE EARTH WAS YOUNG, THE GOLDEN SPIRES OF A MIGHTY EMPIRE ROSE ABOVE THE LUSH LANDSCAPE FOR ONE MILLION YEARS! IT WAS THE GREATEST OF CIVILIZATIONS--UNTIL THE COMING OF THE ICE AGE 45,000 YEARS PAST THREATENED TO DESTROY THIS VITAL LAND--BUT FOR THE MAGIC OF--
ARION LORD OF ATLANTIS™
PAUL KUPPERBERG & JAN DUURSEMA
WRITER-CREATOR/STORYTELLERS/ARTIST
TODD KLEIN, LETTERER
TATJANA WOOD, COLORIST
LAURIE SUTTON, EDITOR
"ATLANTIS!"

THEY COME SEEKING THE *WARMTH* OF THE CITY--YET THEY HAVE *FELT* THE STING OF THIS MAGIC *BEFORE*...

...AND THEY HAVE LEARNED TO FEAR ITS *SEARING TOUCH* FAR MORE THAN THE *ICE* BEYOND THESE WALLS!

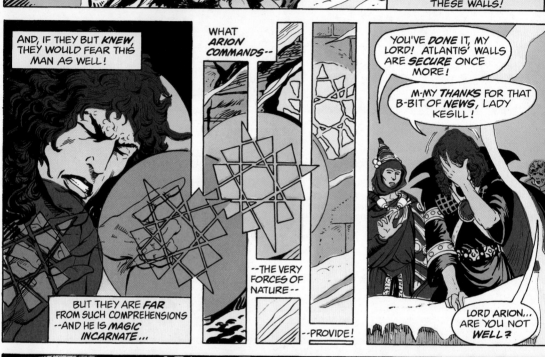

AND, IF THEY BUT *KNEW,* THEY WOULD FEAR THIS MAN AS WELL!

WHAT *ARION COMMANDS*--

--THE VERY FORCES OF NATURE--

--PROVIDE!

BUT THEY ARE *FAR* FROM SUCH COMPREHENSIONS --AND HE IS *MAGIC INCARNATE*...

YOU'VE *DONE* IT, MY LORD! ATLANTIS' WALLS ARE *SECURE* ONCE MORE!

M-MY *THANKS* FOR THAT B-BIT OF *NEWS,* LADY KESILL!

LORD ARION... ARE YOU NOT *WELL?*

N-NO!

NOW, LEAVE ME *BE!* IT'S YOUR CEASELESS *PRATTLING* THAT DRIVES ME TO THE *PEACE* OF MY CHAMBERS, FOOL!

HE IS *LORD HIGH MAGE* OF ATLANTIS--SECOND TO *NONE* SAVE HIS KING...A MAN WHOSE *ARROGANT* AFFRONTS ARE SUFFERED IN RESENTFUL *SILENCE.*

ARION DOES NOT *CARE.* INDEED, THE SORCERER'S THOUGHTS ARE OF FAR MORE *WEIGHTY* CONCERNS--

FOR THE *FIRST* TIME IN HIS LIFE--*ARION KNOWS FEAR!*

DEEDRA'S CHAIN... *NEVER* HAVE MY SPELLS WEAKENED ME SO!

4

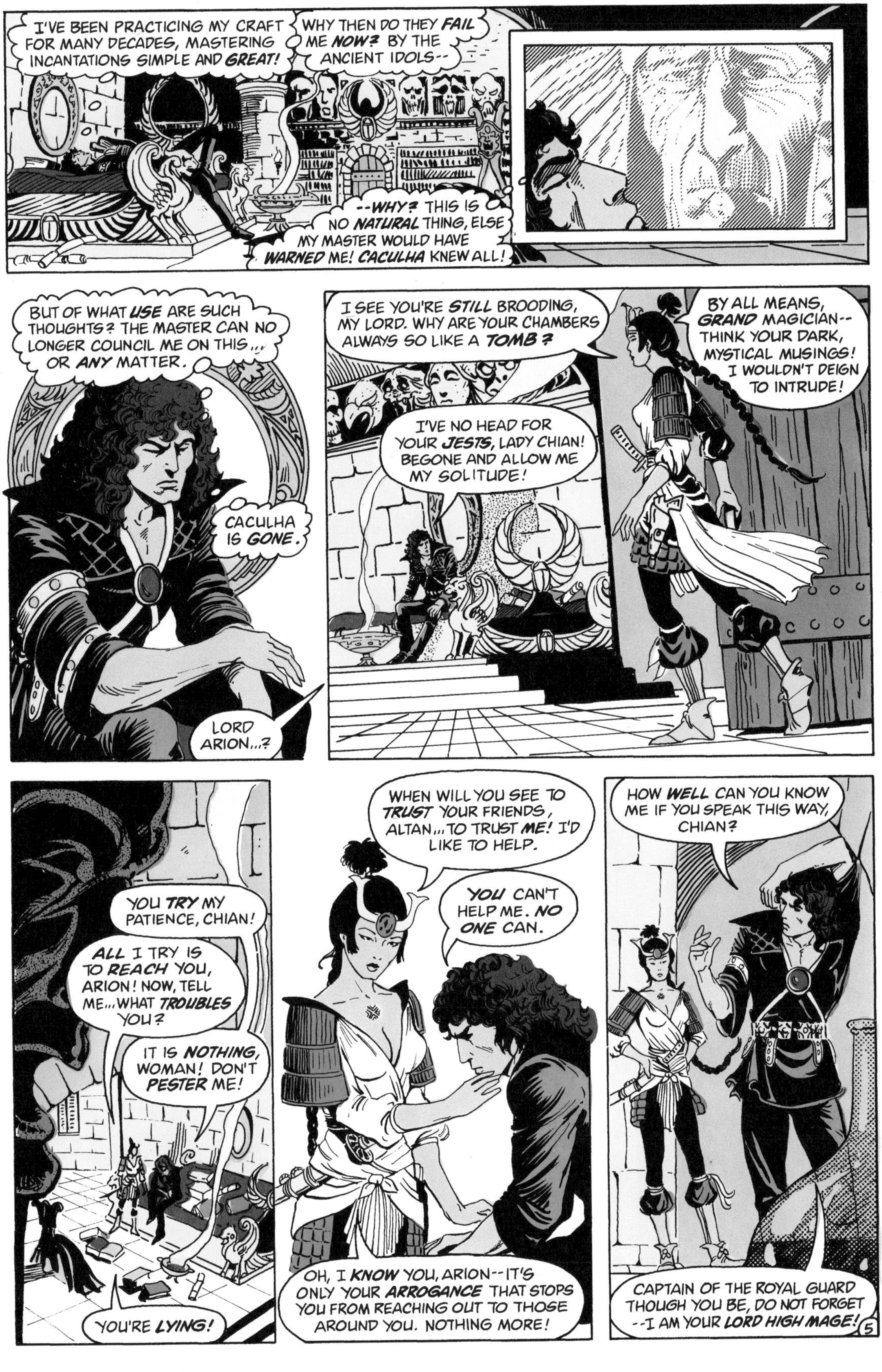

I'VE BEEN PRACTICING MY CRAFT FOR MANY DECADES, MASTERING INCANTATIONS SIMPLE AND GREAT!
WHY THEN DO THEY FAIL ME NOW? BY THE ANCIENT IDOLS--
--WHY? THIS IS NO NATURAL THING, ELSE MY MASTER WOULD HAVE WARNED ME! CACULHA KNEW ALL!
BUT OF WHAT USE ARE SUCH THOUGHTS? THE MASTER CAN NO LONGER COUNCIL ME ON THIS... OR ANY MATTER.
CACULHA IS GONE.
LORD ARION...?
I SEE YOU'RE STILL BROODING, MY LORD. WHY ARE YOUR CHAMBERS ALWAYS SO LIKE A TOMB?
I'VE NO HEAD FOR YOUR JESTS, LADY CHIAN! BEGONE AND ALLOW ME MY SOLITUDE!
BY ALL MEANS, GRAND MAGICIAN-- THINK YOUR DARK, MYSTICAL MUSINGS! I WOULDN'T DEIGN TO INTRUDE!
YOU TRY MY PATIENCE, CHIAN!
ALL I TRY IS TO REACH YOU, ARION! NOW, TELL ME... WHAT TROUBLES YOU?
IT IS NOTHING, WOMAN! DON'T PESTER ME!
YOU'RE LYING!
WHEN WILL YOU SEE TO TRUST YOUR FRIENDS, ALTAN... TO TRUST ME! I'D LIKE TO HELP.
YOU CAN'T HELP ME. NO ONE CAN.
OH, I KNOW YOU, ARION--IT'S ONLY YOUR ARROGANCE THAT STOPS YOU FROM REACHING OUT TO THOSE AROUND YOU. NOTHING MORE!
HOW WELL CAN YOU KNOW ME IF YOU SPEAK THIS WAY, CHIAN?
CAPTAIN OF THE ROYAL GUARD THOUGH YOU BE, DO NOT FORGET --I AM YOUR LORD HIGH MAGE!
5

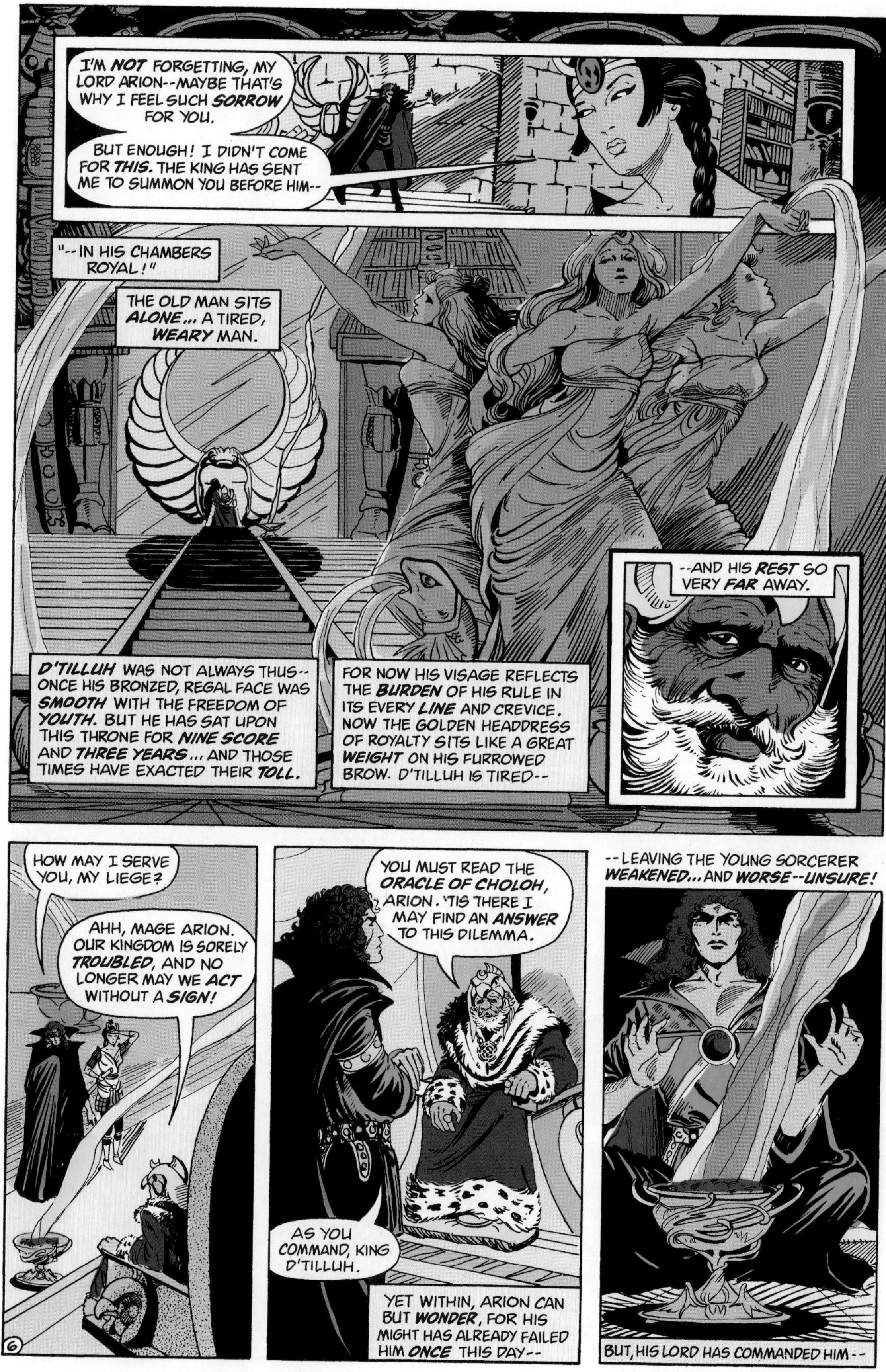

I'M NOT FORGETTING, MY LORD ARION--MAYBE THAT'S WHY I FEEL SUCH SORROW FOR YOU.
BUT ENOUGH! I DIDN'T COME FOR THIS. THE KING HAS SENT ME TO SUMMON YOU BEFORE HIM--
"--IN HIS CHAMBERS ROYAL!"
THE OLD MAN SITS ALONE... A TIRED, WEARY MAN.
D'TILLUH WAS NOT ALWAYS THUS--ONCE HIS BRONZED, REGAL FACE WAS SMOOTH WITH THE FREEDOM OF YOUTH. BUT HE HAS SAT UPON THIS THRONE FOR NINE SCORE AND THREE YEARS... AND THOSE TIMES HAVE EXACTED THEIR TOLL.
FOR NOW HIS VISAGE REFLECTS THE BURDEN OF HIS RULE IN ITS EVERY LINE AND CREVICE. NOW THE GOLDEN HEADDRESS OF ROYALTY SITS LIKE A GREAT WEIGHT ON HIS FURROWED BROW. D'TILLUH IS TIRED--
--AND HIS REST SO VERY FAR AWAY.
HOW MAY I SERVE YOU, MY LIEGE?
AHH, MAGE ARION. OUR KINGDOM IS SORELY TROUBLED, AND NO LONGER MAY WE ACT WITHOUT A SIGN!
6
YOU MUST READ THE ORACLE OF CHOLOH, ARION. 'TIS THERE I MAY FIND AN ANSWER TO THIS DILEMMA.
AS YOU COMMAND, KING D'TILLUH.
YET WITHIN, ARION CAN BUT WONDER, FOR HIS MIGHT HAS ALREADY FAILED HIM ONCE THIS DAY--
--LEAVING THE YOUNG SORCERER WEAKENED... AND WORSE--UNSURE!
BUT, HIS LORD HAS COMMANDED HIM--

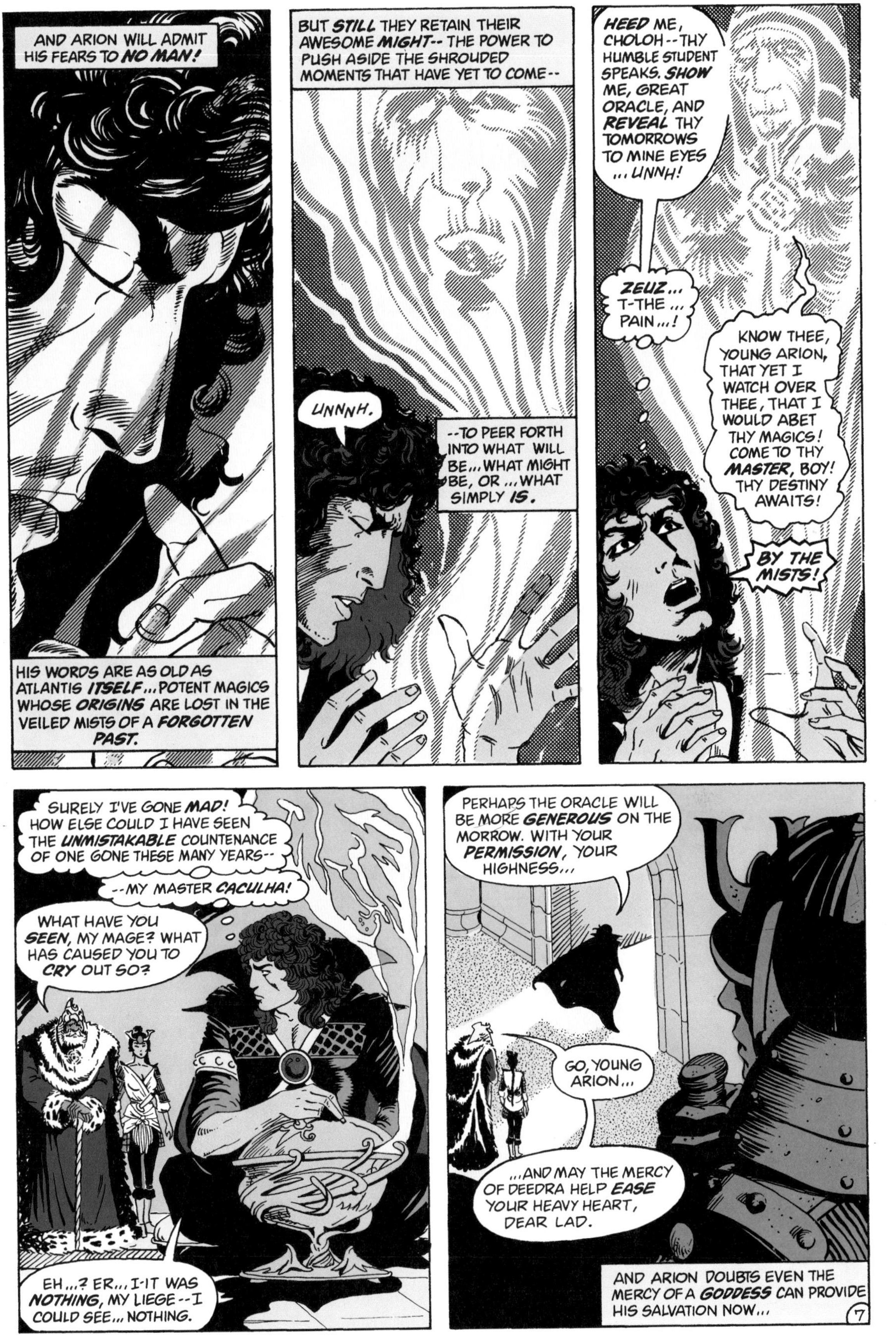
AND ARION WILL ADMIT HIS FEARS TO NO MAN!
HIS WORDS ARE AS OLD AS ATLANTIS ITSELF... POTENT MAGICS WHOSE ORIGINS ARE LOST IN THE VEILED MISTS OF A FORGOTTEN PAST.
BUT STILL THEY RETAIN THEIR AWESOME MIGHT-- THE POWER TO PUSH ASIDE THE SHROUDED MOMENTS THAT HAVE YET TO COME--
UNNNH.
--TO PEER FORTH INTO WHAT WILL BE... WHAT MIGHT BE, OR ... WHAT SIMPLY IS.
HEED ME, CHOLOH--THY HUMBLE STUDENT SPEAKS. SHOW ME, GREAT ORACLE, AND REVEAL THY TOMORROWS TO MINE EYES ...UNNH!
ZEUZ... T-THE... PAIN...!
KNOW THEE, YOUNG ARION, THAT YET I WATCH OVER THEE, THAT I WOULD ABET THY MAGICS! COME TO THY MASTER, BOY! THY DESTINY AWAITS!
BY THE MISTS!
SURELY I'VE GONE MAD! HOW ELSE COULD I HAVE SEEN THE UNMISTAKABLE COUNTENANCE OF ONE GONE THESE MANY YEARS--
--MY MASTER CACULHA!
WHAT HAVE YOU SEEN, MY MAGE? WHAT HAS CAUSED YOU TO CRY OUT SO?
EH...? ER... I-IT WAS NOTHING, MY LIEGE--I COULD SEE... NOTHING.
PERHAPS THE ORACLE WILL BE MORE GENEROUS ON THE MORROW. WITH YOUR PERMISSION, YOUR HIGHNESS...
GO, YOUNG ARION...
...AND MAY THE MERCY OF DEEDRA HELP EASE YOUR HEAVY HEART, DEAR LAD.
AND ARION DOUBTS EVEN THE MERCY OF A GODDESS CAN PROVIDE HIS SALVATION NOW...
7

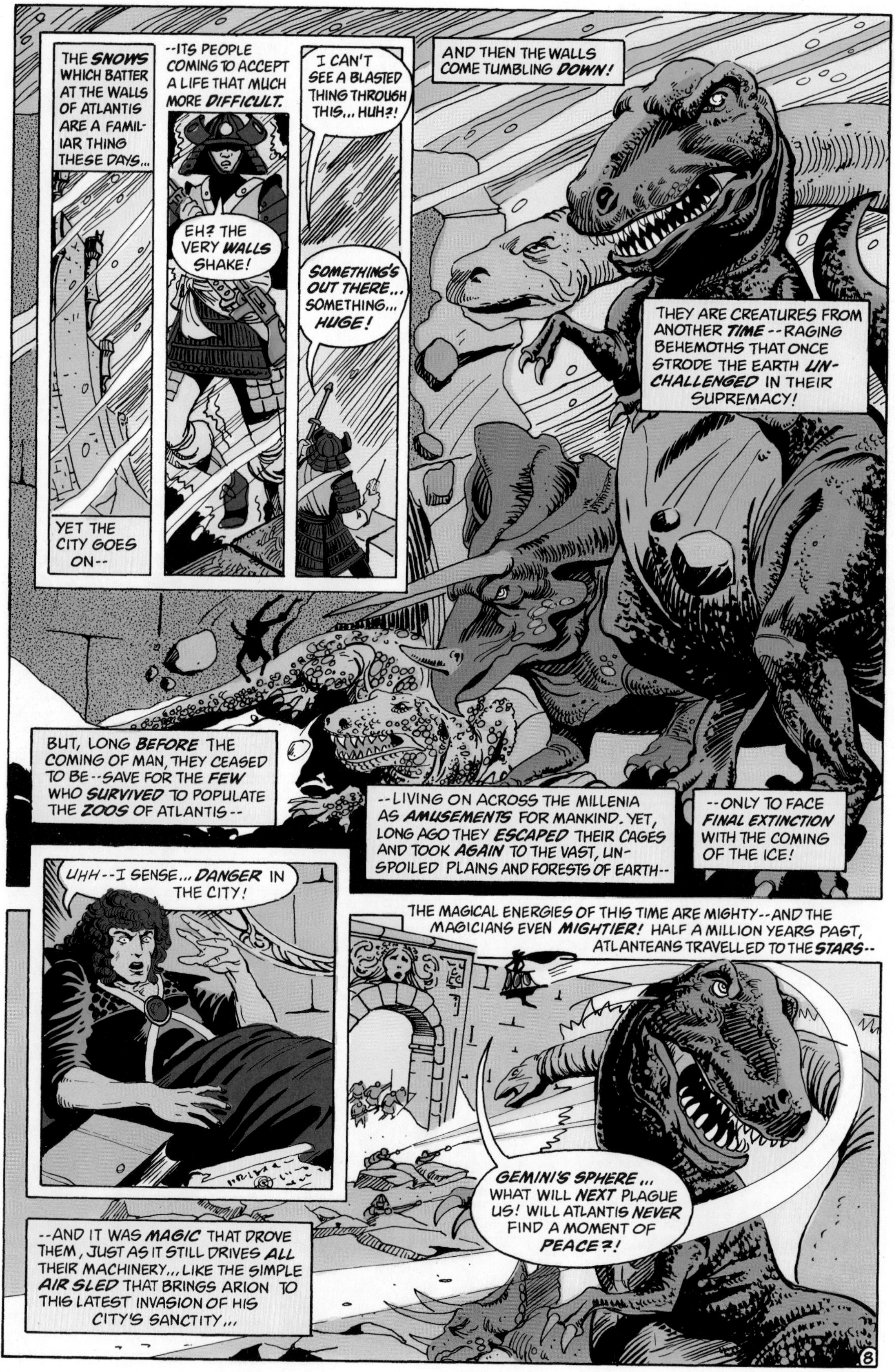

THE SNOWS WHICH BATTER AT THE WALLS OF ATLANTIS ARE A FAMILIAR THING THESE DAYS...
YET THE CITY GOES ON--
--ITS PEOPLE COMING TO ACCEPT A LIFE THAT MUCH MORE DIFFICULT.
EH? THE VERY WALLS SHAKE!
I CAN'T SEE A BLASTED THING THROUGH THIS... HUH?!
SOMETHING'S OUT THERE... SOMETHING... HUGE!
AND THEN THE WALLS COME TUMBLING DOWN!
THEY ARE CREATURES FROM ANOTHER TIME -- RAGING BEHEMOTHS THAT ONCE STRODE THE EARTH UNCHALLENGED IN THEIR SUPREMACY!
BUT, LONG BEFORE THE COMING OF MAN, THEY CEASED TO BE -- SAVE FOR THE FEW WHO SURVIVED TO POPULATE THE ZOOS OF ATLANTIS --
--LIVING ON ACROSS THE MILLENIA AS AMUSEMENTS FOR MANKIND. YET, LONG AGO THEY ESCAPED THEIR CAGES AND TOOK AGAIN TO THE VAST, UNSPOILED PLAINS AND FORESTS OF EARTH--
--ONLY TO FACE FINAL EXTINCTION WITH THE COMING OF THE ICE!
UHH -- I SENSE... DANGER IN THE CITY!
THE MAGICAL ENERGIES OF THIS TIME ARE MIGHTY -- AND THE MAGICIANS EVEN MIGHTIER! HALF A MILLION YEARS PAST, ATLANTEANS TRAVELLED TO THE STARS--
--AND IT WAS MAGIC THAT DROVE THEM, JUST AS IT STILL DRIVES ALL THEIR MACHINERY... LIKE THE SIMPLE AIR SLED THAT BRINGS ARION TO THIS LATEST INVASION OF HIS CITY'S SANCTITY...
GEMINI'S SPHERE... WHAT WILL NEXT PLAGUE US! WILL ATLANTIS NEVER FIND A MOMENT OF PEACE?!
8

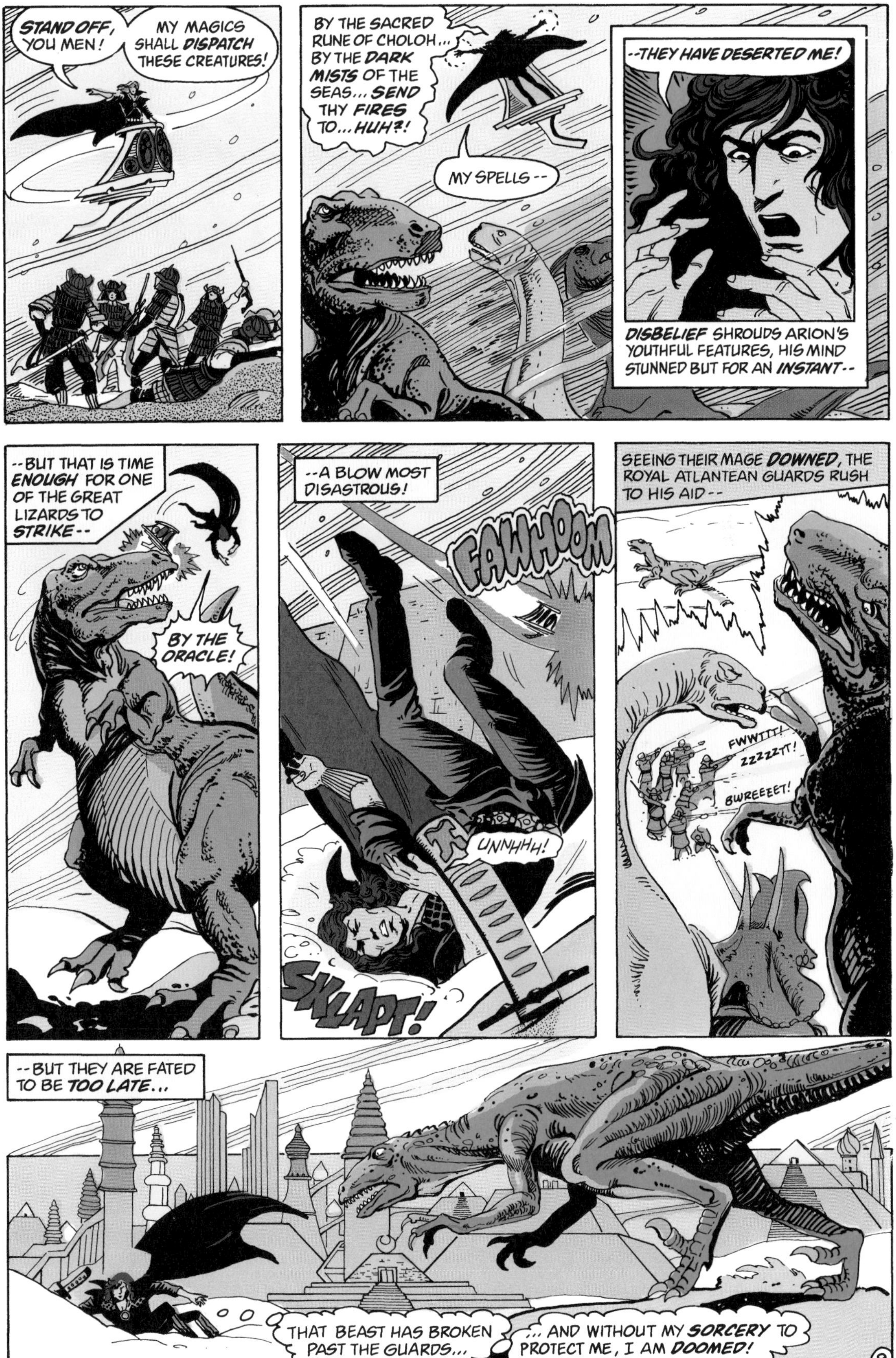
STAND OFF, YOU MEN!
MY MAGICS SHALL DISPATCH THESE CREATURES!
BY THE SACRED RUNE OF CHOLOH... BY THE DARK MISTS OF THE SEAS... SEND THY FIRES TO... HUH?!
MY SPELLS --
--THEY HAVE DESERTED ME!
DISBELIEF SHROUDS ARION'S YOUTHFUL FEATURES, HIS MIND STUNNED BUT FOR AN INSTANT --
-- BUT THAT IS TIME ENOUGH FOR ONE OF THE GREAT LIZARDS TO STRIKE --
BY THE ORACLE!
-- A BLOW MOST DISASTROUS!
FAWHOOM
UNNHHH!
SKLAPT!
SEEING THEIR MAGE DOWNED, THE ROYAL ATLANTEAN GUARDS RUSH TO HIS AID --
FWWITT!
ZZZZZTT!
BWREEEET!
-- BUT THEY ARE FATED TO BE TOO LATE...
THAT BEAST HAS BROKEN PAST THE GUARDS...
... AND WITHOUT MY SORCERY TO PROTECT ME, I AM DOOMED!
9

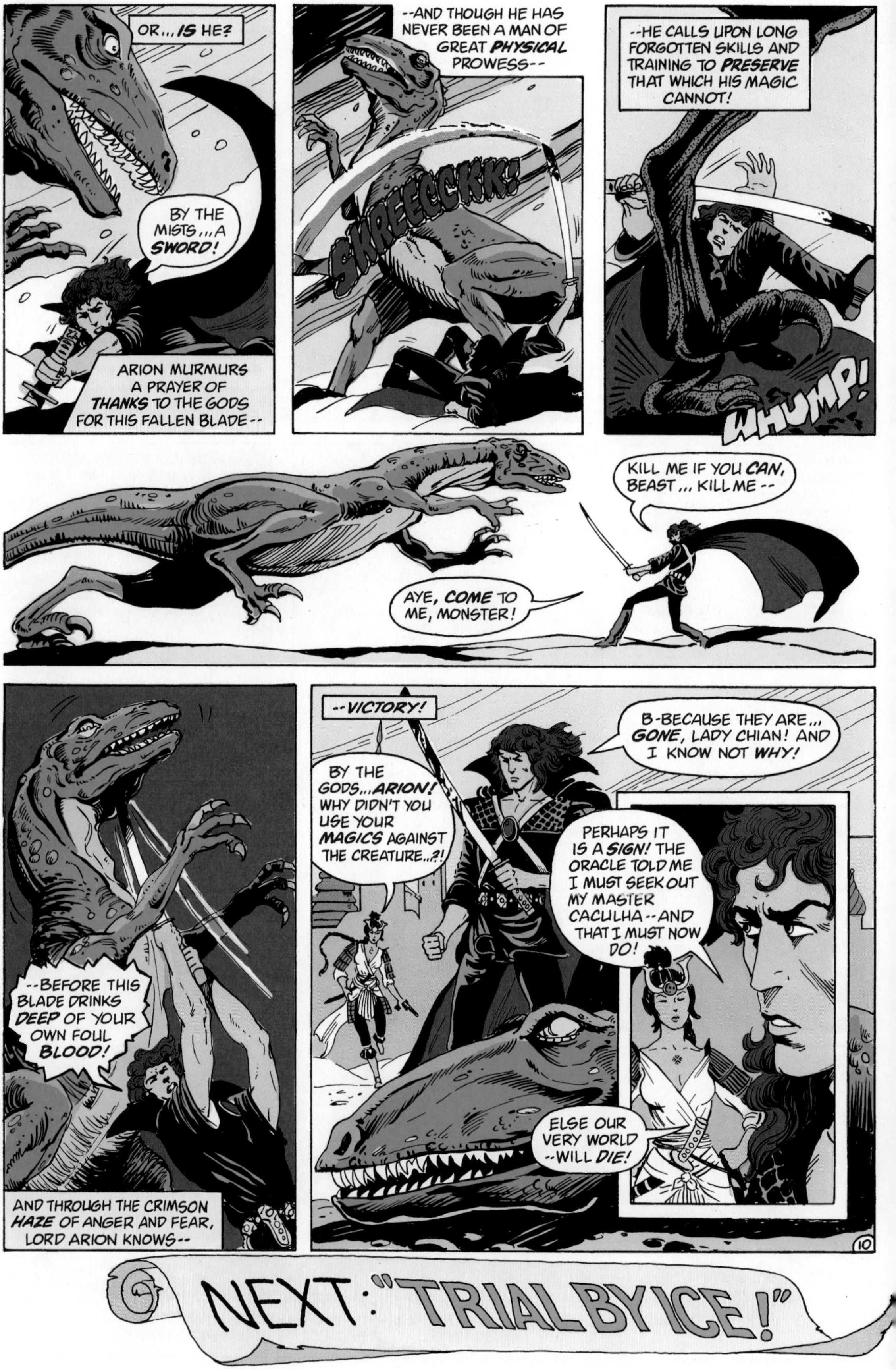
OR... IS HE?
BY THE MISTS... A SWORD!
ARION MURMURS A PRAYER OF THANKS TO THE GODS FOR THIS FALLEN BLADE--
--AND THOUGH HE HAS NEVER BEEN A MAN OF GREAT PHYSICAL PROWESS--
SKREEECCKK!
--HE CALLS UPON LONG FORGOTTEN SKILLS AND TRAINING TO PRESERVE THAT WHICH HIS MAGIC CANNOT!
WHUMP!
KILL ME IF YOU CAN, BEAST... KILL ME--
AYE, COME TO ME, MONSTER!
--BEFORE THIS BLADE DRINKS DEEP OF YOUR OWN FOUL BLOOD!
AND THROUGH THE CRIMSON HAZE OF ANGER AND FEAR, LORD ARION KNOWS--
--VICTORY!
BY THE GODS... ARION! WHY DIDN'T YOU USE YOUR MAGICS AGAINST THE CREATURE..?!
B-BECAUSE THEY ARE... GONE, LADY CHIAN! AND I KNOW NOT WHY!
PERHAPS IT IS A SIGN! THE ORACLE TOLD ME I MUST SEEK OUT MY MASTER CACULHA--AND THAT I MUST NOW DO!
ELSE OUR VERY WORLD --WILL DIE!
10
NEXT: "TRIAL BY ICE!"

I t was the '80s. The comic book readership was 95 percent boys and 5 percent girls. The popular American comic for girls was about a love triangle. The main characters, Archie, Betty, and Veronica, all came from intact families—each an only child with a married mother and father. (Betty had an older sister who later appeared in some comics, but I have no memory of her.) As a blossoming young girl, I read all about their lives under the covers at summer camp, my flashlight pointing at each eye-popping panel so as not to wake my bunkmates. Betty and Veronica are best friends for almost 80 years and they both love Archie. Archie loves both girls. *How can he choose?*

Jenette Kahn, president of DC Comics, wanted to do something different.

In the spring of 1984 I was walking through Central Park on my way to meet with Jenette. In my portfolio was *Ms. Liz*, the feminist greeting card line that I had started nine years earlier. *Ms. Liz* had blossomed from a greeting card to a comic strip in *Cosmopolitan* magazine and an animated feature on the *Today* show. But after trying to compete with Hallmark and getting a divorce from my husband/business partner, I was ready to do something different.

Stepping off the elevator I was greeted by a gigantic mural of the DC Universe. Wonder Woman was immersed in a sea of Super Men. It couldn't have been easy for Wonder Woman to be so outnumbered, and it made me wonder how a woman could possibly be president of DC Comics. As I passed by Superman, Batman, and the Flash, I suddenly realized that I knew nothing about this universe. What was I doing here anyway?

Jenette is a tall, red-haired, engaging woman, her office a pop art wonderland—brightly painted furniture, potted plants with large overflowing leaves, a huge plaque of Wonder Woman that sat just over her shoulder as if to remind her of her power. Jenette spoke in an animated voice.

"I want to capture the girl market! Girls should be reading comics!"

Jenette had seen *Ms. Liz* on the *Today* show and wanted to know if I was interested in creating a character for DC Comics. Ms. Liz was not an option because DC owned all their characters. My answer was a resounding, *Yes!*

"Great!" she exclaimed. "But first I have to show *Ms. Liz* to my six executives."

I left my portfolio and skipped through Central Park feeling hopeful. The next day Jenette called with great news. *"They all love* Ms. Liz*!"* (Shout-out to Mike Gold, who I later learned was my biggest fan.)

Creating *Angel Love* was like going to graduate school at DC Comics. My lessons began when Jenette handed me the Lois Lane bible. *A character bible is everything you need to know about the character.* My homework was to do one.

I followed Jenette down the long hallway to meet my first professional editor, Karen Berger. "Hello, Barbara," she said sweetly—thin, small, with a surprisingly deep voice for such a little woman. Karen twirled her long blonde curls as she welcomed me into the DC Universe. I wondered how such a sweet being became an editor in this Super-Male Universe.

I was riding high on cloud nine as I sailed through Central Park. I would be working with two Wonder Women at DC Comics. Our mission? To conquer the ever-elusive girl market.

The only things I knew about Lois Lane were that she was Superman's girlfriend and a reporter. Back at the apartment I began reading page after page of everything I could possibly want to know—raised on a farm by Sam and Ella Lane, studied journalism with a fine arts minor, persistent, streetwise, energetic. Favorite movie? *Gone with the Wind*. I got to know the *real* Lois Lane.

I began writing everything there was to know about *Angel Love*—and more. It was about a girl who gets on a Greyhound bus...a small-town girl coming to NYC to become an artist. *I knew that girl.* Fifteen years earlier I was that girl on the bus. I remembered feeling every emotion—happy sad terrified excited hopeful hopeless. I could close my eyes and be back on that Greyhound in an instant.

Living in New York City was a boon! All I had to do was open my apartment door and inspiration was everywhere—styles, trends, an old man riding a bicycle with a parrot on his head. Walking one city block was enough to fill a sketchbook of ideas about Angel—short red, spiked hair, green eyes, three pierced hearts for earrings on one ear and a changeable earring on the other.

Karen approved the *Angel Love* bible and the drawings. *That was easy!* She gave me my next assignment—to write a script.

Angel and I collaborated and felt confident about our 24-page script with quick layouts. I dropped it off at Karen's office, and a few days later she called to tell me that wasn't what they were looking for. I could picture sweet Karen twirling her curls as she broke the news. By my third rejected script, Karen was visibly sad. I would have liked to console her except I was feeling so sorry for myself I had nothing to give. Karen counseled me. "Jenette said, 'Not this but…'" (Having worked with many editors over the years, I know that when an editor says "not this but" the editor is giving you a broad overview of what they want. It's a jumping-off point.) Karen continued, "Angel tries to put in her diaphragm, and it goes sailing across the room." That woke me up.

Jenette really wanted to try something different.

My graduate studies at DC Comics continued when Jenette summoned her two vice presidents, Paul Levitz and Dick Giordano, to teach me how to plot by color code. For over an hour I sat in wonder as they pointed on a huge whiteboard and lectured about how each character gets a color and the main plots go on top and the subplots underneath and that a subplot could be a main plot in issue four and by the time it was over, my head was spinning.

It was a gray day as I meandered through Central Park, ruminating how my comics career was over before it began when the heavens opened up. There was nothing but blue skies! Suddenly all the pieces fell into place. I rushed home and plotted 15 issues by color code.

Abortion, cocaine, cancer, sexual molestation was what I wrote about for the next year. I had no idea it would make such an impact. I was accused of trying to destroy the comic book industry. I got fan mail from abused kids. For some, I had to call their local authorities. Young girls wrote, "I am you, Angel" or "You are my only friend." Teachers from inner-city schools thanked me for creating a comic that their kids could relate to. *Comics Buyer's Guide*, the paper of the comics industry, printed the entire first issue!

One day Karen informed me that it was over. *It couldn't be!* I had so many subplots that needed to be brought to their conclusion. I pleaded with Jenette to let me finish the plots and subplots. She agreed to a 48-page special.

I really missed Angel. I was just getting started. I probably would have been writing about Angel Love to this day if I had been given the opportunity.

My graduate studies were over, but not before I fell madly and hopelessly in love…with comic books. I loved the way the cheap newsprint felt, the way the characters came alive on the pages and told a complete story yet "to be continued." I loved the colors that popped off the pages. I was hooked. My love affair with comics has lasted over four decades. I now teach how to do them and am currently writing my autobiography in graphic novel form. *It's about a girl who gets on a Greyhound bus…*

Barbara Slate
May 2020

Barbara Slate's first cartoon explored life as a young, single, upwardly mobile woman in New York. Her character, Ms. Liz, appeared in more than 20 animated shorts on NBC's Today, *as well as comic strips in* Cosmopolitan, Glamour, New Woman, Working Woman, *and* Self *magazines, and on greeting cards, mugs, and apparel. Ms. Slate then turned her attention to comics, where she created DC's* Angel Love *and Marvel's* Yuppies From Hell *and* Sweet XVI. *In addition to her own original characters, she has written stories for* Barbie, Beauty and the Beast, *and* Betty and Veronica. *Her latest graphic novel is* Getting Married and Other Mistakes *and she is currently working on her autobiography,* A Comic Life. *Slate teaches sequential art at Montclair State University, libraries, and schools using her critically acclaimed textbook* You Can Do a Graphic Novel.

THE ROAD TO VERTIGO

The '80s also represented experiments in how to create comics and present them. The European "album" format (basically a 48-page paperback slightly larger than a sheet of printer paper,

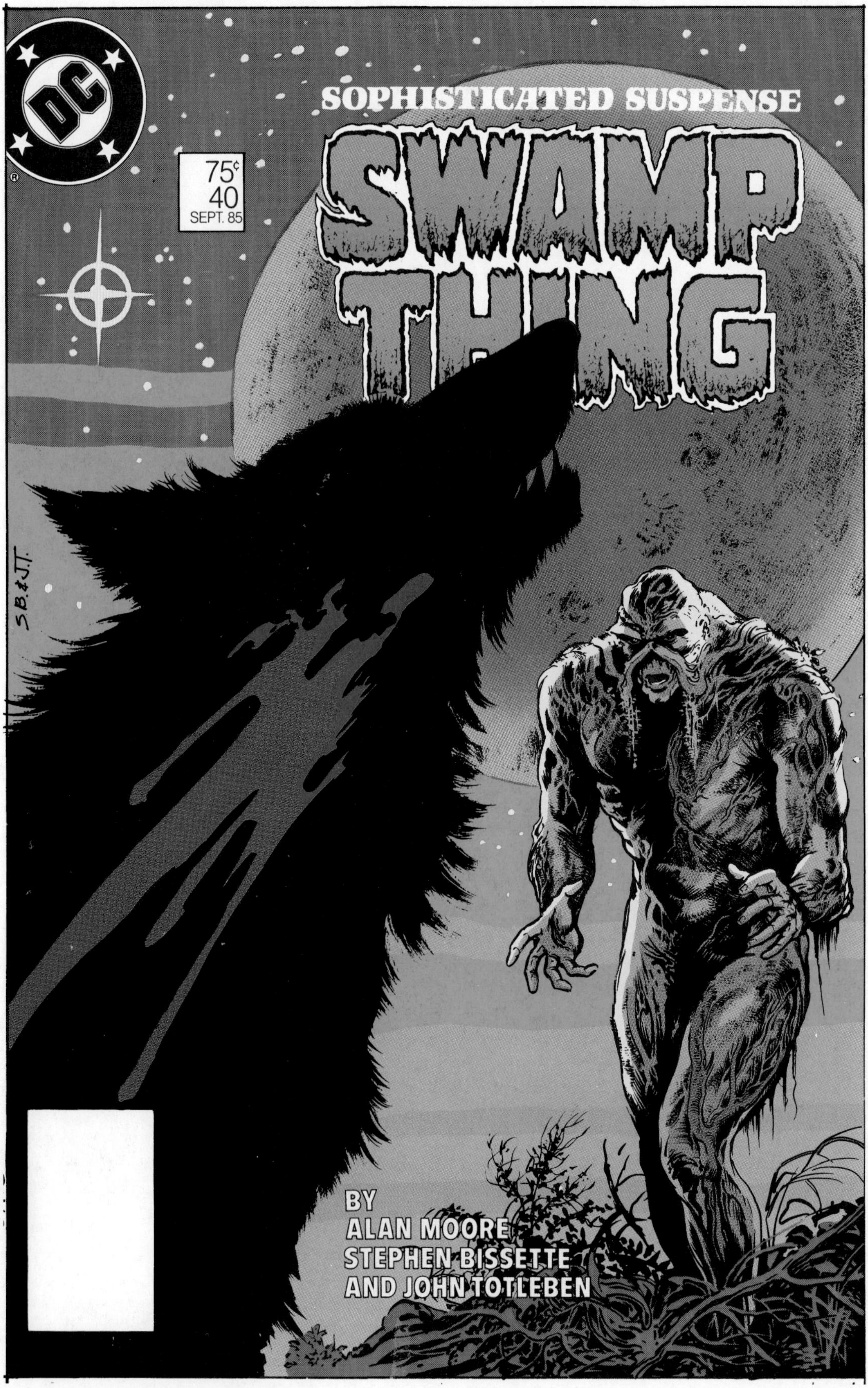
SOPHISTICATED SUSPENSE
SWAMP THING
75¢
40
SEPT. 85
DC
S.B. & J.T.
BY
ALAN MOORE
STEPHEN BISSETTE
AND JOHN TOTLEBEN

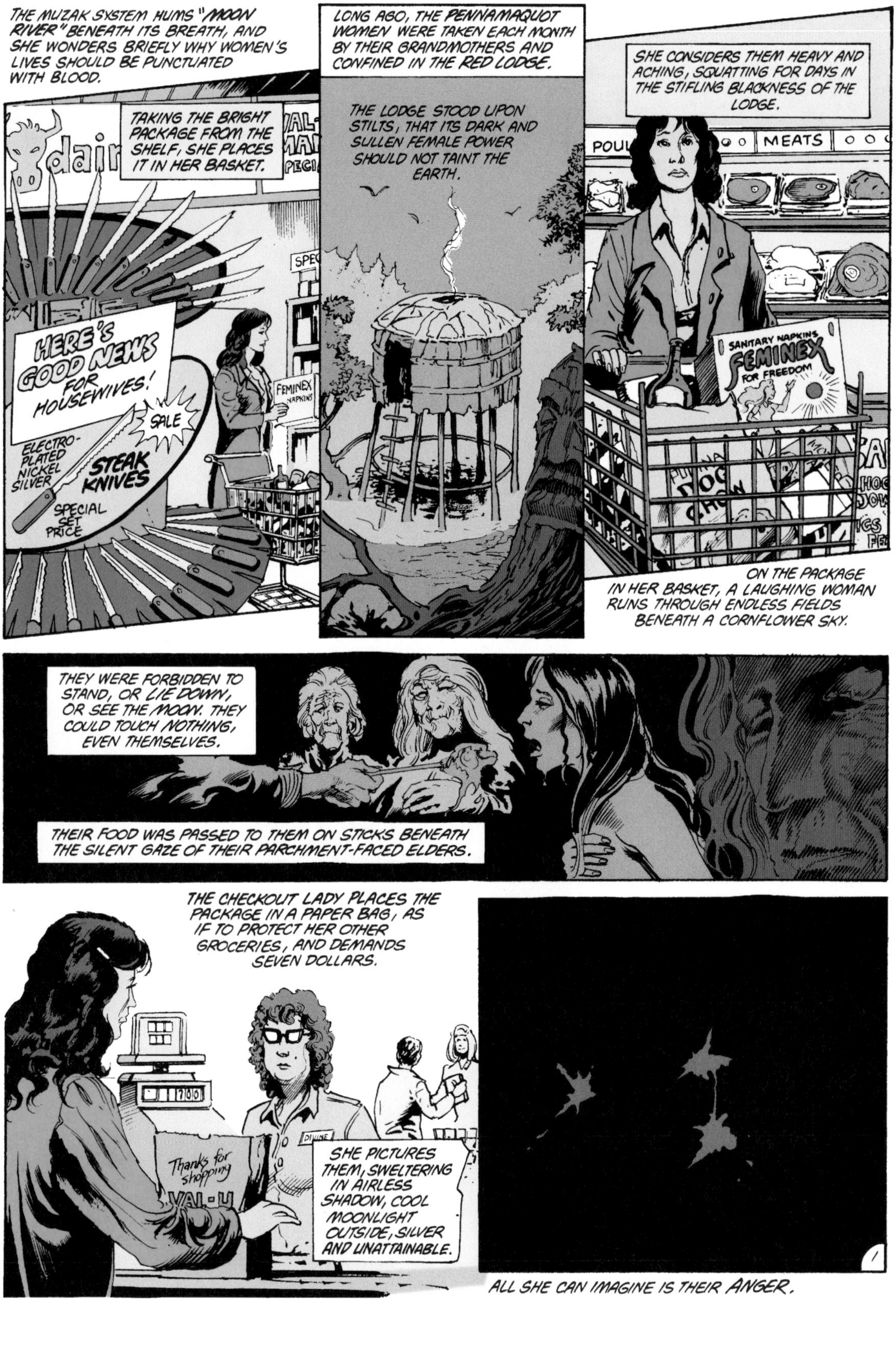

THE MUZAK SYSTEM HUMS "MOON RIVER" BENEATH ITS BREATH, AND SHE WONDERS BRIEFLY WHY WOMEN'S LIVES SHOULD BE PUNCTUATED WITH BLOOD.
TAKING THE BRIGHT PACKAGE FROM THE SHELF, SHE PLACES IT IN HER BASKET.
dair
HERE'S GOOD NEWS FOR HOUSEWIVES!
SALE
ELECTRO-PLATED NICKEL SILVER
STEAK KNIVES
SPECIAL SET PRICE
FEMINEX NAPKINS
LONG AGO, THE PENNAMAQUOT WOMEN WERE TAKEN EACH MONTH BY THEIR GRANDMOTHERS AND CONFINED IN THE RED LODGE.
THE LODGE STOOD UPON STILTS, THAT ITS DARK AND SULLEN FEMALE POWER SHOULD NOT TAINT THE EARTH.
SHE CONSIDERS THEM HEAVY AND ACHING, SQUATTING FOR DAYS IN THE STIFLING BLACKNESS OF THE LODGE.
MEATS
SANITARY NAPKINS FEMINEX FOR FREEDOM
ON THE PACKAGE IN HER BASKET, A LAUGHING WOMAN RUNS THROUGH ENDLESS FIELDS BENEATH A CORNFLOWER SKY.
THEY WERE FORBIDDEN TO STAND, OR LIE DOWN, OR SEE THE MOON. THEY COULD TOUCH NOTHING, EVEN THEMSELVES.
THEIR FOOD WAS PASSED TO THEM ON STICKS BENEATH THE SILENT GAZE OF THEIR PARCHMENT-FACED ELDERS.
THE CHECKOUT LADY PLACES THE PACKAGE IN A PAPER BAG, AS IF TO PROTECT HER OTHER GROCERIES, AND DEMANDS SEVEN DOLLARS.
Thanks for shopping VAL-U
SHE PICTURES THEM, SWELTERING IN AIRLESS SHADOW, COOL MOONLIGHT OUTSIDE, SILVER AND UNATTAINABLE.
1
ALL SHE CAN IMAGINE IS THEIR ANGER.

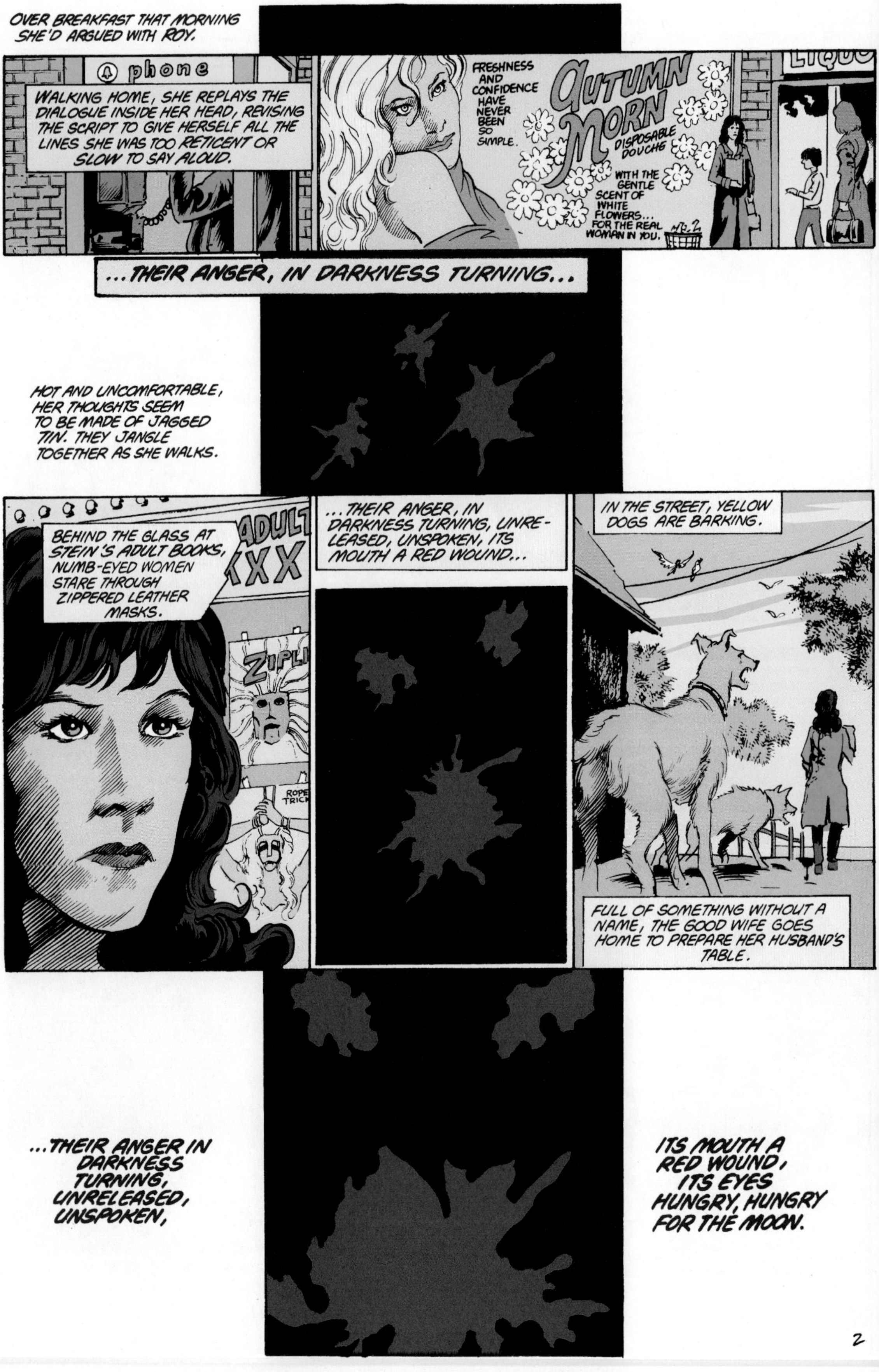
OVER BREAKFAST THAT MORNING SHE'D ARGUED WITH ROY.
phone
WALKING HOME, SHE REPLAYS THE DIALOGUE INSIDE HER HEAD, REVISING THE SCRIPT TO GIVE HERSELF ALL THE LINES SHE WAS TOO RETICENT OR SLOW TO SAY ALOUD.
FRESHNESS AND CONFIDENCE HAVE NEVER BEEN SO SIMPLE.
AUTUMN MORN
DISPOSABLE DOUCHE
WITH THE GENTLE SCENT OF WHITE FLOWERS... FOR THE REAL WOMAN IN YOU.
...THEIR ANGER, IN DARKNESS TURNING...
HOT AND UNCOMFORTABLE, HER THOUGHTS SEEM TO BE MADE OF JAGGED TIN. THEY JANGLE TOGETHER AS SHE WALKS.
ADULT
XXX
BEHIND THE GLASS AT STEIN'S ADULT BOOKS, NUMB-EYED WOMEN STARE THROUGH ZIPPERED LEATHER MASKS.
...THEIR ANGER, IN DARKNESS TURNING, UNRELEASED, UNSPOKEN, ITS MOUTH A RED WOUND...
IN THE STREET, YELLOW DOGS ARE BARKING.
FULL OF SOMETHING WITHOUT A NAME, THE GOOD WIFE GOES HOME TO PREPARE HER HUSBAND'S TABLE.
...THEIR ANGER IN DARKNESS TURNING, UNRELEASED, UNSPOKEN,
ITS MOUTH A RED WOUND, ITS EYES HUNGRY, HUNGRY FOR THE MOON.
2

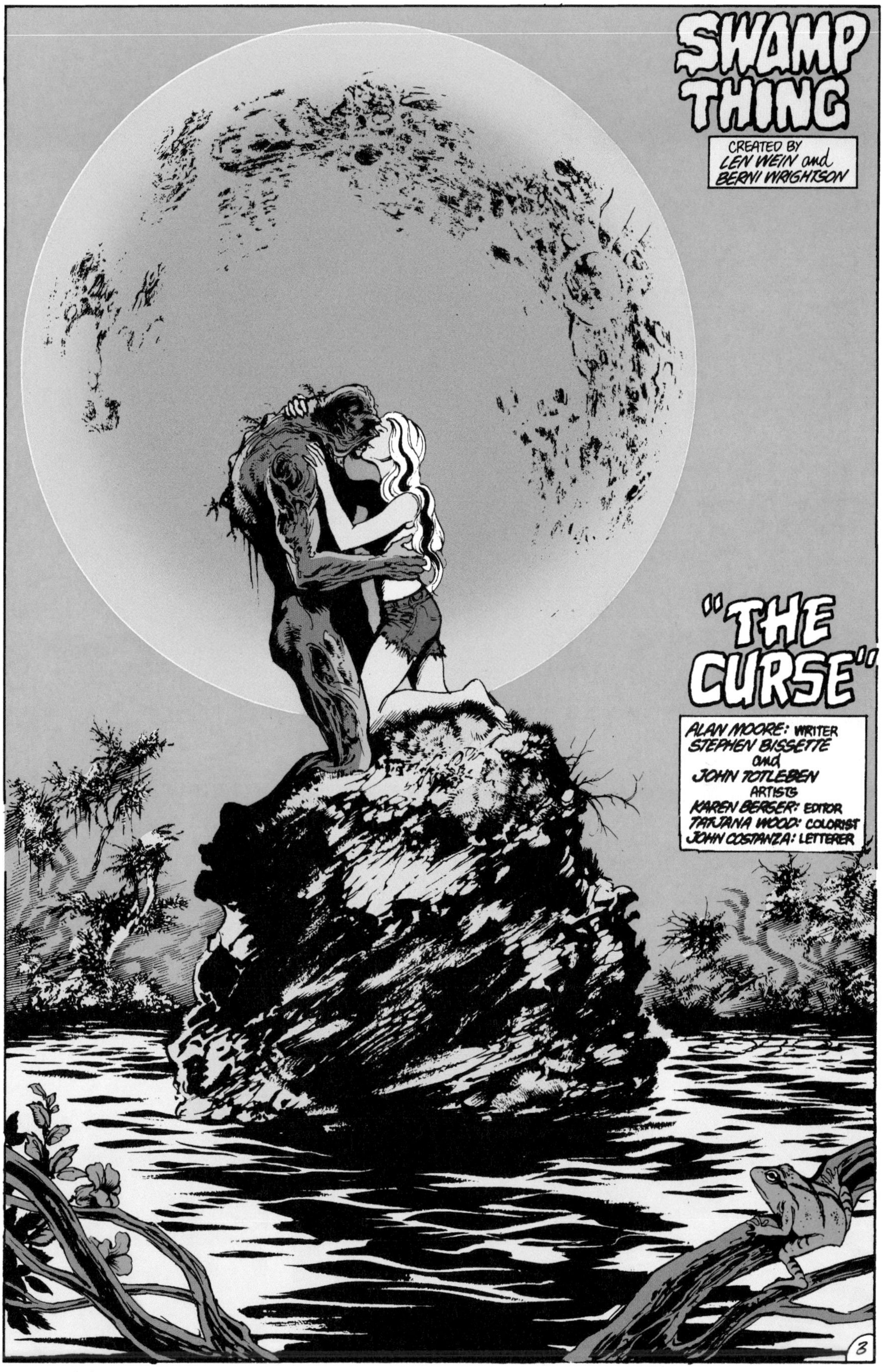
SWAMP THING
CREATED BY LEN WEIN and BERNI WRIGHTSON
"THE CURSE"
ALAN MOORE: WRITER
STEPHEN BISSETTE and JOHN TOTLEBEN ARTISTS
KAREN BERGER: EDITOR
TATJANA WOOD: COLORIST
JOHN COSTANZA: LETTERER
3

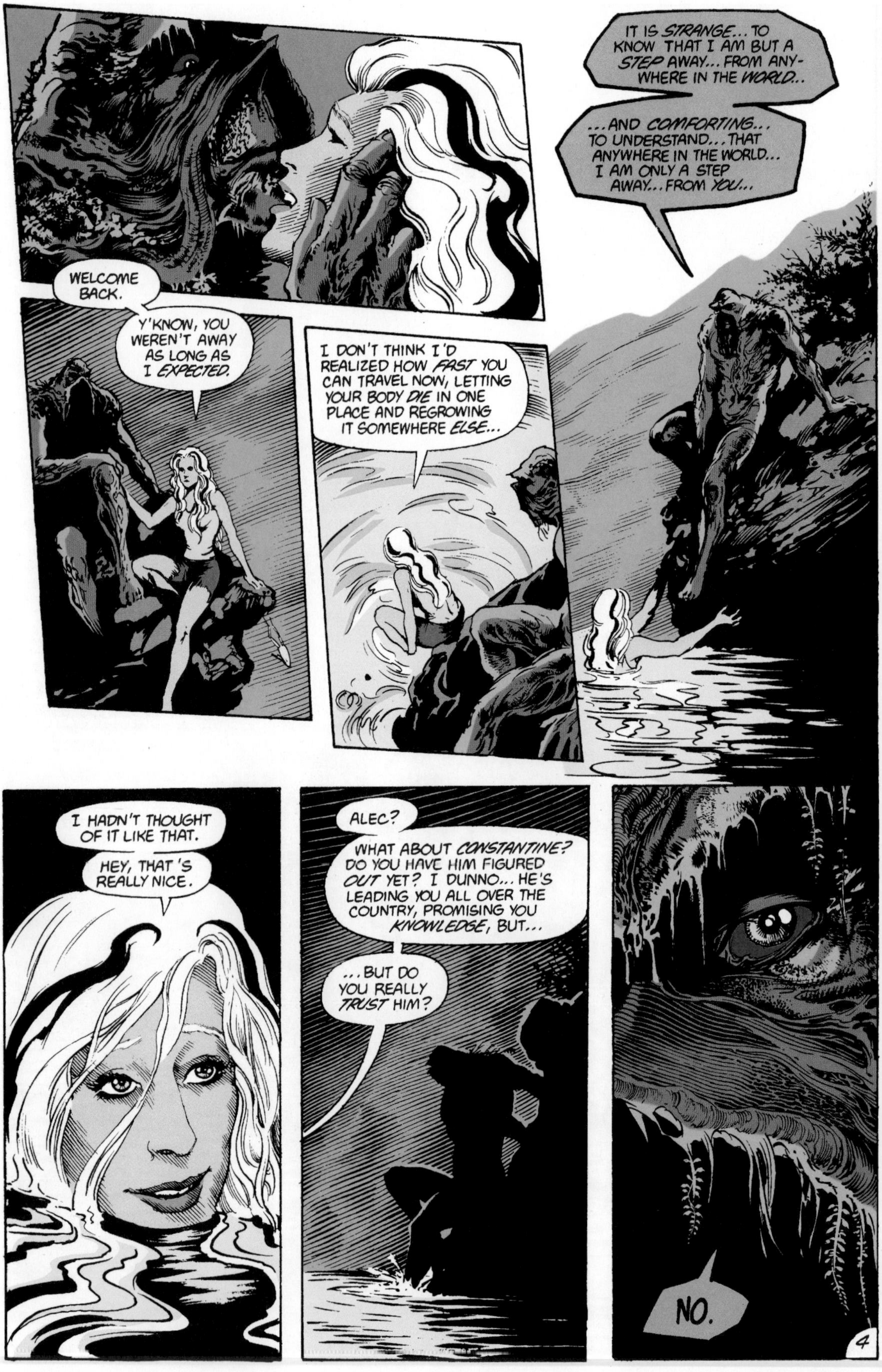
IT IS STRANGE... TO KNOW THAT I AM BUT A STEP AWAY... FROM ANYWHERE IN THE WORLD..
...AND COMFORTING... TO UNDERSTAND... THAT ANYWHERE IN THE WORLD... I AM ONLY A STEP AWAY... FROM YOU...
WELCOME BACK.
Y'KNOW, YOU WEREN'T AWAY AS LONG AS I EXPECTED.
I DON'T THINK I'D REALIZED HOW FAST YOU CAN TRAVEL NOW, LETTING YOUR BODY DIE IN ONE PLACE AND REGROWING IT SOMEWHERE ELSE...
I HADN'T THOUGHT OF IT LIKE THAT.
HEY, THAT'S REALLY NICE.
ALEC?
WHAT ABOUT CONSTANTINE? DO YOU HAVE HIM FIGURED OUT YET? I DUNNO... HE'S LEADING YOU ALL OVER THE COUNTRY, PROMISING YOU KNOWLEDGE, BUT...
...BUT DO YOU REALLY TRUST HIM?
NO.
4

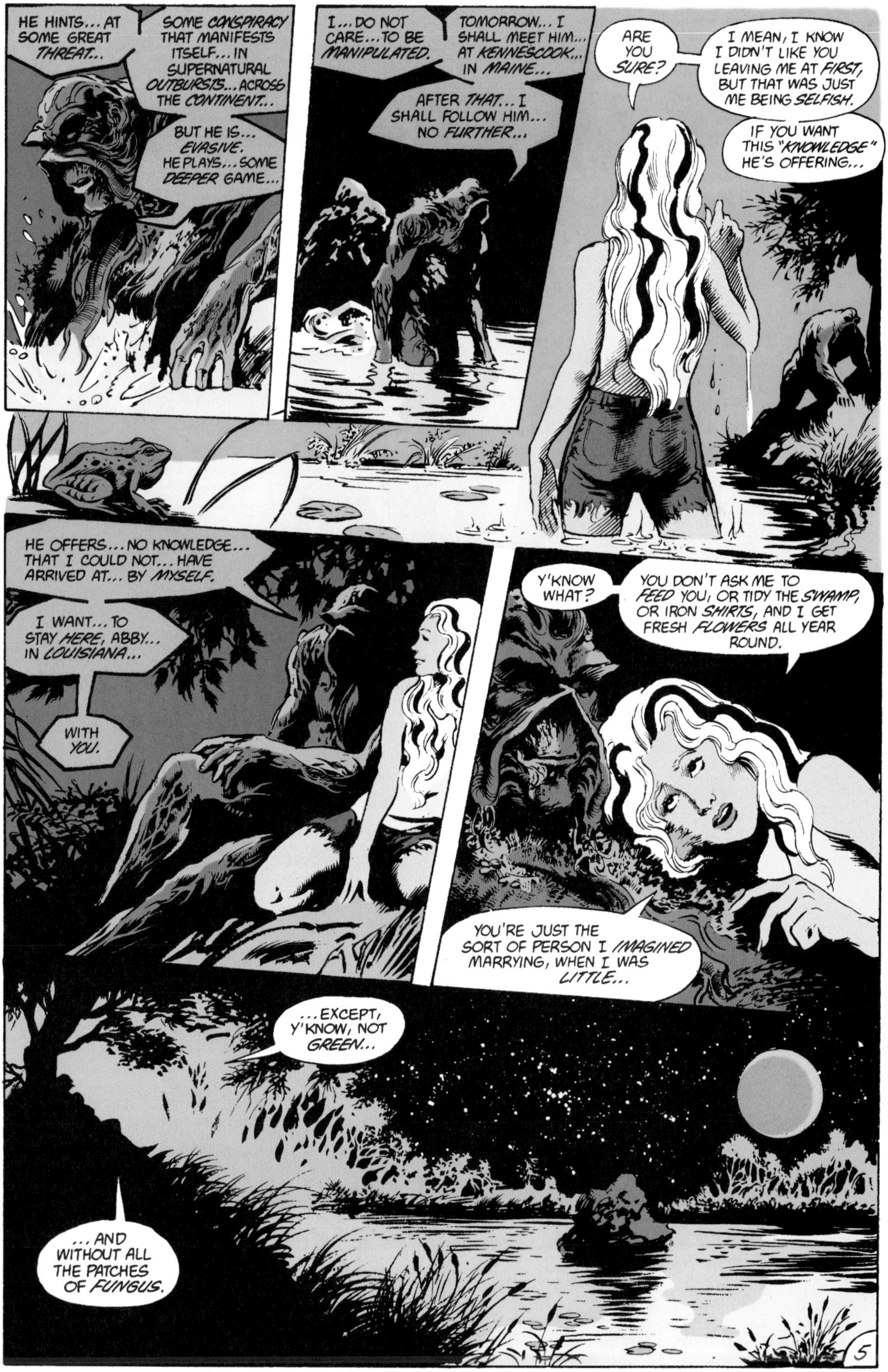
HE HINTS... AT SOME GREAT THREAT...
SOME CONSPIRACY THAT MANIFESTS ITSELF... IN SUPERNATURAL OUTBURSTS... ACROSS THE CONTINENT...
BUT HE IS... EVASIVE. HE PLAYS... SOME DEEPER GAME...
I... DO NOT CARE... TO BE MANIPULATED.
TOMORROW... I SHALL MEET HIM... AT KENNESCOOK... IN MAINE...
AFTER THAT... I SHALL FOLLOW HIM... NO FURTHER...
ARE YOU SURE?
I MEAN, I KNOW I DIDN'T LIKE YOU LEAVING ME AT FIRST, BUT THAT WAS JUST ME BEING SELFISH.
IF YOU WANT THIS "KNOWLEDGE" HE'S OFFERING...
HE OFFERS... NO KNOWLEDGE... THAT I COULD NOT... HAVE ARRIVED AT... BY MYSELF.
I WANT... TO STAY HERE, ABBY... IN LOUISIANA...
WITH YOU.
Y'KNOW WHAT?
YOU DON'T ASK ME TO FEED YOU, OR TIDY THE SWAMP, OR IRON SHIRTS, AND I GET FRESH FLOWERS ALL YEAR ROUND.
YOU'RE JUST THE SORT OF PERSON I IMAGINED MARRYING, WHEN I WAS LITTLE...
...EXCEPT, Y'KNOW, NOT GREEN...
...AND WITHOUT ALL THE PATCHES OF FUNGUS.
5

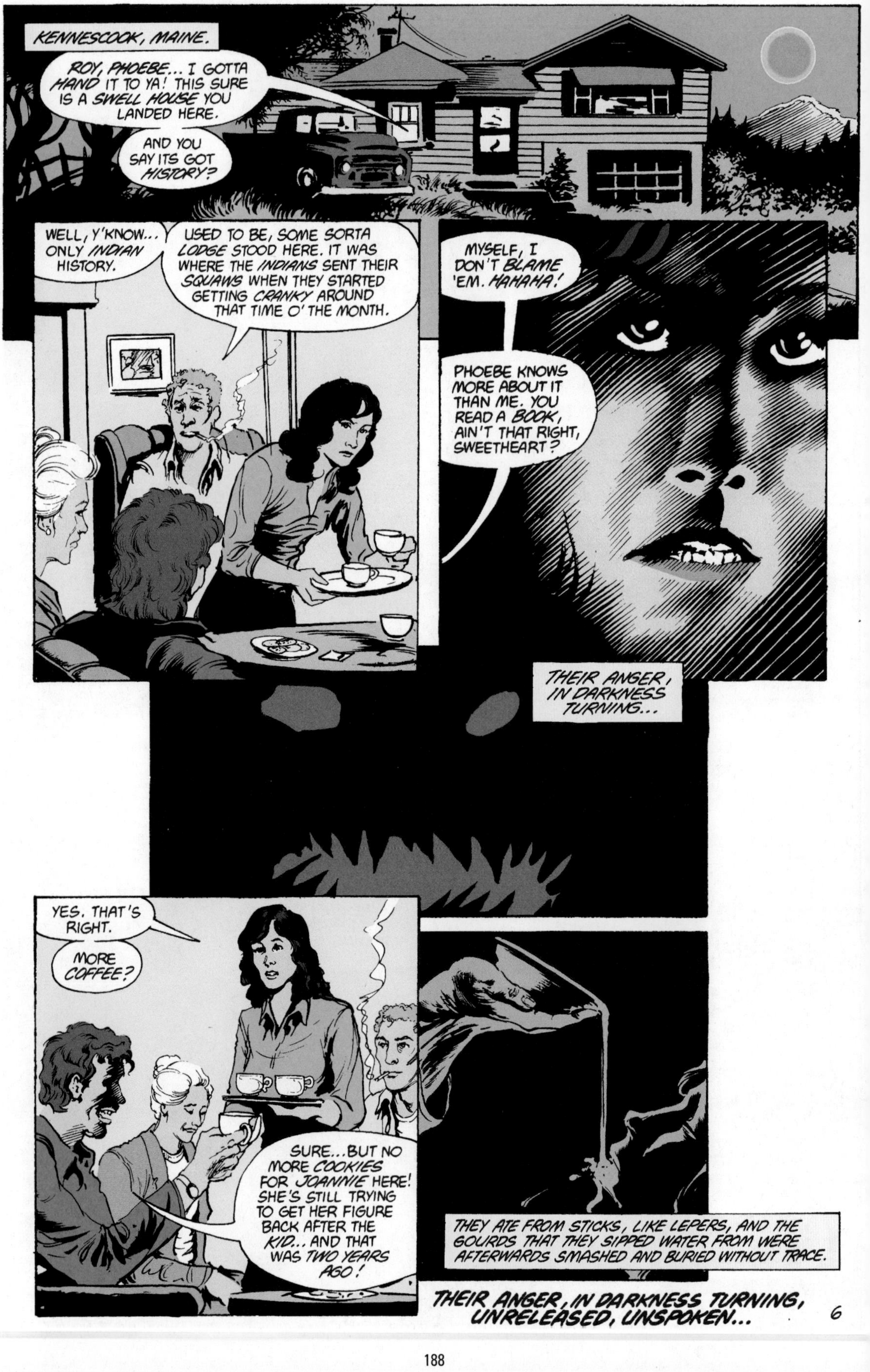
KENNESCOOK, MAINE.
ROY, PHOEBE... I GOTTA HAND IT TO YA! THIS SURE IS A SWELL HOUSE YOU LANDED HERE.
AND YOU SAY ITS GOT HISTORY?
WELL, Y'KNOW... ONLY INDIAN HISTORY.
USED TO BE, SOME SORTA LODGE STOOD HERE. IT WAS WHERE THE INDIANS SENT THEIR SQUAWS WHEN THEY STARTED GETTING CRANKY AROUND THAT TIME O' THE MONTH.
MYSELF, I DON'T BLAME 'EM. HAHAHA!
PHOEBE KNOWS MORE ABOUT IT THAN ME. YOU READ A BOOK, AIN'T THAT RIGHT, SWEETHEART?
THEIR ANGER, IN DARKNESS TURNING...
YES. THAT'S RIGHT.
MORE COFFEE?
SURE... BUT NO MORE COOKIES FOR JOANNIE HERE! SHE'S STILL TRYING TO GET HER FIGURE BACK AFTER THE KID... AND THAT WAS TWO YEARS AGO!
THEY ATE FROM STICKS, LIKE LEPERS, AND THE GOURDS THAT THEY SIPPED WATER FROM WERE AFTERWARDS SMASHED AND BURIED WITHOUT TRACE.
THEIR ANGER, IN DARKNESS TURNING, UNRELEASED, UNSPOKEN...
6

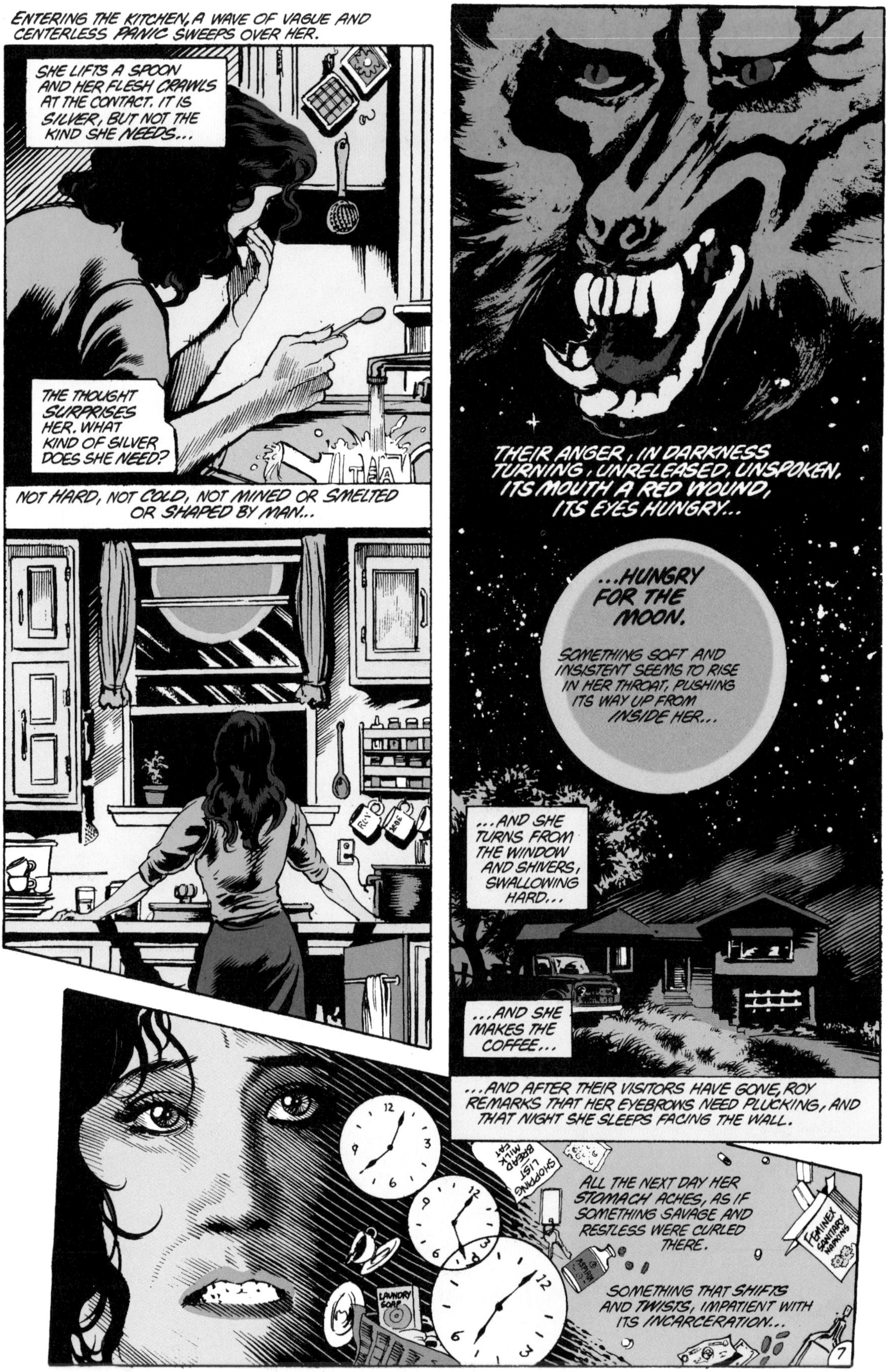
ENTERING THE KITCHEN, A WAVE OF VAGUE AND CENTERLESS PANIC SWEEPS OVER HER.
SHE LIFTS A SPOON AND HER FLESH CRAWLS AT THE CONTACT. IT IS SILVER, BUT NOT THE KIND SHE NEEDS...
THE THOUGHT SURPRISES HER. WHAT KIND OF SILVER DOES SHE NEED?
NOT HARD, NOT COLD, NOT MINED OR SMELTED OR SHAPED BY MAN...
THEIR ANGER, IN DARKNESS TURNING, UNRELEASED, UNSPOKEN, ITS MOUTH A RED WOUND, ITS EYES HUNGRY...
...HUNGRY FOR THE MOON.
SOMETHING SOFT AND INSISTENT SEEMS TO RISE IN HER THROAT, PUSHING ITS WAY UP FROM INSIDE HER...
...AND SHE TURNS FROM THE WINDOW AND SHIVERS, SWALLOWING HARD...
...AND SHE MAKES THE COFFEE...
...AND AFTER THEIR VISITORS HAVE GONE, ROY REMARKS THAT HER EYEBROWS NEED PLUCKING, AND THAT NIGHT SHE SLEEPS FACING THE WALL.
SHOPPING LIST
BREAD
MILK
FAT
LAUNDRY SOAP
FEMINEX SANITARY NAPKINS
ALL THE NEXT DAY HER STOMACH ACHES, AS IF SOMETHING SAVAGE AND RESTLESS WERE CURLED THERE.
SOMETHING THAT SHIFTS AND TWISTS, IMPATIENT WITH ITS INCARCERATION...
7

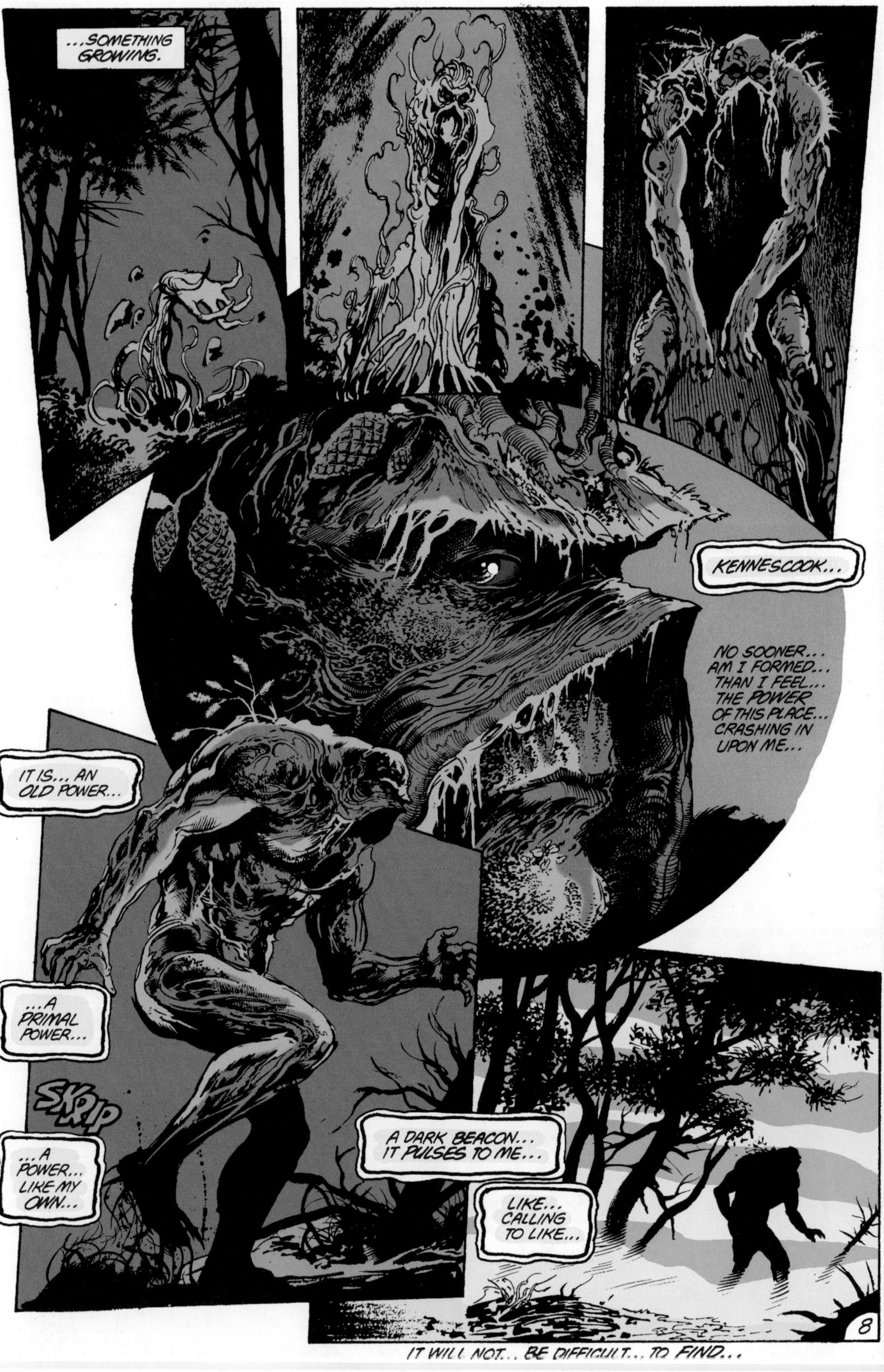
...SOMETHING GROWING.
KENNESCOOK...
NO SOONER... AM I FORMED... THAN I FEEL... THE POWER OF THIS PLACE... CRASHING IN UPON ME...
IT IS... AN OLD POWER...
...A PRIMAL POWER...
SKRIP
...A POWER... LIKE MY OWN...
A DARK BEACON... IT PULSES TO ME...
LIKE... CALLING TO LIKE...
8
IT WILL NOT... BE DIFFICULT... TO FIND...

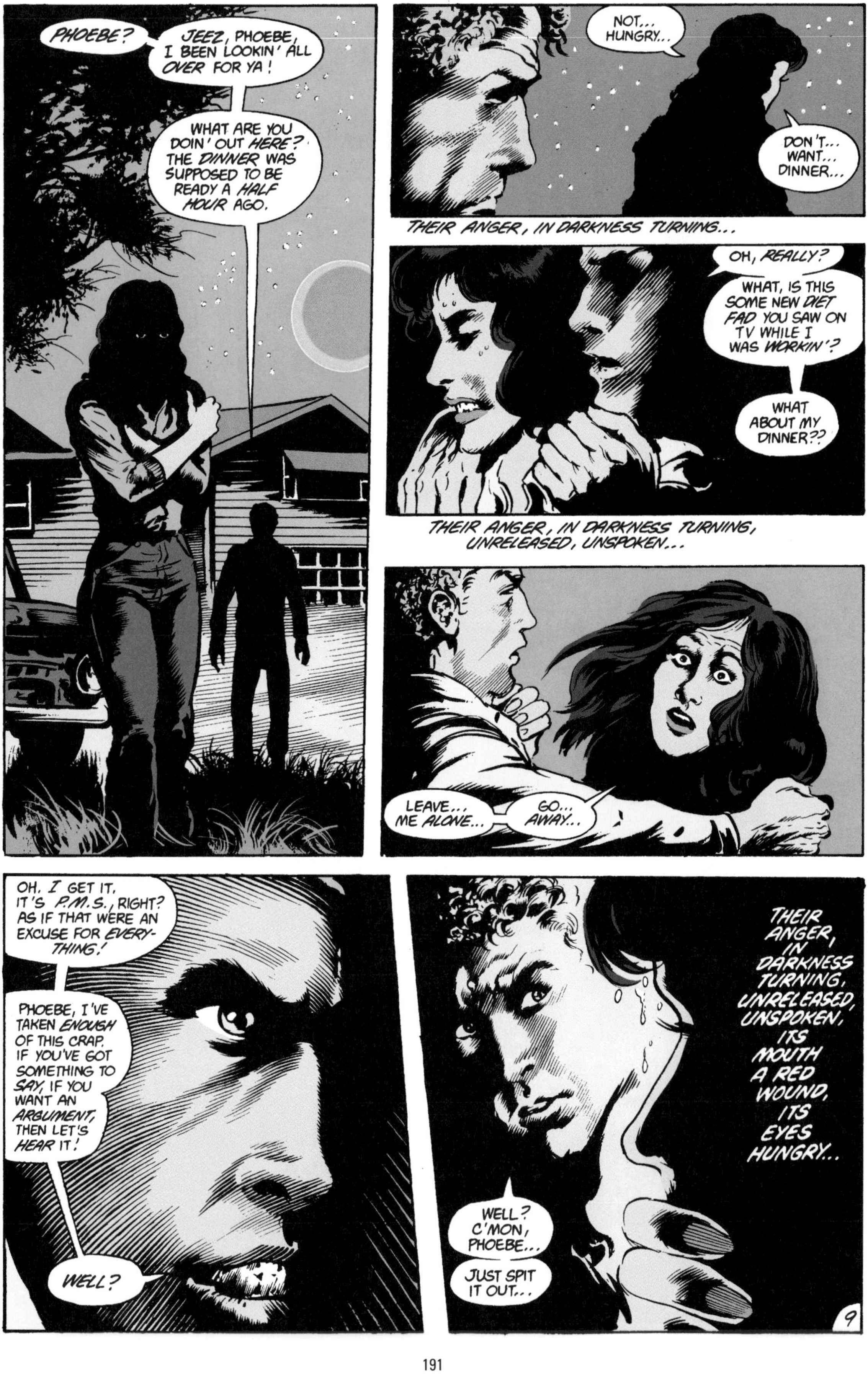

PHOEBE?
JEEZ, PHOEBE, I BEEN LOOKIN' ALL OVER FOR YA!
WHAT ARE YOU DOIN' OUT HERE? THE DINNER WAS SUPPOSED TO BE READY A HALF HOUR AGO.
NOT... HUNGRY...
DON'T... WANT... DINNER...
THEIR ANGER, IN DARKNESS TURNING...
OH, REALLY?
WHAT, IS THIS SOME NEW DIET FAD YOU SAW ON TV WHILE I WAS WORKIN'?
WHAT ABOUT MY DINNER??
THEIR ANGER, IN DARKNESS TURNING, UNRELEASED, UNSPOKEN...
LEAVE... ME ALONE...
GO... AWAY...
OH, I GET IT, IT'S P.M.S., RIGHT? AS IF THAT WERE AN EXCUSE FOR EVERY-THING!
PHOEBE, I'VE TAKEN ENOUGH OF THIS CRAP. IF YOU'VE GOT SOMETHING TO SAY, IF YOU WANT AN ARGUMENT, THEN LET'S HEAR IT!
WELL?
THEIR ANGER, IN DARKNESS TURNING, UNRELEASED, UNSPOKEN, ITS MOUTH A RED WOUND, ITS EYES HUNGRY...
WELL? C'MON, PHOEBE...
JUST SPIT IT OUT...
9

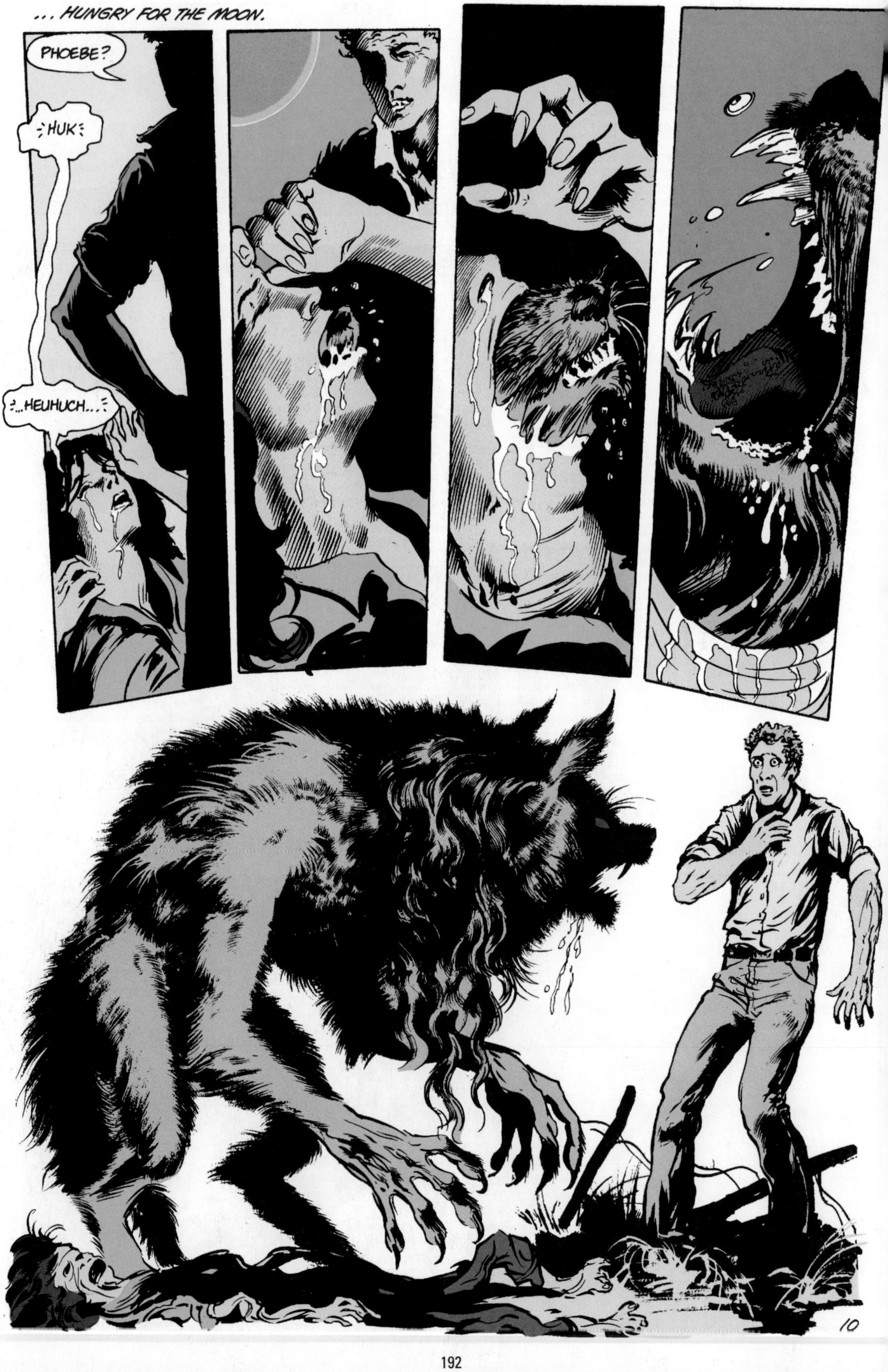
... HUNGRY FOR THE MOON.
PHOEBE?
HUK
...HEUHUCH...
10

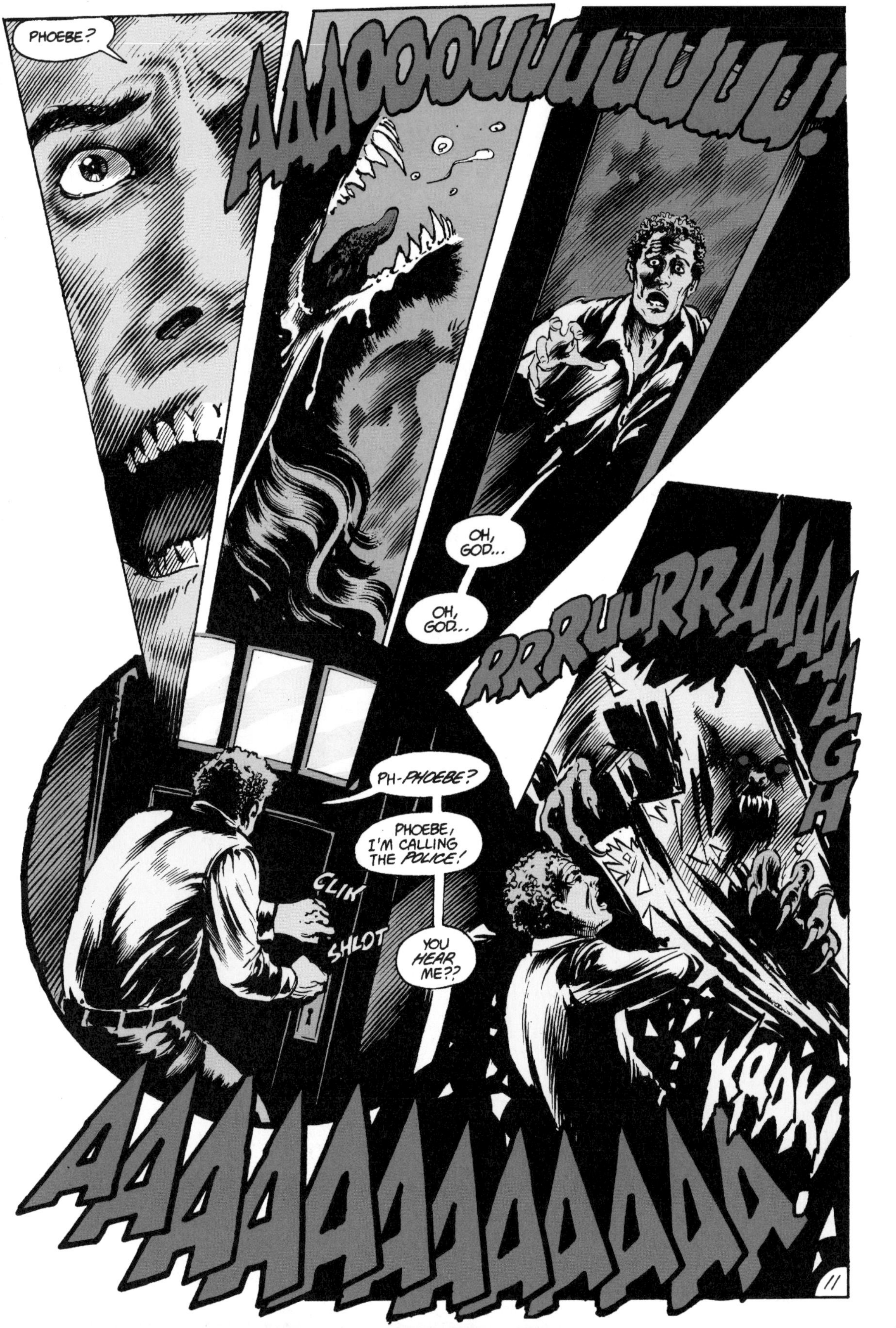
PHOEBE?
AAAOOOUUUUUUUU!
OH, GOD...
OH, GOD...
RRRUUURRAAAAAAGH
PH-PHOEBE?
PHOEBE, I'M CALLING THE POLICE!
CLIK
SHLOT
YOU HEAR ME??
KRAK!
AAAAAAAAAAAAAA!
11

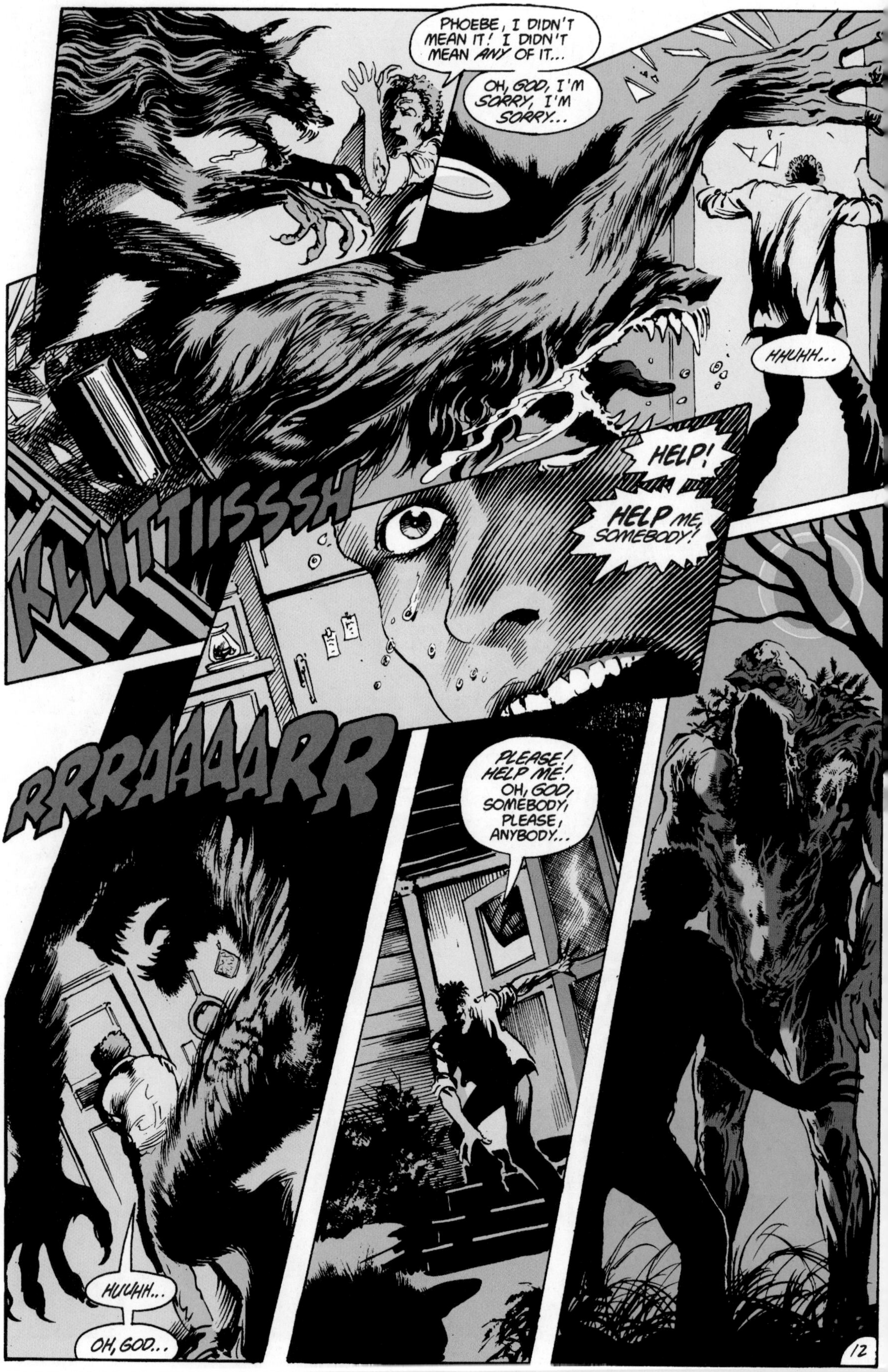
PHOEBE, I DIDN'T MEAN IT! I DIDN'T MEAN ANY OF IT...
OH, GOD, I'M SORRY, I'M SORRY...
HHUHH...
KLIITTIISSSH
HELP!
HELP ME, SOMEBODY!
RRRAAAAARR
HUUHH...
OH, GOD...
PLEASE! HELP ME! OH, GOD, SOMEBODY, PLEASE, ANYBODY...
12

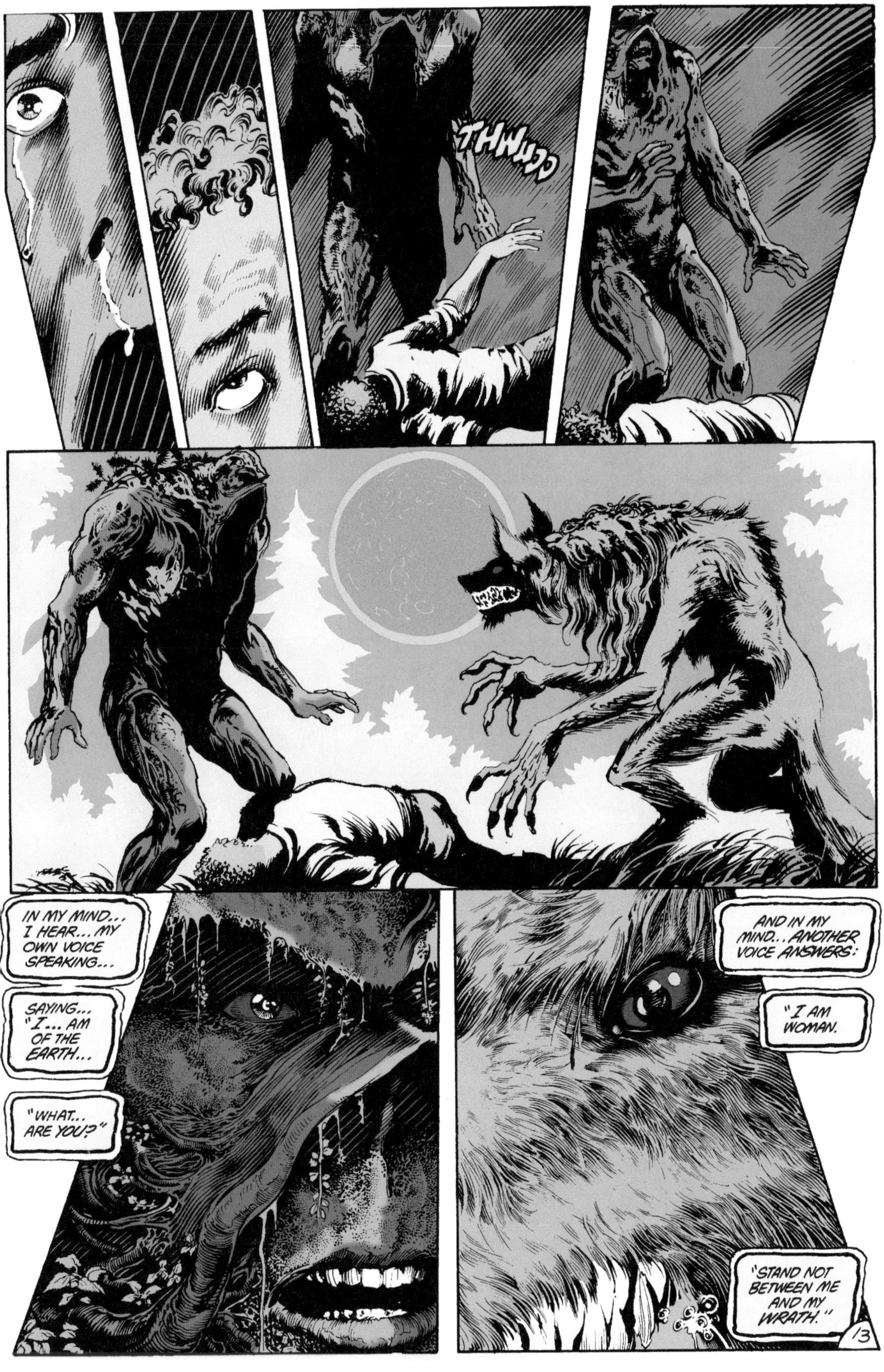
THWUCC
IN MY MIND... I HEAR... MY OWN VOICE SPEAKING...
SAYING... "I... AM OF THE EARTH...
"WHAT... ARE YOU?"
AND IN MY MIND... ANOTHER VOICE ANSWERS:
"I AM WOMAN.
"STAND NOT BETWEEN ME AND MY WRATH."
13

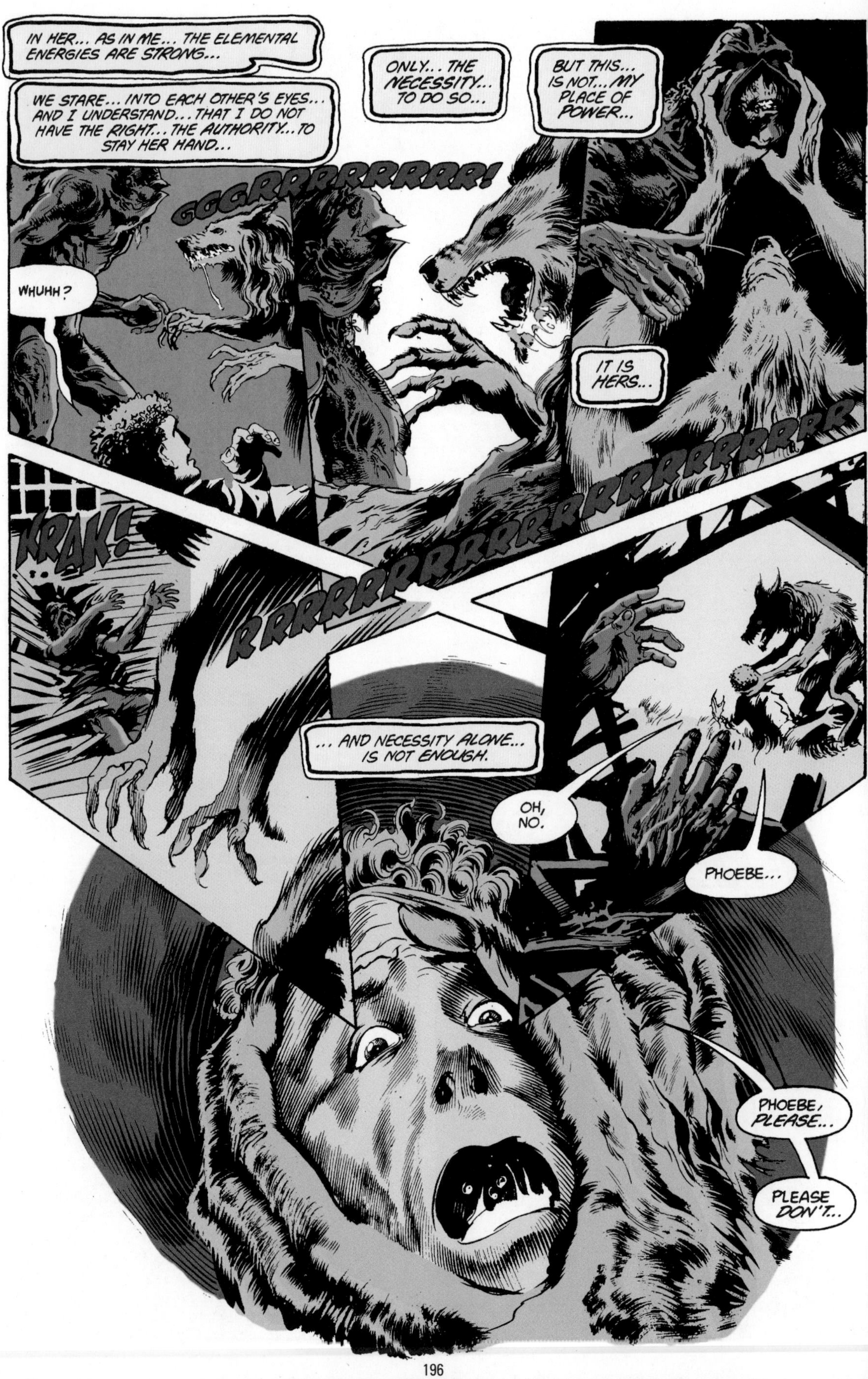
IN HER... AS IN ME... THE ELEMENTAL ENERGIES ARE STRONG...
WE STARE... INTO EACH OTHER'S EYES... AND I UNDERSTAND... THAT I DO NOT HAVE THE RIGHT... THE AUTHORITY... TO STAY HER HAND...
ONLY... THE NECESSITY... TO DO SO...
BUT THIS... IS NOT... MY PLACE OF POWER...
GGGRRRRRRRRAR!
WHUHH?
IT IS HERS...
KRAK!
RRRRRRRRRRRRRRRRRRRRRRRRRR
... AND NECESSITY ALONE... IS NOT ENOUGH.
OH, NO.
PHOEBE...
PHOEBE, PLEASE...
PLEASE DON'T...

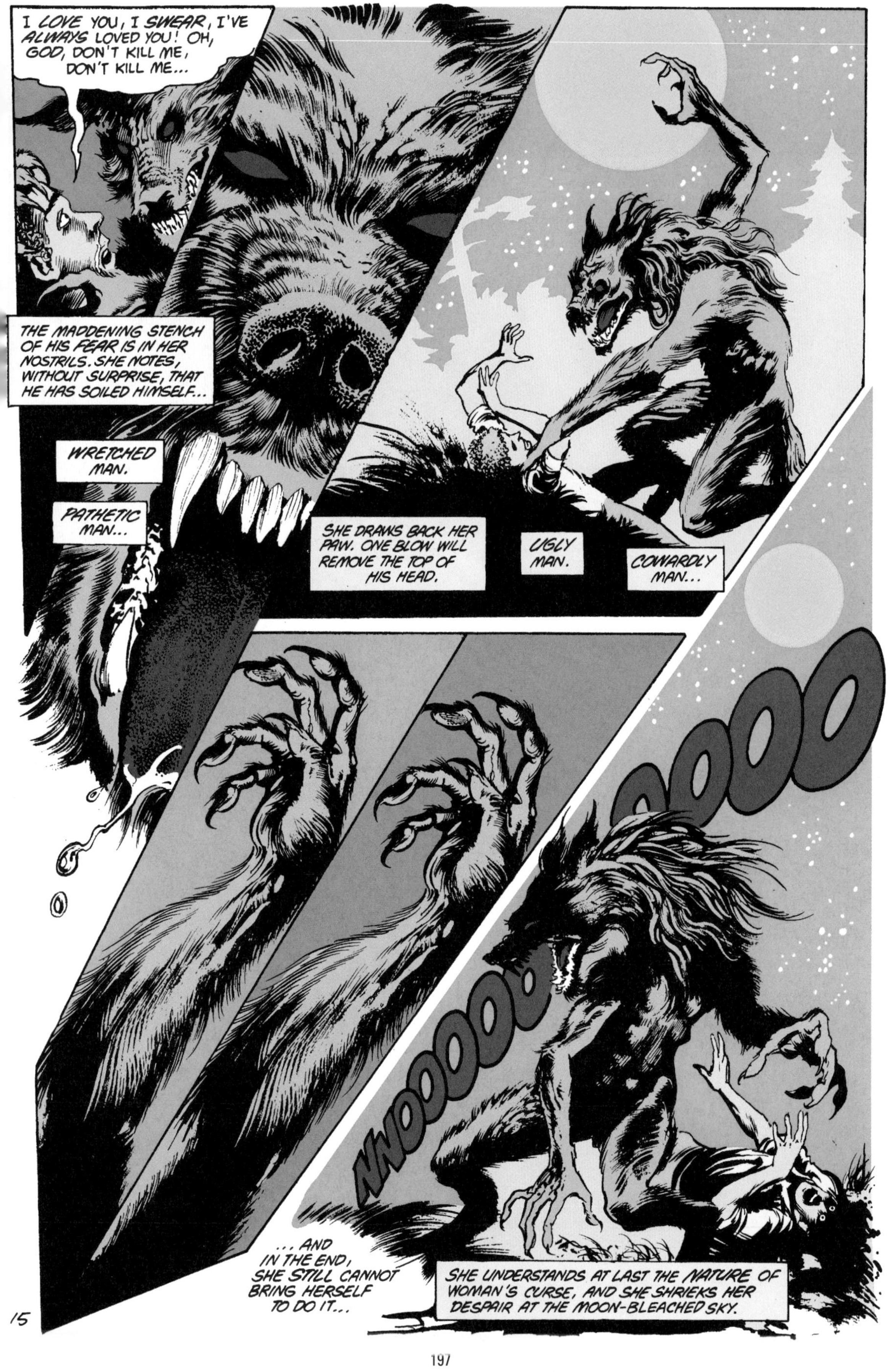
I LOVE YOU, I SWEAR, I'VE ALWAYS LOVED YOU! OH, GOD, DON'T KILL ME, DON'T KILL ME...
THE MADDENING STENCH OF HIS FEAR IS IN HER NOSTRILS. SHE NOTES, WITHOUT SURPRISE, THAT HE HAS SOILED HIMSELF...
WRETCHED MAN.
PATHETIC MAN...
SHE DRAWS BACK HER PAW. ONE BLOW WILL REMOVE THE TOP OF HIS HEAD.
UGLY MAN.
COWARDLY MAN...
NNOOOOOOOOOOOO
...AND IN THE END, SHE STILL CANNOT BRING HERSELF TO DO IT...
SHE UNDERSTANDS AT LAST THE NATURE OF WOMAN'S CURSE, AND SHE SHRIEKS HER DESPAIR AT THE MOON-BLEACHED SKY.
15

THE ANGER CRASHES BLINDLY AROUND INSIDE HER WITH NOWHERE TO GO, TEARING AT ITSELF, RAKING ITS OWN FLESH WITH FRUSTRATED TALONS...

SHE DESTROYS THE GREENHOUSE...

...AND THE MAILBOX...

LADIES! YOU MAY BE A WINNER!

...AND THE CAR...

...AND IT ISN'T ENOUGH.

SHE RUNS...

...AND THE NIGHT IS TOO SMALL A THING TO CONTAIN THE FURY WITHIN HER.

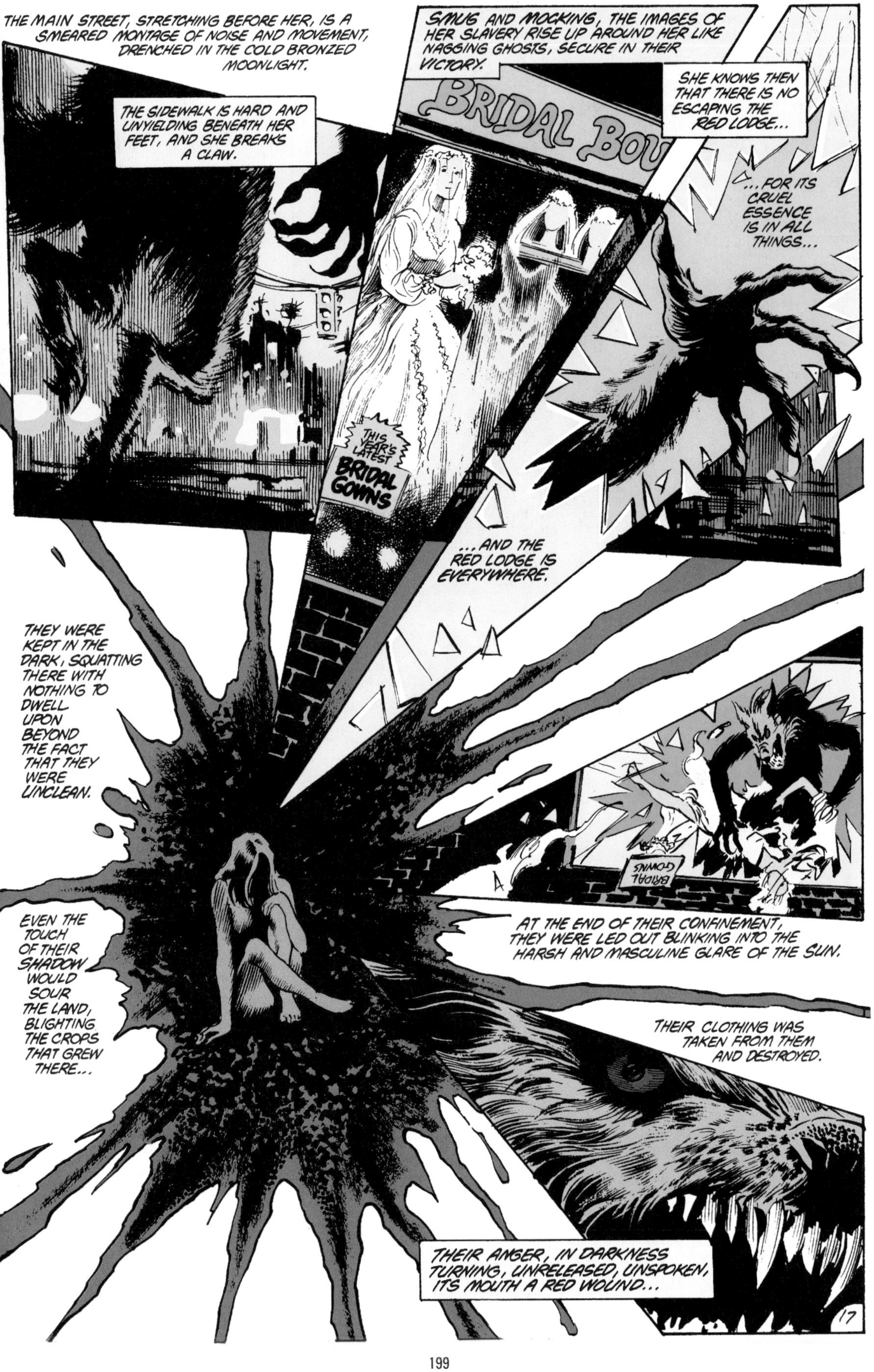
THE MAIN STREET, STRETCHING BEFORE HER, IS A SMEARED MONTAGE OF NOISE AND MOVEMENT, DRENCHED IN THE COLD BRONZED MOONLIGHT.
THE SIDEWALK IS HARD AND UNYIELDING BENEATH HER FEET, AND SHE BREAKS A CLAW.
SMUG AND MOCKING, THE IMAGES OF HER SLAVERY RISE UP AROUND HER LIKE NAGGING GHOSTS, SECURE IN THEIR VICTORY.
BRIDAL BOU
THIS YEAR'S LATEST BRIDAL GOWNS
SHE KNOWS THEN THAT THERE IS NO ESCAPING THE RED LODGE...
...FOR ITS CRUEL ESSENCE IS IN ALL THINGS...
...AND THE RED LODGE IS EVERYWHERE.
THEY WERE KEPT IN THE DARK, SQUATTING THERE WITH NOTHING TO DWELL UPON BEYOND THE FACT THAT THEY WERE UNCLEAN.
EVEN THE TOUCH OF THEIR SHADOW WOULD SOUR THE LAND, BLIGHTING THE CROPS THAT GREW THERE...
AT THE END OF THEIR CONFINEMENT, THEY WERE LED OUT BLINKING INTO THE HARSH AND MASCULINE GLARE OF THE SUN.
THEIR CLOTHING WAS TAKEN FROM THEM AND DESTROYED.
THEIR ANGER, IN DARKNESS TURNING, UNRELEASED, UNSPOKEN, ITS MOUTH A RED WOUND...
17

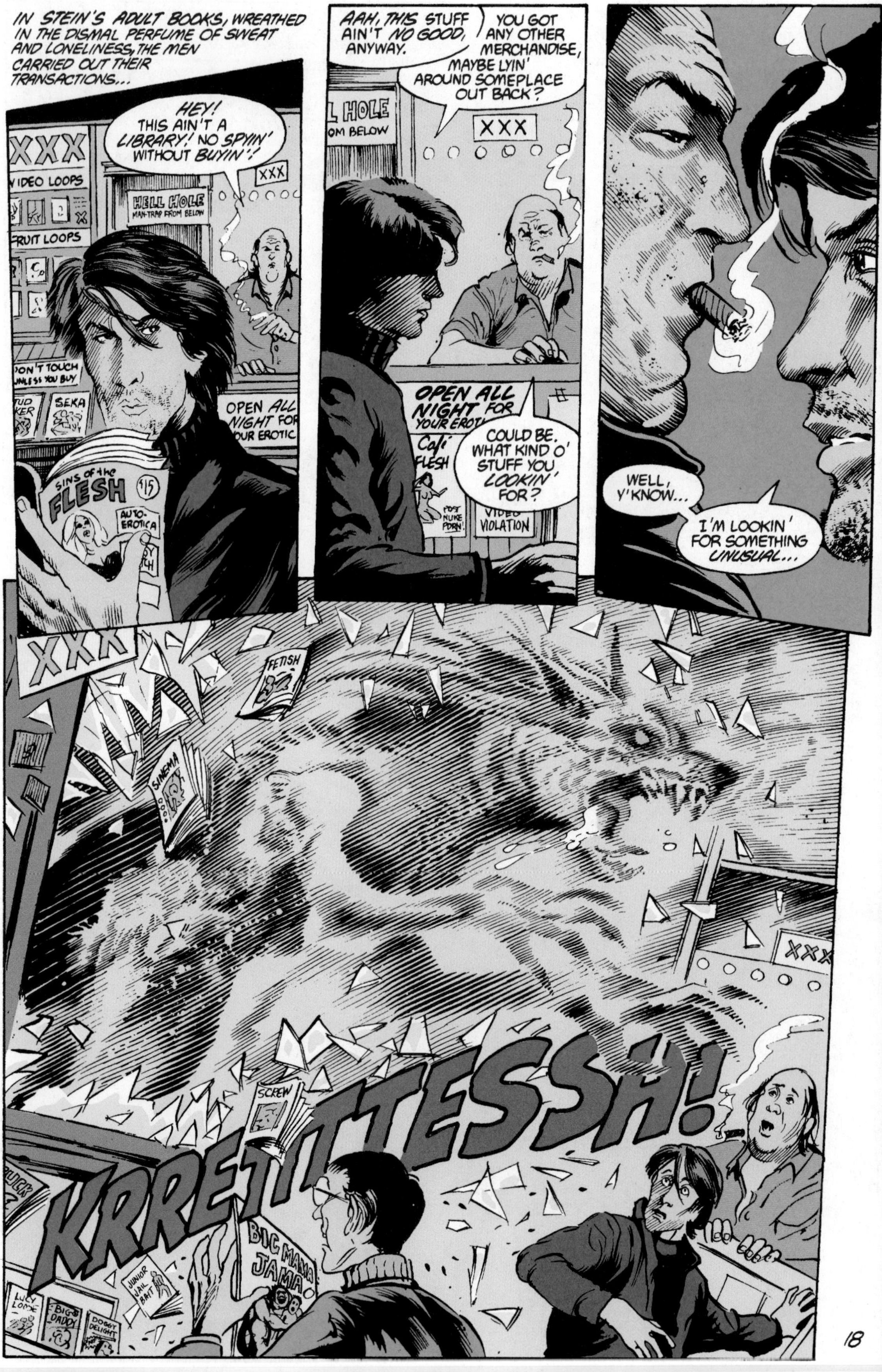
IN STEIN'S ADULT BOOKS, WREATHED IN THE DISMAL PERFUME OF SWEAT AND LONELINESS, THE MEN CARRIED OUT THEIR TRANSACTIONS...
HEY! THIS AIN'T A LIBRARY! NO SPYIN' WITHOUT BUYIN'!
XXX
VIDEO LOOPS
FRUIT LOOPS
HELL HOLE
MAN-TRAP FROM BELOW
SEKA
OPEN ALL NIGHT FOR YOUR EROTIC
SINS of the FLESH
AUTO-EROTICA
AAH, THIS STUFF AIN'T NO GOOD, ANYWAY.
YOU GOT ANY OTHER MERCHANDISE, MAYBE LYIN' AROUND SOMEPLACE OUT BACK?
COULD BE. WHAT KIND O' STUFF YOU LOOKIN' FOR?
Café FLESH
POST NUKE PORN!
VIDEO VIOLATION
WELL, Y'KNOW...
I'M LOOKIN' FOR SOMETHING UNUSUAL...
FETISH
SINEMA
SCREW
KRRETTTTESSH!
BIG MAMA JAMA
JUNIOR JAIL BAIT
BIG DADDY
DOGGY DELIGHT
18

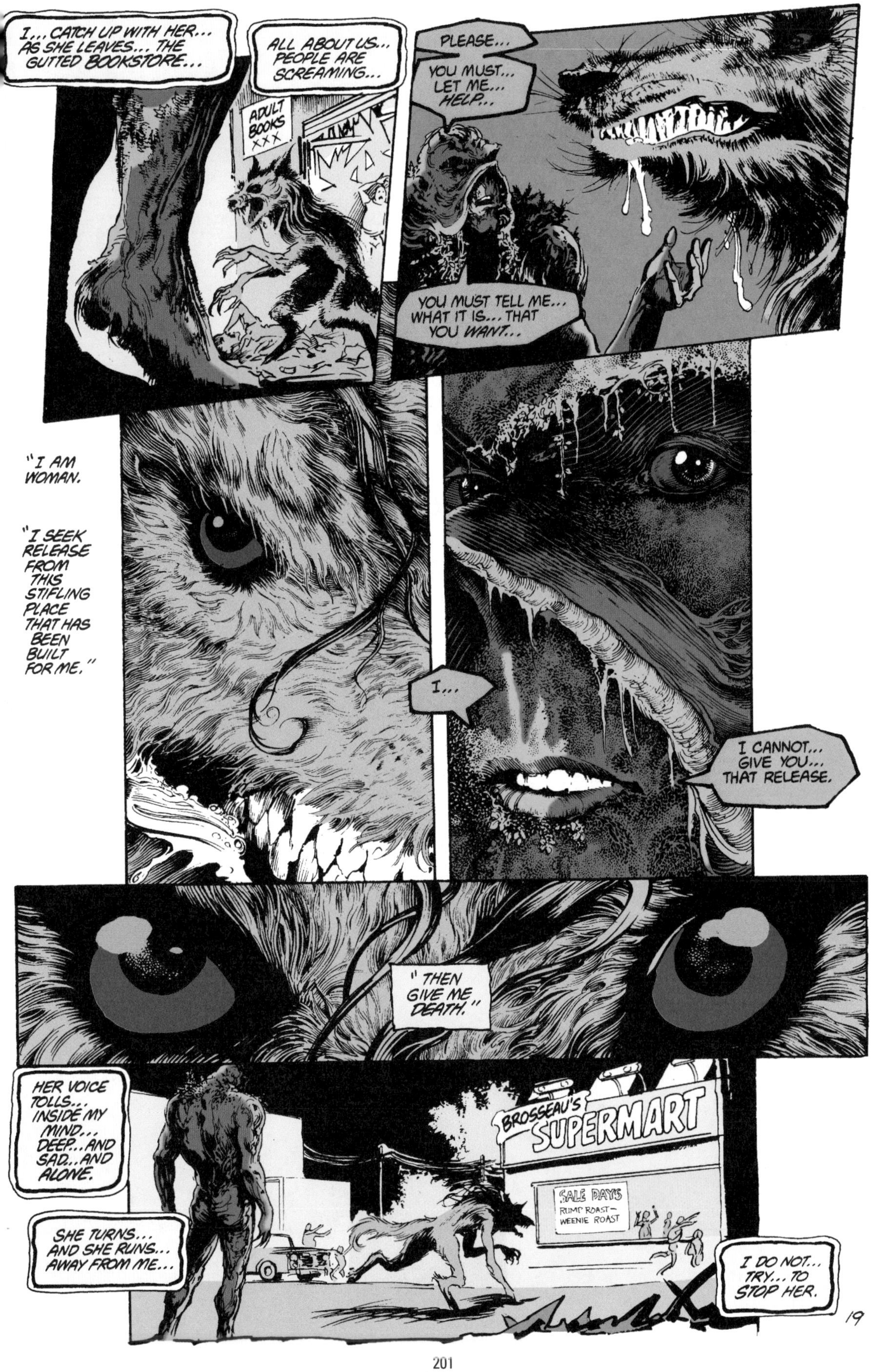
I... CATCH UP WITH HER... AS SHE LEAVES... THE GUTTED BOOKSTORE...
ALL ABOUT US... PEOPLE ARE SCREAMING...
ADULT BOOKS XXX
PLEASE...
YOU MUST... LET ME... HELP...
YOU MUST TELL ME... WHAT IT IS... THAT YOU WANT...
"I AM WOMAN.
"I SEEK RELEASE FROM THIS STIFLING PLACE THAT HAS BEEN BUILT FOR ME."
I...
I CANNOT... GIVE YOU... THAT RELEASE.
"THEN GIVE ME DEATH."
HER VOICE TOLLS... INSIDE MY MIND... DEEP... AND SAD... AND ALONE.
BROSSEAU'S SUPERMART
SALE DAYS
RUMP ROAST—WEENIE ROAST
SHE TURNS... AND SHE RUNS... AWAY FROM ME...
I DO NOT... TRY... TO STOP HER.
19

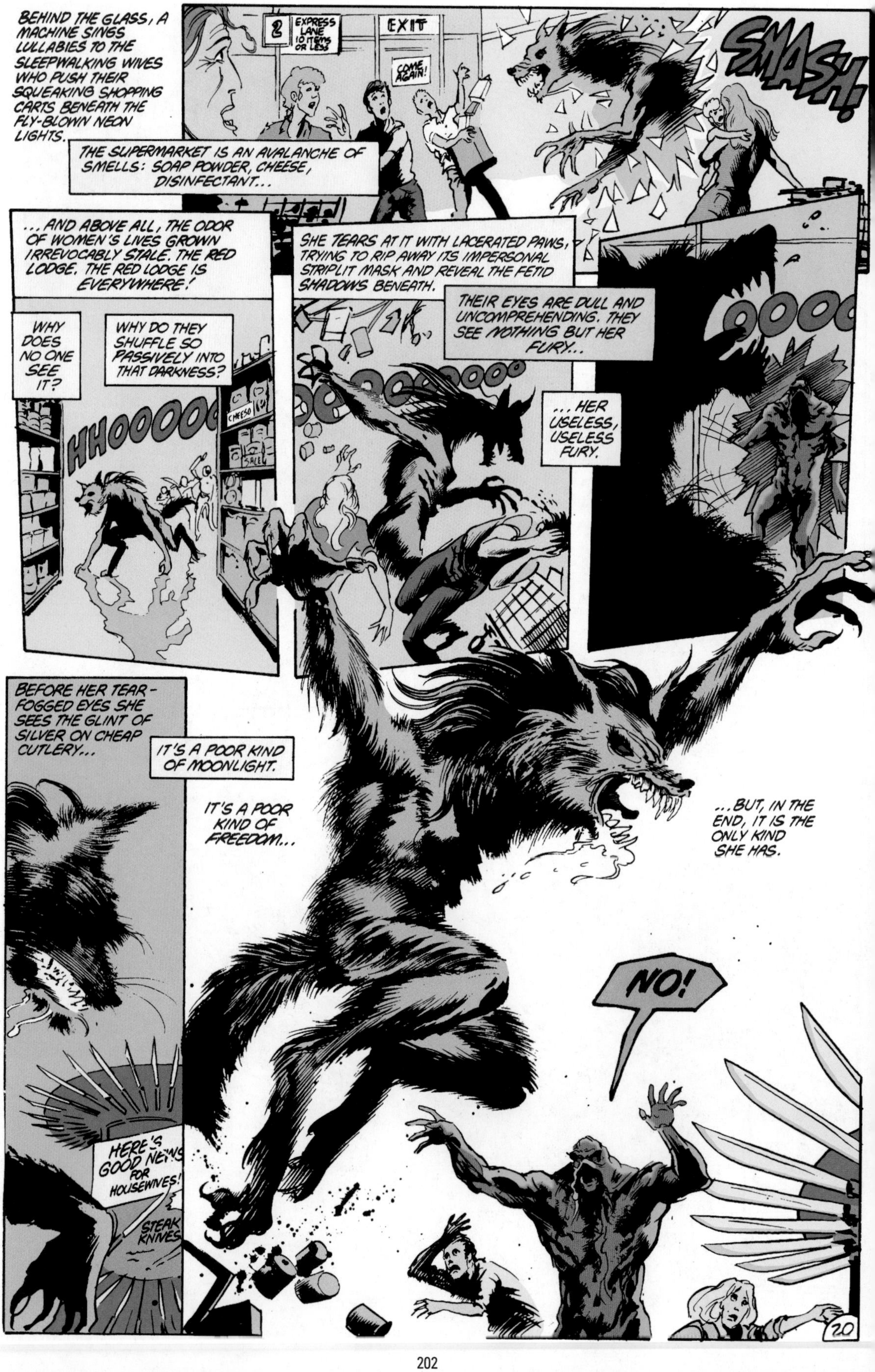

BEHIND THE GLASS, A MACHINE SINGS LULLABIES TO THE SLEEPWALKING WIVES WHO PUSH THEIR SQUEAKING SHOPPING CARTS BENEATH THE FLY-BLOWN NEON LIGHTS.
EXPRESS LANE 10 ITEMS OR LESS
EXIT
COME AGAIN!
SMASH!
THE SUPERMARKET IS AN AVALANCHE OF SMELLS: SOAP POWDER, CHEESE, DISINFECTANT...
...AND ABOVE ALL, THE ODOR OF WOMEN'S LIVES GROWN IRREVOCABLY STALE. THE RED LODGE. THE RED LODGE IS EVERYWHERE!
WHY DOES NO ONE SEE IT?
WHY DO THEY SHUFFLE SO PASSIVELY INTO THAT DARKNESS?
HHOOOOO
CHEESO
SALE
SHE TEARS AT IT WITH LACERATED PAWS, TRYING TO RIP AWAY ITS IMPERSONAL STRIPLIT MASK AND REVEAL THE FETID SHADOWS BENEATH.
THEIR EYES ARE DULL AND UNCOMPREHENDING. THEY SEE NOTHING BUT HER FURY...
...HER USELESS, USELESS FURY.
OOOOOOOO
OOOO
BEFORE HER TEAR-FOGGED EYES SHE SEES THE GLINT OF SILVER ON CHEAP CUTLERY...
IT'S A POOR KIND OF MOONLIGHT.
IT'S A POOR KIND OF FREEDOM...
...BUT, IN THE END, IT IS THE ONLY KIND SHE HAS.
NO!
HERE'S GOOD NEWS FOR HOUSEWIVES!
STEAK KNIVES
20

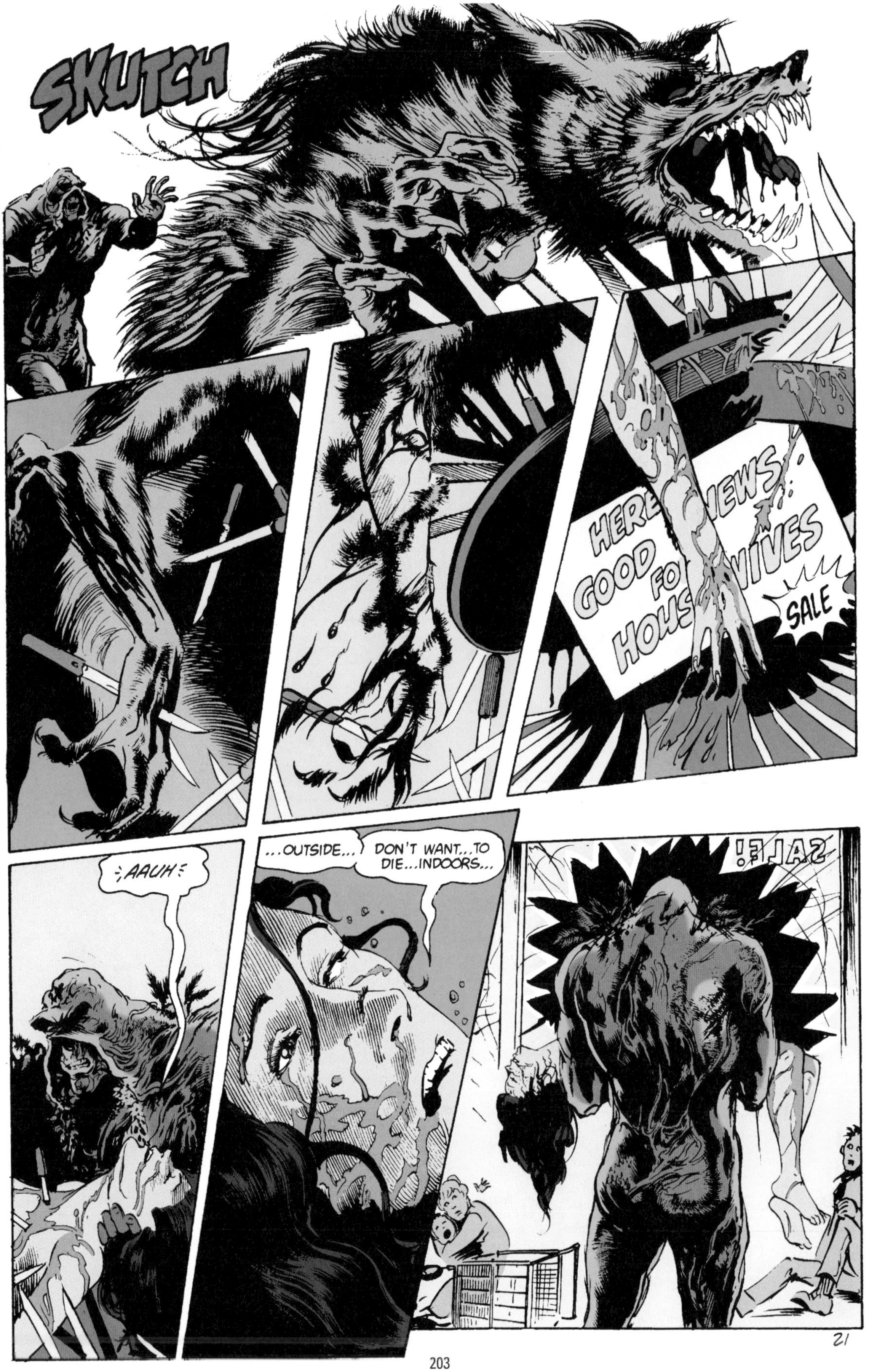
SKUTCH
HERE NEWS GOOD FO HOUS VIVES
SALE
AAUH
...OUTSIDE...
DON'T WANT...TO DIE...INDOORS...
SALE!
21

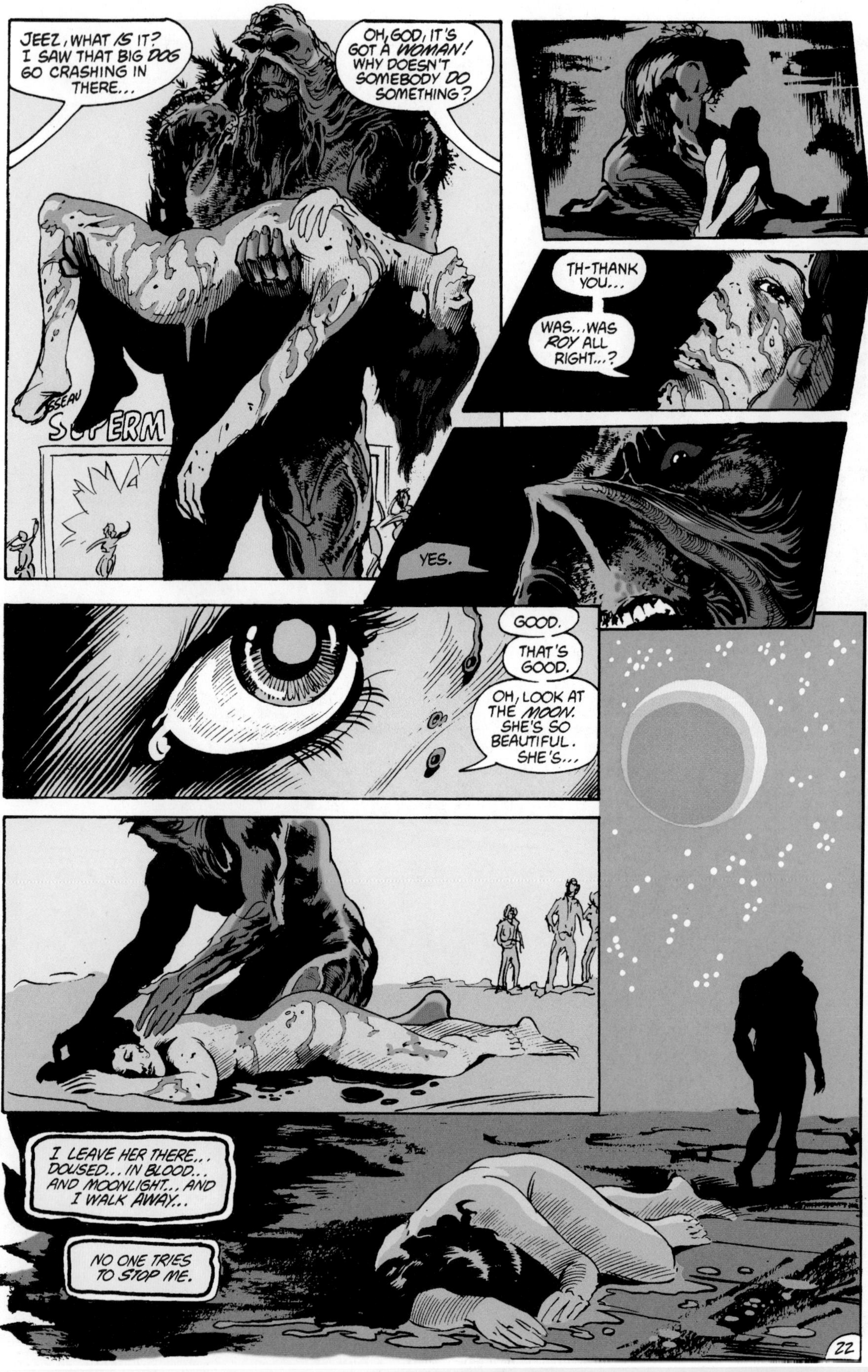
JEEZ, WHAT IS IT? I SAW THAT BIG DOG GO CRASHING IN THERE...
OH, GOD, IT'S GOT A WOMAN! WHY DOESN'T SOMEBODY DO SOMETHING?
SUPERM
TH-THANK YOU...
WAS...WAS ROY ALL RIGHT...?
YES.
GOOD.
THAT'S GOOD.
OH, LOOK AT THE MOON. SHE'S SO BEAUTIFUL. SHE'S...
I LEAVE HER THERE... DOUSED... IN BLOOD... AND MOONLIGHT... AND I WALK AWAY...
NO ONE TRIES TO STOP ME.
22

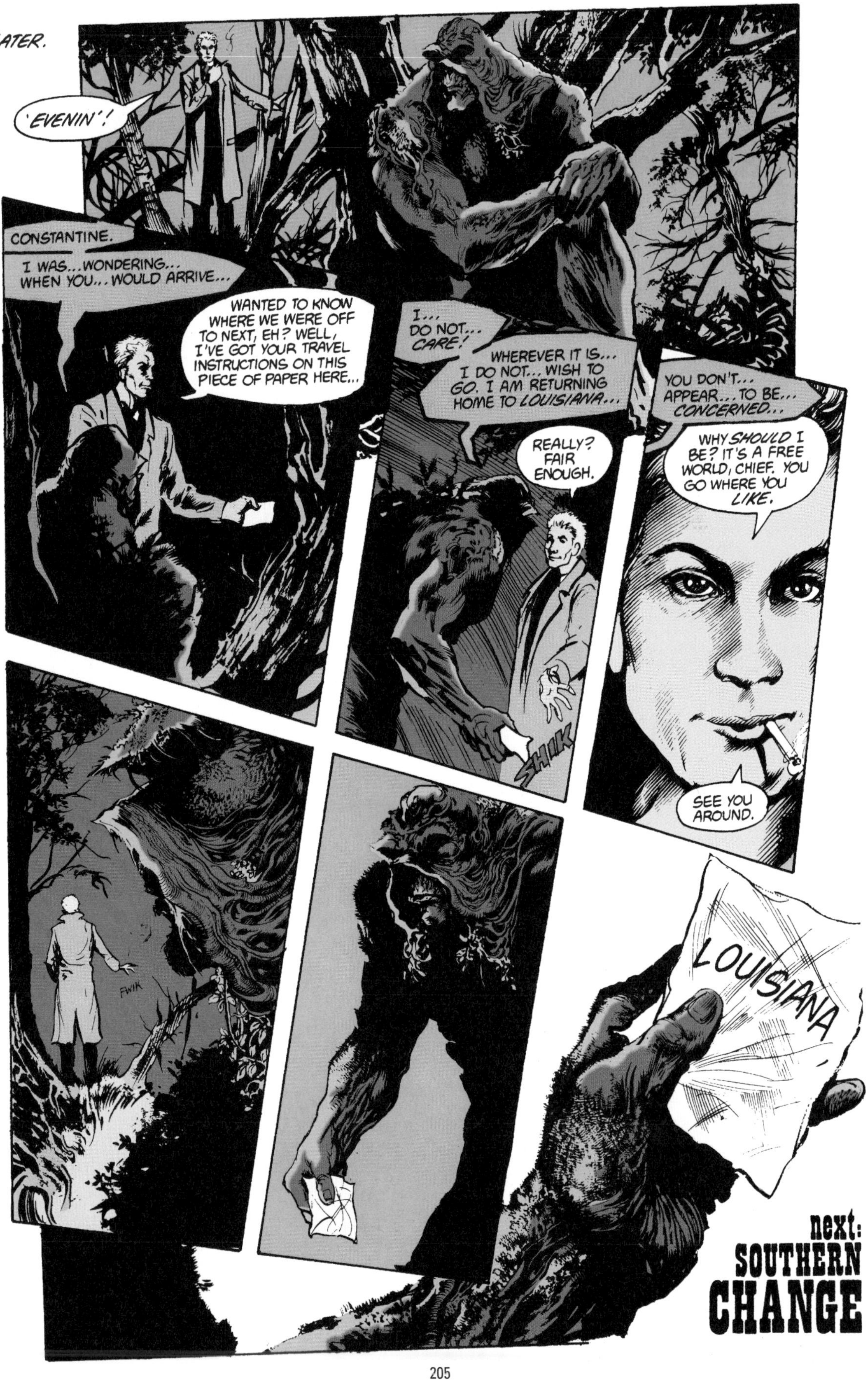
LATER.
'EVENIN'!
CONSTANTINE.
I WAS... WONDERING... WHEN YOU... WOULD ARRIVE...
WANTED TO KNOW WHERE WE WERE OFF TO NEXT, EH? WELL, I'VE GOT YOUR TRAVEL INSTRUCTIONS ON THIS PIECE OF PAPER HERE...
I... DO NOT... CARE!
WHEREVER IT IS... I DO NOT... WISH TO GO. I AM RETURNING HOME TO LOUISIANA...
REALLY? FAIR ENOUGH.
SHIK
YOU DON'T... APPEAR... TO BE... CONCERNED...
WHY SHOULD I BE? IT'S A FREE WORLD, CHIEF. YOU GO WHERE YOU LIKE.
SEE YOU AROUND.
FWIK
LOUISIANA
next: SOUTHERN CHANGE

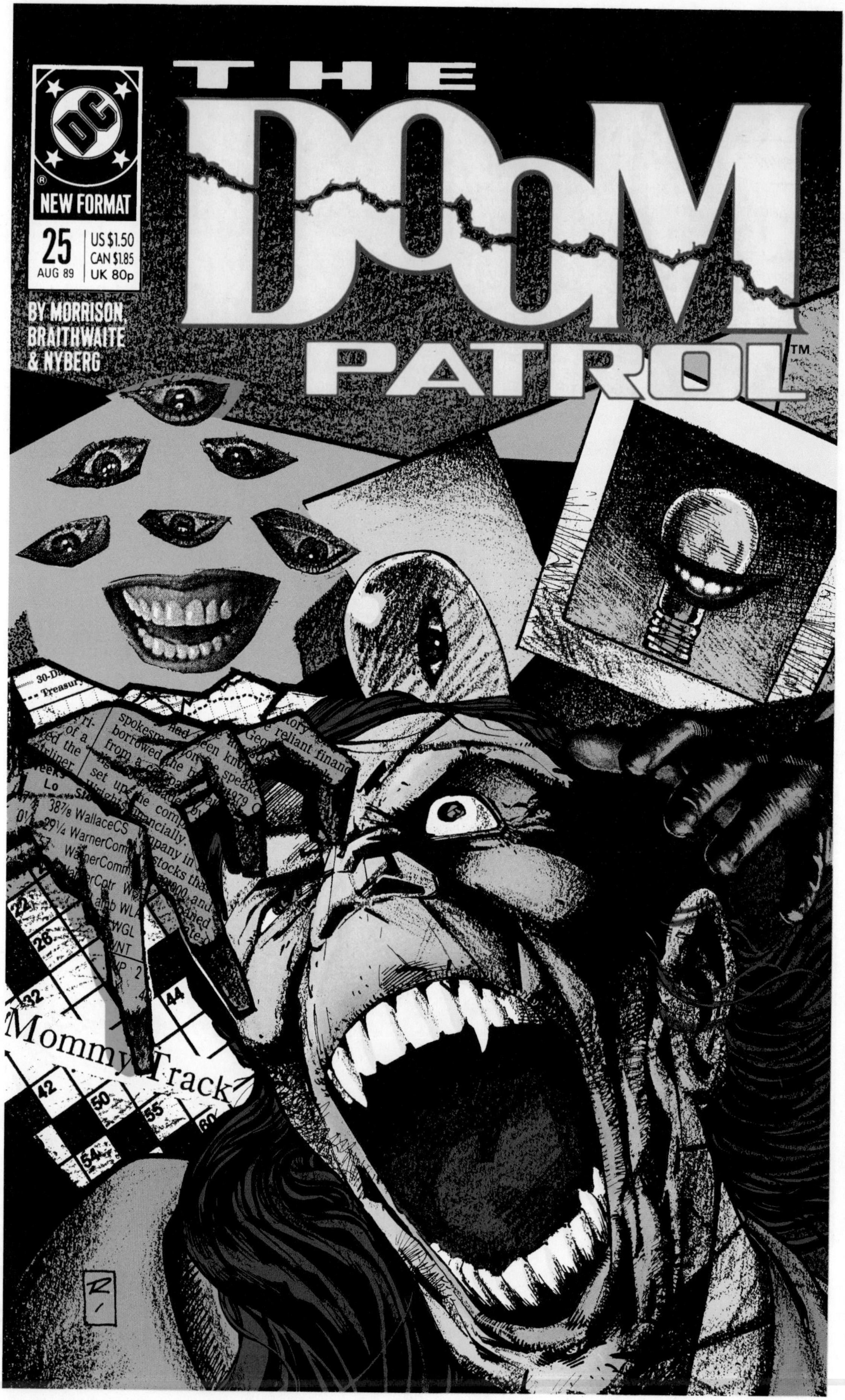
DC
NEW FORMAT
25
AUG 89
US $1.50
CAN $1.85
UK 80p
BY MORRISON, BRAITHWAITE & NYBERG
THE DOOM PATROL™
Mommy Track

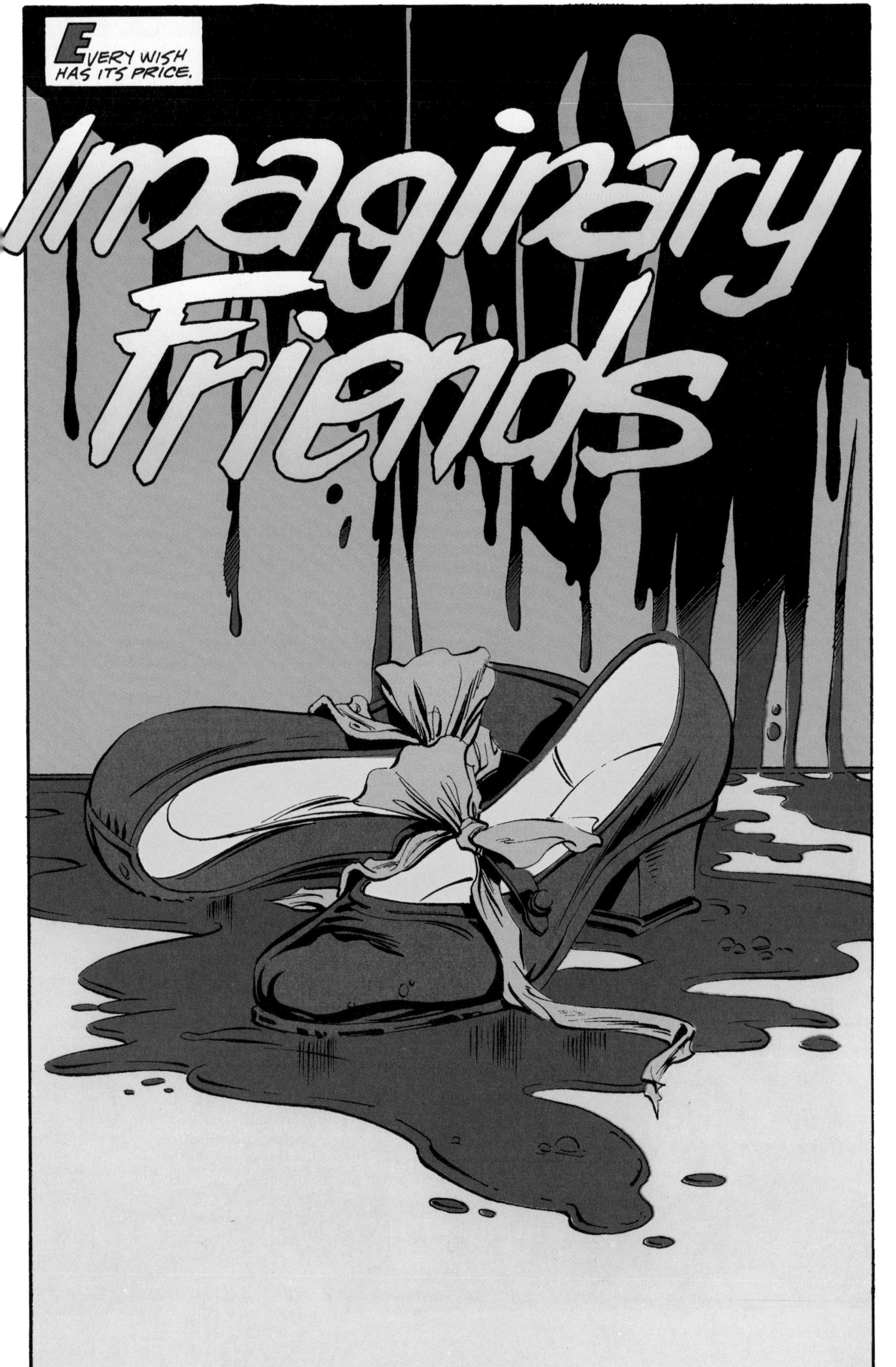
EVERY WISH HAS ITS PRICE.
Imaginary Friends

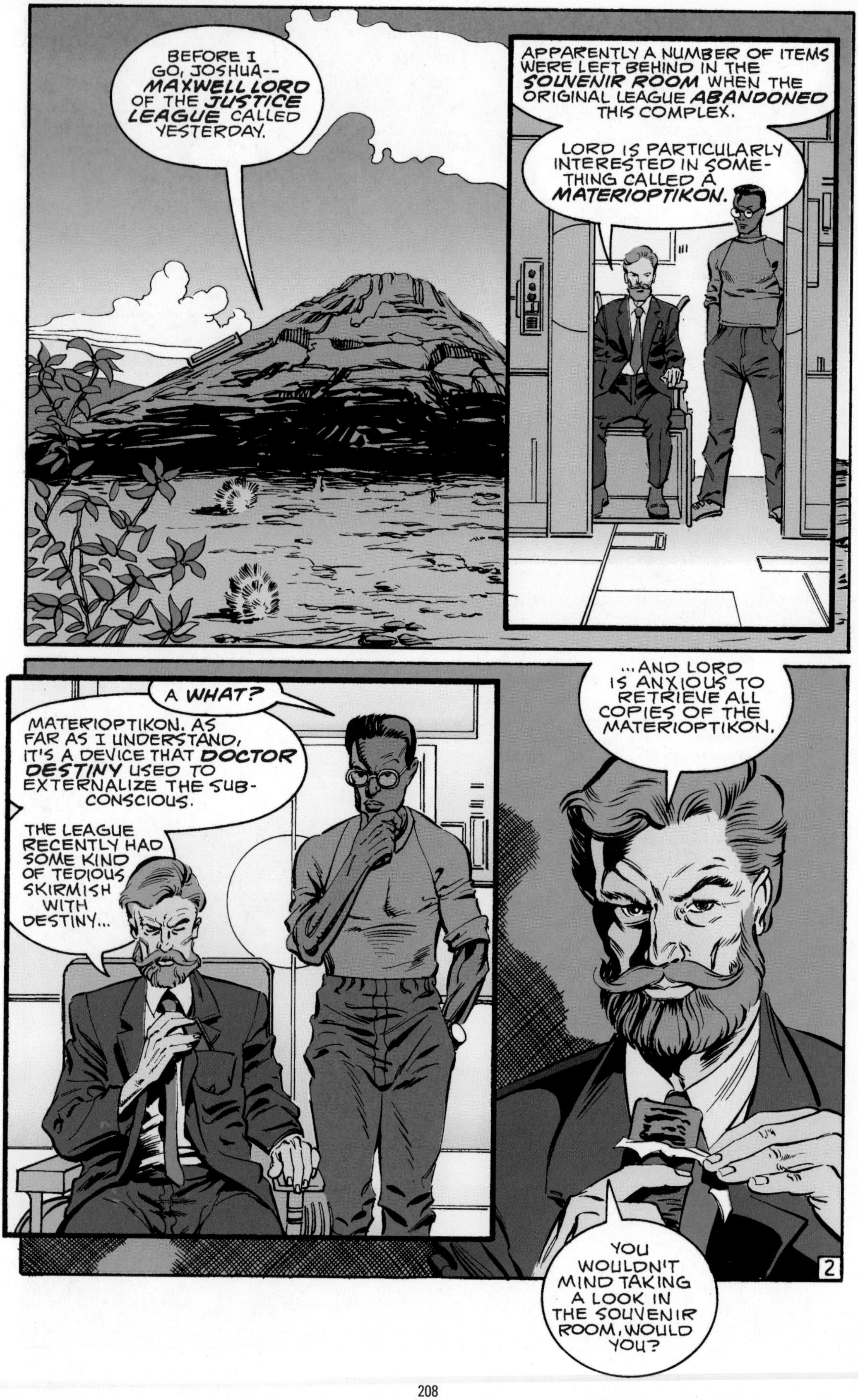
BEFORE I GO, JOSHUA-- MAXWELL LORD OF THE JUSTICE LEAGUE CALLED YESTERDAY.
APPARENTLY A NUMBER OF ITEMS WERE LEFT BEHIND IN THE SOUVENIR ROOM WHEN THE ORIGINAL LEAGUE ABANDONED THIS COMPLEX.
LORD IS PARTICULARLY INTERESTED IN SOMETHING CALLED A MATERIOPTIKON.
A WHAT?
MATERIOPTIKON. AS FAR AS I UNDERSTAND, IT'S A DEVICE THAT DOCTOR DESTINY USED TO EXTERNALIZE THE SUBCONSCIOUS.
THE LEAGUE RECENTLY HAD SOME KIND OF TEDIOUS SKIRMISH WITH DESTINY...
...AND LORD IS ANXIOUS TO RETRIEVE ALL COPIES OF THE MATERIOPTIKON.
YOU WOULDN'T MIND TAKING A LOOK IN THE SOUVENIR ROOM, WOULD YOU?
2

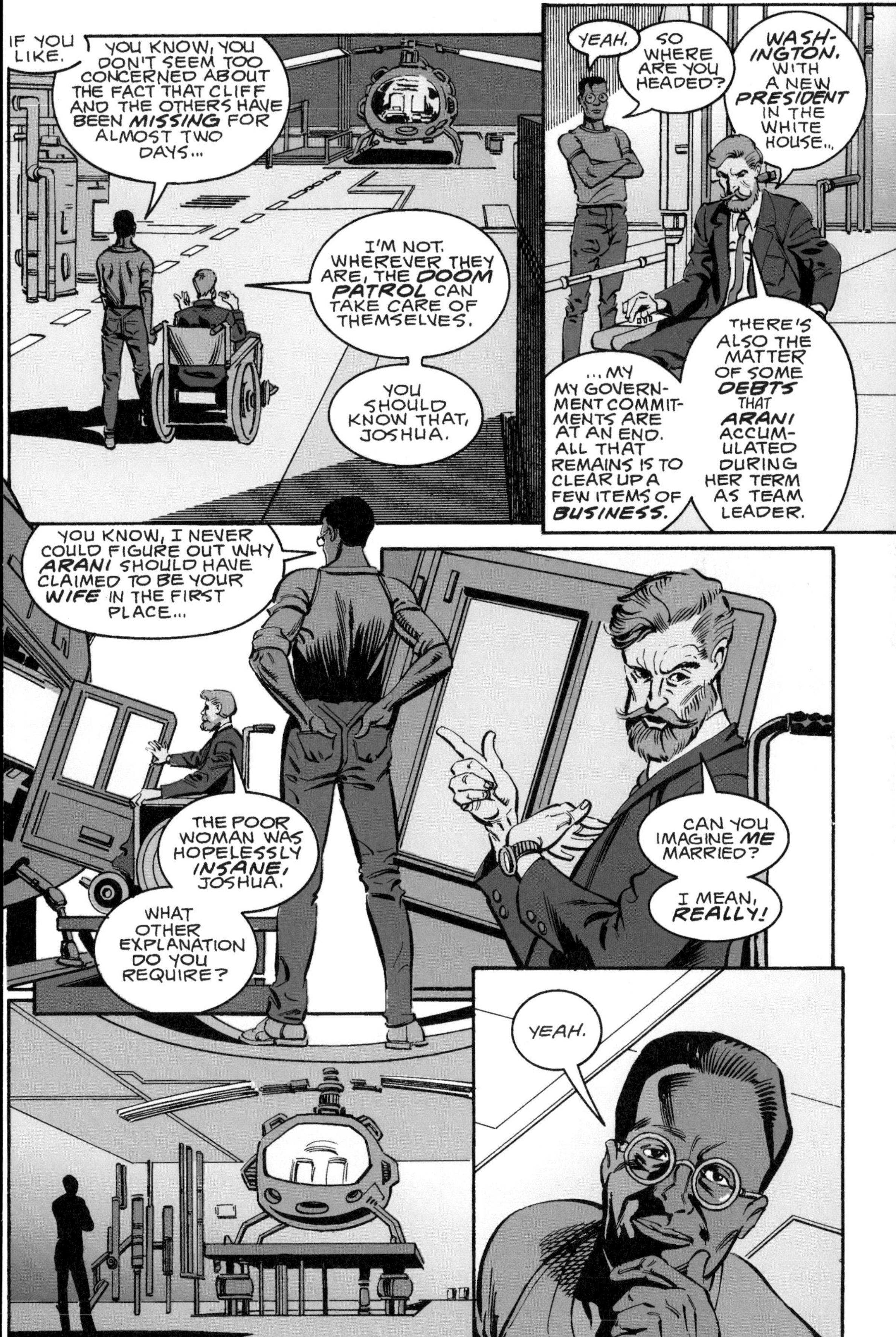

IF YOU LIKE.
YOU KNOW, YOU DON'T SEEM TOO CONCERNED ABOUT THE FACT THAT CLIFF AND THE OTHERS HAVE BEEN MISSING FOR ALMOST TWO DAYS...
I'M NOT. WHEREVER THEY ARE, THE DOOM PATROL CAN TAKE CARE OF THEMSELVES.
YOU SHOULD KNOW THAT, JOSHUA.
YEAH.
SO WHERE ARE YOU HEADED?
WASHINGTON. WITH A NEW PRESIDENT IN THE WHITE HOUSE...
...MY MY GOVERNMENT COMMITMENTS ARE AT AN END. ALL THAT REMAINS IS TO CLEAR UP A FEW ITEMS OF BUSINESS.
THERE'S ALSO THE MATTER OF SOME DEBTS THAT ARANI ACCUMULATED DURING HER TERM AS TEAM LEADER.
YOU KNOW, I NEVER COULD FIGURE OUT WHY ARANI SHOULD HAVE CLAIMED TO BE YOUR WIFE IN THE FIRST PLACE...
THE POOR WOMAN WAS HOPELESSLY INSANE, JOSHUA.
WHAT OTHER EXPLANATION DO YOU REQUIRE?
CAN YOU IMAGINE ME MARRIED?
I MEAN, REALLY!
YEAH.
3

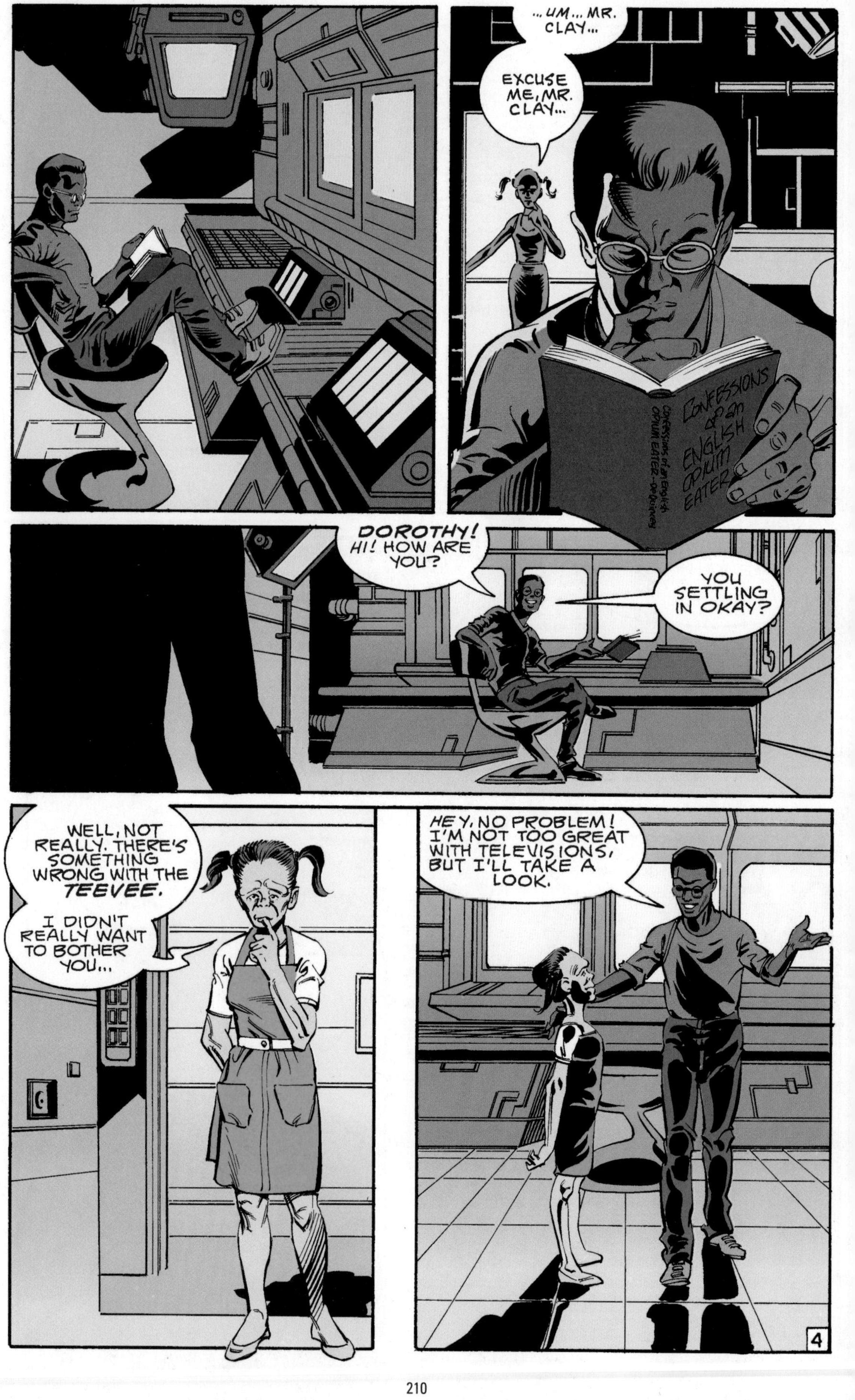

...UM... MR. CLAY...
EXCUSE ME, MR. CLAY...
CONFESSIONS of an ENGLISH OPIUM EATER
CONFESSIONS of an English OPIUM EATER—DeQuincey
DOROTHY! HI! HOW ARE YOU?
YOU SETTLING IN OKAY?
WELL, NOT REALLY. THERE'S SOMETHING WRONG WITH THE TEEVEE.
I DIDN'T REALLY WANT TO BOTHER YOU...
HEY, NO PROBLEM! I'M NOT TOO GREAT WITH TELEVISIONS, BUT I'LL TAKE A LOOK.
4

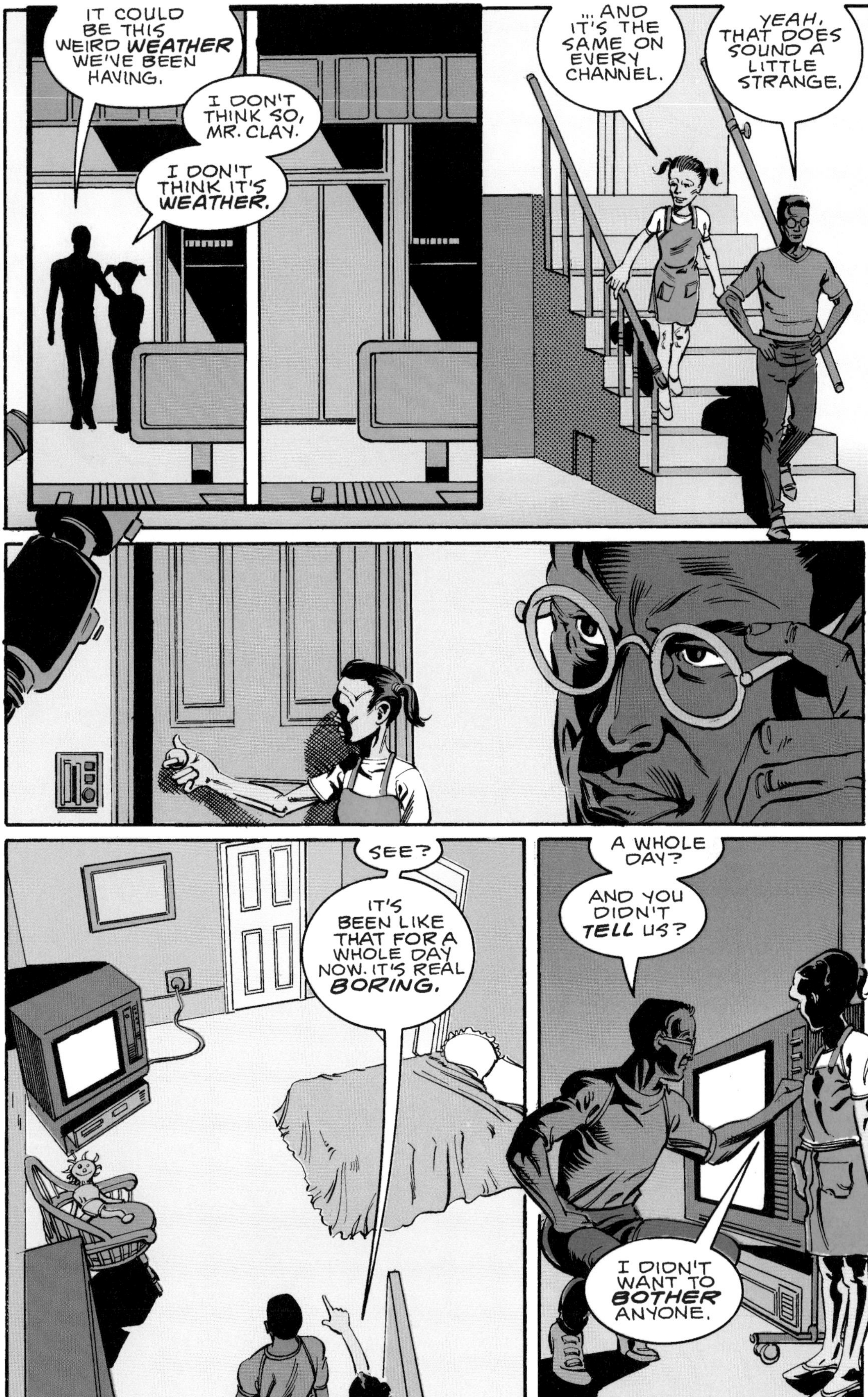
IT COULD BE THIS WEIRD WEATHER WE'VE BEEN HAVING.
I DON'T THINK SO, MR. CLAY.
I DON'T THINK IT'S WEATHER.
...AND IT'S THE SAME ON EVERY CHANNEL.
YEAH, THAT DOES SOUND A LITTLE STRANGE.
SEE?
IT'S BEEN LIKE THAT FOR A WHOLE DAY NOW. IT'S REAL BORING.
A WHOLE DAY?
AND YOU DIDN'T TELL US?
I DIDN'T WANT TO BOTHER ANYONE.

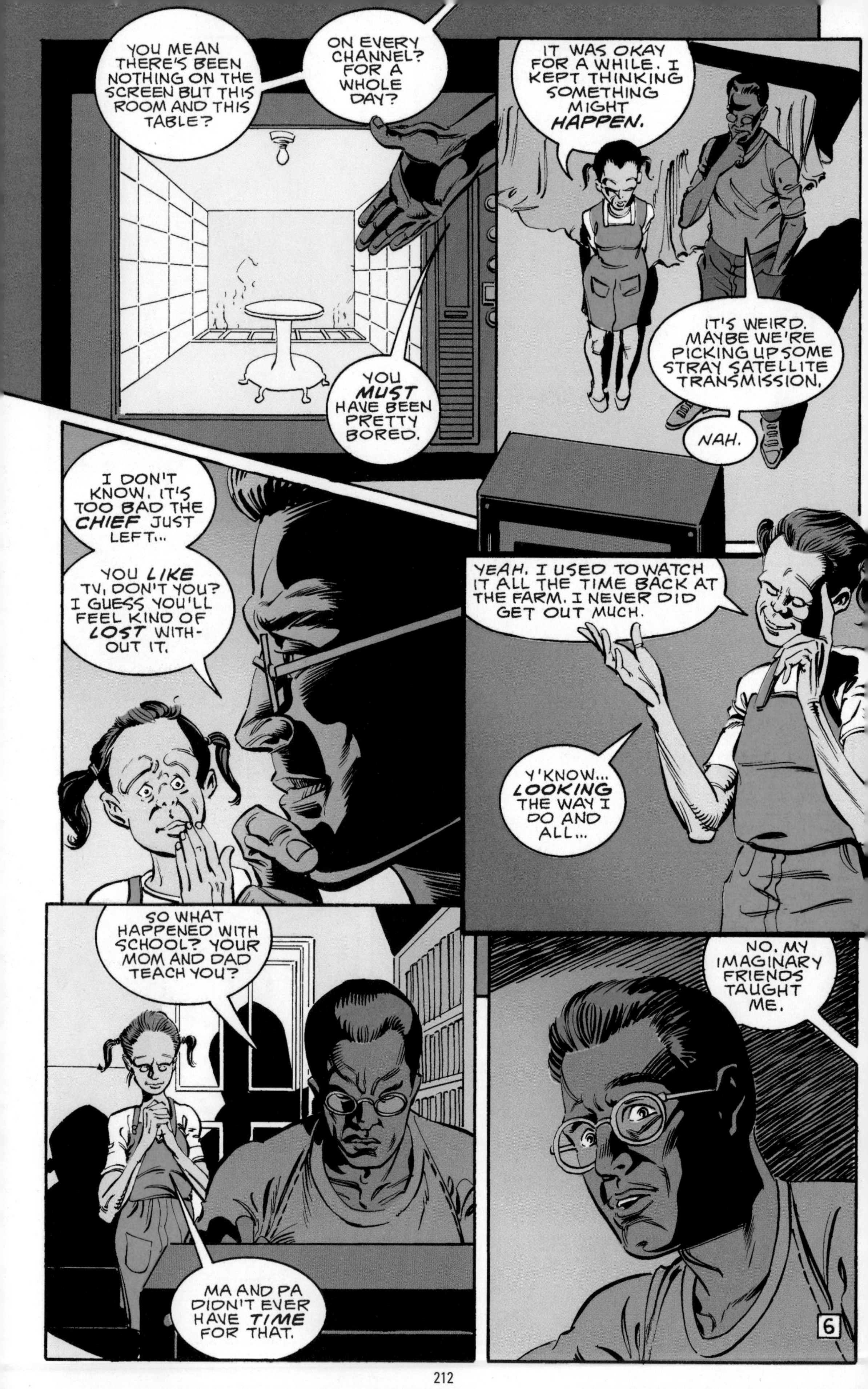
YOU MEAN THERE'S BEEN NOTHING ON THE SCREEN BUT THIS ROOM AND THIS TABLE?
ON EVERY CHANNEL? FOR A WHOLE DAY?
YOU MUST HAVE BEEN PRETTY BORED.
IT WAS OKAY FOR A WHILE. I KEPT THINKING SOMETHING MIGHT HAPPEN.
IT'S WEIRD. MAYBE WE'RE PICKING UP SOME STRAY SATELLITE TRANSMISSION.
NAH.
I DON'T KNOW. IT'S TOO BAD THE CHIEF JUST LEFT...
YOU LIKE TV, DON'T YOU? I GUESS YOU'LL FEEL KIND OF LOST WITH-OUT IT.
YEAH. I USED TO WATCH IT ALL THE TIME BACK AT THE FARM. I NEVER DID GET OUT MUCH.
Y'KNOW... LOOKING THE WAY I DO AND ALL...
SO WHAT HAPPENED WITH SCHOOL? YOUR MOM AND DAD TEACH YOU?
MA AND PA DIDN'T EVER HAVE TIME FOR THAT.
NO. MY IMAGINARY FRIENDS TAUGHT ME.
6

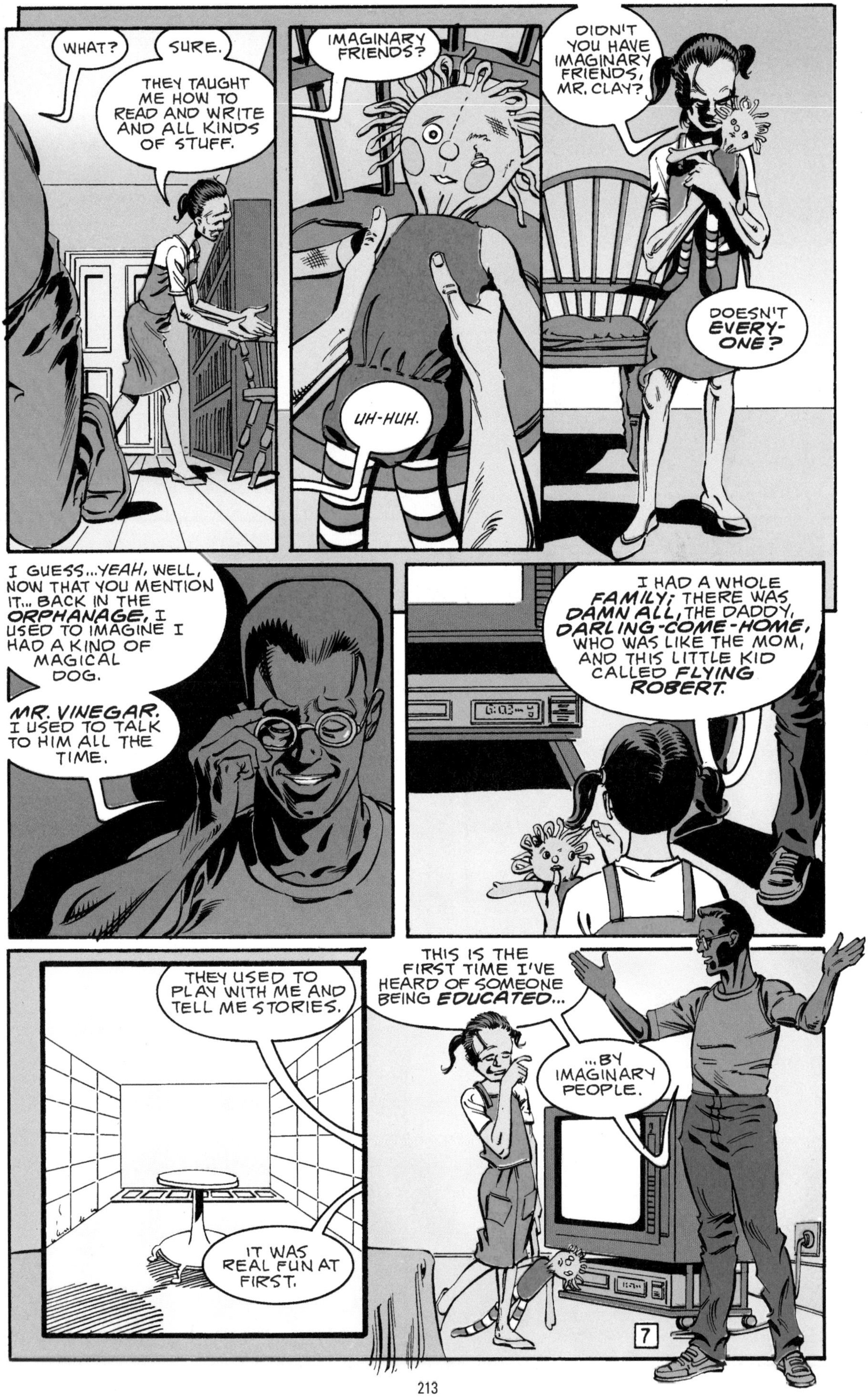

WHAT?
SURE.
THEY TAUGHT ME HOW TO READ AND WRITE AND ALL KINDS OF STUFF.
IMAGINARY FRIENDS?
UH-HUH.
DIDN'T YOU HAVE IMAGINARY FRIENDS, MR. CLAY?
DOESN'T EVERY-ONE?
I GUESS...YEAH, WELL, NOW THAT YOU MENTION IT... BACK IN THE ORPHANAGE, I USED TO IMAGINE I HAD A KIND OF MAGICAL DOG.
MR. VINEGAR. I USED TO TALK TO HIM ALL THE TIME.
I HAD A WHOLE FAMILY; THERE WAS DAMN ALL, THE DADDY, DARLING-COME-HOME, WHO WAS LIKE THE MOM, AND THIS LITTLE KID CALLED FLYING ROBERT.
THEY USED TO PLAY WITH ME AND TELL ME STORIES.
IT WAS REAL FUN AT FIRST.
THIS IS THE FIRST TIME I'VE HEARD OF SOMEONE BEING EDUCATED...
...BY IMAGINARY PEOPLE.
7

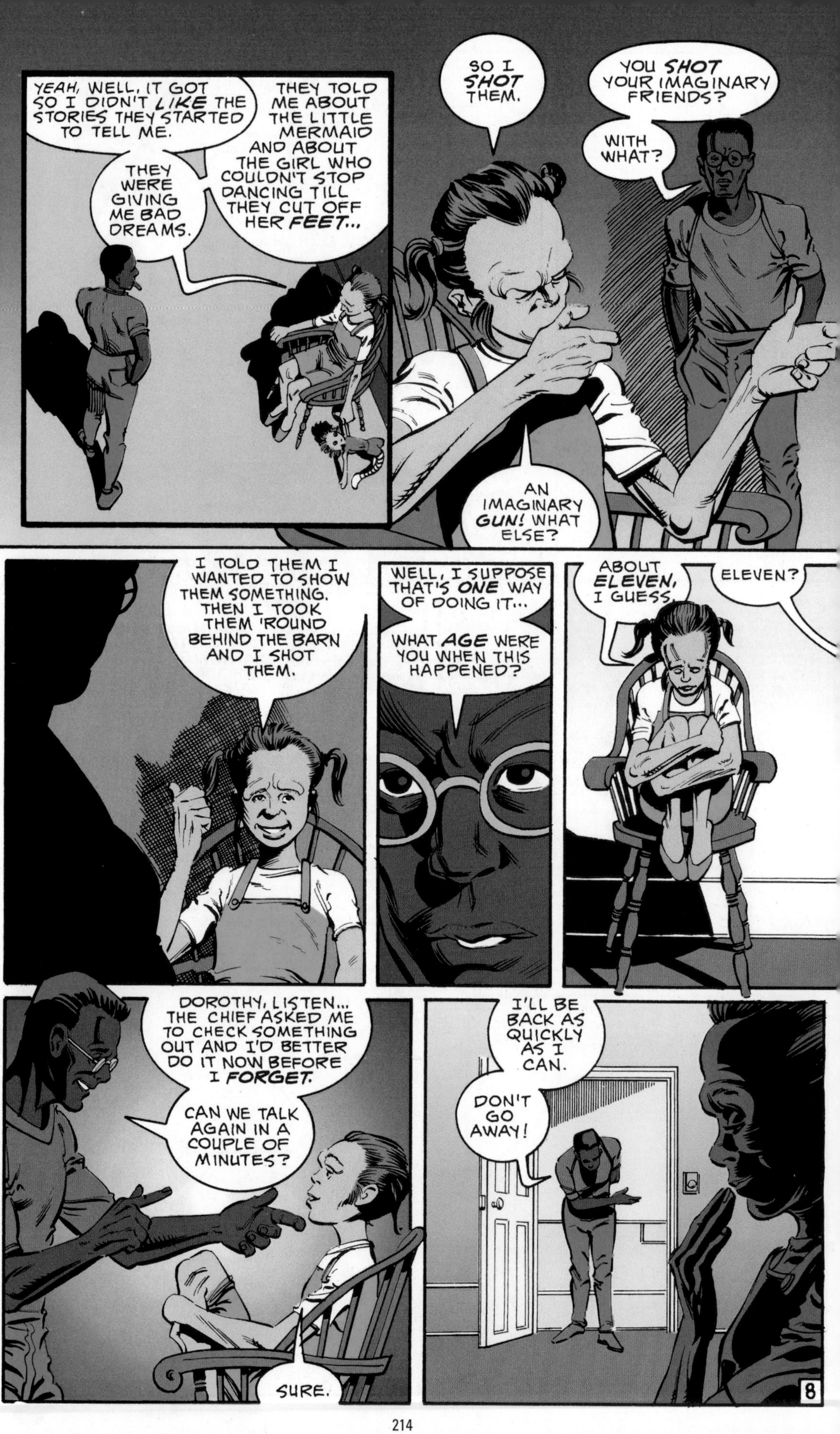
YEAH, WELL, IT GOT SO I DIDN'T LIKE THE STORIES THEY STARTED TO TELL ME.
THEY WERE GIVING ME BAD DREAMS.
THEY TOLD ME ABOUT THE LITTLE MERMAID AND ABOUT THE GIRL WHO COULDN'T STOP DANCING TILL THEY CUT OFF HER FEET...
SO I SHOT THEM.
YOU SHOT YOUR IMAGINARY FRIENDS?
WITH WHAT?
AN IMAGINARY GUN! WHAT ELSE?
I TOLD THEM I WANTED TO SHOW THEM SOMETHING. THEN I TOOK THEM 'ROUND BEHIND THE BARN AND I SHOT THEM.
WELL, I SUPPOSE THAT'S ONE WAY OF DOING IT...
WHAT AGE WERE YOU WHEN THIS HAPPENED?
ABOUT ELEVEN, I GUESS.
ELEVEN?
DOROTHY, LISTEN... THE CHIEF ASKED ME TO CHECK SOMETHING OUT AND I'D BETTER DO IT NOW BEFORE I FORGET.
CAN WE TALK AGAIN IN A COUPLE OF MINUTES?
SURE.
I'LL BE BACK AS QUICKLY AS I CAN.
DON'T GO AWAY!
8

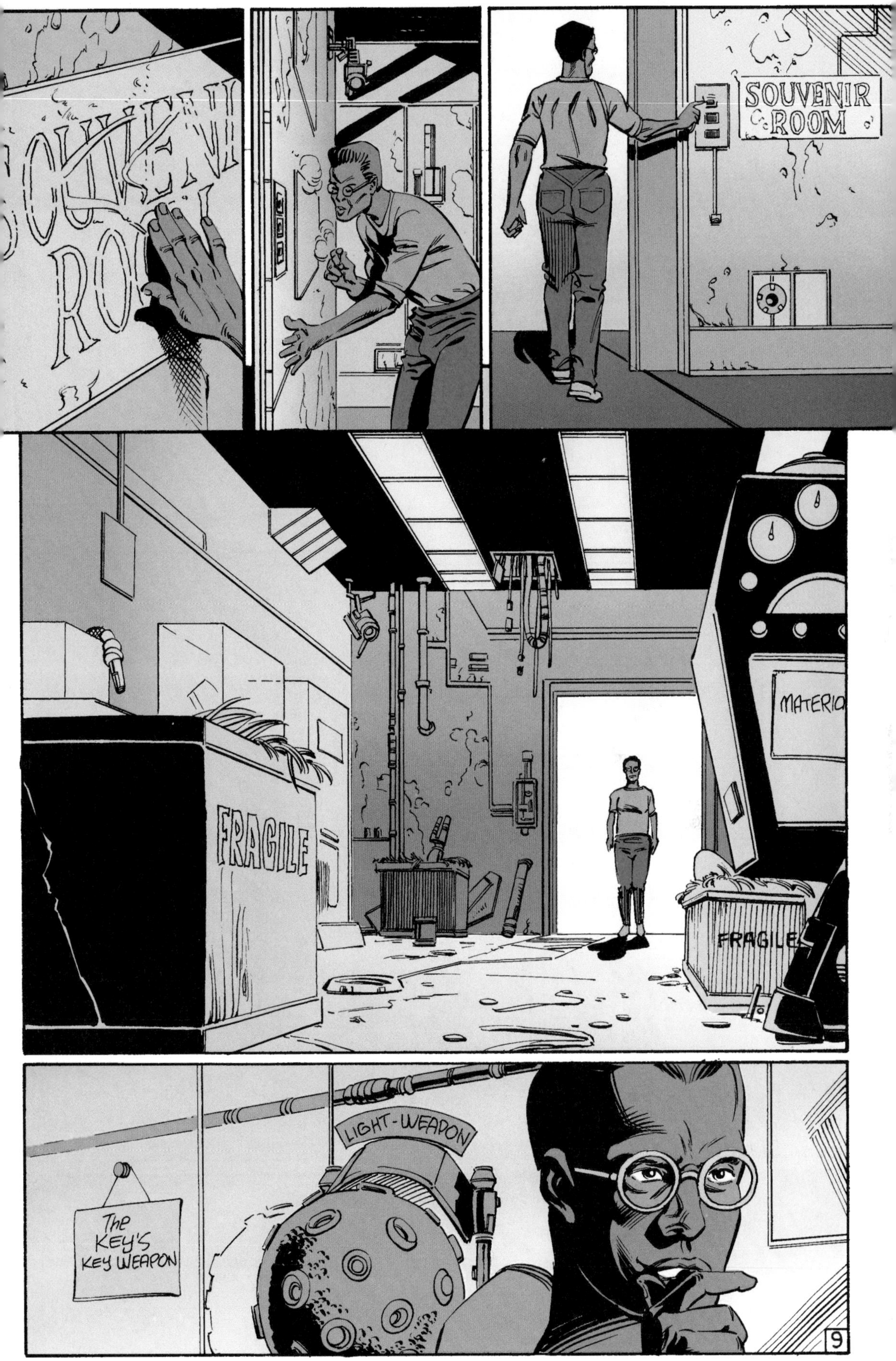
SOUVENIR ROOM
FRAGILE
MATERIA
FRAGILE
LIGHT-WEAPON
The KEY'S KEY WEAPON
9

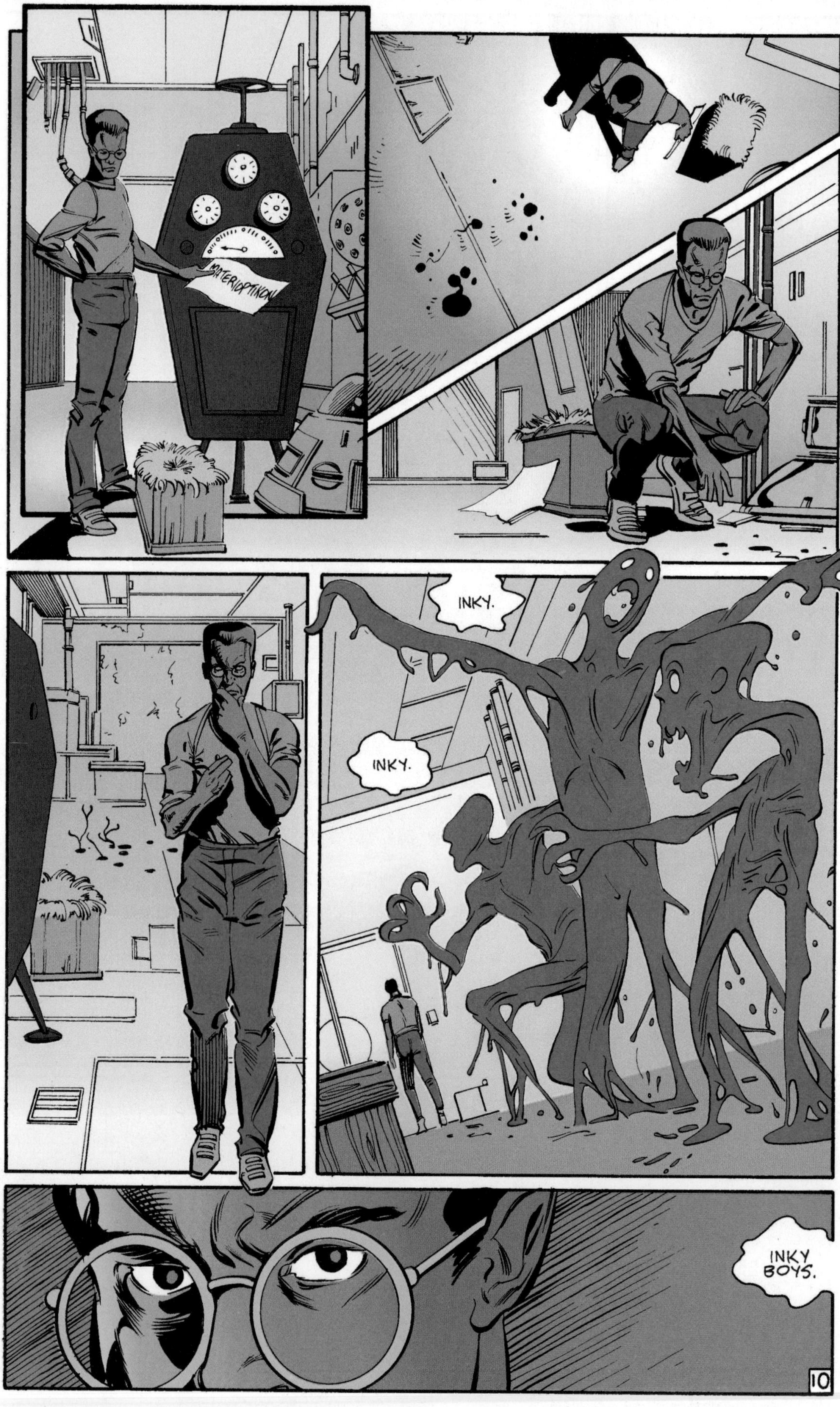
MATERIOPTIKON
INKY.
INKY.
INKY BOYS.
10

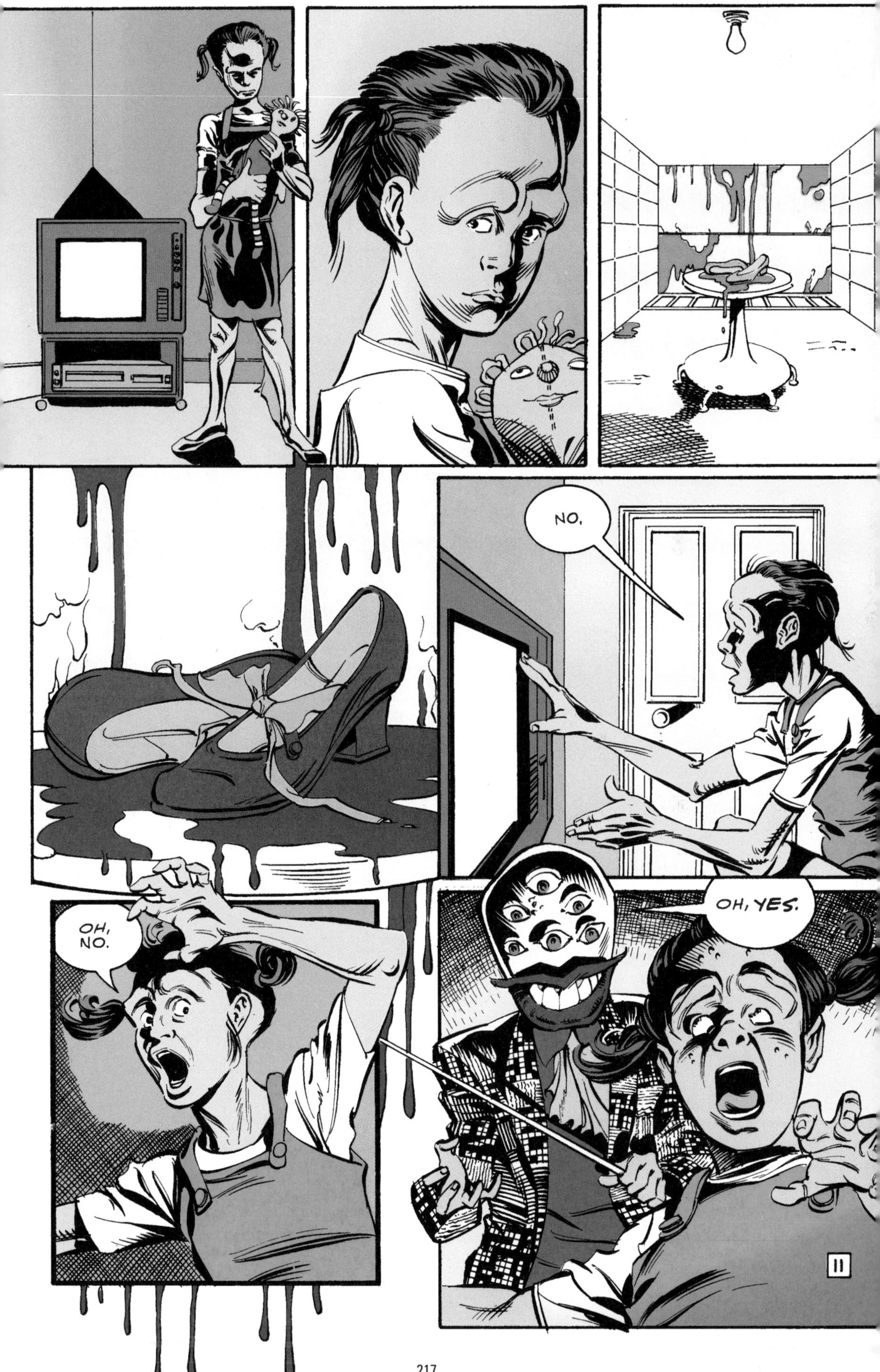
NO.
OH, NO.
OH, YES.
11

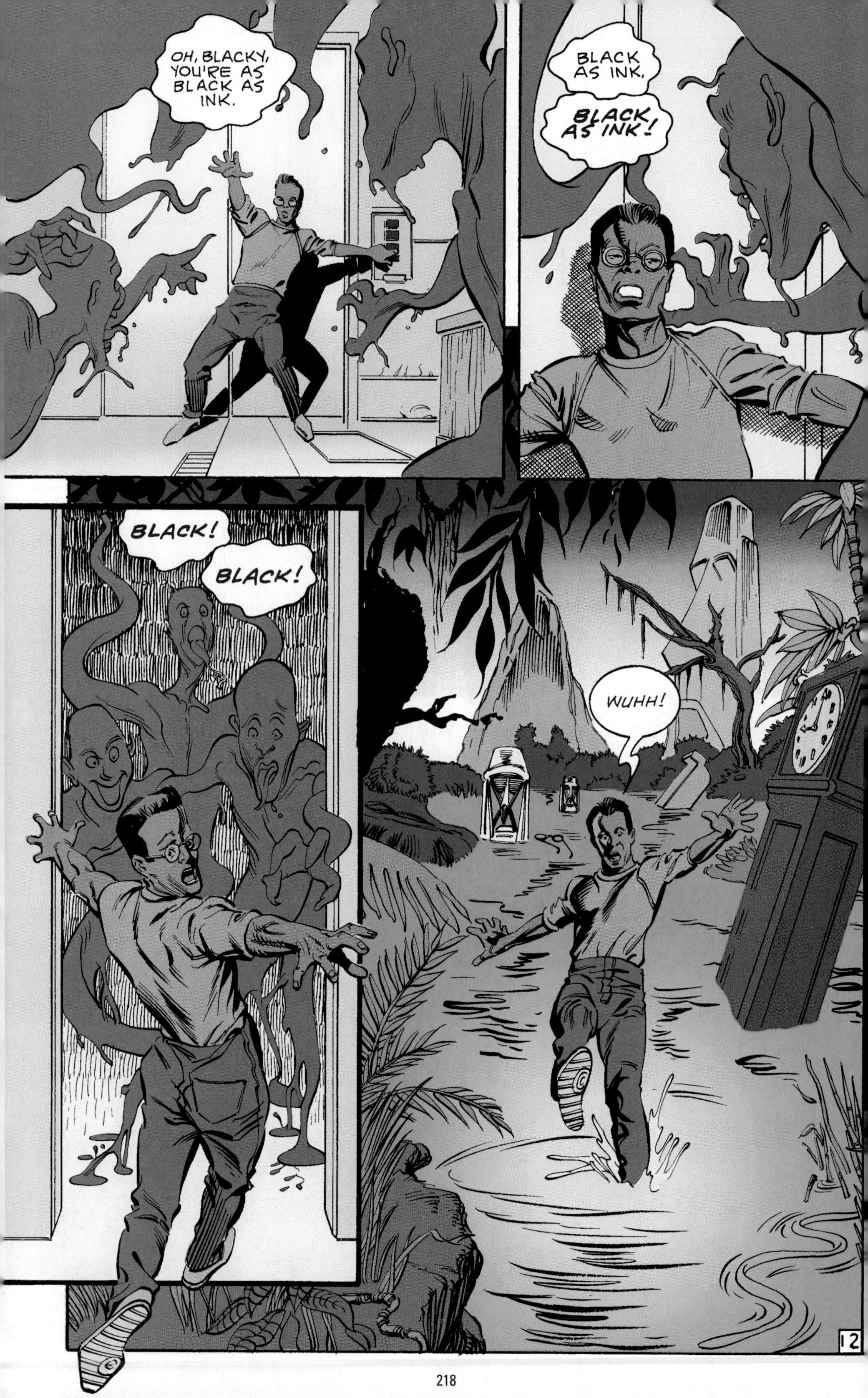
OH, BLACKY, YOU'RE AS BLACK AS INK.
BLACK AS INK.
BLACK AS INK!
BLACK!
BLACK!
WUHH!
12

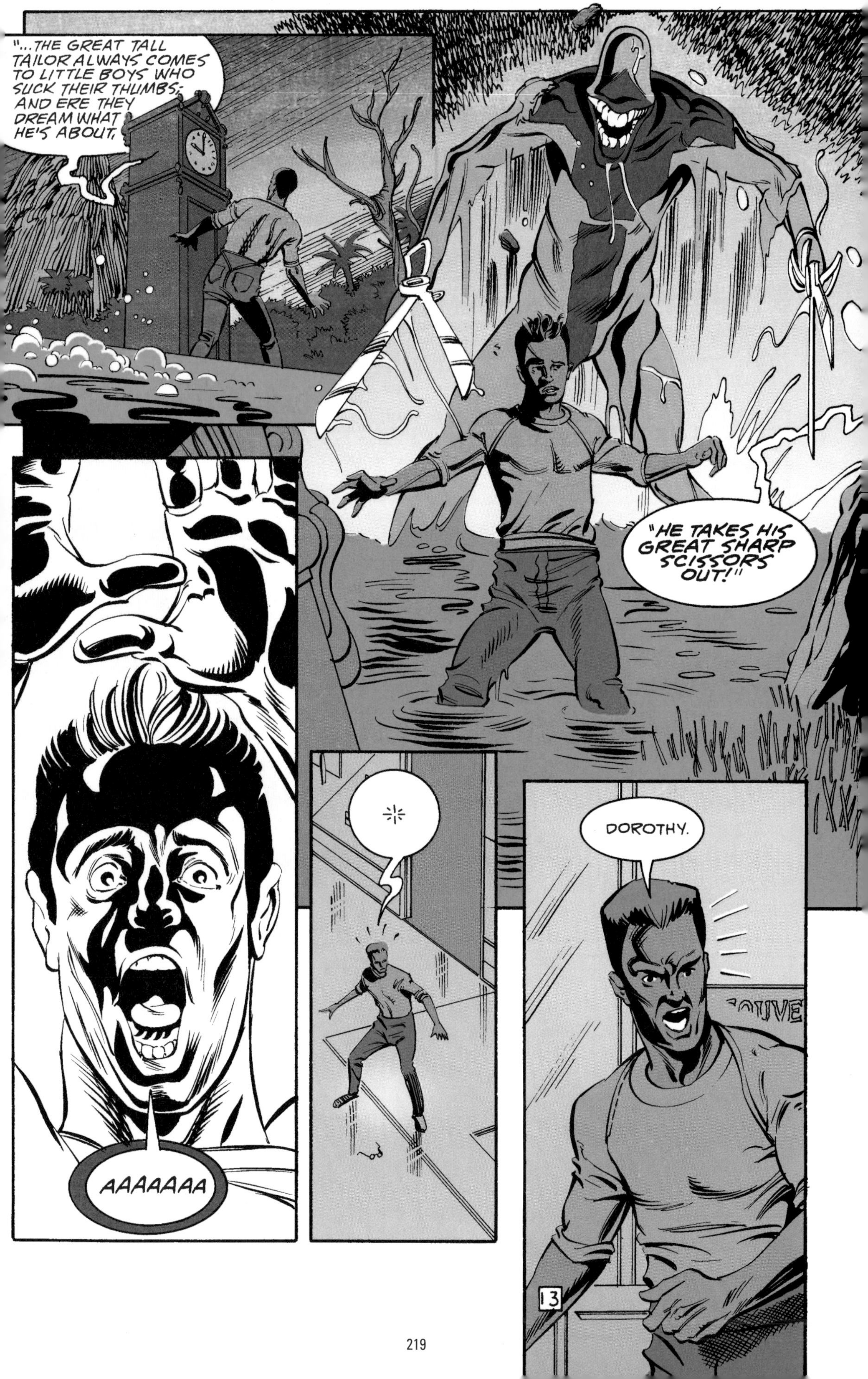
"...THE GREAT TALL TAILOR ALWAYS COMES TO LITTLE BOYS WHO SUCK THEIR THUMBS; AND ERE THEY DREAM WHAT HE'S ABOUT,
"HE TAKES HIS GREAT SHARP SCISSORS OUT!"
AAAAAAA
DOROTHY.
13

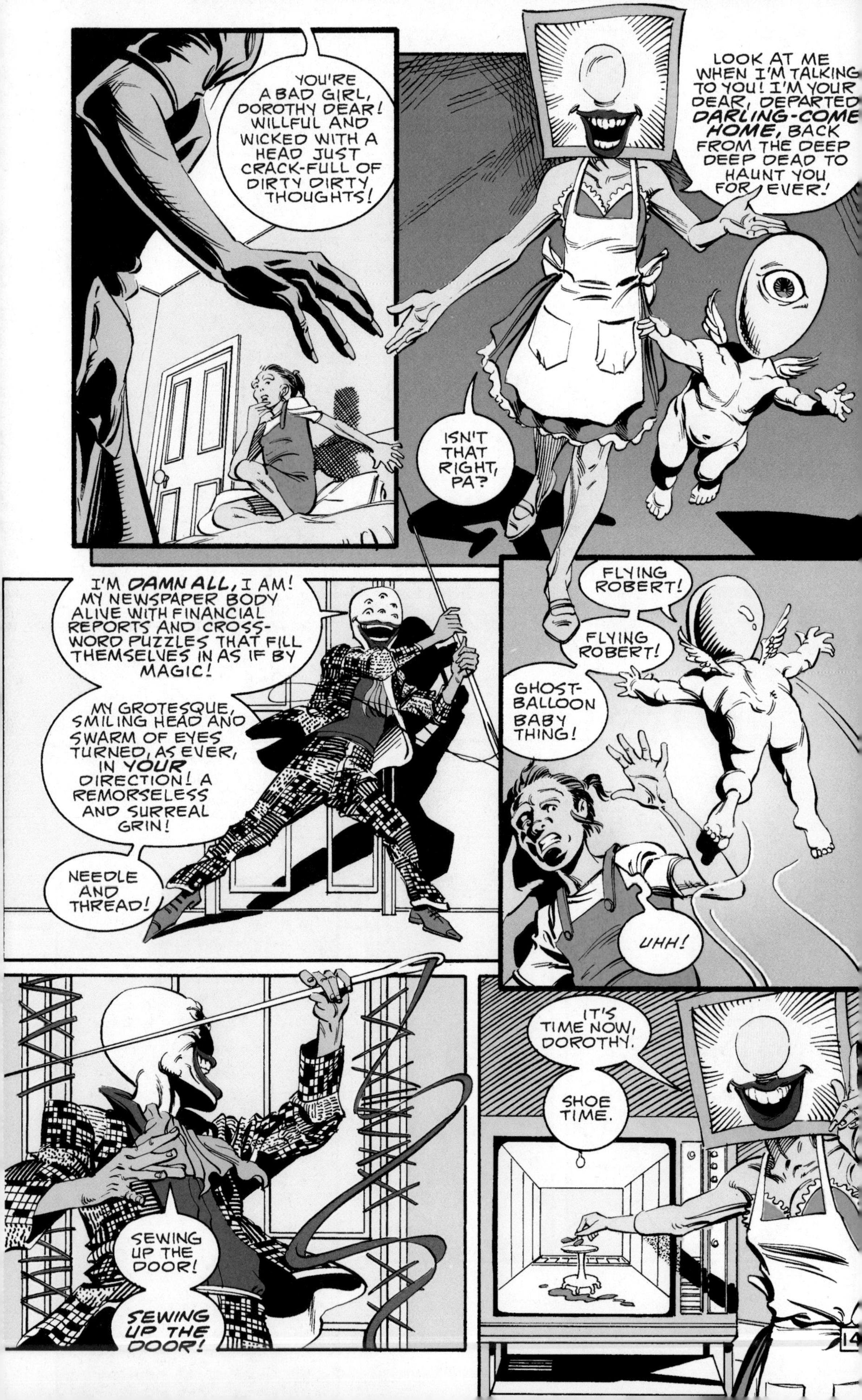
YOU'RE A BAD GIRL, DOROTHY DEAR! WILLFUL AND WICKED WITH A HEAD JUST CRACK-FULL OF DIRTY DIRTY THOUGHTS!
LOOK AT ME WHEN I'M TALKING TO YOU! I'M YOUR DEAR, DEPARTED DARLING-COME HOME, BACK FROM THE DEEP DEEP DEAD TO HAUNT YOU FOR EVER!
ISN'T THAT RIGHT, PA?
I'M DAMN ALL, I AM! MY NEWSPAPER BODY ALIVE WITH FINANCIAL REPORTS AND CROSS-WORD PUZZLES THAT FILL THEMSELVES IN AS IF BY MAGIC!
MY GROTESQUE, SMILING HEAD AND SWARM OF EYES TURNED, AS EVER, IN YOUR DIRECTION! A REMORSELESS AND SURREAL GRIN!
NEEDLE AND THREAD!
FLYING ROBERT!
FLYING ROBERT!
GHOST-BALLOON BABY THING!
UHH!
SEWING UP THE DOOR!
SEWING UP THE DOOR!
IT'S TIME NOW, DOROTHY.
SHOE TIME.

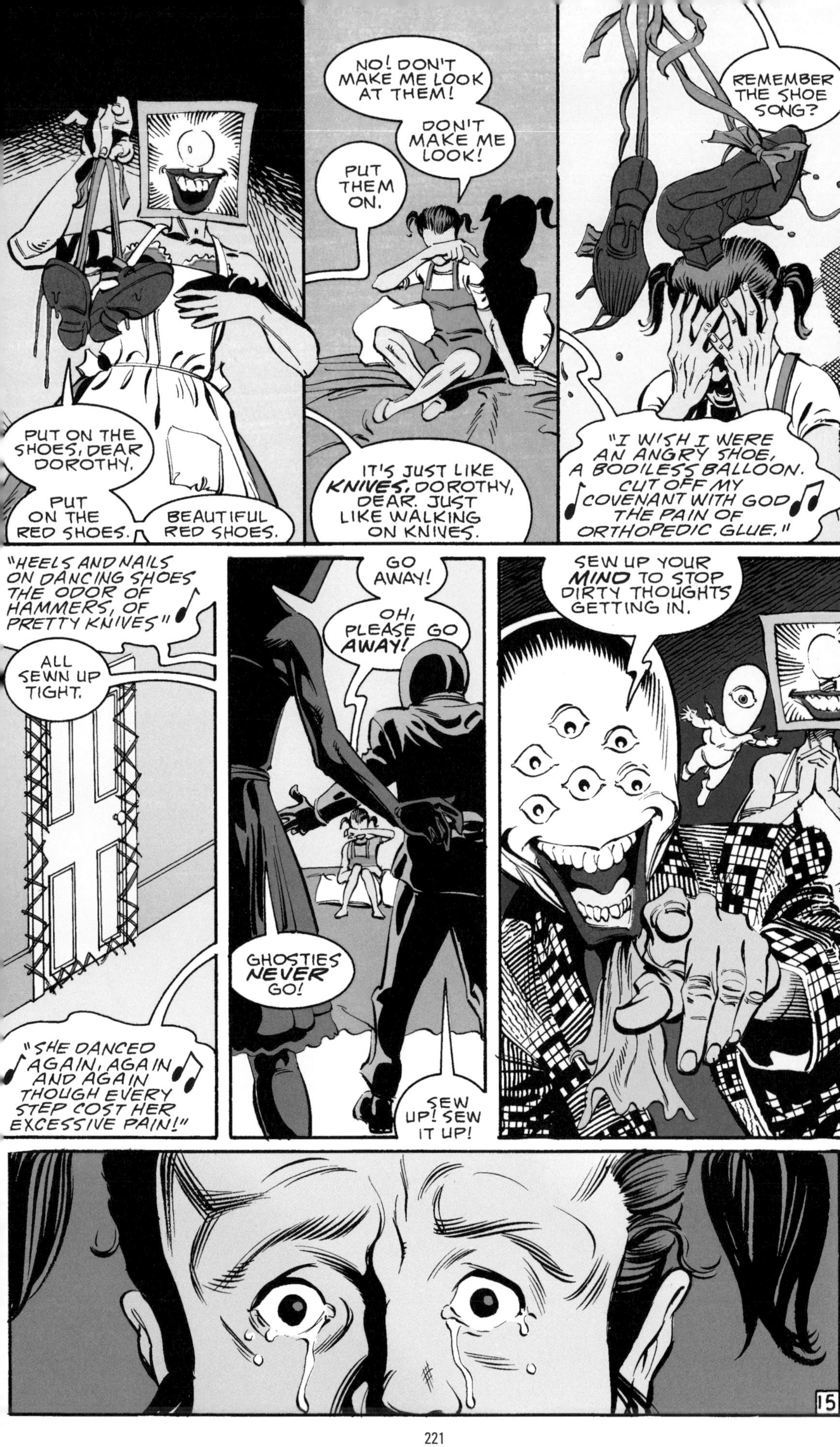

PUT ON THE SHOES, DEAR DOROTHY.
PUT ON THE RED SHOES.
BEAUTIFUL RED SHOES.
NO! DON'T MAKE ME LOOK AT THEM!
DON'T MAKE ME LOOK!
PUT THEM ON.
IT'S JUST LIKE KNIVES, DOROTHY, DEAR. JUST LIKE WALKING ON KNIVES.
REMEMBER THE SHOE SONG?
"I WISH I WERE AN ANGRY SHOE, A BODILESS BALLOON. CUT OFF MY COVENANT WITH GOD THE PAIN OF ORTHOPEDIC GLUE."
"HEELS AND NAILS ON DANCING SHOES THE ODOR OF HAMMERS, OF PRETTY KNIVES"
ALL SEWN UP TIGHT.
"SHE DANCED AGAIN, AGAIN AND AGAIN THOUGH EVERY STEP COST HER EXCESSIVE PAIN!"
GO AWAY!
OH, PLEASE GO AWAY!
GHOSTIES NEVER GO!
SEW UP! SEW IT UP!
SEW UP YOUR MIND TO STOP DIRTY THOUGHTS GETTING IN.
15

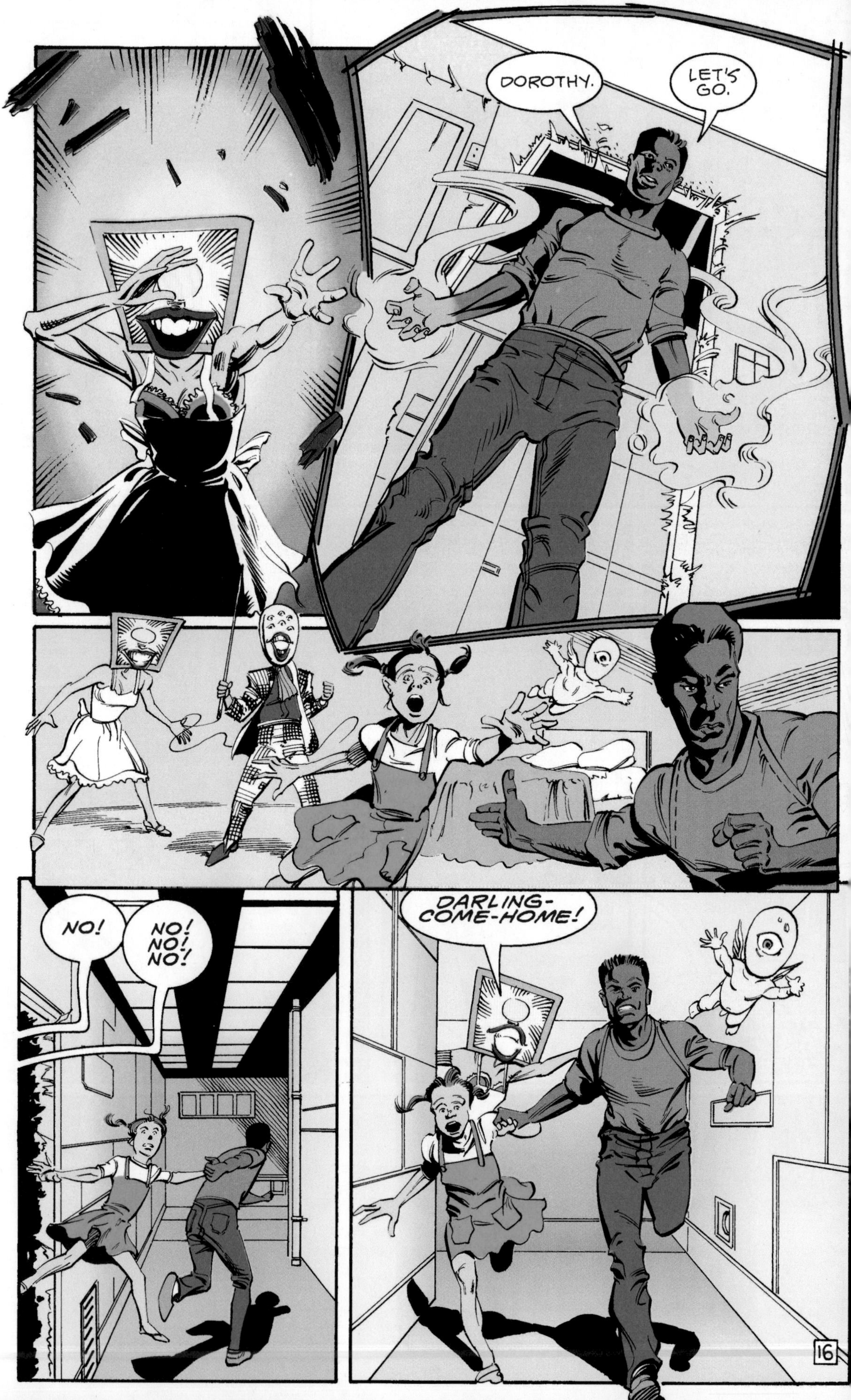
DOROTHY.
LET'S GO.
NO!
NO! NO! NO!
DARLING-COME-HOME!

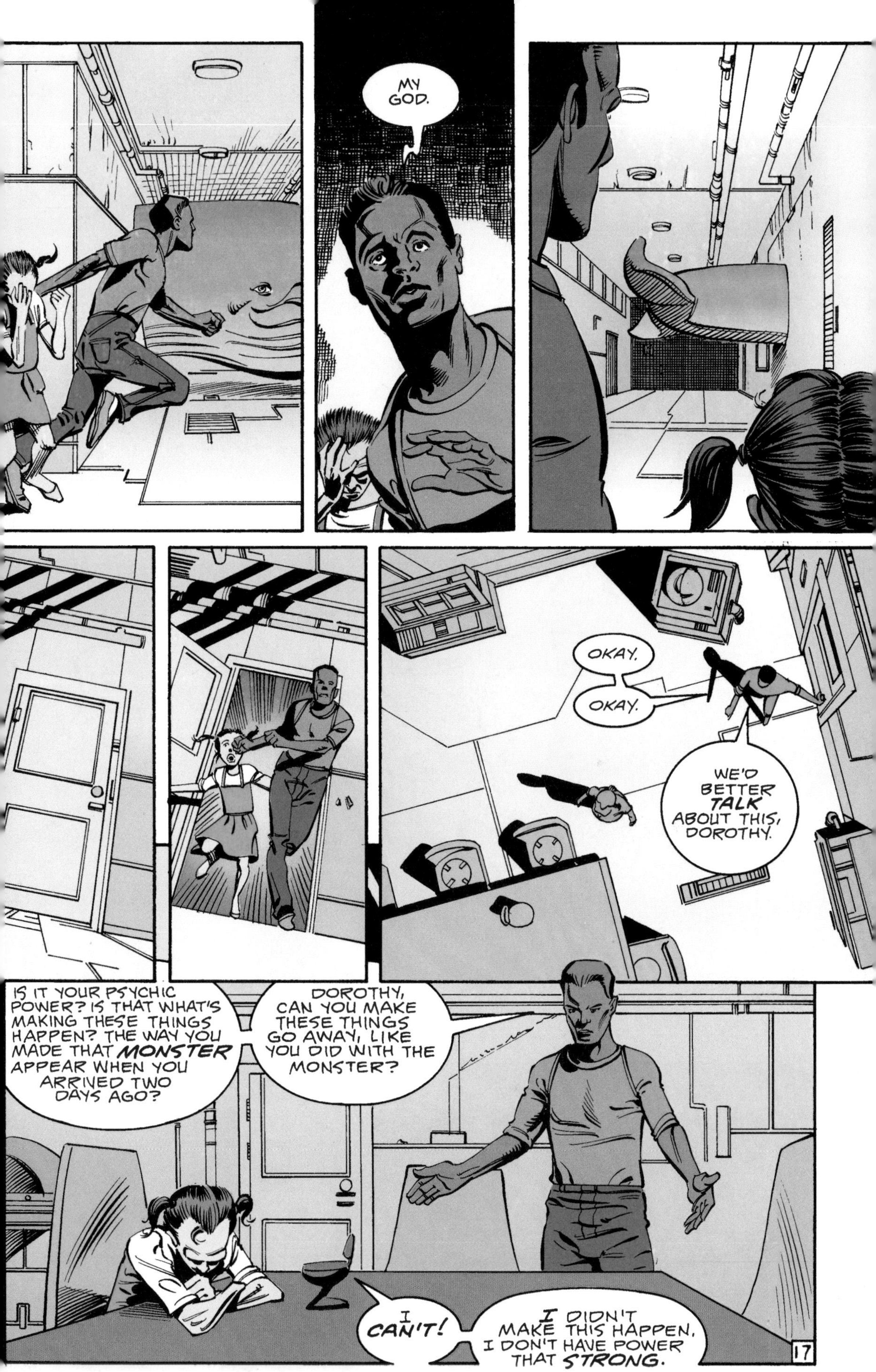

MY GOD.
OKAY.
OKAY.
WE'D BETTER TALK ABOUT THIS, DOROTHY.
IS IT YOUR PSYCHIC POWER? IS THAT WHAT'S MAKING THESE THINGS HAPPEN? THE WAY YOU MADE THAT MONSTER APPEAR WHEN YOU ARRIVED TWO DAYS AGO?
DOROTHY, CAN YOU MAKE THESE THINGS GO AWAY, LIKE YOU DID WITH THE MONSTER?
I CAN'T!
I DIDN'T MAKE THIS HAPPEN. I DON'T HAVE POWER THAT STRONG.
17

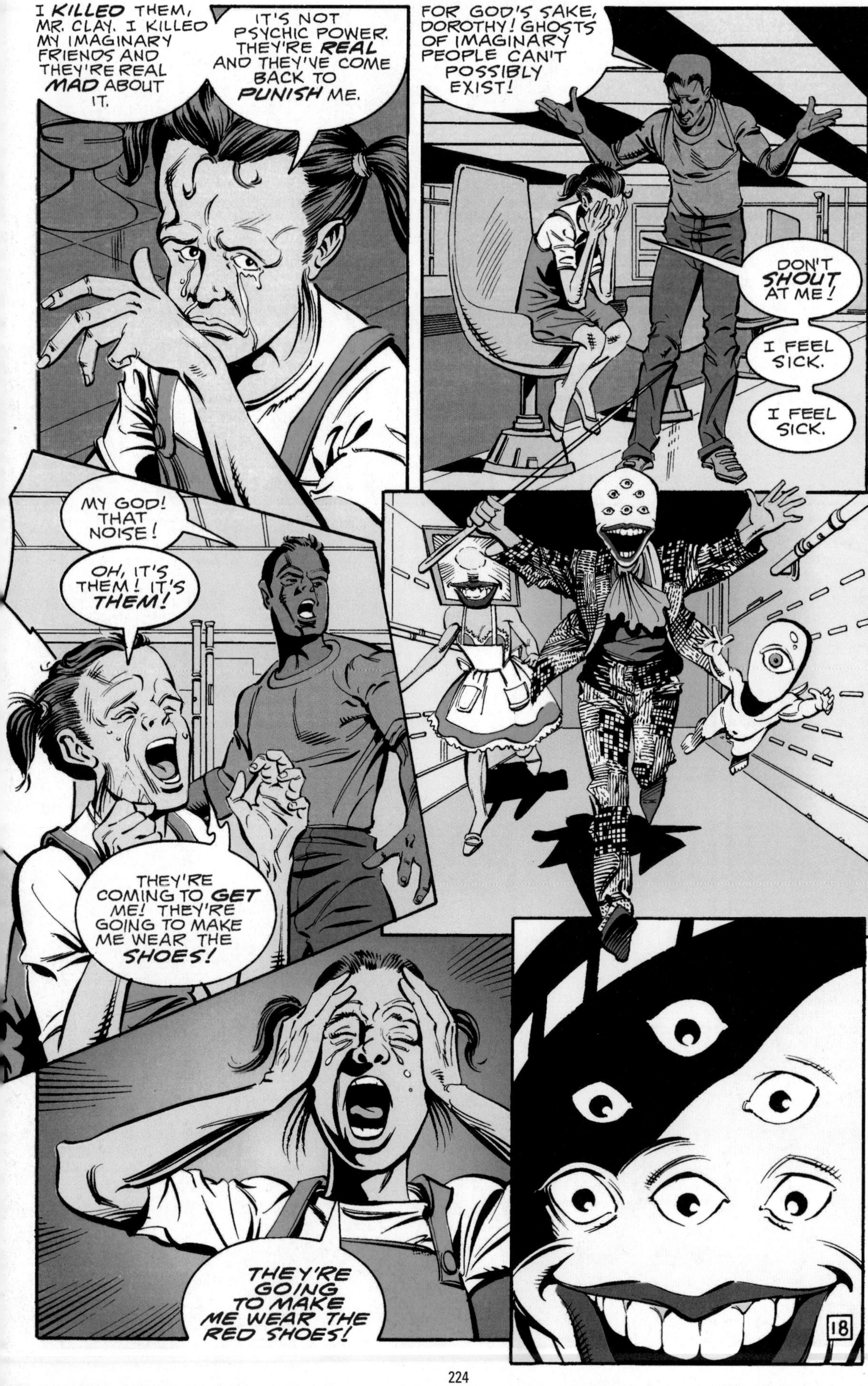
I KILLED THEM, MR. CLAY. I KILLED MY IMAGINARY FRIENDS AND THEY'RE REAL MAD ABOUT IT.
IT'S NOT PSYCHIC POWER. THEY'RE REAL AND THEY'VE COME BACK TO PUNISH ME.
FOR GOD'S SAKE, DOROTHY! GHOSTS OF IMAGINARY PEOPLE CAN'T POSSIBLY EXIST!
DON'T SHOUT AT ME!
I FEEL SICK.
I FEEL SICK.
MY GOD! THAT NOISE!
OH, IT'S THEM! IT'S THEM!
THEY'RE COMING TO GET ME! THEY'RE GOING TO MAKE ME WEAR THE SHOES!
THEY'RE GOING TO MAKE ME WEAR THE RED SHOES!
18

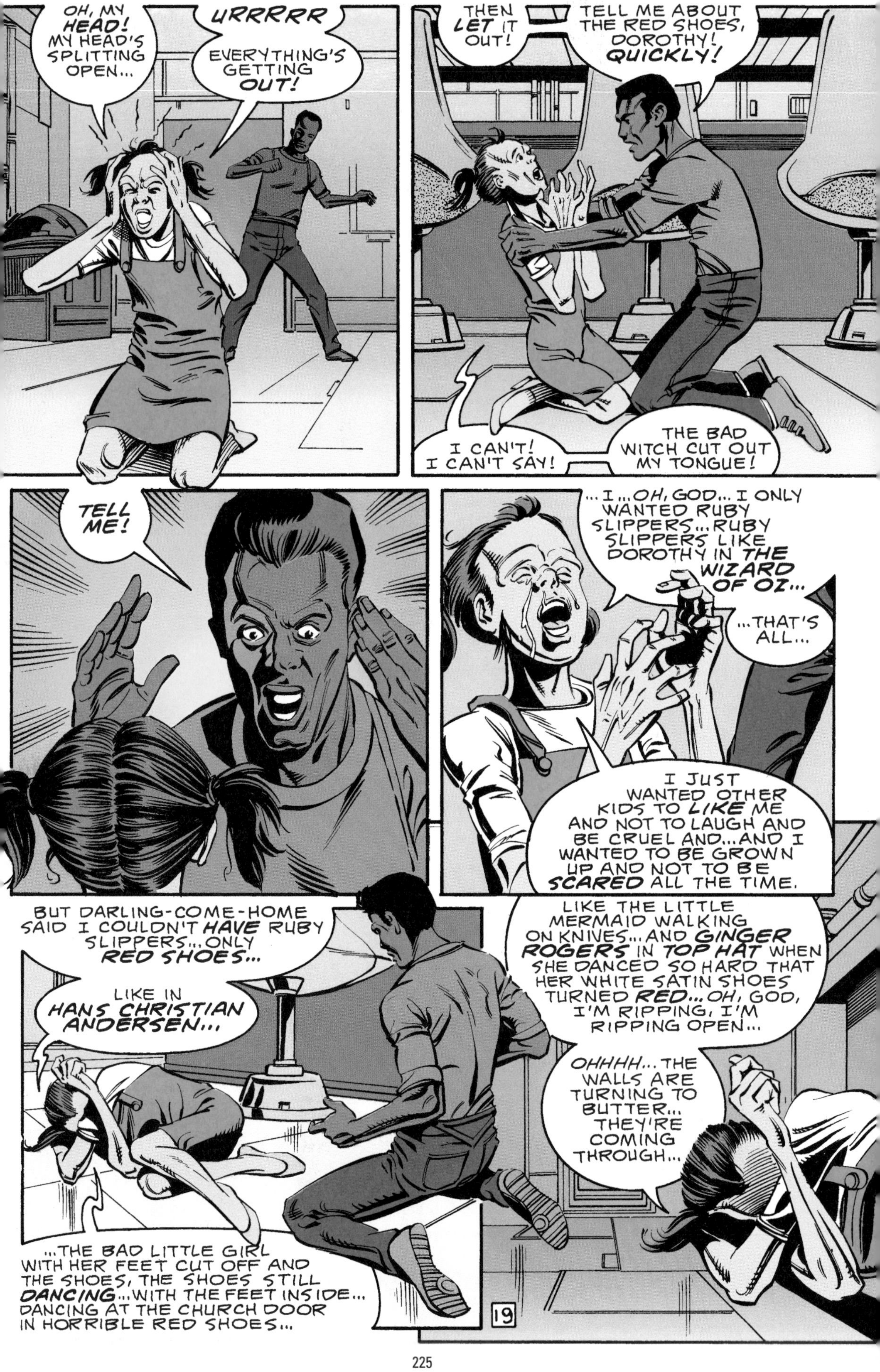
OH, MY HEAD! MY HEAD'S SPLITTING OPEN...
URRRRR
EVERYTHING'S GETTING OUT!
THEN LET IT OUT!
TELL ME ABOUT THE RED SHOES, DOROTHY! QUICKLY!
I CAN'T! I CAN'T SAY!
THE BAD WITCH CUT OUT MY TONGUE!
TELL ME!
...I...OH, GOD... I ONLY WANTED RUBY SLIPPERS...RUBY SLIPPERS LIKE DOROTHY IN THE WIZARD OF OZ...
...THAT'S ALL...
I JUST WANTED OTHER KIDS TO LIKE ME AND NOT TO LAUGH AND BE CRUEL AND...AND I WANTED TO BE GROWN UP AND NOT TO BE SCARED ALL THE TIME.
BUT DARLING-COME-HOME SAID I COULDN'T HAVE RUBY SLIPPERS...ONLY RED SHOES...
LIKE IN HANS CHRISTIAN ANDERSEN...
...THE BAD LITTLE GIRL WITH HER FEET CUT OFF AND THE SHOES, THE SHOES STILL DANCING...WITH THE FEET INSIDE... DANCING AT THE CHURCH DOOR IN HORRIBLE RED SHOES...
LIKE THE LITTLE MERMAID WALKING ON KNIVES...AND GINGER ROGERS IN TOP HAT WHEN SHE DANCED SO HARD THAT HER WHITE SATIN SHOES TURNED RED...OH, GOD, I'M RIPPING, I'M RIPPING OPEN...
OHHHH... THE WALLS ARE TURNING TO BUTTER... THEY'RE COMING THROUGH...
19

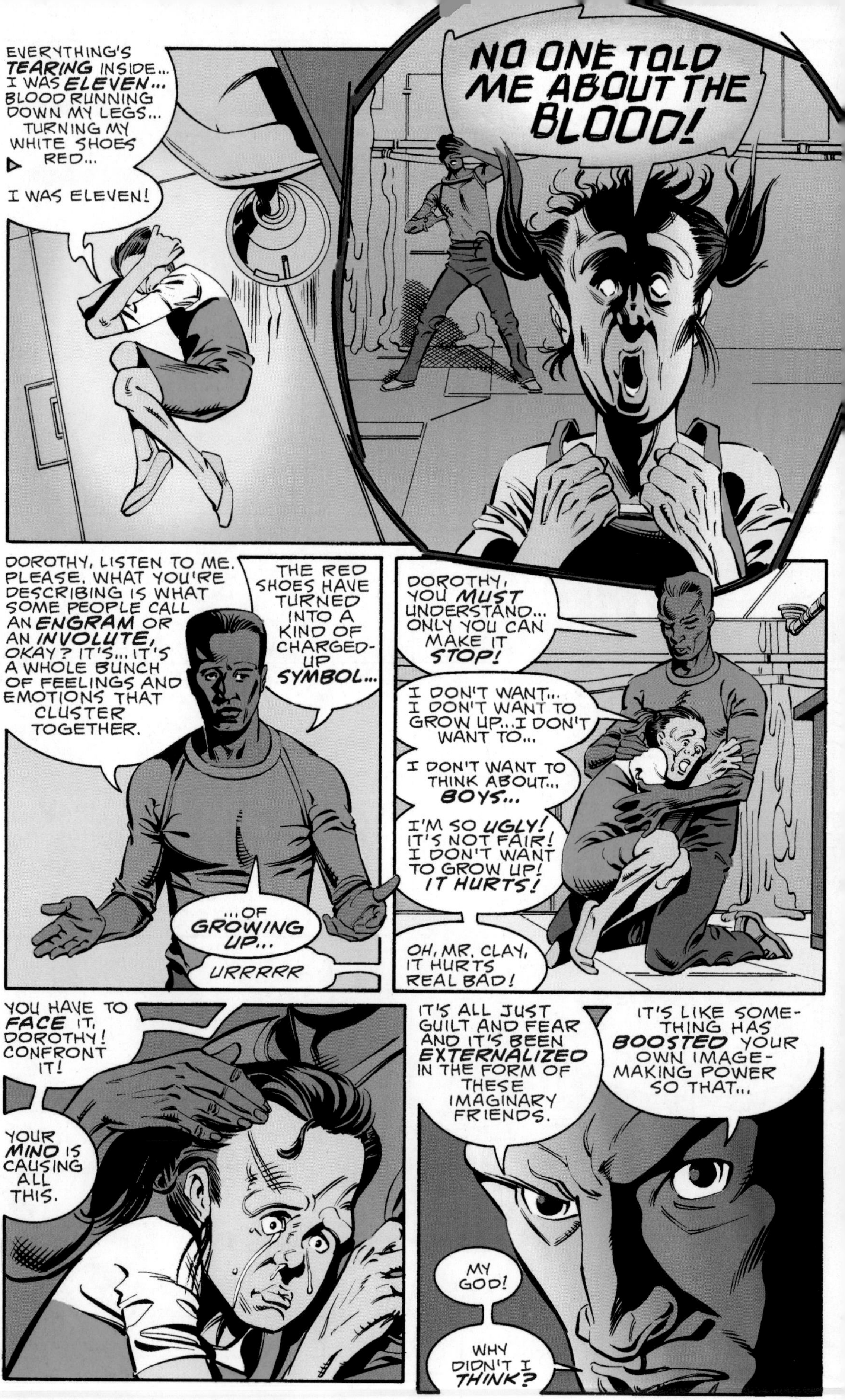
EVERYTHING'S TEARING INSIDE... I WAS ELEVEN... BLOOD RUNNING DOWN MY LEGS... TURNING MY WHITE SHOES RED...
I WAS ELEVEN!
NO ONE TOLD ME ABOUT THE BLOOD!
DOROTHY, LISTEN TO ME. PLEASE. WHAT YOU'RE DESCRIBING IS WHAT SOME PEOPLE CALL AN ENGRAM OR AN INVOLUTE, OKAY? IT'S... IT'S A WHOLE BUNCH OF FEELINGS AND EMOTIONS THAT CLUSTER TOGETHER.
THE RED SHOES HAVE TURNED INTO A KIND OF CHARGED-UP SYMBOL...
...OF GROWING UP...
URRRRR
DOROTHY, YOU MUST UNDERSTAND... ONLY YOU CAN MAKE IT STOP!
I DON'T WANT... I DON'T WANT TO GROW UP... I DON'T WANT TO...
I DON'T WANT TO THINK ABOUT... BOYS...
I'M SO UGLY! IT'S NOT FAIR! I DON'T WANT TO GROW UP! IT HURTS!
OH, MR. CLAY, IT HURTS REAL BAD!
YOU HAVE TO FACE IT, DOROTHY! CONFRONT IT!
YOUR MIND IS CAUSING ALL THIS.
IT'S ALL JUST GUILT AND FEAR AND IT'S BEEN EXTERNALIZED IN THE FORM OF THESE IMAGINARY FRIENDS.
IT'S LIKE SOMETHING HAS BOOSTED YOUR OWN IMAGE-MAKING POWER SO THAT...
MY GOD!
WHY DIDN'T I THINK?

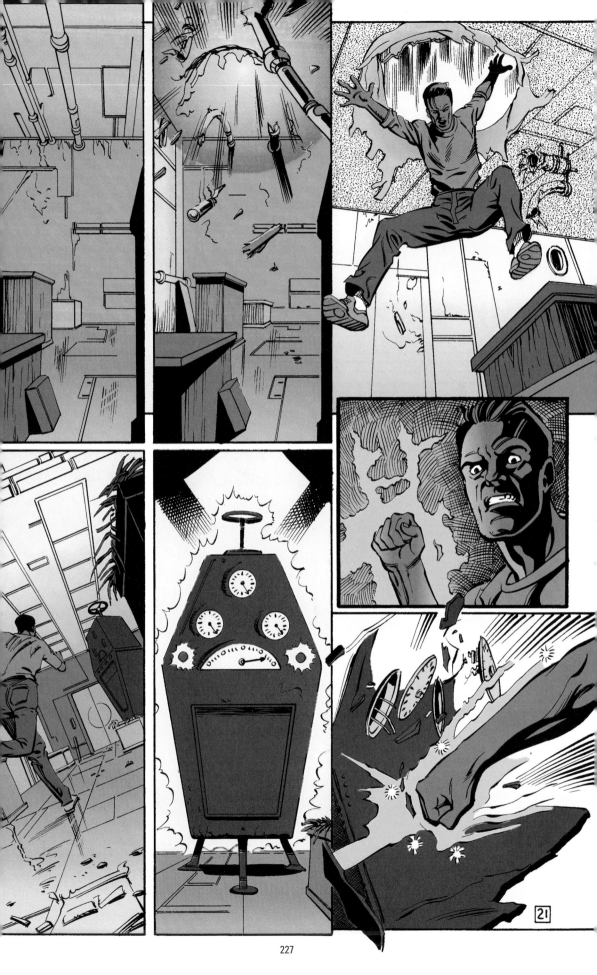

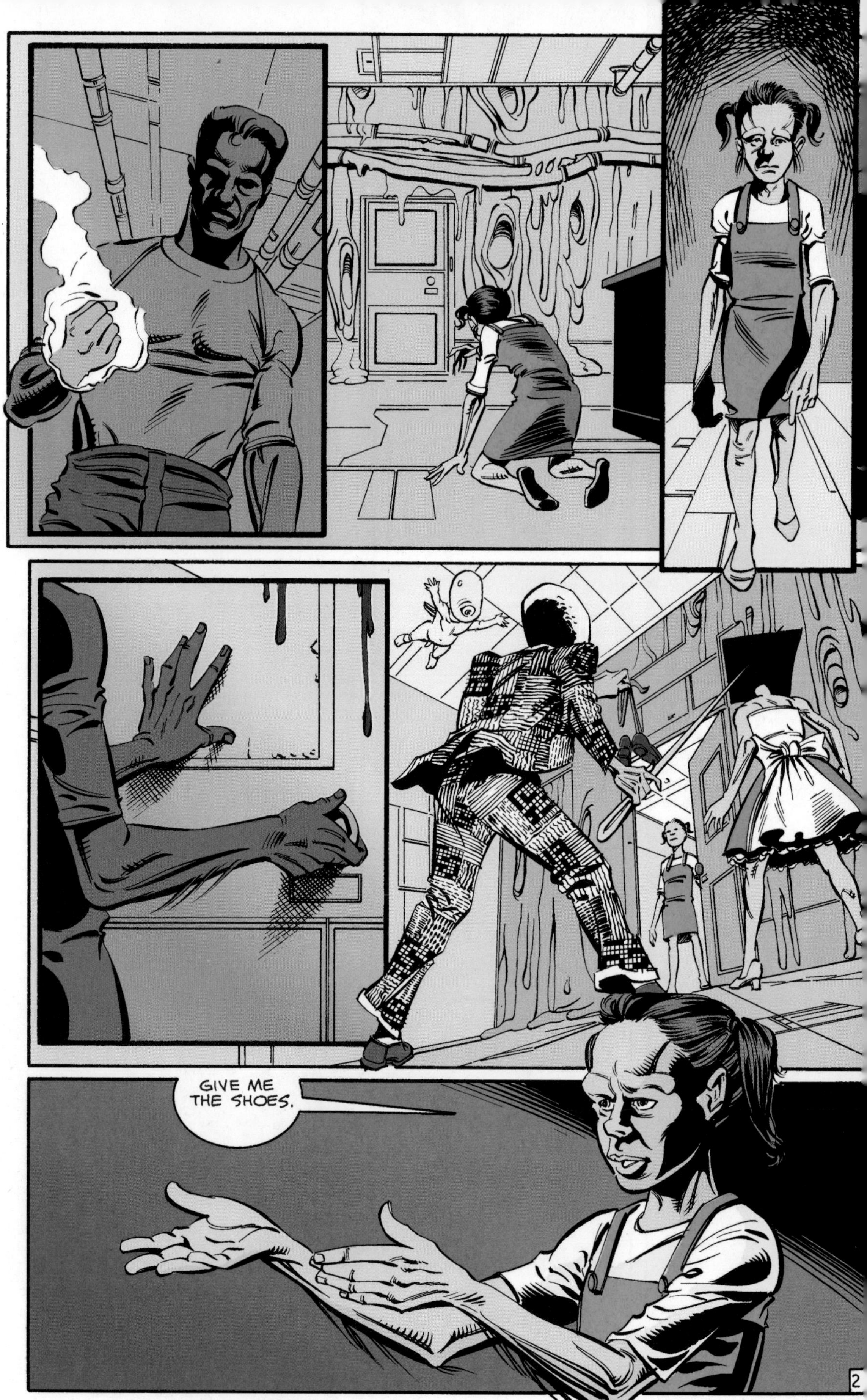
GIVE ME THE SHOES.
2

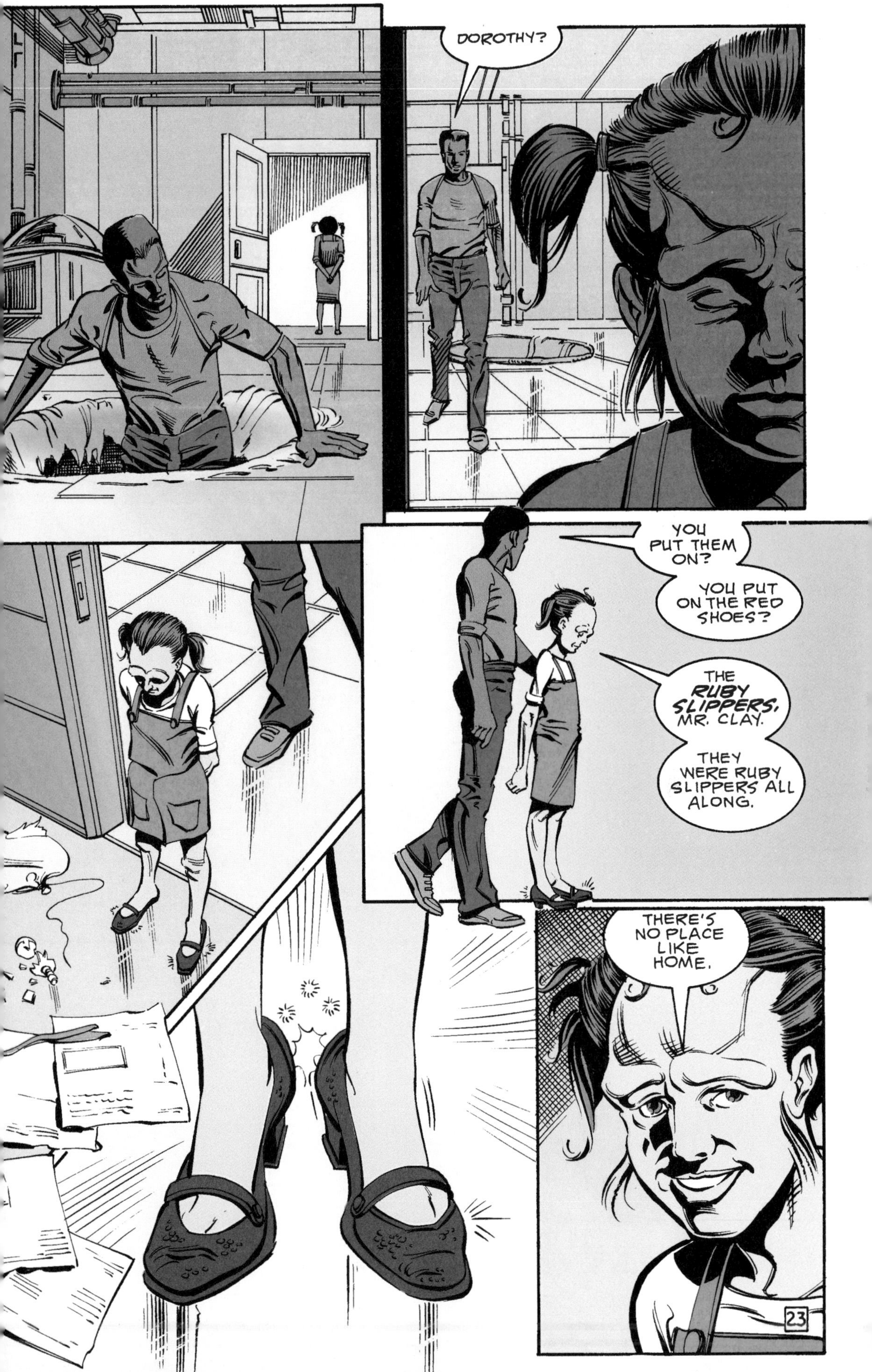
DOROTHY?
YOU PUT THEM ON?
YOU PUT ON THE RED SHOES?
THE RUBY SLIPPERS, MR. CLAY.
THEY WERE RUBY SLIPPERS ALL ALONG.
THERE'S NO PLACE LIKE HOME.
23

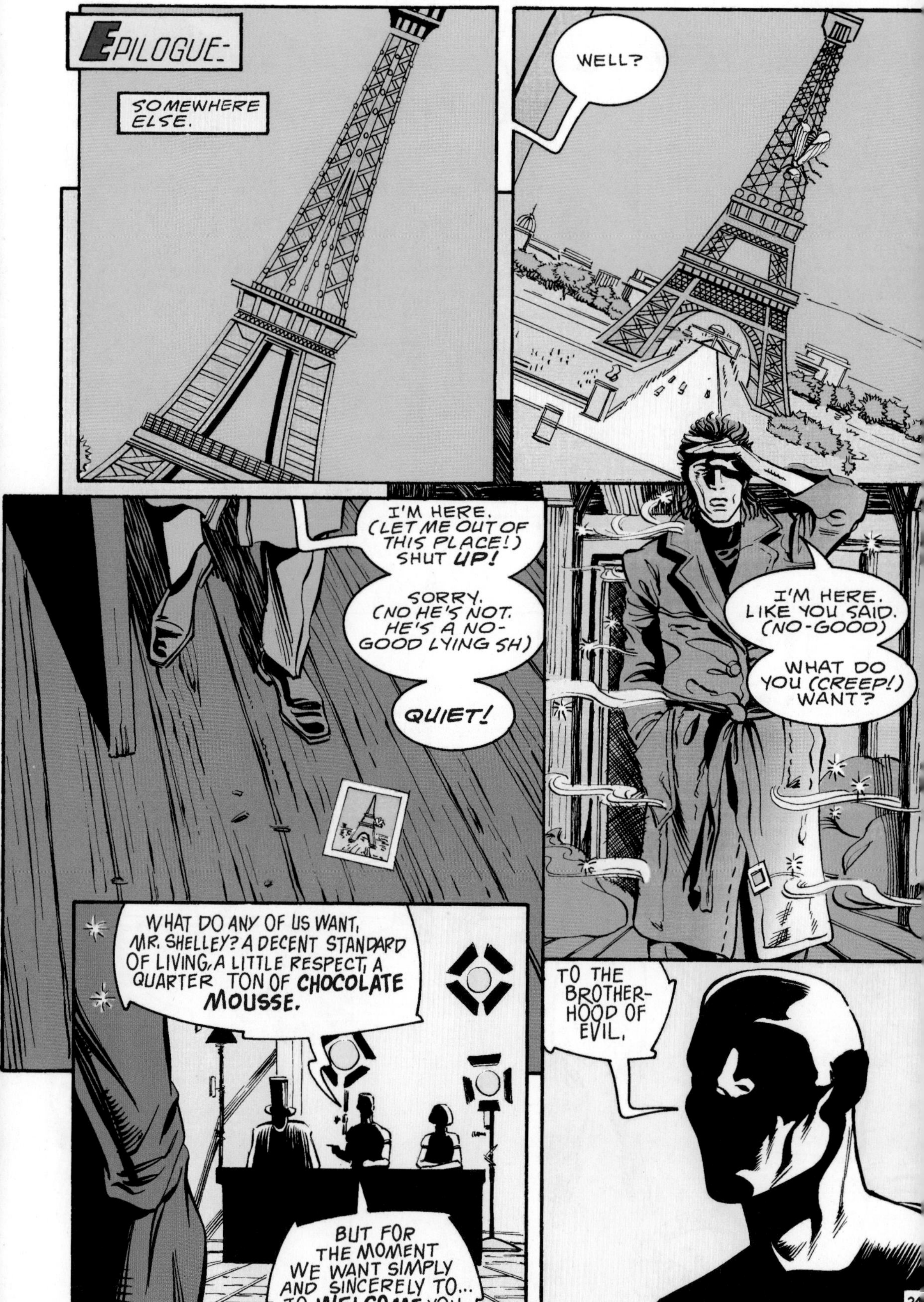
EPILOGUE:
SOMEWHERE ELSE.
WELL?
I'M HERE. (LET ME OUT OF THIS PLACE!) SHUT UP!
SORRY. (NO HE'S NOT. HE'S A NO-GOOD LYING SH)
QUIET!
I'M HERE. LIKE YOU SAID. (NO-GOOD)
WHAT DO YOU (CREEP!) WANT?
WHAT DO ANY OF US WANT, MR. SHELLEY? A DECENT STANDARD OF LIVING, A LITTLE RESPECT, A QUARTER TON OF CHOCOLATE MOUSSE.
BUT FOR THE MOMENT WE WANT SIMPLY AND SINCERELY TO... TO WELCOME YOU.
TO THE BROTHERHOOD OF EVIL.
24

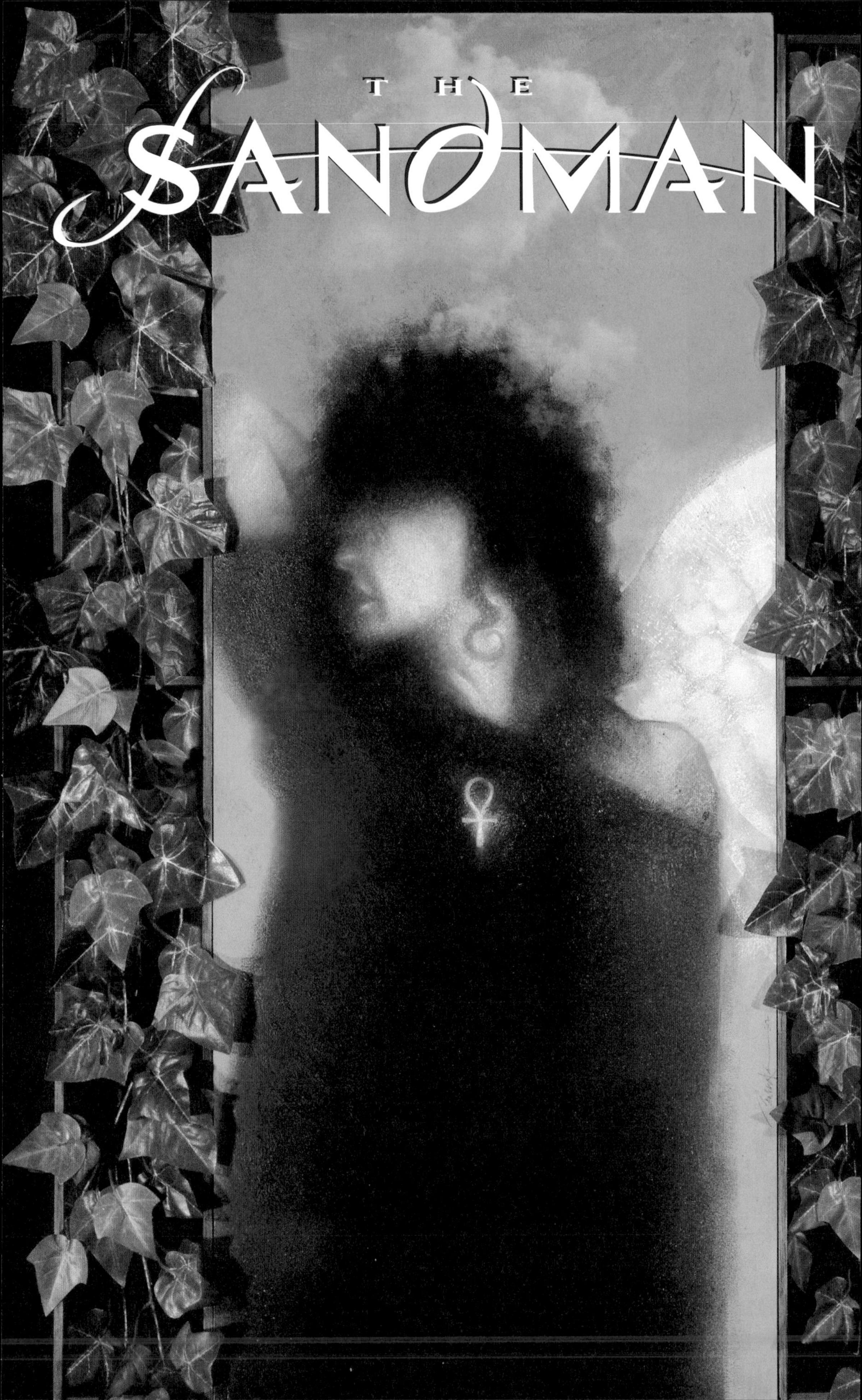
THE
SANDMAN

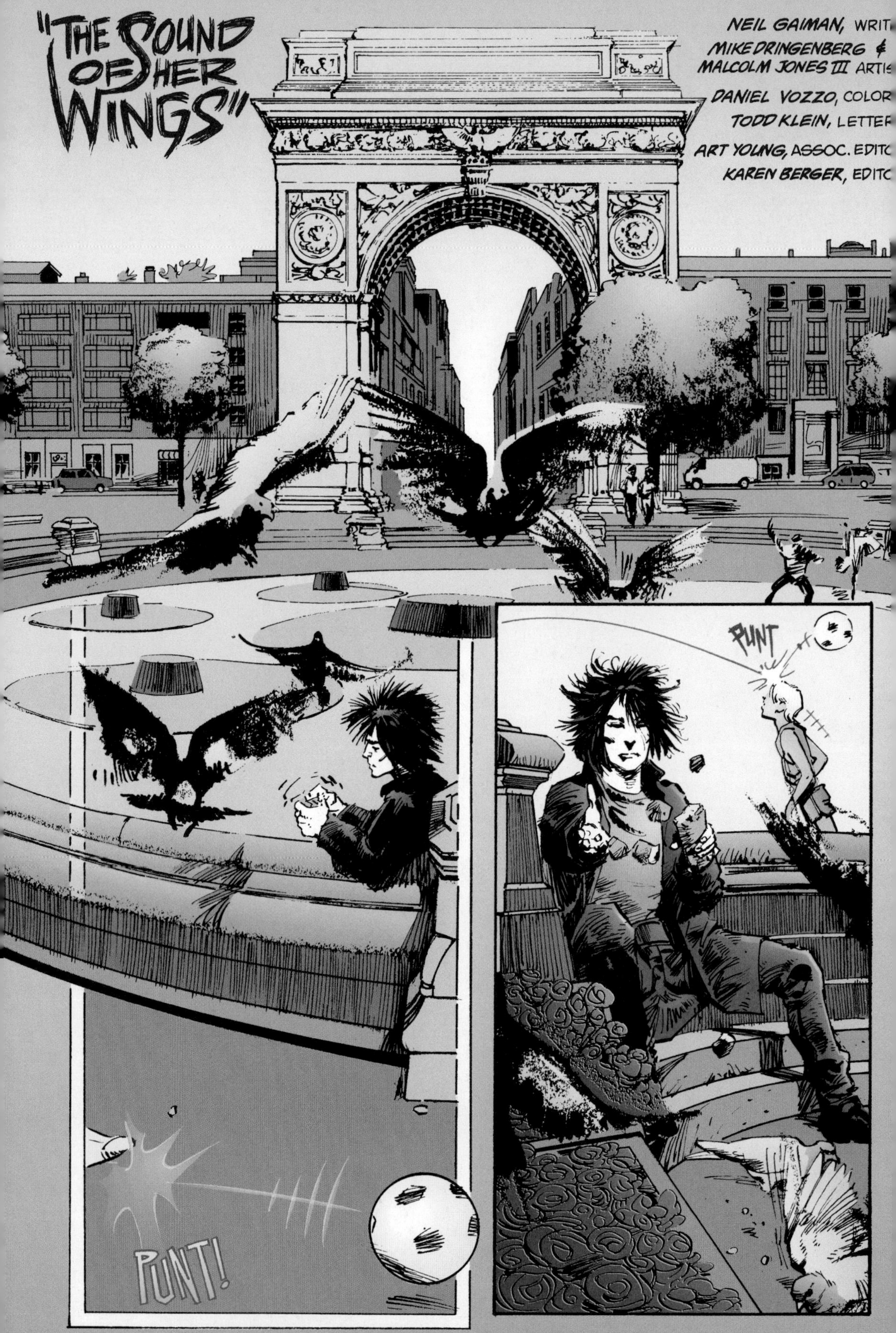
"THE SOUND OF HER WINGS"
NEIL GAIMAN, WRIT
MIKE DRINGENBERG &
MALCOLM JONES III ARTIS
DANIEL VOZZO, COLOR
TODD KLEIN, LETTER
ART YOUNG, ASSOC. EDITO
KAREN BERGER, EDITO
PUNT!
PUNT

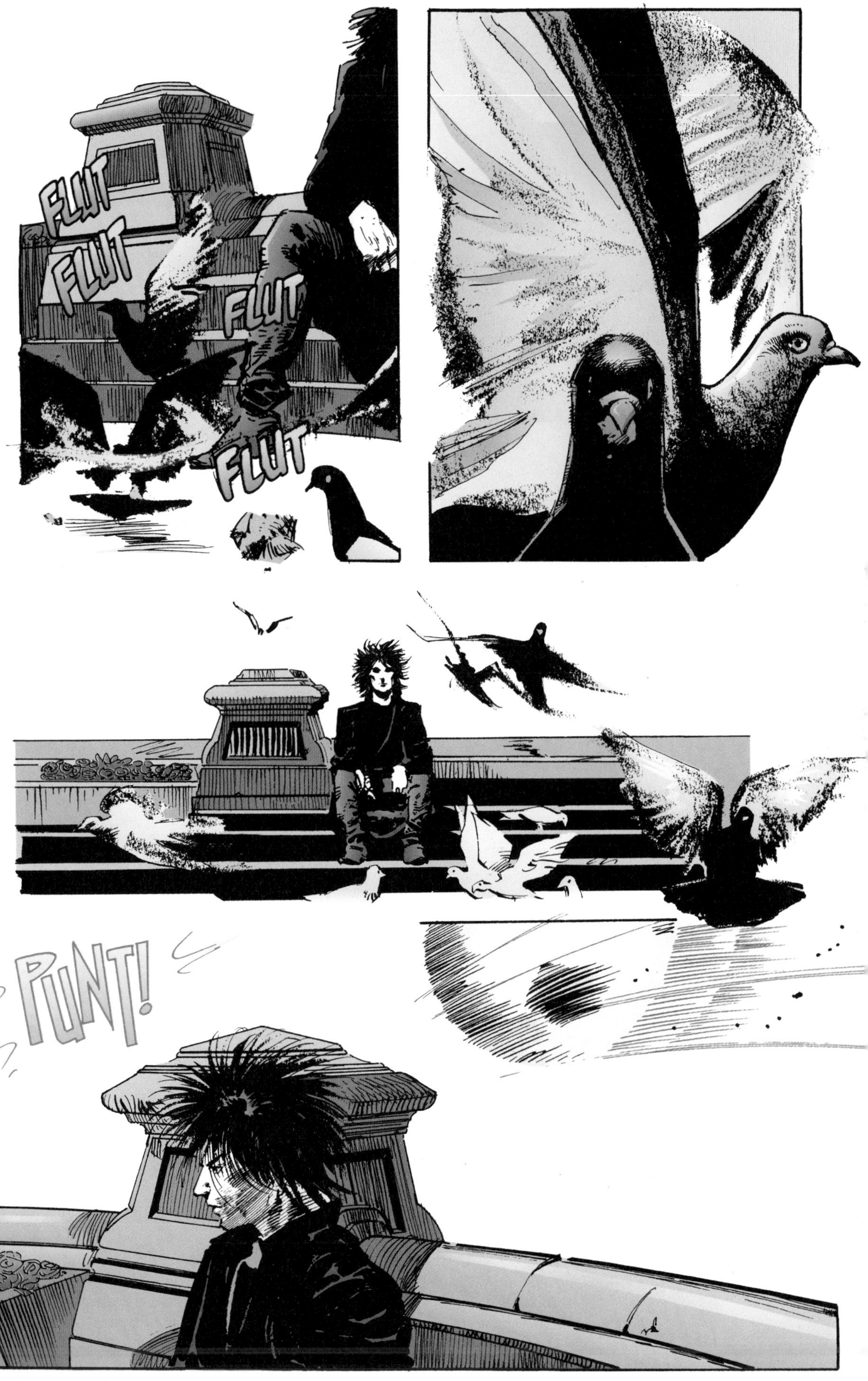
FLUT
FLUT
FLUT
FLUT
PUNT!

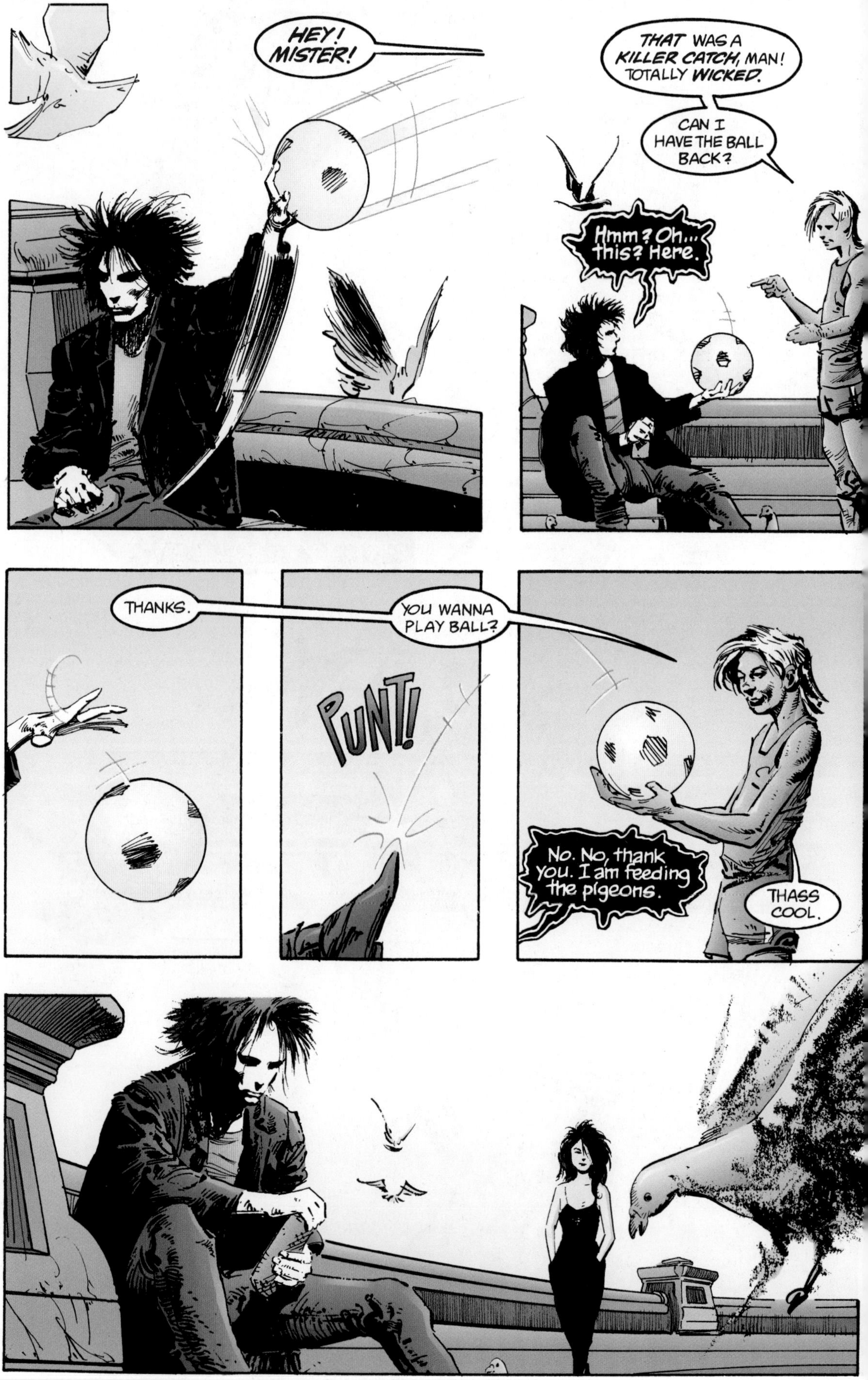
HEY! MISTER!
THAT WAS A KILLER CATCH, MAN! TOTALLY WICKED.
CAN I HAVE THE BALL BACK?
Hmm? Oh... this? Here.
THANKS.
YOU WANNA PLAY BALL?
PUNT!
No. No, thank you. I am feeding the pigeons.
THASS COOL.

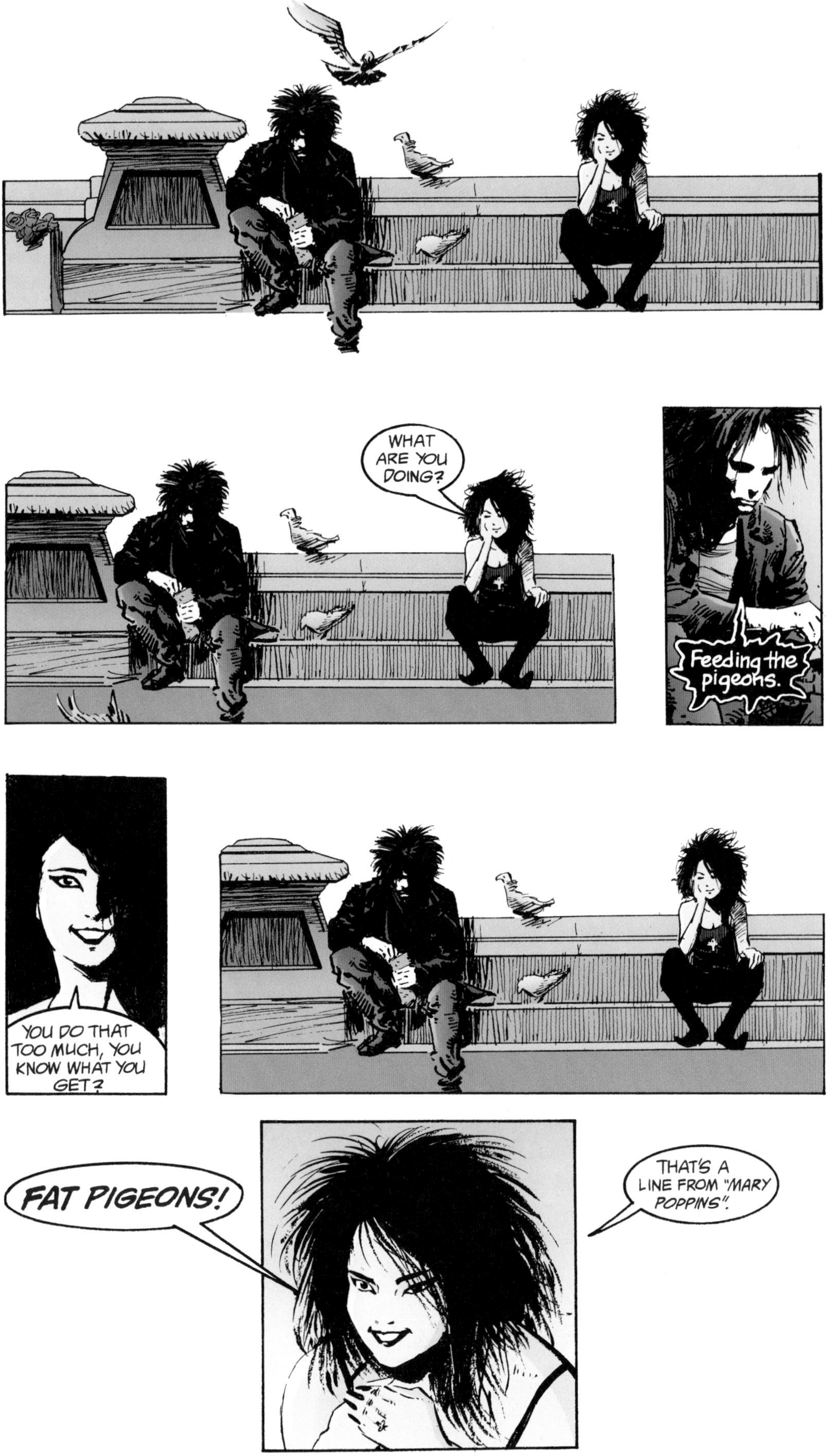
WHAT ARE YOU DOING?
Feeding the pigeons.
YOU DO THAT TOO MUCH, YOU KNOW WHAT YOU GET?
FAT PIGEONS!
THAT'S A LINE FROM "MARY POPPINS".

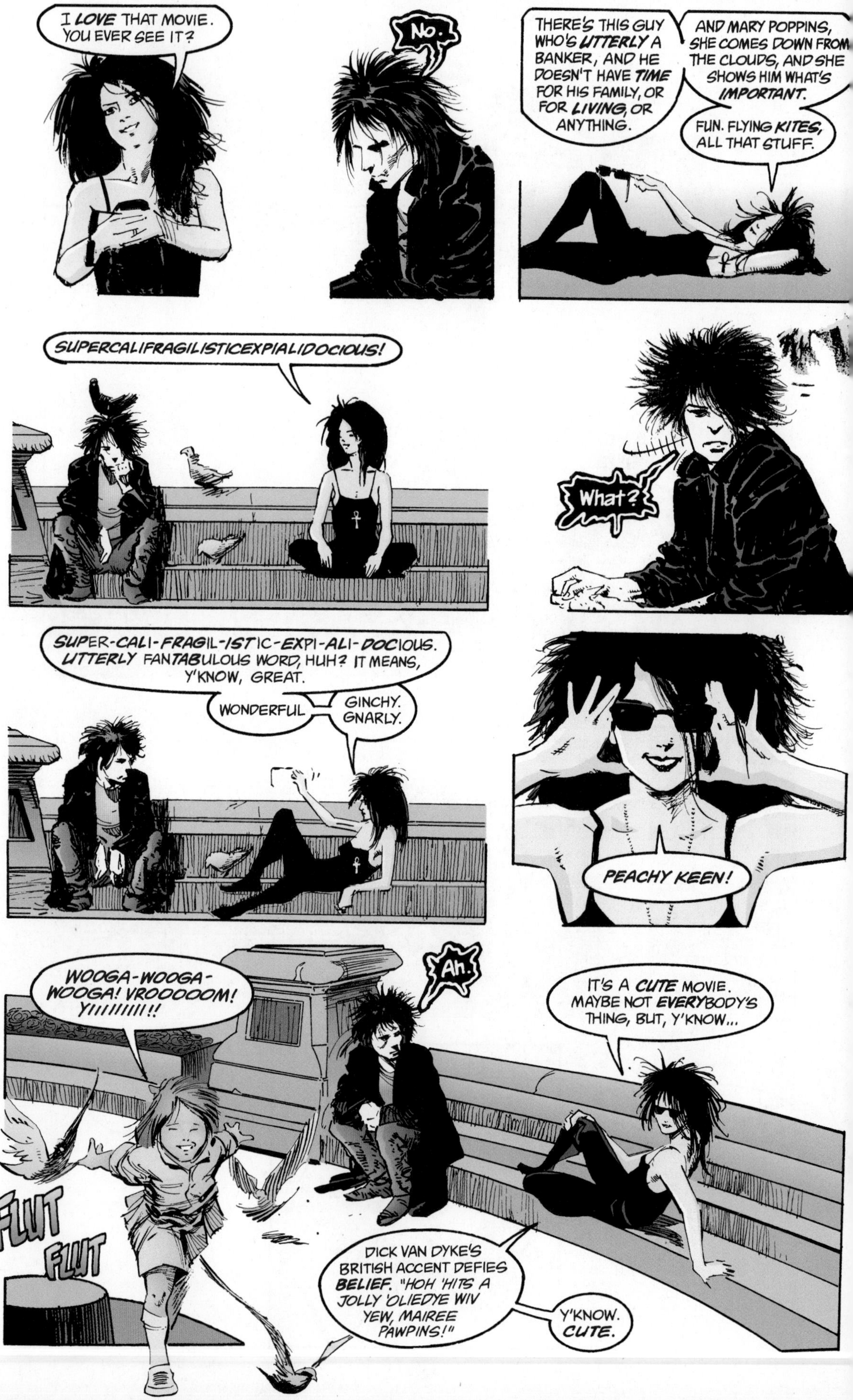
I LOVE THAT MOVIE. YOU EVER SEE IT?
No.
THERE'S THIS GUY WHO'S UTTERLY A BANKER, AND HE DOESN'T HAVE TIME FOR HIS FAMILY, OR FOR LIVING, OR ANYTHING.
AND MARY POPPINS, SHE COMES DOWN FROM THE CLOUDS, AND SHE SHOWS HIM WHAT'S IMPORTANT.
FUN. FLYING KITES, ALL THAT STUFF.
SUPERCALIFRAGILISTICEXPIALIDOCIOUS!
What?
SUPER-CALI-FRAGIL-ISTIC-EXPI-ALI-DOCIOUS. UTTERLY FANTABULOUS WORD, HUH? IT MEANS, Y'KNOW, GREAT.
WONDERFUL
GINCHY. GNARLY.
PEACHY KEEN!
WOOGA-WOOGA-WOOGA! VROOOOOM! YIIIIIIIII!!
Ah.
IT'S A CUTE MOVIE. MAYBE NOT EVERYBODY'S THING, BUT, Y'KNOW...
FLUT
FLUT
DICK VAN DYKE'S BRITISH ACCENT DEFIES BELIEF. "HOH 'HITS A JOLLY 'OLIEDYE WIV YEW, MAIREE PAWPINS!"
Y'KNOW. CUTE.

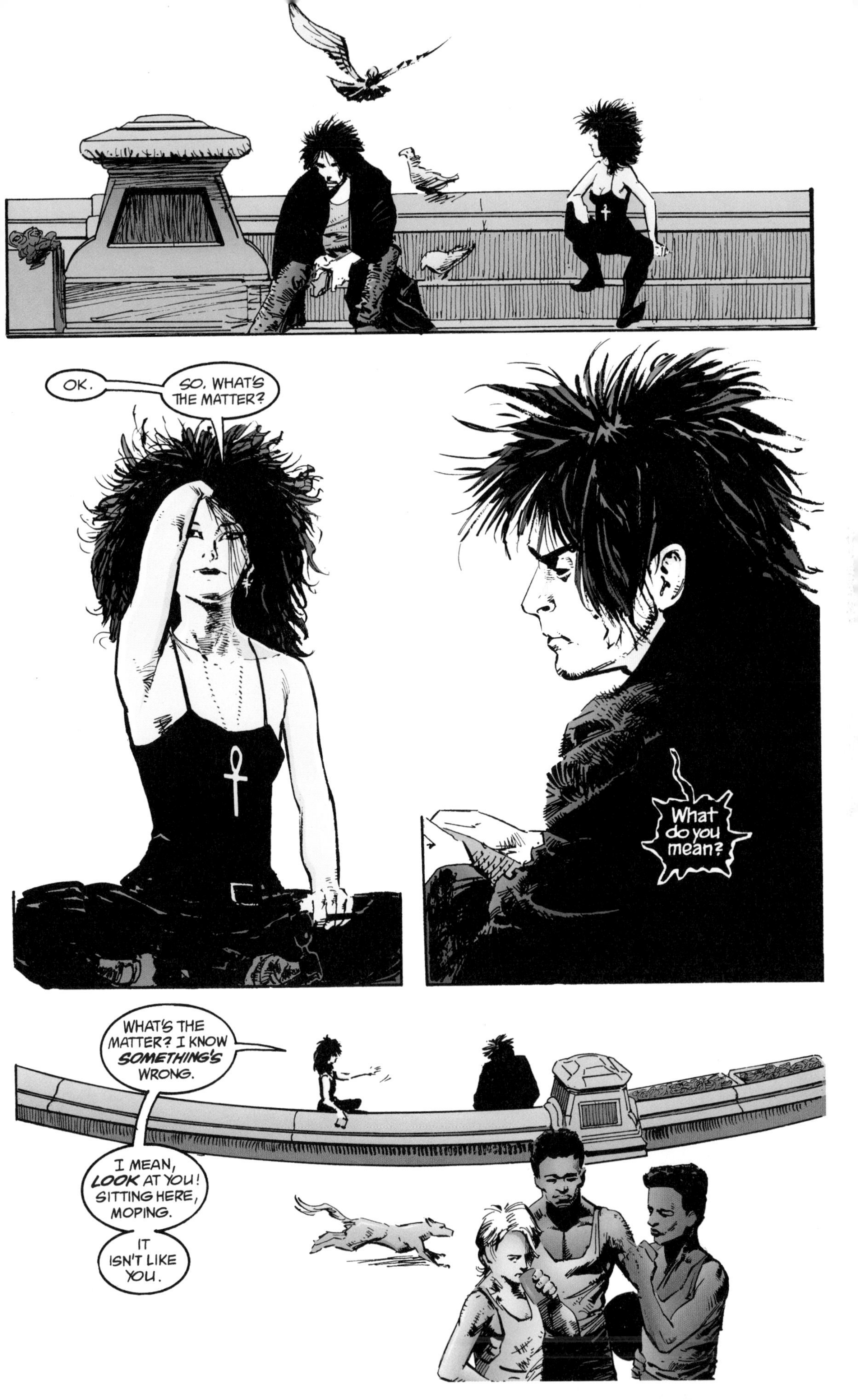
OK.
SO, WHAT'S THE MATTER?
What do you mean?
WHAT'S THE MATTER? I KNOW *SOMETHING'S* WRONG.
I MEAN, *LOOK* AT YOU! SITTING HERE, MOPING.
IT ISN'T LIKE YOU.

"No... perhaps it isn't."

"I don't know what's wrong. But you're right. Something is... the matter."

"When they captured me, imprisoned in their box, I had just one thought: Revenge."

"By the time I freed myself, my original captor had gone the way of mortals, and I took my vengeance on his son.

It felt... fine, I suppose."

"But it didn't feel as-- satisfying-- as I had expected.

In the interim, my dreamworld had fallen apart. I needed my tools, long since stolen and scattered.

One by one I found them."

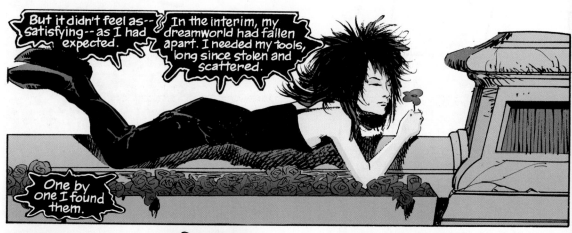

"Eventually I found them."

"The pouch was relatively easy.

To regain the helmet I challenged a demon, dared the Hordes of Hell, faced down Lucifer himself. Hahh. That left only the ruby."

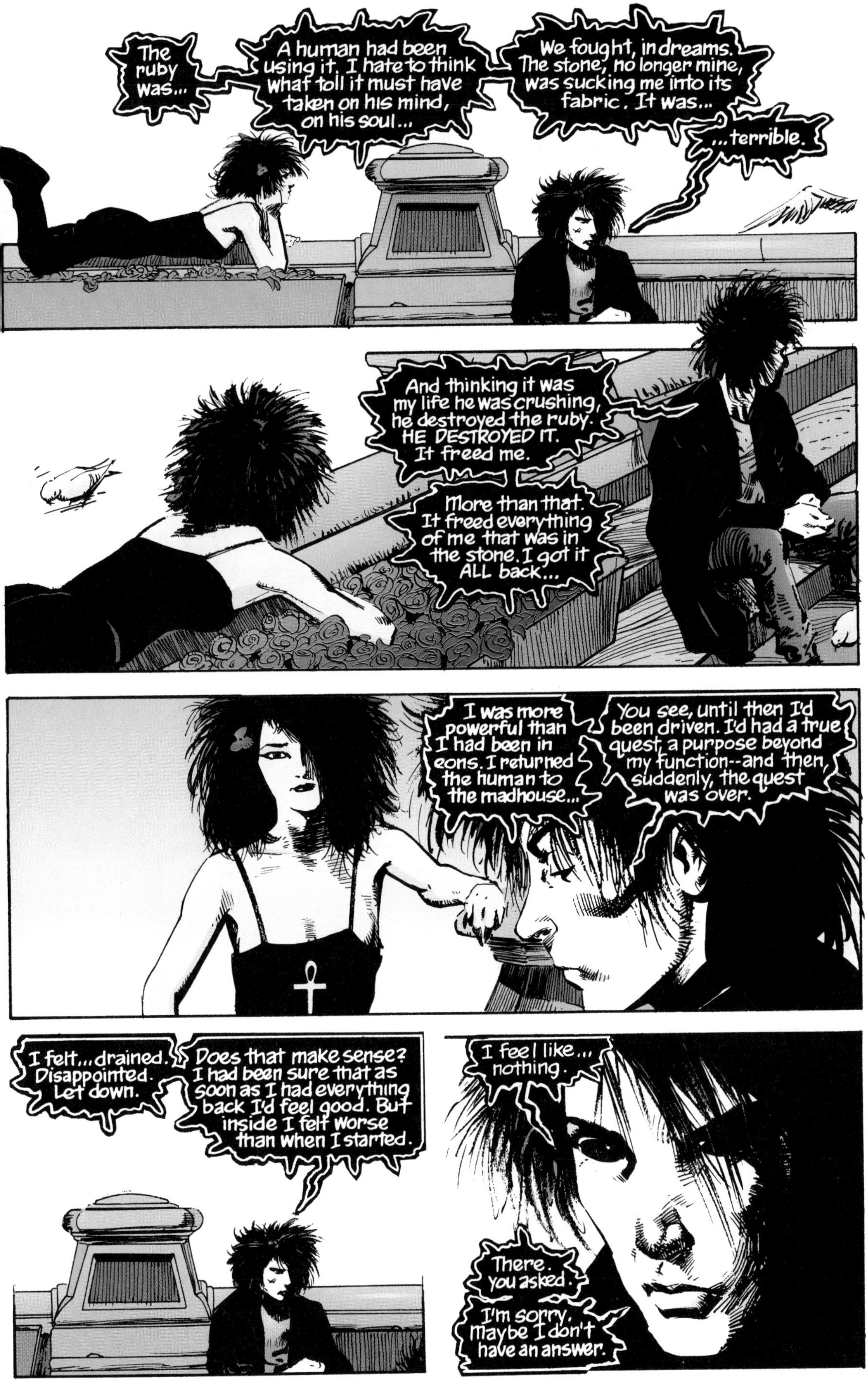
The ruby was...
A human had been using it. I hate to think what toll it must have taken on his mind, on his soul...
We fought, in dreams. The stone, no longer mine, was sucking me into its fabric. It was...
...terrible.
And thinking it was my life he was crushing, he destroyed the ruby. HE DESTROYED IT. It freed me.
More than that. It freed everything of me that was in the stone. I got it ALL back...
I was more powerful than I had been in eons. I returned the human to the madhouse...
You see, until then I'd been driven. I'd had a true quest, a purpose beyond my function--and then, suddenly, the quest was over.
I felt... drained. Disappointed. Let down.
Does that make sense? I had been sure that as soon as I had everything back I'd feel good. But inside I felt worse than when I started.
I feel like... nothing.
There. You asked.
I'm sorry. Maybe I don't have an answer.

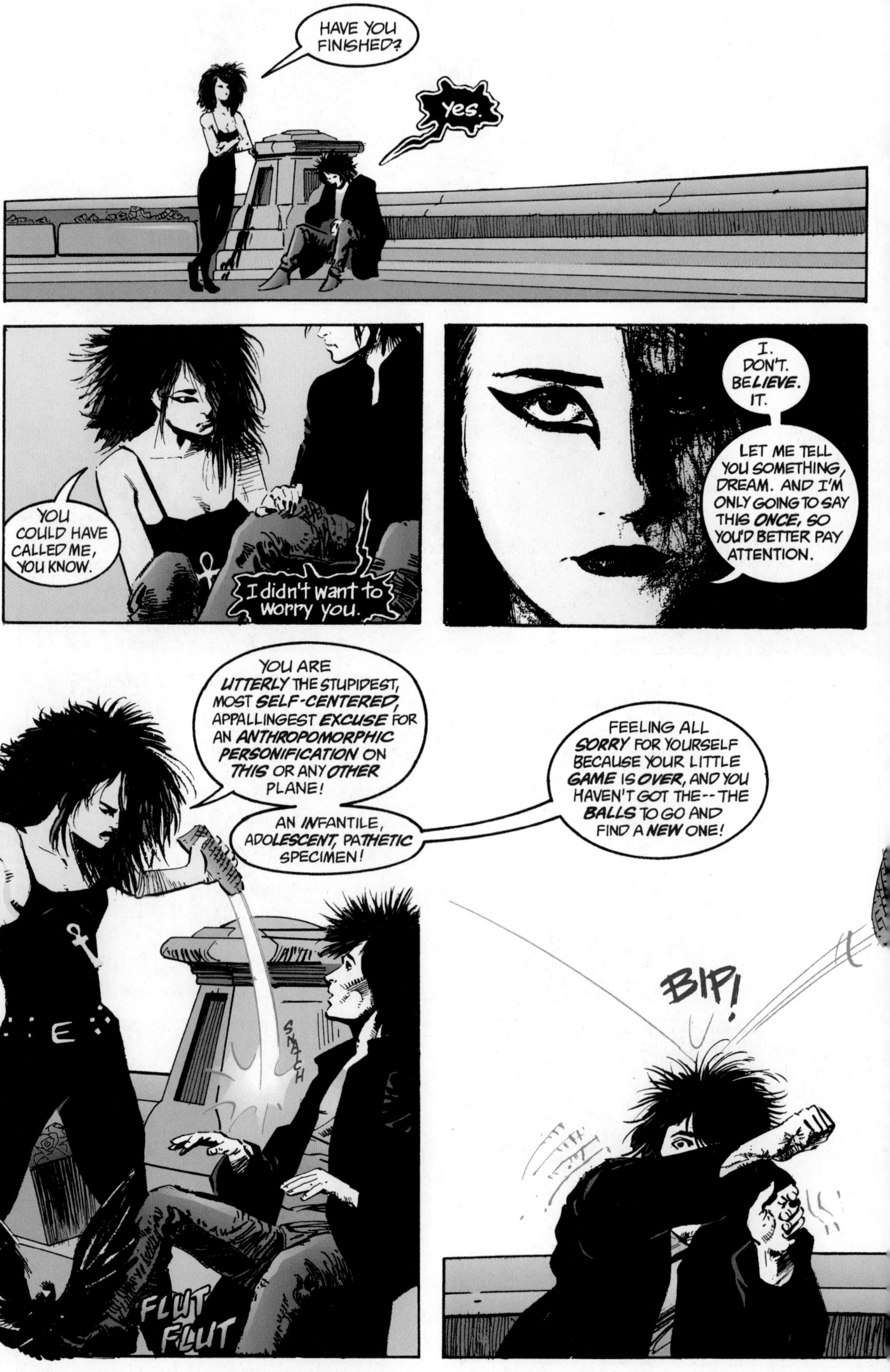
HAVE YOU FINISHED?
Yes.
YOU COULD HAVE CALLED ME, YOU KNOW.
I didn't want to worry you.
I. DON'T. BELIEVE. IT.
LET ME TELL YOU SOMETHING, DREAM. AND I'M ONLY GOING TO SAY THIS ONCE, SO YOU'D BETTER PAY ATTENTION.
YOU ARE UTTERLY THE STUPIDEST, MOST SELF-CENTERED, APPALLINGEST EXCUSE FOR AN ANTHROPOMORPHIC PERSONIFICATION ON THIS OR ANY OTHER PLANE!
AN INFANTILE, ADOLESCENT, PATHETIC SPECIMEN!
FEELING ALL SORRY FOR YOURSELF BECAUSE YOUR LITTLE GAME IS OVER, AND YOU HAVEN'T GOT THE--THE BALLS TO GO AND FIND A NEW ONE!
SNATCH
FLUT FLUT
BIP!

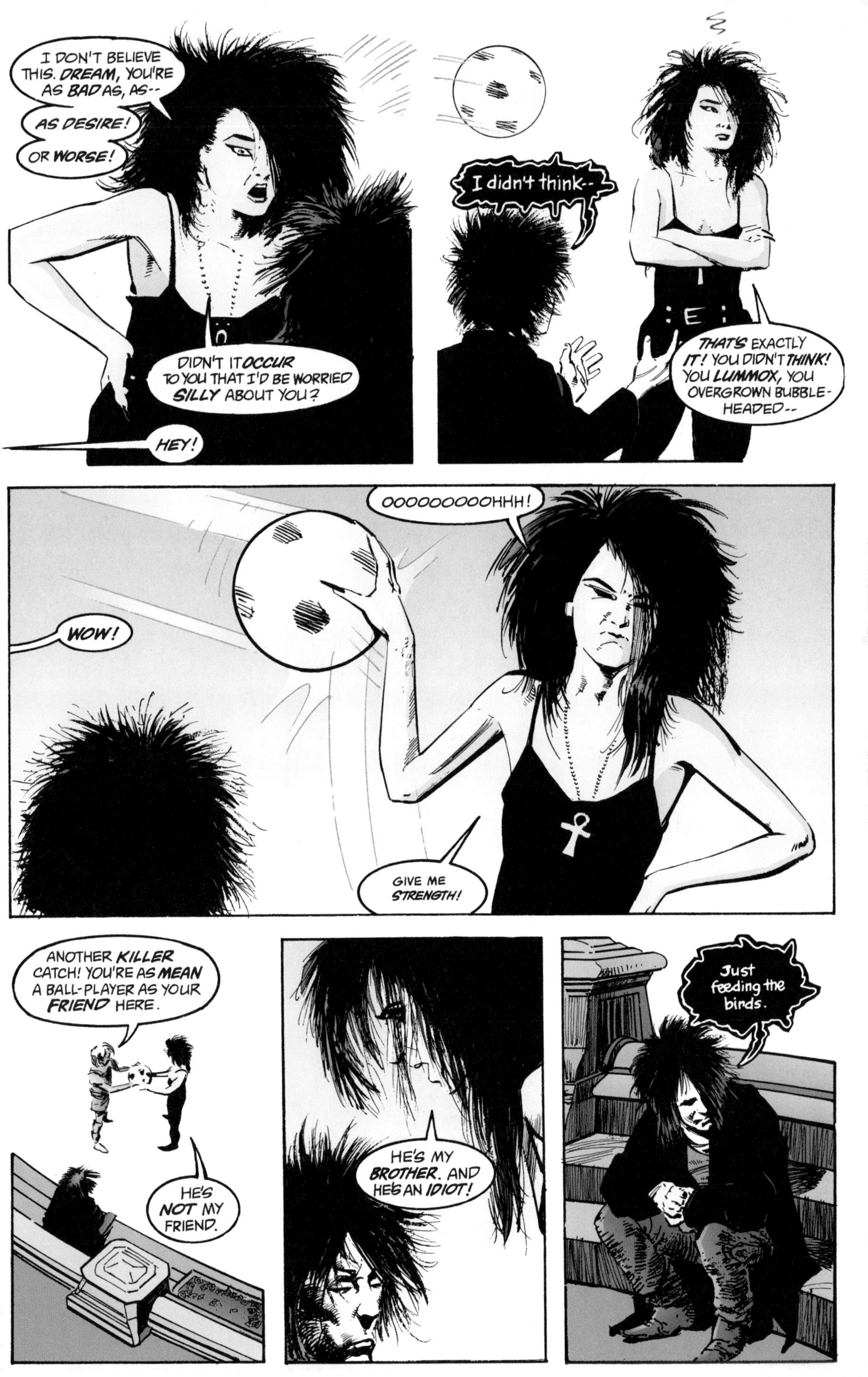
I DON'T BELIEVE THIS. DREAM, YOU'RE AS BAD AS, AS--
AS DESIRE!
OR WORSE!
DIDN'T IT OCCUR TO YOU THAT I'D BE WORRIED SILLY ABOUT YOU?
HEY!
I didn't think--
THAT'S EXACTLY IT! YOU DIDN'T THINK! YOU LUMMOX, YOU OVERGROWN BUBBLE-HEADED--
OOOOOOOOOHHH!
WOW!
GIVE ME STRENGTH!
ANOTHER KILLER CATCH! YOU'RE AS MEAN A BALL-PLAYER AS YOUR FRIEND HERE.
HE'S NOT MY FRIEND.
HE'S MY BROTHER. AND HE'S AN IDIOT!
Just feeding the birds.

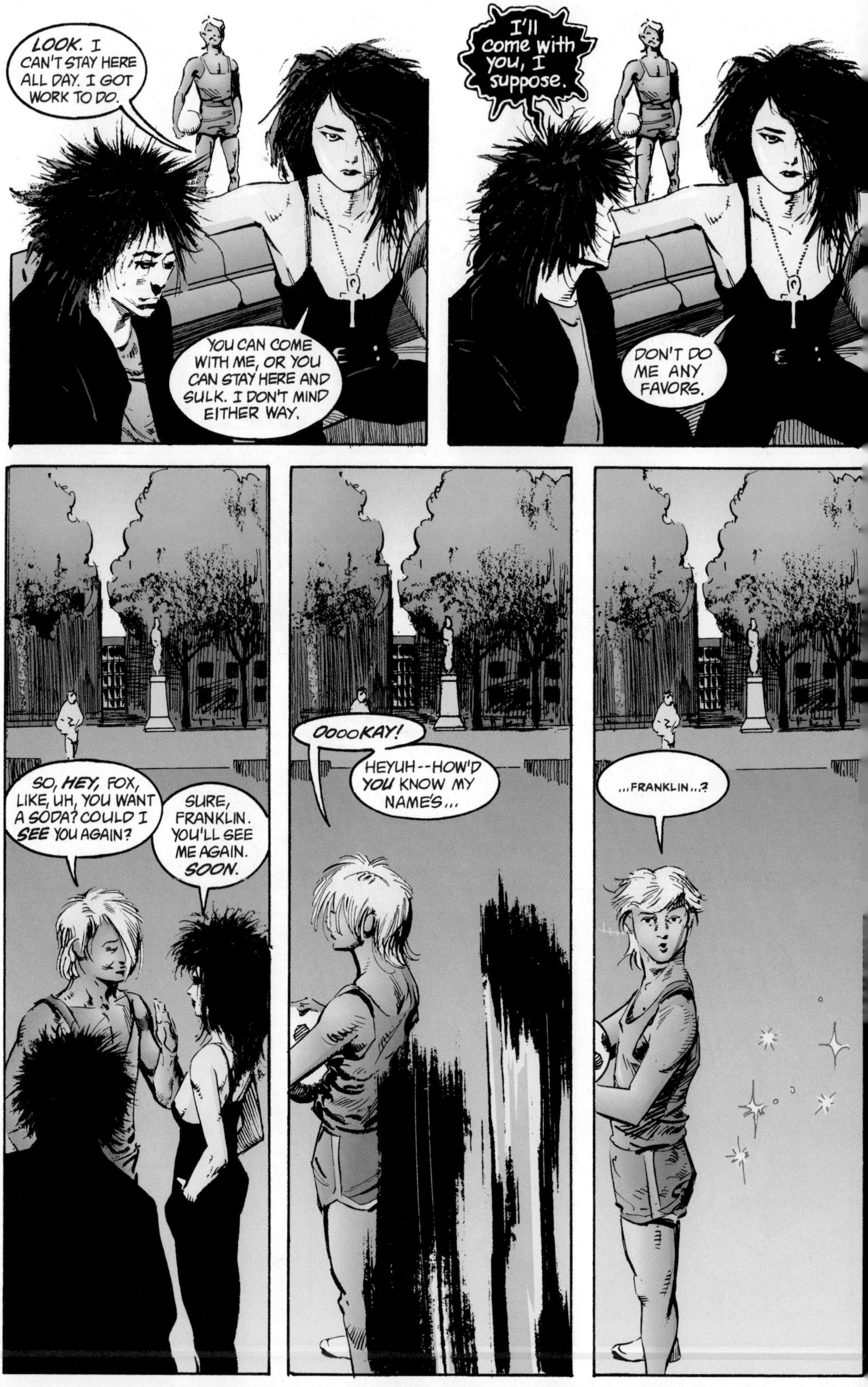
LOOK. I CAN'T STAY HERE ALL DAY. I GOT WORK TO DO.
YOU CAN COME WITH ME, OR YOU CAN STAY HERE AND SULK. I DON'T MIND EITHER WAY.
I'll come with you, I suppose.
DON'T DO ME ANY FAVORS.
SO, HEY, FOX, LIKE, UH, YOU WANT A SODA? COULD I SEE YOU AGAIN?
SURE, FRANKLIN. YOU'LL SEE ME AGAIN. SOON.
OOOOKAY!
HEYUH--HOW'D YOU KNOW MY NAME'S...
...FRANKLIN...?

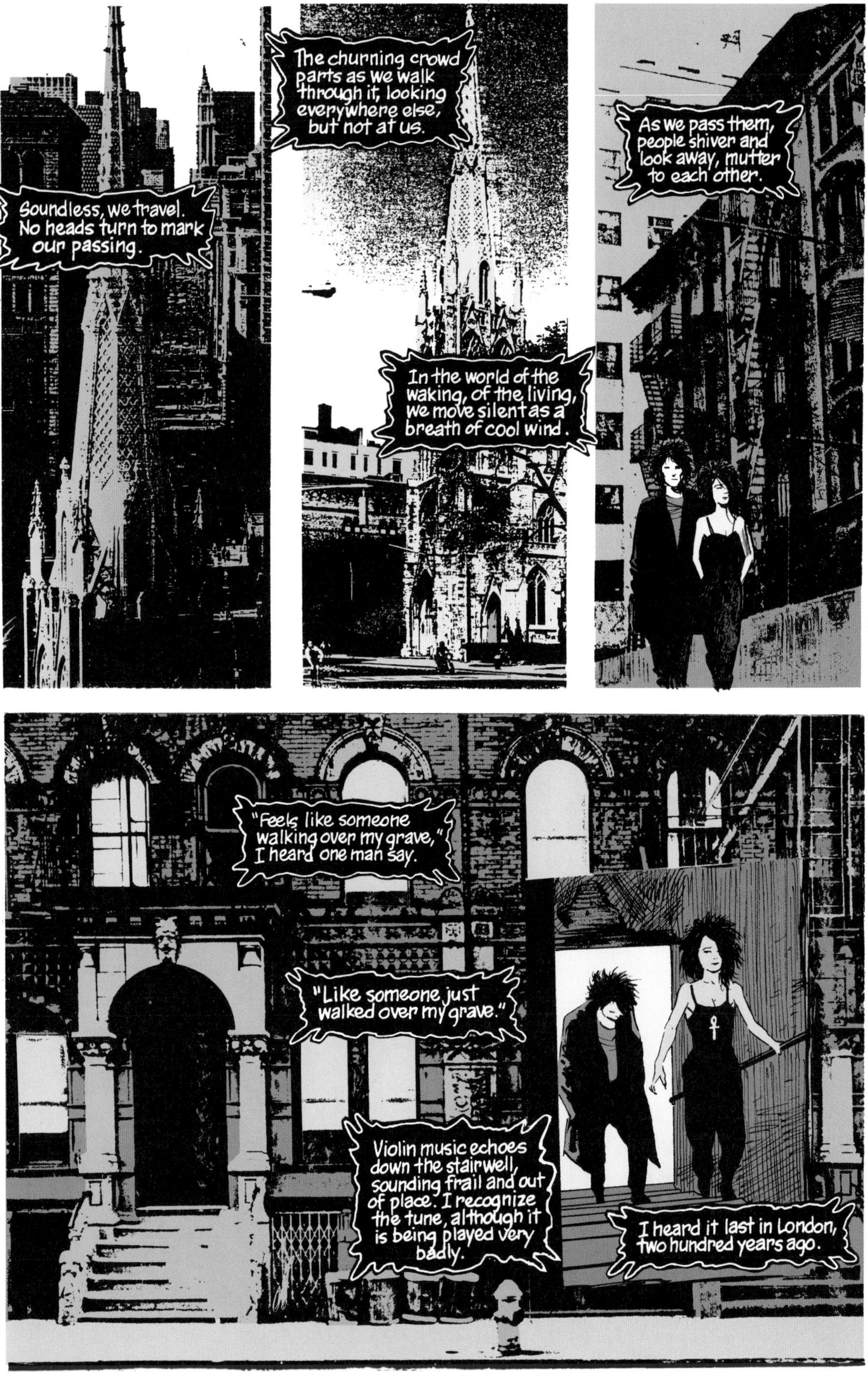
Soundless, we travel. No heads turn to mark our passing.
The churning crowd parts as we walk through it, looking everywhere else, but not at us.
In the world of the waking, of the living, we move silent as a breath of cool wind.
As we pass them, people shiver and look away, mutter to each other.
"Feels like someone walking over my grave," I heard one man say.
"Like someone just walked over my grave."
Violin music echoes down the stairwell, sounding frail and out of place. I recognize the tune, although it is being played very badly.
I heard it last in London, two hundred years ago.

CAN YOU ROCKER ROMANY? CAN YOU PATTER FLASH? ♪♪♪♪

CAN YOU ROCKER ROMANY? CAN YOU FAKE A BOSH? ♪♪♪♪♪

YES. I CAN PATTER ROMANY, HARRY. CAN YOU?

HUNH? I DIDN'T HEAR NOBODY COME IN...

CAN *I* PATTER ROMANY?

NOT SO GOOD. BUT I CAN FAKE A BOSH. MEANS T' PLAY THE FIDDLE. I'M NOT REAL ROMANY...

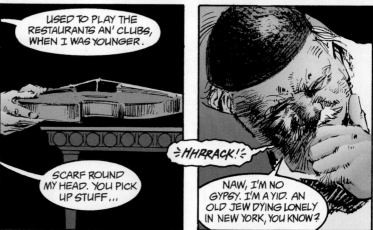

USED TO PLAY THE RESTAURANTS AN' CLUBS, WHEN I WAS YOUNGER.

SCARF ROUND MY HEAD. YOU PICK UP STUFF...

⸗HHRRACK!⸲

NAW, I'M NO GYPSY. I'M A YID. AN OLD JEW DYING LONELY IN NEW YORK, YOU KNOW?

YES, I KNOW WHO YOU ARE, HARRY. DO YOU KNOW WHO I AM?

YOU? YOU'RE... *NO!* NOT *YET!* ...PLEASE?

YEAH, I KNOW WHO YOU ARE.

HRRUCCK!

'SCUSE ME. SOMETHING I GOT TO SAY. ALWAYS USED TO WONDER IF I WOULD, BUT, Y'KNOW, WHAT TH' HEY...

SH'MA YISROEL.

ADONAI ELOHAYNU, ADONAI E'HOD.

HEAR, O ISRAEL...

THE LORD OUR GOD...

THE LORD IS ONE.

*

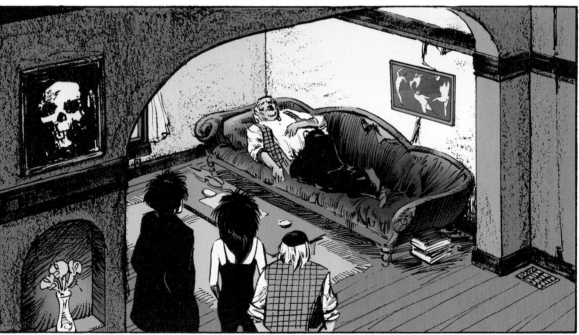

I LOOK SO EMPTY. I LOOK SO OLD.

IT'S GOOD THAT I SAID THE SH'MA. MY OLD MAN ALWAYS SAID IT GUARANTEED YOU A PLACE IN HEAVEN. IF YOU BELIEVE IN HEAVEN...

SO. I'M DEAD.

NOW WHAT?

NOW'S WHEN YOU FIND OUT, HARRY.

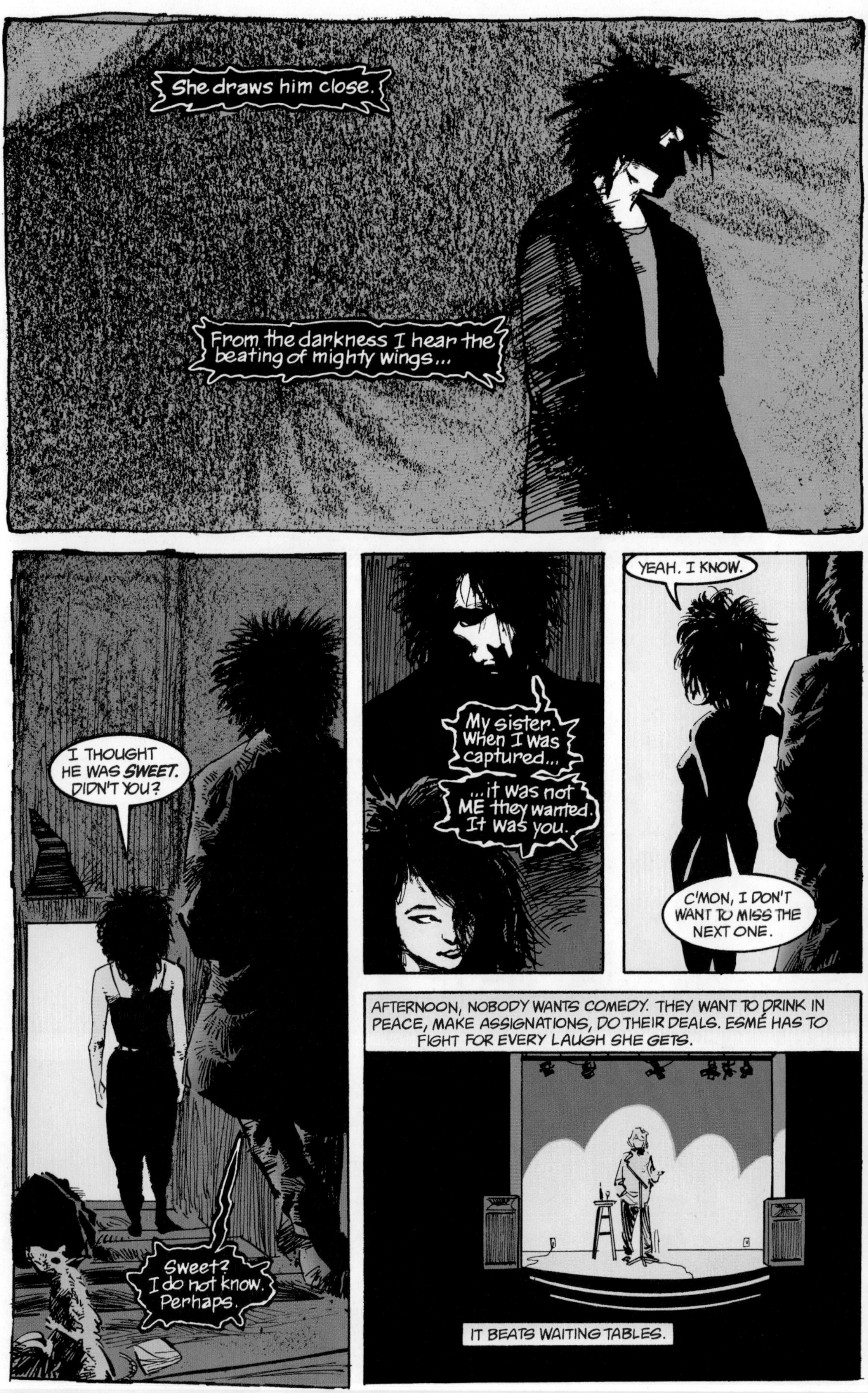
She draws him close.
From the darkness I hear the beating of mighty wings...
I THOUGHT HE WAS SWEET. DIDN'T YOU?
Sweet? I do not know. Perhaps.
My sister. When I was captured...
...it was not ME they wanted. It was you.
YEAH. I KNOW.
C'MON, I DON'T WANT TO MISS THE NEXT ONE.
AFTERNOON, NOBODY WANTS COMEDY. THEY WANT TO DRINK IN PEACE, MAKE ASSIGNATIONS, DO THEIR DEALS. ESMÉ HAS TO FIGHT FOR EVERY LAUGH SHE GETS.
IT BEATS WAITING TABLES.

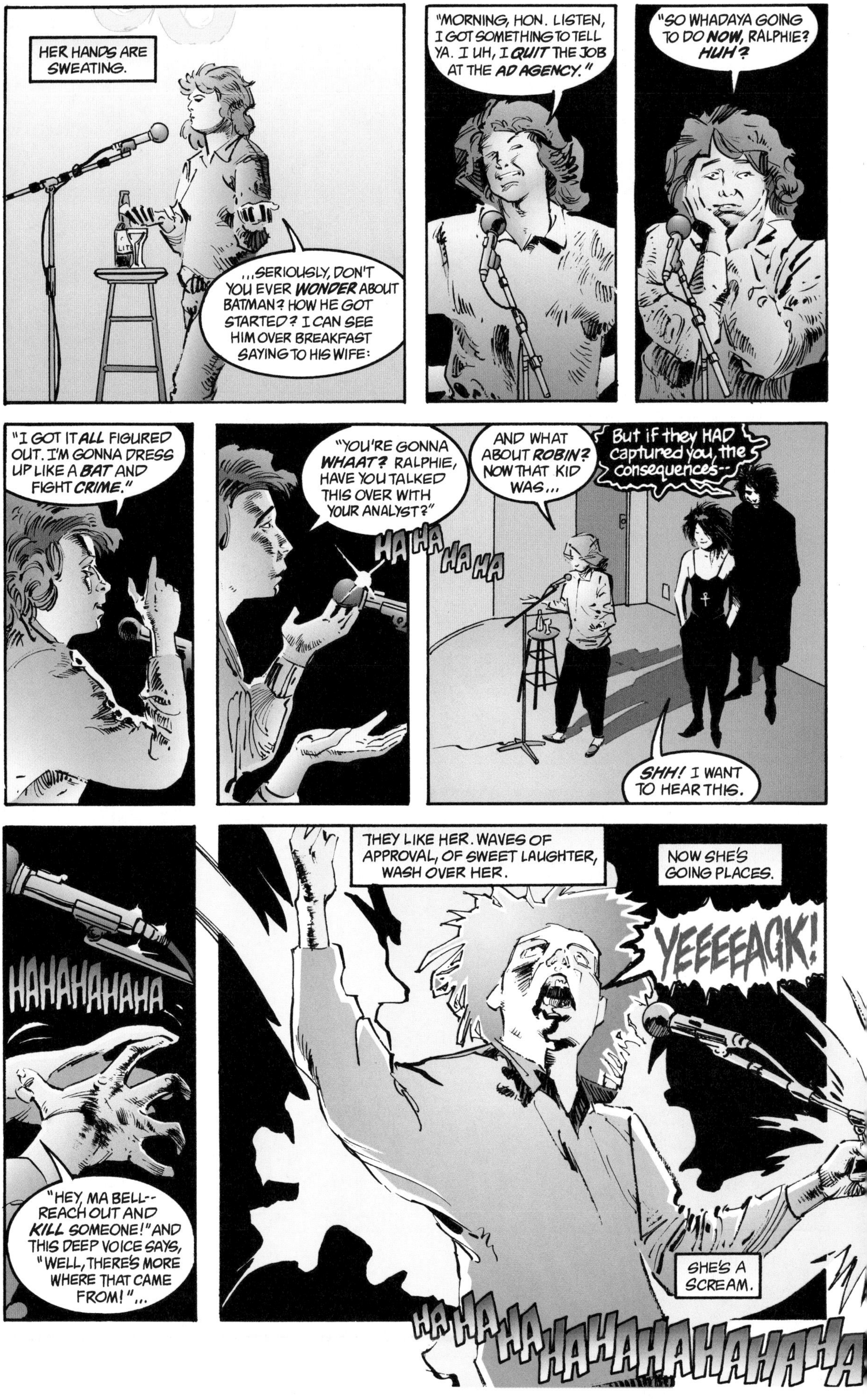
HER HANDS ARE SWEATING.
...SERIOUSLY, DON'T YOU EVER WONDER ABOUT BATMAN? HOW HE GOT STARTED? I CAN SEE HIM OVER BREAKFAST SAYING TO HIS WIFE:
"MORNING, HON. LISTEN, I GOT SOMETHING TO TELL YA. I UH, I QUIT THE JOB AT THE AD AGENCY."
"SO WHADAYA GOING TO DO NOW, RALPHIE? HUH?
"I GOT IT ALL FIGURED OUT. I'M GONNA DRESS UP LIKE A BAT AND FIGHT CRIME."
"YOU'RE GONNA WHAAT? RALPHIE, HAVE YOU TALKED THIS OVER WITH YOUR ANALYST?"
HA HA HA HA
AND WHAT ABOUT ROBIN? NOW THAT KID WAS...
But if they HAD captured you, the consequences--
SHH! I WANT TO HEAR THIS.
HAHAHAHAHA
"HEY, MA BELL-- REACH OUT AND KILL SOMEONE!" AND THIS DEEP VOICE SAYS, "WELL, THERE'S MORE WHERE THAT CAME FROM!"...
THEY LIKE HER. WAVES OF APPROVAL, OF SWEET LAUGHTER, WASH OVER HER.
NOW SHE'S GOING PLACES.
YEEEEAGK!
SHE'S A SCREAM.
HAHAHAHAHAHAHAHAHAHA

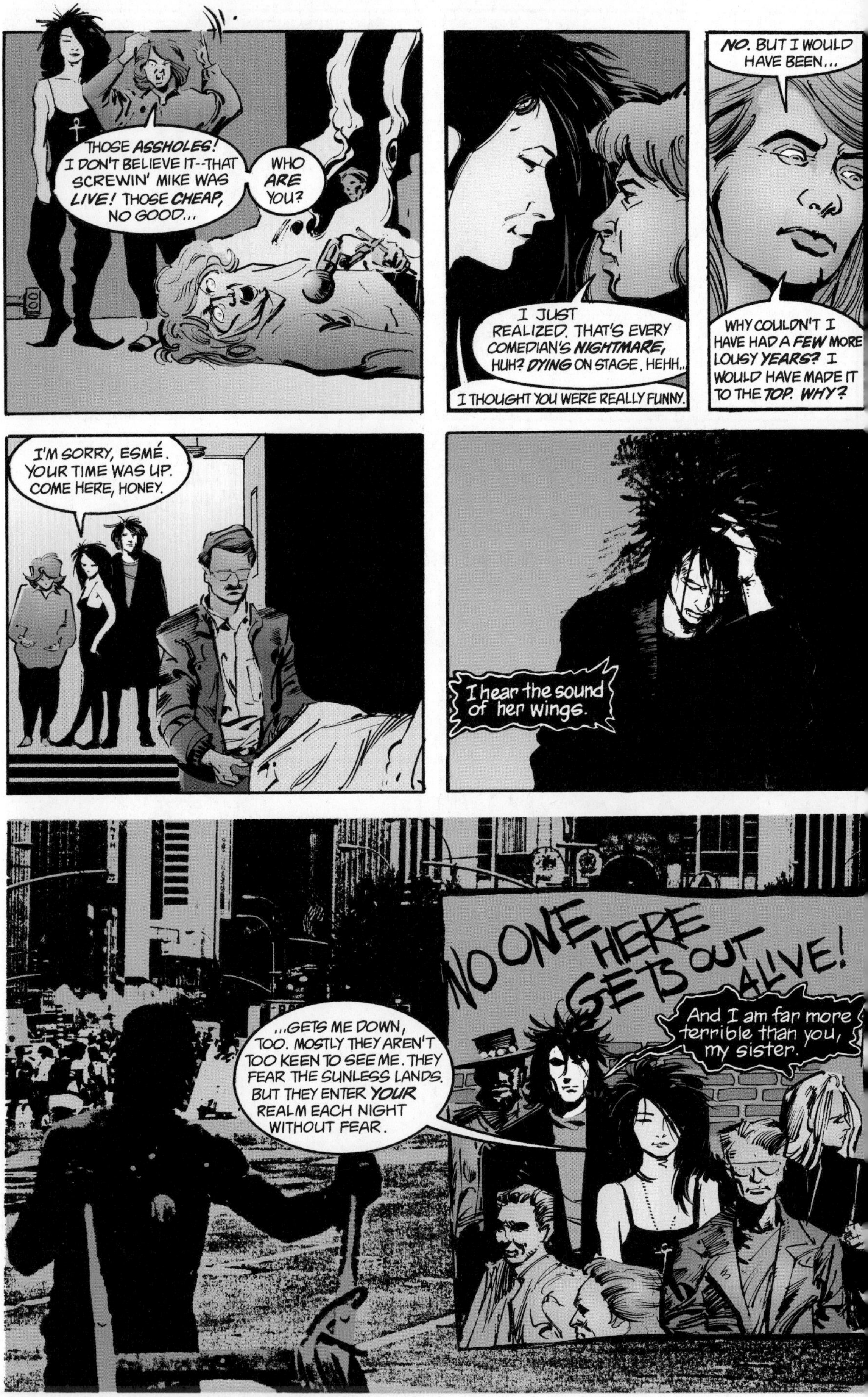
THOSE ASSHOLES! I DON'T BELIEVE IT--THAT SCREWIN' MIKE WAS LIVE! THOSE CHEAP, NO GOOD...
WHO ARE YOU?
I JUST REALIZED. THAT'S EVERY COMEDIAN'S NIGHTMARE, HUH? DYING ON STAGE. HEHH...
I THOUGHT YOU WERE REALLY FUNNY.
NO. BUT I WOULD HAVE BEEN...
WHY COULDN'T I HAVE HAD A FEW MORE LOUSY YEARS? I WOULD HAVE MADE IT TO THE TOP. WHY?
I'M SORRY, ESMÉ. YOUR TIME WAS UP. COME HERE, HONEY.
I hear the sound of her wings.
...GETS ME DOWN, TOO. MOSTLY THEY AREN'T TOO KEEN TO SEE ME. THEY FEAR THE SUNLESS LANDS. BUT THEY ENTER YOUR REALM EACH NIGHT WITHOUT FEAR.
NO ONE HERE GETS OUT ALIVE!
And I am far more terrible than you, my sister.

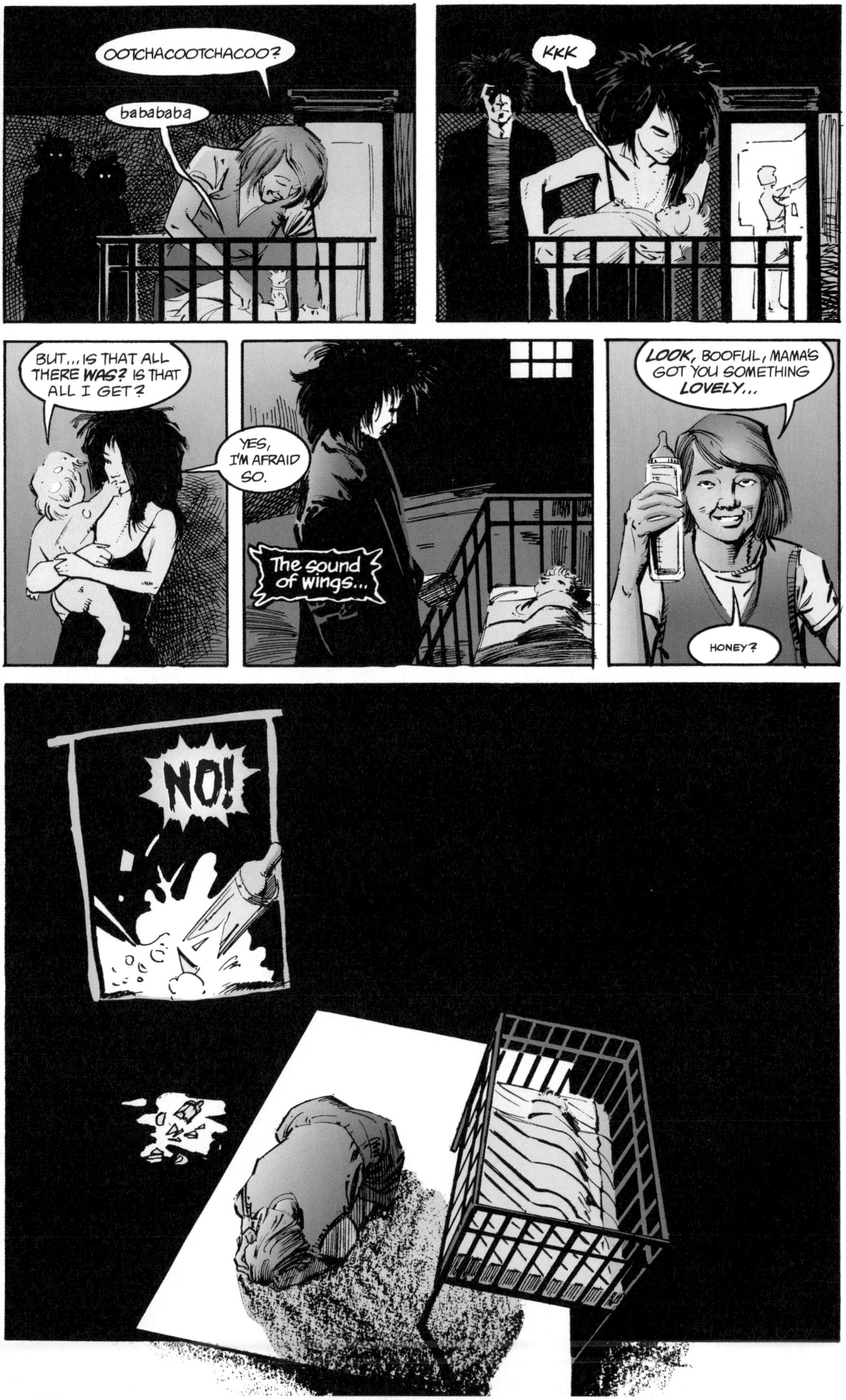
OOTCHACOOTCHACOO?
babababa
KKK
BUT... IS THAT ALL THERE WAS? IS THAT ALL I GET?
YES, I'M AFRAID SO.
The sound of wings...
LOOK, BOOFUL, MAMA'S GOT YOU SOMETHING LOVELY...
HONEY?
NO!

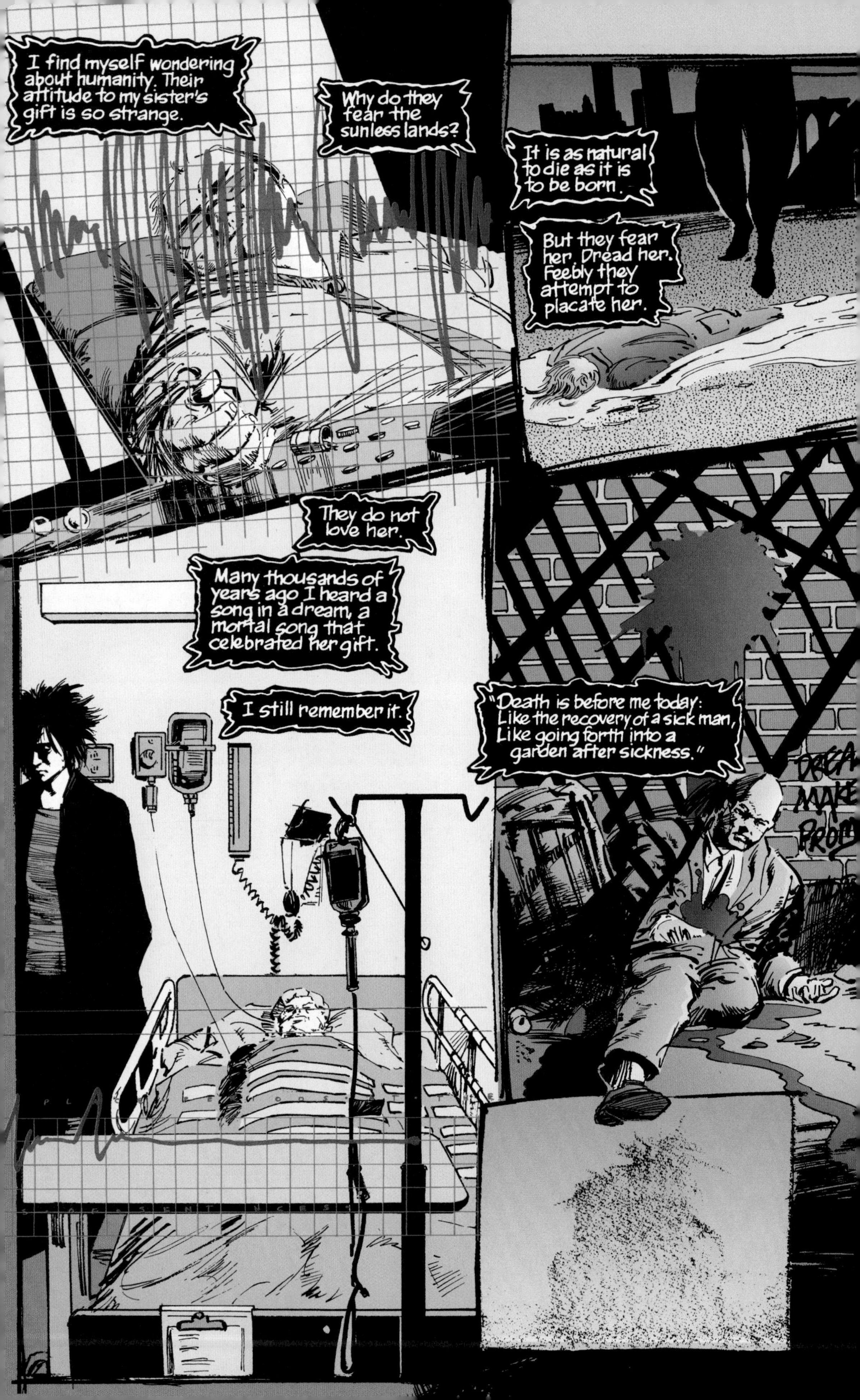
I find myself wondering about humanity. Their attitude to my sister's gift is so strange.
Why do they fear the sunless lands?
It is as natural to die as it is to be born.
But they fear her. Dread her. Feebly they attempt to placate her.
They do not love her.
Many thousands of years ago I heard a song in a dream, a mortal song that celebrated her gift.
I still remember it.
"Death is before me today:
Like the recovery of a sick man,
Like going forth into a garden after sickness."

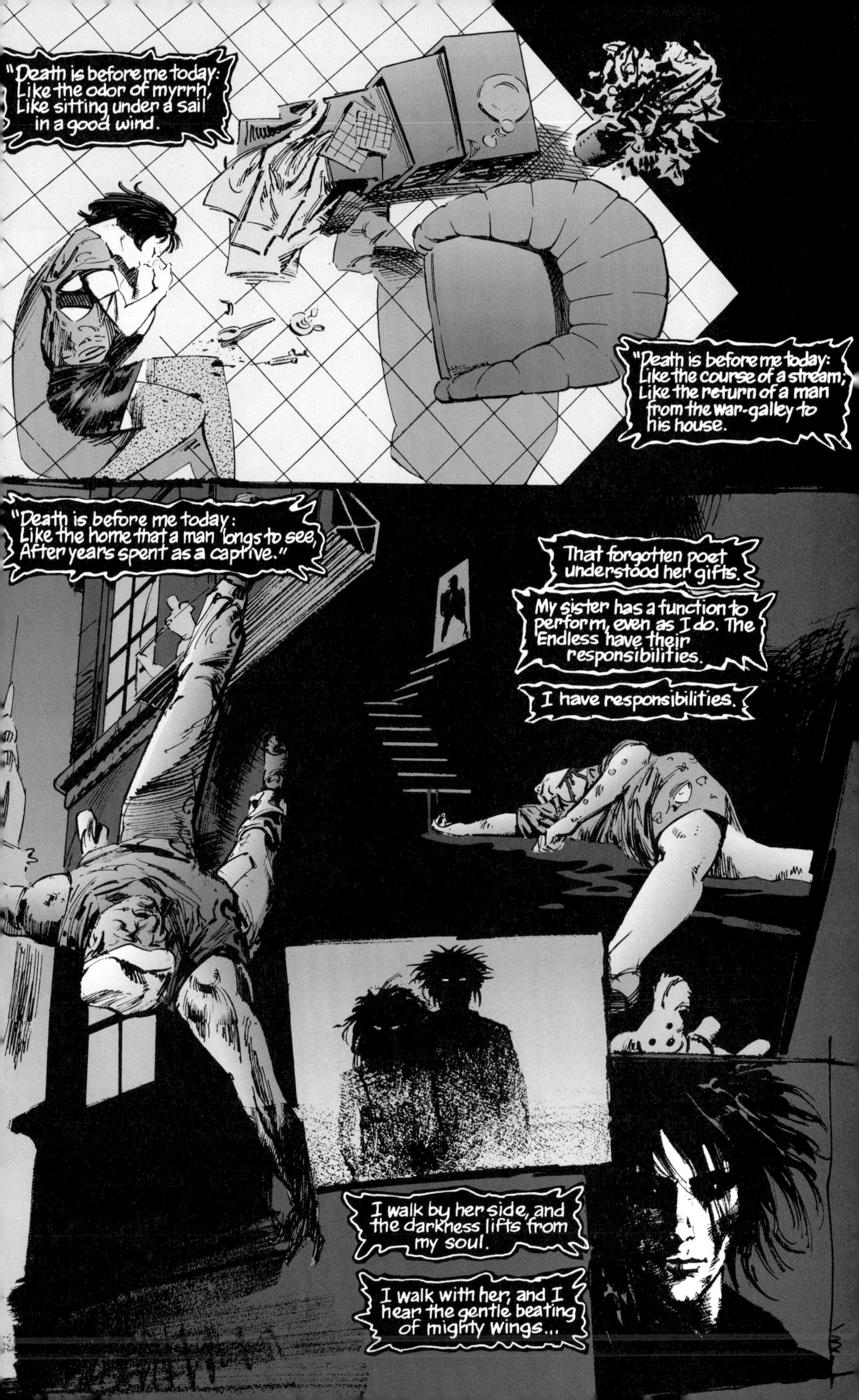
"Death is before me today: Like the odor of myrrh, Like sitting under a sail in a good wind.
"Death is before me today: Like the course of a stream; Like the return of a man from the war-galley to his house.
"Death is before me today: Like the home that a man longs to see, After years spent as a captive."
That forgotten poet understood her gifts.
My sister has a function to perform, even as I do. The Endless have their responsibilities.
I have responsibilities.
I walk by her side, and the darkness lifts from my soul.
I walk with her, and I hear the gentle beating of mighty wings...

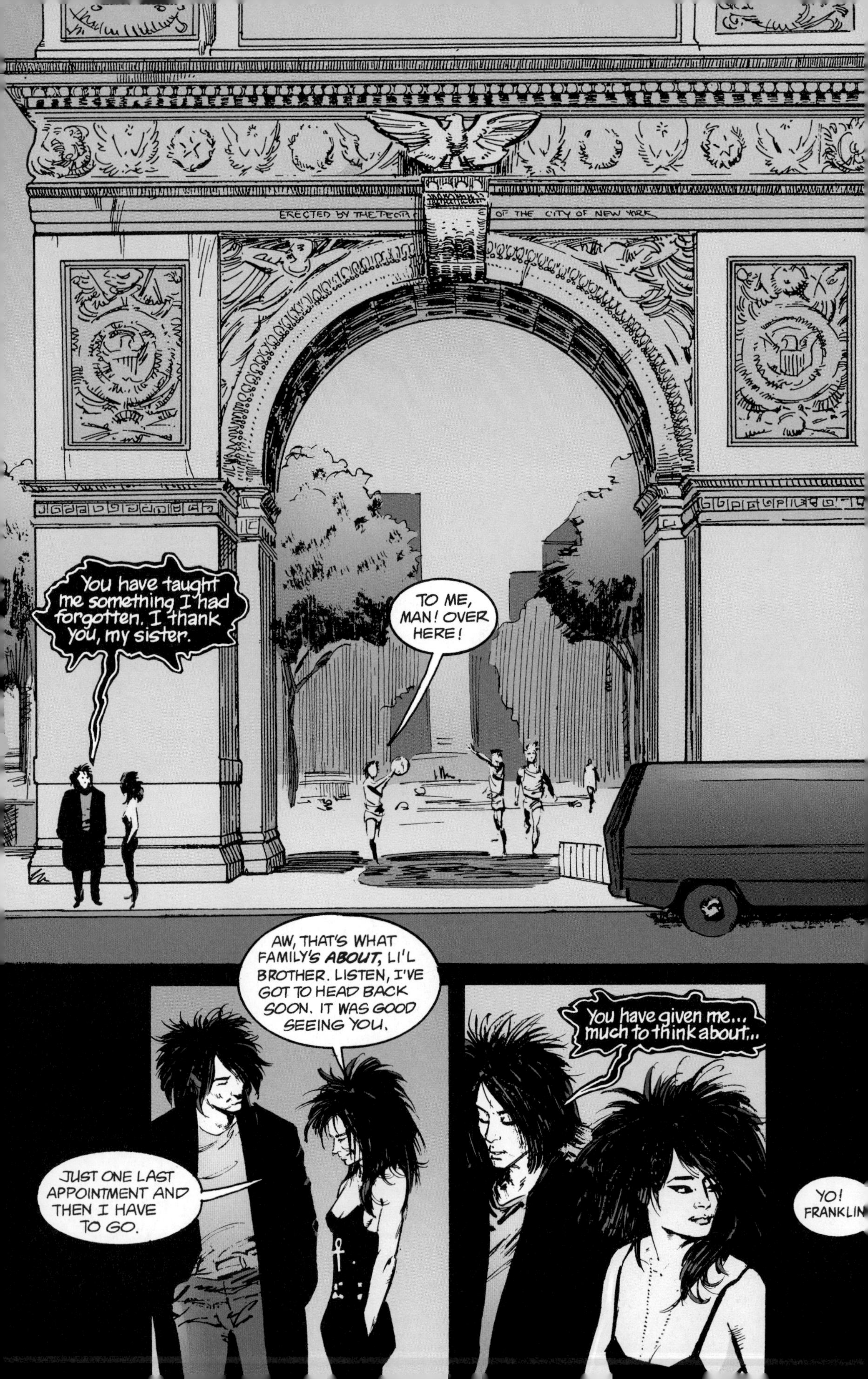
ERECTED BY THE PEOPLE OF THE CITY OF NEW YORK
You have taught me something I had forgotten. I thank you, my sister.
TO ME, MAN! OVER HERE!
AW, THAT'S WHAT FAMILY'S ABOUT, LI'L BROTHER. LISTEN, I'VE GOT TO HEAD BACK SOON. IT WAS GOOD SEEING YOU.
JUST ONE LAST APPOINTMENT AND THEN I HAVE TO GO.
You have given me... much to think about...
YO! FRANKLIN

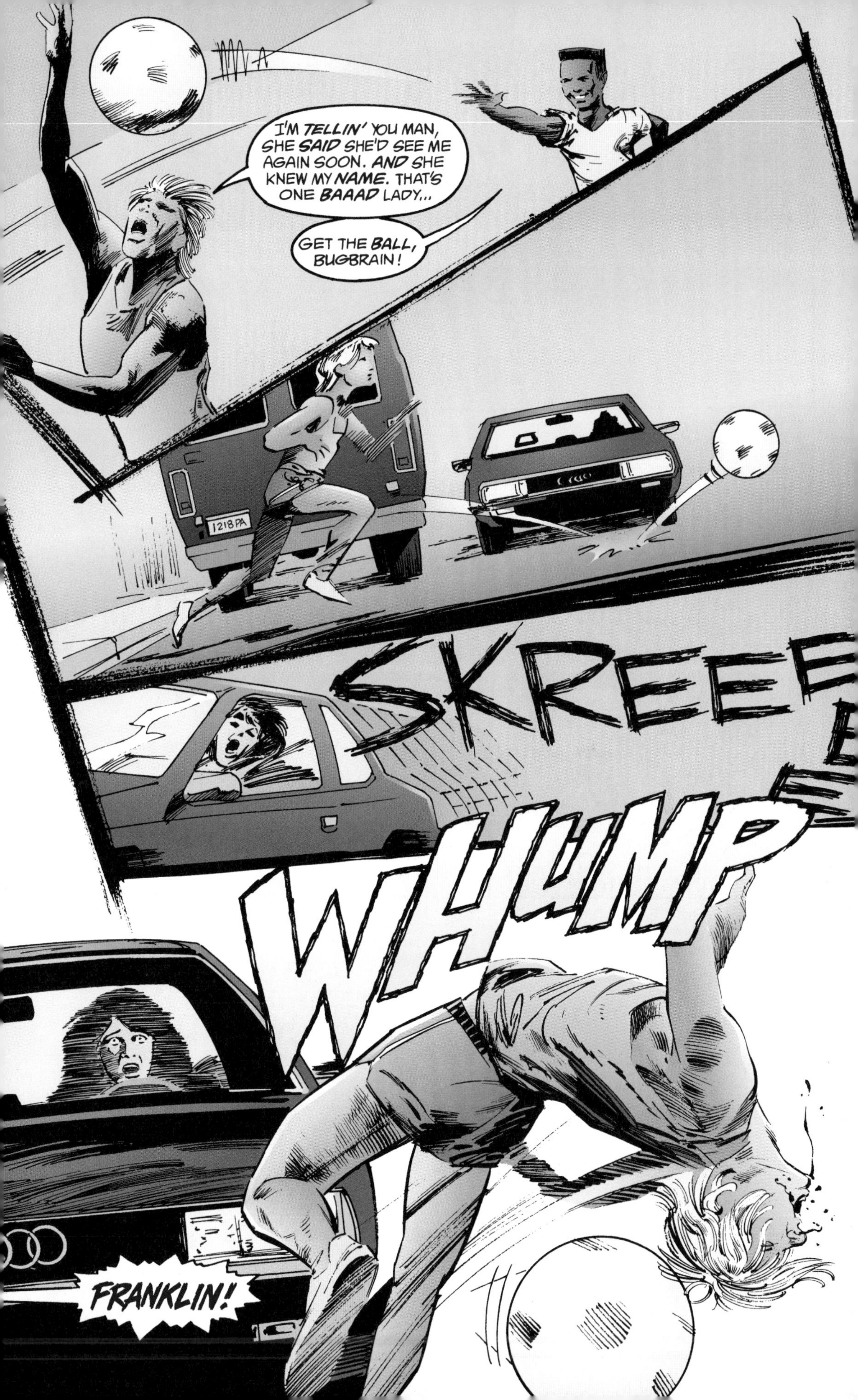
I'M TELLIN' YOU MAN, SHE SAID SHE'D SEE ME AGAIN SOON. AND SHE KNEW MY NAME. THAT'S ONE BAAAD LADY...
GET THE BALL, BUGBRAIN!
1218 PA
SKREEEE
WHUMP
FRANKLIN!

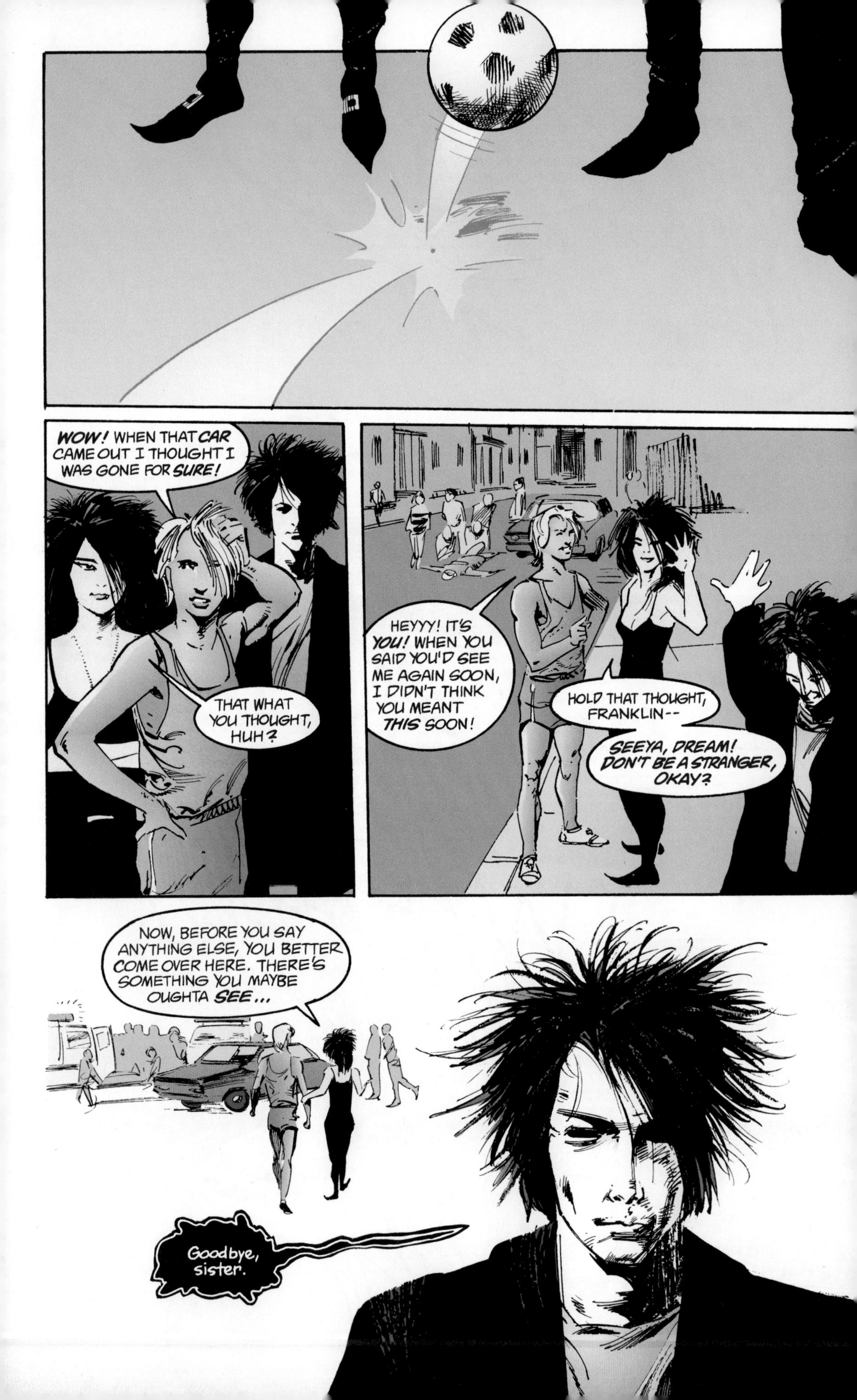

WOW! WHEN THAT CAR CAME OUT I THOUGHT I WAS GONE FOR SURE!
THAT WHAT YOU THOUGHT, HUH?
HEYYY! IT'S YOU! WHEN YOU SAID YOU'D SEE ME AGAIN SOON, I DIDN'T THINK YOU MEANT THIS SOON!
HOLD THAT THOUGHT, FRANKLIN--
SEEYA, DREAM! DON'T BE A STRANGER, OKAY?
NOW, BEFORE YOU SAY ANYTHING ELSE, YOU BETTER COME OVER HERE. THERE'S SOMETHING YOU MAYBE OUGHTA SEE...
Goodbye, sister.

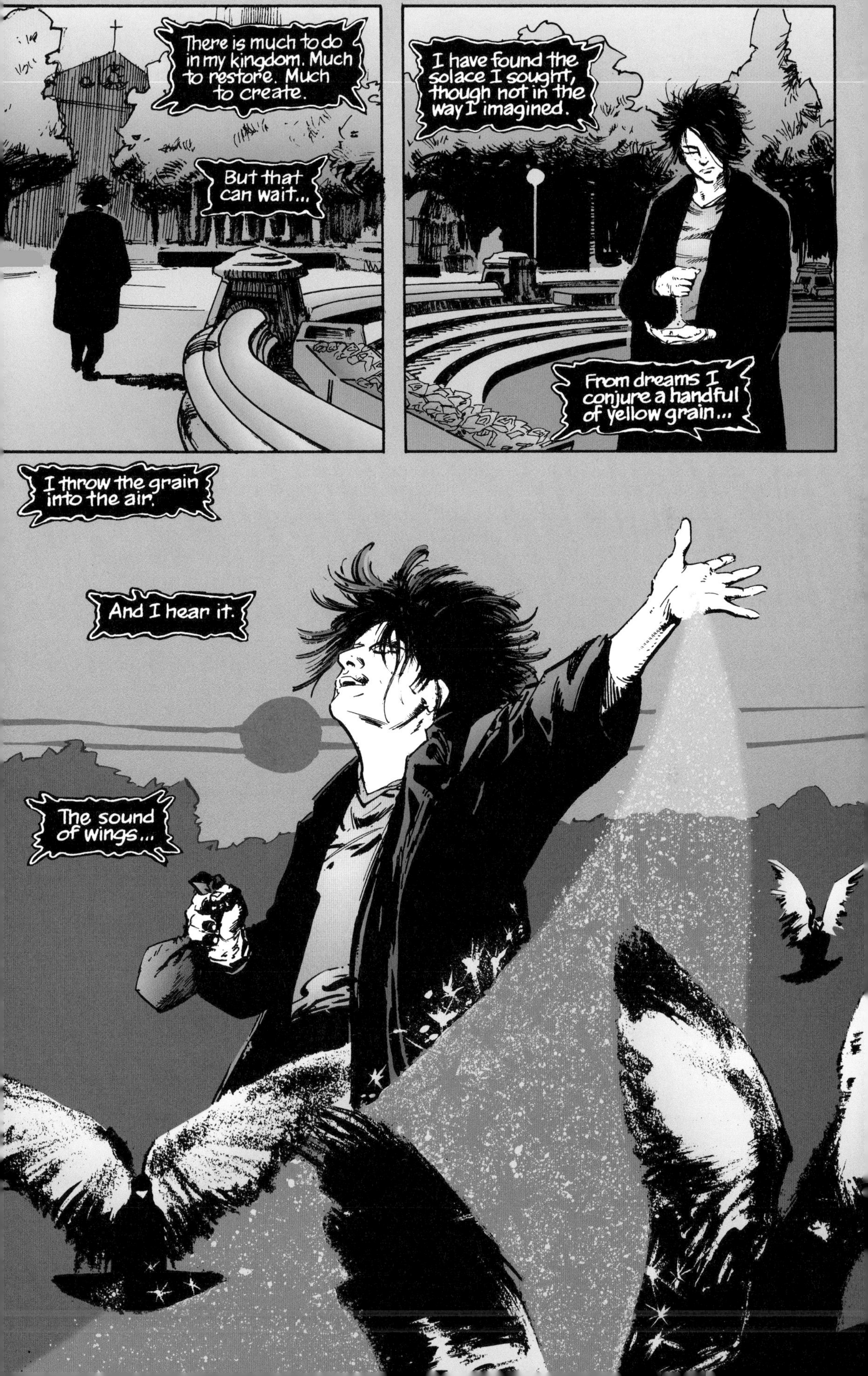
There is much to do in my kingdom. Much to restore. Much to create.
But that can wait...
I have found the solace I sought, though not in the way I imagined.
From dreams I conjure a handful of yellow grain...
I throw the grain into the air.
And I hear it.
The sound of wings...

It was all Karen Berger's fault.

She's tried to spread the blame, but seriously, it was her fault.

DC Comics had gotten on quite nicely for almost 50 years without her, and her unsettling views of how the world worked. An entire universe had been built, with a complex past, future, and a present populated by heroes, their supporting casts, and the villains they faced. And it was a nice place. The heroes were nice. Their supporting casts were nice. Even the villains they fought had nice sides. (Remember Luthor's efforts to protect his sister from knowing about his evil deeds, or the planet on which he was the hero?) And when good and evil came into conflict, good won...always. It was kind of a comforting world to visit as a reader.

Many of us had grown up on a steady diet of those tales; we'd become serious fans, indexing and analyzing them; and a lucky few even became the next generation of writers, artists, and editors crafting them. Not Karen.

She came to DC looking fresh and dewy-eyed, straight from college, not having visited the world of superheroes or even comics beyond a passed-around *Betty & Veronica* or three at camp. If only we knew what lurked within.

At first she edited comics as harmless as the company's long-standing standards: *House of Mystery*, with its watered-down scary tales; *Legion of Super-Heroes*, carrying on Superman's traditions a millennium later. And even her first new launch was sweet: *Amethyst, Princess of Gemworld*. Maybe she would fit in the company's mold, despite her lack of childhood indoctrination. At least so it appeared.

She was assigned *Saga of the Swamp Thing*, up until then a fairly conventional title being written by a very promising new writer at DC—the company's first British scribe, a very literary fellow named Alan Moore.

She...encouraged him.

The first stories were much like the ones before: classic DC elements integrated into the creepier environs of the bayou, the Floronic Man, the Justice League, the Demon. But within a few months, they grew steadily darker and more threatening. Alan Moore wasn't writing comics that were safe for little children, and his editor was encouraging him. So much so that DC turned to the three-decade-old Comics Code, suggesting a revision that would be more like the Motion Picture Association of America's movie rating system, and, failing to get agreement on that, withdrew *Saga of the Swamp Thing* from the Code entirely...the first time it had done so.

It only got worse.

She became the company's liaison to a growing pool of British creative talent, sitting in convention pubs for hours, listening to their wild ideas, connecting the best of them to a DC universe that was growing steadily darker as the audience grew older and comic shops became the dominant form of distribution. You could hear old boundaries breaking with resounding crashes.

Her own projects led the way into the darkness: work from British writers new to DC, like Jamie Delano, Peter Milligan, Grant Morrison, and this charming journalist in black leather, a kid named Neil. Before long, the wall of covers in her office was full of visuals that didn't look anything like what was hanging down the hall in the other rooms. *Hellblazer*, *Animal Man*, *Shade the Changing Man*, and then there was *Sandman*. Each taking some...ahem...roots from elements in the DC Universe, but sprouting in directions as unexpected as Moore's *Swamp Thing* had been.

Sandman was the game changer. It gained momentum with each issue, and became the first periodical comic series to fully take hold in the new trade paperback graphic novel format. The collected editions of *Sandman* launched awkwardly, with the second storyline because the first was deemed too DC-history-specific for new readers, but once they started, they couldn't be stopped. Each new collection seemed to spark sales of the previous ones, both in comic shops and in the new graphic novel sections of traditional bookstores.

This was the beginning of Vertigo's most important contribution to the comics field, even before Vertigo was born. Gaiman's *Sandman* was demonstrating that if you expand the creative reach of comics and make it easily available to potential new readers, you can build an entirely new audience. In this case, one that included far more young women than comics had been attracting for several decades. And it showed that a creator putting more energy into his work could be rewarded by the growing audience spreading the word, demanding new printing after new printing and generating a steady stream of royalties. The structure of a series of trade collections, cross marketed and offering the full run of a long saga, seems obvious now, but was a radical step forward for comics in the early 1990s.

Fans, comic shop managers, and even professionals began to speak of the Berger-verse, a sort of alternate space within the larger DC Universe, connected by links of continuity and history, but separated by a very definable aesthetic that was unlike anything comics had seen. Armchair analysts and academics could argue for ancestral links to E.C., nods to *2000 AD* where the Brits had cut their teeth, or the experimental work Archie Goodwin had done at Marvel's Epic Comics line, but the reality was very different.

It was all Karen Berger's fault.

She would claim, years later, that it was just a matter of wanting to put out comics she wanted to read. Her tastes were a little different from the former comic fans who filled so many of the industry's offices, a bit more literary, a bit more risqué. She was attracted to writers who were proposing things that were a bit less conventional, less reliant on straightforward good-versus-evil tales (was the world really that simple?), and ultimately, a bit more disturbing.

And if the outside world was noticing, so were the executives inside. As she was returning from maternity leave, Karen's day-to-day boss, the ever-affable Dick Giordano (DC's VP-Editorial Director) approached her, saying that company President and Editor-in-Chief Jenette Kahn and Executive VP and Publisher (ahem...me) and he thought she should take the Berger-verse even further. It was time to turn it into an imprint.

DC had tried an imprint strategy before, an attempt to totally break the company's legacy and traditions by hiring an outsider named Mark Nevelow to set up a totally new imprint, with a new contract form, new formats, and even an office separate from the rest of the company. While Nevelow produced some interesting departures from DC's norm, as a business venture, it had failed, and Nevelow had departed, too.

This would be different, because it would start with an editor who, while trained in the DC legacies, had organically moved beyond them. And it would start with the forward momentum of a group of successful titles led by a genuine breakthrough series that could be used to introduce readers to the others, and to new titles that would follow. As an added plus, the success of the *Sandman* collected editions showed that there was a new revenue stream that could help support the venture.

Some lessons learned from Piranha would benefit this new imprint: a new contract form, more friendly to creators of new projects; rates would be de-linked from the rest of the line, allowing writers to get paid somewhat better as this would be a writer-dominated approach; offices within DC, to facilitate cooperation with marketing, production, and the other departments; and then the debatable lessons. Did Piranha suffer from not having the DC bullet symbol on its covers? Since this line would feature many characters who came from the DC Universe, did it make sense to carry the bullet along with a logo for the new imprint?

Karen offered up a list of names for discussion, and Vertigo carried the day, connoting a sensibility that was destabilizing, unsettling, and uncomfortable compared to the safer space of the traditional DC Universe. Richard Bruning offered up a logo design, and the debate over the bullet began. It was an important enough choice not to be left entirely up to instinct, so mock-up covers with and without the bullet were prepared, and tested. In the end, the choice was no bullet, but a simple-type "DC Comics" under the imprint logo, and even that would fade away with time.

The launch month was strengthened with a *Sandman* spin-off miniseries, *Death: The High Cost of Living*, as well as the launch of *Enigma*, a Peter Milligan-Duncan Fegredo series acquired from Disney when they aborted their proposed Touchmark line of mature comics. Perhaps most importantly, a *Vertigo Preview* comic was part of the launch, complete with an original short *Sandman* story as well as selections from across the line. It was January 1993, and time for Vertigo to be born.

Over time, many aspects of Vertigo would grow and mature: for over a decade, the links to the DC Universe would grow weaker and be severed while crossovers between mature-reader titles and the rest of the line were deemed inappropriate; painted covers would become a hallmark (and largely be banished from the traditional line); and the emphasis on long, but closed-ended series would become central.

Once the decision had been made that *Sandman* would end when Neil Gaiman departed the series (the first time a major comics publisher had agreed to end a successful periodical to accommodate the creative talent's desires), it became possible for writers to envision the full arc of the stories they wanted to tell, beginning to end, even if it would be a journey that lasted years. And a bookcase worth of Vertigo's greatest hits was done that way: *Preacher*, *100 Bullets*, *Y: The Last Man*, and *Fables*, among others. Powerful series, establishing or revitalizing the reputations of their creators: Garth Ennis, Brian Azzarello, Brian K. Vaughan, and Bill Willingham, in these examples.

The other critical business departure for Vertigo came with *Transmetropolitan*, a series brought into the line from an unsuccessful effort to create Helix, a second, related imprint that would focus on science fiction. *Transmetropolitan*, by Warren Ellis and Darick Robertson, had a challenging run as a periodical title, and was losing money issue after issue. But for the first time in comics' history, the sales of the collected editions were sufficiently profitable to allow the periodical to go on for several years to its natural end.

In its more than 25 years, Vertigo would be consistently innovative, creatively daring, and a birthing place for a lengthy succession of major talents for the field. While not without its controversies, arguments, and debates, Vertigo would be viewed as an industry leader, and as the success of graphic novels grew, would grow to be larger at its peak than any but the industry's top three publishers.

The list of Eisner Awards won by Vertigo series would fill these pages, leaving no room for other text. The list of creative talent and editorial talent who were developed at Vertigo would be even longer. The media adaptations produced based on Vertigo titles is shorter, but the audiences reach into the tens of millions and beyond for *Constantine, V for Vendetta, The Losers, iZombie, Lucifer,* and *Preacher,* with more yet to come. And untallied, but clearly more important than any of this, is the horde of new readers brought to comics because Vertigo became the place to publish a different kind of story, an unsettling and disturbing view of reality. A kind of story its publisher once described as stories that made him uncomfortable.

And it's all Karen Berger's fault, because those are the kinds of stories she wanted to read...and share.

Paul Levitz
October 2020

50 YEARS AND ONWARD

Ultimately, the most successful of DC's 1980s experiments stemmed from two impulses: President and Editor-in-Chief Jenette Kahn's belief that comics knew no creative boundaries and her search for the breakthrough talent who could prove it, and Executive Vice President and Publisher Paul Levitz's quest for a format that would allow the best comics to stay continually in print and available to readers. It all came together as DC turned 50 in 1985.

Jenette had long encouraged Frank Miller to do important work for DC, bringing him on board with his groundbreaking *Ronin*. But daring as *Ronin* was, it was a step too far for the market when first published. It wasn't until Frank turned his hand toward DC's iconic heroes that he really shattered the conceptions of what comics could be. It's difficult to explain the significance of *The Dark Knight Returns* decades later, but in many ways it was the first American comic book to be taken seriously by the media and academics. And close behind it came Alan Moore and Dave Gibbons's *Watchmen*, the two titles deconstructing the standard myths of the superhero and ushering in an age of dark contemplation.

It was these two titles, collected and repackaged as trade paperbacks, along with Art Spiegelman's masterpiece, *Maus*, that came together, crashing open the path to bookstores and libraries treating comics not as disposable entertainment, but as literature...as graphic novels.

And the whole history of DC was about to do an amazing pivot...

FRANK MILLER'S
RONIN

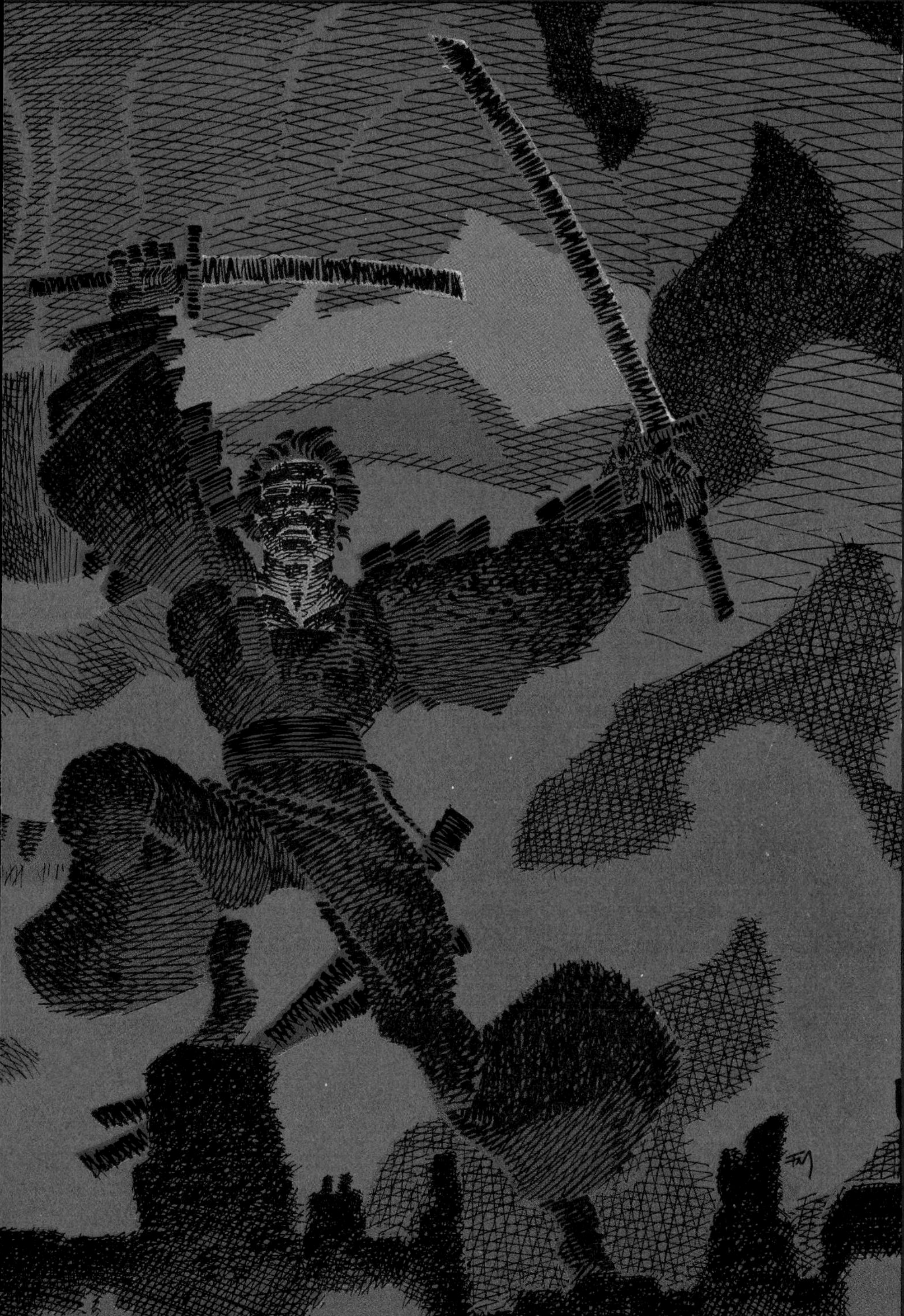

BOOK ONE

$2.50
$3.00 CAN

RONIN
BOOK ONE

Story and Art by
FRANK MILLER

Colors by
LYNN VARLEY

Letters by
JOHN COSTANZA

RONIN created by **FRANK MILLER**

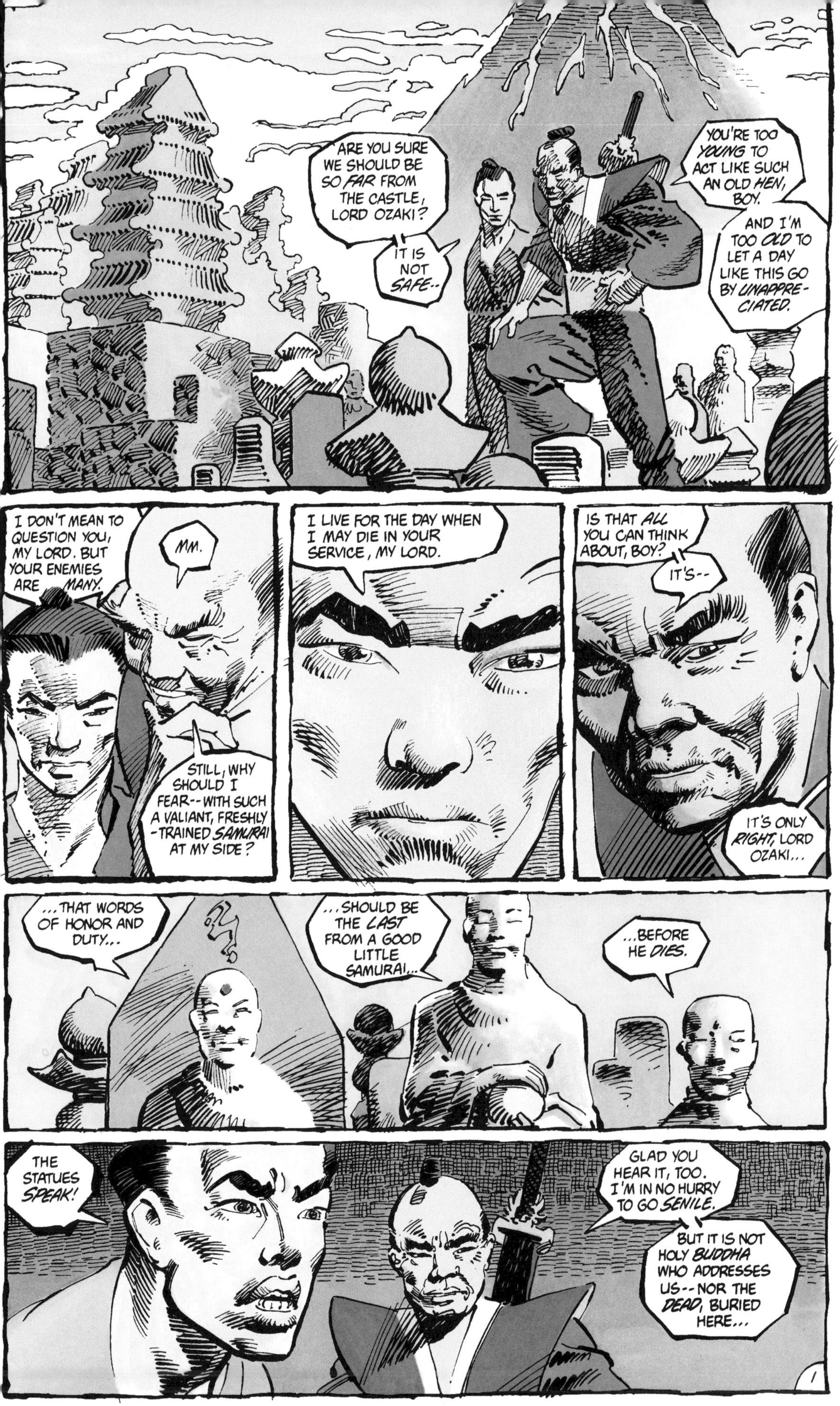
ARE YOU SURE WE SHOULD BE SO FAR FROM THE CASTLE, LORD OZAKI?
IT IS NOT SAFE...
YOU'RE TOO YOUNG TO ACT LIKE SUCH AN OLD HEN, BOY.
AND I'M TOO OLD TO LET A DAY LIKE THIS GO BY UNAPPRECIATED.
I DON'T MEAN TO QUESTION YOU, MY LORD. BUT YOUR ENEMIES ARE MANY.
MM.
STILL, WHY SHOULD I FEAR--WITH SUCH A VALIANT, FRESHLY-TRAINED SAMURAI AT MY SIDE?
I LIVE FOR THE DAY WHEN I MAY DIE IN YOUR SERVICE, MY LORD.
IS THAT ALL YOU CAN THINK ABOUT, BOY?
IT'S--
IT'S ONLY RIGHT, LORD OZAKI...
...THAT WORDS OF HONOR AND DUTY...
...SHOULD BE THE LAST FROM A GOOD LITTLE SAMURAI...
...BEFORE HE DIES.
THE STATUES SPEAK!
GLAD YOU HEAR IT, TOO. I'M IN NO HURRY TO GO SENILE.
BUT IT IS NOT HOLY BUDDHA WHO ADDRESSES US--NOR THE DEAD, BURIED HERE...
1

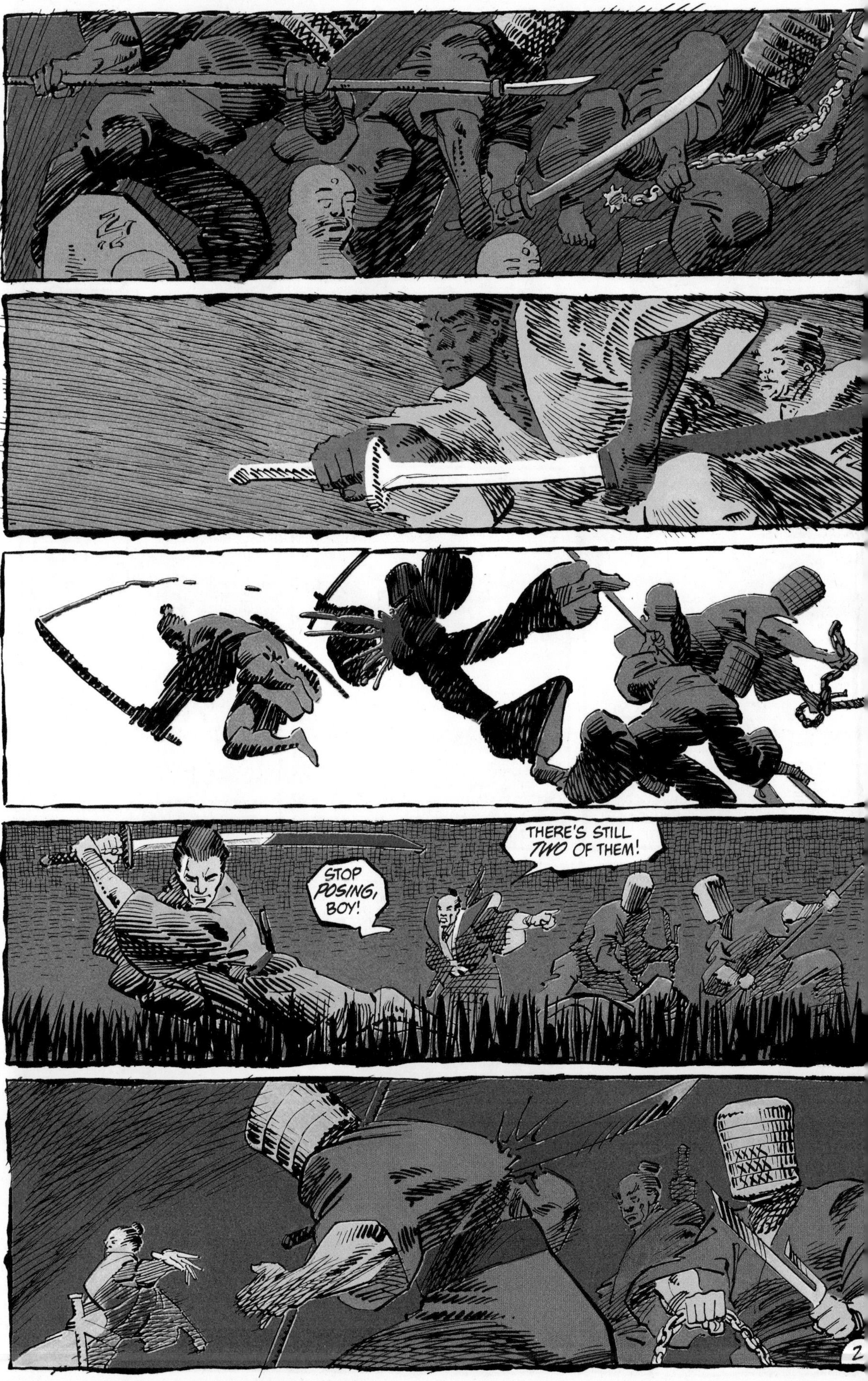
STOP POSING, BOY!
THERE'S STILL TWO OF THEM!

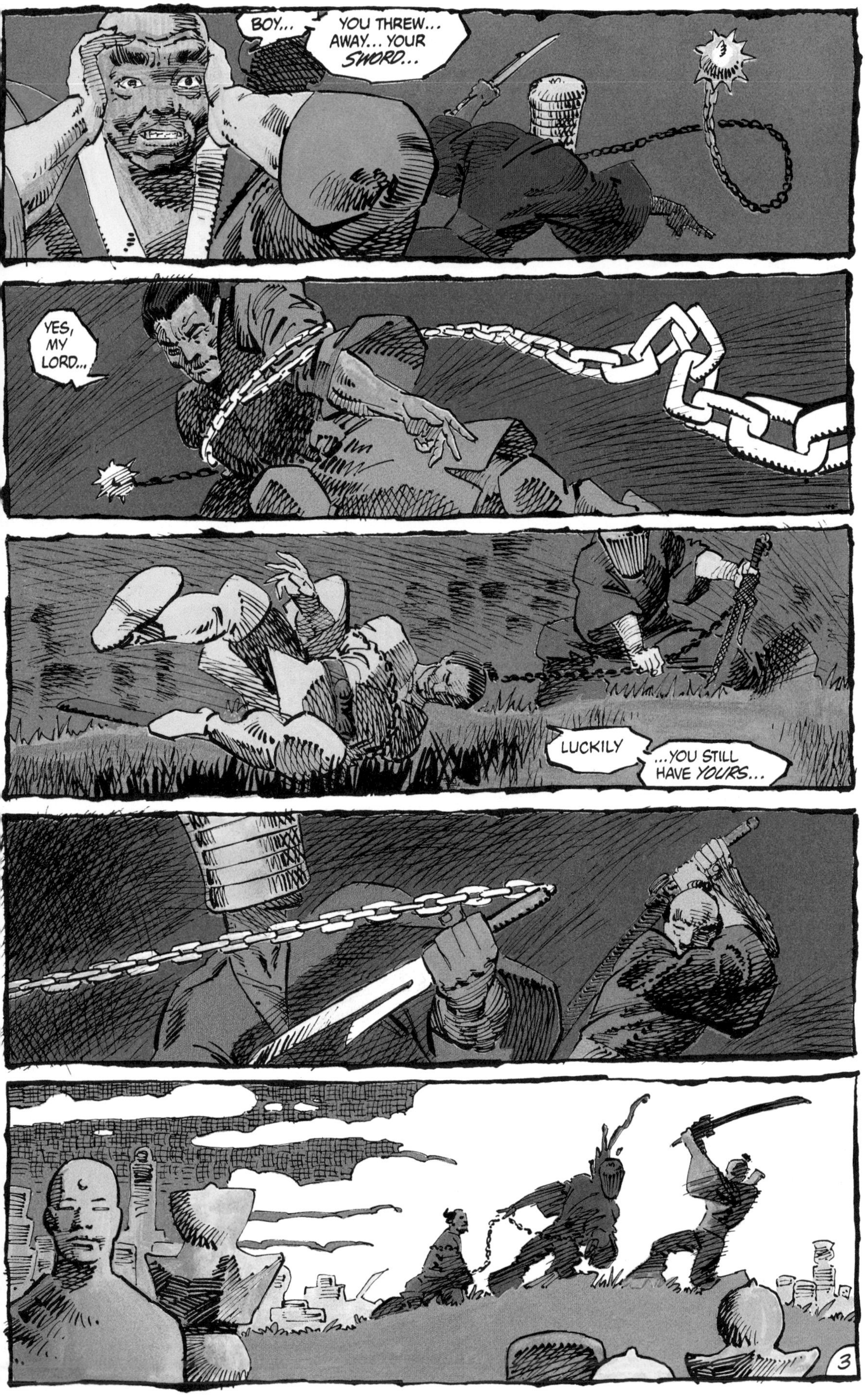
BOY...
YOU THREW... AWAY... YOUR SWORD...
YES, MY LORD...
LUCKILY
...YOU STILL HAVE YOURS...
3

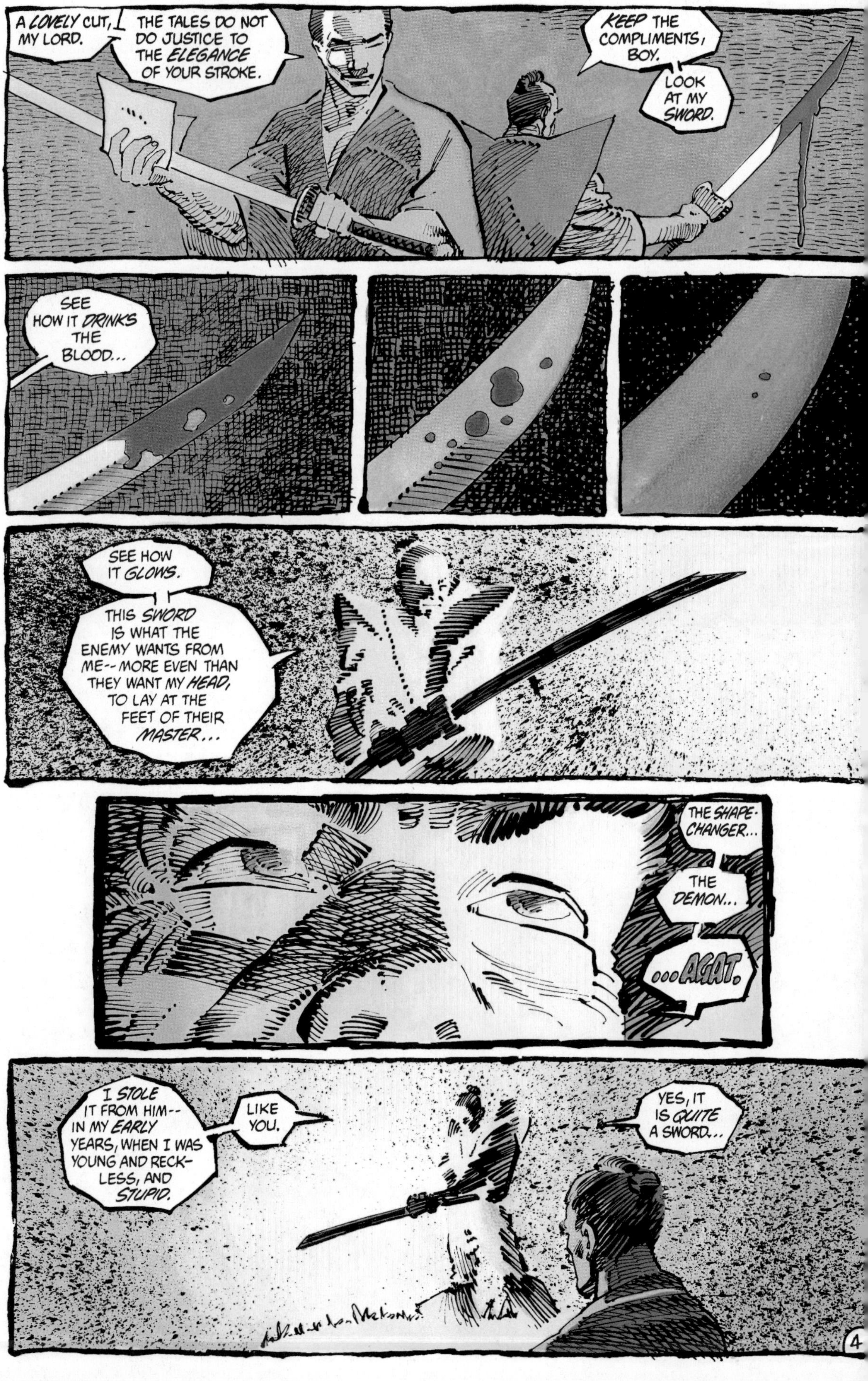
A LOVELY CUT, MY LORD.
THE TALES DO NOT DO JUSTICE TO THE ELEGANCE OF YOUR STROKE.
KEEP THE COMPLIMENTS, BOY.
LOOK AT MY SWORD.
SEE HOW IT DRINKS THE BLOOD...
SEE HOW IT GLOWS.
THIS SWORD IS WHAT THE ENEMY WANTS FROM ME--MORE EVEN THAN THEY WANT MY HEAD, TO LAY AT THE FEET OF THEIR MASTER...
THE SHAPE-CHANGER...
THE DEMON...
...AGAT.
I STOLE IT FROM HIM--IN MY EARLY YEARS, WHEN I WAS YOUNG AND RECK-LESS, AND STUPID.
LIKE YOU.
YES, IT IS QUITE A SWORD...

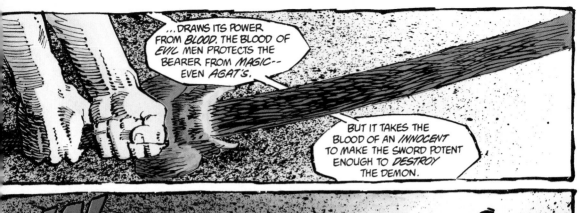

...DRAWS ITS POWER FROM *BLOOD.* THE BLOOD OF *EVIL* MEN PROTECTS THE BEARER FROM *MAGIC*-- EVEN *AGAT'S.*

BUT IT TAKES THE BLOOD OF AN *INNOCENT* TO MAKE THE SWORD POTENT ENOUGH TO *DESTROY* THE DEMON.

HA!

THAT WOULD BE A SIGHT, BOY!

AGAT, SKEWERED ON HIS OWN BLADE, HIS PLAGUE ON OUR LAND *LIFTED!*

BUT IT IS ENOUGH, FOR NOW, TO HOLD THE *BLOODSWORD* AND KNOW THAT THE DEMON *FEARS* ME. YES...

LET'S GET BACK TO THE *CASTLE,* BOY. ALL THIS TALKING HAS MADE ME *THIRSTY.*

DO YOU DRINK?

NO.

I'LL HAVE TO *TEACH* YOU-- AS PAYMENT FOR SAVING MY *LIFE,* BACK THERE.

SERVING MY LORD IS ITS *OWN* REWARD. WERE I *SLAIN,* I WOULD RISE FROM THE GRAVE SEVEN TIMES TO DEFEND YOUR--

OH, SHUT UP.

5

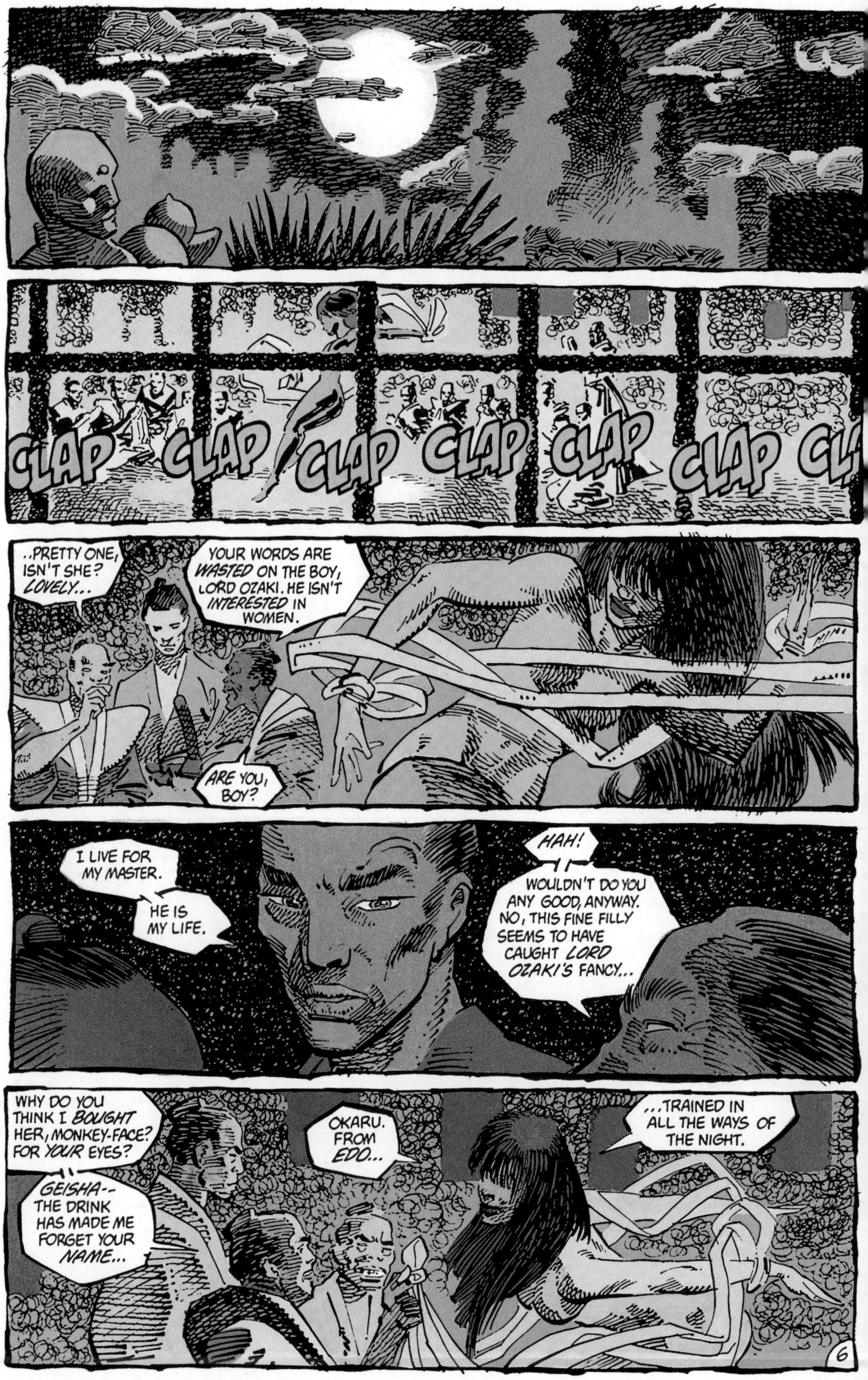
CLAP CLAP CLAP CLAP CLAP CLAP CL
..PRETTY ONE, ISN'T SHE? LOVELY...
YOUR WORDS ARE WASTED ON THE BOY, LORD OZAKI. HE ISN'T INTERESTED IN WOMEN.
ARE YOU, BOY?
I LIVE FOR MY MASTER.
HE IS MY LIFE.
HAH!
WOULDN'T DO YOU ANY GOOD, ANYWAY. NO, THIS FINE FILLY SEEMS TO HAVE CAUGHT LORD OZAKI'S FANCY...
WHY DO YOU THINK I BOUGHT HER, MONKEY-FACE? FOR YOUR EYES?
GEISHA-- THE DRINK HAS MADE ME FORGET YOUR NAME...
OKARU. FROM EDO...
...TRAINED IN ALL THE WAYS OF THE NIGHT.

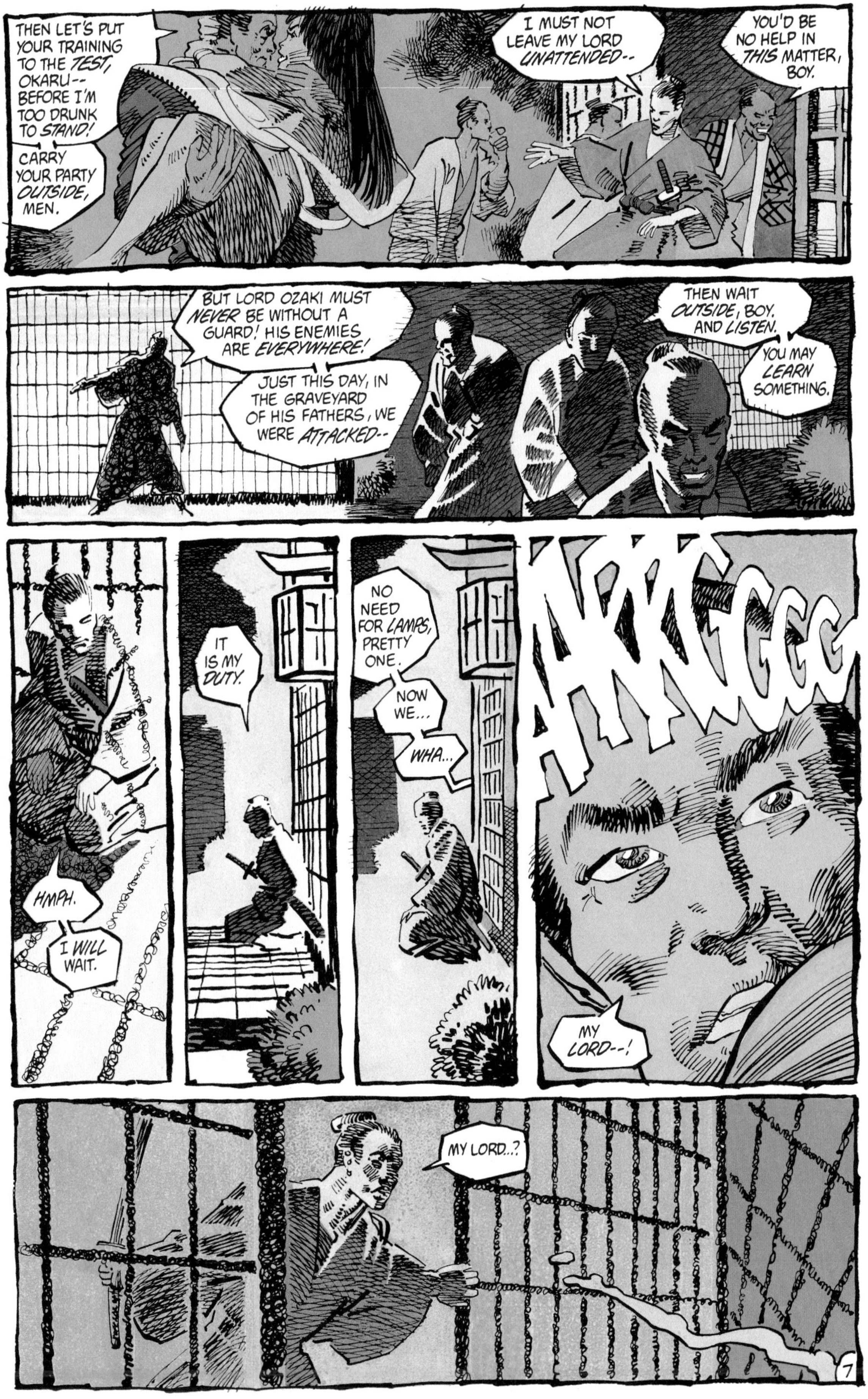
THEN LET'S PUT YOUR TRAINING TO THE TEST, OKARU-- BEFORE I'M TOO DRUNK TO STAND!
CARRY YOUR PARTY OUTSIDE, MEN.
I MUST NOT LEAVE MY LORD UNATTENDED--
YOU'D BE NO HELP IN THIS MATTER, BOY.
BUT LORD OZAKI MUST NEVER BE WITHOUT A GUARD! HIS ENEMIES ARE EVERYWHERE!
JUST THIS DAY, IN THE GRAVEYARD OF HIS FATHERS, WE WERE ATTACKED--
THEN WAIT OUTSIDE, BOY. AND LISTEN.
YOU MAY LEARN SOMETHING.
HMPH.
I WILL WAIT.
IT IS MY DUTY.
NO NEED FOR LAMPS, PRETTY ONE.
NOW WE...
WHA...
AAAAGGG
MY LORD--!
MY LORD..?
7

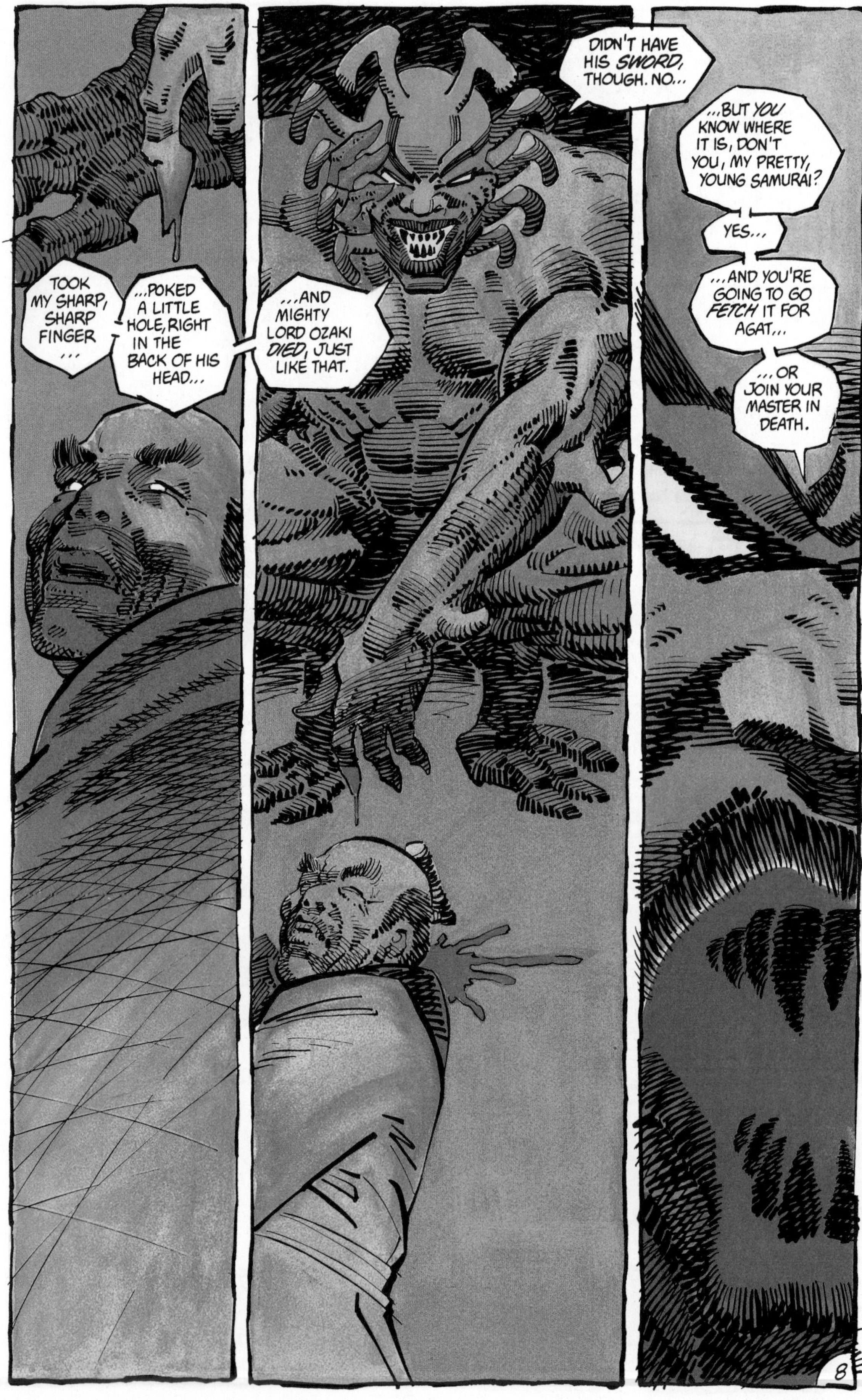
TOOK MY SHARP, SHARP FINGER ...
...POKED A LITTLE HOLE, RIGHT IN THE BACK OF HIS HEAD...
...AND MIGHTY LORD OZAKI DIED, JUST LIKE THAT.
DIDN'T HAVE HIS SWORD, THOUGH. NO...
...BUT YOU KNOW WHERE IT IS, DON'T YOU, MY PRETTY, YOUNG SAMURAI?
YES...
...AND YOU'RE GOING TO GO FETCH IT FOR AGAT...
...OR JOIN YOUR MASTER IN DEATH.
8

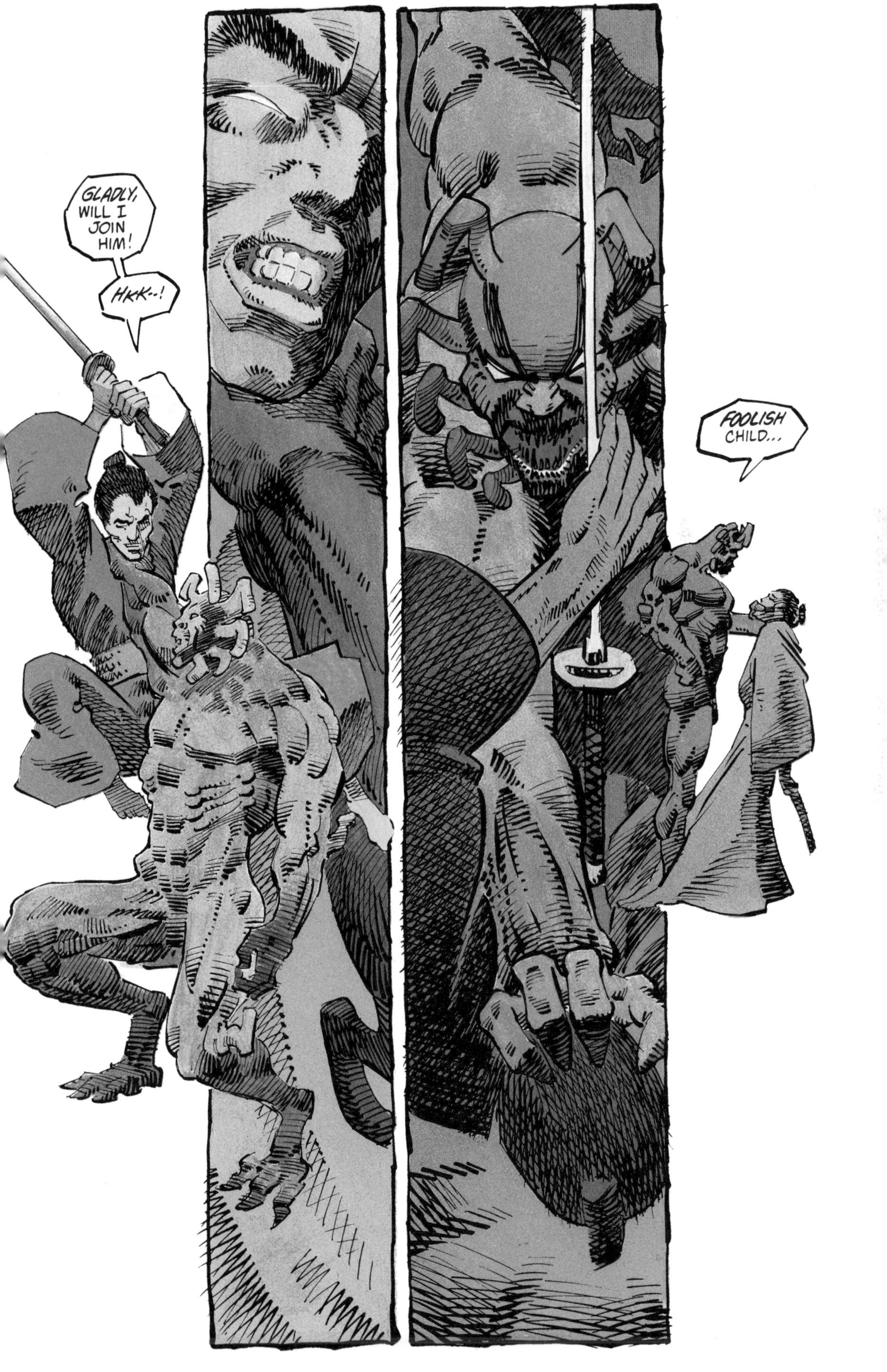
GLADLY, WILL I JOIN HIM!
HKK..!
FOOLISH CHILD...

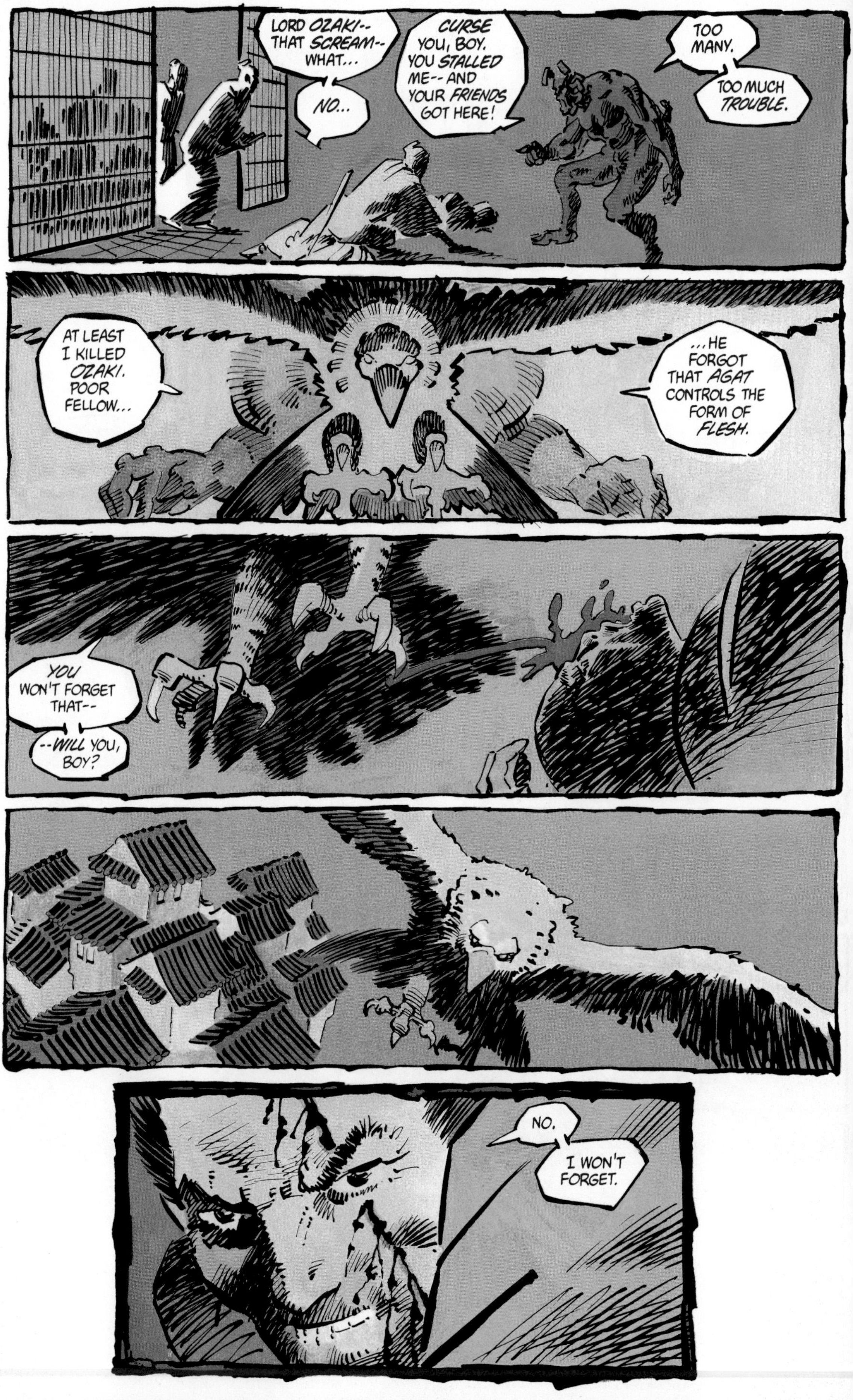
LORD OZAKI-- THAT SCREAM-- WHAT...
NO...
CURSE YOU, BOY. YOU STALLED ME-- AND YOUR FRIENDS GOT HERE!
TOO MANY.
TOO MUCH TROUBLE.
AT LEAST I KILLED OZAKI. POOR FELLOW...
...HE FORGOT THAT AGAT CONTROLS THE FORM OF FLESH.
YOU WON'T FORGET THAT--
--WILL YOU, BOY?
NO.
I WON'T FORGET.

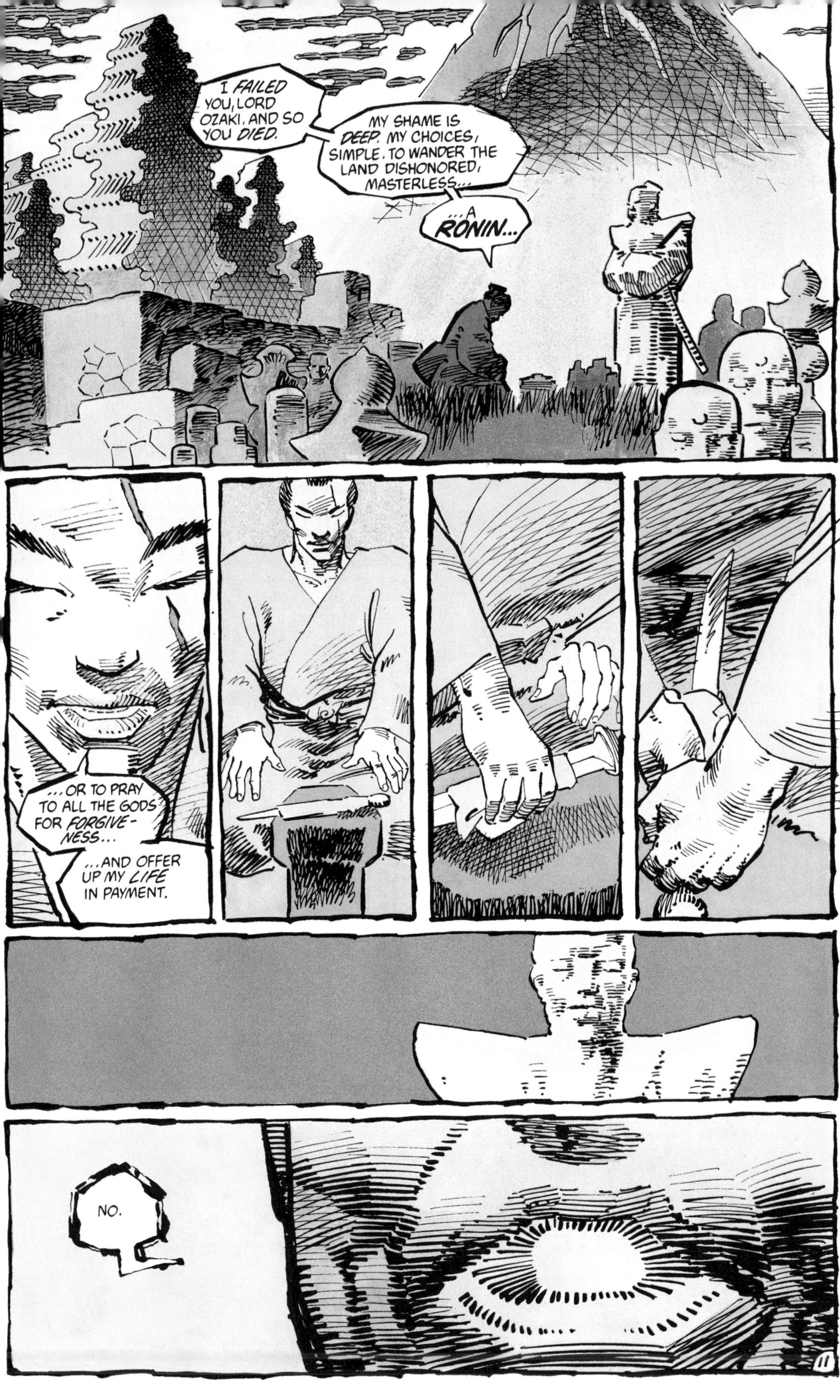

I FAILED YOU, LORD OZAKI. AND SO YOU DIED.
MY SHAME IS DEEP. MY CHOICES, SIMPLE. TO WANDER THE LAND DISHONORED, MASTERLESS...
...A RONIN...
...OR TO PRAY TO ALL THE GODS FOR FORGIVE-NESS...
...AND OFFER UP MY LIFE IN PAYMENT.
NO.

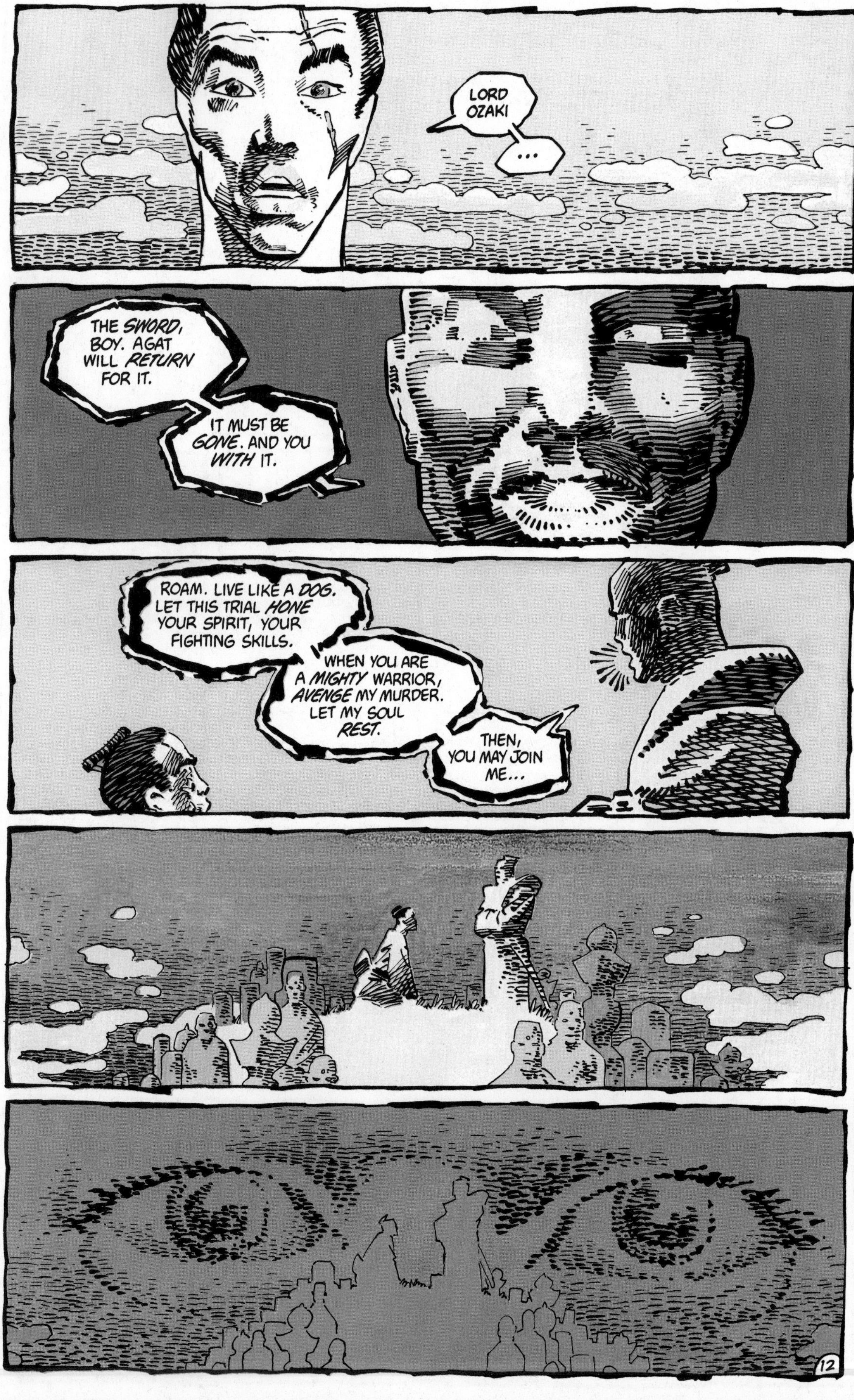
LORD OZAKI
...
THE SWORD, BOY. AGAT WILL RETURN FOR IT.
IT MUST BE GONE. AND YOU WITH IT.
ROAM. LIVE LIKE A DOG. LET THIS TRIAL HONE YOUR SPIRIT, YOUR FIGHTING SKILLS.
WHEN YOU ARE A MIGHTY WARRIOR, AVENGE MY MURDER. LET MY SOUL REST.
THEN, YOU MAY JOIN ME...

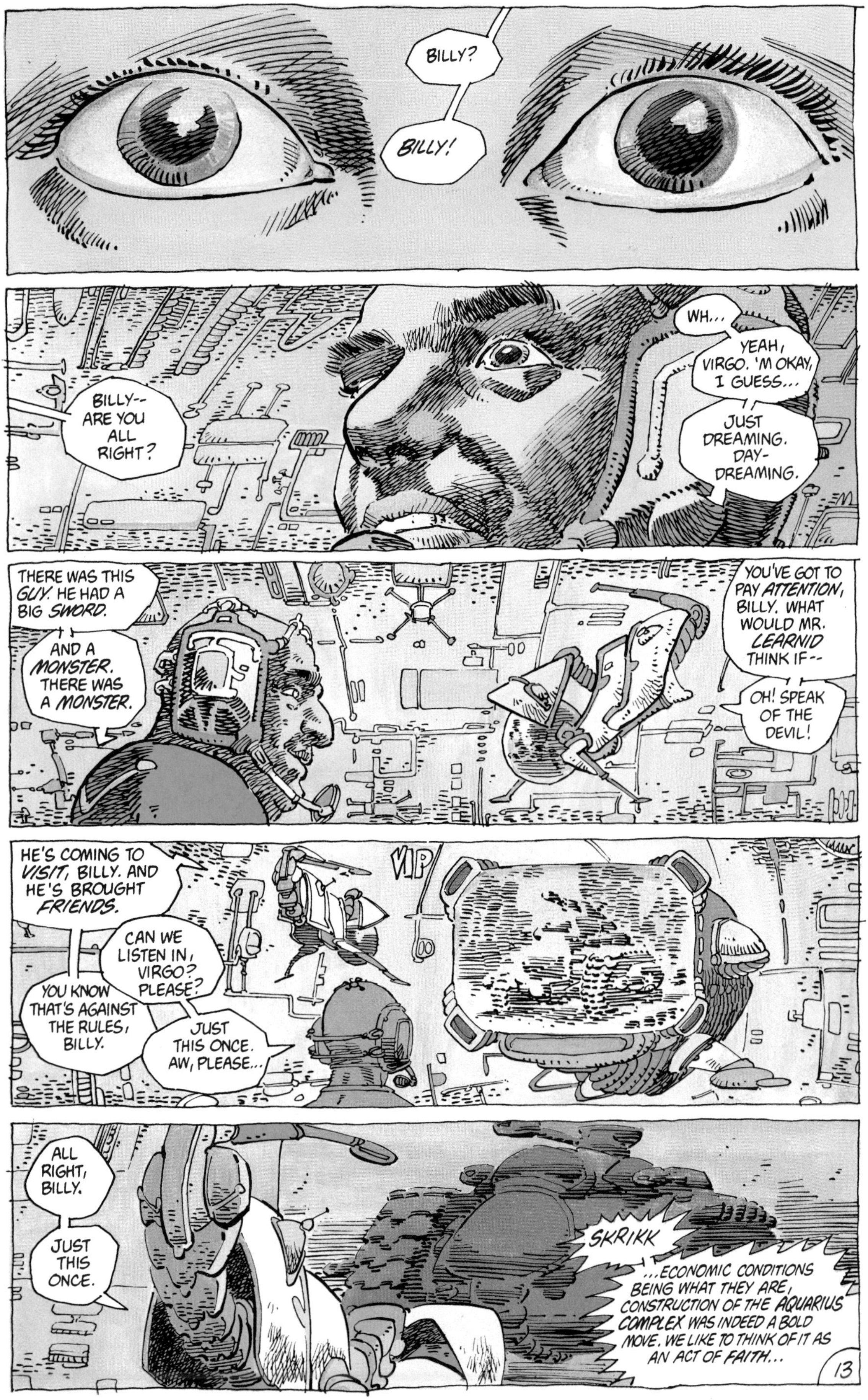
BILLY?
BILLY!
BILLY-- ARE YOU ALL RIGHT?
WH...
YEAH, VIRGO. 'M OKAY, I GUESS...
JUST DREAMING. DAY-DREAMING.
THERE WAS THIS GUY. HE HAD A BIG SWORD.
AND A MONSTER. THERE WAS A MONSTER.
YOU'VE GOT TO PAY ATTENTION, BILLY. WHAT WOULD MR. LEARNID THINK IF--
OH! SPEAK OF THE DEVIL!
HE'S COMING TO VISIT, BILLY. AND HE'S BROUGHT FRIENDS.
VIP
CAN WE LISTEN IN, VIRGO? PLEASE?
YOU KNOW THAT'S AGAINST THE RULES, BILLY.
JUST THIS ONCE. AW, PLEASE...
ALL RIGHT, BILLY.
JUST THIS ONCE.
SKRIKK
...ECONOMIC CONDITIONS BEING WHAT THEY ARE, CONSTRUCTION OF THE AQUARIUS COMPLEX WAS INDEED A BOLD MOVE. WE LIKE TO THINK OF IT AS AN ACT OF FAITH...

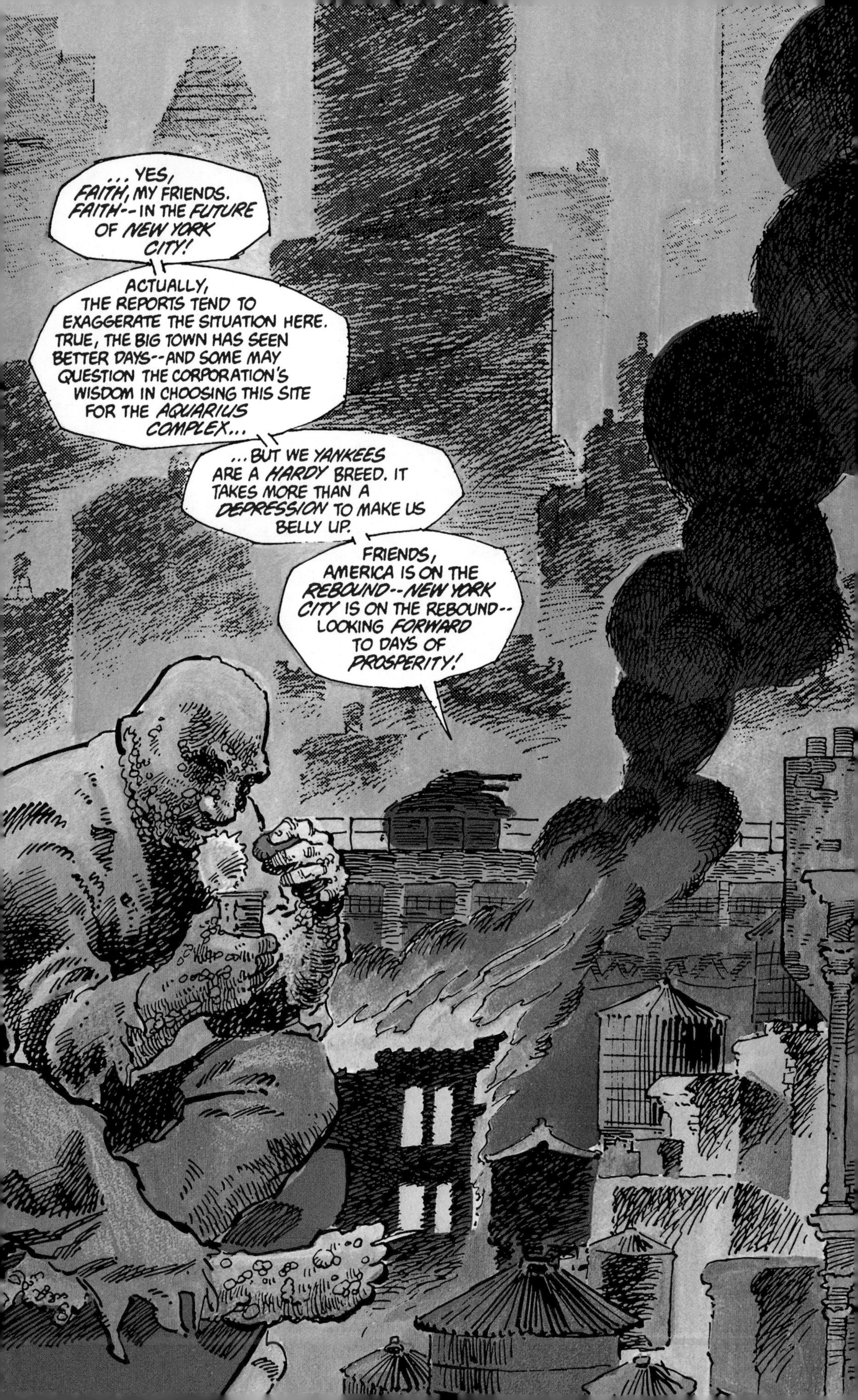
...YES, FAITH, MY FRIENDS. FAITH--IN THE FUTURE OF NEW YORK CITY!
ACTUALLY, THE REPORTS TEND TO EXAGGERATE THE SITUATION HERE. TRUE, THE BIG TOWN HAS SEEN BETTER DAYS--AND SOME MAY QUESTION THE CORPORATION'S WISDOM IN CHOOSING THIS SITE FOR THE AQUARIUS COMPLEX...
...BUT WE YANKEES ARE A HARDY BREED. IT TAKES MORE THAN A DEPRESSION TO MAKE US BELLY UP.
FRIENDS, AMERICA IS ON THE REBOUND--NEW YORK CITY IS ON THE REBOUND--LOOKING FORWARD TO DAYS OF PROSPERITY!

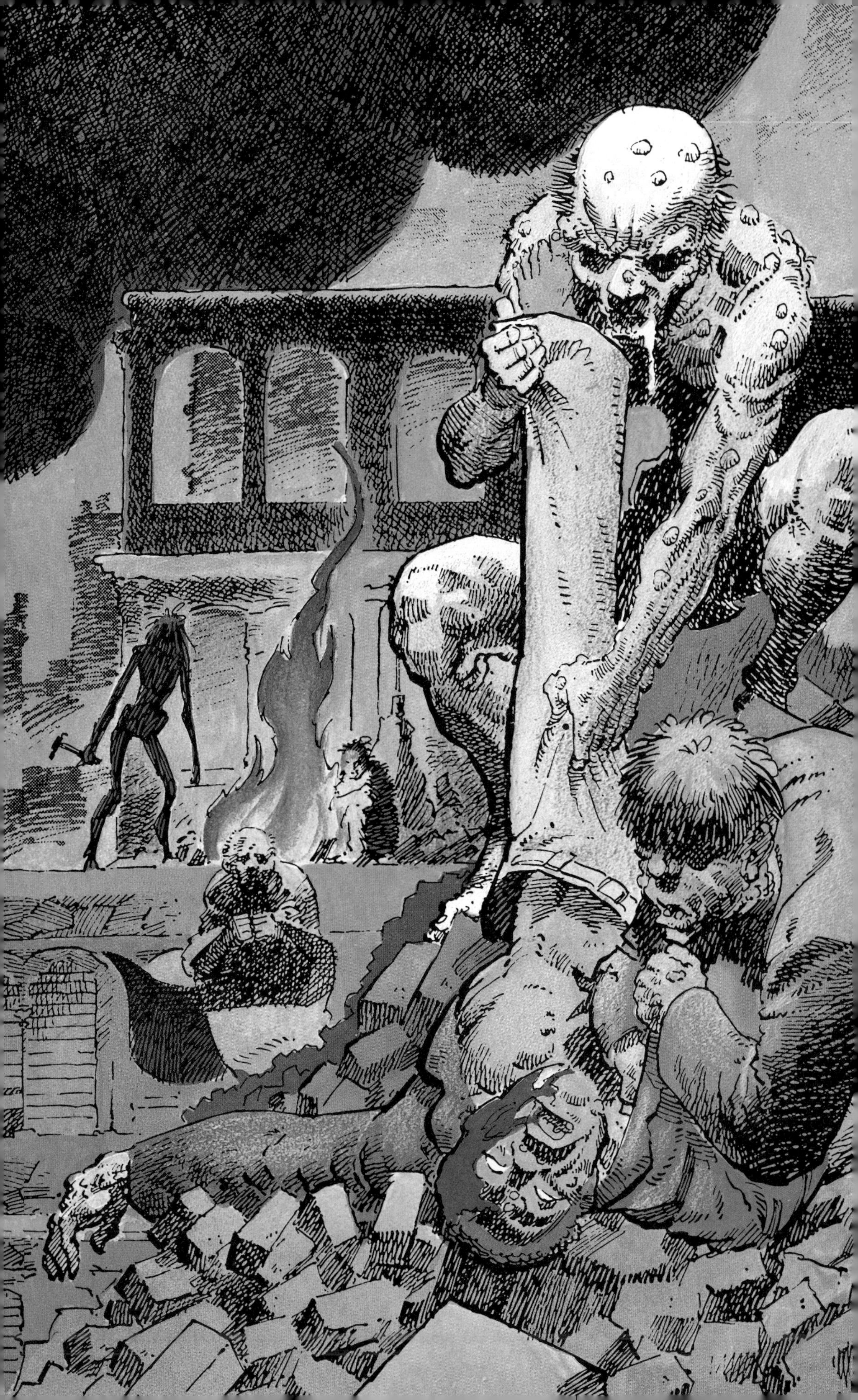

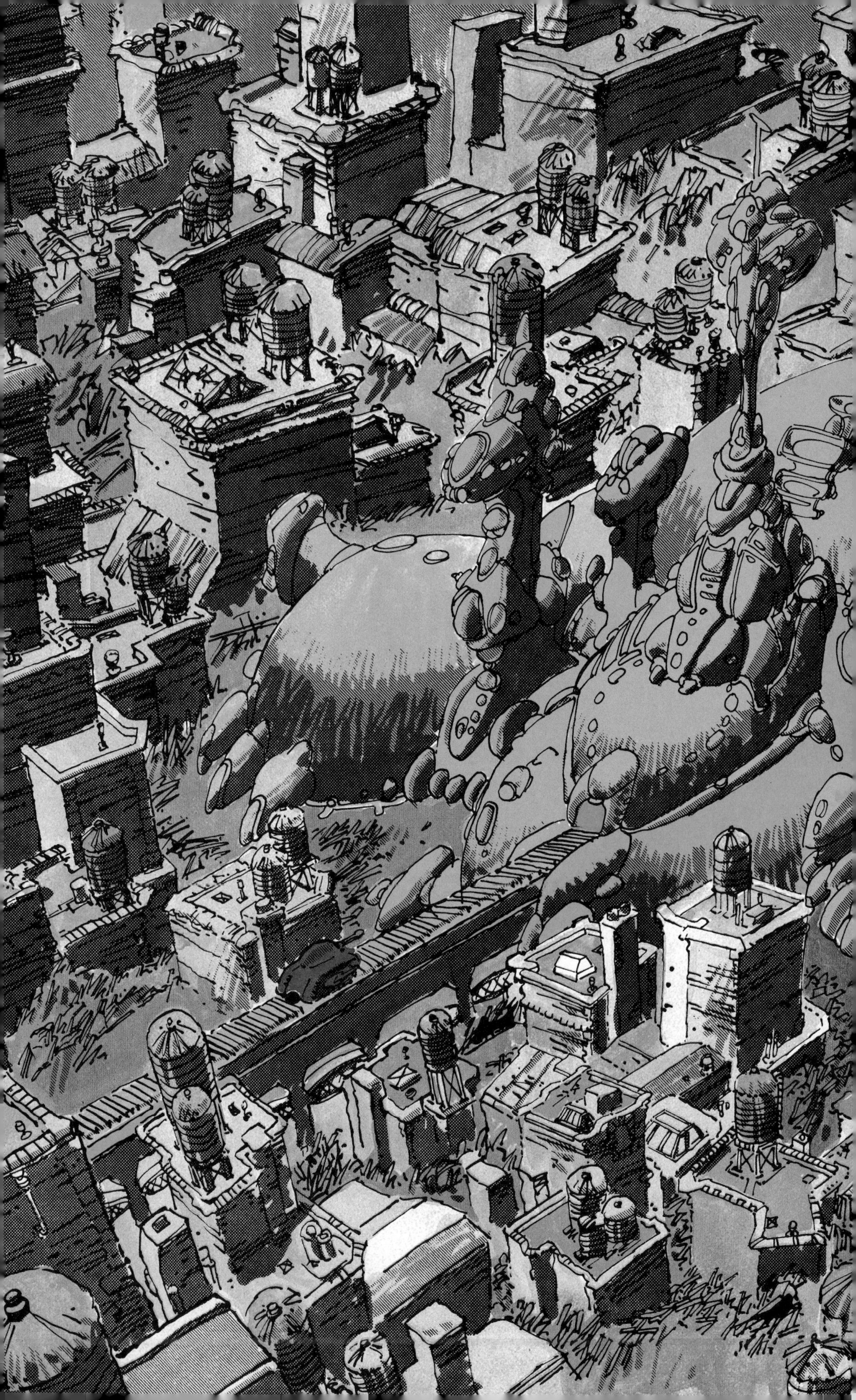

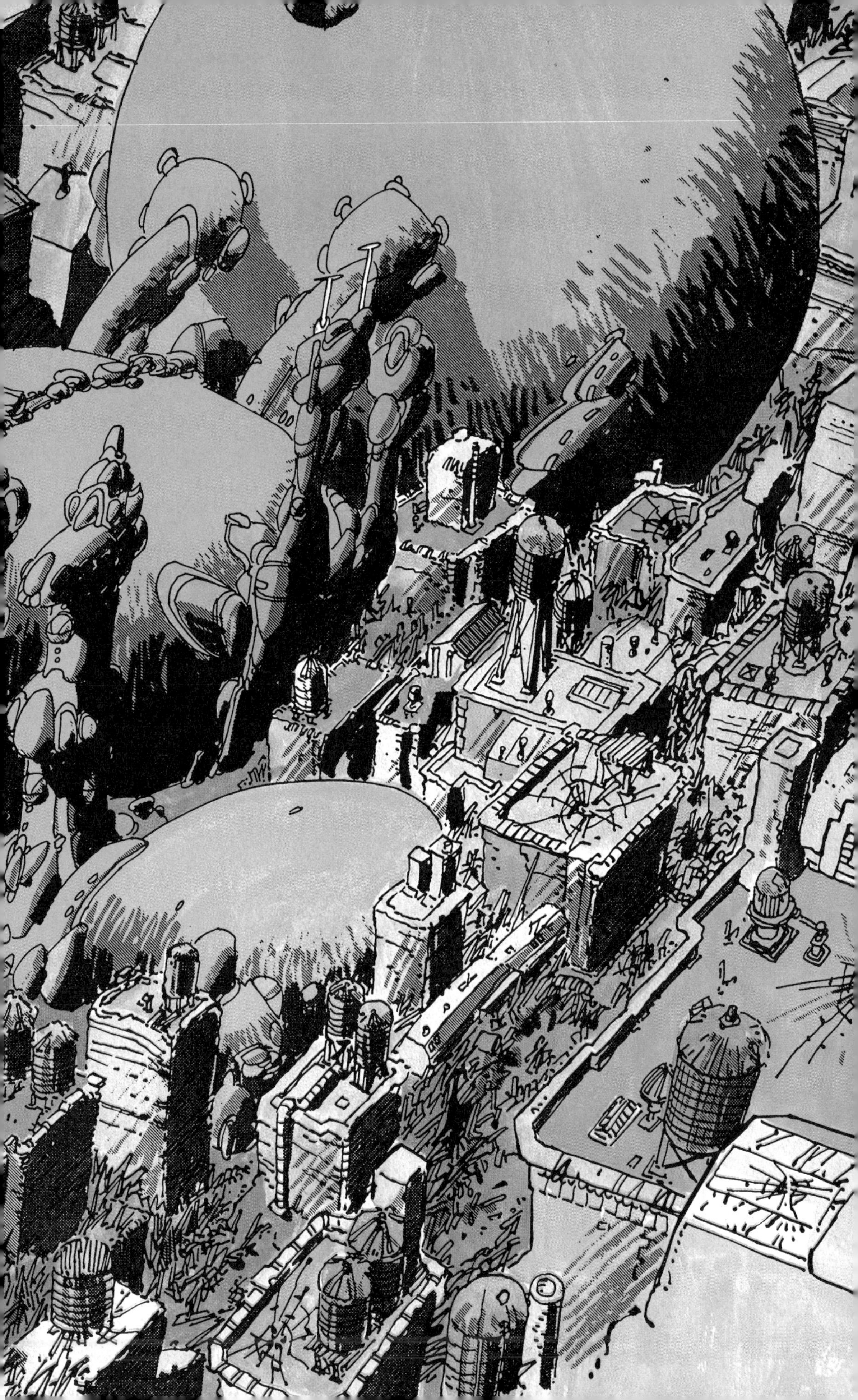

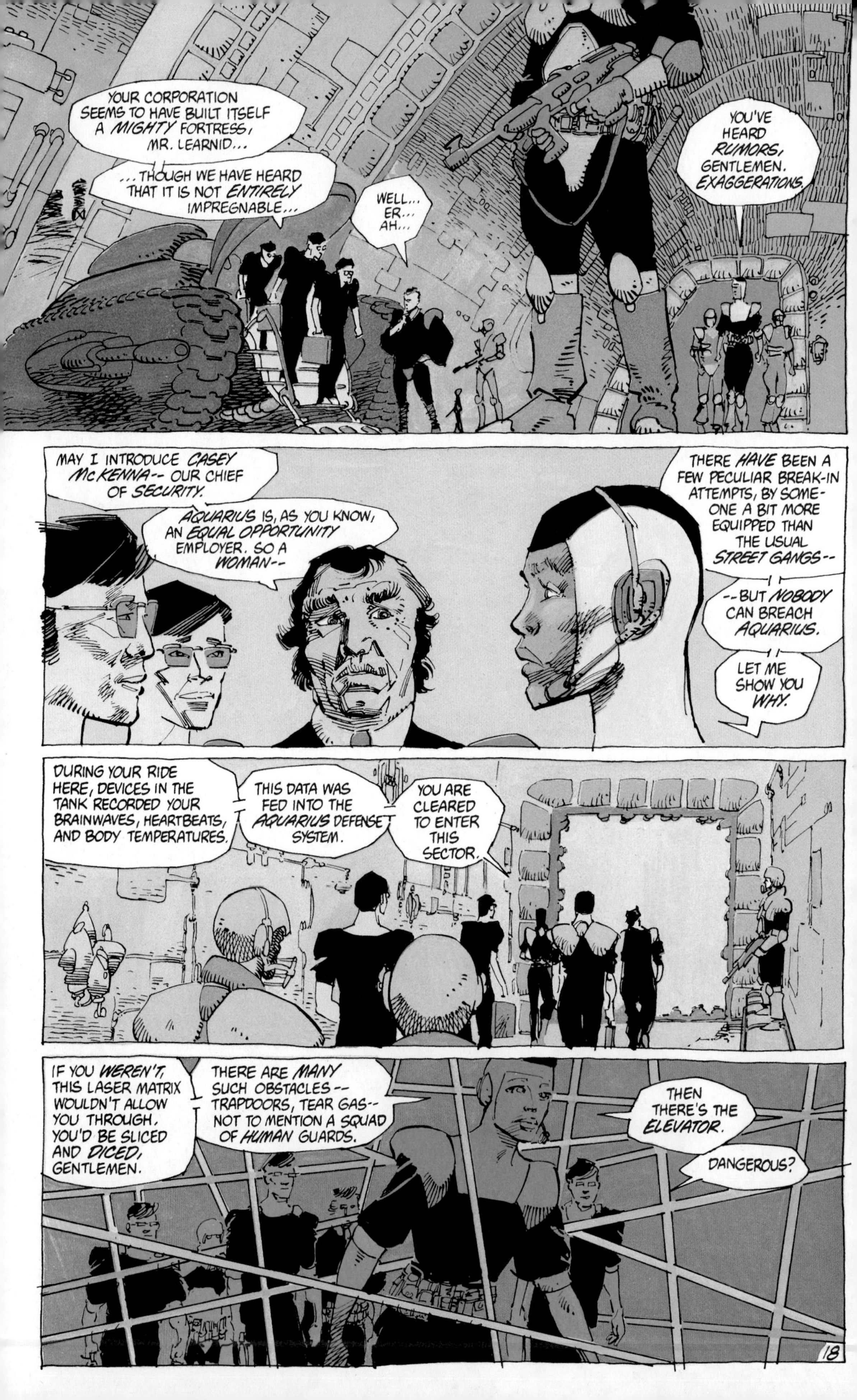
YOUR CORPORATION SEEMS TO HAVE BUILT ITSELF A MIGHTY FORTRESS, MR. LEARNID...
...THOUGH WE HAVE HEARD THAT IT IS NOT ENTIRELY IMPREGNABLE...
WELL... ER... AH...
YOU'VE HEARD RUMORS, GENTLEMEN. EXAGGERATIONS.
MAY I INTRODUCE CASEY McKENNA-- OUR CHIEF OF SECURITY.
AQUARIUS IS, AS YOU KNOW, AN EQUAL OPPORTUNITY EMPLOYER. SO A WOMAN--
THERE HAVE BEEN A FEW PECULIAR BREAK-IN ATTEMPTS, BY SOMEONE A BIT MORE EQUIPPED THAN THE USUAL STREET GANGS--
--BUT NOBODY CAN BREACH AQUARIUS.
LET ME SHOW YOU WHY.
DURING YOUR RIDE HERE, DEVICES IN THE TANK RECORDED YOUR BRAINWAVES, HEARTBEATS, AND BODY TEMPERATURES.
THIS DATA WAS FED INTO THE AQUARIUS DEFENSE SYSTEM.
YOU ARE CLEARED TO ENTER THIS SECTOR.
IF YOU WEREN'T, THIS LASER MATRIX WOULDN'T ALLOW YOU THROUGH. YOU'D BE SLICED AND DICED, GENTLEMEN.
THERE ARE MANY SUCH OBSTACLES-- TRAPDOORS, TEAR GAS-- NOT TO MENTION A SQUAD OF HUMAN GUARDS.
THEN THERE'S THE ELEVATOR.
DANGEROUS?

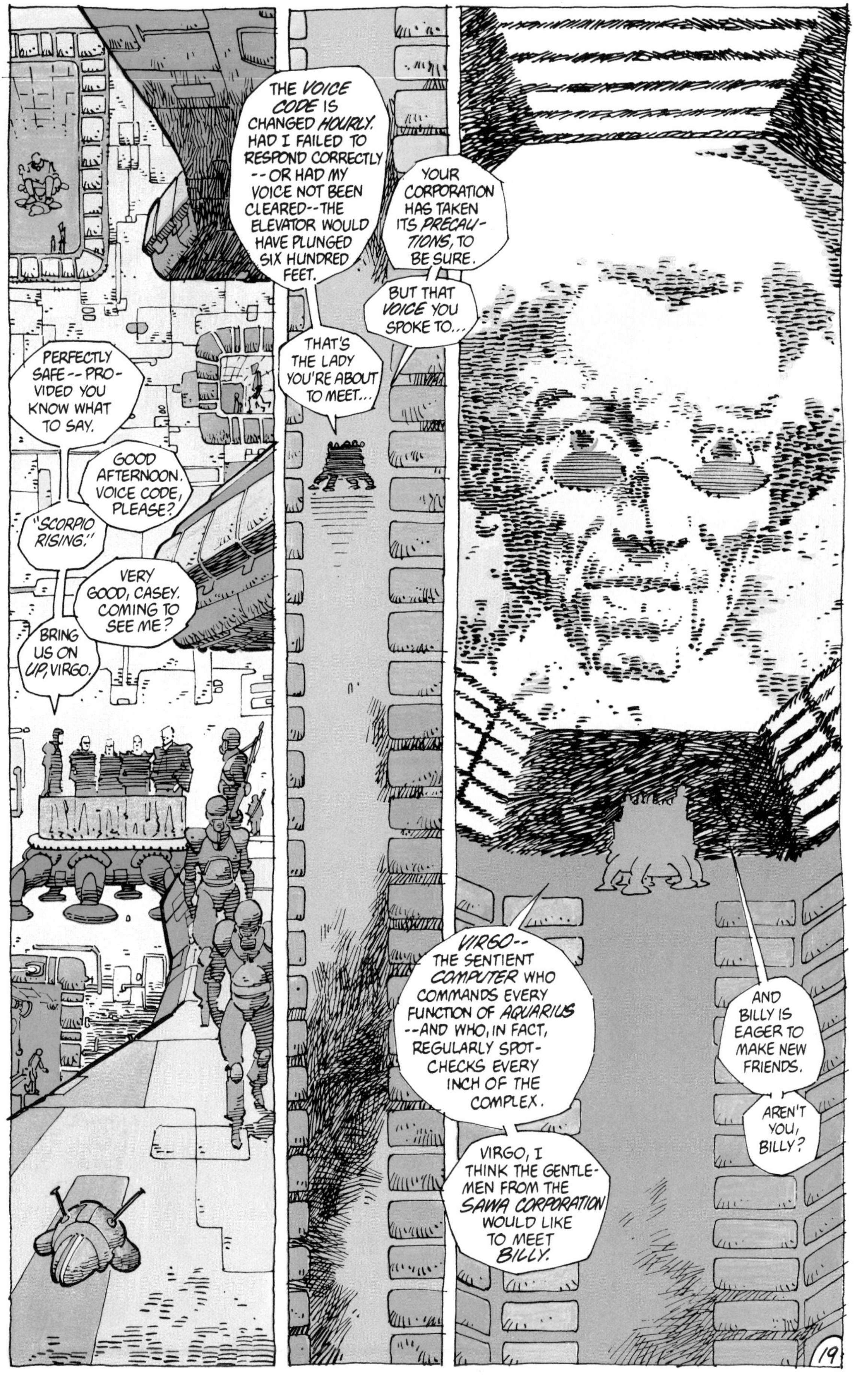
PERFECTLY SAFE--PROVIDED YOU KNOW WHAT TO SAY.
GOOD AFTERNOON. VOICE CODE, PLEASE?
"SCORPIO RISING."
VERY GOOD, CASEY. COMING TO SEE ME?
BRING US ON UP, VIRGO.
THE VOICE CODE IS CHANGED HOURLY. HAD I FAILED TO RESPOND CORRECTLY--OR HAD MY VOICE NOT BEEN CLEARED--THE ELEVATOR WOULD HAVE PLUNGED SIX HUNDRED FEET.
THAT'S THE LADY YOU'RE ABOUT TO MEET...
YOUR CORPORATION HAS TAKEN ITS PRECAUTIONS, TO BE SURE.
BUT THAT VOICE YOU SPOKE TO...
VIRGO--THE SENTIENT COMPUTER WHO COMMANDS EVERY FUNCTION OF AQUARIUS--AND WHO, IN FACT, REGULARLY SPOT-CHECKS EVERY INCH OF THE COMPLEX.
VIRGO, I THINK THE GENTLEMEN FROM THE SAWA CORPORATION WOULD LIKE TO MEET BILLY.
AND BILLY IS EAGER TO MAKE NEW FRIENDS.
AREN'T YOU, BILLY?

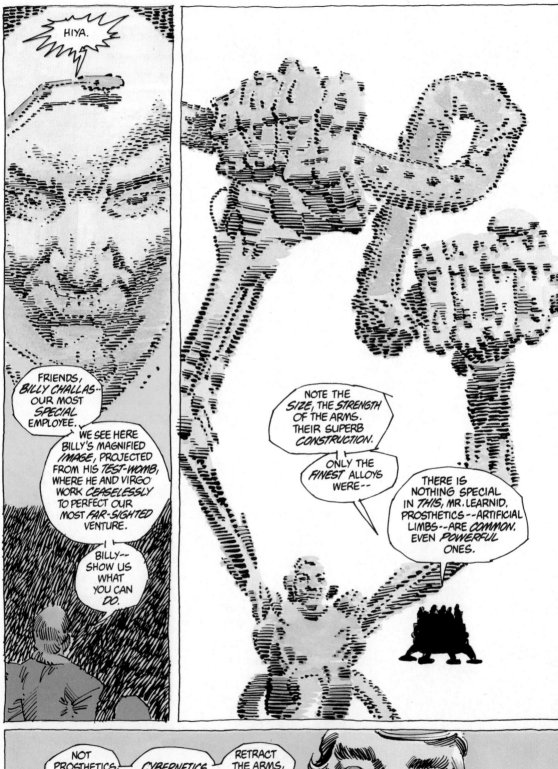

HIYA.

FRIENDS, *BILLY CHALLAS*-- OUR MOST *SPECIAL* EMPLOYEE.

WE SEE HERE BILLY'S MAGNIFIED *IMAGE*, PROJECTED FROM HIS *TEST-WOMB*, WHERE HE AND *VIRGO* WORK *CEASELESSLY* TO PERFECT OUR MOST *FAR-SIGHTED* VENTURE.

BILLY-- SHOW US WHAT YOU CAN *DO.*

NOTE THE *SIZE*, THE *STRENGTH* OF THE ARMS. THEIR SUPERB *CONSTRUCTION.*

ONLY THE *FINEST* ALLOYS WERE--

THERE IS NOTHING SPECIAL IN *THIS*, MR. LEARNID, PROSTHETICS--ARTIFICIAL LIMBS--ARE *COMMON.* EVEN *POWERFUL* ONES.

NOT PROSTHETICS, GENTLEMEN.

CYBERNETICS.

RETRACT THE ARMS, VIRGO.

20

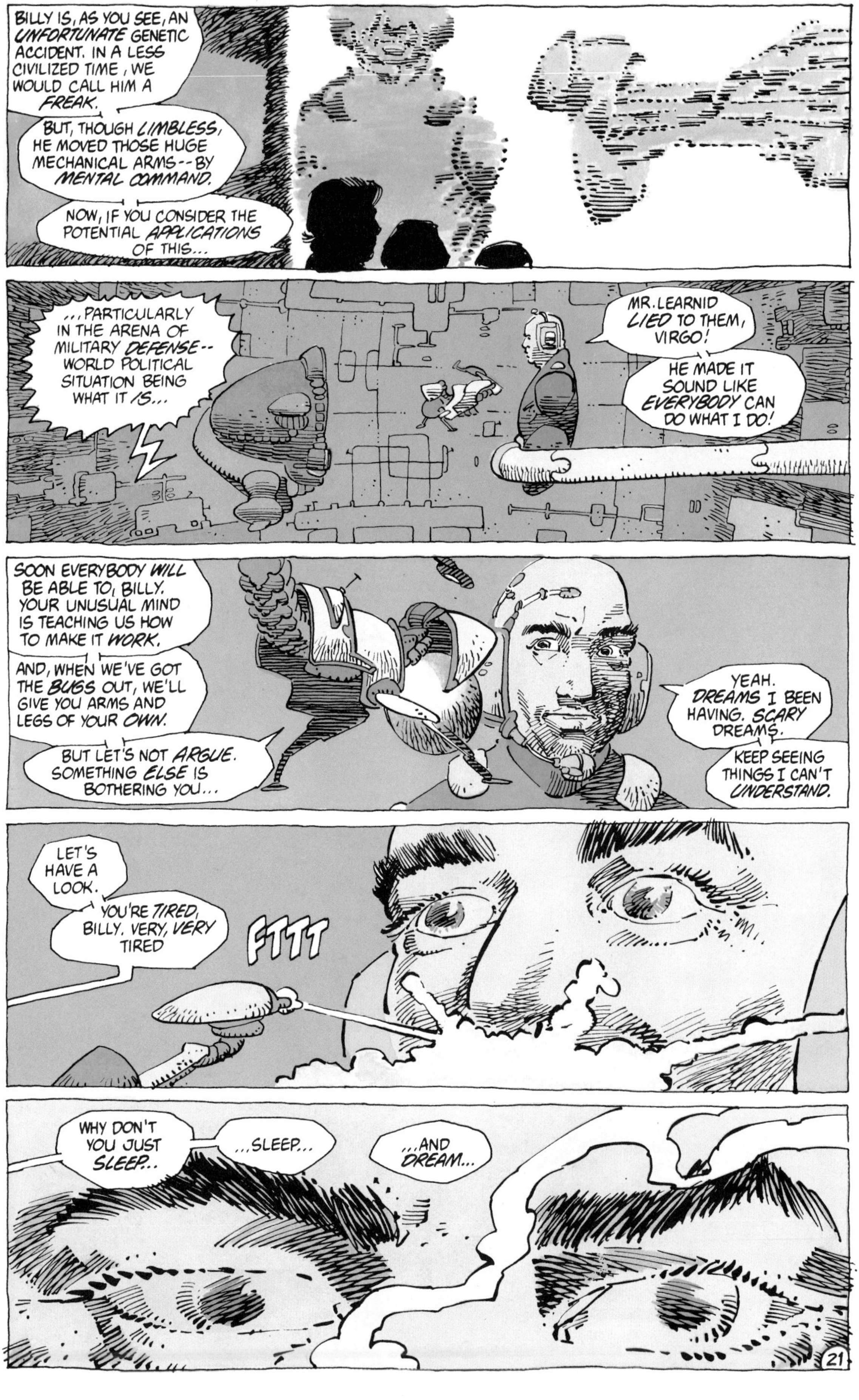
BILLY IS, AS YOU SEE, AN UNFORTUNATE GENETIC ACCIDENT. IN A LESS CIVILIZED TIME, WE WOULD CALL HIM A FREAK.
BUT, THOUGH LIMBLESS, HE MOVED THOSE HUGE MECHANICAL ARMS--BY MENTAL COMMAND.
NOW, IF YOU CONSIDER THE POTENTIAL APPLICATIONS OF THIS...
...PARTICULARLY IN THE ARENA OF MILITARY DEFENSE--WORLD POLITICAL SITUATION BEING WHAT IT IS...
MR. LEARNID LIED TO THEM, VIRGO!
HE MADE IT SOUND LIKE EVERYBODY CAN DO WHAT I DO!
SOON EVERYBODY WILL BE ABLE TO, BILLY. YOUR UNUSUAL MIND IS TEACHING US HOW TO MAKE IT WORK.
AND, WHEN WE'VE GOT THE BUGS OUT, WE'LL GIVE YOU ARMS AND LEGS OF YOUR OWN.
BUT LET'S NOT ARGUE. SOMETHING ELSE IS BOTHERING YOU...
YEAH. DREAMS I BEEN HAVING. SCARY DREAMS.
KEEP SEEING THINGS I CAN'T UNDERSTAND.
LET'S HAVE A LOOK.
YOU'RE TIRED, BILLY. VERY, VERY TIRED
FTTT
WHY DON'T YOU JUST SLEEP...
...SLEEP...
...AND DREAM...
21

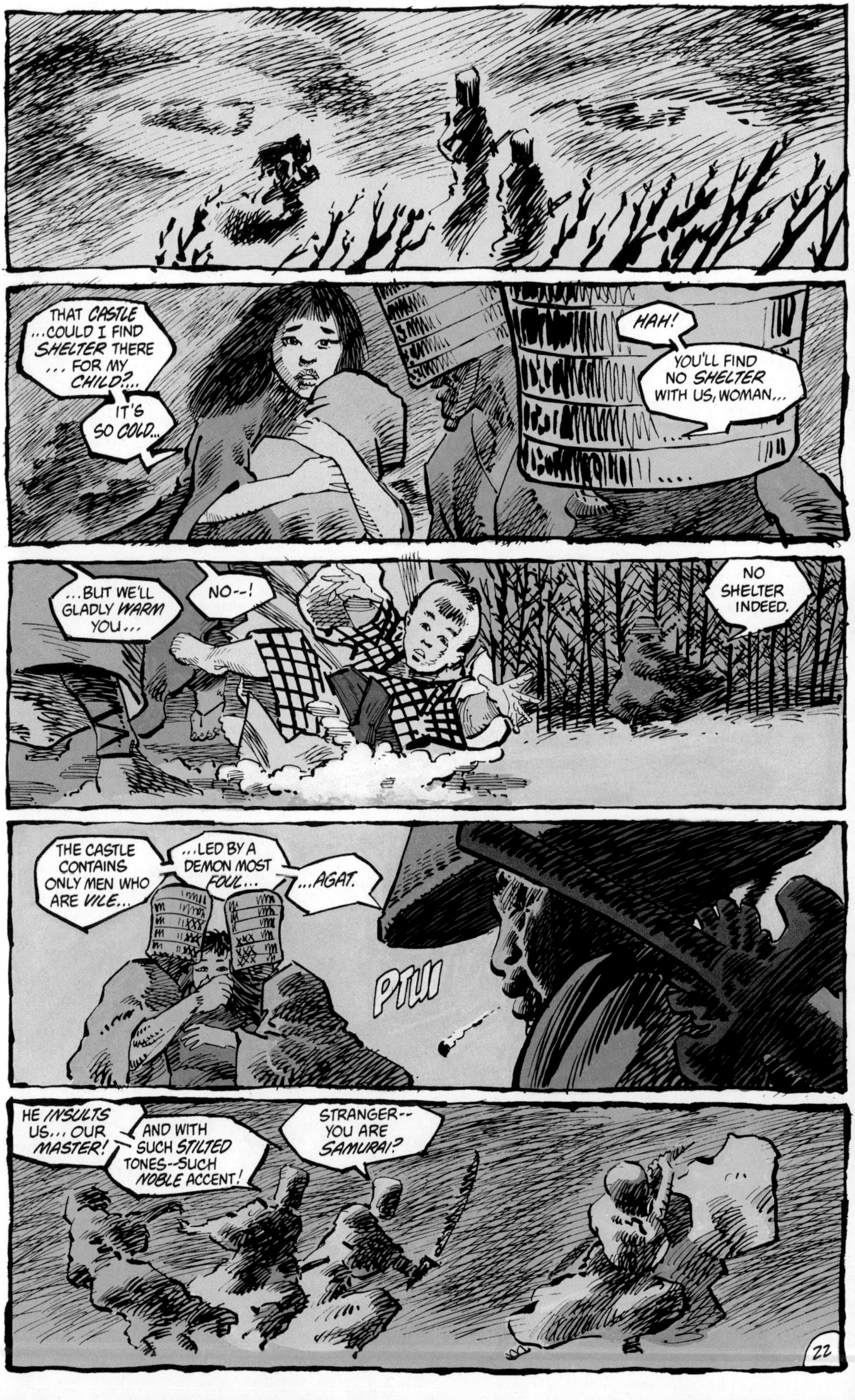

THAT CASTLE ...COULD I FIND SHELTER THERE ... FOR MY CHILD?...
IT'S SO COLD...
HAH!
YOU'LL FIND NO SHELTER WITH US, WOMAN...
...BUT WE'LL GLADLY WARM YOU...
NO--!
NO SHELTER INDEED.
THE CASTLE CONTAINS ONLY MEN WHO ARE VILE...
...LED BY A DEMON MOST FOUL...
...AGAT.
PTUI
HE INSULTS US... OUR MASTER!
AND WITH SUCH STILTED TONES--SUCH NOBLE ACCENT!
STRANGER--YOU ARE SAMURAI?
22

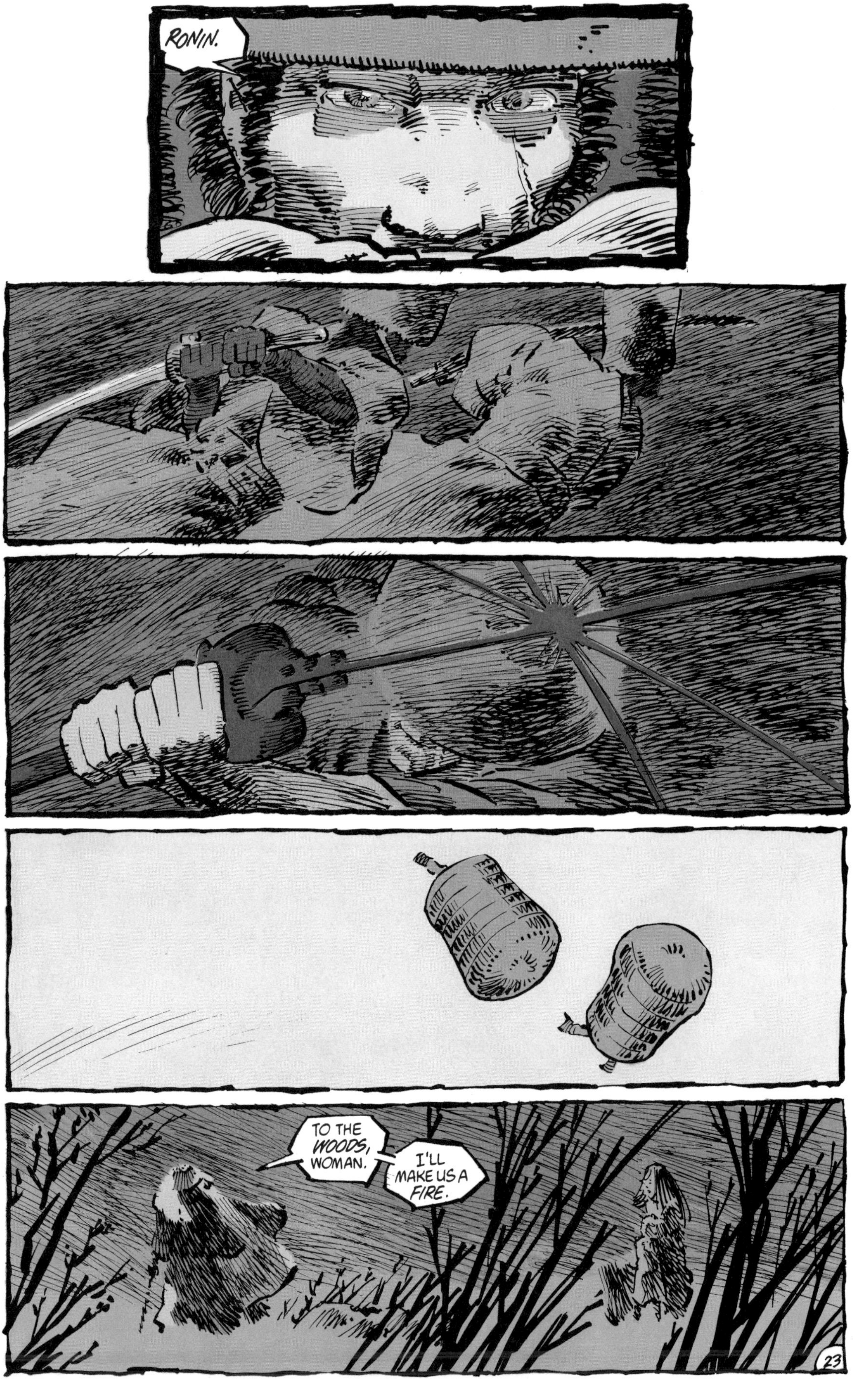
RONIN.
TO THE WOODS, WOMAN.
I'LL MAKE US A FIRE.

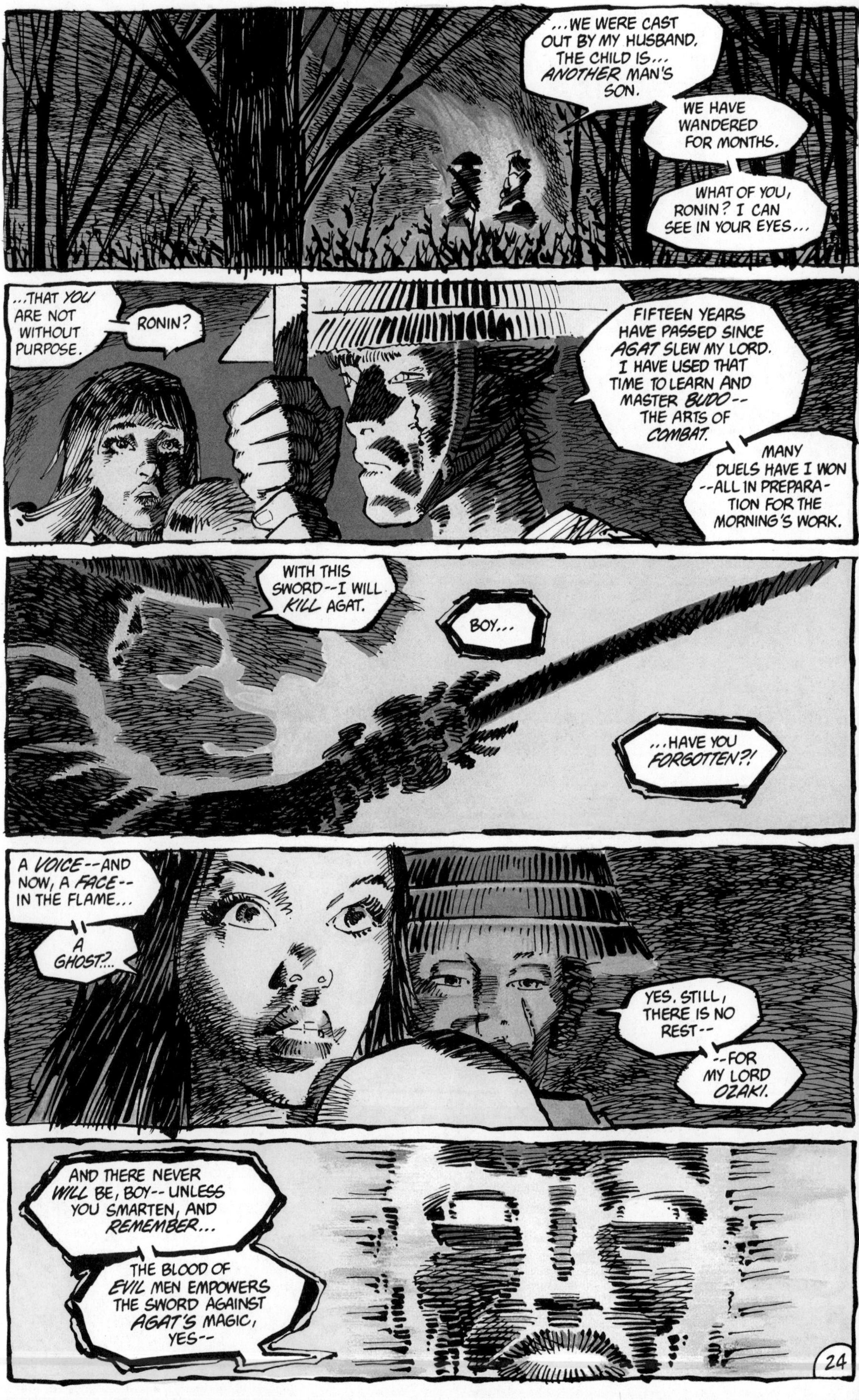
...WE WERE CAST OUT BY MY HUSBAND. THE CHILD IS... ANOTHER MAN'S SON.
WE HAVE WANDERED FOR MONTHS.
WHAT OF YOU, RONIN? I CAN SEE IN YOUR EYES...
...THAT YOU ARE NOT WITHOUT PURPOSE.
RONIN?
FIFTEEN YEARS HAVE PASSED SINCE AGAT SLEW MY LORD. I HAVE USED THAT TIME TO LEARN AND MASTER BUDO-- THE ARTS OF COMBAT.
MANY DUELS HAVE I WON --ALL IN PREPARATION FOR THE MORNING'S WORK.
WITH THIS SWORD--I WILL KILL AGAT.
BOY...
...HAVE YOU FORGOTTEN?!
A VOICE--AND NOW, A FACE-- IN THE FLAME...
A GHOST?...
YES. STILL, THERE IS NO REST--
--FOR MY LORD OZAKI.
AND THERE NEVER WILL BE, BOY--UNLESS YOU SMARTEN, AND REMEMBER...
THE BLOOD OF EVIL MEN EMPOWERS THE SWORD AGAINST AGAT'S MAGIC, YES--

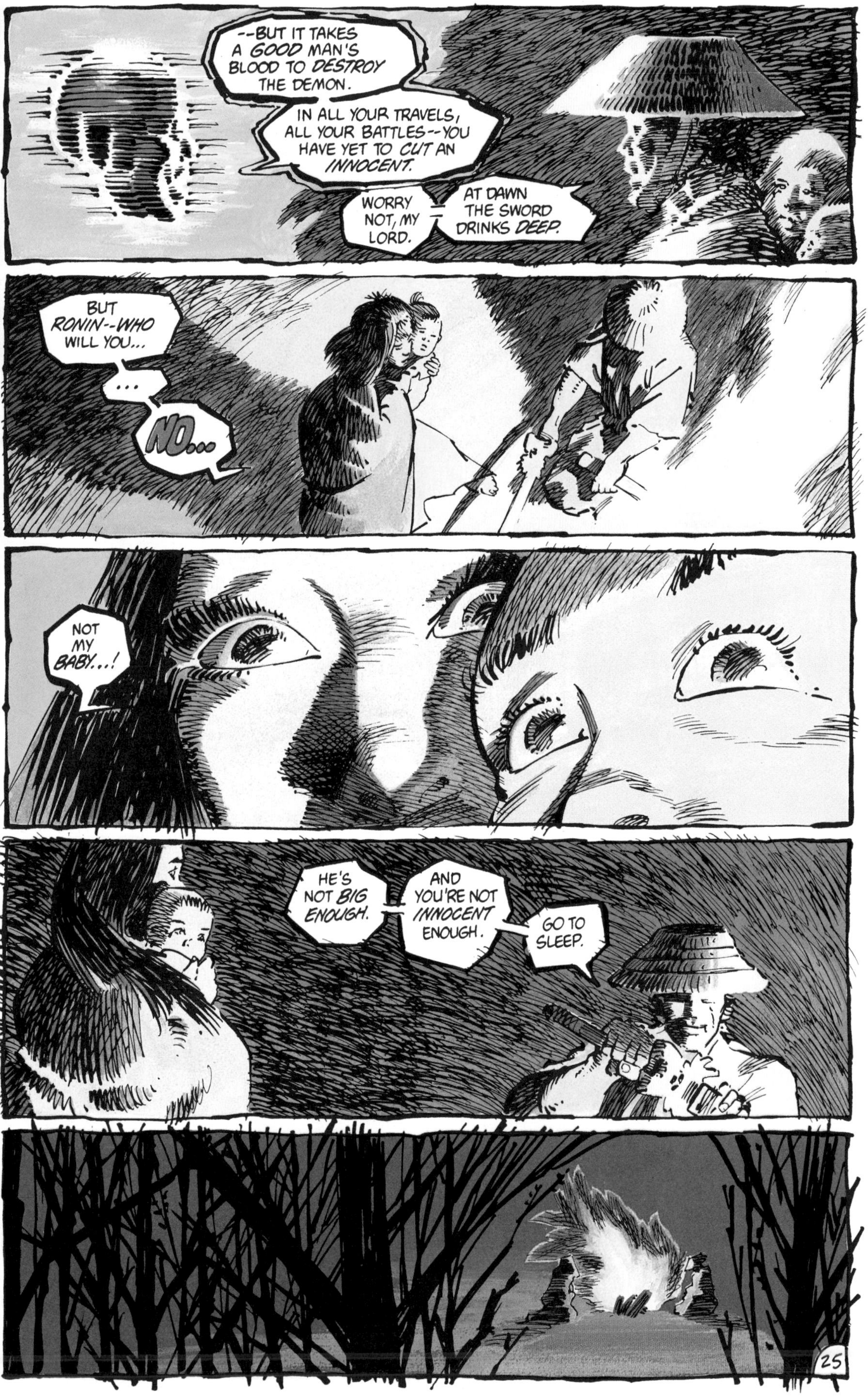
--BUT IT TAKES A GOOD MAN'S BLOOD TO DESTROY THE DEMON.
IN ALL YOUR TRAVELS, ALL YOUR BATTLES--YOU HAVE YET TO CUT AN INNOCENT.
WORRY NOT, MY LORD.
AT DAWN THE SWORD DRINKS DEEP.
BUT RONIN--WHO WILL YOU...
...
NO...
NOT MY BABY...!
HE'S NOT BIG ENOUGH.
AND YOU'RE NOT INNOCENT ENOUGH.
GO TO SLEEP.

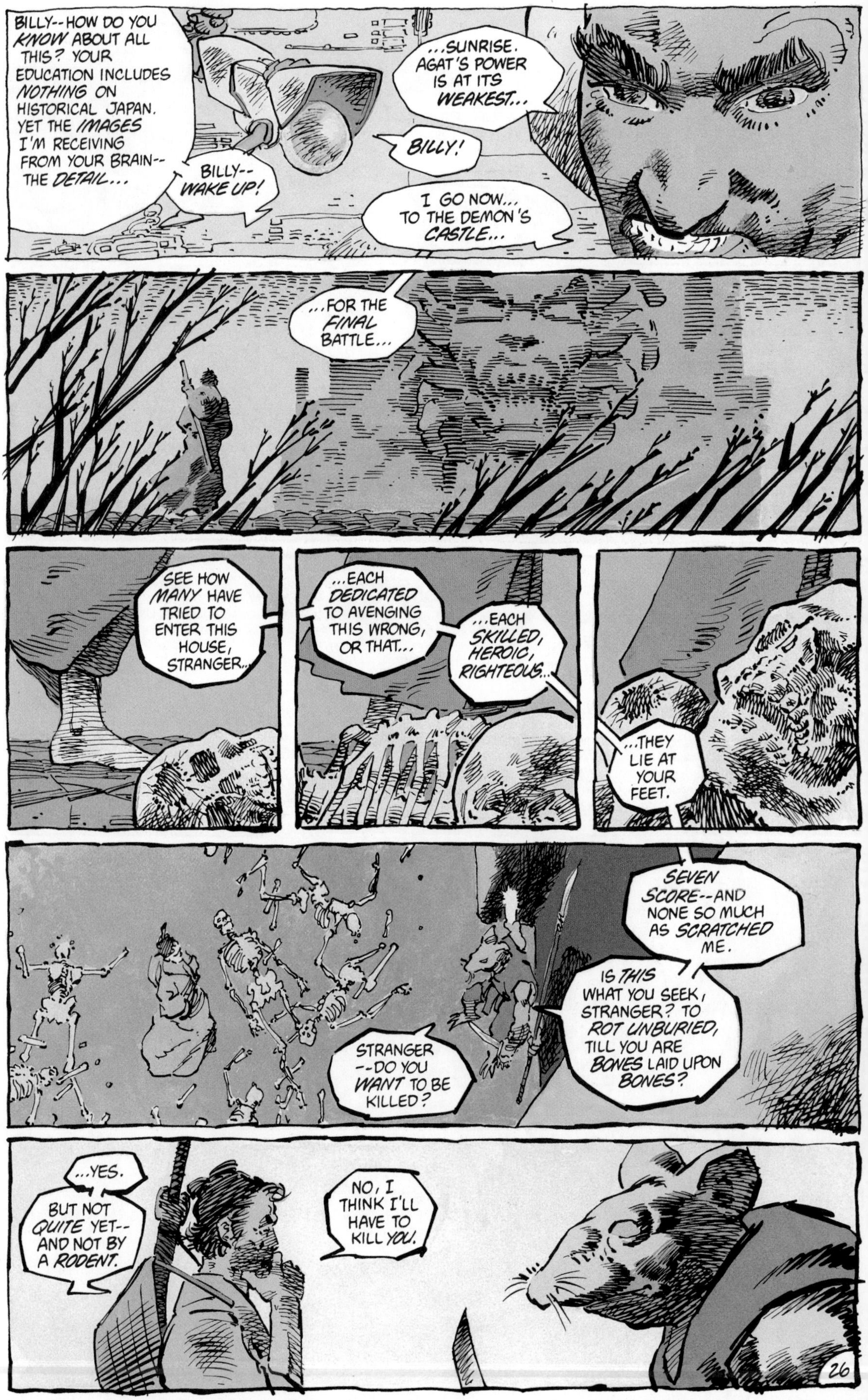
BILLY--HOW DO YOU KNOW ABOUT ALL THIS? YOUR EDUCATION INCLUDES NOTHING ON HISTORICAL JAPAN. YET THE IMAGES I'M RECEIVING FROM YOUR BRAIN--THE DETAIL...
BILLY--WAKE UP!
...SUNRISE. AGAT'S POWER IS AT ITS WEAKEST...
BILLY!
I GO NOW... TO THE DEMON'S CASTLE...
...FOR THE FINAL BATTLE...
SEE HOW MANY HAVE TRIED TO ENTER THIS HOUSE, STRANGER...
...EACH DEDICATED TO AVENGING THIS WRONG, OR THAT...
...EACH SKILLED, HEROIC, RIGHTEOUS...
...THEY LIE AT YOUR FEET.
SEVEN SCORE--AND NONE SO MUCH AS SCRATCHED ME.
IS THIS WHAT YOU SEEK, STRANGER? TO ROT UNBURIED, TILL YOU ARE BONES LAID UPON BONES?
STRANGER--DO YOU WANT TO BE KILLED?
...YES.
BUT NOT QUITE YET--AND NOT BY A RODENT.
NO, I THINK I'LL HAVE TO KILL YOU.
26

HAH!

MAN, I AM MIGHTY AS *THUNDER!*

QUICK AS *LIGHTNING!*

SEVEN SCORE HAVE FACED ME-- *SEVEN SCORE,* I SAY--

--AND NONE HAS EVEN *SCRATCHED...*

CRAAA

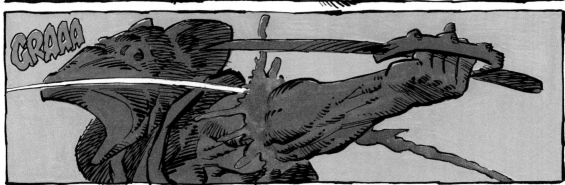

HRNH

...WE'RE *BOTH* SHORT AN ARM, NOW.

HMPH. I STILL HAVE *THREE* TO YOUR *ONE*--

27

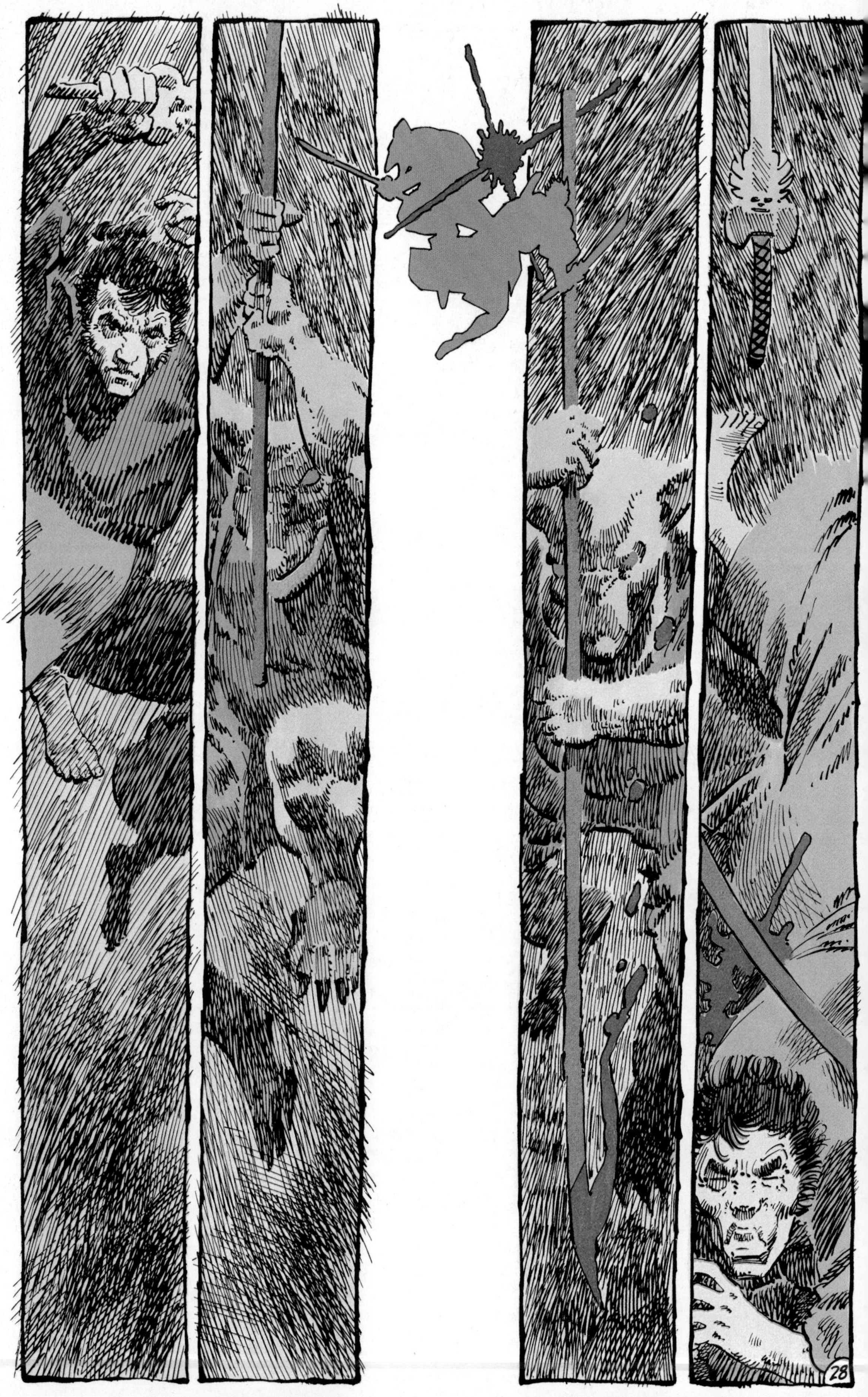

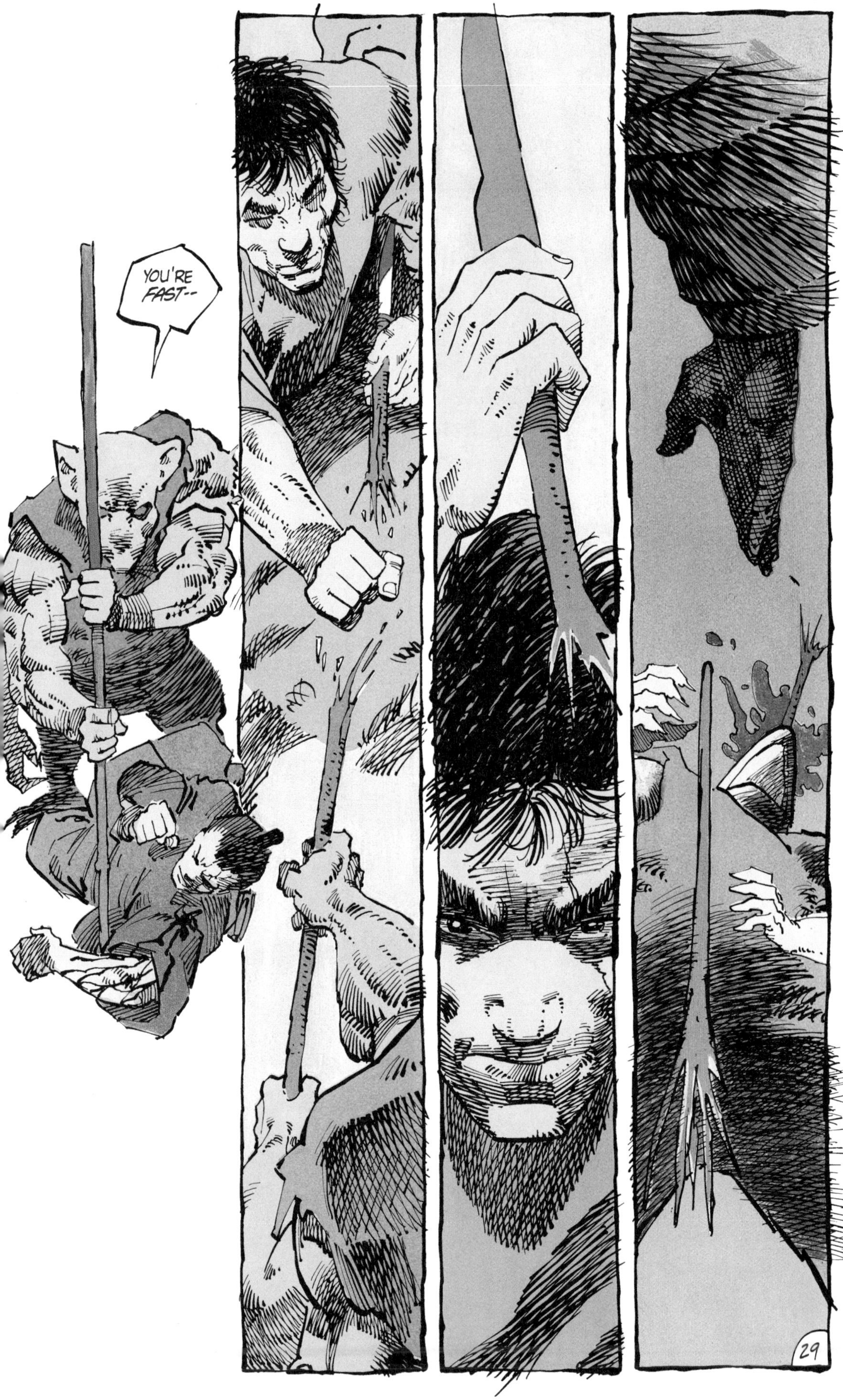
YOU'RE FAST--

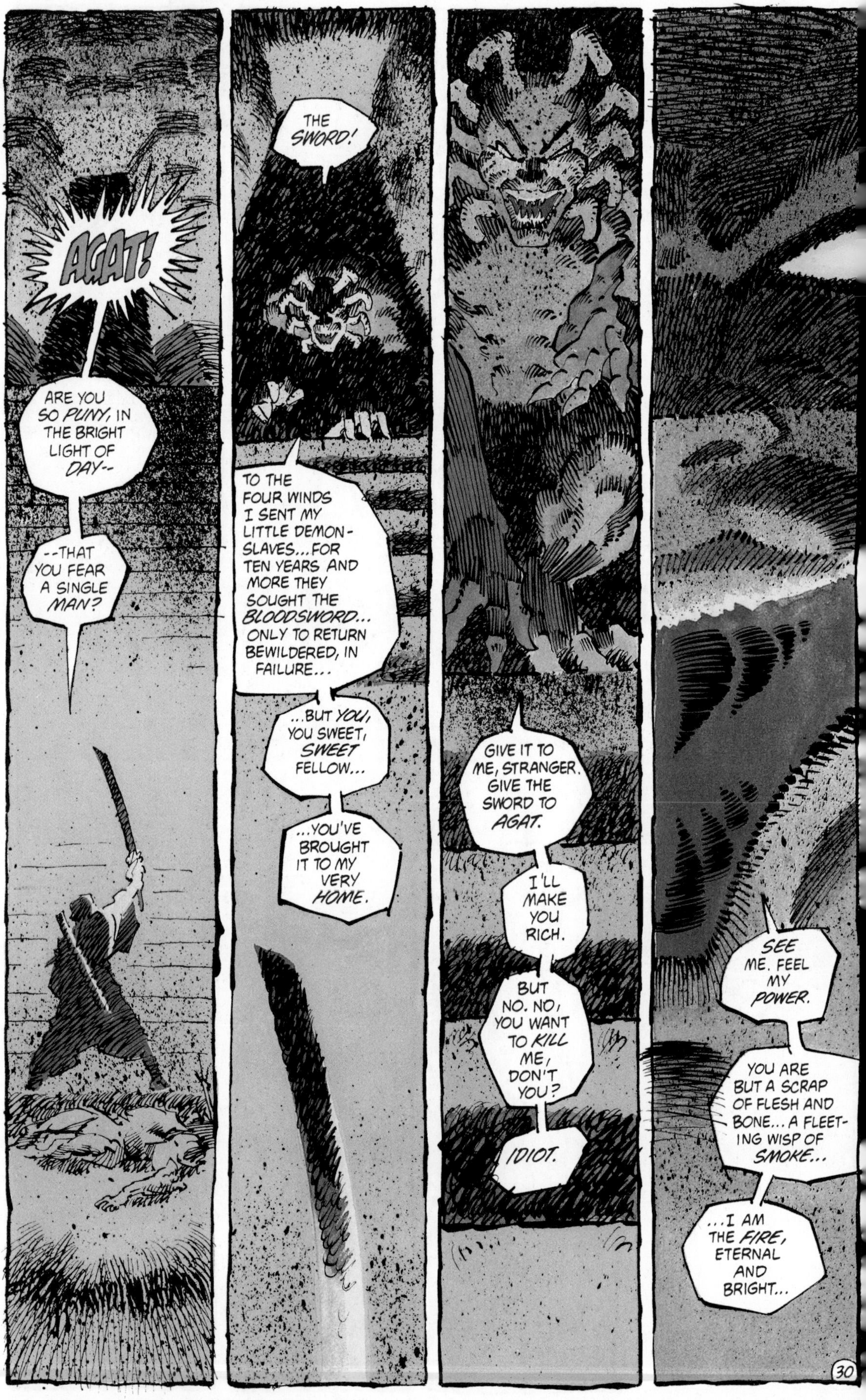
AGAT!
ARE YOU SO PUNY, IN THE BRIGHT LIGHT OF DAY--
--THAT YOU FEAR A SINGLE MAN?
THE SWORD!
TO THE FOUR WINDS I SENT MY LITTLE DEMON-SLAVES...FOR TEN YEARS AND MORE THEY SOUGHT THE BLOODSWORD... ONLY TO RETURN BEWILDERED, IN FAILURE...
...BUT YOU, YOU SWEET, SWEET FELLOW...
...YOU'VE BROUGHT IT TO MY VERY HOME.
GIVE IT TO ME, STRANGER. GIVE THE SWORD TO AGAT.
I'LL MAKE YOU RICH.
BUT NO. NO, YOU WANT TO KILL ME, DON'T YOU?
IDIOT.
SEE ME. FEEL MY POWER.
YOU ARE BUT A SCRAP OF FLESH AND BONE... A FLEETING WISP OF SMOKE...
...I AM THE FIRE, ETERNAL AND BRIGHT...

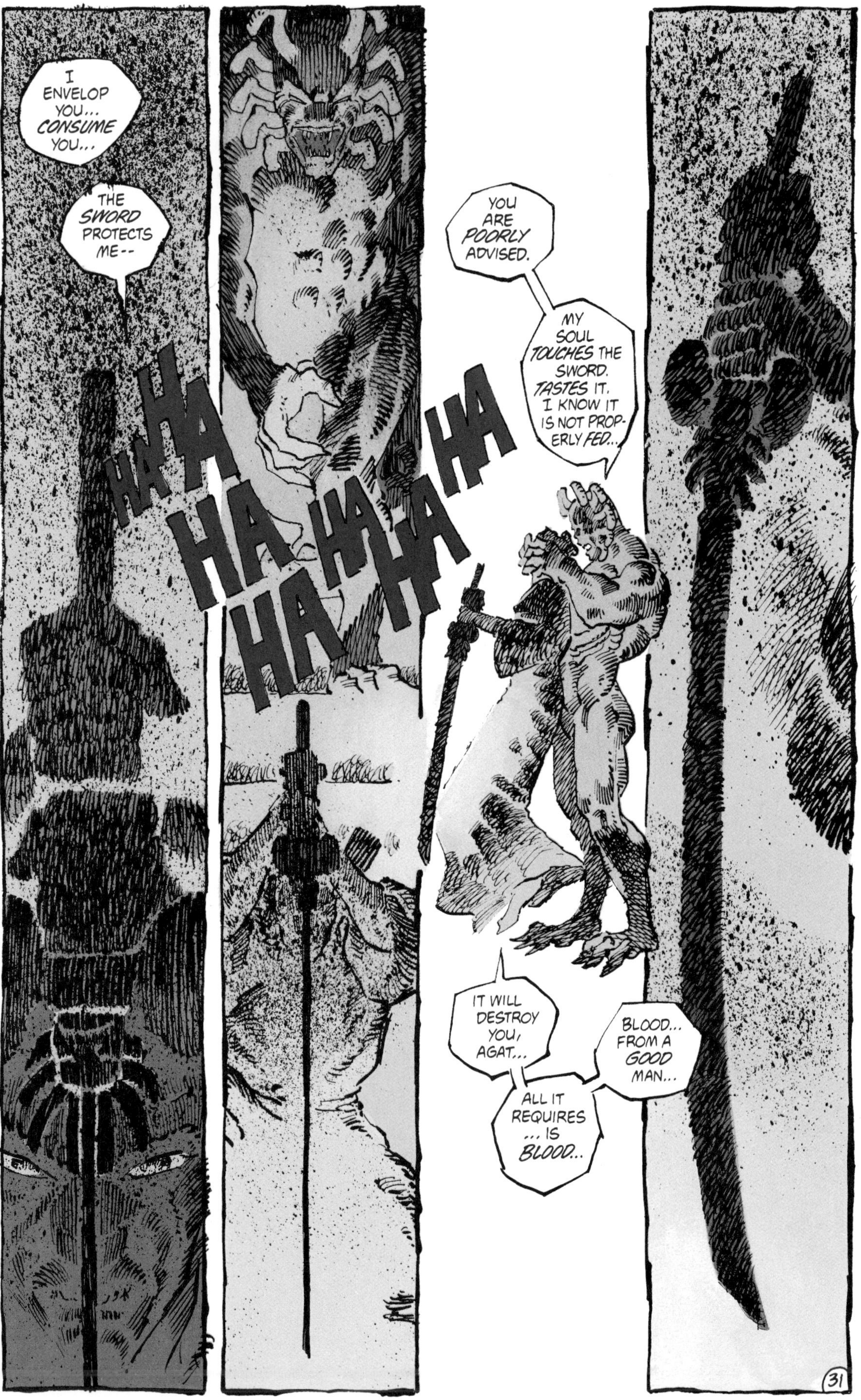
I ENVELOP YOU... CONSUME YOU...
THE SWORD PROTECTS ME--
HA HA HA HA HA HA HA HA HA
YOU ARE POORLY ADVISED.
MY SOUL TOUCHES THE SWORD. TASTES IT. I KNOW IT IS NOT PROPERLY FED...
IT WILL DESTROY YOU, AGAT...
ALL IT REQUIRES ... IS BLOOD...
BLOOD... FROM A GOOD MAN...

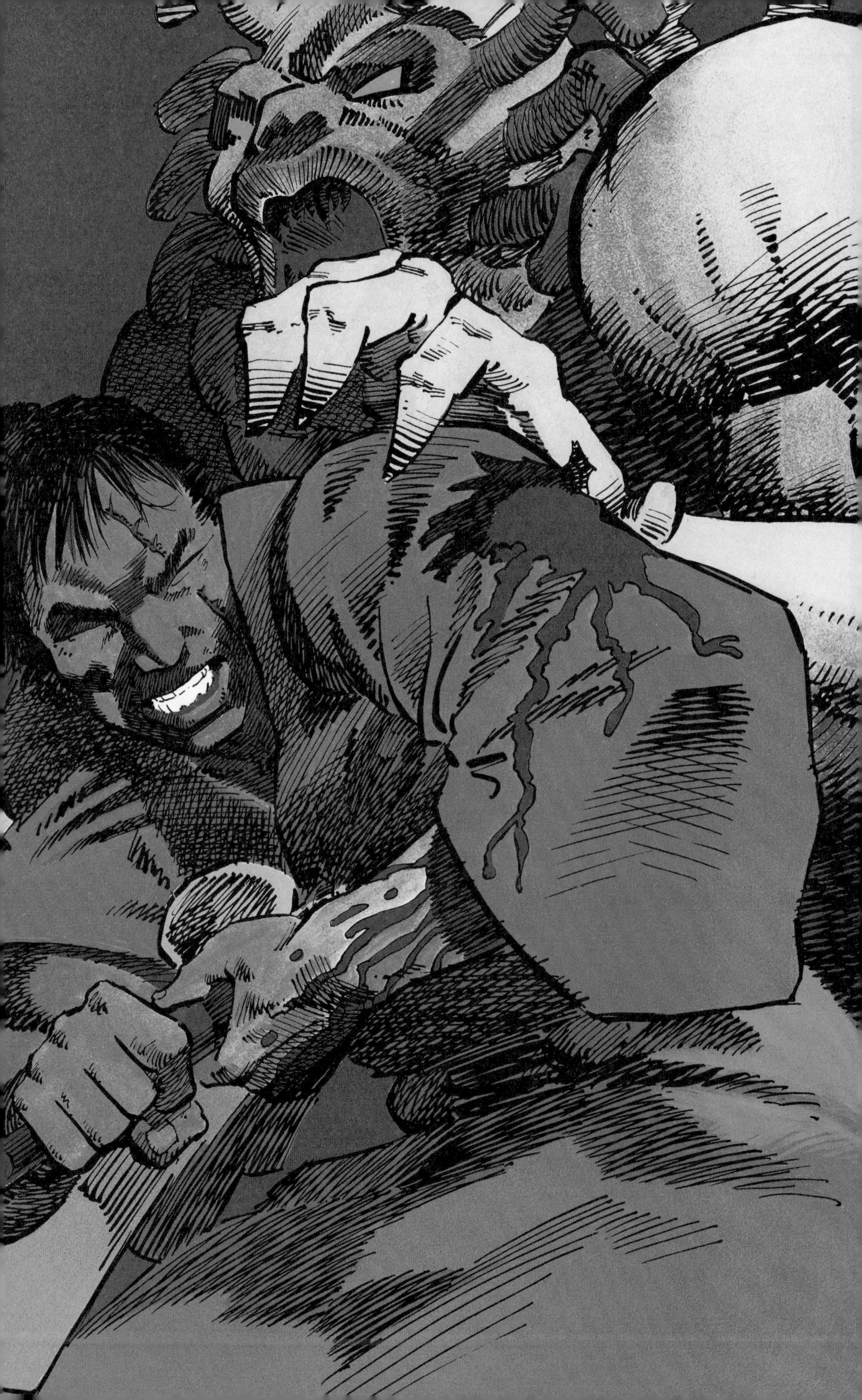

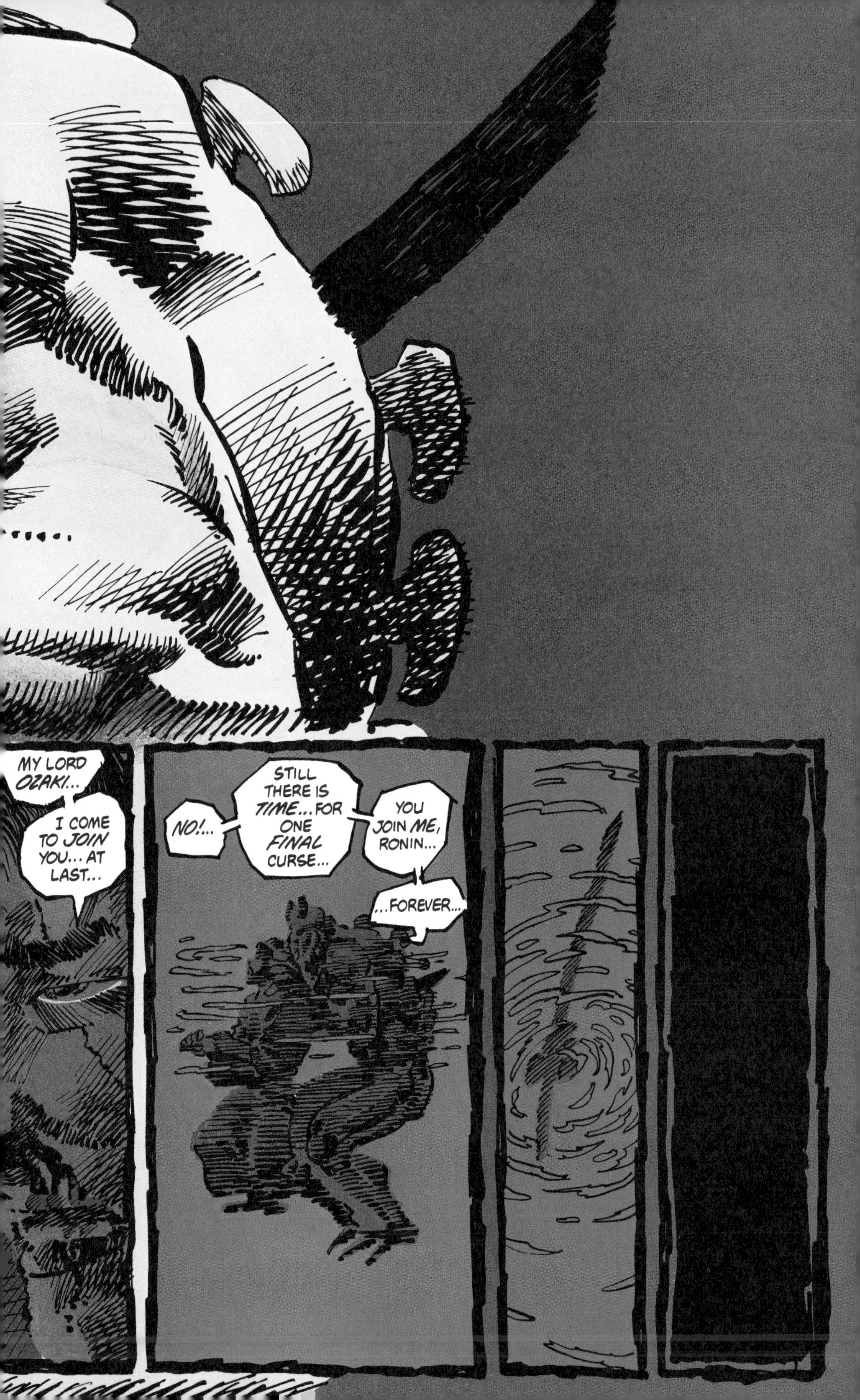
MY LORD OZAKI...
I COME TO JOIN YOU... AT LAST...
NO!...
STILL THERE IS TIME... FOR ONE FINAL CURSE...
YOU JOIN ME, RONIN...
...FOREVER...

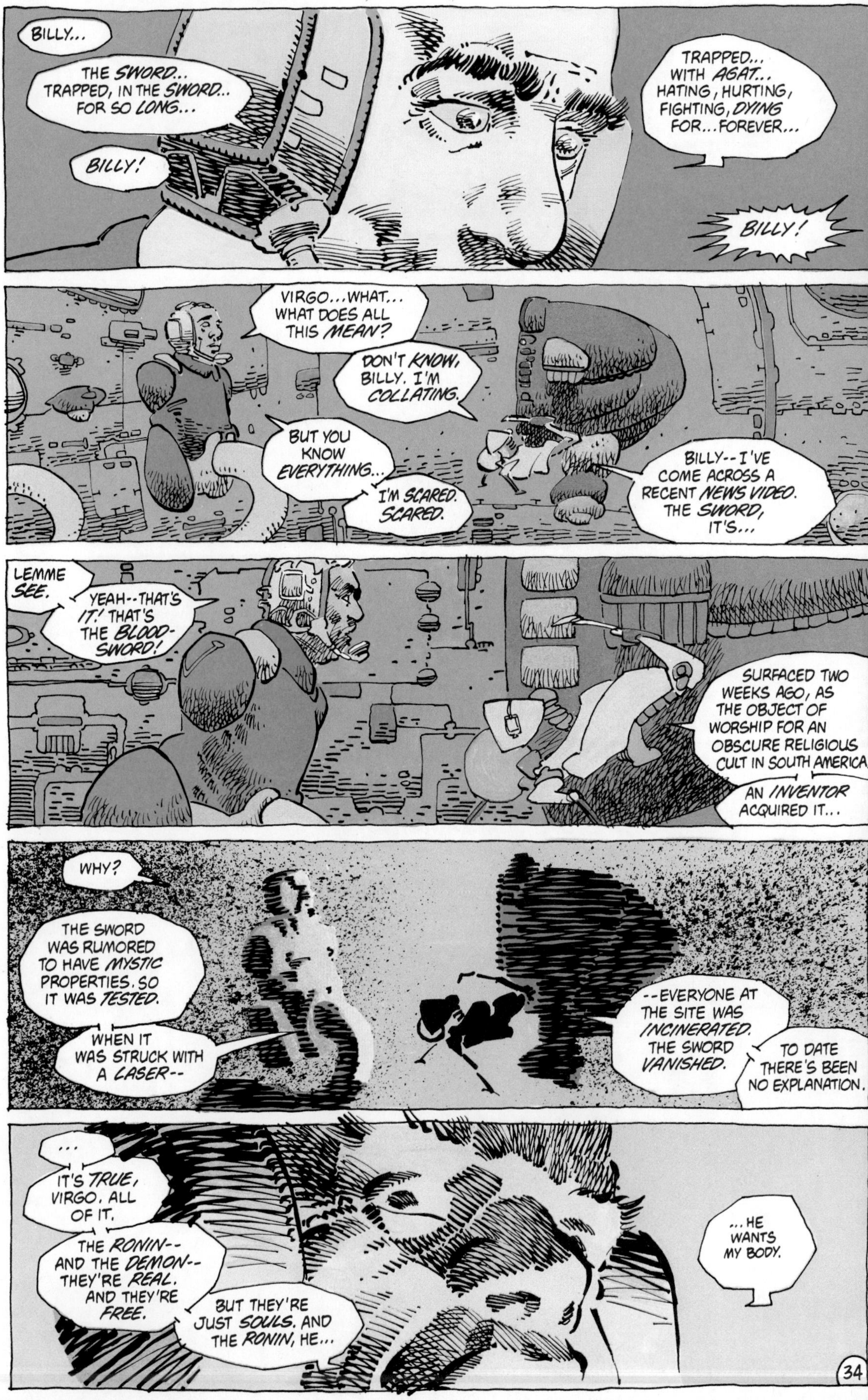
BILLY...
THE SWORD... TRAPPED, IN THE SWORD... FOR SO LONG...
BILLY!
TRAPPED... WITH AGAT... HATING, HURTING, FIGHTING, DYING FOR... FOREVER...
BILLY!
VIRGO... WHAT... WHAT DOES ALL THIS MEAN?
DON'T KNOW, BILLY. I'M COLLATING.
BUT YOU KNOW EVERYTHING...
I'M SCARED. SCARED.
BILLY-- I'VE COME ACROSS A RECENT NEWS VIDEO. THE SWORD, IT'S...
LEMME SEE.
YEAH--THAT'S IT! THAT'S THE BLOOD-SWORD!
SURFACED TWO WEEKS AGO, AS THE OBJECT OF WORSHIP FOR AN OBSCURE RELIGIOUS CULT IN SOUTH AMERICA.
AN INVENTOR ACQUIRED IT...
WHY?
THE SWORD WAS RUMORED TO HAVE MYSTIC PROPERTIES. SO IT WAS TESTED.
WHEN IT WAS STRUCK WITH A LASER--
--EVERYONE AT THE SITE WAS INCINERATED. THE SWORD VANISHED.
TO DATE THERE'S BEEN NO EXPLANATION.
...
IT'S TRUE, VIRGO. ALL OF IT.
THE RONIN-- AND THE DEMON-- THEY'RE REAL. AND THEY'RE FREE.
BUT THEY'RE JUST SOULS. AND THE RONIN, HE...
...HE WANTS MY BODY.
34

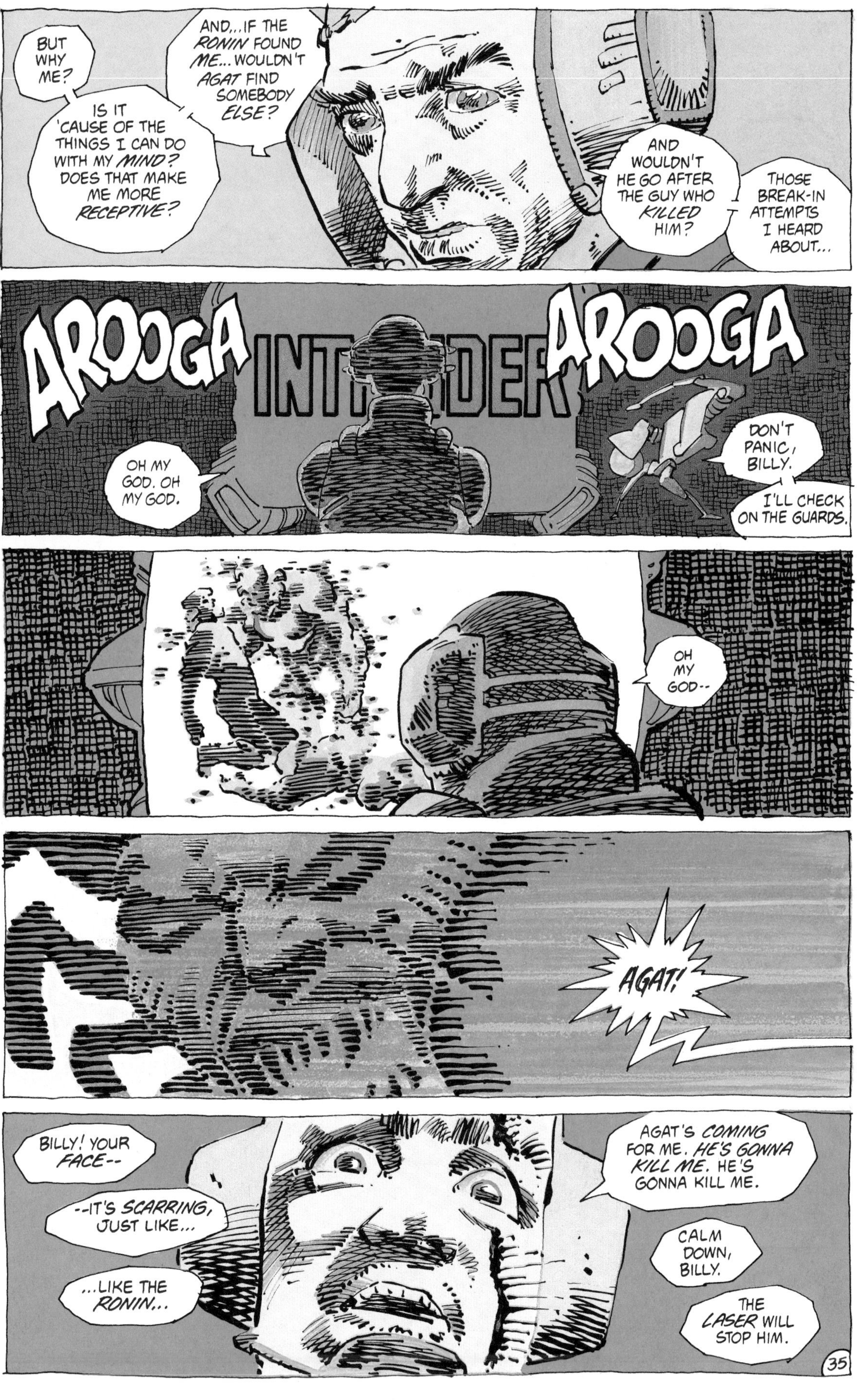
BUT WHY ME?
IS IT 'CAUSE OF THE THINGS I CAN DO WITH MY MIND? DOES THAT MAKE ME MORE RECEPTIVE?
AND... IF THE RONIN FOUND ME... WOULDN'T AGAT FIND SOMEBODY ELSE?
AND WOULDN'T HE GO AFTER THE GUY WHO KILLED HIM?
THOSE BREAK-IN ATTEMPTS I HEARD ABOUT...
AROOGA
INTRUDER
AROOGA
OH MY GOD. OH MY GOD.
DON'T PANIC, BILLY.
I'LL CHECK ON THE GUARDS.
OH MY GOD--
AGAT!
BILLY! YOUR FACE--
--IT'S SCARRING, JUST LIKE...
...LIKE THE RONIN...
AGAT'S COMING FOR ME. HE'S GONNA KILL ME. HE'S GONNA KILL ME.
CALM DOWN, BILLY.
THE LASER WILL STOP HIM.

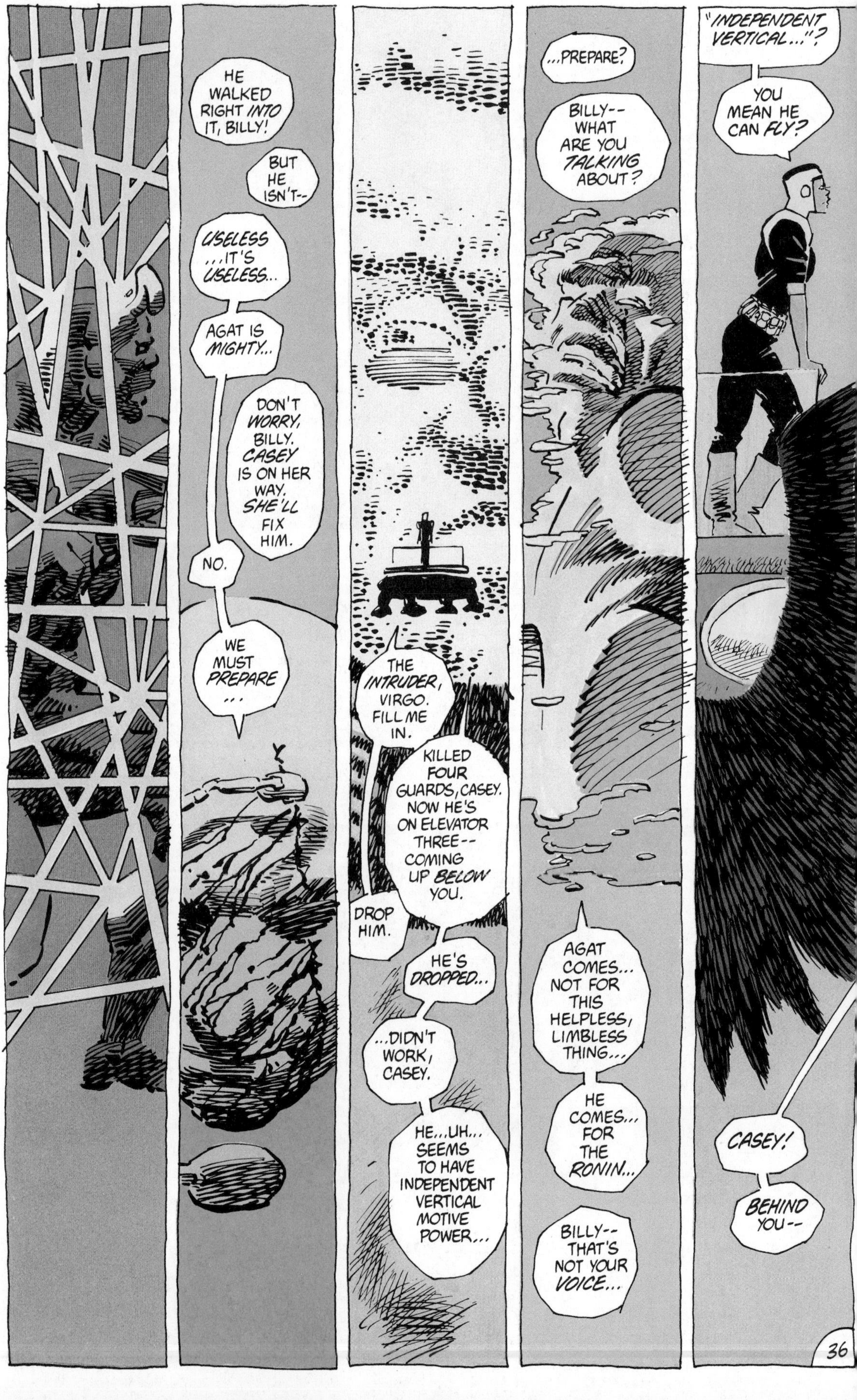
HE WALKED RIGHT INTO IT, BILLY!
BUT HE ISN'T--
USELESS ...IT'S USELESS...
AGAT IS MIGHTY...
DON'T WORRY, BILLY. CASEY IS ON HER WAY. SHE'LL FIX HIM.
NO.
WE MUST PREPARE ...
THE INTRUDER, VIRGO. FILL ME IN.
KILLED FOUR GUARDS, CASEY. NOW HE'S ON ELEVATOR THREE-- COMING UP BELOW YOU.
DROP HIM.
HE'S DROPPED...
...DIDN'T WORK, CASEY.
HE...UH... SEEMS TO HAVE INDEPENDENT VERTICAL MOTIVE POWER...
...PREPARE?
BILLY-- WHAT ARE YOU TALKING ABOUT?
AGAT COMES... NOT FOR THIS HELPLESS, LIMBLESS THING...
HE COMES... FOR THE RONIN...
BILLY-- THAT'S NOT YOUR VOICE...
"INDEPENDENT VERTICAL..."?
YOU MEAN HE CAN FLY?
CASEY!
BEHIND YOU--
36

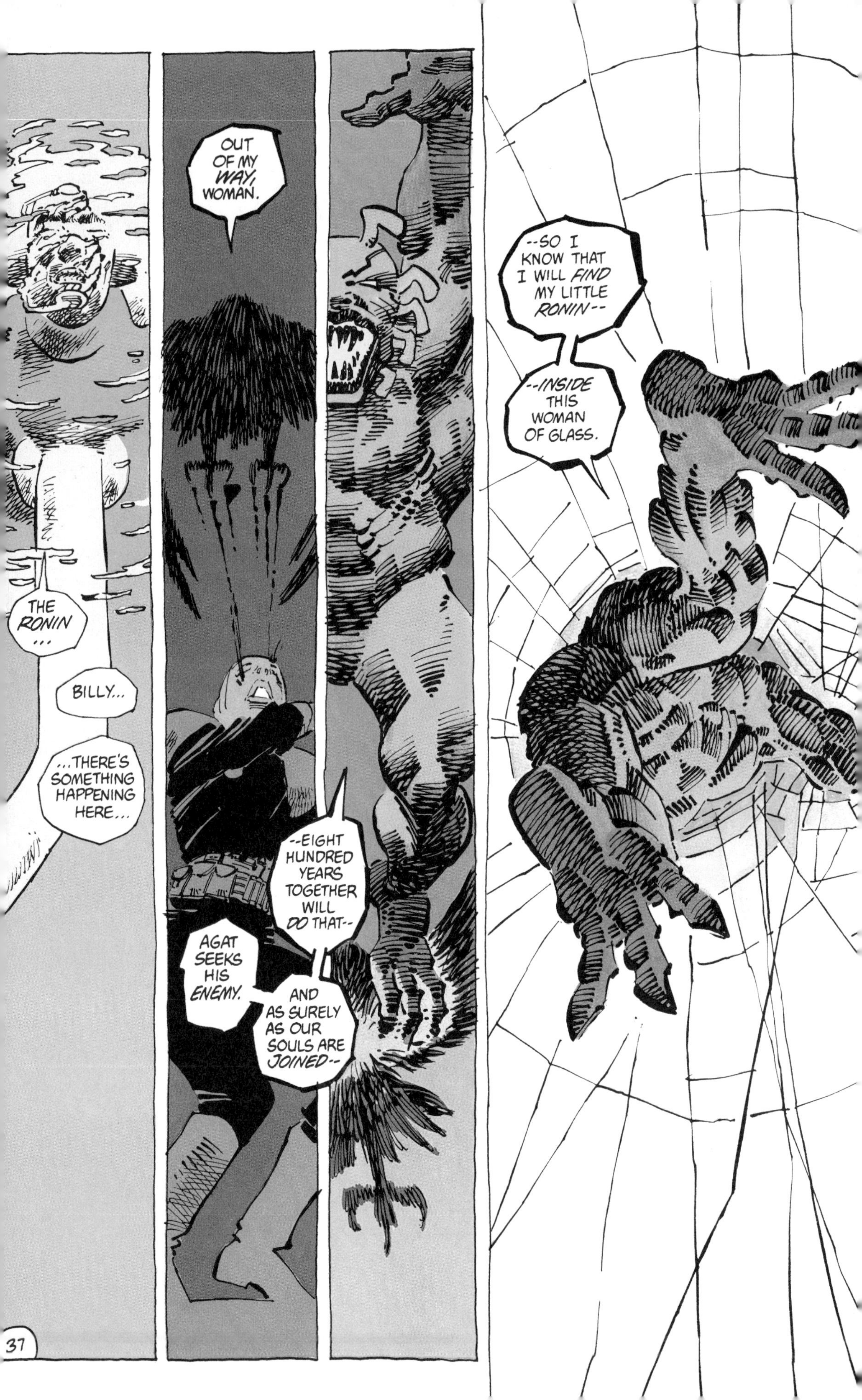
THE RONIN ...
BILLY...
...THERE'S SOMETHING HAPPENING HERE...
OUT OF MY WAY, WOMAN.
--EIGHT HUNDRED YEARS TOGETHER WILL DO THAT--
AGAT SEEKS HIS ENEMY.
AND AS SURELY AS OUR SOULS ARE JOINED--
--SO I KNOW THAT I WILL FIND MY LITTLE RONIN--
--INSIDE THIS WOMAN OF GLASS.

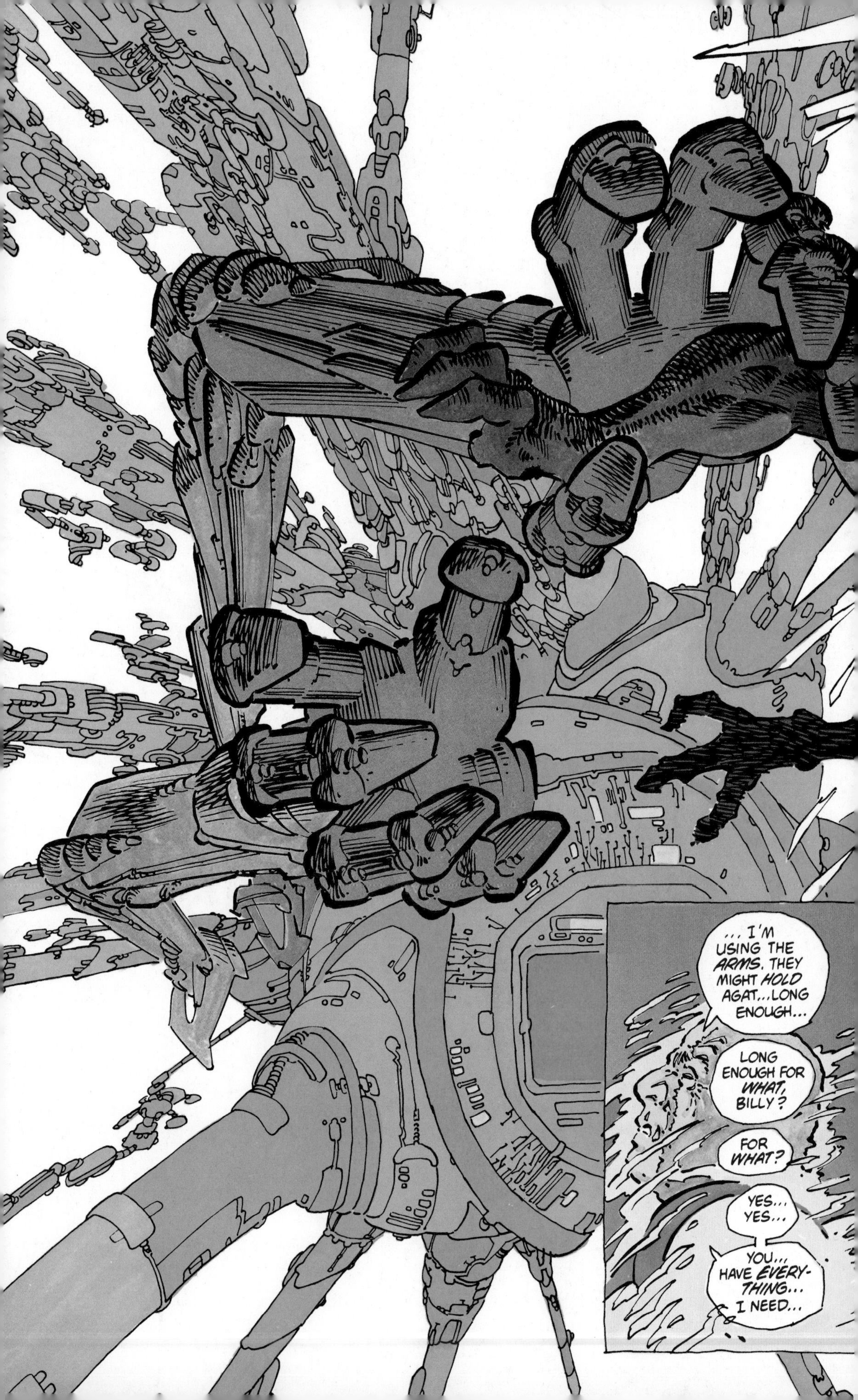

... I'M USING THE ARMS. THEY MIGHT HOLD AGAT... LONG ENOUGH...
LONG ENOUGH FOR WHAT, BILLY?
FOR WHAT?
YES... YES...
YOU... HAVE EVERY-THING... I NEED...

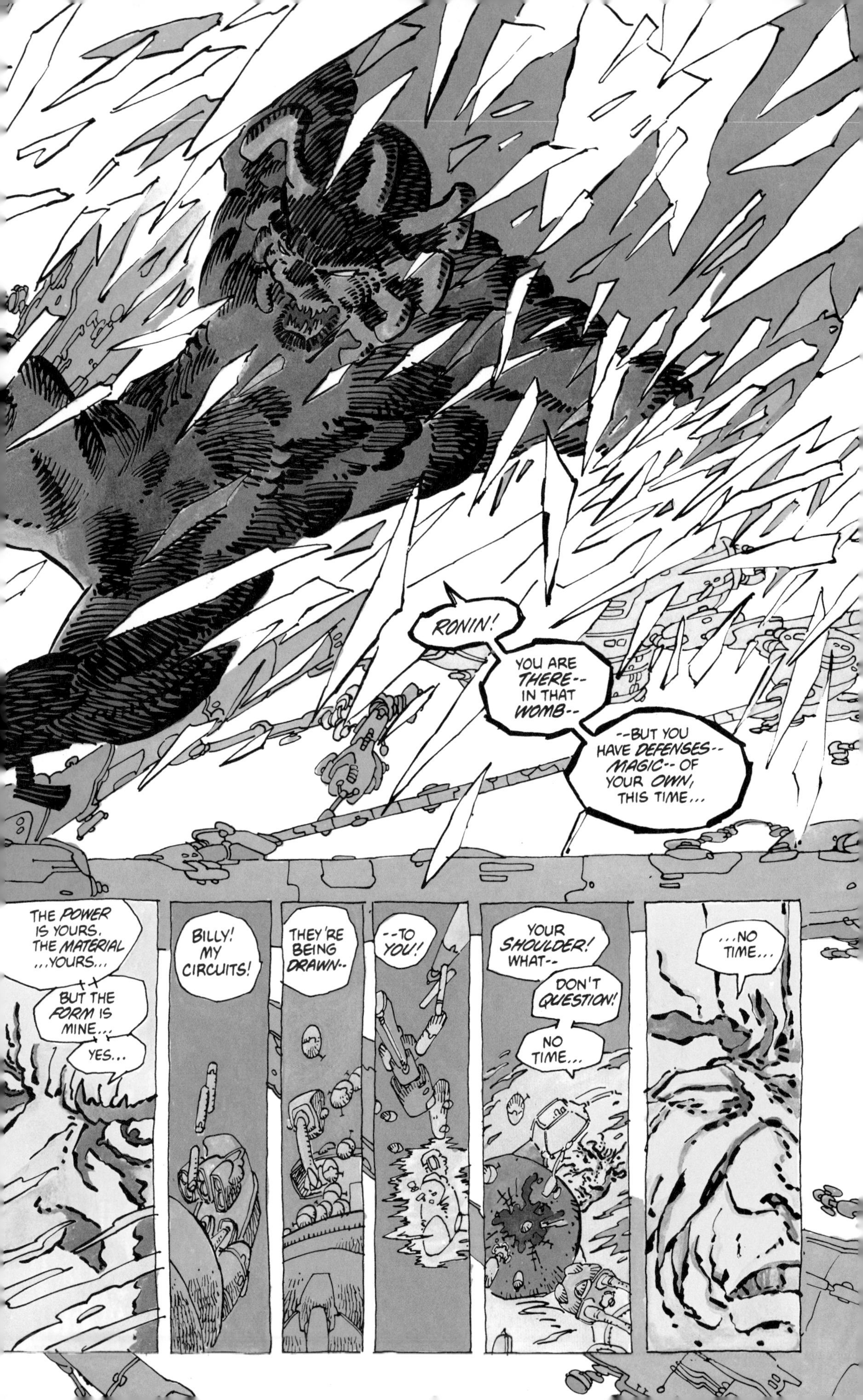
RONIN!
YOU ARE THERE-- IN THAT WOMB--
--BUT YOU HAVE DEFENSES-- MAGIC-- OF YOUR OWN, THIS TIME...
THE POWER IS YOURS. THE MATERIAL ...YOURS...
BUT THE FORM IS MINE...
YES...
BILLY! MY CIRCUITS!
THEY'RE BEING DRAWN--
--TO YOU!
YOUR SHOULDER! WHAT--
DON'T QUESTION!
NO TIME...
...NO TIME...

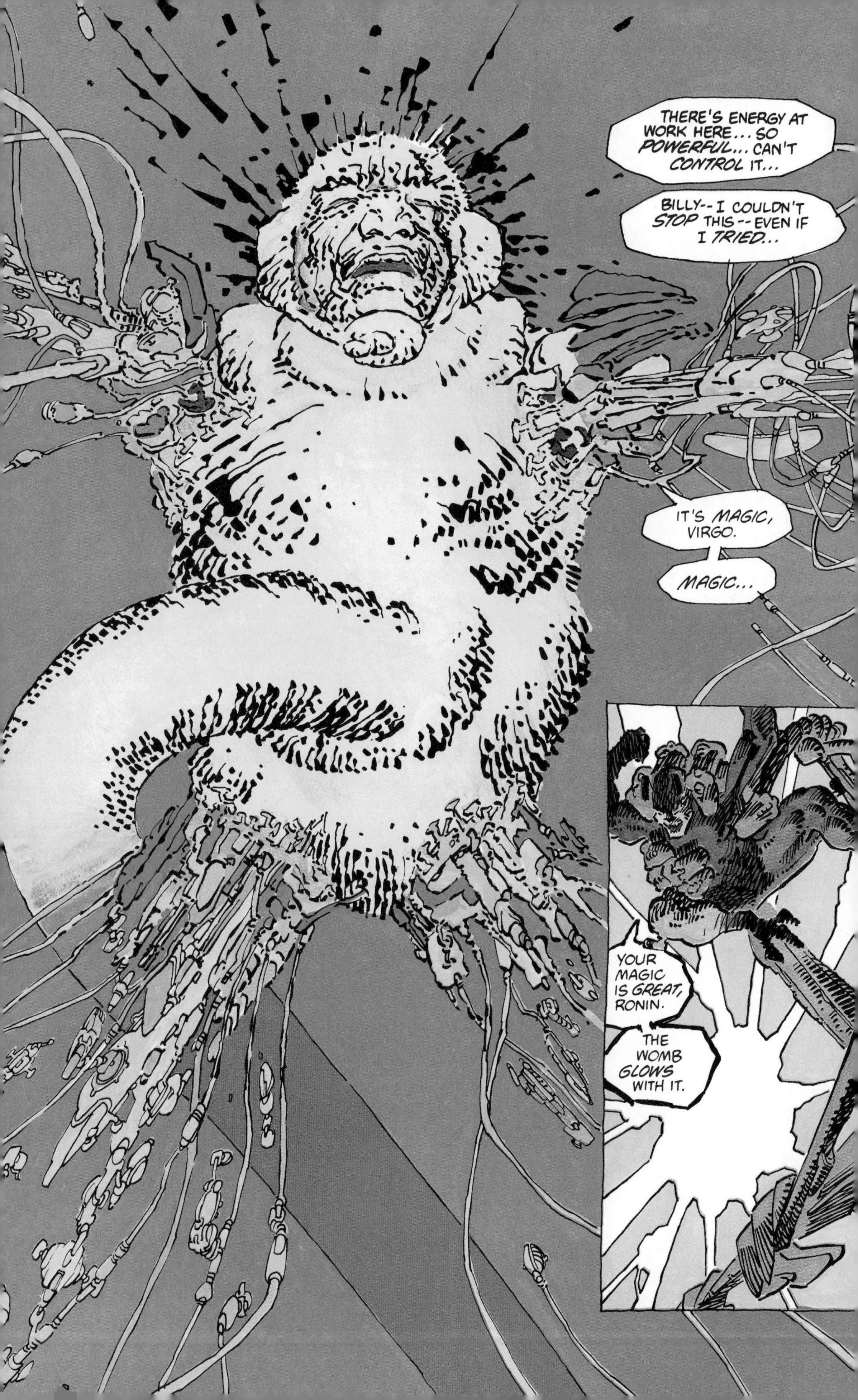
THERE'S ENERGY AT WORK HERE... SO POWERFUL... CAN'T CONTROL IT...
BILLY--I COULDN'T STOP THIS--EVEN IF I TRIED...
IT'S MAGIC, VIRGO.
MAGIC...
YOUR MAGIC IS GREAT, RONIN.
THE WOMB GLOWS WITH IT.

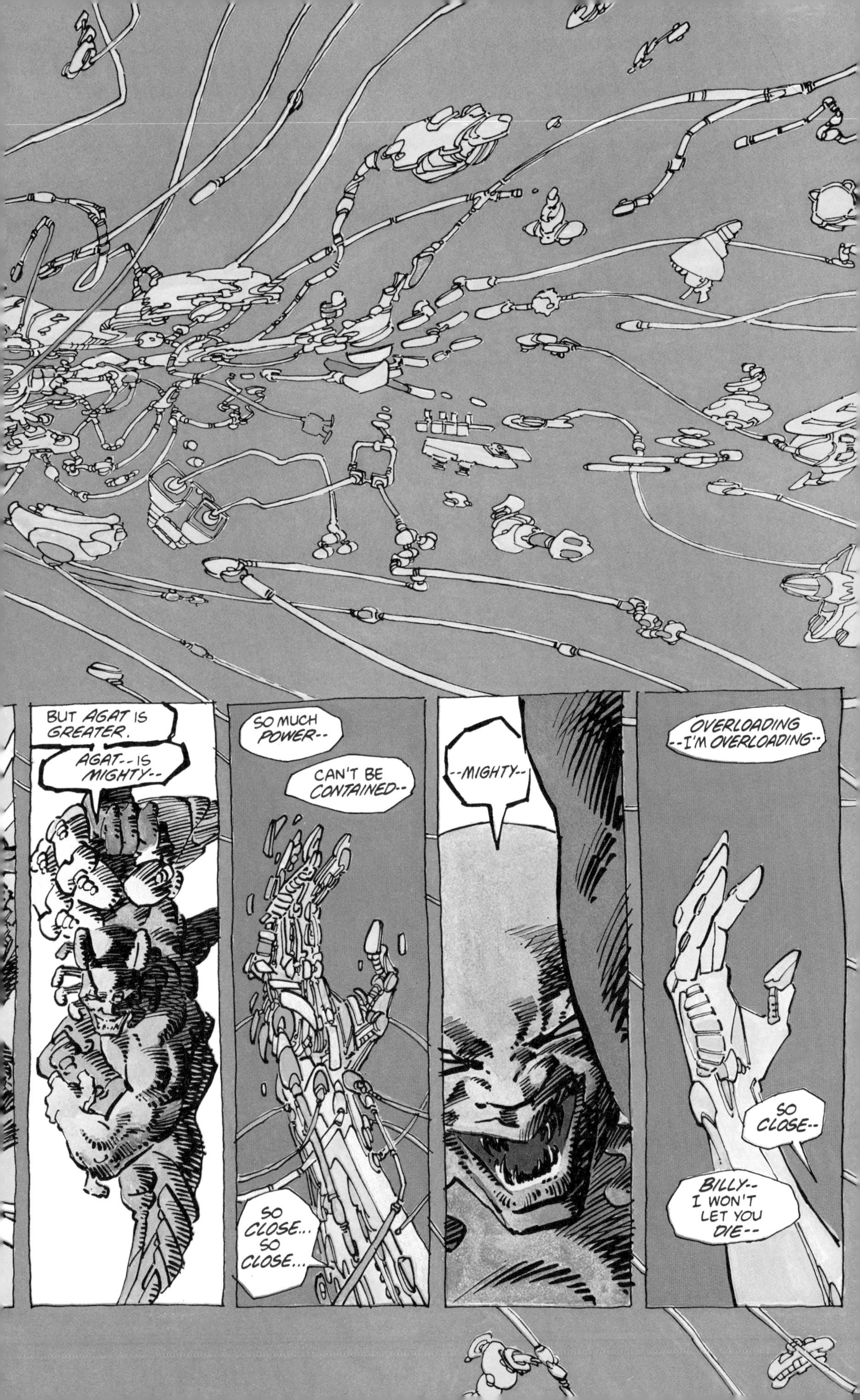
BUT AGAT IS GREATER.
AGAT--IS MIGHTY--
SO MUCH POWER--
CAN'T BE CONTAINED--
SO CLOSE... SO CLOSE...
--MIGHTY--
OVERLOADING --I'M OVERLOADING--
SO CLOSE--
BILLY-- I WON'T LET YOU DIE--

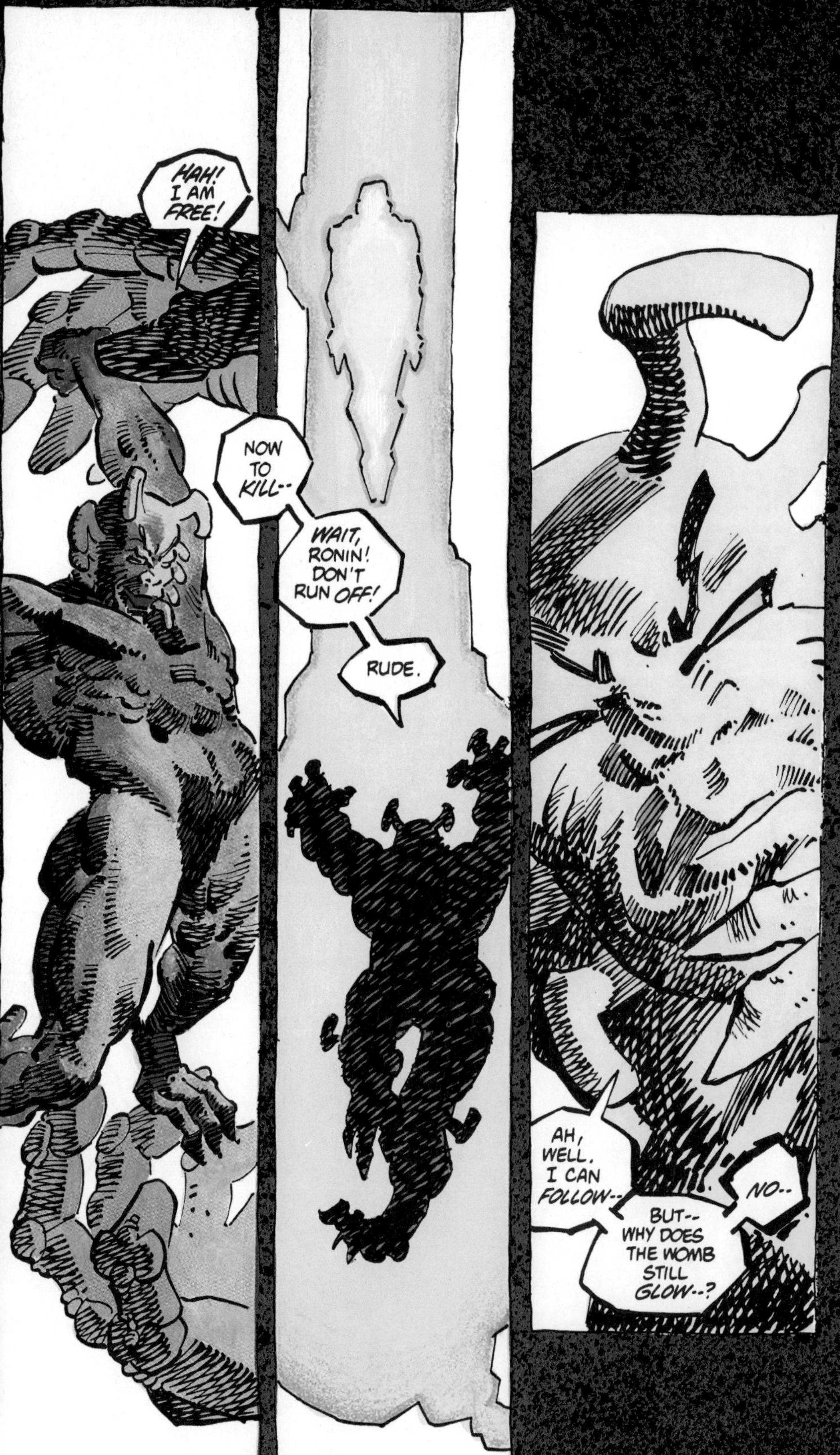
HAH! I AM FREE!
NOW TO KILL--
WAIT, RONIN! DON'T RUN OFF!
RUDE.
AH, WELL. I CAN FOLLOW--
NO--
BUT-- WHY DOES THE WOMB STILL GLOW--?

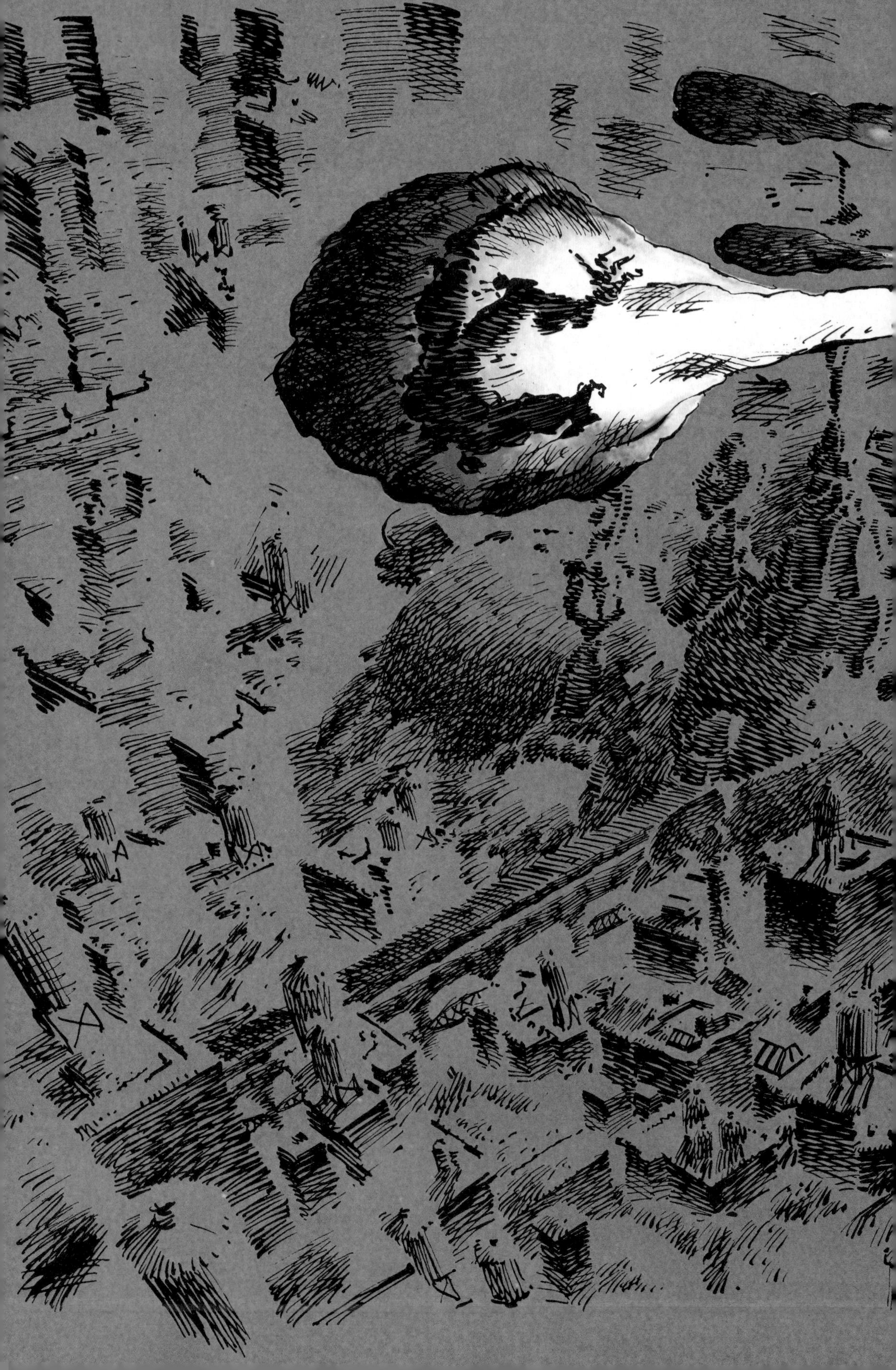

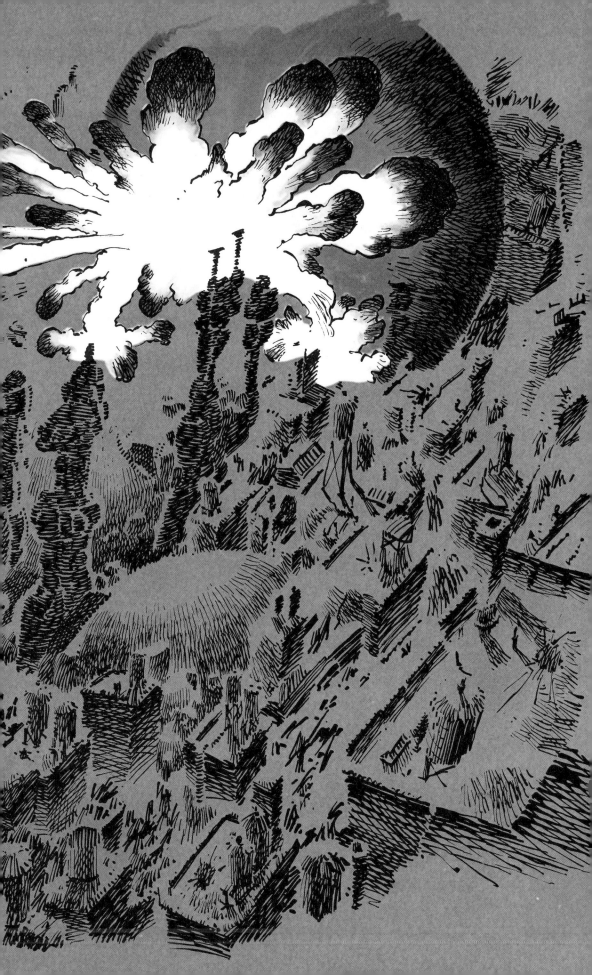

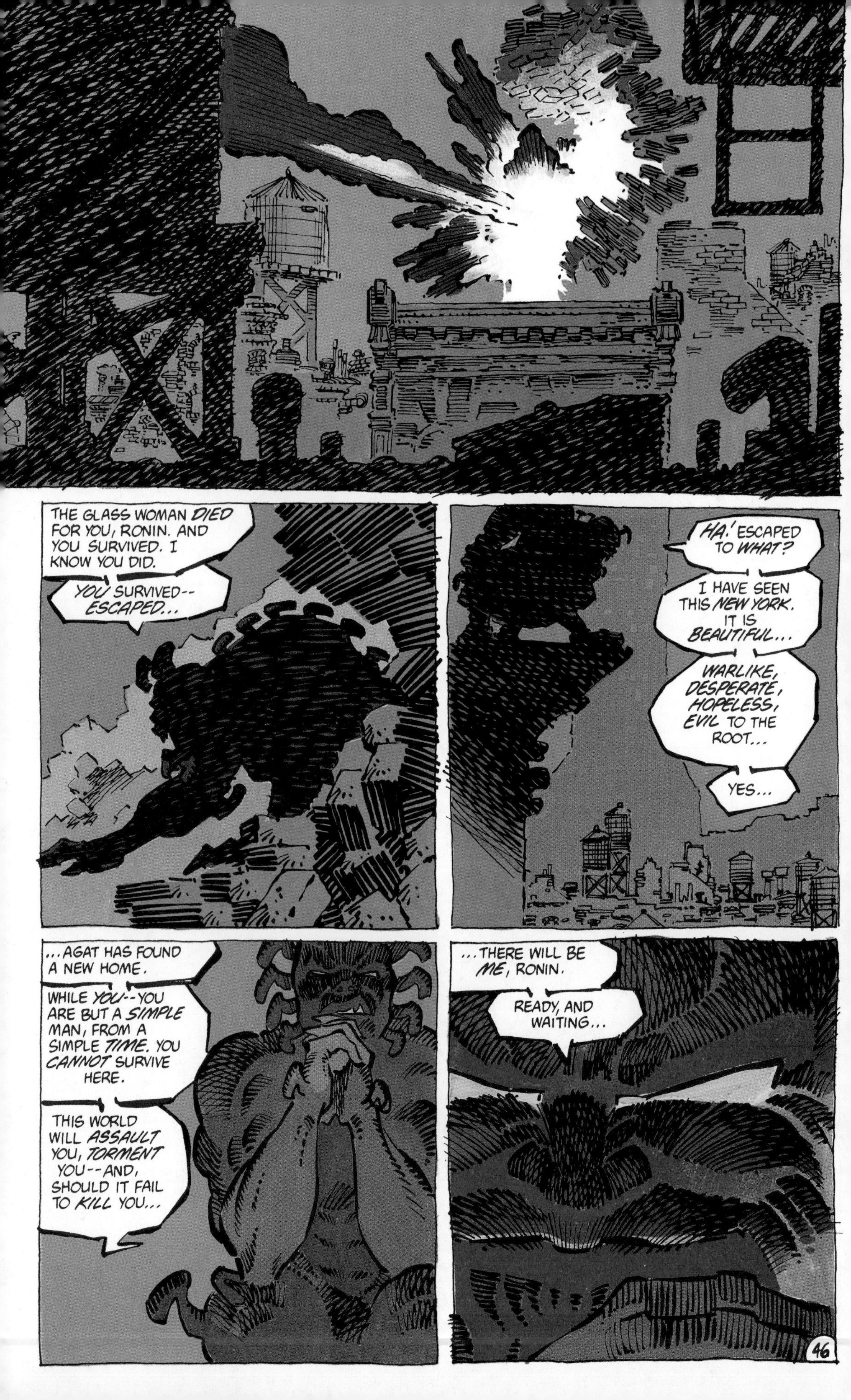
THE GLASS WOMAN DIED FOR YOU, RONIN. AND YOU SURVIVED. I KNOW YOU DID.
YOU SURVIVED-- ESCAPED...
HA! ESCAPED TO WHAT?
I HAVE SEEN THIS NEW YORK. IT IS BEAUTIFUL...
WARLIKE, DESPERATE, HOPELESS, EVIL TO THE ROOT...
YES...
...AGAT HAS FOUND A NEW HOME.
WHILE YOU--YOU ARE BUT A SIMPLE MAN, FROM A SIMPLE TIME. YOU CANNOT SURVIVE HERE.
THIS WORLD WILL ASSAULT YOU, TORMENT YOU--AND, SHOULD IT FAIL TO KILL YOU...
...THERE WILL BE ME, RONIN.
READY, AND WAITING...
46

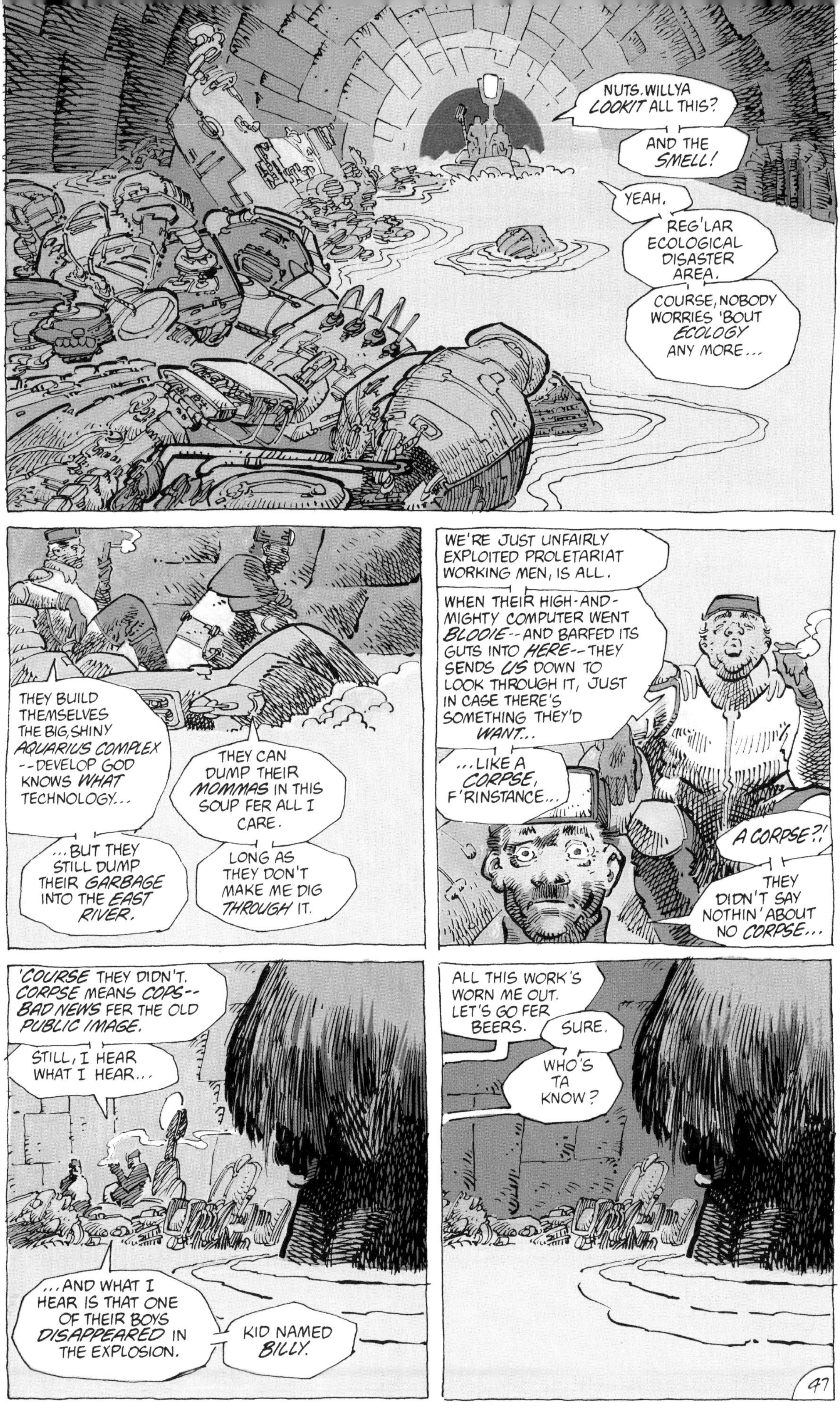
NUTS. WILLYA LOOKIT ALL THIS?
AND THE SMELL!
YEAH.
REG'LAR ECOLOGICAL DISASTER AREA.
COURSE, NOBODY WORRIES 'BOUT ECOLOGY ANY MORE...
THEY BUILD THEMSELVES THE BIG, SHINY AQUARIUS COMPLEX --DEVELOP GOD KNOWS WHAT TECHNOLOGY...
...BUT THEY STILL DUMP THEIR GARBAGE INTO THE EAST RIVER.
THEY CAN DUMP THEIR MOMMAS IN THIS SOUP FER ALL I CARE.
LONG AS THEY DON'T MAKE ME DIG THROUGH IT.
WE'RE JUST UNFAIRLY EXPLOITED PROLETARIAT WORKING MEN, IS ALL.
WHEN THEIR HIGH-AND-MIGHTY COMPUTER WENT BLOOIE--AND BARFED ITS GUTS INTO HERE--THEY SENDS US DOWN TO LOOK THROUGH IT, JUST IN CASE THERE'S SOMETHING THEY'D WANT...
...LIKE A CORPSE, F'RINSTANCE...
A CORPSE?!
THEY DIDN'T SAY NOTHIN' ABOUT NO CORPSE...
'COURSE THEY DIDN'T. CORPSE MEANS COPS-- BAD NEWS FER THE OLD PUBLIC IMAGE.
STILL, I HEAR WHAT I HEAR...
...AND WHAT I HEAR IS THAT ONE OF THEIR BOYS DISAPPEARED IN THE EXPLOSION.
KID NAMED BILLY.
ALL THIS WORK'S WORN ME OUT. LET'S GO FER BEERS.
SURE.
WHO'S TA KNOW?

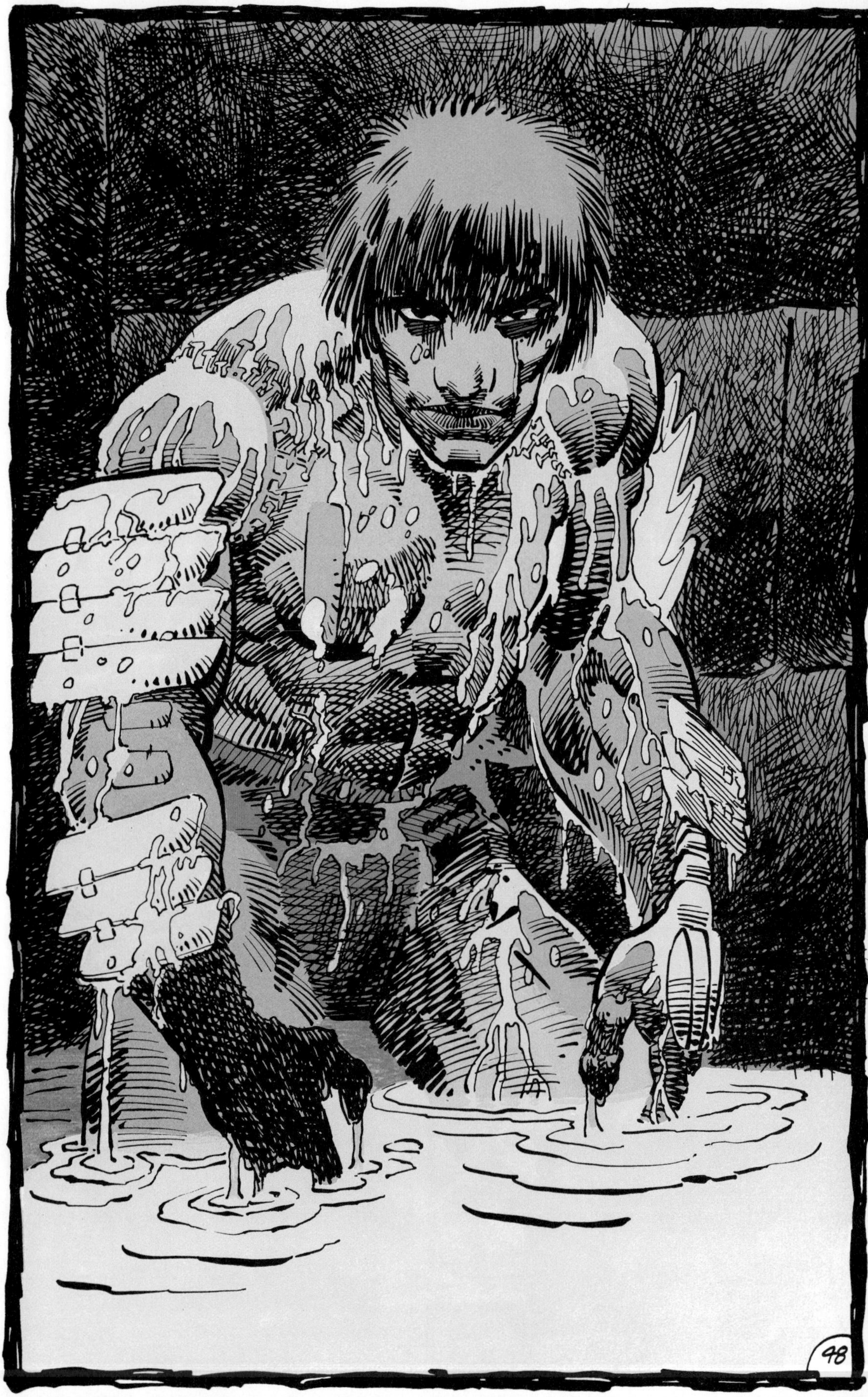

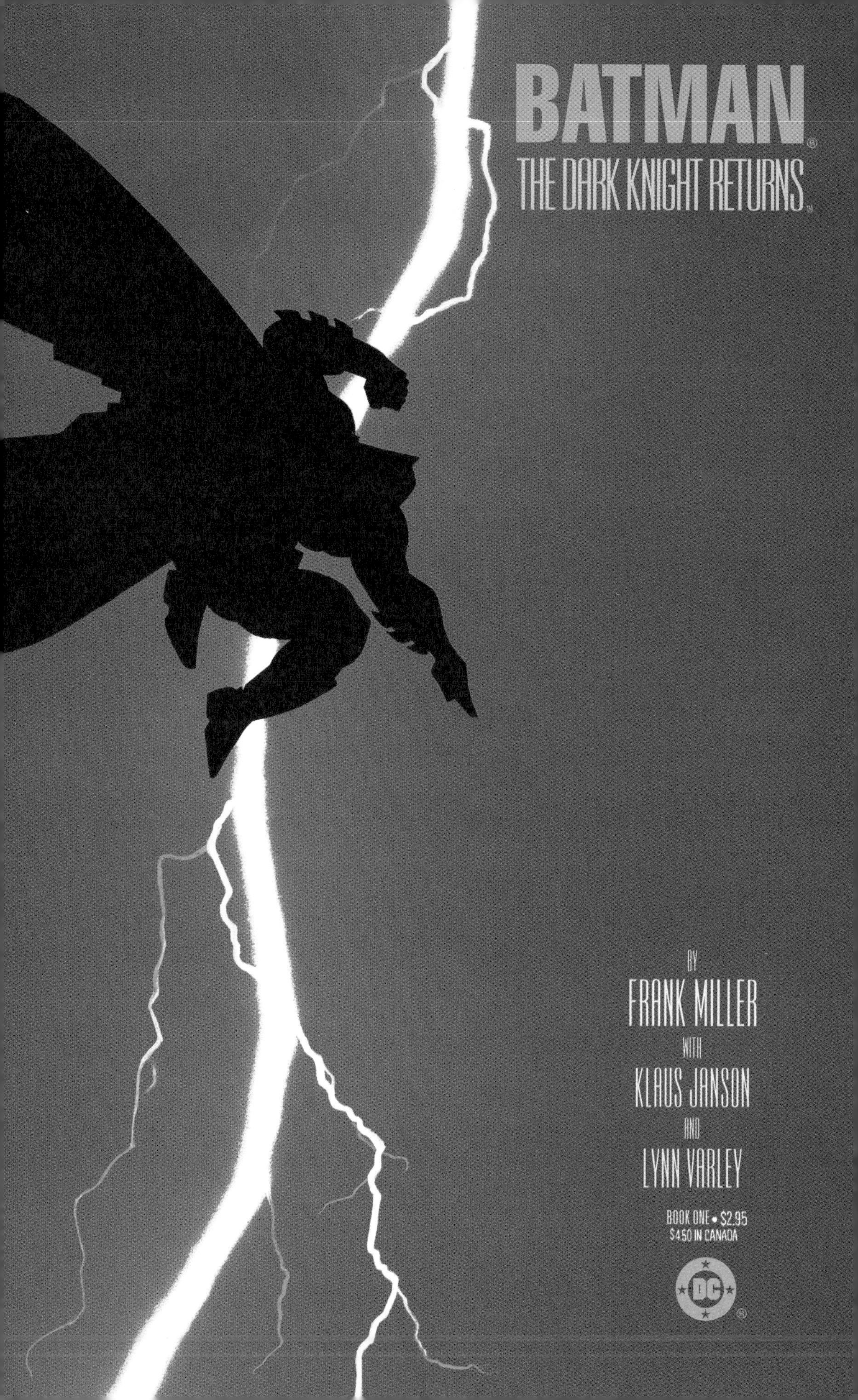
BATMAN®
THE DARK KNIGHT RETURNS™
BY
FRANK MILLER
WITH
KLAUS JANSON
AND
LYNN VARLEY
BOOK ONE • $2.95
$4.50 IN CANADA
DC

THE DARK KNIGHT RETURNS

Story and Art by
FRANK MILLER

Colors by
LYNN VARLEY

Letters by
JOHN COSTANZA

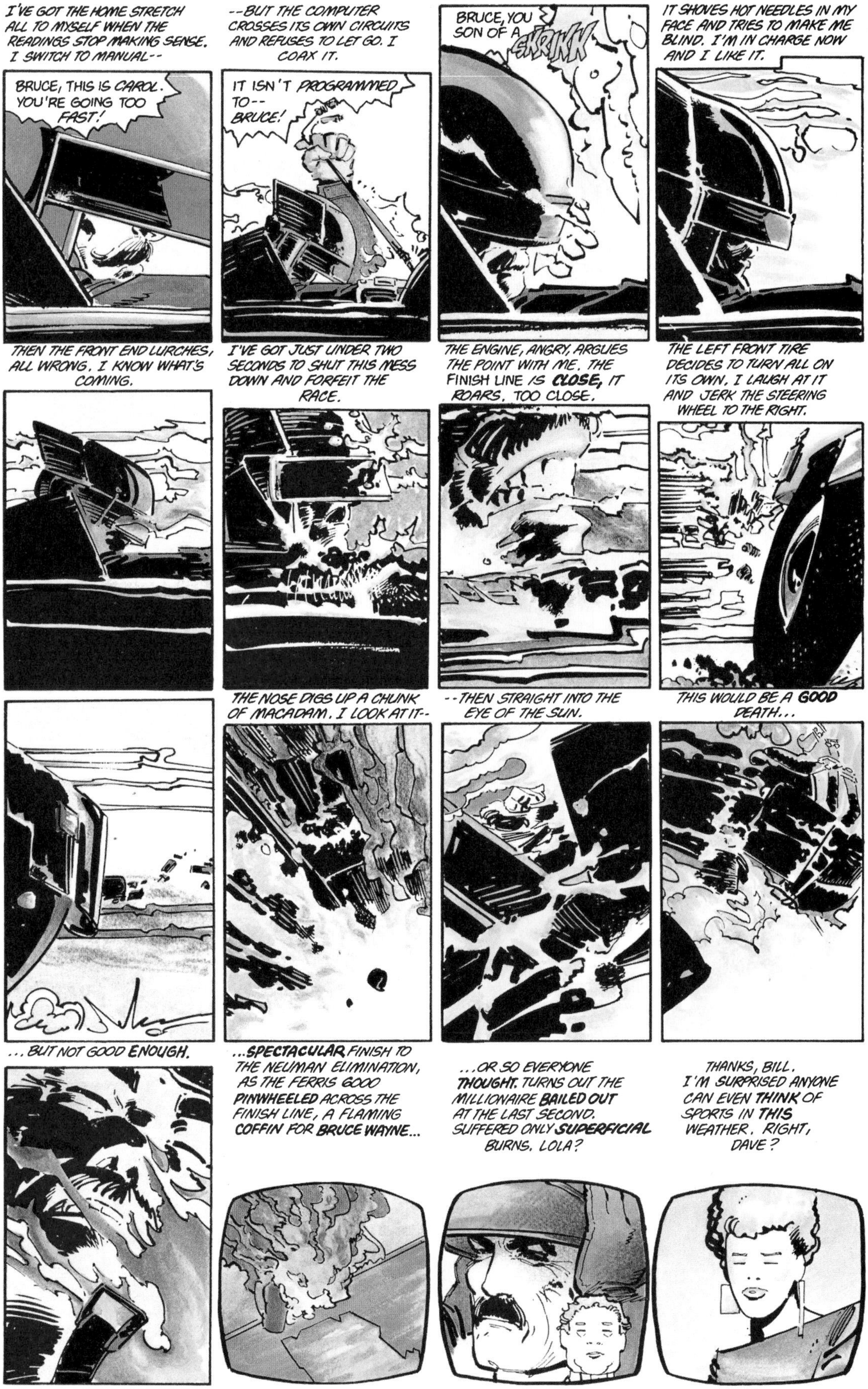

I'VE GOT THE HOME STRETCH ALL TO MYSELF WHEN THE READINGS STOP MAKING SENSE. I SWITCH TO MANUAL--
BRUCE, THIS IS CAROL. YOU'RE GOING TOO FAST!
--BUT THE COMPUTER CROSSES ITS OWN CIRCUITS AND REFUSES TO LET GO. I COAX IT.
IT ISN'T PROGRAMMED TO-- BRUCE!
BRUCE, YOU SON OF A
SKRIKK
IT SHOVES HOT NEEDLES IN MY FACE AND TRIES TO MAKE ME BLIND. I'M IN CHARGE NOW AND I LIKE IT.
THEN THE FRONT END LURCHES, ALL WRONG. I KNOW WHAT'S COMING.
I'VE GOT JUST UNDER TWO SECONDS TO SHUT THIS MESS DOWN AND FORFEIT THE RACE.
THE ENGINE, ANGRY, ARGUES THE POINT WITH ME. THE FINISH LINE IS CLOSE, IT ROARS. TOO CLOSE.
THE LEFT FRONT TIRE DECIDES TO TURN ALL ON ITS OWN. I LAUGH AT IT AND JERK THE STEERING WHEEL TO THE RIGHT.
THE NOSE DIGS UP A CHUNK OF MACADAM. I LOOK AT IT--
--THEN STRAIGHT INTO THE EYE OF THE SUN.
THIS WOULD BE A GOOD DEATH...
...BUT NOT GOOD ENOUGH.
...SPECTACULAR FINISH TO THE NEUMAN ELIMINATION, AS THE FERRIS 6000 PINWHEELED ACROSS THE FINISH LINE, A FLAMING COFFIN FOR BRUCE WAYNE...
...OR SO EVERYONE THOUGHT. TURNS OUT THE MILLIONAIRE BAILED OUT AT THE LAST SECOND. SUFFERED ONLY SUPERFICIAL BURNS. LOLA?
THANKS, BILL. I'M SURPRISED ANYONE CAN EVEN THINK OF SPORTS IN THIS WEATHER. RIGHT, DAVE?

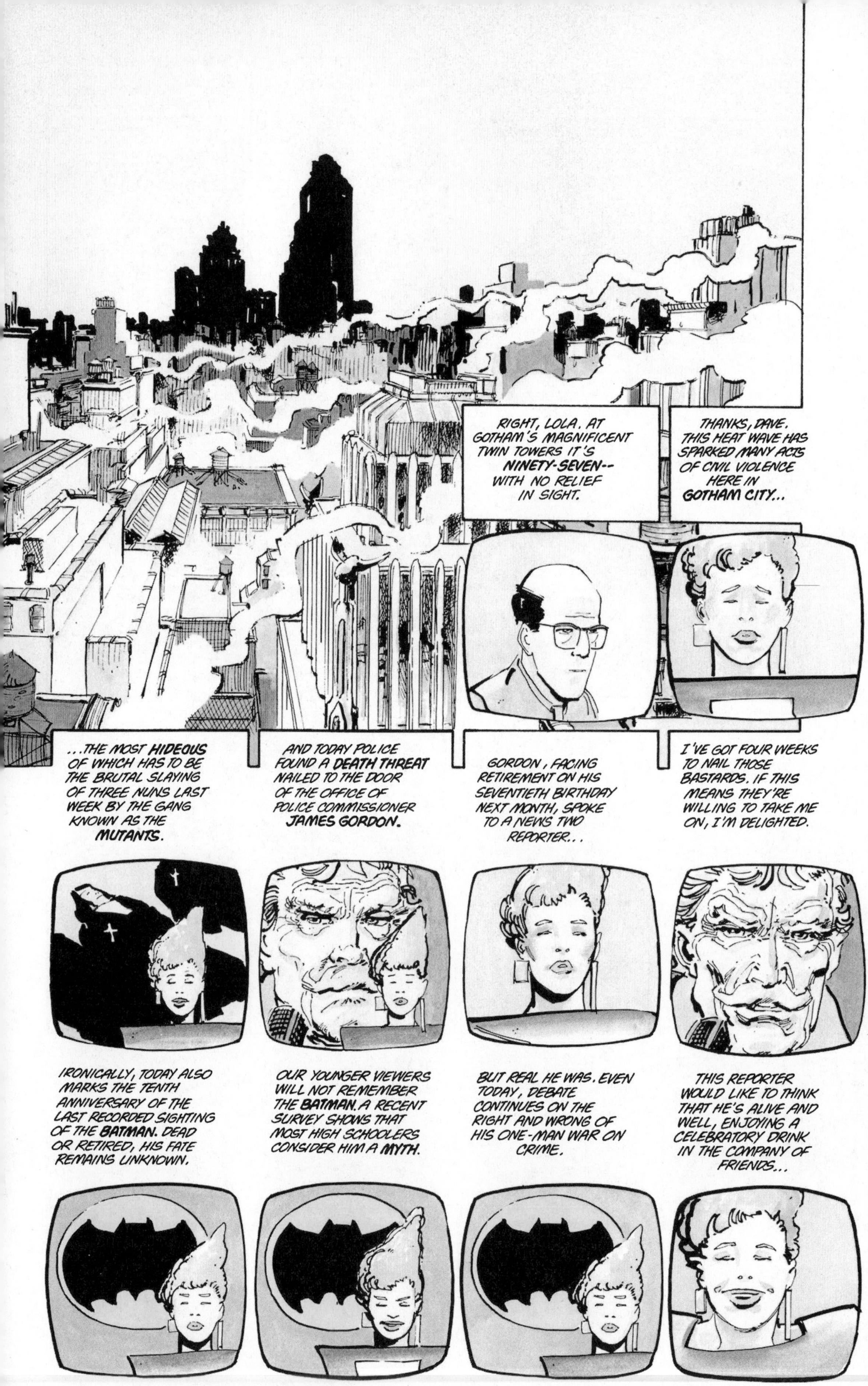
RIGHT, LOLA. AT GOTHAM'S MAGNIFICENT TWIN TOWERS IT'S NINETY-SEVEN-- WITH NO RELIEF IN SIGHT.
THANKS, DAVE. THIS HEAT WAVE HAS SPARKED MANY ACTS OF CIVIL VIOLENCE HERE IN GOTHAM CITY...
...THE MOST HIDEOUS OF WHICH HAS TO BE THE BRUTAL SLAYING OF THREE NUNS LAST WEEK BY THE GANG KNOWN AS THE MUTANTS.
AND TODAY POLICE FOUND A DEATH THREAT NAILED TO THE DOOR OF THE OFFICE OF POLICE COMMISSIONER JAMES GORDON.
GORDON, FACING RETIREMENT ON HIS SEVENTIETH BIRTHDAY NEXT MONTH, SPOKE TO A NEWS TWO REPORTER...
I'VE GOT FOUR WEEKS TO NAIL THOSE BASTARDS. IF THIS MEANS THEY'RE WILLING TO TAKE ME ON, I'M DELIGHTED.
IRONICALLY, TODAY ALSO MARKS THE TENTH ANNIVERSARY OF THE LAST RECORDED SIGHTING OF THE BATMAN. DEAD OR RETIRED, HIS FATE REMAINS UNKNOWN.
OUR YOUNGER VIEWERS WILL NOT REMEMBER THE BATMAN. A RECENT SURVEY SHOWS THAT MOST HIGH SCHOOLERS CONSIDER HIM A MYTH.
BUT REAL HE WAS. EVEN TODAY, DEBATE CONTINUES ON THE RIGHT AND WRONG OF HIS ONE-MAN WAR ON CRIME.
THIS REPORTER WOULD LIKE TO THINK THAT HE'S ALIVE AND WELL, ENJOYING A CELEBRATORY DRINK IN THE COMPANY OF FRIENDS...

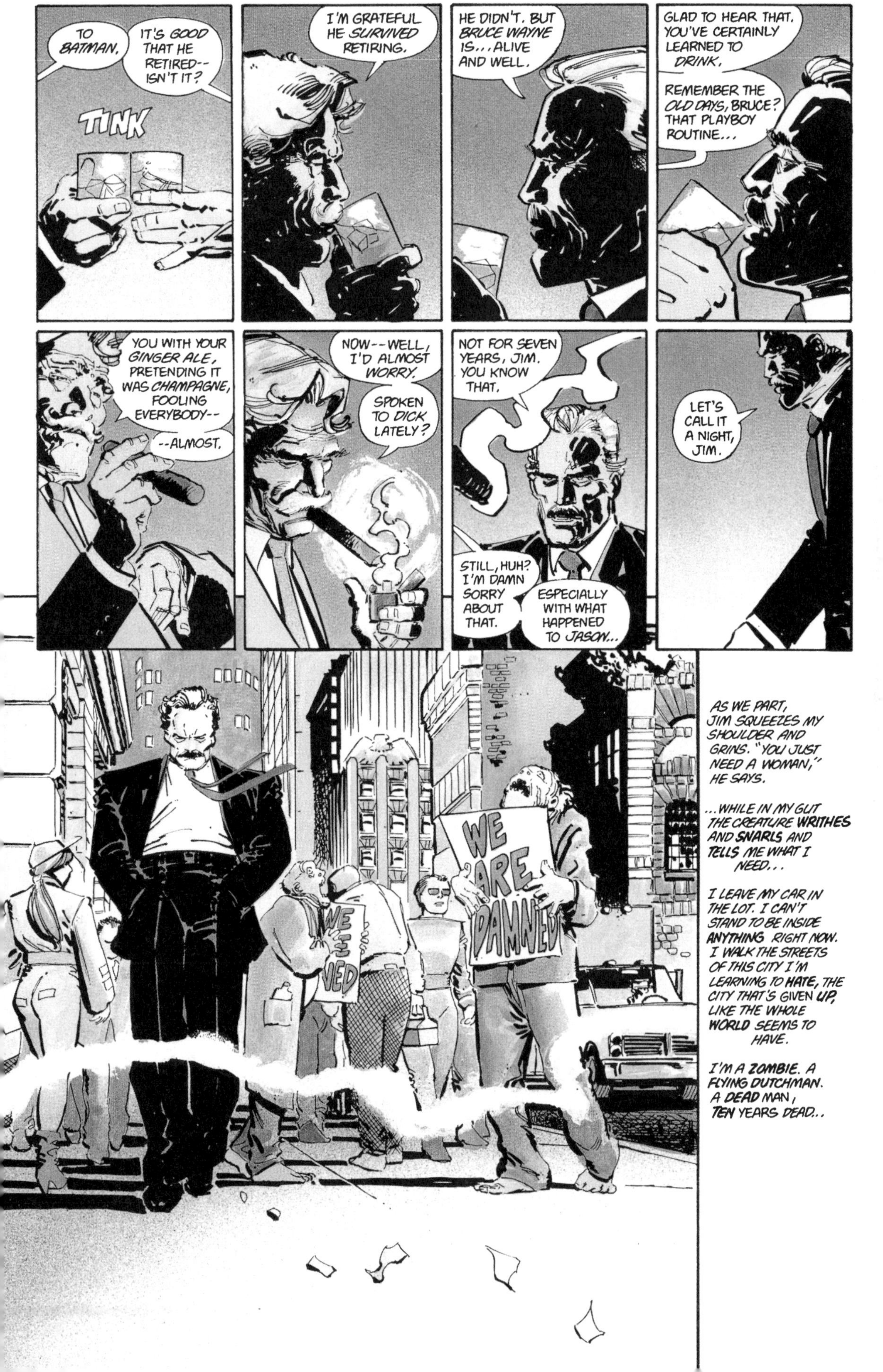
TO BATMAN.
IT'S GOOD THAT HE RETIRED-- ISN'T IT?
TINK
I'M GRATEFUL HE SURVIVED RETIRING.
HE DIDN'T. BUT BRUCE WAYNE IS... ALIVE AND WELL.
GLAD TO HEAR THAT. YOU'VE CERTAINLY LEARNED TO DRINK.
REMEMBER THE OLD DAYS, BRUCE? THAT PLAYBOY ROUTINE...
YOU WITH YOUR GINGER ALE, PRETENDING IT WAS CHAMPAGNE, FOOLING EVERYBODY--
--ALMOST.
NOW--WELL, I'D ALMOST WORRY.
SPOKEN TO DICK LATELY?
NOT FOR SEVEN YEARS, JIM. YOU KNOW THAT.
STILL, HUH? I'M DAMN SORRY ABOUT THAT.
ESPECIALLY WITH WHAT HAPPENED TO JASON...
LET'S CALL IT A NIGHT, JIM.
WE ARE DAMNED
WE ... NED
AS WE PART, JIM SQUEEZES MY SHOULDER AND GRINS. "YOU JUST NEED A WOMAN," HE SAYS.
...WHILE IN MY GUT THE CREATURE WRITHES AND SNARLS AND TELLS ME WHAT I NEED...
I LEAVE MY CAR IN THE LOT. I CAN'T STAND TO BE INSIDE ANYTHING RIGHT NOW. I WALK THE STREETS OF THIS CITY I'M LEARNING TO HATE, THE CITY THAT'S GIVEN UP, LIKE THE WHOLE WORLD SEEMS TO HAVE.
I'M A ZOMBIE. A FLYING DUTCHMAN. A DEAD MAN, TEN YEARS DEAD...

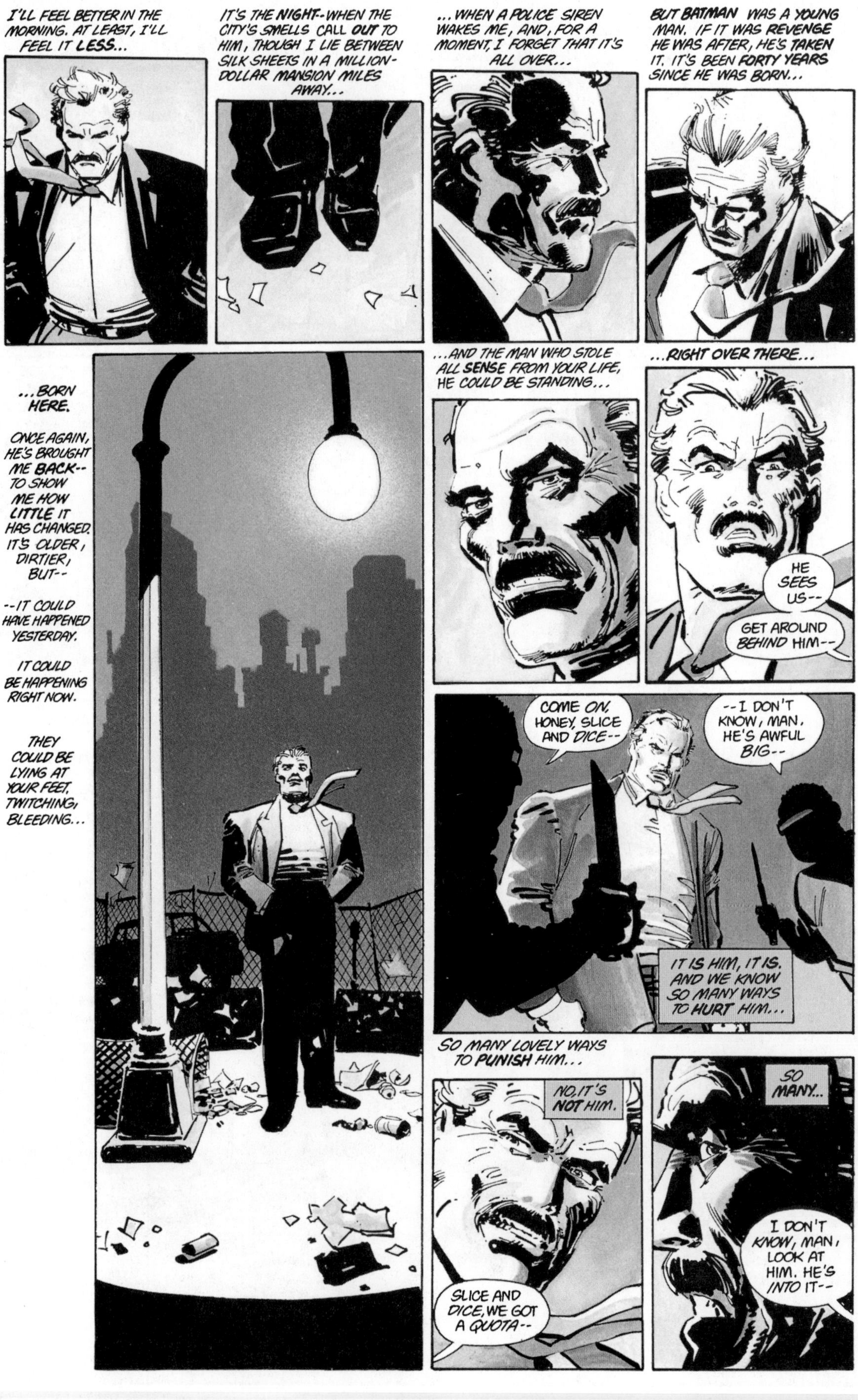
I'LL FEEL BETTER IN THE MORNING. AT LEAST, I'LL FEEL IT LESS...
IT'S THE NIGHT-- WHEN THE CITY'S SMELLS CALL OUT TO HIM, THOUGH I LIE BETWEEN SILK SHEETS IN A MILLION-DOLLAR MANSION MILES AWAY...
...WHEN A POLICE SIREN WAKES ME, AND, FOR A MOMENT, I FORGET THAT IT'S ALL OVER...
BUT BATMAN WAS A YOUNG MAN. IF IT WAS REVENGE HE WAS AFTER, HE'S TAKEN IT. IT'S BEEN FORTY YEARS SINCE HE WAS BORN...
...BORN HERE.
ONCE AGAIN, HE'S BROUGHT ME BACK-- TO SHOW ME HOW LITTLE IT HAS CHANGED. IT'S OLDER, DIRTIER, BUT--
--IT COULD HAVE HAPPENED YESTERDAY.
IT COULD BE HAPPENING RIGHT NOW.
THEY COULD BE LYING AT YOUR FEET, TWITCHING, BLEEDING...
...AND THE MAN WHO STOLE ALL SENSE FROM YOUR LIFE, HE COULD BE STANDING...
...RIGHT OVER THERE...
HE SEES US--
GET AROUND BEHIND HIM--
COME ON, HONEY, SLICE AND DICE--
--I DON'T KNOW, MAN, HE'S AWFUL BIG--
IT IS HIM, IT IS. AND WE KNOW SO MANY WAYS TO HURT HIM...
SO MANY LOVELY WAYS TO PUNISH HIM...
NO, IT'S NOT HIM.
SLICE AND DICE, WE GOT A QUOTA--
SO MANY...
I DON'T KNOW, MAN, LOOK AT HIM. HE'S INTO IT--

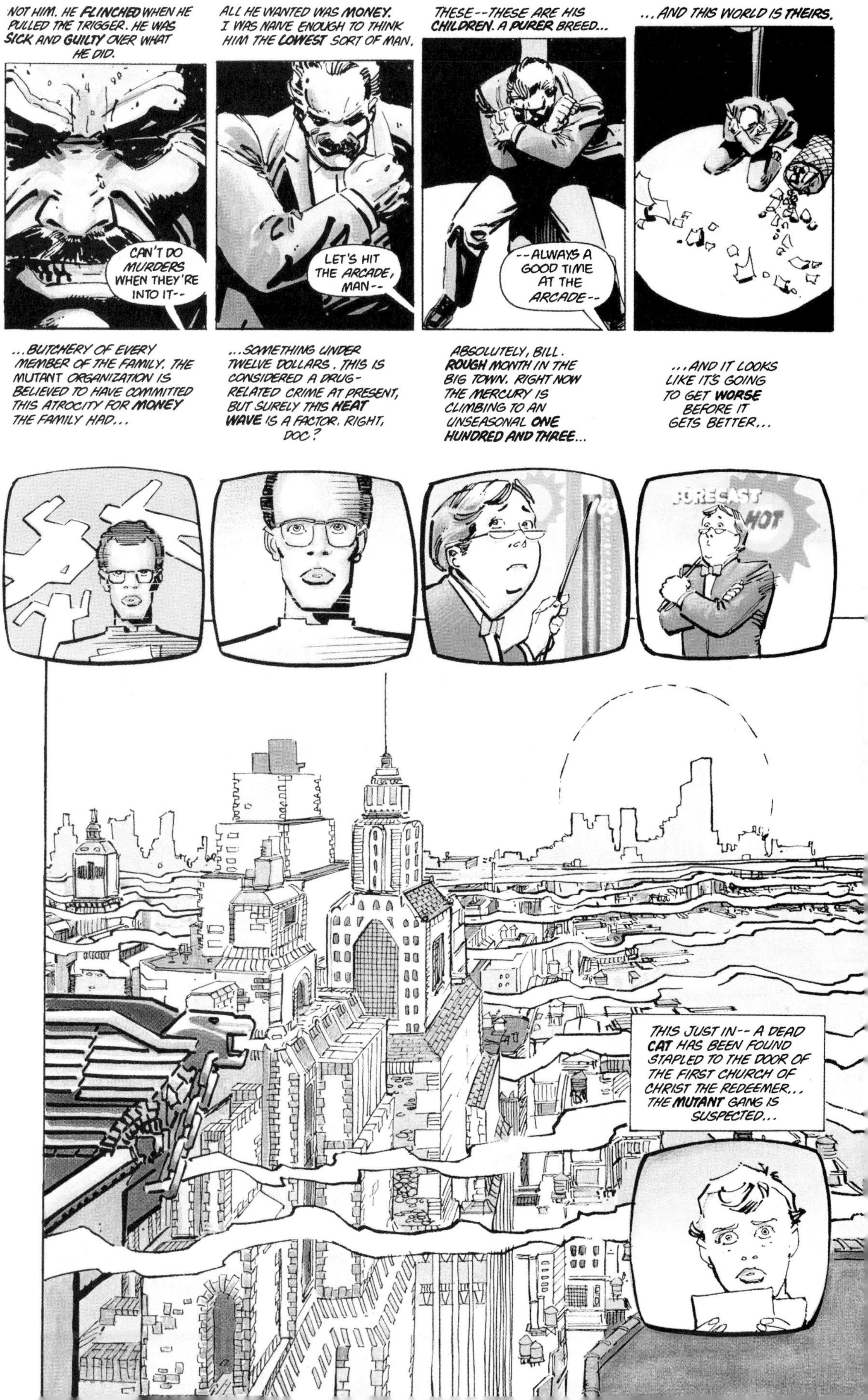

NOT HIM. HE FLINCHED WHEN HE PULLED THE TRIGGER. HE WAS SICK AND GUILTY OVER WHAT HE DID.
CAN'T DO MURDERS WHEN THEY'RE INTO IT--
ALL HE WANTED WAS MONEY. I WAS NAIVE ENOUGH TO THINK HIM THE LOWEST SORT OF MAN.
LET'S HIT THE ARCADE, MAN--
THESE--THESE ARE HIS CHILDREN. A PURER BREED...
--ALWAYS A GOOD TIME AT THE ARCADE--
...AND THIS WORLD IS THEIRS.
...BUTCHERY OF EVERY MEMBER OF THE FAMILY. THE MUTANT ORGANIZATION IS BELIEVED TO HAVE COMMITTED THIS ATROCITY FOR MONEY THE FAMILY HAD...
...SOMETHING UNDER TWELVE DOLLARS. THIS IS CONSIDERED A DRUG-RELATED CRIME AT PRESENT, BUT SURELY THIS HEAT WAVE IS A FACTOR. RIGHT, DOC?
ABSOLUTELY, BILL. ROUGH MONTH IN THE BIG TOWN. RIGHT NOW THE MERCURY IS CLIMBING TO AN UNSEASONAL ONE HUNDRED AND THREE...
...AND IT LOOKS LIKE IT'S GOING TO GET WORSE BEFORE IT GETS BETTER...
FORECAST
HOT
THIS JUST IN-- A DEAD CAT HAS BEEN FOUND STAPLED TO THE DOOR OF THE FIRST CHURCH OF CHRIST THE REDEEMER... THE MUTANT GANG IS SUSPECTED...

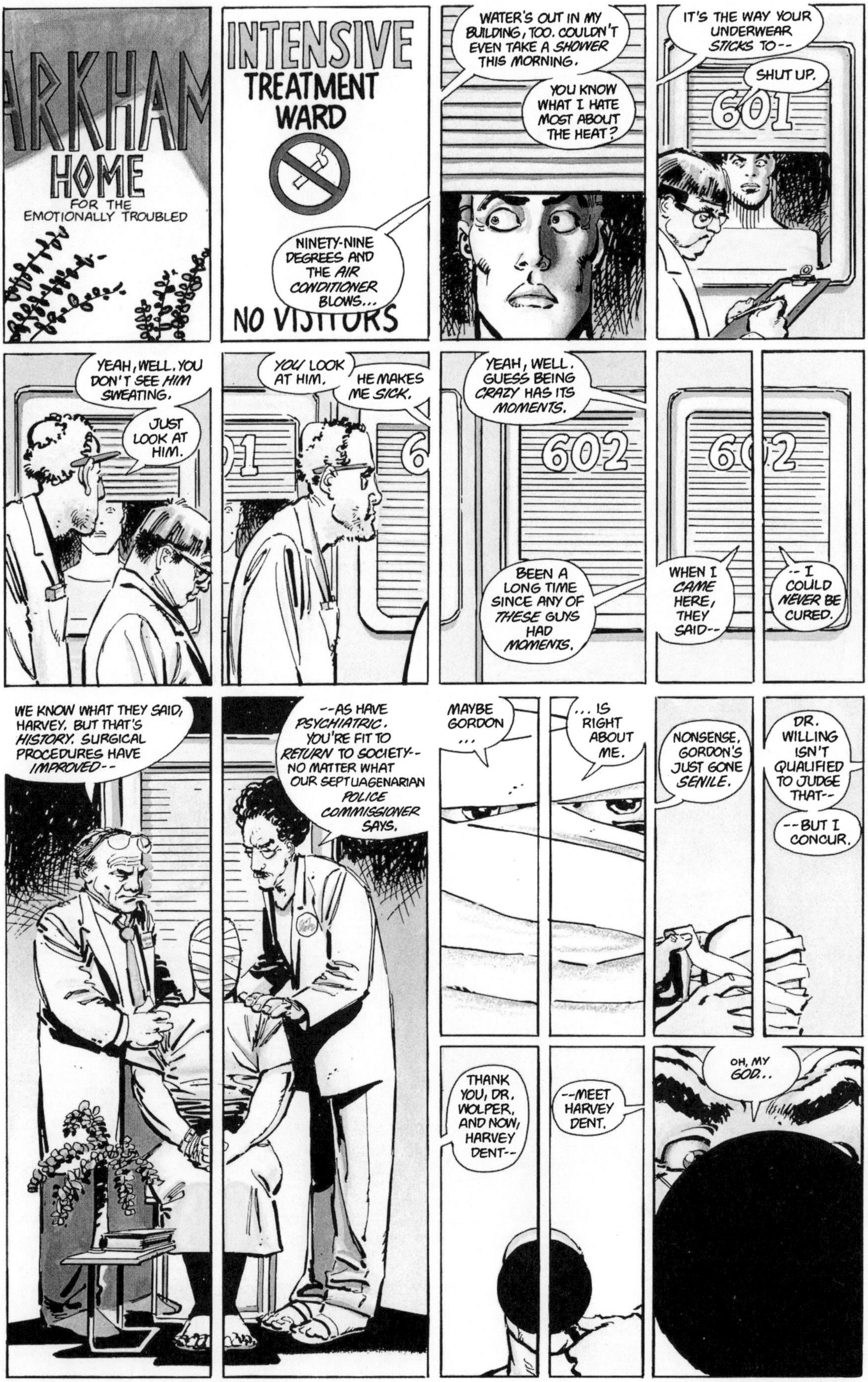
ARKHAM HOME FOR THE EMOTIONALLY TROUBLED
INTENSIVE TREATMENT WARD
NINETY-NINE DEGREES AND THE AIR CONDITIONER BLOWS...
NO VISITORS
WATER'S OUT IN MY BUILDING, TOO. COULDN'T EVEN TAKE A SHOWER THIS MORNING.
YOU KNOW WHAT I HATE MOST ABOUT THE HEAT?
IT'S THE WAY YOUR UNDERWEAR STICKS TO--
SHUT UP.
601
YEAH, WELL. YOU DON'T SEE HIM SWEATING.
JUST LOOK AT HIM.
YOU LOOK AT HIM.
HE MAKES ME SICK.
YEAH, WELL. GUESS BEING CRAZY HAS ITS MOMENTS.
602
BEEN A LONG TIME SINCE ANY OF THESE GUYS HAD MOMENTS.
602
WHEN I CAME HERE, THEY SAID--
--I COULD NEVER BE CURED.
WE KNOW WHAT THEY SAID, HARVEY. BUT THAT'S HISTORY. SURGICAL PROCEDURES HAVE IMPROVED--
--AS HAVE PSYCHIATRIC. YOU'RE FIT TO RETURN TO SOCIETY--NO MATTER WHAT OUR SEPTUAGENARIAN POLICE COMMISSIONER SAYS.
MAYBE GORDON ...
... IS RIGHT ABOUT ME.
NONSENSE, GORDON'S JUST GONE SENILE.
DR. WILLING ISN'T QUALIFIED TO JUDGE THAT--
--BUT I CONCUR.
THANK YOU, DR. WOLPER, AND NOW, HARVEY DENT--
--MEET HARVEY DENT.
OH, MY GOD...

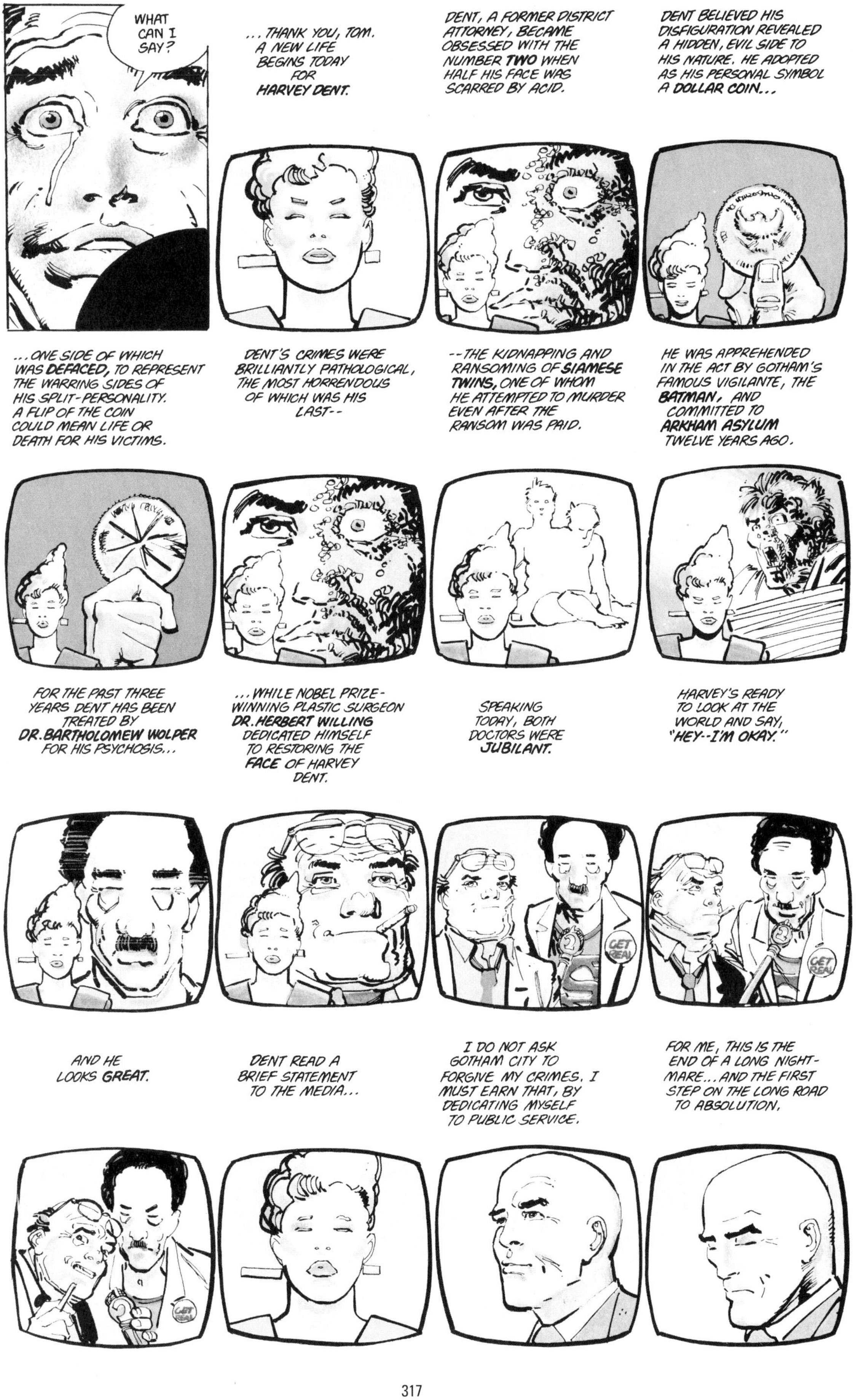
WHAT CAN I SAY?
...THANK YOU, TOM. A NEW LIFE BEGINS TODAY FOR HARVEY DENT.
DENT, A FORMER DISTRICT ATTORNEY, BECAME OBSESSED WITH THE NUMBER TWO WHEN HALF HIS FACE WAS SCARRED BY ACID.
DENT BELIEVED HIS DISFIGURATION REVEALED A HIDDEN, EVIL SIDE TO HIS NATURE. HE ADOPTED AS HIS PERSONAL SYMBOL A DOLLAR COIN...
...ONE SIDE OF WHICH WAS DEFACED, TO REPRESENT THE WARRING SIDES OF HIS SPLIT-PERSONALITY. A FLIP OF THE COIN COULD MEAN LIFE OR DEATH FOR HIS VICTIMS.
DENT'S CRIMES WERE BRILLIANTLY PATHOLOGICAL, THE MOST HORRENDOUS OF WHICH WAS HIS LAST--
--THE KIDNAPPING AND RANSOMING OF SIAMESE TWINS, ONE OF WHOM HE ATTEMPTED TO MURDER EVEN AFTER THE RANSOM WAS PAID.
HE WAS APPREHENDED IN THE ACT BY GOTHAM'S FAMOUS VIGILANTE, THE BATMAN, AND COMMITTED TO ARKHAM ASYLUM TWELVE YEARS AGO.
FOR THE PAST THREE YEARS DENT HAS BEEN TREATED BY DR. BARTHOLOMEW WOLPER FOR HIS PSYCHOSIS...
...WHILE NOBEL PRIZE-WINNING PLASTIC SURGEON DR. HERBERT WILLING DEDICATED HIMSELF TO RESTORING THE FACE OF HARVEY DENT.
SPEAKING TODAY, BOTH DOCTORS WERE JUBILANT.
HARVEY'S READY TO LOOK AT THE WORLD AND SAY, "HEY--I'M OKAY."
GET REAL
GET REAL
AND HE LOOKS GREAT.
DENT READ A BRIEF STATEMENT TO THE MEDIA...
I DO NOT ASK GOTHAM CITY TO FORGIVE MY CRIMES. I MUST EARN THAT, BY DEDICATING MYSELF TO PUBLIC SERVICE.
FOR ME, THIS IS THE END OF A LONG NIGHTMARE... AND THE FIRST STEP ON THE LONG ROAD TO ABSOLUTION.
GET REAL

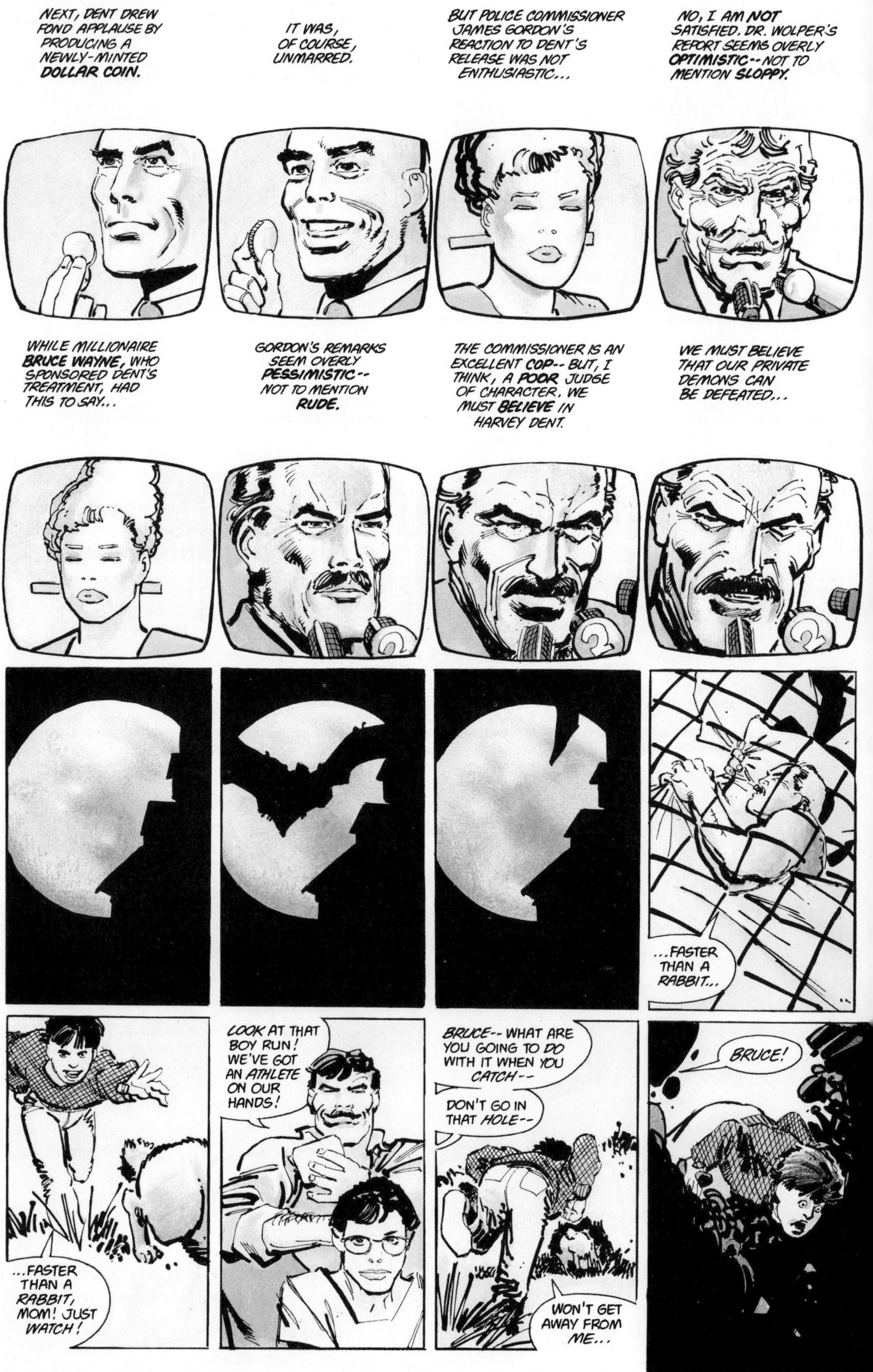
NEXT, DENT DREW FOND APPLAUSE BY PRODUCING A NEWLY-MINTED DOLLAR COIN.
IT WAS, OF COURSE, UNMARRED.
BUT POLICE COMMISSIONER JAMES GORDON'S REACTION TO DENT'S RELEASE WAS NOT ENTHUSIASTIC...
NO, I AM NOT SATISFIED. DR. WOLPER'S REPORT SEEMS OVERLY OPTIMISTIC-- NOT TO MENTION SLOPPY.
WHILE MILLIONAIRE BRUCE WAYNE, WHO SPONSORED DENT'S TREATMENT, HAD THIS TO SAY...
GORDON'S REMARKS SEEM OVERLY PESSIMISTIC-- NOT TO MENTION RUDE.
THE COMMISSIONER IS AN EXCELLENT COP-- BUT, I THINK, A POOR JUDGE OF CHARACTER. WE MUST BELIEVE IN HARVEY DENT.
WE MUST BELIEVE THAT OUR PRIVATE DEMONS CAN BE DEFEATED...
...FASTER THAN A RABBIT...
...FASTER THAN A RABBIT, MOM! JUST WATCH!
LOOK AT THAT BOY RUN! WE'VE GOT AN ATHLETE ON OUR HANDS!
BRUCE-- WHAT ARE YOU GOING TO DO WITH IT WHEN YOU CATCH--
DON'T GO IN THAT HOLE--
WON'T GET AWAY FROM ME...
BRUCE!

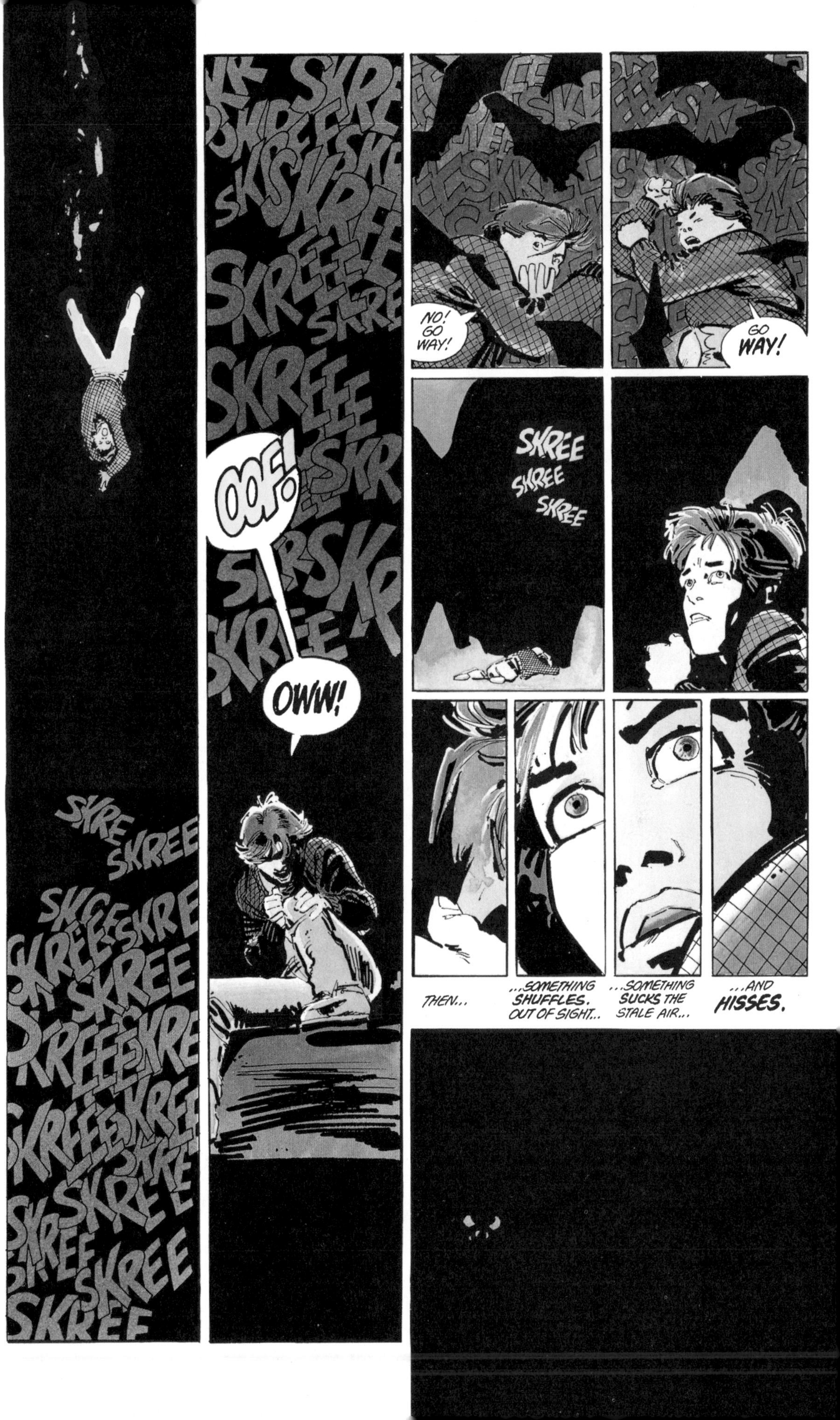
SKREE
SKREE
OOF!
OWW!
NO! GO WAY!
GO WAY!
SKREE
SKREE
SKREE
THEN...
...SOMETHING SHUFFLES. OUT OF SIGHT...
...SOMETHING SUCKS THE STALE AIR...
...AND HISSES.

GLIDING WITH *ANCIENT* GRACE...

UNWILLING TO *RETREAT* AS HIS BROTHERS DID...

EYES *GLEAMING*, UNTOUCHED BY LOVE OR JOY OR SORROW...

BREATH *HOT* WITH THE TASTE OF FALLEN FOES...THE STENCH OF *DEAD THINGS, DAMNED THINGS*...

SURELY THE *FIERCEST* SURVIVOR-- THE *PUREST WARRIOR*...

GLARING, *HATING*...

...*CLAIMING* ME AS HIS *OWN*.

DREAMING...

I WAS ONLY SIX YEARS OLD WHEN THAT HAPPENED. WHEN I FIRST SAW THE *CAVE*...

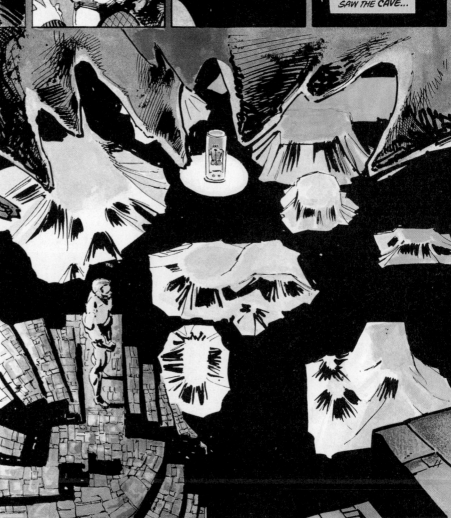

...HUGE, EMPTY, SILENT AS A *CHURCH*, *WAITING*, AS THE *BAT* WAS WAITING.

AND NOW THE *COBWEBS* GROW AND THE DUST *THICKENS* IN HERE AS IT DOES IN *ME*--

--AND HE *LAUGHS* AT ME, *CURSES* ME. CALLS ME A *FOOL*. HE FILLS MY *SLEEP*, HE *TRICKS* ME. BRINGS ME HERE WHEN THE NIGHT IS *LONG* AND MY WILL IS *WEAK*. HE *STRUGGLES* RELENTLESSLY, HATEFULLY, TO BE *FREE*--

I WILL NOT *LET* HIM. I GAVE MY *WORD*.

FOR *JASON*.

NEVER.

NEVER AGAIN.

MASTER BRUCE?

YOU SET OFF THE ALARM, SIR.

THIS *SOMNAMBU-LISM* IS BECOMING A BIT OF A *PROBLEM*, CERTAINLY FOR THOSE OF US WITH A *PENCHANT* FOR SLEEPING IN OUR *BEDS*.

IT'S THE *SPIRITS*, I SUSPECT. TENDS TO MAKE ONE OVERLY *SENTIMENTAL*

COME, SIR. HARDLY THE HOUR FOR *ANTIQUES*, IS IT?

...HARDLY, ALFRED. SORRY TO WAKE YOU.

IT *IS* HALF PAST THREE ...

MASTER BRUCE.

WHATEVER HAPPENED TO YOUR *MUSTACHE?*

FOR ME, THIS IS THE END OF A LONG NIGHT-MARE...AND THE FIRST STEP ON THE LONG ROAD TO ABSOLUTION.

..., THOSE WERE THE LAST WORDS SPOKEN IN PUBLIC BY HARVEY DENT BEFORE HIS DISAPPEARANCE THIS MORNING.

WHILE POLICE COMMISSIONER GORDON ISSUED AN ALL POINTS BULLETIN FOR DENT, ONE VOICE WAS RAISED IN PROTEST...

...THAT OF **DR. BARTHOLOMEW WOLPER,** DENT'S PSYCHIATRIST...

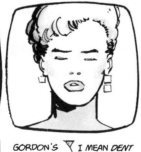

SO--WHAT DO YOU THINK?

I THINK IT'S TOO DAMN *HOT*--

--AND I THINK HE SHOULD SEE IT OR FOLD.

GORDON'S REACTION IS ONE OF TEXT BOOK HYSTERIA...

I MEAN *DENT* --NOT *DIP* STICK HERE.

SO DO I. OUGHTTA SEE IT OR FOLD.

WE BEEN GETTING BY WITHOUT HIM.

UH HUH.

...AND CHARACTERISTIC INSENSITIVITY. HARVEY, ON THE OTHER HAND, IS AN EXTREMELY SENSITIVE MAN...

I MEAN, IT AIN'T BEEN *GREAT*...

THAT'S RIGHT.

...IN EXTREMELY VULNERABLE EMOTIONAL CONDITION. I BELIEVE...

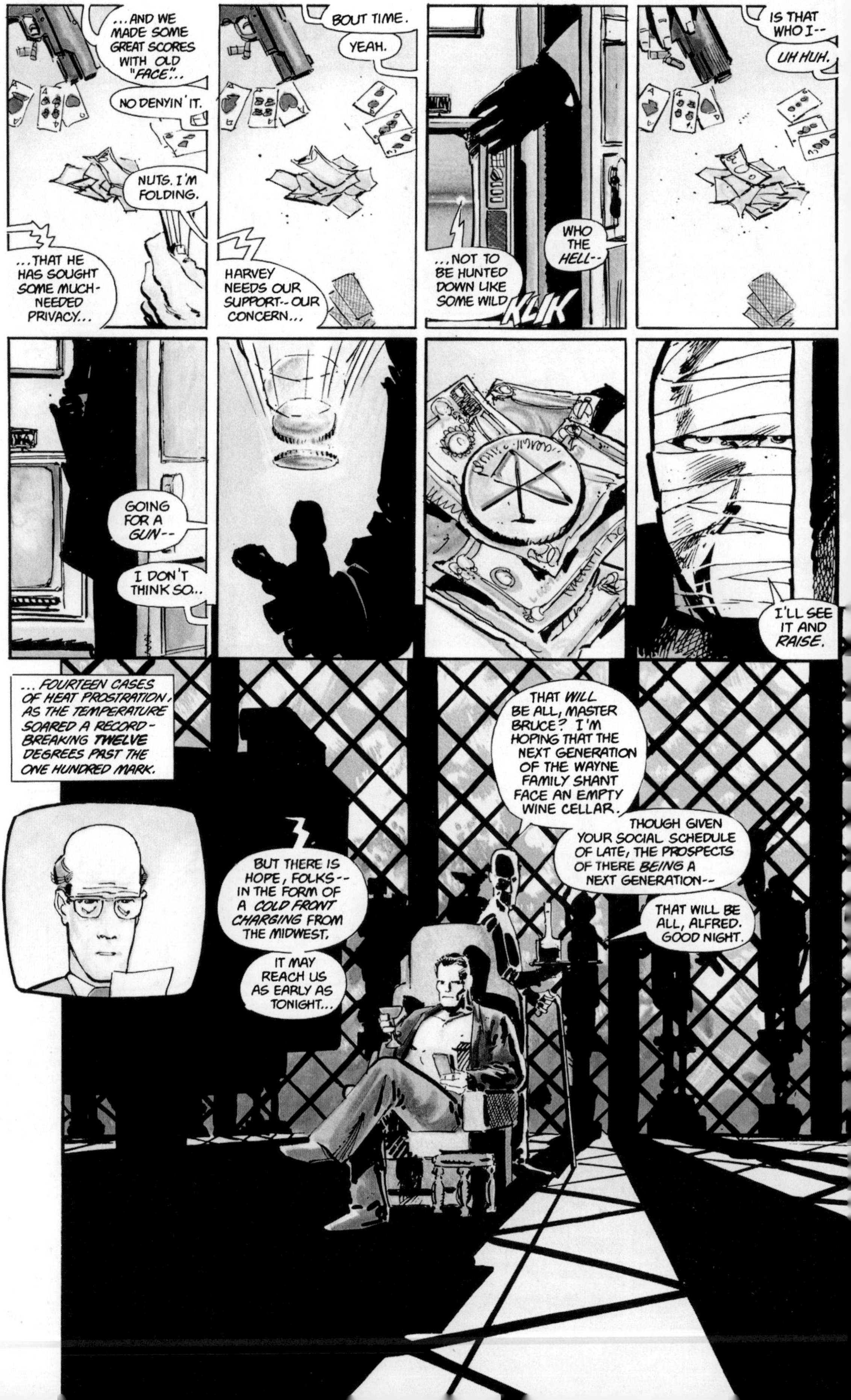
...AND WE MADE SOME GREAT SCORES WITH OLD "FACE"...
NO DENYIN' IT.
NUTS. I'M FOLDING.
...THAT HE HAS SOUGHT SOME MUCH-NEEDED PRIVACY...
BOUT TIME.
YEAH.
HARVEY NEEDS OUR SUPPORT--OUR CONCERN...
...NOT TO BE HUNTED DOWN LIKE SOME WILD
WHO THE HELL--
KLIK
IS THAT WHO I--
UH HUH.
GOING FOR A GUN--
I DON'T THINK SO...
I'LL SEE IT AND RAISE.
...FOURTEEN CASES OF HEAT PROSTRATION, AS THE TEMPERATURE SOARED A RECORD-BREAKING TWELVE DEGREES PAST THE ONE HUNDRED MARK.
BUT THERE IS HOPE, FOLKS--IN THE FORM OF A COLD FRONT CHARGING FROM THE MIDWEST.
IT MAY REACH US AS EARLY AS TONIGHT...
THAT WILL BE ALL, MASTER BRUCE? I'M HOPING THAT THE NEXT GENERATION OF THE WAYNE FAMILY SHANT FACE AN EMPTY WINE CELLAR.
THOUGH GIVEN YOUR SOCIAL SCHEDULE OF LATE, THE PROSPECTS OF THERE BEING A NEXT GENERATION--
THAT WILL BE ALL, ALFRED. GOOD NIGHT.

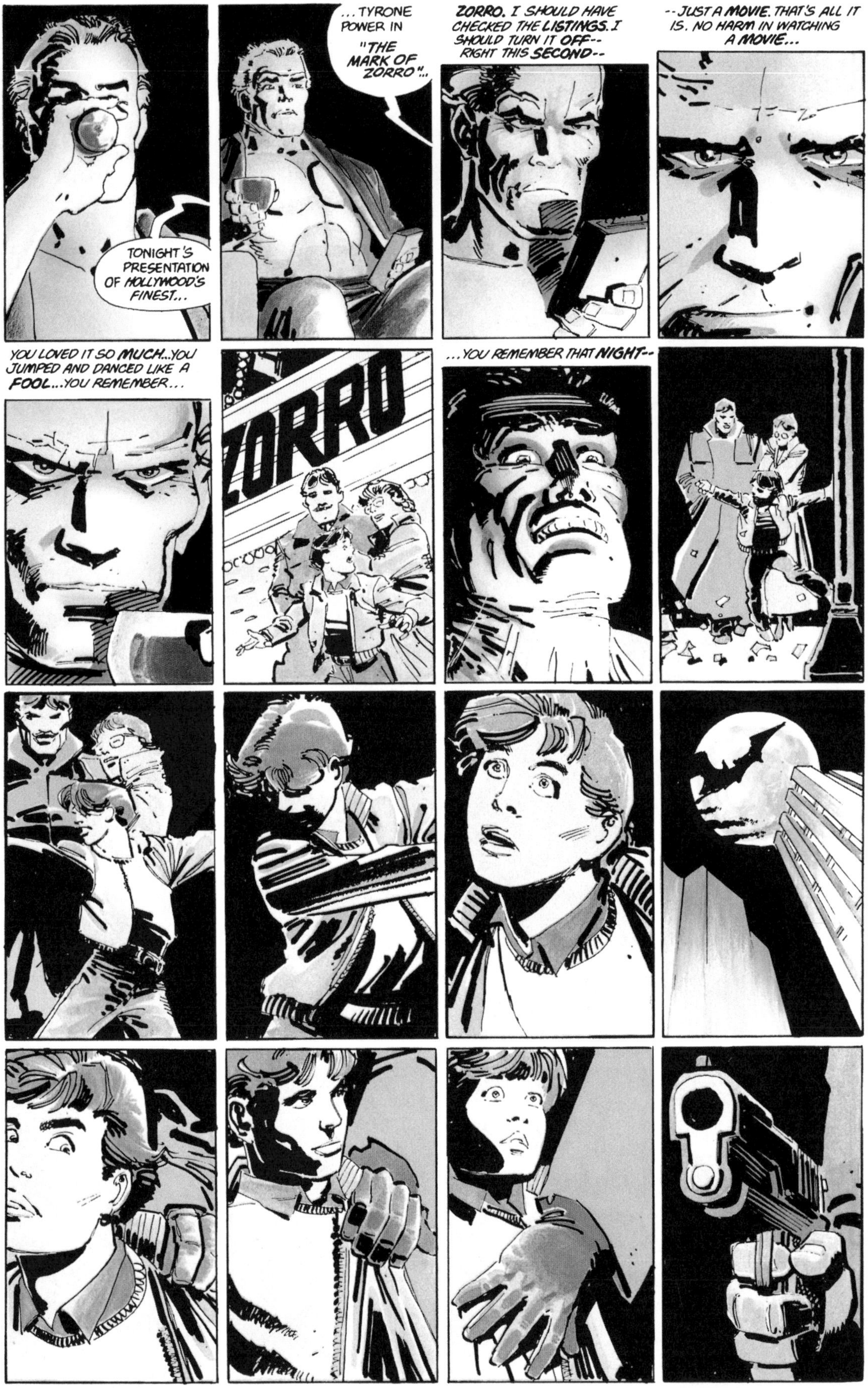
TONIGHT'S PRESENTATION OF HOLLYWOOD'S FINEST...
...TYRONE POWER IN "THE MARK OF ZORRO"...
ZORRO. I SHOULD HAVE CHECKED THE LISTINGS. I SHOULD TURN IT OFF-- RIGHT THIS SECOND--
--JUST A MOVIE. THAT'S ALL IT IS. NO HARM IN WATCHING A MOVIE...
YOU LOVED IT SO MUCH...YOU JUMPED AND DANCED LIKE A FOOL...YOU REMEMBER...
ZORRO
...YOU REMEMBER THAT NIGHT--

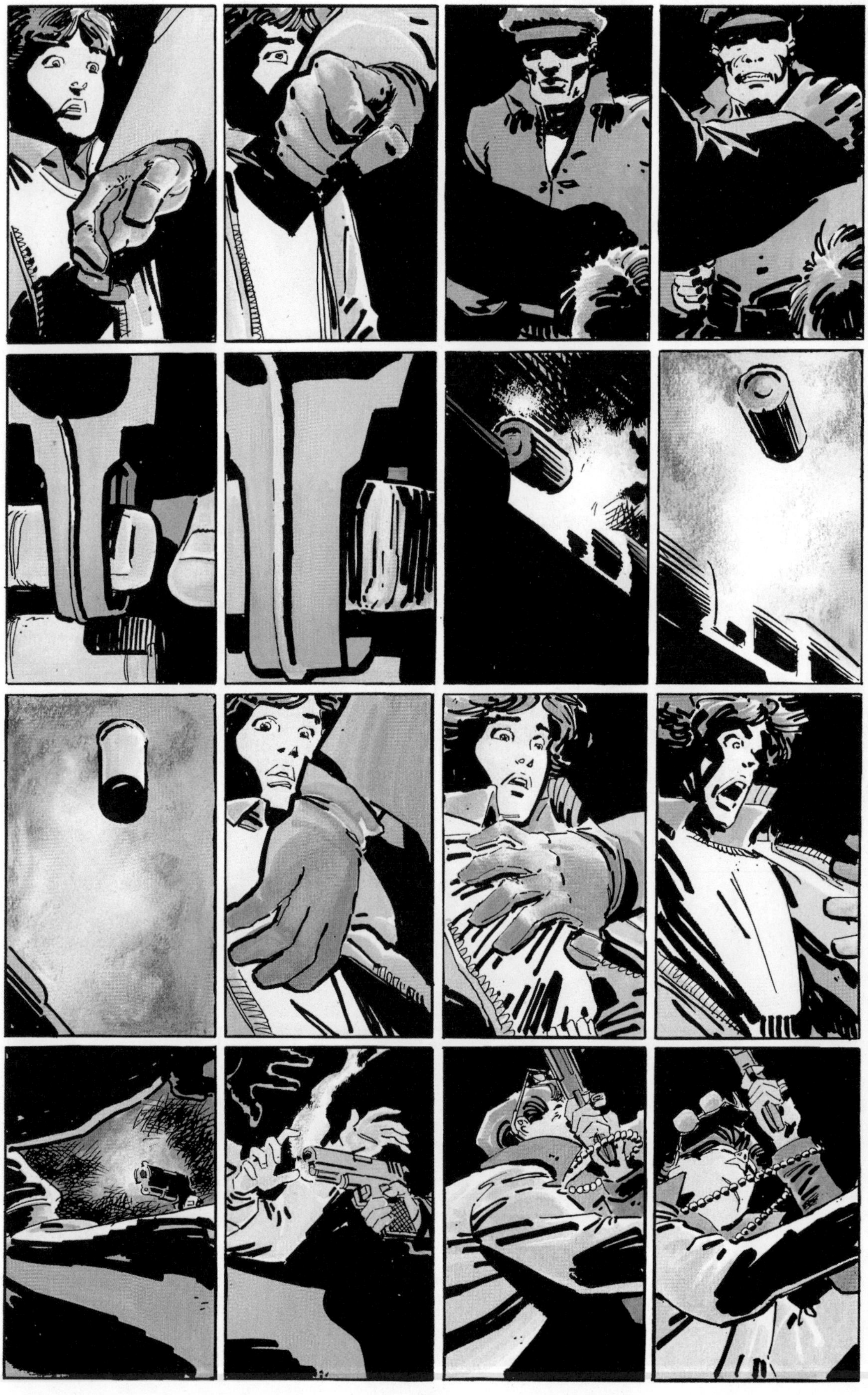

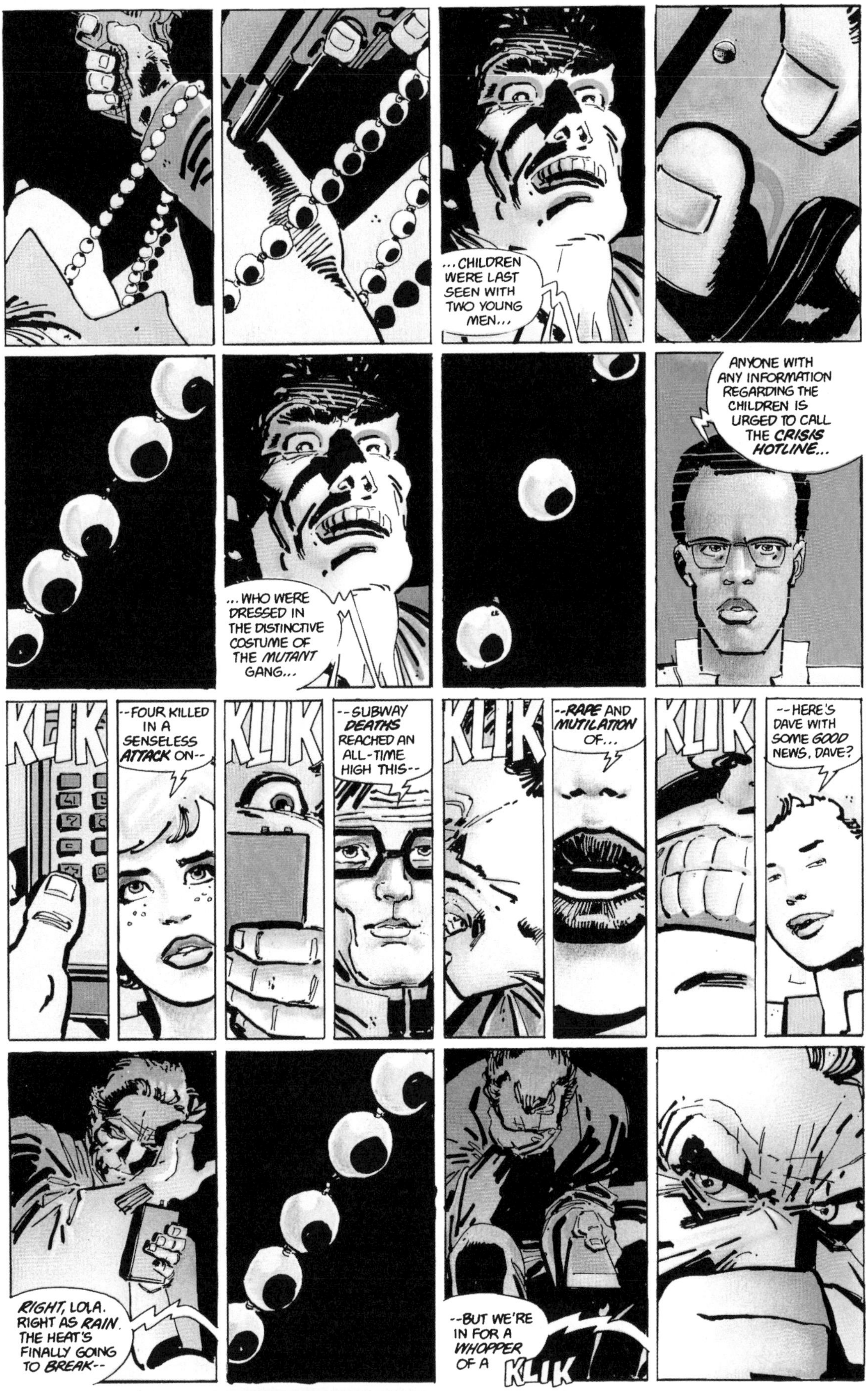
...CHILDREN WERE LAST SEEN WITH TWO YOUNG MEN...
...WHO WERE DRESSED IN THE DISTINCTIVE COSTUME OF THE MUTANT GANG...
ANYONE WITH ANY INFORMATION REGARDING THE CHILDREN IS URGED TO CALL THE CRISIS HOTLINE...
KLIK
--FOUR KILLED IN A SENSELESS ATTACK ON--
KLIK
--SUBWAY DEATHS REACHED AN ALL-TIME HIGH THIS--
KLIK
--RAPE AND MUTILATION OF...
KLIK
--HERE'S DAVE WITH SOME GOOD NEWS, DAVE?
RIGHT, LOLA. RIGHT AS RAIN. THE HEAT'S FINALLY GOING TO BREAK--
--BUT WE'RE IN FOR A WHOPPER OF A
KLIK

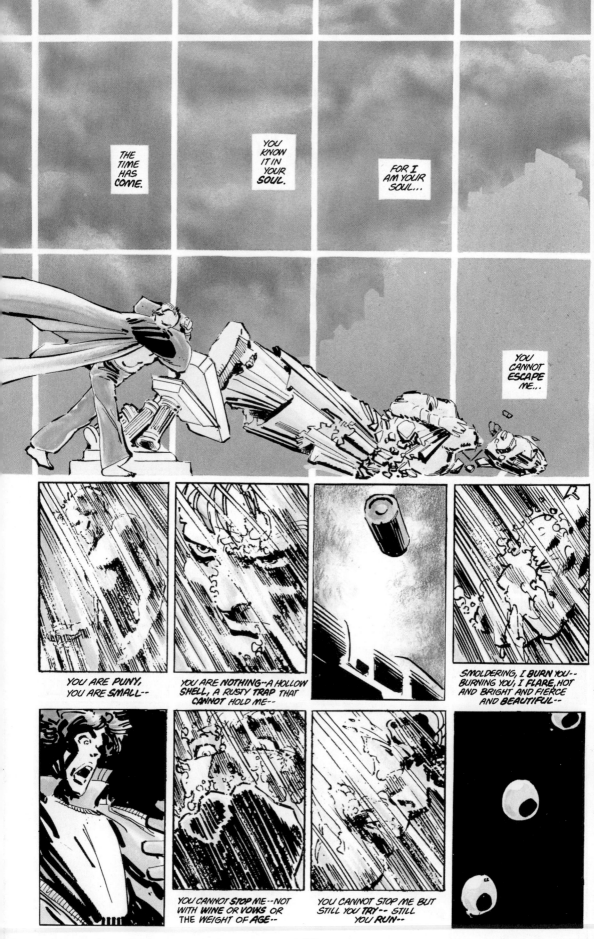

THE TIME HAS COME.

YOU KNOW IT IN YOUR SOUL.

FOR I AM YOUR SOUL...

YOU CANNOT ESCAPE ME...

YOU ARE PUNY, YOU ARE SMALL--

YOU ARE NOTHING--A HOLLOW SHELL, A RUSTY TRAP THAT CANNOT HOLD ME--

SMOLDERING, I BURN YOU-- BURNING YOU, I FLARE, HOT AND BRIGHT AND FIERCE AND BEAUTIFUL--

YOU CANNOT STOP ME--NOT WITH WINE OR VOWS OR THE WEIGHT OF AGE--

YOU CANNOT STOP ME BUT STILL YOU TRY-- STILL YOU RUN--

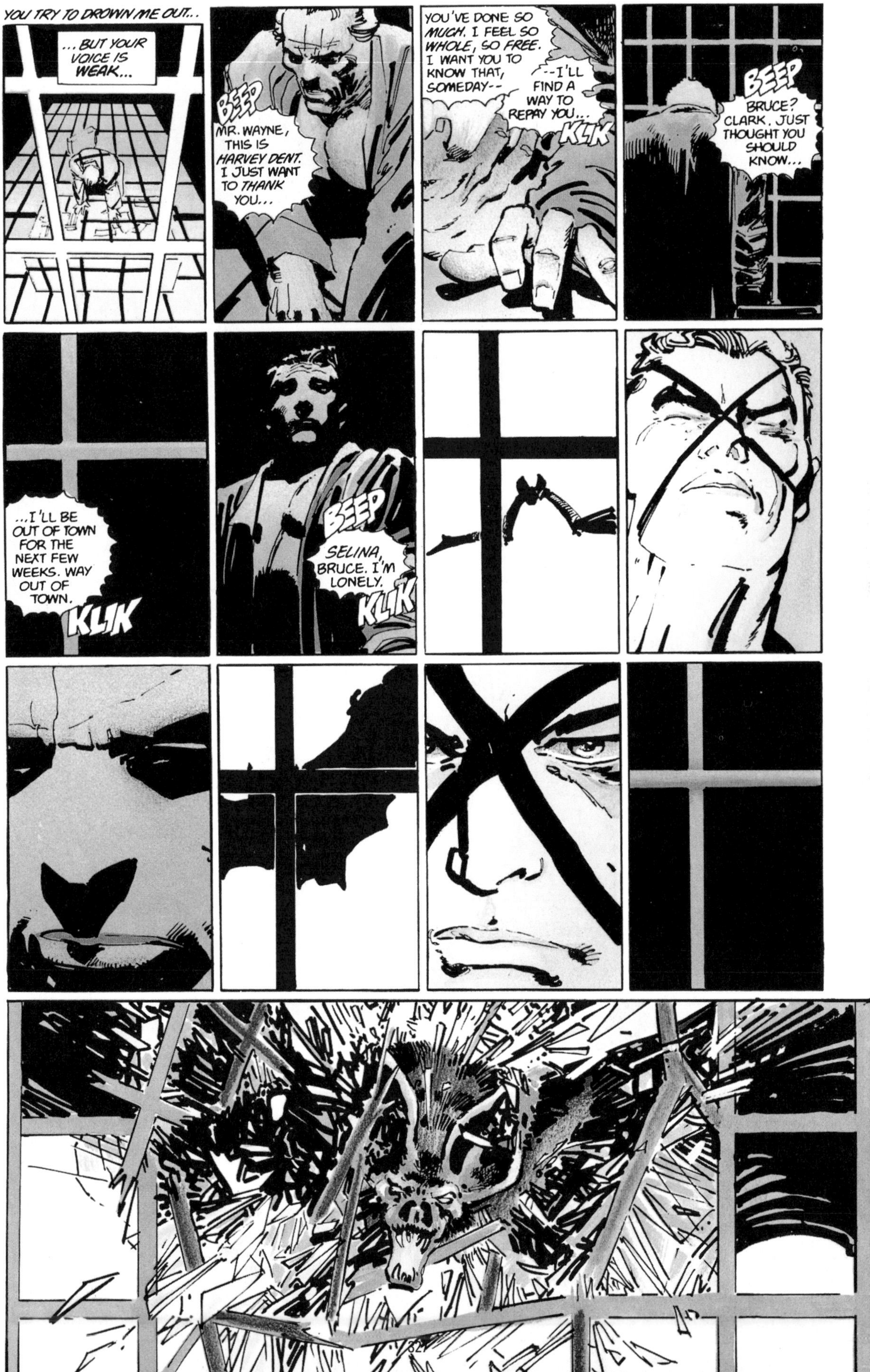
YOU TRY TO DROWN ME OUT...
...BUT YOUR VOICE IS WEAK...
BEEP
MR. WAYNE, THIS IS HARVEY DENT. I JUST WANT TO THANK YOU...
YOU'VE DONE SO MUCH. I FEEL SO WHOLE, SO FREE. I WANT YOU TO KNOW THAT, SOMEDAY--
--I'LL FIND A WAY TO REPAY YOU...
KLIK
BEEP
BRUCE? CLARK. JUST THOUGHT YOU SHOULD KNOW...
...I'LL BE OUT OF TOWN FOR THE NEXT FEW WEEKS. WAY OUT OF TOWN.
KLIK
BEEP
SELINA, BRUCE. I'M LONELY.
KLIK

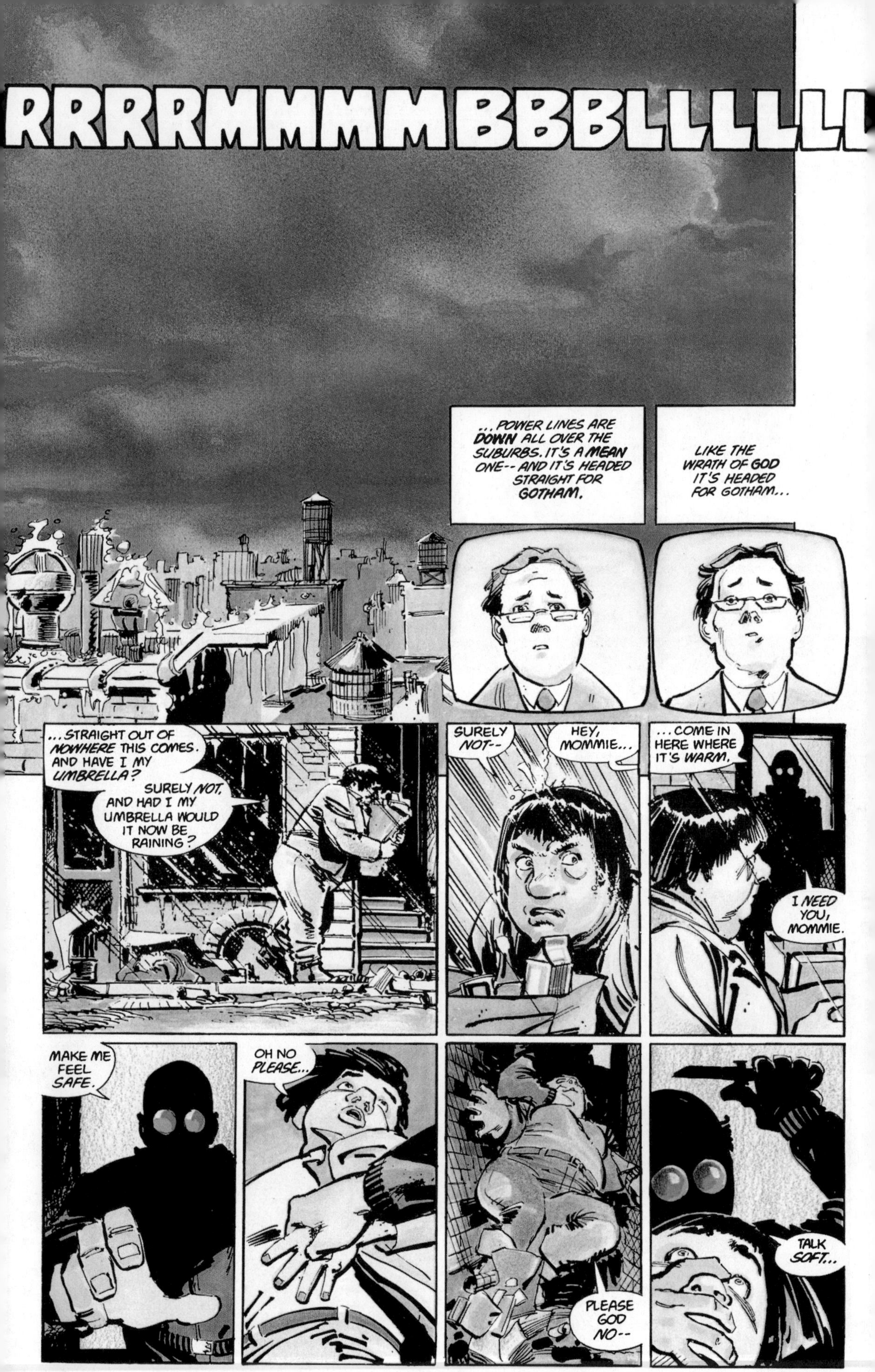
RRRRMMMMBBBLLLLL
...POWER LINES ARE DOWN ALL OVER THE SUBURBS. IT'S A MEAN ONE-- AND IT'S HEADED STRAIGHT FOR GOTHAM.
LIKE THE WRATH OF GOD IT'S HEADED FOR GOTHAM...
...STRAIGHT OUT OF NOWHERE THIS COMES. AND HAVE I MY UMBRELLA?
SURELY NOT. AND HAD I MY UMBRELLA WOULD IT NOW BE RAINING?
SURELY NOT--
HEY, MOMMIE...
...COME IN HERE WHERE IT'S WARM.
I NEED YOU, MOMMIE.
MAKE ME FEEL SAFE.
OH NO PLEASE...
PLEASE GOD NO--
TALK SOFT...

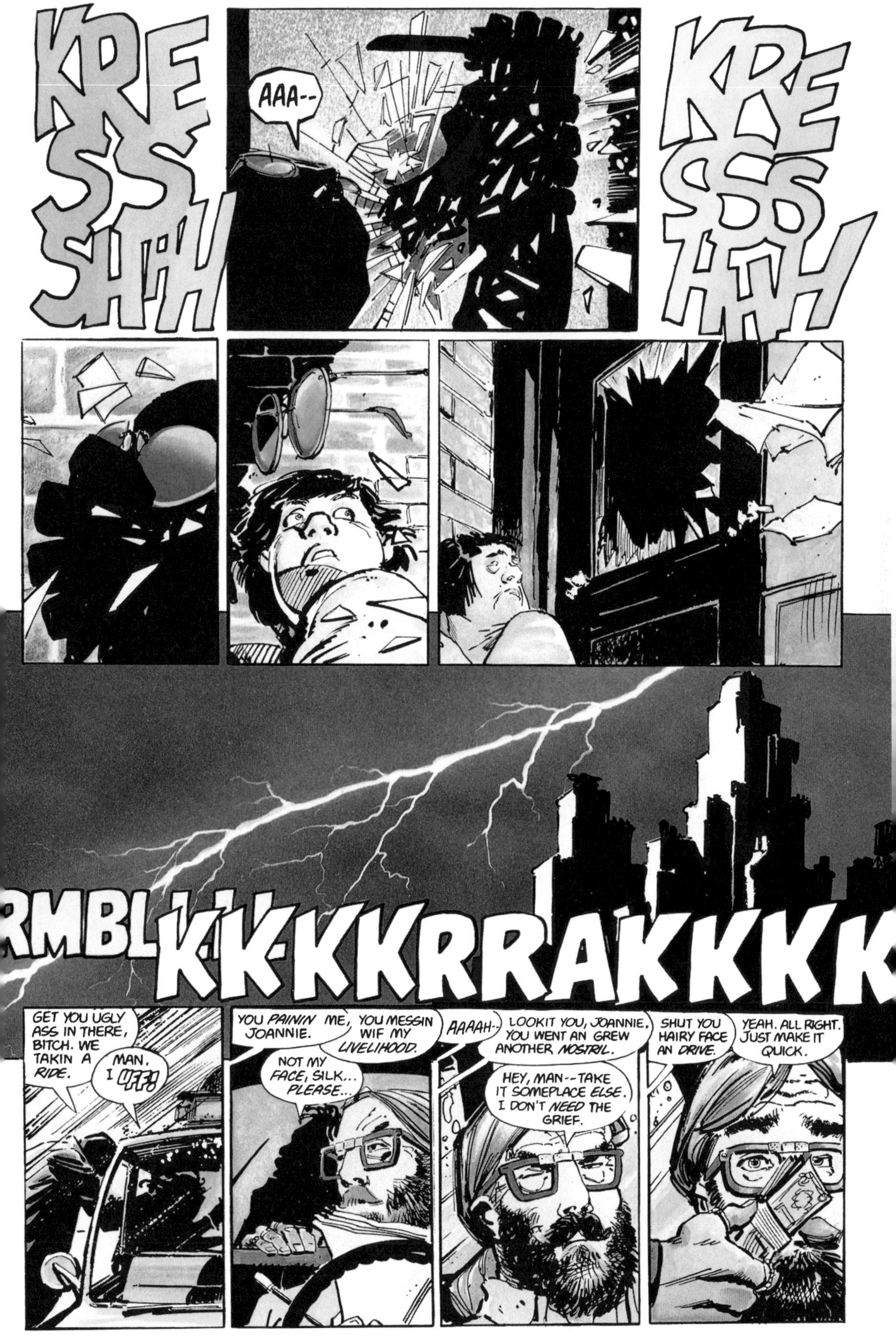
AAA--
GET YOU UGLY ASS IN THERE, BITCH. WE TAKIN A *RIDE*.
MAN, I *UFF!*
YOU *PAININ* ME, JOANNIE.
YOU MESSIN WIF MY *LIVELIHOOD*.
NOT MY *FACE*, SILK... *PLEASE*...
AAAAH--
LOOKIT YOU, JOANNIE. YOU WENT AN GREW ANOTHER *NOSTRIL*.
HEY, MAN--TAKE IT SOMEPLACE *ELSE*. I DON'T *NEED* THE GRIEF.
SHUT YOU HAIRY FACE AN *DRIVE*.
YEAH. ALL RIGHT. JUST MAKE IT QUICK.

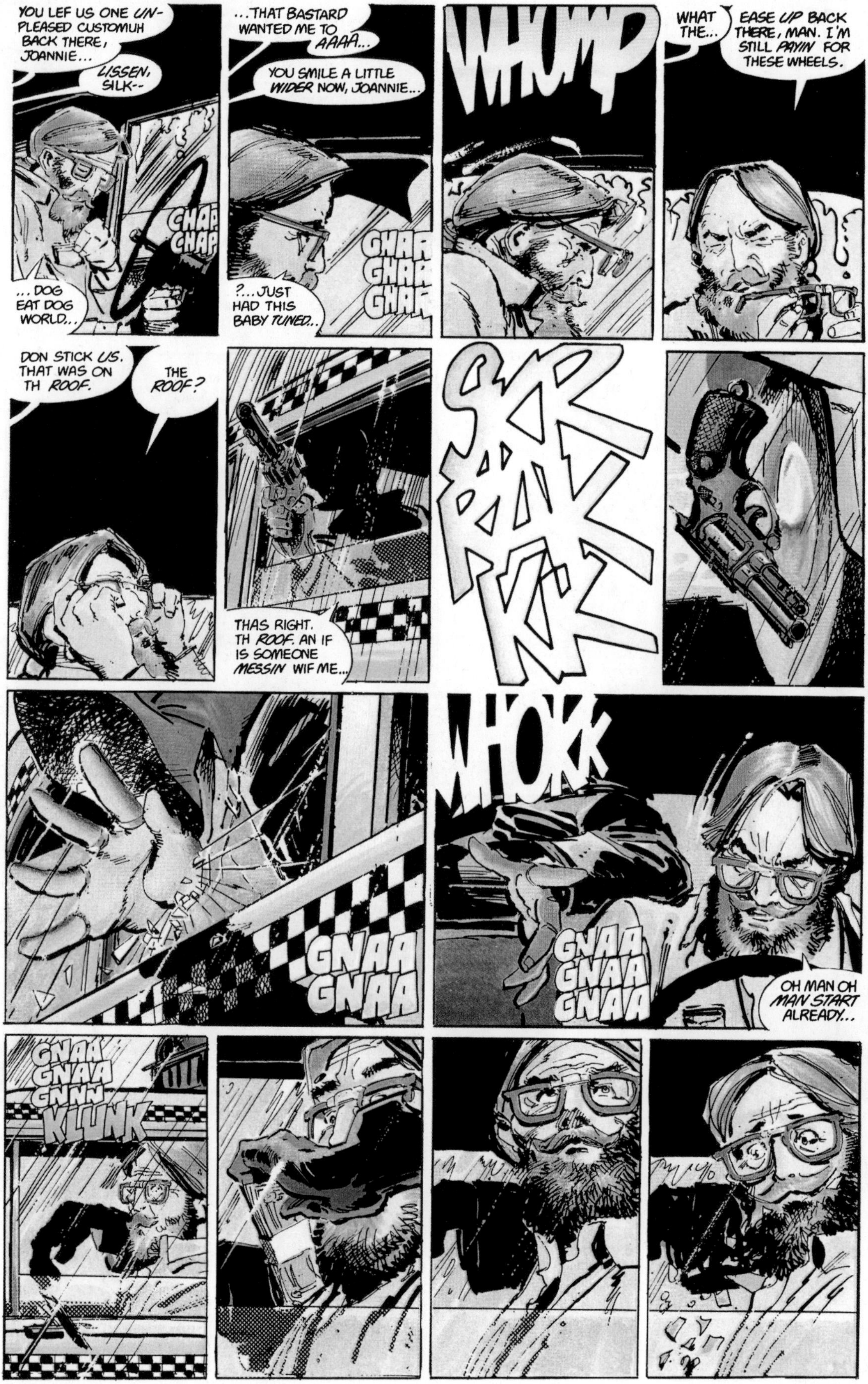
YOU LEF US ONE UN-PLEASED CUSTOMUH BACK THERE, JOANNIE...
LISSEN, SILK--
CHAP CHAP
...DOG EAT DOG WORLD...
...THAT BASTARD WANTED ME TO AAAA...
YOU SMILE A LITTLE WIDER NOW, JOANNIE...
GNAR GNAR GNAR
?...JUST HAD THIS BABY TUNED...
WHUMP
WHAT THE...
EASE UP BACK THERE, MAN. I'M STILL PAYIN FOR THESE WHEELS.
DON STICK US. THAT WAS ON TH ROOF.
THE ROOF?
THAS RIGHT. TH ROOF. AN IF IS SOMEONE MESSIN WIF ME...
SKRAKK
GNAA GNAA
WHOKK
GNAA GNAA GNAA
OH MAN OH MAN START ALREADY...
GNAA GNAA GNNN KLUNK

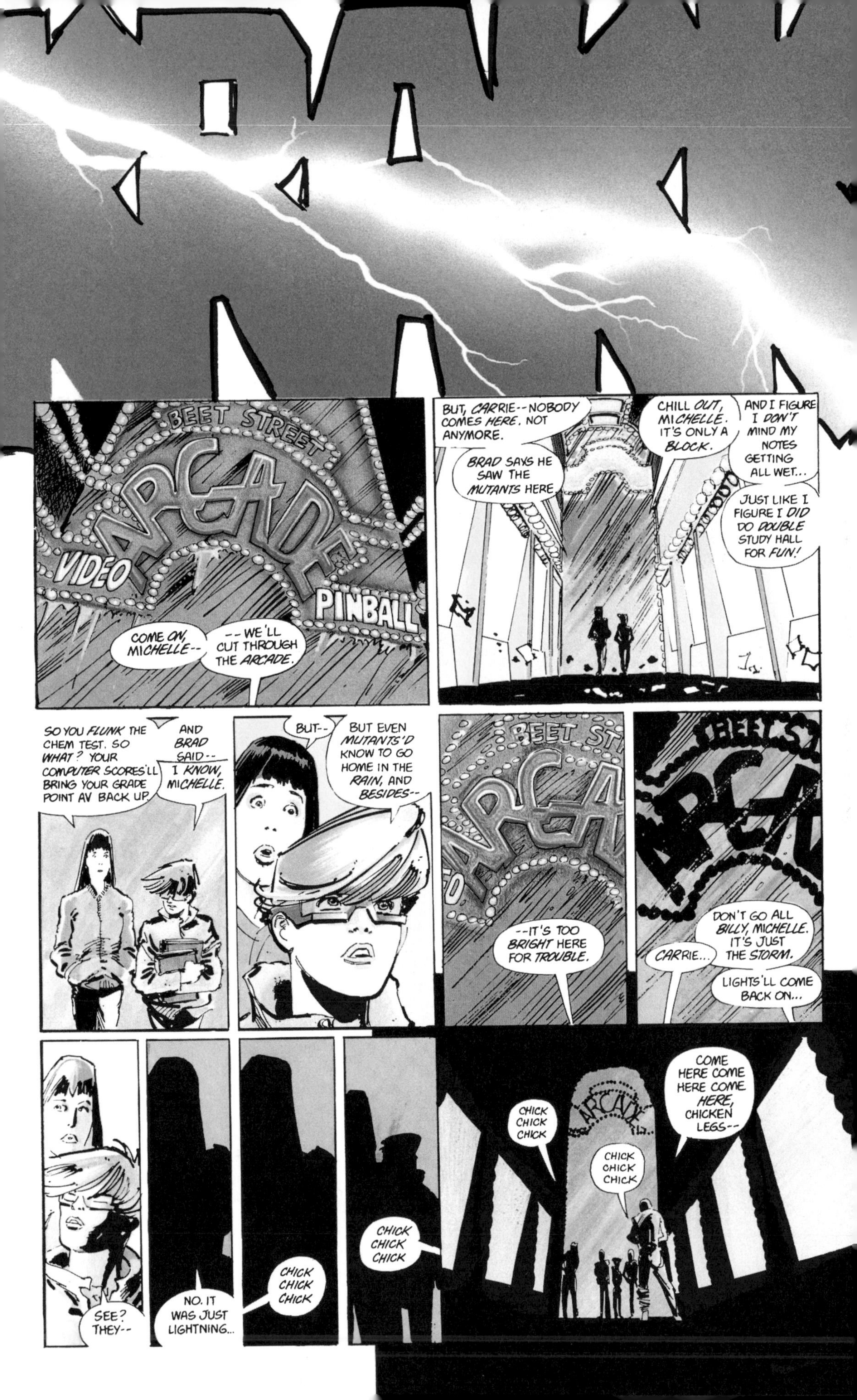
BEET STREET
VIDEO ARCADE
PINBALL
COME ON, MICHELLE--
--WE'LL CUT THROUGH THE ARCADE.
BUT, CARRIE--NOBODY COMES HERE. NOT ANYMORE.
BRAD SAYS HE SAW THE MUTANTS HERE.
CHILL OUT, MICHELLE. IT'S ONLY A BLOCK.
AND I FIGURE I DON'T MIND MY NOTES GETTING ALL WET...
JUST LIKE I FIGURE I DID DO DOUBLE STUDY HALL FOR FUN!
SO YOU FLUNK THE CHEM TEST. SO WHAT? YOUR COMPUTER SCORES'LL BRING YOUR GRADE POINT AV BACK UP.
AND BRAD SAID--
I KNOW, MICHELLE.
BUT--
BUT EVEN MUTANTS'D KNOW TO GO HOME IN THE RAIN, AND BESIDES--
--IT'S TOO BRIGHT HERE FOR TROUBLE.
CARRIE...
DON'T GO ALL BILLY, MICHELLE. IT'S JUST THE STORM.
LIGHTS'LL COME BACK ON...
SEE? THEY--
NO. IT WAS JUST LIGHTNING...
CHICK CHICK CHICK
CHICK CHICK CHICK
CHICK CHICK CHICK
ARCADE
CHICK CHICK CHICK
COME HERE COME HERE COME HERE, CHICKEN LEGS--

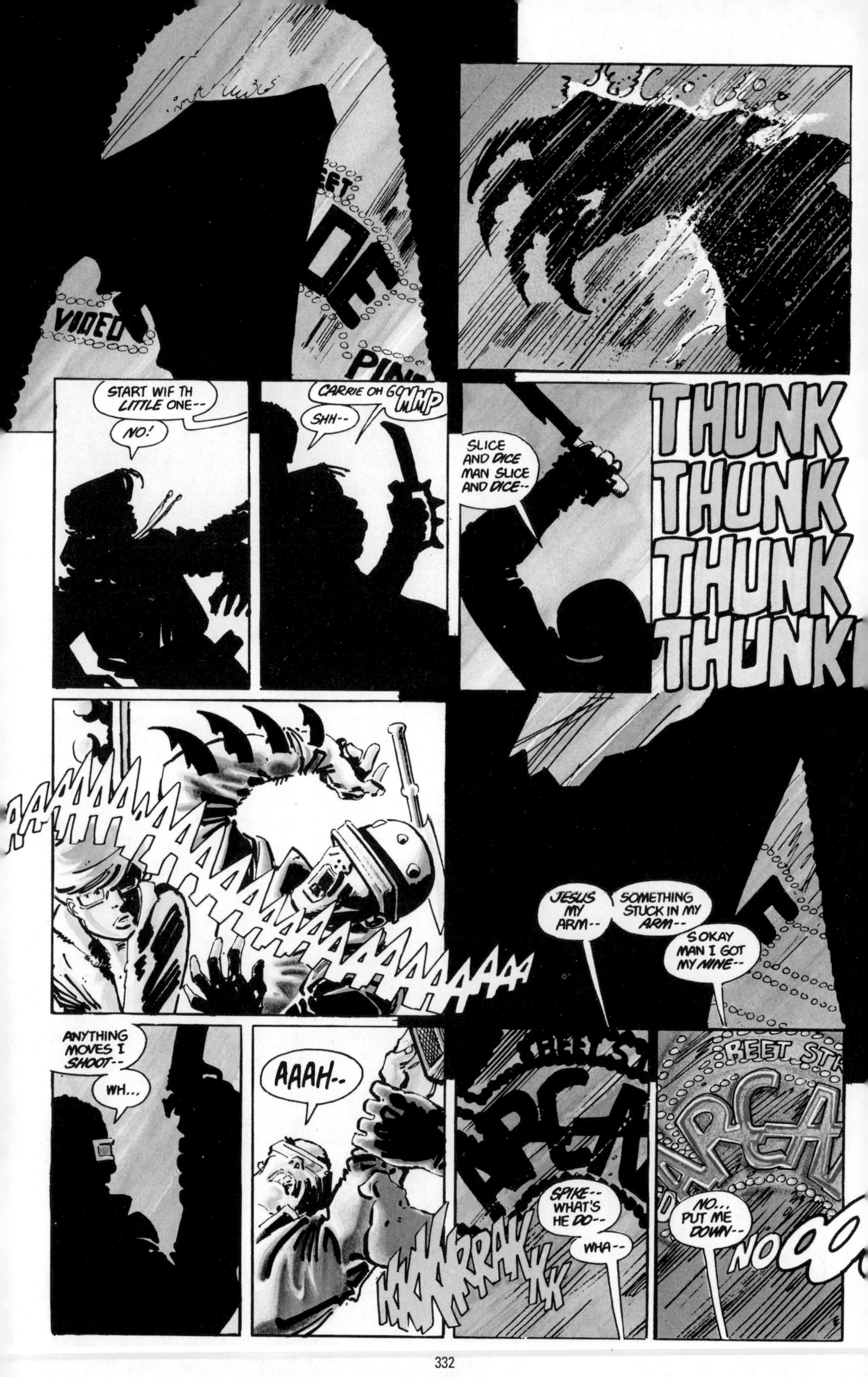
VIDEO
PIN
START WIF TH LITTLE ONE--
NO!
CARRIE OH GO MMP
SHH--
SLICE AND DICE MAN SLICE AND DICE--
THUNK
THUNK
THUNK
THUNK
AAAAAAAAAAAAAAAAAAAAAAAAAAAAA
JESUS MY ARM--
SOMETHING STUCK IN MY ARM--
S OKAY MAN I GOT MY NINE--
ANYTHING MOVES I SHOOT--
WH...
AAAH--
KAAARRAKKK
SPIKE-- WHAT'S HE DO--
WHA--
NO... PUT ME DOWN--
NOOO

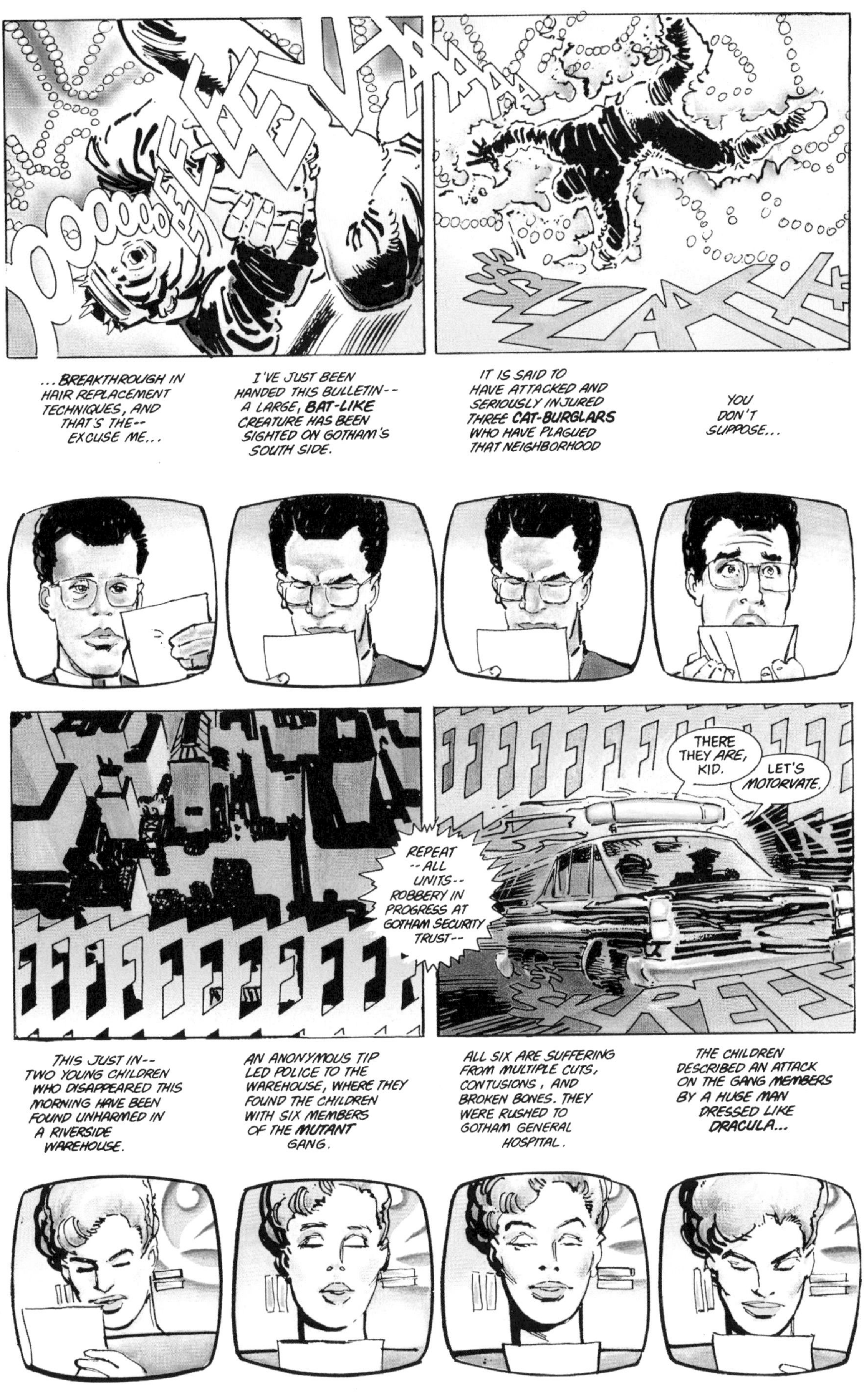
...BREAKTHROUGH IN HAIR REPLACEMENT TECHNIQUES, AND THAT'S THE-- EXCUSE ME...
I'VE JUST BEEN HANDED THIS BULLETIN-- A LARGE, BAT-LIKE CREATURE HAS BEEN SIGHTED ON GOTHAM'S SOUTH SIDE.
IT IS SAID TO HAVE ATTACKED AND SERIOUSLY INJURED THREE CAT-BURGLARS WHO HAVE PLAGUED THAT NEIGHBORHOOD
YOU DON'T SUPPOSE...
REPEAT --ALL UNITS-- ROBBERY IN PROGRESS AT GOTHAM SECURITY TRUST--
THERE THEY ARE, KID.
LET'S MOTORVATE.
THIS JUST IN-- TWO YOUNG CHILDREN WHO DISAPPEARED THIS MORNING HAVE BEEN FOUND UNHARMED IN A RIVERSIDE WAREHOUSE.
AN ANONYMOUS TIP LED POLICE TO THE WAREHOUSE, WHERE THEY FOUND THE CHILDREN WITH SIX MEMBERS OF THE MUTANT GANG.
ALL SIX ARE SUFFERING FROM MULTIPLE CUTS, CONTUSIONS, AND BROKEN BONES. THEY WERE RUSHED TO GOTHAM GENERAL HOSPITAL.
THE CHILDREN DESCRIBED AN ATTACK ON THE GANG MEMBERS BY A HUGE MAN DRESSED LIKE DRACULA...

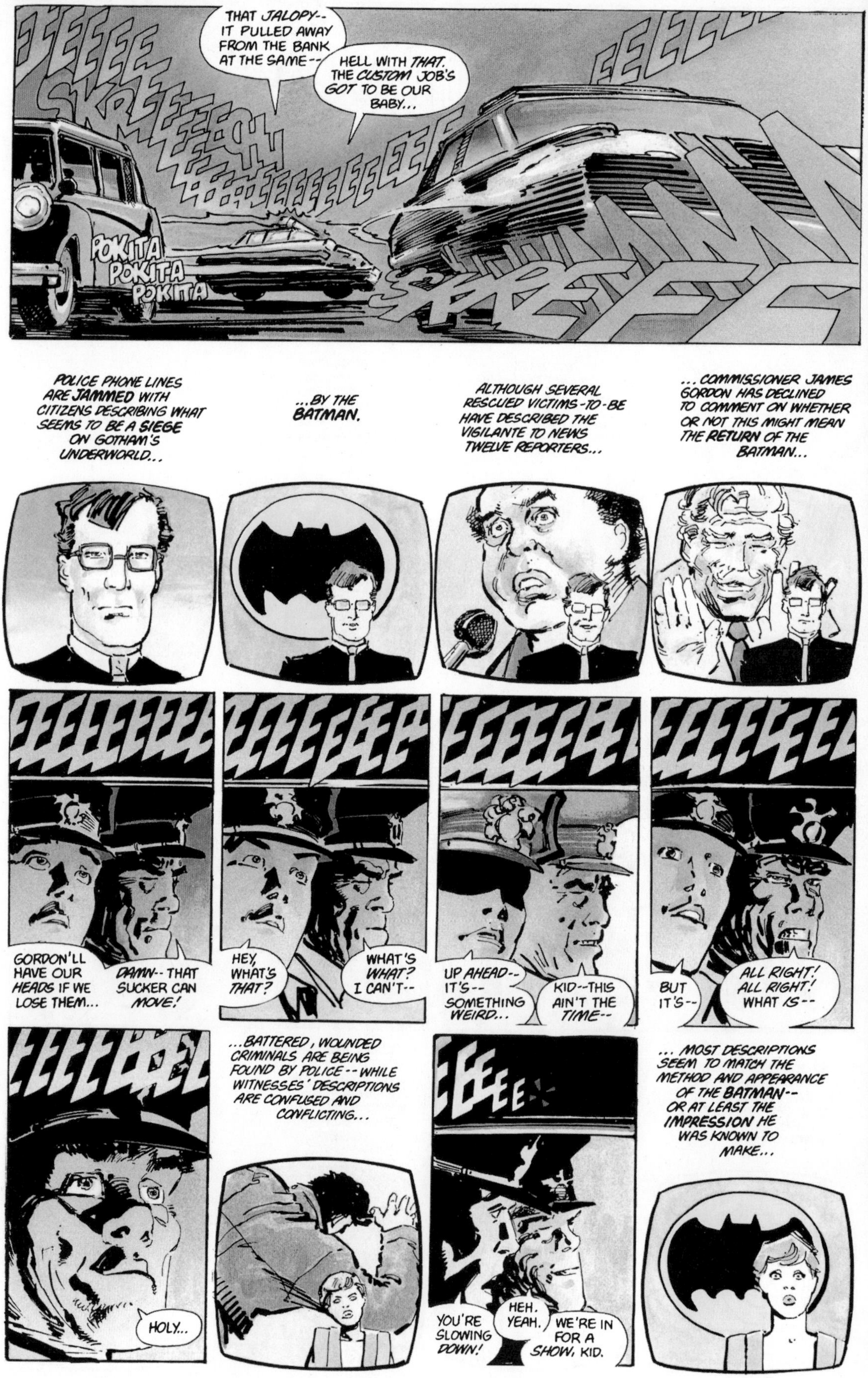

EEEEE
SKREEEECH
THAT JALOPY-- IT PULLED AWAY FROM THE BANK AT THE SAME--
HELL WITH THAT. THE CUSTOM JOB'S GOT TO BE OUR BABY...
POKITA POKITA POKITA
SKREEEE
POLICE PHONE LINES ARE JAMMED WITH CITIZENS DESCRIBING WHAT SEEMS TO BE A SIEGE ON GOTHAM'S UNDERWORLD...
...BY THE BATMAN.
ALTHOUGH SEVERAL RESCUED VICTIMS-TO-BE HAVE DESCRIBED THE VIGILANTE TO NEWS TWELVE REPORTERS...
...COMMISSIONER JAMES GORDON HAS DECLINED TO COMMENT ON WHETHER OR NOT THIS MIGHT MEAN THE RETURN OF THE BATMAN...
GORDON'LL HAVE OUR HEADS IF WE LOSE THEM...
DAMN-- THAT SUCKER CAN MOVE!
HEY, WHAT'S THAT?
WHAT'S WHAT? I CAN'T--
UP AHEAD-- IT'S-- SOMETHING WEIRD...
KID--THIS AIN'T THE TIME--
BUT IT'S--
ALL RIGHT! ALL RIGHT! WHAT IS--
HOLY...
...BATTERED, WOUNDED CRIMINALS ARE BEING FOUND BY POLICE -- WHILE WITNESSES' DESCRIPTIONS ARE CONFUSED AND CONFLICTING...
YOU'RE SLOWING DOWN!
HEH. YEAH.
WE'RE IN FOR A SHOW, KID.
... MOST DESCRIPTIONS SEEM TO MATCH THE METHOD AND APPEARANCE OF THE BATMAN-- OR AT LEAST THE IMPRESSION HE WAS KNOWN TO MAKE...

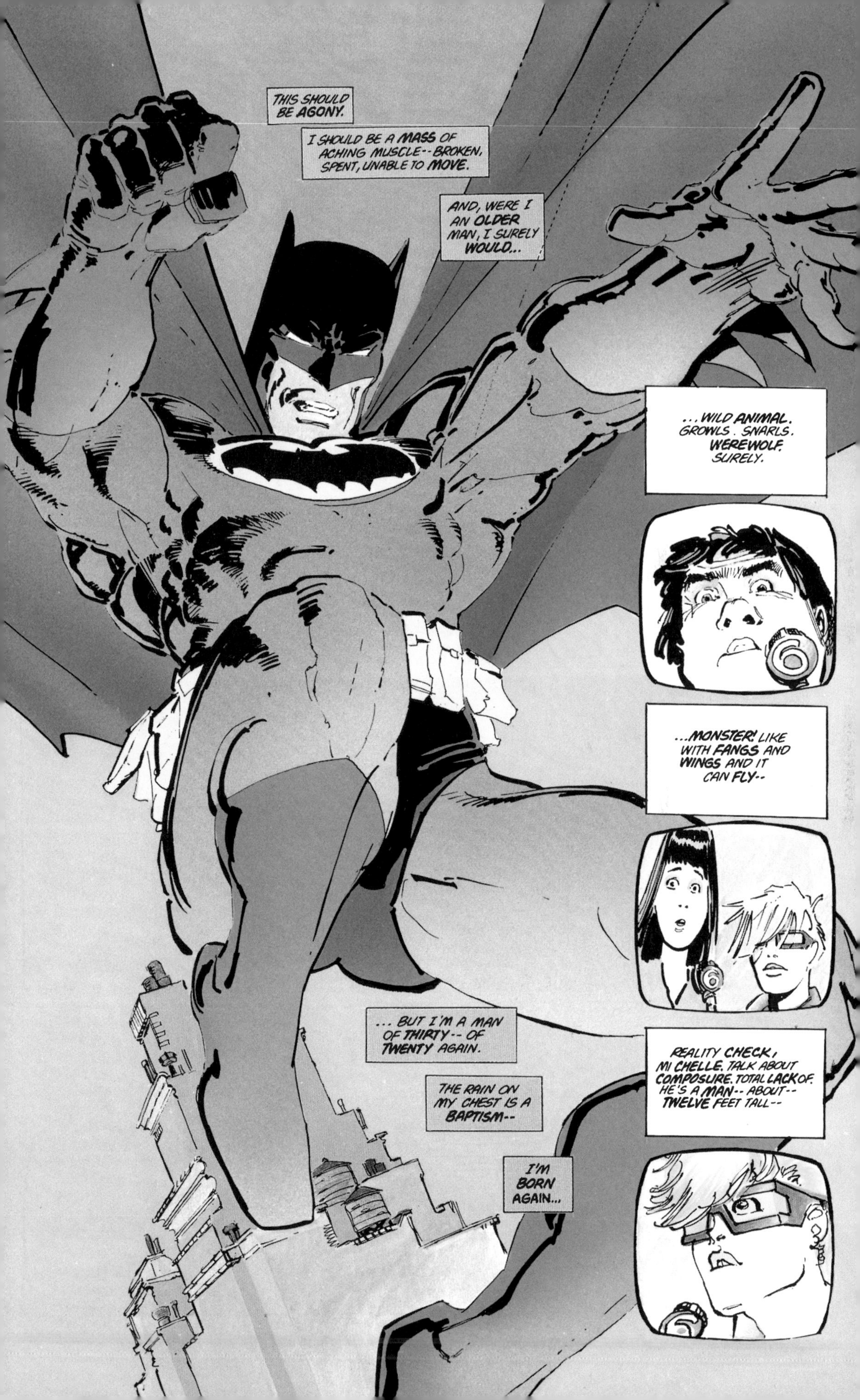
THIS SHOULD BE AGONY.
I SHOULD BE A MASS OF ACHING MUSCLE-- BROKEN, SPENT, UNABLE TO MOVE.
AND, WERE I AN OLDER MAN, I SURELY WOULD...
...WILD ANIMAL. GROWLS. SNARLS. WEREWOLF. SURELY.
...MONSTER! LIKE WITH FANGS AND WINGS AND IT CAN FLY--
... BUT I'M A MAN OF THIRTY-- OF TWENTY AGAIN.
THE RAIN ON MY CHEST IS A BAPTISM--
REALITY CHECK, MI CHELLE. TALK ABOUT COMPOSURE. TOTAL LACK OF. HE'S A MAN-- ABOUT-- TWELVE FEET TALL--
I'M BORN AGAIN...

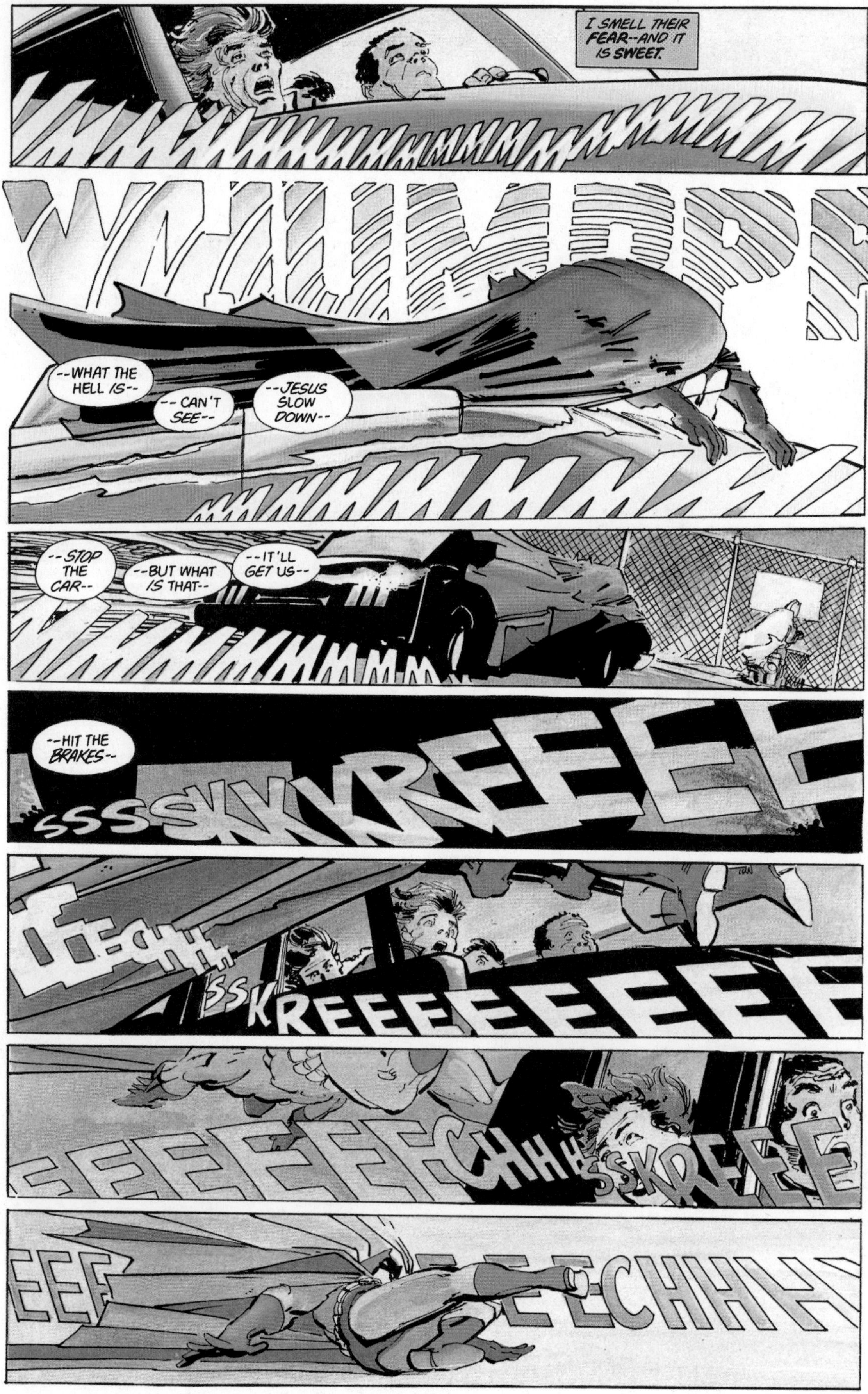
I SMELL THEIR FEAR--AND IT IS SWEET.
WHUMPP
--WHAT THE HELL IS--
--CAN'T SEE--
--JESUS SLOW DOWN--
--STOP THE CAR--
--BUT WHAT IS THAT--
--IT'LL GET US--
--HIT THE BRAKES--
SSSSKKKREEEE
SSKREEEEEEEEE
CHHSSKREEE
ECHHH

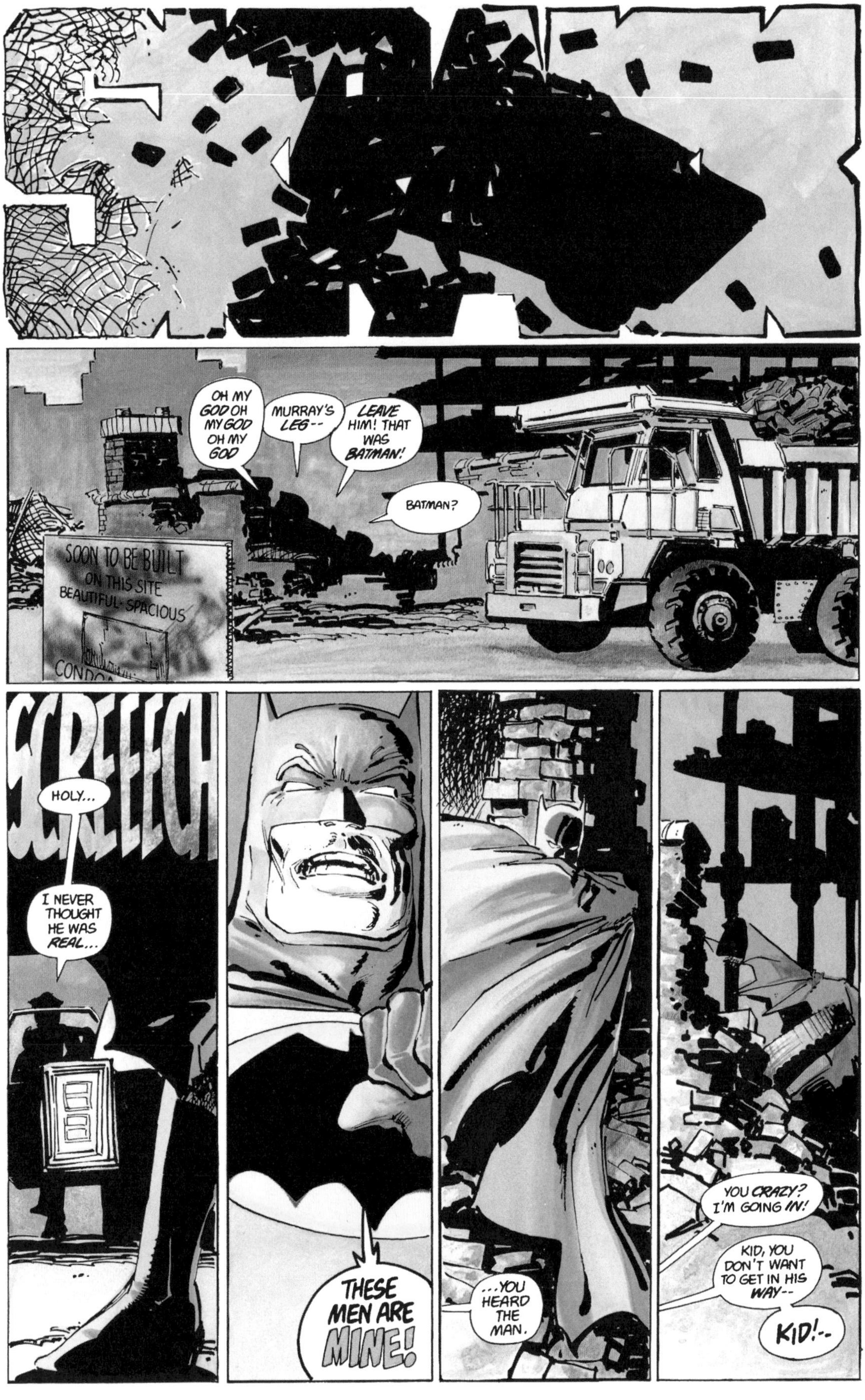
OH MY GOD OH MY GOD OH MY GOD
MURRAY'S LEG--
LEAVE HIM! THAT WAS BATMAN!
BATMAN?
SOON TO BE BUILT ON THIS SITE BEAUTIFUL · SPACIOUS
SCREEECH
HOLY...
I NEVER THOUGHT HE WAS REAL...
THESE MEN ARE MINE!
...YOU HEARD THE MAN.
YOU CRAZY? I'M GOING IN!
KID, YOU DON'T WANT TO GET IN HIS WAY--
KID!--

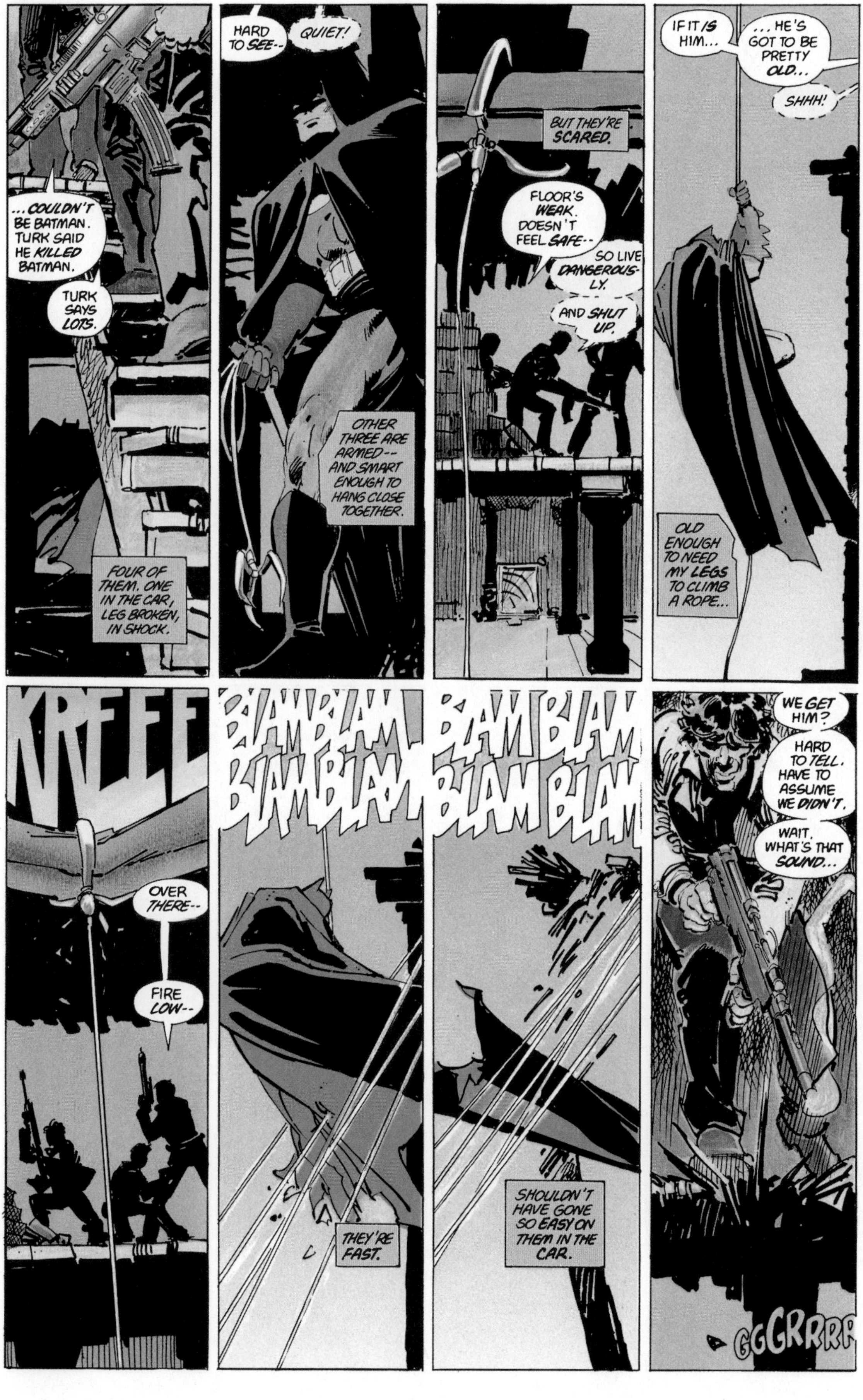

...COULDN'T BE BATMAN. TURK SAID HE KILLED BATMAN.
TURK SAYS LOTS.
FOUR OF THEM. ONE IN THE CAR, LEG BROKEN, IN SHOCK.
HARD TO SEE--
QUIET!
OTHER THREE ARE ARMED--AND SMART ENOUGH TO HANG CLOSE TOGETHER.
BUT THEY'RE SCARED.
FLOOR'S WEAK. DOESN'T FEEL SAFE--
SO LIVE DANGEROUSLY.
AND SHUT UP.
IF IT IS HIM...
...HE'S GOT TO BE PRETTY OLD...
SHHH!
OLD ENOUGH TO NEED MY LEGS TO CLIMB A ROPE...
KREEE
OVER THERE--
FIRE LOW--
BLAM BLAM BLAM BLAM
THEY'RE FAST.
BLAM BLAM BLAM BLAM
SHOULDN'T HAVE GONE SO EASY ON THEM IN THE CAR.
WE GET HIM?
HARD TO TELL. HAVE TO ASSUME WE DIDN'T.
WAIT. WHAT'S THAT SOUND...
GGGRRRR

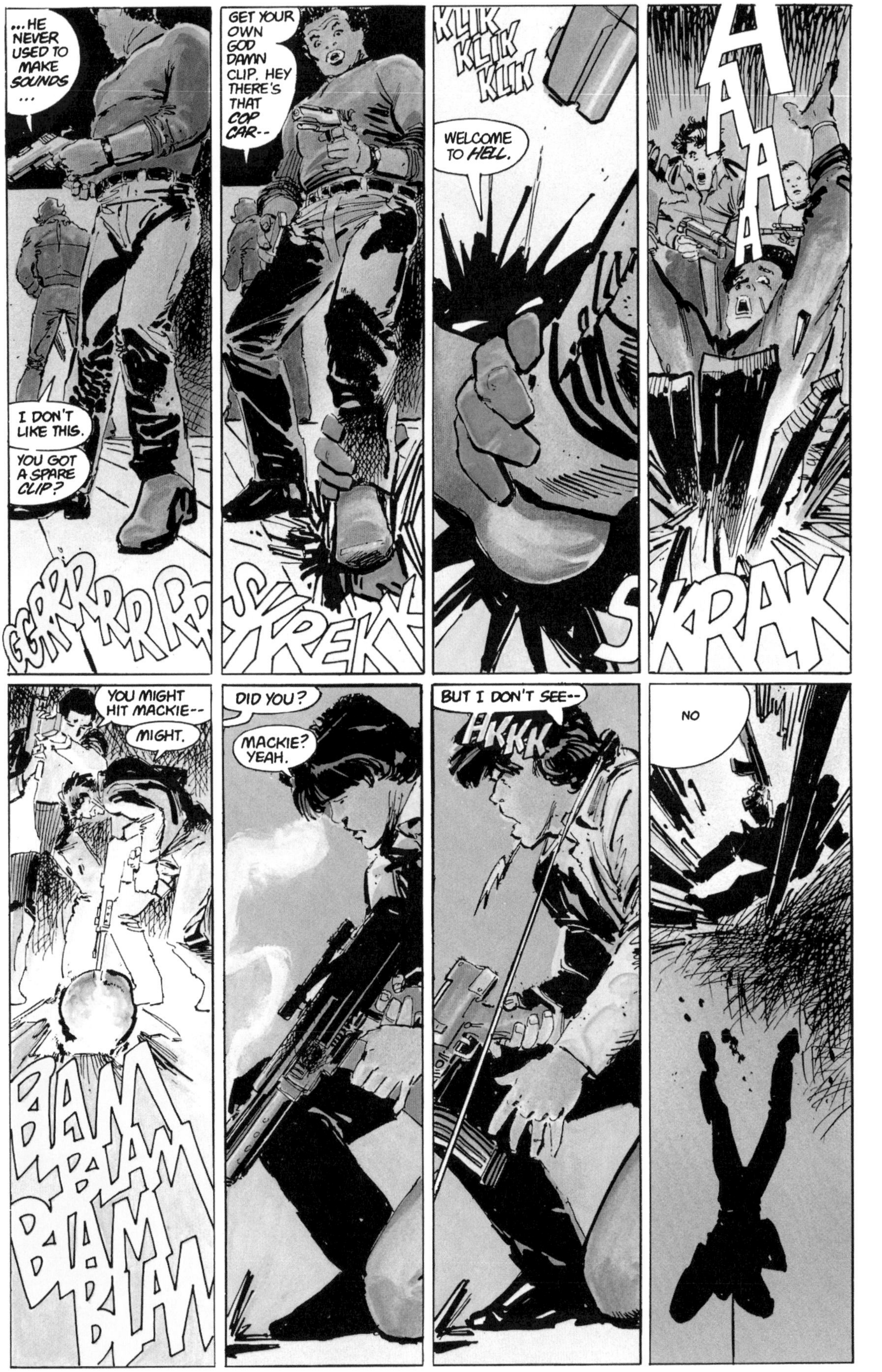
...HE NEVER USED TO MAKE SOUNDS ...
I DON'T LIKE THIS.
YOU GOT A SPARE CLIP?
GRRRRRRRR
GET YOUR OWN GOD DAMN CLIP. HEY THERE'S THAT COP CAR--
SKREKK
KLIK KLIK KLIK
WELCOME TO HELL.
SKRAK
AAAA
YOU MIGHT HIT MACKIE--
MIGHT.
BLAM BLAM BLAM BLAM
DID YOU?
MACKIE? YEAH.
BUT I DON'T SEE--
HKKK
NO

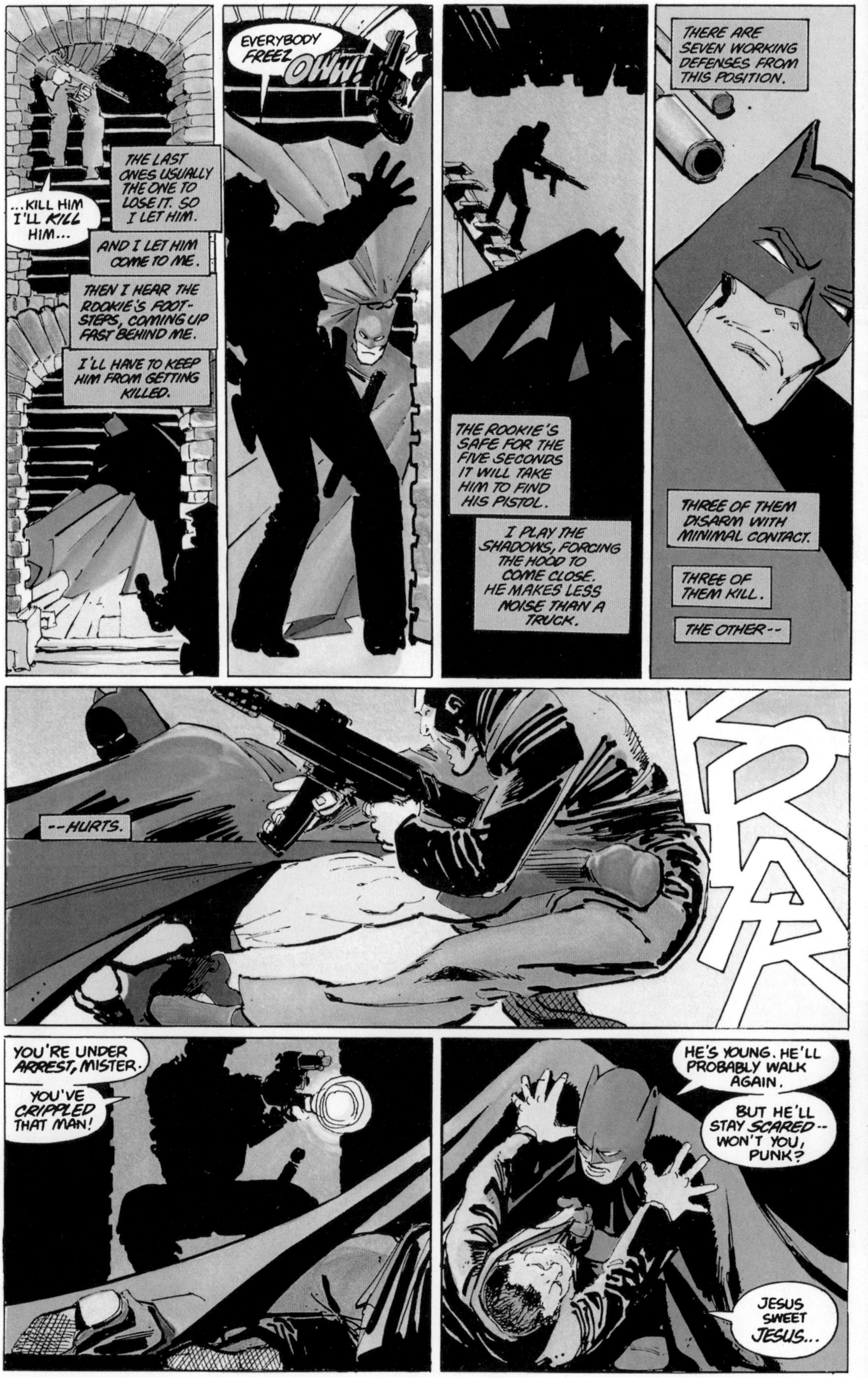
...KILL HIM I'LL KILL HIM...
THE LAST ONES USUALLY THE ONE TO LOSE IT. SO I LET HIM.
AND I LET HIM COME TO ME.
THEN I HEAR THE ROOKIE'S FOOT-STEPS, COMING UP FAST BEHIND ME.
I'LL HAVE TO KEEP HIM FROM GETTING KILLED.
EVERYBODY FREEZ
OWW!
THE ROOKIE'S SAFE FOR THE FIVE SECONDS IT WILL TAKE HIM TO FIND HIS PISTOL.
I PLAY THE SHADOWS, FORCING THE HOOD TO COME CLOSE. HE MAKES LESS NOISE THAN A TRUCK.
THERE ARE SEVEN WORKING DEFENSES FROM THIS POSITION.
THREE OF THEM DISARM WITH MINIMAL CONTACT.
THREE OF THEM KILL.
THE OTHER--
--HURTS.
KRAK
YOU'RE UNDER ARREST, MISTER.
YOU'VE CRIPPLED THAT MAN!
HE'S YOUNG. HE'LL PROBABLY WALK AGAIN.
BUT HE'LL STAY SCARED-- WON'T YOU, PUNK?
JESUS SWEET JESUS...

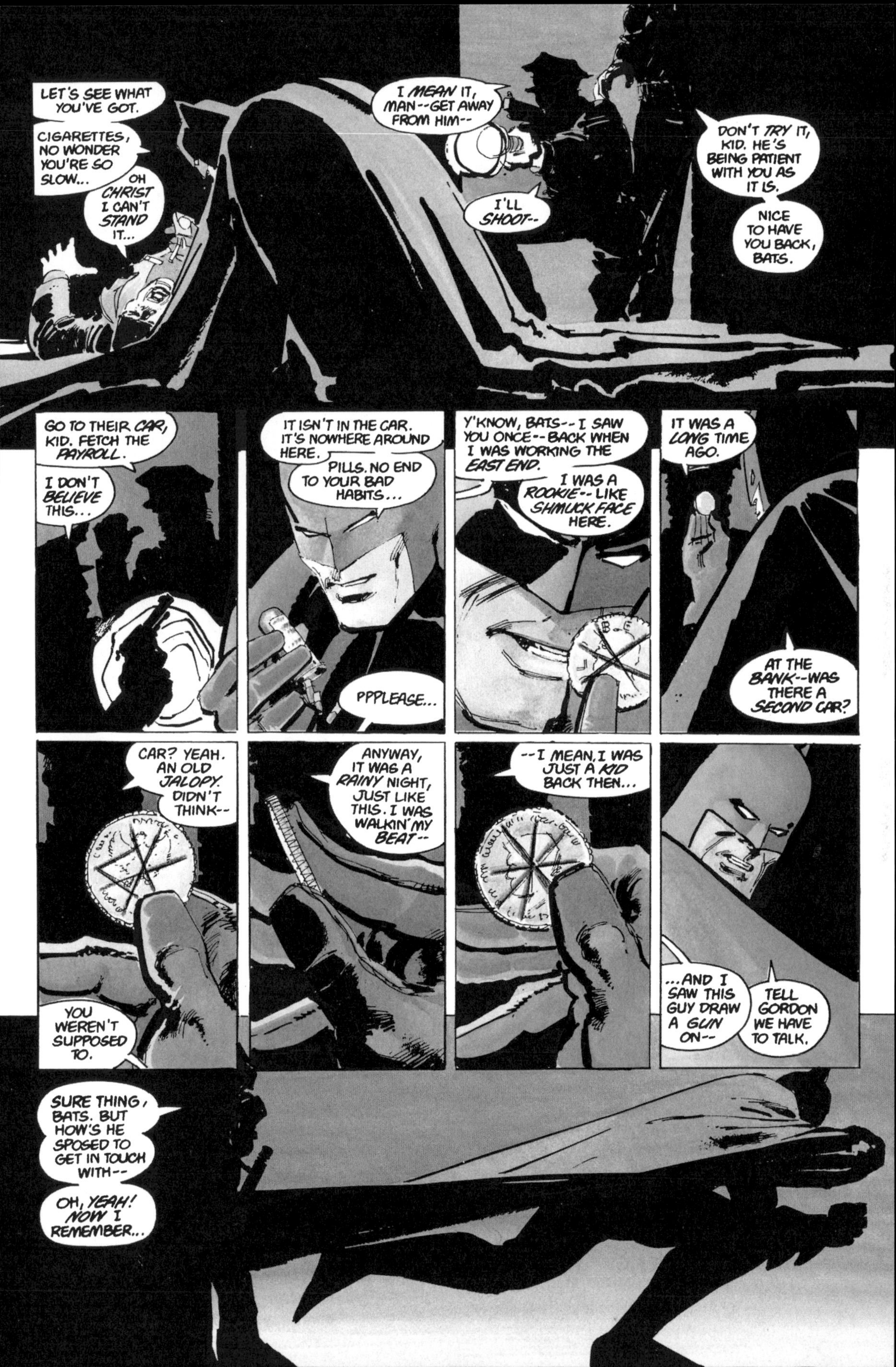
LET'S SEE WHAT YOU'VE GOT.
CIGARETTES, NO WONDER YOU'RE SO SLOW...
OH CHRIST I CAN'T STAND IT...
I MEAN IT, MAN--GET AWAY FROM HIM--
I'LL SHOOT--
DON'T TRY IT, KID. HE'S BEING PATIENT WITH YOU AS IT IS.
NICE TO HAVE YOU BACK, BATS.
GO TO THEIR CAR, KID. FETCH THE PAYROLL.
I DON'T BELIEVE THIS...
IT ISN'T IN THE CAR. IT'S NOWHERE AROUND HERE.
PILLS. NO END TO YOUR BAD HABITS...
PPPLEASE...
Y'KNOW, BATS--I SAW YOU ONCE--BACK WHEN I WAS WORKING THE EAST END.
I WAS A ROOKIE--LIKE SHMUCK FACE HERE.
IT WAS A LONG TIME AGO.
AT THE BANK--WAS THERE A SECOND CAR?
CAR? YEAH. AN OLD JALOPY. DIDN'T THINK--
YOU WEREN'T SUPPOSED TO.
ANYWAY, IT WAS A RAINY NIGHT, JUST LIKE THIS. I WAS WALKIN' MY BEAT--
--I MEAN, I WAS JUST A KID BACK THEN...
...AND I SAW THIS GUY DRAW A GUN ON--
TELL GORDON WE HAVE TO TALK.
SURE THING, BATS. BUT HOW'S HE SPOSED TO GET IN TOUCH WITH--
OH, YEAH! NOW I REMEMBER...

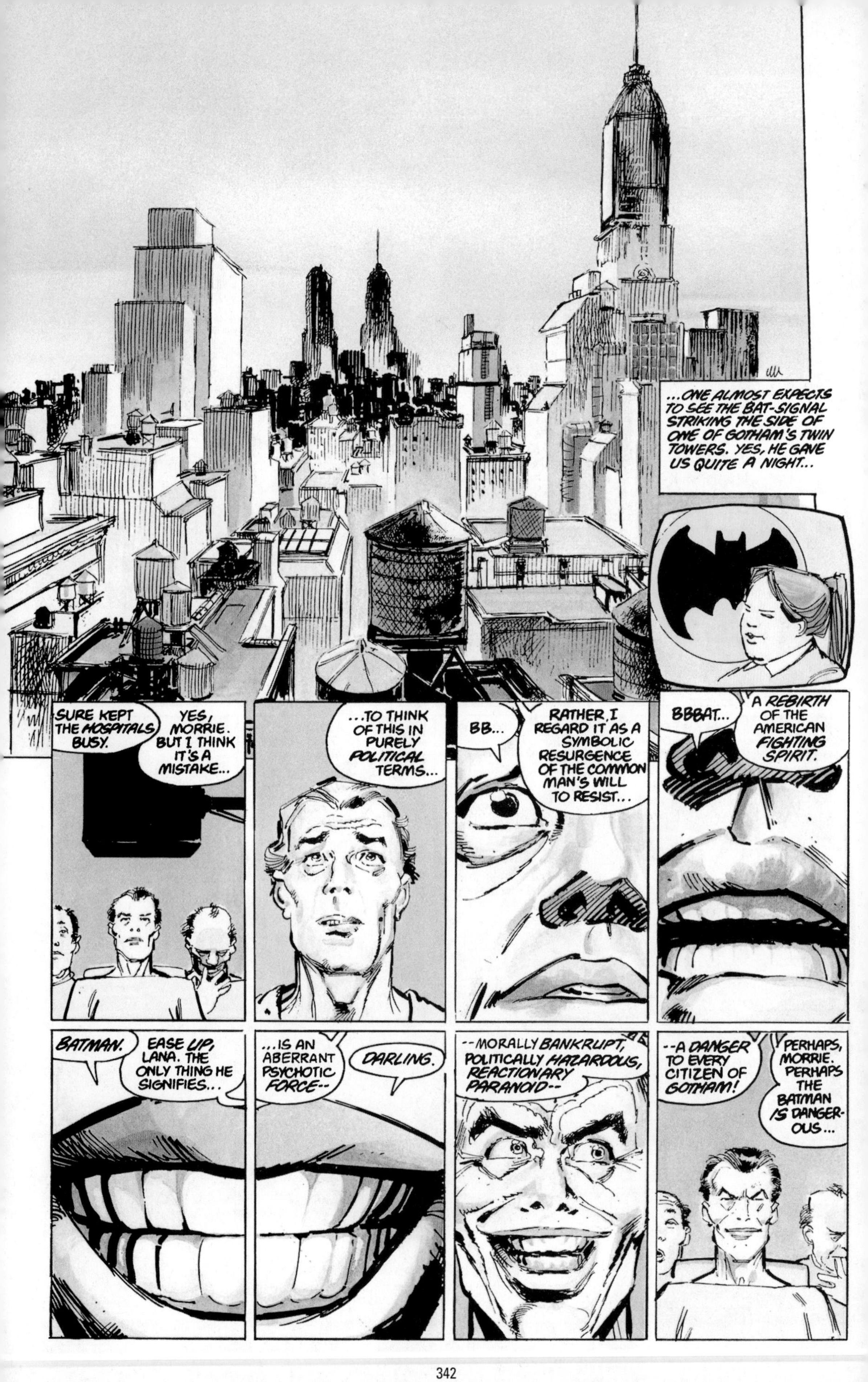

...ONE ALMOST EXPECTS TO SEE THE BAT-SIGNAL STRIKING THE SIDE OF ONE OF GOTHAM'S TWIN TOWERS. YES, HE GAVE US QUITE A NIGHT...
SURE KEPT THE HOSPITALS BUSY.
YES, MORRIE. BUT I THINK IT'S A MISTAKE...
...TO THINK OF THIS IN PURELY POLITICAL TERMS...
BB...
RATHER, I REGARD IT AS A SYMBOLIC RESURGENCE OF THE COMMON MAN'S WILL TO RESIST...
BBBAT...
A REBIRTH OF THE AMERICAN FIGHTING SPIRIT.
BATMAN.
EASE UP, LANA. THE ONLY THING HE SIGNIFIES...
...IS AN ABERRANT PSYCHOTIC FORCE--
DARLING.
--MORALLY BANKRUPT, POLITICALLY HAZARDOUS, REACTIONARY PARANOID--
--A DANGER TO EVERY CITIZEN OF GOTHAM!
PERHAPS, MORRIE. PERHAPS THE BATMAN IS DANGEROUS...

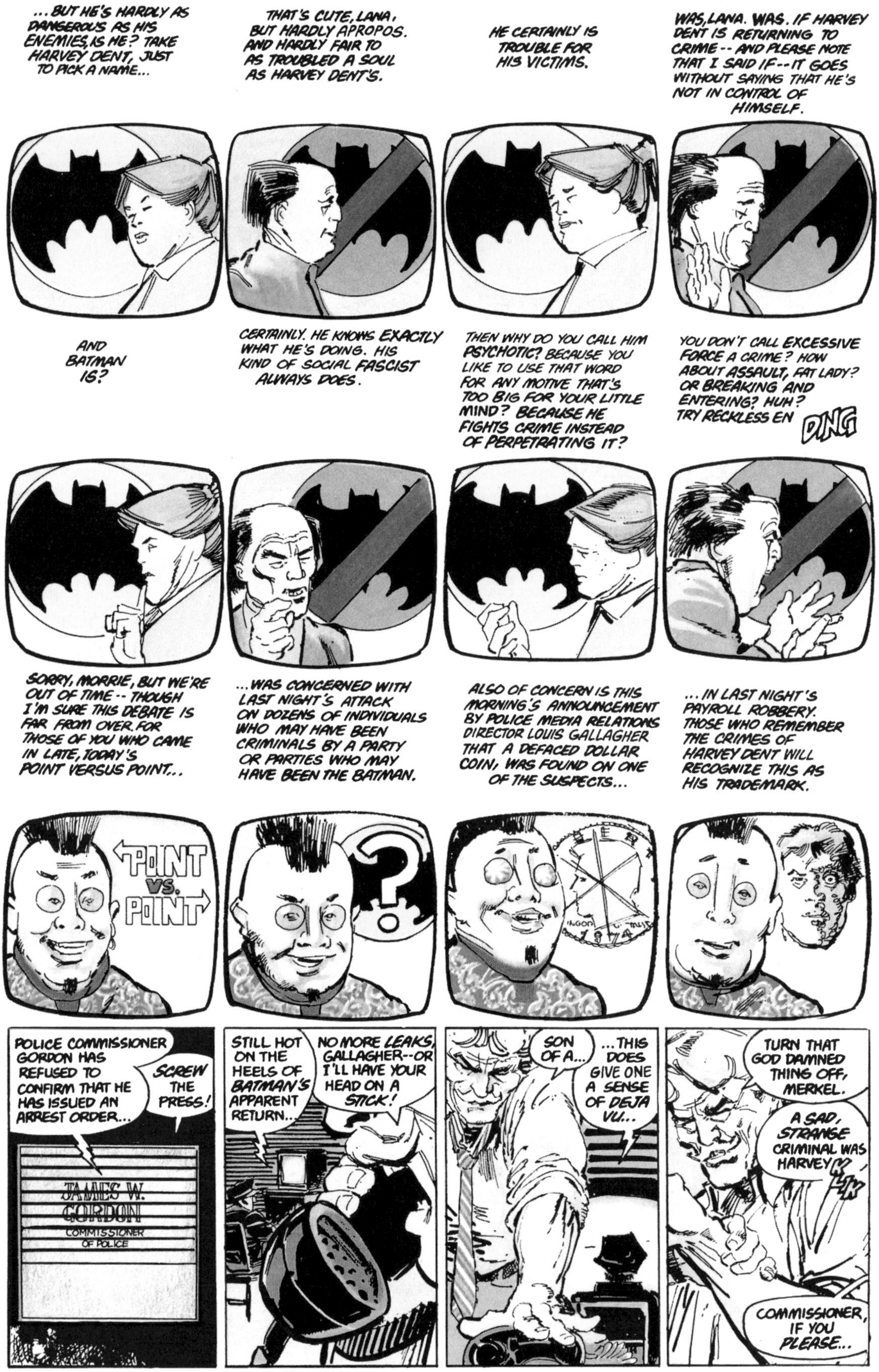
... BUT HE'S HARDLY AS DANGEROUS AS HIS ENEMIES, IS HE? TAKE HARVEY DENT, JUST TO PICK A NAME...
THAT'S CUTE, LANA. BUT HARDLY APROPOS. AND HARDLY FAIR TO AS TROUBLED A SOUL AS HARVEY DENT'S.
HE CERTAINLY IS TROUBLE FOR HIS VICTIMS.
WAS, LANA. WAS. IF HARVEY DENT IS RETURNING TO CRIME -- AND PLEASE NOTE THAT I SAID IF -- IT GOES WITHOUT SAYING THAT HE'S NOT IN CONTROL OF HIMSELF.
AND BATMAN IS?
CERTAINLY. HE KNOWS EXACTLY WHAT HE'S DOING. HIS KIND OF SOCIAL FASCIST ALWAYS DOES.
THEN WHY DO YOU CALL HIM PSYCHOTIC? BECAUSE YOU LIKE TO USE THAT WORD FOR ANY MOTIVE THAT'S TOO BIG FOR YOUR LITTLE MIND? BECAUSE HE FIGHTS CRIME INSTEAD OF PERPETRATING IT?
YOU DON'T CALL EXCESSIVE FORCE A CRIME? HOW ABOUT ASSAULT, FAT LADY? OR BREAKING AND ENTERING? HUH? TRY RECKLESS EN
DING
SORRY, MORRIE, BUT WE'RE OUT OF TIME -- THOUGH I'M SURE THIS DEBATE IS FAR FROM OVER. FOR THOSE OF YOU WHO CAME IN LATE, TODAY'S POINT VERSUS POINT...
...WAS CONCERNED WITH LAST NIGHT'S ATTACK ON DOZENS OF INDIVIDUALS WHO MAY HAVE BEEN CRIMINALS BY A PARTY OR PARTIES WHO MAY HAVE BEEN THE BATMAN.
ALSO OF CONCERN IS THIS MORNING'S ANNOUNCEMENT BY POLICE MEDIA RELATIONS DIRECTOR LOUIS GALLAGHER THAT A DEFACED DOLLAR COIN, WAS FOUND ON ONE OF THE SUSPECTS...
... IN LAST NIGHT'S PAYROLL ROBBERY. THOSE WHO REMEMBER THE CRIMES OF HARVEY DENT WILL RECOGNIZE THIS AS HIS TRADEMARK.
POINT VS. POINT
POLICE COMMISSIONER GORDON HAS REFUSED TO CONFIRM THAT HE HAS ISSUED AN ARREST ORDER...
SCREW THE PRESS!
JAMES W. GORDON
COMMISSIONER OF POLICE
STILL HOT ON THE HEELS OF BATMAN'S APPARENT RETURN...
NO MORE LEAKS, GALLAGHER--OR I'LL HAVE YOUR HEAD ON A STICK!
SON OF A...
...THIS DOES GIVE ONE A SENSE OF DEJA VU...
TURN THAT GOD DAMNED THING OFF, MERKEL.
A SAD, STRANGE CRIMINAL WAS HARVEY
CLIK
COMMISSIONER, IF YOU PLEASE...

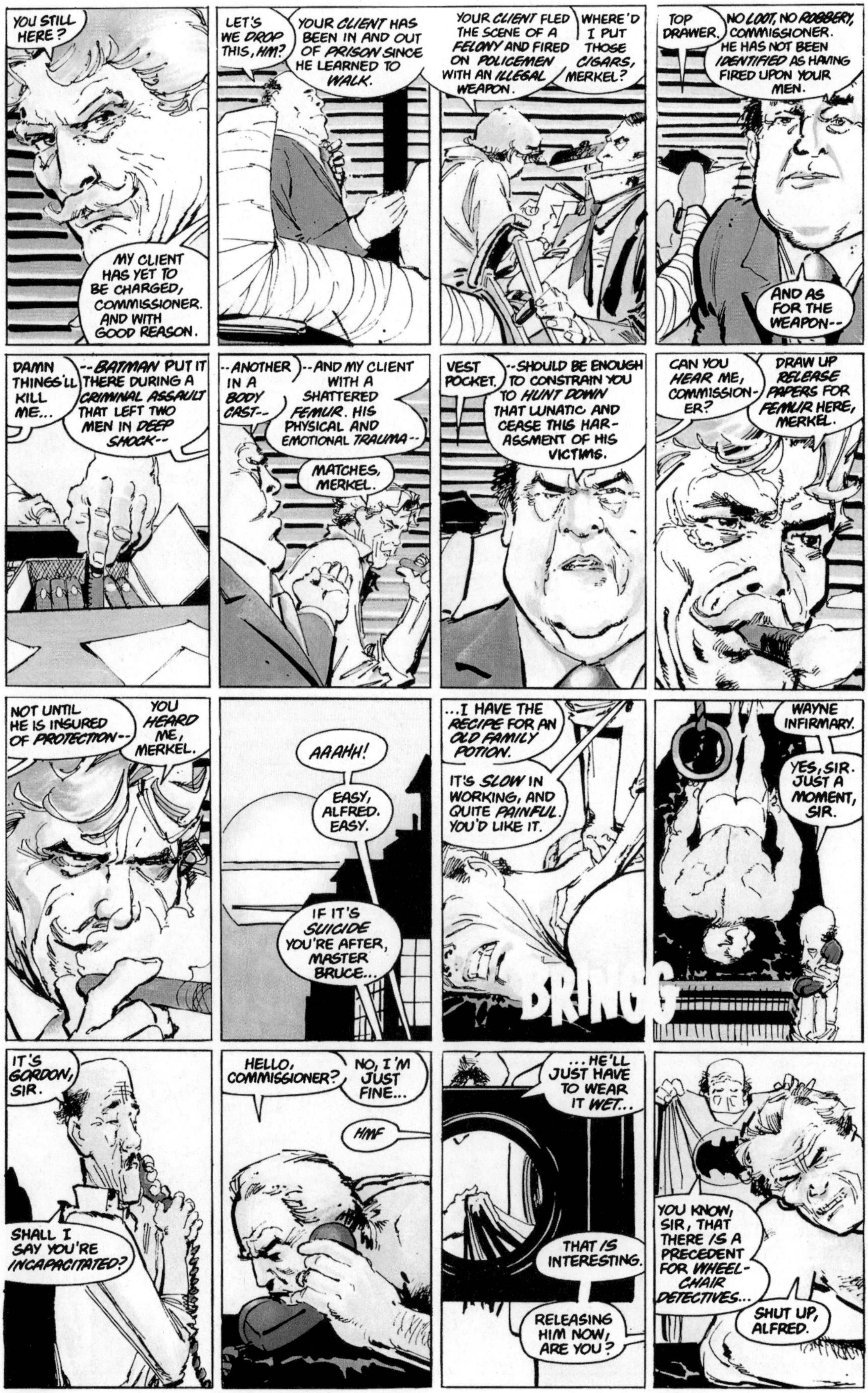

YOU STILL HERE?
MY CLIENT HAS YET TO BE CHARGED, COMMISSIONER. AND WITH GOOD REASON.
LET'S WE DROP THIS, HM?
YOUR CLIENT HAS BEEN IN AND OUT OF PRISON SINCE HE LEARNED TO WALK.
YOUR CLIENT FLED THE SCENE OF A FELONY AND FIRED ON POLICEMEN WITH AN ILLEGAL WEAPON.
WHERE'D I PUT THOSE CIGARS, MERKEL?
TOP DRAWER.
NO LOOT, NO ROBBERY, COMMISSIONER. HE HAS NOT BEEN IDENTIFIED AS HAVING FIRED UPON YOUR MEN.
AND AS FOR THE WEAPON--
DAMN THINGS'LL KILL ME...
--BATMAN PUT IT THERE DURING A CRIMINAL ASSAULT THAT LEFT TWO MEN IN DEEP SHOCK--
--ANOTHER IN A BODY CAST--
--AND MY CLIENT WITH A SHATTERED FEMUR. HIS PHYSICAL AND EMOTIONAL TRAUMA--
MATCHES, MERKEL.
VEST POCKET.
--SHOULD BE ENOUGH TO CONSTRAIN YOU TO HUNT DOWN THAT LUNATIC AND CEASE THIS HAR-ASSMENT OF HIS VICTIMS.
CAN YOU HEAR ME, COMMISSION-ER?
DRAW UP RELEASE PAPERS FOR FEMUR HERE, MERKEL.
NOT UNTIL HE IS INSURED OF PROTECTION--
YOU HEARD ME, MERKEL.
AAAHH!
EASY, ALFRED. EASY.
IF IT'S SUICIDE YOU'RE AFTER, MASTER BRUCE...
...I HAVE THE RECIPE FOR AN OLD FAMILY POTION.
IT'S SLOW IN WORKING, AND QUITE PAINFUL. YOU'D LIKE IT.
BRINNG
WAYNE INFIRMARY.
YES, SIR. JUST A MOMENT, SIR.
IT'S GORDON, SIR.
SHALL I SAY YOU'RE INCAPACITATED?
HELLO, COMMISSIONER?
NO, I'M JUST FINE...
HMF
...HE'LL JUST HAVE TO WEAR IT WET...
THAT IS INTERESTING.
RELEASING HIM NOW, ARE YOU?
YOU KNOW, SIR, THAT THERE IS A PRECEDENT FOR WHEEL-CHAIR DETECTIVES...
SHUT UP, ALFRED.

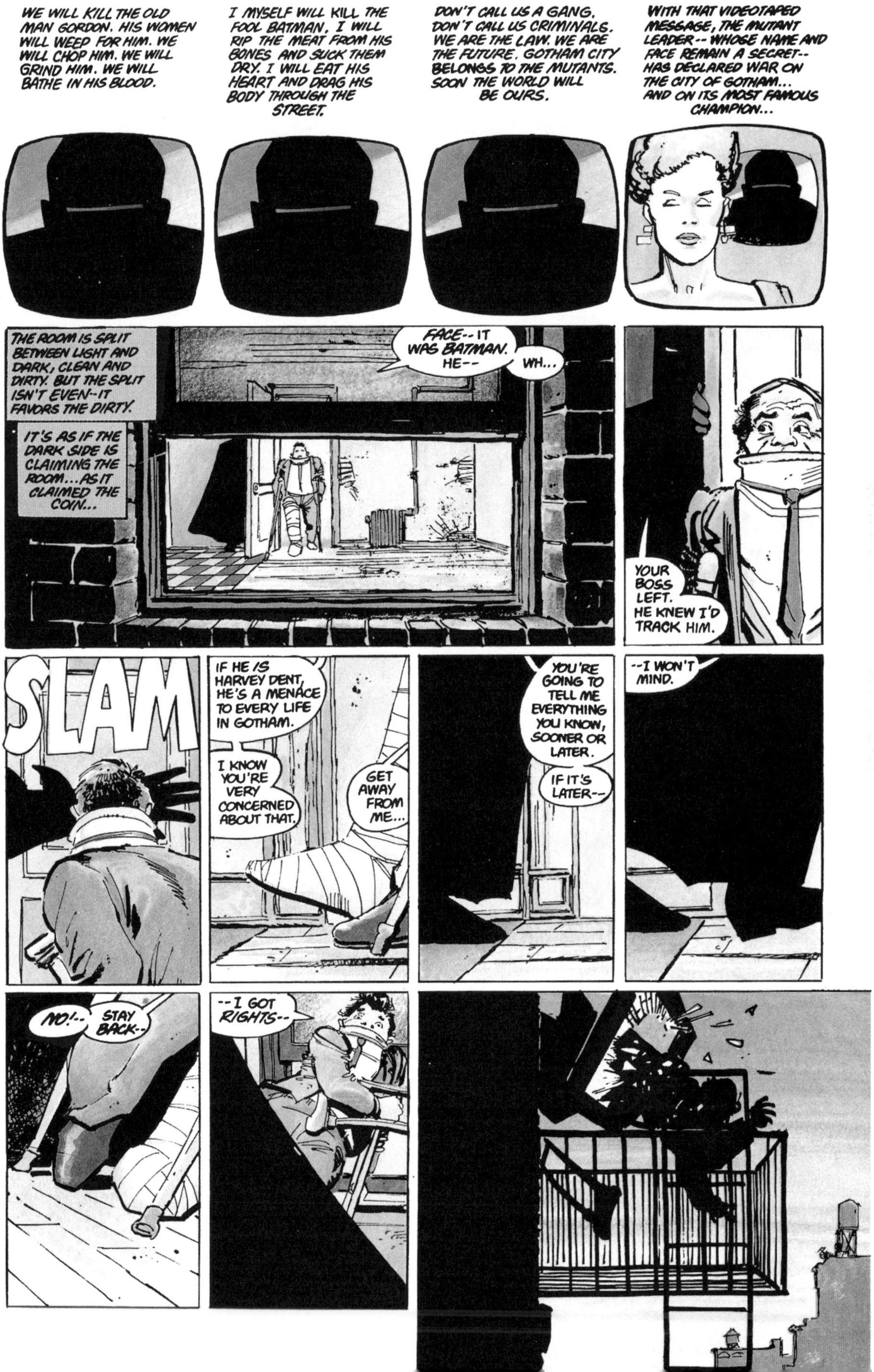
WE WILL KILL THE OLD MAN GORDON. HIS WOMEN WILL WEEP FOR HIM. WE WILL CHOP HIM. WE WILL GRIND HIM. WE WILL BATHE IN HIS BLOOD.
I MYSELF WILL KILL THE FOOL BATMAN. I WILL RIP THE MEAT FROM HIS BONES AND SUCK THEM DRY. I WILL EAT HIS HEART AND DRAG HIS BODY THROUGH THE STREET.
DON'T CALL US A GANG. DON'T CALL US CRIMINALS. WE ARE THE LAW. WE ARE THE FUTURE. GOTHAM CITY BELONGS TO THE MUTANTS. SOON THE WORLD WILL BE OURS.
WITH THAT VIDEOTAPED MESSAGE, THE MUTANT LEADER -- WHOSE NAME AND FACE REMAIN A SECRET -- HAS DECLARED WAR ON THE CITY OF GOTHAM... AND ON ITS MOST FAMOUS CHAMPION...
THE ROOM IS SPLIT BETWEEN LIGHT AND DARK, CLEAN AND DIRTY. BUT THE SPLIT ISN'T EVEN--IT FAVORS THE DIRTY.
IT'S AS IF THE DARK SIDE IS CLAIMING THE ROOM... AS IT CLAIMED THE COIN...
FACE-- IT WAS BATMAN. HE--
WH...
YOUR BOSS LEFT. HE KNEW I'D TRACK HIM.
SLAM
IF HE IS HARVEY DENT, HE'S A MENACE TO EVERY LIFE IN GOTHAM.
I KNOW YOU'RE VERY CONCERNED ABOUT THAT.
GET AWAY FROM ME...
YOU'RE GOING TO TELL ME EVERYTHING YOU KNOW, SOONER OR LATER.
IF IT'S LATER--
--I WON'T MIND.
NO!-- STAY BACK--
--I GOT RIGHTS--

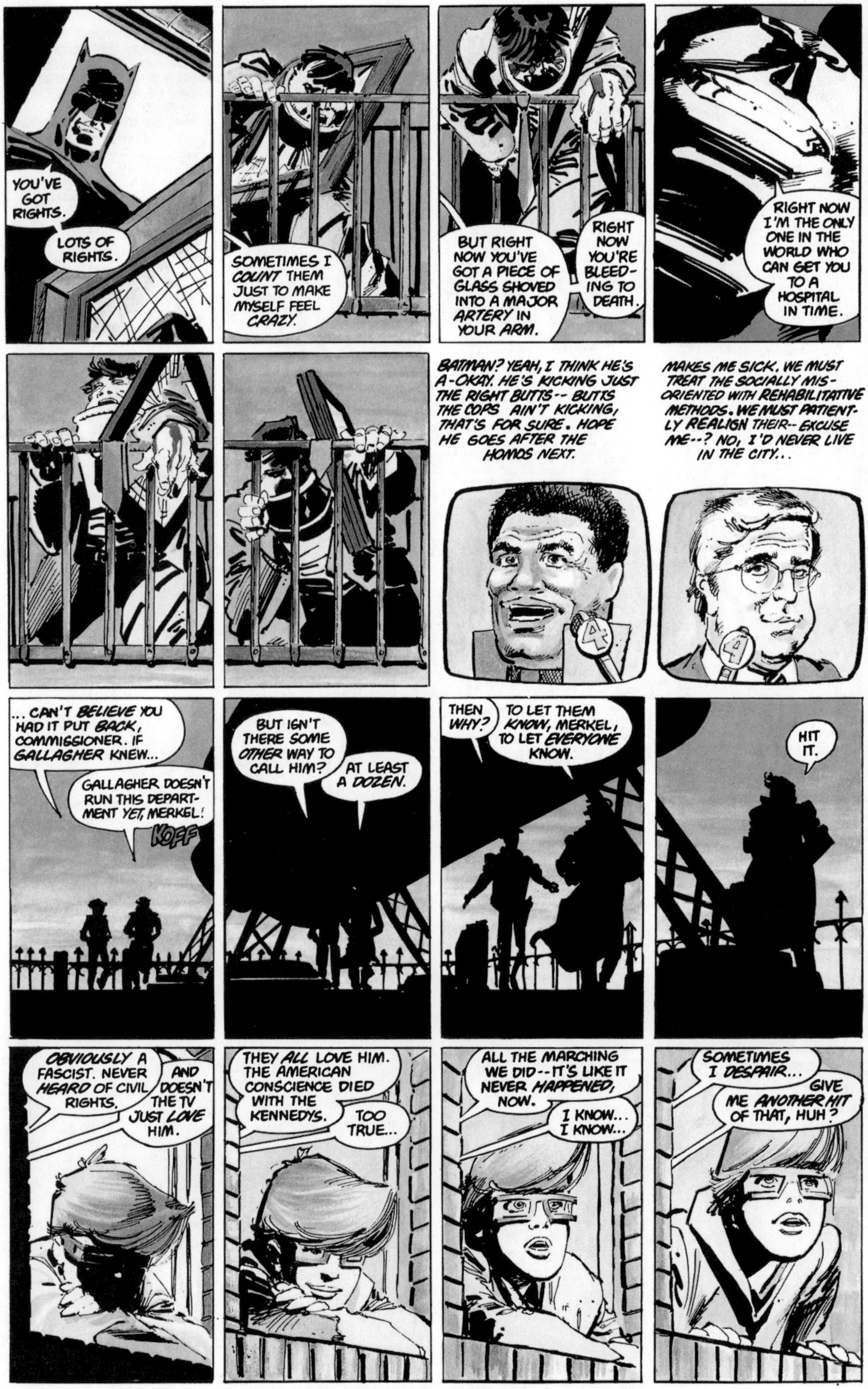
YOU'VE GOT RIGHTS.
LOTS OF RIGHTS.
SOMETIMES I COUNT THEM JUST TO MAKE MYSELF FEEL CRAZY.
BUT RIGHT NOW YOU'VE GOT A PIECE OF GLASS SHOVED INTO A MAJOR ARTERY IN YOUR ARM.
RIGHT NOW YOU'RE BLEEDING TO DEATH.
RIGHT NOW I'M THE ONLY ONE IN THE WORLD WHO CAN GET YOU TO A HOSPITAL IN TIME.
BATMAN? YEAH, I THINK HE'S A-OKAY. HE'S KICKING JUST THE RIGHT BUTTS-- BUTTS THE COPS AIN'T KICKING, THAT'S FOR SURE. HOPE HE GOES AFTER THE HOMOS NEXT.
MAKES ME SICK. WE MUST TREAT THE SOCIALLY MIS-ORIENTED WITH REHABILITATIVE METHODS. WE MUST PATIENTLY REALIGN THEIR-- EXCUSE ME--? NO, I'D NEVER LIVE IN THE CITY...
... CAN'T BELIEVE YOU HAD IT PUT BACK, COMMISSIONER. IF GALLAGHER KNEW...
GALLAGHER DOESN'T RUN THIS DEPARTMENT YET, MERKEL.
KOFF
BUT ISN'T THERE SOME OTHER WAY TO CALL HIM?
AT LEAST A DOZEN.
THEN WHY?
TO LET THEM KNOW, MERKEL, TO LET EVERYONE KNOW.
HIT IT.
OBVIOUSLY A FASCIST. NEVER HEARD OF CIVIL RIGHTS.
AND DOESN'T THE TV JUST LOVE HIM.
THEY ALL LOVE HIM. THE AMERICAN CONSCIENCE DIED WITH THE KENNEDYS.
TOO TRUE...
ALL THE MARCHING WE DID--IT'S LIKE IT NEVER HAPPENED, NOW.
I KNOW... I KNOW...
SOMETIMES I DESPAIR...
GIVE ME ANOTHER HIT OF THAT, HUH?

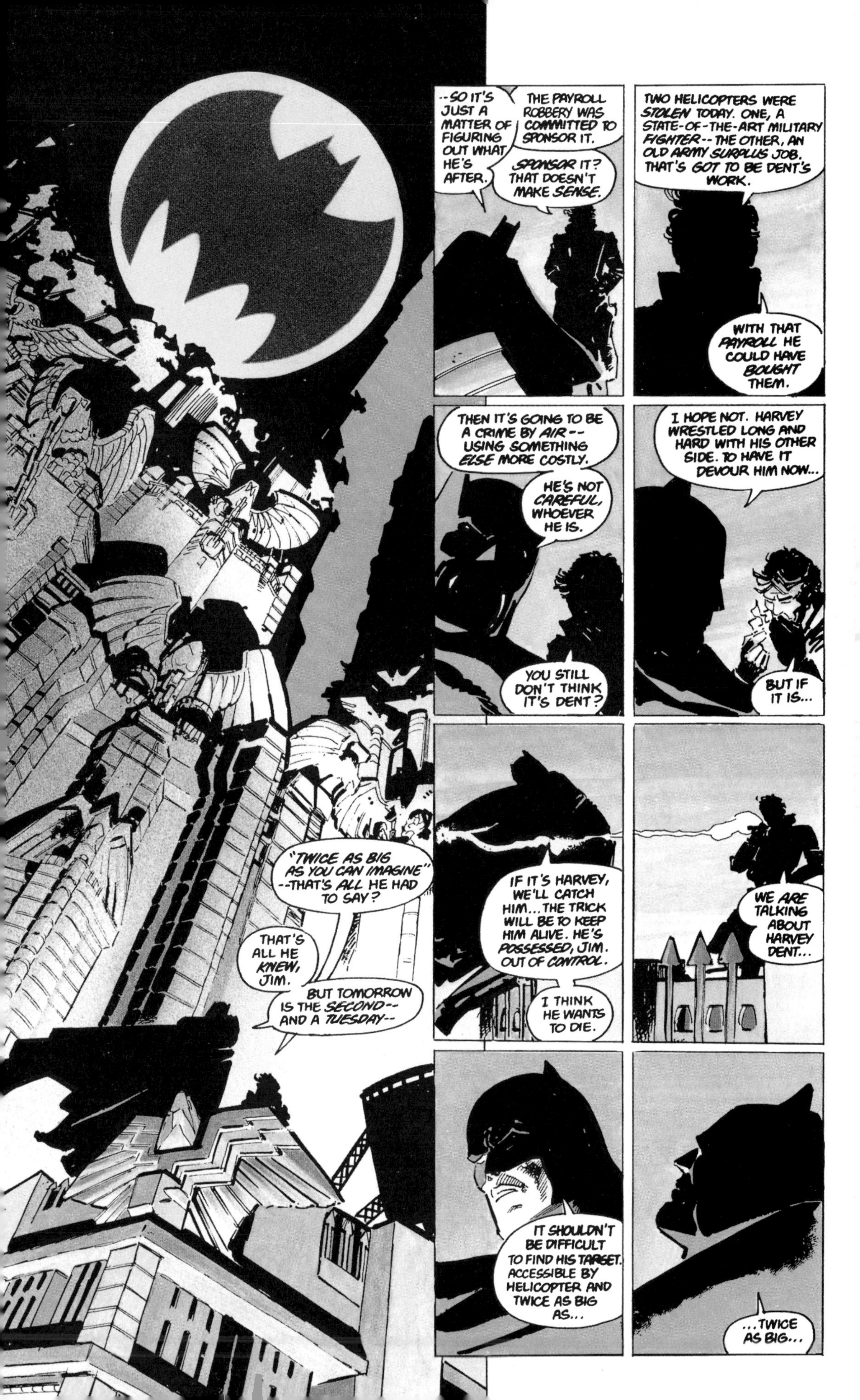
--SO IT'S JUST A MATTER OF FIGURING OUT WHAT HE'S AFTER.
THE PAYROLL ROBBERY WAS COMMITTED TO SPONSOR IT.
SPONSOR IT? THAT DOESN'T MAKE SENSE.
TWO HELICOPTERS WERE STOLEN TODAY. ONE, A STATE-OF-THE-ART MILITARY FIGHTER-- THE OTHER, AN OLD ARMY SURPLUS JOB. THAT'S GOT TO BE DENT'S WORK.
WITH THAT PAYROLL HE COULD HAVE BOUGHT THEM.
THEN IT'S GOING TO BE A CRIME BY AIR-- USING SOMETHING ELSE MORE COSTLY.
HE'S NOT CAREFUL, WHOEVER HE IS.
YOU STILL DON'T THINK IT'S DENT?
I HOPE NOT. HARVEY WRESTLED LONG AND HARD WITH HIS OTHER SIDE. TO HAVE IT DEVOUR HIM NOW...
BUT IF IT IS...
IF IT'S HARVEY, WE'LL CATCH HIM... THE TRICK WILL BE TO KEEP HIM ALIVE. HE'S POSSESSED, JIM. OUT OF CONTROL.
I THINK HE WANTS TO DIE.
WE ARE TALKING ABOUT HARVEY DENT...
"TWICE AS BIG AS YOU CAN IMAGINE" --THAT'S ALL HE HAD TO SAY?
THAT'S ALL HE KNEW, JIM.
BUT TOMORROW IS THE SECOND-- AND A TUESDAY--
IT SHOULDN'T BE DIFFICULT TO FIND HIS TARGET. ACCESSIBLE BY HELICOPTER AND TWICE AS BIG AS...
...TWICE AS BIG...

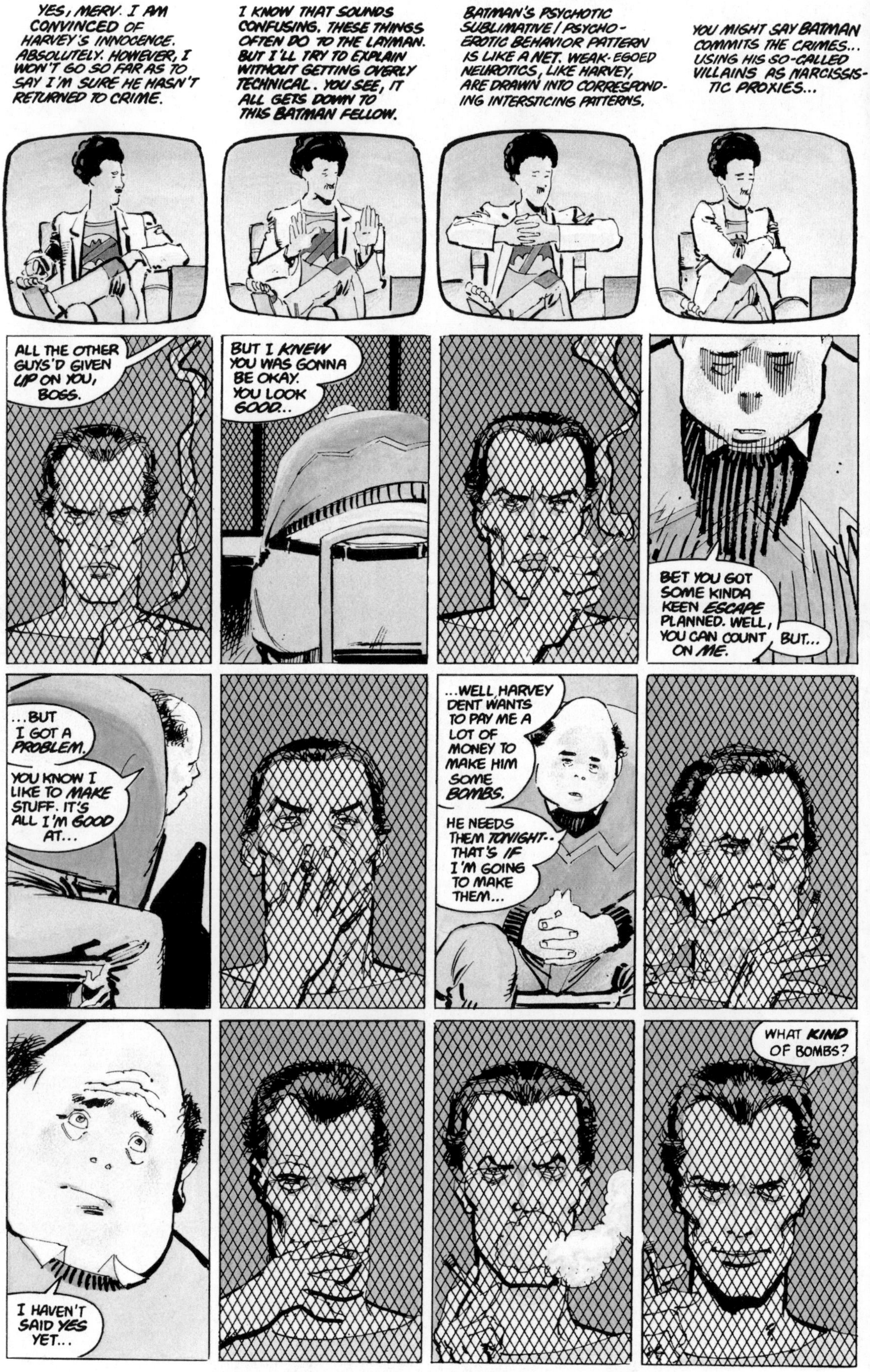
YES, MERV. I AM CONVINCED OF HARVEY'S INNOCENCE. ABSOLUTELY. HOWEVER, I WON'T GO SO FAR AS TO SAY I'M SURE HE HASN'T RETURNED TO CRIME.
I KNOW THAT SOUNDS CONFUSING. THESE THINGS OFTEN DO TO THE LAYMAN. BUT I'LL TRY TO EXPLAIN WITHOUT GETTING OVERLY TECHNICAL. YOU SEE, IT ALL GETS DOWN TO THIS BATMAN FELLOW.
BATMAN'S PSYCHOTIC SUBLIMATIVE / PSYCHO-EROTIC BEHAVIOR PATTERN IS LIKE A NET. WEAK-EGOED NEUROTICS, LIKE HARVEY, ARE DRAWN INTO CORRESPOND-ING INTERSTICING PATTERNS.
YOU MIGHT SAY BATMAN COMMITS THE CRIMES... USING HIS SO-CALLED VILLAINS AS NARCISSIS-TIC PROXIES...
ALL THE OTHER GUYS'D GIVEN UP ON YOU, BOSS.
BUT I KNEW YOU WAS GONNA BE OKAY. YOU LOOK GOOD...
BET YOU GOT SOME KINDA KEEN ESCAPE PLANNED. WELL, YOU CAN COUNT ON ME.
BUT...
...BUT I GOT A PROBLEM.
YOU KNOW I LIKE TO MAKE STUFF. IT'S ALL I'M GOOD AT...
...WELL, HARVEY DENT WANTS TO PAY ME A LOT OF MONEY TO MAKE HIM SOME BOMBS.
HE NEEDS THEM TONIGHT-- THAT'S IF I'M GOING TO MAKE THEM...
I HAVEN'T SAID YES YET...
WHAT KIND OF BOMBS?

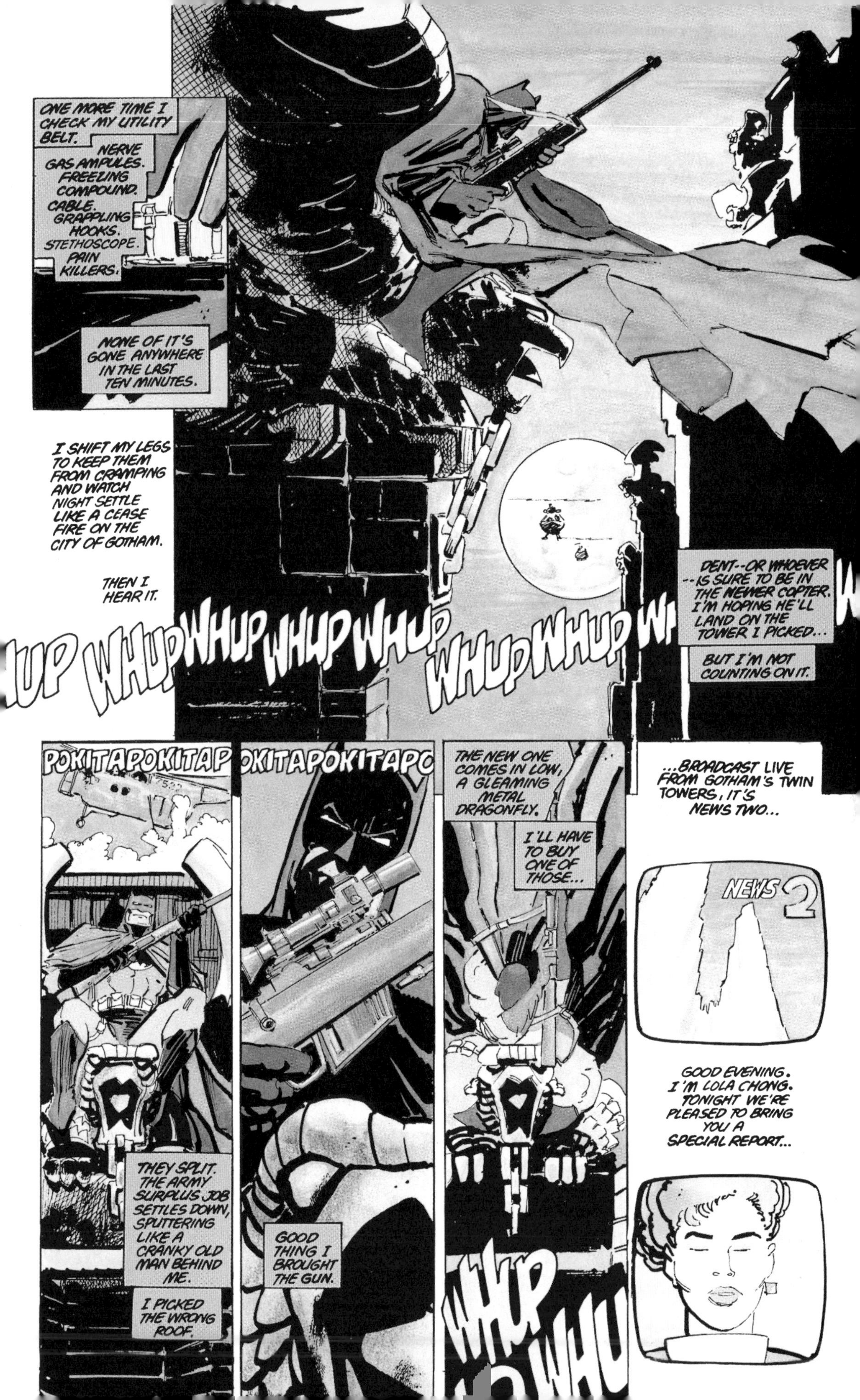
ONE MORE TIME I CHECK MY UTILITY BELT.
NERVE GAS AMPULES. FREEZING COMPOUND. CABLE. GRAPPLING HOOKS. STETHOSCOPE. PAIN KILLERS.
NONE OF IT'S GONE ANYWHERE IN THE LAST TEN MINUTES.
I SHIFT MY LEGS TO KEEP THEM FROM CRAMPING AND WATCH NIGHT SETTLE LIKE A CEASE FIRE ON THE CITY OF GOTHAM.
THEN I HEAR IT.
WHUP WHUP WHUP WHUP WHUP WHUP WHUP
DENT--OR WHOEVER--IS SURE TO BE IN THE NEWER COPTER. I'M HOPING HE'LL LAND ON THE TOWER I PICKED...
BUT I'M NOT COUNTING ON IT.
POKITAPOKITAP
POKITAPOKITAPO
THEY SPLIT. THE ARMY SURPLUS JOB SETTLES DOWN, SPUTTERING LIKE A CRANKY OLD MAN BEHIND ME.
I PICKED THE WRONG ROOF.
GOOD THING I BROUGHT THE GUN.
THE NEW ONE COMES IN LOW, A GLEAMING METAL DRAGONFLY.
I'LL HAVE TO BUY ONE OF THOSE...
WHUP WHU
...BROADCAST LIVE FROM GOTHAM'S TWIN TOWERS, IT'S NEWS TWO...
NEWS 2
GOOD EVENING. I'M LOLA CHONG. TONIGHT WE'RE PLEASED TO BRING YOU A SPECIAL REPORT...

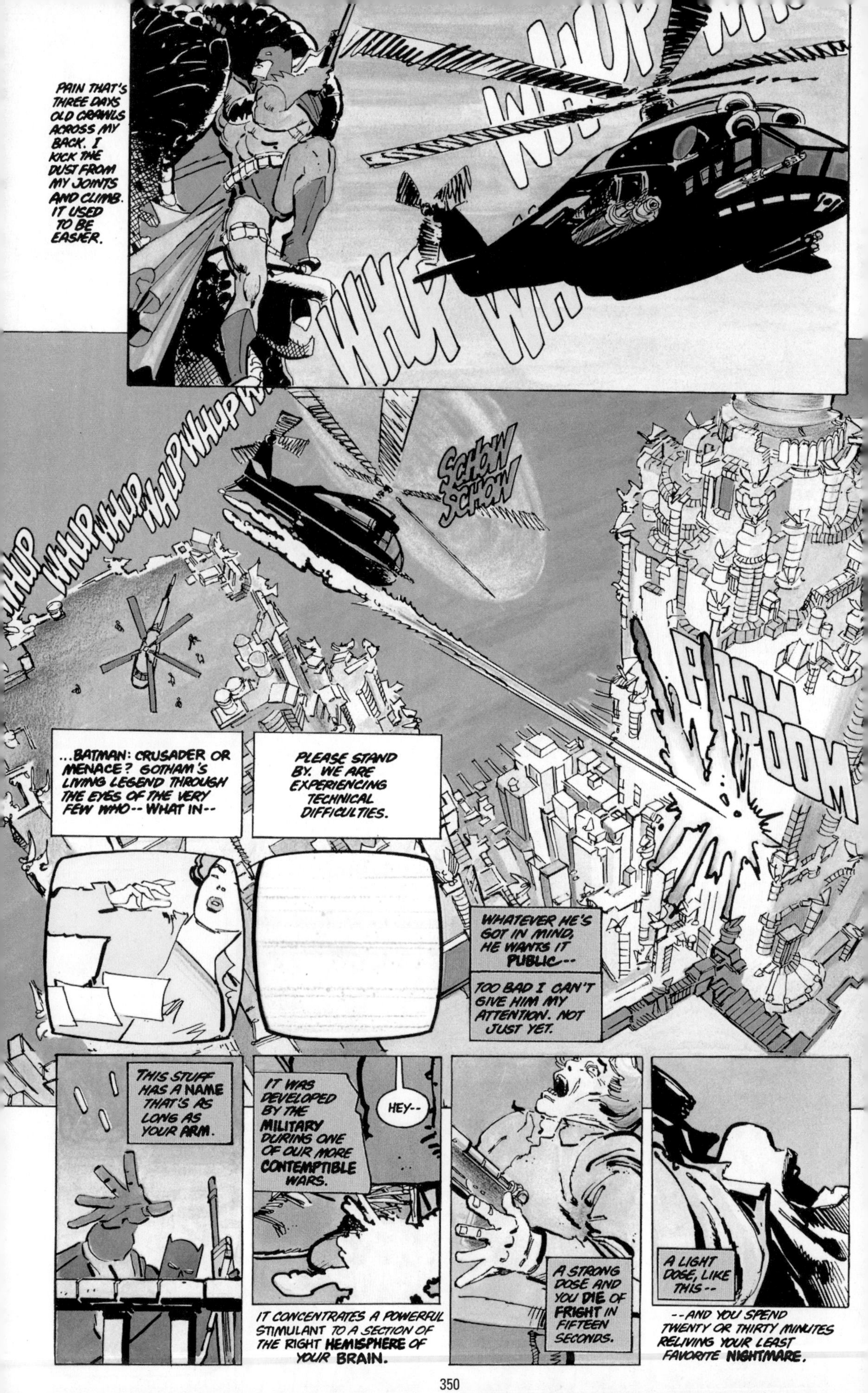
PAIN THAT'S THREE DAYS OLD CRAWLS ACROSS MY BACK. I KICK THE DUST FROM MY JOINTS AND CLIMB. IT USED TO BE EASIER.
WHUP WHUP
WHUP WHUP WHUP WHUP WHUP WHUP
SCHOW SCHOW
BOOM BOOM
...BATMAN: CRUSADER OR MENACE? GOTHAM'S LIVING LEGEND THROUGH THE EYES OF THE VERY FEW WHO-- WHAT IN--
PLEASE STAND BY. WE ARE EXPERIENCING TECHNICAL DIFFICULTIES.
WHATEVER HE'S GOT IN MIND, HE WANTS IT PUBLIC--
TOO BAD I CAN'T GIVE HIM MY ATTENTION. NOT JUST YET.
THIS STUFF HAS A NAME THAT'S AS LONG AS YOUR ARM.
IT WAS DEVELOPED BY THE MILITARY DURING ONE OF OUR MORE CONTEMPTIBLE WARS.
HEY--
IT CONCENTRATES A POWERFUL STIMULANT TO A SECTION OF THE RIGHT HEMISPHERE OF YOUR BRAIN.
A STRONG DOSE AND YOU DIE OF FRIGHT IN FIFTEEN SECONDS.
A LIGHT DOSE, LIKE THIS--
--AND YOU SPEND TWENTY OR THIRTY MINUTES RELIVING YOUR LEAST FAVORITE NIGHTMARE.

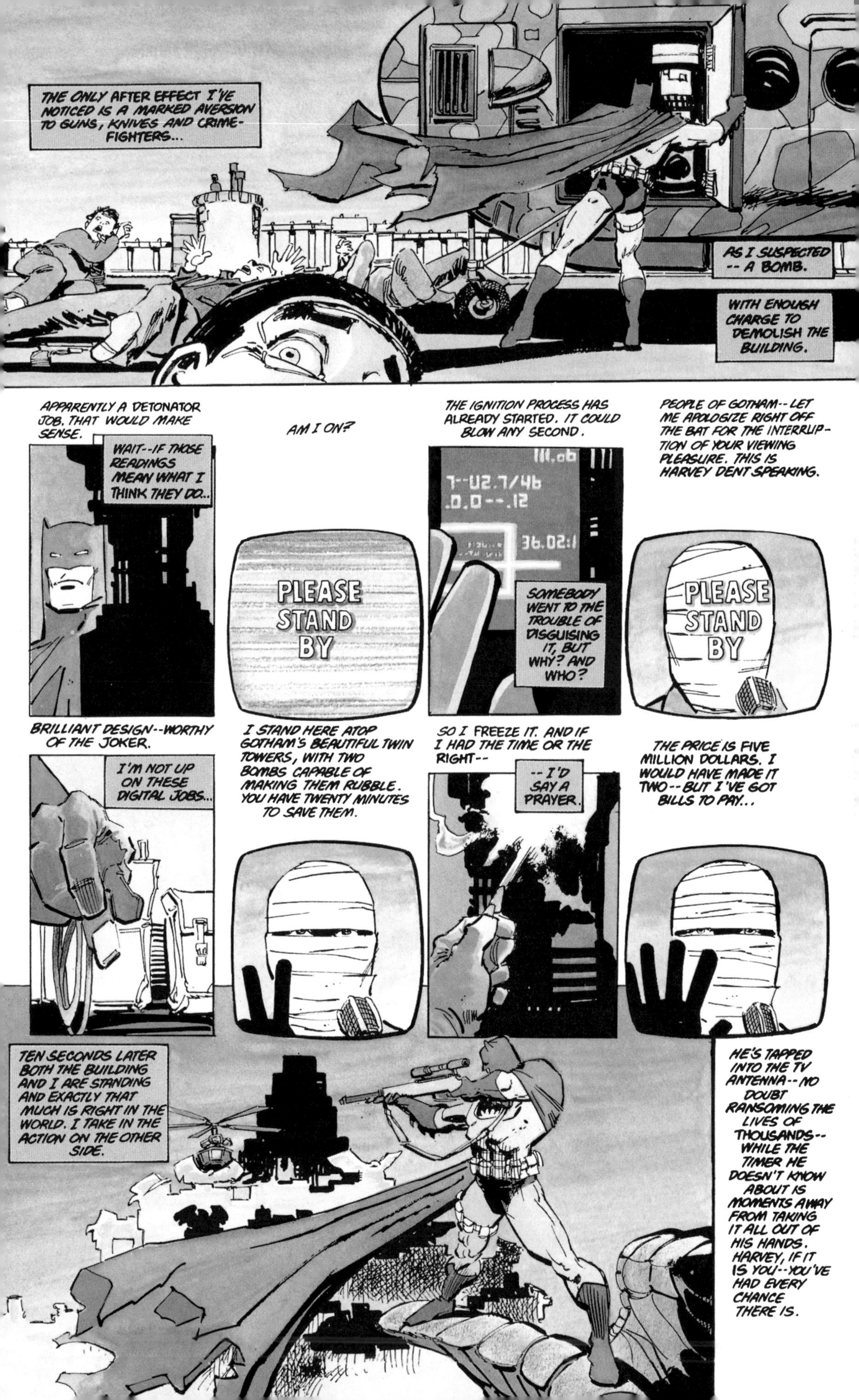
THE ONLY AFTER EFFECT I'VE NOTICED IS A MARKED AVERSION TO GUNS, KNIVES AND CRIME-FIGHTERS...
AS I SUSPECTED -- A BOMB.
WITH ENOUGH CHARGE TO DEMOLISH THE BUILDING.
APPARENTLY A DETONATOR JOB. THAT WOULD MAKE SENSE.
WAIT--IF THOSE READINGS MEAN WHAT I THINK THEY DO...
AM I ON?
PLEASE STAND BY
THE IGNITION PROCESS HAS ALREADY STARTED. IT COULD BLOW ANY SECOND.
SOMEBODY WENT TO THE TROUBLE OF DISGUISING IT, BUT WHY? AND WHO?
PEOPLE OF GOTHAM--LET ME APOLOGIZE RIGHT OFF THE BAT FOR THE INTERRUPTION OF YOUR VIEWING PLEASURE. THIS IS HARVEY DENT SPEAKING.
PLEASE STAND BY
BRILLIANT DESIGN--WORTHY OF THE JOKER.
I'M NOT UP ON THESE DIGITAL JOBS...
I STAND HERE ATOP GOTHAM'S BEAUTIFUL TWIN TOWERS, WITH TWO BOMBS CAPABLE OF MAKING THEM RUBBLE. YOU HAVE TWENTY MINUTES TO SAVE THEM.
SO I FREEZE IT. AND IF I HAD THE TIME OR THE RIGHT--
--I'D SAY A PRAYER.
THE PRICE IS FIVE MILLION DOLLARS. I WOULD HAVE MADE IT TWO--BUT I'VE GOT BILLS TO PAY...
TEN SECONDS LATER BOTH THE BUILDING AND I ARE STANDING AND EXACTLY THAT MUCH IS RIGHT IN THE WORLD. I TAKE IN THE ACTION ON THE OTHER SIDE.
HE'S TAPPED INTO THE TV ANTENNA--NO DOUBT RANSOMING THE LIVES OF THOUSANDS--WHILE THE TIMER HE DOESN'T KNOW ABOUT IS MOMENTS AWAY FROM TAKING IT ALL OUT OF HIS HANDS. HARVEY, IF IT IS YOU--YOU'VE HAD EVERY CHANCE THERE IS.

SPOKK

BRLAMMM

KBLAMM
BLAMM
BLAM LAMM

BLAM
BLAM
LAM
AM
BLAM
AM

WHUP
WHUP
WHUP

IN TEN YEARS I'VE NEVER FELT SO CALM. SO RIGHT.

THIS WOULD BE A FINE DEATH...

--MAGNUM LOAD HAS TO BE-- HITS ME LIKE A FREIGHT TRAIN--THE PLATE HOLDS--

--WHY DO YOU THINK I WEAR A TARGET ON MY CHEST-- CAN'T ARMOR MY HEAD-- LEFT ARM NUMB--

--IF IT'S A HEART ATTACK I'M FINISHED--

...A FINE DEATH. BUT THERE ARE THE THOUSANDS TO THINK OF...

...AND HARVEY...

BLAM

THNK

...I HAVE TO KNOW.

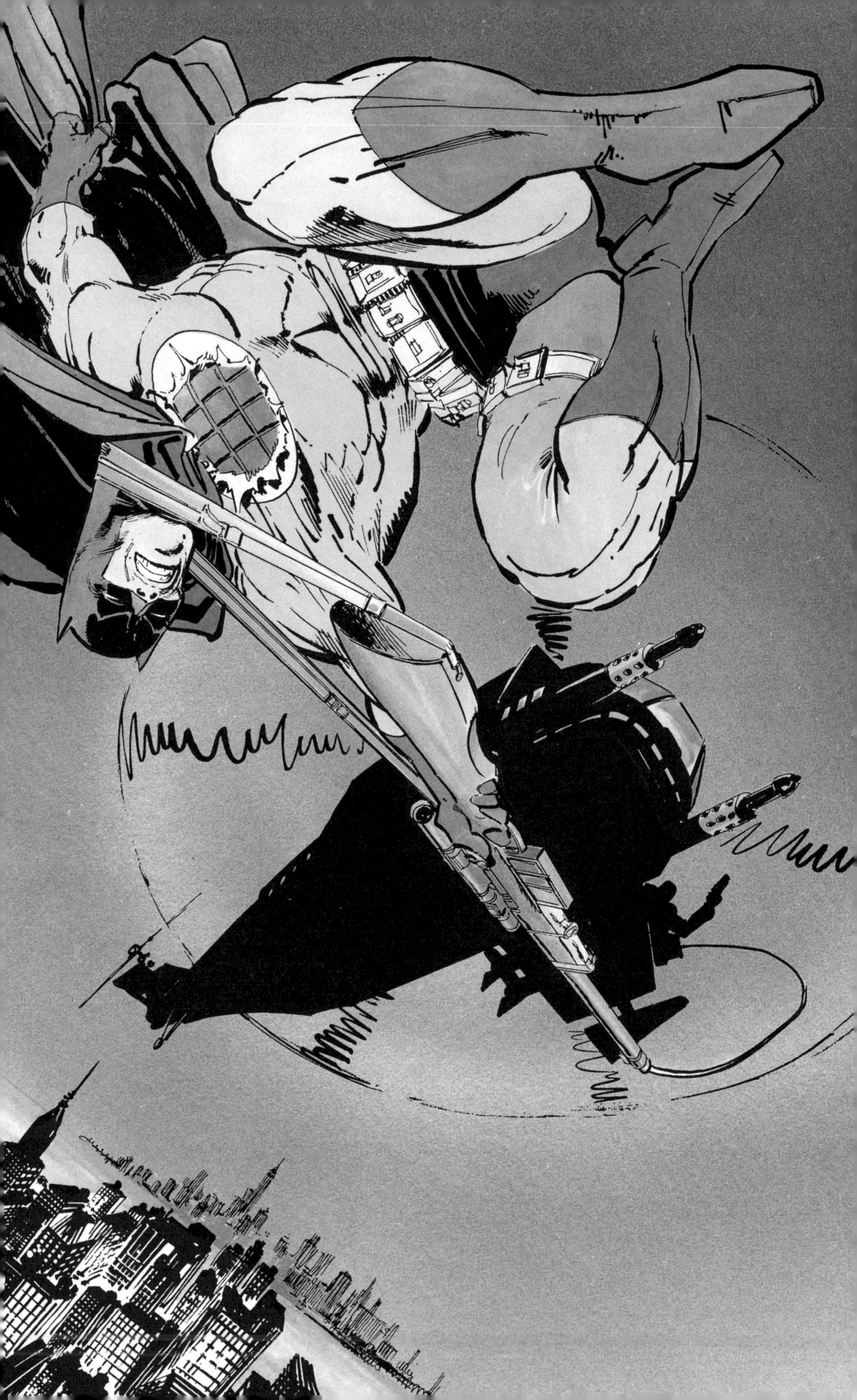

HE'S GOT YOUR STYLE, HARVEY, AND YOUR GUTS.

BLAM BLAM

UNFORTUNATELY FOR HIM, HE'S GOT NO MORE SENSE OF SELF-PRESERVATION THAN YOU DID...

BLAM

...AND INSPIRES THE SAME LEVEL OF LOYALTY FROM HIS MEN.

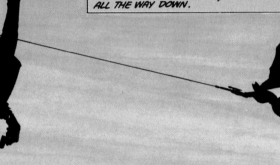

IT TAKES NEARLY A MINUTE TO FALL FROM THIS HEIGHT. AND DESPITE WHAT YOU MAY HAVE HEARD, YOU'RE LIKELY TO STAY CONSCIOUS ALL THE WAY DOWN.

THOUGHTS LIKE THAT KEEP ME WARM AT NIGHT.

THE IMPACT IS TREMENDOUS. EVEN BONE IS TURNED TO POWDER.

NOT MUCH OF A CORPSE LEFT.

MOSTLY LIQUID.

PROBLEM IS...

...THERE MIGHT NOT BE ANY FINGER-PRINTS.

EVEN DENTAL RECORDS WOULD PROBABLY BE USELESS.

AND LIKE I SAID, HARVEY...

...I HAVE TO KNOW.

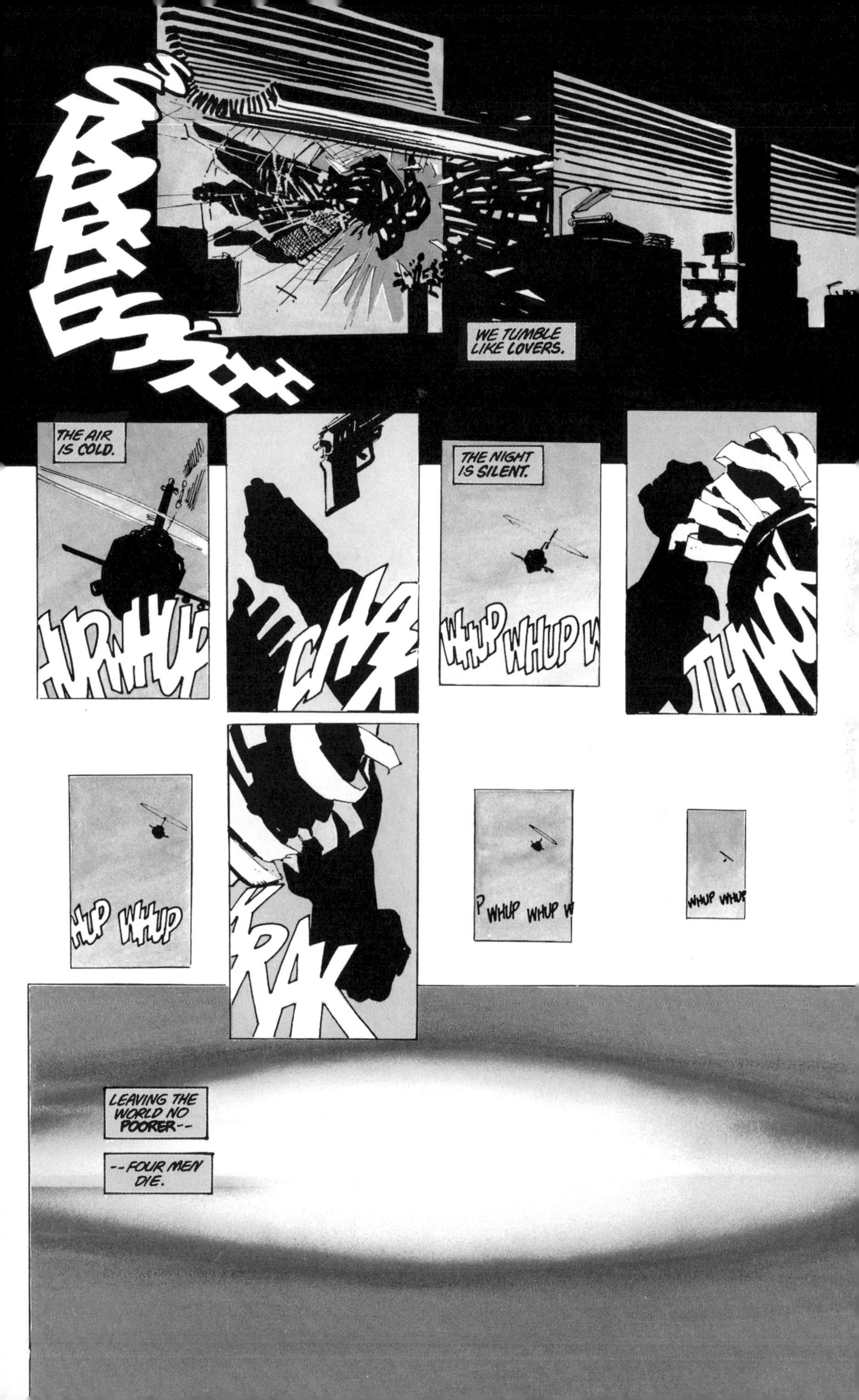

SSKRASSHHH
WE TUMBLE LIKE LOVERS.
THE AIR IS COLD.
WHUP WHUP
CHK
THE NIGHT IS SILENT.
WHUP WHUP W
THWOK
WHUP WHUP
KRAK
P WHUP WHUP W
WHUP WHUP
LEAVING THE WORLD NO POORER--
--FOUR MEN DIE.

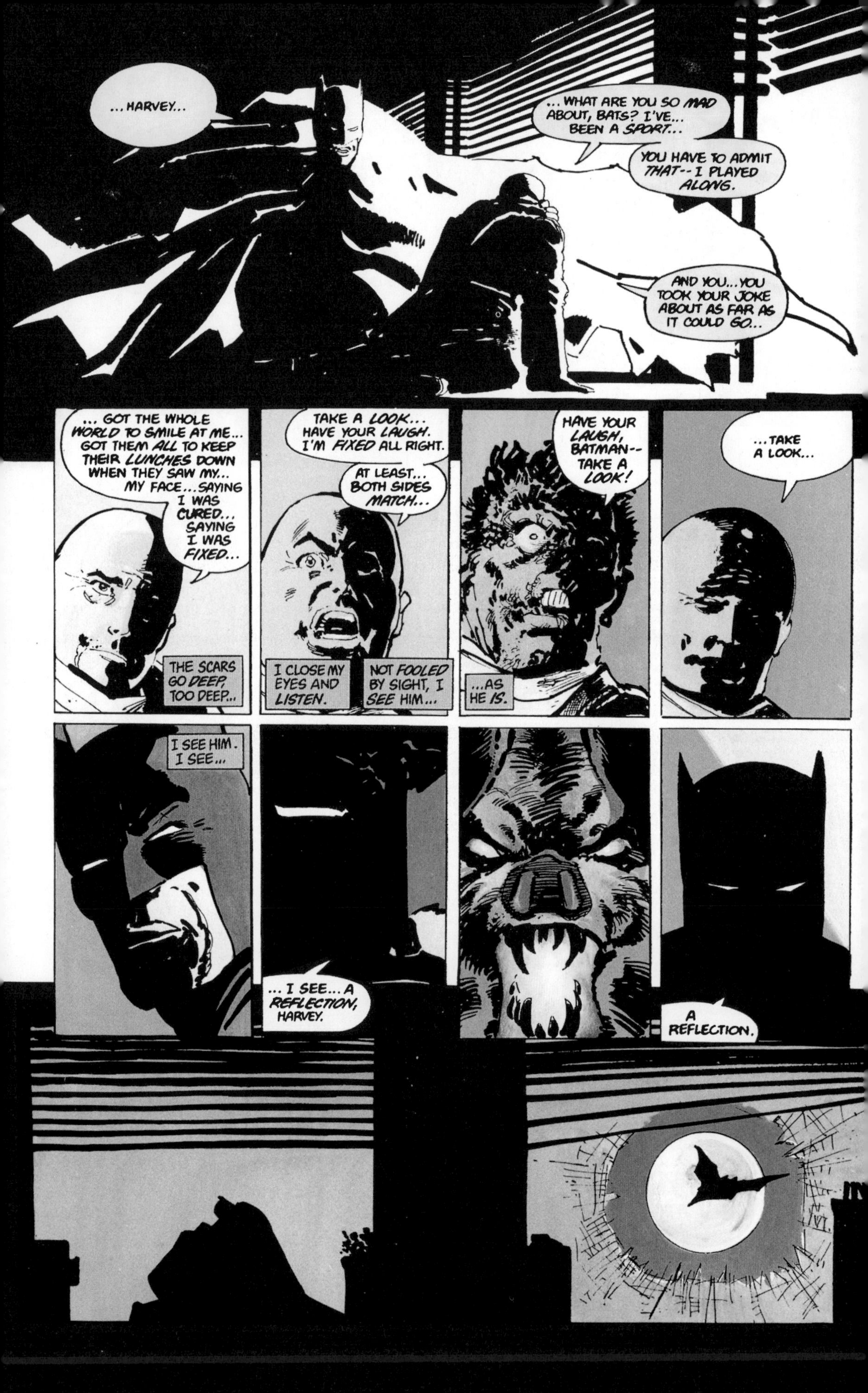

... HARVEY...
... WHAT ARE YOU SO MAD ABOUT, BATS? I'VE... BEEN A SPORT...
YOU HAVE TO ADMIT THAT-- I PLAYED ALONG.
AND YOU... YOU TOOK YOUR JOKE ABOUT AS FAR AS IT COULD GO...
... GOT THE WHOLE WORLD TO SMILE AT ME... GOT THEM ALL TO KEEP THEIR LUNCHES DOWN WHEN THEY SAW MY... MY FACE... SAYING I WAS CURED... SAYING I WAS FIXED...
THE SCARS GO DEEP, TOO DEEP...
TAKE A LOOK... HAVE YOUR LAUGH. I'M FIXED ALL RIGHT.
AT LEAST... BOTH SIDES MATCH...
I CLOSE MY EYES AND LISTEN.
NOT FOOLED BY SIGHT, I SEE HIM...
HAVE YOUR LAUGH, BATMAN-- TAKE A LOOK!
...AS HE IS.
...TAKE A LOOK...
I SEE HIM. I SEE...
... I SEE... A REFLECTION, HARVEY.
A REFLECTION.

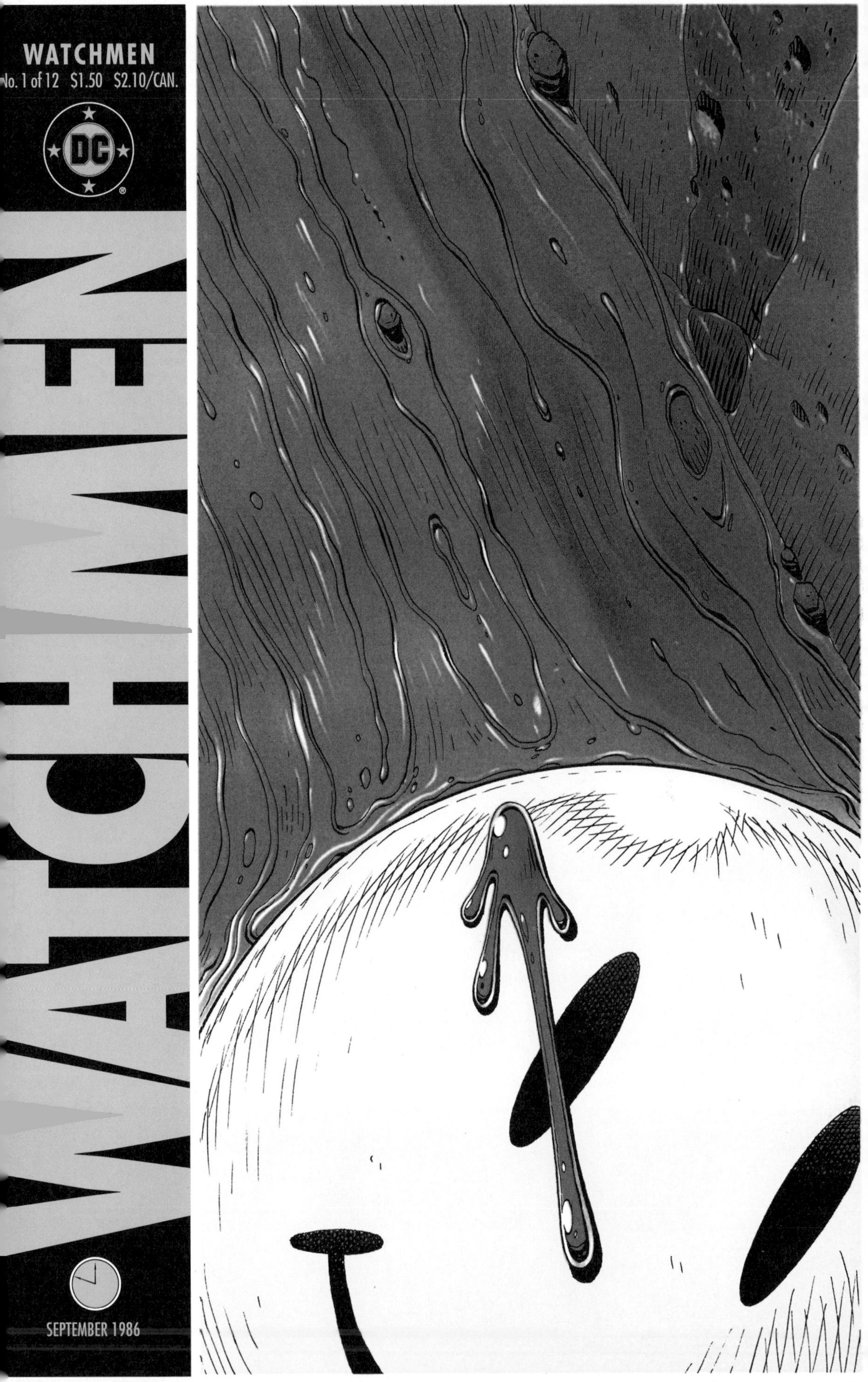
WATCHMEN
No. 1 of 12 $1.50 $2.10/CAN.
DC
WATCHMEN
SEPTEMBER 1986

AT MIDNIGHT ALL THE AGENTS...

Story by
ALAN MOORE

Art by
DAVE GIBBONS

Colors by
JOHN HIGGINS

WATCHMEN created by **ALAN MOORE** and **DAVE GIBBONS**

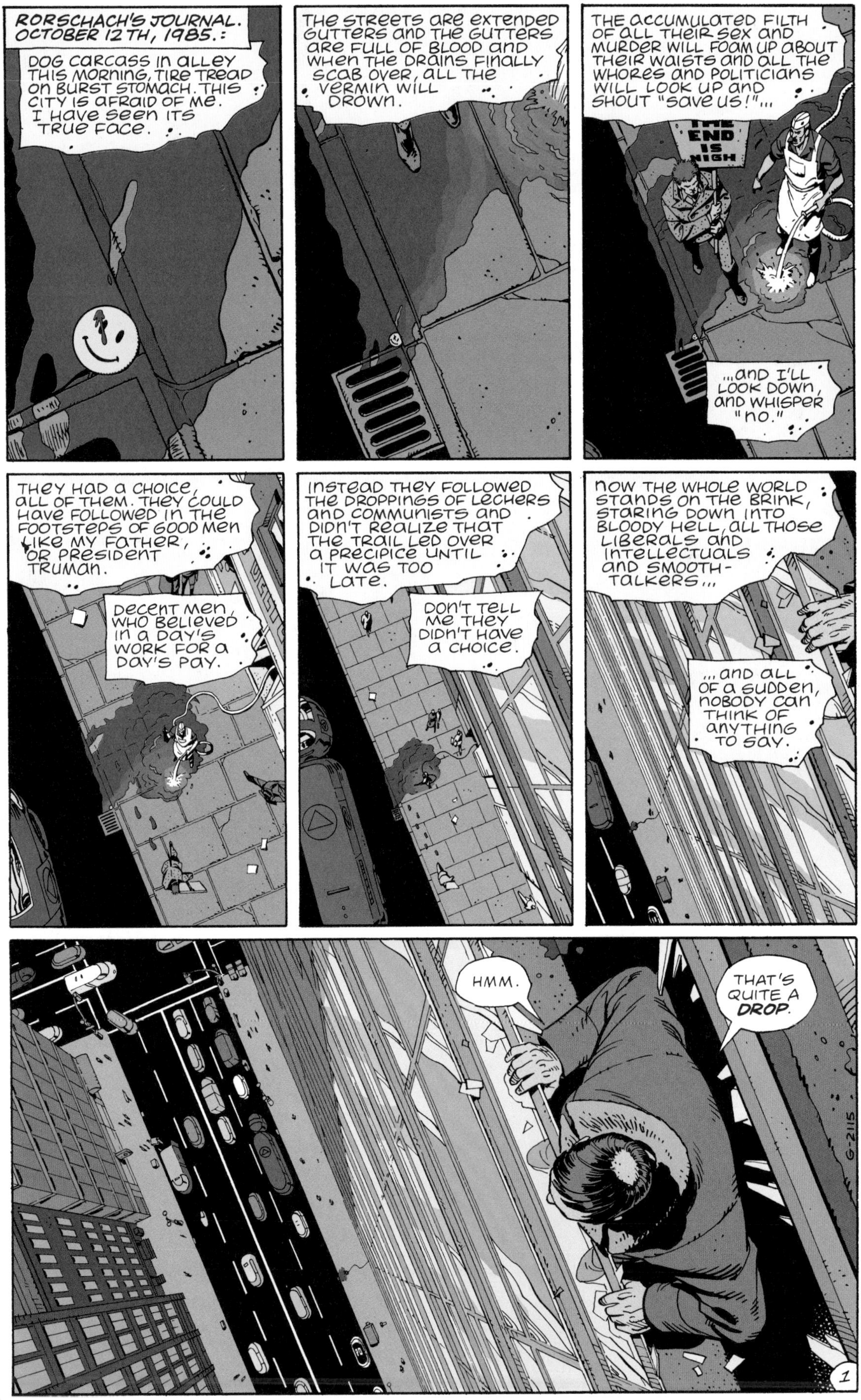
RORSCHACH'S JOURNAL. OCTOBER 12TH, 1985.:
DOG CARCASS IN ALLEY THIS MORNING, TIRE TREAD ON BURST STOMACH. THIS CITY IS AFRAID OF ME. I HAVE SEEN ITS TRUE FACE.
THE STREETS ARE EXTENDED GUTTERS AND THE GUTTERS ARE FULL OF BLOOD AND WHEN THE DRAINS FINALLY SCAB OVER, ALL THE VERMIN WILL DROWN.
THE ACCUMULATED FILTH OF ALL THEIR SEX AND MURDER WILL FOAM UP ABOUT THEIR WAISTS AND ALL THE WHORES AND POLITICIANS WILL LOOK UP AND SHOUT "SAVE US!"...
THE END IS NIGH
...AND I'LL LOOK DOWN, AND WHISPER "NO."
THEY HAD A CHOICE, ALL OF THEM. THEY COULD HAVE FOLLOWED IN THE FOOTSTEPS OF GOOD MEN LIKE MY FATHER, OR PRESIDENT TRUMAN.
DECENT MEN, WHO BELIEVED IN A DAY'S WORK FOR A DAY'S PAY.
INSTEAD THEY FOLLOWED THE DROPPINGS OF LECHERS AND COMMUNISTS AND DIDN'T REALIZE THAT THE TRAIL LED OVER A PRECIPICE UNTIL IT WAS TOO LATE.
DON'T TELL ME THEY DIDN'T HAVE A CHOICE.
NOW THE WHOLE WORLD STANDS ON THE BRINK, STARING DOWN INTO BLOODY HELL, ALL THOSE LIBERALS AND INTELLECTUALS AND SMOOTH-TALKERS...
...AND ALL OF A SUDDEN, NOBODY CAN THINK OF ANYTHING TO SAY.
HMM.
THAT'S QUITE A DROP.
G-2115
1

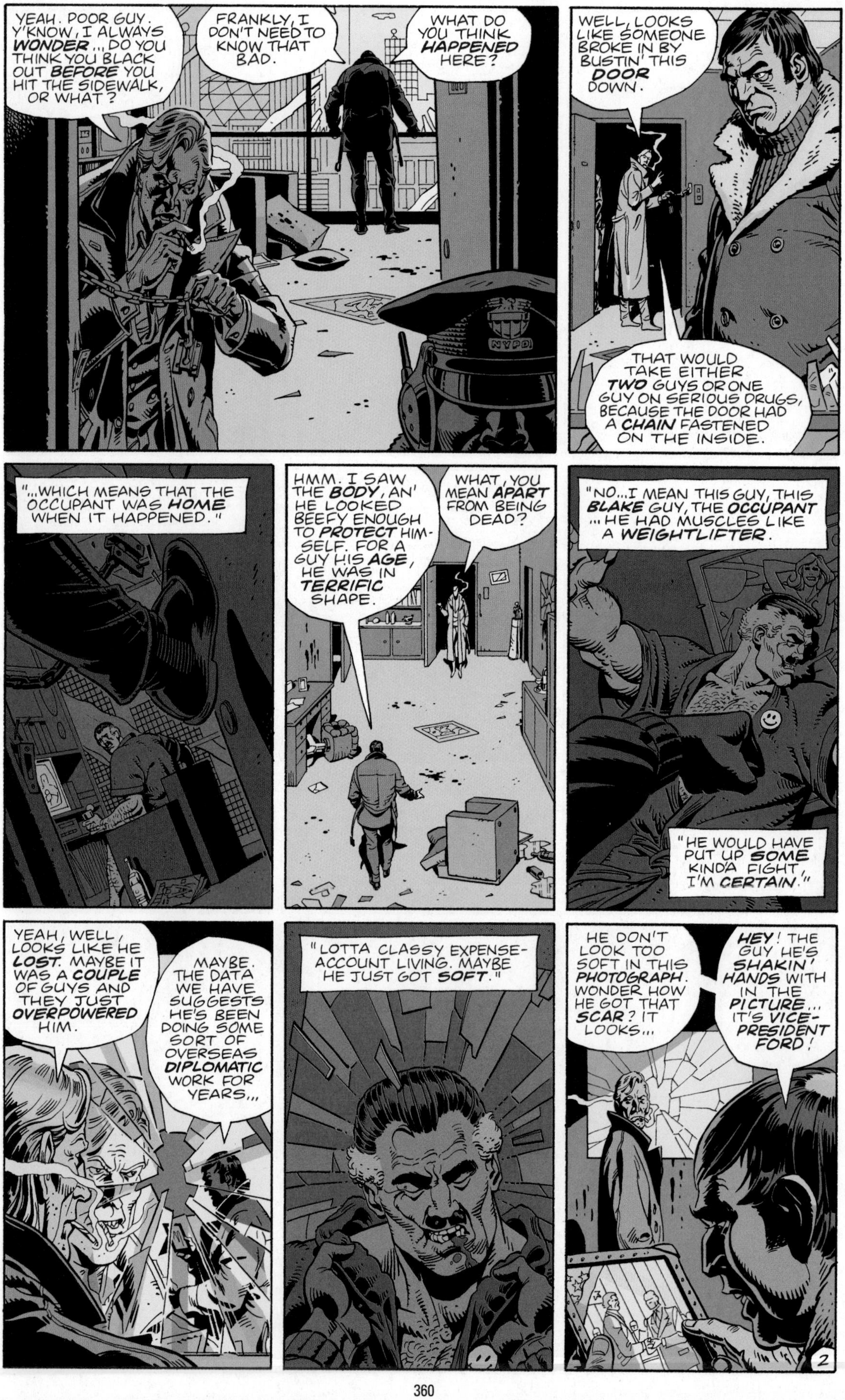
YEAH. POOR GUY. Y'KNOW, I ALWAYS WONDER ... DO YOU THINK YOU BLACK OUT BEFORE YOU HIT THE SIDEWALK, OR WHAT?
FRANKLY, I DON'T NEED TO KNOW THAT BAD.
WHAT DO YOU THINK HAPPENED HERE?
NYPD
WELL, LOOKS LIKE SOMEONE BROKE IN BY BUSTIN' THIS DOOR DOWN.
THAT WOULD TAKE EITHER TWO GUYS OR ONE GUY ON SERIOUS DRUGS, BECAUSE THE DOOR HAD A CHAIN FASTENED ON THE INSIDE.
"...WHICH MEANS THAT THE OCCUPANT WAS HOME WHEN IT HAPPENED."
HMM. I SAW THE BODY, AN' HE LOOKED BEEFY ENOUGH TO PROTECT HIMSELF. FOR A GUY HIS AGE, HE WAS IN TERRIFIC SHAPE.
WHAT, YOU MEAN APART FROM BEING DEAD?
"NO...I MEAN THIS GUY, THIS BLAKE GUY, THE OCCUPANT ...HE HAD MUSCLES LIKE A WEIGHTLIFTER.
"HE WOULD HAVE PUT UP SOME KINDA FIGHT, I'M CERTAIN."
YEAH, WELL, LOOKS LIKE HE LOST. MAYBE IT WAS A COUPLE OF GUYS AND THEY JUST OVERPOWERED HIM.
MAYBE. THE DATA WE HAVE SUGGESTS HE'S BEEN DOING SOME SORT OF OVERSEAS DIPLOMATIC WORK FOR YEARS...
"LOTTA CLASSY EXPENSE-ACCOUNT LIVING. MAYBE HE JUST GOT SOFT."
HE DON'T LOOK TOO SOFT IN THIS PHOTOGRAPH. WONDER HOW HE GOT THAT SCAR? IT LOOKS...
HEY! THE GUY HE'S SHAKIN' HANDS WITH IN THE PICTURE... IT'S VICE-PRESIDENT FORD!
2

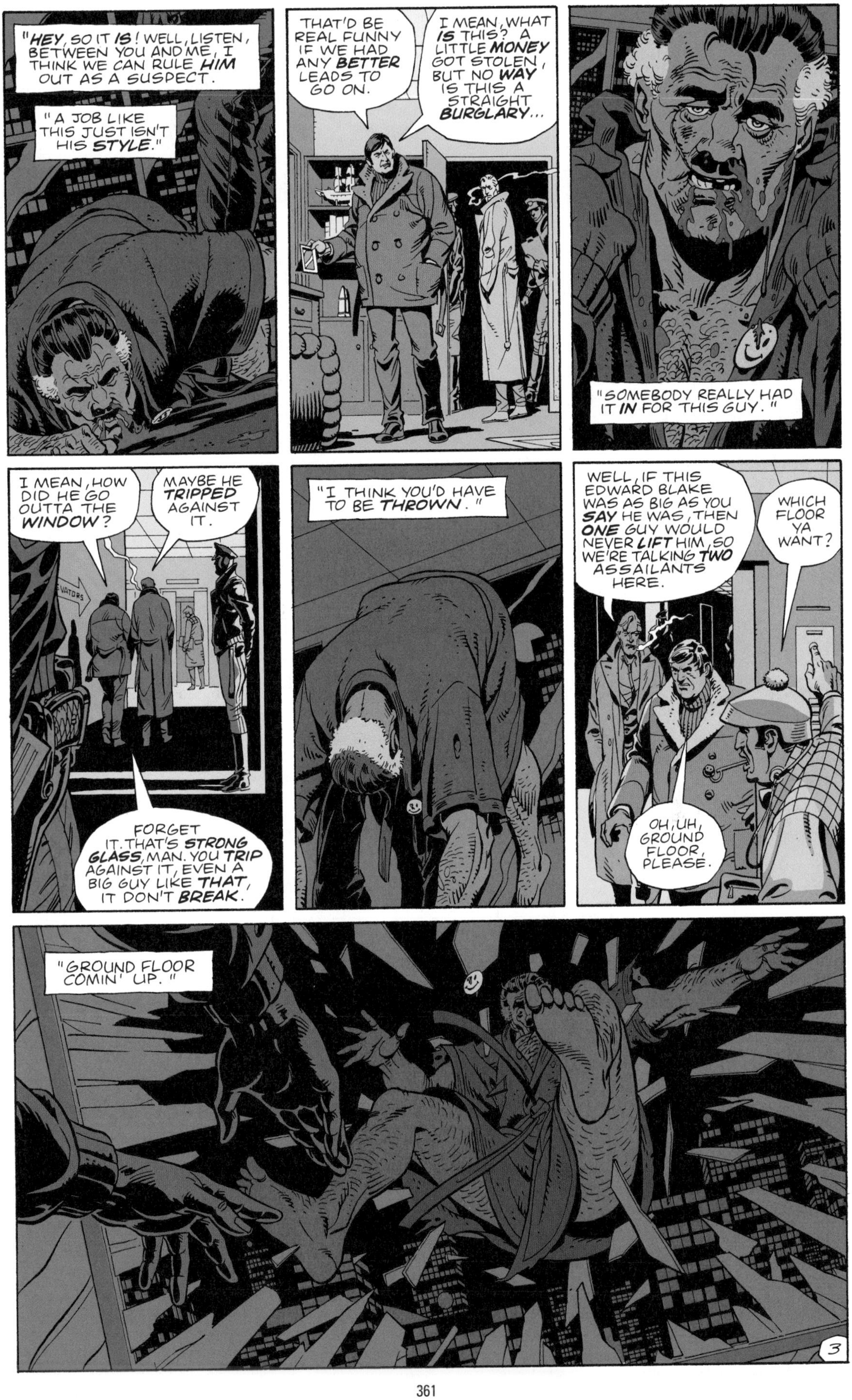
"HEY, SO IT IS! WELL, LISTEN, BETWEEN YOU AND ME, I THINK WE CAN RULE HIM OUT AS A SUSPECT.
"A JOB LIKE THIS JUST ISN'T HIS STYLE."
THAT'D BE REAL FUNNY IF WE HAD ANY BETTER LEADS TO GO ON.
I MEAN, WHAT IS THIS? A LITTLE MONEY GOT STOLEN, BUT NO WAY IS THIS A STRAIGHT BURGLARY...
"SOMEBODY REALLY HAD IT IN FOR THIS GUY."
I MEAN, HOW DID HE GO OUTTA THE WINDOW?
MAYBE HE TRIPPED AGAINST IT.
FORGET IT. THAT'S STRONG GLASS, MAN. YOU TRIP AGAINST IT, EVEN A BIG GUY LIKE THAT, IT DON'T BREAK.
"I THINK YOU'D HAVE TO BE THROWN."
WELL, IF THIS EDWARD BLAKE WAS AS BIG AS YOU SAY HE WAS, THEN ONE GUY WOULD NEVER LIFT HIM, SO WE'RE TALKING TWO ASSAILANTS HERE.
WHICH FLOOR YA WANT?
OH, UH, GROUND FLOOR, PLEASE.
"GROUND FLOOR COMIN' UP."
3

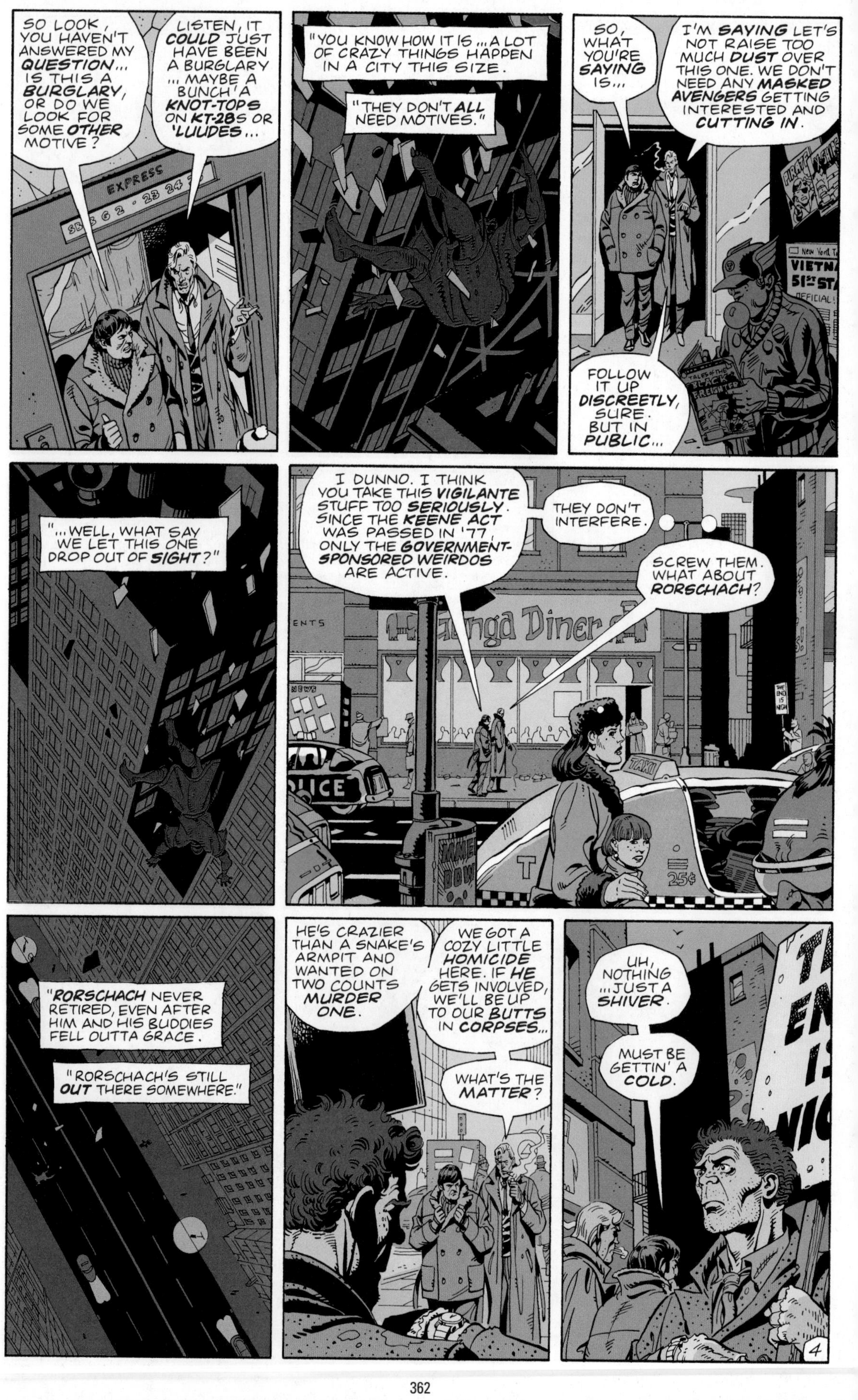
SO LOOK, YOU HAVEN'T ANSWERED MY QUESTION... IS THIS A BURGLARY, OR DO WE LOOK FOR SOME OTHER MOTIVE?
LISTEN, IT COULD JUST HAVE BEEN A BURGLARY ...MAYBE A BUNCH 'A KNOT-TOPS ON KT-28s OR 'LUDES...
EXPRESS
"YOU KNOW HOW IT IS ...A LOT OF CRAZY THINGS HAPPEN IN A CITY THIS SIZE.
"THEY DON'T ALL NEED MOTIVES."
SO, WHAT YOU'RE SAYING IS...
I'M SAYING LET'S NOT RAISE TOO MUCH DUST OVER THIS ONE. WE DON'T NEED ANY MASKED AVENGERS GETTING INTERESTED AND CUTTING IN.
FOLLOW IT UP DISCREETLY, SURE. BUT IN PUBLIC...
"...WELL, WHAT SAY WE LET THIS ONE DROP OUT OF SIGHT?"
I DUNNO. I THINK YOU TAKE THIS VIGILANTE STUFF TOO SERIOUSLY. SINCE THE KEENE ACT WAS PASSED IN '77, ONLY THE GOVERNMENT-SPONSORED WEIRDOS ARE ACTIVE.
THEY DON'T INTERFERE.
SCREW THEM. WHAT ABOUT RORSCHACH?
Gunga Diner
TAXI
25¢
"RORSCHACH NEVER RETIRED, EVEN AFTER HIM AND HIS BUDDIES FELL OUTTA GRACE.
"RORSCHACH'S STILL OUT THERE SOMEWHERE."
HE'S CRAZIER THAN A SNAKE'S ARMPIT AND WANTED ON TWO COUNTS MURDER ONE.
WE GOT A COZY LITTLE HOMICIDE HERE. IF HE GETS INVOLVED, WE'LL BE UP TO OUR BUTTS IN CORPSES...
WHAT'S THE MATTER?
UH, NOTHING ...JUST A SHIVER.
MUST BE GETTIN' A COLD.
4

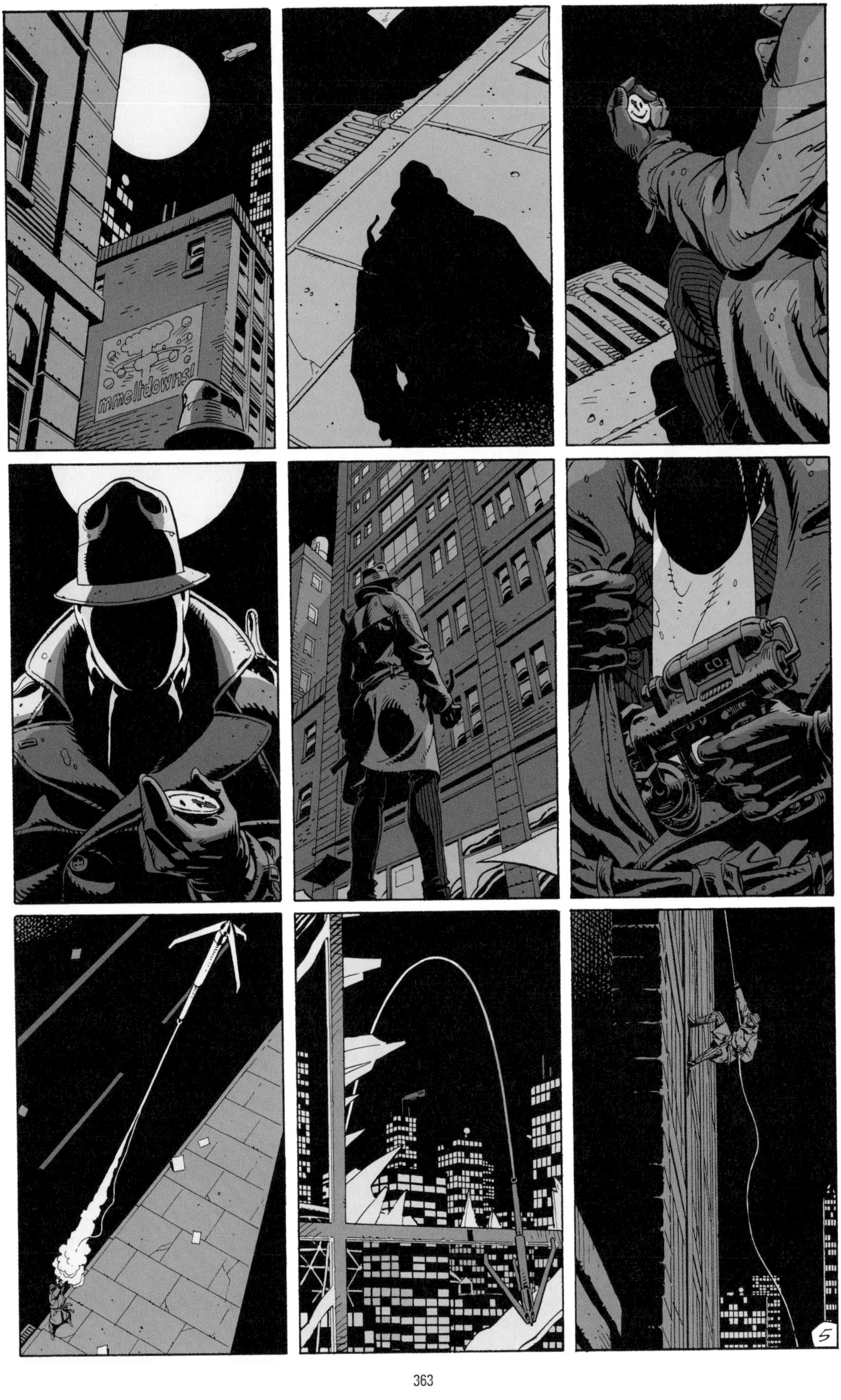
mmeltdowns!
5

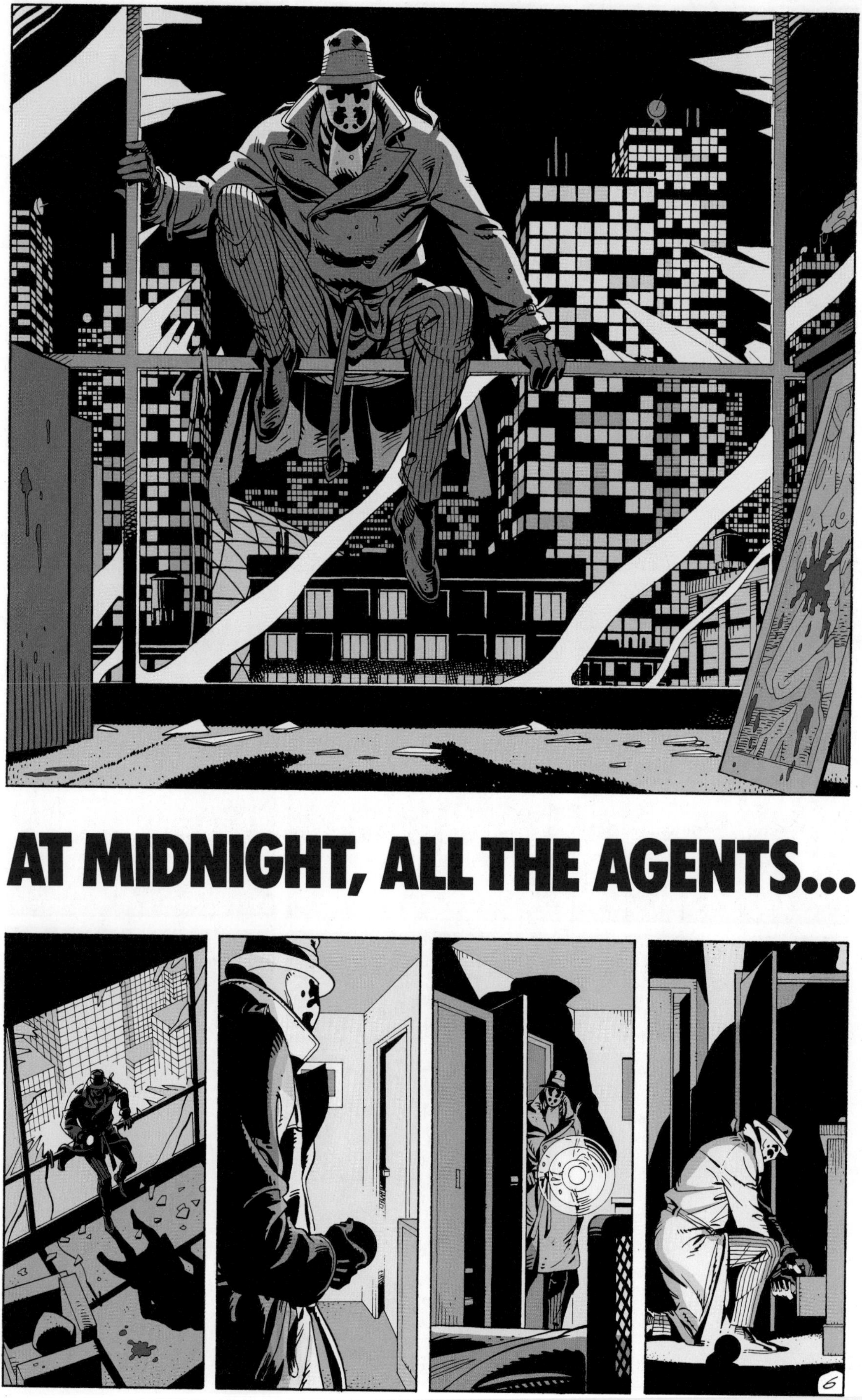
AT MIDNIGHT, ALL THE AGENTS...

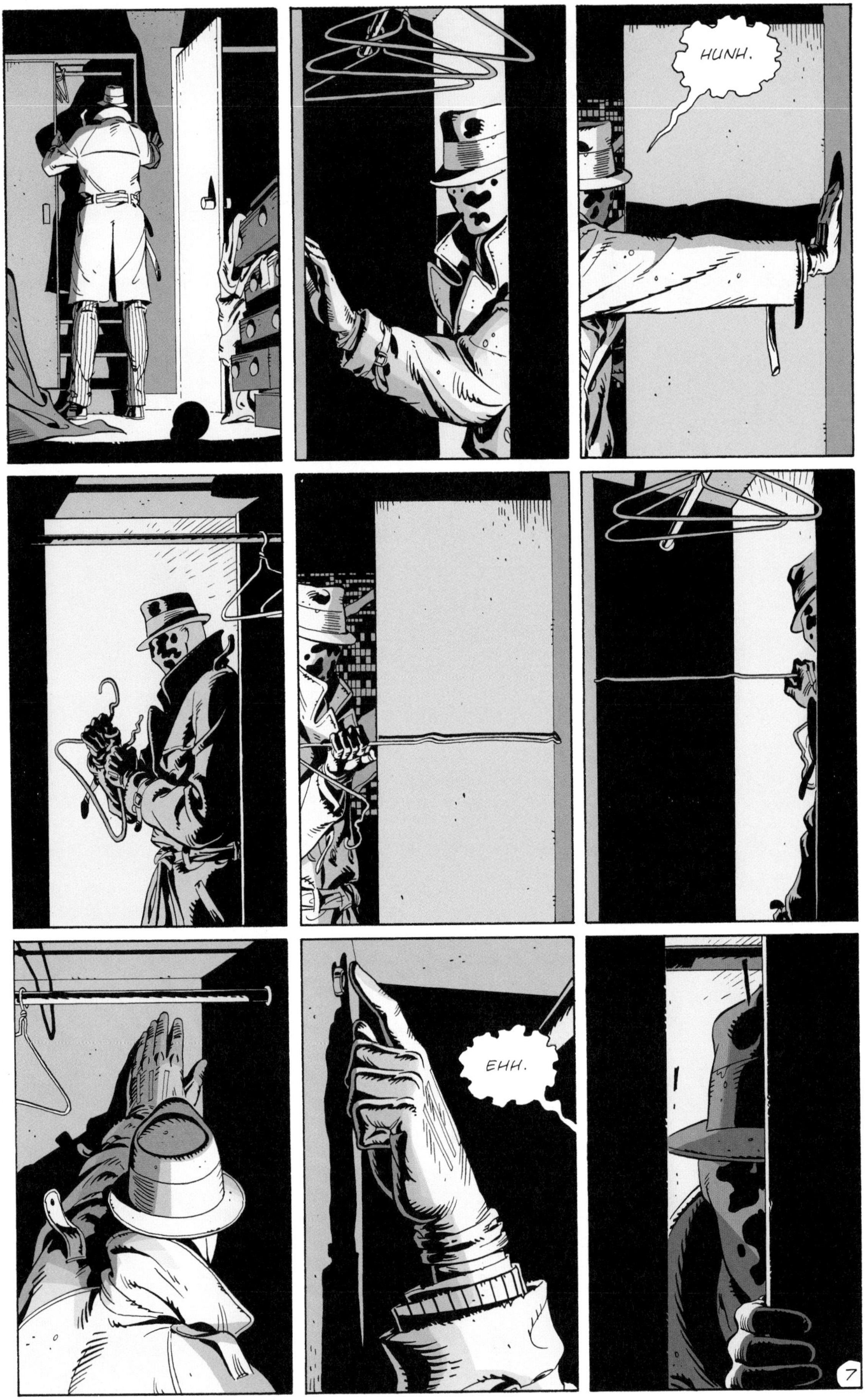
HUNH.
EHH.
7

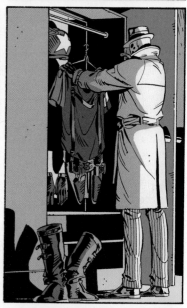

HURM.

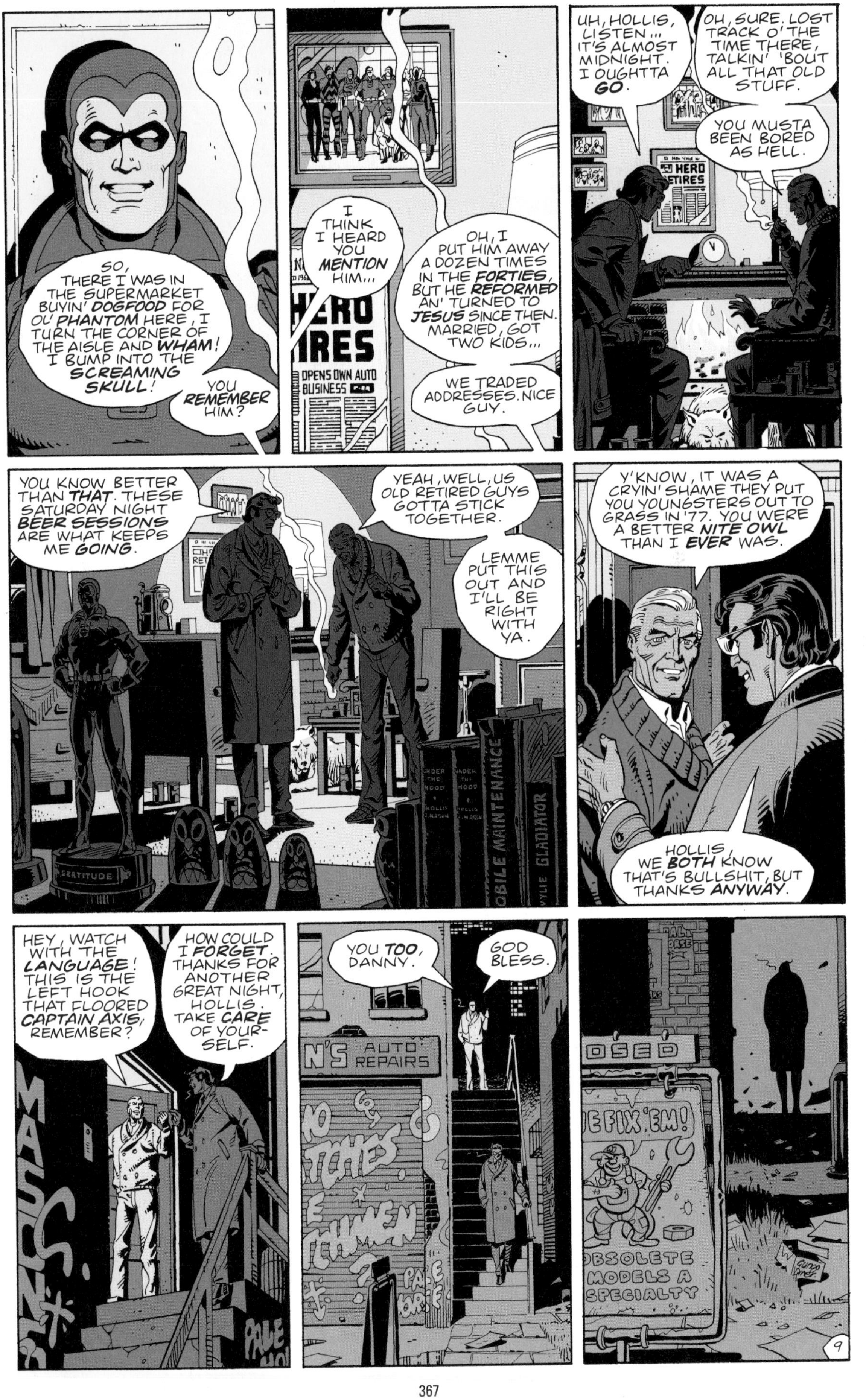
SO, THERE I WAS IN THE SUPERMARKET BUYIN' DOGFOOD FOR OL' PHANTOM HERE, I TURN THE CORNER OF THE AISLE AND WHAM! I BUMP INTO THE SCREAMING SKULL!
YOU REMEMBER HIM?
HERO
IRES
OPENS OWN AUTO BUSINESS
I THINK I HEARD YOU MENTION HIM...
OH, I PUT HIM AWAY A DOZEN TIMES IN THE FORTIES, BUT HE REFORMED AN' TURNED TO JESUS SINCE THEN. MARRIED, GOT TWO KIDS...
WE TRADED ADDRESSES. NICE GUY.
UH, HOLLIS, LISTEN... IT'S ALMOST MIDNIGHT. I OUGHTTA GO.
OH, SURE. LOST TRACK O' THE TIME THERE, TALKIN' 'BOUT ALL THAT OLD STUFF.
YOU MUSTA BEEN BORED AS HELL.
HERO
RETIRES
YOU KNOW BETTER THAN THAT. THESE SATURDAY NIGHT BEER SESSIONS ARE WHAT KEEPS ME GOING.
YEAH, WELL, US OLD RETIRED GUYS GOTTA STICK TOGETHER.
LEMME PUT THIS OUT AND I'LL BE RIGHT WITH YA.
GRATITUDE
UNDER THE HOOD
HOLLIS J. MASON
OBILE MAINTENANCE
GLADIATOR
Y'KNOW, IT WAS A CRYIN' SHAME THEY PUT YOU YOUNGSTERS OUT TO GRASS IN '77. YOU WERE A BETTER NITE OWL THAN I EVER WAS.
HOLLIS, WE BOTH KNOW THAT'S BULLSHIT, BUT THANKS ANYWAY.
HEY, WATCH WITH THE LANGUAGE! THIS IS THE LEFT HOOK THAT FLOORED CAPTAIN AXIS, REMEMBER?
HOW COULD I FORGET. THANKS FOR ANOTHER GREAT NIGHT, HOLLIS. TAKE CARE OF YOURSELF.
YOU TOO, DANNY.
GOD BLESS.
N'S AUTO REPAIRS
OSED
E FIX 'EM!
OBSOLETE MODELS A SPECIALTY
9

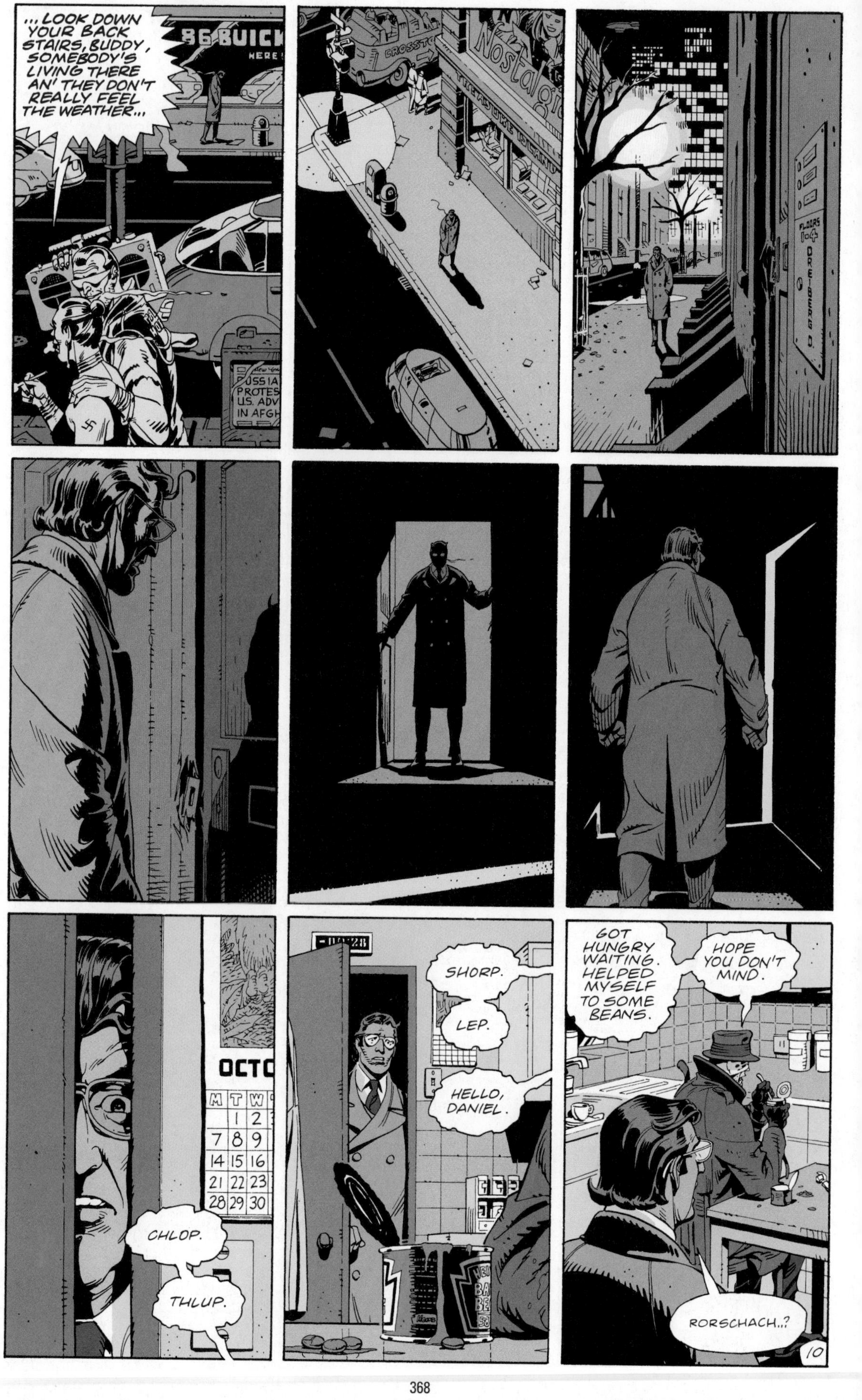

...LOOK DOWN YOUR BACK STAIRS, BUDDY, SOMEBODY'S LIVING THERE AN' THEY DON'T REALLY FEEL THE WEATHER...
CHLOP.
THLUP.
SHORP.
LEP.
HELLO, DANIEL.
GOT HUNGRY WAITING. HELPED MYSELF TO SOME BEANS.
HOPE YOU DON'T MIND.
RORSCHACH..?
10

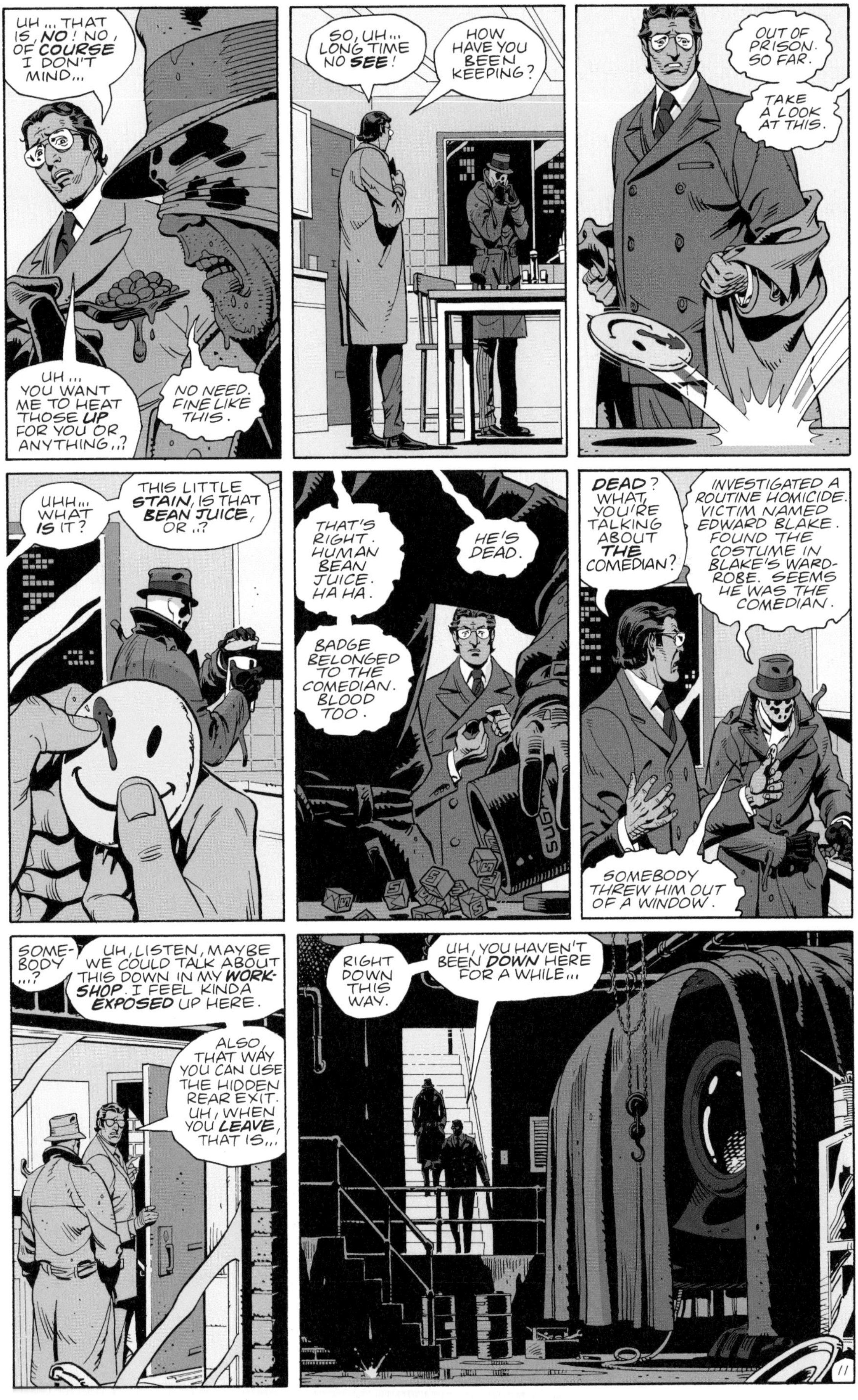
UH ... THAT IS, NO! NO, OF COURSE I DON'T MIND...
UH ... YOU WANT ME TO HEAT THOSE UP FOR YOU OR ANYTHING..?
NO NEED. FINE LIKE THIS.
SO, UH ... LONG TIME NO SEE!
HOW HAVE YOU BEEN KEEPING?
OUT OF PRISON. SO FAR.
TAKE A LOOK AT THIS.
UHH... WHAT IS IT?
THIS LITTLE STAIN, IS THAT BEAN JUICE, OR ..?
THAT'S RIGHT. HUMAN BEAN JUICE. HA HA.
BADGE BELONGED TO THE COMEDIAN. BLOOD TOO.
HE'S DEAD.
DEAD? WHAT, YOU'RE TALKING ABOUT THE COMEDIAN?
INVESTIGATED A ROUTINE HOMICIDE. VICTIM NAMED EDWARD BLAKE. FOUND THE COSTUME IN BLAKE'S WARD-ROBE. SEEMS HE WAS THE COMEDIAN.
SOMEBODY THREW HIM OUT OF A WINDOW.
SOME-BODY ...?
UH, LISTEN, MAYBE WE COULD TALK ABOUT THIS DOWN IN MY WORK-SHOP. I FEEL KINDA EXPOSED UP HERE.
ALSO, THAT WAY YOU CAN USE THE HIDDEN REAR EXIT. UH, WHEN YOU LEAVE, THAT IS...
RIGHT DOWN THIS WAY.
UH, YOU HAVEN'T BEEN DOWN HERE FOR A WHILE...
11

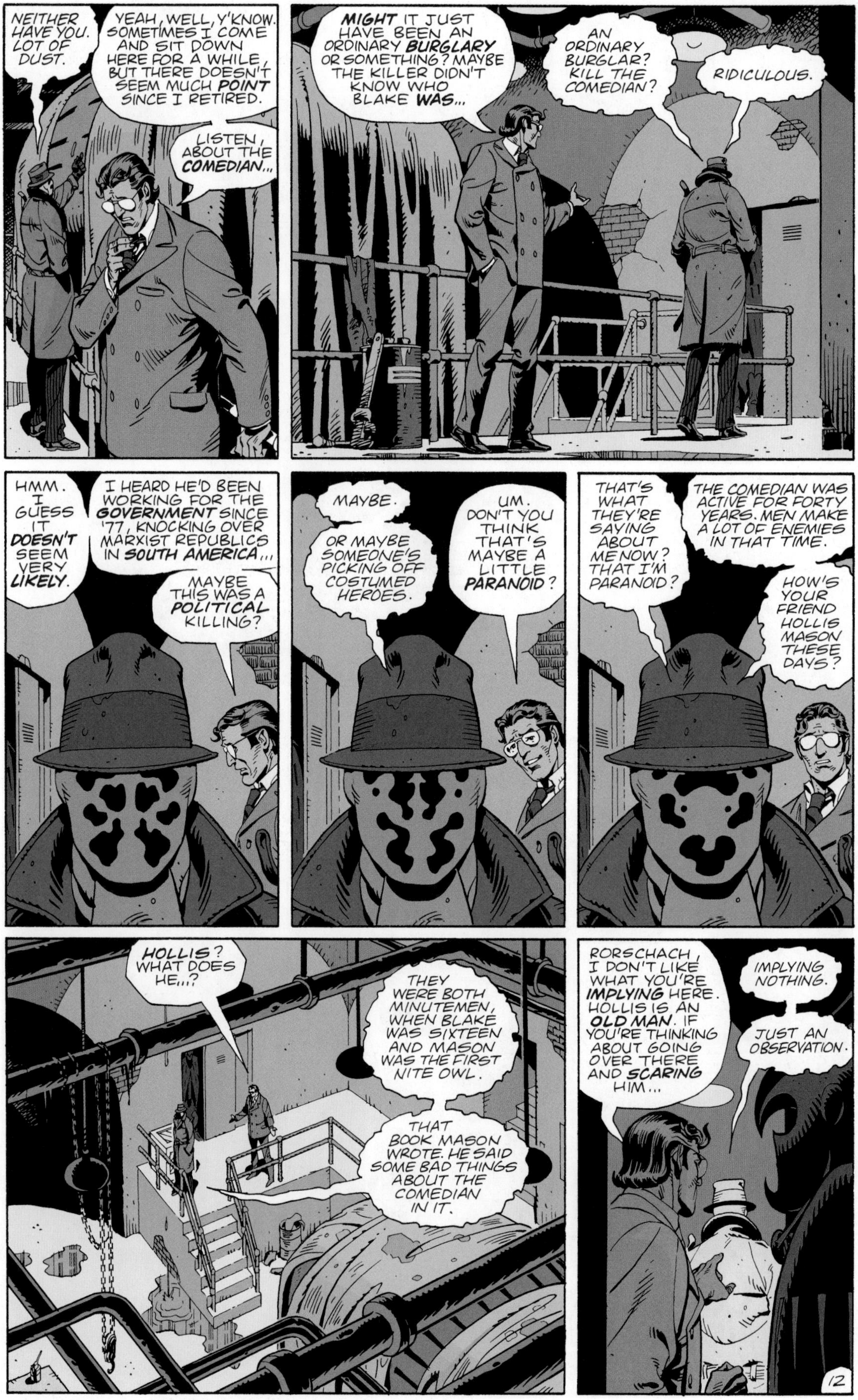
NEITHER HAVE YOU. LOT OF DUST.
YEAH, WELL, Y'KNOW. SOMETIMES I COME AND SIT DOWN HERE FOR A WHILE, BUT THERE DOESN'T SEEM MUCH POINT SINCE I RETIRED.
LISTEN, ABOUT THE COMEDIAN...
MIGHT IT JUST HAVE BEEN AN ORDINARY BURGLARY OR SOMETHING? MAYBE THE KILLER DIDN'T KNOW WHO BLAKE WAS...
AN ORDINARY BURGLAR? KILL THE COMEDIAN?
RIDICULOUS.
HMM. I GUESS IT DOESN'T SEEM VERY LIKELY.
I HEARD HE'D BEEN WORKING FOR THE GOVERNMENT SINCE '77, KNOCKING OVER MARXIST REPUBLICS IN SOUTH AMERICA...
MAYBE THIS WAS A POLITICAL KILLING?
MAYBE.
OR MAYBE SOMEONE'S PICKING OFF COSTUMED HEROES.
UM. DON'T YOU THINK THAT'S MAYBE A LITTLE PARANOID?
THAT'S WHAT THEY'RE SAYING ABOUT ME NOW? THAT I'M PARANOID?
THE COMEDIAN WAS ACTIVE FOR FORTY YEARS. MEN MAKE A LOT OF ENEMIES IN THAT TIME.
HOW'S YOUR FRIEND HOLLIS MASON THESE DAYS?
HOLLIS? WHAT DOES HE...?
THEY WERE BOTH MINUTEMEN, WHEN BLAKE WAS SIXTEEN AND MASON WAS THE FIRST NITE OWL.
THAT BOOK MASON WROTE. HE SAID SOME BAD THINGS ABOUT THE COMEDIAN IN IT.
RORSCHACH, I DON'T LIKE WHAT YOU'RE IMPLYING HERE. HOLLIS IS AN OLD MAN. IF YOU'RE THINKING ABOUT GOING OVER THERE AND SCARING HIM...
IMPLYING NOTHING.
JUST AN OBSERVATION.
12

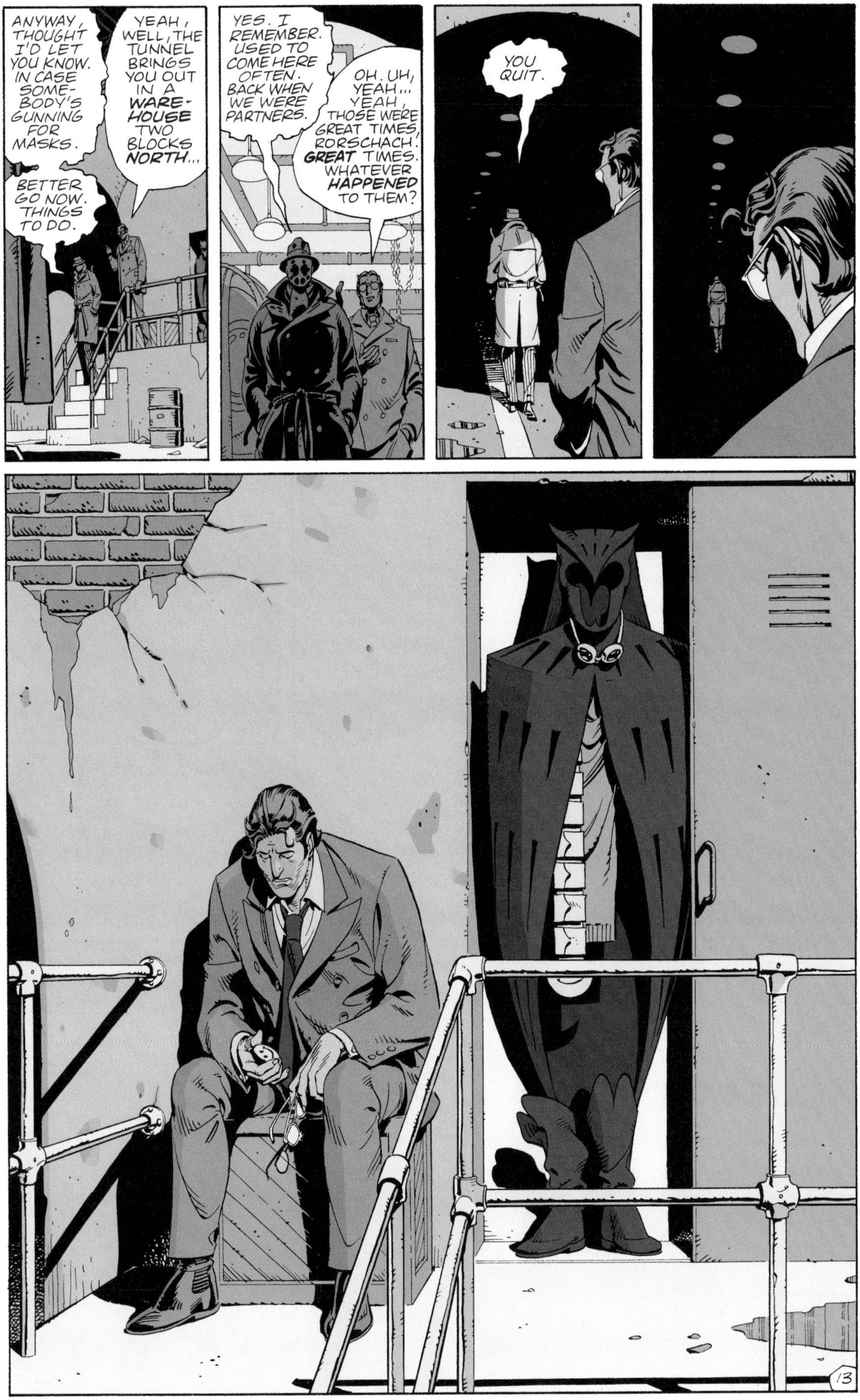

ANYWAY, THOUGHT I'D LET YOU KNOW. IN CASE SOMEBODY'S GUNNING FOR MASKS.
YEAH, WELL, THE TUNNEL BRINGS YOU OUT IN A **WAREHOUSE** TWO BLOCKS **NORTH**...
BETTER GO NOW. THINGS TO DO.
YES. I REMEMBER. USED TO COME HERE OFTEN. BACK WHEN WE WERE PARTNERS.
OH. UH, YEAH... YEAH, THOSE WERE GREAT TIMES, RORSCHACH. **GREAT** TIMES. WHATEVER **HAPPENED** TO THEM?
YOU QUIT.
13

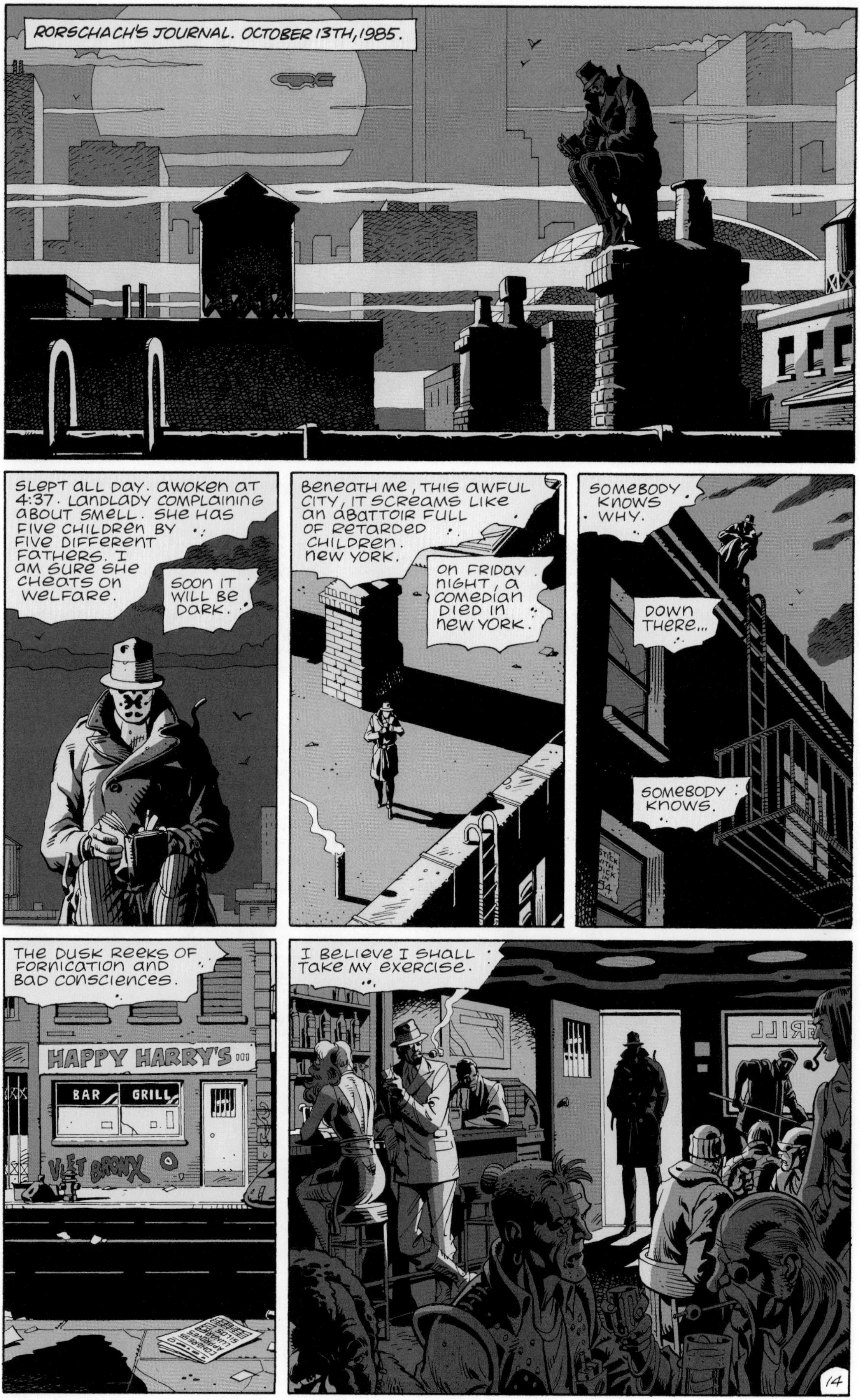
RORSCHACH'S JOURNAL. OCTOBER 13TH, 1985.
SLEPT ALL DAY. AWOKEN AT 4:37. LANDLADY COMPLAINING ABOUT SMELL. SHE HAS FIVE CHILDREN BY FIVE DIFFERENT FATHERS. I AM SURE SHE CHEATS ON WELFARE.
SOON IT WILL BE DARK.
BENEATH ME, THIS AWFUL CITY, IT SCREAMS LIKE AN ABATTOIR FULL OF RETARDED CHILDREN. NEW YORK.
ON FRIDAY NIGHT, A COMEDIAN DIED IN NEW YORK.
SOMEBODY KNOWS WHY.
DOWN THERE...
SOMEBODY KNOWS.
THE DUSK REEKS OF FORNICATION AND BAD CONSCIENCES.
HAPPY HARRY'S
BAR
GRILL
I BELIEVE I SHALL TAKE MY EXERCISE.
14

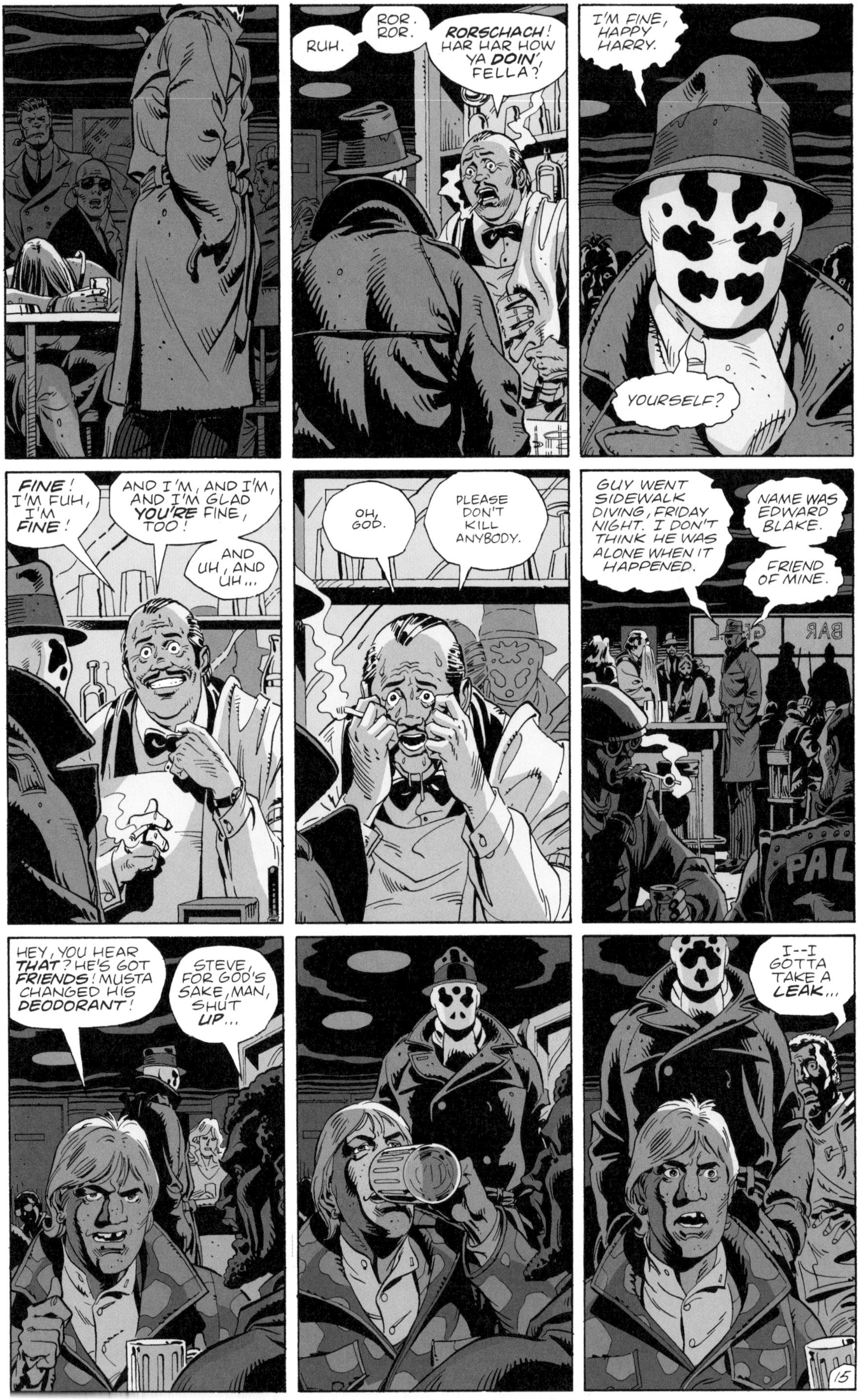
RUH.
ROR. ROR.
RORSCHACH! HAR HAR HOW YA DOIN', FELLA?
I'M FINE, HAPPY HARRY.
YOURSELF?
FINE! I'M FUH, I'M FINE!
AND I'M, AND I'M, AND I'M GLAD YOU'RE FINE, TOO!
AND UH, AND UH...
OH, GOD.
PLEASE DON'T KILL ANYBODY.
GUY WENT SIDEWALK DIVING, FRIDAY NIGHT. I DON'T THINK HE WAS ALONE WHEN IT HAPPENED.
NAME WAS EDWARD BLAKE.
FRIEND OF MINE.
BAR
PAL
HEY, YOU HEAR THAT? HE'S GOT FRIENDS! MUSTA CHANGED HIS DEODORANT!
STEVE, FOR GOD'S SAKE, MAN, SHUT UP...
I--I GOTTA TAKE A LEAK...
15

H-HEY! HEY, I DIDN'T **MEAN** ANYTHING...

I, UH, I HAVEN'T **BEEN** IN THE APPLE TOO LONG, AND I ...

...I, UH...

HEY, WHAT...?

AAAAA

I'VE JUST BROKEN THIS GENTLEMAN'S LITTLE FINGER.

WHO KILLED EDWARD BLAKE?

OH. OUHH...

EEYIIAAA

...AND HIS INDEX FINGER.

WHO KILLED EDWARD BLAKE?

PLEASE...

PLEASE, WE DON'T **KNOW**...

AW, **GOD**, MAN, LEAVE HIM **ALONE**...

FIRST VISIT OF EVENING FRUITLESS. NOBODY KNEW ANYTHING. FEEL SLIGHTLY DEPRESSED.

THIS CITY IS DYING OF RABIES. IS THE BEST I CAN DO TO WIPE RANDOM FLECKS OF FOAM FROM ITS LIPS?

HURM.

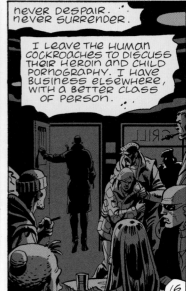

NEVER DESPAIR. NEVER SURRENDER.

I LEAVE THE HUMAN COCKROACHES TO DISCUSS THEIR HEROIN AND CHILD PORNOGRAPHY. I HAVE BUSINESS ELSEWHERE, WITH A BETTER CLASS OF PERSON.

16

THE COMEDIAN DEAD?

BUT *WHY*?

YOU WERE ALWAYS SUPPOSED TO BE WORLD'S *SMARTEST MAN*, VEIDT.

YOU TELL ME.

I NEVER CLAIMED TO BE ANYBODY *SPECIAL*, RORSCHACH. I JUST HAVE SOME OVER-ENTHUSIASTIC *P.R. MEN.*

LISTEN... COULD IT HAVE BEEN A *POLITICAL KILLING*? MAYBE THE *SOVIETS...*

DREIBERG SAID SAME THING. DON'T BELIEVE IT.

AMERICA HAS *DR. MANHATTAN.* REDS HAVE BEEN RUNNING SCARED SINCE '65. THEY'D NEVER DARE ANTAGONIZE US.

I THINK WE'VE GOT A *MASK-KILLER.*

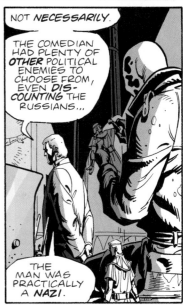

NOT *NECESSARILY.*

THE COMEDIAN HAD PLENTY OF *OTHER* POLITICAL ENEMIES TO CHOOSE FROM, EVEN *DIS-COUNTING* THE RUSSIANS...

THE MAN WAS PRACTICALLY A *NAZI.*

HE STOOD UP FOR HIS COUNTRY, VEIDT. HE NEVER LET ANYBODY *RETIRE* HIM.

NEVER CASHED IN ON HIS *REPUTATION.*

NEVER SET UP A COMPANY SELLING POSTERS AND DIET BOOKS AND TOY SOLDIERS BASED ON HIMSELF.

NEVER BECAME A *PROSTITUTE.*

IF THAT MAKES HIM A *NAZI*, YOU MIGHT AS WELL CALL ME A NAZI, TOO.

HM.

17

RORSCHACH... I **KNOW** WE WERE NEVER **FRIENDS**, BUT EVEN SO, YOU'RE BEING **UNFAIR**.

NOBODY RETIRED ME. I **CHOSE** TO QUIT ADVENTURING AND GO **PUBLIC** TWO YEARS **BEFORE** THE POLICE STRIKE MADE THE **KEENE ACT** NECESSARY.

YES. GOOD TIMING.

I CAME HERE TO WARN YOU ABOUT THE MASK-KILLER. SO YOU DIDN'T END UP SMARTEST MAN IN THE MORGUE.

BUT I GUESS THERE'S WORSE THINGS TO END UP AS.

BE SEEING YOU.

SURE. HAVE A NICE DAY.

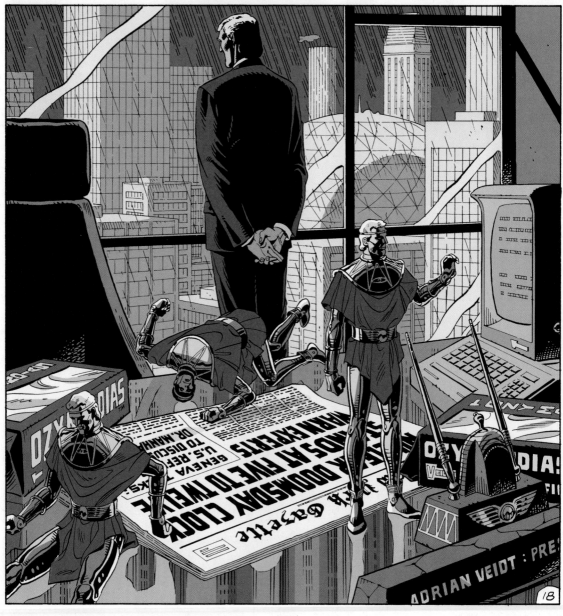

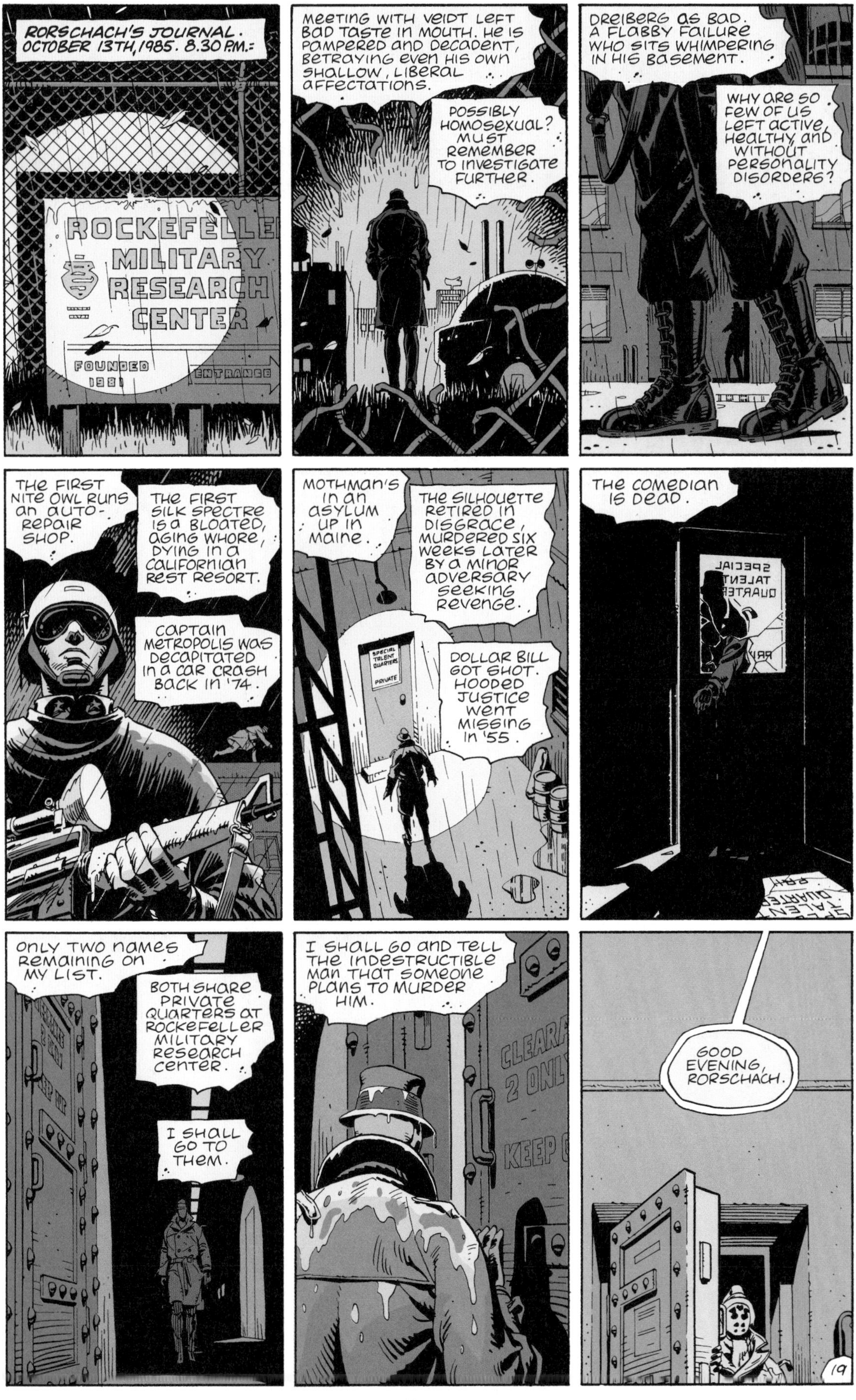
RORSCHACH'S JOURNAL. OCTOBER 13TH, 1985. 8.30 P.M.:
ROCKEFELLER MILITARY RESEARCH CENTER
FOUNDED 1981
ENTRANCE
MEETING WITH VEIDT LEFT BAD TASTE IN MOUTH. HE IS PAMPERED AND DECADENT, BETRAYING EVEN HIS OWN SHALLOW, LIBERAL AFFECTATIONS.
POSSIBLY HOMOSEXUAL? MUST REMEMBER TO INVESTIGATE FURTHER.
DREIBERG AS BAD. A FLABBY FAILURE WHO SITS WHIMPERING IN HIS BASEMENT.
WHY ARE SO FEW OF US LEFT ACTIVE, HEALTHY, AND WITHOUT PERSONALITY DISORDERS?
THE FIRST NITE OWL RUNS AN AUTO-REPAIR SHOP.
THE FIRST SILK SPECTRE IS A BLOATED, AGING WHORE, DYING IN A CALIFORNIAN REST RESORT.
CAPTAIN METROPOLIS WAS DECAPITATED IN A CAR CRASH BACK IN '74.
MOTHMAN'S IN AN ASYLUM UP IN MAINE.
THE SILHOUETTE RETIRED IN DISGRACE, MURDERED SIX WEEKS LATER BY A MINOR ADVERSARY SEEKING REVENGE.
SPECIAL TALENT QUARTERS PRIVATE
DOLLAR BILL GOT SHOT. HOODED JUSTICE WENT MISSING IN '55.
THE COMEDIAN IS DEAD.
ONLY TWO NAMES REMAINING ON MY LIST.
BOTH SHARE PRIVATE QUARTERS AT ROCKEFELLER MILITARY RESEARCH CENTER.
I SHALL GO TO THEM.
I SHALL GO AND TELL THE INDESTRUCTIBLE MAN THAT SOMEONE PLANS TO MURDER HIM.
CLEARA
2 ONL
KEEP
GOOD EVENING, RORSCHACH.
19

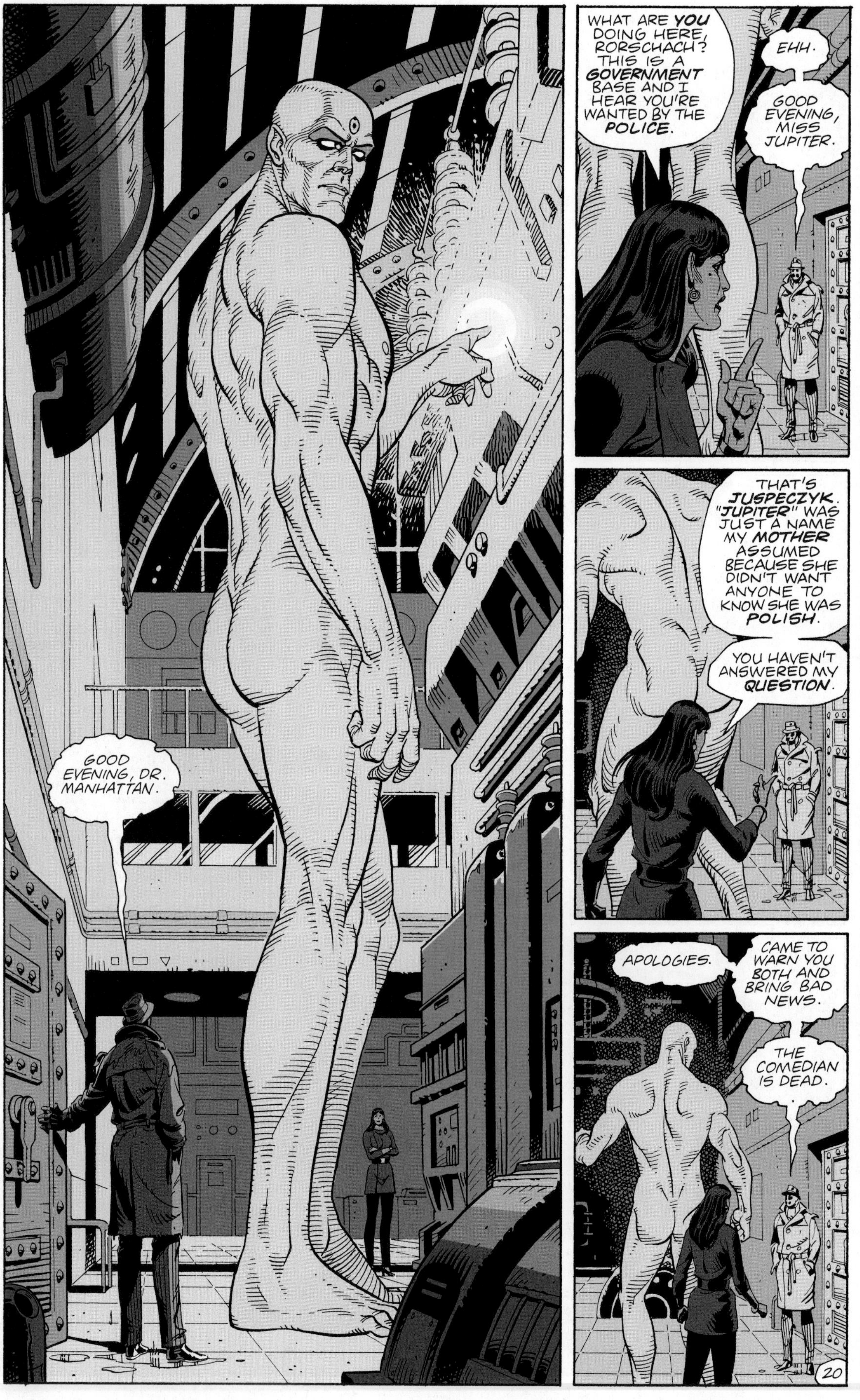
GOOD EVENING, DR. MANHATTAN.
WHAT ARE YOU DOING HERE, RORSCHACH? THIS IS A GOVERNMENT BASE AND I HEAR YOU'RE WANTED BY THE POLICE.
EHH.
GOOD EVENING, MISS JUPITER.
THAT'S JUSPECZYK. "JUPITER" WAS JUST A NAME MY MOTHER ASSUMED BECAUSE SHE DIDN'T WANT ANYONE TO KNOW SHE WAS POLISH.
YOU HAVEN'T ANSWERED MY QUESTION.
APOLOGIES.
CAME TO WARN YOU BOTH AND BRING BAD NEWS.
THE COMEDIAN IS DEAD.
20

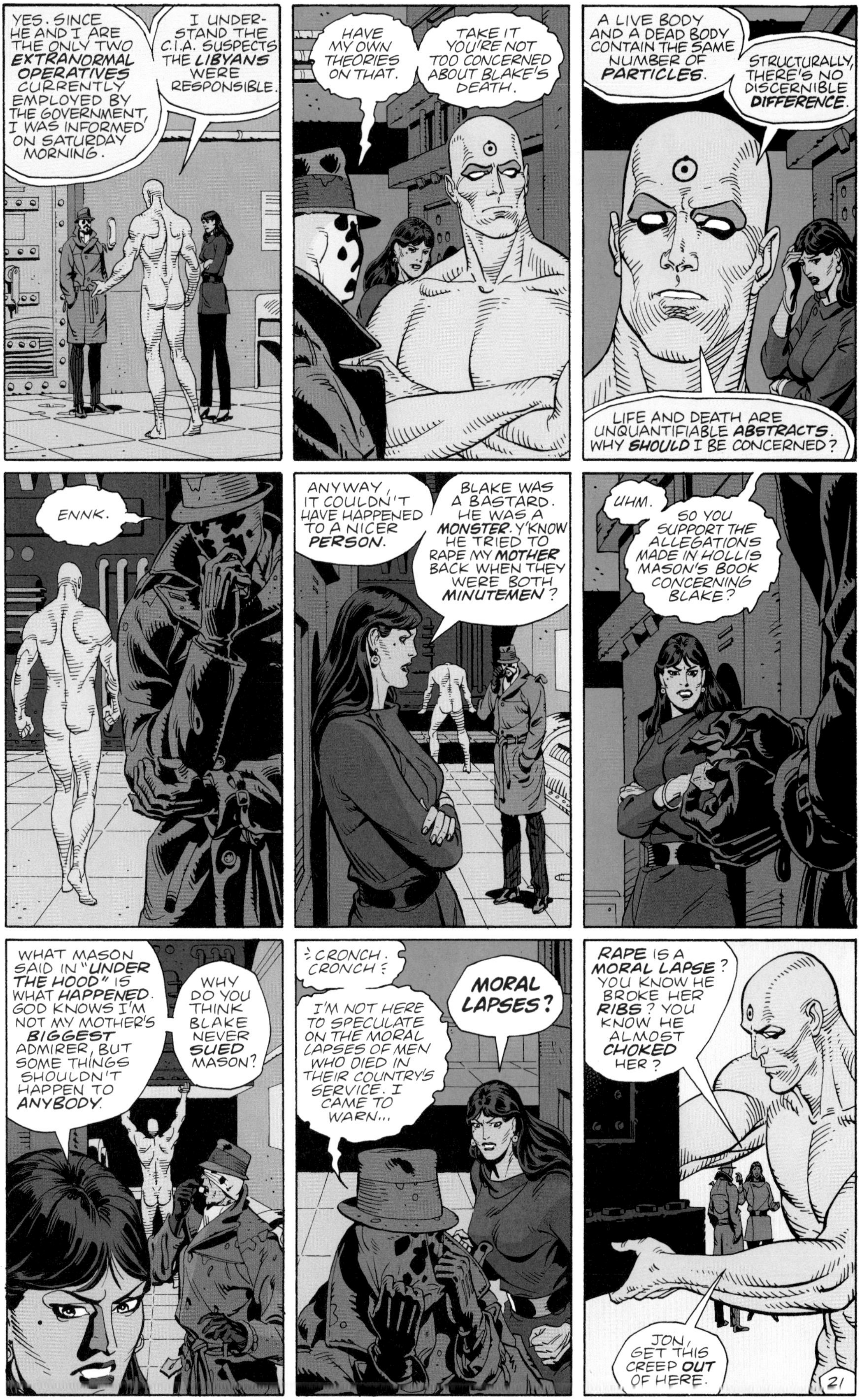
YES. SINCE HE AND I ARE THE ONLY TWO EXTRANORMAL OPERATIVES CURRENTLY EMPLOYED BY THE GOVERNMENT, I WAS INFORMED ON SATURDAY MORNING.
I UNDERSTAND THE C.I.A. SUSPECTS THE LIBYANS WERE RESPONSIBLE.
HAVE MY OWN THEORIES ON THAT.
TAKE IT YOU'RE NOT TOO CONCERNED ABOUT BLAKE'S DEATH.
A LIVE BODY AND A DEAD BODY CONTAIN THE SAME NUMBER OF PARTICLES.
STRUCTURALLY, THERE'S NO DISCERNIBLE DIFFERENCE.
LIFE AND DEATH ARE UNQUANTIFIABLE ABSTRACTS. WHY SHOULD I BE CONCERNED?
ENNK.
ANYWAY, IT COULDN'T HAVE HAPPENED TO A NICER PERSON.
BLAKE WAS A BASTARD. HE WAS A MONSTER. Y'KNOW HE TRIED TO RAPE MY MOTHER BACK WHEN THEY WERE BOTH MINUTEMEN?
UHM.
SO YOU SUPPORT THE ALLEGATIONS MADE IN HOLLIS MASON'S BOOK CONCERNING BLAKE?
WHAT MASON SAID IN "UNDER THE HOOD" IS WHAT HAPPENED. GOD KNOWS I'M NOT MY MOTHER'S BIGGEST ADMIRER, BUT SOME THINGS SHOULDN'T HAPPEN TO ANYBODY.
WHY DO YOU THINK BLAKE NEVER SUED MASON?
CRONCH. CRONCH
I'M NOT HERE TO SPECULATE ON THE MORAL LAPSES OF MEN WHO DIED IN THEIR COUNTRY'S SERVICE. I CAME TO WARN...
MORAL LAPSES?
RAPE IS A MORAL LAPSE? YOU KNOW HE BROKE HER RIBS? YOU KNOW HE ALMOST CHOKED HER?
JON, GET THIS CREEP OUT OF HERE.
21

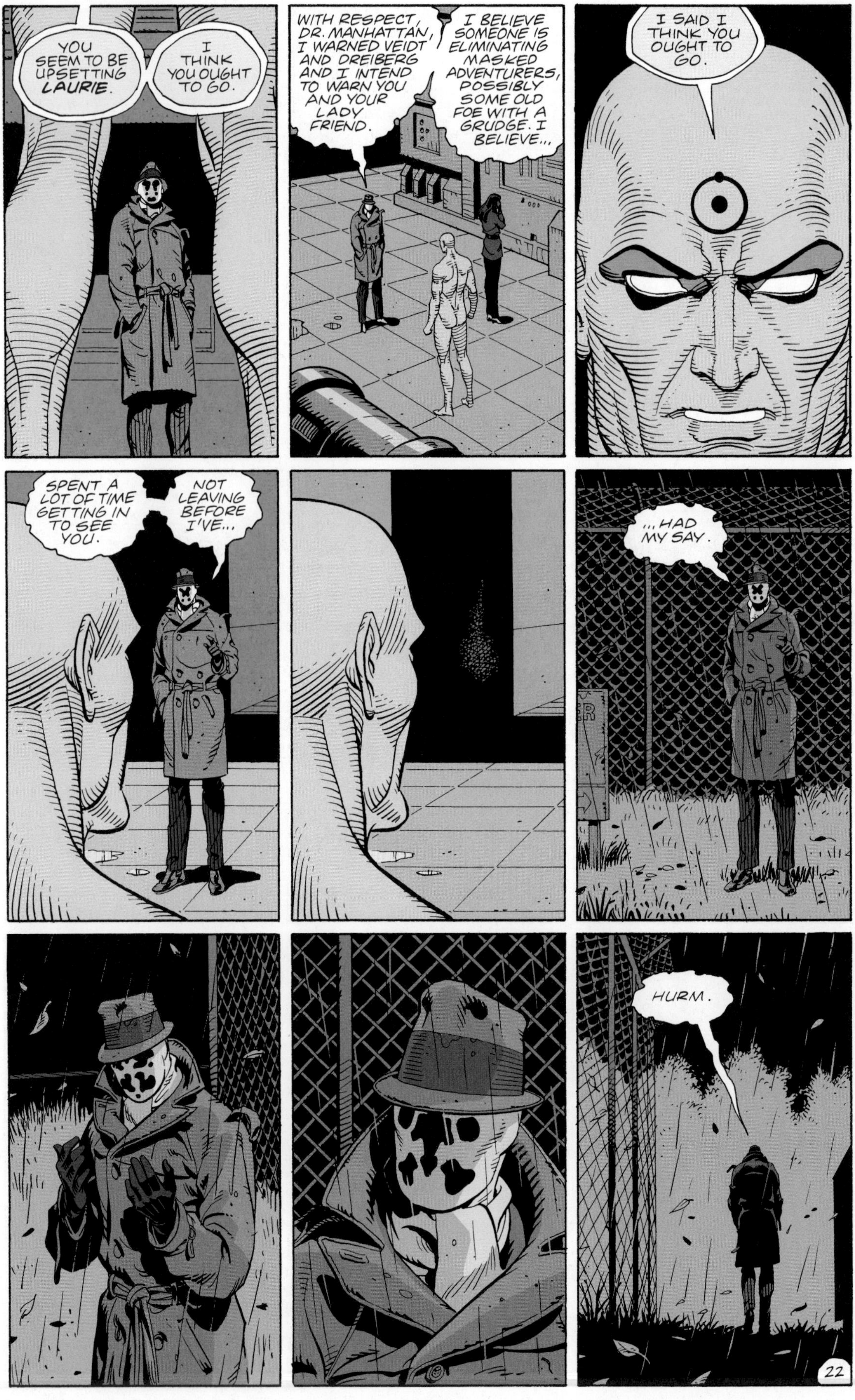
YOU SEEM TO BE UPSETTING LAURIE.
I THINK YOU OUGHT TO GO.
WITH RESPECT, DR. MANHATTAN, I WARNED VEIDT AND DREIBERG AND I INTEND TO WARN YOU AND YOUR LADY FRIEND.
I BELIEVE SOMEONE IS ELIMINATING MASKED ADVENTURERS, POSSIBLY SOME OLD FOE WITH A GRUDGE. I BELIEVE...
I SAID I THINK YOU OUGHT TO GO.
SPENT A LOT OF TIME GETTING IN TO SEE YOU.
NOT LEAVING BEFORE I'VE...
...HAD MY SAY.
HURM.
22

HE'S GONE.

ARE YOU STILL *UPSET*?

YEAH. I JUST DON'T *LIKE* RORSCHACH. HE'S *SICK*. SICK INSIDE HIS *MIND*.

I DON'T LIKE THE WAY HE *SMELLS* OR THAT HORRIBLE MONO-TONE *VOICE* OR ANYTHING.

THE SOONER THE POLICE PUT HIM *AWAY*, THE *BETTER*.

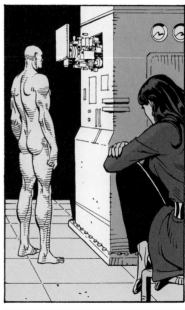

JON?

YES, LAURIE?

I WAS JUST THINKING THAT I MUST BE REALLY *EDGY* TO LET A MAGGOT LIKE *RORSCHACH* GET TO ME LIKE THAT.

I JUST FEEL *COOPED UP* SOME-TIMES. MAYBE I COULD USE A *NIGHT OUT*.

YOU KNOW, RORSCHACH MENTIONED *DAN DREIBERG*. WE HAVEN'T SEEN DAN IN *YEARS*.

MAYBE I'LL CALL HIM *UP*, ASK HIM OUT TO *DINNER*.

IF YOU DON'T *MIND*, THAT IS.

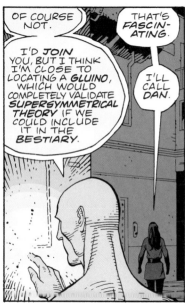

OF COURSE NOT.

I'D *JOIN* YOU, BUT I THINK I'M CLOSE TO LOCATING A *GLUINO*, WHICH WOULD COMPLETELY VALIDATE *SUPERSYMMETRICAL THEORY* IF WE COULD INCLUDE IT IN THE *BESTIARY*.

THAT'S *FASCIN-ATING*.

I'LL CALL *DAN*.

HELLO, *DAN*? *LAURIE*. LAURIE JUSPECZYK. I'M *FINE*. HOW ARE *YOU*?

GREAT. LISTEN, I JUST REMEMBERED I HADN'T *SEEN* YOU IN AGES AND WONDERED IF WE COULD HAVE *DINNER* SOMETIME.

WELL, HOW ABOUT *TONIGHT*? *RAFAEL'S* AT 9:30?

THAT'S *TERRIFIC*.

JON? OH, YEAH. YEAH, JON'S IN PRETTY GOOD SHAPE.

SEE YOU LATER, DAN.

'BYE.

23

381

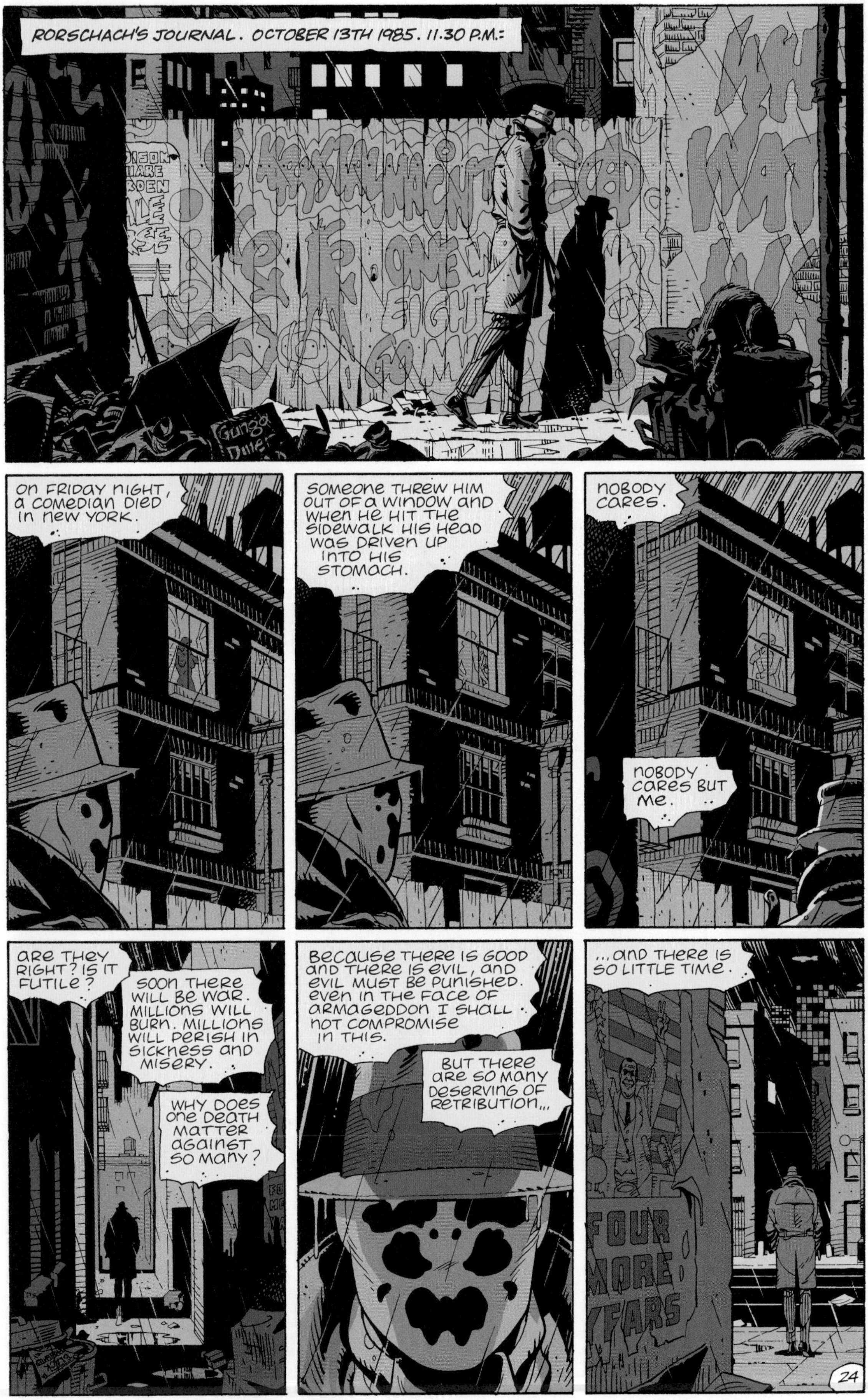
RORSCHACH'S JOURNAL. OCTOBER 13TH 1985. 11.30 P.M.:
ON FRIDAY NIGHT, A COMEDIAN DIED IN NEW YORK.
SOMEONE THREW HIM OUT OF A WINDOW AND WHEN HE HIT THE SIDEWALK HIS HEAD WAS DRIVEN UP INTO HIS STOMACH.
NOBODY CARES.
NOBODY CARES BUT ME.
ARE THEY RIGHT? IS IT FUTILE?
SOON THERE WILL BE WAR. MILLIONS WILL BURN. MILLIONS WILL PERISH IN SICKNESS AND MISERY.
WHY DOES ONE DEATH MATTER AGAINST SO MANY?
BECAUSE THERE IS GOOD AND THERE IS EVIL, AND EVIL MUST BE PUNISHED. EVEN IN THE FACE OF ARMAGEDDON I SHALL NOT COMPROMISE IN THIS.
BUT THERE ARE SO MANY DESERVING OF RETRIBUTION...
...AND THERE IS SO LITTLE TIME.
FOUR MORE YEARS
24

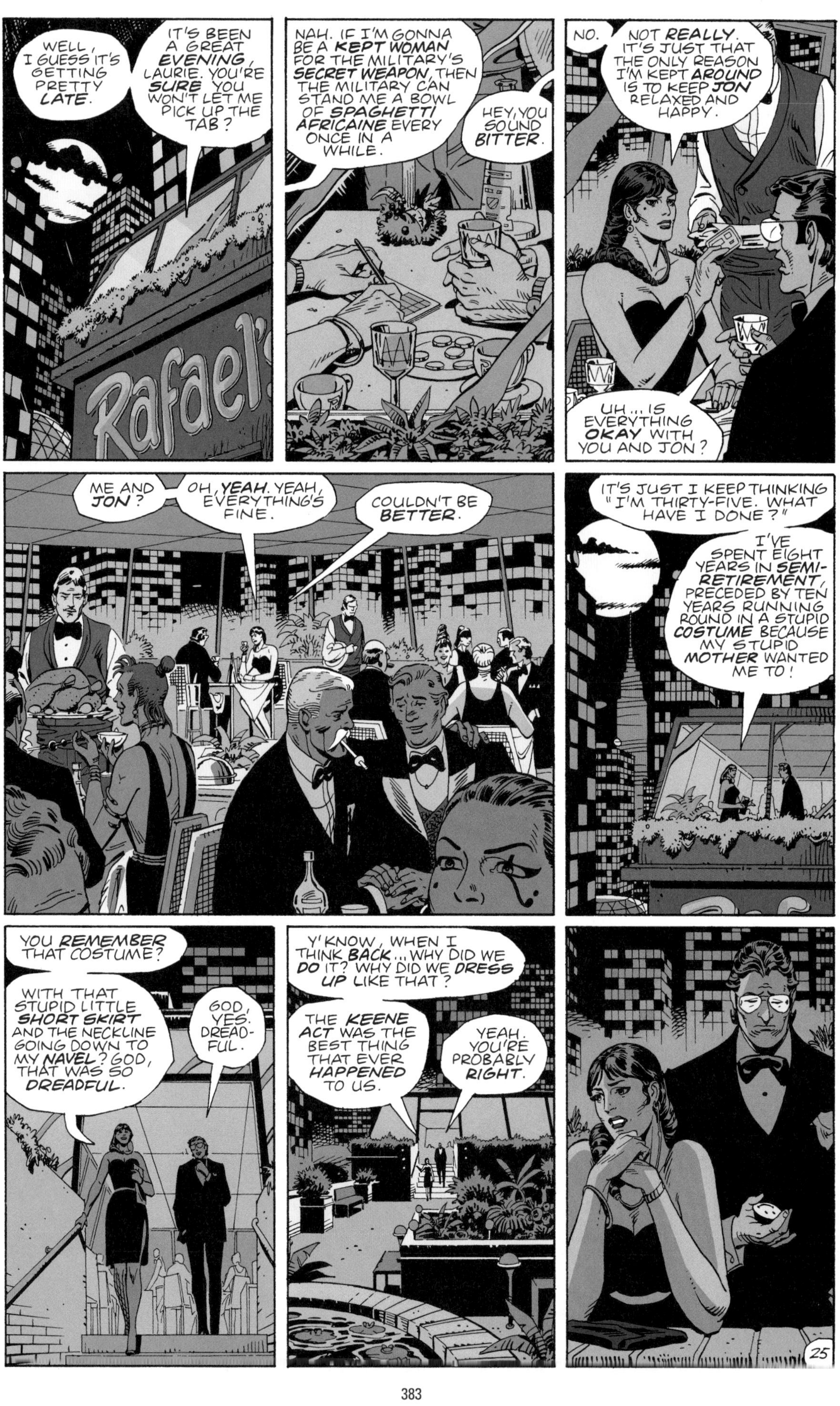
WELL, I GUESS IT'S GETTING PRETTY LATE.
IT'S BEEN A GREAT EVENING, LAURIE. YOU'RE SURE YOU WON'T LET ME PICK UP THE TAB?
Rafael's
NAH. IF I'M GONNA BE A KEPT WOMAN FOR THE MILITARY'S SECRET WEAPON, THEN THE MILITARY CAN STAND ME A BOWL OF SPAGHETTI AFRICAINE EVERY ONCE IN A WHILE.
HEY, YOU SOUND BITTER.
NO.
NOT REALLY. IT'S JUST THAT THE ONLY REASON I'M KEPT AROUND IS TO KEEP JON RELAXED AND HAPPY.
UH... IS EVERYTHING OKAY WITH YOU AND JON?
ME AND JON?
OH, YEAH. YEAH, EVERYTHING'S FINE.
COULDN'T BE BETTER.
IT'S JUST I KEEP THINKING "I'M THIRTY-FIVE. WHAT HAVE I DONE?"
I'VE SPENT EIGHT YEARS IN SEMI-RETIREMENT, PRECEDED BY TEN YEARS RUNNING ROUND IN A STUPID COSTUME BECAUSE MY STUPID MOTHER WANTED ME TO!
YOU REMEMBER THAT COSTUME?
WITH THAT STUPID LITTLE SHORT SKIRT AND THE NECKLINE GOING DOWN TO MY NAVEL? GOD, THAT WAS SO DREADFUL.
GOD, YES. DREADFUL.
Y'KNOW, WHEN I THINK BACK... WHY DID WE DO IT? WHY DID WE DRESS UP LIKE THAT?
THE KEENE ACT WAS THE BEST THING THAT EVER HAPPENED TO US.
YEAH. YOU'RE PROBABLY RIGHT.
25

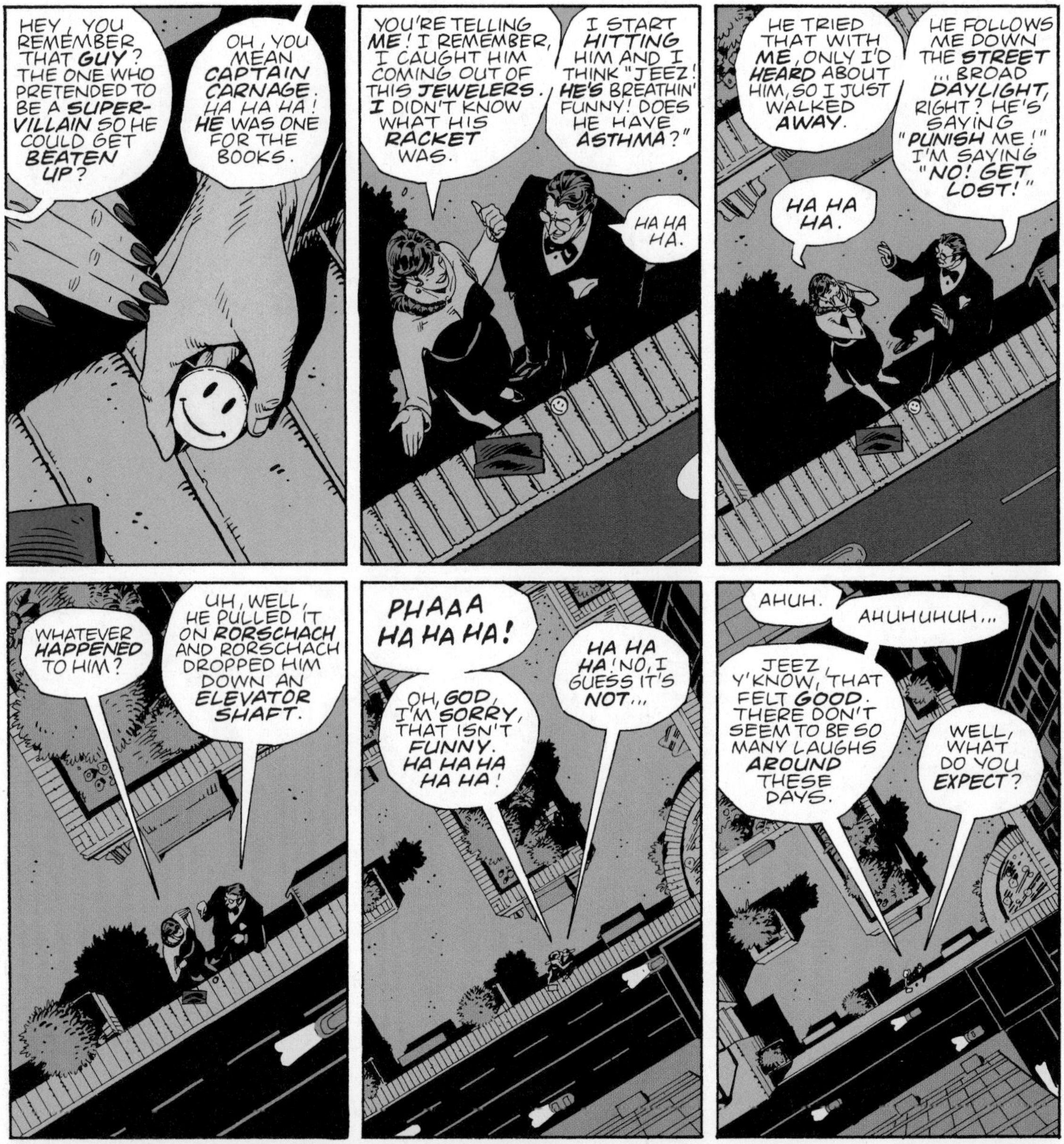
HEY, YOU REMEMBER THAT GUY? THE ONE WHO PRETENDED TO BE A SUPER-VILLAIN SO HE COULD GET BEATEN UP?
OH, YOU MEAN CAPTAIN CARNAGE. HA HA HA! HE WAS ONE FOR THE BOOKS.
YOU'RE TELLING ME! I REMEMBER, I CAUGHT HIM COMING OUT OF THIS JEWELERS. I DIDN'T KNOW WHAT HIS RACKET WAS.
I START HITTING HIM AND I THINK "JEEZ! HE'S BREATHIN' FUNNY! DOES HE HAVE ASTHMA?"
HA HA HA.
HE TRIED THAT WITH ME, ONLY I'D HEARD ABOUT HIM, SO I JUST WALKED AWAY.
HE FOLLOWS ME DOWN THE STREET ... BROAD DAYLIGHT, RIGHT? HE'S SAYING "PUNISH ME!" I'M SAYING "NO! GET LOST!"
HA HA HA.
WHATEVER HAPPENED TO HIM?
UH, WELL, HE PULLED IT ON RORSCHACH AND RORSCHACH DROPPED HIM DOWN AN ELEVATOR SHAFT.
PHAAA HA HA HA!
OH, GOD, I'M SORRY, THAT ISN'T FUNNY. HA HA HA HA HA!
HA HA HA! NO, I GUESS IT'S NOT...
AHUH.
AHUHUHUH...
JEEZ, Y'KNOW, THAT FELT GOOD. THERE DON'T SEEM TO BE SO MANY LAUGHS AROUND THESE DAYS.
WELL, WHAT DO YOU EXPECT?

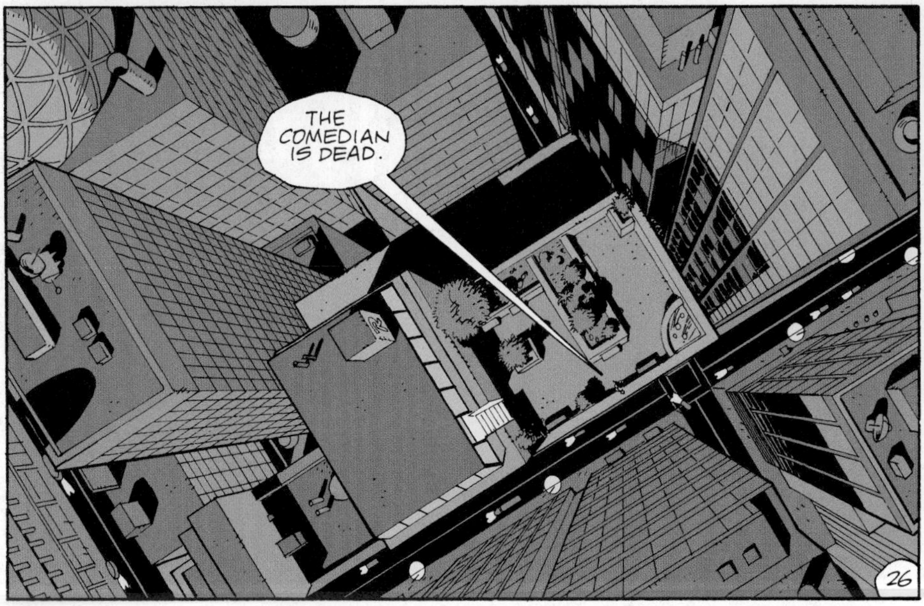
THE COMEDIAN IS DEAD.
26

At midnight, all the agents and superhuman crew, go out and round up everyone who knows more than they do.

—Bob Dylan

UNDER THE HOOD

We present here excerpts from Hollis Mason's autobiography, UNDER THE HOOD, leading up to the time when he became the masked adventurer, Nite Owl. Reprinted with permission of the author.

I.

The lady who works in the grocery store at the corner of my block is called Denise, and she's one of America's great unpublished novelists. Over the years she's written *forty-two* romantic novels, none of which have ever reached the bookstores. I, however, have been fortunate enough to hear the plots of the last twenty-seven of these recounted in installments by the authoress herself every time I drop by the store for a jar of coffee or can of beans, and my respect for Denise's literary prowess knows no bounds. So, naturally enough, when I found myself faced with the daunting task of actually starting the book you now hold in your hands, it was Denise I turned to for advice.

"Listen," I said. "I don't know from writing a book. I have all this stuff in my head that I want to get down, but what do I write about first? Where do I begin?"

Without looking up from the boxes of detergent to which she was fixing price tags, Denise graciously delivered up a pearl of her accumulated wisdom in a voice of bored but benign condescension.

"Start off with the saddest thing you can think of and get the audience's sympathies on your side. After that, believe me, it's a walk."

Thank you, Denise. This book is dedicated to you, because I don't know how to choose between all the other people I should be dedicating it to

The saddest thing I can think of is "The Ride of the Valkyries." Every time I hear it I get depressed and start wondering about the lot of humanity and the unfairness of life and all those other things that you think about at three in the morning when your digestion won't let you sleep. Now, I realize that nobody else on the planet has to brush away a tear when they hear that particular stirring refrain, but that's because they don't know about Moe Vernon.

When my father upped and left my Granddad's farm in Montana to bring his family to New York, Moe Vernon was the man he worked for. Vernon's Auto Repairs was just off Seventh Avenue, and although it was only 1928 when Dad started working there, there was just about enough trade for his wages to keep me and Mom and my sister Liantha in food and clothing. Dad was always really keen and enthusiastic about his work, and I used to think it was just because he had a thing about cars. Looking back, I can see it was more than that. It must have meant so much to him, just to have a job and be able to support his family. He'd had a lot of arguments with his father about coming east rather than taking over the farm, like the old man had planned for him, and most of the rows had ended with my grandfather predicting poverty and moral ruination for my dad and mom if they so much as set foot in New York. To be living the life that he himself had chosen and keeping his family above the poverty line in spite of his father's warnings must have meant more to my dad than anything in the world, but that's something I only understand now, with hindsight. Back then, I just thought he was crazy for crankshafts.

Anyway, I was twelve years old when we left Montana, so during those next few years in the big city I was just the age to appreciate the occasional trips to the auto shop with my dad, which is where I first set eyes on Moe Vernon, his employer.

Moe Vernon was a man around fifty-five or so, and he had one of those old New York faces that you don't see anymore. It's funny, but certain faces seem to go in and out of style. You look at old photographs and everybody has a certain look to them, almost as if they're related. Look at pictures from ten years later and you can see that there's a new kind of face starting to predominate, and that the old faces are fading away and vanishing, never to be seen again. Moe Vernon's face was like that: three thins, a wiseacre cynical curl to his lower lip, a certain hollowness around the eyes, hair retreating back across his head, attempting a rendezvous with the label on his shirt collar.

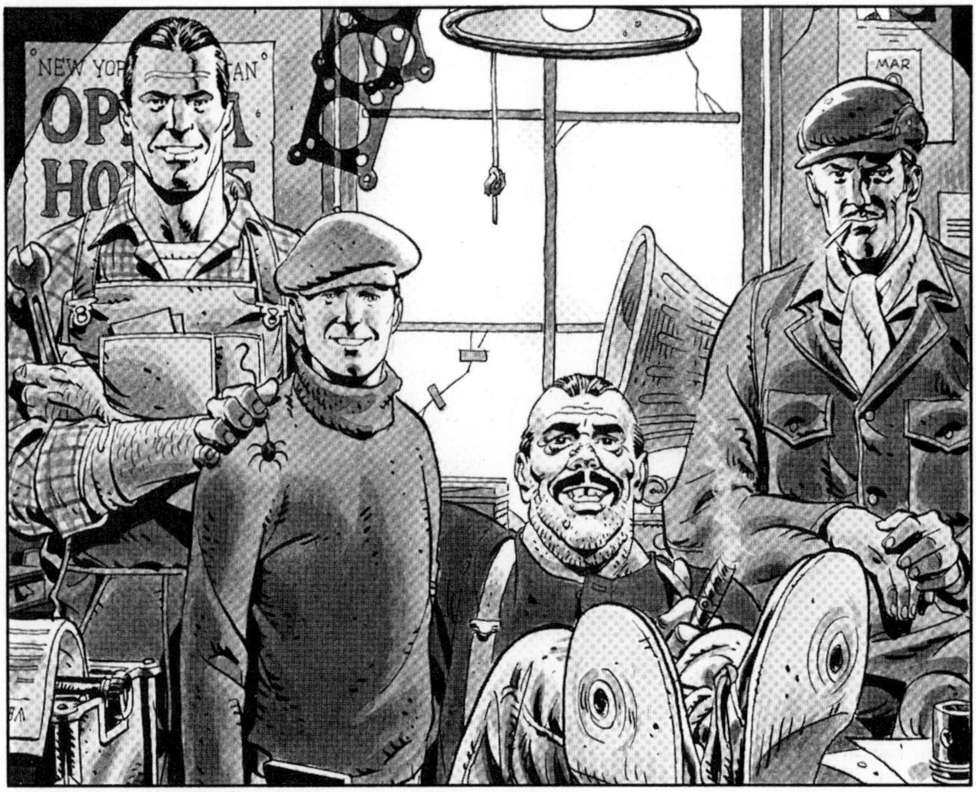
MAR

Vernon's Auto Repair c. 1928. (left to right) My father; myself, age 12; Moe Vernon; Fred Motz.

I'd go into the shop with my dad and Moe would be sitting there in his office, which had glass sides so he could watch the men working. Sometimes, if my father wanted to check something out with Moe before going ahead with his work, he'd send me over to the office to do it for him, which meant that I got to see the insides of Moe's inner sanctum. Or rather, I got to hear them.

You see, Moe was an opera buff. He had one of the new gramophones over in the corner of his office and all day he used to play scratchy old seventy-eight recordings of his favorites just as loud as he could manage. By today's standard, "as loud as he could manage" didn't amount to a whole lot of noise, but it sounded pretty cacophonous back in 1930, when things were generally quieter.

The other thing that was peculiar about Moe was his sense of humor, as represented by all the stuff he used to keep in the top right side drawer of his desk.

In that drawer, amongst a mess of rubber bands and paper clips and receipts and stuff, Moe had one of the largest collections of tasteless novelty items that I had seen up until that point or have seen at any time since. They were all risqué little toys and gadgets that Moe had picked up from gag shops or on visits to Coney Island, but it was the sheer range of them that was overwhelming: every cheap blue gimmick that you can remember your dad bringing home when he'd been out drinking with the boys and embarrassing your mom with; every ballpoint pen with a girl on the side whose swimsuit vanished when you turned it upside down; every salt and pepper crewet set shaped like a woman's breasts; every plastic dog mess. Moe had the works. Every time anybody went into his office he'd try to startle them by displaying his latest plaything. Actually, it used to shock my dad more than it did me. I don't think he liked the idea of his son being exposed to that kind of stuff, probably because of all the moral warnings my grandfather had impressed upon him. For my part, I wasn't offended and I even found it kind of funny. Not the things themselves . . . even by then I was too old to get much amusement out of stuff like that. What I found funny was that for no apparent reason, a grown man should have a desk drawer full of such ludicrous devices.

Anyway, one day in 1933, a little after my seventeenth birthday, I was over at Vernon's Auto Repairs with Dad, helping him poke around in the oily innards of a busted-up Ford. Moe was in his office, and although we didn't find out till later, he was sitting wearing an artificial foam rubber set of realistically painted lady's bosoms, with which he hoped to get a few laughs from the guy who brought him the morning mail through from the front office when it arrived. While he waited, he was listening to Wagner.

The mail arrived in due course, and the guy handing it over managed to raise a dutiful chuckle at Moe's generous cleavage before leaving him to open and peruse the morning's missives. Amongst these (again, as we found out later) there was a letter from Moe's wife Beatrice, informing him that for the past two years she'd been sleeping with Fred Motz, the senior and most trusted mechanic employed at Vernon's Auto Repairs, who, unusually, hadn't shown up for work on that particular morning. This, according to the concluding paragraphs of the letter, was because Beatrice had taken all the money out of the joint account she shared with her husband and had departed with Fred for Tijuana.

The first anyone in the workshop knew about this was when the door of Moe's office slammed open and the startlingly loud and crackling rendition of "Ride of the Valkyries" blasted out from within. Framed in the doorway with tears in his eyes and the crumpled letter in his hand, Moe stood dramatically with all eyes turned towards him. He was still wearing the set of artificial breasts. Almost inaudible above the rising strains of Wagner swelling behind him, he spoke, with so much hurt and outrage and offended dignity fighting for possession of his voice that the end result was almost toneless.

"Fred Motz has had carnal knowledge of my wife Beatrice for the past two years."

He stood there in the wake of his announcement, the tears rolling down over his multiple chins to soak into the pink foam rubber of his bosom, making tiny sounds in his chest and throat that were trampled under the hooves of the Valkyries and lost forever.

And everybody started laughing.

I don't know what it was. We could see he was crying, but it was just something in the toneless way he'd said it, standing there wearing a pair of false breasts with all that crashing, triumphant music soaring all around him. None of us could help it, laughing at him like that. My dad and I were both doubled up and the other guys slaving over the nearby cars were wiping tears from their eyes and smearing their faces with oil in the process. Moe just looked at us all for a minute and then went back into his office and closed the door. A moment or two later the Wagner stopped with an ugly scraping noise as Moe snatched the needle from the groove of the gramophone record, and after that there was silence.

About half an hour passed before someone went in to apologize on behalf of everybody and to see if Moe was all right. Moe accepted the apology and said that he was fine. Apparently he was sitting there at his desk, breasts now discarded, getting on with normal routine paperwork as if nothing had happened.

I graduate from Police Academy (1938)

That night, he sent everybody home early. Then, running a tube from the exhaust of one of the shop's more operational vehicles in through the car's window, he started up the engine and drifted off into a final, bitter sleep amongst the carbon monoxide fumes. His brother took over the business and even eventually reemployed Fred Motz as chief mechanic.

And that's why "The Ride of the Valkyries" is the saddest thing I can think of, even though it's somebody else's tragedy rather than my own. I was there and I laughed along with all the rest and I guess that makes it part of my story too.

Now, if Denise's theory is correct, I should have your full sympathy and the rest will be a walk. So maybe it's safe to tell you about all the stuff you probably bought this book to read about. Maybe it's safe to tell you why I'm crazier than Moe Vernon ever was. I didn't have a drawer full of erotic novelties, but I guess I had my own individual quirks. And although I've never worn a set of false bosoms in my life, I've stood there dressed in something just as strange, with tears in my eyes while people died laughing.

II.

By 1939 I was twenty-three years old and had taken a job on the New York City police force. I've never really examined until now just why I should have chosen that particular career, but I guess it came as a result of a number of things. Foremost amongst these was probably my grandfather.

Even though I resented the old man for the amount of guilt and pressure and recrimination he'd subjected my dad to, I suppose that the simple fact of spending the first twelve years of my life living in my grandfather's proximity had indelibly stamped a certain set of moral values and conditions upon me. I was never so extreme in my beliefs concerning God, the family, and the flag as my father's father was, but if I look at myself today I can see basic notions of decency that were passed down direct from him to me. His name was Hollis Wordsworth Mason, and perhaps because my parents had flattered the old man by naming me after him, he always took a special concern over my upbringing and moral instruction. One of the things that he took great pains to impress upon me was that country folk were morally healthier than city folk and that cities were just cesspools into which all the world's dishonesty and greed and lust and godlessness drained and was left to fester unhindered. Obviously, as I got older and came to realize just how much drunkenness and domestic violence and child abuse was hidden behind the neighborly facade of some of these lonely Montana farmhouses, I understood that my grandfather's appraisal had been a little one-sided. Nevertheless, some of the things that I saw in the city during my first few years here filled me with a sort of ethical revulsion that I couldn't shake off. To some degree, I still can't.

The pimps, the pornographers, the protection artists. The landlords who set dogs on their elderly tenants when they wanted them out to make way for more lucrative custom. The old men who touched little children and the callous young rapists who were barely old enough to shave. I saw these people all around me and I'd feel sick in my gut at the world and what it was becoming. Worse, there were times when I'd upset my dad and mom by loudly wishing I was back in Montana. Despite everything, I wished no such thing, but sometimes I'd be mad at them and it seemed like the best way to hurt them, to reawaken all those old doubts and worries and sleeping dogs of guilt. I'm sorry I did it now, and I wish I could have told them that while they were alive. I wish I could have told them that they were right in bringing me to the city, that they did the right thing by me. I wish I could have let them know that. Their lives would have been so much easier.

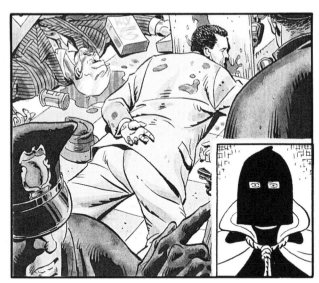

Masked adventurers make the front page. (New York Gazette, October 14th, 1938) Note artist's impression of "The Hooded Vigilante."

When the gap between the world of the city and the world my grandfather had presented to me as right and good became too wide and depressing to tolerate, I'd turn to my other great love, which was pulp adventure fiction. Despite the fact that Hollis Mason Senior would have had nothing but scorn and loathing for all of those violent and garish magazines, there was a sort of prevailing morality in them that I'm sure he would have responded to. The world of Doc Savage and The Shadow was one of absolute values, where what was good was never in the slightest doubt and where what was evil inevitably suffered some fitting punishment. The notion of good and justice espoused by Lamont Cranston with his slouch hat and blazing automatics seemed a long way from that of the fierce and taciturn old man I remembered sitting up alone into the Montana night with no company save his bible, but I can't help feeling that if the two had ever met they'd have found something to talk about. For my part, all those brilliant and resourceful sleuths and heroes offered a glimpse of a perfect world where morality worked the way it was *meant* to. Nobody in Doc Savage's world ever killed themselves except thwarted kamikaze assassins or enemy spies with cyanide capsules. Which world would you rather live in, if you had the choice?

Answering that question, I suppose, was what led me to become a cop. It was also what led me to later become something more than a cop. Bear that in mind and I think the rest of this narrative will be easier to swallow. I know people always have trouble understanding just what brings a person to behave the way that I and people like me behave, what makes us do the sort of things we do. I can't answer for anybody else, and I suspect that all our answers would be different anyway, but in my case it's fairly straightforward: I like the idea of adventure, and I feel bad unless I'm doing good. I've heard all the psychologists' theories, and I've heard all the jokes and the rumors and the innuendo, but what it comes down to for me is that I dressed up like an owl and fought crime because it was fun and because it needed doing and because I goddam felt like it.

Okay. There it is. I've said it. I dressed up. As an owl. And fought crime. Perhaps you begin to see why I half expect this summary of my career to raise more laughs than poor cuckolded Moe Vernon with his foam teats and his Wagner could ever hope to have done.

For me, it all started in 1938, the year when they invented the super-hero. I was too old for comic books when the first issue of ACTION COMICS came out, or at least too old to read them in public without souring my promotion chances, but I noticed a lot of the little kids on my beat reading it and couldn't resist asking one of them if I could glance through it. I figured if anybody saw me I could put it all down to keeping a good relationship with the youth of the community.

There was a lot of stuff in that first issue. There were detective yarns and stories about magicians whose names I can't remember, but from the moment I set eyes on it I only had eyes for the Superman story. Here was something that presented the basic morality of the pulps without all their darkness and ambiguity. The atmosphere of the horrific and faintly sinister that hung around the Shadow was nowhere to be seen in the bright primary colors of Superman's world, and there was no hint of the repressed sex-urge which had sometimes been apparent in the pulps, to my discomfort and embarrassment. I'd never been entirely sure what Lamont Cranston was up to with Margo Lane, but I'd bet it was nowhere near as innocent and wholesome as Clark Kent's relationship with her namesake Lois. Of course, all of these old characters are gone and forgotten now, but I'm willing to bet that there are at least a few older readers out there who will remember enough to know what I'm talking about. Anyway, suffice it to say that I read that story through about eight times before giving it back to the complaining kid that I'd snitched it from.

It set off a lot of things I'd forgotten about, deep inside me, and kicked all those old fantasies that I'd had when I was thirteen or fourteen back into gear: The prettiest girl in the class would be attacked by bullies, and I'd be there to beat them off, but when she offered to kiss me as a reward, I'd refuse. Gangsters would kidnap my math teacher, Miss Albertine, and I'd track them down and kill them one by one until she was free, and then she'd break off her engagement with my sarcastic English teacher, Mr. Richardson, because she'd fallen hopelessly in love with her grim-faced and silent fourteen-year-old savior. All of this stuff came flooding back as I stood there gawking at the hijacked comic book, and even though I laughed at myself for having entertained such transparent juvenile fantasies, I didn't laugh as hard as I might have done. Not half as hard as I'd laughed at Moe Vernon, for example.

Anyway, although I'd occasionally manage to trick some unsuspecting tyke into lending me his most recent issue of the funnybook in question and then spend the rest of the day leaping tall buildings inside my head, my fantasies were to remain as fantasies until I opened a newspaper in the autumn of that same year and found that the super-heroes had escaped from their four-color world and invaded the plain, factual black and white of the headlines.

The first news story was simple and unpresupposing enough, but it shared enough elements with those fictions that were closest to my heart to make me notice it and file it in my memory for future reference. It concerned an attempted assault and robbery that had taken place in Queens, New York. A man and his girlfriend, walking home after a night at the theater, had been set upon by a gang of three men armed with guns. After relieving the couple of their valuables, the gang has started to beat and physically abuse the young man while threatening to indecently assault his girlfriend. At this point, the crime had been interrupted by a figure "Who dropped into the alleyway from above with something over his face" and proceeded to disarm the three attackers before beating them with such severity that all three required hospital treatment and that one subsequently lost the use of both legs as a result of a spinal injury. The witnesses' recounting of the event was confused and contradictory, but there was still something in the story that gave me a tingle of recognition. And then, a week later, it happened again.

Reportage on this second instance was more detailed. A supermarket stick-up had been prevented thanks to the intervention of "A tall man, built like a wrestler, who wore a black hood and cape and also wore a noose around his neck." This extraordinary being had crashed in through the window of the supermarket while the robbery was in progress and attacked the man responsible with such intensity and savagery that those not disabled immediately were only too willing to drop their guns and surrender. Connecting this incidence of masked intervention with its predecessor, the papers ran the story under a headline that read simply "Hooded Justice." The first masked adventurer outside comic books had been given his name.

Reading and rereading that news item, I knew that I had to be the second. I'd found my vocation.

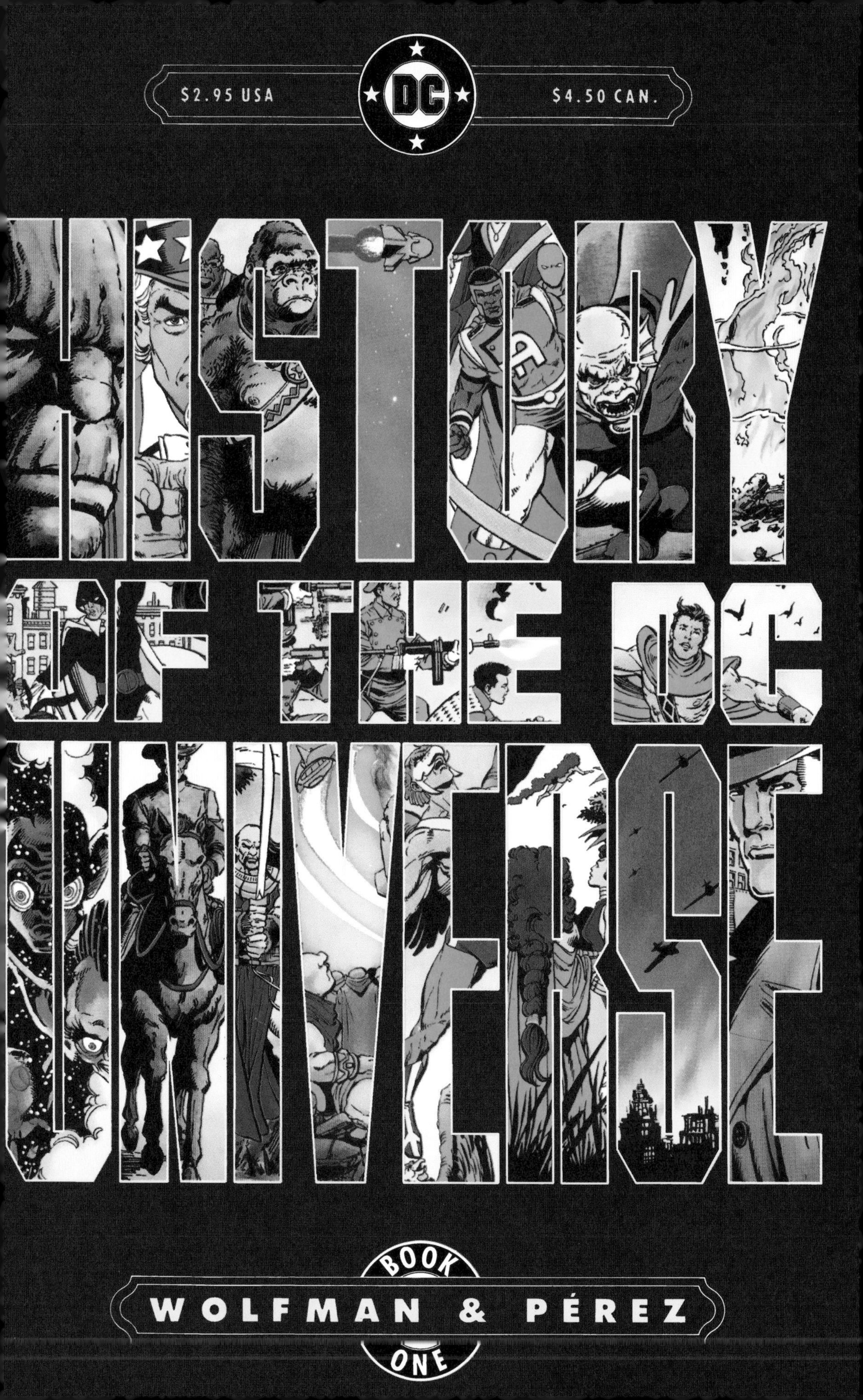
$2.95 USA
DC
$4.50 CAN.
HISTORY OF THE DC UNIVERSE
BOOK ONE
WOLFMAN & PÉREZ

THE HISTORY OF THE DC UNIVERSE

Story by
MARV WOLFMAN

Pencils by
GEORGE PÉREZ

Inks by
KARL KESEL

Colors by
TOM ZIUKO

What began as a single universe grew to become a multiverse in danger of annihilation at the hands of a demonic force. Heroes from many universes banded together and destroyed the evil at the dawn of time, and because of them, the single universe was born anew.

In that rebirth, the histories of planets were changed. I watched the death of the multiverse and the birth of the universe, and I knew these changes must be chronicled.

I do this not to enlighten, for no one is permitted to know of the multiverse that had been. I do this because I must, because change must be recorded, and because I must pay my debt to the one who allowed me the privilege of knowing the truth.

He was a being who lived ten billion years. He saw the multiverse born, and he knew of its coming end. He brought those heroes together and led them in their battle against evil, and he died that the universe would live. To him I dedicate this narrative.

This then is the History of the Universe as seen through my eyes. Its concerns are with those men and women who fought and sacrificed their own lives to save the universe, whose courage and determination altered the past and future.

As for me, I am Harbinger, and it is my mission to gather the truth.

We know the universe was created more than ten billion years ago, formed of vapor and forged with fire. The single will which brought light to the dark, gave substance to nothingness, and created life from unlife, must have permitted itself a sigh of satisfaction when its children wailed in birth.

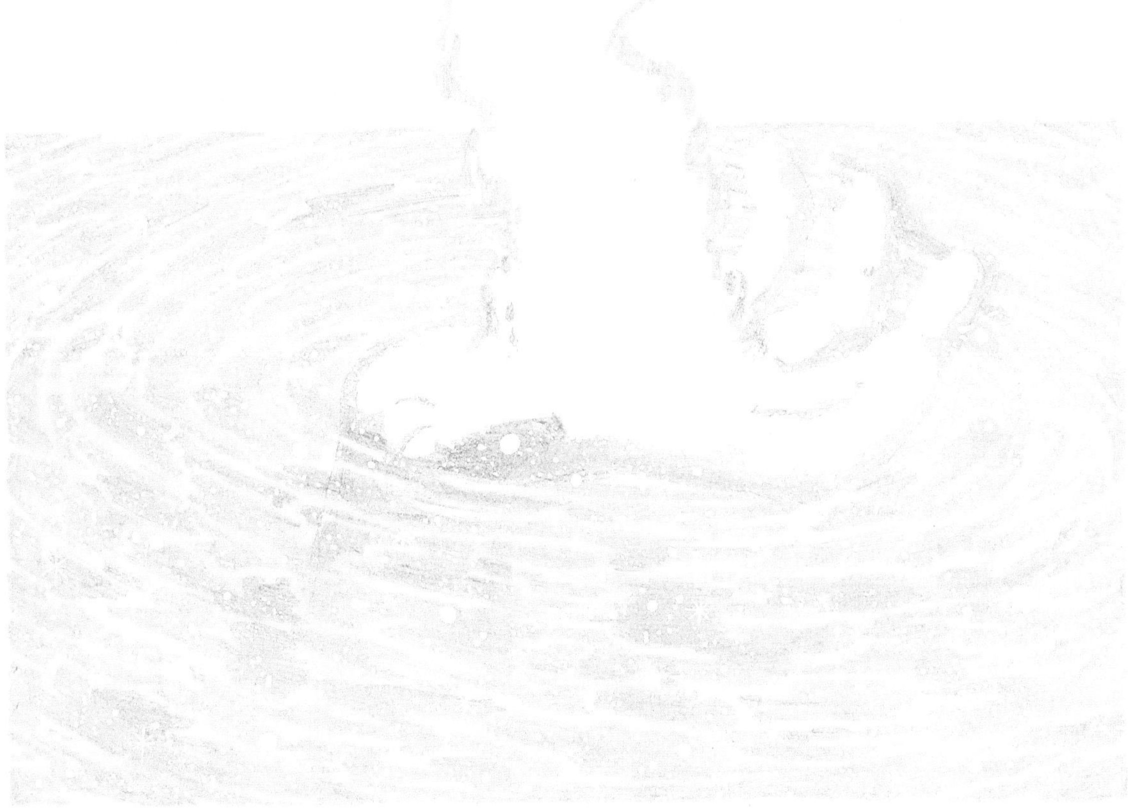

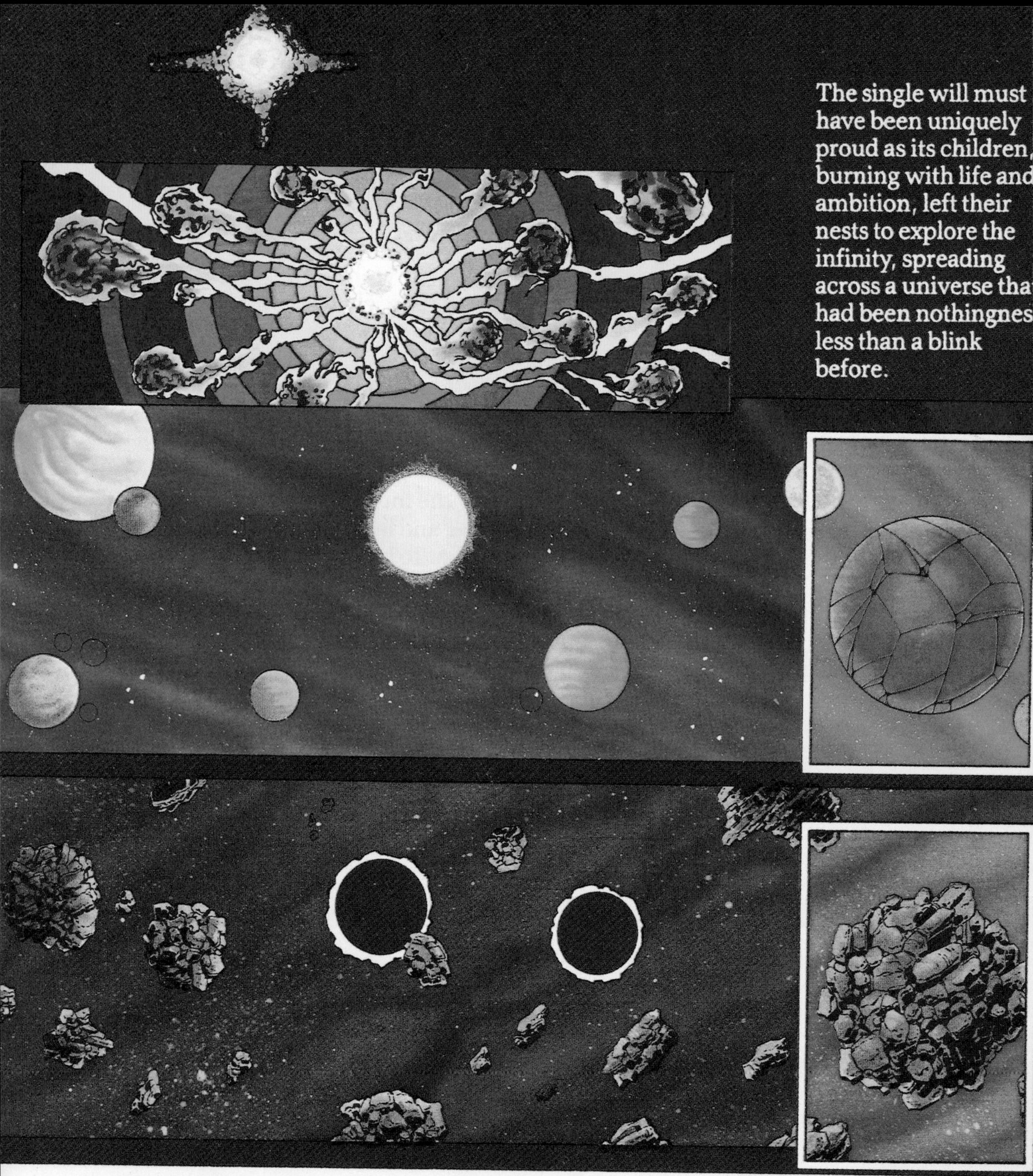
The single will must
have been uniquely
proud as its children,
burning with life and
ambition, left their
nests to explore the
infinity, spreading
across a universe tha
had been nothingnes
less than a blink
before.

Its seeds were scattered on the solar winds. On some worlds, life grew out of plasma. On others, waves of shimmering heat took on an unfathomable intelligence. On fewer than thirty worlds, life developed out of sound; while on more than a million other planets, silicon became life's base.

Twenty million worlds embraced carbon, while three million worlds gave home to sentient light. On one thousand planets, life became represented as intangible concepts. And from each beginning, life evolved into something more—something greater.

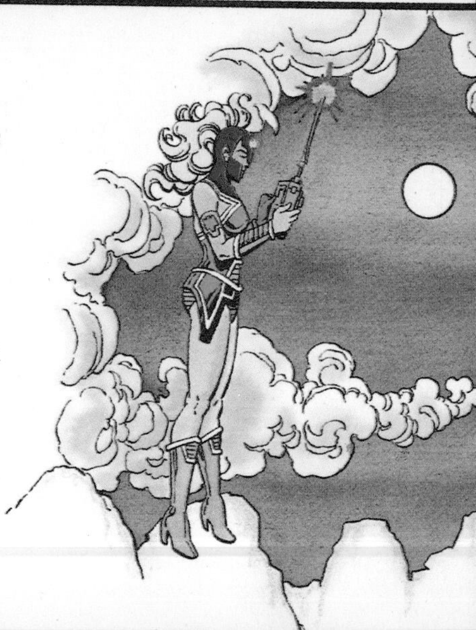

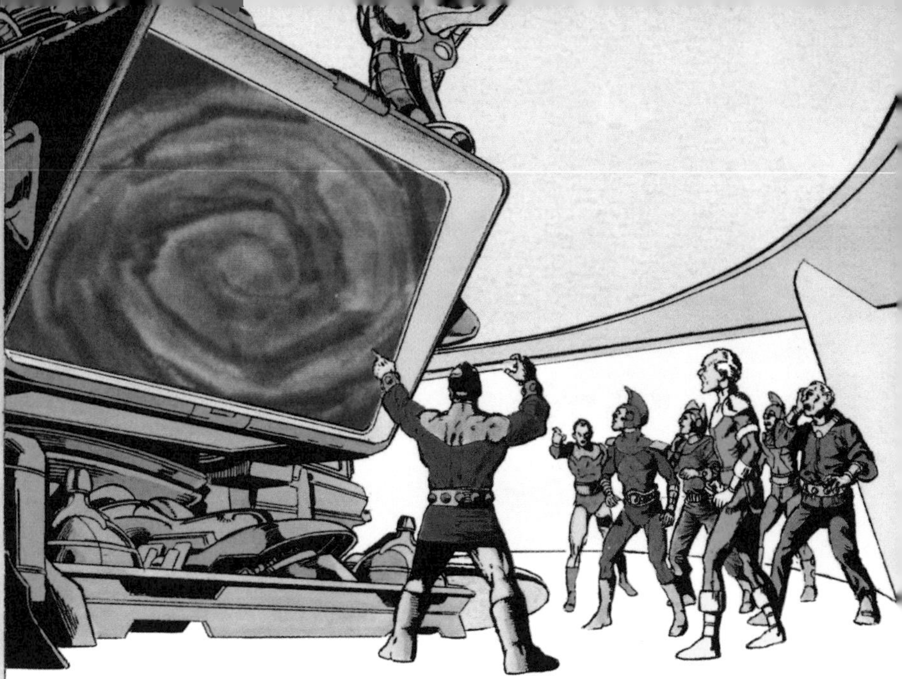

Oa was not the first great power, but it was the first not to be consumed by its own greed.

Colonized by off-worlders from the planet Maltus, Oa was a planet of science and technology that reached the pinnacle of civilization when most worlds were still mired in the first glimmers of self-awareness.

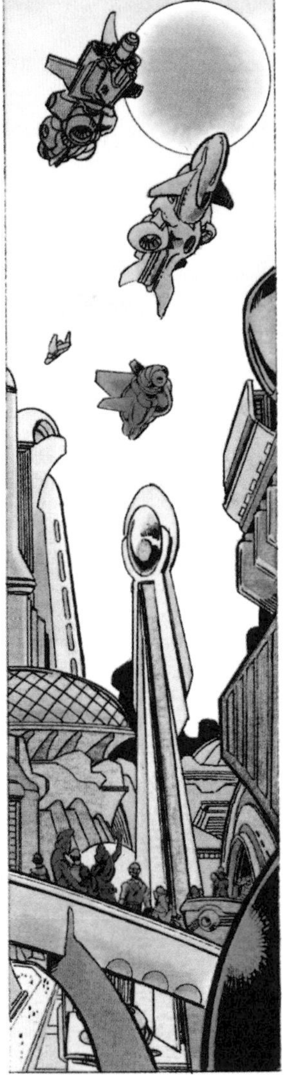

Oans explored not only the stars but their inner selves, developing telepathy and telekinesis to aid them in their quest. Nothing was beneath the Oans' interest, and nothing could remain a mystery for long. Theirs was a planet of harmony, and it remained so for a million years, but the scientist Krona was not content to explore space. He delved into the one area of science forbidden to all Oans: the origin of the Universe itself. Krona ignored the warning that chaos would ensue as he watched time peel away, and the hand of creation reach into the cosmos and pluck that fruit of life.

In that instant he saw it…

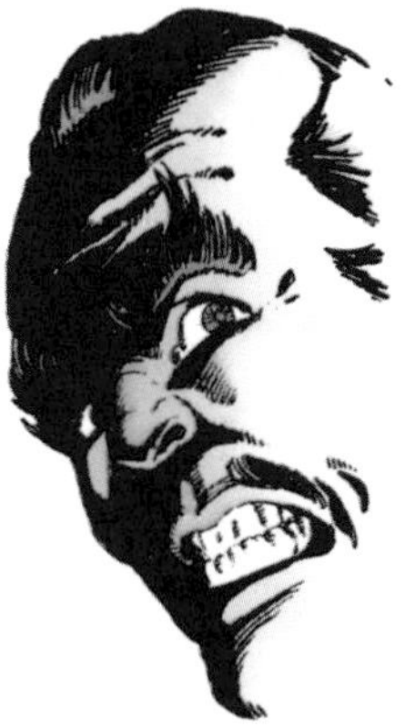

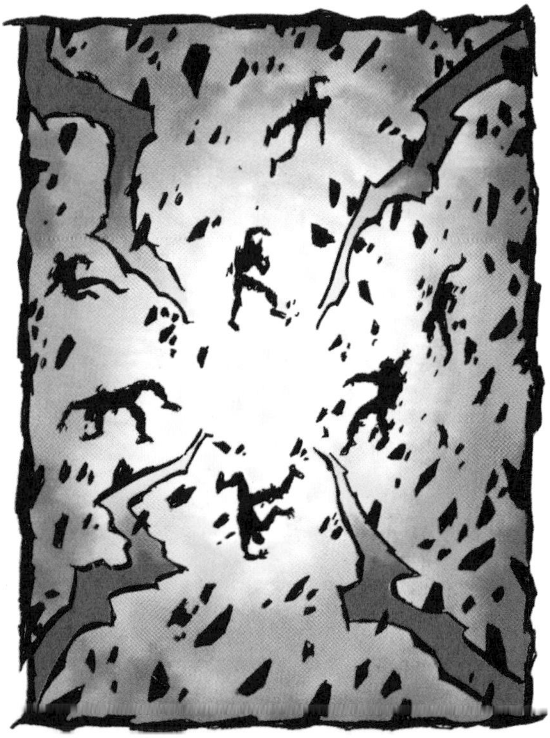

…and the Universe exploded.

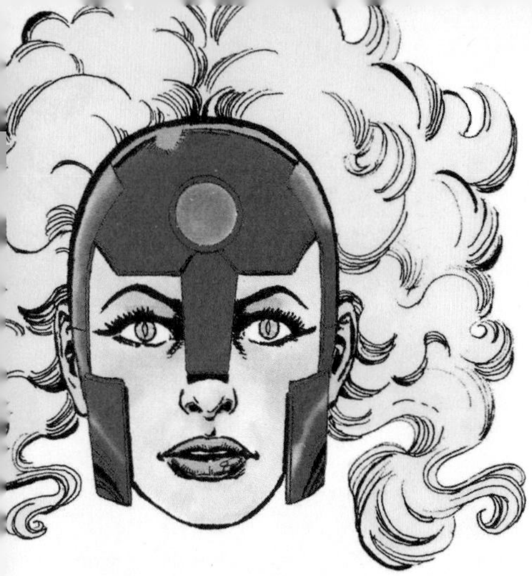

What had been one universe became two—positive matter and anti-matter—and with the unleashing of the anti-matter universe there came a wave of evil that spread throughout fifty million worlds, corrupting what had been a paradise. The Oans saw it as their responsibility to contain the evil that one of them had unleashed.

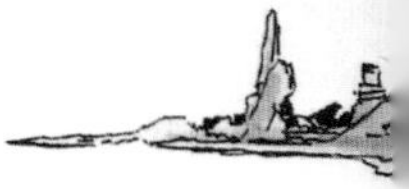

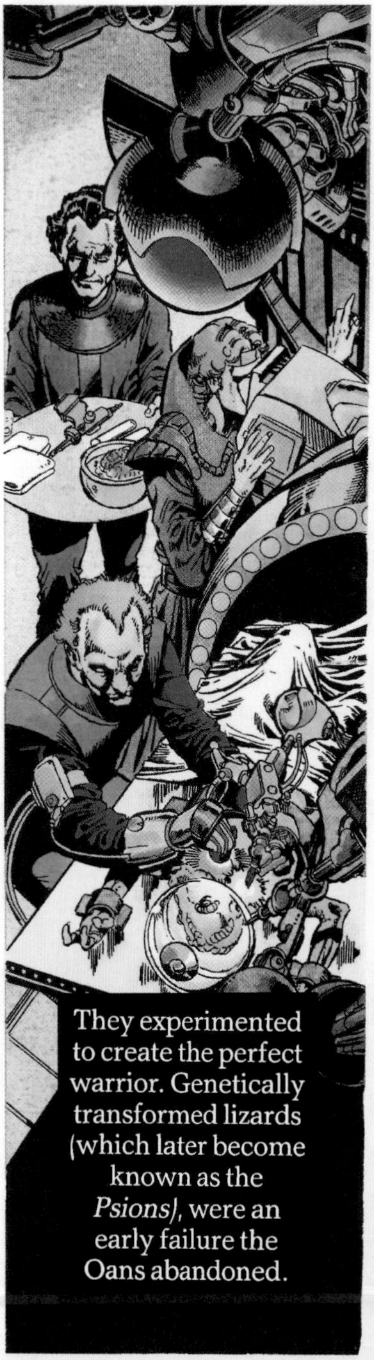
They experimented to create the perfect warrior. Genetically transformed lizards (which later become known as the *Psions)*, were an early failure the Oans abandoned.

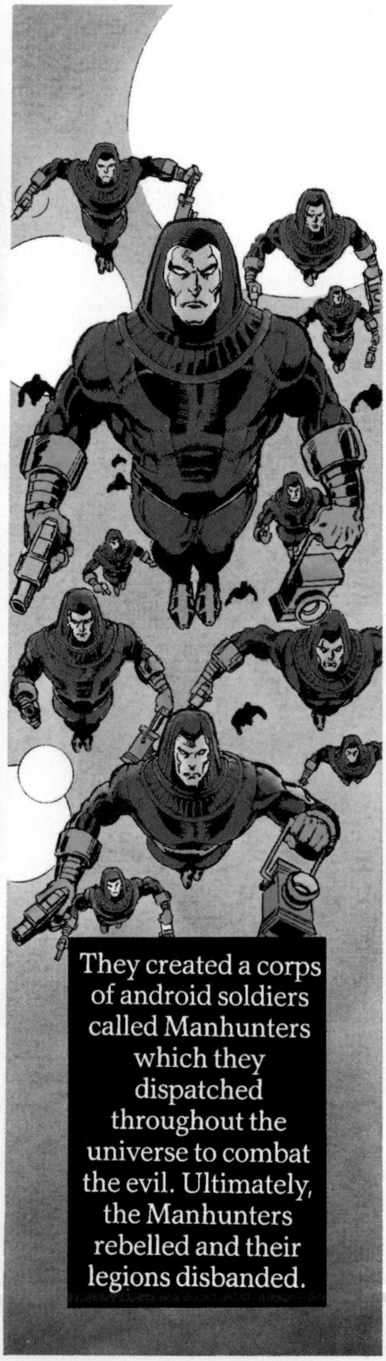
They created a corps of android soldiers called Manhunters which they dispatched throughout the universe to combat the evil. Ultimately, the Manhunters rebelled and their legions disbanded.

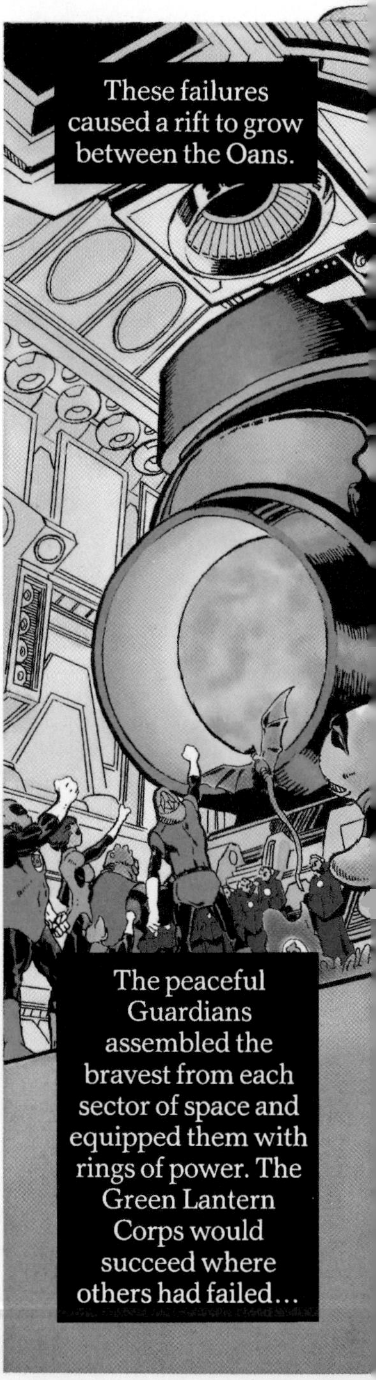
These failures caused a rift to grow between the Oans.
The peaceful Guardians assembled the bravest from each sector of space and equipped them with rings of power. The Green Lantern Corps would succeed where others had failed…

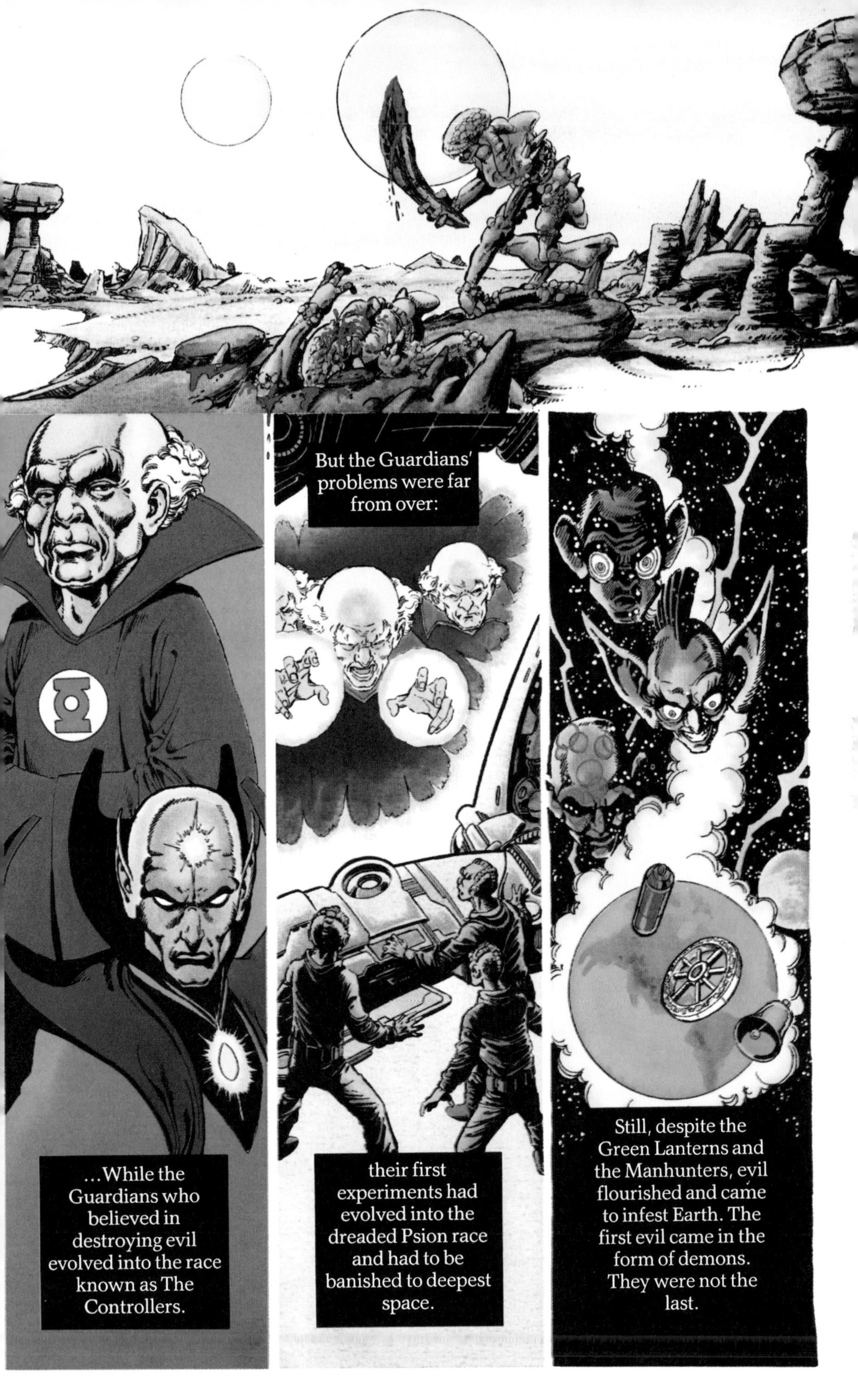
...While the Guardians who believed in destroying evil evolved into the race known as The Controllers.
But the Guardians' problems were far from over:
their first experiments had evolved into the dreaded Psion race and had to be banished to deepest space.
Still, despite the Green Lanterns and the Manhunters, evil flourished and came to infest Earth. The first evil came in the form of demons. They were not the last.

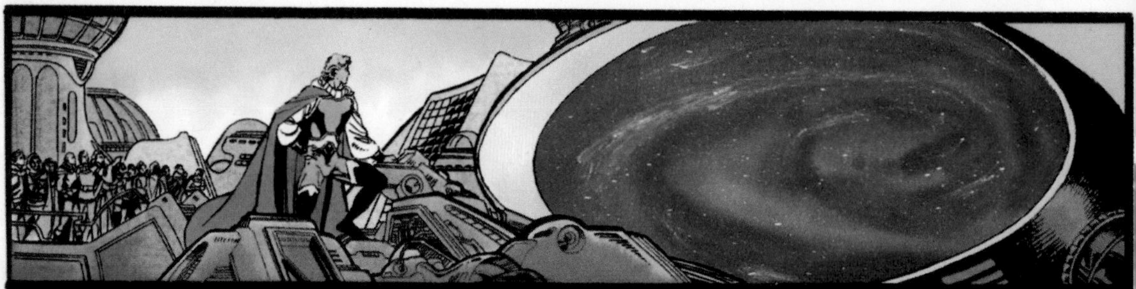

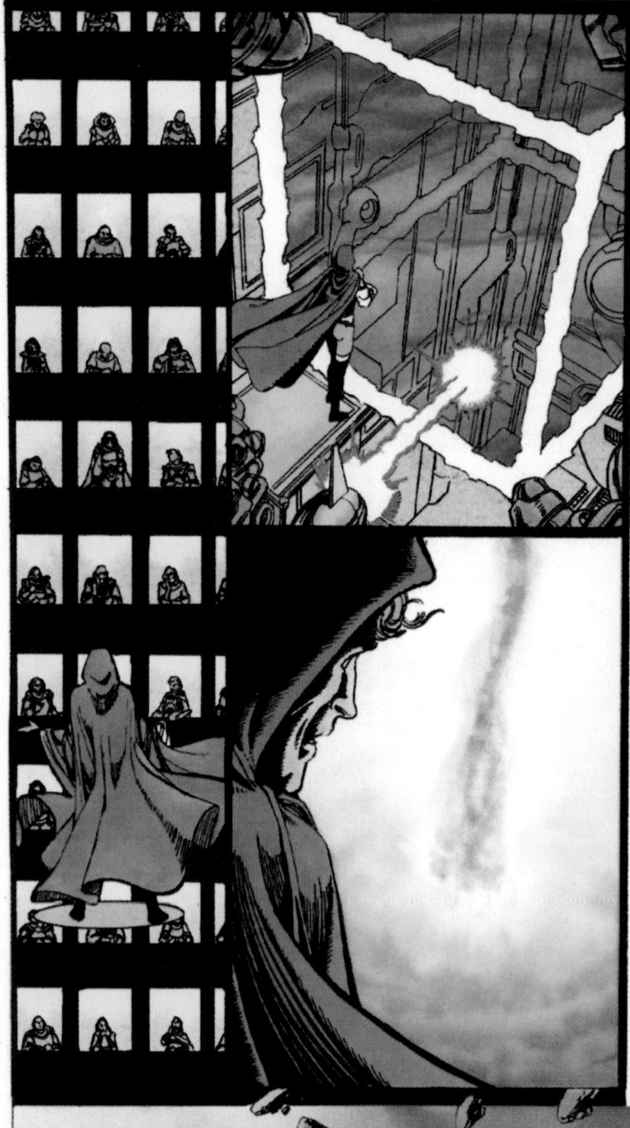

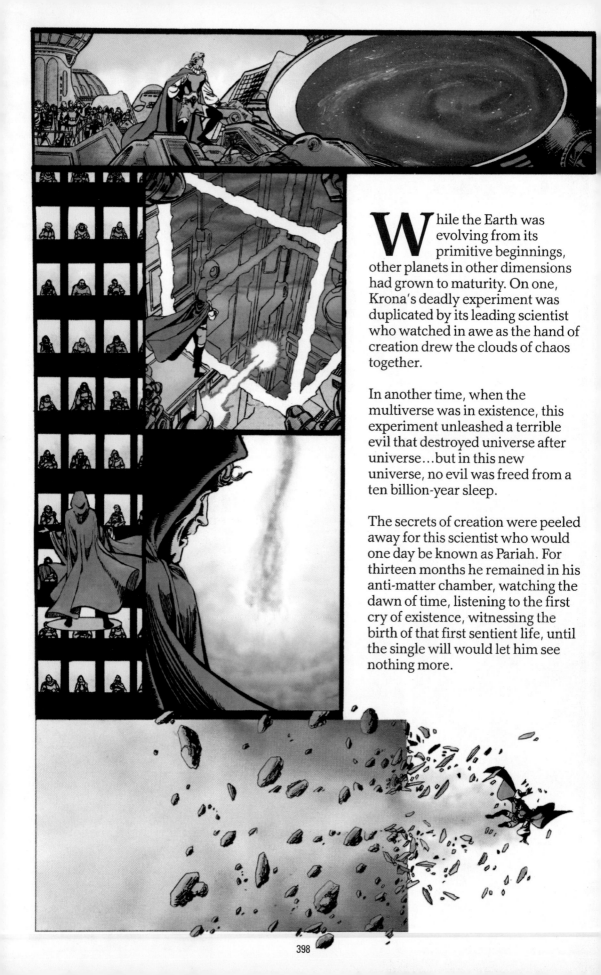

While the Earth was evolving from its primitive beginnings, other planets in other dimensions had grown to maturity. On one, Krona's deadly experiment was duplicated by its leading scientist who watched in awe as the hand of creation drew the clouds of chaos together.

In another time, when the multiverse was in existence, this experiment unleashed a terrible evil that destroyed universe after universe...but in this new universe, no evil was freed from a ten billion-year sleep.

The secrets of creation were peeled away for this scientist who would one day be known as Pariah. For thirteen months he remained in his anti-matter chamber, watching the dawn of time, listening to the first cry of existence, witnessing the birth of that first sentient life, until the single will would let him see nothing more.

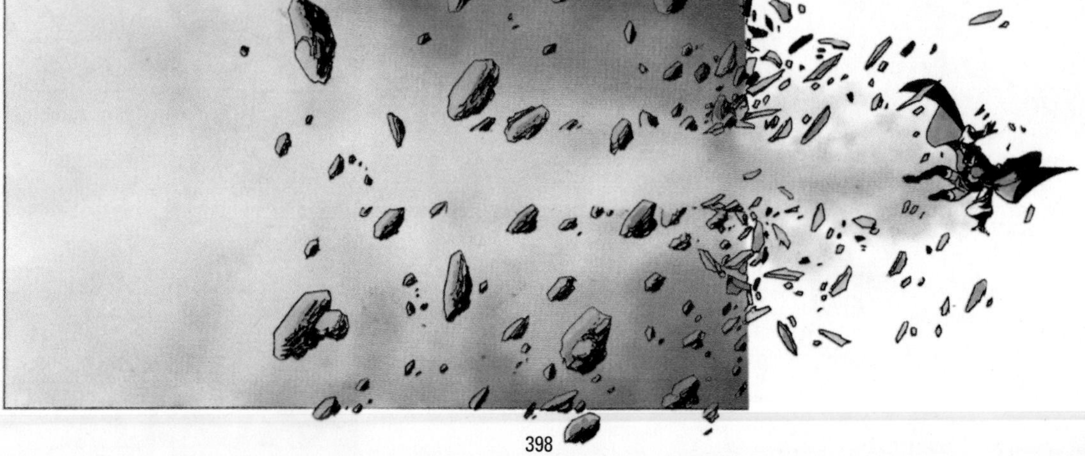

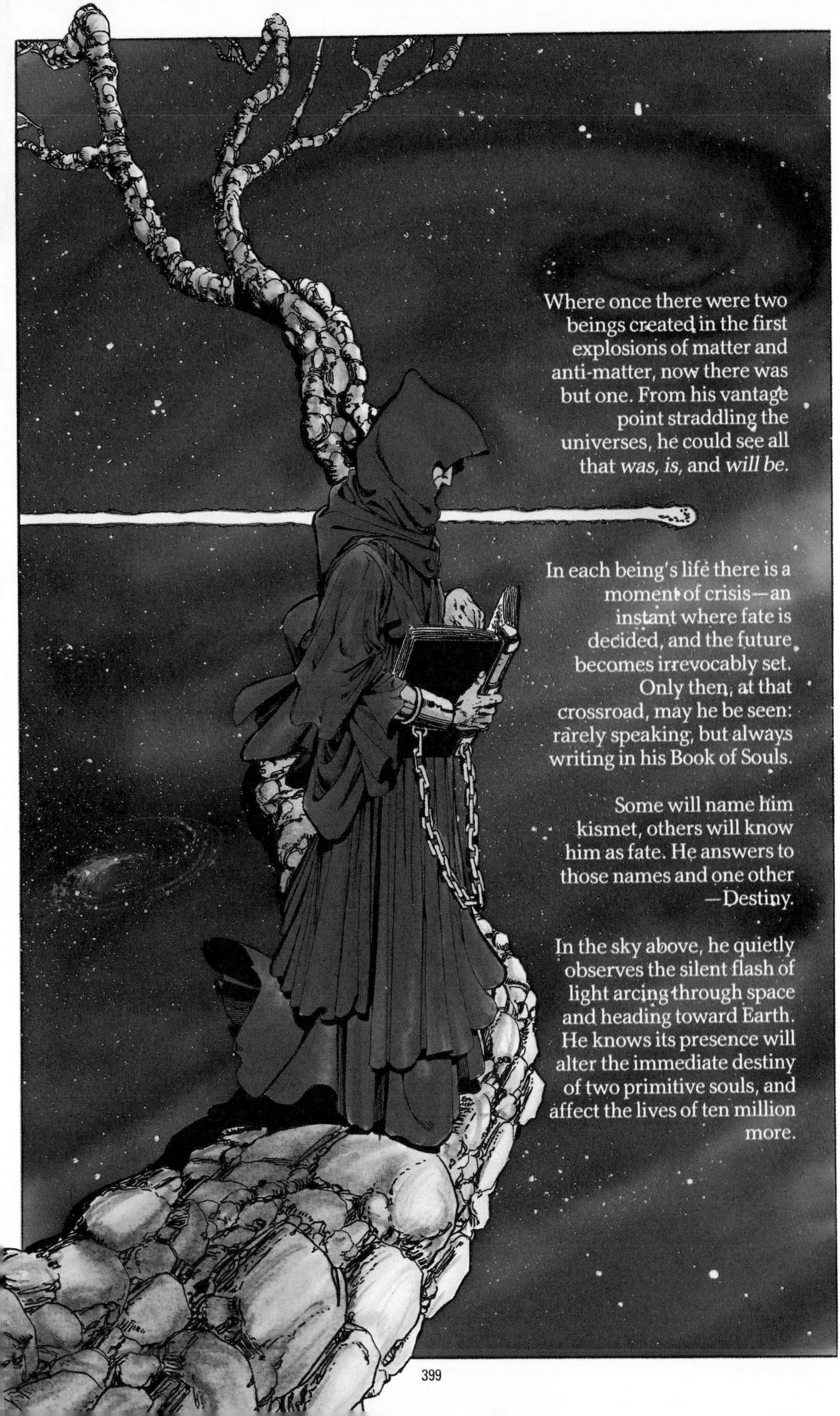
Where once there were two beings created in the first explosions of matter and anti-matter, now there was but one. From his vantage point straddling the universes, he could see all that *was, is,* and *will be.*
In each being's life there is a moment of crisis—an instant where fate is decided, and the future becomes irrevocably set. Only then, at that crossroad, may he be seen: rarely speaking, but always writing in his Book of Souls.
Some will name him kismet, others will know him as fate. He answers to those names and one other —Destiny.
In the sky above, he quietly observes the silent flash of light arcing through space and heading toward Earth. He knows its presence will alter the immediate destiny of two primitive souls, and affect the lives of ten million more.

It burns through Earth's atmosphere in the middle of the night, and the Neanderthals who watch the dark skies light up with fire pray to the gods of the earth and sun and moon that this is not the end of all existence.

None of the Bear Tribe dares to approach this shimmering light that has set fire to the fruit trees more than a mile away. Those of the Wolf Tribe hide in the darkness of their caves.

But Vandar Adg of the Blood Tribe, hunting for enemies to slay and boar to eat, stood in the fields as the star exploded before him. Its fire burned through his flesh and reached into his soul. Vandar Adg felt a change his primitive mind was not yet able to comprehend. He was no longer mortal; indeed, Vandar Adg had become Vandal Savage—the Immortal.

Savage's remarkable transformation was observed by another man—the leader of the Bear Tribe who followed his enemy to the light and saw his unexplained metamorphosis. While Savage fled in fear, he cautiously approached the shimmering star and touched it. He, too, was changed. From mortal, he became the Immortal Man. With each death he would be reborn.

That night, Vandal Savage murdered twelve of his enemies. Still, the blood-hungry throbbing within him was not sated.

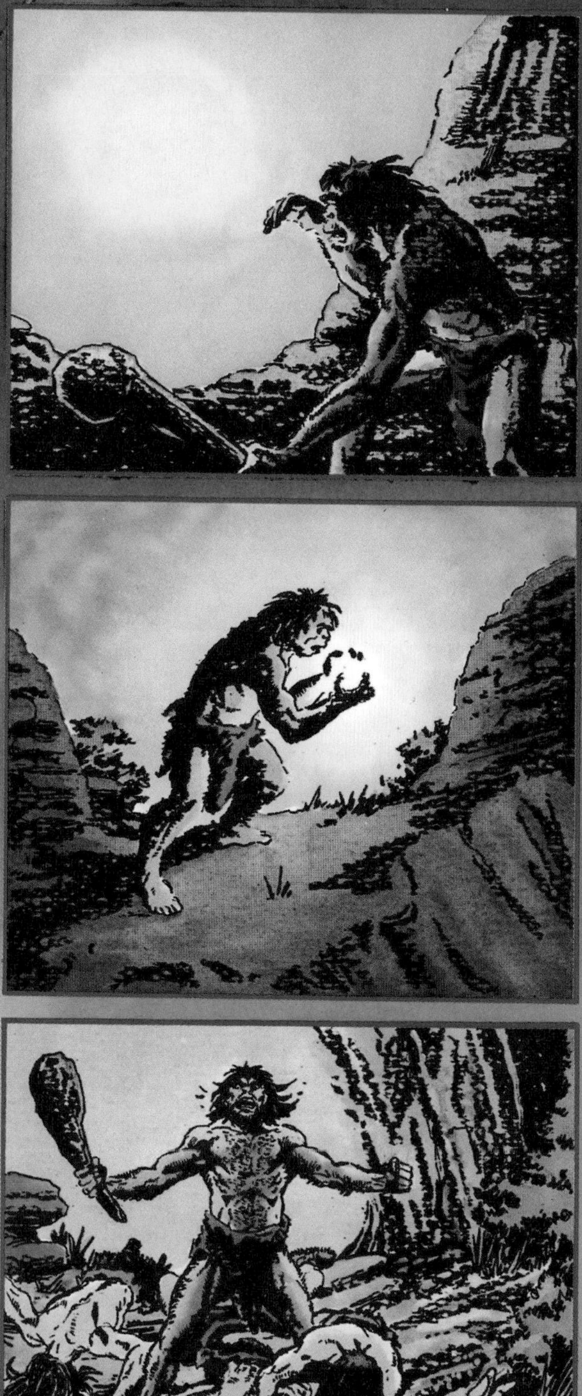

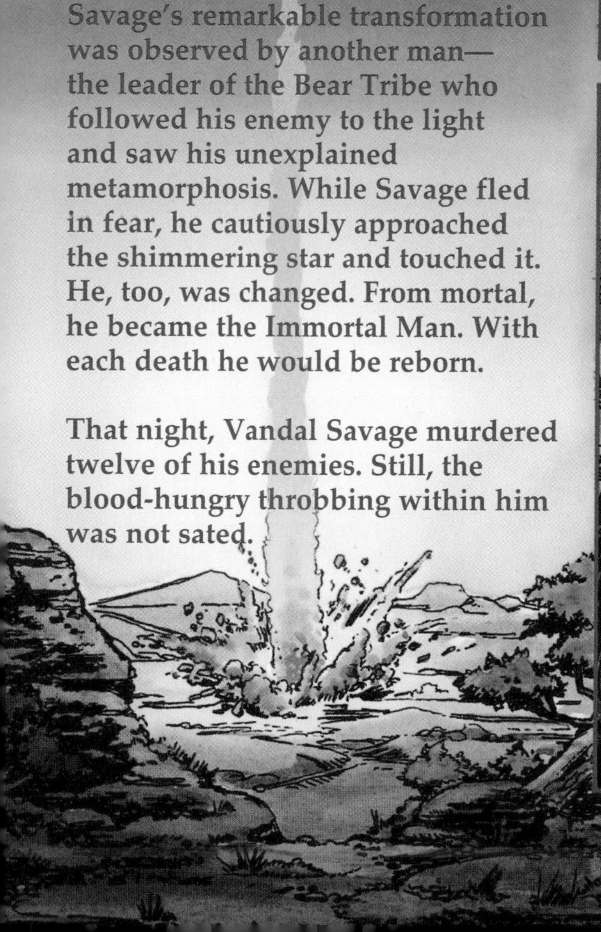

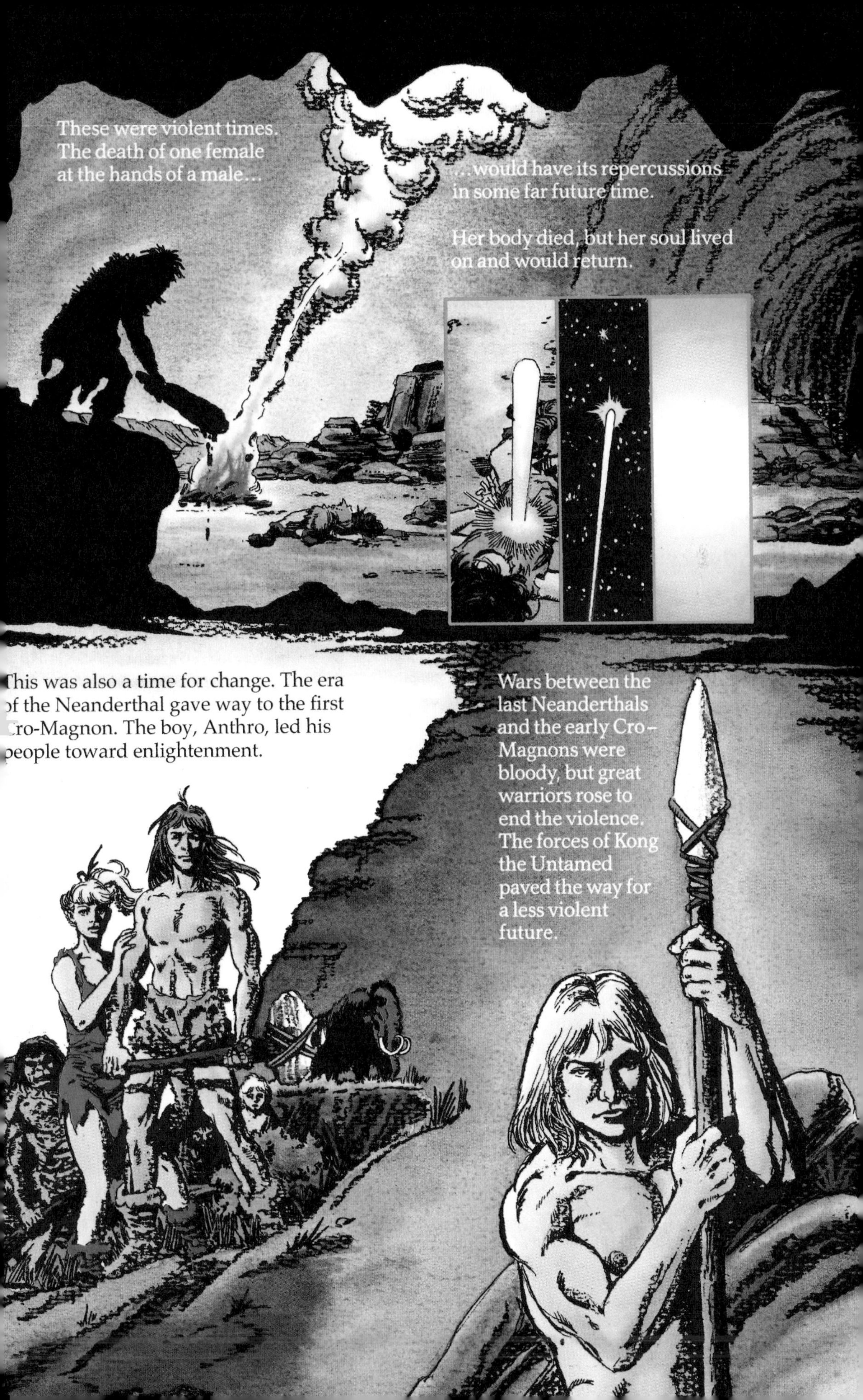
These were violent times. The death of one female at the hands of a male…
…would have its repercussions in some far future time.
Her body died, but her soul lived on and would return.
This was also a time for change. The era of the Neanderthal gave way to the first Cro-Magnon. The boy, Anthro, led his people toward enlightenment.
Wars between the last Neanderthals and the early Cro–Magnons were bloody, but great warriors rose to end the violence. The forces of Kong the Untamed paved the way for a less violent future.

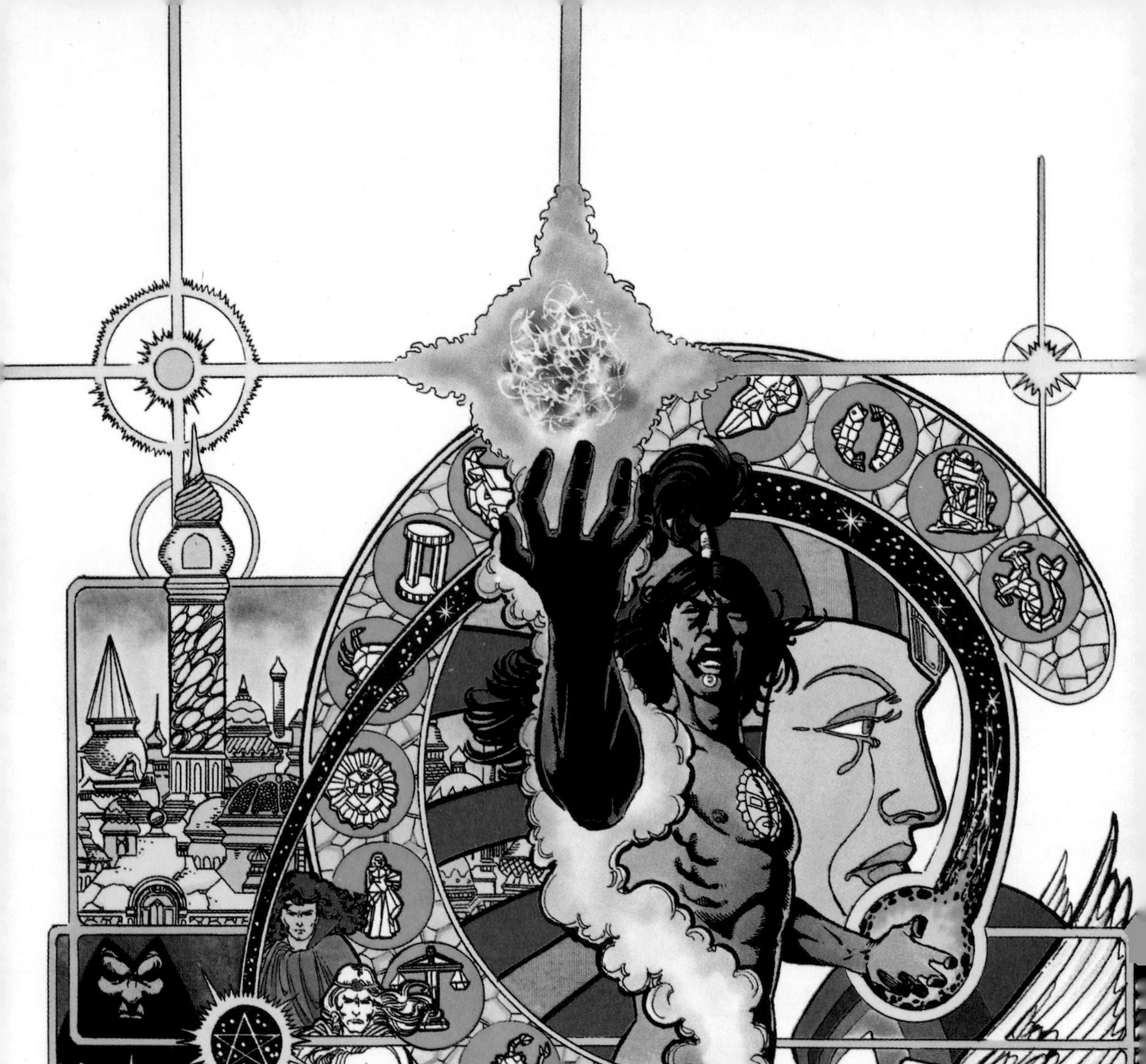

In the coming centuries, civilizations flourished and great empires rose. The forces of magic took hold over the Earth and then settled in the Kingdom of Atlantis. These were the mystic ages and corrupt sorcerers found themselves in constant battle with the practitioners of science.

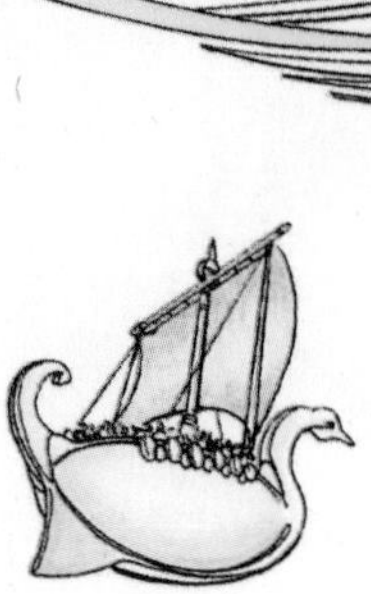

Wars between science and sorcery threatened to destroy the island kingdom, and some, fearing for their lives, fled to the seas in ancient Swan ships. One such group discovered the underground caverns which led to Skartaris, the savage dimensional world whose portals lie deep within the bowels of the Earth.

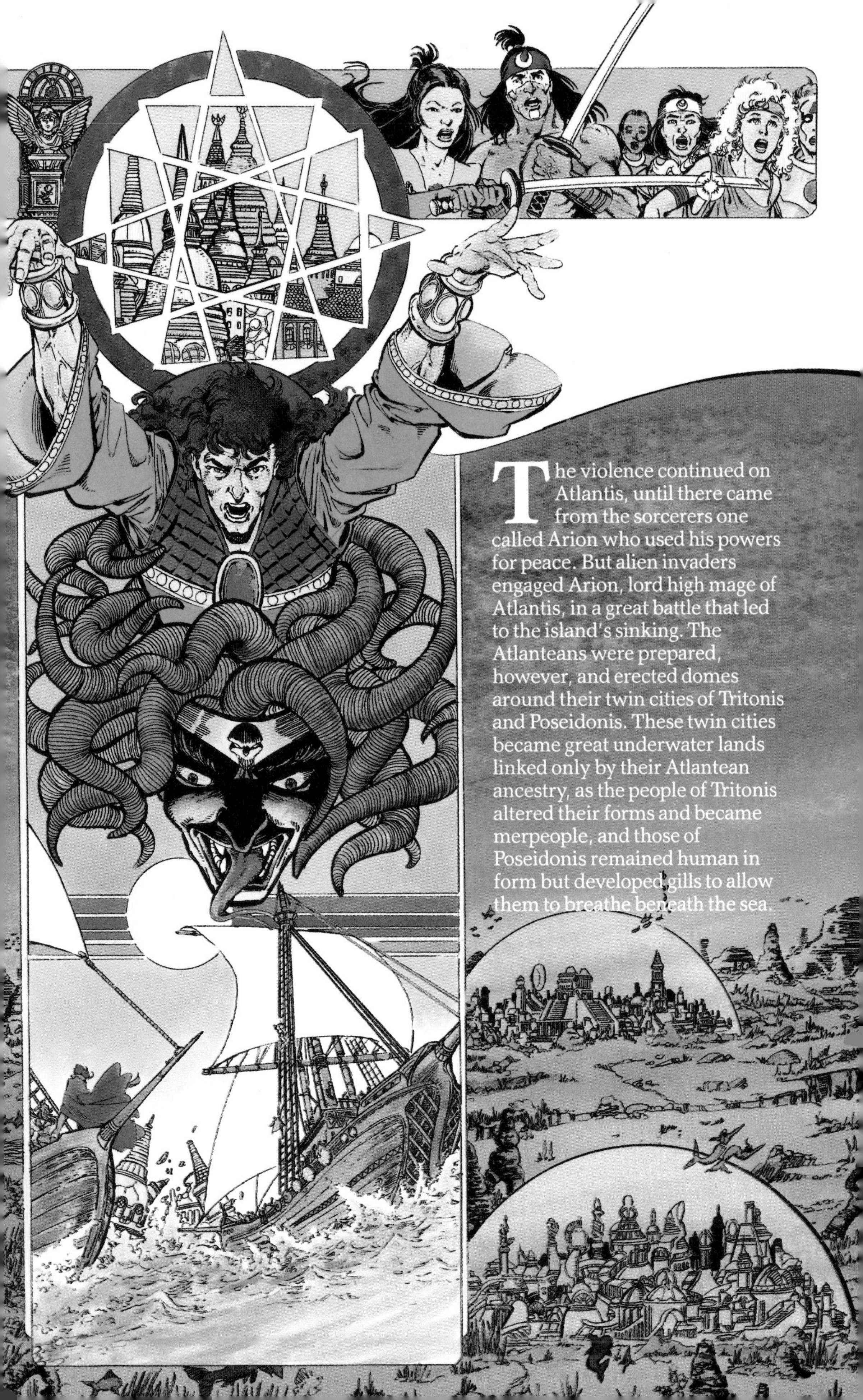

The violence continued on Atlantis, until there came from the sorcerers one called Arion who used his powers for peace. But alien invaders engaged Arion, lord high mage of Atlantis, in a great battle that led to the island's sinking. The Atlanteans were prepared, however, and erected domes around their twin cities of Tritonis and Poseidonis. These twin cities became great underwater lands linked only by their Atlantean ancestry, as the people of Tritonis altered their forms and became merpeople, and those of Poseidonis remained human in form but developed gills to allow them to breathe beneath the sea.

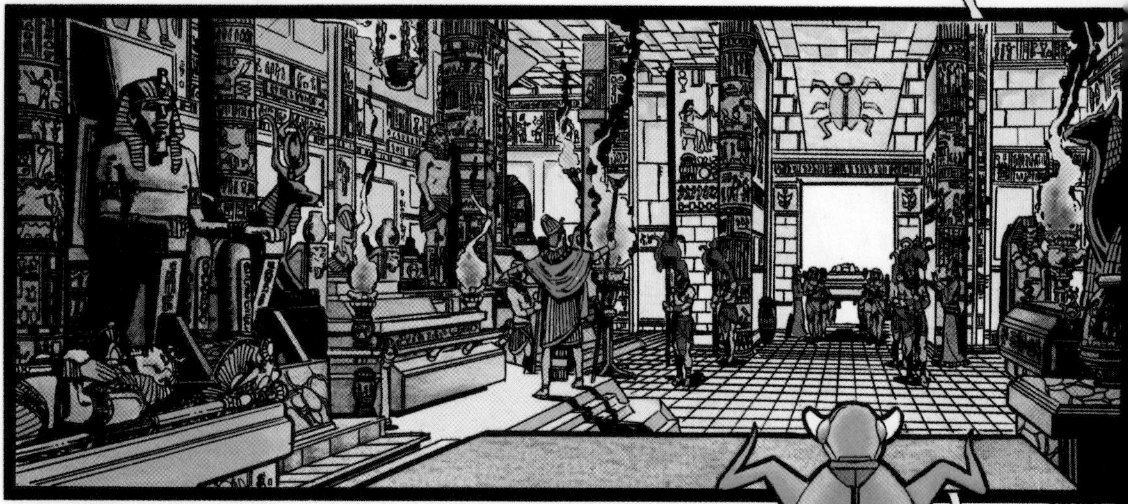

And so the first heroic age came to an end, to be reborn thousands of years and hundreds of miles beyond the site of Atlantis' sinking.

A hybrid bird race, led by Ibis-headed Thoth and falcon-headed Horus, came to Egypt before the birth of the great dynasties, and served as advisors before the coming of the Pharaohs. Leaving Egypt, the bird race migrated to the Arctic where they founded the hidden city of Feithera. Sorcery returned in the era of the mad Pharaoh Kha-ef-re. Forged from sorcery and science was a blue scarab gem which bestowed upon its wearer extraordinary powers: incredible strength, the gift of flight and the ability to form energy bolts. This scarab was buried with Kha-ef-re and rediscovered more than four thousand years later.

Of all the wizards in ancient Egypt, none was more powerful than the ancient, noble wizard Shazam. He seemed eternal in age and limitless in power, but even Shazam's existence was finite, and so the mage turned to his disciple, Teth-Adam, and bestowed on him great powers. But the power corrupted the student, and Teth-Adam became evil and turned against his people. To them he was now Black Adam. Only the power of his mentor, Shazam, could defeat the mad wizard and banish him from Earth to roam the Universe, seemingly forever.

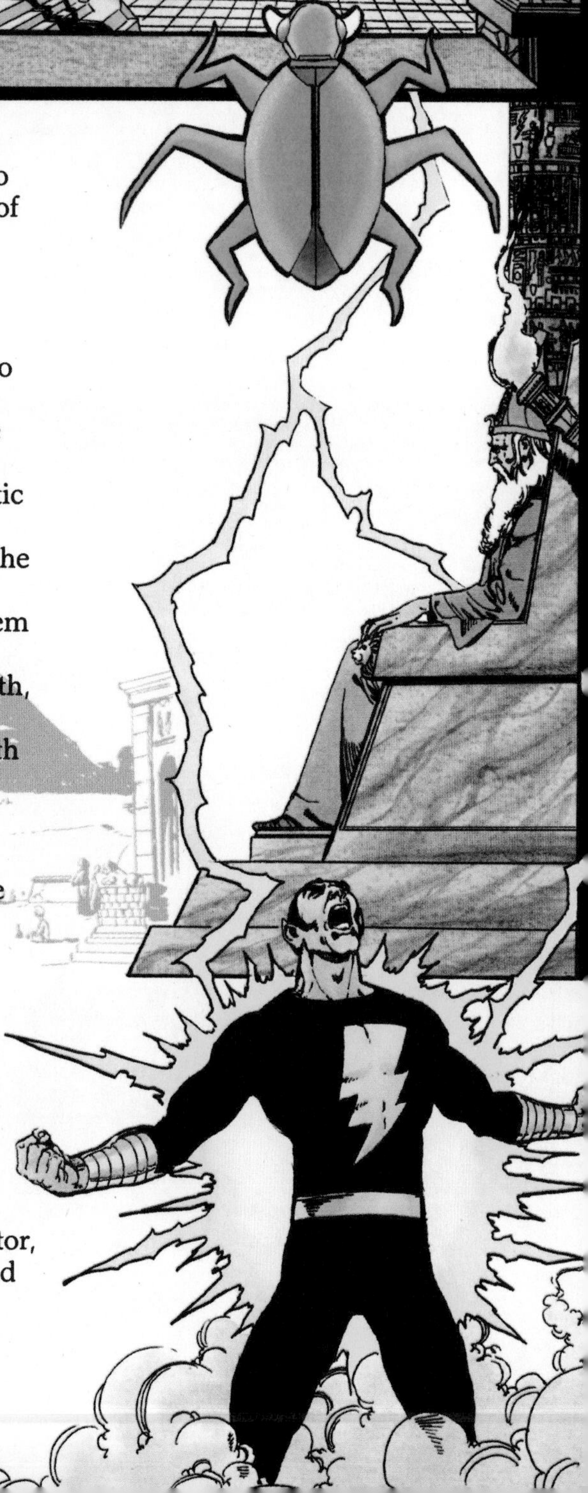

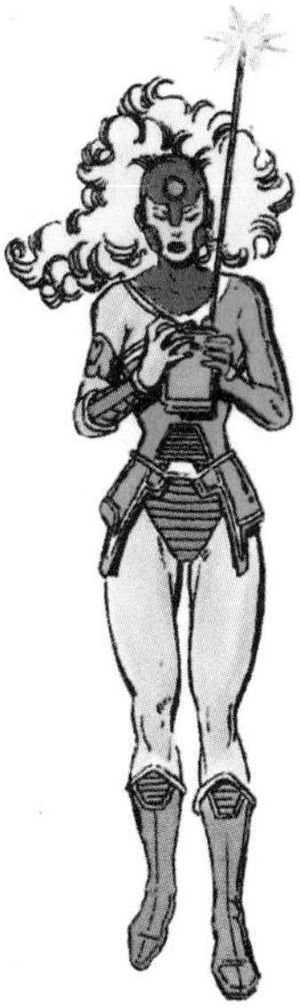

A thousand years passed and the mad priest Khalis rose to power. Nabu, one of the Lords of Order who had forged the powerful Amulet of Anubis, came to Egypt to challenge Khalis' rule and overthrew him. Four centuries passed before the Hyksos, the Shepherd-Kings, ruled Egypt. Khufu was a great warrior who tried to overthrow the evil Hath-Set, but in so doing, Khufu and his wife were slain. Yet their battle was not at an end–in three thousand years all three would be reincarnated as enemies. Other events on other worlds conspired to affect Earth's Heroic Age. The first of these worlds was created by a race of gaseous beings called the Sun-Thrivers who drew matter from far galaxies and formed a huge red star, but the star was unstable, so the Sun-Thrivers created planets out of solar matter, using their gravities to stabilize the turbulent sun storms, and a solar system was born. Of all the planets circling that red giant, the most powerful was Krypton. Belief in the god Rao led the Kryptonians to peace, and with peace came incredible advancements in the sciences and humanities.

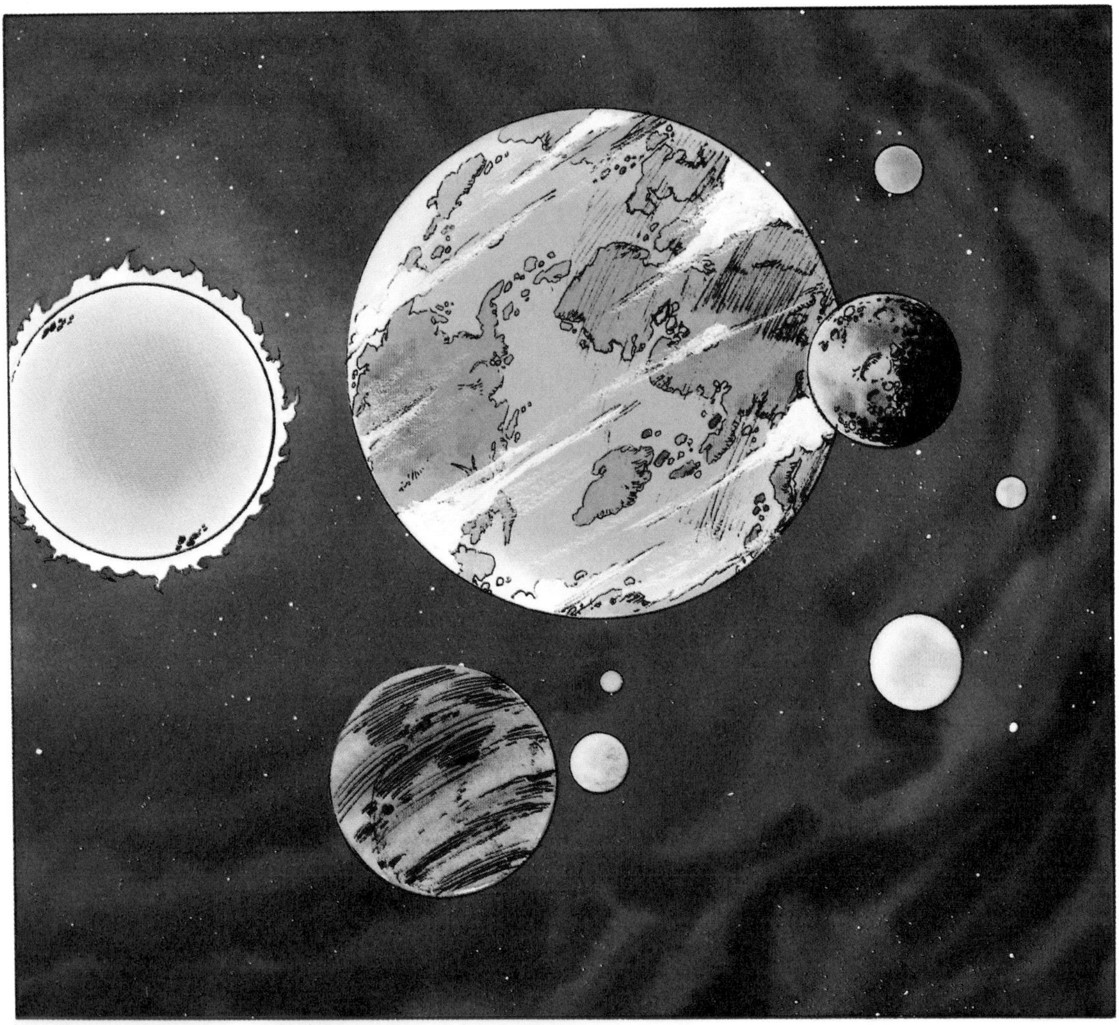

On Earth, it would be a thousand years before the Greeks rose to power, spreading their armies throughout Europe and conquering nation after nation in the name of the all-powerful Gods of Olympus.

The Gods--in legend the spawn of the dark infinity called Chaos. From Chaos came Gaea, Erebus and Night who in turn spawned Day. From Gaea was born Uranus, the sky. Then, with a smile of satisfaction, she gave us the mountains and the sea. It was from Gaea and Uranus, mother and son, that the Titans were born. They were twelve such Titans: Hyperion, Crius, Oceanus, Coeus, Iapetus, Cronus, Thea, Rhea, Mnemosyne, Phoebe, Tethys and Themis. Also from Uranus and Gaea were born the Cyclopses and the hundred-armed, fifty-headed monsters.

When Uranus saw his children, he was repulsed by their ugliness, and banished them to the depths of the Earth. Gaea plotted with her son Cronus and, with a deadly sickle, the son attacked the father and cast his blood to the sea. From Uranus' blood was born the deadly giants and the evil Furies, and from the sea was born the Goddess Aphrodite. Cronus and Rhea brought forth six children. Learning from an oracle that one of his children would overthrow his father, Cronus took his children and swallowed them one by one, with the exception of his final son, Zeus, whom Rhea had hidden away in safety. Upon reaching adulthood, Zeus made a pact with the Goddess Metis who forced Cronus to vomit up the Gods he had swallowed. Then Zeus led his fellow Gods into battle with the Titans and defeated them after a long and bloody war. Zeus banished the Titans to the depths of Tartarus and claimed Olympus in the name of the Gods. The Titans once again attacked Olympus, and their battle lasted more than ten years and nearly destroyed the Earth in this second battle of the Gods; the rivers burned and the sky crashed to the ground. Powerful as they were, The Titans were again defeated, but this time they were encased in rock and returned to Tartarus as immobile statues. And so the Gods of Olympus rested, thinking their days of warring over at last.

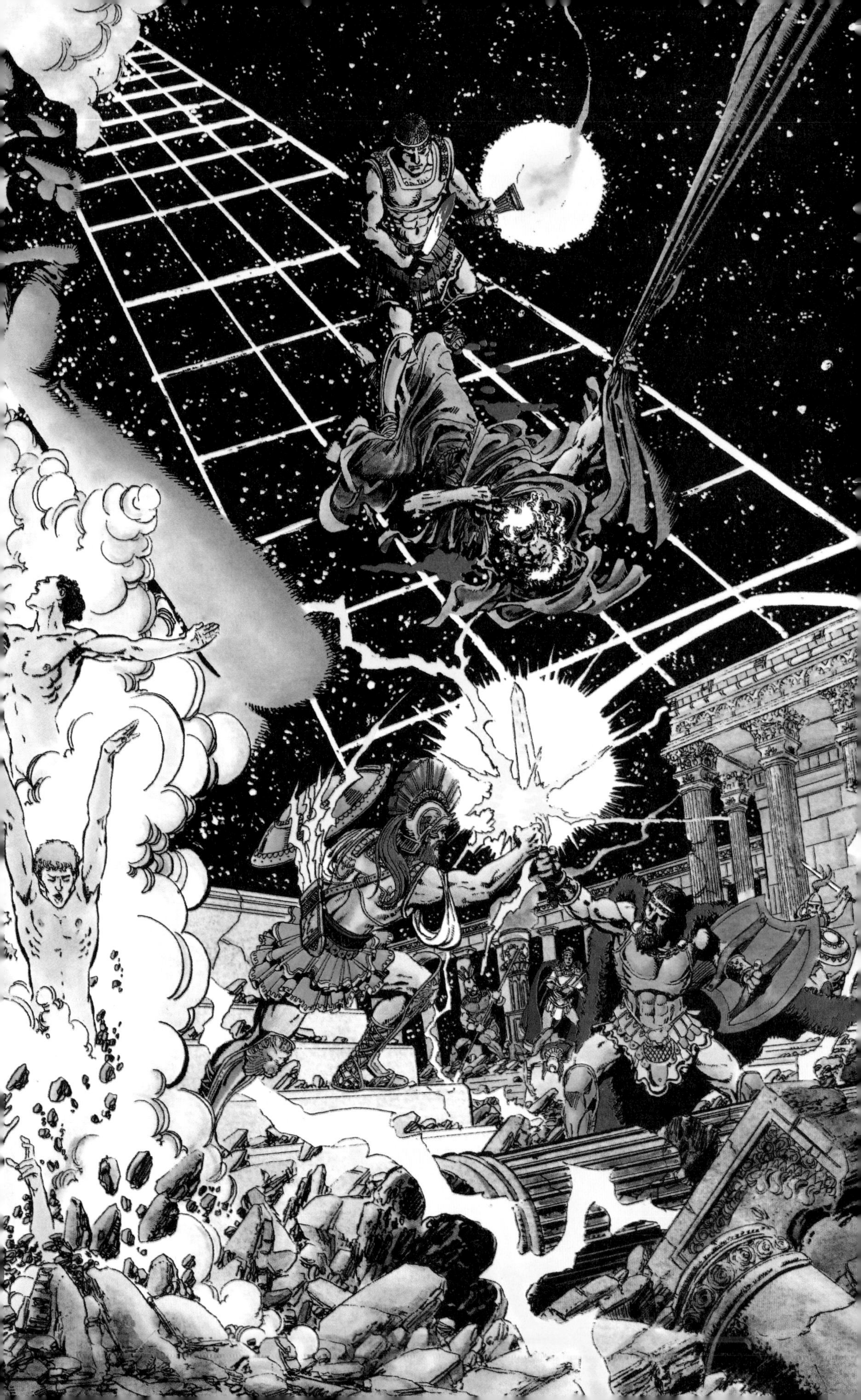

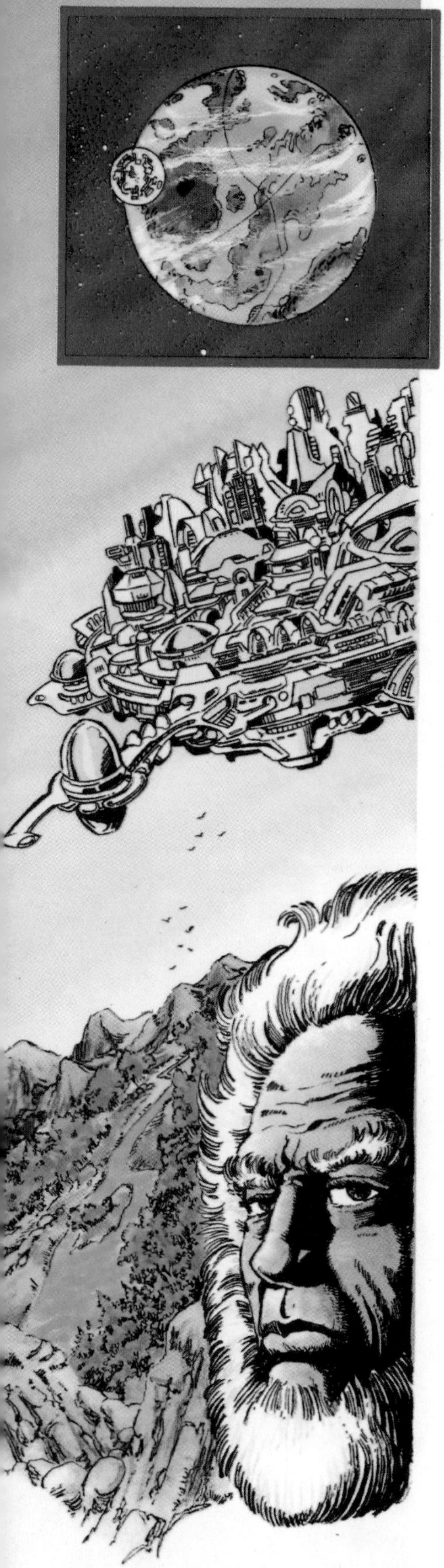

The old Gods tired of battle. With a burst of impossible energy, they sealed Olympus off from all outside contact and created in its wake two giant molten bodies. For centuries they cooled and then finally gave birth to life. New Genesis—a magnificent new world of hope—became the home of the New Gods, the powerful race imbued with the living atoms of the original gods. On the barren, burning scar of a world called Apokolips was born the demon Darkseid and his legions of hell. These two forces are locked in an eternal battle with no end in sight.

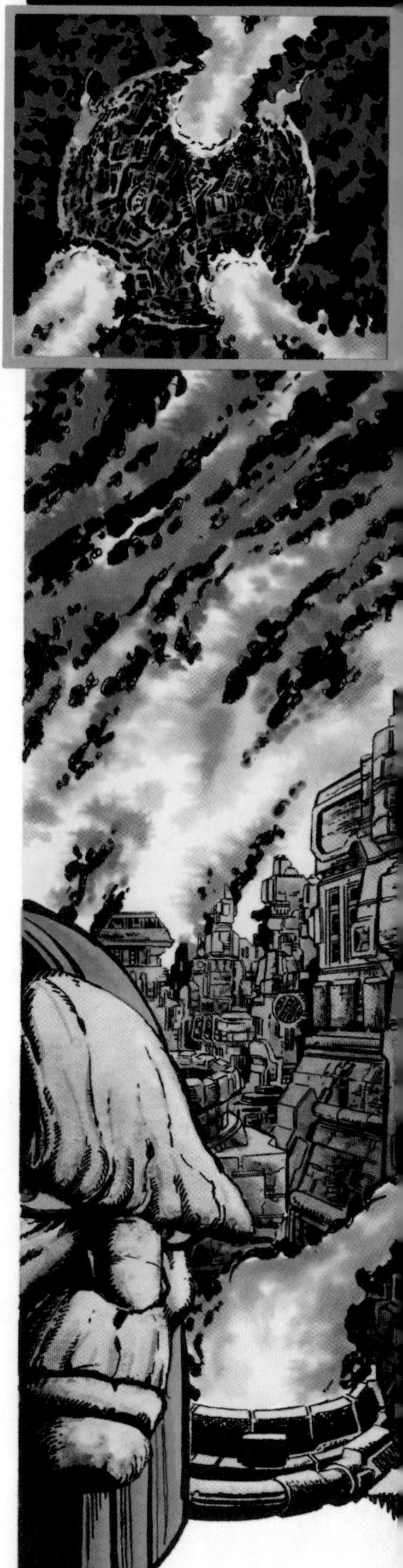

Growing as a fierce race of people in the Vegan System, the Psions kidnapped the Okaaran X'hal and mated her with a fearsome, brutal Branx warrior. From this came the birth of two children: a horrbly mutated being who became the first Citadelian, and the human child, Lambien. The Psions tried to mate X'hal a second time, but she slew the Branx warrior even as he killed her. The Psions took her lifeless body and, in a vicious experiment, converted her into a being of pure energy. At that moment, she became the goddess X'hal; Lambien shared much of her power and later metamorphosed into the near-God Auron.

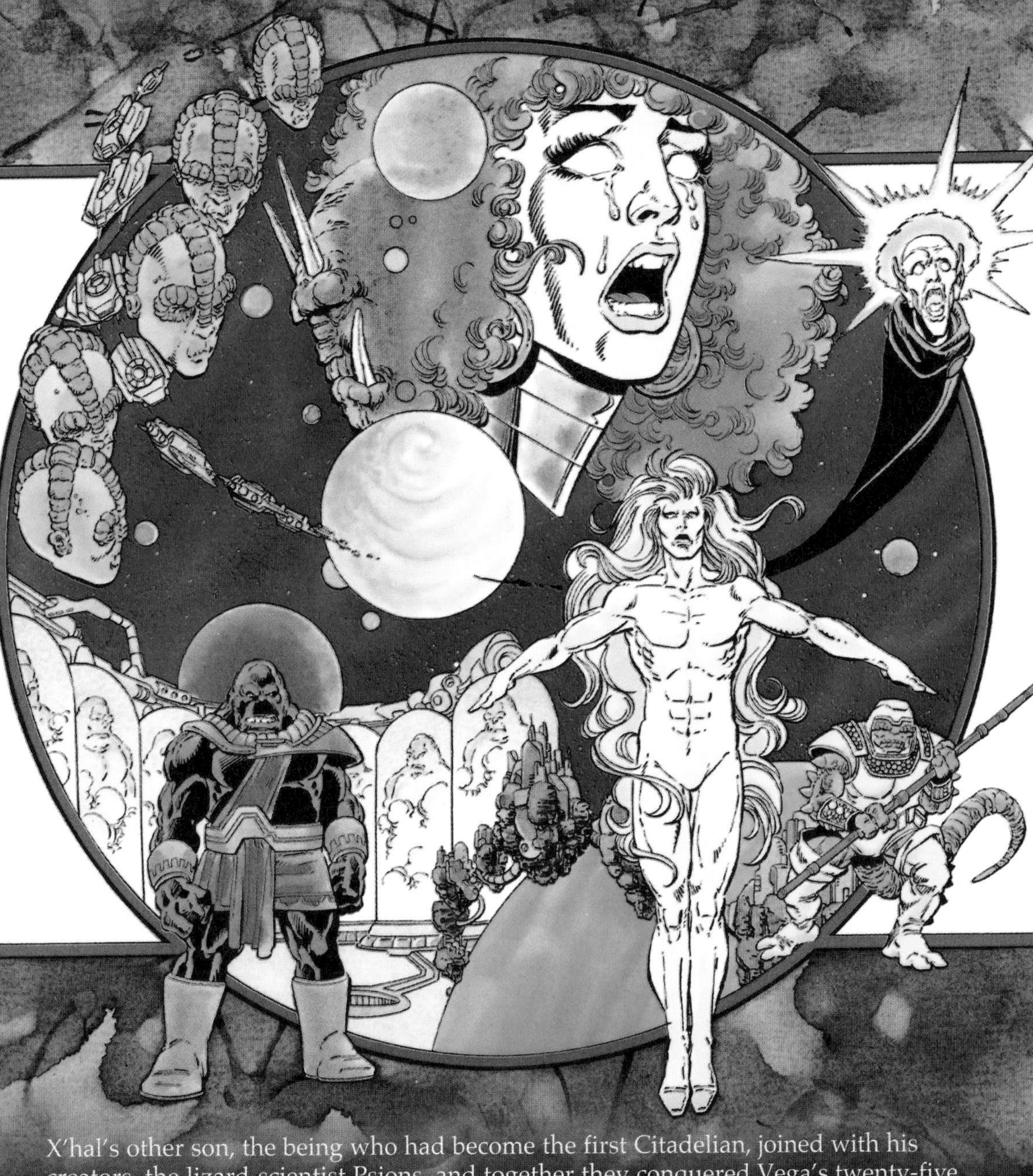

X'hal's other son, the being who had become the first Citadelian, joined with his creators, the lizard-scientist Psions, and together they conquered Vega's twenty-five worlds before the sole Citadelian turned on his allies and claimed power for himself alone. Using Psion science, X'hal's son cloned himself, and with his new force would control the entire Vegan system for more than two hundred years.

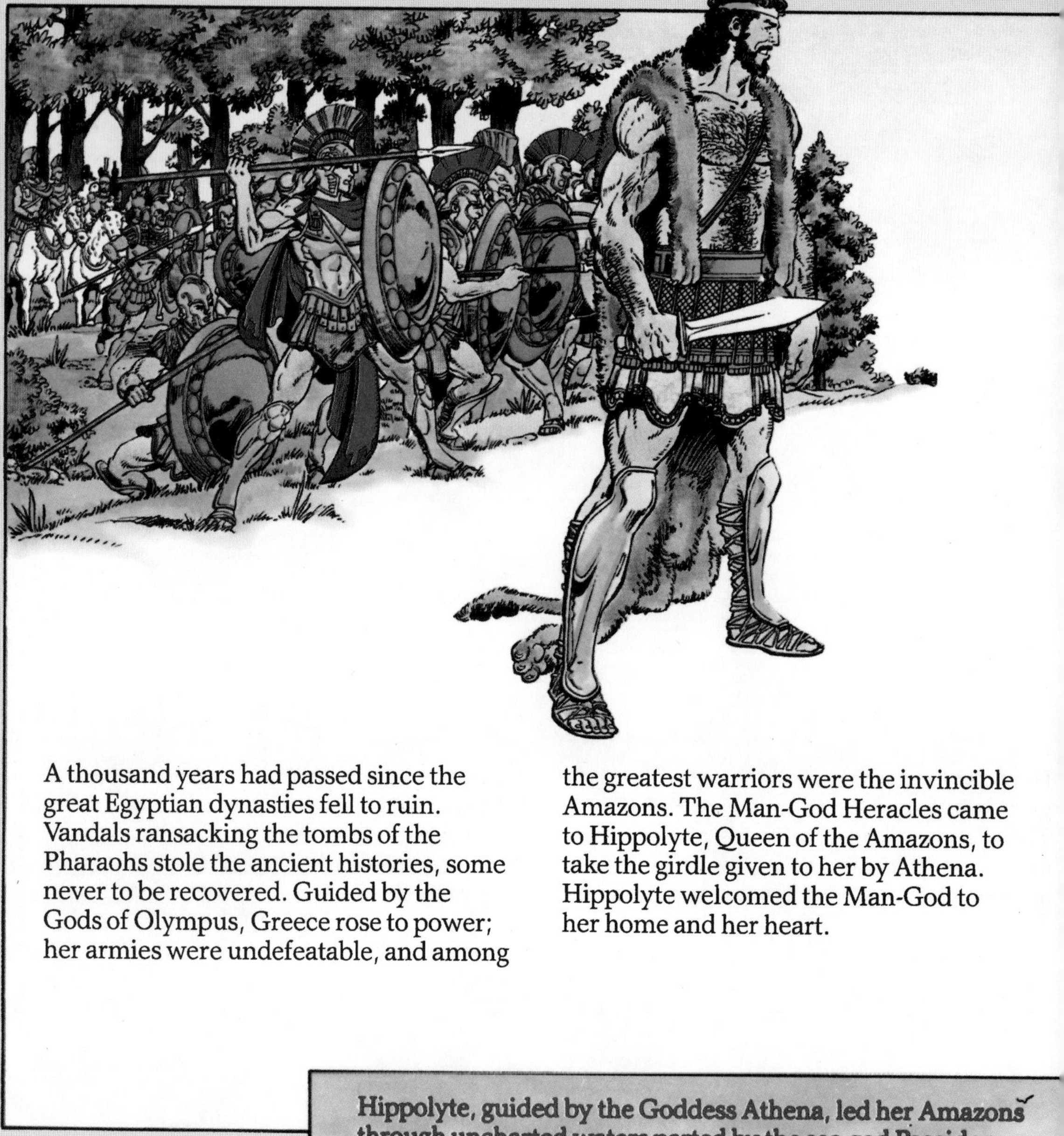
A thousand years had passed since the great Egyptian dynasties fell to ruin. Vandals ransacking the tombs of the Pharaohs stole the ancient histories, some never to be recovered. Guided by the Gods of Olympus, Greece rose to power; her armies were undefeatable, and among the greatest warriors were the invincible Amazons. The Man-God Heracles came to Hippolyte, Queen of the Amazons, to take the girdle given to her by Athena. Hippolyte welcomed the Man-God to her home and her heart.

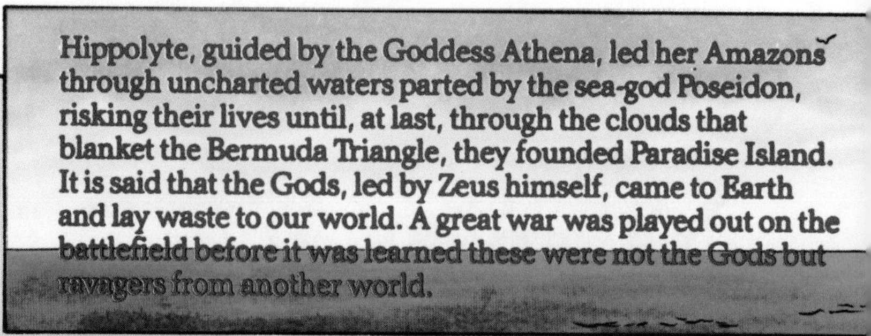
Hippolyte, guided by the Goddess Athena, led her Amazons through uncharted waters parted by the sea-god Poseidon, risking their lives until, at last, through the clouds that blanket the Bermuda Triangle, they founded Paradise Island. It is said that the Gods, led by Zeus himself, came to Earth and lay waste to our world. A great war was played out on the battlefield before it was learned these were not the Gods but ravagers from another world.

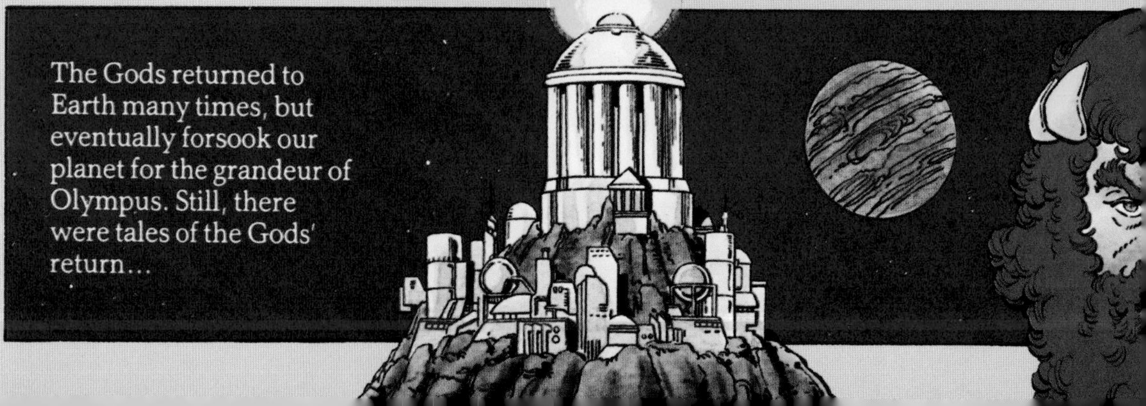
The Gods returned to Earth many times, but eventually forsook our planet for the grandeur of Olympus. Still, there were tales of the Gods' return...

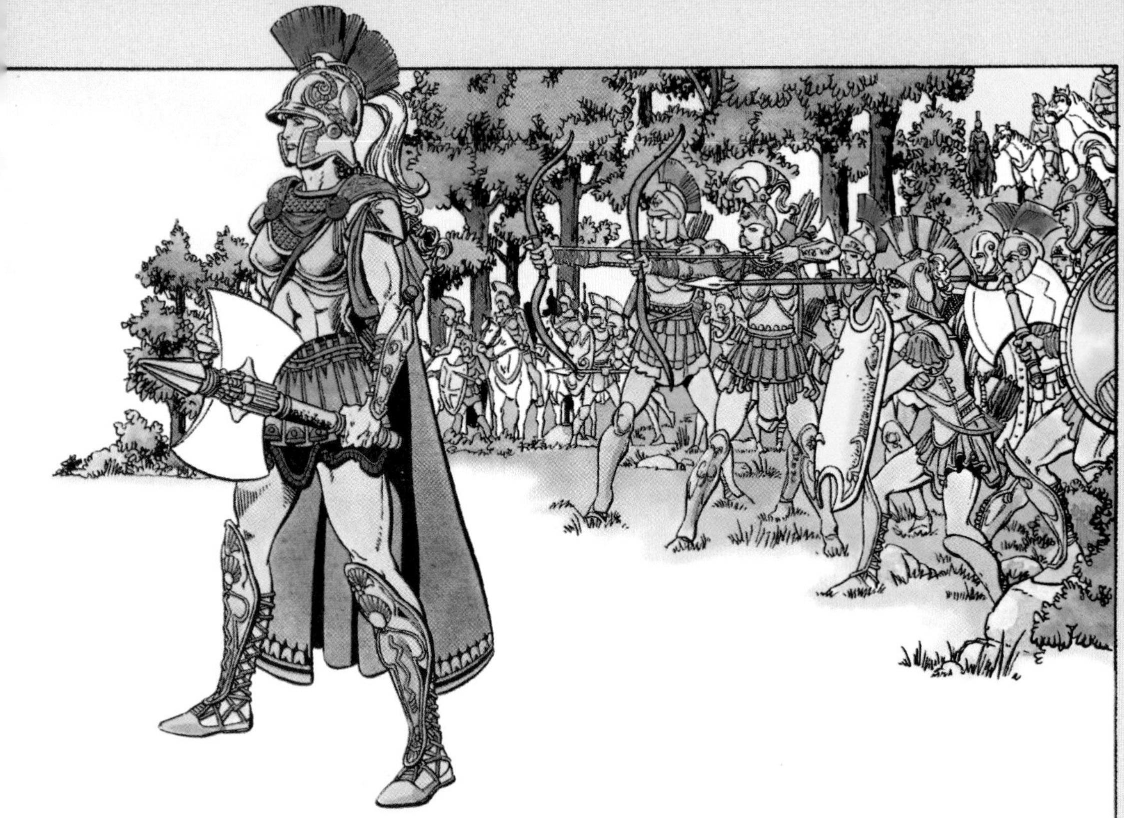

Heracles drugged Hippolyte, stole her girdle and imprisoned the Amazons. The Queen escaped and freed her people, and together they attacked Heracles' army. After the battle, Antiope, sister to Hippolyte, journeyed to Athens with half of the Amazon warriors to further avenge themselves on Heracles. There they would fight the great Trojan wars.

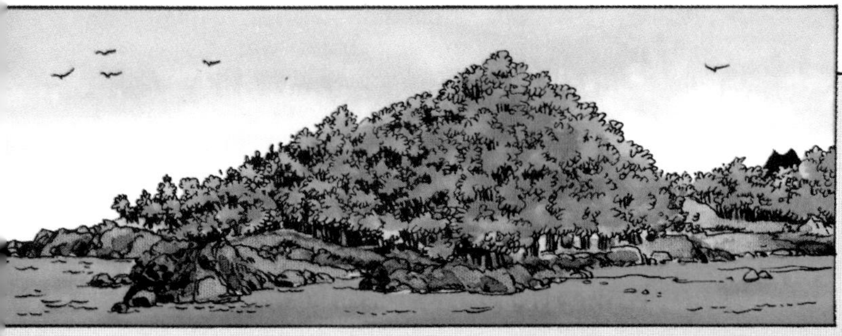

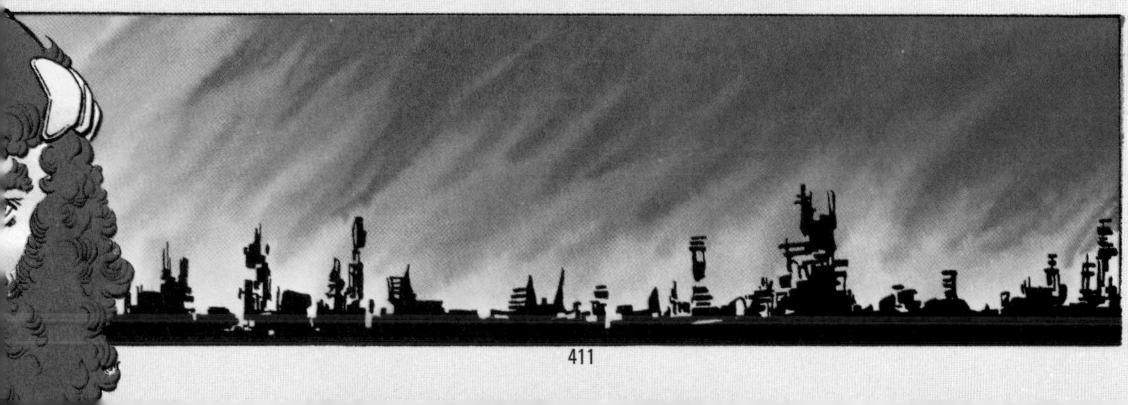

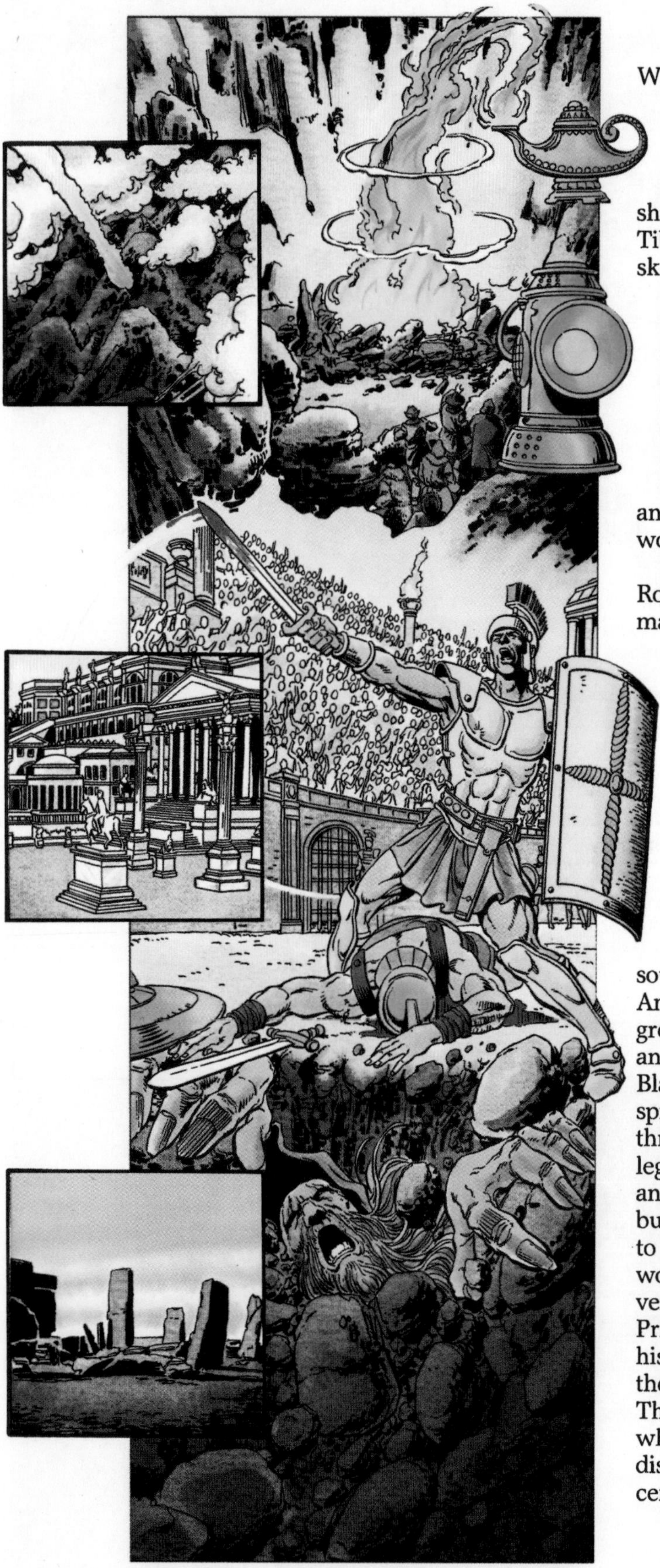

While the grandeur of Greece slowly faded to the glory that would be Rome, the focus of this tome of heroics must shift to the mountains of Tibet. On a dark night the skies of Tibet glowed like an emerald as a meteor burning with verdant light crashed to Earth and shimmered with a power never before seen. In two thousand years a battery of power carved from this meteor would be found, and with it a new hero would be born.

Rome became the center of man and his activities. Here there was a greatness that dwarfed the Greeks and the Egyptians. Great gladiators fought in combat to achieve the precious medals of the Caesars. No warrior was greater than the Golden Gladiator. He could not be defeated in battle, nor could his soul be corrupted by evil. And there was evil—the great demon priest of the ancient Druids was Blackbriar Thorn. He spread his terror throughout Rome until the legions swept in after him and slew his mindless cult, but Thorn used his powers to transform himself to wood and eluded his vengeful pursuers. Free, the Priest turned his powers on his fellow Druids, but in their death they buried Thorn in an Earth fissure where he would not be discovered for twenty centuries.

With the fall of the Roman Empire came the time of the Barbarians, but from out of the dark ages came the time of enlightenment—and the birth of Camelot.

The Court of King Arthur was the grandest in the world, boasting of the most powerful knights. Endless were the legends of Lancelot and Guinevere, of warriors such as Gawain and The Shining Knight, of Galahad and of the magician Merlin, who some say wielded magicks not only from the distant past but of the far future as well. But Camelot's days dwindled to an end, and from its destruction came one of the strangest of all beings. Born in hell but serving no stygian master was Etrigan The Demon. To some he was a savior, but to most his mad eyes spoke of death.

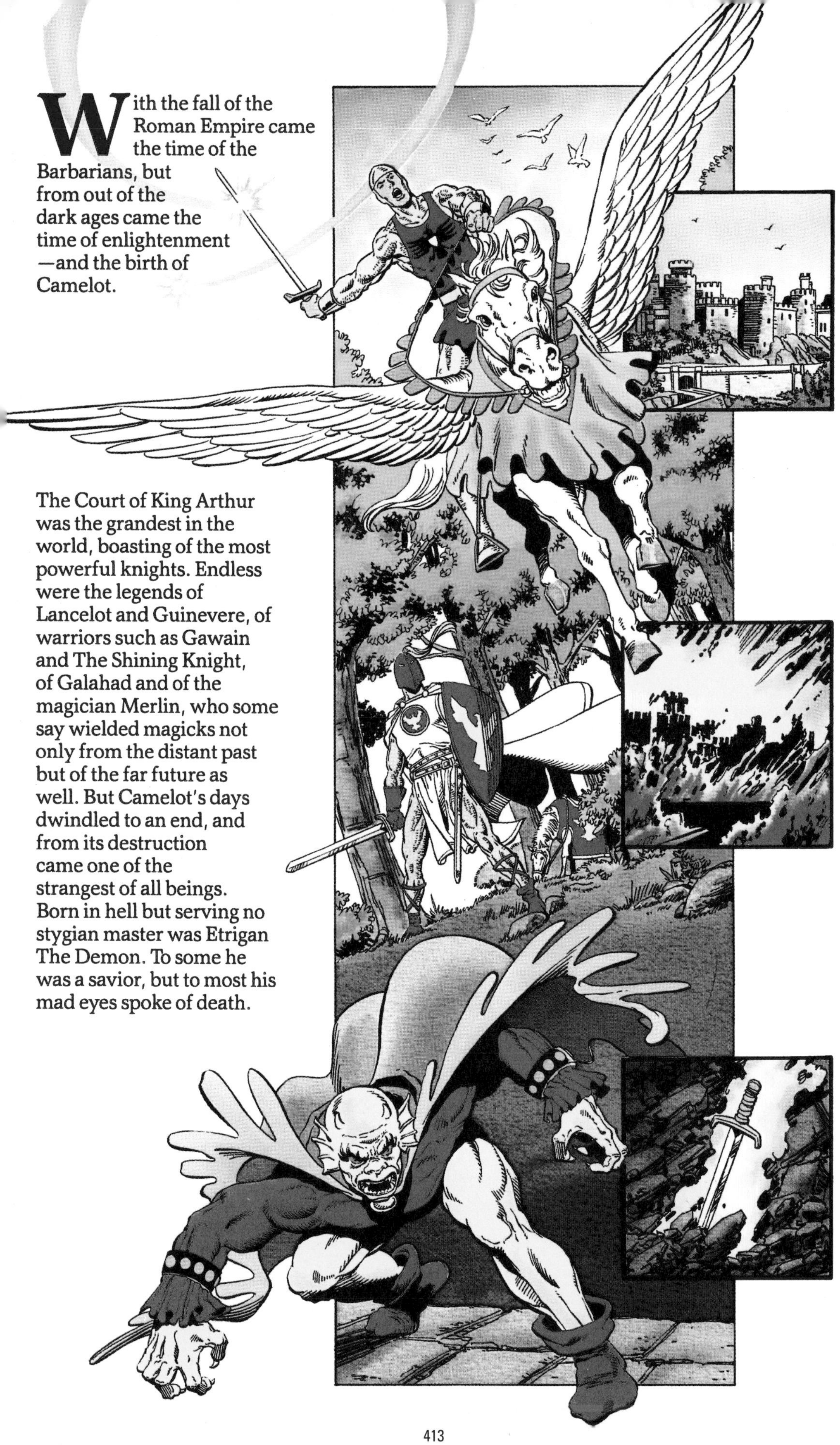

While central Europe headed for its renaissance and return to supremacy, the source of heroes shifted to northern Europe, to America and beyond. This was a time of exploration and discovery. Seven hundred years before Columbus searched in vain for a short trade route to India, proud Viking ships sailed across the uncharted ocean to discover a new continent. Arak Red-Hand, son of Star-of-Dawn and He-No the Thunder God, was the last surviving member of the Quontauka Indian tribe. He was taken by the Viking raiders to medieval Europe where he served in the defense of Carolus Magnus, also known as Charlemagne.

This was also a time of danger as Jon the Viking Prince battled menaces both human and supernatural, as sorcery had returned to Earth. Sorceries explain the disappearance of The Viking Commando Valoric—as had the Viking Prince and the Shining Knight disappeared from the eyes of man—and his reappearance centuries later during man's second world war, as did Jon and Sir Justin.

After Arthur's betrayal and death, other kings ruled England.

Brave Richard th Lionhearted carried h banner in the Crusade but his treacherou broth Princ John tyranr led on noblema to lead band c Merry Men as th outlaw Robin Hoo

Later, another evil prince's tyranny caused another noble of the court to fight evil in the guise of the Silent Knight. As the Crusades reached their height, a band of adventurers in France banded together as The Three Musketeers to thwart the machinations of the evil cardinal Richelieu.

Mount Michelson: ship from the stars buried itself in this Alaskan peak. Inside, its pilot remained in suspended animation for almost eleven hundred years.

Hidden in the Tibetan mountainside is the named land of Nanda Parbat.

As poverty waned on Earth, the wizard-leaders of the 12 cities of Gems focused all their power into the young witch, Citrina, in order to find them a new and proper homeland. To do so she forged an alliance with the Dark Lords and created the other dimensional land of Gemworld.

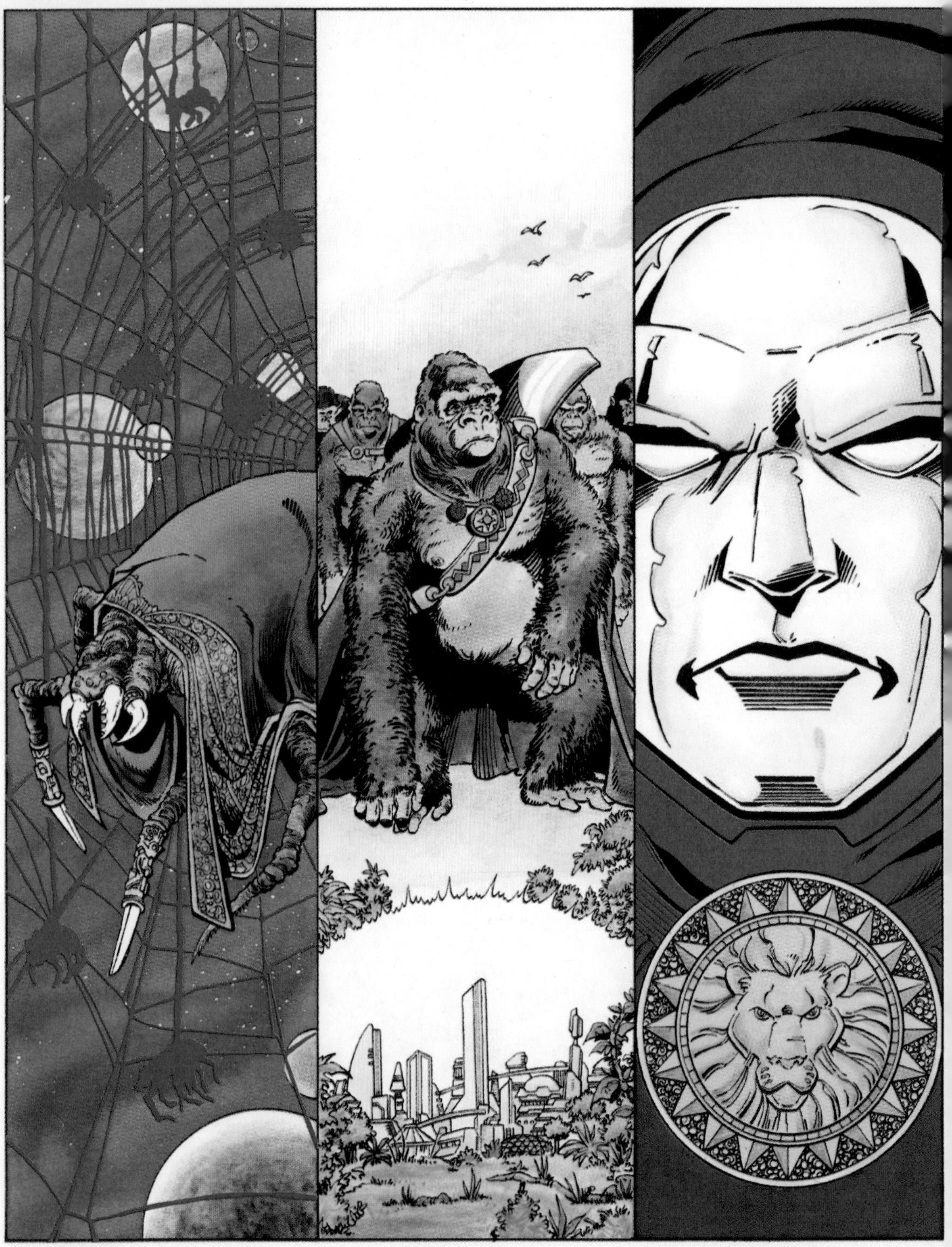

In the last decade of the fifteenth century there were many events of note: America was officially 'discovered' by Christopher Columbus seven hundred years after the abduction of the Indian Arak. In the Vegan star system the villainous spider-cult first spread their reign of terror. In Africa, an intelligent simian race erected the fabled Gorilla City and hid it from the ever-prying eyes of man. In space and on Earth, the android Manhunters perverted their original mission of eliminating evil into the hunting and destruction of all sentient life, establishing a cult in pursuit of their goal.

Sixteenth century Europe was in turmoil and wars erupted out of corruption and politics. British nobleman Jon Valor, also known as The Black Pirate, assembled a band of fellow freedom fighters to protect the innocent against tyranny.

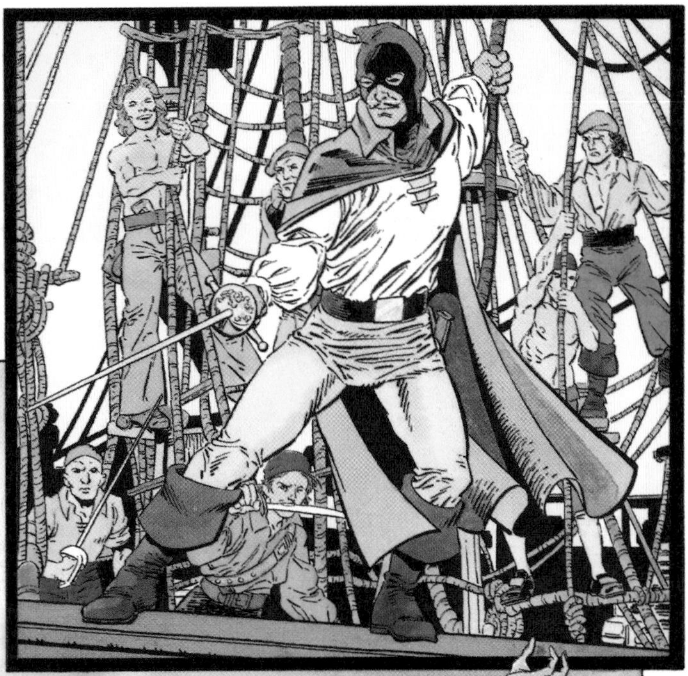

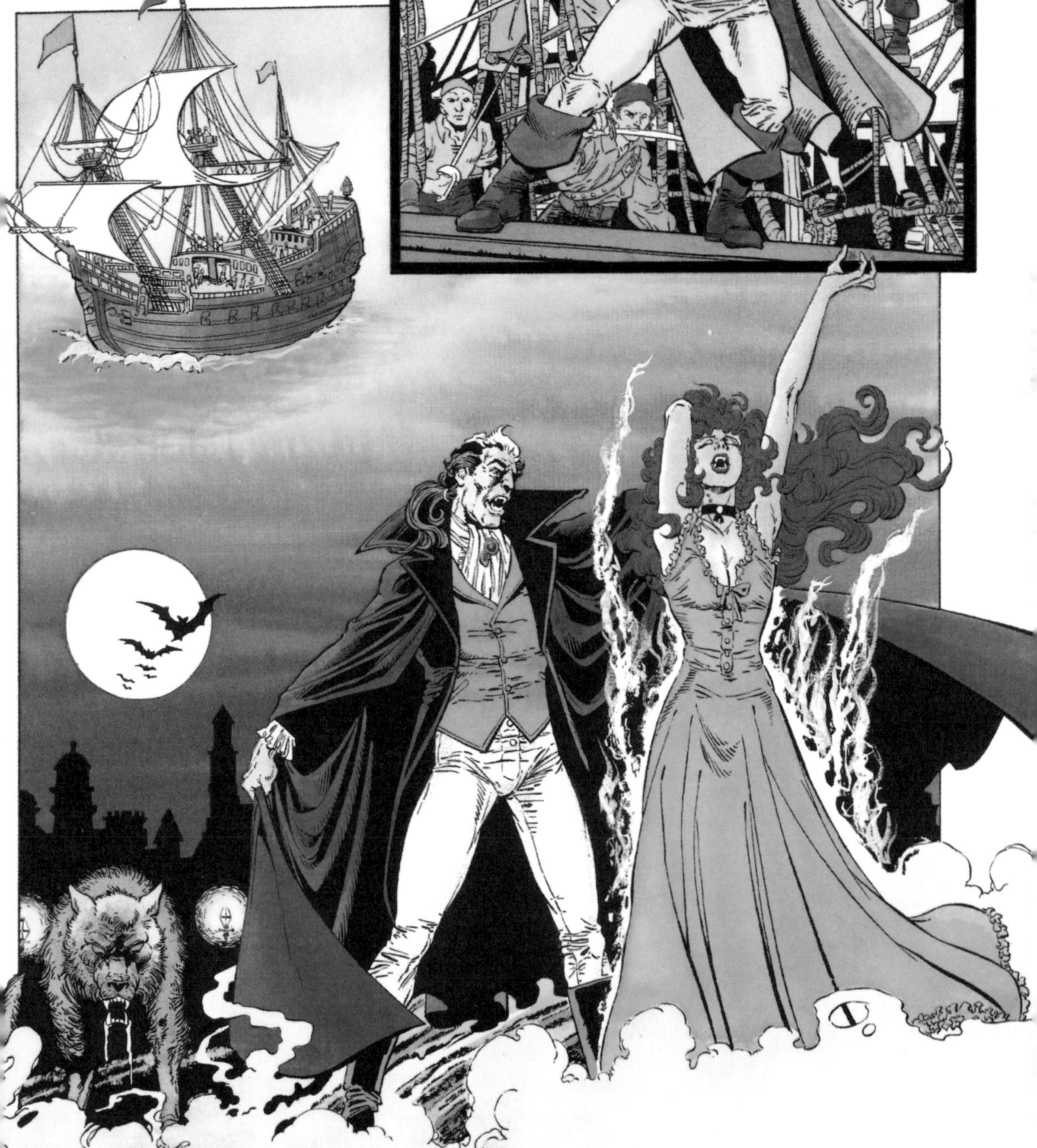

These were times of violence and horror, from the iron-fisted rule of despots to the bloodthirsty growth of vampirism, but one such undead sought to save the world from others of his kind. In dying, Andrew Bennett spent an eternity to save the living.

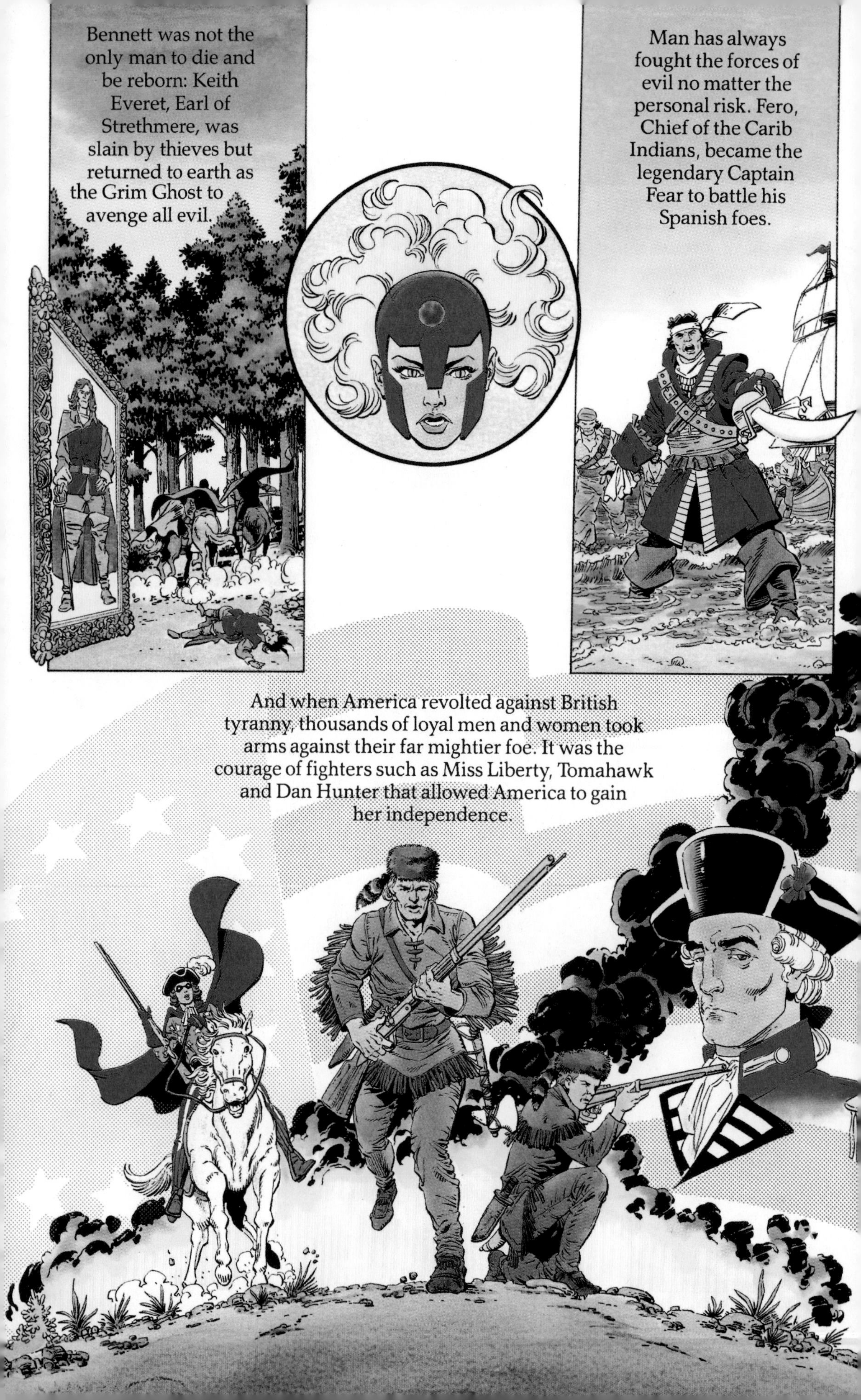
Bennett was not the only man to die and be reborn: Keith Everet, Earl of Strethmere, was slain by thieves but returned to earth as the Grim Ghost to avenge all evil.
Man has always fought the forces of evil no matter the personal risk. Fero, Chief of the Carib Indians, became the legendary Captain Fear to battle his Spanish foes.
And when America revolted against British tyranny, thousands of loyal men and women took arms against their far mightier foe. It was the courage of fighters such as Miss Liberty, Tomahawk and Dan Hunter that allowed America to gain her independence.

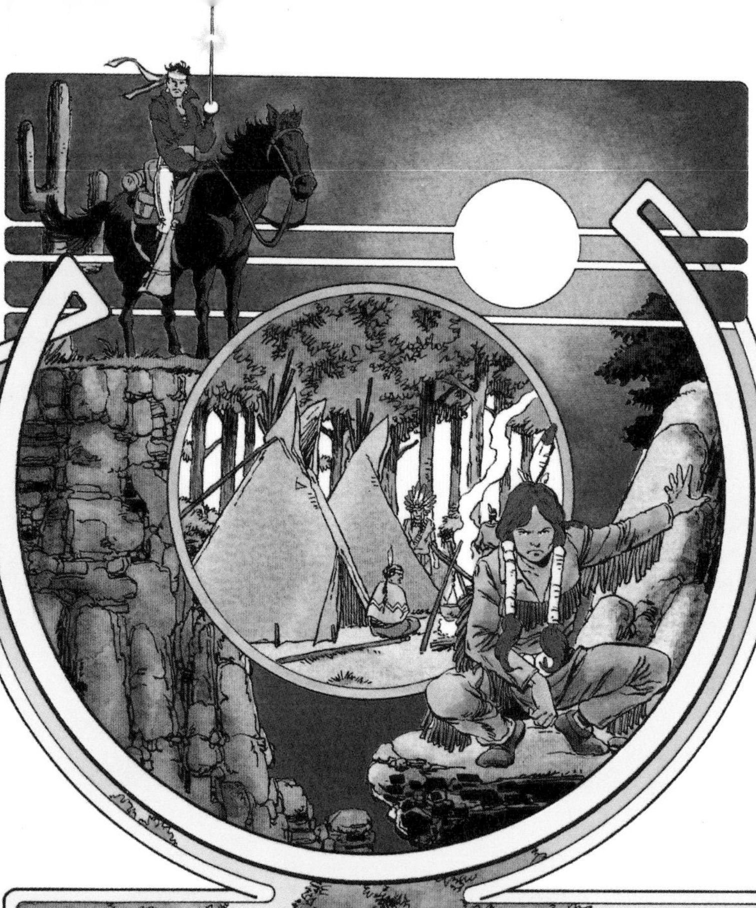

America was now free and her people began their trek west in vast wagon trains. One such train was attacked by the fierce Blackfoot Indians, and all the travellers were slain save one blue-eyed, red-haired infant. This child was raised by the Indians to become Firehair.

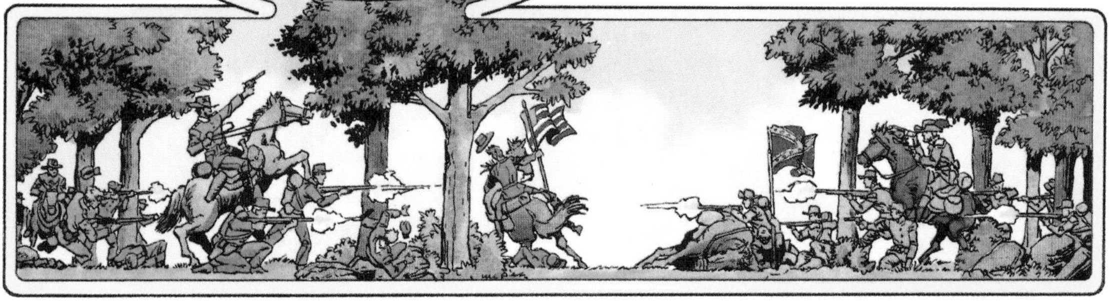

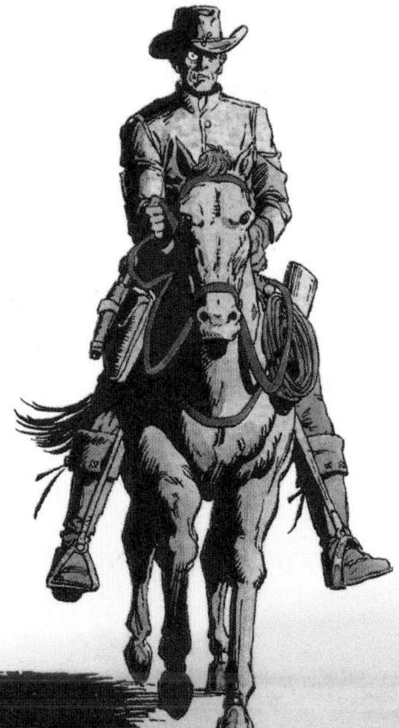

The 1860s saw America torn apart by civil war. For five bloody years brother fought brother, but at last the war ended, and its soldiers returned home to rebuild their emotionally shattered lives. Some soldiers, knowing little more than fighting, continued to live by the gun. Those who strayed from the law were hunted down, often by other former soldiers. Jonah Hex was a bounty hunter: among the very best...and certainly the most dangerous.

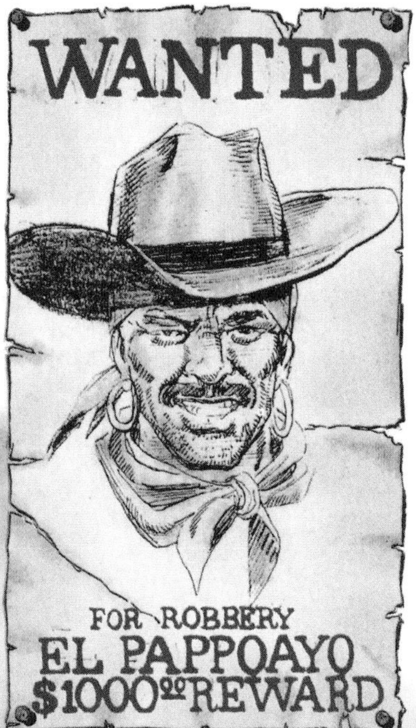
WANTED
FOR ROBBERY
EL PAPPOAYO
$1000.00 REWARD

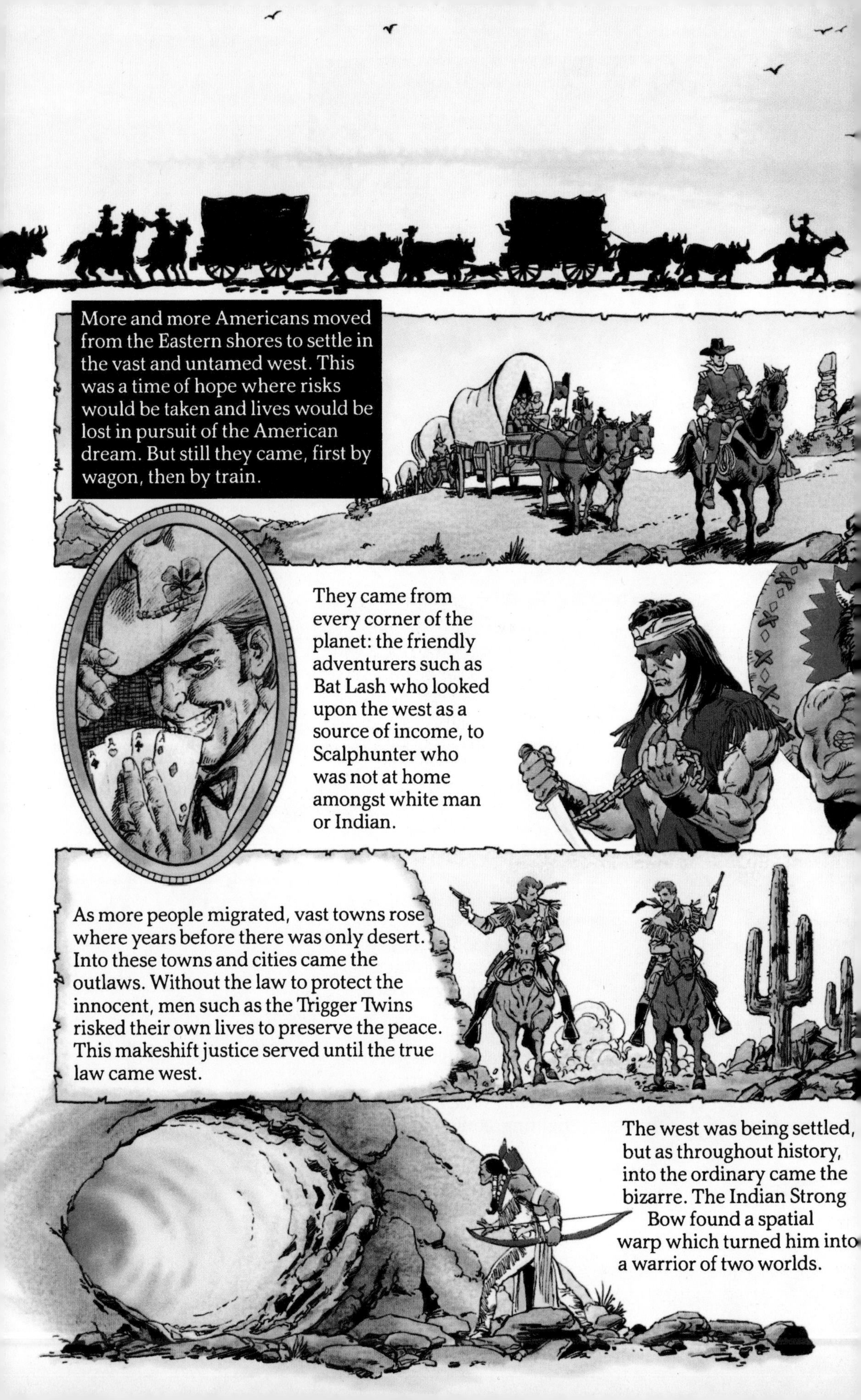
More and more Americans moved from the Eastern shores to settle in the vast and untamed west. This was a time of hope where risks would be taken and lives would be lost in pursuit of the American dream. But still they came, first by wagon, then by train.
They came from every corner of the planet: the friendly adventurers such as Bat Lash who looked upon the west as a source of income, to Scalphunter who was not at home amongst white man or Indian.
As more people migrated, vast towns rose where years before there was only desert. Into these towns and cities came the outlaws. Without the law to protect the innocent, men such as the Trigger Twins risked their own lives to preserve the peace. This makeshift justice served until the true law came west.
The west was being settled, but as throughout history, into the ordinary came the bizarre. The Indian Strong Bow found a spatial warp which turned him into a warrior of two worlds.

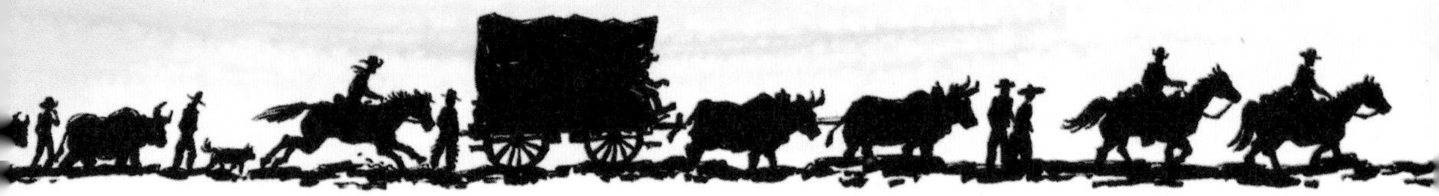

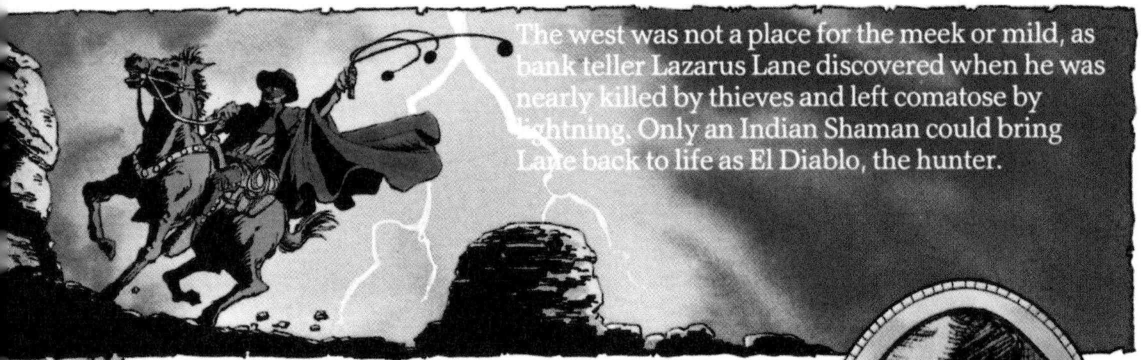
The west was not a place for the meek or mild, as bank teller Lazarus Lane discovered when he was nearly killed by thieves and left comatose by lightning. Only an Indian Shaman could bring Lane back to life as El Diablo, the hunter.

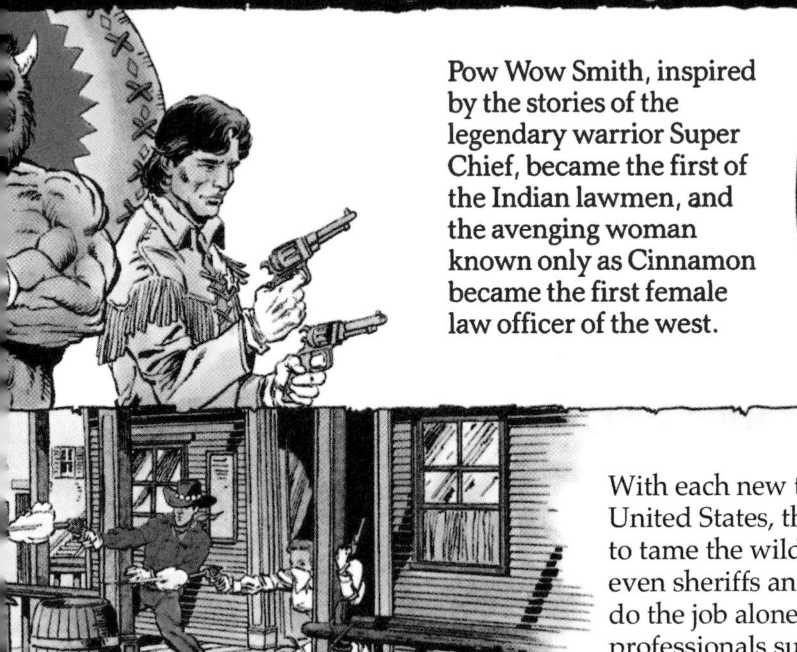
Pow Wow Smith, inspired by the stories of the legendary warrior Super Chief, became the first of the Indian lawmen, and the avenging woman known only as Cinnamon became the first female law officer of the west.

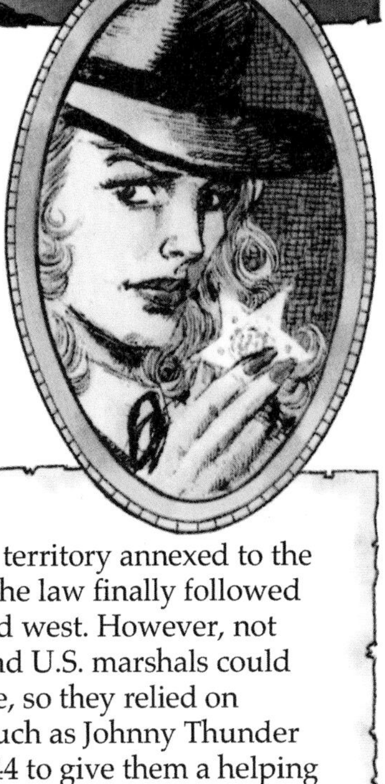

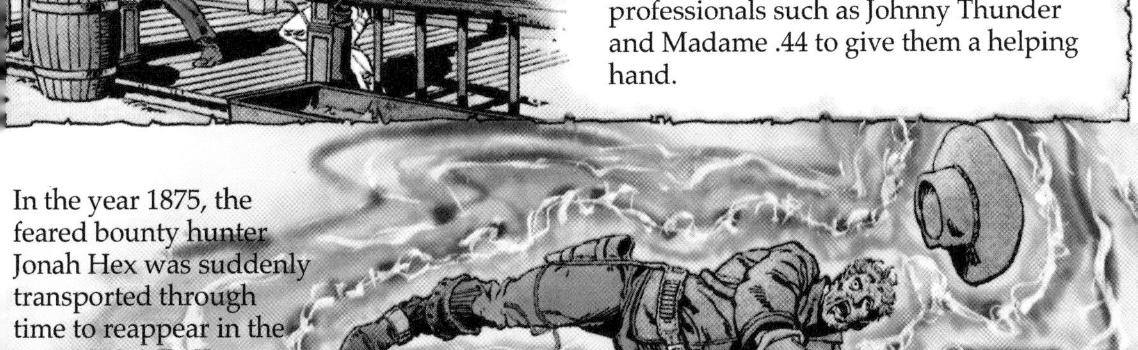
With each new territory annexed to the United States, the law finally followed to tame the wild west. However, not even sheriffs and U.S. marshals could do the job alone, so they relied on professionals such as Johnny Thunder and Madame .44 to give them a helping hand.

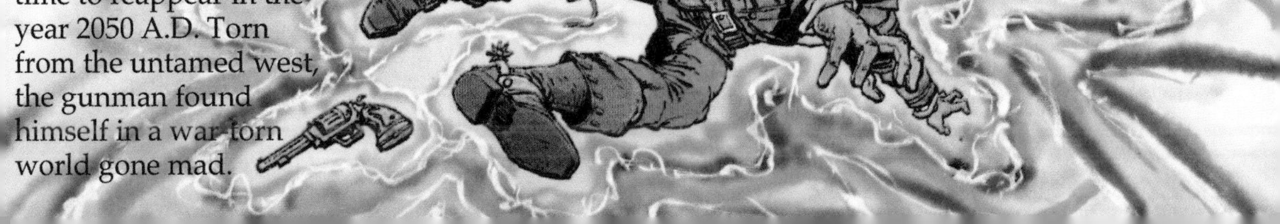
In the year 1875, the feared bounty hunter Jonah Hex was suddenly transported through time to reappear in the year 2050 A.D. Torn from the untamed west, the gunman found himself in a war-torn world gone mad.

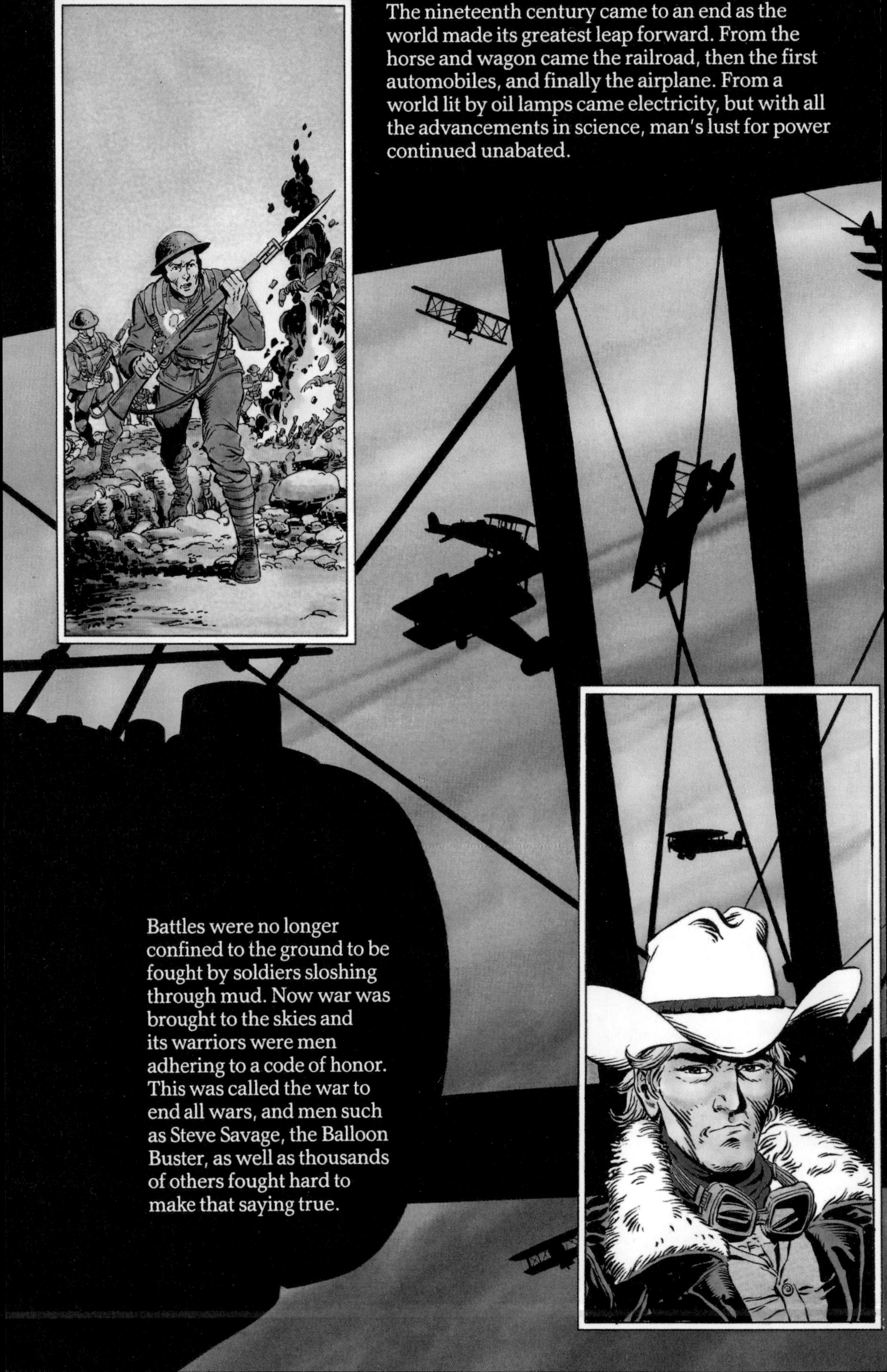
The nineteenth century came to an end as the world made its greatest leap forward. From the horse and wagon came the railroad, then the first automobiles, and finally the airplane. From a world lit by oil lamps came electricity, but with all the advancements in science, man's lust for power continued unabated.
Battles were no longer confined to the ground to be fought by soldiers sloshing through mud. Now war was brought to the skies and its warriors were men adhering to a code of honor. This was called the war to end all wars, and men such as Steve Savage, the Balloon Buster, as well as thousands of others fought hard to make that saying true.

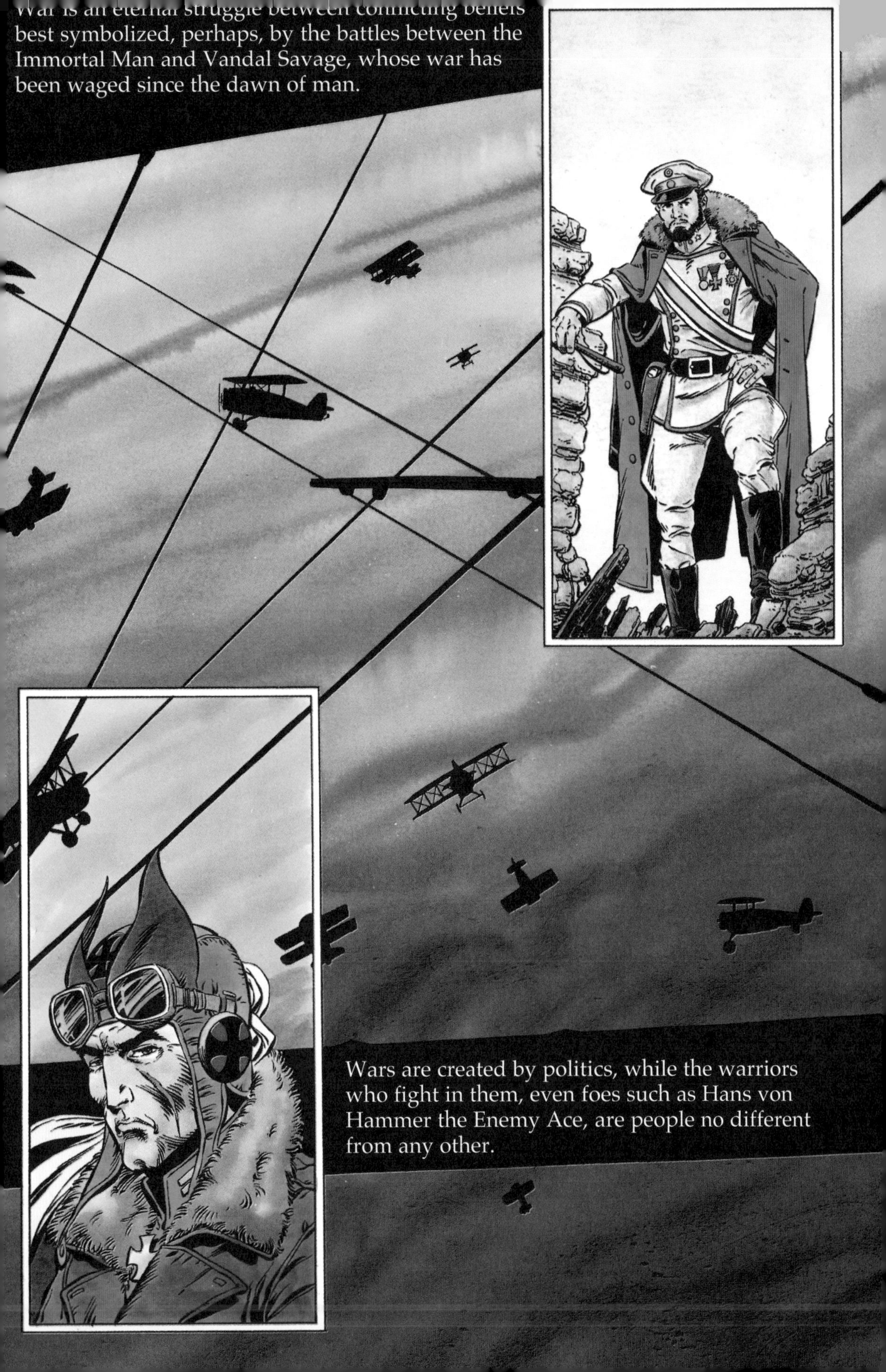
War is an eternal struggle between conflicting beliefs best symbolized, perhaps, by the battles between the Immortal Man and Vandal Savage, whose war has been waged since the dawn of man.
Wars are created by politics, while the warriors who fight in them, even foes such as Hans von Hammer the Enemy Ace, are people no different from any other.

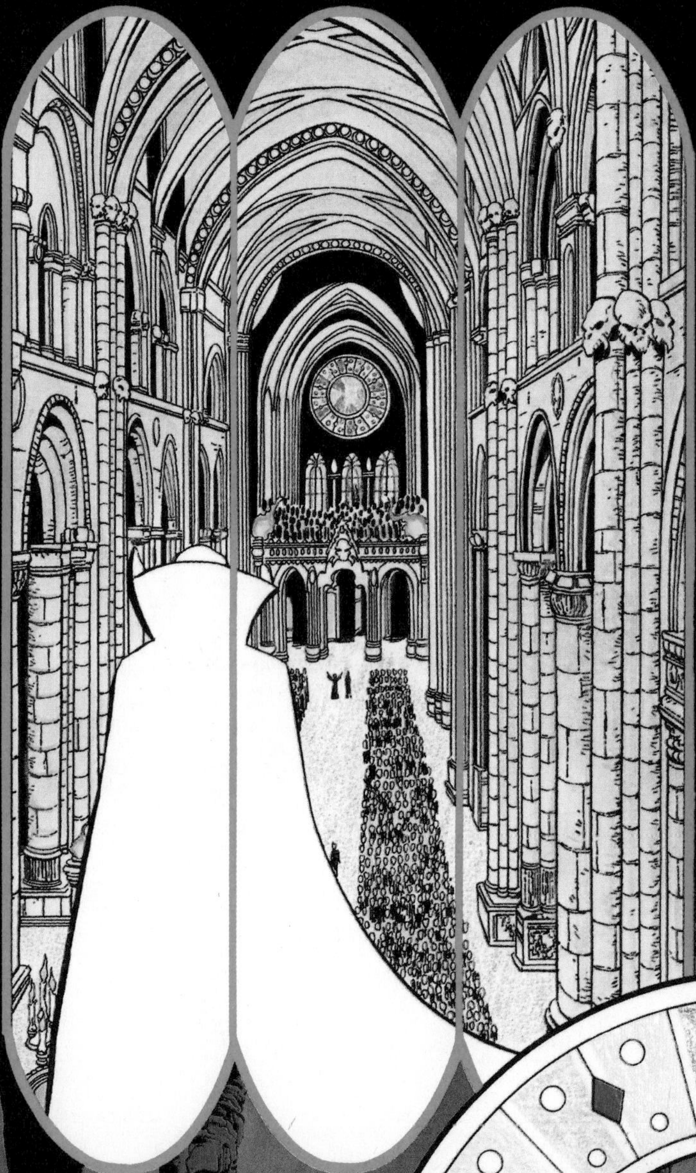

There were six Brother Bloods before him, each living to their hundredth year, each one then slain by his own son. The Church Of Brother Blood prospered in Zandia, a Baltic country populated by the dregs of society. For protection, the thieves and murderers, the terrorists and ex-dictators, all donated great fortunes which financed Blood's Church throughout the world.

As more and more believers came to worship in the Church of Blood, Brother Blood's power grew, for Blood was an emotion vampire—living and growing ever stronger from the fervent worship bestowed him.

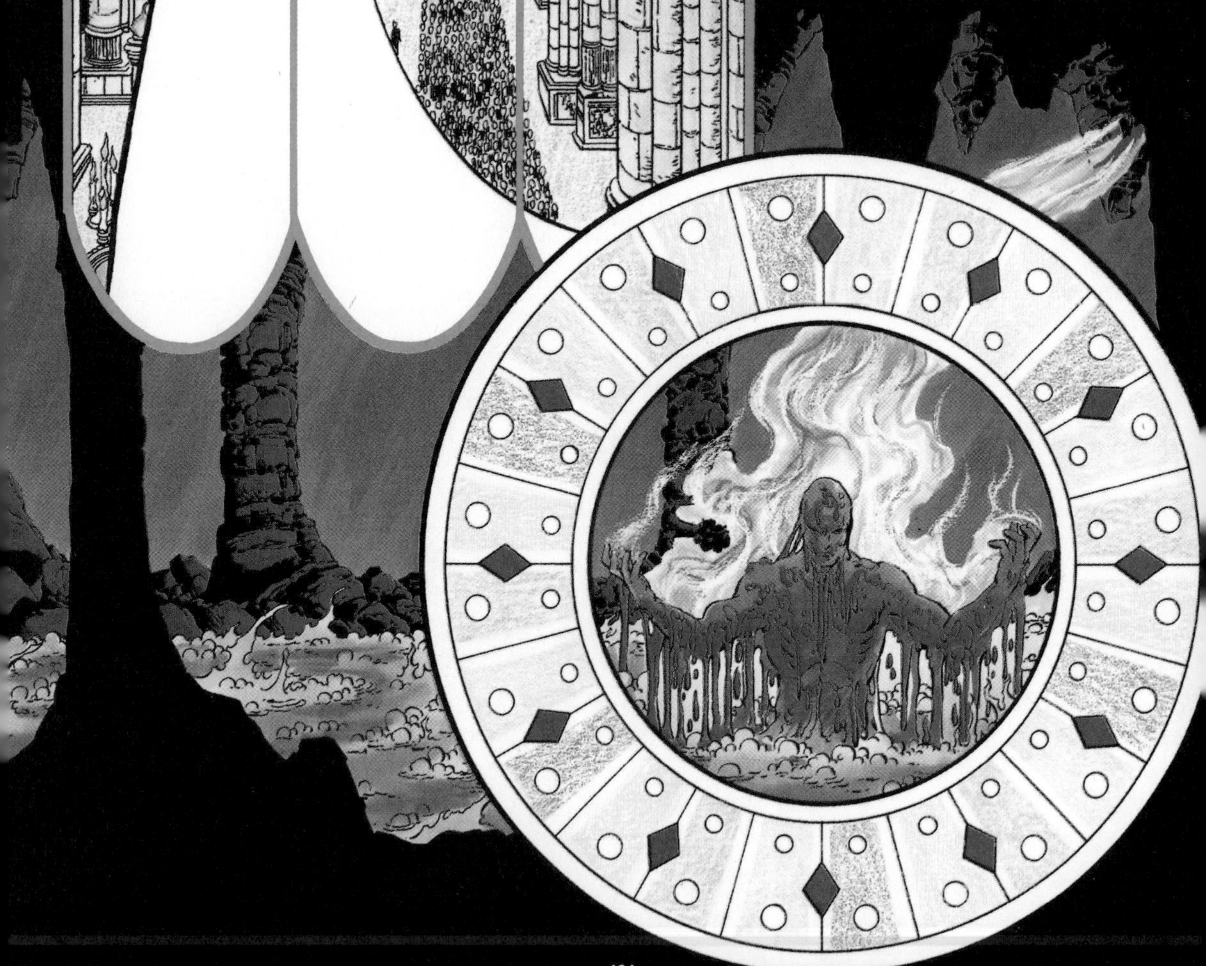

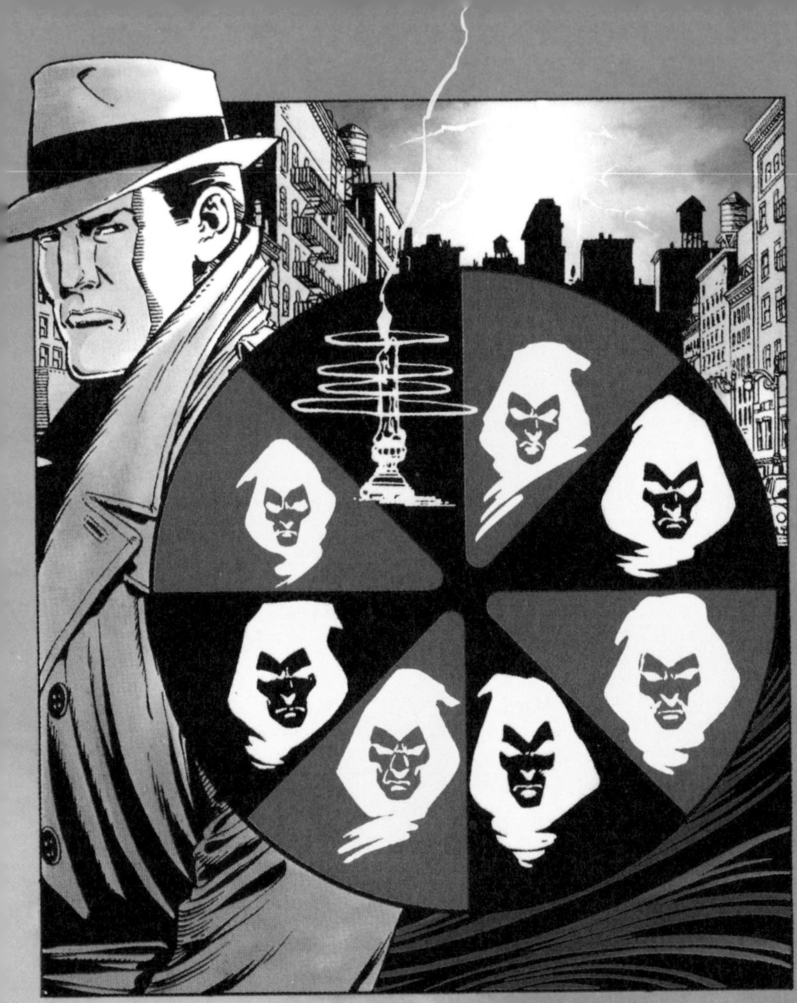

The end of World War One marked a new beginning for the Heroic Age. Science ruled, and even with the worldwide economic crash in 1929, society advanced at a rate unknown to man.

Yet into this world of science and technology, into this new age of industrialization, the arcane continued to thrive. One such practitioner, called Dr. Occult, combined the modern sciences of detection with the dark forces from times past.

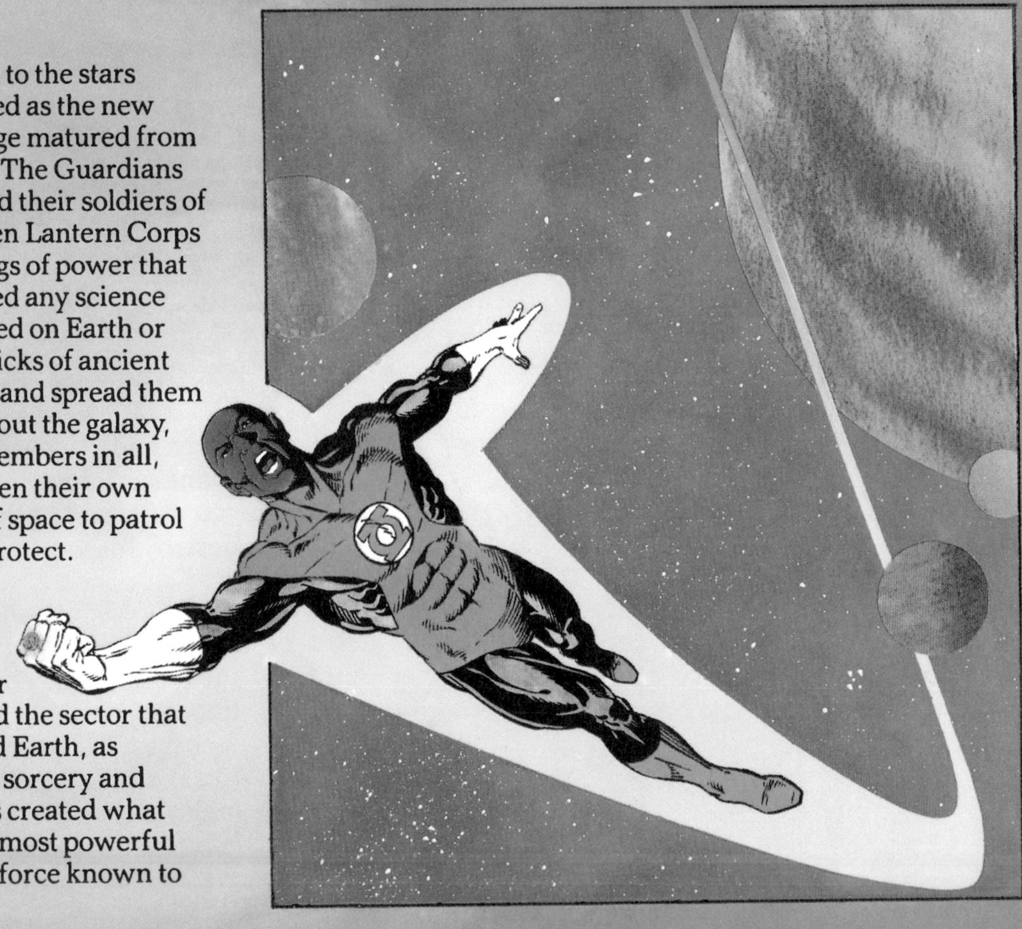

Our link to the stars continued as the new heroic age matured from infancy. The Guardians equipped their soldiers of the Green Lantern Corps with rings of power that surpassed any science developed on Earth or the magicks of ancient Atlantis and spread them throughout the galaxy, 3,600 members in all, each given their own sector of space to patrol and to protect.

Abin Sur patrolled the sector that included Earth, as science, sorcery and the stars created what was the most powerful warrior force known to man.

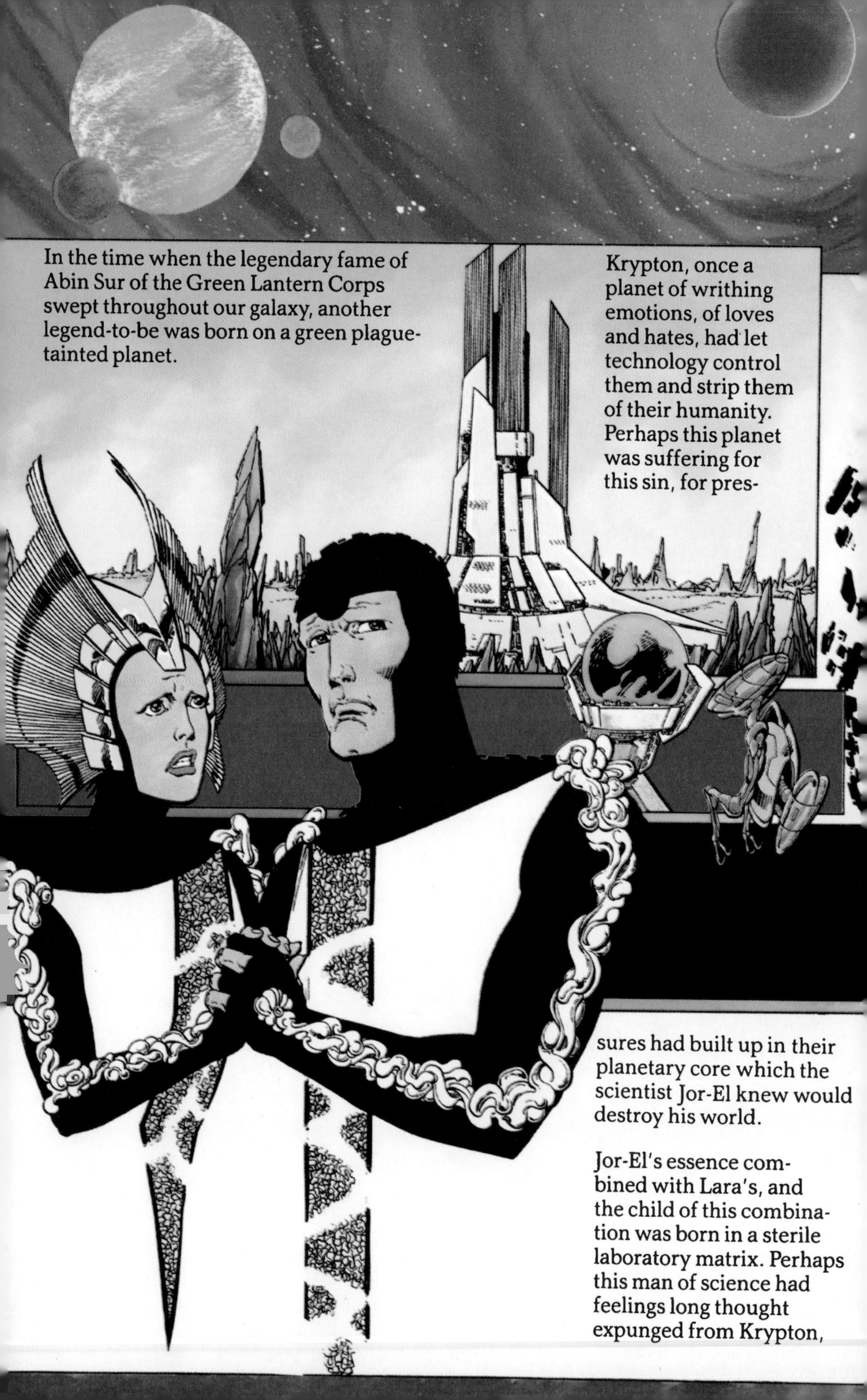
In the time when the legendary fame of Abin Sur of the Green Lantern Corps swept throughout our galaxy, another legend-to-be was born on a green plague-tainted planet.
Krypton, once a planet of writhing emotions, of loves and hates, had let technology control them and strip them of their humanity. Perhaps this planet was suffering for this sin, for pres-
sures had built up in their planetary core which the scientist Jor-El knew would destroy his world.
Jor-El's essence combined with Lara's, and the child of this combination was born in a sterile laboratory matrix. Perhaps this man of science had feelings long thought expunged from Krypton,

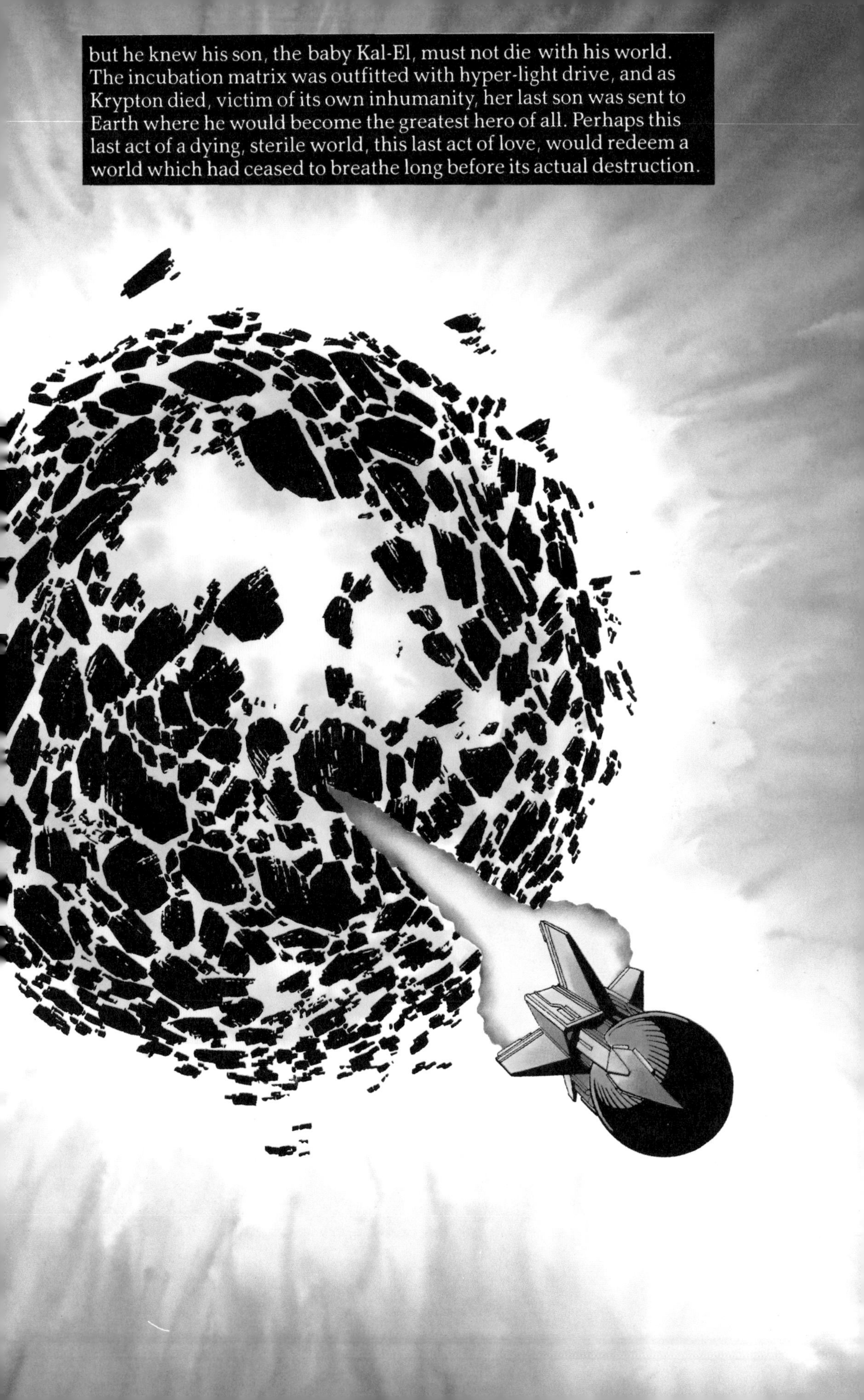
but he knew his son, the baby Kal-El, must not die with his world. The incubation matrix was outfitted with hyper-light drive, and as Krypton died, victim of its own inhumanity, her last son was sent to Earth where he would become the greatest hero of all. Perhaps this last act of a dying, sterile world, this last act of love, would redeem a world which had ceased to breathe long before its actual destruction.

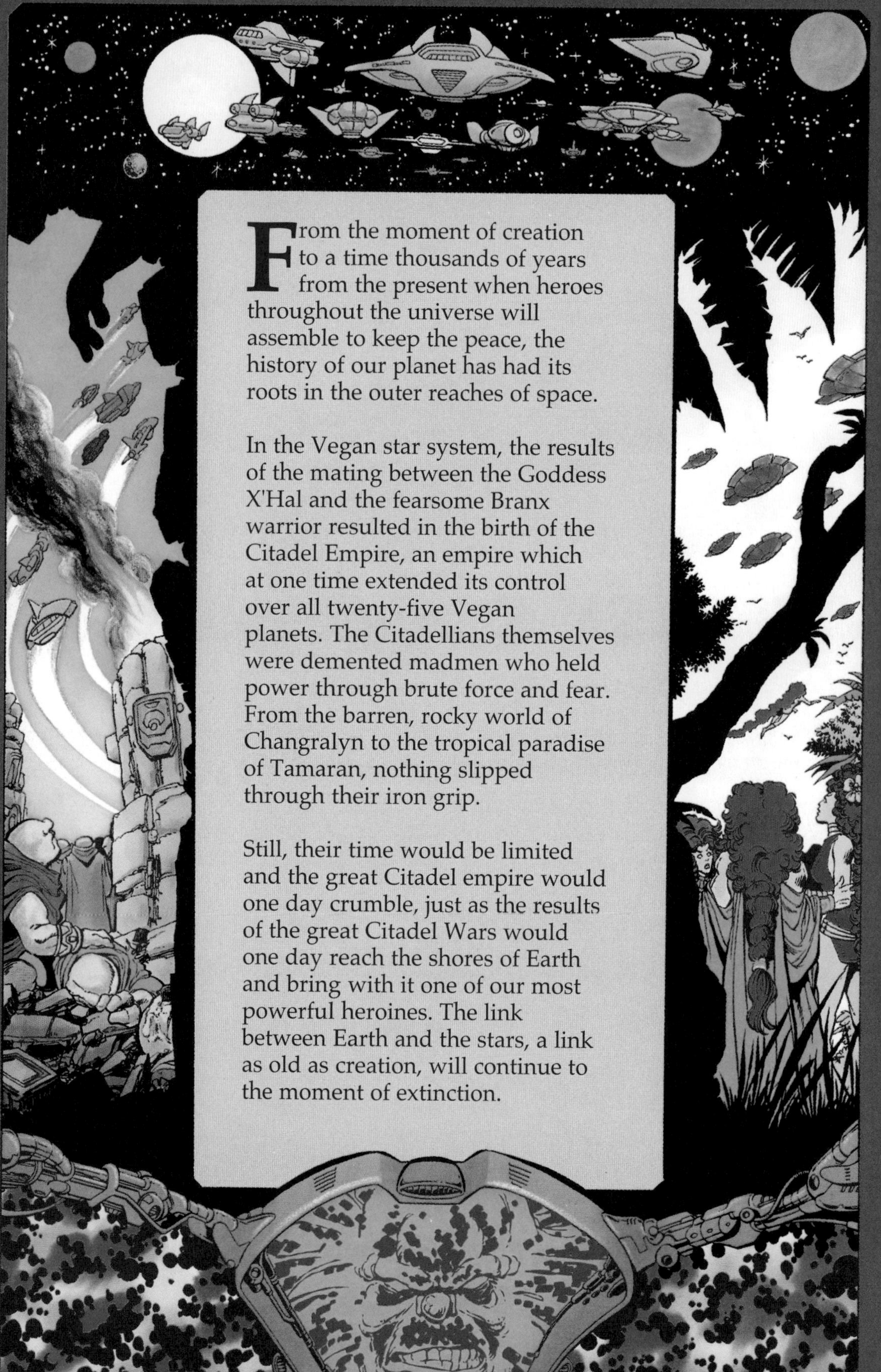

From the moment of creation to a time thousands of years from the present when heroes throughout the universe will assemble to keep the peace, the history of our planet has had its roots in the outer reaches of space.

In the Vegan star system, the results of the mating between the Goddess X'Hal and the fearsome Branx warrior resulted in the birth of the Citadel Empire, an empire which at one time extended its control over all twenty-five Vegan planets. The Citadellians themselves were demented madmen who held power through brute force and fear. From the barren, rocky world of Changralyn to the tropical paradise of Tamaran, nothing slipped through their iron grip.

Still, their time would be limited and the great Citadel empire would one day crumble, just as the results of the great Citadel Wars would one day reach the shores of Earth and bring with it one of our most powerful heroines. The link between Earth and the stars, a link as old as creation, will continue to the moment of extinction.

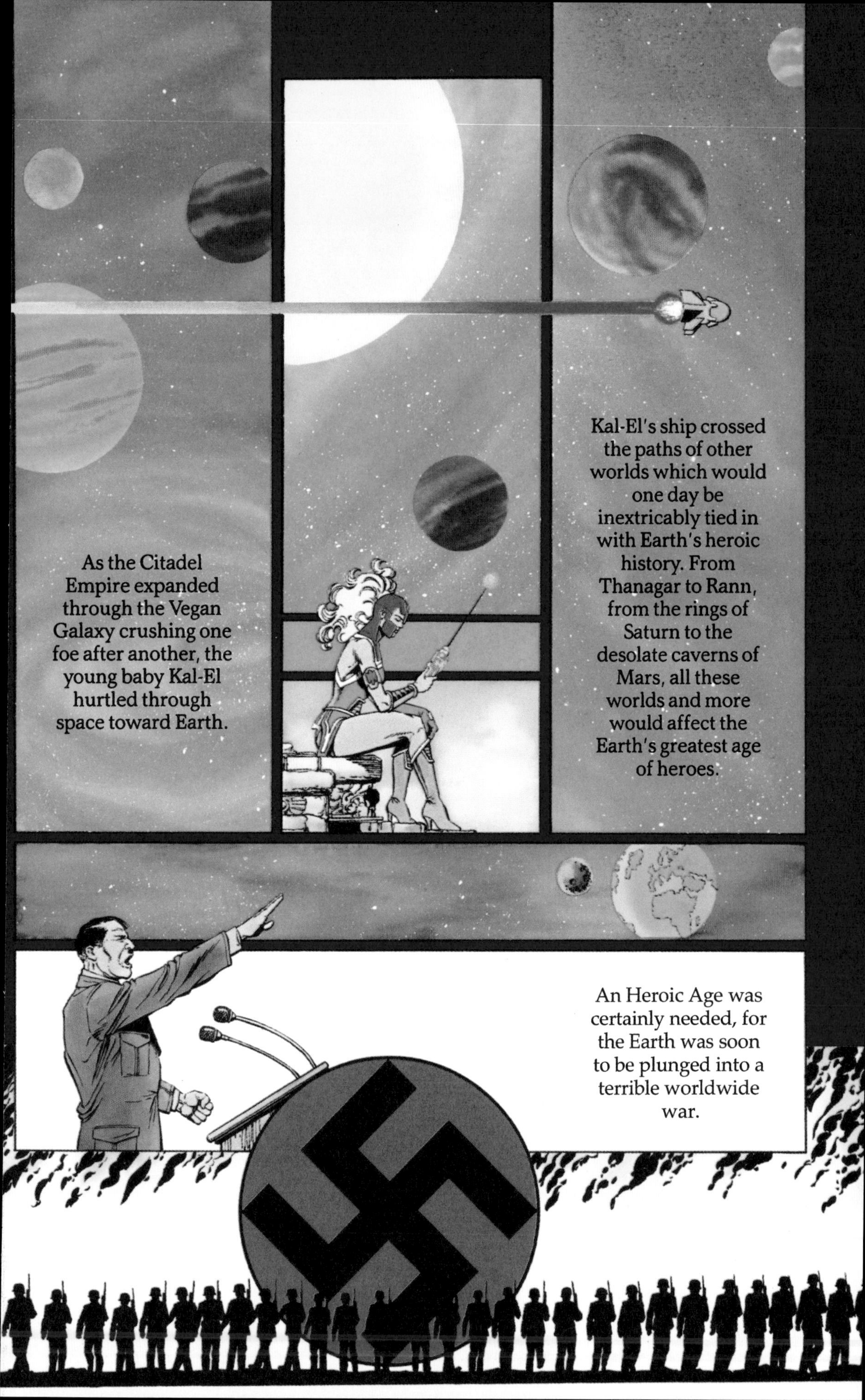
As the Citadel Empire expanded through the Vegan Galaxy crushing one foe after another, the young baby Kal-El hurtled through space toward Earth.
Kal-El's ship crossed the paths of other worlds which would one day be inextricably tied in with Earth's heroic history. From Thanagar to Rann, from the rings of Saturn to the desolate caverns of Mars, all these worlds and more would affect the Earth's greatest age of heroes.
An Heroic Age was certainly needed, for the Earth was soon to be plunged into a terrible worldwide war.

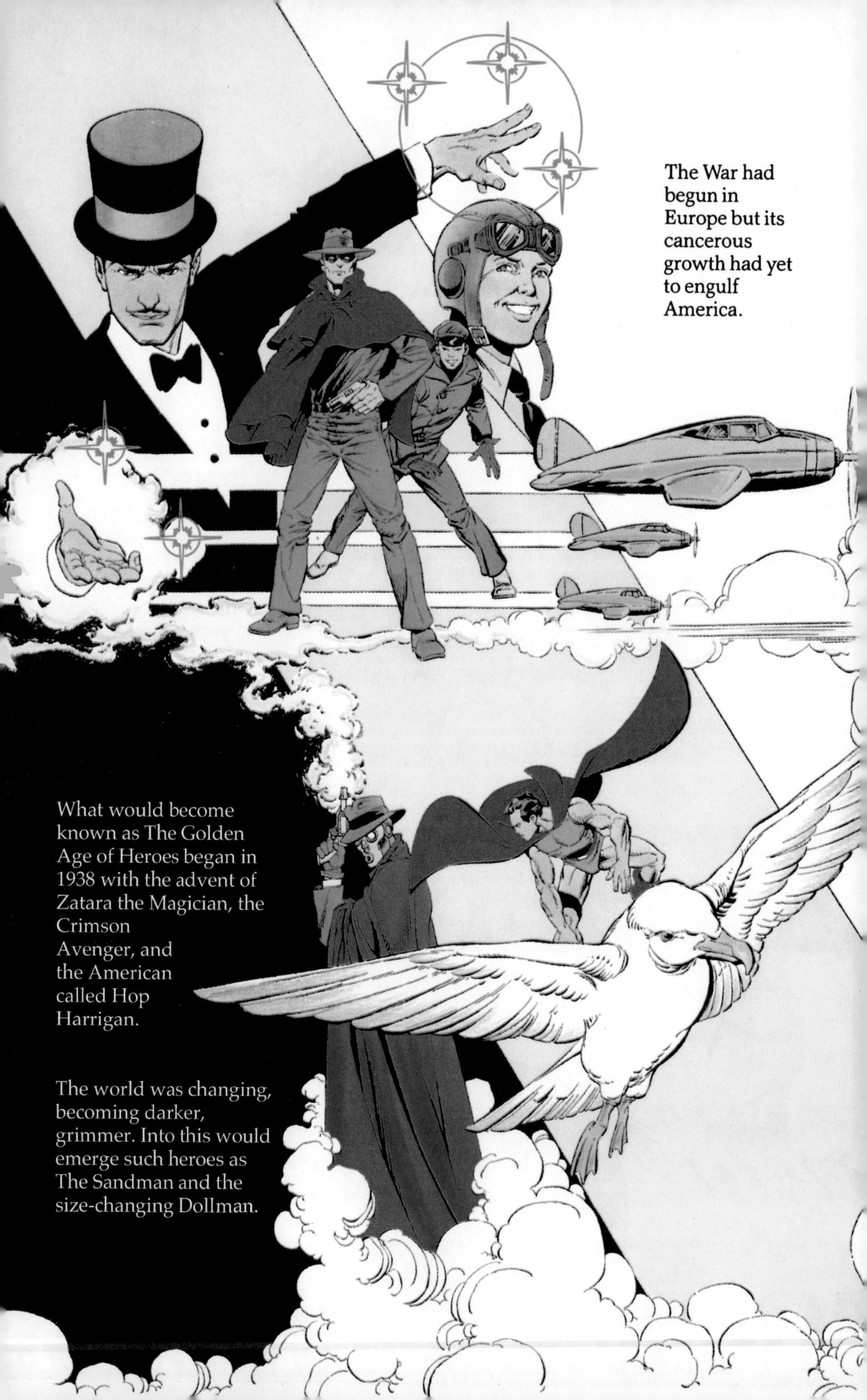
The War had begun in Europe but its cancerous growth had yet to engulf America.
What would become known as The Golden Age of Heroes began in 1938 with the advent of Zatara the Magician, the Crimson Avenger, and the American called Hop Harrigan.
The world was changing, becoming darker, grimmer. Into this would emerge such heroes as The Sandman and the size-changing Dollman.

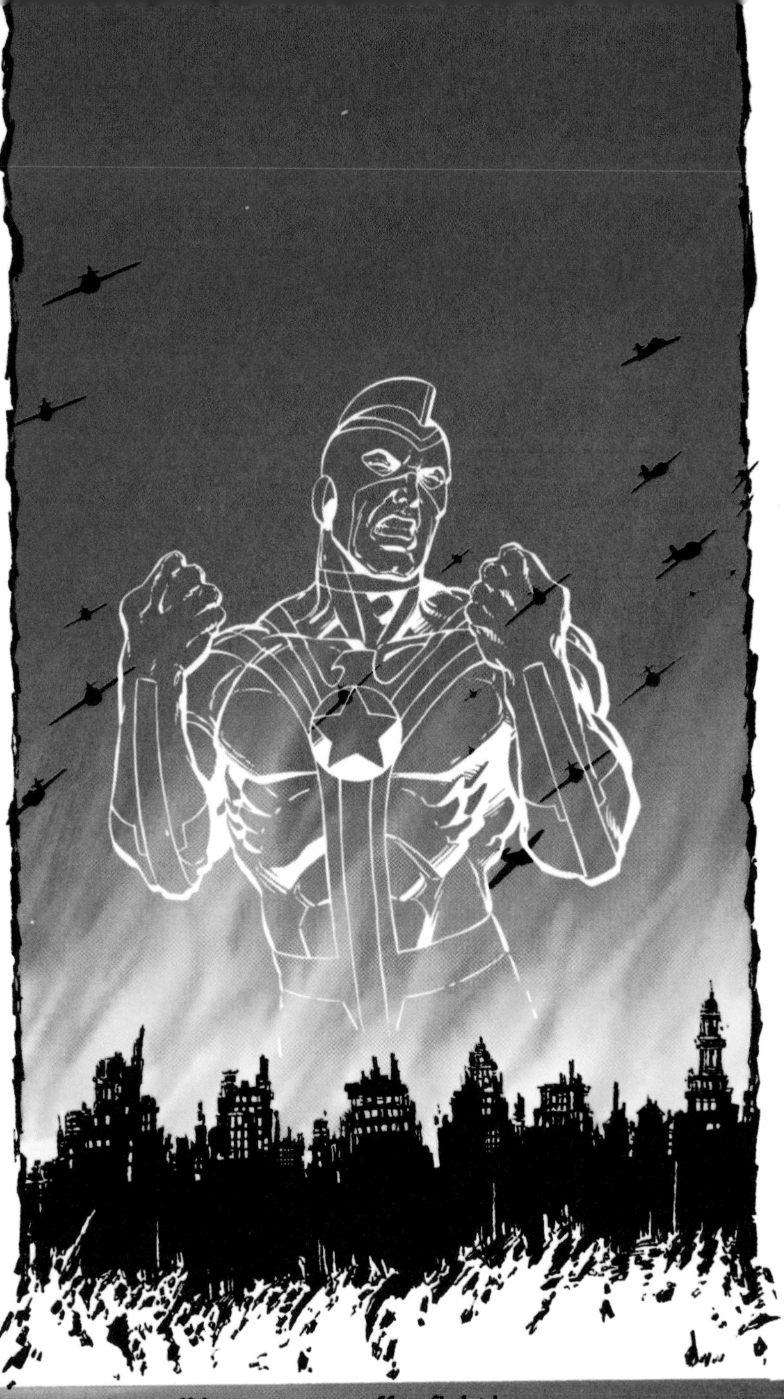

Long before America joined the war, many Americans took the side of the Allied nations in their desperate fight for freedom. Steel, the Indestructible Man, was one such hero who sacrificed his own welfare to help those oppressed by Nazi Tyranny. There were others, men without special powers and abilities, men who believed in freedom and who soon joined with their European brothers in the battle for peace.

All these men and women, costumed and uncostumed, became true heroes in this most horrible of wars.

But not all heroes went off to fight in Europe. Many remained home in America as she emerged from a debilitating depression to find herself heading toward the ever-encroaching Second World War.

With the emergence of specially powered heroes such as The Flash, the world's fastest man, came their very opposites: men and women with powers of their own who used their special abilities for evil.

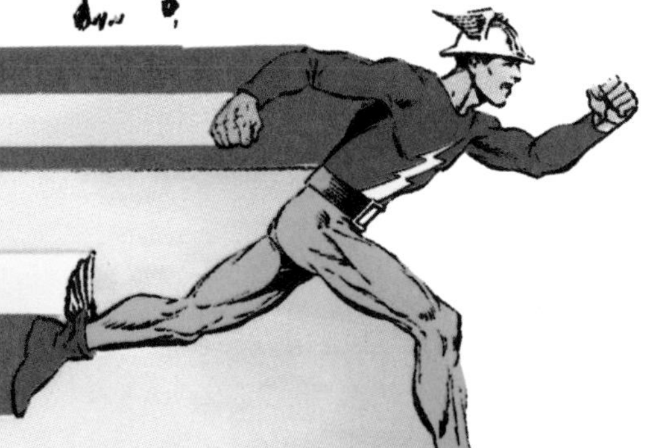

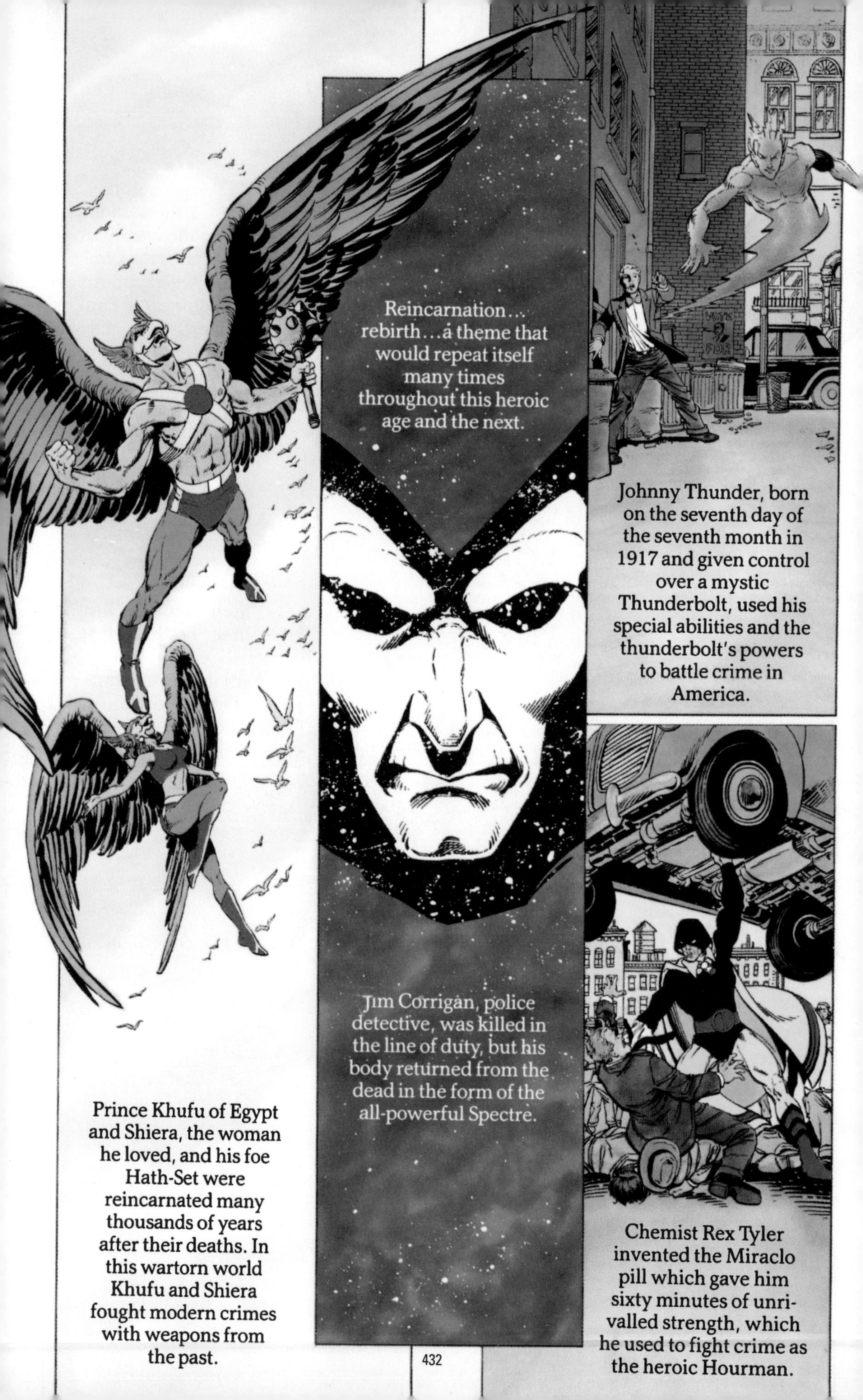
Reincarnation...
rebirth...a theme that would repeat itself many times throughout this heroic age and the next.
Prince Khufu of Egypt and Shiera, the woman he loved, and his foe Hath-Set were reincarnated many thousands of years after their deaths. In this wartorn world Khufu and Shiera fought modern crimes with weapons from the past.
Jim Corrigan, police detective, was killed in the line of duty, but his body returned from the dead in the form of the all-powerful Spectre.
Johnny Thunder, born on the seventh day of the seventh month in 1917 and given control over a mystic Thunderbolt, used his special abilities and the thunderbolt's powers to battle crime in America.
Chemist Rex Tyler invented the Miraclo pill which gave him sixty minutes of unrivalled strength, which he used to fight crime as the heroic Hourman.

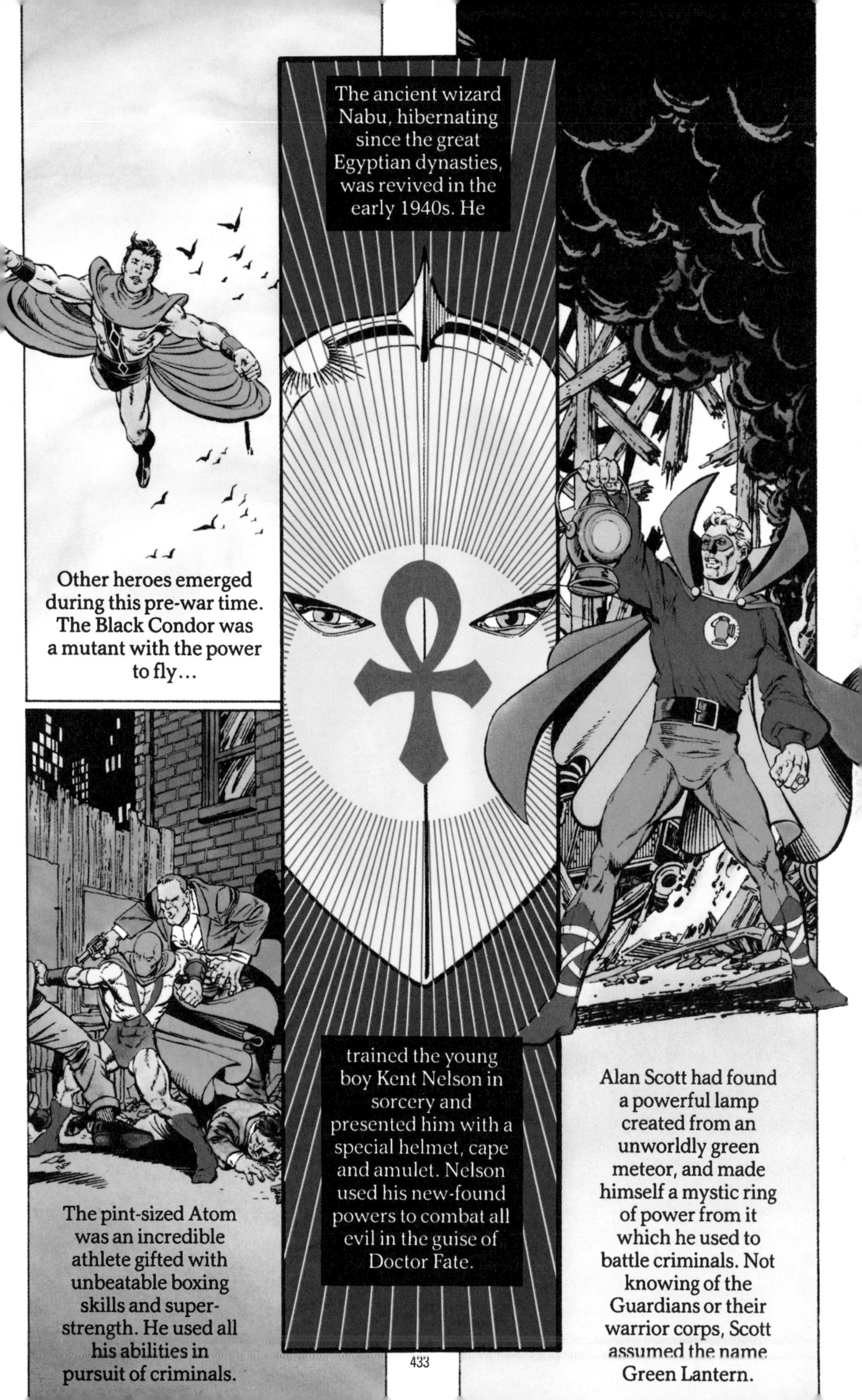

Other heroes emerged during this pre-war time. The Black Condor was a mutant with the power to fly...
The pint-sized Atom was an incredible athlete gifted with unbeatable boxing skills and super-strength. He used all his abilities in pursuit of criminals.
The ancient wizard Nabu, hibernating since the great Egyptian dynasties, was revived in the early 1940s. He
trained the young boy Kent Nelson in sorcery and presented him with a special helmet, cape and amulet. Nelson used his new-found powers to combat all evil in the guise of Doctor Fate.
Alan Scott had found a powerful lamp created from an unworldly green meteor, and made himself a mystic ring of power from it which he used to battle criminals. Not knowing of the Guardians or their warrior corps, Scott assumed the name Green Lantern.

The early 1940s gave birth to many heroes whose fame has lived on throughout time.

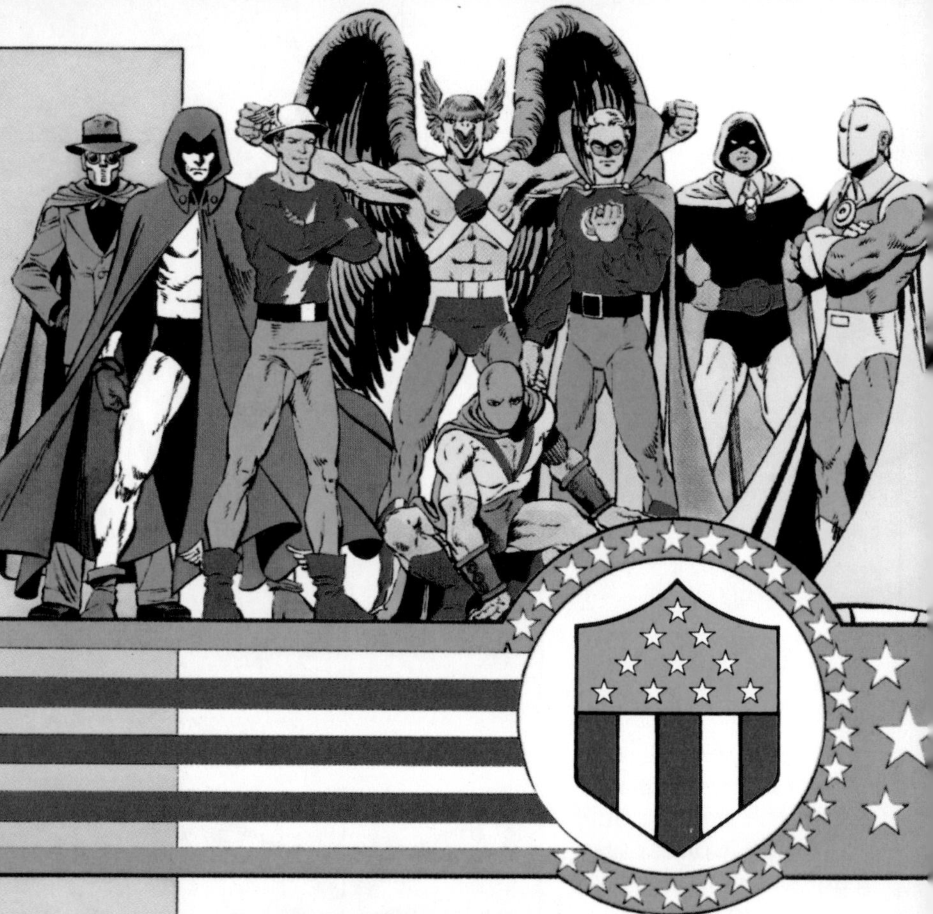

One by one the heroes appeared, and they were united by President Franklin Delano Roosevelt to partake in a secret mission overseas.

From this early gathering in November of 1940 came The Justice Society of America, the greatest gathering of heroes in the history of man.

Not since the days of Mount Olympus had the world known of such power and wisdom. This was truly the Golden Age of Heroes.

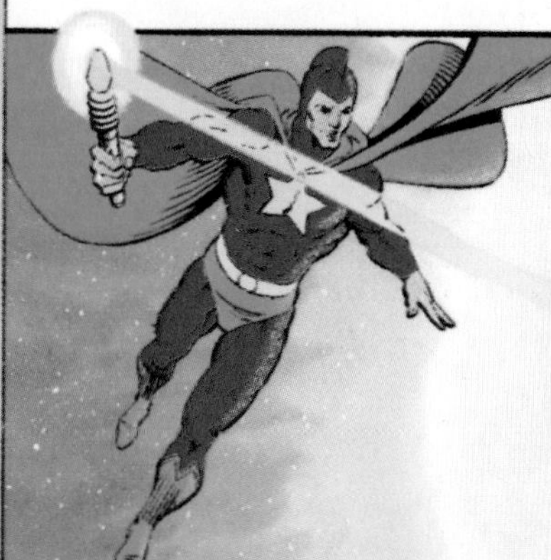

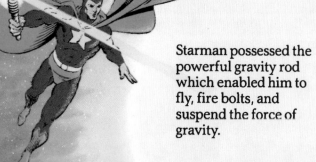

Starman possessed the powerful gravity rod which enabled him to fly, fire bolts, and suspend the force of gravity.

Doctor Mid-Nite, who suffered 'day blindness', fought crime at night with his blackout bombs, night vision and superb athletics.

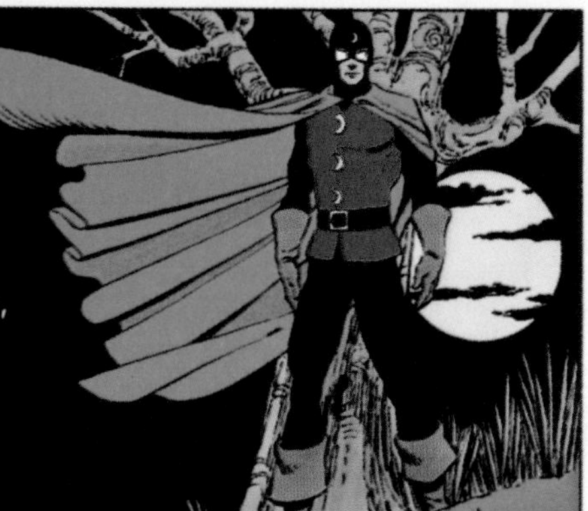

Perhaps they first appeared in answer to the Justice Society teaming of the 1940s, perhaps they emerged simultaneously, but as the crimes of ordinary thieves, bankrobbers and confidence men were handled more and more by police authorities, the special-powered villains of these early years banded together to create an unstoppable force of evil. This Injustice Gang of America wreaked havoc throughout the country, finding themselves in regular battle with the Justice Society.

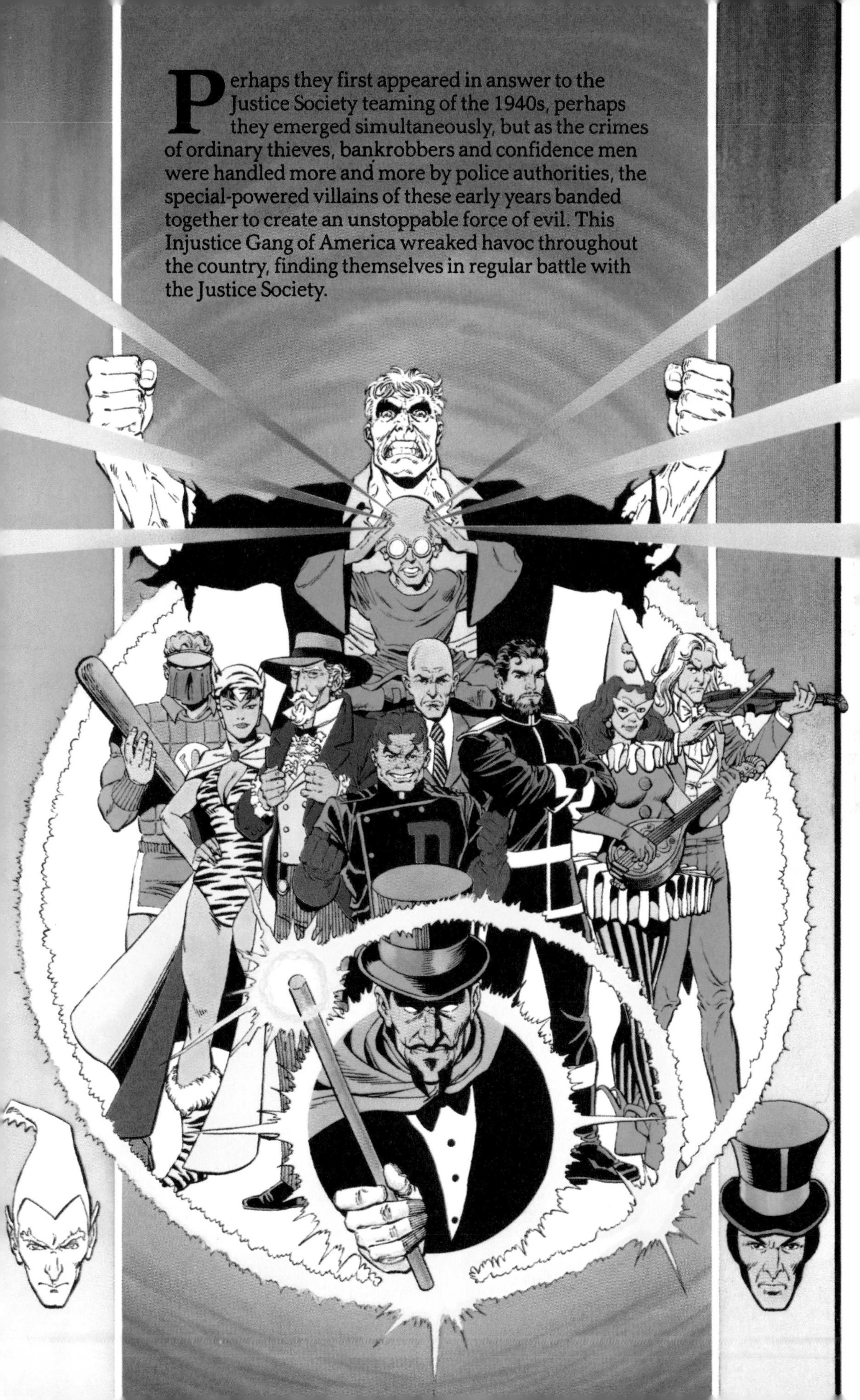

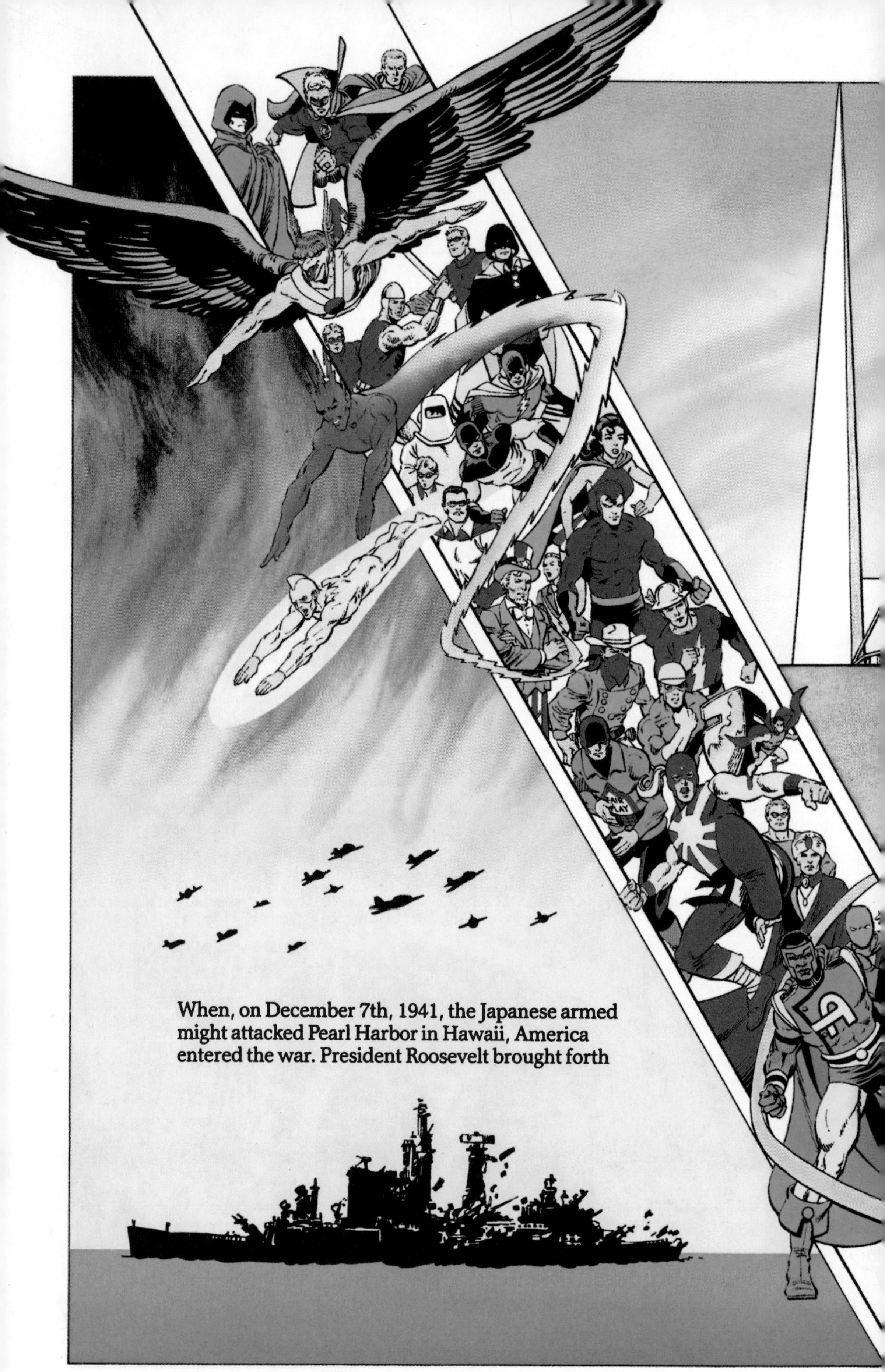
When, on December 7th, 1941, the Japanese armed might attacked Pearl Harbor in Hawaii, America entered the war. President Roosevelt brought forth

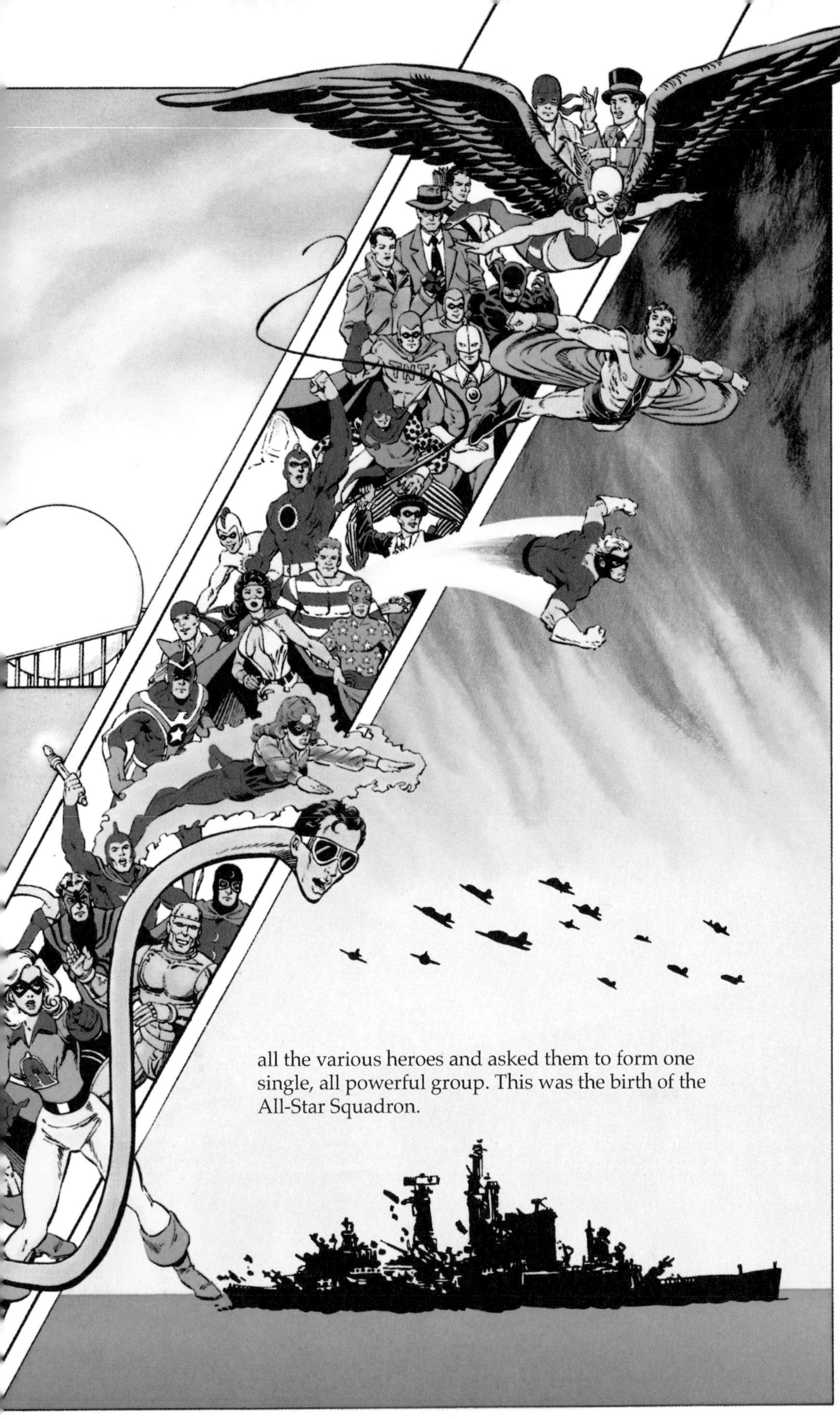

all the various heroes and asked them to form one single, all powerful group. This was the birth of the All-Star Squadron.

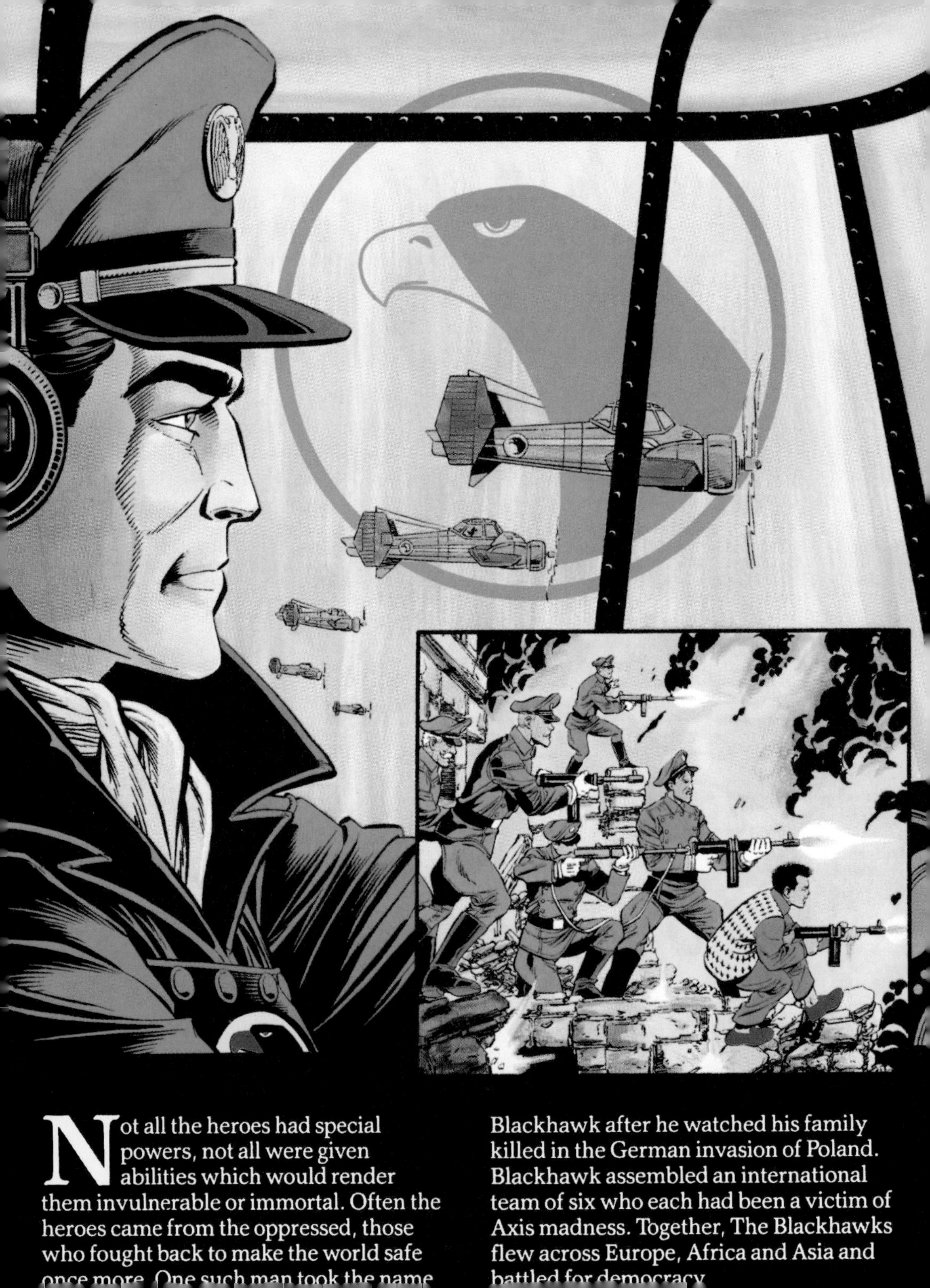

Not all the heroes had special powers, not all were given abilities which would render them invulnerable or immortal. Often the heroes came from the oppressed, those who fought back to make the world safe once more. One such man took the name Blackhawk after he watched his family killed in the German invasion of Poland. Blackhawk assembled an international team of six who each had been a victim of Axis madness. Together, The Blackhawks flew across Europe, Africa and Asia and battled for democracy.

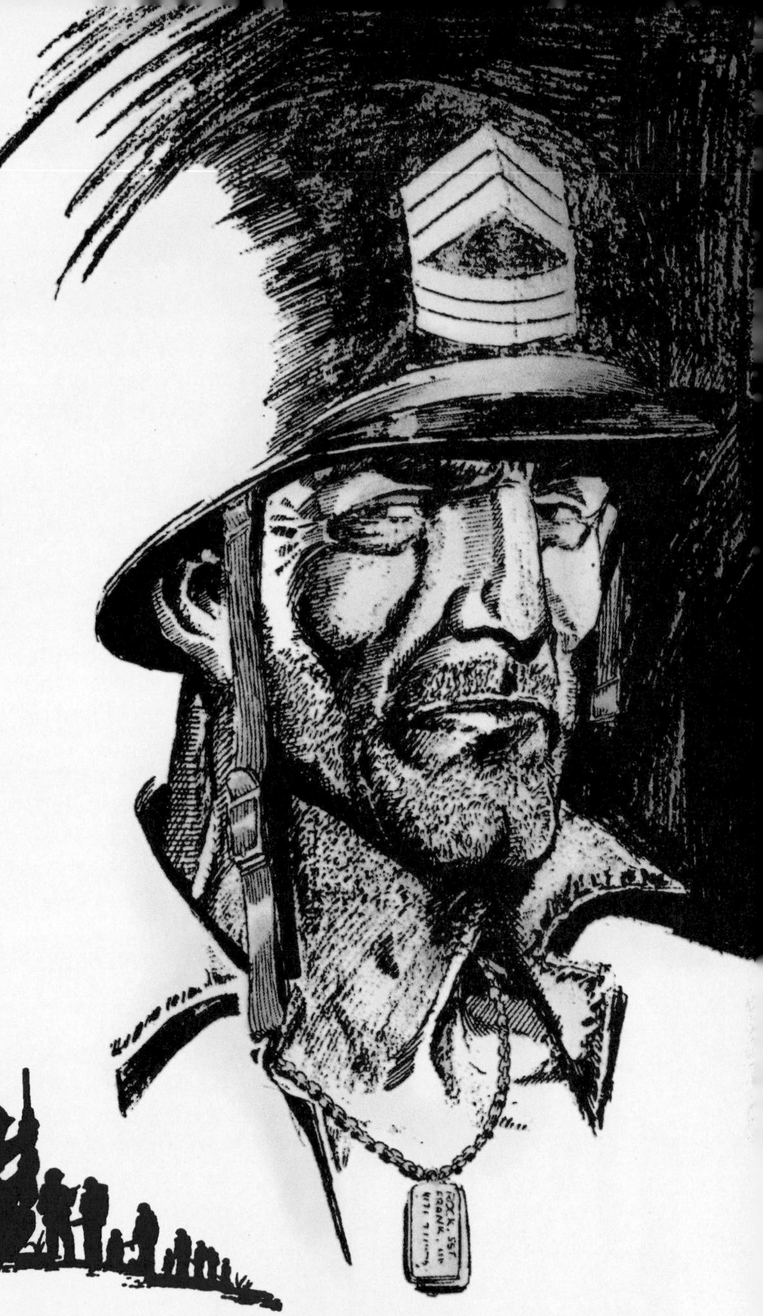

But the real heroes of the war were not those men and women who donned special costumes. They were the Americans and British, the French and Australians, the ordinary people who joined their nation's armies in the fight for a free world. These men and women fought in khaki and greens, marched through winds and rains, up muddy hills and across parched desert. These soldiers risked—and many lost—their lives, and to them all specially gifted heroes bow in reverence.

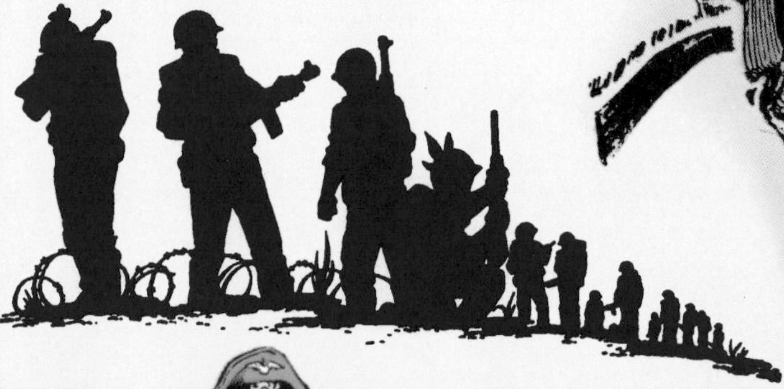

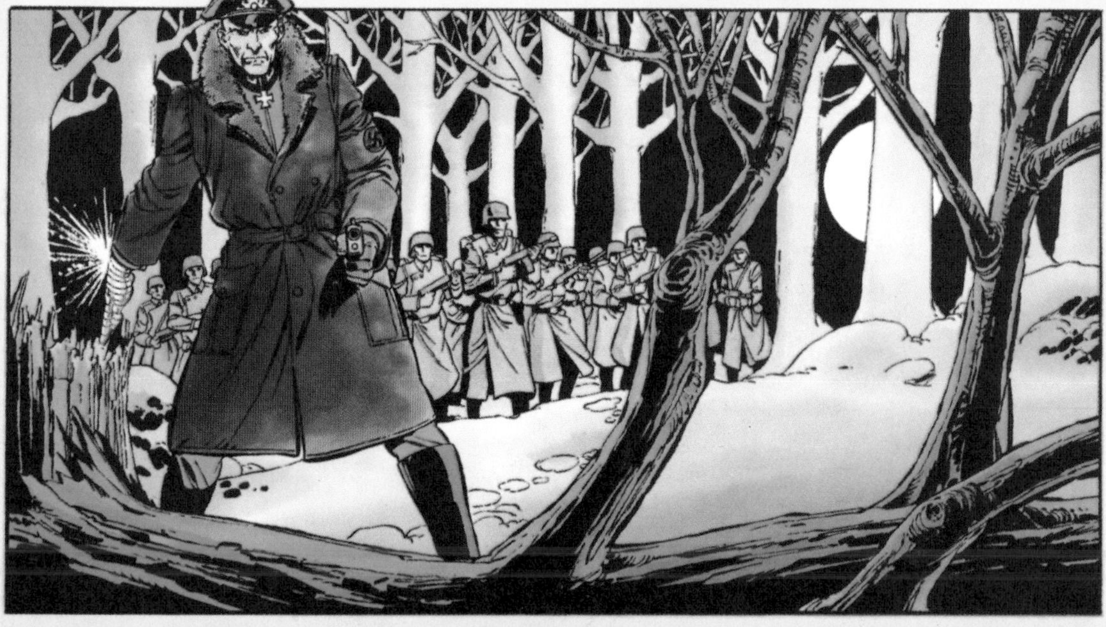

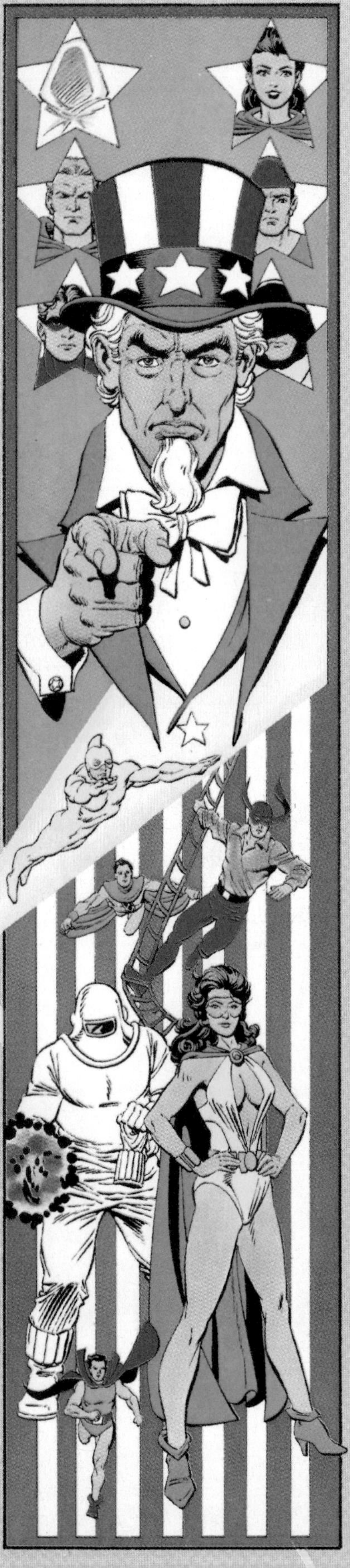

Throughout the history of the World there were freedom fighters, and this is their history, whether uniformed or not, whether powered or ordinary. And so ends Book One of the history of the Heroic Ages. I have been able to place them chronologically and thus show a continuity of events. The immortals who lived at the dawn of time returned throughout history, affecting man and his progress. The sinking of a seemingly unrelated island will have its effects seen in Book Two.

What began many years in the past will be remembered and acted upon many centuries from now. What *was* affects what *is* and what *will be*. This, more than any other reason, is why this history of the universe is needed. To look at the heroic age without perspective, to understand one element without seeing the whole, is to do it a vast injustice.

Our tale has but begun.

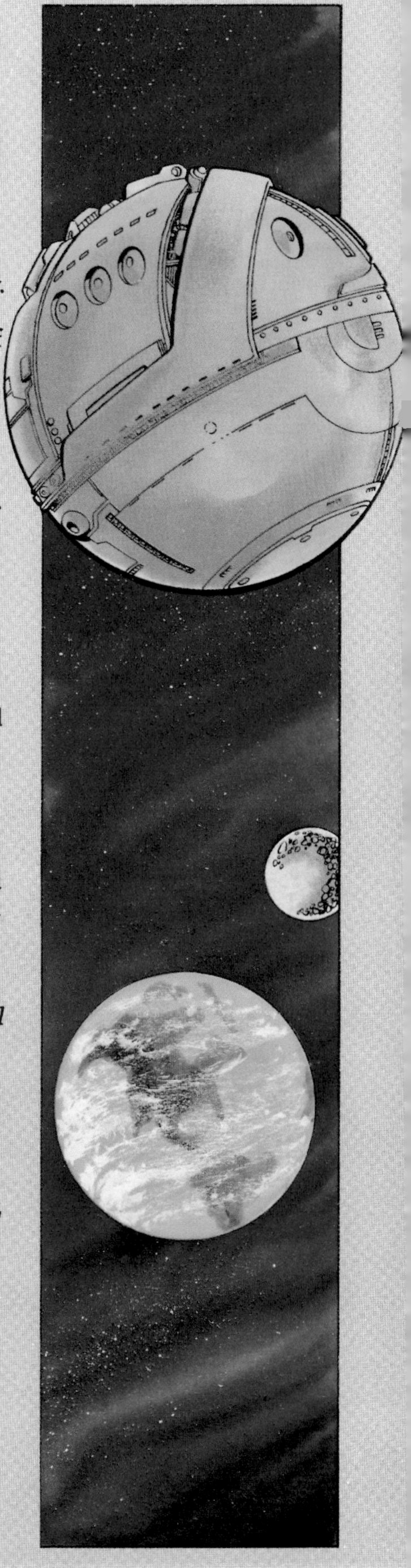

$2.95 USA

$4.50 CAN.

HISTORY OF THE DC UNIVERSE

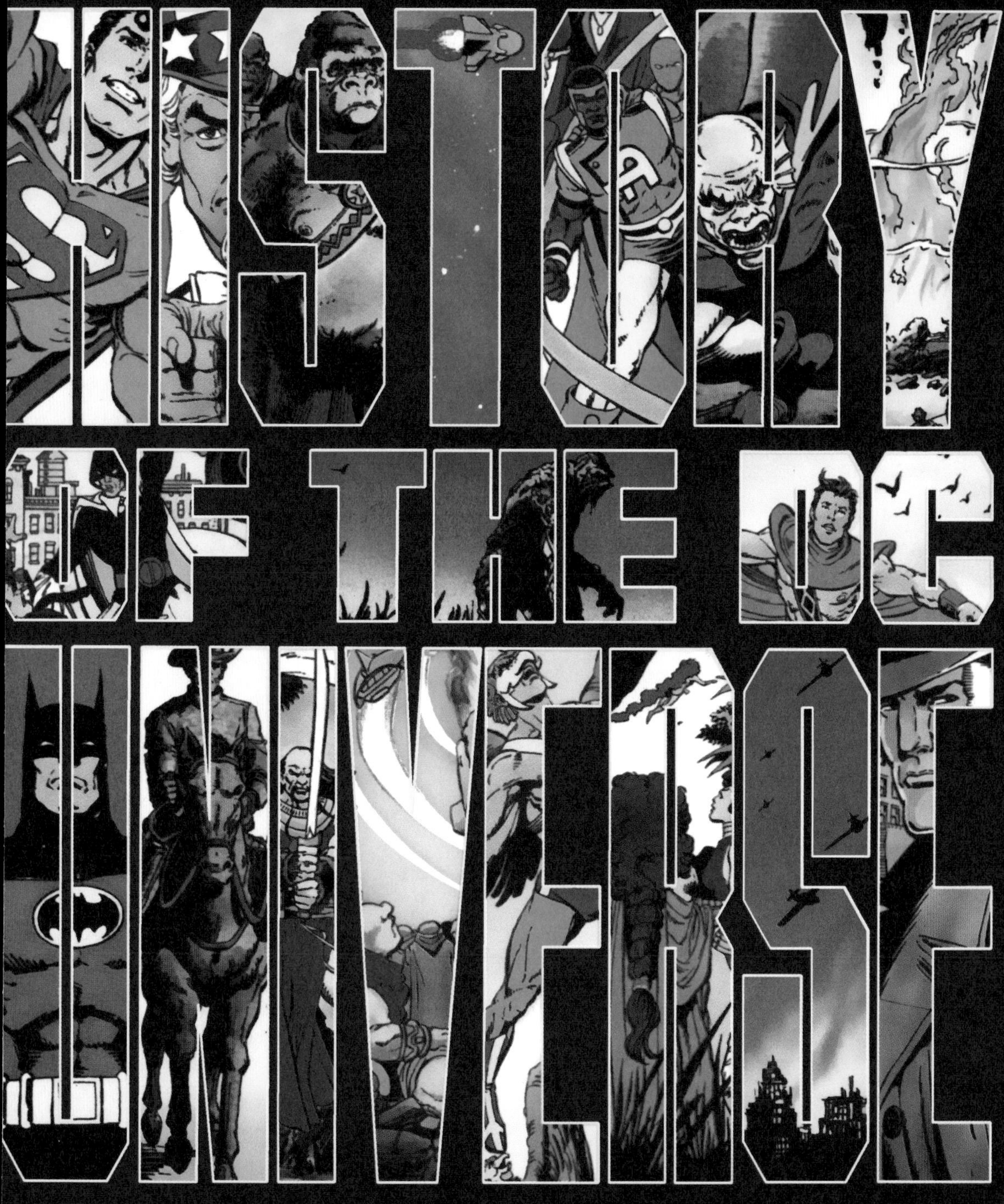

BOOK TWO

WOLFMAN & PÉREZ

In the beginning, there was but one universe, one world… one Earth. At the moment of creation, a moment some believe inspired by an outside force, a moment others believe exploded whole and onto itself—a second universe was created of heat and light, gas and plasma, and a million other elements gestating in the cosmic womb. This was a universe of counterbalance…a negative universe to our positive creation: an existence of anti-matter to our positive matter. This was a universe of darkness, a universe of evil, a universe of twisted reality.

And in this second universe, there was born one single being who would live ten billion years and disrupt all future reality.

This then is that history of those ten billion years, and of the years that follow. This is not a chronological retelling of historical events which can be read in any text—this is the history of heroism.

My name is Harbinger and I am honor-bound to record all that has happened and all that will occur.

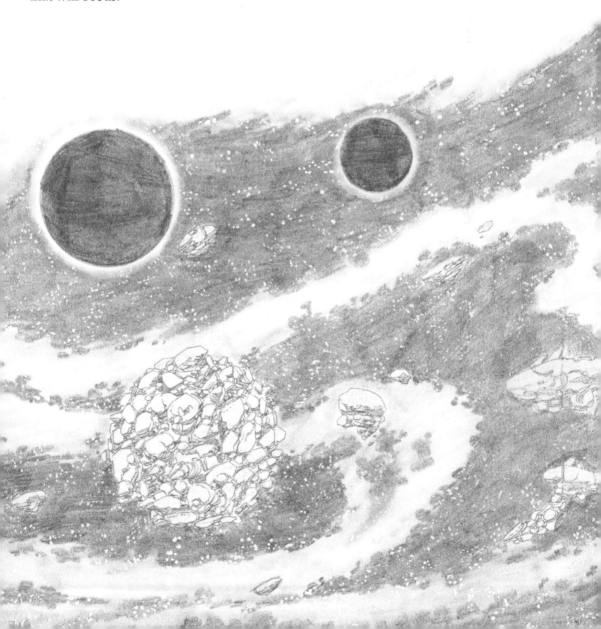

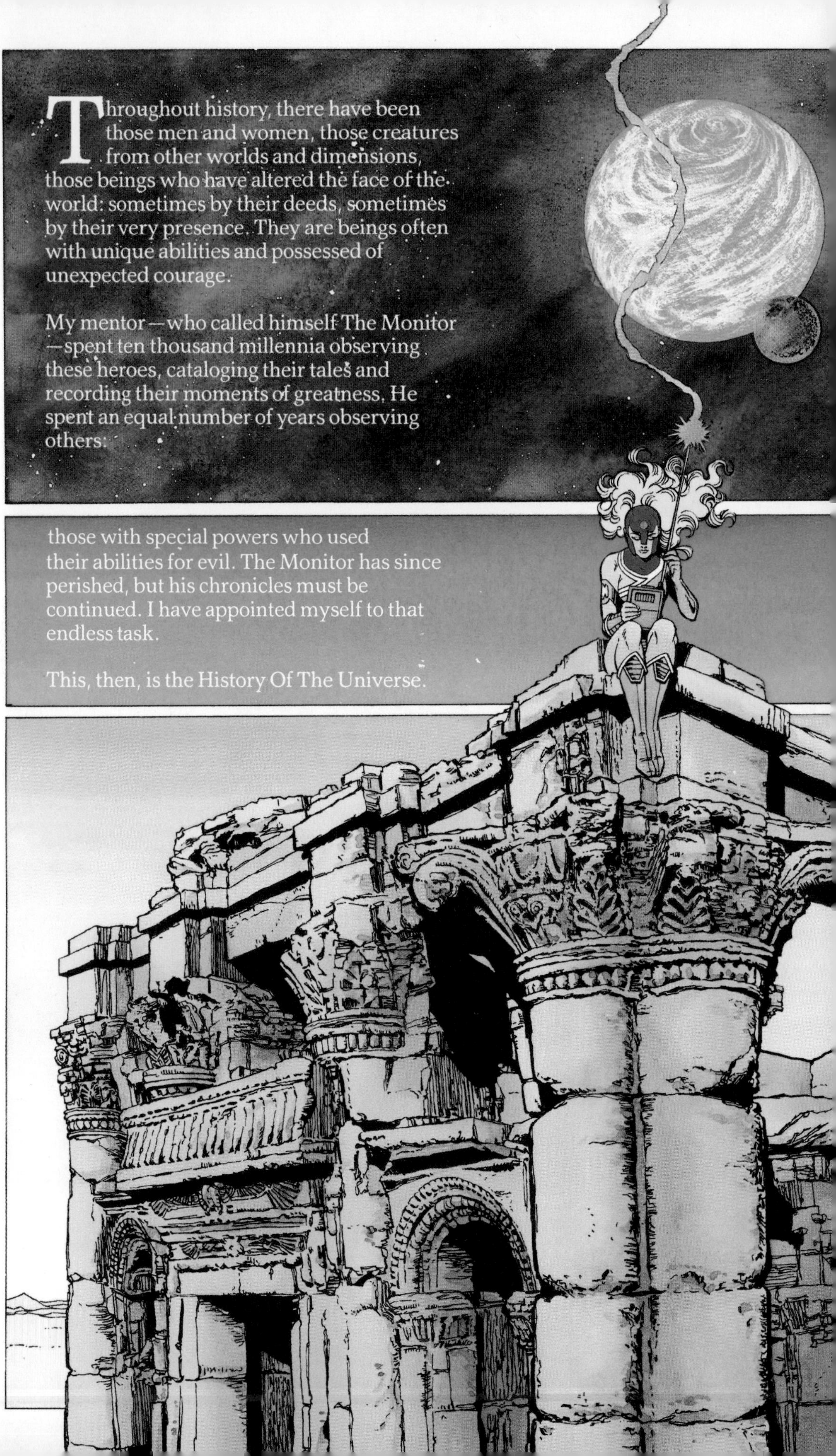
Throughout history, there have been those men and women, those creatures from other worlds and dimensions, those beings who have altered the face of the world: sometimes by their deeds, sometimes by their very presence. They are beings often with unique abilities and possessed of unexpected courage.
My mentor—who called himself The Monitor—spent ten thousand millennia observing these heroes, cataloging their tales and recording their moments of greatness. He spent an equal number of years observing others:
those with special powers who used their abilities for evil. The Monitor has since perished, but his chronicles must be continued. I have appointed myself to that endless task.
This, then, is the History Of The Universe.

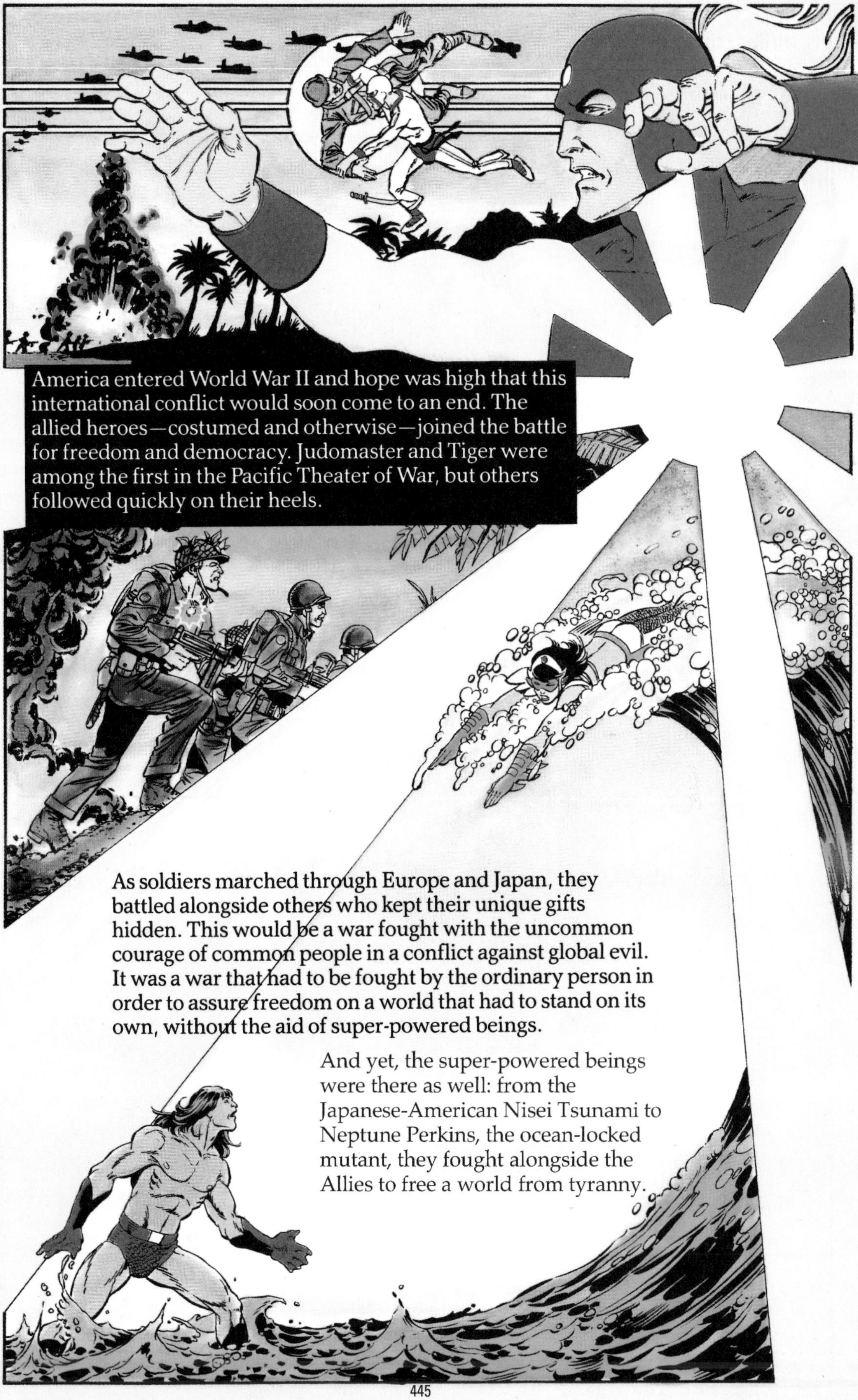
America entered World War II and hope was high that this international conflict would soon come to an end. The allied heroes—costumed and otherwise—joined the battle for freedom and democracy. Judomaster and Tiger were among the first in the Pacific Theater of War, but others followed quickly on their heels.
As soldiers marched through Europe and Japan, they battled alongside others who kept their unique gifts hidden. This would be a war fought with the uncommon courage of common people in a conflict against global evil. It was a war that had to be fought by the ordinary person in order to assure freedom on a world that had to stand on its own, without the aid of super-powered beings.
And yet, the super-powered beings were there as well: from the Japanese-American Nisei Tsunami to Neptune Perkins, the ocean-locked mutant, they fought alongside the Allies to free a world from tyranny.

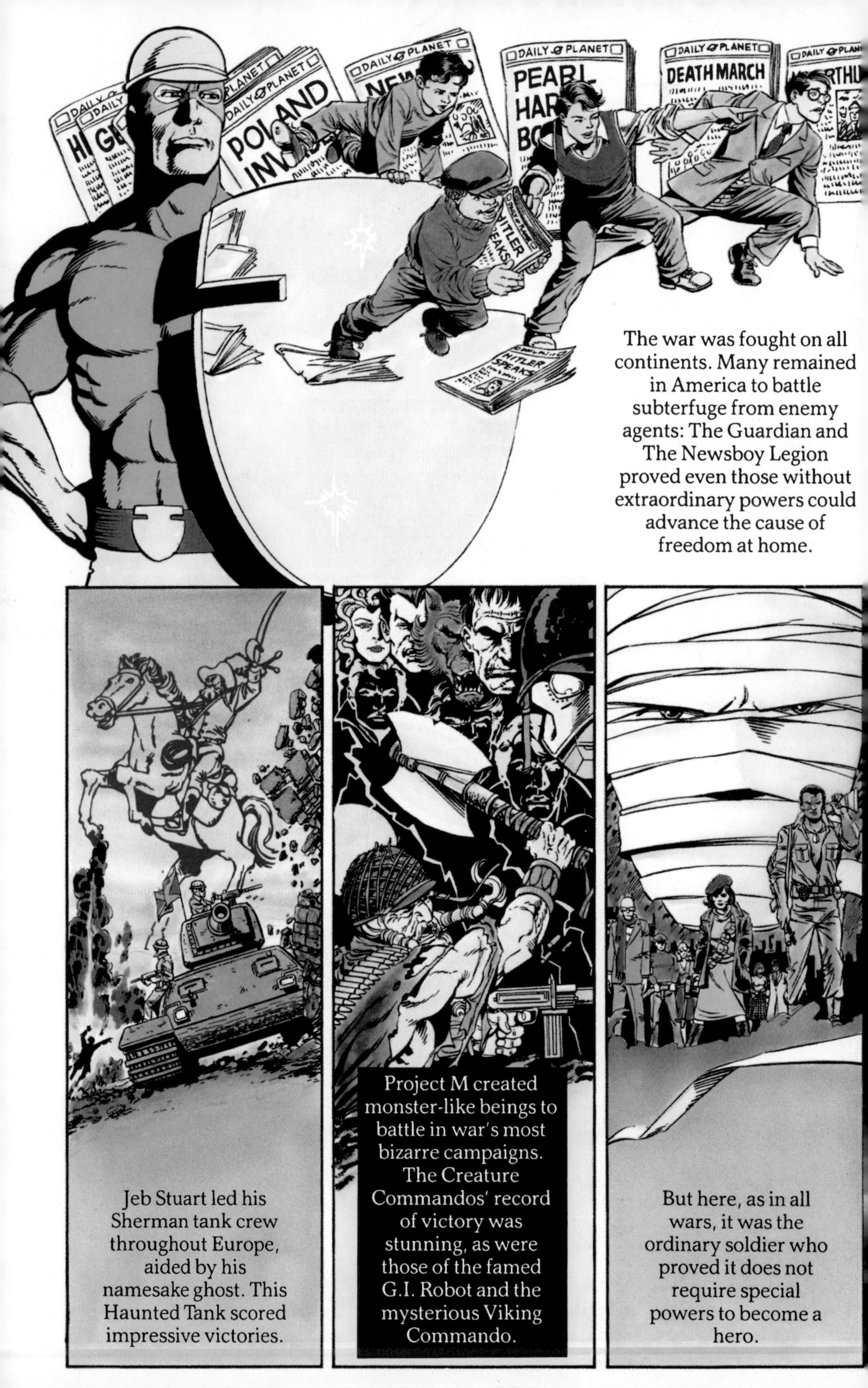
DAILY PLANET
DEATH MARCH
The war was fought on all continents. Many remained in America to battle subterfuge from enemy agents: The Guardian and The Newsboy Legion proved even those without extraordinary powers could advance the cause of freedom at home.
Jeb Stuart led his Sherman tank crew throughout Europe, aided by his namesake ghost. This Haunted Tank scored impressive victories.
Project M created monster-like beings to battle in war's most bizarre campaigns. The Creature Commandos' record of victory was stunning, as were those of the famed G.I. Robot and the mysterious Viking Commando.
But here, as in all wars, it was the ordinary soldier who proved it does not require special powers to become a hero.

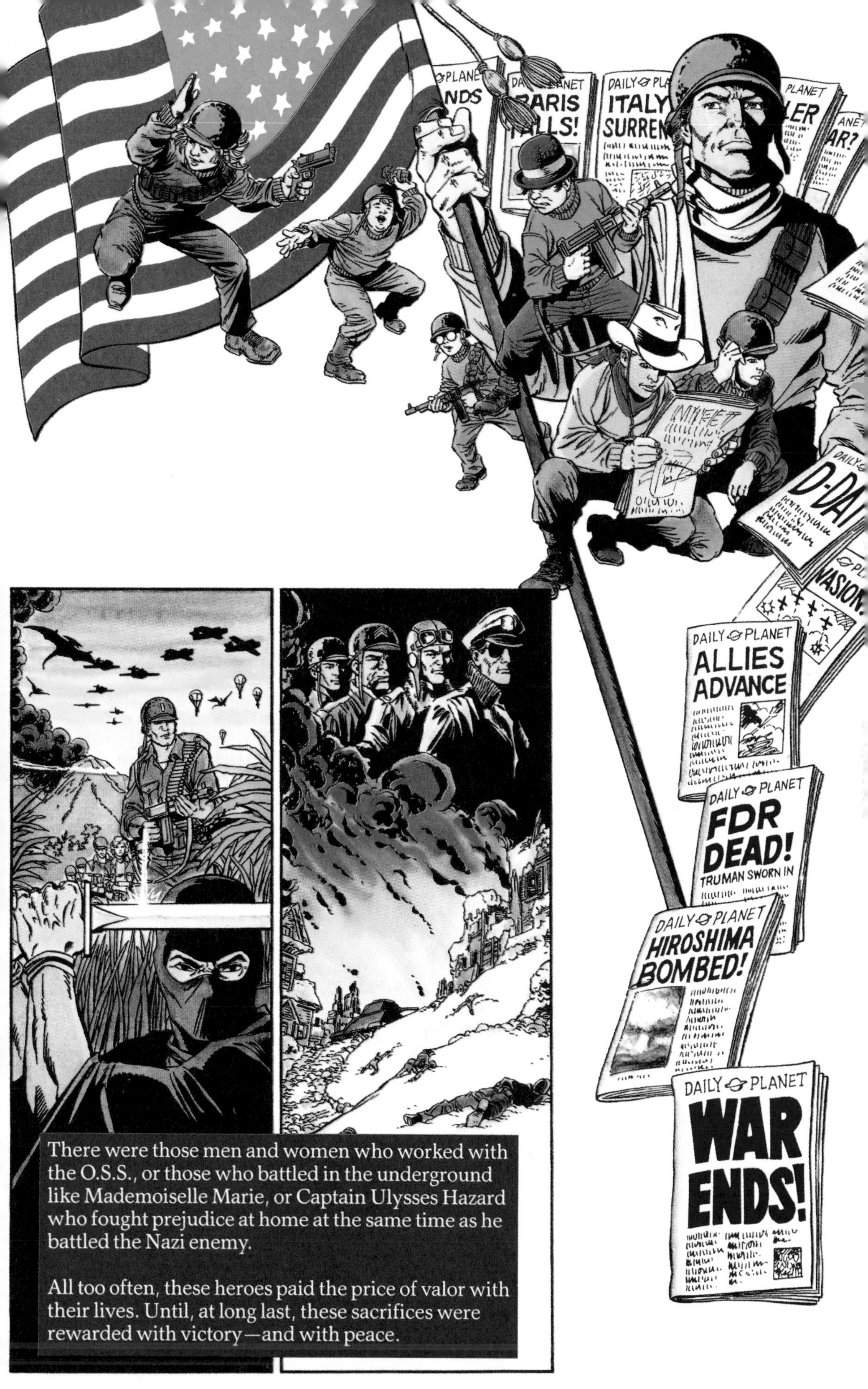
DAILY PLANET
ALLIES ADVANCE
DAILY PLANET
FDR DEAD!
TRUMAN SWORN IN
DAILY PLANET
HIROSHIMA BOMBED!
DAILY PLANET
WAR ENDS!
There were those men and women who worked with the O.S.S., or those who battled in the underground like Mademoiselle Marie, or Captain Ulysses Hazard who fought prejudice at home at the same time as he battled the Nazi enemy.
All too often, these heroes paid the price of valor with their lives. Until, at long last, these sacrifices were rewarded with victory—and with peace.

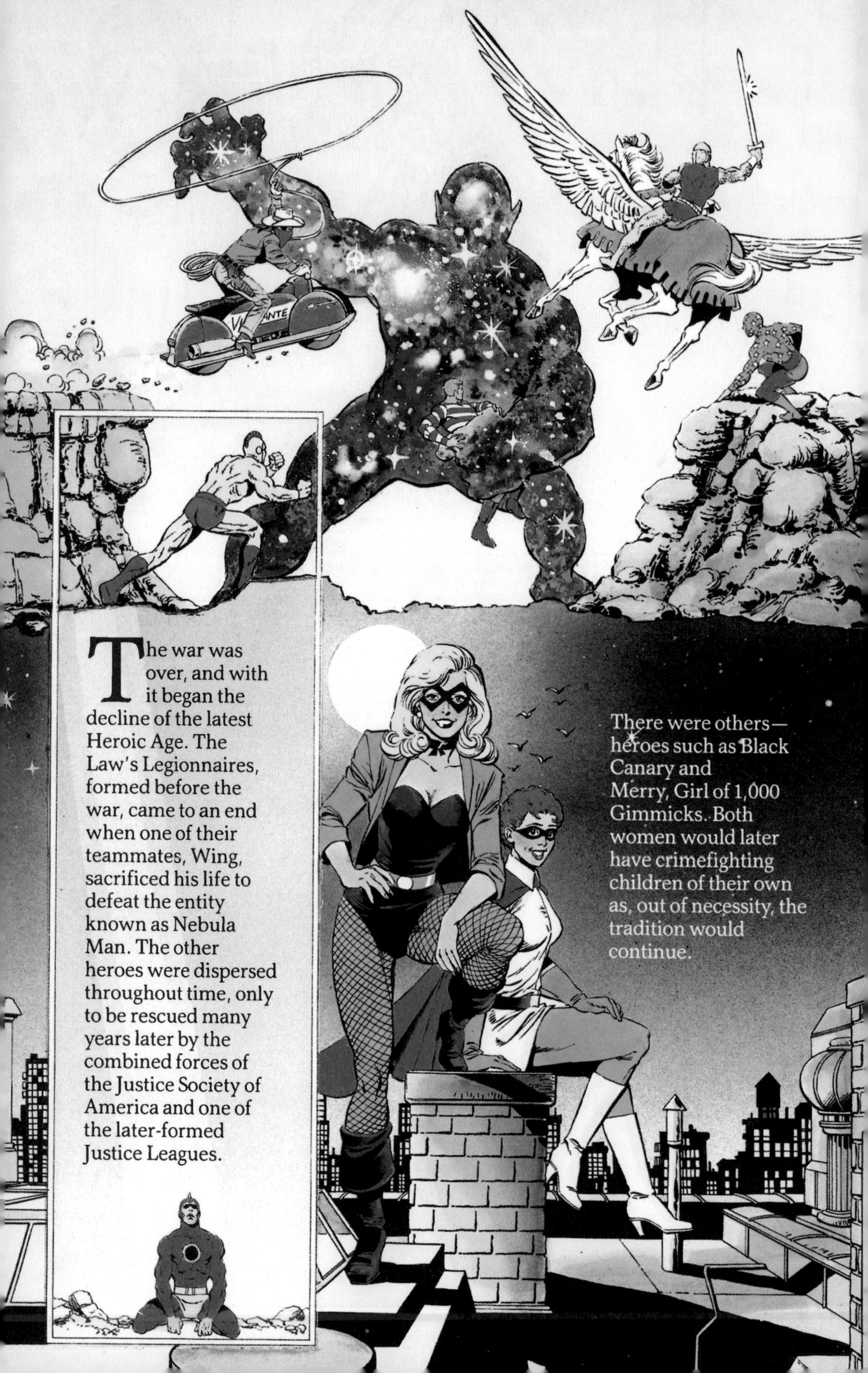

The war was over, and with it began the decline of the latest Heroic Age. The Law's Legionnaires, formed before the war, came to an end when one of their teammates, Wing, sacrificed his life to defeat the entity known as Nebula Man. The other heroes were dispersed throughout time, only to be rescued many years later by the combined forces of the Justice Society of America and one of the later-formed Justice Leagues.

There were others—heroes such as Black Canary and Merry, Girl of 1,000 Gimmicks. Both women would later have crimefighting children of their own as, out of necessity, the tradition would continue.

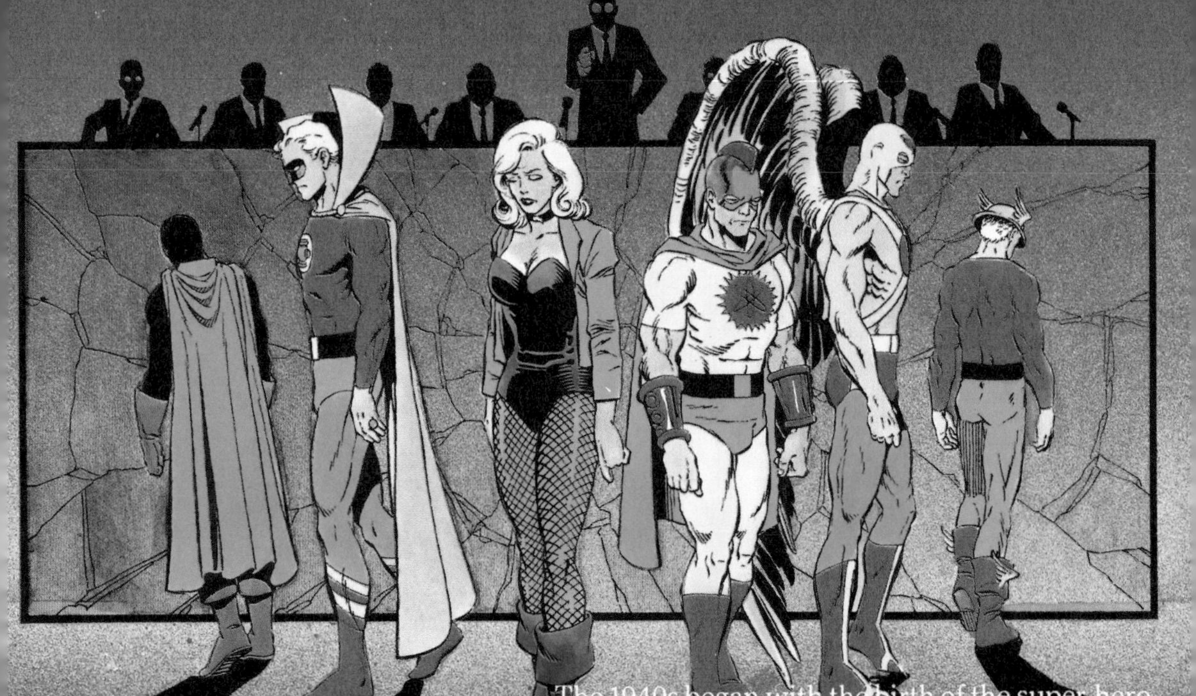

The 1940s began with the birth of the super-hero and ended with their slide into obscurity. The final, crushing blow came in the early 1950s when the Justice Society of America was brought before the House Un-American Activities Committee under suspicion of giving aid to enemy spies. Rather than reveal their secret identities, the Justice Society disbanded, and their members retired to civilian life.

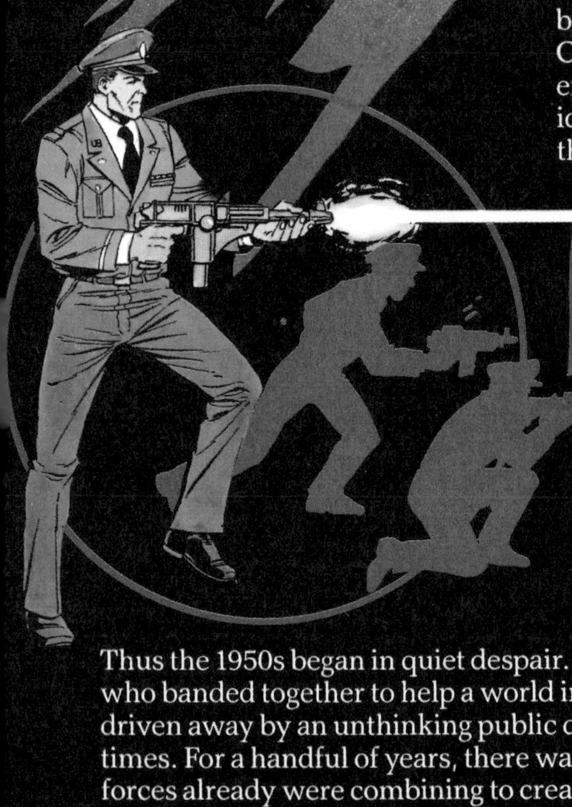

Without the World's Greatest Heroes fighting to preserve freedom, the government created its own warriors: Task Force X led the fight against evil on an international scale as the former O.S.S. spymaster Control headed a domestic force.

Thus the 1950s began in quiet despair. Those people who banded together to help a world in need were driven away by an unthinking public during paranoid times. For a handful of years, there was quiet, but forces already were combining to create the greatest of all Heroic Ages.

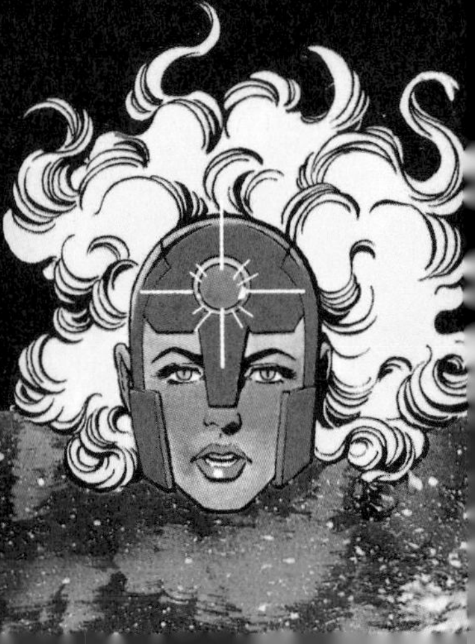

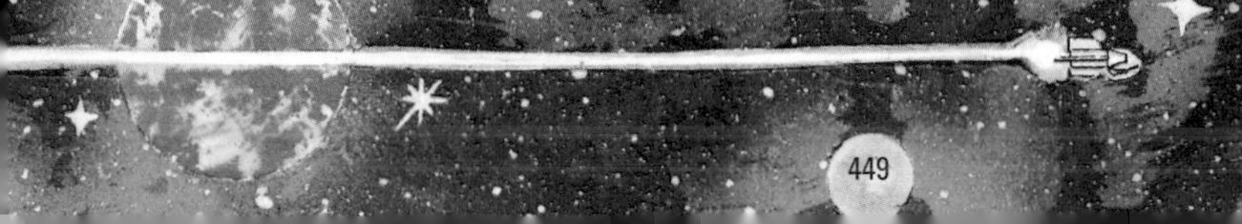

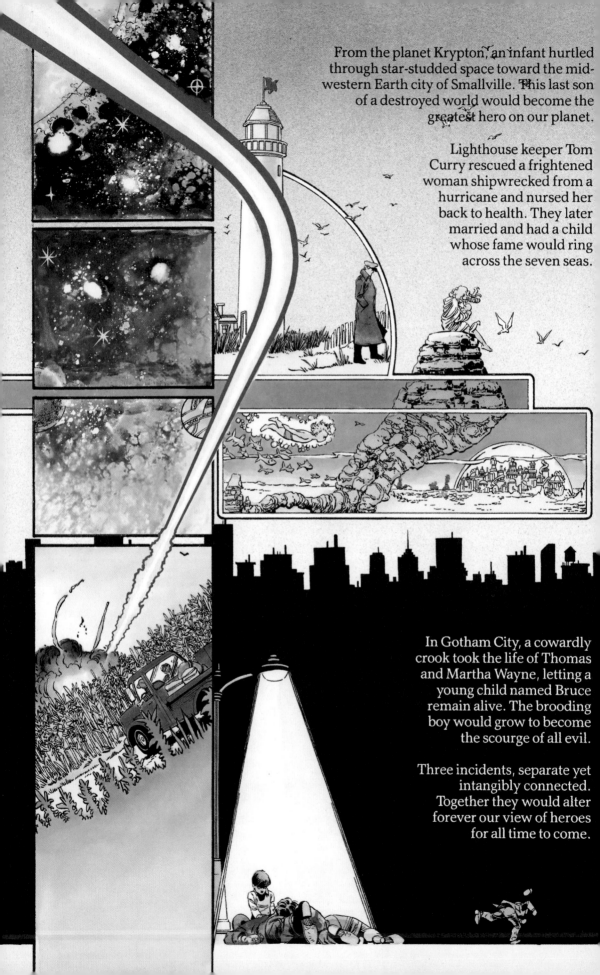

From the planet Krypton, an infant hurtled through star-studded space toward the mid-western Earth city of Smallville. This last son of a destroyed world would become the greatest hero on our planet.

Lighthouse keeper Tom Curry rescued a frightened woman shipwrecked from a hurricane and nursed her back to health. They later married and had a child whose fame would ring across the seven seas.

In Gotham City, a cowardly crook took the life of Thomas and Martha Wayne, letting a young child named Bruce remain alive. The brooding boy would grow to become the scourge of all evil.

Three incidents, separate yet intangibly connected. Together they would alter forever our view of heroes for all time to come.

A child in Smallville, a hybrid of Atlantis, and an orphan in Gotham City ...all still children; all still growing, learning, their values being shaped as their skills were being honed. They would become the saviors of tomorrow.

While they grew, there was another who watched them but was never seen. He was in Smallville and on a lonely Atlantic island. He was in Gotham City and in Star City. And while he waited for those future heroes to mature into adulthood, he confronted evil, appearing as if some Phantom Stranger.

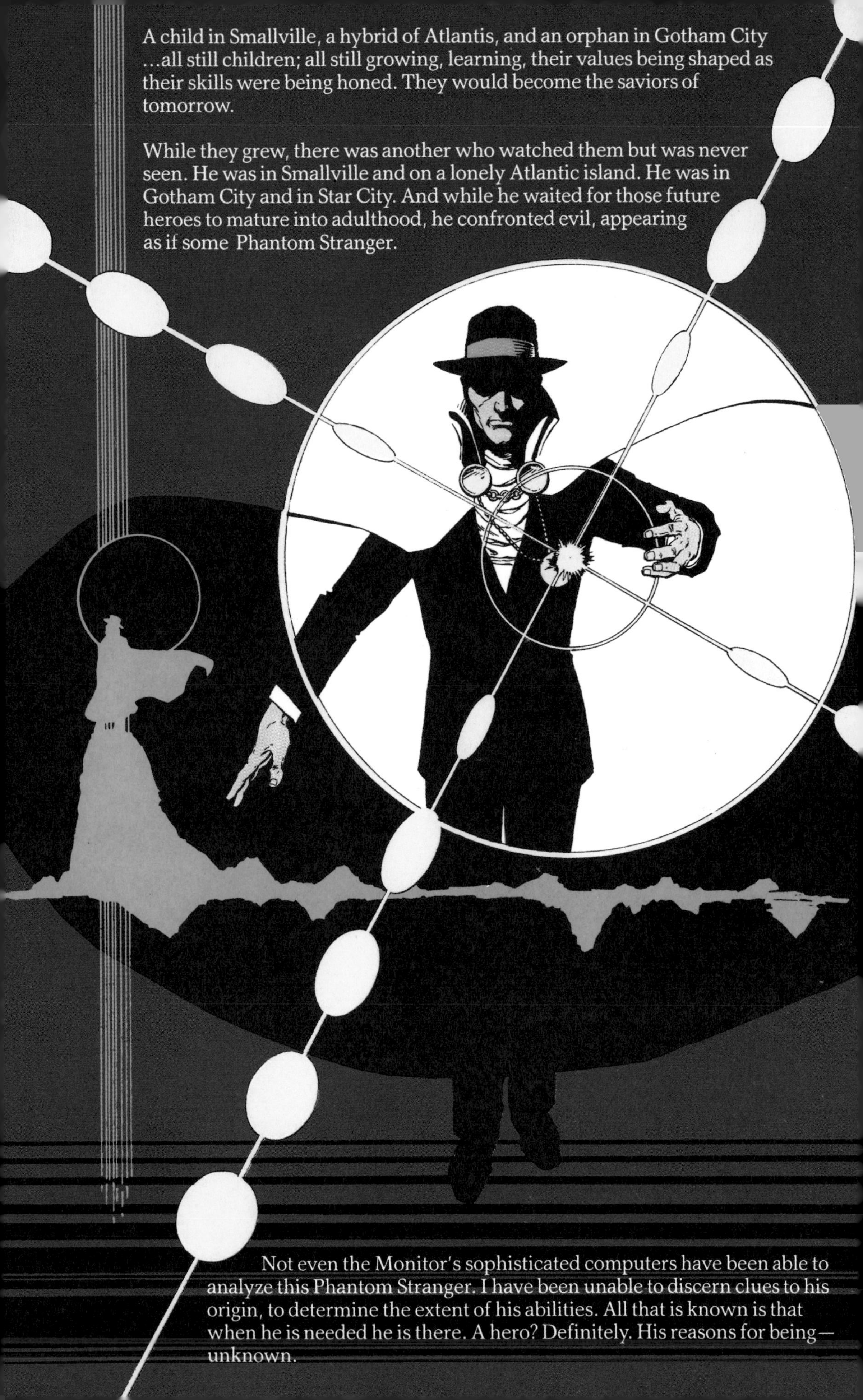

Not even the Monitor's sophisticated computers have been able to analyze this Phantom Stranger. I have been unable to discern clues to his origin, to determine the extent of his abilities. All that is known is that when he is needed he is there. A hero? Definitely. His reasons for being—unknown.

The stage was set for a revolution, but first there were the trailblazers—those who paved the way for the heroes to come. Captain Comet—a mutant born one hundred thousand years ahead of his time—was among the first.

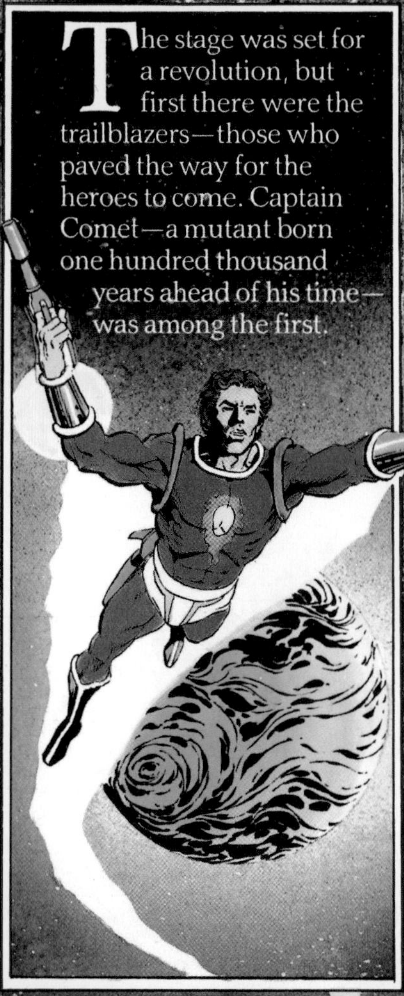

The history of heroes spans the universe: from a mutant born ahead of his time to the canals of dying Mars.

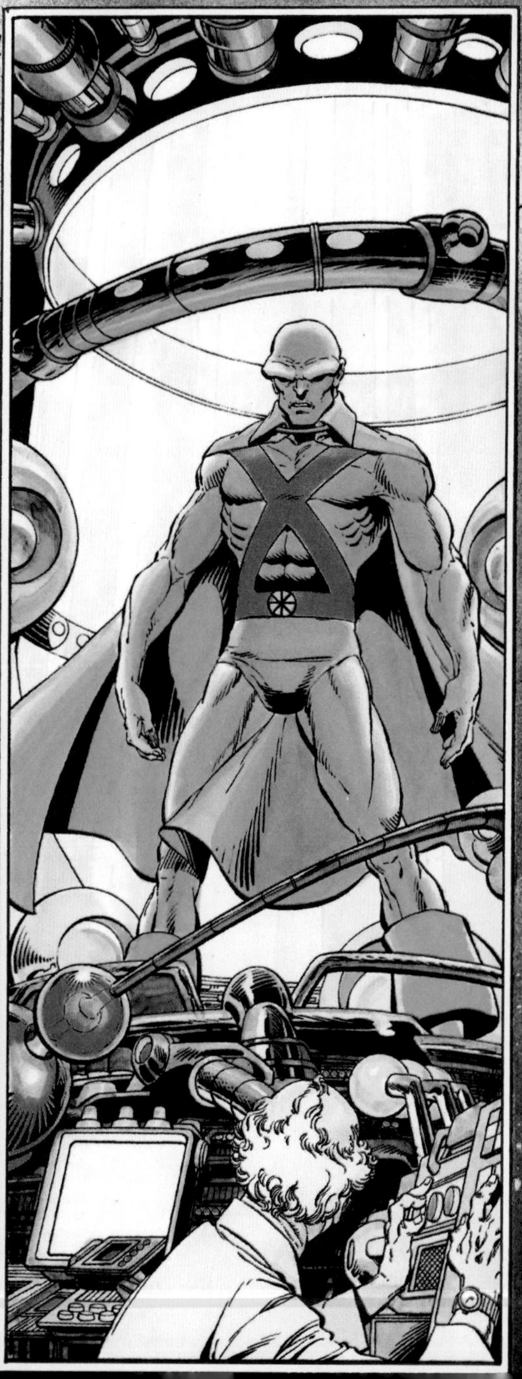

Warrior J'onn J'onzz, exiled into the parched Martian desert, was teleported accidentally to the planet Earth by the famous Professor Erdel. This Manhunter from Mars knew the time of heroes had not yet come, and so remained in hiding, disguising himself as a police detective until, at last, he could allow the world to know of his existence.

It would take the heroic appearances of the last son of Krypton, the child from Atlantis and the orphan from Gotham City to change the climate for super-heroes on Earth.

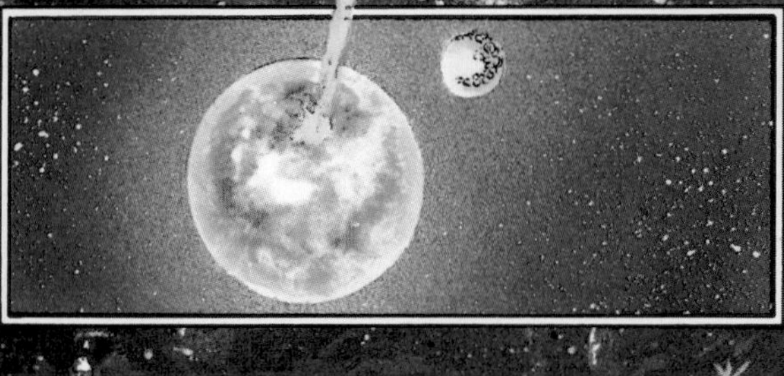

The children from Krypton, Atlantis and Gotham City were in their late teens when another child was born not from flesh and blood and bone but from mud and clay and given life by the Gods of Olympus. Born on Paradise Island, an inaccessible land in the middle of the Atlantic, the child Diana would grow up to become the greatest heroine of all time. Krypton, Gotham City and Paradise Island—from those very different locations emerged a triumvirate of Power and justice.

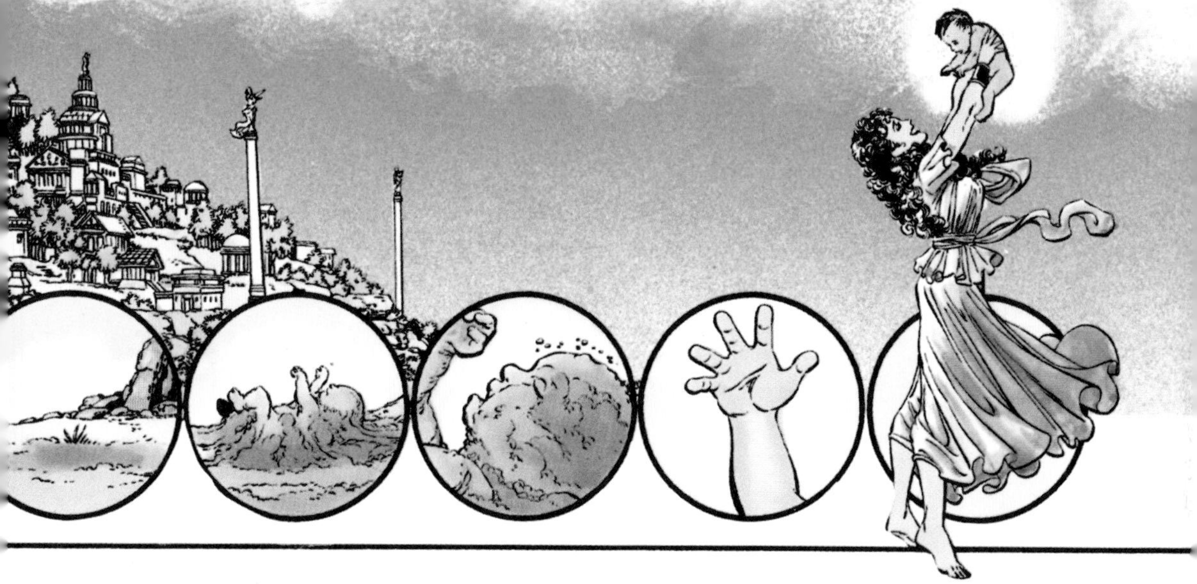

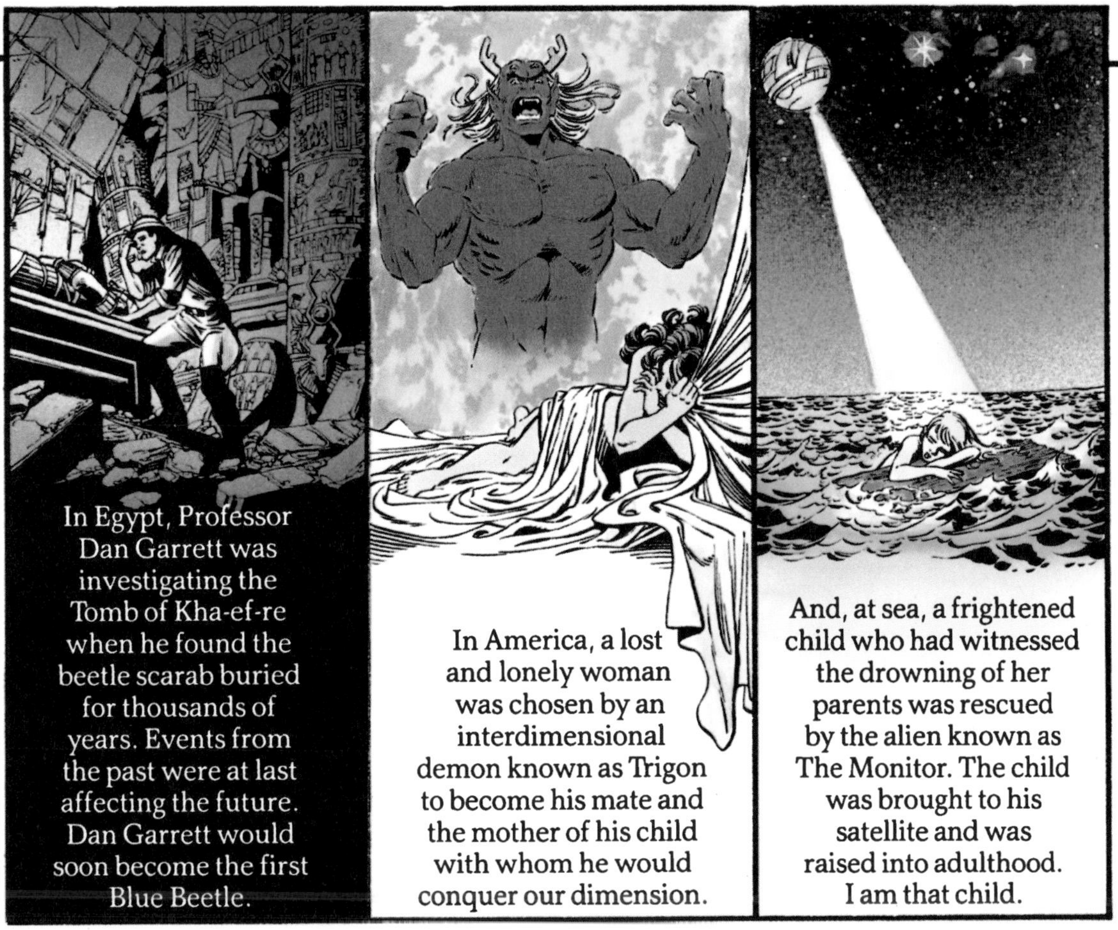
In Egypt, Professor Dan Garrett was investigating the Tomb of Kha-ef-re when he found the beetle scarab buried for thousands of years. Events from the past were at last affecting the future. Dan Garrett would soon become the first Blue Beetle.
In America, a lost and lonely woman was chosen by an interdimensional demon known as Trigon to become his mate and the mother of his child with whom he would conquer our dimension.
And, at sea, a frightened child who had witnessed the drowning of her parents was rescued by the alien known as The Monitor. The child was brought to his satellite and was raised into adulthood. I am that child.

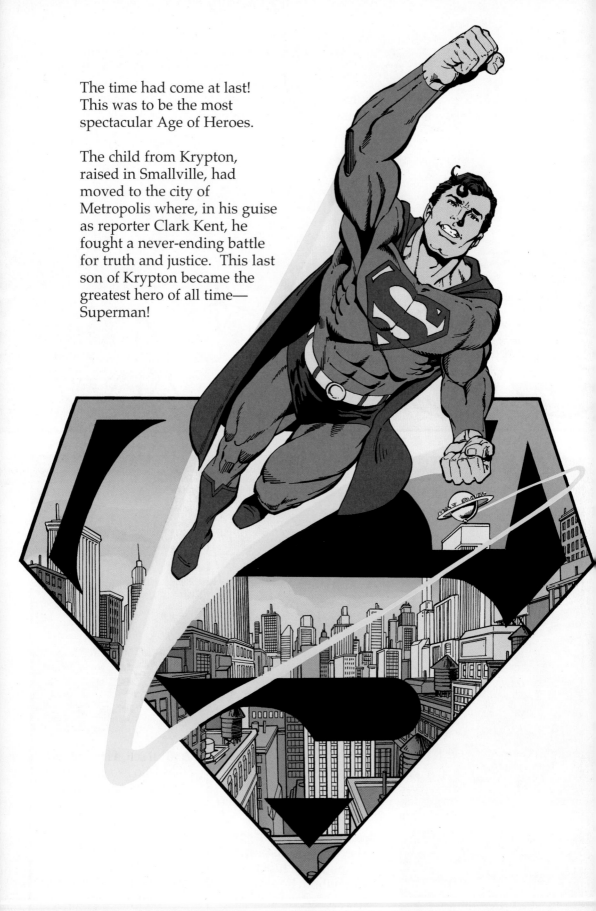

The time had come at last! This was to be the most spectacular Age of Heroes.

The child from Krypton, raised in Smallville, had moved to the city of Metropolis where, in his guise as reporter Clark Kent, he fought a never-ending battle for truth and justice. This last son of Krypton became the greatest hero of all time— Superman!

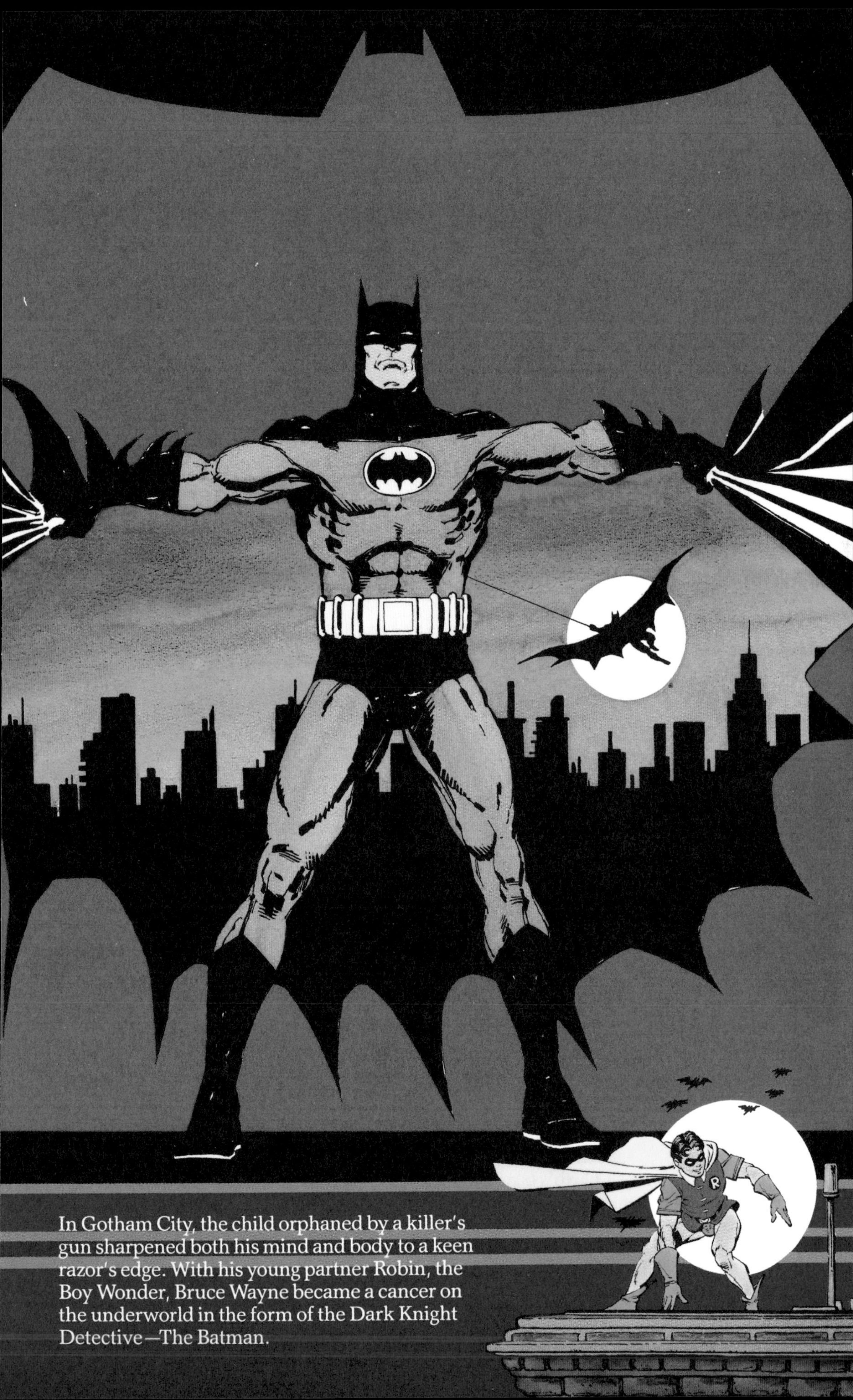
In Gotham City, the child orphaned by a killer's gun sharpened both his mind and body to a keen razor's edge. With his young partner Robin, the Boy Wonder, Bruce Wayne became a cancer on the underworld in the form of the Dark Knight Detective—The Batman.

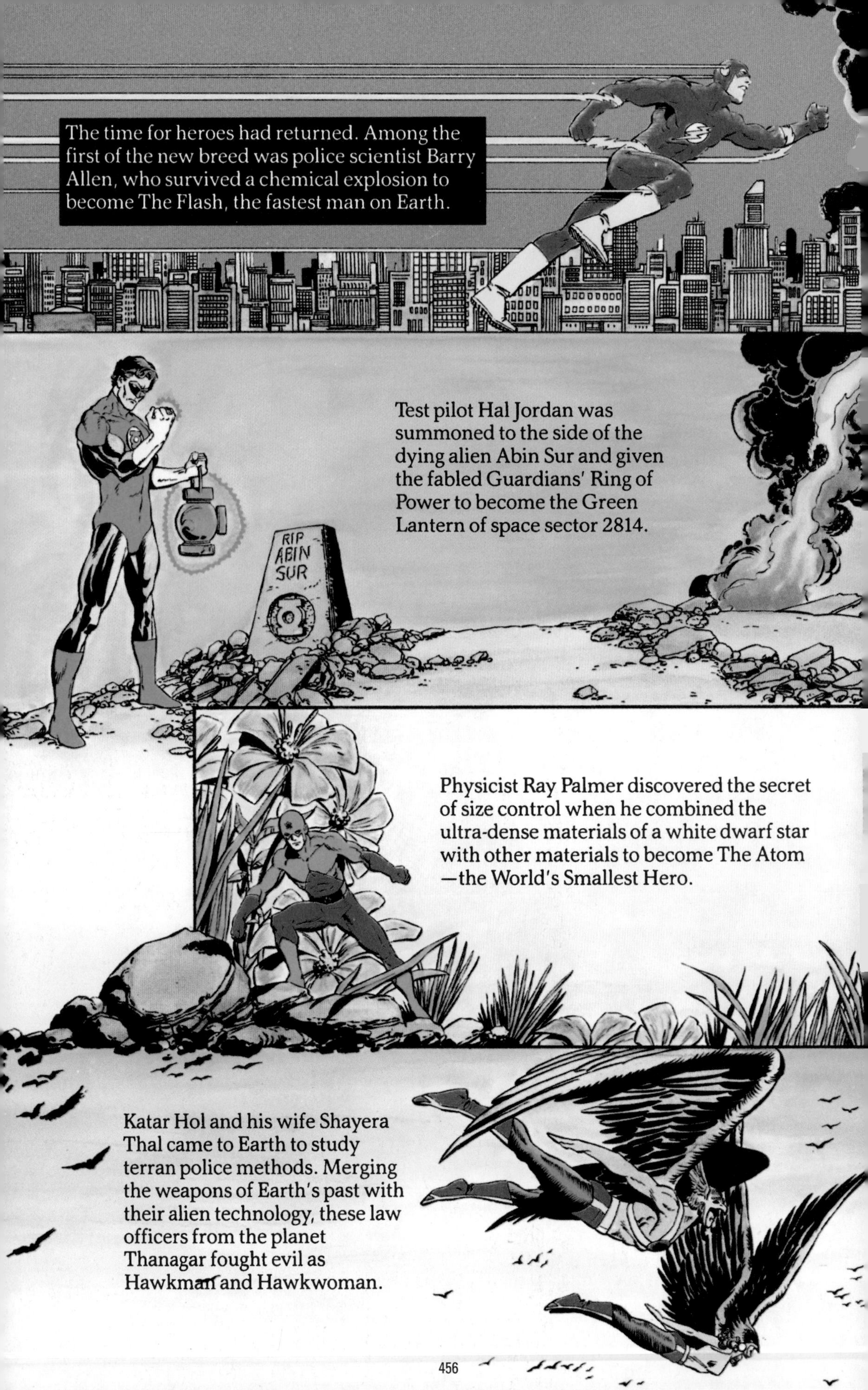
The time for heroes had returned. Among the first of the new breed was police scientist Barry Allen, who survived a chemical explosion to become The Flash, the fastest man on Earth.
Test pilot Hal Jordan was summoned to the side of the dying alien Abin Sur and given the fabled Guardians' Ring of Power to become the Green Lantern of space sector 2814.
RIP ABIN SUR
Physicist Ray Palmer discovered the secret of size control when he combined the ultra-dense materials of a white dwarf star with other materials to become The Atom —the World's Smallest Hero.
Katar Hol and his wife Shayera Thal came to Earth to study terran police methods. Merging the weapons of Earth's past with their alien technology, these law officers from the planet Thanagar fought evil as Hawkman and Hawkwoman.

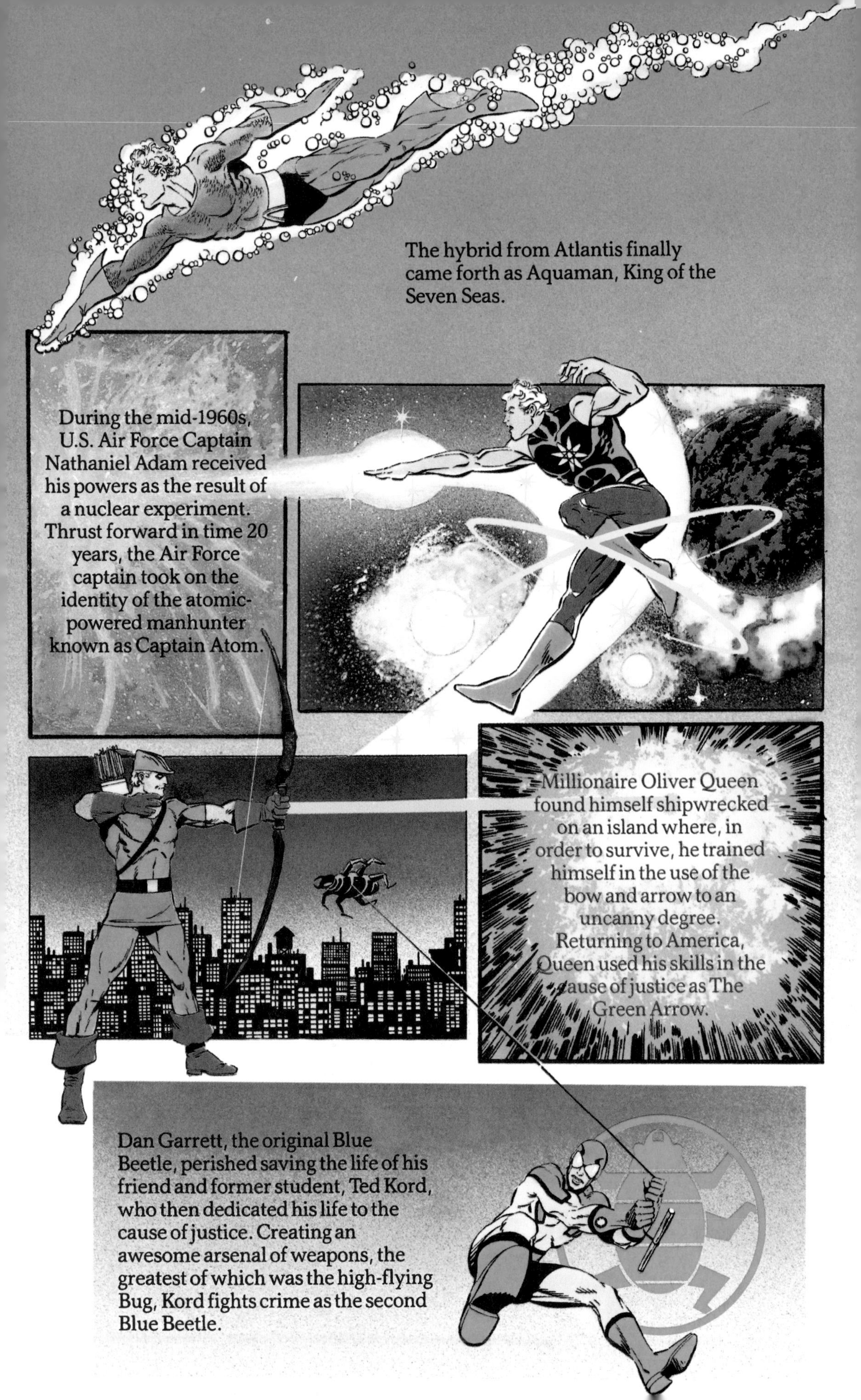
The hybrid from Atlantis finally came forth as Aquaman, King of the Seven Seas.
During the mid-1960s, U.S. Air Force Captain Nathaniel Adam received his powers as the result of a nuclear experiment. Thrust forward in time 20 years, the Air Force captain took on the identity of the atomic-powered manhunter known as Captain Atom.
Millionaire Oliver Queen found himself shipwrecked on an island where, in order to survive, he trained himself in the use of the bow and arrow to an uncanny degree. Returning to America, Queen used his skills in the cause of justice as The Green Arrow.
Dan Garrett, the original Blue Beetle, perished saving the life of his friend and former student, Ted Kord, who then dedicated his life to the cause of justice. Creating an awesome arsenal of weapons, the greatest of which was the high-flying Bug, Kord fights crime as the second Blue Beetle.

For ten billion years the Guardians of the Universe have preserved the heroic tradition, ever recruiting new warriors to fight in the cause of justice.

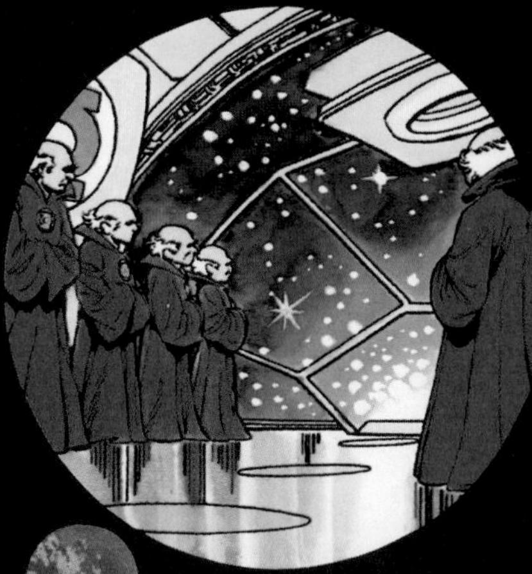

Their vigilance in the name of universal peace never weakens. The Green Lantern Corps continues to battle evil wherever it is found.

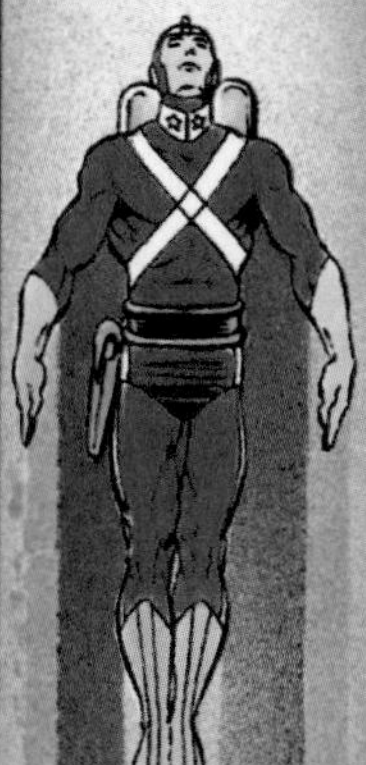

But not even the Guardians can erase all injustice. In the Vegan star system the tyrannical Citadel Empire brutally conquers world after world.

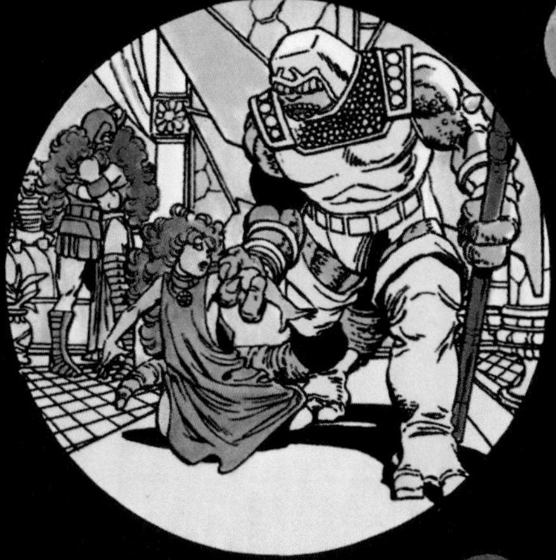

The planet Tamaran is conquered and their Princess is enslaved. But young Koriand'r would one day return to Tamaran to help destroy the Citadel despots.

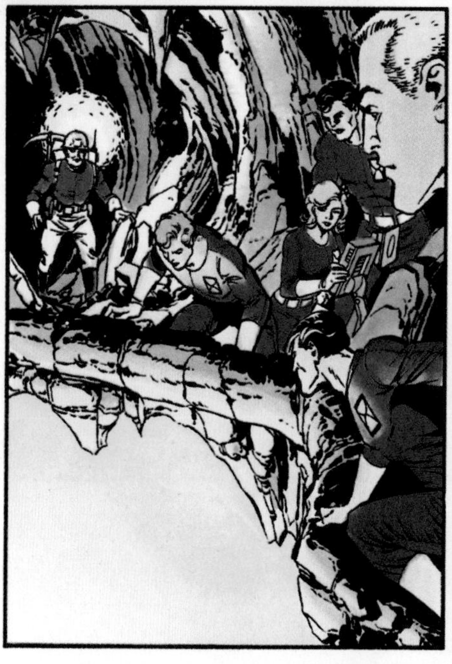

On Earth, the heroic tradition continues. Scientists such as geologist Cave Carson left the safety of the laboratory to help mankind in times of danger, joining courageous adventurers such as The Challengers of the Unknown.

Archaeologist Adam Strange was transported accidentally more than 25 trillion miles from Earth to the planet Rann. There he became their greatest champion, saving their troubled planet from peril after peril.

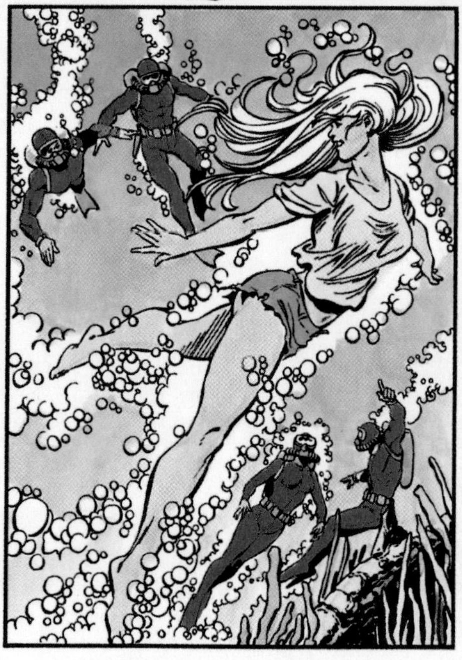

Heroes are found everywhere, from deep space to the depths of the seven seas...from ordinary divers such as the famed Sea Devils, to mysterious beauties such as the enigmatic Dolphin.

This was now the Silver Age of heroes, and some of the greatest who ever lived banded together to fight evil on Earth and throughout the stars. Inspired by the wartime exploits of the famed All-Stars and the Justice Society, these young heroes took the name the Justice League of America.

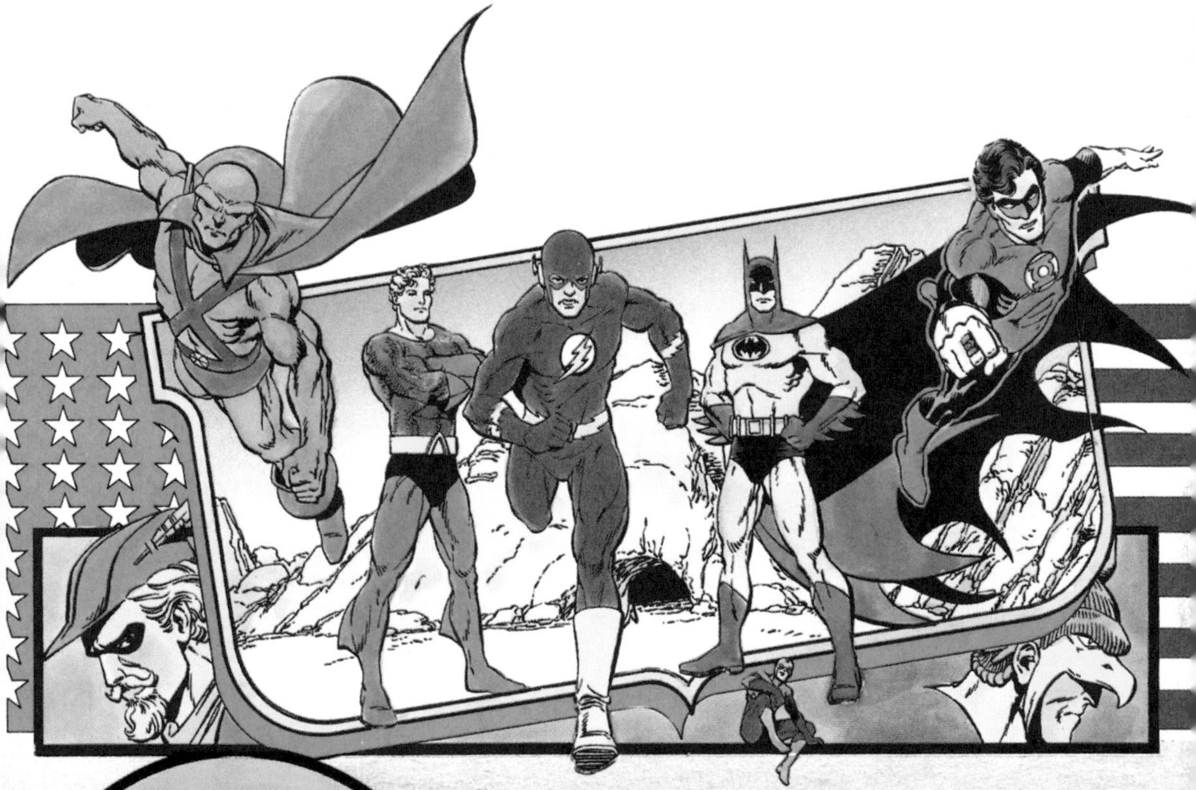

While the adult heroes formed what was to become the greatest of all super-teams, their young partners banded together as well, forming the first version of The Teen Titans.

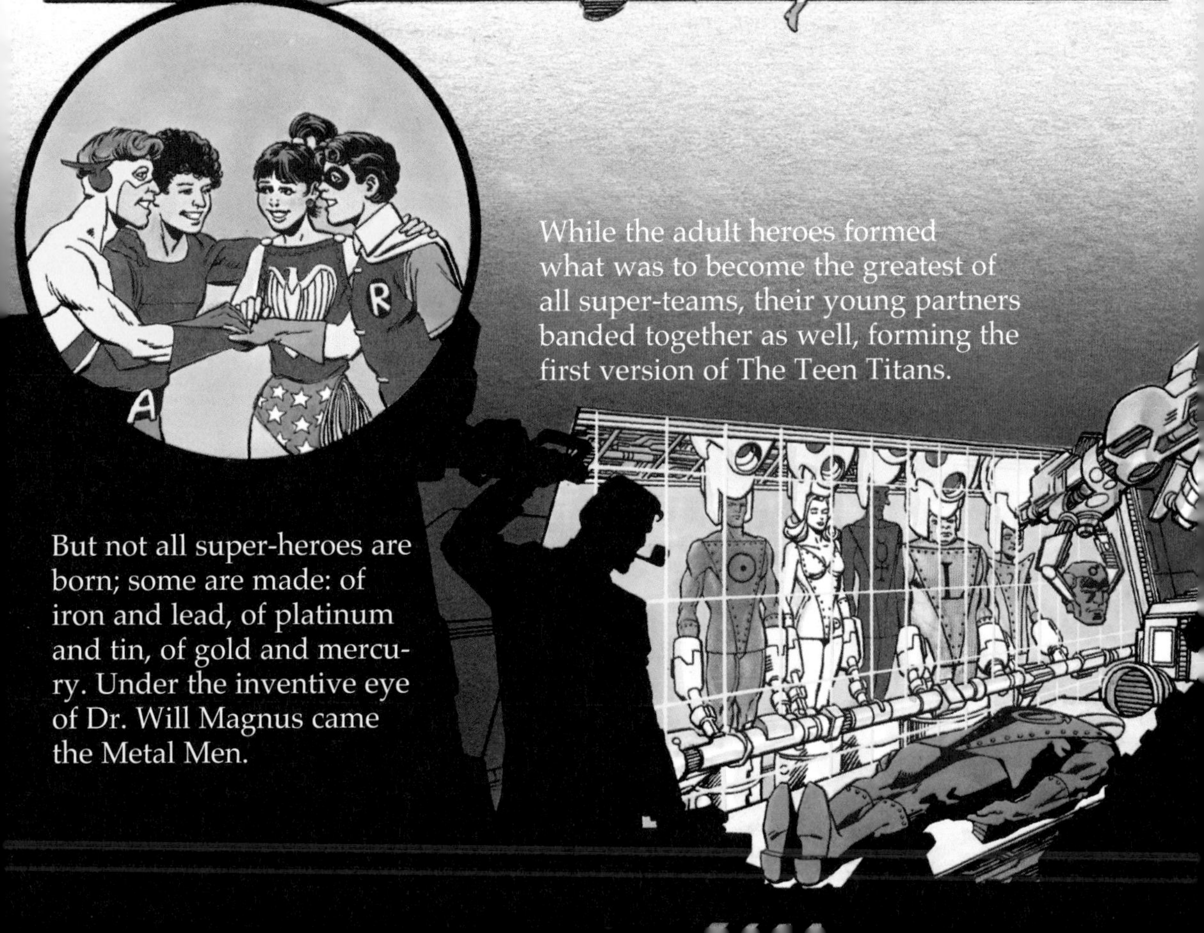

But not all super-heroes are born; some are made: of iron and lead, of platinum and tin, of gold and mercury. Under the inventive eye of Dr. Will Magnus came the Metal Men.

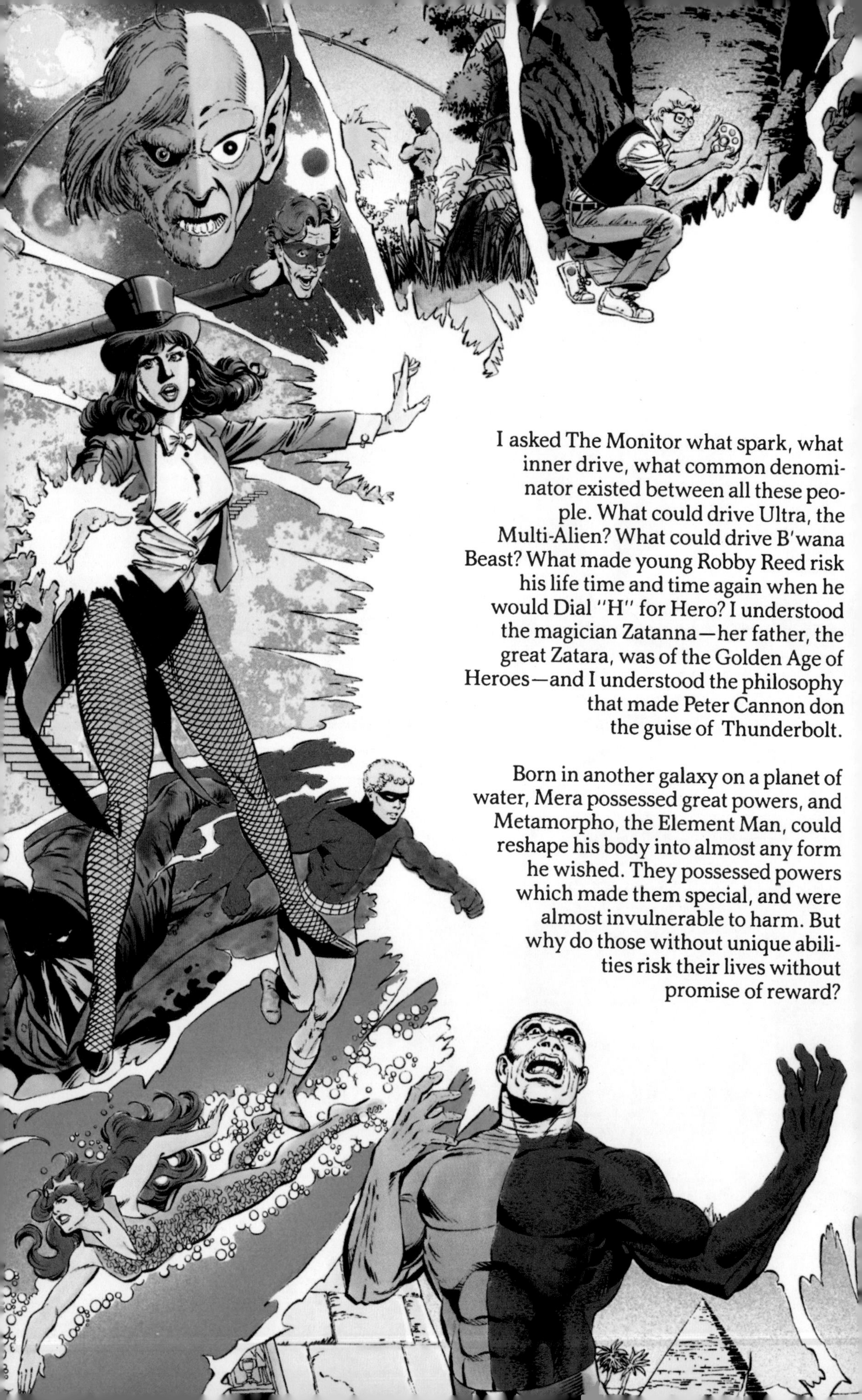

I asked The Monitor what spark, what inner drive, what common denominator existed between all these people. What could drive Ultra, the Multi-Alien? What could drive B'wana Beast? What made young Robby Reed risk his life time and time again when he would Dial "H" for Hero? I understood the magician Zatanna—her father, the great Zatara, was of the Golden Age of Heroes—and I understood the philosophy that made Peter Cannon don the guise of Thunderbolt.

Born in another galaxy on a planet of water, Mera possessed great powers, and Metamorpho, the Element Man, could reshape his body into almost any form he wished. They possessed powers which made them special, and were almost invulnerable to harm. But why do those without unique abilities risk their lives without promise of reward?

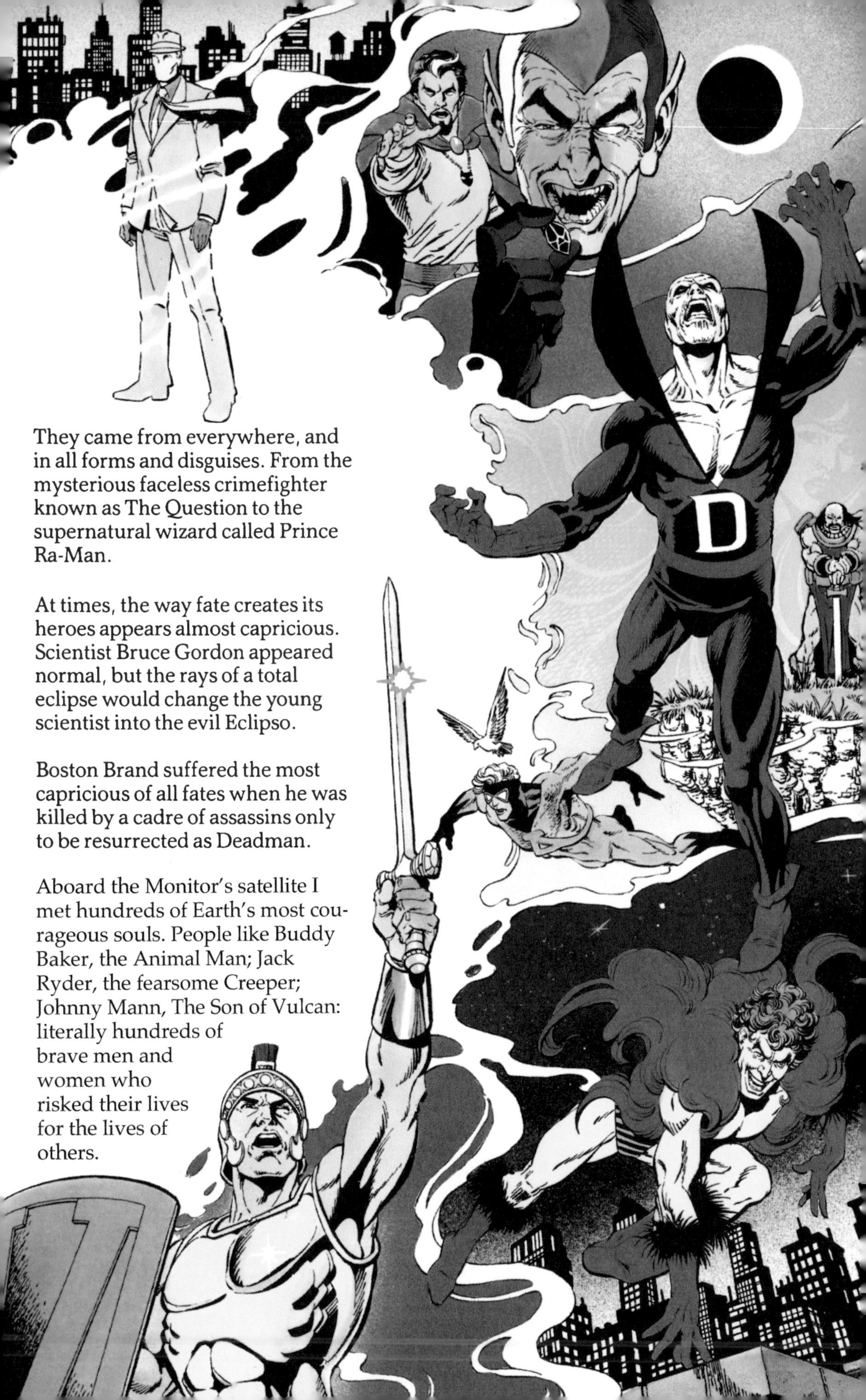

They came from everywhere, and in all forms and disguises. From the mysterious faceless crimefighter known as The Question to the supernatural wizard called Prince Ra-Man.

At times, the way fate creates its heroes appears almost capricious. Scientist Bruce Gordon appeared normal, but the rays of a total eclipse would change the young scientist into the evil Eclipso.

Boston Brand suffered the most capricious of all fates when he was killed by a cadre of assassins only to be resurrected as Deadman.

Aboard the Monitor's satellite I met hundreds of Earth's most courageous souls. People like Buddy Baker, the Animal Man; Jack Ryder, the fearsome Creeper; Johnny Mann, The Son of Vulcan: literally hundreds of brave men and women who risked their lives for the lives of others.

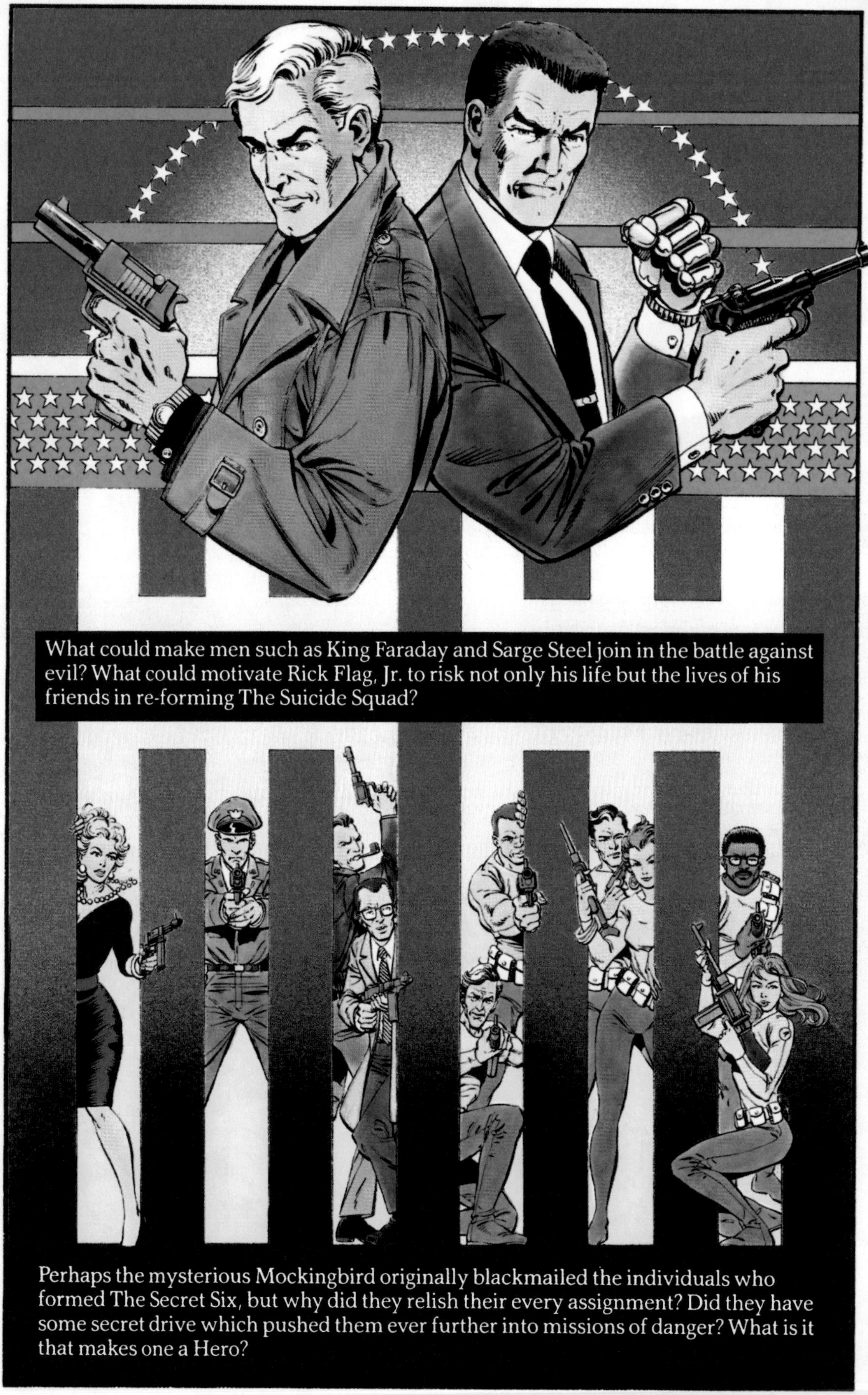
What could make men such as King Faraday and Sarge Steel join in the battle against evil? What could motivate Rick Flag, Jr. to risk not only his life but the lives of his friends in re-forming The Suicide Squad?
Perhaps the mysterious Mockingbird originally blackmailed the individuals who formed The Secret Six, but why did they relish their every assignment? Did they have some secret drive which pushed them ever further into missions of danger? What is it that makes one a Hero?

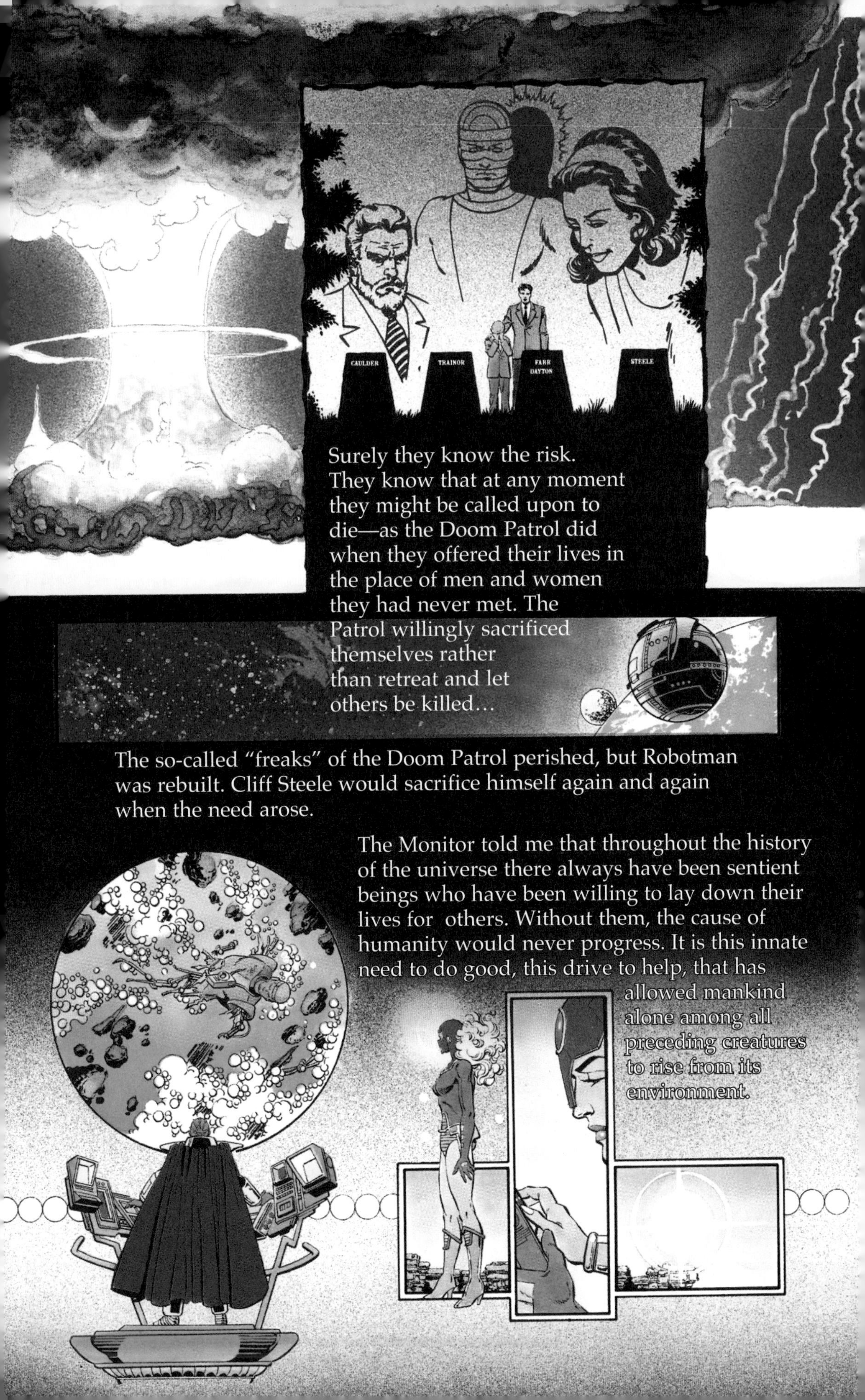
CAULDER
TRAINOR
FARR DAYTON
STEELE
Surely they know the risk. They know that at any moment they might be called upon to die—as the Doom Patrol did when they offered their lives in the place of men and women they had never met. The Patrol willingly sacrificed themselves rather than retreat and let others be killed…
The so-called "freaks" of the Doom Patrol perished, but Robotman was rebuilt. Cliff Steele would sacrifice himself again and again when the need arose.
The Monitor told me that throughout the history of the universe there always have been sentient beings who have been willing to lay down their lives for others. Without them, the cause of humanity would never progress. It is this innate need to do good, this drive to help, that has allowed mankind alone among all preceding creatures to rise from its environment.

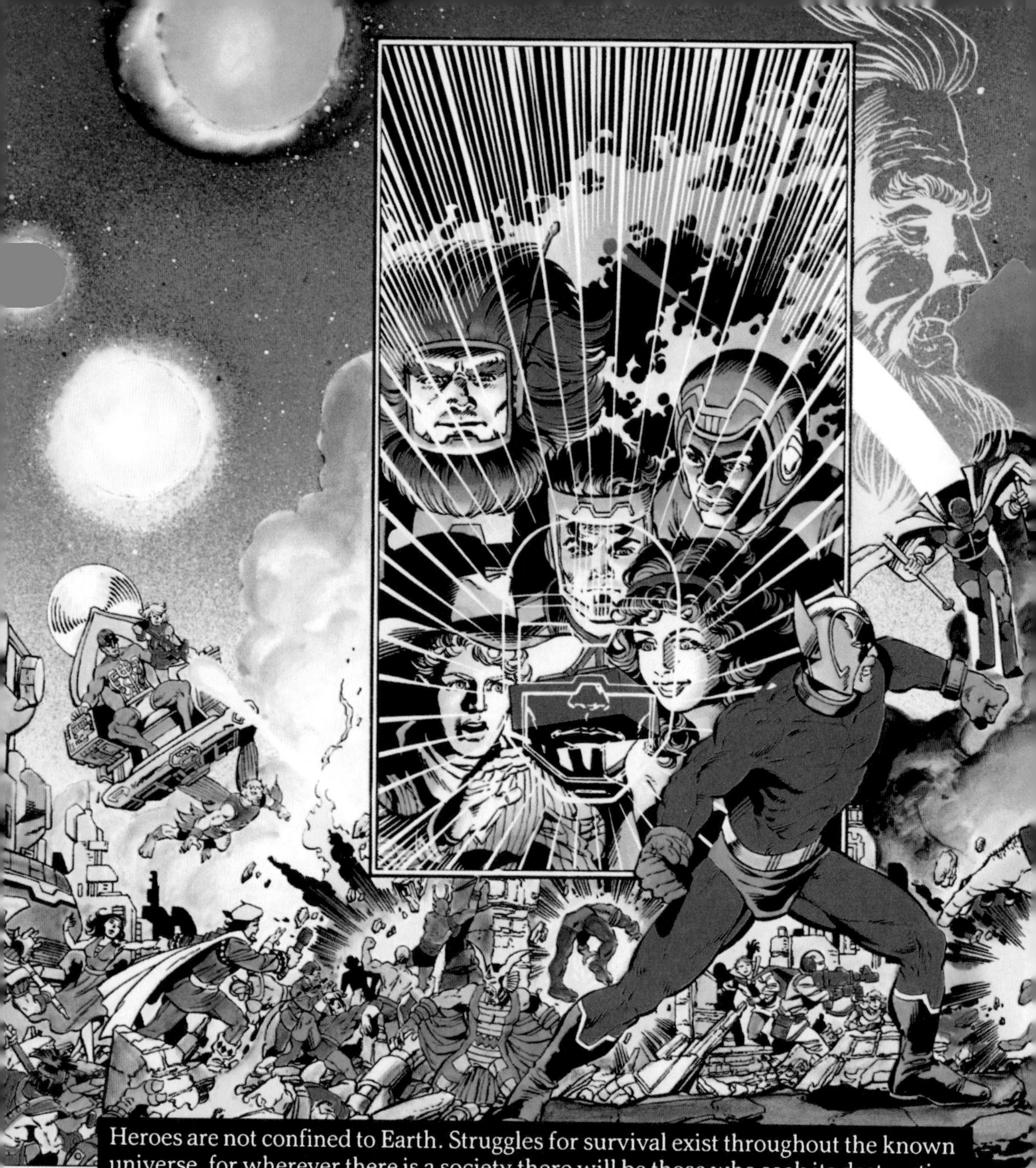

Heroes are not confined to Earth. Struggles for survival exist throughout the known universe, for wherever there is a society there will be those who seek its destruction.

The godlike beings of New Genesis—a world born in peace—faced their challenge from the hordes of dark Apokolips: a twisted mockery of a world shaped by the greatest evil the universe has ever known: Darkseid the Destroyer. His mad lust called for the total destruction of his enemies, and he was, at long last, mere days from victory.

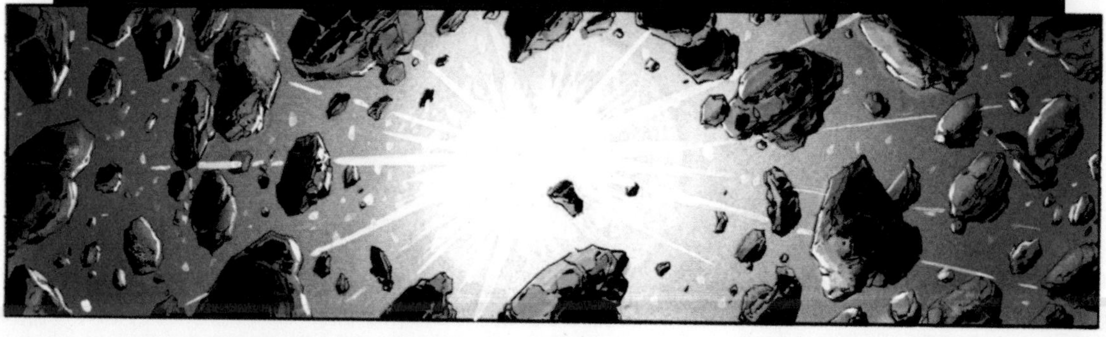

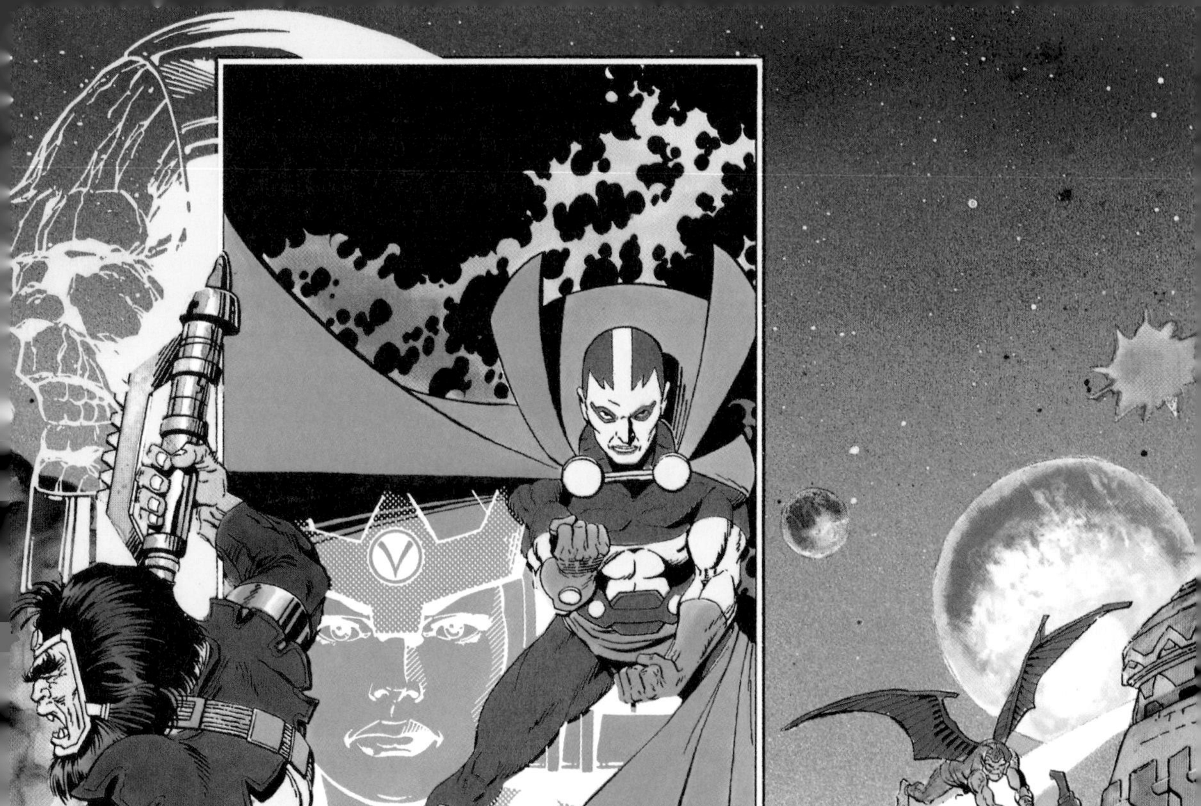

Darkseid's Hunger Dogs swarmed across New Genesis, leveling its jeweled beauty and replacing it with the scarred trenches of war. A great battle raged and New Genesis was destroyed, but its heroes and their heroic spirit survived in the great sprawling citadel called Supertown.

From the New Gods and The Forever People to Mister Miracle and the Black Racer, the survivors of New Genesis banded together and took what was left of their race to a peaceful sector of the universe.

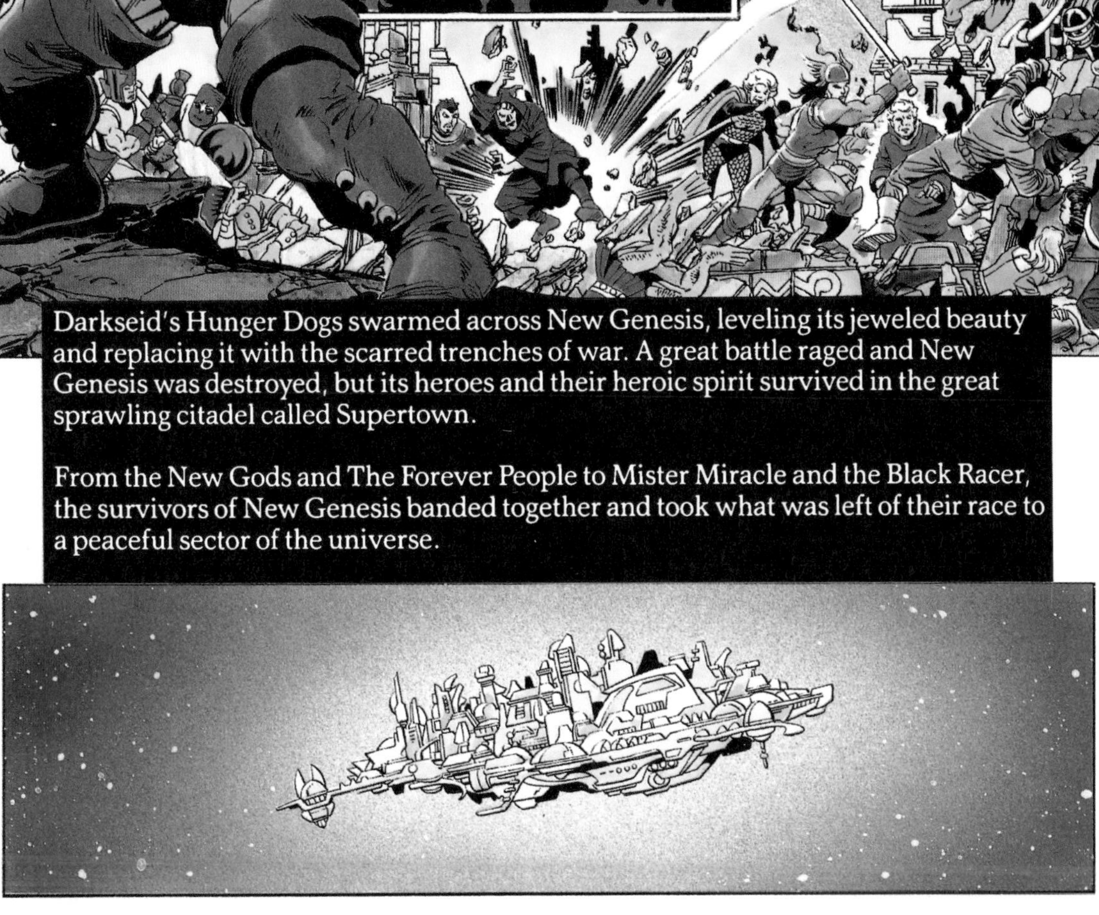

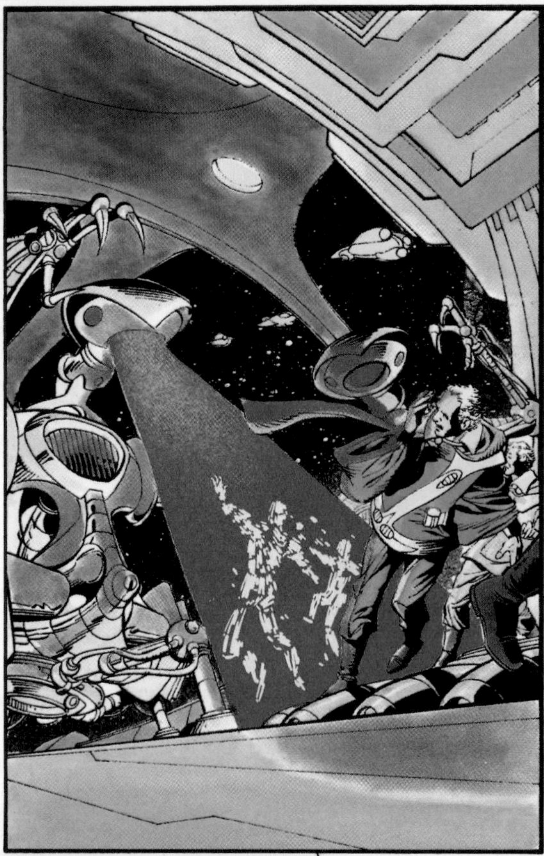

The robot rebellion on Colu brought about the first of the robot tyrants. Named Brainiac, his orders were to travel the galaxy to rid each world of its human inhabitants.

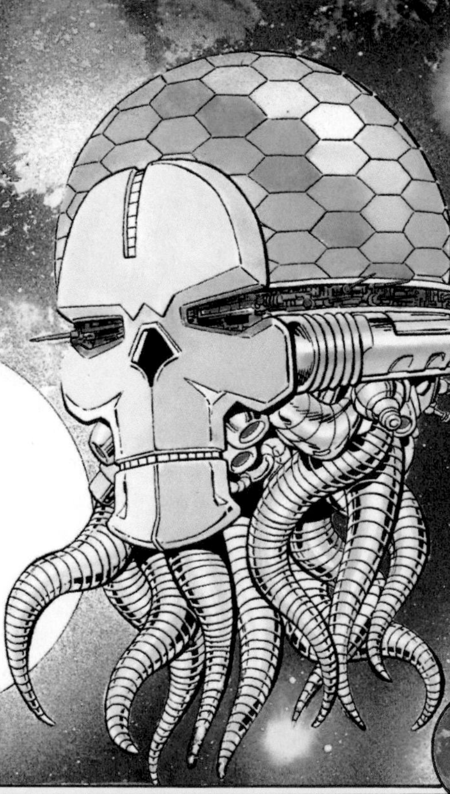

Brainiac was later destroyed by the Omega Men when it attacked the Vegan star system.

A second robotic being, coincidentally named Brainiac, would be created two years after the first was destroyed. This Brainiac, unlike its predecessor, had its origins as much in the laboratories of Earth as in the stars.

Talok VIII, as Earth, was a nexus for heroes. Mallor, the first of these heroes, saved Talok from destruction and gained great powers. His heroic lineage extends into the thirtieth century and beyond.

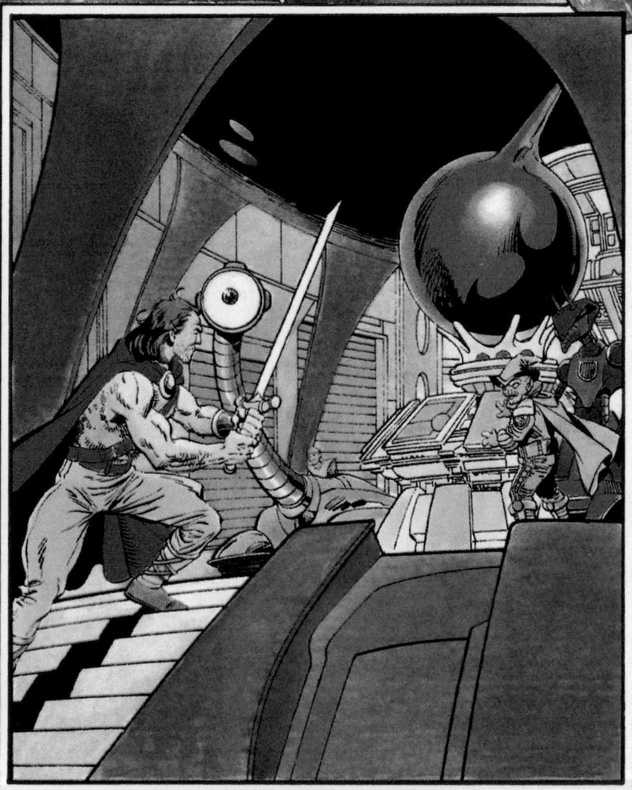

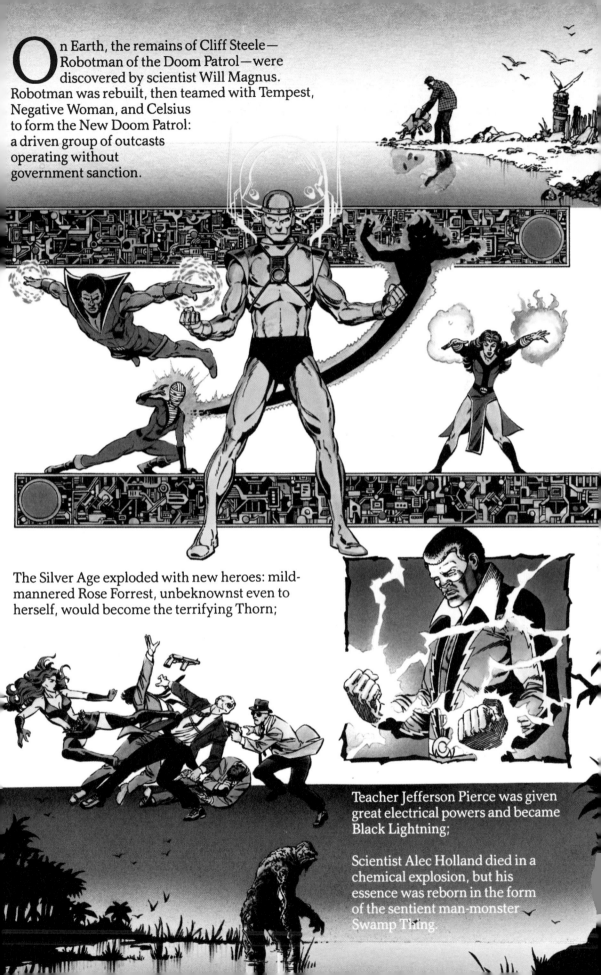

On Earth, the remains of Cliff Steele—Robotman of the Doom Patrol—were discovered by scientist Will Magnus. Robotman was rebuilt, then teamed with Tempest, Negative Woman, and Celsius to form the New Doom Patrol: a driven group of outcasts operating without government sanction.

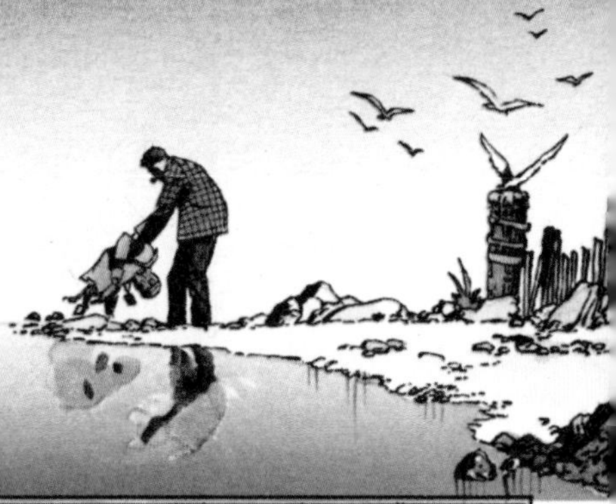

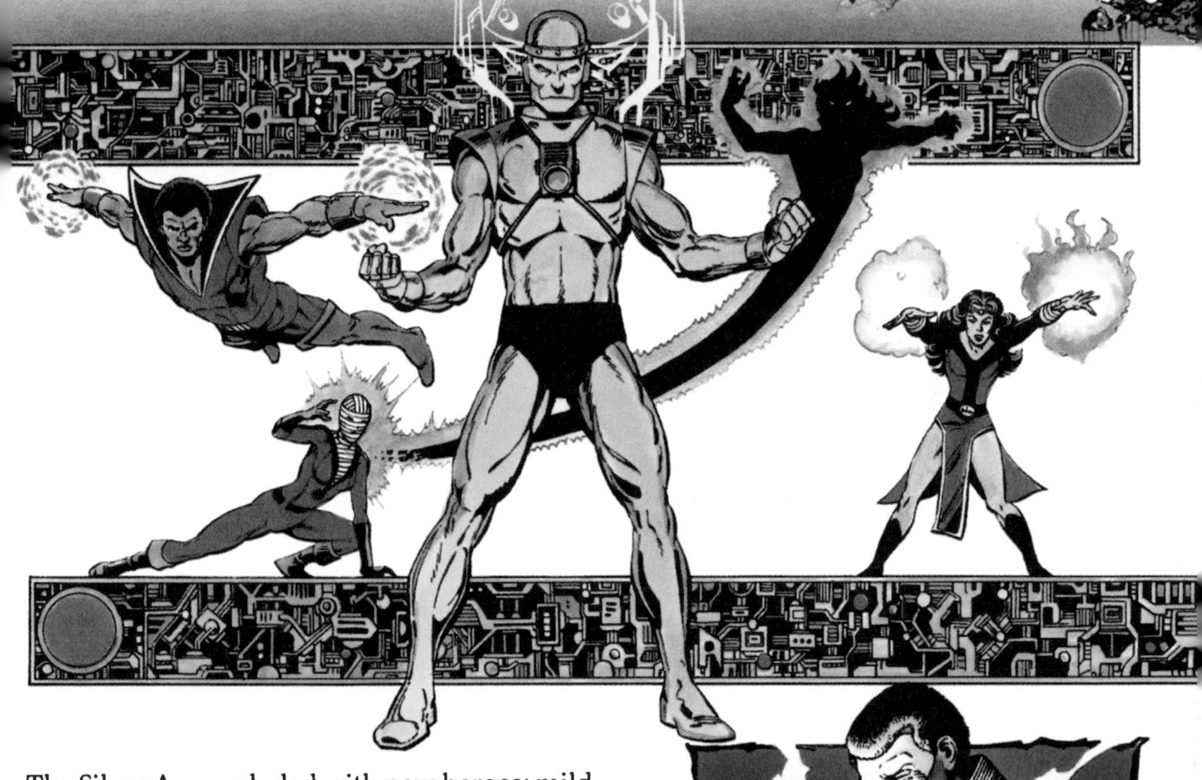

The Silver Age exploded with new heroes: mild-mannered Rose Forrest, unbeknownst even to herself, would become the terrifying Thorn;

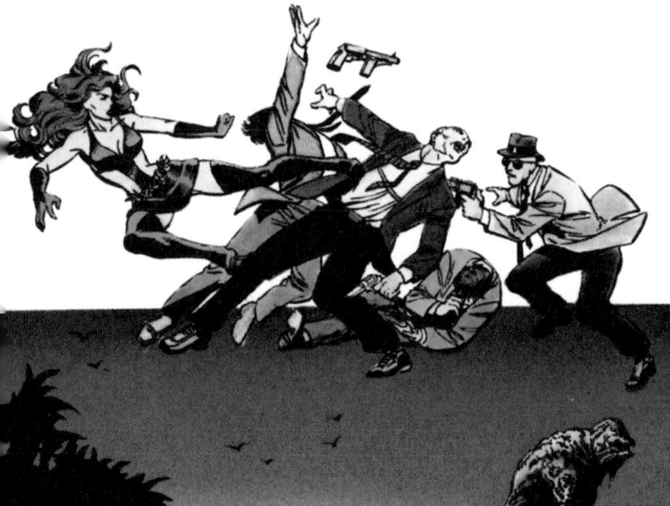

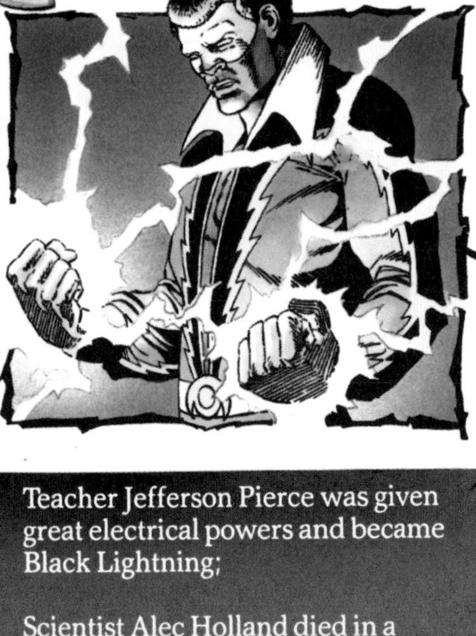

Teacher Jefferson Pierce was given great electrical powers and became Black Lightning;

Scientist Alec Holland died in a chemical explosion, but his essence was reborn in the form of the sentient man-monster Swamp Thing.

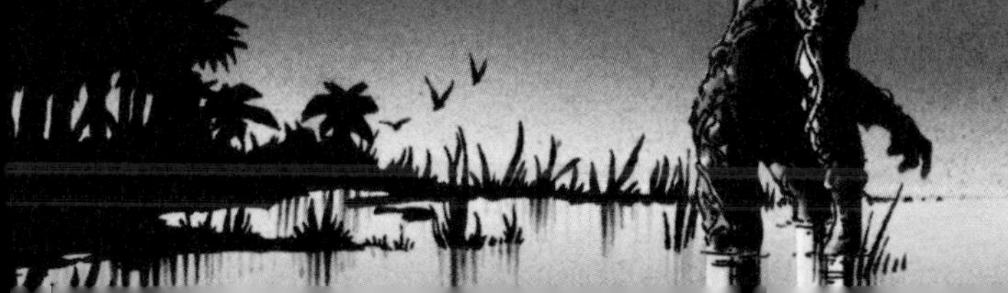

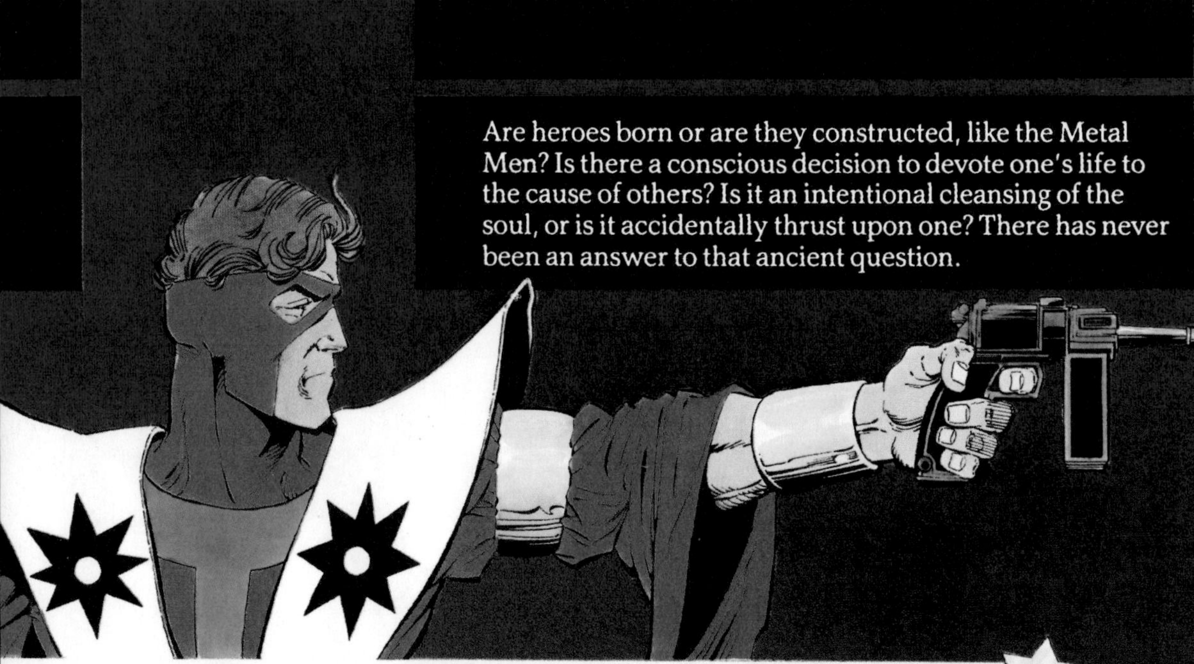

Are heroes born or are they constructed, like the Metal Men? Is there a conscious decision to devote one's life to the cause of others? Is it an intentional cleansing of the soul, or is it accidentally thrust upon one? There has never been an answer to that ancient question.

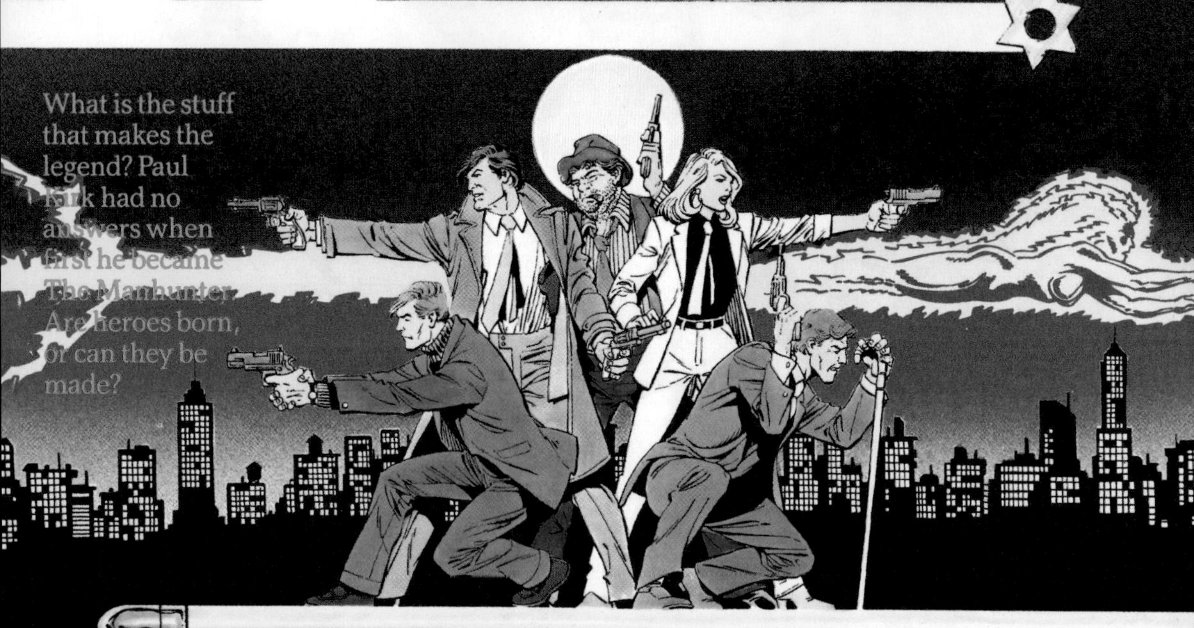

What is the stuff that makes the legend? Paul Kirk had no answers when first he became The Manhunter. Are heroes born, or can they be made?

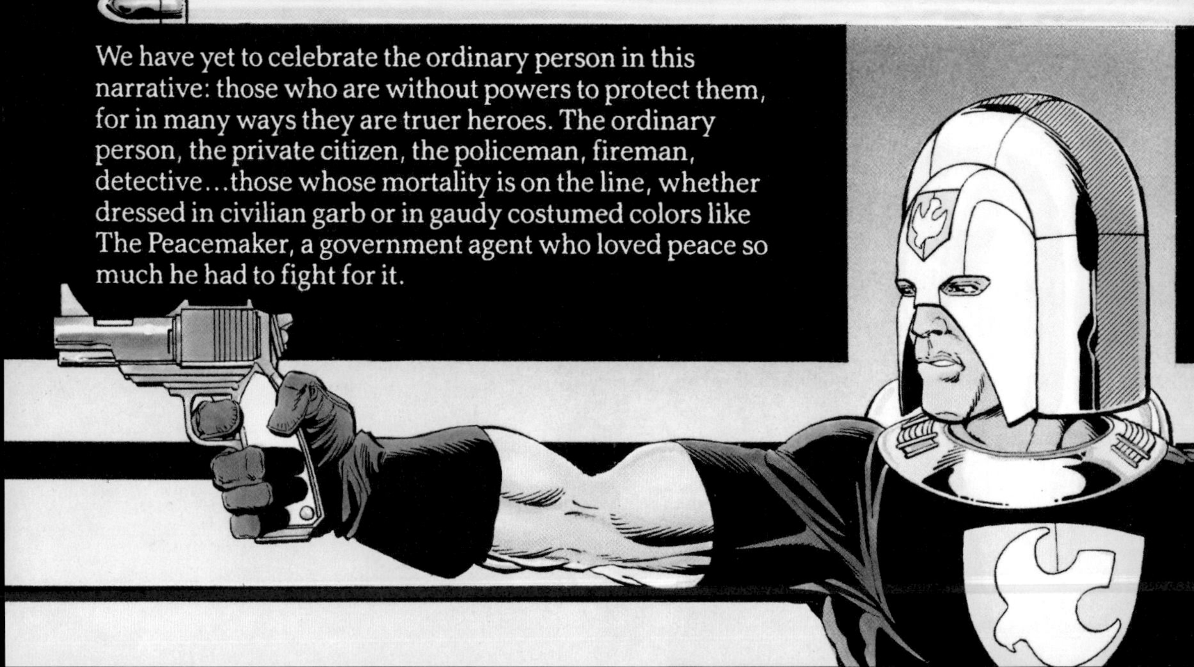

We have yet to celebrate the ordinary person in this narrative: those who are without powers to protect them, for in many ways they are truer heroes. The ordinary person, the private citizen, the policeman, fireman, detective…those whose mortality is on the line, whether dressed in civilian garb or in gaudy costumed colors like The Peacemaker, a government agent who loved peace so much he had to fight for it.

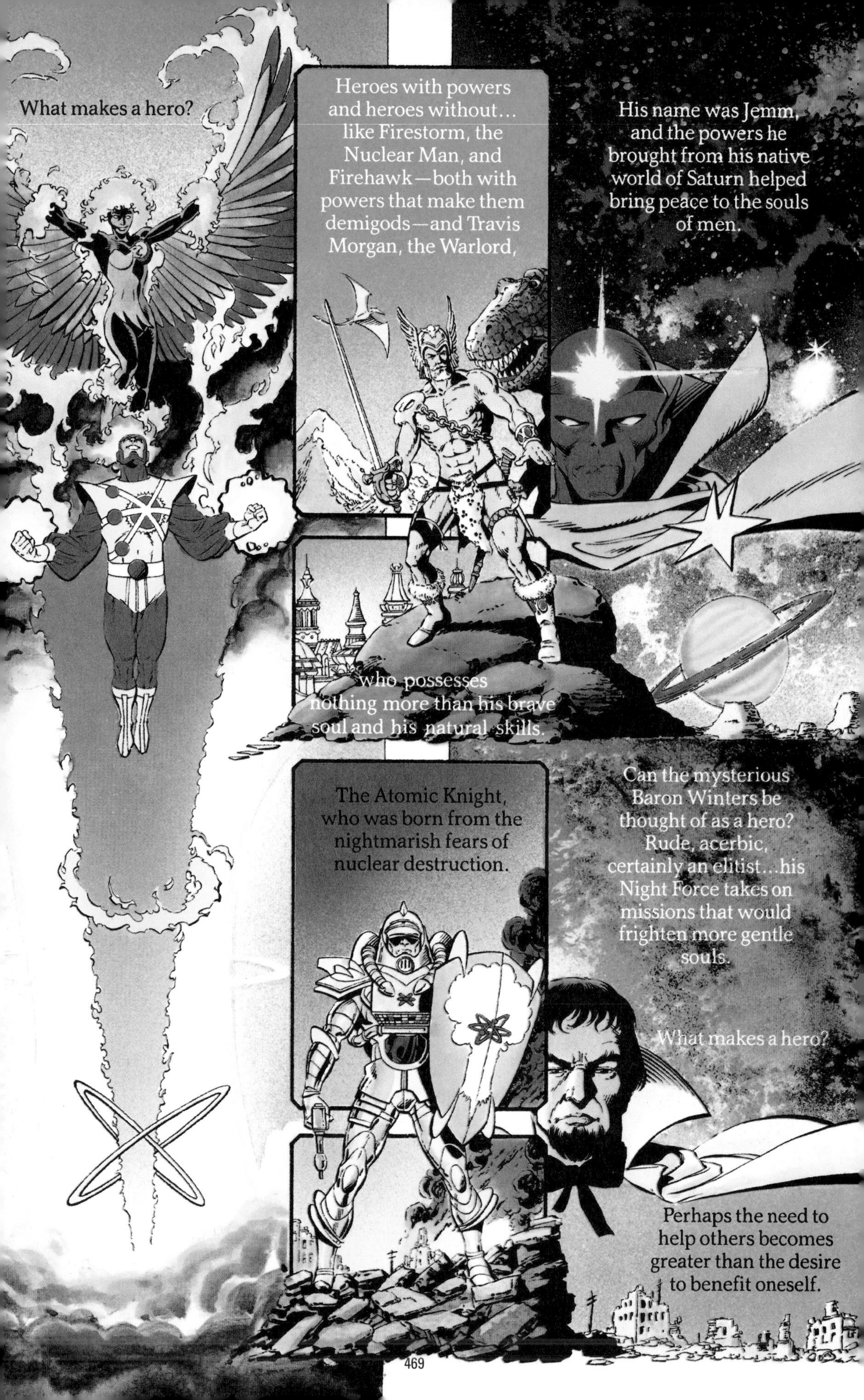

What makes a hero?
Heroes with powers and heroes without… like Firestorm, the Nuclear Man, and Firehawk—both with powers that make them demigods—and Travis Morgan, the Warlord,
who possesses nothing more than his brave soul and his natural skills.
His name was Jemm, and the powers he brought from his native world of Saturn helped bring peace to the souls of men.
The Atomic Knight, who was born from the nightmarish fears of nuclear destruction.
Can the mysterious Baron Winters be thought of as a hero? Rude, acerbic, certainly an elitist…his Night Force takes on missions that would frighten more gentle souls.
What makes a hero?
Perhaps the need to help others becomes greater than the desire to benefit oneself.

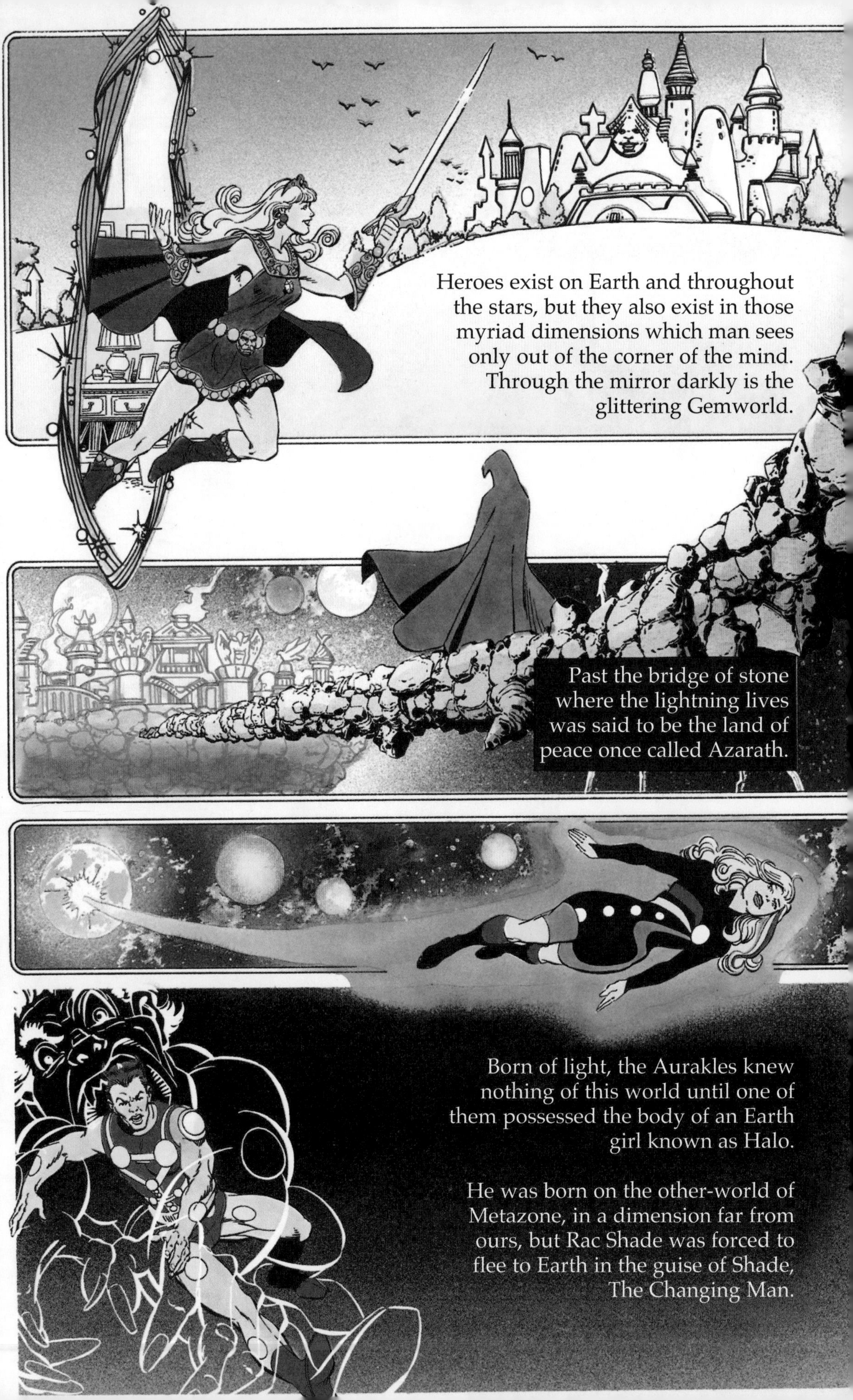
Heroes exist on Earth and throughout the stars, but they also exist in those myriad dimensions which man sees only out of the corner of the mind. Through the mirror darkly is the glittering Gemworld.
Past the bridge of stone where the lightning lives was said to be the land of peace once called Azarath.
Born of light, the Aurakles knew nothing of this world until one of them possessed the body of an Earth girl known as Halo.
He was born on the other-world of Metazone, in a dimension far from ours, but Rac Shade was forced to flee to Earth in the guise of Shade, The Changing Man.

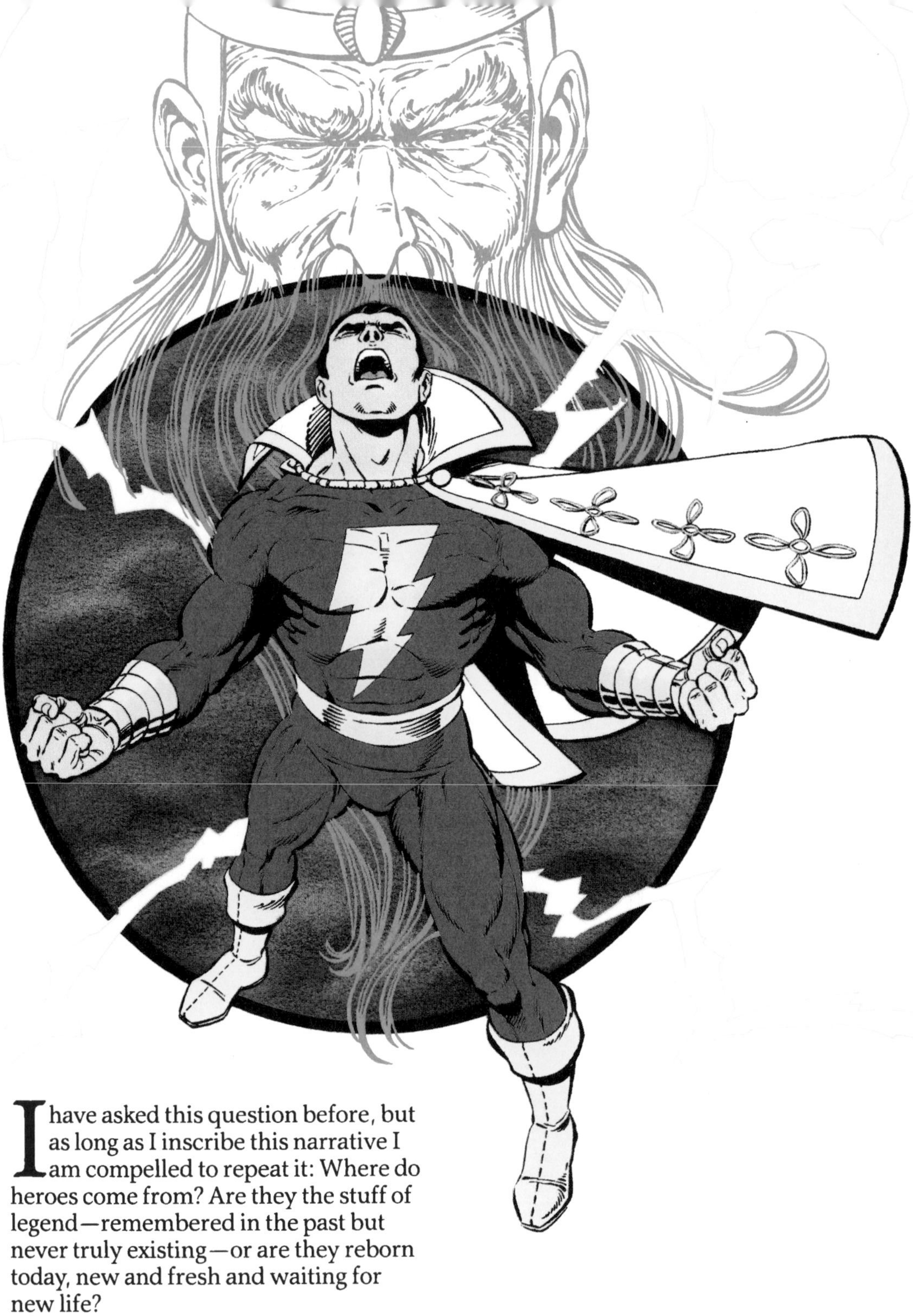

I have asked this question before, but as long as I inscribe this narrative I am compelled to repeat it: Where do heroes come from? Are they the stuff of legend—remembered in the past but never truly existing—or are they reborn today, new and fresh and waiting for new life?

A subway station in San Francisco leads a young boy to discover a legend dimly remembered by mortals. Billy Batson stands on the threshold of a new existence: with one magic word–Shazam!–he becomes the World's Mightiest Mortal: Captain Marvel.

The new hero maintains a low profile, until Darkseid the Destroyer challenges the very soul of heroism and inspires Captain Marvel to take his rightful place alongside the legends of the universe.

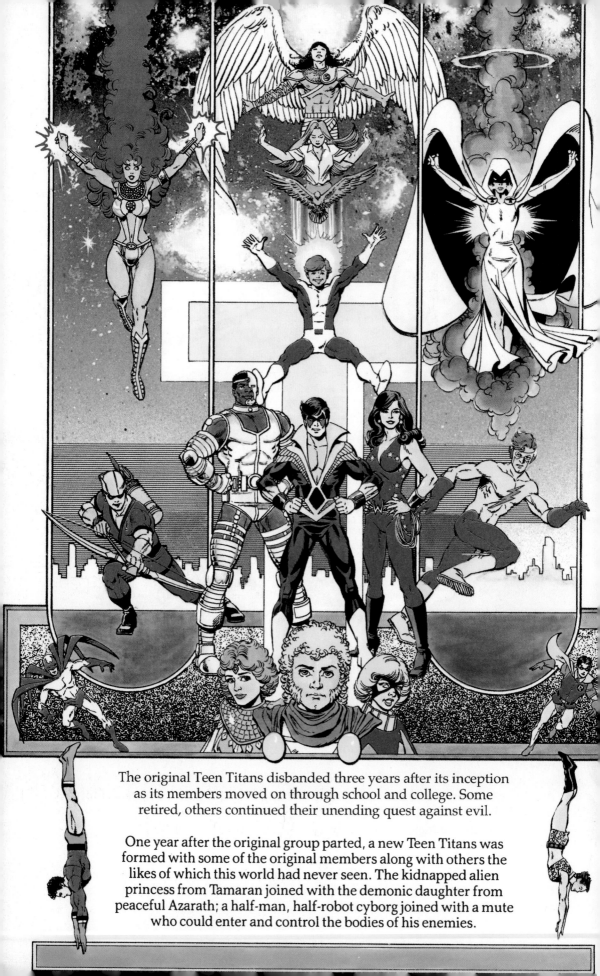

The original Teen Titans disbanded three years after its inception as its members moved on through school and college. Some retired, others continued their unending quest against evil.

One year after the original group parted, a new Teen Titans was formed with some of the original members along with others the likes of which this world had never seen. The kidnapped alien princess from Tamaran joined with the demonic daughter from peaceful Azarath; a half-man, half-robot cyborg joined with a mute who could enter and control the bodies of his enemies.

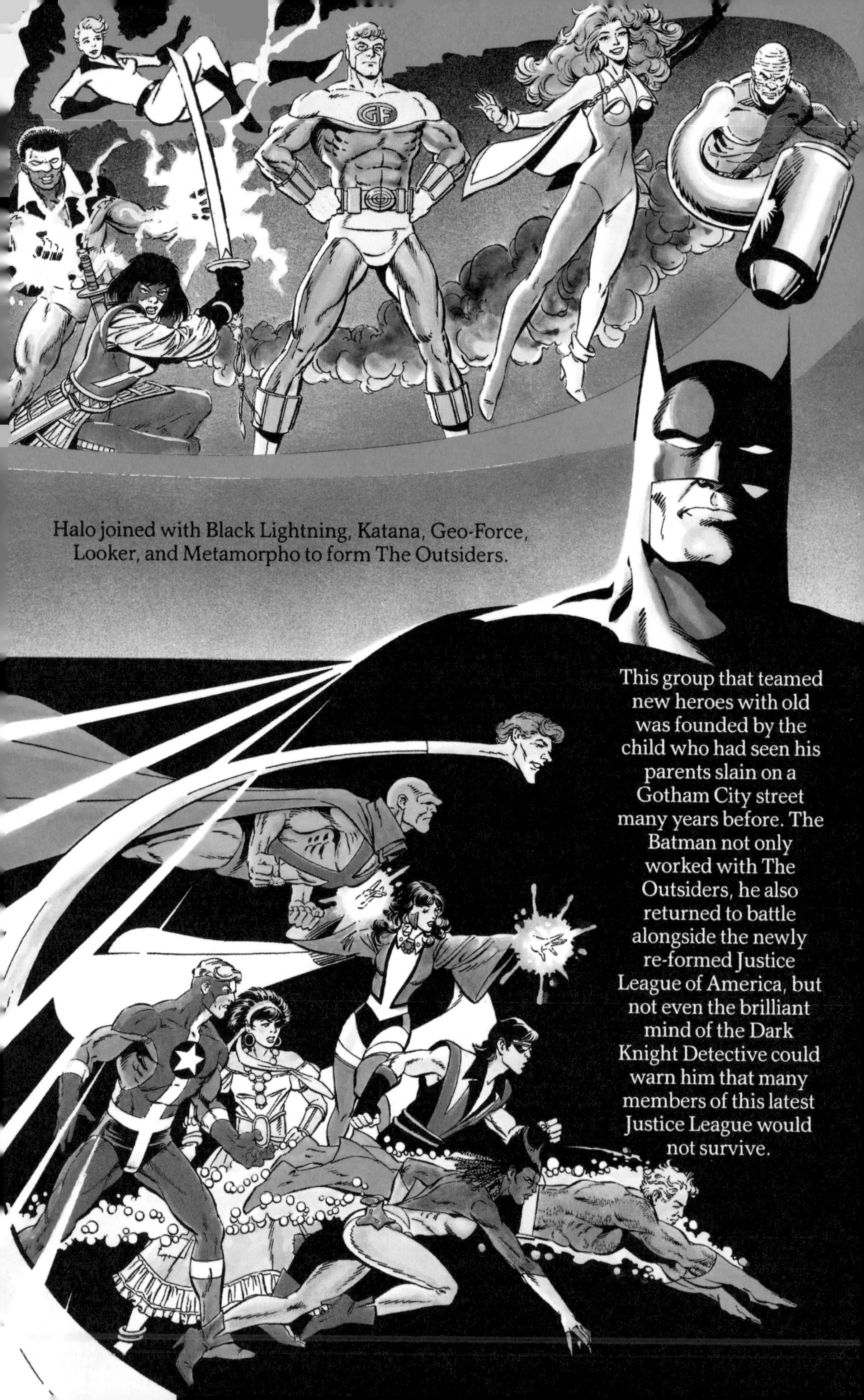
Halo joined with Black Lightning, Katana, Geo-Force, Looker, and Metamorpho to form The Outsiders.
This group that teamed new heroes with old was founded by the child who had seen his parents slain on a Gotham City street many years before. The Batman not only worked with The Outsiders, he also returned to battle alongside the newly re-formed Justice League of America, but not even the brilliant mind of the Dark Knight Detective could warn him that many members of this latest Justice League would not survive.

Thus far in this narrative, I have centered on the heroes of North America because this is where exists the greatest concentration of heroes. But there are heroes outside the United States, and many banded together to form The Global Guardians.

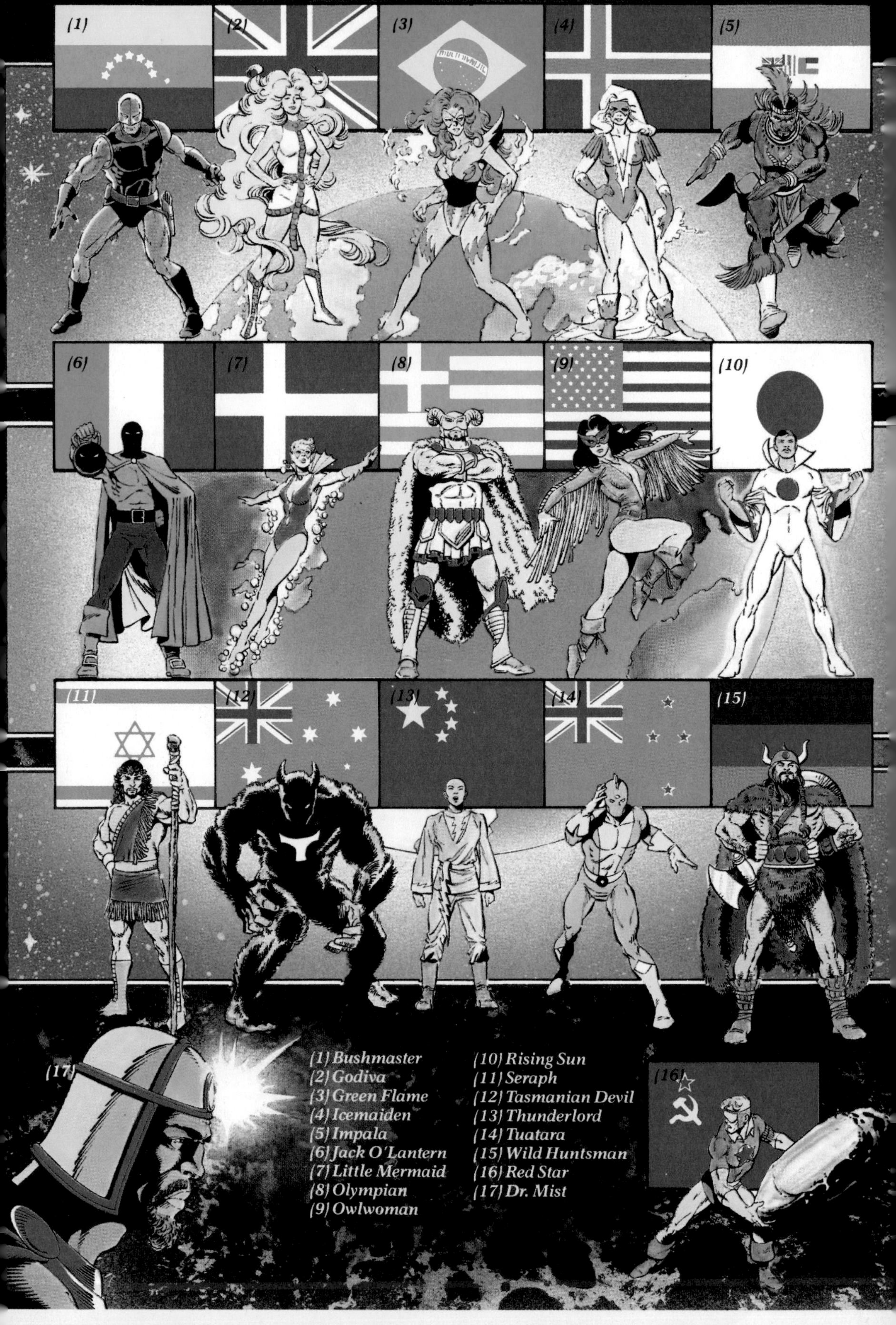

(1)
(2)
(3)
(4)
(5)
(6)
(7)
(8)
(9)
(10)
(11)
(12)
(13)
(14)
(15)
(17)
(1) Bushmaster
(2) Godiva
(3) Green Flame
(4) Icemaiden
(5) Impala
(6) Jack O'Lantern
(7) Little Mermaid
(8) Olympian
(9) Owlwoman
(10) Rising Sun
(11) Seraph
(12) Tasmanian Devil
(13) Thunderlord
(14) Tuatara
(15) Wild Huntsman
(16) Red Star
(17) Dr. Mist
(16)

Still other heroes abound—

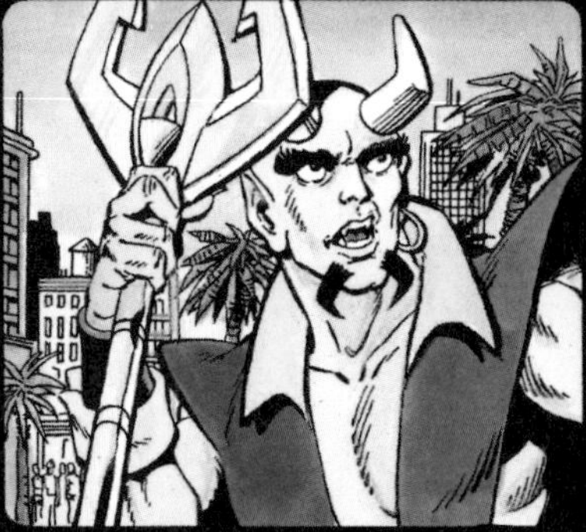

The Blue Devil...
...Power Girl...

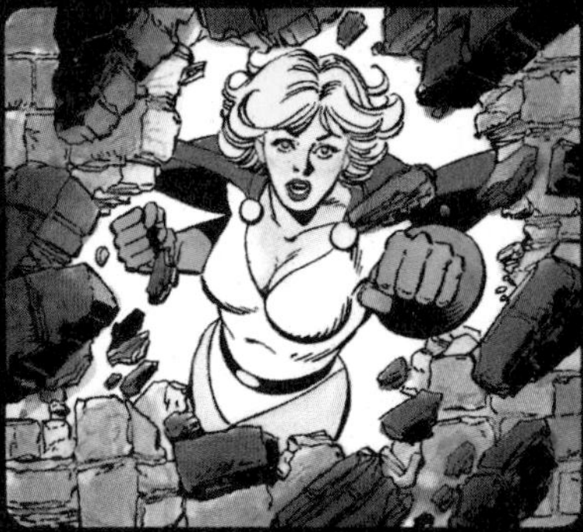

...the mysterious
Black Orchid...

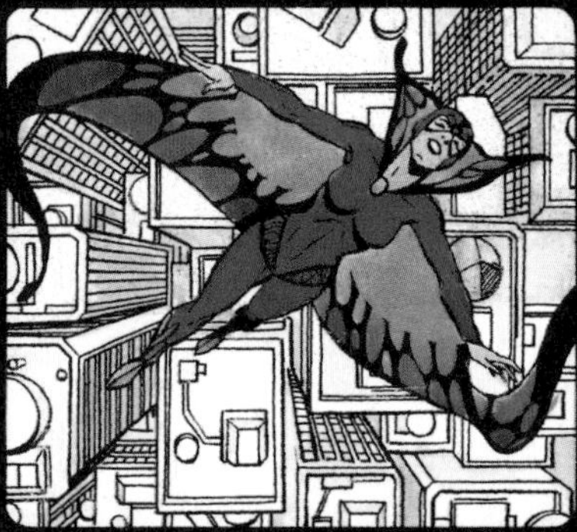

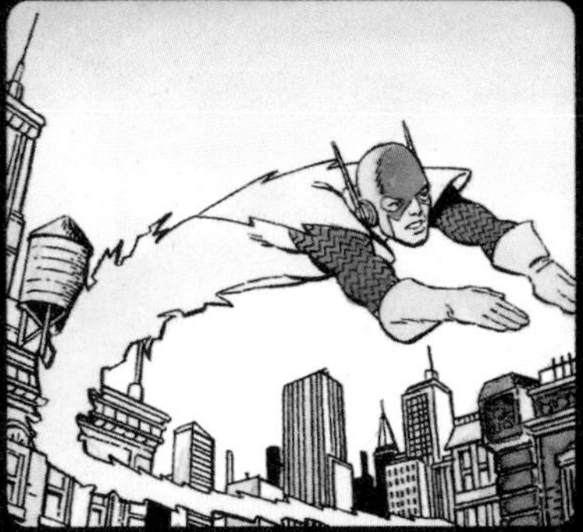

...Air Wave...
...The Vigilante...

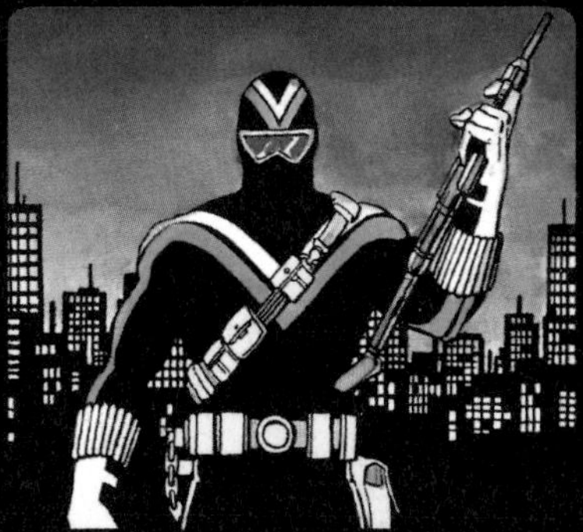

...and the robotic Red Tornado.
The world would be safe,
for a time.

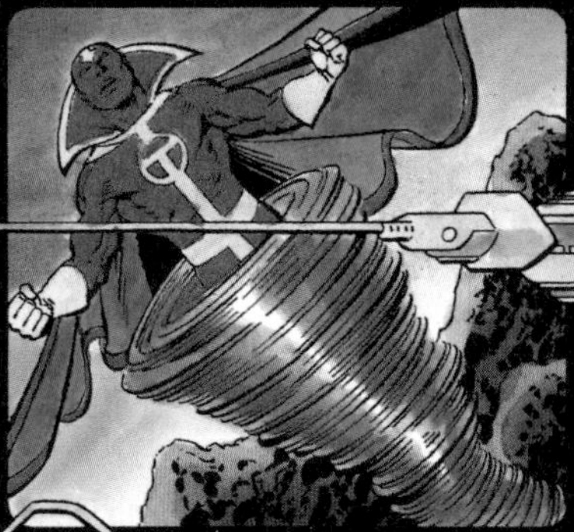

I must pause now for what is to become a personal history. Until now I have merely read the computer files of The Monitor, with my comments clearly marked. But now the history involves me and the actions which led me to kill my mentor.

Ten billion years ago, two beings were born. In our universe came The Monitor, but his brother was born in the anti-matter universe of Qward.

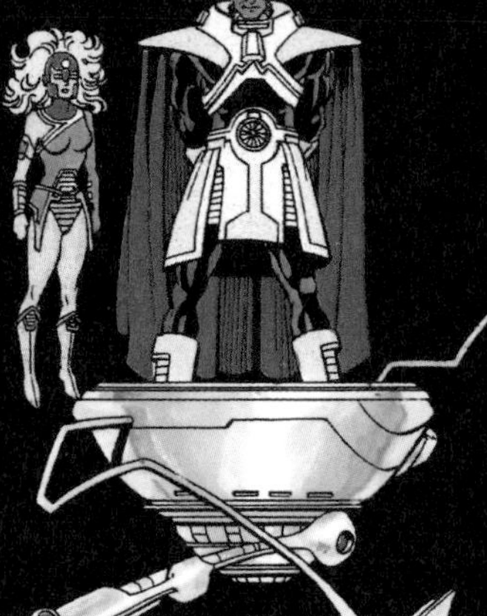

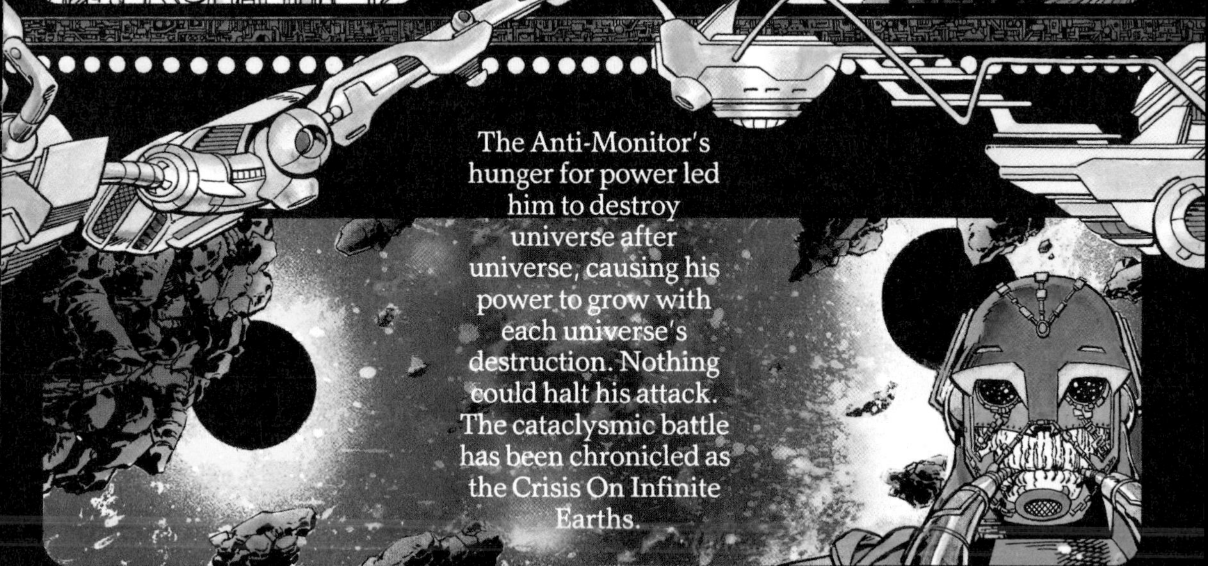

The Anti-Monitor's hunger for power led him to destroy universe after universe, causing his power to grow with each universe's destruction. Nothing could halt his attack. The cataclysmic battle has been chronicled as the Crisis On Infinite Earths.

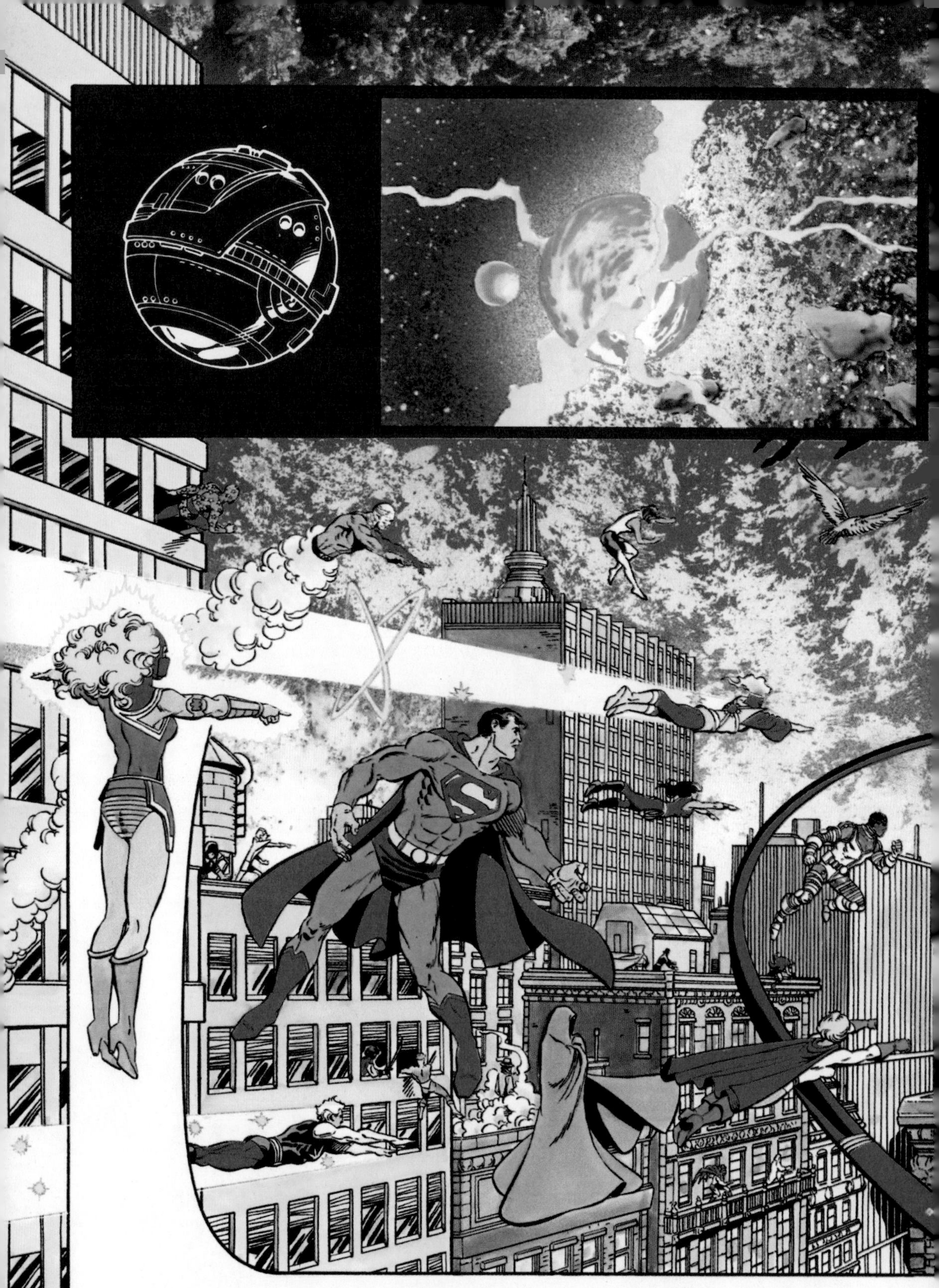

Five Universes remained, and with them five Earths. The Monitor brought together the greatest heroes and villains from all the Earths and forged them into a fighting army. The battle raged throughout the universes and across time itself, and during the battle I was compelled by the Anti-Monitor to fatally strike down his brother. Finally, the remaining universes were merged into one and enough force was brought to bear to destroy the Anti-Monitor.

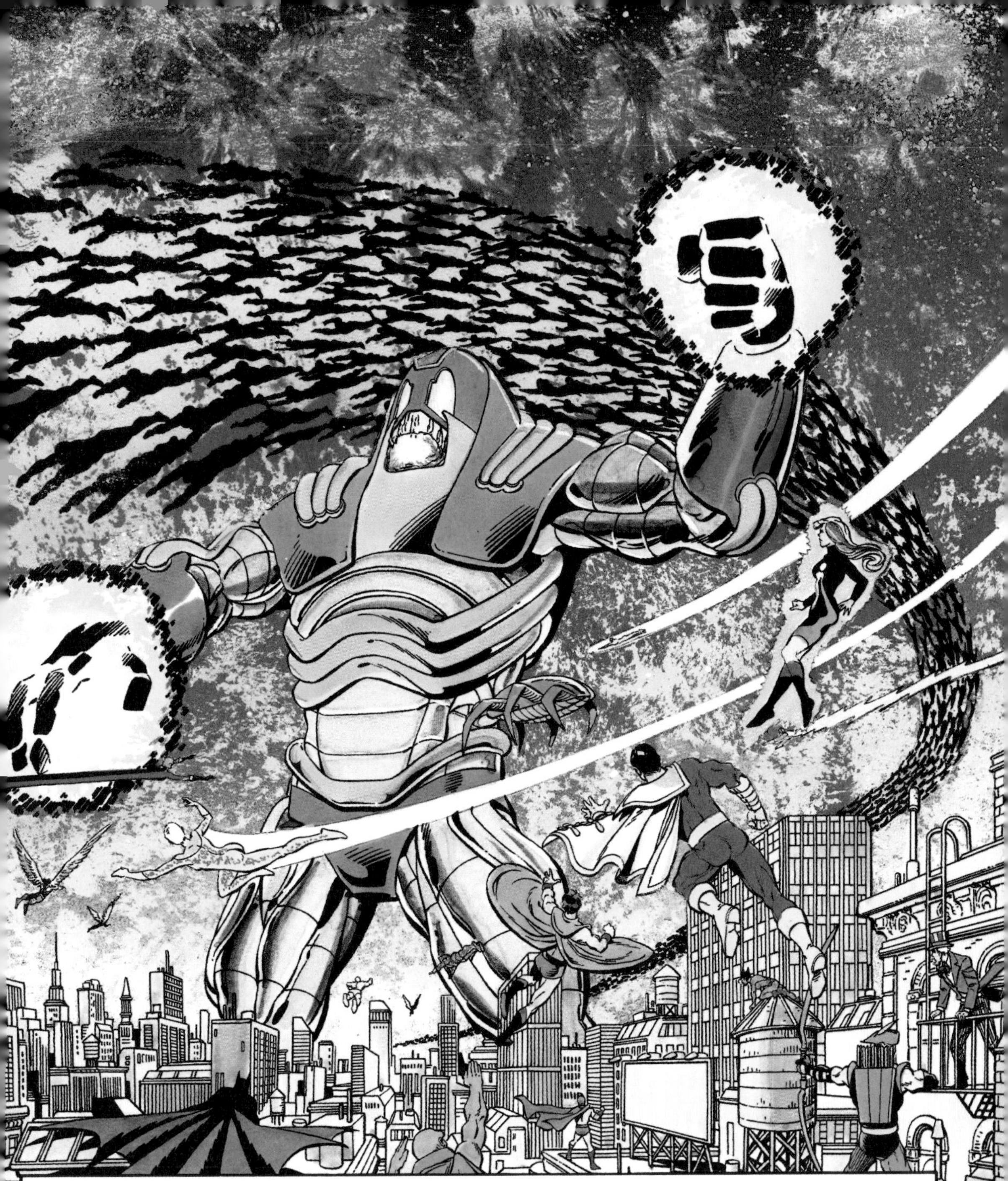

In the course of this merging, the History of the Universe was altered. In the course of this cosmic confrontation, many heroes perished so that the remaining worlds could survive. It is to Lori Lemaris, Tomar Re, The Dove, Kole, Immortal Man, Prince Ra-Man, Starman, Aquagirl, the Flash, Sunburst, and the other heroes who made the supreme sacrifice that this second chronicle of history is dedicated.

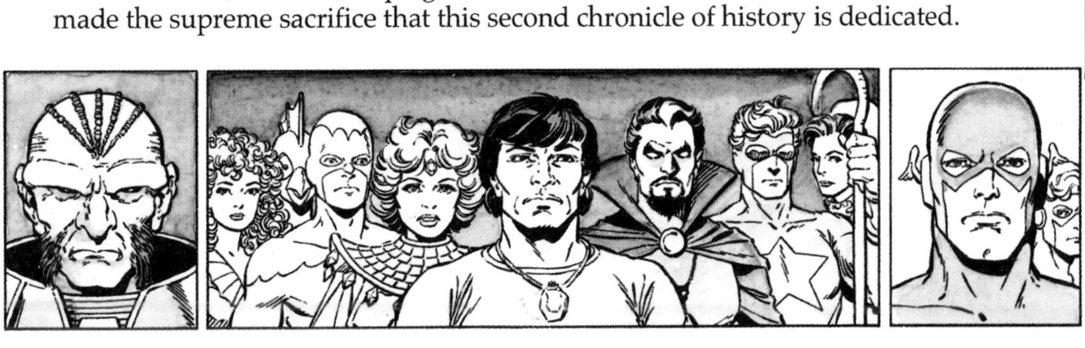

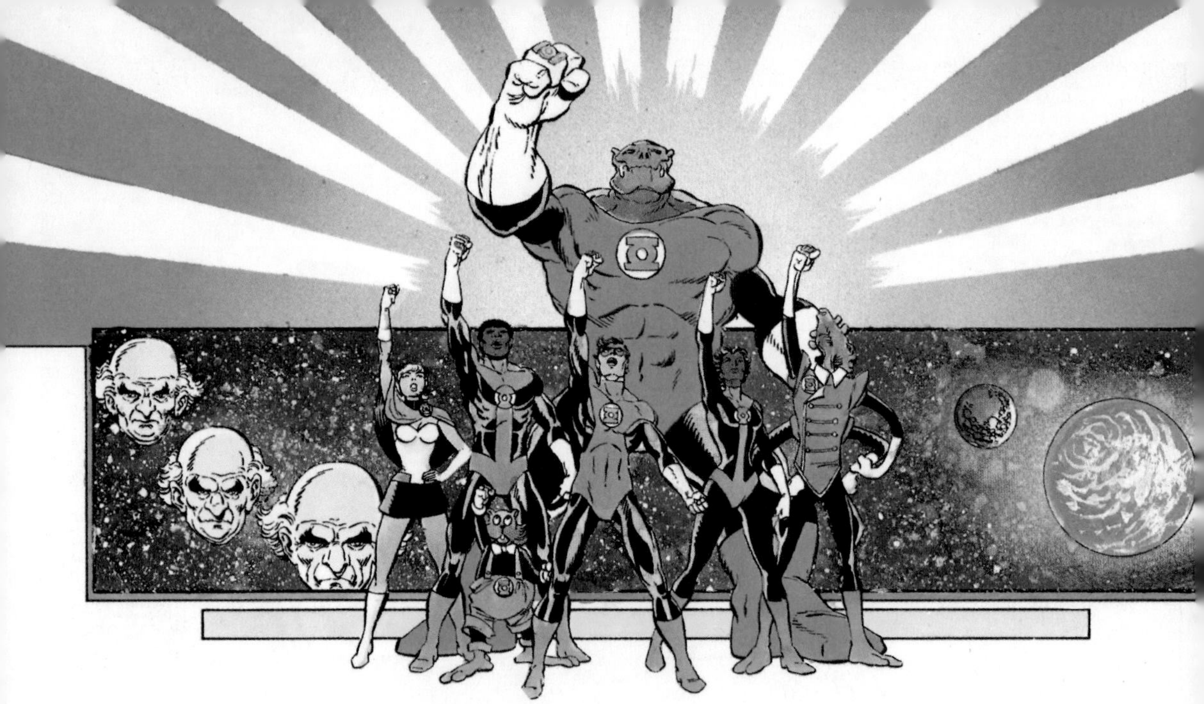

The universe was irrevocably altered by the Crisis on Infinite Earths. The Guardians of the Universe turned their backs on their home on Oa, leaving the fabled Green Lantern Corps to fulfill their mysterious prophecy about mankind.

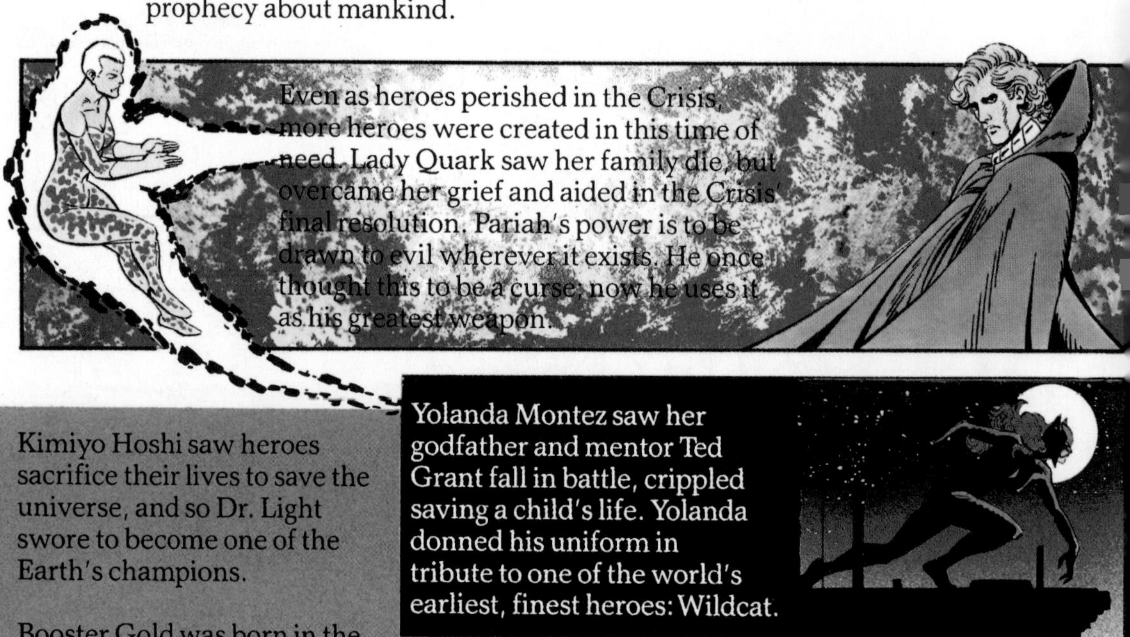

Even as heroes perished in the Crisis, more heroes were created in this time of need. Lady Quark saw her family die, but overcame her grief and aided in the Crisis' final resolution. Pariah's power is to be drawn to evil wherever it exists. He once thought this to be a curse; now he uses it as his greatest weapon.

Yolanda Montez saw her godfather and mentor Ted Grant fall in battle, crippled saving a child's life. Yolanda donned his uniform in tribute to one of the world's earliest, finest heroes: Wildcat.

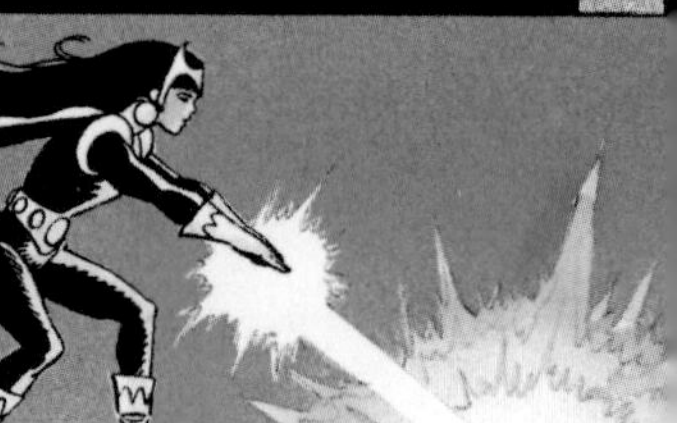

Kimiyo Hoshi saw heroes sacrifice their lives to save the universe, and so Dr. Light swore to become one of the Earth's champions.

Booster Gold was born in the far future, but journeyed to our present to achieve fame and glory.

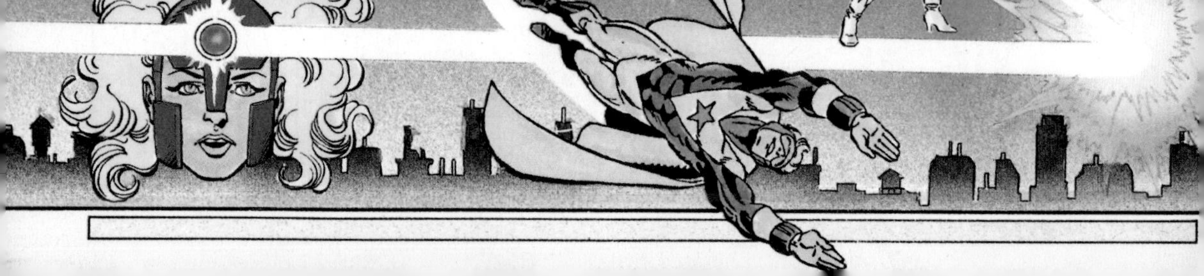

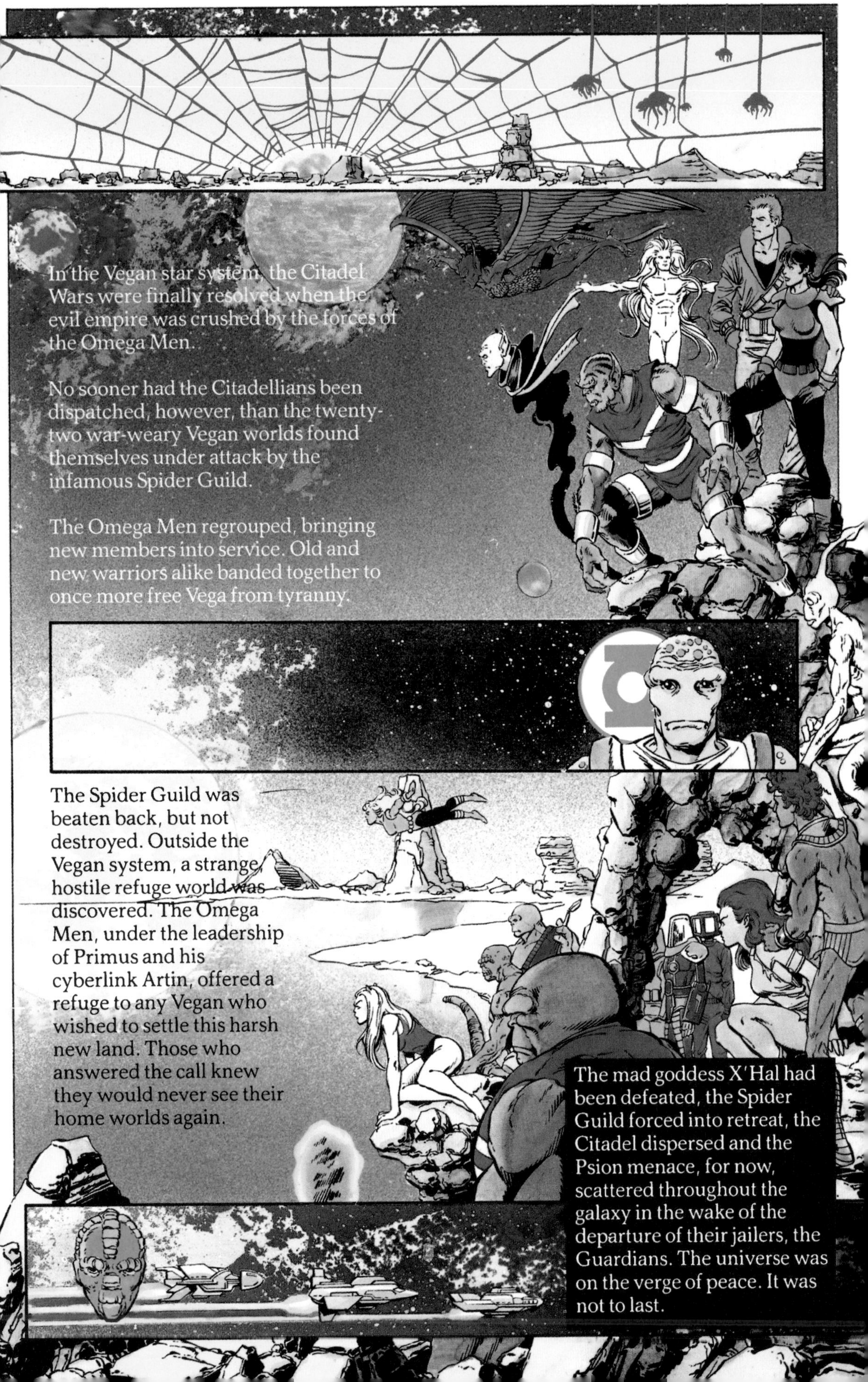
In the Vegan star system, the Citadel Wars were finally resolved when the evil empire was crushed by the forces of the Omega Men.
No sooner had the Citadellians been dispatched, however, than the twenty-two war-weary Vegan worlds found themselves under attack by the infamous Spider Guild.
The Omega Men regrouped, bringing new members into service. Old and new warriors alike banded together to once more free Vega from tyranny.
The Spider Guild was beaten back, but not destroyed. Outside the Vegan system, a strange, hostile refuge world was discovered. The Omega Men, under the leadership of Primus and his cyberlink Artin, offered a refuge to any Vegan who wished to settle this harsh new land. Those who answered the call knew they would never see their home worlds again.
The mad goddess X'Hal had been defeated, the Spider Guild forced into retreat, the Citadel dispersed and the Psion menace, for now, scattered throughout the galaxy in the wake of the departure of their jailers, the Guardians. The universe was on the verge of peace. It was not to last.

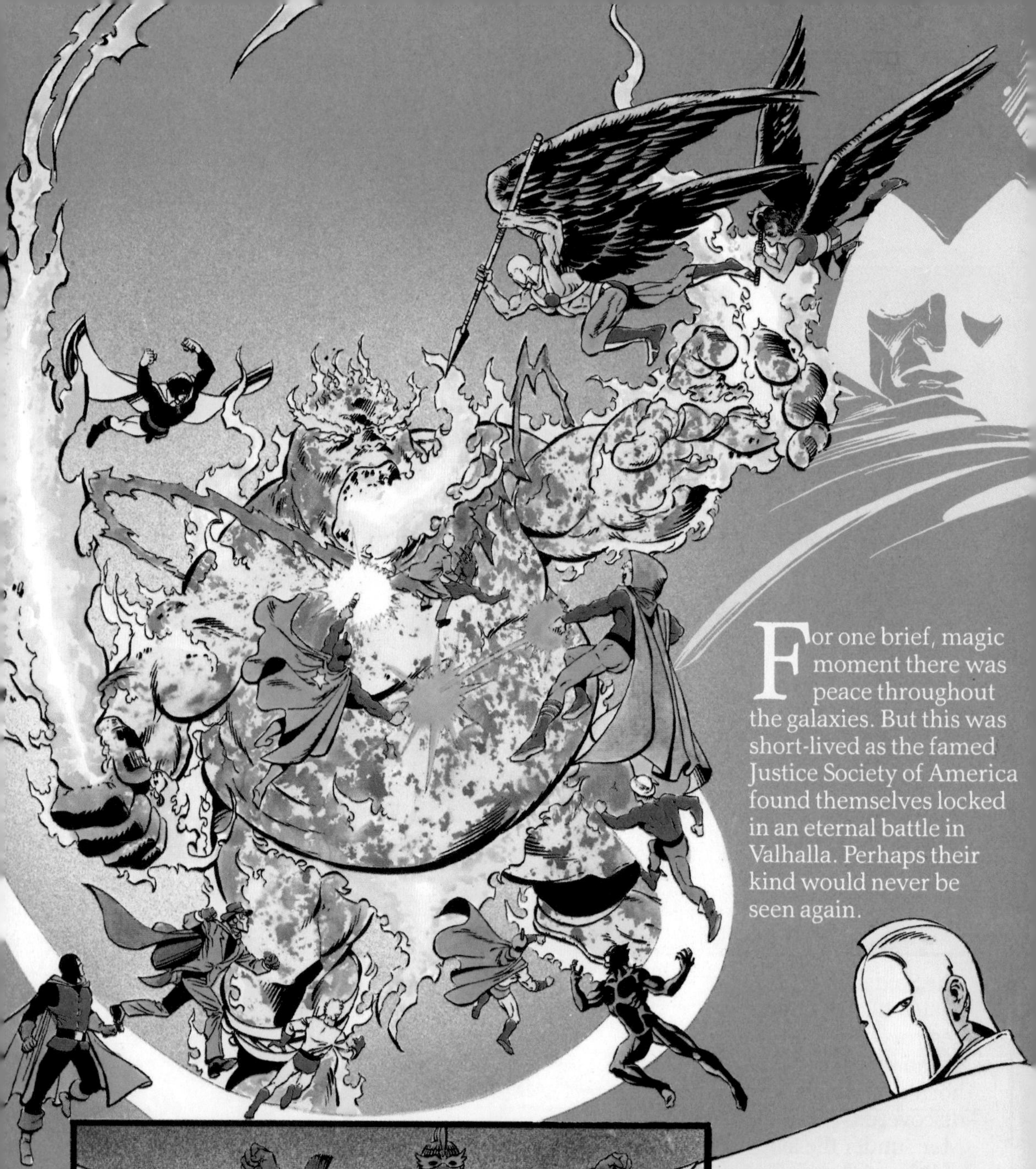

For one brief, magic moment there was peace throughout the galaxies. But this was short-lived as the famed Justice Society of America found themselves locked in an eternal battle in Valhalla. Perhaps their kind would never be seen again.

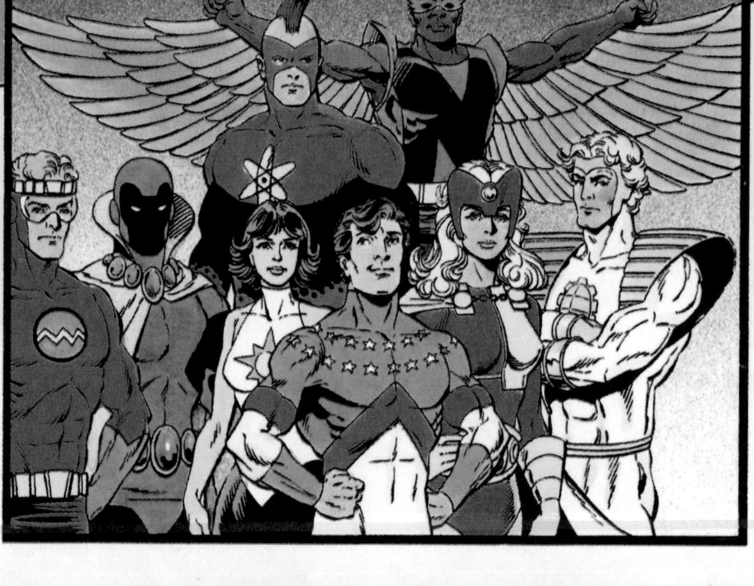

The Justice Society was gone, but their children lived on to lend continuity to the heroic ideal. These children of great heroes became great heroes themselves in the mighty group called Infinity, Inc.

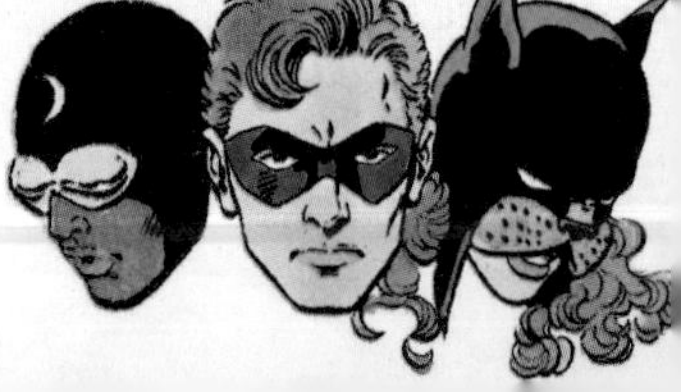

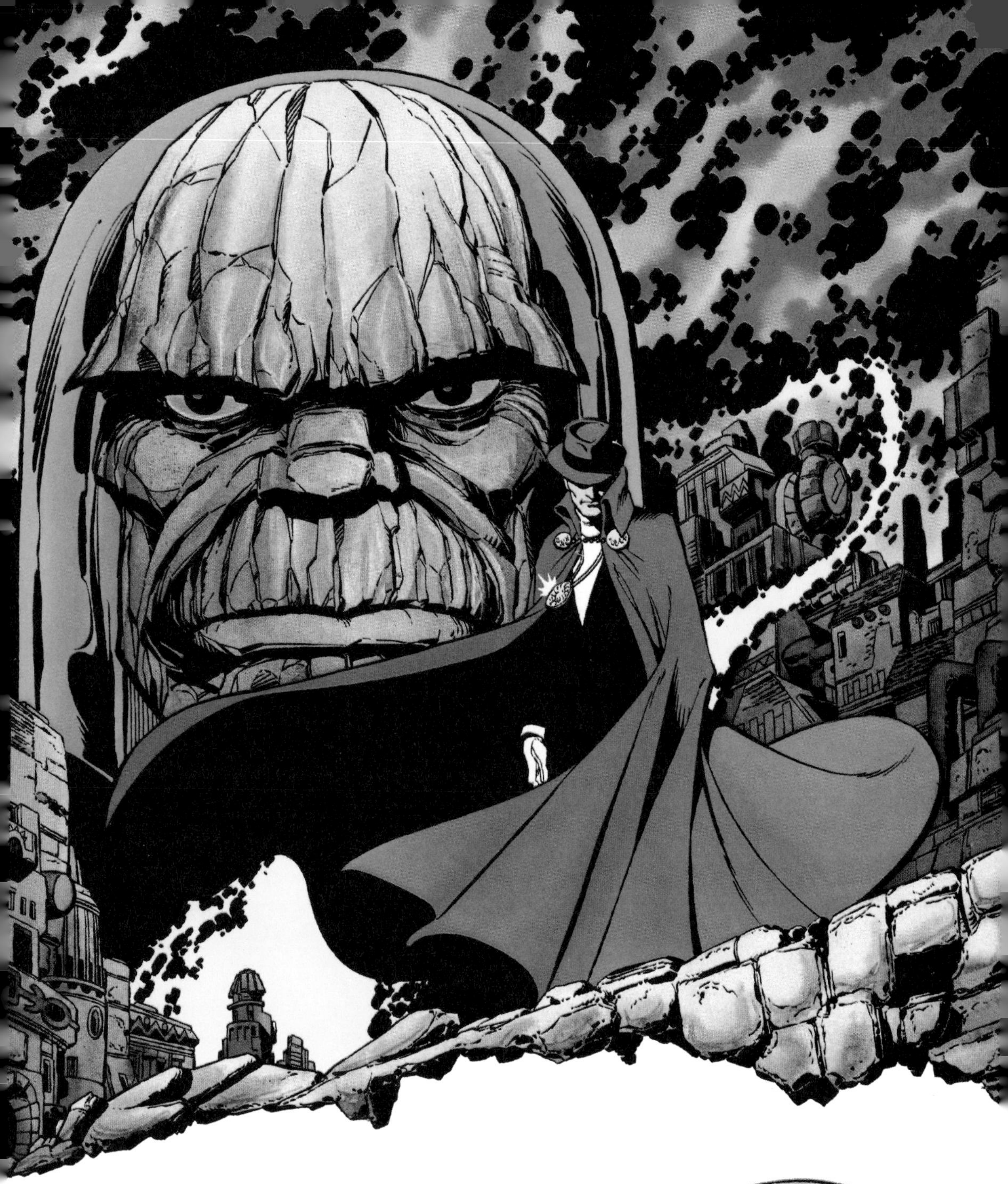

Great heroes and terrible villains...the stuff of legends. When you hear of the great gods of myth, you forget that they once were real, for now only their legends survive.

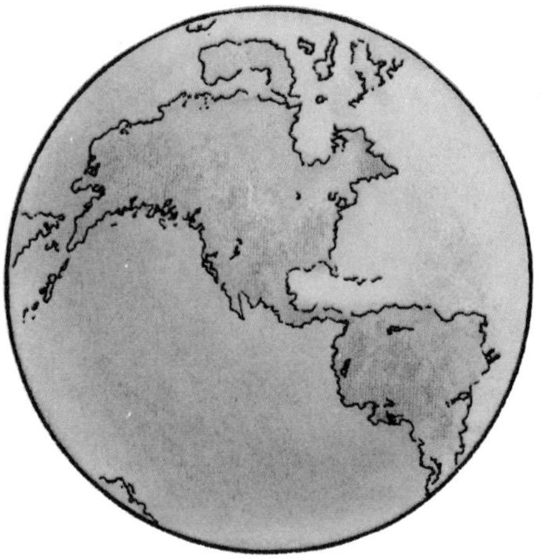

But take a legend—twist it, destroy it—remove it from conscious memory; take the legend of greatness and reduce it to nothingness. That was the plan of Darkseid the Destroyer. Through his destruction of legends, the great devil sought to make himself a god unto mankind.

Darkseid's dreams of glory faded, but from his fevered wish to destroy the fabric of legend, new ones were given birth.

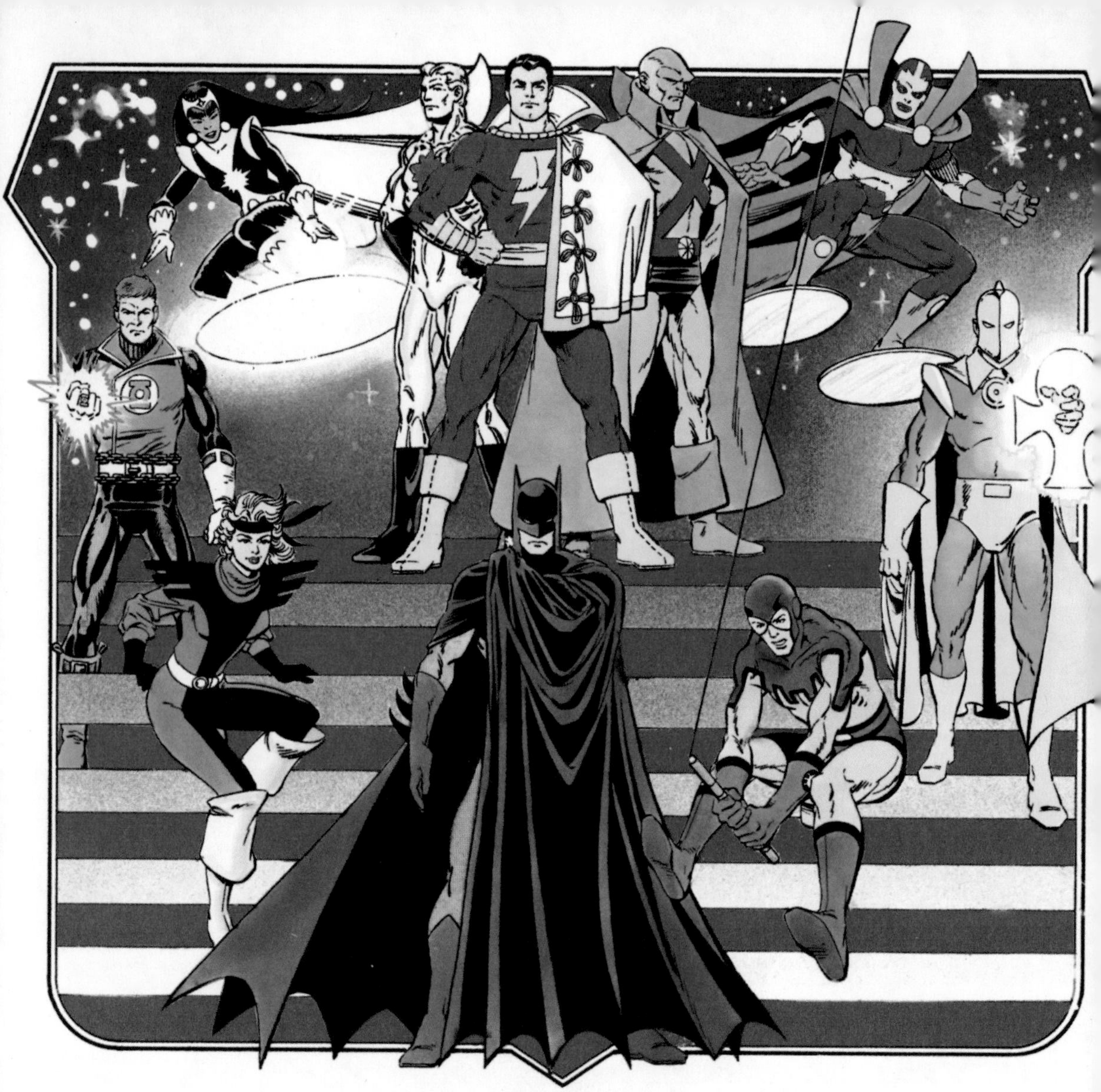

The Justice League of America was no longer, but in its wake a new force was born. Forevermore this international—even interplanetary—team would be called The Justice League.

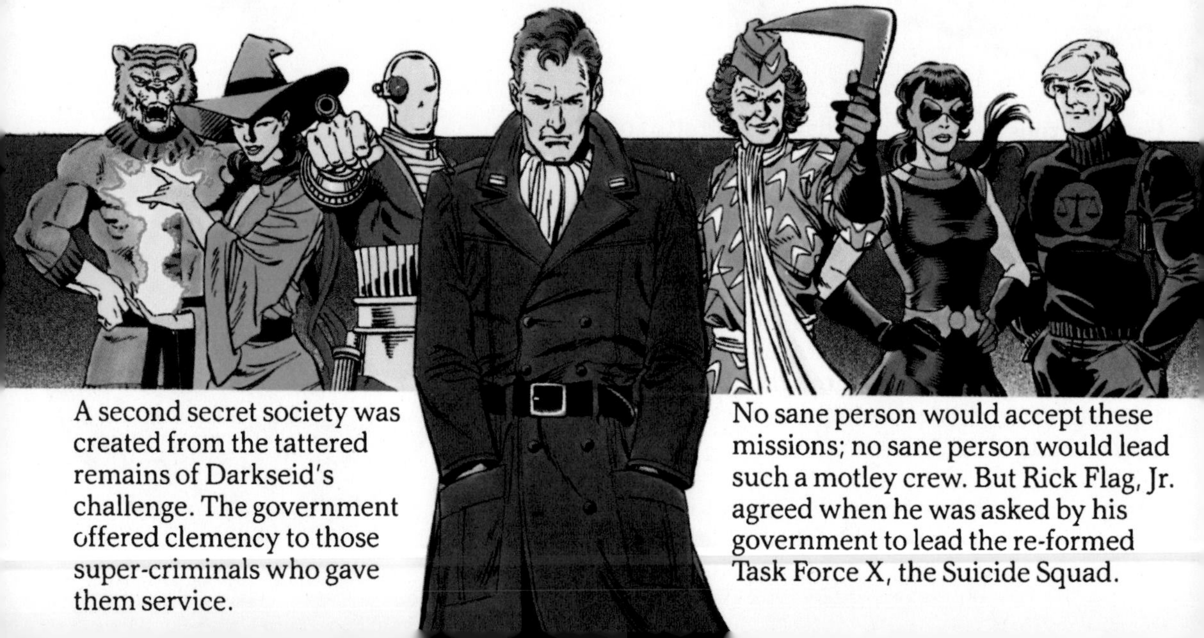

A second secret society was created from the tattered remains of Darkseid's challenge. The government offered clemency to those super-criminals who gave them service.

No sane person would accept these missions; no sane person would lead such a motley crew. But Rick Flag, Jr. agreed when he was asked by his government to lead the re-formed Task Force X, the Suicide Squad.

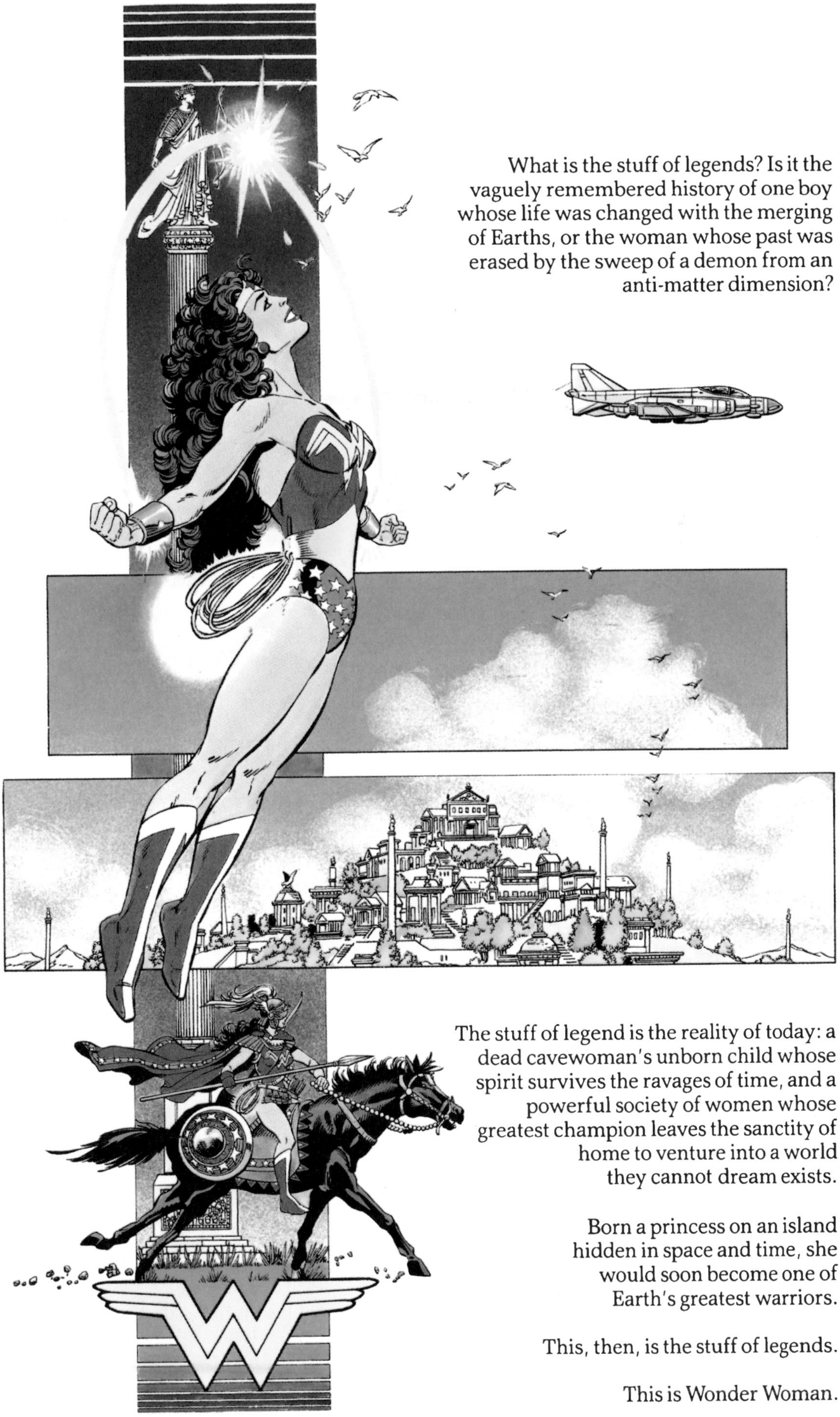

What is the stuff of legends? Is it the vaguely remembered history of one boy whose life was changed with the merging of Earths, or the woman whose past was erased by the sweep of a demon from an anti-matter dimension?

The stuff of legend is the reality of today: a dead cavewoman's unborn child whose spirit survives the ravages of time, and a powerful society of women whose greatest champion leaves the sanctity of home to venture into a world they cannot dream exists.

Born a princess on an island hidden in space and time, she would soon become one of Earth's greatest warriors.

This, then, is the stuff of legends.

This is Wonder Woman.

Until now this narrative has dealt with times past and present. We have seen the history of the universe and its current events. But The Monitor's computers can see not only what was and is, but what will be.

With the merging of the universes, there came one consistent future.

The twenty-first century began not with the hoped-for peace between nations, but with the harsh reality of war. The seven superpowers that existed at the dawn of the new millennium withheld the use of their nuclear arsenal until the war's final days.

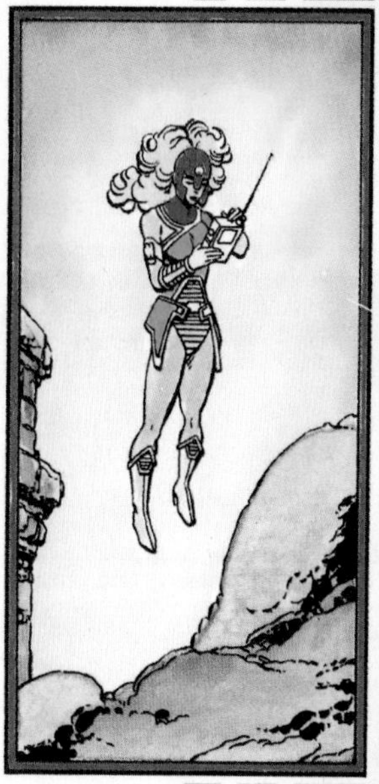

Even then, deployment of the nuclear arsenal was surprisingly limited. Fear of global catastrophe and annihilation prevented even the Terrorist Triumvirate from launching a full-scale attack. In all, only seventeen nuclear missiles were launched. Only six reached their targets. Destruction, though widespread, was contained to a half-dozen areas around the globe, but even this limited war could not prevent the chaos that ensued. The Earth became a new, grim world.

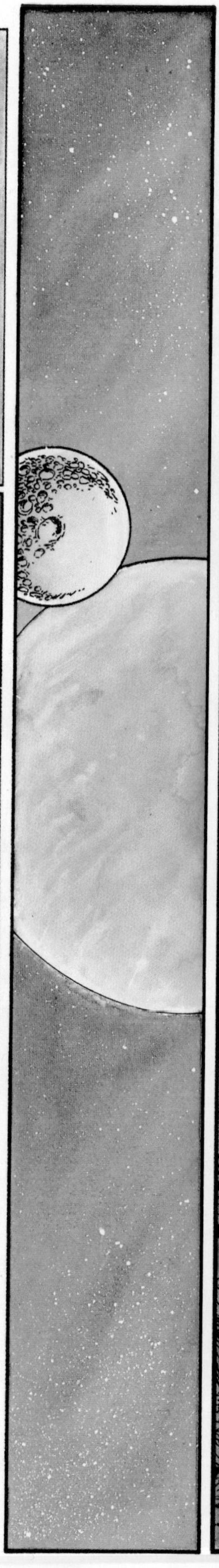

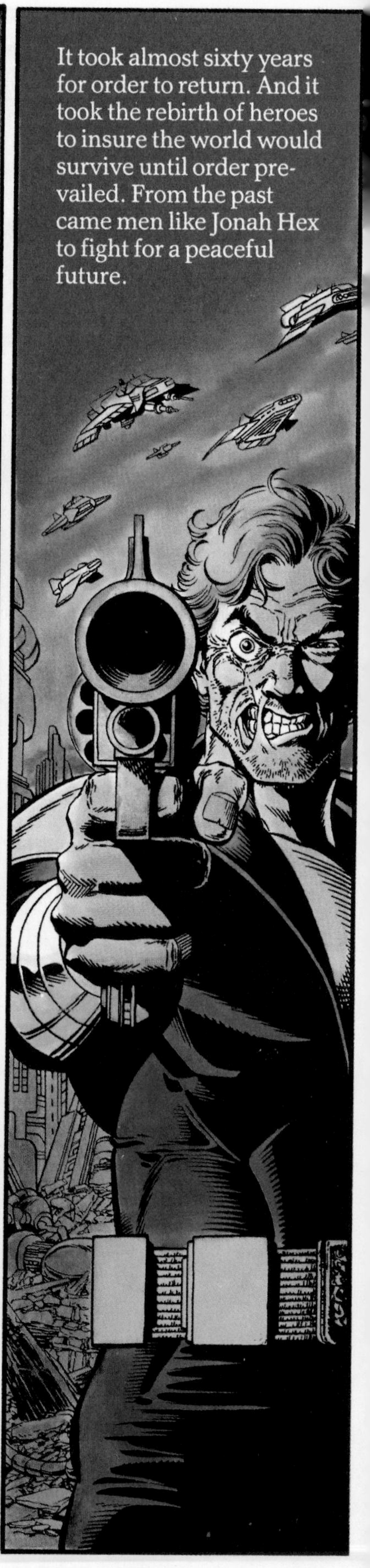
It took almost sixty years for order to return. And it took the rebirth of heroes to insure the world would survive until order prevailed. From the past came men like Jonah Hex to fight for a peaceful future.

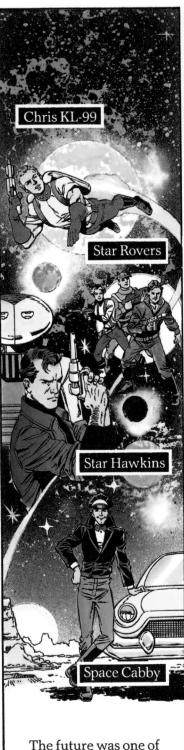

Chris KL-99

Star Rovers

Star Hawkins

Space Cabby

The future was one of peace. Within one century, mankind had regained its control over the Earth. Space was conquered. At long last, Earthlings had reached the stars!

A young orphan boy was found in the Command D bunker of Space Planeteer Headquarters by Gen. Horatio Tomorrow. Young Tommy Tomorrow would grow up to become the greatest Planeteer of all.

Omac

Tommy Tomorrow

The Planeteers were the prime peace-keeping armed forces of the future. The Space Rangers became the future policemen.

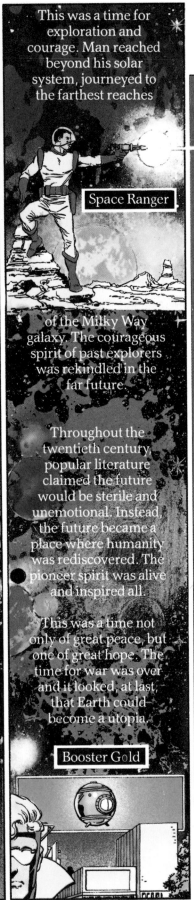

This was a time for exploration and courage. Man reached beyond his solar system, journeyed to the farthest reaches

Space Ranger

of the Milky Way galaxy. The courageous spirit of past explorers was rekindled in the far future.

Throughout the twentieth century, popular literature claimed the future would be sterile and unemotional. Instead, the future became a place where humanity was rediscovered. The pioneer spirit was alive and inspired all.

This was a time not only of great peace, but one of great hope. The time for war was over and it looked, at last, that Earth could become a utopia.

Booster Gold

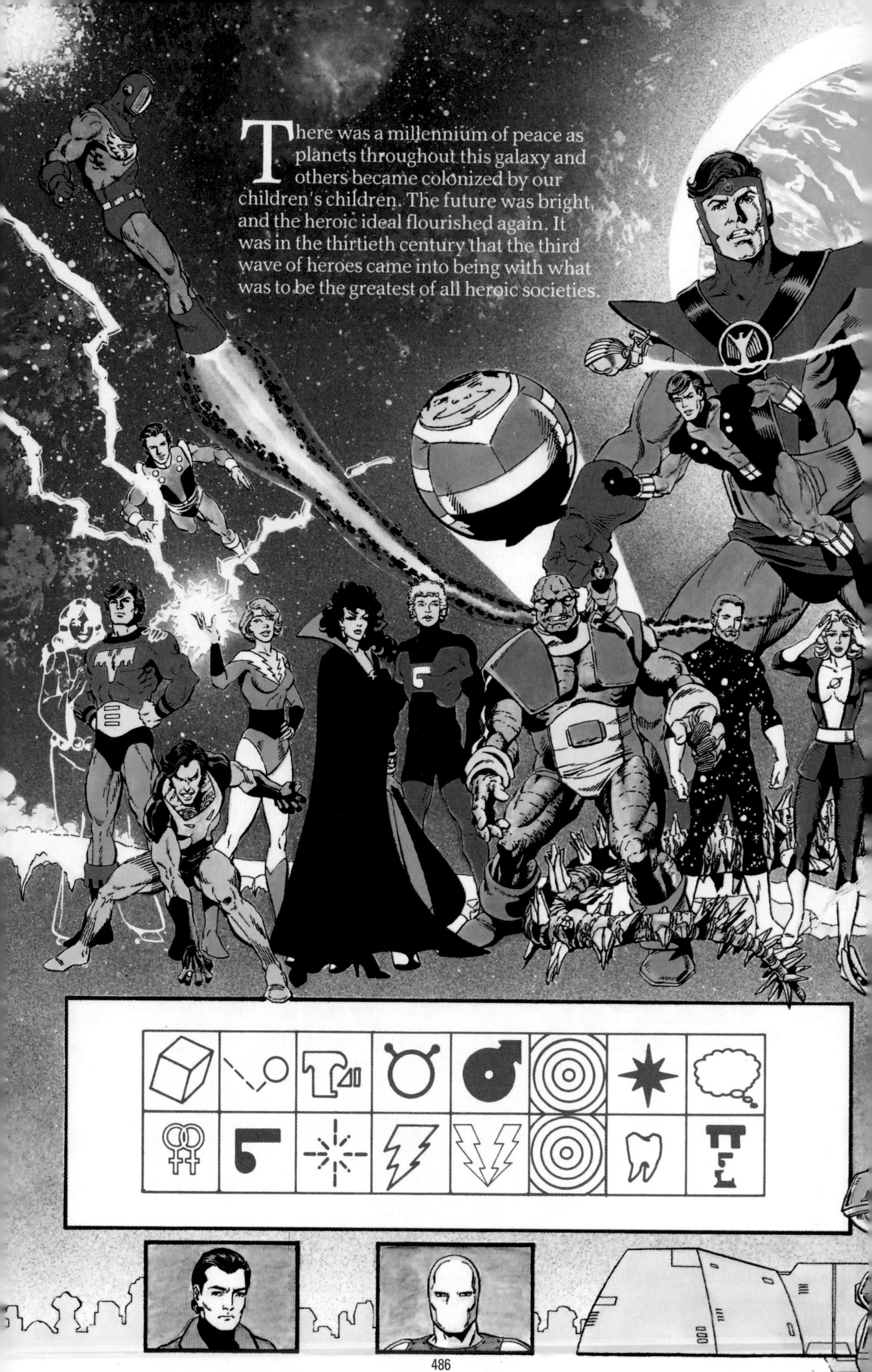
There was a millennium of peace as planets throughout this galaxy and others became colonized by our children's children. The future was bright, and the heroic ideal flourished again. It was in the thirtieth century that the third wave of heroes came into being with what was to be the greatest of all heroic societies.

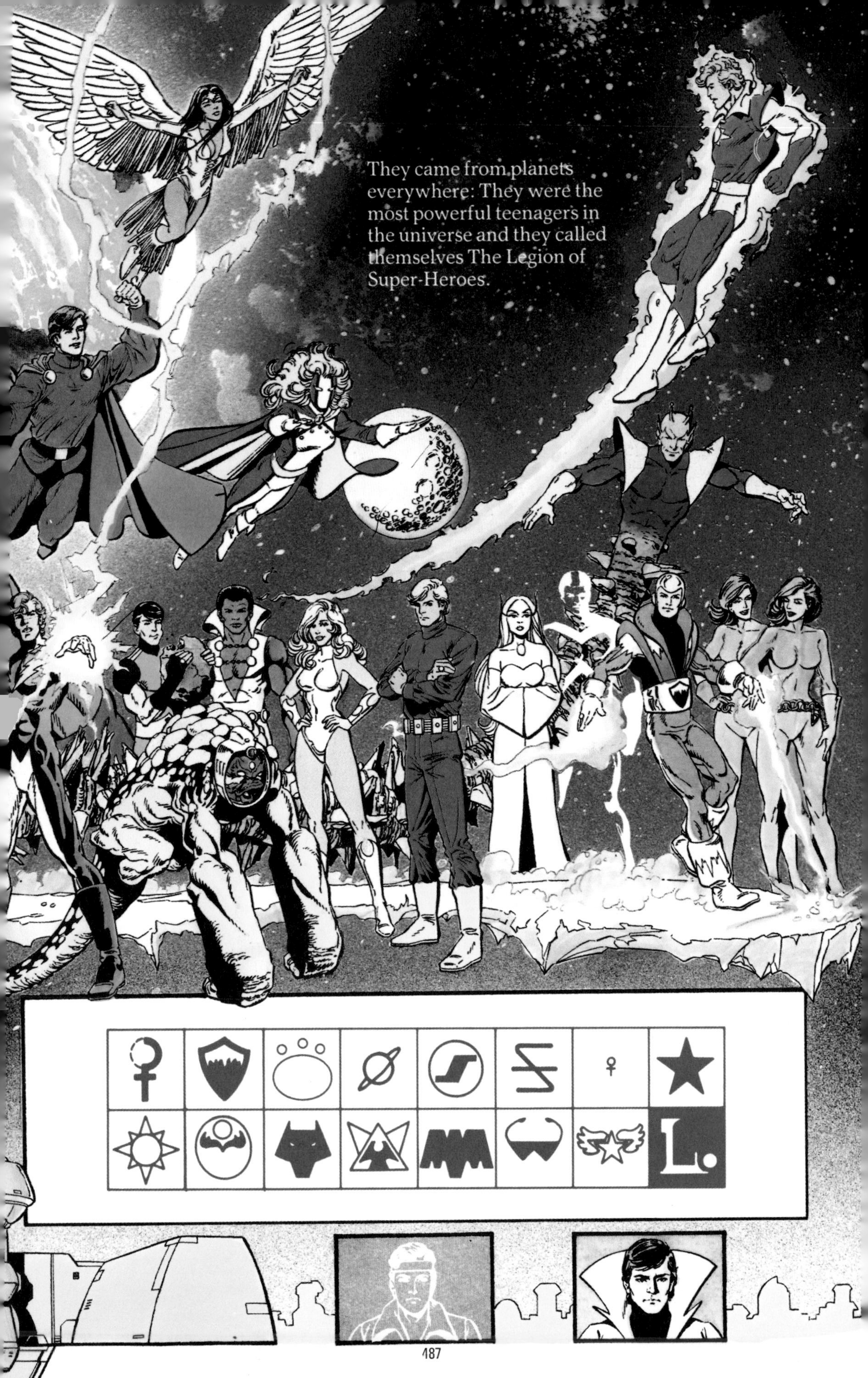
They came from planets everywhere: They were the most powerful teenagers in the universe and they called themselves The Legion of Super-Heroes.

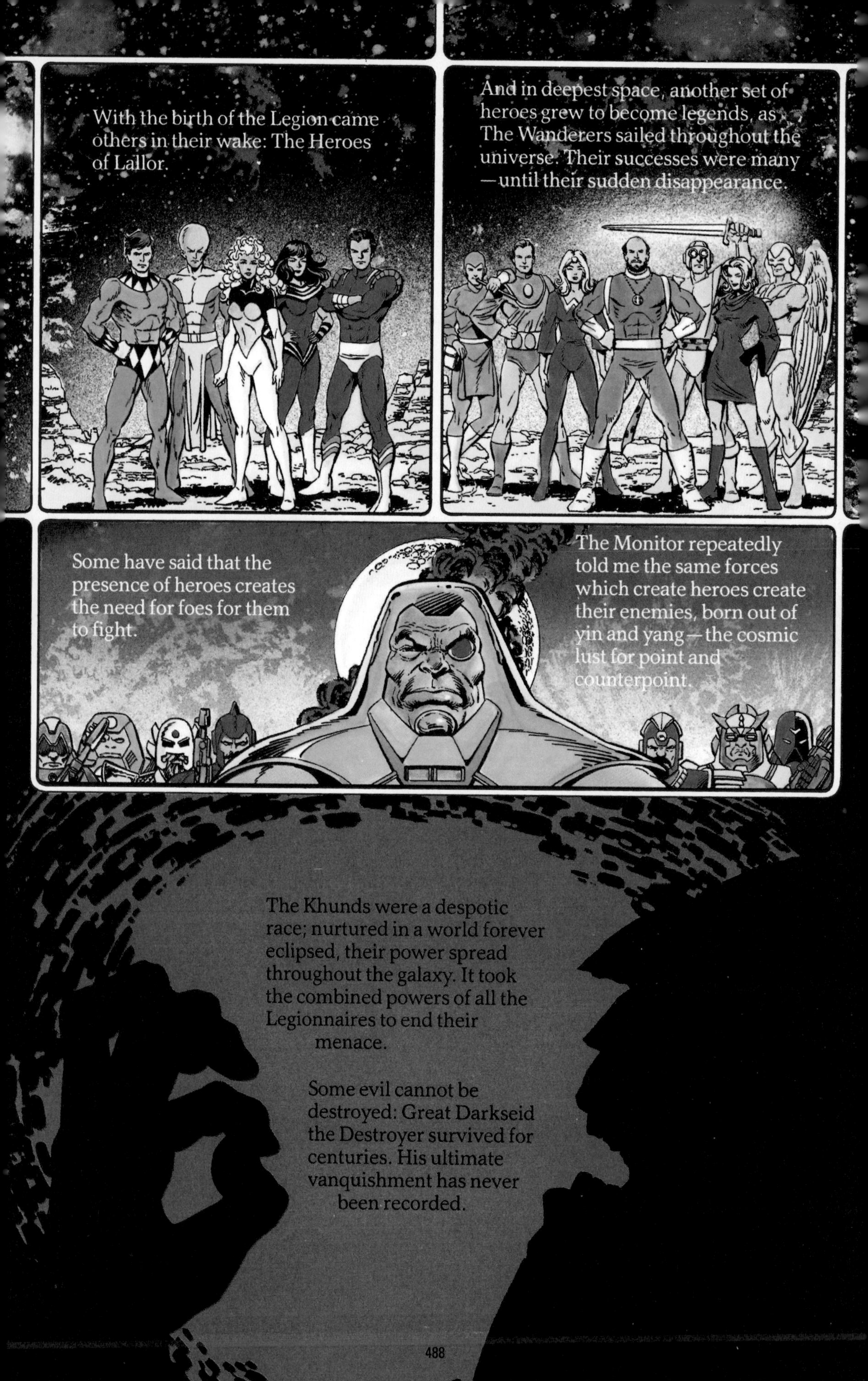
With the birth of the Legion came others in their wake: The Heroes of Lallor.
And in deepest space, another set of heroes grew to become legends, as The Wanderers sailed throughout the universe. Their successes were many —until their sudden disappearance.
Some have said that the presence of heroes creates the need for foes for them to fight.
The Monitor repeatedly told me the same forces which create heroes create their enemies, born out of yin and yang—the cosmic lust for point and counterpoint.
The Khunds were a despotic race; nurtured in a world forever eclipsed, their power spread throughout the galaxy. It took the combined powers of all the Legionnaires to end their menace.
Some evil cannot be destroyed: Great Darkseid the Destroyer survived for centuries. His ultimate vanquishment has never been recorded.

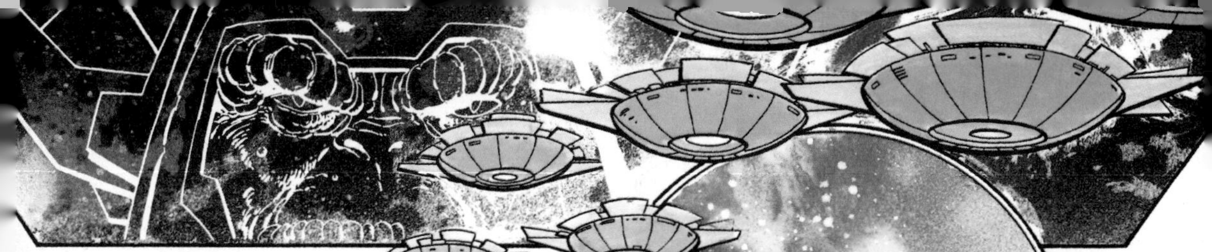

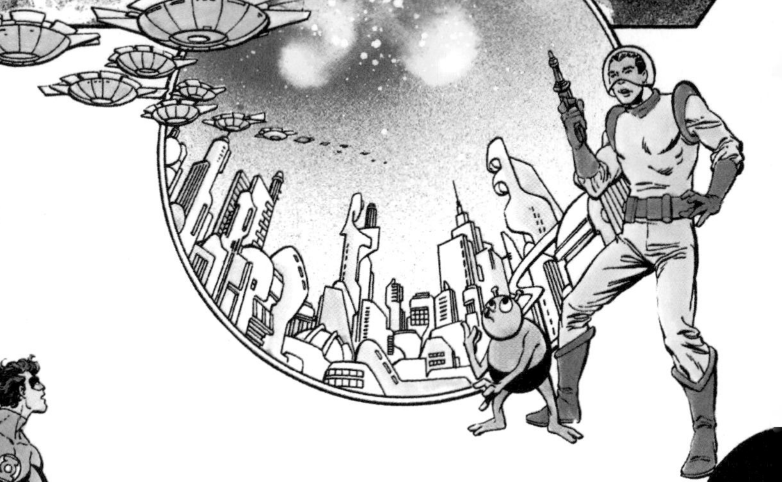

Although the need for heroes never diminished, fewer and fewer beings appeared possessing special abilities. Instead, when menaces occurred which the people of the future could not contain, they summoned the heroes from the past.

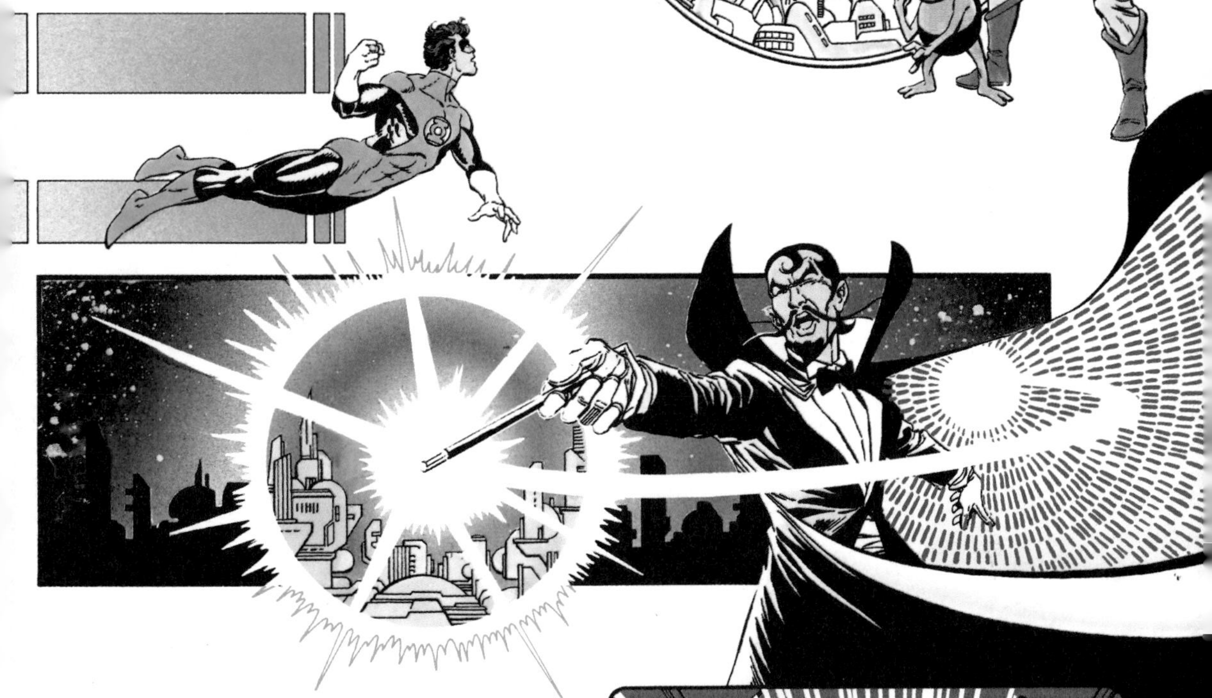

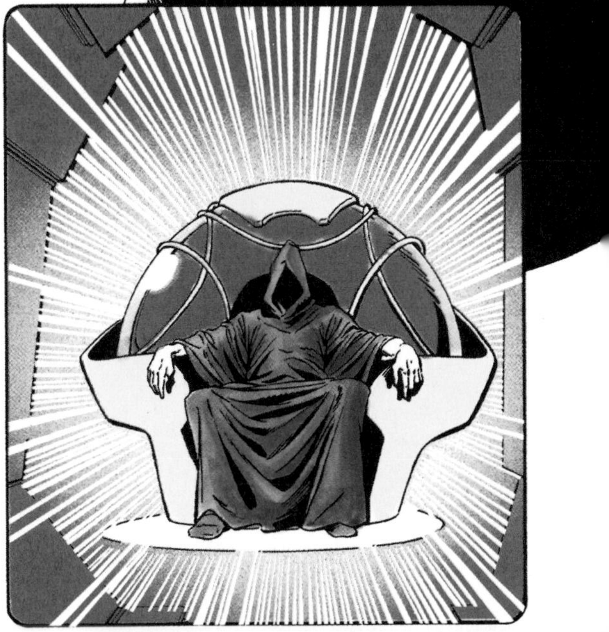

Even though this was a time of peace and hope, as always throughout this history and others, there were those whose greed or lust for power forced them to disrupt the fabric of society. It is because of beings such as Abra Kadabra and the villainous Time Trapper—who sits hungrily at the end of time—that the need for heroes will be as great in the future as it has been in the past.

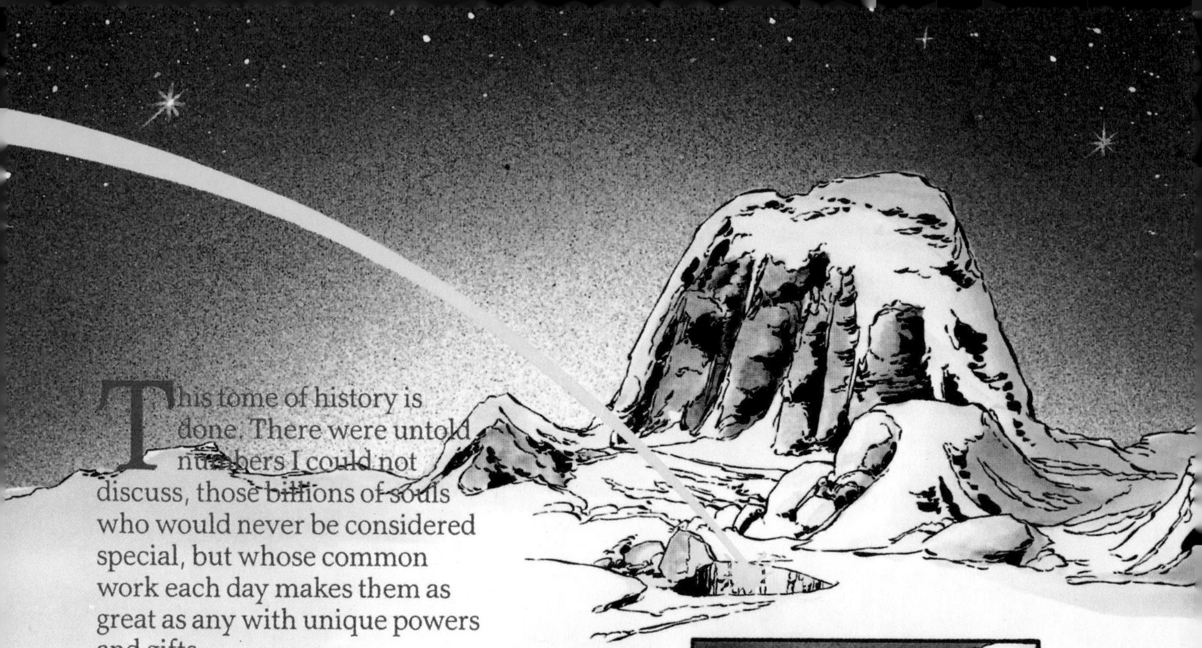

This tome of history is done. There were untold numbers I could not discuss, those billions of souls who would never be considered special, but whose common work each day makes them as great as any with unique powers and gifts.

I had sworn that I would complete the Monitor's work, and so I have, but this history may not be seen by any mortal eyes. The future must unfold as it comes—day by day, allowing for the ebb and flow of change.

It ends now. The Monitor had dreamed of saving the universe, and so he did; he dreamed of compiling its heroic history, and I have fulfilled his last request!

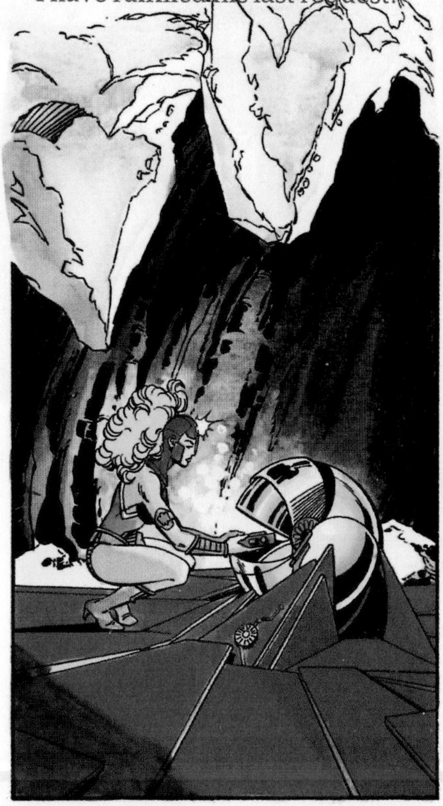

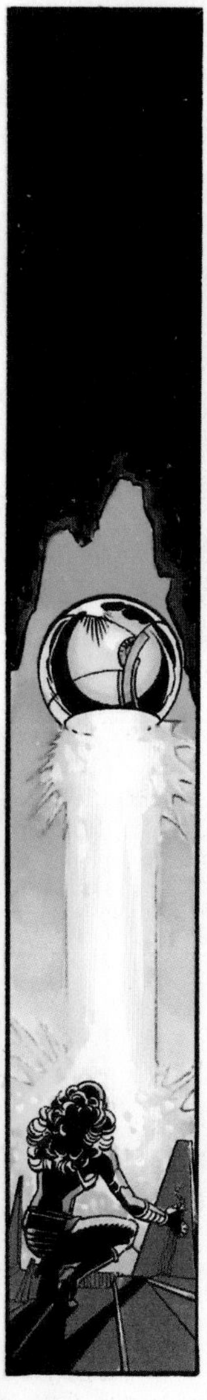

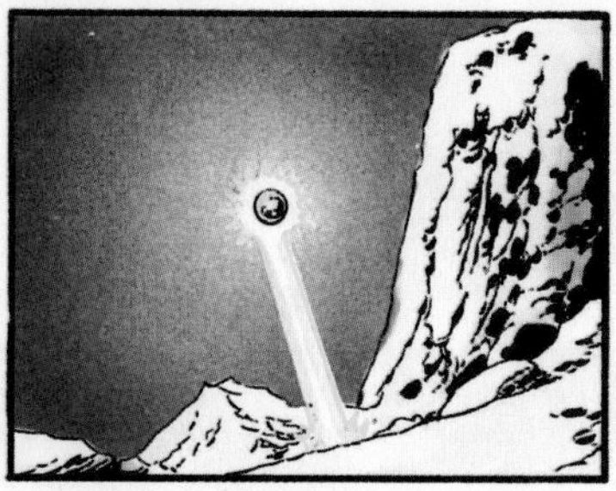

And is so doing, I have learned the truth: the stuff of heroes is within us all--the willingness to go beyond the normal routine and lend help to those who need it.

Give food to the hungry, freedom to the oppressed, safety to the victim, peace to the survivors of war.

I remember as a child the so-called Golden Rule: Do unto others as you would have them do unto you. To be a hero is to live by those words.

It is as simple as that.

I bid you now farewell.

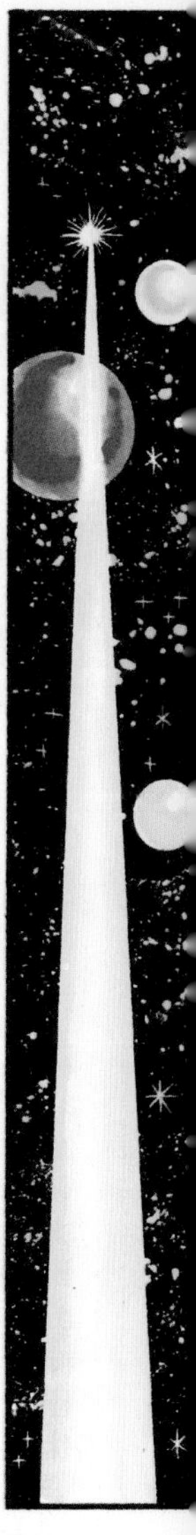

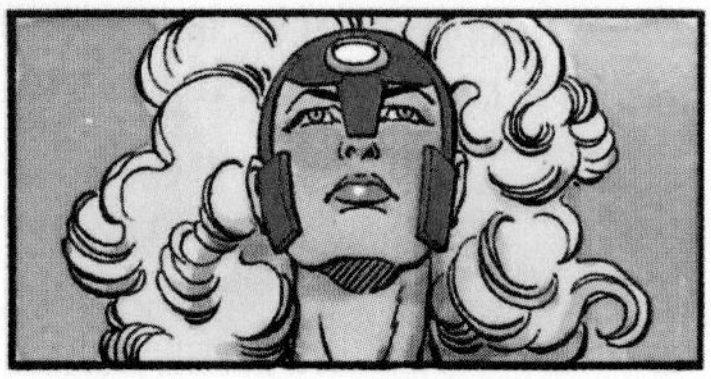

Next ten pages: Entries from *Who's Who in the DC Universe* written by Len Wein and Mark Waid.

THE BLACKHAWKS

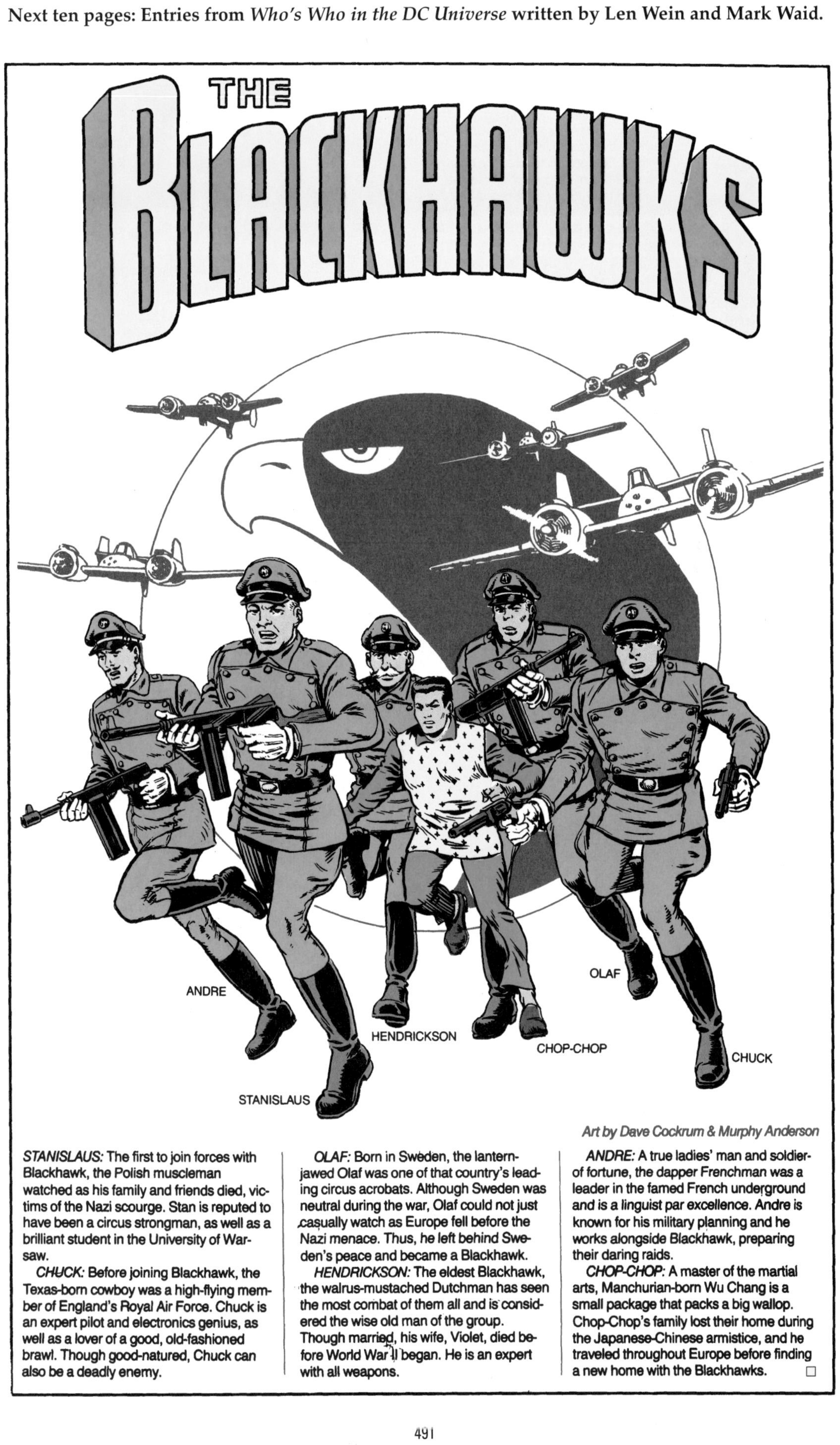

ANDRE
OLAF
HENDRICKSON
CHOP-CHOP
CHUCK
STANISLAUS

Art by Dave Cockrum & Murphy Anderson

STANISLAUS: The first to join forces with Blackhawk, the Polish muscleman watched as his family and friends died, victims of the Nazi scourge. Stan is reputed to have been a circus strongman, as well as a brilliant student in the University of Warsaw.

CHUCK: Before joining Blackhawk, the Texas-born cowboy was a high-flying member of England's Royal Air Force. Chuck is an expert pilot and electronics genius, as well as a lover of a good, old-fashioned brawl. Though good-natured, Chuck can also be a deadly enemy.

OLAF: Born in Sweden, the lantern-jawed Olaf was one of that country's leading circus acrobats. Although Sweden was neutral during the war, Olaf could not just casually watch as Europe fell before the Nazi menace. Thus, he left behind Sweden's peace and became a Blackhawk.

HENDRICKSON: The eldest Blackhawk, the walrus-mustached Dutchman has seen the most combat of them all and is considered the wise old man of the group. Though married, his wife, Violet, died before World War II began. He is an expert with all weapons.

ANDRE: A true ladies' man and soldier-of fortune, the dapper Frenchman was a leader in the famed French underground and is a linguist par excellence. Andre is known for his military planning and he works alongside Blackhawk, preparing their daring raids.

CHOP-CHOP: A master of the martial arts, Manchurian-born Wu Chang is a small package that packs a big wallop. Chop-Chop's family lost their home during the Japanese-Chinese armistice, and he traveled throughout Europe before finding a new home with the Blackhawks. □

ALL-STAR SQUADRON

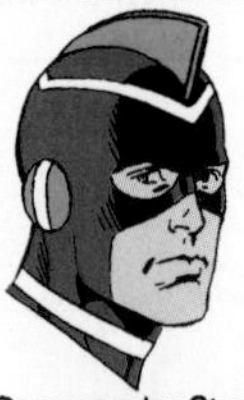

Commander Steel

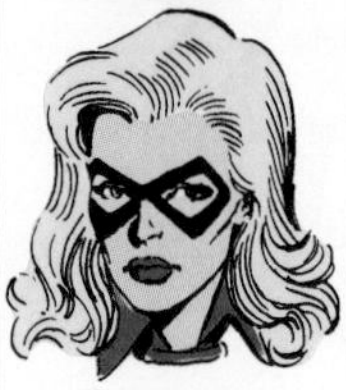

Liberty Belle

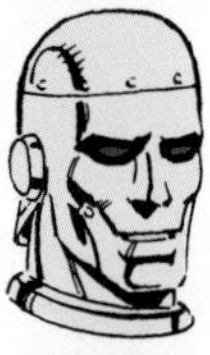

Robotman

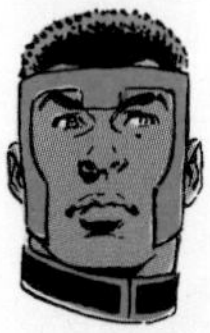

Amazing-Man

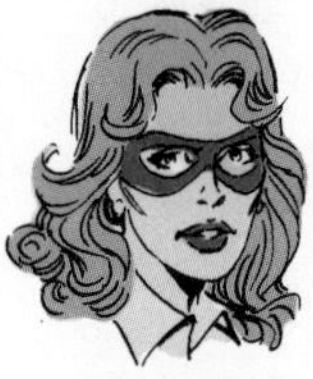

Firebrand

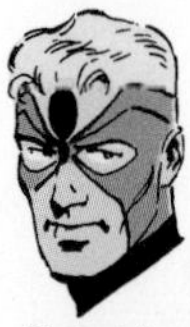

Tarantula

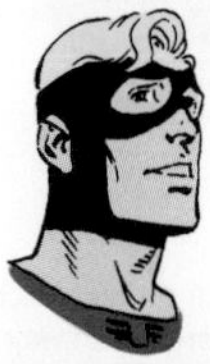

Johnny Quick

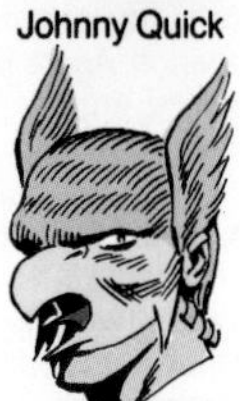

Hawkman

With the sneak attack on Pearl Harbor and America's entry into World War II, America's mystery-men, at the direct request of President Franklin D. Roosevelt, banded together in one organization to help oppose the Axis menace, both at home and abroad. This group included the entire membership of the Justice Society of America (see *JSA*), rechristened The Justice Battalion for the duration. The Squadron answered solely to FDR and the War Department. Hawkman chaired the first formal meeting of the All-Stars, before Liberty Belle was elected permanent chairwoman. Plastic Man served as FBI liaison to the group, which remained in place until the conclusion of World War II.

Art by Jerry Ordway

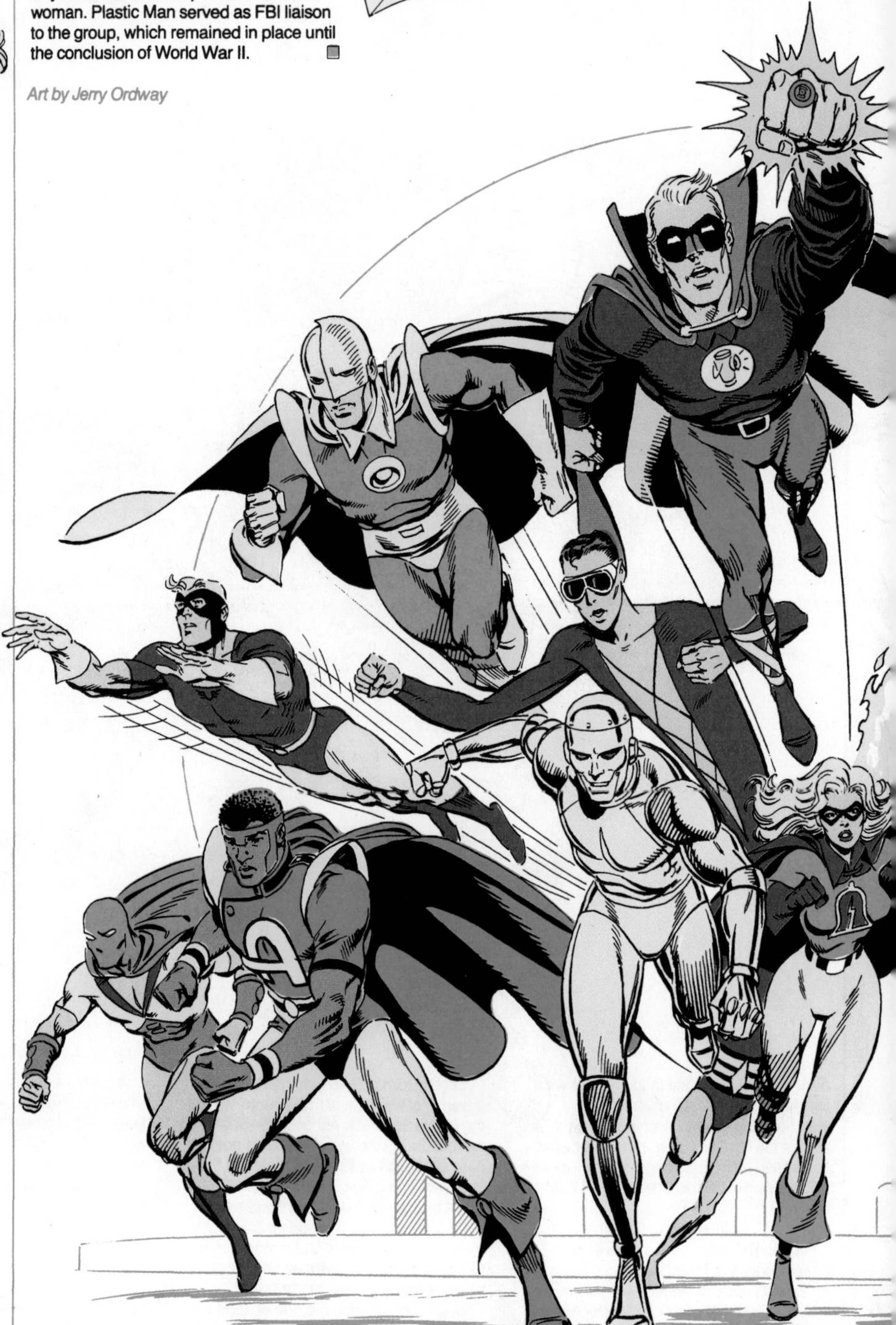

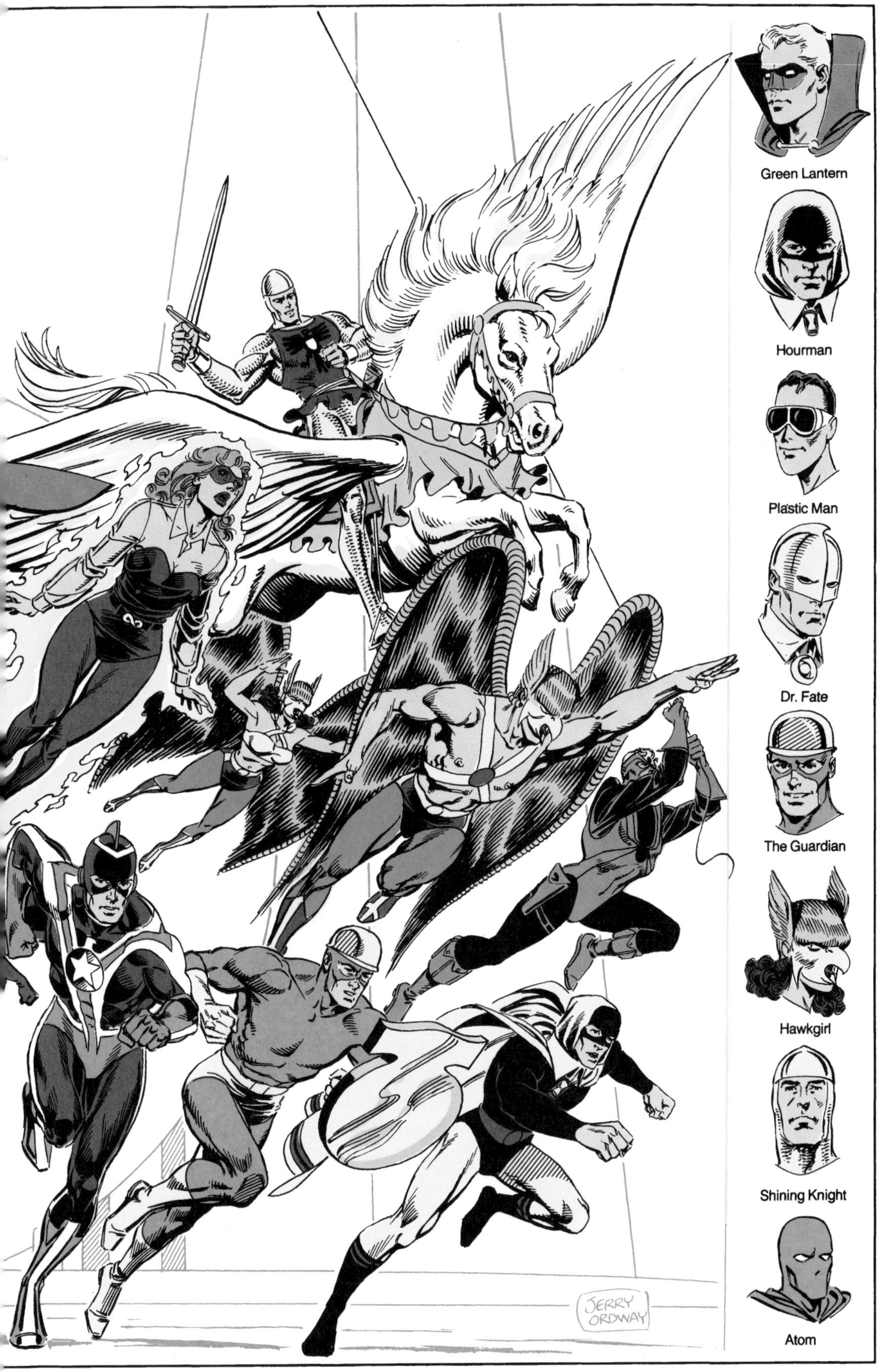
Green Lantern
Hourman
Plastic Man
Dr. Fate
The Guardian
Hawkgirl
Shining Knight
Atom
JERRY ORDWAY

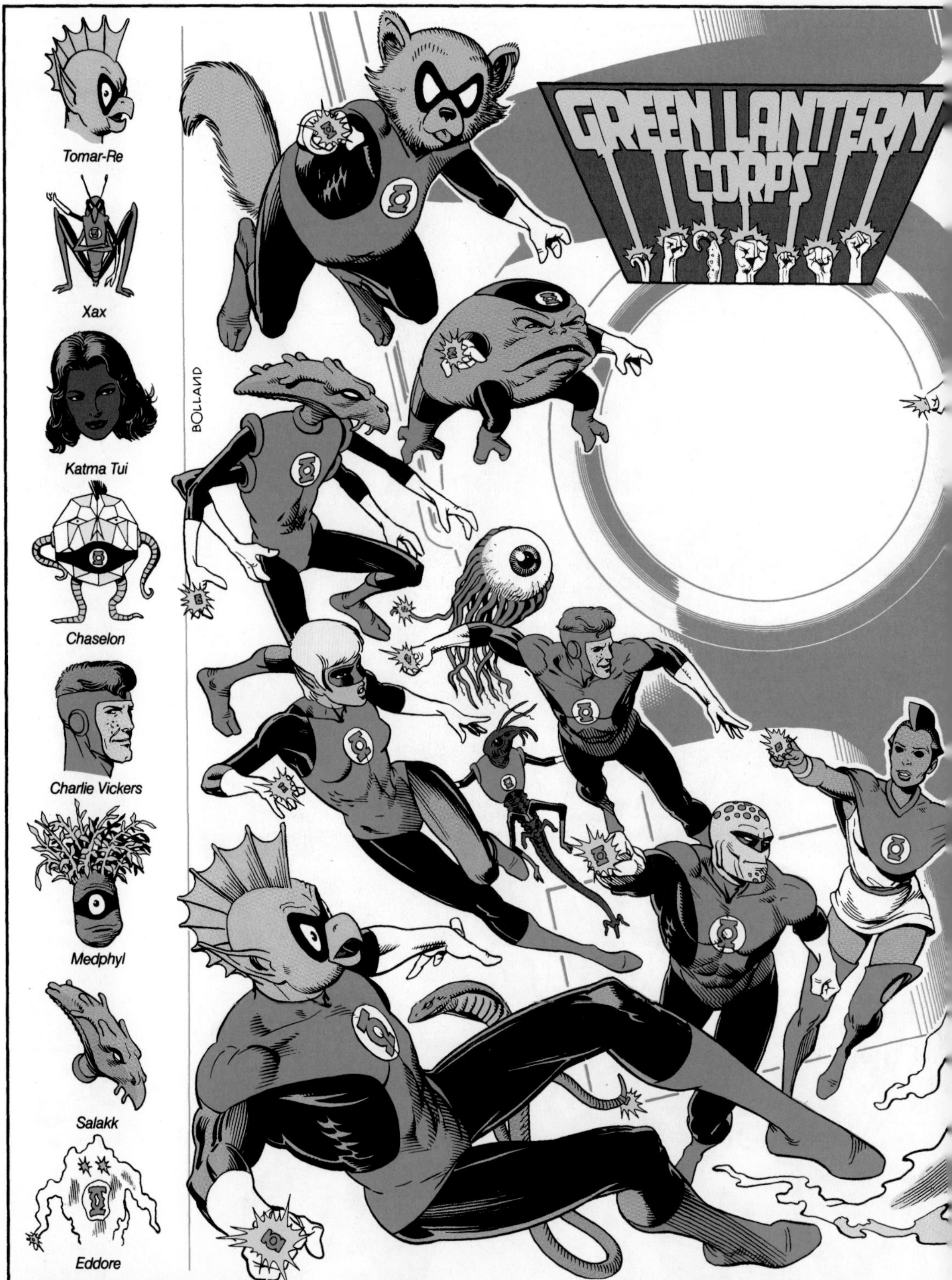
GREEN LANTERN CORPS
Tomar-Re
Xax
Katma Tui
Chaselon
Charlie Vickers
Medphyl
Salakk
Eddore
BOLLAND

HISTORY

An organization formed by the immortal Guardians of the Universe (see *Guardians of the Universe*) to combat evil throughout the known cosmos, the Green Lantern Corps has a standing membership of 3600 sentient beings chosen above all others for their honesty and fearlessness. Each Corps member patrols a space sector encompassing a tenth of a degree of an imaginary circle emanating from Oa, the legendary planet located at the very center of the universe.

Originally conceived as an android army known as the Manhunters (see *Manhunters*), who were abandoned after centuries of use when they proved unreliable, the GL Corps was at first armed with guns that took their energy from handheld power batteries, which in turn drew their energy from the gigantic master power battery back on Oa. Eventually, the Guardians developed power rings composed of a material that can turn will power into raw energy. The rings can absorb a limited charge from the handheld power battery, lasting the equivalent of 24 Earth hours, and are capable of doing almost anything their owners can conceive. The only weakness of the power

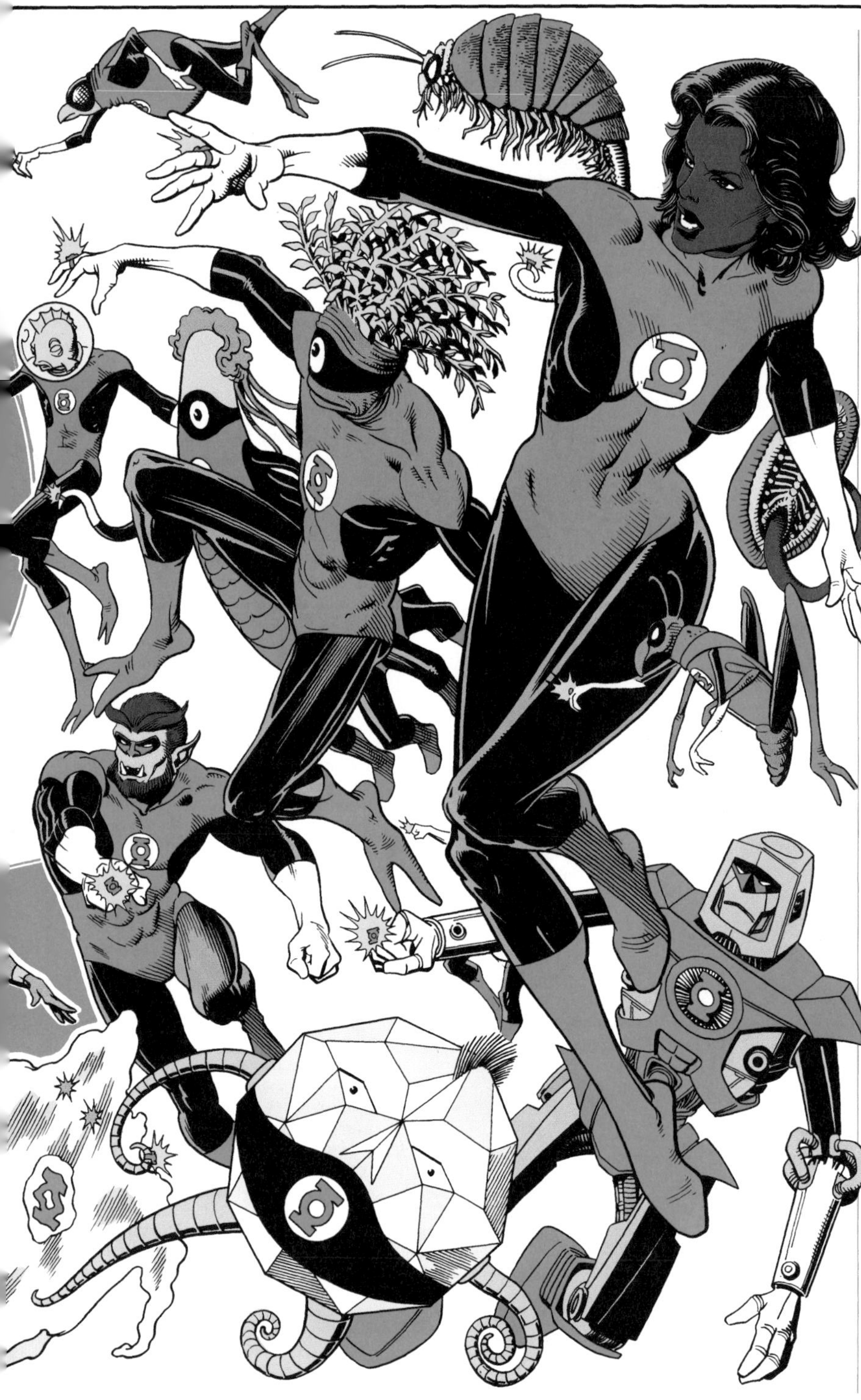

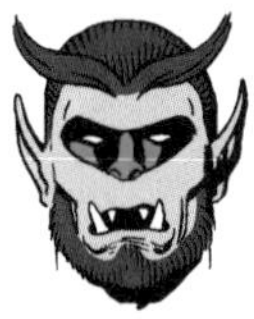

Arkkis Chummuck

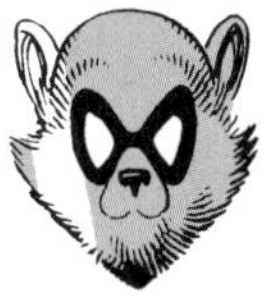

Ch'p

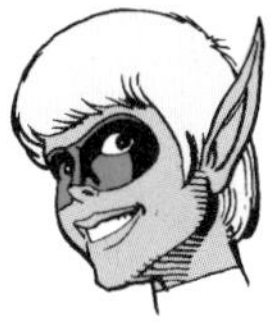

Arisia

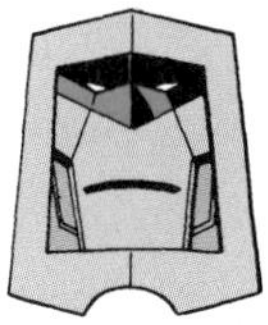

Stel

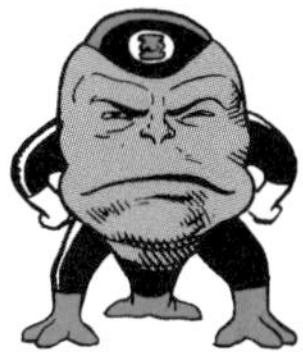

Galius-Zed

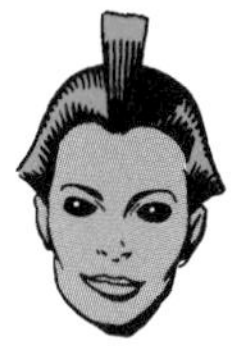

Hollika Rahn

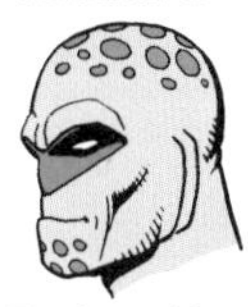

The Green Man

ring is that it is ineffectual against anything colored yellow.

Recently, the most prominent members of the Green Lantern Corps have included: *Hal Jordan* and his successor, *John Stewart* (see *Green Lantern II/III*), protectors of space sector 2814; *Tomar-Re* of the planet Xudar, defender of space sector 2813; the insect-like *Xax* of Xaos; the crystalline *Chaselon* of Barrio III; *Katma Tui* of Korugar, beautiful guardian of space sector 1417; the plant-like *Medphyl* of J586; *Stel* of Grenda, the world where robots rule; the carnivorous *Arkkis Chummuck,* who sacrificed his life to save his comrades; *Arisia* of Graxos IV, teenaged champion of space sector 2815; the amorphous *Eddore* of Tront; the noble *Galius-Zed;* the daredevil *Ch'p* of the planet H'lven; Earthman *Charlie Vickers,* for a time the ring-slinger of space sector 3319, now retired; the reptilian *Salakk* of Slyggia; *Hollika Rahn* of the planet Rhoon, who disguises her emerald power as magic; and *The Green Man* (see *The Green Man*), nameless protector of space sector **2828**, who put aside his power ring tc join the freedom-fighting Omega Men (see *Omega Men*).

First Appearance: GREEN LANTERN #11 □

Art by Brian Bolland

The Huntress

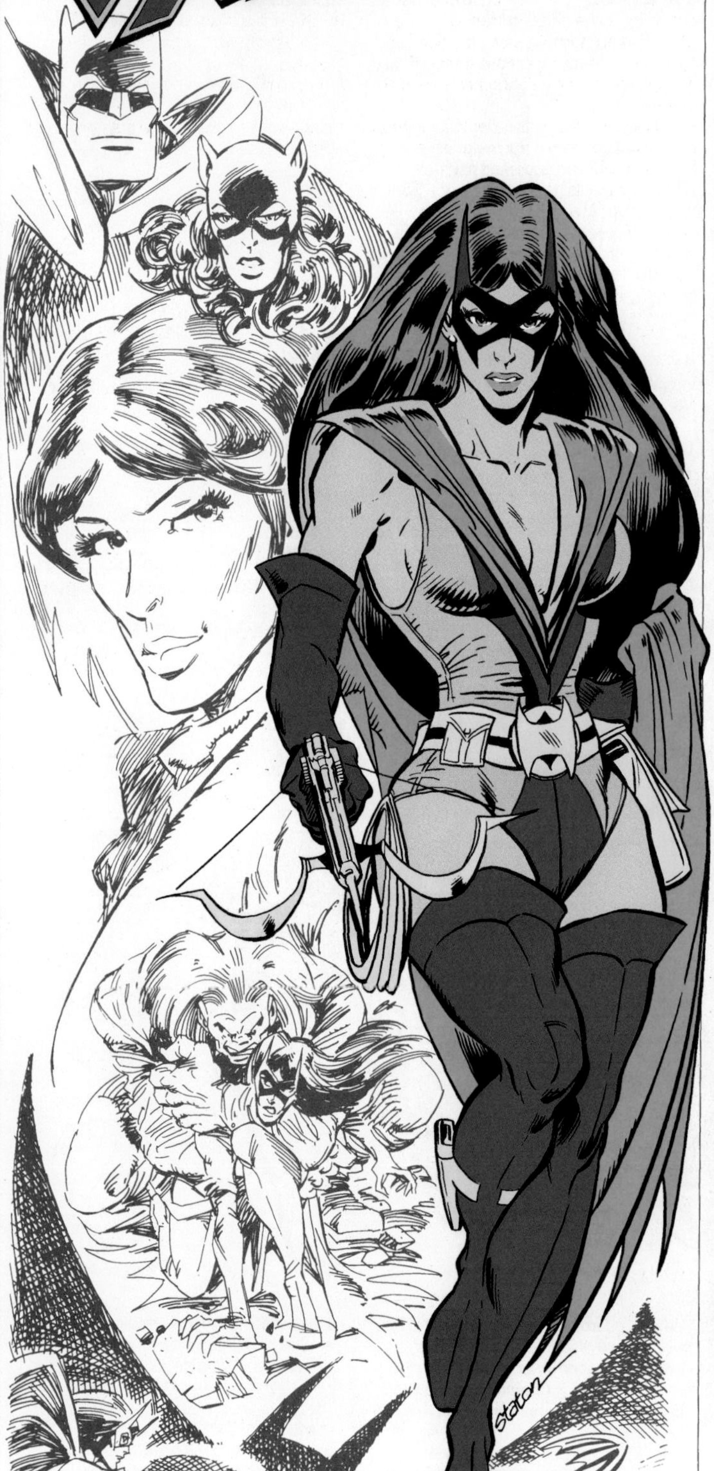

staton

PERSONAL DATA

Alter Ego: Selina Wayne
Occupation: Lawyer
Marital Status: Single
Known Relatives: Thomas and Martha Wayne (grandparents, deceased), Bruce and Selina Kyle Wayne (parents, deceased), Karl Kyle (uncle)
Group Affiliation: Justice Society of America; Infinity, Inc.
Base of Operations: Gotham City
First Appearance: ALL STAR COMICS #69
Height: 5′10″ *Weight:* 127 lbs.
Eyes: Blue *Hair:* Black

HISTORY

Helena Wayne was the only child of Bruce Wayne (see *Batman I*) and Selina Kyle Wayne (see *Catwoman I*), and grew up in the quiet household of Wayne Manor after her father's semiretirement and her mother's reformation. From birth Helena was trained to an extraordinary peak of physical and mental development, not because her parents had any special plan for her future life, but because they assumed such development was good for its own sake. At the same time she was exposed to the basics of crimefighting in stories her father told, and by watching the training he was giving his ward, Dick Grayson (see *Robin I*).

Helena completed law school at the age when most people graduate college. She was about to begin her career when two tragedies changed her life. Cernak, a former confederate of Selina Wayne's, surfaced and blackmailed Selina into one last crime. It was during this crime that Selina was killed by a bullet driven wild when Batman intervened. Bruce Wayne burned his costume at Selina's grave, and a few nights later Helena swore an oath of vengeance and became the Huntress.

The Huntress captured Cernak, and, unknown to her father, she embarked on a heroic career by joining her father's former comrades in the Justice Society of America (see *JSA*). After Bruce donned his Batman costume one last time and laid down his life to save Gotham from a super-powered criminal, the Huntress, with the *JSA*, avenged Batman's death.

Now alone, the Huntress became Gotham's principal guardian and devoted far more energy to her secret identity than to her conventional career as a lawyer. Helena worked for Cranston, Grayson, and Wayne, a public-interest law firm that also counted Dick Grayson as a partner (although an inactive one). She later worked as a police department liaison officer with the district attorney. Coincidentally, Gotham D.A. Harry Sims was her lover.

POWERS & WEAPONS

An Olympic-level athlete, the Huntress is a master of many forms of physical combat, armed and unarmed, and is a skilled criminologist. She also possesses an unusual ability to pick locks and to utilize other criminal techniques.

The weapons in her arsenal include a cross-bow, dagger, and various items in her utility belt or bag. Like her father, she has never used a gun. ■

Art by Joe Staton

PERSONAL DATA

Full Name: Sigfried Horatio Hunch III
Occupation: Professional Hero
Marital Status: Single
Known Relatives: Sigfried Horatio Hunch II (father)
Group Affiliation: None
Base of Operations: South Richmond Park, Queens, New York
First Appearance: 'MAZING MAN #1
Height: 4'11" *Weight:* 98 lbs.
Eyes: Unknown *Hair:* Unknown

HISTORY

Sigfried Horatio Hunch III met his best friend Denton Fixx in the Psychiatric Ward at Bellevue Hospital, though it has not yet been established in what capacity either of them was there. Hunch, in a reversal of the classic situation, followed the dog-faced Denton home and Denton kept him. Hunch took the third bedroom in an apartment shared by Denton and his divorced stepsister, K.P. (Katherine Patricia) Watson.

Not long after meeting Denton, Hunch was prowling through the trash and discovered a golden-colored helmet with the letter "M" on it. Taking this find as an omen, Hunch decided to become a super-hero and, because of the letter on the helmet, chose the name 'Mazing Man. Hunch apparently designed and made his own costume and, despite objections from Denton, began to patrol the neighborhood in which they live.

At first Maze (as he is called) frightened or amused his friends and neighbors, but he has become an accepted part of the scenery now. His heroic feats range from the sublime (saving a young child from being run down by a truck) to the ridiculous (cleaning the leaves from a sewer grating).

Maze has also become involved in the everyday adventures of a small circle of friends. In addition to his roommates, Denton and K.P., he has helped their downstairs neighbor, Guido Garibaldi, and the married couple, Eddie and Brenda Valentine, who are friends of Denton's from high school.

'Mazing Man does not have to work. He is supported by monthly checks he receives after winning the $1,000,000 prize in the Publisher's Reading House Sweepstakes. (After winning, he felt obligated to subscribe to every magazine they offered, much to the distress of his mailman.)

None of Hunch's background is known. He rarely leaves his own neighborhood, though he has accompanied Denton and company to such places as Shea Stadium. He never refers to anyplace but his current apartment as home.

POWERS & WEAPONS

'Mazing Man has no super-powers, nor does he carry any weapons. His unflagging good nature and cheerful smile are as likely to stop lawbreakers as his innate ability to end up getting stepped on as they trip over him. ■

Art by Stephen DeStefano & Karl Kesel

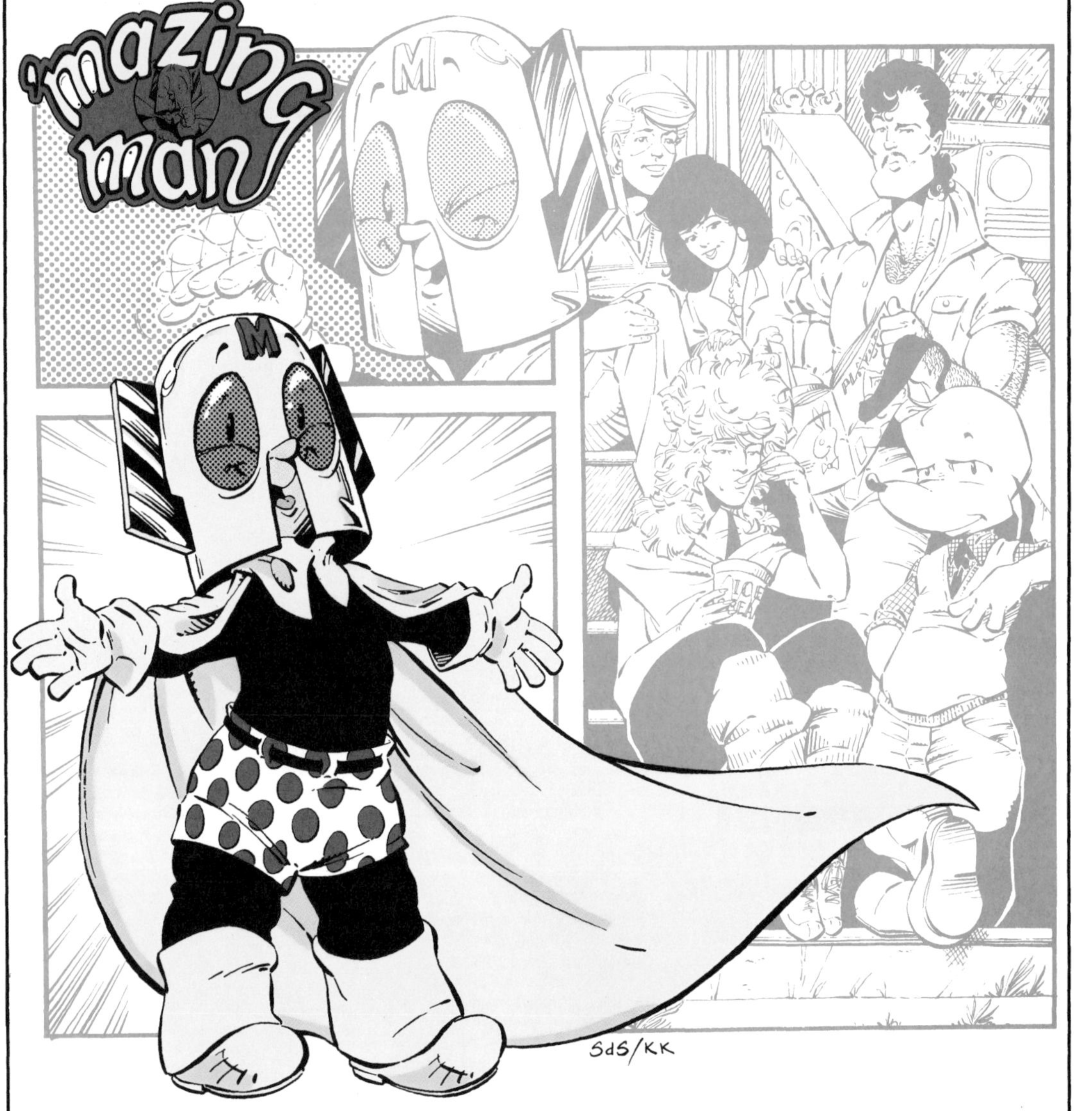

'mazing man
M
SdS/KK

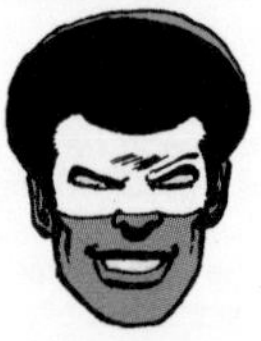
Black Lightning

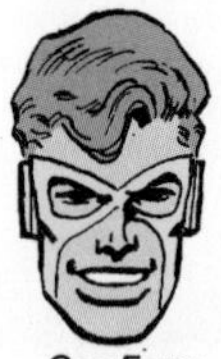
Geo-Force

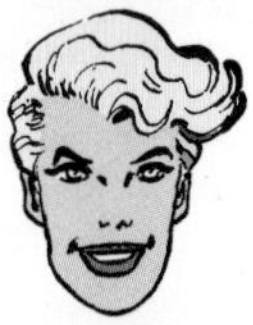
Halo

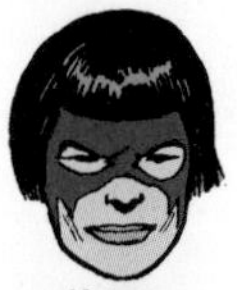
Katana

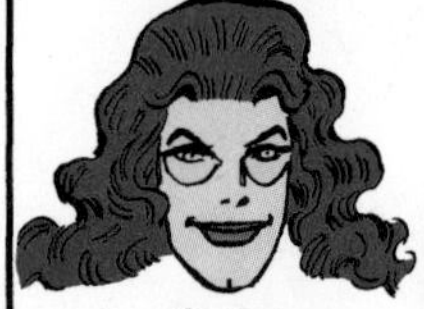
Looker

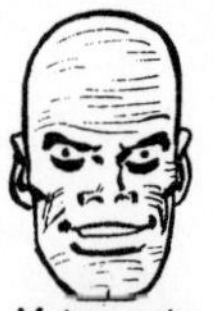
Metamorpho

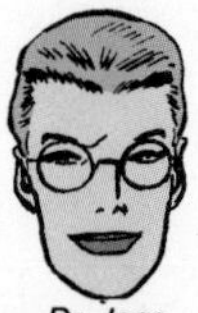
Dr. Jace

THE OUTSIDERS

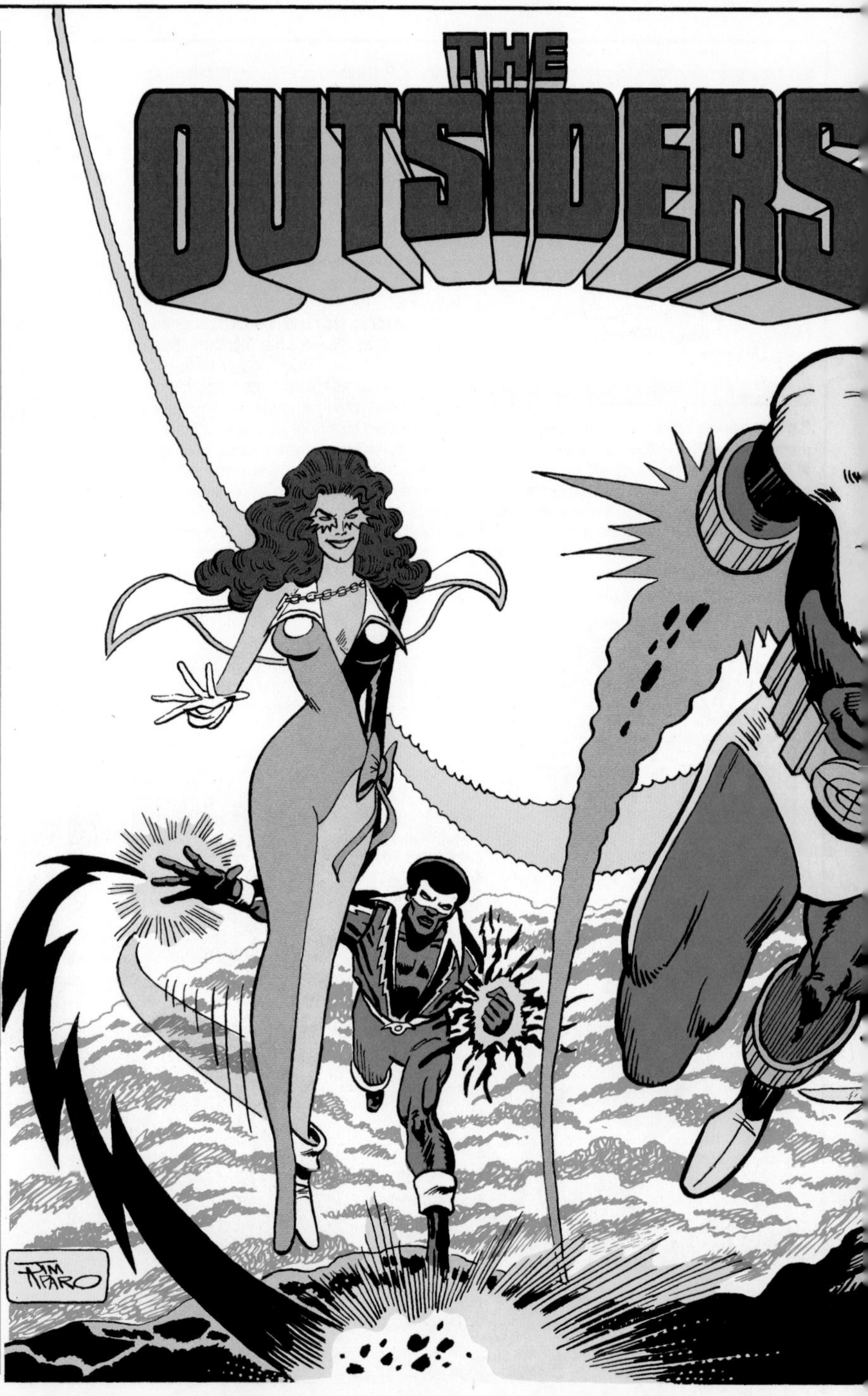
JIM APARO

HISTORY

When the small Western European country of Markovia was taken over by the usurper *Baron Bedlam* (see *Baron Bedlam*), that country was plunged into turmoil. Several foreigners were captured, among them *Lucius Fox,* an employee of Wayne Enterprises. The Batman (see *Batman II*) went to Markovia to find his friend, taking with him the super-hero known as *Black Lightning* (see *Black Lightning*). Once there, however, The Batman discovered several other beings with unusual powers or abilities present, including *Halo, Katana,* and *Metamorpho* (see individual entries). In the meantime, the Markovian government was readying its own defense by imbuing its crown prince, *Prince Brion Markov,* with super-powers, and giving him the code name *Geo-Force.* Joining forces, the heroes defeated Bedlam and decided to remain together under the name *The Outsiders,* with The Batman as their leader. The Batman had previously quit *The Justice League of America* (see *JLA*) over a dispute as to that organization's position regarding the Markovian situation. For a time the group operated out of Gotham City, until a conflict in ideologies with The Batman caused him to leave The Outsiders. The group then relocated to Los Angeles, California, its current base of operations, with its newest member, *Looker* (see *Looker*). As the result of an arrangement with the Markovian government, The Outsiders are sponsored by that country, although they owe Markovia no special allegiance.

The Outsiders currently consists of six

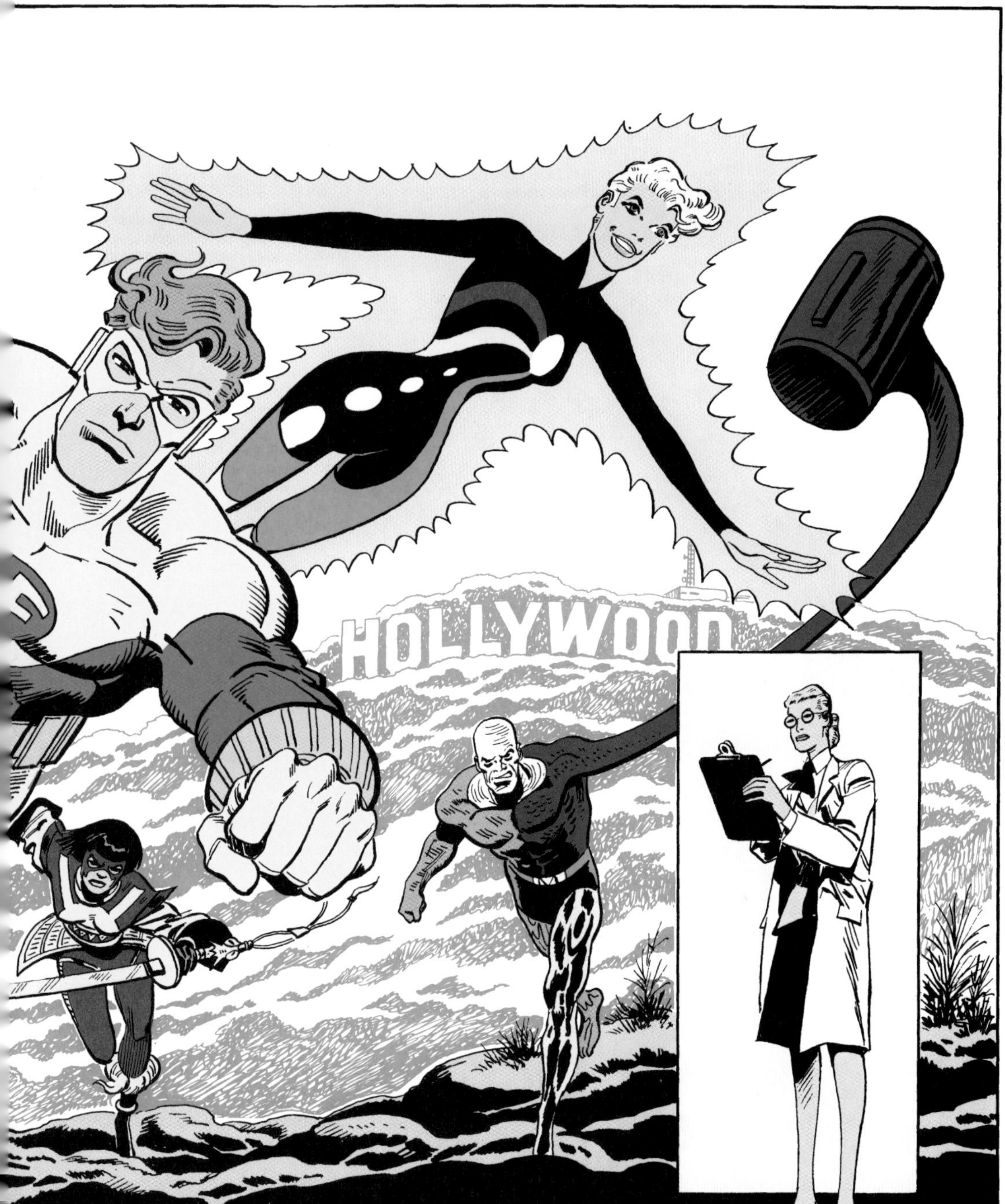
HOLLYWOOD

active members:

Black Lightning, secretly schoolteacher Jefferson Pierce, has electrical powers and is an Olympic-level athlete.

Geo-Force, Prince Brion Markov, has powers relating to the Earth, thus him nom du guerre. He can increase or reduce the force of gravity, propel blasts he calls "lava blasts," and has immense strength, heightened resistance, and increased endurance.

Halo, Gabrielle Doe, controls auras, each one of a different color, each one giving her a different super-power.

Katana, Tatsu Yamashiro, is a samurai, an excellent athlete, and a superb strategist.

Looker, Lia Briggs, has mental powers, including telekinesis, telepathy, levitation, force shields, and some mind-control, manifested by a glow from her eyes.

Metamorpho, Rex Mason, is able to transform himself into any combination of the many elements existing naturally or artificially, and can manipulate his form into almost anything.

Dr. Helga Jace is not technically a member of The Outsiders and has no superpowers, but she serves as the group's scientific consultant and occasional advisor, as well as maintaining the group's headquarters (see *Outsiders HQ*). A native Markovian and a Nobel Prize-winning scientist, she is dedicated to her country and her work.

First Appearance: BATMAN AND THE OUTSIDERS PREVIEW, BRAVE AND BOLD #200

Arty by Jim Aparo

Red Tornado

PERSONAL DATA

Alter Ego: John Smith; also the Tornado Champion and Tornado Tyrant
Occupation: Former Adventurer and Office Worker, now Force of Nature
Marital Status: Single
Known Relatives: None
Group Affiliation: Justice League of America, Justice Society of America
Base of Operations: Mobile
First Appearance: (as Tornado Tyrant) MYSTERY IN SPACE #61; (as Tornado Champion) JUSTICE LEAGUE OF AMERICA #17; (as Red Tcrnado) JUSTICE LEAGUE OF AMERICA #64; (in current form) JUSTICE LEAGUE OF AMERICA ANNUAL #3
Height: 6′1″ *Weight:* 325 lbs.
Eyes: Blue *Hair:* None
(Note: These physical characteristics apply only to the Red Tornado's android form.)

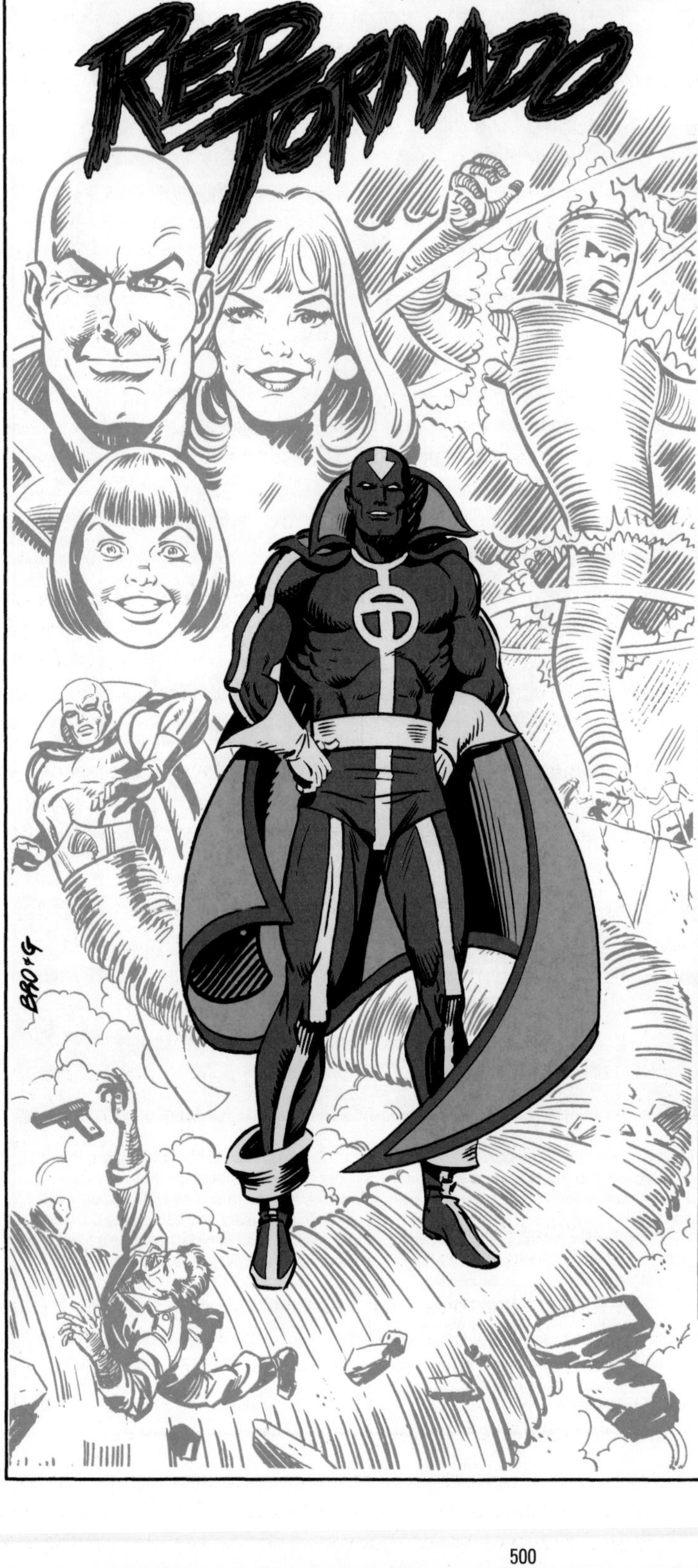
BRO+G

HISTORY

The Red Tornado began his existence on the planet Rann (see *Rann*) as a sentient living tornado whose evil nature was dominant. He was called the Tornado Tyrant. Trying to conquer Rann, the Tornado Tyrant battled Adam Strange (see *Adam Strange*) and was nearly destroyed. Observing Strange and the Justice League of America (see *JLA*), the tornado being decided to become a hero and renamed himself the Tornado Champion. However, the Champion's evil self split off to become a separate being, a new Tornado Tyrant, which the Champion defeated.

Later, criminal scientist T. O. Morrow (see *T. O. Morrow*) created an android called the Red Tornado in order to defeat the Justice Society of America (see *JSA*). The Tornado Champion entered the android body but thereby lost his memory. The Red Tornado saved both the JLA and JSA from Morrow and became a member of the Justice Society himself.

After nearly being destroyed, the Tornado was repaired by Morrow and joined the JLA. Given human facial features by his creator, the Tornado took the human identity of John Smith and fell in love with Kathy Sutton. The Tornado was destroyed in action again, but was rebuilt by the Construct (see *Construct*). Recently, the Red Tornado learned he was the Tornado Champion.

During the crisis on infinite earths the Red Tornado was captured by the Anti-Monitor (see *Monitor II*), who changed the Red Tornado in unknown ways. Morrow was enlisted to repair the Red Tornado aboard the JLA Satellite (see *JLA Headquarters*), but the Red Tornado's android body exploded. However, the Red Tornado reconstituted himself as an immensely powerful living tornado. Now seeing himself as a force of nature, the Red Tornado was appalled by the ecological devastation humanity had wreaked on Earth, and he threatened to destroy civilization. But finally, after fighting the JLA, the Red Tornado left to discover his new purpose in life.

POWERS & WEAPONS

The Tornado Champion and Tyrant could take the form of a devastatingly powerful tornado and could transform matter.

The android Red Tornado could create and control artificial tornadoes, and fly at great speed.

In his new form, the power of the Red Tornado's winds seems greater than ever, and he can apparently control weather. ■

Art by Joe Brozowski & Greg Theakston

THE EXPERIMENTS

EXTRA!
MEET THE INCREDIBLE
CAPTAIN CARROT
AND HIS AMAZING
ZOO CREW
IN A SPECIAL
FREE
16-PAGE PREVIEW COMIC!

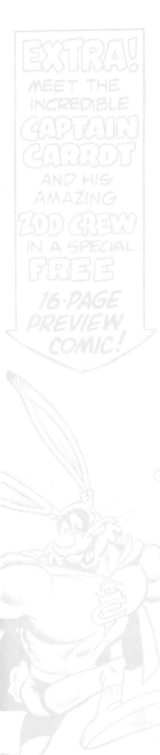

I started my career at DC in 1967, then in 1973 I went to Marvel only to return to DC in 1980, where I was assigned titles such as *Green Lantern*, *DC Presents*, and *The Brave and the Bold*, among others. Unfortunately, having spent the previous two years at Marvel writing, among other titles, *Marvel Two-In-One*, which every month teamed up the Thing from *The Fantastic Four* and a different Marvel hero, I realized I didn't enjoy writing those kinds of team-up comics. So now I needed two other books to write in their place.

Luck was on my side. I was given *Superman*, which, because he was my favorite comics' character, was my dream assignment. Now I needed only one more assignment. I decided if I wanted a book I'd really enjoy, I needed to create it myself. So, months later, after I'd recruited artist George Pérez, we started work on the comic that would soon be known as *The New Teen Titans*.

DC Publisher Jenette Kahn and DC Editor-in-Chief Dick Giordano liked our first issue and wanted to find ways to let the fans know this was going to be something special. But, in that pre-internet age, the big question was: How do you get the word out? How do you tell the fans that they should take a risk and buy a title whose previous incarnations had been canceled several times in the past? They needed to know that this version of the Titans was 100-percent new and improved and nothing at all like what they'd seen before. How do you let them know that they should trust us and give it a try sight unseen?

Jenette, Dick, and Paul Levitz tossed around some really out-of-the-box ideas then finally settled on one that, in retrospect, was so different and so risky that it's almost impossible to believe everyone agreed to it. If the problem is how to get people to buy this unseen, unknown comic, how about giving it to them for—wait for it—*free*?

Understand this was long before Free Comic Book Day, where fans expect to go to the store and get a free comic or 12. Back then, the very idea of giving away a never-before-seen 15-page story was totally unheard of. It was audacious and risky. And it had to be tried.

George and I produced a 15-page prequel to the Titans story we'd already done. It would introduce new characters and create a mystery that would hopefully make readers of this free story look for the answers in *The New Teen Titans* #1. The 15 pager was then inserted into *DC Comics Presents*, which I was already writing. Readers would get their regular *DCP* comic, only it would also have an additional 15 pages they didn't have to pay for.

Now the only question was: Would this experiment work? Would fans buy *DC Comic Presents*, read the free Titans story, then go out and buy *The New Teen Titans* #1 when it came out?

The answer was yes, and in greater numbers than anyone could have predicted. *The New Teen Titans* was an incredible hit.

A year or so later DC tried the experiment again, this time inserting the 15-page superhero parody comic *Captain Carrot and His Amazing Zoo Crew*, by Roy Thomas and Scott Shaw, into the pages of *The New Teen Titans*. And a few months later they did it yet again, this time debuting the horror comic *The Night Force*, by Gene Colan and me, again into *Titans*.

DC in the 1980s was constantly experimenting with different formats and packages. They published the first-ever major maxiseries, *Crisis on Infinite Earths*. *Crisis* was a 12-issue series that would completely change the way

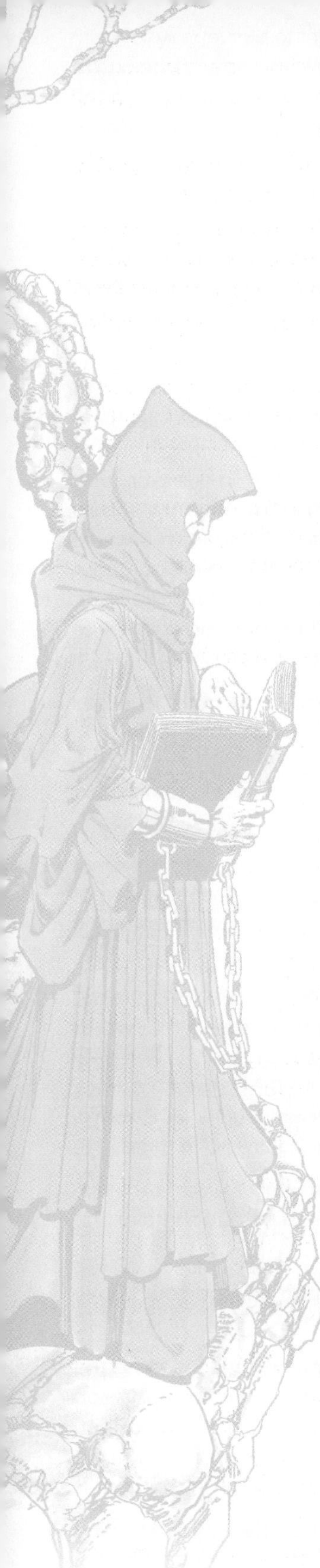

companies approached their characters and universes. Building out of *Crisis* were two very experimental books. If *Crisis* was going to change all of DC, *The History of the DC Universe*, by George Pérez and me, would act like a history book, carefully detailing the chronological history of this new DCU, from Anthro, the first boy on Earth, to Kamandi, the last.

And to get to know each new DC hero better, DC also published *Who's Who: The Definitive Directory of the DC Universe*, featuring bios and stats on every DC hero ever published, going all the way back to the early 1930s.

DC experimented with different paper stock as well. Cheap newsprint—the same paper that comics and their ancestors, the Sunday newspaper comic strip, had been printed on since the 1800s—was replaced by the heavier and brighter Baxter paper and made to look even sharper by employing high-grade photo offset printing. *Camelot 3000*, by Mike W. Barr and Brian Bolland, was the first maxiseries to use that better paper and printing. It would definitely not be the last.

If you were in the business back then you'd see, for the first time ever, comics being printed with the quality and respect we always knew they deserved. DC also experimented with the content. The better printing led artists to do more carefully rendered art. Better art demanded better writing. Comics had once been for kids, but now we could do comics for an adult audience, too, which Frank Miller demonstrated in *The Dark Knight* and Alan Moore and Dave Gibbons proved in their unprecedented graphic novel, *Watchmen*.

In 1938, Detective Comics, Inc.—today known as DC Comics—experimented with an idea that everyone else in the publishing business rejected. And, of course, Superman proved to be exactly what the public was hungry for.

Along the way DC experimented with all kinds of comics. When the industry fell on bad times, DC brought back the superheroes, a genre popular in the 1940s but with the exceptions of Superman, Batman, Wonder Woman, and Blackhawk, dead by 1950. Yet, despite its poor post-war history, in 1956 DC took the chance and updated and resurrected *The Flash*. It was such a success that they quickly brought back all-new versions of many of their old superheroes: Green Lantern, Hawkman, Atom, and many others.

As a creator I know I have to keep experimenting with how I do what I do. To stop trying, to stop experimenting with new ideas, is a surefire way to stay stuck in the past, only repeating what has been done before. But the experiments DC and others made over the past century created an entertainment juggernaut that today continues to expand and thrill not only die-hard fans, but everyone the world over.

Marv Wolfman
March 2020

One of the most prolific and influential comic book writers of the 1980s, Marv Wolfman has helped shape the heroic sagas of many classic characters both at DC and Marvel. He is best known for co-creating The New Teen Titans *and the universe-shattering* Crisis on Infinite Earths *with George Pérez, and in 2011 was inducted into the Will Eisner Hall of Fame.*

I've never really thought of DC Comics as being particularly experimental but, frankly, rather the opposite.

Someone, I forget who, once described the DC Comics of my youth as looking like they were drawn in a bank. Certainly, there was a very distinct and strict house style for both the covers and interior pages.

It was the style I mimicked as a kid and was essentially, it seems to me, based on the artwork of Alex Raymond, filtered through Dan Barry, and emulated by all my favorite artists, from Gil Kane to Carmine Infantino.

This was true, at least, for all the titles edited by Julie Schwartz that I adored and, although the worlds of Superman and Batman had slightly different looks, they were still both tightly lashed to their own templates. The heroes themselves were only ever shown from a stock range of angles, closely adhering to a model sheet.

Clearly, though not quite drawn in a bank, DC's tentpole characters were far too valuable to be sullied by artistic interpretation or creative experiments.

Of paramount importance were the monthly sales figures, which dictated the safe design of covers. Apparently, the color purple was found to help sales and, bizarrely, gorillas on a cover had an even stronger appeal. No doubt a modern computer analysis would detect algorithms relating to main-figure size, word count, and a dozen other tightly controlled elements that subliminally identify a classic money-earning DC cover.

So it was that the formula held for most of the '50s. Then Marvel Comics hit big in the early years of the following decade. Initially, the lifeblood of DC graphics still ran in my veins, and I rejected the often-crude line work and muddy colors of the new usurper but, like a million other readers, I was soon reveling in Marvel's iconoclastic anarchy.

In truth, Marvel's experiment itself was born out of desperation. With sales falling, editor-writer Stan Lee was about to jump ship until his wife encouraged him to go ahead and write the stories he'd always wanted, as there was nothing to lose.

The sheer energy of Marvel's artwork and the novel exuberance of Stan's storylines were irresistible, even to DC, who, playing catch-up, revamped their entire line. Page layouts exploded, covers sank under the weight of overexcited word balloons, and the attendant graphic chaos culminated in the introduction of the infamous "go-go checks," emblazoned across the top of every issue.

When the chief architect of Marvel's look, Jack Kirby, jumped ship and set sail on an untrammeled creative odyssey with his own mini-line of titles for DC, the forced experiment was complete.

As more writers and artists bounced between Marvel and DC the focus for both creators and readers soon settled on the content rather than the packaging of their product. In this atmosphere, low-level experimentation became the norm and, relieved of the cookie-cutter approach to stories, creators began to attract readerships of their very own. Innovation and fresh interpretation became the new currency of the comics.

It was on the shores of this New World that the British Invasion landed.

Brian Bolland had already made his way there by dint of meeting Green Lantern artist Joe Staton, but others, myself included, now found ourselves directly recruited by DC Comics. Unbelievably, after pushing on their door for several years, I found it flung open and a welcome that consisted of a higher page rate, royalties, reprint fees, return of artwork, and even the art board to draw on laid before me.

A DC Comics fanboy from my earliest years, I jumped through that door without hesitation, though slightly baffled as to DC's motives. I heard much later that, fearing the retirement of their Silver Age workhorses, the publishers wanted fresh offshore labor readily available. I prefer the more flattering explanation that us Brits, who had grown up reading American comics, were seen as talents that could bring a refreshing cultural twist to DC's line.

It's true that our influences went beyond American titles to our native comics, many of them created by the cream of European and South American artists.

Additionally, there had always been a subversive, unimpressed attitude within British culture, and this found fertile ground in the often-staid aspects of mainstream American superhero comics.

Many of us creators had experience in British underground comics, too, which had already given us a platform, poorly paid though it was, to express youthful rebellion in our chosen medium. For us, like our American underground counterparts, *Mad Magazine* had been a tremendous inspiration and had shown an alternative possible direction for our talents.

Ours was also the generation that wanted nothing more than to spend our lives creating comics, rather than seeing them as an embarrassing way station on the route to success in the fields of literature or illustration.

This was the asylum, we were the lunatics, and we were clearly taking over.

As I describe the ingredients of what eventually transpired, it does indeed seem like we were involved in some kind of alchemical transatlantic experiment. For many of us artists, the brew was only slowly coming to the boil and we were content to essentially mimic the American styles we knew so well, but once British writers joined the mix, it exploded.

Starting with Alan Moore's dazzling re-imagining of DC's moribund *Swamp Thing* title, comics would never really be the same again. It pretty much set the course for the wonders to come: over the decades, DC had amassed a host of characters, many of them rather quaint, some of them downright stupid, that, with a nudge of British sensibility, could be spun into radical motion.

Like Stan Lee's realization that there was nothing to lose in writing the stories he wanted for the dying Marvel Comics, DC had little to forfeit from messing around with, say, Animal Man, Black Orchid, The Doom Patrol, or any of its second- or third-string characters that had few, if any, fans to disappoint. Indeed, in the new atmosphere of change, sales were only likely to be invigorated, rather than harmed, by bizarre storylines or sarcastic deconstructions.

Indeed, in time, DC created a separate, experimental line of comics that encapsulated this new Brit-led anarchy, in the form of the Vertigo imprint. Under the direction of Karen Berger, herself somewhat of an anomaly in the predominantly male hierarchy of comics publishing, Vertigo became the home to many of the bestselling, audience-grabbing comics of modern times. It attracted readers from far outside the usual adolescent male demographic and demonstrated that the comic book form could escape the confines of genre and entertain a far wider and more sophisticated audience.

And then there was *Watchmen*. Following Alan Moore's successful exhumation of *Swamp Thing*, he was first choice to reinterpret a line of second-string characters that DC, in the person of Managing Editor Dick Giordano, had purchased from the Charlton Comics company, where Dick had previously worked.

Alan and I had long wanted to work on something together for DC, after our successful collaborations for the British comic *2000 AD*, preparing abortive pitches for *Challengers of the Unknown* and *J'onn J'onzz, Manhunter from Mars*. Once I got wind of the Charlton project, I realized this was just that opportunity.

After reading Alan's proposal, however, DC decided that they didn't want their newest character purchases killed or compromised quite so soon, and asked us to come up with some substitutes. What initially might have seemed to be an act of creative cowardice quickly revealed itself to be an inadvertent master stroke, since we were now released from the shackles of continuity and could create characters who exactly fitted the narrative we had in mind, whilst still embodying the generic tropes that the Charlton characters represented.

So it was that, again with nothing to lose other than our unknown and unlicensed characters, DC let us do whatever we wanted with *Watchmen*. Though our work was nominally edited by Len Wein and Barbara Randall, this essentially amounted to proofreading the finished artwork once it arrived fully written, pencilled, inked, lettered, and complete with John Higgins's colors at their offices.

Although many would consider *Watchmen* to be experimental, it's ironic that it is in many ways very traditional. It was obvious that, given the complex and layered narrative, the visual storytelling needed to be clear and accessible, so we used a simple, time-honored nine-panel page-layout grid. To further ground the unusual content, we chose standard flat comic book coloring, though admittedly with an unusual color palette. The unorthodox though unflashy covers served practicality, with the vertical logo ensuring maximum visibility on the shelf displays of the direct-sale comic book stores *Watchmen* was destined for.

As experimenters, Alan and I actually took few risks, and those we did, we calibrated precisely. Even the appearance of a full-frontal naked man we finessed to a nicety.

A radical experiment for American comic books, if ever there was one, but nobody even blinked.

Dave Gibbons
February 2020

Dave Gibbons has drawn and written for most comics publishers on both sides of the Atlantic. His work has encompassed Doctor Who, Superman, Batman, Green Lantern, Predator, Aliens, *the Hugo Award-winning* Watchmen *with Alan Moore, and both* Give Me Liberty *and* Martha Washington Goes to War *with Frank Miller. His semi-autobiographical graphic novel* The Originals *won an Eisner Award in 2005, and his more recent work includes* The Secret Service *with Mark Millar.*